CHAPTER	FOCUS COMPANY	MANAGERIAL FOCUS	CONTRAST COMPANIES	KEY RATIOS
8	Reporting and Interpreting Cost of Sales and Inventory	**NOKIA** Nokia Corporation (Manufacturer of telecommunications software and hardware)	Manufacturing management	Ericsson Telestra	**Inventory Turnover**
9	Reporting and Interpreting Property, Plant, and Equipment; Natural Resources; and Intangibles	WESTJET WestJet Airlines Ltd. (Major Canadian airline)	Planning productive capacity	Southwest Airlines Ryanair	**Fixed Asset Turnover**
10	Reporting and Interpreting Current Liabilities	UNITED COLORS OF BENETTON. Benetton (Manufacturing, distribution, and sale of garments)	Capital structure	Burberry Guess	**Current Ratio Trades Payable Turnover**
11	Reporting and Interpreting Non-Current Liabilities	Nestlé Good Food, Good Life Nestlé S.A. (Manufacturer of nutrition, health, and wellness foods and drinks)	Long-term debt financing	ConAgra Foods Kraft Foods	**Financial Leverage Times Interest Earned**
12	Reporting and Interpreting Owners' Equity	**BCE** Bell Canada Enterprises Inc. (Communications company)	Corporate ownership	Rogers Communications Telus	**Earnings per Share Dividend Yield**
13	Analyzing Financial Statements	THE HOME DEPOT The Home Depot Inc. (Home improvement retailer)	Financial statement analysis	Canadian Tire RONA	**Ratio Summary**
14	Reporting and Interpreting Investments in Other Corporations (online)	**NOKIA** Nokia Corporation (Manufacturer of telecommunications software and hardware)	Investment strategies		

FINANCIAL ACCOUNTING

FOURTH CANADIAN EDITION

ACCOUNTING

Robert Libby

Cornell University

Patricia A. Libby

Ithaca University

Daniel Short

Texas Christian University

George Kanaan

Concordia University

Maureen Gowing

University of Windsor

McGraw-Hill Ryerson

Connect. Learn. Succeed.

Financial Accounting
Fourth Canadian Edition

ISBN-13: 978-0-07-000149-7
ISBN-10: 0-07-000149-9

1 2 3 4 5 6 7 8 9 0 DOW 1 9 8 7 6 5 4 3 2 1

Printed and bound in the United States of America

Vice-President and Editor-in-Chief: *Joanna Cotton*
Executive Sponsoring Editor: *Rhondda McNabb*
Executive Marketing Manager: *Joy Armitage Taylor*
Senior Developmental Editor: *Suzanne Simpson Millar*
Senior Editorial Associate: *Christine Lomas*
Manager, Editorial Services: *Margaret Henderson*
Supervising Editor: *Cathy Biribauer*
Copy Editor: *Julie van Tol*
Proofreader: *Deborah Cooper-Bullock*
Production Coordinator: *Lena Keating*
Inside Design: *Greg Devitt Design*
Composition: *SR Nova Pvt Ltd. Bangalore, India*
Cover Design: *Greg Devitt Design*
Cover Photos: *ULTRA.F/Getty; Ingram publishing/SuperStock; iStock Photo*
Printer: *R.R. Donnelley*

Library and Archives Canada Cataloguing in Publication Data

Financial accounting / Robert Libby ... [et al.]. — 4th Canadian ed.

Includes index.
ISBN 978-0-07-000149-7

1. Accounting—Textbooks. 2. Corporations—Accounting–Textbooks.
3. Financial statements—Textbooks. I. Libby, Robert

HF5636.F54 2011   657   C2010-905432-6

About the Authors

Robert Libby

Robert Libby is the David A. Thomas Professor of Management at the Johnson Graduate School of Management at Cornell University, where he teaches the introductory financial accounting course. He has previously taught at the University of Illinois, Pennsylvania State University, University of Texas at Austin, University of Chicago, and University of Michigan. He received his B.S. from Pennsylvania State University and his M.A.S. and Ph.D. from the University of Illinois; he is also a CPA. Bob is a widely published author specializing in behavioural accounting.

Patricia A. Libby

Patricia Libby is Chair of the Department of Accounting and Associate Professor of Accounting at Ithaca College, where she teaches the undergraduate financial accounting course. She has previously taught graduate and undergraduate financial accounting at Eastern Michigan University and the University of Texas. Before entering academe, she was an auditor with Price Waterhouse (now Pricewaterhouse-Coopers) and a financial administrator at the University of Chicago. She received her B.S. from Pennsylvania State University, her M.B.A. from DePaul University, and her Ph.D. from the University of Michigan; she is also a CPA. Pat conducts research on using cases in the introductory course and other parts of the accounting curriculum.

Daniel G. Short

Daniel Short is Professor of Accounting and Dean of the M.J. Neeley School of Business at Texas Christian University in Fort Worth, Texas. Formerly, he was Dean at the Richard T. Farmer School of Business at Miami University (Ohio) and the College of Business at Kansas State University. Prior to that, he was Associate Dean at the University of Texas at Austin, where he taught the undergraduate and graduate financial accounting courses. He has also taught at the University of Michigan and the University of Chicago. Dan received his undergraduate degree from Boston University and his M.B.A. and Ph.D. from the University of Michigan. He has won numerous awards for his outstanding teaching abilities and has published articles.

George Kanaan

George Kanaan is Associate Professor of Accountancy and Associate Dean at the John Molson School of Business at Concordia University, where he teaches the introductory financial accounting course. George previously taught undergraduate and graduate courses at other universities in Canada, China, and Lebanon. He received his B.A. from the Lebanese University, his M.A. from Southern Illinois University at Carbondale, and his Ph.D. from the University of Wisconsin–Madison. He has conducted research on disclosures related to pension accounting, deferred income taxes, and the effects of changing prices. George's research has been published in *The Journal of Accounting, Auditing and Finance,* and *Managerial Finance*.

Maureen Gowing

Maureen Gowing is Associate Professor of Accounting at the Odette School of Business at the University of Windsor. She has developed and taught Ph.D. research seminars, MBA and undergraduate courses in both managerial and financial accounting. She acquired extensive experience in valuation working as a financial analyst in the oil and securities industries, and did forensic work at the Vancouver Stock Exchange. Maureen obtained her B.A. from Carleton University, her M.B.A. from the University of Toronto, and her Ph.D. from Queen's University. She is also a CMA. Maureen is a member of the Academic Advisory Committee of the Canadian Institute of Chartered Accountants (CICA) and a member of the editorial board of Contemporary Accounting Research. She has conducted research on the effects of personal values on ethical reasoning, and has published in academic journals such as the *Journal of Business Ethics* and *Business Ethics: A European Review*. She is also a co-author of a managerial accounting text.

Contents in Brief

Contents

CHAPTER **THREE**

Operating Decisions and the Income Statement   **103**

FOCUS COMPANY: NESTLÉ S.A.—OFFERING
PRODUCTS TAILORED TO CLIENTS' NEEDS

CHAPTER SIX

Communicating and Interpreting Accounting Information   291

FOCUS COMPANY: THOMSON REUTERS CORPORATION—COMMUNICATING FINANCIAL INFORMATION AND CORPORATE STRATEGY

CHAPTER **NINE**

Reporting and Interpreting Property, Plant, and Equipment; Natural Resources; and Intangibles   461

FOCUS COMPANY: WESTJET AIRLINES—MANAGING PROFITS THROUGH CONTROL OF PRODUCTIVE CAPACITY

CHAPTER **TEN**

Reporting and Interpreting Current Liabilities 529

CHAPTER **ELEVEN**

Reporting and Interpreting Non-current Liabilities 574

CHAPTER **FOURTEEN**

Reporting and Interpreting Investments in Other Corporations   Online

A Trusted Leader

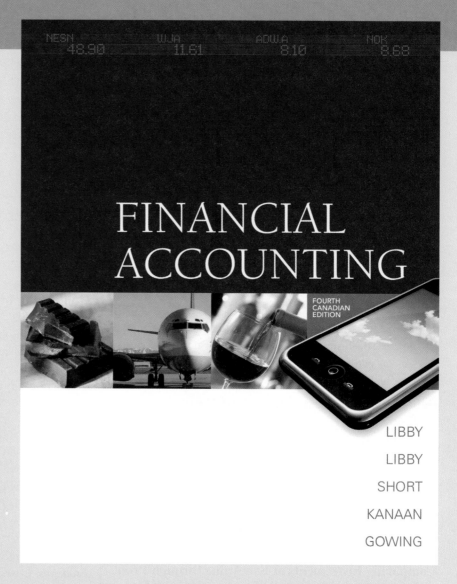

FINANCIAL ACCOUNTING

FOURTH CANADIAN EDITION

LIBBY
LIBBY
SHORT
KANAAN
GOWING

Since it was first published, *Financial Accounting* has grown to be the market-leading financial accounting textbook on which both students and instructors rely. The authors of the Fourth Canadian Edition continue to make financial accounting more relevant and interesting to students. How? By helping the instructor and student become partners in learning, using a remarkable learning approach that keeps students engaged and involved in the material from the first day of class.

Financial Accounting's distinctive focus-company approach motivates students by involving them in the business decisions of a real company and demonstrating how financial accounting makes a difference in the success of a firm. That, combined with pedagogical features and technology tools that serve a variety of learning styles, makes *Financial Accounting* the textbook that both students and instructors agree is the best of its kind on the market today.

For Both Students and Instructors

Financial Accounting maintains its leadership by focusing on

CURRENCY. *Financial Accounting* keeps your students' learning up to date, preparing them for the courses and jobs they will have in the future. International Financial Reporting Standards (IFRS) are completely integrated within each chapter (or throughout the text), and an Accounting Standards for Private Enterprises box concludes each chapter. In addition, the annual reports, financial data, and articles used in both the instruction and the problem material continue to be updated.

RELEVANCE—THE PIONEERING FOCUS-COMPANY

APPROACH. The authors first introduced their focus-company approach as the best method for helping students understand financial statements and real-world implications of financial accounting for future managers. This approach shows how relevent accounting is and motivates students by explaining accounting in a real-world context. Throughout each chapter, the material focuses on a familiar company, its decisions, and its financial statements. This provides the perfect setting for discussing the importance of accounting and how businesses use accounting information. Furthering their real-world applicability, the end-of-chapter cases tie directly to the Financial Statements of the Nestlé Group, conveniently located in Appendix A, and the Annual Report of Cadbury plc, available online. These reports give students valuable practice reading and interpreting real financial data. In addition, real-world excerpts expand on topics, with insight into how real firms use financial accounting to their competitive advantage.

CLARITY. Do students complain that their textbook is hard to read? They don't if they're reading *Financial Accounting*. It is the proven choice for presenting financial accounting with a clear, relevant approach that keeps students engaged throughout the course. To continue to meet the changing needs of financial accounting instructors and students, the organization of the material has been refined to ensure maximum readability for students and flexibility for instructors.

TECHNOLOGY—POWERFUL TOOLS FOR

TEACHING AND STUDY. Today's students have diverse learning styles and conflicting time commitments, so they need technology tools that will help them study more efficiently and effectively. Every new copy of the text includes *Connect*, a web-based assignment and assessment platform that gives students the opportunity to better connect with their coursework. Connect also includes a fully integrated eBook and other study tools that will help them maximize their study time and make their learning experience more enjoyable. The powerful course management tool on Connect also offers a wide range of exclusive features that help instructors spend less time managing and more time teaching.

Inside the Textbook

Financial Accounting offers a host of pedagogical tools that complement the way you like to teach and the ways your students like to learn. Some offer information and tips that help you present a complex subject, while others highlight issues relevant to what your students read online and in the papers, or see on TV. Either way, *Financial Accounting*'s pedagogical support will make a real difference in your course and in your students' learning.

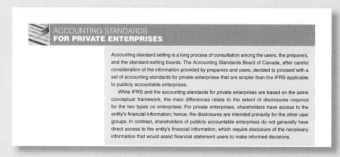

ACCOUNTING STANDARDS FOR PRIVATE ENTERPRISES

Not all companies are public, and not all students will end up working in one. Because of this, and because private enterprises are not required to use IFRS, a new box has been developed for this edition. **Accounting Standards for Private Enterprises** addresses the differences between the two types of reporting, such as why a statement of changes in equity isn't necessary or what details aren't reported in financial statements and related notes.

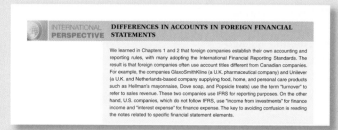

INTERNATIONAL PERSPECTIVE

The **International Perspective** sections make students aware of accounting methods used around the world. Financial statements and real-world excerpts related to international companies are included in the end-of-chapter material as well.

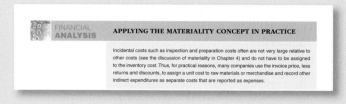

FINANCIAL ANALYSIS

These features tie important chapter concepts to real-world decision-making examples. They also highlight alternative viewpoints and add to the critical thinking and decision-making focus of the text.

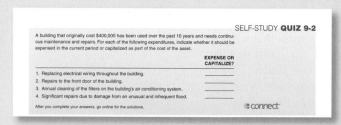

SELF-STUDY QUIZZES

Research shows that students learn best when they are actively engaged in the learning process. This active learning feature engages the student, provides interactivity, and promotes efficient learning. These quizzes ask students to pause at strategic points throughout each chapter to ensure they understand key points before moving ahead.

A Complete Learning System

FOCUS ON CASH FLOWS

The early and consistent coverage of cash flows encourages students to think more critically about the decisions they will face as managers and the impact those decisions will have on the company's cash flow. Each of Chapters 2 through 12 includes a discussion and analysis of changes in the cash flow of the focus company and an exploration of the decisions that caused those changes.

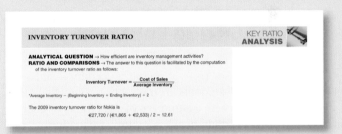

TRADE RECEIVABLES — FOCUS ON CASH FLOWS

The change in trade receivables can be a major determinant of a company's cash flow from operations. The income statement reflects the revenues earned during the period, whereas the cash flow from operating activities reflects the cash collections from customers for the same period. Since sales on account increase the balance in trade receivables, and cash collections from customers decrease the balance in trade receivables, the change in trade receivables from the beginning to the end of the period is the difference between sales and cash collections.

EFFECT ON STATEMENT OF CASH FLOWS

In General → When a net *decrease in trade receivables* for the period occurs, the amount of cash collected from customers exceeds revenue; thus, the decrease must be *added* to revenue or to profit (since revenue is a component of profit) in computing cash flows from operations. When a net *increase in trade receivables* occurs, cash collected from customers is less than revenue; thus, the increase must be *subtracted* from profit in computing cash flows from operations.

KEY RATIO ANALYSIS

Students will be better prepared to use financial information if they understand how to evaluate elements of financial performance while learning how to measure and report them. For this reason, we include relevant key ratios in the **Key Ratio Analysis** sections. Each box presents a ratio analysis for the focus company in the chapter as well as for comparative companies. Cautions are also provided to help students understand the limitations of certain ratios.

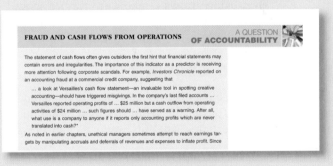

INVENTORY TURNOVER RATIO — KEY RATIO ANALYSIS

ANALYTICAL QUESTION → How efficient are inventory management activities?
RATIO AND COMPARISONS → The answer to this question is facilitated by the computation of the inventory turnover ratio as follows:

$$\text{Inventory Turnover} = \frac{\text{Cost of Sales}}{\text{Average Inventory}^*}$$

*Average Inventory = (Beginning Inventory + Ending Inventory) ÷ 2

The 2009 inventory turnover ratio for Nokia is

€27,720 / (€1,865 + €2,533) / 2 = 12.61

A QUESTION OF ACCOUNTABILITY

The more students are exposed to ethical situations, the more likely they will be to consider the effects their choices will have on others. These boxes appear throughout the text, conveying to students the importance and consequences of acting responsibly in business practice.

FRAUD AND CASH FLOWS FROM OPERATIONS — A QUESTION OF ACCOUNTABILITY

The statement of cash flows often gives outsiders the first hint that financial statements may contain errors and irregularities. The importance of this indicator as a predictor is receiving more attention following corporate scandals. For example, *Investors Chronicle* reported on an accounting fraud at a commercial credit company, suggesting that

... a look at Versailles's cash flow statement—an invaluable tool in spotting creative accounting—should have triggered misgivings. In the company's last filed accounts ... Versailles reported operating profits of ... $25 million but a cash outflow from operating activities of $24 million ... such figures should ... have served as a warning. After all, what use is a company to anyone if it reports only accounting profits which are never translated into cash?*

As noted in earlier chapters, unethical managers sometimes attempt to reach earnings targets by manipulating accruals and deferrals of revenues and expenses to inflate profit. Since

A Complete Learning System

ORGANIZATION OF THE CHAPTER

This framework, at the beginning of each chapter, provides a powerful visual schematic of the content and of what questions will be answered.

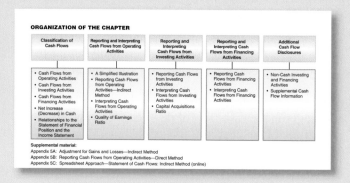

ALL JOURNAL ENTRIES TIED TO THE ACCOUNTING EQUATION

In early chapters, all journal entries marked with (A), (L), (SE), (R), (E), or (X)—if a contra account—and + and − signs assist students in transaction analysis. All journal entries end with a summary of the effects of each transaction on the fundamental accounting equation.

T-accounts (when appropriate) in the margin show the effect a transaction has on cash and profit. **New to the fourth edition** is a small box using arrows (↑ and ↓) to further show the effect on transactions.

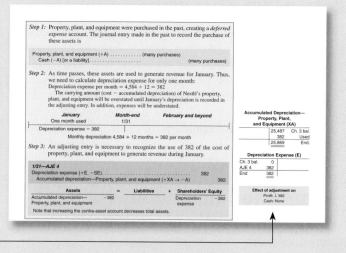

REAL WORLD EXCERPT

These excerpts appear throughout the text and include annual report information from focus companies and others, news articles, analysts' reports, and press releases.

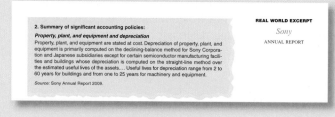

ICONS

Easily identifiable margin icons indicate what types of skills are being addressed in the end-of-chapter material.

 International coverage

 An ethical dilemma

 Cash flow analysis

 Ratio analysis

 Written work, for developing communication skills

 eXcel Exercises to be solved using the Excel template provided

Problems and cases requiring analysis, for developing the ability to use financial information to guide business decisions.

Flexible End-of-Chapter Content and Organization

Each chapter is followed by an extensive selection of end-of-chapter material that examines and integrates multiple concepts presented in the chapter. To maintain the real-world emphasis, they are often based on real Canadian, U.S., and international companies, and require analysis, conceptual thought, calculation, and written communication. Assignments suitable for written individual or group projects and oral presentations are also included.

Chapter Take-Aways   Bulleted end-of-chapter summaries complement the learning objectives outlined at the beginning of the chapter.

Key Ratios   Summary of the key ratios presented in the chapter.

Finding Financial Information   Highlights where to find the financial data discussed in the chapter in an easy-to-review graphic.

Key Terms   Include page references to the location of the term in the chapter text.

Questions   Allow students and faculty to ensure that chapter concepts have been grasped.

Exercises   Assignments that cover multiple learning objectives from the chapter.

Problems   Detailed assignments that integrate various topics discussed in the chapter. Cross-references to the Alternate Problems appear in the blue.

Alternate Problems   Similar in level and content to the end-of-chapter problems, and include cross-references to the Problems in blue.

Cases and Projects   This section includes Finding and Interpreting Financial Information, Financial Reporting and Analysis Cases, Critical Thinking Cases, and Financial Reporting and Analysis Team Project.

Annual Reports   The annual reports of two dynamic companies, the Nestlé Group and Cadbury plc, are referenced in the text's problem material. Excerpts from the annual report for the Nestlé Group appear in Appendix A in the text, and Cadbury's annual report is available online.

What's New in the Fourth Canadian Edition?

Based on market feedback, the primary goals of the fourth edition are:

- to simplify explanations of complex topics;
- to provide a better match of end-of-chapter material to instructor and student needs;
- to accurately reflect the exciting changes taking place in the accounting environment;
- to provide real-world excerpts from financial statements of European and Canadian companies prepared in conformity with International Financial Reporting Standards; and
- to provide instructors with more flexibility in key topical coverage.

As a result, the authors have made the detailed revisions noted in the following sections.

Chapter One

- Changed the focus company to Nestlé S.A., the world's leading nutrition, health, and wellness company.
- Updated material with a focus on IFRS.
- Revised the coverage of the financial statements by including the statement of comprehensive income and the statement of changes in equity.
- Shortened the discussion related to the price earnings ratio.
- Added a box on accounting standards for private enterprises in all chapters.
- Revised the end-of-chapter exercises, problems, and cases, and all new annual report cases.

Chapter Two

- Changed the focus company to Nestlé S.A.
- Simplified Exhibit 2.1.
- Renamed the box on Ethics as A Question of Accountability and updated its content.
- Modified transaction analysis illustration to be clearer and more systematic.
- Added explanation boxes for analytical tools (journal entries and T-accounts).
- Added explanations for journal entries.
- Substantially revised the end-of- chapter exercises, problems, and cases, and added new exercises, problems, and annual report cases.

Chapter Three

- Changed the focus company to Nestlé S.A.
- Updated the International Perspectives box with a focus on IFRS.
- Expanded on the criteria for revenue recognition in conformity with IFRS.
- Clearer exhibit on the transaction analysis model.
- Added explanations for journal entries.
- Added a new pedagogical feature in the margin showing the effect of transactions on profit and cash.
- Revised the Financial Analysis boxes.
- Revised the computation of the Return on Assets to conform to the formulation in Chapter 13.
- Revised the end-of-chapter exercises and problems, and all new annual report cases.

Chapter Four

- Changed the focus company to Nestlé S.A.
- Revised the learning objectives.
- Reorganized discussion of the adjustment process.
- Clarified and simplified illustration of the adjustment process.
- Converted one of the illustrations to a demonstration case.
- Added a new pedagogical feature in the margin showing the effect of transactions on profit and cash.

- Added a self-study quiz on adjusting entries.
- Revised the end-of-chapter exercises and problems, and all new annual report cases.

Chapter Five

- Updated the focus and comparison companies.
- Added a simplified illustration of the direct and indirect methods of computing cash flows from operations.
- Transferred detailed reporting of cash flows from operations using the direct method to an end-of-chapter appendix.
- Moved discussion of spreadsheet approach to preparing a cash flow statement to an online appendix.
- Updated discussion of classification of interest paid or received, and dividends paid or received.
- Revised the end-of-chapter exercises, problems, and cases, and all new annual report cases.

Chapter Six

- Changed the focus company to Thomson Reuters Corporation, the world's leading source of intelligent information for businesses and professionals.
- Revised the coverage of the qualitative characteristics of accounting information.
- Added a new section on profit measurement, and a brief discussion of the statement of comprehensive income and the statement of changes in equity.
- Updated the demonstration case.
- Significantly revised the end-of-chapter material, adding new problems, cases, and all new annual report cases.

Chapter Seven

- Updated focus and comparison companies.
- Reorganized the section Estimating Bad Debts with a focus on the Aging of Trade Receivables method.
- Updated the discussion of ethics in relation to internal control in the box: A Question of Accountability.

- Revised the discussion on revenue recognition rules for specific circumstances.
- Updated the online appendix covering the accounting for passive investments in securities.
- Substantially revised the end-of-chapter exercises and problems, and all new annual report cases.

Chapter Eight

- Changed the focus company to Nokia Corporation, a leading provider of telecommunication solutions.
- Integrated the recording of journal entries under both the periodic and perpetual inventory systems within the discussion of cost-flow assumptions.
- Provided clearer layout of the cost flow computations in Exhibits 8.5, 8.6, 8.9, and 8.10.
- Moved discussion of LIFO from the text to an online appendix.
- Revised the discussion of the lower of cost and net realizable value rule.
- Revised the end-of-chapter exercises, problems, and cases, and all new annual report cases.

Chapter Nine

- Updated focus and comparison companies.
- Expanded on the discussion of asset impairment.
- Updated financial disclosure examples.
- Substantially revised the end-of-chapter exercises, problems, and cases, and all new annual report cases.

Chapter Ten

- Changed the focus company to Benetton Group.
- Revised the section on contingent liabilities to conform to IFRS.
- Added a new section on provisions.
- Revised the information related to the various exhibits and real-world excerpts.
- Revised the end-of-chapter exercises, problems, and cases, and all new annual report cases.

Chapter Eleven

- Changed the focus company to Nestlé S.A.
- Restructured the discussion of amortization of bond discount or premium to focus on the effective interest method.
- Updated the discussion of lease liabilities.
- Added an appendix covering the straight-line method of amortizing bond discount or premium.
- Added a new section on provisions.
- Added an online appendix showing present value computations using Excel.
- Revised the end-of-chapter exercises, problems, and cases, and all new annual report cases.

Chapter Twelve

- Changed the focus company to BCE Inc., Canada's largest telecommunications company.
- Incorporated the discussion of repurchase of shares into the chapter.
- Added a new section on measuring and reporting changes in shareholders' equity.

- Eliminated discussion of restrictions on retained earnings.
- Eliminated discussion of accounting and reporting for income trusts.
- Revised the end-of-chapter exercises, problems, and cases, and all new annual report cases.

Chapter Thirteen

- Updated the information and financial analysis related to the focus company, Home Depot.
- Updated comparison companies and the information related to the various exhibits and real-world excerpts.
- Substantially revised the end-of-chapter exercises, problems, and cases, and added new assignment material.

Chapter Fourteen

- Changed the focus company to Nokia Corporation.
- Updated the discussion on passive investments in conformity with IFRS.
- Revised the end-of-chapter exercises, problems, and cases, and all new annual report cases.

Teaching and Learning with Technology

CONNECT

Connect is a web-based assignment and assessment platform that gives students the means to better connect with their coursework, with their instructors, and with the important concepts they will need to know for success now and in the future. Connect embraces diverse study behaviours and preferences with breakthrough features that help students master course content and achieve better results. The powerful course management tool in Connect also offers a wide range of exclusive features that help instructors spend less time managing and more time teaching.

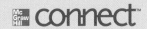

With Connect, you can deliver assignments, quizzes, and tests online. A robust set of questions and problems are presented and tied to the textbook's learning objectives. Track individual student performance—by question, by assignment, or in relation to the class overall—with detailed grade reports. Integrate grade reports easily with Learning Management Systems such as WebCT and Blackboard. And much more.

Connect helps you teach for today's needs:

UNLIMITED PRACTICE, INSTANT FEEDBACK

Provide instant feedback to unlimited textbook practice problems, acknowledging correct answers and pointing to areas that need more work.

AUTOMATIC GRADING

Focus on teaching instead of administrating with electronic access to the class roster and gradebook, which easily sync with your school's course management system.

DIRECT TEXTBOOK AND TEST BANK QUESTIONS

Assign students online homework as well as test and quiz questions with multiple problem types, algorithmic variation, and randomized question order.

INTEGRATED eBOOKS

Connect directly integrates the McGraw-Hill Ryerson textbooks you already use into the engaging, easy-to-use interface.

DEDICATED CANADIAN SUPPORT AND TRAINING

The Connect development team and customer service groups are located in our Canadian offices and work closely together to provide expert technical support and training for both instructors and students.

Lyryx

Lyryx Assessment Financial Accounting is an online assessment system designed to support both students and instructors. The assessment takes the form of a homework assignment called a Lab. The Labs are algorithmically generated and automatically graded. Students get unlimited opportunities to practice, and after they submit a Lab for marking, students receive extensive feedback on their work, thus promoting their learning experience. Recent research shows that when Labs are tied to assessment, even if they are worth only a small percentage of the total grade for the course, students will do their homework – and the result is improved student success.

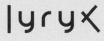

Services and Support

INSTRUCTOR SUPPORT

The following resources are available online to support instructors:

- **Instructor's Manual.** Includes a chapter outline, detailed lecture notes, suggested activities, and a reading list for each chapter.
- **Solutions Manual.** Provides solutions for end-of-chapter questions, exercises, problems, and cases.
- **PowerPoint® Presentations.** These slides for use in your classroom are completely customized for the fourth Canadian edition of *Financial Accounting*.
- **Computerized Test Bank.** Includes more than 1,800 True/False, Multiple Choice, and Essay questions.
- **Instructor's Excel® Template Solutions.** These Excel template solutions accompany the templates available to students online.

OTHER SERVICES AND SUPPORT

*i*LEARNING SERVICES

At McGraw-Hill Ryerson, we take great pride in developing high-quality learning resources while working hard to provide you with the tools necessary to utilize them. We want to help bring your teaching to life, and we do this by integrating technology, events, conferences, training, and other services. We call it *i*Services. For more information, visit **www.mcgrawhill.ca/olc/iservices**.

BLACKBOARD AND WebCT

McGraw-Hill Ryerson offers a range of flexible integration solutions for **WebCT** and **Blackboard** platforms. Please contact your McGraw-Hill Ryerson *i*Learning Sales Specialist for details.

COURSESMART

CourseSmart brings together thousands of textbooks across hundreds of courses in an eTextbook format, providing unique benefits to students and faculty. By purchasing an eTextbook, students can save up to 50 percent of the cost of a print textbook, reduce their impact on the environment, and gain access to powerful Web tools for learning, including full-text search, notes and highlighting, and email tools for sharing notes between classmates. For faculty, CourseSmart provides instant access for reviewing and comparing textbooks and course materials in their discipline area without the time, cost, and environmental impact of mailing print examination copies. For further details, contact your *i*Learning Sales Specialist or go to **www.coursesmart.com**.

CREATE

McGraw-Hill's Create Online gives you access to the most abundant resource at your fingertips–literally. With a few mouse clicks, you can create customized learning tools simply and affordably. McGraw-Hill Ryerson has included many of our market-leading textbooks within Create Online for eBook and print customization as well as many licensed readings and cases. For more information, go to **www.mcgrawhillcreate.com**.

Acknowledgements

Writing and adapting a successful textbook requires a team effort and we have enjoyed working with excellent teammates. Throughout the process of writing this textbook, many people stepped forward with tremendous efforts that enabled us to accomplish our goals. First and foremost, we are deeply indebted to Robert Libby, Patricia Libby, and Daniel Short, authors of the U.S. edition, for developing the pedagogical approach used in this text. Their approach helped us tremendously in shaping this fourth Canadian edition.

We would like to recognize the sincere and devoted efforts of the many people who added their input to the process of developing this book. We received invaluable advice and suggestions during the manuscript development and revision process. For this assistance, we thank the following colleagues:

FOURTH EDITION REVIEWERS

Ann Clarke-Okah	*Carleton University*
Sandra Daga	*University of Toronto, Scarborough*
Robert Ducharme	*University of Waterloo*
Allan W. Foerster	*Wilfrid Laurier University*
Gordon Holyer	*Vancouver Island University*
Ian Hutchinson	*Acadia University*
Marg Johnson	*Thompson Rivers University*
Stuart H. Jones	*University of Calgary*
Camillo Lento	*Lakehead University*
Ken MacAulay	*St. Francis Xavier University*
Marie Madill-Payne	*George Brown College*
Debbie Musil	*Kwantlen Polytechnic University*
S.M. Khalid Nainar	*McMaster University*
Catherine Seguin	*University of Toronto, Mississauga*
Vicki Sweeney	*University of Western Ontario*
Shu-Lun Wong	*Memorial University of Newfoundland*

We also received invaluable input and support through the years from present and former colleagues and students. We are indebted to the following individuals who helped adapt, critique, and shape the ancillary package for the Canadian market: Terry Anderson; Karen Congo, University of Western Ontario; Robert Ducharme, University of Waterloo; Ian Feltmate, Acadia University; Allan Foerster, Wilfrid Laurier University; and Richard Michalski from McMaster University.

The extraordinary efforts of a talented group of individuals at McGraw-Hill Ryerson made all of this come together. We especially thank Rhondda McNabb for her guidance throughout this project; Suzanne Simpson Millar for initiating the developmental work for this edition and for tirelessly following the whole process through until the final printing; Cathy Biribauer, who managed the final production of this book, and all the marketing and sales people who helped bring this book to both instructors and students. We also thank all those who worked behind the scenes to ensure the successful completion of this book. Special thanks to Julie van Tol who edited our work and Deborah Cooper-Bullock for proofreading the entire manuscript.

We thank the Nestlé Group and Cadbury plc for permitting us to use their financial statements to provide students with real-world examples of financial statements and accompanying notes. We are also grateful to all the focus companies that allowed us to use excerpts from their financial statements and notes to illustrate the main ideas in each chapter.

Special thanks go to our families for their support, patience, and understanding while we worked on completing this fourth Canadian edition of the book. We dedicate the book to them.

George Kanaan
Maureen Gowing

To Our Student Readers

This book is aimed at two groups of readers:

1. *Future managers*, who will need to interpret and use financial statement information in business decisions.

2. *Future accountants*, who will prepare financial statements for those managers.

Future managers need a firm basis for using financial statement information in their careers in marketing, finance, banking, manufacturing, human resources, sales, information systems, or other areas of management. Future accountants need a solid foundation for further professional study.

Both managers and accountants must understand how to *use financial statements in making real business decisions* to perform their duties successfully. The best way to learn this is to study accounting in real business contexts. This is the key idea behind our focus-company approach, which we introduce in the first chapter. Each chapter's material is integrated with a focus company, its decisions, and its financial statements. The focus companies are drawn from different industries, providing you with a broad range of experience in realistic business and financial accounting practices. In each chapter, you *will actually work with these real companies' statements* and those of additional contrast companies.

When you complete this course, you will be able to read and understand financial statements of real companies. We help you achieve this goal by

1. Selecting learning objectives and content based on the way that seasoned managers use financial statements in modern businesses. We emphasize the topics that count.

2. Recognizing that students using this book have no previous exposure to accounting and financial statements and often little exposure to the business world. We take you through the financial statements three times at increasing levels of detail (in Chapter 1, Chapters 2 through 5, and Chapters 6 through 13). This is the secret to our "building-block approach."

3. Helping you "learn how to learn" by teaching efficient and effective approaches for learning the material. Keep these learning hints in mind throughout.

4. Providing regular feedback in Self-Study Quizzes, which occur throughout each chapter. Complete the quizzes before you move on. Check your answers against the solutions provided online. If you are still unclear about any of the answers, refer back to the chapter material before moving on.

5. Repeating the key terms and their definitions in the margins. You should pay special attention to the definitions of these terms and review them at the end of the chapter. A handy index is provided at the end of the book.

6. Introducing the Key Financial Ratios used to assess different elements of financial performance at the same time you are learning how to measure and report those elements. These will show you what kinds of accounting information managers use and how they interpret it.

7. At the end of each chapter, test what you have learned by working through the Demonstration Cases. *Working problems is one of the keys to learning accounting.*

Good luck in your financial accounting course.

George Kanaan
Maureen Gowing

Financial Statements and Business Decisions

After studying this chapter, you should be able to do the following:

FOCUS COMPANY: **Nestlé S.A.**

VALUING AN INVESTMENT USING FINANCIAL STATEMENT INFORMATION

Nestlé S.A., based in Vevey, Switzerland, is the world's leading nutrition, health, and wellness company. It was founded in 1866 by Henri Nestlé, a pharmacist who developed a baby formula that offered a safe and more nutritious alternative to existing breast milk substitutes for mothers who were unable to provide breast milk. People quickly recognized the value of the new product after Nestlé's new formula saved children's lives.

Nestlé grew over the next 40 years and set up factories in the United States, Britain, Germany, and Spain. In the 1920s, Nestlé expanded into new products, with chocolate production becoming the company's second most important activity. Nestlé continued to grow over the years through innovation and acquisition of other companies. Today, Nestlé has an impressive list of products, including such well-known brand names as Nestlé, KitKat, Nescafé, Coffee-Mate, Smarties, Cheerios, and Perrier.

Nestlé became a public company in 1873. Its shares currently trade on the SIX Swiss Exchange. Anyone who has invested in Nestlé must have taken into consideration the value of the company's economic resources, its debts to others, its ability to sell goods for more than the cost of producing them, and its ability to generate the cash necessary to pay its current bills. Much of this assessment was based on financial information that Nestlé provided to investors in the form of financial statements.

UNDERSTANDING THE BUSINESS

The Players

The success story of Nestlé began in 1866 when the Company's founder, Henri Nestlé, by investing a major portion of his savings, became the sole owner of the company. As is common in new businesses, the founder also functioned as manager of the business (he was *owner-manager*).

When he started the company, Henri Nestlé needed additional money to build manufacturing facilities and to develop the business. So he borrowed money from a local bank and other lenders, or *creditors*, and used the funds to expand the business. Henri Nestlé's leadership in developing the baby formula and then expanding into other milk products and baby foods helped Nestlé become the leading international nutrition, health, and wellness company.

Investors—individuals who buy small percentages of large corporations—make their purchases hoping to gain in two ways. They hope to receive a portion of what the company earns in the form of cash payments called *dividends*, and they hope to eventually sell their share of the company at a higher price than they paid.

Creditors lend money to a company for a specific length of time. They gain by charging interest on the money they lend. When Nestlé exchanges money with its lenders and owners, these are called *financing activities*. When Nestlé buys or sells property, such as roasting equipment used in producing coffee products, these are called *investing activities*.

The Business Operations

To understand any company's financial statements, you must first understand its operations. As noted, Nestlé produces and markets nutrition and health foods for personal consumption. Nestlé's products are manufactured from natural ingredients. To produce the nutrition and health foods for sale, Nestlé needs raw materials such as milk, cocoa, and cereals. Nestlé purchases these ingredients and accessories from other companies, referred to as *suppliers*.

Nestlé distributes its many products through its own distribution network throughout the world. It sells its products to retail stores, or *customers*, through wholesale distributors.

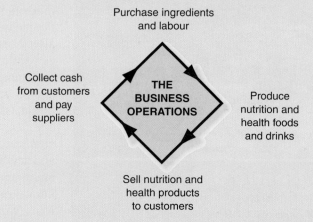

The Accounting System

Like all businesses, Nestlé has an accounting system that collects and processes financial information about an organization and reports that information to decision makers. Nestlé's managers (often called *internal decision makers*) and parties outside the firm (often called *external decision makers*), such as the investors in Nestlé's shares and the bank's loan officer, use reports produced by this system. Exhibit 1.1 outlines the two parts of the accounting system. Internal managers typically require continuous detailed information because they must plan and manage the day-to-day operations of the organization. Developing accounting information for internal decision makers is called *managerial* or *management accounting* and is the subject of a separate accounting course. The focus of this text is accounting for external decision makers, called *financial accounting*, and the four basic financial statements and related disclosures that are the output of that system.

We begin this process with a brief but comprehensive overview of the four basic financial statements and the people and organizations involved in their preparation and

LO¹

Recognize the information conveyed in each of the four basic financial statements and how it is used by different decision makers (investors, creditors, and managers).

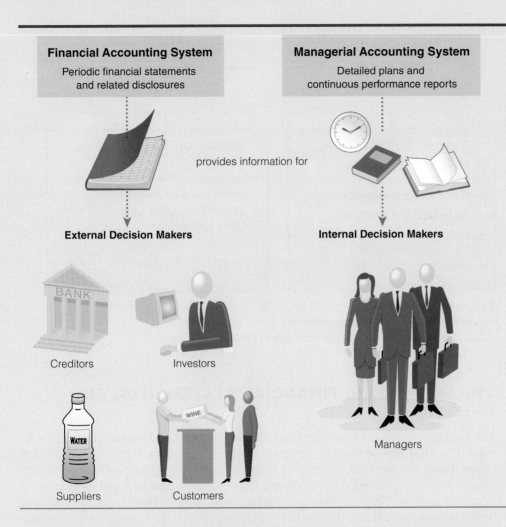

Exhibit **1.1**
The Accounting System and
Decision Makers

use. This overview provides you with a context in which you can learn the more detailed material that is presented in the following chapters. In particular, we focus on how two primary users of the statements, investors (owners) and creditors (lenders) relied on each of Nestlé's four basic financial statements in their decisions to invest in or lend money to Nestlé. Later in the chapter, we discuss a broader range of uses of financial statement data in marketing, management, human resources, and other business contexts.

To understand the way that investors and creditors use Nestlé's financial statements in their decisions, we must first understand what specific information is presented in the four basic financial statements for a company such as Nestlé.

We present many new business and financial statement terms in this chapter. **Instead of trying to memorize the definitions of every term used in this chapter, focus your attention on learning the general structure and content of the statements.** Specifically, you should focus on these questions:

1. What categories of items (often called *elements*) are reported on each of the four statements? (What type of information does a statement convey, and where can you find it?)

2. How are the elements within a statement related? These *relationships* are usually described by an equation that tells you how the elements fit together.

3. Why is each element important to managers', owners', or creditors' decisions? (How important is the information to decision makers?)

The *Self-Study Quizzes* that occur throughout the chapter will test your ability to answer these questions. Remember that since this chapter is an overview, each concept discussed in this chapter will be discussed again in Chapters 2 through 5.

ORGANIZATION OF THE CHAPTER

The Basic Financial Statements	Responsibilities for the Accounting Communication Process
• Statement of Financial Position • Statement of Comprehensive Income • Statement of Changes in Equity • Statement of Cash Flows • Relationships among the Four Statements • Notes to Financial Statements	• International Financial Reporting Standards (IFRS) • Management Responsibility and the Demand for Auditing • Ethics, Reputation, and Legal Liability

Supplemental material:
Appendix 1A: Types of Business Entities
Appendix 1B: Employment in the Accounting Profession Today

THE FOUR BASIC FINANCIAL STATEMENTS: AN OVERVIEW

The four basic financial statements include the statement of financial position, statement of comprehensive income, statement of changes in equity, and statement of cash flows. These are the basic statements normally prepared by for-profit corporations. The statements are intended primarily to inform investors, creditors, and other external decisions makers. They summarize the financial activities of the business. They can be prepared at any point in time and can apply to any time span (such as one year, one quarter, or one month). Like most companies, Nestlé prepares financial statements for investors and creditors at the end of each quarter (known as *quarterly reports*) and at the end of the year (known as *annual reports*).

The Statement of Financial Position[1]

A **STATEMENT OF FINANCIAL POSITION (BALANCE SHEET)** reports the financial position (assets, liabilities, and shareholders' equity) of an accounting entity at a point in time.

The purpose of the statement of financial position is to report the financial position (amount of assets, liabilities, and shareholders' equity) of an accounting entity at a particular point in time. We can learn a lot about what the statement of financial position reports just by reading the statement from the top. The statement of financial position of Nestlé is shown in Exhibit 1.2.

Structure   The *heading* of the statement of financial position identifies four significant items related to the statement:

1. *name of the entity*—The Nestlé Group
2. *title of the statement*—Statement of Financial Position
3. *specific date of the statement*—At December 31, 2009
4. *unit of measure*—(in millions of Swiss francs)

Statement of Financial Position

Assets = Liabilities + Shareholders' Equity

---

[1]Some companies refer to this statement as a "balance sheet," a title that was commonly used prior to the adoption of IFRS in Canada.

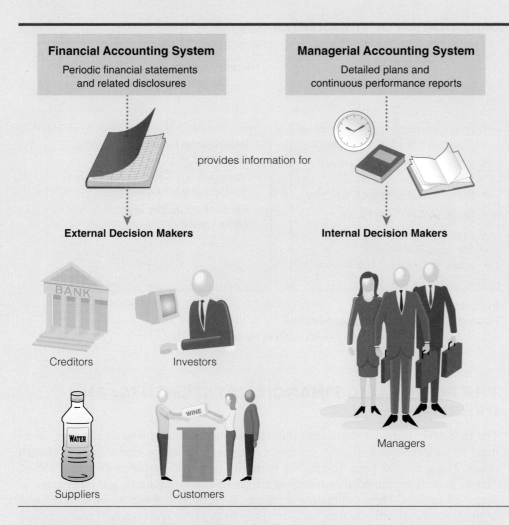

Exhibit **1.1**
The Accounting System and
Decision Makers

use. This overview provides you with a context in which you can learn the more detailed material that is presented in the following chapters. In particular, we focus on how two primary users of the statements, investors (owners) and creditors (lenders) relied on each of Nestlé's four basic financial statements in their decisions to invest in or lend money to Nestlé. Later in the chapter, we discuss a broader range of uses of financial statement data in marketing, management, human resources, and other business contexts.

To understand the way that investors and creditors use Nestlé's financial statements in their decisions, we must first understand what specific information is presented in the four basic financial statements for a company such as Nestlé.

We present many new business and financial statement terms in this chapter. **Instead of trying to memorize the definitions of every term used in this chapter, focus your attention on learning the general structure and content of the statements**. Specifically, you should focus on these questions:

1. What categories of items (often called *elements*) are reported on each of the four statements? (What type of information does a statement convey, and where can you find it?)

2. How are the elements within a statement related? These *relationships* are usually described by an equation that tells you how the elements fit together.

3. Why is each element important to managers', owners', or creditors' decisions? (How important is the information to decision makers?)

The *Self-Study Quizzes* that occur throughout the chapter will test your ability to answer these questions. Remember that since this chapter is an overview, each concept discussed in this chapter will be discussed again in Chapters 2 through 5.

ORGANIZATION OF THE CHAPTER

The Basic Financial Statements	Responsibilities for the Accounting Communication Process

The Basic Financial Statements
- Statement of Financial Position
- Statement of Comprehensive Income
- Statement of Changes in Equity
- Statement of Cash Flows
- Relationships among the Four Statements
- Notes to Financial Statements

Responsibilities for the Accounting Communication Process
- International Financial Reporting Standards (IFRS)
- Management Responsibility and the Demand for Auditing
- Ethics, Reputation, and Legal Liability

Supplemental material:
Appendix 1A: Types of Business Entities
Appendix 1B: Employment in the Accounting Profession Today

THE FOUR BASIC FINANCIAL STATEMENTS: AN OVERVIEW

The four basic financial statements include the statement of financial position, statement of comprehensive income, statement of changes in equity, and statement of cash flows. These are the basic statements normally prepared by for-profit corporations. The statements are intended primarily to inform investors, creditors, and other external decisions makers. They summarize the financial activities of the business. They can be prepared at any point in time and can apply to any time span (such as one year, one quarter, or one month). Like most companies, Nestlé prepares financial statements for investors and creditors at the end of each quarter (known as *quarterly reports*) and at the end of the year (known as *annual reports*).

The Statement of Financial Position[1]

The purpose of the statement of financial position is to report the financial position (amount of assets, liabilities, and shareholders' equity) of an accounting entity at a particular point in time. We can learn a lot about what the statement of financial position reports just by reading the statement from the top. The statement of financial position of Nestlé is shown in Exhibit 1.2.

Structure   The *heading* of the statement of financial position identifies four significant items related to the statement:

1. *name of the entity*—The Nestlé Group
2. *title of the statement*—Statement of Financial Position
3. *specific date of the statement*—At December 31, 2009
4. *unit of measure*—(in millions of Swiss francs)

A **STATEMENT OF FINANCIAL POSITION (BALANCE SHEET)** reports the financial position (assets, liabilities, and shareholders' equity) of an accounting entity at a point in time.

---

[1]Some companies refer to this statement as a "balance sheet," a title that was commonly used prior to the adoption of IFRS in Canada.

Exhibit **1.2**
Statement of Financial Position

THE NESTLÉ GROUP Statement of Financial Position At December 31, 2009 (in millions of CHF)			Name of the entity Title of the statement Accounting period Unit of measure
Assets			
Cash and cash equivalents		5,825	Amount of cash and short-term deposits in the company's bank accounts
Trade receivables		12,309	Amounts owed by customers from prior sales
Inventories		7,734	Food and drink products, and production materials
Prepayments		589	Rent and insurance paid in advance
Property, plant, and equipment		21,599	Factories and production equipment
Investments		11,278	Amounts invested in shares of other corporations
Intangible assets		34,160	Economic resources that lack physical substance
Other assets		17,422	A variety of assets that are covered in future chapters
Total assets		110,916	
Liabilities			
Trade payables	13,033		Amounts owed to suppliers for prior purchases
Short-term borrowings	14,438		Amounts owed to lenders within one year
Income taxes payable	1,173		Amount of taxes owed to the government
Accrued liabilities	2,779		Amounts owed to various suppliers of services
Long-term borrowings	8,966		Amounts owed on written debt contracts after one year
Provisions	3,865		Estimated liabilities whose amounts and timing of payment are not Known with certainty
Other liabilities	13,031		A variety of liabilities that are covered in future chapters
Total liabilities		57,285	
Shareholders' Equity			
Share capital	6,248		Amounts invested in the business by shareholders
Retained earnings	64,660		Past earnings not distributed to shareholders
Other components	(17,277)		Adjustments to assets and liabilities that are explained in future chapters
Total shareholders' equity		53,631	
Total liabilities and shareholders' equity		110,916	

The notes are an integral part of these financial statements. This statement is an adaptation of Nestlé's actual statement of financial position. A more detailed statement of financial position is presented in Chapter 2.
Source: Nesté S.A.

The organization for which financial data are to be collected and reported is called an accounting entity. The accounting entity must be precisely defined and is often called the business or the corporation. On the statement of financial position, the accounting entity itself, not the business owners, is viewed as owning the resources it uses and as owing its debts.

An **ACCOUNTING ENTITY** is the organization for which financial data are to be collected.

The heading of the statement indicates the time dimension of the report. The statement of financial position is like a financial snapshot clearly stating the entity's financial position *at a specific point in time*—in this case, December 31, 2009—which is stated clearly on the statement. Financial reports are normally denominated in the currency of the country in which they are legally required to report their financial results. In this case, Nestlé reports in Swiss francs (abbreviated as CHF). Similarly, Canadian companies report in Canadian dollars and Mexican companies in Mexican pesos. Large-sized companies often report their financial figures in millions; that is, they round the last six digits to the nearest million. The inventories amount of CHF 7,734 on Nestlé's statement of financial position actually means CHF 7,734,000,000.

Nestlé's statement of financial position first lists the company's assets. Assets are economic resources legally controlled by the entity. Assets are followed by liabilities and shareholders' equity. These are the sources of financing or claims against the company's economic resources. Financing provided by creditors creates a liability. Financing provided by owners creates owners' equity. Because Nestlé is a corporation, its

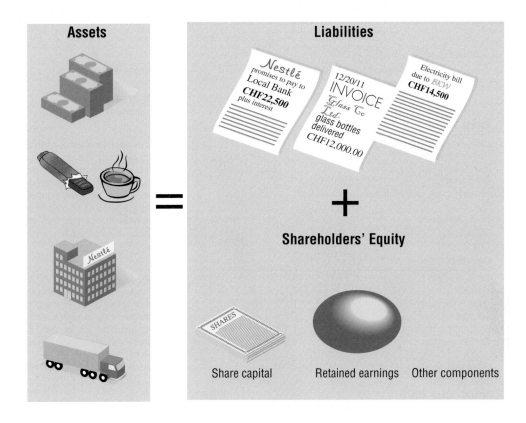

owners' equity is designated shareholders' equity. Since each asset must have a source of financing, a company's assets must, by definition, equal the sum of its liabilities and shareholders' equity.[2] The basic accounting equation, is written as

Assets	=	**Liabilities + Shareholders' Equity**
Economic resources (e.g., cash, inventory)		Sources of financing for the economic resources Liabilities: from creditors Shareholders' Equity: from shareholders

The basic accounting equation shows what we mean when we refer to a company's *financial position*: the economic resources that the company owns and the sources of financing for those resources.

Elements   *Assets* are economic resources controlled by the entity as a result of past business events and from which future economic benefits can be obtained. Nestlé lists eight items under the category *assets*. The specific items listed as assets on a company's statement of financial position depend on the nature of its operations. The eight items listed by Nestlé are the economic resources needed to provide future benefit to Nestlé through the production and sale of nutrition and health products to its customers. Each of these economic resources is expected to provide future benefits to the company. To prepare for the production process, Nestlé first needed *cash* to purchase *land* on which to build manufacturing facilities and install production machinery (*plant and equipment*). Nestlé needs to have insurance to protect its resources against potential losses; advance payment of any insurance premiums gave rise to *prepayments* that reflect future economic benefits (i.e., insurance protection). Nestlé then began making its baby

---

[2]A corporation is a business that is incorporated under the federal or provincial laws. The owners are called *shareholders* or *stockholders*. Ownership is represented by shares of capital that usually can be bought and sold freely. The corporation operates as a separate legal entity, separate and apart from its owners. The shareholders enjoy limited liability; they are liable for the debts of the corporation only to the extent of their investments. Appendix 1A discusses forms of ownership in more detail.

food products, which led to the value assigned to *inventories*. When Nestlé sells its nutrition and health products to retailers and wholesalers, it often sells them on credit and receives promises to pay called *trade receivables*, which are collected in cash later. As the company grew, it made *investments* in other companies. Nestlé also owns brands, trademarks, and intellectual property rights. These are called *intangible assets* because they do not have physical existence. Because of the complexity of Nestlé's operations, its resources include many *other assets*, which are explained in future chapters.

Every asset on the statement of financial position is initially measured at the total cost incurred to acquire it. Subsequent to acquisition, assets are reported on the statement of financial position at values that reflect the benefits the company expects to realize from these assets through use or sale.

Liabilities are the entity's legal obligations that result from past business events. They arise primarily from the purchase of goods or services on credit and through cash borrowings to finance the business.

There are seven types of liabilities listed on Nestlé's statement of financial position. The *trade payables* arise from the purchase of goods and services from suppliers on credit, without a formal written contract (or note). *Short-term borrowings* represent amounts borrowed from banks and other creditors, to be repaid in the near future. The *income taxes payable* represent an amount due to the government's tax authorities as a result of the company's profitable operations. The *accrued liabilities* are amounts owed to suppliers of various types of services, such as rent and utilities.

Long-term borrowings result from cash borrowings based on formal written debt contracts with lending institutions such as banks. The *provisions* are estimated amounts payable in the future, but the exact amount and timing of the payment depends on actual future events. Nestlé is a very large global company that incurs many *other liabilities*, which are identified and described in future chapters.

Shareholders' equity indicates the amount of financing provided by owners of shares in the business as well as earnings over time. Shareholders' equity arises from three sources: (1) *share capital*, or the investment of cash and other assets in the business by the owners in exchange for shares; (2) *retained earnings*, or the amount of earnings reinvested in the business (and thus not distributed to shareholders in the form of dividends); and (3) *other components* that essentially reflect the changes in the values of assets and liabilities over time.

In Exhibit 1.2, the Shareholders' Equity section reports three items. Nestlé's shareholders contributed cash and received shares of capital in exchange for their contributions. This is reported as share capital. Nestlé's profit less all dividends paid to the shareholders since formation of the corporation equalled CHF 64,660 and is reported as retained earnings. Total shareholders' equity is the sum of the proceeds received on issuing shares to owners, plus the retained earnings, and the valuation adjustments to the company's assets and liabilities at year-end.

INTERPRETING ASSETS, LIABILITIES, AND SHAREHOLDERS' EQUITY ON THE STATEMENT OF FINANCIAL POSITION

 FINANCIAL ANALYSIS

Assessment of Nestlé's assets is important to its creditors and to its owners because assets provide a basis for judging whether the company has sufficient resources available to operate the business. Assets are also important because they could be sold for cash in the event that Nestlé goes out of business.

Creditors are interested in Nestlé's debts because of their concern as to whether or not the company has sufficient sources of cash to pay its debt obligations. Nestlé's debts are also relevant to its bankers' decisions to lend money to the company because existing creditors share the bankers' claims against Nestlé's assets. Legal ownership of assets remains with the creditors to secure Nestlé's repayment of debt. If a business does not pay its creditors, the creditors may force the sale of assets sufficient to meet their claims. In some situations, the sale of assets may not cover the company's current debts, thus creditors often take a loss. This is because the assets were acquired with the intent of producing benefits in the context of other resources under the legal control of Nestlé. The assets, when taken out of that context, rarely will be seen by external parties as having the same potential benefit for them as the assets had for Nestlé. Thus, creditors may not be able to sell the assets for the amount of the debt.

Nestlé's shareholders' equity or net worth is important to creditors because, legally, their claims for repayment of obligations must be settled before those of the owners. If Nestlé goes out of business and its assets are sold, the proceeds of that sale must be used to pay back creditors before the shareholders receive any money. Shareholders provide resources for the company to use in future, with no promise of any future repayment. They are entitled to what is left only after all other claims have been settled. Thus, creditors consider shareholders' equity a protective cushion.

A Note on Format   A few additional formatting conventions are worth noting here. Assets may be listed on the statement of financial position in either increasing or decreasing order of their convertibility to cash. Some international companies, like Nestlé, list their assets beginning with the most liquid asset, cash, and ending with the least liquid assets that are not readily convertible to cash, such as patents. In contrast, other companies list their least liquid assets, such as intangibles, first and most liquid assets last. Similarly, liabilities may be listed by either increasing or decreasing order of maturity (due date). International Accounting Standard 1 allows companies to use either format to report their assets and liabilities.

Most financial statements include the monetary unit sign (in Canada, the $) beside the first amount in a group of items (e.g., share capital in Shareholders' equity). Also, it is common to place a single underline below the last item in a group before a total or subtotal (e.g., Other assets). A double underline is also placed below group totals (e.g., Total assets). The same conventions are followed in all four basic financial statements.

SELF STUDY **QUIZ 1-1**

1. Nestlé's *assets* are listed in one section and *liabilities* and *shareholders' equity* in another. Notice that the two sections balance, in conformity with the basic accounting equation. In the following chapters, you will learn that the accounting equation is the basic building block for the entire accounting process. Your task here is to verify that the shareholders' equity of CHF 53,631 is correct, using the numbers for assets and liabilities presented in Exhibit 1.2 and the basic accounting equation in the form

Assets − Liabilities = Shareholders' Equity

2. Learning which items belong in each of the categories on the statement of financial position is an important first step in understanding their meaning. Mark each item in the following list as an asset (A), a liability (L), or shareholders' equity (SE), without referring to Exhibit 1.2.

_____ Trade payables   _____ Inventories

_____ Trade receivables   _____ Bank borrowings

_____ Cash   _____ Provisions

_____ Share capital   _____ Retained earnings

_____ Property, plant, and equipment

After you complete your answers, go online for the solutions.

The Statement of Comprehensive Income

Structure   The statement of comprehensive income reports the change in shareholders' equity, during a period, from business activities other than investments by shareholders or distributions to shareholders. It includes all changes in equity during a period except those resulting from investments by owners (such as the issuance of shares) and distributions to owners (such as dividends). The statement of comprehensive income has two parts. The first part reports the accountant's primary measure of a company's performance: revenues generated less expenses incurred during the accounting period. Accountants label this measure of performance "profit." The second part reports other comprehensive income, which comprises income and expense items that are not recognized in the income statement in accordance with International Financial Reporting Standards.

Companies can present all items of income and expenses either in one statement of comprehensive income or in two related statements—an income statement reporting the revenues and expenses that have already affected profit, and a statement of comprehensive income reporting income and expense items that will affect profit in the future. We discuss the income statement in this chapter and the statement of comprehensive income in Chapters 6 and 12.

Nestlé uses the two-statement approach. A quick reading of Nestlé's income statement (Exhibit 1.3) provides an indication about its purpose and content. The heading of the income statement again identifies the name of the entity, title of the statement, and unit of measure used in the statement. Unlike the statement of financial position,

The **STATEMENT OF COMPREHENSIVE INCOME** reports the change in shareholders' equity, during a period, from business activities, excluding exchanges with shareholders.

The **INCOME STATEMENT** reports the revenues less the expenses of the accounting period.

Statement of Comprehensive Income

Revenues
– Expenses

Profit
+ Other comprehensive income

Comprehensive income

Exhibit **1.3**

Income Statement

THE NESTLÉ GROUP Income Statement For the Year Ended December 31, 2009 (in thousands of CHF, except for EPS)			
Revenues			Name of the entity Title of the statement Accounting period Unit of measure
Sales revenue	107,618		Revenue earned from sale of food and drink products
Other income	1,309		Income from investments and profit on sale of assets
Total revenues		108,927	
Expenses			
Cost of goods sold	45,208		Cost to produce food and drink products that have been sold
Distribution	8,420		Expenses related to distribution of Nestlé's products
Marketing and administration	36,270		Expenses related to marketing and promotion of Nestlé's products, and administration of the company's business activities
Research and development	2,021		Expenses related to research and development of new products
Other expenses	1,238		A variety of expenses that are covered in future chapters
Interest expense	615		Cost of using borrowed funds
Total expenses		93,772	
Profit before income taxes		15,155	
Income tax expense		3,362	Income taxes on the period's pretax profit
Profit for the year		11,793	
Earnings per share		2.92	

The notes are an integral part of these financial statements.
This income statement is an adaptation of Nestlé's actual income statement for 2009.
Source: Nestlé S.A.

The **ACCOUNTING PERIOD** is the time period covered by the financial statements.

which reports financial information as of a certain date, the income statement reports information for a *specified period of time* (for the year ended December 31, 2009). The time period covered by the financial statements (one year in this case) is called an accounting period.

Revenues   –   Expenses   =   Profit

Notice that Nestlé's income statement has three major captions: revenues, expenses, and profit. The income statement equation that describes this relationship is

$$\textbf{Revenues} - \textbf{Expenses} = \textbf{Profit}$$

Elements   Companies earn *revenues* from the sale of goods or services to customers (in Nestlé's case, from the sale of nutrition and health products). Revenues are normally reported on the income statement when the goods or services are sold to customers **whether or not they have been paid for**. Retail stores such as Walmart or McDonald's often receive cash at the time of sale. However, when Nestlé sells its nutrition and health products to wholesale distributors, it receives a promise of future payment called a trade receivable, which is collected in cash at a later date. In either case, the business recognizes the total of cash and credit sales made during a specific accounting period as revenue for that period. Various terms are used in financial statements to describe different sources of revenue (e.g., provision of services, sale of goods, rental of property). Nestlé lists two sources: *sales revenue*, from selling nutrition and health products, and *other income* from its investments as well as profit from selling property, plant, and equipment.

Expenses represent the monetary value of resources the entity used up, or consumed, to earn revenues during the period. Nestlé lists seven items as expenses on the income statement. The ***cost of sales*** (or *cost of goods sold*) is Nestlé's total cost to produce the nutrition and health products sold to customers during the year. These include the costs of ingredients, wages paid to the factory workers, and even a portion of the cost of buildings, equipment, and tools used (called ***depreciation***) to produce the goods that were sold. ***Distribution expenses*** include a variety of expenses such as the salaries of sales staff and expenses related to distribution of the company's products. ***Marketing and administrative expenses*** include items such as the salaries of marketing and management personnel, promotion of the company's products through print and electronic media, rental of office space, insurance, utilities, plus other general costs of operating the company not directly related to production. ***Research and development expenses*** relate to the research and development of new products. The ***other expenses*** consist of a variety of expenses that are not included in the previous categories.

Nestlé also reported ***interest expense***, which reflects the cost of using borrowed funds. Finally, as a corporation, Nestlé must pay income tax to the government. Nestlé's ***income tax expense*** for 2009 is approximately 16.5 percent of its pretax profit.

Expenses may require immediate payment of cash, payment of cash at a future date, or use of some other resource, such as an inventory item, that may have been paid for in a previous period. For accounting purposes, the expense reported in one accounting period may actually be paid for in cash in another accounting period. Nevertheless, the company recognizes all expenses (cash and credit) incurred during a specific accounting period regardless of the timing of the cash payment. For example, let us assume that Nestlé owes CHF 50,000 in sales commissions to salespeople who sold nutrition and health items to retailers in December 2009, but it did not pay the CHF 50,000 until January 2010. In this case, the sales commissions would be recognized as expenses for the accounting period ending on December 31, 2009, because during December 2009 the salespeople exerted the efforts resulting in commissions for successfully selling the company's various products.

Profit (also called *net income* or *net earnings*) is the excess of total revenues over total expenses incurred to generate revenue during a specific period. Nestlé's profit for the year measures its success in selling nutrition and health goods for more than it cost to generate those sales. If total expenses exceed total revenues, a loss is reported. (Losses are normally noted by parentheses around the reported figure.) When revenues and expenses are equal for the period, the business has operated at breakeven.

We noted earlier that revenues are not necessarily the same as collections from customers, and expenses are not necessarily the same as payments to suppliers. As a result, profit normally **does not equal** the net cash generated by operations. This latter amount is reported on the statement of cash flows discussed later in the chapter.

ANALYZING THE INCOME STATEMENT

FINANCIAL
ANALYSIS

Investors and creditors closely monitor a firm's profit because it indicates the firm's ability to sell goods and services for more than they cost to produce and deliver. Investors buy the company's shares when they believe that profit will improve and lead to a higher share price. Lenders also rely on future earnings to provide the resources to repay loans. The details of the statement also are important. For example, Nestlé had to sell CHF 107,618 million worth of nutrition and health products to earn CHF 11,793 million. If a competitor were to lower prices just by 10 percent, forcing Nestlé to do the same in order to retain its market share, or if Nestlé had to triple market development to catch up to a competitor, its profit could be reduced significantly and may turn into a loss. These factors and others help investors and creditors estimate the company's future profit based on past information.

SELF STUDY **QUIZ 1-2**

1. Learning which items belong in each of the income statement categories is an important first step in understanding their meaning. Mark each income statement item in the following list as a revenue (R) or an expense (E), without referring to Exhibit 1.3.

    _____ Cost of goods sold   _____ Selling and administrative

    _____ Sales

2. During the year 2009, Nestlé delivered nutrition and health products to customers for which the customers paid, or promised to pay in the future, amounts totalling CHF 107,618 million. During the same period, it collected CHF 110,060 million in cash from its customers. Without referring to Exhibit 1.3, indicate which of the two amounts will be shown on Nestlé's income statement as *sales revenue* for 2009. Explain.

3. During the year 2009, Nestlé *produced* nutrition and health items with a total production cost of CHF 43,515 million. During the same period, it *delivered* to customers goods that had cost a total of CHF 45,208 million to produce. Without referring to Exhibit 1.3, indicate which of the two amounts will be shown on Nestlé's income statement as *cost of goods sold* for 2009. Explain.

After you complete your answers, go online for the solutions.

connect

The Statement of Changes in Equity

The **STATEMENT OF CHANGES IN EQUITY** reports all changes to shareholders' equity during the accounting period.

Structure   Nestlé prepares a separate statement of changes in equity, shown in Exhibit 1.4 in a condensed format.[3] The heading identifies the name of the entity, title of the statement, and unit of measure used. Like the income statement, the statement of changes in equity covers a specific period of time (the accounting period), which in this case is one year. This statement reports the way that profit, distribution of profit (dividends), and other changes to shareholders' equity affected the company's financial position during the accounting period. We focus on retained earnings in this chapter and discuss the other components of equity in later chapters.

RETAINED EARNINGS reflect the profits that have been earned since the creation of the company but not distributed yet to shareholders as dividends.

Profit earned during the year increases the balance of retained earnings. The declaration of dividends to the shareholders decreases retained earnings.[4] The retained earnings equation that describes these relationships is

Beginning retained earnings + Profit − Dividends = Ending retained earnings

Statement of Changes in Equity

Equity, beginning of the period
+ Profit for the year
+ Other comprehensive income
− Dividends
+/− Other changes, net

Equity, end of the period

Elements   The statement begins with Nestlé's balances to share capital, retained earnings, and other equity components at January 1, 2009 (the beginning of the accounting period). The profit reported on the income statement for the current period is added to the beginning balance of retained earnings, and dividends declared during the year are subtracted from this amount. During 2009, Nestlé earned CHF 11,793 million, as shown in Exhibit 1.3. Also during 2009, Nestlé declared and paid a total of CHF 5,779 million in dividends to its shareholders. The net result is that retained earnings at December 31, 2009, (the end of the accounting period) increased by CHF 6,014 million (=11,793 million − 5,779 million), or the portion of the 2009 profit reinvested in the business.

The ending retained earnings amount of CHF 64,660 million is the same as that reported in Exhibit 1.2 on Nestlé's statement of financial position. The ending balances of share capital and other components are also reported on the statement of financial position. Thus, the statement of changes in equity shows how the income

---

Exhibit **1.4**

Statement of Changes in Equity

	THE NESTLÉ GROUP		
	Statement of Changes in Equity		
	For the Year Ended December 31, 2009		
	(in millions of CHF)		
	Share Capital	Retained Earnings	Other Components
Balance as at Jan. 1, 2009	6,266	58,646	(9,996)
Profit for the year		11,793	
Distribution of dividends		(5,779)	
Decrease in share capital	(18)		
Other comprehensive income			(834)
Other changes, net			(6,447)
Balance as at Dec. 31, 2009	6,248	64,660	(17,277)

Name of the entity → THE NESTLÉ GROUP
Title of the statement → Statement of Changes in Equity
Accounting period → For the Year Ended December 31, 2009
Unit of measure → (in millions of CHF)

Last period ending balances → Balance as at Jan. 1, 2009
Profit reported on the income statement → Profit for the year
Dividends declared during the period → Distribution of dividends
Issuance of additional share capital during the year → Decrease in share capital
Adjustments to the balances of specific assets and liabilities → Other changes, net
Ending balances reported on the statement of financial position → Balance as at Dec. 31, 2009

The notes are an integral part of these financial statements.
This statement is an adaptation of Nestlé's actual statement of changes in equity for 2009.
Source: Nestlé S.A.

---

[3] A detailed version of the statement of changes in equity is discussed in Chapter 6.

[4] Retained earnings decrease when expenses exceed revenues, resulting in a loss. The complete process of declaring and paying dividends is discussed in a later chapter.

statement and the statement of financial position are linked through the retained earnings section of shareholders' equity.

INTERPRETING RETAINED EARNINGS

FINANCIAL ANALYSIS

Reinvestment of profit, or retained earnings, is an important source of financing for Nestlé, representing over one-half of its financing. Creditors closely monitor a firm's retained earnings because the firm's policy on dividend payments to its shareholders affects its ability to repay its debts. Every Swiss franc Nestlé pays to shareholders as a dividend is not available for use in paying back its debt to creditors. The reverse is also true; every Swiss franc used to repay creditors is unavailable either for distribution to investors as dividends or for retention and reinvestment in the company's future growth. Investors examine retained earnings to determine whether the company is reinvesting a sufficient portion of profit to support future growth.

SELF STUDY QUIZ 1-3

Nestlé's retained earnings reflect the way that the profit and distribution of dividends affected the financial position of the company during the accounting period. In a prior period, Nestlé's financial statements reported the following amounts: beginning retained earnings, CHF 52,827 million; total assets, CHF 109,908 million; dividends, CHF 4,982 million; cost of goods sold, CHF 47,339 million; and profit, CHF 19,051 million. Without referring to Exhibit 1.4, compute ending retained earnings.

After you complete your answers, go online for the solutions.

connect

The Statement of Cash Flows

Structure Nestlé's statement of cash flows, presented in Exhibit 1.5, divides Nestlé's cash inflows (receipts) and outflows (payments) into three primary categories of cash flows in a typical business: cash flows from operating, investing, and financing activities. The heading identifies the name of the entity, title of the statement, and unit of measure used. Like the income statement, the statement of cash flows covers a specified period of time (the accounting period), which in this case is one year.

As discussed earlier in this chapter, reported revenues do not always equal cash collected from customers because some sales may be on credit. Also, expenses reported on the income statement may not be equal to cash paid out during the period because expenses may be incurred in one period and paid for in another. As a result, profit (revenues minus expenses) does *not* usually equal the amount of cash received minus the amount paid during the period. Because the income statement does not provide any information concerning cash flows, accountants prepare the statement of cash flows to report inflows and outflows of cash.

The statement of cash flows equation describes the causes of the change in cash reported on the statement of financial position from the end of the last period to the end of the current period:

> $+/-$ **Cash flows from operating activities**
> $+/-$ **Cash flows from investing activities**
> $+/-$ **Cash flows from financing activities**
> **Change in cash**

Note that each of the three cash flow sources can be either positive or negative.

Elements *Cash flows from operating activities* are cash flows that are directly related to earning income. For example, when retailers pay Nestlé for the nutrition and health products it delivered to them, Nestlé lists the amounts collected as cash

The **STATEMENT OF CASH FLOWS** reports cash inflows and outflows that are related to operating, investing, and financing activities during the accounting period.

Statement of Cash Flows

$+/-$ CFO
$+/-$ CFI
$+/-$ CFF

Change in cash

Exhibit **1.5**

Statement of Cash Flows

Name of the entity	**THE NESTLÉ GROUP**
Title of the statement	**Statement of Cash Flows**
Accounting period	**For the year ended December 31, 2009**
Unit of measure	**(in millions of CHF)**
Directly related to earning income	**Cash flows from operating activities**
	Cash collected from customers ... 110,060
	Cash paid to trade suppliers ... (43,175)
	Cash paid to employees ... (16,333)
	Cash paid for general and administrative expenses ... (29,294)
	Cash paid for interest ... (566)
	Cash paid for taxes ... (2,758)
	Net cash flow from operating activities ... 17,934
Purchase/sale of financial and productive assets	**Cash flows from investing activities**
	Cash paid to purchase property, plant, and equipment ... (4,641)
	Cash paid to purchase intangible assets ... (400)
	Cash received for sale of property, plant, and equipment ... 111
	Cash paid to purchase businesses ... (796)
	Cash received for sale of businesses ... 242
	Cash received from other investing activities ... 85
	Net cash flow used for investing activities ... (5,399)
From investors and creditors	**Cash flows from financing activities**
	Cash paid for dividends ... (5,779)
	Cash paid to repurchase issued share capital ... (6,721)
	Cash received from long-term borrowings ... 3,957
	Repayment of long-term borrowings ... (1,744)
	Repayment of short-term bank borrowings ... (446)
	Cash paid for purchase of short-term investments ... (1,759)
	Cash paid for other financing activities ... (53)
	Net cash flow used for financing activities ... (12,545)
Change in cash during the period	**Net decrease in cash during the year** ... (10)
Last period's ending cash balance	**Cash at beginning of year** ... 5,835
Ending cash on the statement of financial position	**Cash at end of year** ... 5,825

The notes are an integral part of these financial statements.
This statement is an adaptation of Nestlé's actual statement of cash flows.
Source: Nestlé S.A.

collected from customers. When Nestlé pays salaries or bills received for materials, it includes the amounts in cash paid to employees and trade suppliers.[5]

Cash flows from investing activities include cash flows related to the acquisition or sale of the company's productive assets. This year, Nestlé had three cash outflows for investing activities: purchase of additional property, plant, and equipment to meet the growing demand for its products; purchase of intangible assets; and acquisition of other businesses. It also received cash for selling some of its businesses and old equipment.

Cash flows from financing activities are directly related to the financing of the company itself. They involve both receipts and payments of cash to investors and creditors. During 2009, Nestlé paid CHF 5,779 million in dividends to the company's shareholders as well as CHF 6,721 million to buy back shares that were previously issued to shareholders. It also paid CFH 2,190 million to reduce both short-term and long-term borrowings, and CHF 1,759 million to purchase short-term investments. Nestlé received CHF 3,957 million by signing on long-term borrowings.

---

[5]Alternative ways to present cash flows from operating activities are discussed in Chapter 5.

INTERPRETING THE STATEMENT OF CASH FLOWS

FINANCIAL
ANALYSIS

Many analysts believe that the statement of cash flows is particularly useful for predicting future cash flows that may be available for payment of debt to creditors and dividends to investors. Bankers often consider the operating activities section to be the most important because it indicates the company's ability to generate cash from sales to meet its current cash needs. Any amount left can be used to repay the bank debt or expand the company.

Shareholders will invest in a company if they believe that it will eventually generate more cash from operations than it uses, so that cash will become available to pay dividends and to expand. The investing activities section shows that Nestlé has made significant investments in new manufacturing capacity, a good sign if demand continues to increase. The financing activities section indicates that Nestlé was able to pay dividends to shareholders and repay part of its short-term and long-term borrowings because it generated cash from operating activities.

SELF STUDY **QUIZ 1-4**

1. During the period 2009, Nestlé delivered nutrition and health products to customers that paid, or promised to pay in the future, amounts totalling CHF 107,618 million. During the same period, it collected CHF 110,060 million in cash from its customers. Without referring to Exhibit 1.5, indicate which of the two numbers will be shown on Nestlé's statement of cash flows for 2009.

2. Learning which items belong in each category on the statement of cash flows is an important first step in understanding their meaning. Mark each item in the following list as a cash flow from operating activities (O), investing activities (I), or financing activities (F), without referring to Exhibit 1.5. Also place parentheses around the letter only if it is a cash *outflow*.

   _____ Cash paid for dividends

   _____ Cash paid for interest

   _____ Cash received from bank borrowings

   _____ Cash paid for taxes

   _____ Cash paid to purchase property, plant, and equipment

   _____ Cash collected from customers

After you complete your answers, go online for the solutions.

connect

Relationships among the Four Financial Statements

Our discussion of the four basic financial statements focused on the different elements reported on each of the statements, how the elements are related through the equation for each statement, and how the elements are important to the decisions of investors, creditors, and other external users. We have also discovered how the statements, all of which are outputs from the same system, are related to one another. In particular, we learned that

1. Profit from the income statement results in an increase in ending retained earnings on the statement of changes in equity.

2. Ending retained earnings from the statement of changes in equity is one of the three components of shareholders' equity on the statement of financial position.

3. The change in cash on the statement of cash flows added to the cash balance at the beginning of the year equals the balance of cash at the end of the year, which appears on the statement of financial position.

Thus, as external users, we can think of the income statement (and the statement of comprehensive income) as explaining, through the statement of changes in equity, how the operations of the company changed its financial position during the year. The statement of cash flows explains how the operating, investing, and financing activities of the company affected the cash balance on the statement of financial position during the year. These relationships are illustrated in Exhibit 1.6 for Nestlé's financial statements.

Exhibit **1.6**

Relationships among Nestlé's Statements

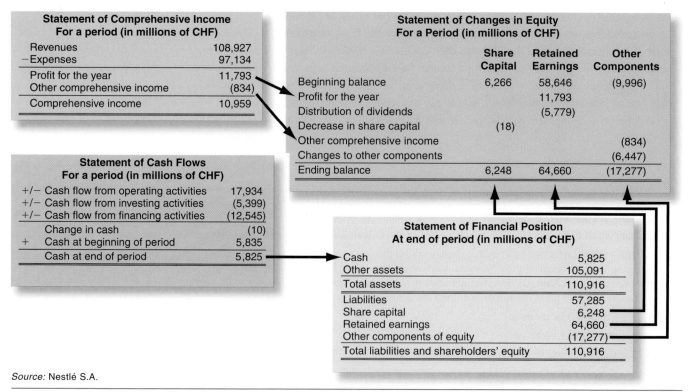

Statement of Comprehensive Income For a period (in millions of CHF)	
Revenues	108,927
−Expenses	97,134
Profit for the year	11,793
Other comprehensive income	(834)
Comprehensive income	10,959

Statement of Cash Flows For a period (in millions of CHF)	
+/− Cash flow from operating activities	17,934
+/− Cash flow from investing activities	(5,399)
+/− Cash flow from financing activities	(12,545)
Change in cash	(10)
+ Cash at beginning of period	5,835
Cash at end of period	5,825

Statement of Changes in Equity For a Period (in millions of CHF)	Share Capital	Retained Earnings	Other Components
Beginning balance	6,266	58,646	(9,996)
Profit for the year		11,793	
Distribution of dividends		(5,779)	
Decrease in share capital	(18)		
Other comprehensive income			(834)
Changes to other components			(6,447)
Ending balance	6,248	64,660	(17,277)

Statement of Financial Position At end of period (in millions of CHF)	
Cash	5,825
Other assets	105,091
Total assets	110,916
Liabilities	57,285
Share capital	6,248
Retained earnings	64,660
Other components of equity	(17,277)
Total liabilities and shareholders' equity	110,916

Source: Nestlé S.A.

FINANCIAL ANALYSIS

MANAGEMENT USES OF FINANCIAL STATEMENTS

In our discussion of financial analysis thus far, we have focused on the perspectives of investors and creditors. In addition, managers within the firm often make direct use of financial statements. For example, Nestlé's *marketing managers* and *credit managers* use customers' financial statements to decide whether to extend credit to them for their purchases of nutrition and health goods. Nestlé's *purchasing managers* analyze financial statements of suppliers to judge whether the suppliers have the resources to meet Nestlé's demand for ingredients and invest in the development of new ingredients. Both Nestlé's *human resource managers* and the *employees' union* use the company's financial statements as a basis for contract negotiations over pay rates. The profit figure even serves as a basis for computing *employee bonuses*.

When Nestlé's managers examine the financial statements of the company's customers and suppliers, they rely on these statements as the best source of financial information available to external users because they do not have access to internal financial information produced by their customers and their suppliers. However, when they make internal decisions regarding Nestlé's operations, they rely on more detailed financial information obtained through the company's managerial accounting system.

Notes to Financial Statements

At the bottom of each of the four basic financial statements you will typically find the following statement: ***"The notes are an integral part of these financial statements."*** This is the accounting equivalent of the nutritional content on pre-packaged food. It warns users that failure to read the notes (or footnotes) to these financial statements will result in incomplete knowledge of the company's financial health. Notes provide supplemental information about the financial condition of a company, without which the financial statements cannot be fully understood.

NOTES (FOOTNOTES) provide supplemental information about the financial condition of a company, without which the financial statements cannot be fully understood.

There are three basic types of notes. The first type provides descriptions of the accounting rules applied in the company's statements. The second presents additional detail about a line on the financial statements. For example, Nestlé's inventory note indicates the costs of raw materials and supplies, nutrition and health items that are in the process of being completed, and finished products that are ready for sale to customers. The third type of note presents additional financial disclosures about items not listed on the statements themselves. For example, Nestlé is exposed to significant risks; the risks related to credit and fluctuations in exchange rates are disclosed in a note. We will discuss many note disclosures throughout the book because understanding their content is critical to understanding the company.[6]

Summary of the Four Basic Financial Statements

We learned a lot about the content of the four basic statements. Exhibit 1.7 summarizes this information. Take a few minutes to review the information in the exhibit before you move on to the next section of the chapter.

DETERMINING NESTLÉ'S PURCHASE PRICE

FINANCIAL ANALYSIS

Even at this early stage of your study of accounting, we can illustrate part of the process that investors may use to determine the price they are willing to pay for Nestlé. The price is decided by considering a variety of factors, including the value of Nestlé's assets, its debts to others, its ability to sell goods for more than their production cost, and its ability to generate the cash necessary to pay its current bills. These factors are the subject matter of Nestlé's financial statements.

In general, investors use prior years' financial performance to make projections about future performance. They may be willing to pay for a firm that reported high profit in the past if they believe it will produce higher profit in the future.

One method for estimating the value of a company that relies on net earnings and growth in earnings is with a ***price/earnings ratio*** (or *P/E ratio* or *P/E multiple*). The P/E ratio measures the multiple of current year's earnings that investors are willing to pay for the company's shares. A high P/E ratio means that investors have confidence in the company's ability to produce higher profits in future years.

---

[6]The basic financial statements and related notes are part of more elaborate documents called *annual reports* that are produced by public companies. Annual reports are normally split into two sections. The first is non-financial and usually includes a letter to shareholders from the chairperson of the company's board of directors and the chief executive officer; descriptions of the company's management philosophy, products, successes (and occasionally failures); exciting prospects and challenges for the future; as well as beautiful photographs of products, facilities, and personnel.

The second section includes the core of the report. The principal components of this financial section include summarized financial data for five or ten years, management's discussion and analysis of the company's financial condition and results of operations, four financial statements and related notes, auditor's report, recent stock price information, a summary of quarterly financial data, and a list of directors and officers of the company.

Competitors' P/E ratios often serve as a starting point in analyzing the price that should be paid for a company or its shares. If we assume that other companies in the same industry with similar performance and past growth were selling for 15 times their current year's earnings, then the price per share could be determined by using the following computation:

$$\text{Price/Earnings ratio} = \frac{\text{Market Price}}{\text{Earnings per share (EPS)}}$$
$$\text{Market (Purchase) price} = \text{P/E ratio} \times \text{EPS}$$
$$= 15 \times \text{CHF } 2.92$$
$$= \text{CHF } 43.80 \text{ per share}$$

The role of net earnings in determining the value of a company will be discussed in more detail in your corporate finance course and more advanced courses in financial statement analysis.

Exhibit **1.7**

Summary of Four Basic Financial Statements

Financial Statement	Purpose	Structure	Examples of Content
Statement of Financial Position	Reports the financial position (economic resources and sources of financing) of an accounting entity *at a point in time*.	Statement of Financial Position Assets = Liabilities + Shareholders' Equity	Cash, trade receivables, plant and equipment, notes payable, share capital
Statement of Comprehensive Income (including the Income Statement)	Reports the profit achieved *during the accounting period*, as well as income and expense items that are not recognized in profit.	Statement of Comprehensive Income Revenues − Expenses Profit + Other comprehensive income Comprehensive income	Sales revenue, cost of sales, selling expense, interest expense
Statement of Changes in Equity	Reports the way that elements of comprehensive income, dividends, and changes to share capital affected the financial position of the company *during the accounting period*.	Statement of Changes in Equity Equity, beginning of the period + Profit for the year + Other comprehensive income − Dividends +/− Other changes, net Equity, end of the period	Retained earnings, elements of comprehensive income, distributions of dividends, increase in share capital
Statement of Cash Flows	Reports inflows (receipts) and outflows (payments) of cash *during the accounting period* in the categories operating, investing, and financing.	Statement of Cash Flows +/− CFO +/− CFI +/− CFF Change in cash	Cash collected from customers, cash paid to suppliers, cash paid to purchase equipment, cash borrowed from banks

LO²

Identify the role of International Financial Reporting Standards (IFRS) in determining the content of financial statements.

RESPONSIBILITIES FOR THE ACCOUNTING COMMUNICATION PROCESS

Effective communication means that the recipient understands what the sender intends to convey. For decision makers to use the information in Nestlé's financial statements effectively, they have to understand what information each statement conveys.

They also need to know that the amounts reported in the statements fairly represent what is claimed. Financial statements that do not represent what they claim to are meaningless and cannot be used effectively to make decisions. For example, if the statement of financial position lists $2,000,000 for a factory that does not exist, that part of the statement does not convey useful information.

Decision makers also need to understand the ***measurement rules*** applied in computing the numbers on the statements. A swim coach would never try to evaluate a swimmer's time in the "100 freestyle" without first asking whether the time was for a race in metres or in yards. Likewise, a decision maker should never attempt to use accounting information without first understanding the measurement rules that were used to develop the information. These measurement rules are based on International Financial Reporting Standards (IFRS). These encompass broad principles, specific rules, practices, and conventions of general application that are used by organizations to record transactions and report financial statement information to interested users.

> **INTERNATIONAL FINANCIAL REPORTING STANDARDS (IFRS)** are guidelines for the measurement rules used to develop the information in financial statements.

International Financial Reporting Standards (IFRS)

How are Accounting Standards Determined?   The accounting system that we use today has a long history. Its foundations are normally traced back to the works of an Italian monk and mathematician, Fr. Luca Pacioli. In 1494, he described an approach developed by Italian merchants to account for their activities as owner-managers of business ventures. Many others wrote works on accounting after Pacioli, but prior to 1933, each company's management largely determined its own financial reporting practices. Thus, little uniformity in practice existed among companies.

Following the dramatic stock market decline of 1929, the *Securities Act* of 1933 and the *Securities Exchange Act* of 1934 were passed into law by the U.S. Congress. These acts created the Securities and Exchange Commission (SEC) and gave it broad powers to determine the measurement rules for financial statements that companies must provide to shareholders. In Canada, provincial securities legislation created securities commissions, most notably the Ontario Securities Commission (OSC), to regulate the flow of financial information provided by publicly traded companies whose shares trade on Canadian stock exchanges, such as the Toronto Stock Exchange. Similar to the SEC, the OSC plays an influential role in promotion, surveillance, and enforcement of sound accounting practices by publicly traded companies. The OSC is one of 13 securities regulators of Canada's provinces and territories. These regulators have formed the Canadian Securities Administrators, which coordinates and harmonizes regulation of the Canadian capital markets among them.

> The **SECURITIES AND EXCHANGE COMMISSION (SEC)** is the U.S. government agency that determines the financial statements that public companies must provide to shareholders and the measurement rules that they must use in producing those statements.

> The **ONTARIO SECURITIES COMMISSION (OSC)** is the most influential Canadian regulator of the flow of financial information provided by publicly traded companies in Canada.

Since their establishment, these securities commissions have worked with organizations of professional accountants to establish groups that are given the primary responsibilities to work out the detailed rules that become generally accepted accounting principles. The current Canadian group that has this responsibility is the Accounting Standards Board (AcSB) of the Canadian Institute of Chartered Accountants. The AcSB is responsible for establishing standards of accounting and reporting by publicly accountable enterprises, private enterprises, government organizations, and not-for-profit organizations. These standards or recommendations, which are published in the *CICA Handbook*, have expanded over time because of the increasing diversity and complexity of business practices. The OSC performs surveillance and enforcement functions for legal requirements arising from standards in the *CICA Handbook*.

> The **ACCOUNTING STANDARDS BOARD (AcSB)** is the private-sector body given the primary responsibility to work out the detailed rules that become accepted accounting standards.

In January 2006, the AcSB publicized the strategic plan that guided the Board in carrying out its standard-setting mandate for the next five years:[7]

---

[7]*Accounting Standards in Canada: New Directions—Strategic Plan*, Canadian Institute of Chartered Accountants, 2006, page 1.

For public companies, the AcSB's objective is to move to a single set of globally accepted high-quality standards. The AcSB has concluded that this objective is best accomplished by converging Canadian GAAP with International Financial Reporting Standards (IFRSs) over a transitional period. Australia and the European Union have already adopted IFRS and other countries have convergence programs underway. The AcSB will develop and publish a detailed implementation plan for achieving convergence later this year.... The AcSB expects that the transition period will take approximately five years, but the precise timing will depend on many factors, and will be continuously monitored throughout the process. At the end of that period, Canadian GAAP will cease to exist as a separate, distinct basis of financial reporting for public companies.

The AcSB implemented its plan by requiring all publicly accountable enterprises to use IFRS in reporting their financial statements for fiscal years (annual accounting periods) that start on or after January 1, 2011. Some Canadian companies, such as Thomson Reuters Corporation, adopted IFRS for financial reporting prior to 2011, but the majority of public companies adopted IFRS in 2011.

The **INTERNATIONAL ACCOUNTING STANDARDS BOARD** is an independent standard-setting board that is responsible for the development and publication of International Financial Reporting Standards.

International Financial Accounting Standards are produced by the International Accounting Standards Board (IASB), which is an independent standard-setting board consisting of 15 members from nine countries. The IASB co-operates with national accounting standard-setters to achieve convergence in accounting standards around the world.[8] The IASB initially issued International Accounting Standards (IAS). New IASs are known as International Financial Reporting Standards.

This book focuses on the accounting and financial reporting by publicly accountable enterprises. The accounting and financial reporting standards used by other types of organizations are covered in advanced accounting courses. Differences between the accounting standards applicable to Canadian private enterprises and Canadian publicly accountable enterprises are highlighted at the end of each chapter.

Most managers do not need to learn all of the details included in all accounting standards. Our approach is to focus on standards appropriate to an introductory course, which have the greatest effect on the numbers presented in financial statements.

Why Are Accounting Standards Important to Managers and External Users?

Accounting standards are of great interest to the companies that must prepare the statements and to the readers of these statements. IFRS provide guidance to companies in selecting the accounting methods that best reflect the results of their operations and financial situation. These globally accepted accounting standards also prevent managers from deliberately manipulating and reporting values that serve their personal interests by using accounting practices not in conformity with IFRS. Widely divergent accounting practices reduce the comparability of financial information from different companies operating in the same line of business. IFRS enhances the comparability by limiting the number of acceptable alternative accounting methods across companies and over time. Furthermore, understanding IFRS enables external users to assess the quality of the information presented in the financial statements and related notes.

Companies, their managers, and their owners are most directly affected by the information presented in the financial statements. Companies incur the cost of preparing the statements and bear the major economic consequences of their publication. These economic consequences include, among others,

1. changes to the selling price of a company's shares,

2. changes to the amount of bonuses received by management and employees, and

3. loss of competitive advantage over other companies.

---

[8]The IASB's website (www.ifrs.org) provides more details about the process of producing IFRS.

THE INTERNATIONAL ACCOUNTING STANDARDS BOARD AND GLOBAL CONVERGENCE OF ACCOUNTING STANDARDS

REAL WORLD EXCERPT

Deloitte IAS Plus Website

(www.iasplus.com)

Financial accounting standards and disclosure requirements are set by national regulatory agencies and standard-setting bodies. However, since 2002, the International Accounting Standards Board (IASB) has progressed quickly to fulfill its responsibility to produce International Financial Reporting Standards (IFRS). More than 100 countries have adopted the international standards. Countries currently requiring use of IFRS include

All countries in the European Union

Australia and New Zealand

India, Hong Kong, and South Korea

Brazil and Chile

China

Canada

In the United States, the SEC allows foreign companies whose shares are traded on U.S. exchange markets to use IFRS and is considering allowing the same for domestic companies in the future.

Source: Deloitte IAS PLUS website.

Recall that Nestlé's share price can be determined in part based on the profit computed in compliance with IFRS. This presents the possibility that changes in accounting standards can affect the price buyers are willing to pay for companies. Employees who receive part of their pay based on reaching stated profit targets are directly concerned with any changes in how profit is determined. Managers and owners often are concerned that publishing more information in financial statements will give away trade secrets to other companies that compete with them. As a consequence of these and other concerns, changes in accounting standards are actively debated, political lobbying often takes place, and the accounting standards that are eventually issued are often a compromise among the conflicting wishes of interested parties.

Management Responsibility and the Demand for Auditing

Who is responsible for the accuracy of the numbers in Nestlé's financial statements? Primary responsibility lies with management, as represented by the highest officer of the company and its highest financial officer.[9] Companies take three important steps to assure investors that the company's records are accurate: (1) they develop and maintain a system of internal controls over both the records and the assets of the company, (2) they hire outside independent auditors to attest to the fairness of the statement presentations, and (3) they form a committee of the board of directors to oversee the integrity of these two safeguards. These responsibilities are often reiterated in a formal report to management or management certification in the annual report. These three safeguards and a management certification are required for all Canadian companies with publicly traded shares. Managers of companies that prepare fraudulent financial statements are subject to criminal and civil penalties.

LO3

Identify the roles of managers and auditors in the accounting communication process.

The **REPORT TO MANAGEMENT (MANAGEMENT CERTIFICATION)** indicates management's primary responsibility for financial statement information and the steps to ensure the accuracy of the company's records.

---

[9]Legally this is enforced by the OSC through National Instrument 52-109 - *Certification of Disclosure in Issuers' Annual and Interim Filings.* Chief executive and chief financial officers must sign a legal document with every financial report filed with the OSC. That document certifies that the CEO and CFO have designed or supervised the design of a financial data collection and reporting system that will result in financial statements free of material misstatement and fraud. This is an assurance of the quality of financial information disclosed by companies listed on Canadian stock exchanges.

Three steps to ensure the accuracy of records:

System of Controls   External Auditors   Board of Directors

The **AUDIT REPORT (REPORT OF INDEPENDENT AUDITORS)** describes the auditors' opinion of the fairness of the financial statement presentations and the evidence gathered to support that opinion.

The role of the independent auditor is described in more detail in the audit report, or report of independent auditors (Exhibit 1.8). The audit report describes the auditor's opinion of the fairness of the financial statements, and the evidence gathered to support that opinion. It is important to note that the main difference between the report of management and the report of the independent auditors concerns the responsibility for the financial information included in the company's annual report. As the report of the independent auditors indicates, the auditor's responsibility is to express an opinion on Nestlé's financial statements that have been prepared by its accounting personnel and reviewed by the **audit committee** of the **board of directors**, which assumes responsibility for the quality of the content of these financial statements.[10]

In Canada, an accountant may be designated as a **Chartered Accountant (CA)**, a **Certified General Accountant (CGA)**, or a **Certified Management Accountant (CMA)**. These accounting designations are granted by the respective professional accounting organizations on completion of specific educational programs and experience requirements.[11] Professional accountants can offer various accounting services to the public, but only CAs and CGAs (in most Canadian provinces[12]) are permitted to issue audit reports of publicly traded companies because they have certain responsibilities that extend to the general public as well as to the specific business that pays for their services.

An **AUDIT** is an examination of the financial reports to ensure that they represent what they claim and conform with International Financial Reporting Standards.

An audit involves the examination of the financial reports (prepared by the management of the company) to ensure that they represent what they claim and conform with IFRS. In performing an audit, the independent auditor examines the underlying transactions and the accounting methods used to account for these transactions. Because of the enormous number of transactions that total billions of dollars each year for a major enterprise, such as Air Canada, the auditor does not examine each transaction. Rather, professional approaches are used to ascertain beyond reasonable doubt that transactions were measured and reported properly.[13]

Many opportunities exist for managers to intentionally prepare misleading financial reports. An audit performed by an independent auditor is the best protection available to the public. When that protection fails, however, the independent auditor is sometimes found liable for losses incurred by those who rely on the statements. In this regard, the Canadian Public Accountability Board was created in 2003 to provide public oversight for auditors of public companies.

---

[10]A typical audit report for Canadian public companies consists of the auditor's responsibility and opinion.
[11]Refer to the following websites for details of the educational and experience requirements for the respective designations:

    Chartered Accountant: www.cica.ca
    Certified General Accountant: www.cga-canada.org
    Certified Management Accountant: www.cma-canada.org

[12]CGAs and CMAs have the right to practice public accounting in Quebec if they meet stringent competency criteria. In British Columbia, CMAs are permitted to do assurance audits upon successful application to the Audit Certification Board.
[13]The Auditing and Assurance Standards Board (AASB) of the Canadian Institute of Chartered Accountants sets standards for auditing of public companies. The AASB has recently produced new Canadian Auditing Standards that are essentially the International Standards on Auditing issued by the International Auditing and Assurance Standards Board.

Exhibit **1.8**
Auditors' Report

REAL WORLD EXCERPT

The Nestlé Group

ANNUAL REPORT

REPORT OF THE STATUTORY AUDITOR ON THE CONSOLIDATED FINANCIAL STATEMENTS
to the General Meeting of Nestle S.A.

As Statutory auditor we have audited the Consolidated Financial Statements (income statement, balance sheet, cash flow statement, statement of recognised income and expense, changes in equity and notes on pages 44 to 113) of the Nestle Group for the year ended 31 December 2009.

Board of Directors' responsibility

The Board of Directors is responsible for the preparation and fair presentation of the Consolidated Financial Statements in accordance with International Financial Reporting Standards (IFRS) and the requirements of Swiss law. This responsibility Includes designing, Implementing and maintaining an internal control system relevant to the preparation and fair presentation of Consolidated Financial Statements that are free from material misstatement, whether due to fraud or error. The Board of Directors is further responsible for selecting and applying appropriate accounting policies and making accounting estimates that are reasonable in the circumstances.

Auditor's responsibility

Our responsibility Is to express an opinion on these Consolidated Financial Statements based on our audit. We conducted our audit in accordance with Swiss law and Swiss Auditing Standards and International Standards on Auditing. Those standards require that we plan and perform the audit to obtain reasonable assurance whether the Consolidated Financial Statements are free from material misstatement.

An audit involves performing procedures to obtain audit evidence about the amounts and disclosures in the Consolidated Financial Statements. The procedures selected depend on the auditor's Judgment, including the assessment of the risks of material misstatement of the Consolidated Financial Statements, whether due to fraud or a error. In making those risk assessments, the auditor considers the Internal control system relevant to the entity's preparation and fair presentation of the Consolidated Financial Statements in order to design audit procedures that are appropriate in the circumstances, but not for the purpose of expressing an opinion on the effectiveness of the entity's internal control system. An audit also includes evaluating the appropriateness of the accounting policies used and the reasonableness of accounting estimates made, as well as evaluating the overall presentation of the Consolidated Financial Statements. We believe that the audit evidence we have obtained is sufficient and appropriate to provide a basis for our audit opinion.

Opinion

In our opinion, the Consolidated Financial Statements for the year ended 31 December 2009 give a true and fair view of the financial position, the result or operations and the cash flows in accordance with IFRS and comply with Swiss law.

Report on other legal requirements

We confirm that we meet the legal requirements on licensing according to the Auditor Oversight Act (AOA) and Independence (article 72B CO and article 11 AOA) and that there are no circumstances Incompatible with our independence.

In accordance with article723a paragraph 1 Item 3 CO and Swiss Auditing Standard 890, we confirm that an internal control system exists, which has been designed for the preparation of Consolidated Financial Statements according to the instructions of the Board of Directors.

We recommend that the Consolidated Financial Statements submitted to you be approved.

 Klynveld Peat Marwick Goerdeler SA

Mark Balllache
Licensed Audit Expert
Auditor in charge

Stephane Gard
Licensed Audit Expert

Zurich, 18 February 2010

Source: Nestlé, 2009 Financial Statements.

Ethics, Reputation, and Legal Liability

LO⁴

Appreciate the importance of ethics, reputation, and legal liability in accounting.

If financial statements are to be of any value to decision makers, users must have confidence in the fairness of the information. These users will have greater confidence in the information if they know that the people who were associated with auditing the financial statements were required to meet professional standards of ethics and competence.

The three Canadian professional accounting organizations require all of their members to adhere to professional codes of ethics. These broad principles are supported by specific rules governing the performance of audits by members of these organizations. These organizations stress how important it is for each member to behave in ways that enhance the reputation of the profession by voluntarily complying with codes of ethical conduct. For example, the Canadian Institute of Chartered Accountants places ethical behaviour and professionalism as the most important of the pervasive competencies possessed by its members.[14] The Certified General Accountants Association of Canada notes in its *Code of Ethical Principles and Rules of Conduct* that an accountant's actions will have an influence not only on the welfare of society but also on that of the profession.[15] The Society of Management Accountants of Canada has also issued a few publications related to ethical conduct, such as *Codes of Ethics, Practice and Conduct* and *Implementing Ethics Strategies within Organizations*.[16]

Failure to comply with professional rules of conduct can result in serious penalties for professional accountants, including rescinding the professional designation of an offending member. The potential economic effects of damage to reputation and malpractice liability, however, provide even stronger incentives to abide by professional standards. Thus, the profession recognizes that its members' reputations for ethical conduct and competence are their most important assets. Finally, recent changes in laws and securities regulation permit the assessment of personal financial penalties on professional accountants who are found guilty of non-compliance, and they must compensate for the financial harm done to others.

Financial statement fraud is a fairly rare event, due in part to the diligent efforts of practising professional accountants. In fact, many such frauds are first identified by the firm's accounting staff or its external auditors who advise regulatory authorities of possible wrongdoing. In doing so, these "whistle blowers" place the interest of the public at large ahead of their own interests and act accordingly. However, in case of malpractice, independent auditors may be held liable for losses suffered by those who relied on the audited financial statements.

It is important to note that the vast majority of managers and owners do act in an honest and responsible manner. However, when the top officers in an organization collude to deceive other parties, they may temporarily succeed. In many cases, even the most diligent audit may not immediately uncover the results of fraud involving collusion of the top officers of a corporation, such as occurred in a number of well-publicized cases such as YBM Magnex International Inc. and Livent Inc. in Canada, American Investment Group Inc. (AIG) in the United States, Siemens AG in Germany, and Parmalat S.p.A in Italy. However, those who were involved in fraudulent behaviour were eventually identified and were sanctioned by the appropriate legal authorities.

Misrepresentations by managers highlight the importance of ensuring the integrity of the financial reporting system by the public accounting profession. Disclosure of financial information that does not conform to existing accounting standards imposes significant costs on the shareholders, creditors, and employees of companies affected by fraudulent activities. Recent reforms of the accounting profession and the imposition of new government regulations both in Canada and the United States make it more difficult and costly for company managers to engage in fraudulent activities.

---

[14]*The UFE Candidates' Competency Map.* The Canadian Institute of Chartered Accountants, Toronto: Canada, 2009, pp. 11–16, accessible through the CICA's website: www.cica.ca.
[15]*Code of Ethical Principles and Rules of Conduct.* Certified General Accountants Association of Canada, Vancouver: Canada, 2010, accessible through the CGA's website: www.cga-canada.org.
[16]These publications are accessible through the society's website: www.cma-canada.org.

ACCOUNTING STANDARDS
FOR PRIVATE ENTERPRISE

The use of International Financial Reporting Standards is required of all Canadian publicly accountable enterprises. However, corporations that do not have their shares traded on organized exchange markets and other private for-profit enterprises (proprietorships and partnerships) are not required to use IFRS. Instead, Canadian private enterprises may prepare their financial statements in accordance with a set of Canadian accounting standards that excludes inappropriate financial reporting complexities.[17]

The AcSB's decision to allow Canadian private enterprises to use accounting standards that deviate from IFRS recognizes that the information needs of external users of the financial statements of private enterprises differ from the information needs of users of the financial statements of publicly accountable enterprises. The major difference between the two types of enterprises is that external users of the private enterprise's financial statements do not include the many individual investors that typically purchase shares of publicly accountable enterprises. Hence, lenders are often the major external stakeholders in private enterprises and may obtain additional information from these companies upon request.

The financial statements prepared by both types of companies are based on the same conceptual framework, but they may differ with respect to the details that are reported in the financial statements and related notes. For example, the concept of other comprehensive income is not applicable to private enterprises. Hence, they are not required to prepare a statement of comprehensive income or a statement of changes in equity.

It should be noted that private enterprises may choose to use IFRS for external reporting. On the other hand, they may choose to not follow either IFRS or the accounting standards prescribed for private enterprises, particularly if they are not dependent on significant external sources of financing for their operations.

DEMONSTRATION **CASE**

At the end of most chapters, one or more demonstration cases are presented. These cases provide an overview of the primary issues discussed in the chapter. Each demonstration case is followed by a recommended solution. You should read the case carefully and then prepare your own solution before you study the recommended solution. **This self-evaluation is highly recommended**.

The introductory case presented here reviews the elements reported on the income statement and statement of financial position and how the elements within each are related.

ABC Service Corporation was organized by Able, Baker, and Casella on January 1, 2011. On that date, the investors exchanged $36,000 cash for all shares of the company. On the same day, the corporation borrowed $10,000 from a local bank and signed a three-year note, payable on December 31, 2013. Interest of 10 percent is payable each December 31. On January 1, 2011, the corporation purchased supplies for $20,000 cash. Operations started immediately.

At the end of 2011, the corporation had completed the following additional business transactions (summarized):

a. Performed services and billed customers for $100,000, of which $94,000 was collected by year-end.
b. Used up $5,000 of supplies while rendering services.
c. Paid $54,000 for other service expenses.
d. Paid $1,000 in annual interest expense on the note payable.
e. Paid $8,000 of income taxes to Canada Revenue Agency.

Required:
Complete the following two financial statements for 2011 by entering the correct amounts. The suggested solution follows the blank statements.

---

[17]Not-for-profit organizations and pension plans are subject to different sets of accounting standards. The accounting standards applicable to the various types of organizations are compiled in different parts of the *CICA Handbook*. Part I of the Handbook includes IFRS. Part II includes accounting standards for private enterprises.

ABC SERVICE CORPORATION
Income Statement
_____ (date)
(in dollars)

		Computation
Revenues		
Service revenue	$ _____	_____
Expenses		
Service expenses	$ _____	_____
Interest expense	_____	_____
Total pretax expenses		
Profit before income tax	$ _____	
Income tax expense	_____	_____
Profit for the year	$ _____	

ABC SERVICE CORPORATION
Statement of Financial Position
_____ (date)
(in dollars)

		Computation
Assets		
Cash	$ _____	
Trade receivables	_____	_____
Supplies	_____	_____
Total assets	$ _____	
Liabilities		
Note payable (10%)	$ _____	
Total liabilities	$ _____	_____
Shareholders' Equity		
Share capital	$ _____	_____
Retained earnings	_____	_____
Total shareholders' equity		
Total liabilities and shareholders' equity	$ _____	

We strongly recommend that you prepare your own answers to these requirements and then check your answers with the suggested solution.

SUGGESTED **SOLUTION**

ABC SERVICE CORPORATION
Income Statement
For the Year Ended December 31, 2011
(in dollars)

			Computation
Revenues			
Service revenue		$100,000	Total billed to customers
Expenses			
Service expenses	$59,000		$5,000 + $54,000
Interest expense	1,000*		
Total pretax expenses		60,000	
Profit before income tax		$ 40,000	
Income tax expense		8,000	
Profit		$ 32,000	

*This amount equals 10 percent of the amount borrowed ($10,000 × 10%).
Note that the *profit before income tax* is the difference between revenues and pretax expenses, and that income tax expense is deducted from profit before income tax to arrive at *profit* for the year.

ABC SERVICE CORPORATION
Statement of Financial Position
At December 31, 2011
(in dollars)

		Computation
Assets		
Cash	$57,000	$36,000 + $10,000
		− $20,000 + $94,000
		− $54,000 − $1,000
		− $8,000
Trade receivables	6,000	$100,000 − $94,000
Supplies	15,000	$20,000 − $5,000
Total assets	$78,000	
Liabilities		
Note payable (10%)	$10,000	Proceeds of bank loan
Total liabilities	$10,000	
Shareholders' Equity		
Share capital	$36,000	Investment by owners
Retained earnings	32,000*	From income statement
Total shareholders' equity	68,000	
Total liabilities and shareholders' equity	$78,000	

*Given that ABC Service Corporation started on January 1, 2011, and there were no dividends declared in 2011, the ending balance of retained earnings equals the profit for 2011. Hence, there is no need to prepare the statement of change in equity for 2011.

Appendix 1A

Types of Business Entities

This textbook emphasizes *accounting for profit-making business entities*. The three main types of business entities are sole proprietorship, partnership, and corporation. A **sole proprietorship** is an unincorporated business owned by one person; it usually is small in size and is common in the service, retailing, and farming industries. Often the owner is the manager. Legally, the business and the owner are not separate entities. However, accounting views the business as a separate entity that must be accounted for separately from its owner.

A **partnership** is an unincorporated business owned by two or more persons known as *partners*. Some partnerships are large in size (e.g., international public accounting firms and law firms). The agreements between the owners are specified in a partnership contract that deals with matters such as division of profit among partners and distribution of resources of the business on termination of its operations. A partnership is not legally separate from its owners. Legally, each partner in a general partnership is responsible for the debts of the business (each general partner has *unlimited liability*). The partnership, however, is a separate business entity to be accounted for separately from its several owners.

A **corporation** is a business incorporated federally under the *Canada Business Corporations Act* or provincially under similar provincial acts. The owners are called shareholders or stockholders. Ownership is represented by shares of capital that usually can be bought and sold freely. When an approved application for incorporation is filed by the organizers, a charter is issued by either the federal or the provincial government. This charter gives the corporation the right to operate as a legal entity, separate from its owners. The shareholders enjoy *limited liability*. Shareholders cannot lose more than they paid for their shares. The corporate charter specifies the types and amounts of share capital that can be issued. Most provinces require a minimum of two shareholders and a minimum amount of resources to be contributed at the time of organization. The shareholders elect a governing board of directors, which in turn employs managers and exercises general supervision of the corporation.

Exhibit **1.9**

Comparison of Three Types of Business Entities

	Proprietorship	Partnership	Corporation
Number of owners	One owner	Two or more owners	Many owners
Legal status of entity	Not separate from that of its owner	Not separate from that of its owner(s)	Separate legal entity
Responsibility of owners for debts of business entity	Unlimited legal liability	Unlimited legal liability	Owners' liability is limited to their investment
Accounting status	Each entity is separate from its owner(s) for accounting purposes		

Members of the board of directors, executives, and officers of companies as well as employees do not enjoy limited liability for any damage caused by their willful wrongdoing. Because a corporation is considered a legally separate entity, directors and executives may find themselves being sued for damages by their former employer. Accounting also views the corporation as a separate business entity that must be accounted for separately from its owners.

In terms of economic importance, the corporation is the dominant form of business organization in Canada. This dominance is caused by the many advantages of the corporate form: (1) limited liability for the shareholders, (2) continuity of life, (3) ease in transferring ownership (shares), and (4) opportunities to raise large amounts of money by selling shares to a large number of people. The primary disadvantages of a corporation are (1) loss of control by shareholders, (2) complex reporting procedures for a variety of government agencies, and (3) potential for double taxation of profit (it is taxed when it is earned and again when it is distributed to shareholders as dividends). In this textbook, we emphasize the corporate form of business. Nevertheless, the accounting concepts and procedures that we discuss also apply to other types of businesses. The main differences among these three types of entities appear in the equity section of the statement of financial position.

Specific aspects of the three types of business entities are compared in Exhibit 1.9.

Appendix 1B

Employment in the Accounting Profession Today

Since 1900, accounting has attained the stature of professions such as law, medicine, engineering, and architecture. As with all recognized professions, accounting is subject to professional competence requirements, is dedicated to service to the public, requires a high level of academic study, and rests on a common body of knowledge. As indicated earlier, three Canadian accounting designations are available to an accountant: CA, CGA, and CMA. These designations are granted only on completion of requirements specified by the respective professional organizations. Although specific requirements vary among the three professional organizations, they include a university degree with a specified number of accounting courses, good character, a minimum of two years of relevant professional experience, and successful completion of a professional examination. Currently, all accountants must be licensed by the government to engage in professional practice and they must meet ongoing tests of competence to retain their licences. Similar accounting designations exist in other countries, most notably the Certified Public Accountant (CPA) in the United States.

Accountants usually are engaged in professional practice or are employed by businesses, government entities, and not-for-profit organizations. The accounting profession is continuously changing. While many accountants still provide traditional accounting and tax services to businesses, individual clients, and government organizations, other areas of practice have become increasingly common in the accounting profession today. Demand for value-added accounting services (e.g., financial analysis, evaluation and implementation of new information technology and business processes, management advisory and consulting services, forensic accounting, and environmental accounting) is reshaping the nature of educational programs that prepare students to become professional accountants.[18]

Practice of Public Accounting

Although an individual may practice public accounting, usually two or more individuals organize an accounting firm in the form of a partnership (in many cases, a limited liability partnership, or LLP). Accounting firms vary in size from a one-person office to regional firms, to the "Big Four" firms (Deloitte & Touche, Ernst & Young, KPMG, and PricewaterhouseCoopers), which have hundreds of offices worldwide. Accounting firms usually render three types of services: assurance services, management consulting services, and tax services.

Assurance Services   Assurance services are independent professional services that improve the quality of information, or its context, for decision makers. The most important assurance service performed by professional accountants in public practice is financial statement auditing. The audit's purpose is to lend credibility to the financial reports; that is, to ensure that they fairly represent what they claim. An audit involves an examination of the financial reports (prepared by the management of the entity) to ensure that they conform to IFRS. Other areas of assurance services include integrity and security of electronic commerce and reliability of information systems.

Management Consulting Services   Many independent accounting firms offer management consulting services. These services usually are accounting-based and encompass such activities as the design and installation of accounting, data processing, and profit-planning and control (budget) systems; financial advice; forecasting; internal controls; cost-effectiveness studies; and operational analysis. This facet of public accounting practice has grown rapidly. The perceived influence that availability of such services might have on auditor independence has caused large accounting firms to dissociate their consulting practice from their audit function.

Tax Services   Accountants in public practice usually provide income tax services to their clients. These services include both tax planning as a part of the decision-making process and the determination of the income tax liability (reported on the annual income tax return). Because of the increasing complexity of provincial and federal tax laws, a high level of competence is required, which accountants specializing in taxation can provide. The accountant's involvement in tax planning often is quite significant. Most major business decisions have significant tax impacts; in fact, tax-planning considerations often govern certain business decisions.

Employment by Organizations

Many accountants, including CAs, CGAs, and CMAs, are employed by profit-making, not-for-profit and government organizations. An organization, depending on its size and complexity, may employ from a few to hundreds of accountants. In a business enterprise, the chief financial officer (usually a vice-president or controller) is a member of the management team. This responsibility usually entails a wide range of management, financial, and accounting duties.

In a business entity, accountants typically are engaged in a wide variety of activities, such as general management, general accounting, cost accounting, profit planning and

---

[18]Refer to the following website for more details about the types of services and skills that should be provided by accountants in the future: **www.accountemps.com/WhatCanadianEmployersSeek**.

control (budgeting), internal auditing, and computerized data processing. A primary function of the accountants in organizations is to provide data that are useful for internal managerial decision making and for controlling operations. The functions of external reporting, tax planning, control of assets, and a host of related responsibilities normally are also performed by accountants in industry.

Employment in the Public and Not-For-Profit Sectors

The vast and complex operations of governmental units, from the local to the international level, create a need for accountants. The same holds true for other not-for-profit organizations such as charitable organizations, hospitals, and universities. Accountants employed in the public and not-for-profit sectors perform functions similar to those performed by their counterparts in private organizations.

A survey of positions occupied by accounting professionals and related salaries is available at **www.accountemps.com.**

CHAPTER **TAKE-AWAYS**

1. **Recognize the information conveyed in each of the four basic financial statements and how it is used by different decision makers (investors, creditors, and managers). p. 2**
   The *statement of financial position* reports financial values for the assets, liabilities, and shareholders' equity at a specific point in time.
   The *statement of comprehensive income* reports the profit (revenues minus expenses) for a period as well as changes in equity during that period, except those resulting from exchanges with owners.
   The *statement of changes in equity* reports the way that profit, the distribution of profit (dividends), and other changes to shareholders' equity affected the company's financial position during a specific period.
   The *statement of cash flows* reports inflows and outflows of cash for a specific period.
   The statements are used by investors and creditors to evaluate different aspects of the firm's financial position and performance.

2. **Identify the role of International Financial Reporting Standards (IFRS) in determining the content of financial statements. p. 18**
   IFRS are the broad principles, specific rules, and practices used to develop and report the information in financial statements. Knowledge of IFRS is necessary to accurately interpret the numbers in financial statements.

3. **Identify the roles of managers and auditors in the accounting communication process. p. 21**
   Management has primary responsibility for the accuracy of a company's financial information. Auditors are responsible for expressing an opinion on the fairness of the financial statement presentations based on their examination of the reports and records of the company.

4. **Appreciate the importance of ethics, reputation, and legal liability in accounting. p. 24**
   Users will have confidence in the accuracy of financial statement numbers only if the people associated with their preparation and audit have reputations for ethical behaviour and competence. Management and auditors can also be held legally liable for fraudulent financial statements and malpractice.

In this chapter, we studied the basic financial statements that communicate financial information to external users. Chapters 2, 3, 4, and 5 will provide a more detailed look at financial statements and examine how to translate data about business transactions into these statements. Learning the relationship between business transactions and financial statements is the key to using financial statements in planning and decision making. Chapter 2 begins our discussion of how the accounting function collects data about business transactions and processes the data to provide periodic financial statements, with emphasis on the statement of financial position. To accomplish this purpose, Chapter 2 discusses key accounting concepts, the accounting model, transaction analysis, and analytical tools. We examine typical business activities of Nestlé to demonstrate the concepts in Chapters 2, 3, and 4.

FINDING **FINANCIAL INFORMATION**

STATEMENT OF FINANCIAL POSITION

Assets = Liabilities + Shareholders' Equity

STATEMENT OF COMPREHENSIVE INCOME

Revenues
− Expenses
Profit
+ Other comprehensive income
Comprehensive income

STATEMENT OF CHANGES IN EQUITY

Equity, beginning of the period
+ Profit for the year
+ Other comprehensive income
− Dividends
+/− Other changes, net
Equity, end of the period

STATEMENT OF CASH FLOWS

+/− Cash flows from operating activities
+/− Cash flows from investing activities
+/− Cash flows from financing activities
Change in Cash

KEY **TERMS**

Accounting p. 2

Accounting Entity p. 5

Accounting Period p. 10

Accounting Standards Board (AcSB) p. 19

Audit p. 22

Audit Report (Report of Independent Auditors) p. 22

Basic Accounting Equation p. 6

Income Statement p. 9

International Accounting Standards Board (IASB) p. 20

International Financial Reporting Standards (IFRS) p. 19

Notes (Footnotes) p. 17

Ontario Securities Commission (OSC) p. 19

Report to Management (Management Certification) p. 21

Retained Earnings p. 12

Securities and Exchange Commission (SEC) p. 19

Statement of Cash Flows p. 13

Statement of Changes in Equity p. 12

Statement of Comprehensive Income p. 9

Statement of Financial Position (Balance Sheet) p. 4

QUESTIONS

1. Define *accounting*.
2. Briefly distinguish financial accounting from managerial accounting.
3. The accounting process generates financial reports for both internal and external users. Identify some of the groups of users.
4. Briefly distinguish investors from creditors.
5. What is an accounting entity? Why is a business treated as a separate entity for accounting purposes?
6. What information should be included in the heading of each of the four primary financial statements?
7. What are the purposes of the (a) income statement, (b) statement of financial position, (c) statement of cash flows, and (d) statement of changes in equity?
8. Explain why the income statement and statement of cash flows are dated "For the Year Ended December 31, 2011," whereas the statement of financial position is dated "At December 31, 2011."

9. Briefly explain the importance of assets and liabilities to the decisions of investors and creditors.

10. Briefly define *profit* and *loss*.

11. Explain the accounting equation for the income statement. Define the three major items reported on the income statement.

12. Explain the accounting equation for the statement of financial position. Define the three major components reported on the statement of financial position.

13. Explain the accounting equation for the statement of cash flows. Explain the three major components reported on the statement.

14. Explain the accounting equation for retained earnings. Explain the major items that affect the ending balance of retained earnings.

15. Financial statements discussed in this chapter are aimed at *external* users. Briefly explain how a company's *internal* managers in different functional areas (e.g., marketing, purchasing, human resources) might use financial statement information.

16. Briefly describe how accounting standards are determined in Canada, including the roles of the Accounting Standards Board and the Ontario Securities Commission.

17. Briefly explain the responsibility of company management, the board of directors, and the independent auditors in the internal control and financial reporting process.

18. (Appendix 1A) Briefly differentiate among a sole proprietorship, a partnership, and a corporation.

19. (Appendix 1B) List and briefly explain the three primary services that accountants in public practice provide.

EXERCISES

LO1

Honda Motor Co.

E1–1 Preparing a Statement of Financial Position

Established less than 50 years ago, Honda Motor Co. Ltd. of Japan is a leading international manufacturer of automobiles and the largest manufacturer of motorcycles in the world. As a Japanese company, it follows Japanese GAAP and reports its financial statements in millions of yen (¥). A recent statement of financial position contained the following items (in millions). Prepare a statement of financial position as at March 31, 2009, solving for the missing amount.

Trade payables and other current liabilities	¥ 4,237,368
Cash and cash equivalents	690,369
Inventories	1,243,961
Investments	639,069
Long-term borrowings	1,932,637
Net property, plant, and equipment	3,435,520
Other assets	722,868
Other current assets	4,232,916
Other liabilities	1,641,624
Retained earnings	3,704,727
Share capital	302,561
Total assets	11,818,917
Total liabilities and shareholders' equity	?
Trade accounts, notes, and other receivables	854,214

LO1

E1–2 Completing a Statement of Financial Position and Inferring Profit

Terry Lloyd and Joan Lopez organized Read More Store as a corporation; each contributed $50,000 cash to start the business and received 4,000 shares of capital. The store completed its first year of operations on December 31, 2011. On that date, the following financial items were determined: cash on hand and in the bank, $48,900; amounts due from customers from sales of books, $25,000; unused portion of store and office equipment, $49,000; amounts owed to publishers for books purchased, $7,000; one-year note for $3,000, signed on January 15, 2011, and payable to a local bank. No dividends were declared or paid to the shareholders during the year.

Required:

1. Complete the following statement of financial position as at December 31, 2011.
2. What was the amount of profit for the year?

	Assets	**Liabilities**	
Cash	$ _____	Trade payables	$ _____
Trade receivables	_____	Note payable	_____
Store and office equipment	_____	Interest payable	120
		Total liabilities	$ _____
		Shareholders' Equity	
		Share capital	$ _____
		Retained earnings	12,780
		Total shareholders' equity	_____
		Total liabilities and	
Total assets	$ _____	shareholders' equity	$ _____

E1–3 Analyzing Revenues and Expenses and Preparing an Income Statement

LO1

Assume that you are the owner of The University Shop, which specializes in items that interest students. At the end of September 2012, you find (for September only) the following:

a. Sales, per the cash register tapes, of $119,000, plus one sale on credit (a special situation) of $1,000.

b. With the help of a friend (who majored in accounting), you determined that all of the goods sold during September had cost $40,000 to purchase.

c. During the month, according to the chequebook, you paid $38,000 for salaries, rent, supplies, advertising, and other expenses; however, you have not yet paid the $600 monthly utilities for September.

Required:

On the basis of the data given, what was the amount of profit for September (disregard income taxes)? Show computations. (*Hint:* A convenient form to use has the following major side captions: Revenue from Sales, Expenses, and the difference—Profit for the period.)

E1–4 Preparing an Income Statement and Inferring Missing Values

LO1

Geox

Geox S.p.A. is an Italian-based international company that produces and distributes footwear and apparel products for men, women, and children. A recent annual income statement contained the following items (in thousands of euros). Solve for the missing amounts and prepare a condensed income statement for the year ended December 31, 2008. (*Hint:* First order the items as they would appear on the income statement and then solve for the missing values.)

Cost of sales	€424,461
Interest expense	4,297
Profit for the year	?
Net sales	892,513
Selling and distribution expenses	43,248
General and administrative expenses	187,397
Advertising and promotion expenses	66,917
Income tax expense	48,603
Total expenses excluding income taxes	?
Profit before income tax	?

E1–5 Analyzing Revenues and Expenses and Completing an Income Statement

LO1

Home Realty Incorporated has been operating for three years and is owned by three investors. J. Doe owns 60 percent of the 9,000 shares that are outstanding and is the managing executive in charge. On

December 31, 2011, the following financial items for the entire year were determined: commissions earned and collected in cash, $150,000; rental service fees earned and collected, $15,000; expenses paid included salaries, $62,000; commissions, $35,000; payroll taxes, $2,500; rent, $2,200; utilities, $1,600; promotion and advertising, $8,000; income taxes, $18,500; and miscellaneous expenses, $500. At December 31, there were $16,000 of commissions earned but not collected, and the rent for December ($200) was not paid. Complete the following income statement:

Revenues		
Commissions	$	
Rental service fees		
Total revenues		$
Expenses		
Salaries	$	
Commission		
Payroll tax		
Rent		
Utilities		
Promotion and advertising		
Miscellaneous		
Total expenses (excluding income taxes)		
Profit before income taxes		$
Income tax expense		
Profit for the period		$

LO1

E1–6 Inferring Values by Using the Income Statement and Statement of Financial Position Equations

Review the chapter explanations of the income statement and the statement of financial position equations. Apply these equations in each independent case to compute the two missing amounts for each case. Assume that it is the end of 2010, the first full year of operations for the company. (*Hint*: Organize the listed items as they are presented in the statement of financial position and income statement equations and then compute the missing amounts.)

Independent Cases	Total Revenues	Total Expenses	Profit (Loss)	Total Assets	Total Liabilities	Shareholders' Equity
A	$100,000	$82,000		$150,000	$70,000	
B		80,000	$12,000	112,000		$60,000
C	80,000	86,000		104,000	26,000	
D	50,000		13,000		22,000	77,000
E		81,000	(6,000)		73,000	28,000

LO1

E1–7 Preparing an Income Statement and a Statement of Financial Position

Ducharme Corporation was organized by five individuals on January 1, 2011. At the end of January 2011, the following monthly financial data are available:

Total revenues	$150,000
Total expenses (excluding income taxes)	100,000
Income tax expense (all unpaid as at January 31)	15,000
Cash balance, January 31, 2011	20,000
Receivables from customers (all considered collectable)	25,000
Merchandise inventory (by inventory count at cost)	32,000
Payables to suppliers for merchandise purchased from them (will be paid during February 2011)	11,000
Share capital (2,600 shares)	26,000
Dividends declared in January 2011	10,000

Required:
Complete the following two statements:

DUCHARME CORPORATION
Summary Income Statement

Total revenues	$
Less: Total expenses (excluding income tax)	
Profit before income tax	
Less: Income tax expense	
Profit for the year	

DUCHARME CORPORATION
Statement of Financial Position

Assets

Cash	$
Receivables from customers	
Merchandise inventory	
Total assets	$

Liabilities

Payables to suppliers	$
Income taxes payable	
Total liabilities	

Shareholders' equity

Share capital	$	
Retained earnings		
Total shareholders' equity		
Total liabilities and shareholders' equity		$

E1–8 **Computing Ending Balance of Retained Earnings**   LO1

Sultan Inc. was organized on January 1, 2011. It reported the following for its first two years of operations:

Profit for 2011	$ 36,000
Profit for 2012	45,000
Dividends for 2011	15,000
Dividends for 2012	20,000
Total assets at end of 2011	125,000
Total assets at end of 2012	242,000

Required:
Compute the ending balance of retained earnings for Sultan Inc. as at December 31, 2012. Show computations.

E1–9 **Analyzing and Interpreting an Income Statement and the Price/Earnings Ratio**   LO1

Pest Away Corporation was organized by three individuals on January 1, 2011, to provide insect extermination services. At the end of 2011, the following income statement was prepared:

PEST AWAY CORPORATION
Income Statement
For the Year Ended December 31, 2011

Revenues		
Service revenue (cash)	$192,000	
Service revenue (credit)	24,000	
Total revenues		$216,000
Expenses		
Salaries	$ 76,000	
Rent	21,000	
Utilities	12,000	
Advertising	14,000	
Supplies	25,000	
Interest	8,000	
Total expenses		156,000
Profit before income tax		$ 60,000
Income tax expense		21,000
Profit for the year		$ 39,000

Required:

1. What was the average amount of monthly revenue?
2. What was the amount of monthly rent?
3. Explain why supplies are reported as an expense.
4. Explain why interest is reported as an expense.
5. What was the average income tax rate for Pest Away Corporation?
6. Can you determine how much cash the company had on December 31, 2011? Explain.
7. If the company had a market value of $468,000, what is its price/earnings ratio?

LO1

Dell Computer

E1–10   Focusing on Cash Flows: Matching Cash Flow Items to Categories

Dell Computer is a leading designer and manufacturer of personal computers. The following items were taken from its recent statement of cash flows. Note that different companies use slightly different titles for the same item. Without referring to Exhibit 1.5, mark each item in the list as a cash flow from operating activities (O), investing activities (I), or financing activities (F). Place parentheses around the letter only if it is a cash outflow.

_____ (1) Cash paid to suppliers and employees

_____ (2) Cash received from customers

_____ (3) Income taxes paid

_____ (4) Interest and dividends received

_____ (5) Interest paid

_____ (6) Proceeds from sale of investment in Conner Peripherals Inc.

_____ (7) Purchases of property, plant, and equipment

_____ (8) Repayment of borrowings

LO1

E1–11   Preparing a Statement of Cash Flows

NITSU Manufacturing Corporation is preparing the annual financial statements for its shareholders. A statement of cash flows must be prepared. The following data on cash flows were developed for the entire year ended December 31, 2011: cash inflow from operating revenues, $270,000; cash expended for operating expenses, $180,000; sale of unissued NITSU shares for cash, $30,000; cash dividends declared and paid to shareholders during the year, $22,000; and payments on long-term borrowings, $80,000. During the year, a tract of land was sold for $15,000 cash (which was the same price that NITSU had paid for the land in 2010), and $38,000 cash was expended for two new machines. The machines were used in the factory. The beginning-of-the-year cash balance was $63,000.

Required:

Prepare a statement of cash flows for 2011. Follow the format illustrated in the chapter.

E1–12 Comparing Income and Cash Flows from Operations (A Challenging Exercise) LO1

Paul's Painters, a service organization, prepared the following special report for the month of January 2012:

Service Revenue, Expenses, and Profit

Service revenue		
Cash services (per cash register tape)	$105,000	
Credit services (per charge bills; not yet		
collected by end of January)	30,500	
		$135,500
Expenses		
Salaries and wages expense (paid by cheque)	$ 50,000	
Salaries for January not yet paid	3,000	
Supplies used (taken from stock, purchased		
for cash during December)	2,000	
Estimated cost of using company-owned truck		
for the month (called *depreciation*)	500	
Other expenses (paid by cheque)	26,000	81,500
Profit before income tax		54,000
Income tax expense (not yet paid)		13,500
Profit for January		$ 40,500

Required:

1. The owner (who knows little about the financial part of the business) asked you to compute the amount by which cash had increased in January 2012 from the operations of the company. You decided to prepare a detailed report for the owner with the following major captions: Cash inflows (collections), Cash outflows (payments), and the difference—Net increase (or decrease) in cash.

2. Reconcile the difference—net increase (or decrease) in cash—you computed in (1) with the income for January 2012 by filling in the following chart.

Reconciliation with profit:	
Profit	$40,500
Deduct: Non-cash services	(?)
Add: Non-cash expenses (? + ? + ? + ?)	?
Net increase (decrease) in cash	$29,000

PROBLEMS

P1–1 Preparing an Income Statement and a Statement of Financial Position (AP1–1) LO1

Assume that you are the president of Nuclear Company. At December 31, 2011, the end of the first year of operations, the following financial data for the company are available:

Cash	$ 25,000
Receivables from customers (all considered collectable)	12,000
Inventory of merchandise (based on physical count and priced at cost)	90,000
Equipment owned, at cost less used portion	45,000
Payables to suppliers of merchandise	47,370
Salary payable for 2011 (on December 31, 2011, this was owed to an employee who was away because of an emergency and returned to work on January 10, 2012, at which time the payment was made)	2,000
Total sales revenue	140,000
Expenses, including the cost of the merchandise sold (excluding income taxes)	89,100
Income taxes expense (at 30% of pretax profit); all paid during 2011	?
Share capital, 7,000 shares outstanding	87,000
No dividends were declared or paid during 2011.	

Required (show computations):

1. Prepare a summarized income statement for the year ended December 31, 2011.
2. Prepare a statement of financial position at December 31, 2011.

 LO1

P1–2   **Analyzing a Student's Business and Preparing an Income Statement and a Statement of Financial Position** (AP1–2)

While pursuing her undergraduate studies, Brigitte Lebeau needed to earn sufficient money for the coming academic year. Unable to obtain a job with a reasonable salary, she decided to try the lawn care business for three months during the summer. After a survey of the market potential, Brigitte bought a used pick-up truck on June 1 for $1,500. On each door she painted "Brigitte's Lawn Service, Phone 471-4487." She also spent $900 for mowers, trimmers, and tools. To acquire these items, she borrowed $2,500 cash by signing a note payable, promising to pay the $2,500 plus interest of $75 at the end of the three months (ending August 31).

At the end of the summer, Brigitte realized that she had done a lot of work, and her bank account looked good. This fact prompted her to become concerned about how much profit the business had earned.

A review of the cheque stubs showed the following: bank deposits of collections from customers totalled $12,600. The following cheques had been written: gas, oil, and lubrication, $920; truck repairs, $210; mower repair, $75; miscellaneous supplies used, $80; helpers, $4,500; payroll taxes, $175; payment for assistance in preparing payroll tax forms, $25; insurance, $125; telephone, $110; and $2,575 to pay off the note including interest (on August 31). A notebook kept in the truck, plus some unpaid bills, reflected that customers still owed her $800 for lawn services rendered and that she owed $200 for gas and oil (credit card charges). She estimated that the cost for use of the truck and the other equipment (called depreciation) for three months amounted to $500.

Required:

1. Prepare a quarterly income statement for Brigitte's Lawn Service for the months of June, July, and August 2011. Use the following main captions: Revenues from services, Expenses, and Profit. Because this is a sole proprietorship, the company will not be subject to income tax.

2. Prepare a statement of financial position for Brigitte's Lawn Service as at August 31, 2011. Brigitte's business is a proprietorship with one equity item: Brigitte Lebeau, capital.

3. Do you see a need for one or more additional financial reports for this company for 2011 and thereafter? Explain.

 LO1

P1–3   **Comparing Profit with Cash Flow (A Challenging Problem)**

New Delivery Company was organized on January 1, 2012. At the end of the first quarter (three months) of operations, the owner prepared a summary of its operations as shown in the first row of the following tabulation:

	Computation of	
	----------------	----------
Summary of Transactions	**Profit**	**Cash**
a. Services performed for customers, $66,000, of which one-sixth remained uncollected at the end of the quarter.	$66,000	$55,000
b. Cash borrowed from the local bank, $30,000 (one-year note).		
c. Small service truck purchased for use in the business: cost, $9,000; paid 30% down, balance on credit.		
d. Expenses, $36,000, of which one-sixth remained unpaid at the end of the quarter.		
e. Service supplies purchased for use in the business, $3,000, of which one-fourth remained unpaid (on credit) at the end of the quarter. Also, one-fifth of these supplies were unused (still on hand) at the end of the quarter.		
f. Wages earned by employees, $21,000, of which one-half remained unpaid at the end of the quarter		
Based only on the above transactions, compute the following for the quarter:		
Profit (or loss)	=====	
Cash inflow (or outflow)		=====

Required:

1. For each of the six transactions given in this tabulation, enter what you consider to be the correct amounts. Enter a zero when appropriate. The first transaction is illustrated.

2. For each transaction, explain the basis for your responses.

P1–4 Evaluating Data to Support a Loan Application (A Challenging Problem)
On January 1, 2013, three individuals organized West Company as a corporation. Each individual invested $10,000 cash in the business. On December 31, 2013, they prepared a list of resources owned (assets) and a list of the debts (liabilities) to support the company's request for a loan of $70,000 submitted to a local bank. None of the three investors had studied accounting. The two lists prepared were as follows:

▓ **LO1**

Company resources	
Cash	$ 12,000
Service supplies inventory (on hand)	7,000
Service trucks (four practically new)	68,000
Personal residences of organizers (three houses)	190,000
Service equipment used in the business (practically new)	30,000
Amounts due from customers (for services already completed)	15,000
Total	$322,000
Company obligations	
Unpaid wages to employees	$ 19,000
Unpaid taxes	8,000
Owed to suppliers	10,000
Owed on service trucks and equipment (to a finance company)	50,000
Loan from organizer	15,000
Total	$102,000

Required:

Prepare a short memo indicating the following:

1. Which of these items do not belong on the statement of financial position (bear in mind that the company is considered to be separate from the owners)?

2. What additional questions would you raise about measurement of items on the lists? Explain the basis for each question.

3. If you were advising the local bank on its loan decision, which amounts on the lists would create special concerns? Explain the basis for each concern and include any recommendations that you have.

4. In view of your responses to (1) and (2), calculate the amount of shareholders' equity as at December 31, 2013. Show your computations.

LO1

P1–5   Using Financial Reports: Identifying and Correcting Deficiencies in an Income Statement and a Statement of Financial Position

Performance Corporation was organized on January 1, 2011. At the end of 2011, the company had not yet employed an accountant; however, an employee who was "good with numbers" prepared the following statements at that date:

Performance Corporation
December 31, 2011

Income from sales of merchandise	$175,000
Total amount paid for goods sold during 2011	(90,000)
Selling costs	(25,000)
Depreciation (on service vehicles used)	(10,000)
Income from services rendered	52,000
Salaries and wages paid	(62,000)

Performance Corporation
December 31, 2011

Resources		
Cash		$ 32,000
Merchandise inventory (held for resale)		42,000
Service vehicles		50,000
Retained earnings (profit earned in 2011)		30,000
Grand total		$154,000
Debts		
Payable to suppliers		$ 22,000
Note owed to bank		25,000
Due from customers		13,000
Total		$ 60,000
Supplies on hand (to be used in rendering services)	$ 15,000	
Accumulated depreciation** (on service vehicles)	10,000	
Share capital, 6,500 shares	65,000	
Total		90,000
Grand total		$150,000

***Accumulated depreciation* represents the cost related to the used portion of the asset and should be subtracted from the asset balance.

Required:

1. List all of the deficiencies that you can identify in these statements. Give a brief explanation of each one.

2. Prepare a proper income statement for Performance Corporation for 2011 (correct profit is $30,000) and a proper statement of financial position at December 31, 2011 (correct total assets are $142,000).

ALTERNATE PROBLEMS

AP1–1 Preparing an Income Statement and a Statement of Financial Position (P1–1)   ■ **LO1**

Assume that you are the president of McClaren Corporation. At June 30, 2012, the end of the first year of operations, the following financial data for the company are available:

Cash	$13,150
Receivables from customers (all considered collectable)	9,500
Inventory of merchandise (based on physical count and priced at cost)	57,000
Equipment owned, at cost less used portion	36,000
Payables to suppliers of merchandise	31,500
Salary payable for 2012 (on June 30, 2012, this was owed to an employee who was away because of an emergency and will return on July 7, 2012, at which time the payment will be made)	1,500
Total sales revenue	90,000
Expenses, including the cost of the merchandise sold (excluding income taxes)	60,500
Income taxes expense (at 30% of pretax profit); all paid during 2012	?
Share capital, 5,000 shares outstanding	?
No dividends were declared or paid during 2012.	

Required (show computations):

1. Prepare a summarized income statement for the year ended June 30, 2012.
2. Prepare a statement of financial position as at June 30, 2012.

AP1–2 Analyzing a Student's Business and Preparing an Income Statement and a Statement of Financial Position (P1–2)   ■ **LO1**

Upon graduation from high school, John Abel immediately accepted a job as an electrician's assistant for a large local electrical repair company. After three years of hard work, John received an electrician's licence and decided to start his own business. He had saved $12,000, which he invested in the business. His lawyer had advised him to start as a corporation. First, he transferred this amount from his savings account to a business bank account for Abel Electric Repair Company Incorporated and was issued shares. He then purchased a used panel truck for $9,000 cash and second-hand tools for $1,500; rented space in a small building; inserted an ad in the local paper; and opened the doors on October 1, 2011. Immediately, John was very busy; after one month, he employed an assistant.

Although John knew practically nothing about the financial side of the business, he realized that a number of reports were required and that costs and collections had to be controlled carefully. At December 31, 2011, prompted in part by concern about his income tax situation, John recognized the need for financial statements. His wife, Jane, developed some financial statements for the business. On December 31, 2011, with the help of a friend, she gathered the following data for the three months just ended. Bank account deposits of collections for electric repair services totalled $32,000. The following cheques had been written: electrician's assistant, $8,500; payroll taxes, $175; supplies purchased and used on jobs, $9,500; oil, gas, and maintenance on truck, $1,200; insurance, $700; rent, $500; utilities and telephone, $825; and miscellaneous expenses (including advertising), $600. Also, uncollected invoices to customers for electric repair services amounted to $3,000. The $200 rent for December had not been paid. The average income tax rate is 30 percent. John estimated the cost of using the truck and tools (*depreciation*) during the three months to be $1,200.

Required:

1. Prepare a quarterly income statement for Abel Electric Repair Company Incorporated for the three months of October through December 2011. Use the following main captions: Revenue from services, Expenses, Profit before income taxes, and Profit.
2. Prepare a statement of financial position for Abel Electric Repair Company Incorporated as at December 31, 2011.
3. Do you think that John may have a need for one or more additional financial reports for 2011 and thereafter? Explain.

CASES AND PROJECTS

FINDING AND INTERPRETING FINANCIAL INFORMATION

LO1, 3   **CP1–1**   **Finding Financial Information**

The Nestlé Group

Refer to the financial statements of The Nestlé Group. in Appendix A at the end of this book.

Required:

Look at the income statement, statement of financial position, and statement of cash flows closely and attempt to infer the types of information they report. Then answer the following questions based on the report.

1. On what day of the year does its fiscal year end?
2. For how many years does it present complete
       a. statements of financial position?   *b.* income statements?   *c.* statements of cash flows?
3. Are its financial statements audited by independent accountants? How do you know?
4. Did its total assets increase or decrease over the last year?
5. What was the ending balance of inventories?
6. Write out its basic accounting equation in Swiss francs at year-end.

LO1, 3   **CP1–2**   **Finding Financial Information**

Cadbury plc

Refer to the financial statements of Cadbury plc online.

Required:

1. What is the amount of profit for the current fiscal year?
2. What amount of revenue was earned in the current fiscal year?
3. How much inventory does the company have at the end of the current fiscal year?
4. By what amount did cash and cash equivalents* change during the year?
5. Who is the auditor for the company?

LO1   **CP1–3**   **Comparing Companies**

The Nestlé Group
vs.
Cadbury plc

 eXcel

Refer to the financial statements and the accompanying notes of The Nestlé Group given in Appendix A and of Cadbury plc online. Nestlé uses the Swiss franc (CHF) in preparing its financial statements whereas Cadbury reports its financial information by using the pound sterling (£). Use the exchange rates indicated in (1) and (2) below to convert the pounds sterling into Swiss francs so you can compare the specific financial statement elements for both companies.

Required:

1. Total assets is a common measure of the size of a company. Which company had the higher total assets at the end of the most recent year? The exchange rate between the two currencies was £1 = CHF 1.53 at December 31, 2008.
2. Net sales is also a common measure of the size of a company. Which company had the higher net sales for the most recent year? The average exchange rate between the two currencies during 2008 was £1 = CHF 1.99.
3. Growth during a period is calculated as

       Growth rate = [(Ending amount − Beginning amount) / Beginning amount] × 100

Which company had the higher growth rate in total assets during the most recent year? Which company has the higher growth rate in net sales during the most recent year?

FINANCIAL REPORTING AND ANALYSIS CASES

LO1   **CP1–4**   **Using Financial Reports: Applying the Accounting Equation to Liquidate a Company**

On June 1, 2012, Bland Corporation prepared a statement of financial position just prior to going out of business. The totals for the three main components showed the following:

Assets (no cash)	$90,000
Liabilities	50,000
Shareholders' equity	40,000

Shortly thereafter, all of the assets were sold for cash.

---

*Cash equivalents are short-term investments readily convertible into cash and whose value is unlikely to change.

Required:

1. How would the statement of financial position appear immediately after the sale of the assets for cash for each of the following cases? Use the format given here.

	Cash Received for the Assets	Balances Immediately after Sale		
		Assets	− Liabilities	= Shareholders' Equity
Case A	$ 90,000	$ _____	$ _____	$ _____
Case B	80,000	$ _____	$ _____	$ _____
Case C	100,000	$ _____	$ _____	$ _____
Case D	35,000	$ _____	$ _____	$ _____

2. How should the cash be distributed in each separate case? (*Hint*: Creditors must be paid in full before owners receive any payment.) Use the format given here:

	To Creditors	To Shareholders	Total
Case A	$ _____	$ _____	$ _____
Case B	$ _____	$ _____	$ _____
Case C	$ _____	$ _____	$ _____
Case D	$ _____	$ _____	$ _____

CRITICAL THINKING CASES

CP1–5 Making Decisions as a Manager: Reporting the Assets and Liabilities of a Business
Pedro Gonzalez owns and operates Pedro's Shop (a sole proprietorship). An employee prepares a financial report for the business at each year-end. This report lists all of the resources (assets) owned by Gonzalez, including such personal items as the home he owns and occupies. It also lists all of the debts of the business, but not his personal debts.

LO1, 3

Required:

1. From an accounting point of view, do you disagree with what is being included in and excluded from the report of business assets and liabilities? Explain.
2. Upon questioning, Gonzalez responded, "Don't worry about it; we use it only to support a loan from the bank." How would you respond to this comment?

CP1–6 Making Decisions as an Owner: Deciding about a Proposed Audit
You are one of three partners who own and operate Sam's Cleaning Service. The company has been operating for 10 years. One of the other partners has always prepared the company's annual financial statements. Recently you proposed that the statements be audited each year because it would benefit the partners and preclude possible disagreements about the division of profits. The partner who prepares the statements proposed that his nephew Roger, who has a lot of financial experience, can do the job and at little cost. Your other partner remained silent.

LO3

Required:

1. What position would you take on the proposal? Justify your response.
2. What would you strongly recommend? Give the basis for your recommendation.

CP1–7 Evaluating an Ethical Dilemma: Ethics and Auditor Responsibilities
A key factor that an auditor provides is independence. The *codes of professional conduct* typically state that a member in public practice should be independent in fact and appearance when providing auditing and other attestation service.

LO3, 4

Required:

Do you consider the following circumstances to suggest a lack of independence? Justify your position. (Use your imagination. Specific answers are not provided in the chapter.)

1. James Slater is a partner with a large audit firm and is assigned to the CGI audit. James owns 10 shares of CGI.
2. Maria Tsoukas has invested in a mutual fund company that owns 100,000 shares of Sears Canada Inc. She is the auditor of Sears.

3. Bob Fisher is a clerk/typist who works on the audit of the Bank of Montreal. He has just inherited 70,000 shares of the Bank of Montreal. (Bob enjoys his work and plans to continue despite his new wealth.)

4. Nancy Chen worked on weekends as the controller for a small business that a friend started. Nancy quit the job in midyear and now has no association with the company. She works full-time for a large accounting firm and has been assigned to do the audit of her friend's business.

5. Sylvia Bertone borrowed $100,000 for a home mortgage from First City National Bank. The mortgage was granted on normal credit terms. Sylvia is the partner in charge of the First City audit.

FINANCIAL REPORTING AND ANALYSIS TEAM PROJECT

LO1, 3   **CP1–8**   **Team Project: Examining an Annual Report**

As a team, select an industry to analyze. A list of companies classified by industry can be obtained by accessing **www.fpinfomart.ca** and then choosing "Companies by Industry." You can also find a list of industries and companies within each industry via **http://ca.finance.yahoo.com/investing**. A list of industries can be obtained by clicking on "Annual Reports" under "Tools".

Each group member should acquire the annual report for one publicly traded company in the industry, with each member selecting a different company. (Library files, the SEDAR service at **www.sedar.com**, or the company's website are good sources.)

Required:

On an individual basis, each group member should write a short report answering the following questions about the selected company. Discuss any patterns that you observe as a team. Then, as a team, write a short report comparing and contrasting your companies, using the six attributes listed below.

1. What types of products or services does it sell?

2. On what day of the year does its fiscal year end?

3. For how many years does it present complete

    a. statements of financial position (or balance sheets)?

    b. income statements and statements of comprehensive income?

    c. statements of cash flows?

4. Are its financial statements audited by independent auditors? If so, by whom?

5. Did its total assets increase or decrease over the last year?

6. Did its profit increase or decrease over the last year?

Investing and Financing Decisions and the Statement of Financial Position

After studying this chapter, you should be able to do the following:

LEARNING OBJECTIVES

LO1 Understand the objective of financial reporting and the related key accounting assumptions and principles. p. 47

LO2 Define the elements of a classified statement of financial position. p. 50

LO3 Identify what constitutes a business transaction, and recognize common account titles used in business. p. 56

LO4 Apply transaction analysis to simple business transactions in terms of the accounting model: Assets = Liabilities + Shareholders' Equity. p. 58

LO5 Determine the impact of business transactions on the statement of financial position by using two basic tools: journal entries and T-accounts. p. 63

LO6 Prepare a classified statement of financial position and analyze it by using the debt-to-equity ratio. p. 71

LO7 Identify investing and financing transactions and demonstrate how they are reported on the statement of cash flows. p. 74

FOCUS COMPANY: **Nestlé S.A.**

EXPANSION STRATEGY IN THE NUTRITION, HEALTH, AND WELLNESS INDUSTRY

Nestlé S.A. (**www.nestle.com**), founded in 1866, produces and markets a wide assortment of nutrition, health, and wellness products, including baby foods, breakfast cereals, chocolate, coffee, dairy products, ice cream, bottled water, and pet foods. Its products are sold in over 100 countries in the five continents.

Nestlé grew rapidly over the past 60 years to become the leading food company worldwide, with a total of 449 manufacturing facilities in 84 countries by December 31, 2009, including 10 factories in Canada. The company has executed its growth strategy by acquiring or investing in other companies. Since 1998, Nestlé has invested over 50 billion Swiss francs to grow through acquiring other companies. The company's statement of financial position at December 31, 2009, compared to December 31, 1998, (in millions of Swiss francs) highlights its growth:

	Assets	=	Liabilities	+	Shareholders' Equity
December 31, 2009	110,916		57,285		53,631
December 31, 1998	56,441		32,845		23,596
Change	54,475		24,440		30,035

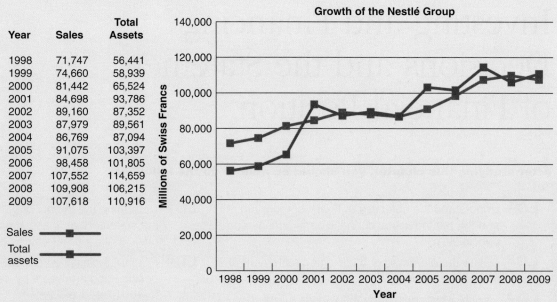

Year	Sales	Total Assets
1998	71,747	56,441
1999	74,660	58,939
2000	81,442	65,524
2001	84,698	93,786
2002	89,160	87,352
2003	87,979	89,561
2004	86,769	87,094
2005	91,075	103,397
2006	98,458	101,805
2007	107,552	114,659
2008	109,908	106,215
2009	107,618	110,916

Source: Nestlé's annual reports

The company's annual growth in sales and total assets since 1998 is highlighted in the graph.

UNDERSTANDING THE BUSINESS

Nutrition, health, and wellness are issues that concern all people. Individuals strive to get proper nutrition and be healthy for as long a period as possible. Governments also exert every effort to help their citizens get proper nutrition to be productive members of society. For this reason, nutrition, health, and wellness have attracted the attention of many businesses worldwide. A large number of companies have emerged over time to meet the needs of people seeking basic nutrition and healthy lifestyles. Nestlé, Kraft Foods, ConAgra Foods, Sara Lee, Le Groupe Danone, and Cadbury among others capture most of the global retail market for nutrition and health foods and drinks. These and other companies compete ferociously, with Nestlé capturing the lion's share of the global market.

Nestlé has been a global food manufacturing giant since the 1900s when it had operations on four continents. The company relies on a strategy of quality for both its products and its services, focusing on research and development to bring innovative products and services to consumers. In 2009, Nestlé invested CHF 2 billion in research and development. The business model that has been so successful for Nestlé rests also on sound scientific evidence of improved nutrition. The company is proud of its history of both developing reliable suppliers in developing countries and creating a safe manufacturing setting, sourcing over two-thirds of its CHF 20 billion of raw materials (milk, coffee, cocoa) from them. Nestlé is committed to sustainable production, socially responsible business practices, and reducing environmental pollution and waste.

The company's financial performance, reported in its audited financial statements, helps users to understand how well Nestlé has implemented its strategy in the past and to evaluate future growth potential.

Financial statements are intended to communicate the economic facts, measured in monetary units, in a standardized, formal way. Therefore, by applying accounting principles consistently, accountants formally communicate comparable estimates that faithfully represent important economic facts about companies like Nestlé and its competitors. As explained in Chapter 1, financial statements include four components: the statement of financial position, the statement of comprehensive income, the statement of changes in equity, and the statement of cash flows. In this chapter, we focus on the statement of financial position, and we examine how this financial statement communicates the results or consequences of Nestlé's strategy by answering the following questions:

- What type of business activities cause changes in amounts reported on the statement of financial position from one period to the next?
- How do specific activities affect each of these amounts?
- How do companies keep track of these amounts?

Once we have answered these questions, we will be able to use the information on the statement of financial position to perform two key analytical tasks:

1. Analyze and predict the effects of business decisions on a company's financial statements.
2. Use the financial statement of other companies to identify and evaluate the activities that managers engaged in during a past period. This is a key task in *financial statement analysis.*

In this chapter, we focus on typical asset acquisition activities (often called *investing activities*) in which Nestlé engages, along with the related *financing activities*, such as borrowing funds from creditors and receiving funds from investors to acquire the assets. We examine only those activities that affect amounts reported on the statement of financial position. Operating activities that affect amounts reported on both the income statement and the statement of financial position are covered in Chapters 3 and 4. Although these activities are all related, we separate them initially to aid your understanding. To begin, let us return to the basic concepts introduced in Chapter 1.

ORGANIZATION OF THE CHAPTER

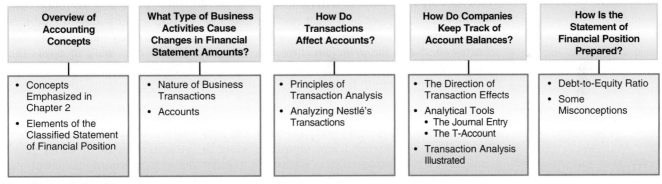

Overview of Accounting Concepts	What Type of Business Activities Cause Changes in Financial Statement Amounts?	How Do Transactions Affect Accounts?	How Do Companies Keep Track of Account Balances?	How Is the Statement of Financial Position Prepared?

• Concepts Emphasized in Chapter 2
• Elements of the Classified Statement of Financial Position
	• Nature of Business Transactions
	• Accounts
		• Principles of Transaction Analysis
		• Analyzing Nestlé's Transactions
			• The Direction of Transaction Effects
			• Analytical Tools
			  • The Journal Entry
			  • The T-Account
			• Transaction Analysis Illustrated
				• Debt-to-Equity Ratio
				• Some Misconceptions

Supplemental material:
Appendix B: The Formal Recordkeeping System (online)

OVERVIEW OF ACCOUNTING CONCEPTS

The key accounting terms and concepts we defined in Chapter 1 are part of a theoretical framework developed over many years. The framework prescribes the nature, function, and limitations of both financial accounting and financial statements. The essential elements of this framework are embodied in the IASB *Framework for the Preparation and Presentation of Financial Statements,*[1] which identifies concepts that form the foundation for financial reporting. This framework is the subject of a major project undertaken jointly by the IASB and the Financial Accounting Standards Board (FASB) of the United States.[2] This conceptual framework is presented in Exhibit 2.1 as

LO1

Understand the objective of financial reporting and the related key accounting assumptions and principles.

---

[1]International Accounting Standards Committee (1989), *Framework for the Preparation and Presentation of Financial Statements.* Adopted by the International Accounting Standards Board, 2001.

[2]Financial Accounting Standards Board, Conceptual Framework for Financial Reporting: The Objective of Financial Reporting and Qualitative Characteristics and Constraints of Decision-Useful Financial Reporting Information, Exposure Draft, May 29, 2008.

an overview, with key concepts discussed in the next five chapters. An understanding of the accounting concepts will be helpful as you study because learning and remembering *how* the accounting process works is much easier if you know *why* it works a certain way. A clear understanding of these concepts will also help you in future chapters as we examine more complex business activities.

Concepts Emphasized in Chapter 2

The **PRIMARY OBJECTIVE OF EXTERNAL FINANCIAL REPORTING** is to provide useful economic information about a business to help external parties make sound financial decisions.

Objective of Financial Reporting   The primary objective of external financial reporting is to provide useful economic information about a business to help external parties, primarily investors and creditors, make sound financial decisions in their capacity as capital providers. The users of accounting information are identified as *decision makers*. These decision makers include average investors, creditors, and experts who provide financial advice. They are all expected to have a reasonable understanding of accounting concepts and procedures (this may be one of the reasons why you are studying accounting). Of course, as we discussed in Chapter 1, many other groups, such as suppliers and customers, also use external financial statements. To achieve this objective, financial reports must enable decision makers not only to assess the amounts, timing, and uncertainty of future cash inflows and outflows but also to understand the financial value of both the assets owned and claims against those assets (liabilities and equity).

All the elements of the financial statements in Exhibit 2.1 are recognized and reported in accordance with the assumptions, principles, and constraints. The objective of financial reporting, however, cannot be achieved simply by reporting any financial value for each element, because the amounts must also conform to specific qualities if they are to be useful to decision makers. These qualities, or qualitative characteristics, appear in the upper part of the exhibit.

Users are most interested in information to assist them in projecting the future cash inflows and outflows of a business. For example, creditors and potential creditors need to assess an entity's ability to pay interest over time and repay the initial amount borrowed, called the *principal*. Investors and potential investors want to assess the entity's ability to pay dividends in the future. They also want to evaluate how successful the company might be in the future, so that as the share price rises, investors can then sell their shares for more than they paid.

The **SEPARATE-ENTITY ASSUMPTION** states that business transactions are separate from the transactions of the owners.

Accounting Assumptions   Three of the four basic assumptions that underlie accounting measurement and reporting relate to the statement of financial position. They were discussed in Chapter 1. Under the separate-entity assumption, the activities of each business must be accounted for as an individual organization that is separate and apart from its owners, all other persons, and other entities. Separation of the owners' resources (and obligations) from those of the business entity is necessary for a proper evaluation of the entity's results of operations and its financial position. For example, a building purchased by the owner of a real estate development and management company for personal use should not be

---

Exhibit **2.1**

Financial Accounting and Reporting– Conceptual Framework

Concepts in red are discussed in Chapters 1 and 2. Those in black will be discussed in Chapters 3, 4, and 6.

Objective of External Financial Reporting:
   To provide useful economic information to external users for decision making
   Qualitative characteristics of useful information:
   • Relevance, faithful representation, comparability, verifiability, timeliness, and understandability

Elements to be Measured and Reported:
   • **Assets, Liabilities, Equity,** Revenues, Expenses, Gains, Losses

Concepts for Measuring and Reporting Information:
   • **Assumptions: Separate-Entity, Unit-of-Measure, Continuity,** Periodicity
   • **Principles:**   **Historical Cost,** Revenue Recognition, Matching, Full Disclosure
   • **Constraints:**   Materiality, Cost

mixed with buildings owned by the company. Under the unit-of-measure assumption, each business entity accounts for and reports its financial results primarily in terms of the national monetary unit (dollars in Canada, euros in European union countries, pesos in Mexico, etc.), even if the entity has business operations in many countries.

The use of a specific unit of measure allows for meaningful aggregation of financial amounts. Furthermore, accountants assume that the unit of measure has a stable value over time, even though we recognize that the price we pay to purchase a specific item, such as a candy bar, tends to increase over time. Nestlé's statement of financial position includes many assets measured in Swiss francs from the 1970s, 1980s, and 1990s. The stable monetary unit assumption allows accountants to combine different amounts, even though the purchasing power of the monetary unit has changed over time.

For accounting purposes, a business normally is assumed to continue operating long enough to carry out its objectives and to meet contractual commitments. This continuity assumption is sometimes called the *going-concern assumption* because we expect a business to continue to operate into the foreseeable future. Violation of this assumption means that assets and liabilities should be valued and reported on the statement of financial position as if the company were to be liquidated (i.e., discontinued, with all assets sold and all debts paid). In all future chapters, unless indicated otherwise, we assume that businesses meet the continuity assumption.

The fourth assumption, periodicity, provides guidance on measuring revenues and expenses that will be discussed in Chapter 3.

Basic Accounting Principle   The historical cost principle states that the cash-equivalent cost needed to acquire an asset (the historical cost) should be used for initial recognition (recording) of all financial statement elements. Under the cost principle, cost is measured on the date of the transaction as the cash paid plus the current monetary value of all non-cash considerations (any assets, privileges, or rights) also given in the exchange. One advantage of this approach is that many assets are acquired according to legal contracts that clearly state the acquisition cost. For example, if you trade your computer plus cash for a new car, the cost of the new car is equal to the cash paid plus the market value of the computer. Thus, in most cases, cost is relatively easy to determine and can be verified. A disadvantage of this approach is that, subsequent to the date of acquisition, the continued reporting of historical cost on the statement of financial position does not reflect any change in market value, usually because market value is a less verifiable measure than historical cost.

> The **UNIT-OF-MEASURE ASSUMPTION** states that accounting information should be measured and reported in the national monetary unit.

> The **CONTINUITY (GOING-CONCERN) ASSUMPTION** states that businesses are assumed to continue to operate into the foreseeable future.

> The **COST PRINCIPLE** requires assets to be recorded at the historical cash-equivalent cost, which is cash paid plus the current monetary value of all non-cash considerations also given in the exchange, on the date of the transaction.

| $15,000 Cash paid | + | $2,000 Market value of computer | = | $17,000 Historical cost of new car |

Nestlé owns land that it acquired several years ago and reports it on the statement of financial position at historical cost. Although the market price or economic value of the land has risen over time, its recorded value remains unchanged at its original cost because this amount is a verifiable measure based on an actual exchange that occurred in the past. It would be desirable to show on the statement of financial position the land's current market value; that is, the price at which it could either be sold or replaced instead of its outdated historical cost. However, the land's current value may not be reliable if different real estate appraisers produce different values for the same piece of land. Accountants continue, therefore, to rely on historical cost measures for reporting purposes because they are factual, although they may not be useful for specific decision-making purposes. Furthermore, as long as Nestlé remains a going concern it is unlikely to sell the land at its current market value. The land retains usefulness, often referred to as the asset's value-in-use, to Nestlé. If Nestlé has no intent to sell the land, then its current market value is not specifically relevant to understanding the financial health of the company. The use of alternative measurement bases for asset valuation will be discussed in Chapter 9.

Assets, liabilities, and equity are the key elements of a corporation's statement of financial position, as we learned in Chapter 1. Let us examine the definitions in more detail.

Elements of the Classified Statement of Financial Position

LO2

Define the elements of a classified statement of financial position.

ASSETS are economic resources controlled by an entity as a result of past transactions or events and from which future economic benefits may be obtained.

Assets are economic resources controlled by an entity as a result of past transactions or events and from which future economic benefits may be obtained. These are the resources that the entity has and can use in its future operations. When Nestlé purchases an asset, it acquires the right for future benefits to be derived from that asset, as well as any future risks and obligations arising from control of the asset. External users of Nestlé's financial statements care about its assets because they embody future financial benefits. For lenders, Nestlé's assets and their productivity are the basis upon which they can generate forecasts about how readily the company can repay its financial obligations. For Nestlé's shareholders, the increase in the value of their investment will depend in large part on the realized future benefits arising from assets under the company's control.

To make financial statements more useful to investors, creditors, and analysts, specific *classifications* of information are included on the statements. Various classifications are used in practice, and you should not be confused when you notice slightly different formats used by different companies.

Let us explore Nestlé's simplified statement of financial position, presented in Exhibit 2.2. First, notice the title of the statement: Consolidated Statement of Financial Position. *Consolidated* means that the classified elements of Nestlé's statement of financial position are combined with those of other companies under its control (e.g., Alcon Inc., Haagen-Dazs Shoppe Company Inc.).[3] For convenience, the amounts for the various elements of the statement of financial position are shown in millions of Swiss francs. Two amounts are shown for each element: one at December 31, 2009, and the other at December 31, 2008, one year earlier. This system allows investors to compare, at a glance, the value of each classified element from year to year, and then analyze these changes to understand whether the company's financial position has improved or deteriorated over time.

Nestlé's statement of financial position is shown in *column* or *report* format, with assets listed first, followed by liabilities, and then shareholders' equity. Other companies may choose an account format with the assets listed on the left-hand side and liabilities and shareholders' equity listed on the right. Both formats are standard ways of communicating the same information. We now explain the various elements that appear on Nestlé's statement of financial position.

Exhibit 2.2 presents Nestlé's statement of financial position, with amounts rounded to the nearest million Swiss francs. Notice that Nestlé's fiscal year ends on December 31. The choice of year-ends will be discussed in Chapter 4.

Typically, the assets of a company include the following:

1. Current assets (short-term)
   a. Cash and cash equivalents
   b. Short-term investments
   c. Trade and other receivables

---

[3]The rules for consolidation of financial statements are covered in advanced accounting courses.

Exhibit **2.2**

Nestlé's Statement of Financial Position

THE NESTLÉ GROUP
Consolidated Statement of Financial Position
As at December 31
(in millions of Swiss francs)

Assets	2009	2008	
Current assets			
Cash and cash equivalents	5,825	5,835	Amount of cash and short-term deposits in the company's bank accounts
Short-term investments	2,585	1,296	Excess cash invested in financial instruments
Trade receivables	9,425	10,552	Amounts owed by customers from prior sales
Notes receivable	2,884	2,890	Amounts to be received from others on specific dates
Inventories	7,734	9,342	Food and drink products, and production materials
Prepayments	589	627	Rent and insurance paid in advance
Other current assets	10,828	2,506	A variety of assets that are covered in future chapters
Total current assets	**39,870**	**33,048**	
Non-current assets			
Property, plant and equipment	21,599	21,097	Factories and production equipment
Investment in associates	8,693	7,796	Amounts invested in shares of associated corporations
Financial assets	4,162	3,868	Amounts invested in term deposits, and securities of other corporations
Goodwill	27,502	30,637	A mix of intangible assets that cannot be identified separately
Intangible assets	6,658	6,867	Economic resources that lack physical substance
Other assets	2,432	2,902	A variety of assets that are covered in future chapters
Total non-current assets	**71,046**	**73,167**	
Total assets	**110,916**	**106,215**	
Liabilities and Equity			
Current liabilities			
Trade payables	13,033	12,608	Amounts owed to suppliers for prior purchases
Short-term borrowings	14,438	15,383	Amounts owed to lenders within one year
Income taxes payable	1,173	824	Amount of taxes owed to the government
Accrued liabilities	2,779	2,931	Amounts owed to various suppliers of services
Other current liabilities	4,017	1,477	A variety of liabilities that are covered in future chapters
Total current liabilities	**35,440**	**33,223**	
Non-current liabilities			
Long-term borrowings	8,966	6,344	Amounts owed on written debt contracts after one year
Deferred income tax liabilities	1,404	1,341	Amount of taxes deferred to future periods
Provisions	3,865	3,663	Estimated liabilities whose amounts and timing of payment are not known with certainty
Other liabilities	7,610	6,728	A variety of liabilities that are covered in future chapters
Total non-current liabilities	**21,845**	**18,076**	
Total liabilities	**57,285**	**51,299**	
Equity			
Share capital	6,248	6,266	Amounts invested in the business by shareholders
Retained earnings	64,660	58,646	Past earnings not distributed to shareholders
Other components	(21,993)	(14,138)	Adjustments to assets and liabilities that are explained in future chapters
Total equity attributable to shareholders of the parent	**48,915**	**50,774**	
Non-controlling interests	4,716	4,142	Equity of other corporations not controlled by Nestlé
Total equity	**53,631**	**54,916**	
Total liabilities and equity	**110,916**	**106,215**	

Note: These statements of financial position are adaptations of Nestlé's actual statements at those dates. Some of the elements of the actual statement were combined for illustrative purposes.
Source: Nestlé S.A.

   d. Inventories

   e. Prepayments (i.e., expenses paid in advance of use)

   f. Other current assets

2. Non-current assets (long-term)

   a. Property, plant, and equipment (at cost less accumulated depreciation)

   b. Investment in associates

   c. Financial assets

   d. Goodwill

   e. Intangible assets

   f. Other (miscellaneous) assets

CURRENT ASSETS are assets that will be used or turned into cash, normally within one year. Inventory is always considered to be a current asset, regardless of the time needed to produce and sell it.

Assets are divided into two subgroups: current and non-current assets. Current assets, also known as *short-term assets*, are those economic resources that Nestlé will typically transform into cash or use within the next year or the operating business cycle of the company, whichever is longer. Nestlé lists its assets *in order of liquidity*, which means how soon they can be transformed into cash. Under current assets, *cash and cash equivalents* (highly liquid investments) appear first because they are the most liquid assets. It should be emphasized that each of the items reported on the statement of financial position, such as cash and cash equivalents, is a combination of a number of similar items. Nestlé's cash equivalents consist of time deposits and placements in commercial paper with original maturities of three months or less. *Short-term investments* represent the reported values for shares of other companies and other financial instruments purchased as investments of excess cash.

Any *receivable* represents an amount of money owed to Nestlé. *Trade and other receivables* consist primarily of *trade receivables*, which are amounts owed by customers who purchased products and services on credit. These amounts are normally collected within one year of the statement's date. *Notes receivable* are written promises by customers and others to pay Nestlé fixed amounts by specific dates.

Inventories refers to goods that (1) are held for sale to customers in the normal course of business, or (2) are used to produce goods or services for sale. Inventory is always considered to be a current asset, no matter how long it takes to produce and sell. Nestlé's inventory would include a variety of nutrition and health foods and drinks not yet sold to distributors; milk, cocoa, sugar, and other ingredients purchased but not yet used for production purposes; and partially completed products. *Prepayments* (e.g., insurance premiums and rent paid in advance for use of a building) reflect available benefits (e.g., monthly insurance protection, office space) that the company will use within one year. *Other current assets*, when reported, will include a number of assets with smaller balances that are combined.

FINANCIAL ANALYSIS

ANALYSIS OF CHANGES IN INVENTORY AND TRADE RECEIVABLES

Investors analyze the financial statements of a company to decide whether or not to purchase its shares or to lend it money. One important decision factor is how easily a company can access cash to pay both debts to its creditors and dividends to its shareholders. In a normal business cycle, Nestlé would produce baby foods, breakfast cereals, chocolate, and coffee products for sale to distributors such as Safeway and Loblaw. These products, called *inventories,* are stored in warehouses until they are sold. The faster these products are sold to customers, the faster these assets are transformed into cash. Let's examine the company's ability to access cash, assuming for simplicity that Nestlé's inventories consist of products held for sale.

Notice the balance of trade receivables decreased from CHF 10,552 million at December 31, 2008, to CHF 9,425 million at December 31, 2009, indicating that the cash collected from customers exceeded the amount of sales on credit. An investor would also observe that cash and cash equivalents decreased from CHF 5,835 million at December 31, 2008, to CHF 5,825 million at December 31, 2009. Investors would examine the statement of cash flows to gain clearer insight on how events in the past year resulted in the change in cash and cash equivalents (see Chapter 5). For the moment, this brief analysis would reassure an investor that the first two elements reported on the statement of financial position are relevant to answering an important question about how easily Nestlé can access cash to pay its debts to creditors and dividends to shareholders.

Following the current assets section, Nestlé reports a number of non-current assets. These assets are considered to be long-term because they will be used or turned into cash over a period longer than the next year. ***Property, plant, and equipment*** includes all land, buildings, machinery, and equipment such as tools, furniture, and other fixtures that will be used for the production, packaging, and storage of Nestlé's foods and drinks. These are also called *fixed assets* or *capital assets*—they have a physical form you can touch, and therefore each asset is *tangible*.

> **NON-CURRENT ASSETS** are considered to be long term because they will be used or turned into cash over a period longer than the next year.

Nestlé may sometimes be interested in purchasing shares issued by other corporations for the purpose of exercising significant influence over their investing, financing, and operating decisions. The investment in shares to achieve such an objective is called ***investment in associates***. For example, Nestlé owned about 30 percent of the shares of L'Oréal as at December 31, 2009, which allows Nestlé's management to influence decisions made by L'Oréal. ***Financial assets*** represent investments in shares or debt instruments issued by other companies that Nestlé intends to keep for longer than one year.

Goodwill is an intangible asset that arises when a company purchases another business to control its operating, investment, and financing decisions. Often, the purchase price of a business exceeds the fair market value of all of the identifiable assets owned by the business minus all of the identifiable liabilities owed to others. Goodwill reflects assets that are not easily identifiable and measured, such as customer confidence, quality products, reputation for good service, and financial standing of the acquired business. The amount of CHF 27,502 million that Nestlé reported at December 31, 2009, resulted from the acquisitions of many businesses over time, particularly its acquisition of Ralston Purina in 2001. ***Intangible assets*** have no physical substance but have a long life. They usually are not acquired for resale but are directly related to the operations of the business. Intangible assets include such items as goodwill, franchises, patents, trademarks, and copyrights. Their values arise from the *legal rights* and *privileges* of ownership, which is recognized if they are purchased from external parties or as a result of internal development. Nestlé's intangibles include brands, intellectual property rights, operating rights, and management information systems. Intangible assets, including goodwill, are discussed in more detail in Chapter 9.

Other assets, when reported, will include a number of assets that are combined because of their relatively small values.

Liabilities are a corporation's debts and obligations arising from past transactions. They represent future outflows of assets (mainly cash) or services to the ***creditors*** that provided the corporation with the resources needed to conduct its business. When the corporation borrows money, creditors receive not only full payment of the amount owed to them, but also interest on the borrowed amount.

> **LIABILITIES** are present debts or obligations of the entity that result from past transactions, which will be paid with assets or services.

Typically, the liabilities of a company include the following:

1. Current liabilities (short-term)
   a. Trade payables
   b. Short-term borrowings
   c. Income taxes payable

    d. Accrued liabilities

    e. Other current liabilities

2. Non-current liabilities (long-term)

    a. Long-term borrowings

    b. Deferred income tax liabilities

    c. Provisions

    d. Other liabilities

> **CURRENT LIABILITIES** are obligations that will be paid in cash (or other current assets) or satisfied by providing service within the coming year.

Like assets, liabilities are divided into two subgroups: current and non-current. They are listed by **order of time to maturity** (how soon an obligation must be paid). Current liabilities, known as short-term liabilities, must be paid within the next year or operating business cycle of the company, whichever is longer. Normally, the cash from converting current assets is used to pay current liabilities. The first current liability is **trade payables**, which represents the total amount owed to suppliers of materials that Nestlé used in producing and packaging its products for sale. The second current liability, **short-term borrowings**, represents short-term loans from banks. Bank loans are common when the company does not have a sufficient amount of cash to pay its creditors. The third liability, **income taxes payable**, is simply an estimate of the amount of taxes Nestlé is expected to pay to taxation authorities. **Accrued liabilities** represent the total amount owed to suppliers for various types of services such as payroll, rent, and other obligations. **Other current liabilities**, when reported, will include a number of liabilities with relatively small amounts that are combined.

FINANCIAL ANALYSIS

ANALYSIS OF CHANGE IN TRADE PAYABLES

Using both current assets and current liabilities for Nestlé, we can improve our analysis of the availability of cash to repay debts to creditors and dividends to shareholders.

The company's current liabilities shows that Nestlé owes CHF 2,217 million more in current liabilities at December 31, 2009, than it did at December 31, 2008. As investors, we would tentatively conclude that the company has increased its reliance on suppliers to finance its current assets. However, investors must learn far more about the business cycle for nutrition and health products, the outlook for the industry sectors in which Nestlé operates, and its main competitors before coming to a firm conclusion.

At the beginning of this chapter, we stated that investors are most interested in relevant information that helps them predict future cash inflows and outflows. From this very preliminary analysis, investors can predict that, because Nestlé has increased its current liabilities by CHF 2,217 million, a larger amount of cash to repay the outstanding debt to creditors is needed next year than in the current year.

> **NON-CURRENT LIABILITIES** are a company's debts that have maturities extending beyond one year from the date of the statement of financial position.

Non-current liabilities are a company's debts having maturities extending beyond one year from the date of the statement of financial position. They include **long-term borrowings** from banks and other lenders, **deferred income tax liabilities** that arise from temporary differences between the profit measured in accordance with IFRS and taxable profit that is determined in conformity with applicable tax laws, **provisions** that are estimated liabilities characterized by uncertainty about the exact amount to be paid and the timing of the payment, and **other liabilities** that include a number of other liabilities. These various types of non-current liabilities will be covered in future chapters.

ENVIRONMENTAL LIABILITIES—THE GREENING OF ACCOUNTING STANDARDS

A QUESTION OF ACCOUNTABILITY

For many years, companies faced growing pressure to estimate and disclose environmental liabilities such as the cleanup of hazardous waste. International Financial Reporting Standards (IFRS) require publicly accountable enterprises to report their best estimate of probable liabilities, including environmental liabilities, in notes to the financial statements. For example, Suncor Energy Inc., which mines oil from the tar sands of northern Alberta, reported environmental liabilities exceeding $2,888 million in its 2009 financial statements, representing approximately 8 percent of its total liabilities at December 31, 2009. It is estimated, however, that a significant percentage of companies under-report or fail to report such liabilities, often because of the way disclosure rules are applied.

A key economic concern for many Canadian companies is how to manage their resources in an economically sustainable way. Nestlé, like many companies, publishes a report on environmental sustainability, which includes both financial and non-financial performance indicators that measure its progress toward meeting its sustainable development targets.

Nestlé's management believes that a business has to create value, not only for its shareholders but also for society at large in order to be successful in the long term. Nestlé's comprehensive report on environmental sustainability provides detailed information about the steps it has taken to reduce the impact of its activities on the environment. The company uses environmental performance indicators to monitor the impact of its activities on greenhouse gas emissions, energy consumption, water consumption, and waste-water management.

Nestlé Canada's Environmental Sustainability Report for 2008 indicates that its management takes its environmental responsibility seriously. The report illustrates how non-financial information is relevant to external decision makers.

Source: Nestlé Canada Environmental Sustainability Report 2008. Nestlé S.A.

Shareholders' equity (owners' equity or stockholders' equity) is the financing provided to the corporation by both its owners and the operations of the business. One key difference between owners and creditors is that creditors are entitled to settlement of their legal claims on the corporation's assets before the owners receive a penny, even if this consumes all the corporation's assets. Consequently, owners have a residual claim on the corporation's assets.

Owners *invest* (purchase shares) in a company because they expect to receive two types of cash flow: dividends, which are a distribution of the corporation's earnings (a return on shareholders' investment), and gains from selling their shares for more than they paid (known as *capital gains*).

Typically the shareholders' equity of a corporation includes the following:

1. Share capital (or capital stock)

2. Retained earnings (accumulated earnings that have not been declared as dividends)

3. Other components

Share capital reflects the proceeds received when the corporation issued the shares. Occasionally, shareholders will contribute in excess of the amount allocated to share capital, such as premiums on shares issued; these contributions are called *contributed surplus*. The sum of share capital and contributed surplus represents the *contributed capital* of the corporation. Nestlé's share capital of CHF 6,248 million has resulted from selling shares to investors at different points in the company's history.[4]

SHAREHOLDERS' EQUITY (OWNERS' EQUITY OR STOCKHOLDERS' EQUITY) is the financing provided by the owners and the operations of the business.

SHARE CAPITAL results from owners providing cash (and sometimes other assets) to the business.

---

[4]In fact, this amount consists of CHF 365 million of share capital and CHF 5,883 million of premiums received from shareholders in exchange of issued shares. We have combined these two amounts for simplicity.

RETAINED EARNINGS refers to the accumulated earnings of a company that are not distributed to the owners and are reinvested in the business.

Most companies that operate profitably retain part of their earnings for reinvestment in their business. The other part is distributed as dividends to shareholders. The annual earnings that are not distributed to shareholders are called retained earnings. Nestlé's retained earnings equalled CHF 64,660 million at December 31, 2009, and represent the net amount of earnings that have not been distributed to shareholders since the company was incorporated in 1873. Nestlé's growth over time has been financed by a substantial reinvestment of retained earnings. In addition to share capital and retained earnings, shareholders' equity includes other components that are explained in Chapter 6.

Nestlé controls other companies and reports all the assets and liabilities of these companies on its consolidated statement of financial position. Because Nestlé does not own all the voting shares issued by these companies, its shareholders' equity is divided between the controlling (parent) and non-controlling (or minority) shareholders, commonly referred to as **non-controlling interest**.

Now that we have reviewed several of the basic accounting concepts and terms, we need to understand the economic activities of a business that result in changes in amounts reported in financial statements and the process used in generating the financial statements.

WHAT TYPE OF BUSINESS ACTIVITIES CAUSE CHANGES IN FINANCIAL STATEMENT AMOUNTS?

Nature of Business Transactions

LO3

Identify what constitutes a business transaction, and recognize common account titles used in business.

Accounting focuses on specific events that have an economic impact on the entity. Those events that are recorded as a part of the accounting process are called transactions. The first step in translating the results of business events to financial statement amounts is determining which events to recognize as transactions; only transactions are reflected in the statements. As the definitions of assets and liabilities indicate, only economic resources and debts *resulting from past transactions* are recorded on the statement of financial position. Transactions include two types of events:

A **TRANSACTION** is (1) an exchange between a business and one or more external parties to a business or (2) a measurable internal event, such as adjustments for the use of assets in operations.

1. **External events** are *exchanges* of assets, goods, or services by one party for assets, services, or promises to pay (liabilities) by one or more other parties. Examples include the purchase of a machine from a supplier, the sale of merchandise to customers, borrowing of cash from a bank, and investment of cash in the business by the owners. Transactions that affect elements of the statement of financial position are discussed in this chapter, and those that affect income statement elements will be covered in Chapter 3.

2. **Internal events** include certain events that are not exchanges between the business and other parties but nevertheless have a direct and measurable effect on the accounting entity. Examples include using up insurance paid in advance and using buildings and equipment over several years. Accounting for internal events will be discussed in Chapter 4.

Throughout this textbook, the word **transaction** will be used in the broad sense to include both types of events.

Some important events that have an economic impact on the company, however, are *not* reflected in Nestlé's statements. In most cases, signing a contract is not considered to be a transaction because it involves *only the exchange of promises*, not of assets such as cash, goods, services, or property. For example, assume that Nestlé signs an employment contract with a new regional manager. From an accounting perspective, no transaction has occurred because no exchange of assets, goods, or services has been made. Each party to the contract has exchanged promises; the manager agrees to work and Nestlé agrees to pay the manager for work rendered. For each day the new manager works, however, the exchange of services for pay results in a transaction that Nestlé must record. Because of their importance, long-term employment contracts, leases, and other commitments may need to be disclosed in notes to the financial statements.

How does the accounting staff at Nestlé record external and internal events that cause changes in the amounts reported on the company's statement of financial position? The recording of transactions has evolved over time. Advances in computer hardware and software technology have paved the way for efficient recording of transactions and instantaneous preparation of financial statements. However, the basic system of recording transactions has withstood the test of time and has been in use for more than 500 years. The basic tenets of manual and computerized recording systems are discussed in this chapter and elaborated on further in Chapters 3 and 4.

Accounts

An account is a standardized record that organizations use to accumulate the monetary effects of transactions on each financial statement item. The cumulative result of all transactions that affect a specific account, or its ending balance, is then reported on the appropriate financial statement. To facilitate the recording of transactions, each company establishes a *chart of accounts*, a list of accounts and their unique numeric codes. The chart of accounts is organized by financial statement element, with asset accounts listed first (by order of liquidity), followed by liabilities (by order of time to maturity), shareholders' equity, revenue, and expense accounts in that order. In formal recordkeeping systems, including computerized accounting systems, use of appropriate account numbers is essential if the monetary effects of similar transactions are to be grouped correctly. Exhibit 2.3 lists account titles that are quite common and used by most companies. This list is helpful when you are completing assignments and are unsure of an account title.

> An **ACCOUNT** is a standardized format that organizations use to accumulate the monetary effects of transactions on each financial statement item.

You have probably already noticed some patterns in how accounts are named:

1. Accounts with "receivable" in the title are always assets, representing amounts owed to the corporation by customers and others, to be collected in the future.

2. Accounts with "payable" in the title are always liabilities, representing amounts owed by the corporation to be paid to others in the future.

3. The account Prepayments is an asset since it represents amounts paid to others for future benefits, such as future insurance coverage or rental of property.

Every company has a variation on this chart of accounts, depending on the nature of its business activities. For example, a small lawn care service may have an asset account called Lawn mowing equipment, but it is unlikely that the Royal Bank of Canada would need such an account. These differences will become more apparent as we examine the statements of financial position of various companies. Because each

Exhibit **2.3**

Typical Account Titles

Assets	Liabilities	Shareholders' Equity	Revenues	Expenses
Cash	Trade payables	Share capital	Sales revenue	Cost of sales
Short-term investments	Accrued liabilities	Contributed surplus	Fee revenue	Wages expense
Trade receivables	Notes payable	Retained earnings	Interest revenue	Rent expense
Notes receivable	Taxes payable		Rent revenue	Interest expense
Inventory (to be sold)	Deferred revenue			Depreciation expense
Supplies	Bonds payable			Advertising expense
Prepayments				Insurance expense
Long-term investments				Repair expense
Equipment				Income tax expense
Buildings				
Land				
Intangibles				

company has a different chart of accounts, you should *not* try to memorize a typical chart of accounts. **When you prepare homework problems, you will either be given the company's account names or be expected to select appropriate descriptive names, similar to the ones in the preceding lists.** Once a name is selected for an account, the exact name must be used in all transactions that affect that account.

The accounts you see in the financial statements are actually summations (or aggregations) of a number of specific accounts. For example, Nestlé keeps separate accounts for the different foods and drinks it produces and sells but combines them as *Inventories* on the statement of financial position. Equipment, buildings, and land are also combined into an account called *Property, plant, and equipment*. Since our aim is to understand financial statements, we focus on aggregated accounts as presented on the statements.

INTERNATIONAL PERSPECTIVE

UNDERSTANDING FOREIGN FINANCIAL STATEMENTS

The adoption of International Financial Reporting Standards (IFRS) by many countries has made it easier to read foreign companies' financial statements. GlaxoSmithKline, the pharmaceutical giant in the United Kingdom, prepares its financial statements under IFRS. However, there are still some differences in the structure of the statements and account titles that may cause confusion. For example, many European companies place non-current assets before current assets and list shareholders' equity before liabilities. Companies in the United States do not use the term "provision" to report estimated liabilities; they do recognize such liabilities, however, under different titles. The key to avoiding confusion is to pay attention to the subheadings in the financial statements and read the notes related to specific financial statement elements.

SELF-STUDY **QUIZ 2-1**

Benetton Group

The following is a list of accounts from a recent statement of financial position for the Italian company Benetton Group, which sells fashion apparel in over 120 countries. Indicate on the line provided whether each of the following is an asset (A), liability (L), or shareholders' equity account (SE).

____ Trades payable	____ Lease financing
____ Buildings	____ Vehicles and aircraft
____ Investments	____ Retained earnings
____ Current portion of long-term loans	____ Financial receivables

 After you complete your answers, go online for the solutions.

HOW DO TRANSACTIONS AFFECT ACCOUNTS?

LO4

Apply transaction analysis to simple business transactions in terms of the accounting model: Assets = Liabilities + Shareholders' Equity.

Managers make business decisions that often result in transactions affecting financial statements. For example, the decisions to expand the number of stores, advertise a new product, change an employee benefit package, and invest excess cash would all affect the financial statements. Sometimes these decisions have unintended consequences as well. For example, the decision to purchase additional inventory for cash in anticipation of a major sales initiative will increase inventory and decrease cash. But, if there is no demand for the additional inventory, the lower cash balance will also reduce the company's ability to pay its other obligations.

Because business decisions often involve an element of risk, business managers should understand how transactions impact the accounts on the financial statements. The process for determining the effects of transactions is called *transaction analysis*.

Principles of Transaction Analysis

Transaction analysis is the process of studying each transaction to determine its economic effect on the entity in terms of the accounting equation (A = L + SE, also known as the *fundamental accounting model*). We outline the process in this section of the chapter and create a visual tool representing the process (the transaction analysis model). The basic accounting equation and two fundamental concepts are the foundation for this model. Recall from Chapter 1 that the accounting equation for a business that is organized as a corporation is as follows:

> **Assets (A) = Liabilities (L) + Shareholders' Equity (SE)**

The two concepts underlying the transaction analysis process follow:

1. Every transaction affects at least two accounts; it is critical to correctly identify the accounts affected and the direction of the effect (increase or decrease).
2. The accounting equation must remain in balance after each transaction.

Success in performing transaction analysis depends on a clear understanding of how the transaction analysis model is constructed, based on these concepts. **Study this material well. You should not move on to a new concept until you understand and can apply all prior concepts.**

Dual Effects   The idea that every transaction has **at least two effects** on the basic accounting equation is known as the **dual effects** concept.[5] Most transactions with external parties involve an **exchange** by which the business entity both receives something and gives up something in return. For example, suppose that Nestlé purchased some office supplies for cash. In this exchange, Nestlé would receive supplies (an increase in an asset) and in return would give up cash (a decrease in an asset).

Transaction	Nestlé Received	Nestlé Gave
Purchased paper for cash	Supplies (increased)	Cash (decreased)

In analyzing this transaction, we determined that the accounts affected were office supplies and cash. As we discussed in Chapter 1, however, most supplies are purchased on credit (i.e., money is owed to suppliers). In that case, Nestlé would engage in *two* transactions:

(1) The purchase of an asset on credit	In the first transaction, Nestlé would receive office supplies (an increase in an asset) and would give in return a promise to pay later, called Accounts Payable (an increase in a liability).
(2) The eventual payment	In the second transaction, Nestlé would eliminate or receive back its promise to pay (a decrease in the Accounts Payable liability) and would give up cash (a decrease in an asset).

---

[5]From this concept, accountants have developed what is known as the **double-entry system** of recordkeeping.

TRANSACTION ANALYSIS is the process of studying a transaction to determine its economic effect on the entity in terms of the accounting equation.

Transaction	Nestlé Received	Nestlé Gave
(1) Purchased paper for credit	Supplies (increased)	Accounts Payable (increased) [a promise to pay]

| (2) Paid on its accounts payable | Accounts Payable (decreased) [a promise was eliminated] | Cash (decreased) |

As noted earlier, not all important business events result in a transaction that affects the financial statements. Most important, signing a contract involving *the exchange of promises to perform a future business transaction does not result in a transaction* that is recorded. For example, if Nestlé sent an order to its paper supplier for more paper without making any payment, and the supplier accepted the order but did not fill it immediately, then no transaction has taken place for accounting purposes because Nestlé and the paper supplier have exchanged only promises.[6] From the supplier's perspective, the same holds true. No transaction has taken place, so the supplier's financial statements are not affected. As soon as the paper is shipped to Nestlé, however, the supplier gives up inventory in exchange for a promise from Nestlé to pay for the paper it receives, and Nestlé exchanges its promise to pay for the paper it receives. Because a *promise* has been exchanged for *goods*, a transaction has taken place, and the financial statements of both Nestlé and the supplier will be affected.

Balancing the Accounting Equation The accounting equation must remain in balance after each transaction. Total assets (resources) must equal total liabilities and shareholders' equity (claims to resources). If the correct accounts have been identified and the appropriate direction of the effect on each account has been determined, then the equation should remain in balance. A systematic transaction analysis includes the following steps, in this order:

Step 1: **Identify and classify accounts and effects**
Identify the accounts affected (by their titles), making sure that at least two accounts change. Ask yourself, what is received and what is given?
Classify each by type of account. Was each account an asset (A), liability (L), or shareholders' equity (SE)?
Determine the direction of the effect. Did the account increase [+] or decrease [−]?

Step 2: **Verify that the accounting equation, A = L + SE, remains in balance.**

Analyzing Nestlé's Transactions

To illustrate the use of the transaction analysis process, let us consider typical Nestlé transactions that are also common to most businesses. This chapter presents transactions affecting accounts reported on the statement of financial position. Assume that Nestlé engaged in the following transactions during January 2010, the month following the statement of financial position in Exhibit 2.2. The month will end on January 31.

---

[6]Contracts of this nature that are likely to result in significant future liabilities must be noted in the financial statements as commitments.

For simplicity, account titles are based on that statement of financial position. Note that all monetary amounts are usually preceded by the symbol of the currency used in the exchange transactions (e.g., $ for Canadian dollars, € for euros, CHF for Swiss francs). In the following illustration, all amounts are in millions of Swiss francs, but we omit including CHF before the monetary amount, for simplicity.

(*a*) Nestlé issues shares to new investors in exchange for 1,300 in cash.

Step 1: **Identify and classify accounts and effects.**

Received: Cash (+A) 1,300   **Given:** Additional share certificates, Share capital (+SE) 1,300.

Step 2: **Is the accounting equation in balance?**

Yes. The left side increased by 1,300 and the right side increased by 1,300.

Assets	=	Liabilities	+	Shareholders' Equity
Cash				Share capital
(*a*) +1,300	=			+1,300

(*b*) The company borrows 1,000 from its local bank, signing a note to be paid in two years.

Step 1: **Identify and classify accounts and effects.**

Received: Cash (+A) 1,000   **Given:** Written promise to bank, Long-term borrowings (+L) 1,000.

Step 2: **Is the accounting equation in balance?**

Yes. The left side increased by 1,000 and the right side increased by 1,000.

Assets	=	Liabilities	+	Shareholders' Equity
		Long-term		
Cash		borrowings		Share capital
(*a*) +1,300	=			+1,300
(*b*) +1,000	=	+1,000		

Transactions (*a*) and (*b*) are *financing* transactions. Companies that need cash for *investing* purposes (to buy or build additional facilities as part of their plans for growth) often seek funds by selling shares to investors, as in transaction (*a*), or borrowing from creditors, usually banks, as in transaction (*b*).

(*c*) For expansion, Nestlé opened a new production facility. The company purchased 2,200 of new coffee roasters, counters, refrigerators, and other equipment, paying 1,500 in cash and signing a note for 700, payable to the equipment manufacturer in two years.

Step 1: **Identify and classify accounts and effects.**

Received: Property, plant and equipment (+A) 2,200.   **Given:** (1) Cash (−A) 1,500 and a written promise to pay the manufacturer, Long-term borrowings (+L) 700.

Step 2: **Is the accounting equation in balance?**

Yes. The left side increased by 2,200 and the right side increased by 2,200.

	Assets		=	Liabilities	+	Shareholders' Equity
	Cash	**Property, plant and equipment**		**Long-term borrowings**		**Share capital**
(a)	+1,300		=			+1,300
(b)	+1,000		=	+1,000		
(c)	−1,500	+2,200	=	+700		

Notice that more than two accounts were affected by transaction (c).

The analysis of transactions (d) through (f) follows. The effects are listed in the chart at the end of Self-Study Quiz 2-2. Space is left in the chart for your answers to the quiz, transactions (g) and (h), that follow transaction (f).

(d) **Nestlé lends 450 to a trade supplier in financial difficulty. The trade supplier signs notes agreeing to repay the amount borrowed in six months.**

Step 1: **Identify and classify accounts and effects.**

Received: Written promise from the trade supplier, Notes receivable (+A) 450.   **Given**: Cash (−A) 450.

Step 2: **Is the accounting equation in balance?**

Yes. The equation remains in balance because assets increase and decrease by the same amount: 450.

(e) **Nestlé purchases shares issued by another company as a long-term investment, paying 3,000 in cash. The number of shares purchased allows Nestlé to exert significant influence over decisions made by that company.**

Step 1: **Identify and classify accounts and effects.**

Received: Share certificates from the other company, Investment in associates (+A) 3,000.   **Given**: Cash (−A) 3,000.

Step 2: **Is the accounting equation in balance?**

Yes. The equation remains in balance because assets increase and decrease by the same amount: 3,000.

(f) **Nestlé's board of directors declares cash dividends of 200 for shareholders. The dividends are paid immediately.**

Step 1: **Identify and classify accounts and effects.**

Received: Earnings retained in the business are distributed to investors, Retained earnings (−SE) 200.   **Given**: Cash (−A) 200.

Step 2: **Is the accounting equation in balance?**

Yes. The left side decreased by 200 and the right side decreased by 200.

The most effective way to develop your transaction analysis skills is to practise with many transactions. Review the analysis in transactions (a) through (f) and complete the transaction analysis steps in the chart following the transactions (g) and (h). **Repeat the steps until they become a natural part of your thought process.**

(g) **Nestlé collects 300 cash on notes receivable from the trade supplier.**
     (*Hint:* **Think about what is received and what is given.**)

Step 1: **Identify and classify accounts and effects.**

Step 2: **Is the accounting equation in balance?**

(h) **Nestlé paid 400 on the note owed to the local bank.**

Step 1: **Identify and classify accounts and effects.**

Step 2: **Is the accounting equation in balance?**

Include these effects on the following chart.

	Cash	**Assets** Notes receivable	Investment in associates	Property, plant and equipment	=	**Liabilities** Long-term borrowings	+	**Shareholders' Equity** Share capital	Retained earnings
(a)	+1,300				=			+1,300	
(b)	+1,000				=	+1,000			
(c)	−1,500			+2,200	=	+700			
(d)	−450	+450			=				
(e)	−3,000		+3,000		=				
(f)	−200				=				−200
(g)	☐	☐			=	☐			
(h)	☐				=				

After you complete your answers, go online for the solutions.   ⊞ connect

(i) **Nestlé's board of directors approved the opening of two new production plants at a meeting in January 2010 and the borrowing of 200 from the local banks to finance the construction of the new plants in February 2010.**

Unlike transactions (a) through (h), which reflect exchanges between Nestlé and external parties, these two decisions of the board of directors are not transactions because no exchanges have taken place yet. The company's board of directors made commitments that will likely translate into actions in February 2010. Specific statement of financial position accounts will be affected only when the actual exchanges occur in February 2010. However, such commitments will normally be disclosed in a financial statement note.

HOW DO COMPANIES KEEP TRACK OF ACCOUNT BALANCES?

For most organizations, recording transaction effects and keeping track of account balances in the manner just presented is impractical. To handle the multitude of daily transactions that businesses generate, companies establish accounting systems, usually computerized, that follow a cycle. The accounting cycle, illustrated in Exhibit 2.4, highlights the primary activities performed during the accounting period to analyze,

LO⁵

Determine the impact of business transactions on the statement of financial position by using two basic tools: journal entries and T-accounts.

Exhibit **2.4**

The Accounting Cycle

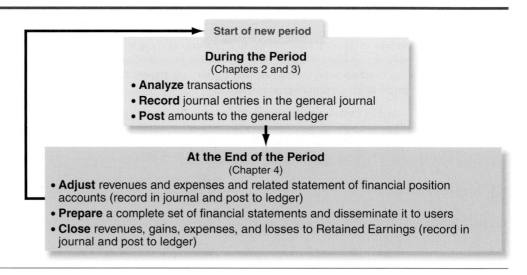

record, and post transactions. In Chapters 2 and 3, we will illustrate these activities *during the period*. In Chapter 4, we will complete the accounting cycle by discussing and illustrating activities *at the end of the period* to adjust the records, prepare financial statements, and close the accounting records.

During the accounting period, transactions that result in exchanges between the company and other external parties are analyzed and recorded in the *general journal* in chronological order, and the related accounts are updated in the *general ledger*. These formal records are based on two very important tools used by accountants: journal entries and T-accounts. From the standpoint of accounting systems design, these analytical tools are more efficient mechanisms for reflecting the effects of transactions and for determining account balances for financial statement preparation. **As future business managers, you should develop your understanding and use of these tools in financial analysis. For those studying accounting, this knowledge is the foundation for understanding the accounting system and future coursework.** After we explain how to perform transaction analysis by using these tools, we illustrate their use in financial analysis.

The Direction of Transaction Effects

As we saw earlier, transactions change the balances of assets, liabilities, and shareholders' equity accounts. To reflect these effects efficiently, we need to structure the transaction analysis model in a manner that shows the *direction* of the effects. One very useful tool for summarizing the transaction effects and determining the balances for individual accounts is a T-account, as shown in Exhibit 2.5. Notice the following:

The **T-ACCOUNT** is a tool for summarizing transaction effects for each account, determining balances, and drawing inferences about a company's activities.

- Each T-account has two sides: a left side, known as the debit side, and a right side, known as the credit side.

- The increase symbol, +, is located on the left side of the T for accounts that appear on the left side of the accounting equation, and on the right side of the T for accounts that are on the right side of the equation.

DEBIT means the left side of an account.

- The term debit (dr) is always written on the left side of each account, and the term credit (cr) is always written on the right side.

From this transaction analysis model, we can observe the following:

CREDIT means the right side of an account.

- Asset accounts increase on the left (debit) side. They have debit balances. It would be highly unusual for an asset account, such as inventories, to have a negative (credit) balance.

- Liabilities and shareholders' equity accounts increase on the right (credit) side, creating credit balances.

To remember which accounts are increased by debit and which accounts are increased by credit, recall that a debit (left) increases asset accounts because assets are

Exhibit **2.5**

Transaction Analysis Model

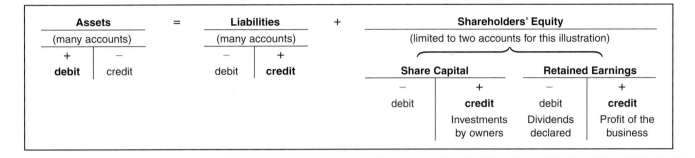

on the left side of the accounting equation (A = L + SE). Similarly, a credit (right) increases liability and shareholders' equity accounts because they are on the right side of the accounting equation.

In summary,

Assets	=	Liabilities	+	Shareholders' Equity
↑ with debits; accounts have debit balances		↑ with credits; accounts have credit balances		↑ with credits; accounts have credit balances

In Chapter 3, we will add revenue and expense account effects. Until then, as you are learning to perform transaction analysis, you should refer to this model often until you can construct it on your own without assistance.

Many students have trouble with accounting because they forget that the only meaning for **debit** is the left side of an account and the only meaning for **credit** is the right side of an account. Perhaps someone once told you that you were a credit to your school or your family. As a result, you may think that credits are good and debits are bad. Such is not the case. Just remember that **debit is on the left** and **credit is on the right**.

If you have identified the correct accounts and effects through transaction analysis, the accounting equation will remain in balance. Moreover, **the total monetary value of all debits equals the total monetary value of all credits** in a transaction. For an extra measure of assurance, add this equality check (debits = credits) to the transaction analysis process.

Analytical Tools

The Journal Entry In a bookkeeping system, transactions are initially recorded in chronological order in a *general journal* (see Appendix B, available online for a detailed illustration of formal recordkeeping procedures). After analyzing the business documents that describe a transaction, the bookkeeper prepares the formal journal entry and enters the effects on the accounts by using debits and credits. The journal entry, then, is an accounting method for expressing the effects of a transaction on various accounts, using the double-entry bookkeeping system explained previously. The journal entry for transaction (*c*) in the Nestlé illustration is written as follows:

A JOURNAL ENTRY provides a summary of a transaction and its effects on various accounts, using the double-entry bookkeeping system.

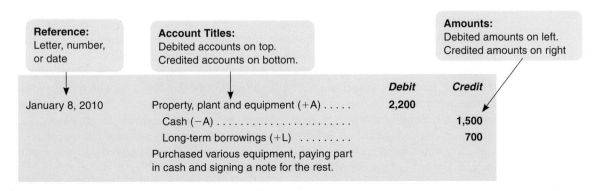

Notice the following:

- It is useful to include a date or some form of reference for each transaction. The debits are written first (on top) with the amounts on the left side of the two columns. The credits are written below the debits and are indented to the right in manual records; the credited amounts are written in the right column. The order of the debited accounts or credited accounts does not matter, as long as the debits are on top and the credits are on the bottom and indented to the right.

    Total debits (2,200) equal total credits (1,500 + 700).

- Three accounts are affected by this transaction. Any journal entry that affects more than two accounts is called a *compound entry*. Although this is the only transaction in the preceding illustration that affects more than two accounts, many transactions in subsequent chapters will require compound journal entries.

Recording external transactions in the journal is based on legal documents that highlight the contractual commitments between Nestlé and other parties. For example, Nestlé signed a contract with a manufacturer to purchase equipment for 2,200. It issued a cheque for 1,500 to transfer cash to the manufacturer and promised to pay 700 in two years. Consequently, the effects of this transaction are recorded in the journal and reflected in Nestlé's financial statements. The equipment manufacturer retains legal control of the equipment until it is fully paid after two years. For accounting purposes, however, Nestlé has control of and will use this resource to generate revenue over the next two years. While recording external transactions in the journal requires legal documents, some legal contracts, such as signing a contract to hire a new employee, are not reflected in the financial statements.

While you are learning to perform transaction analysis, use the symbols A, L, and SE next to each account title, as in the preceding journal entry, for all homework problems. Specifically identifying accounts as assets (A), liabilities (L), or shareholders' equity (SE) clarifies the transaction analysis and makes journal entries easier to write. For example, if Cash is to be increased, we will write Cash (+A). Throughout subsequent chapters, we include the direction of the effect along with the symbol to help you understand the effects of each transaction on the financial statements.

Many students try to memorize journal entries without understanding or using the transaction analysis model. The task becomes increasingly difficult as more detailed transactions are presented in subsequent chapters. In the long run, **memorizing, understanding, and using the transaction analysis model** presented here will save you time and prevent confusion.

The T-Account By themselves, journal entries do not provide the balances in accounts. After the journal entries have been recorded, the bookkeeper posts (transfers) the monetary values to each account affected by the transaction, to determine the new account balances. In most computerized accounting systems, this happens automatically upon recording the journal entry.

As a group, the accounts are called a *general ledger*. In a manual accounting system used by some small organizations, the ledger is often a three-ring binder with a separate page for each account. In a computerized system, accounts are part of a database and stored on a disk. See Exhibit 2.6 for an illustration of a journal page and the related Cash ledger page. Note that the cash effects from the journal entries have been posted to the Cash ledger page. The three digits under the "Ref." column in the general journal are examples of account codes used in the chart of accounts.

Exhibit 2.7 shows the T-accounts for the cash and long-term borrowings accounts for Nestlé, based on transactions (*a*) through (*h*). Notice that for cash, which is an asset, increases are shown on the left and decreases are on the right side of the T-account. For long-term borrowings, however, increases are shown on the right and decreases on the left since notes payable is a liability. Some small businesses still use handwritten or manually maintained accounts in this T-account format. Computerized systems retain the concept but not the format of the T-account.

General Journal Page G1

Date	Account Titles and Explanation (in thousands)	Ref.	Debit	Credit
Jan. 2	Cash	101	1,300	
	Share capital			1,300
	Investment by shareholders.			
Jan. 6	Cash	101	1,000	
	Long-term borrowings	201		1,000
	Borrowed from bank.			
Jan. 8	Property and equipment	140	**2,200**	
	Cash	101		**1,500**
	Long-term borrowings	201		**700**
	Purchased equipment paying part cash			
	and the rest due on a note payable.			

General Ledger **Cash** 101

Date	Explanation	Ref.	Debit	Credit	Balance
	Balance				5,825
Jan. 2		G1	1,300		7,125
Jan. 6		G1	1,000		8,125
Jan. 8		G1		1,500	6,625

General Ledger **Property, Plant and Equipment** 140

Date	Explanation	Ref.	Debit	Credit	Balance
	Balance				21,599
Jan. 8		G1	**2,200**		23,799

General Ledger **Long-term Borrowings** 201

Date	Explanation	Ref.	Debit	Credit	Balance
	Balance				8,966
Jan. 6		G1		1,000	9,966
Jan. 8		G1		**700**	10,666

Exhibit **2.6**

Posting Transaction Effects from the Journal to the Ledger

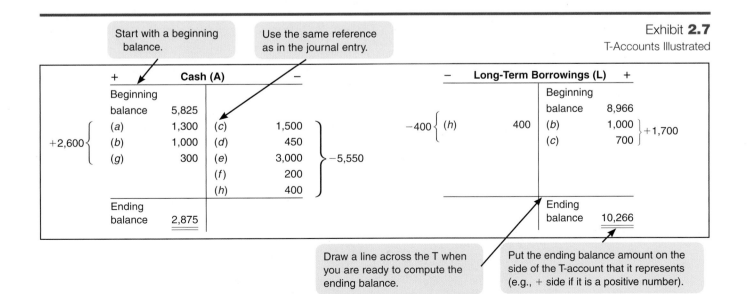

Exhibit **2.7**

T-Accounts Illustrated

Start with a beginning balance.

Use the same reference as in the journal entry.

+	Cash (A)		−
Beginning balance	5,825		
(a)	1,300	(c)	1,500
(b)	1,000	(d)	450
(g)	300	(e)	3,000
		(f)	200
		(h)	400
Ending balance	2,875		

+2,600

−5,550

−	Long-Term Borrowings (L)		+
		Beginning balance	8,966
−400 { (h)	400	(b)	1,000
		(c)	700
		Ending balance	10,266

+1,700

Draw a line across the T when you are ready to compute the ending balance.

Put the ending balance amount on the side of the T-account that it represents (e.g., + side if it is a positive number).

In Exhibit 2.7, notice that the ending balance is indicated on the positive side with a double underline. To find the account balances, we can express the T-accounts as equations:

	Cash	Long-Term Borrowings
Beginning balance	CHF 5,825	CHF 8,966
+ "+" side	+2,600	+1,700
– "–" side	−5,550	−400
Ending balance	CHF 2,875	CHF 10,266

A word on terminology: The words **debit** and **credit** are used as verbs, nouns, and adjectives. For example, we can say that Nestlé's Cash account was debited (verb) when shares were issued to investors, meaning that the amount was entered on the left side of the T-account. Or we can say that a credit (noun) was entered on the right side of an account. Borrowings may be described as a credit account (adjective). These terms will be used instead of *left* and *right* throughout the rest of the textbook.

The next section illustrates the steps to follow in analyzing the effects of transactions, recording the effects in journal entries, and determining account balances by using T-accounts.

Transaction Analysis Illustrated

In this section, we will use the monthly transactions of Nestlé that were presented earlier to demonstrate transaction analysis and the use of journal entries and T-accounts. We analyze each transaction, checking to make sure that the accounting equation remains in balance and that debits equal credits. The amounts from Nestlé's statement of financial position at January 1, 2010, have been inserted as the beginning balances in the T-accounts, located together at the end of the illustration. After reviewing or preparing each journal entry, trace the effects to the appropriate T-accounts by using the transaction letters (*a*) to (*h*) as a reference. The first transaction has been highlighted for you.

Study this illustration carefully, including the explanations of transaction analysis. Careful study is *essential* to the understanding of (1) the accounting model, (2) transaction analysis, (3) the dual effects of each transaction, and (4) the dual-balancing system. **The most effective way to learn these critical concepts that affect material throughout the rest of the textbook is to practise, practise, practise**.

(*a*) **Nestlé issues shares to new investors in exchange for 1,300 in cash.**

Cash (+A) 1,300
    Share capital (+SE) 1,300
Issued share capital for cash

Assets	=	Liabilities	+	Shareholders' Equity	
Cash +1,300				Share capital	+1,300

These effects have been posted to the appropriate T-accounts at the end of the illustration. To post the amounts, transfer or copy the debit or credit amount on each line to the appropriate T-account indicated in order to accumulate balances for each account.
For example, the 1,300 debit is listed in the debit (increase) column of the Cash T-account.

(*b*) **The company borrows 1,000 from its local bank, signing a note to be paid in two years.**

Cash (+A) 1,000
    Long-term borrowings (+L) 1,000
Borrowed money from the local bank, payable in two years.

Assets		=	Liabilities		+	Shareholders' Equity
Cash	+1,100		Long-term borrowings	+1,100		

(c) **For expansion, Nestlé opened a new production facility. The company purchased 2,200 of new coffee roasters, counters, refrigerators, and other equipment, paying 1,500 in cash and signing a note for 700, payable to the equipment manufacturer in two years.**

Property, plant, and equipment (+A)	2,200	
Cash (−A)		1,500
Long-term borrowings (+L)		700
Purchased various equipment, paying part in cash and signing a note for the rest, payable in two years.		

Assets		=	Liabilities		+	Shareholders' Equity
Property, plant, and equipment	+2,200		Long-term borrowings	+700		
Cash	−1,500					

(d) **Nestlé lends 450 to a trade supplier in financial difficulty. The trade supplier signs notes agreeing to repay the amount borrowed within six months.**

Notes receivable (+A)	450	
Cash (−A)		450
Lent money to a trade supplier; to be repaid within six months.		

Assets		=	Liabilities	+	Shareholders' Equity
Cash	−450				
Notes receivable	+450				

(e) **Nestlé purchases shares issued by another corporation as a long-term investment, paying 3,000 in cash. The number of shares purchased allows Nestlé to exert significant influence over decisions made by that company.**

Investment in associates (+A)	3,000	
Cash (−A)		3,000
Purchased shares in another corporation as a long-term investment.		

Assets		=	Liabilities	+	Shareholders' Equity
Cash	−3000				
Investment in associates	+3000				

(f) **Nestlé's board of directors declares cash dividends of 200 for shareholders. The dividends are paid immediately.**

Retained earnings (−SE)	200	
Cash (−A)		200
Declared and paid dividends to shareholders.		

Assets		=	Liabilities	+	Shareholders' Equity	
Cash	−200				Retained earnings	−200

SELF-STUDY **QUIZ 2-3**

For transactions (g) and (h), fill in the missing information, including postings to the T-accounts.

(g) Nestlé collects 300 cash from the trade supplier.

Write the journal entry

[Post to the T-accounts.]

Collection of note from trade supplier.

Assets	=	Liabilities	+	Shareholders' Equity
Cash	+300			
Notes receivable	−300			

(h) Nestlé paid 400 on the note owed to the local bank.

Long-term borrowings (−L)   400   [Post to the
    Cash (−A)   400   T-accounts.]
Partial payment of the amount owed to the local bank.

Assets	=	Liabilities	+	Shareholders' Equity

After you complete your answers, go online for the solutions.

The T-accounts that changed during the period because of these transactions are shown below. The beginning balances are the amounts from Nestlé's statement of financial position at December 31, 2009. The balances of all other accounts remained the same.

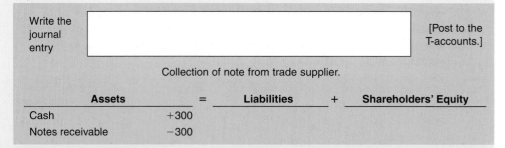

| | **Assets** | | | = | **Liabilities + Shareholders' Equity** | |

+ Cash (A) −

Beg. bal.	5,825		
(a)	1,300	(c)	1,500
(b)	1,000	(d)	450
(g)		(e)	3,000
		(f)	200
		(h)	
End. bal.	2,875		

+ Property, Plant, and Equipment (A) −

Beg. bal.	21,599		
(c)	2,200		
End. bal.	23,799		

+ Investment in Associates (A) −

Beg. bal.	8,693	
(e)	3,000	
End. bal.	11,693	

+ Notes Receivable (A) −

Beg. bal.	2,884		
(d)	450	(g)	
End. bal.	3,034		

− Long-Term Borrowings (L) +

		Beg. bal.	8,966
		(b)	1,000
(h)		(c)	700
		End. bal.	10,266

− Share Capital (SE) +

	Beg. bal.	6,248
	(a)	1,300
	End. bal.	7,548

− Retained Earnings (SE) +

	Beg. bal.	64,660
(f)	200	
	End. bal.	

You can verify that you posted the entries properly by adding the increase side and subtracting the decrease side and then comparing your answer to the ending balance for each T-account. Go online to check your answers.

INFERRING BUSINESS ACTIVITIES FROM T-ACCOUNTS

T-accounts are useful primarily for instructional and analytical purposes. In many cases, we will use T-accounts to determine what transactions a company engaged in during a period. For example, the primary transactions affecting trade payables for a period are purchases of assets on account and cash payments to suppliers. If we know the beginning and ending balances of trade payables and all of the amounts that were purchased on credit during a period, we can determine the amount of cash paid. A T-account will include the following:

–	Trade Payable (L)	+
	Beg. bal.	600
Cash payments to suppliers ?	Purchases on account	1,500
	End. bal.	300

Solution:

Beginning balance	+	Purchases on account	–	Cash payments to suppliers	=	Ending balance
$600	+	$1,500	–	p	=	$300
		$2,100	–	p	=	$300
				p	=	$1,800

HOW IS THE STATEMENT OF FINANCIAL POSITION PREPARED AND ANALYZED?

As discussed in Chapter 1, a statement of financial position is one of the financial statements that will be communicated to users, especially those external to the business. It is possible to prepare a classified statement of financial position at any point in time from the balances in the accounts.

Classified Statement of Financial Position

The statement of financial position in Exhibit 2.8 was prepared by using the new balances shown in the T-accounts in the preceding Nestlé illustration (shaded lines in the exhibit) plus the original balances in the accounts that did not change. It compares the account balances at January 31, 2010, with those at December 31, 2009. Notice that when multiple periods are presented, the most recent amounts on the statement of financial position are usually listed on the left.

At the beginning of the chapter, we presented the changes in Nestlé's total assets from 1998 to 2009. We questioned what made the accounts change and what the process was for reflecting the changes. Now we can see that the assets have changed again in one month, along with liabilities and shareholders' equity, because of the transactions illustrated in this chapter:

	Assets	=	Liabilities	+	Shareholders' Equity
January 31, 2010	113,316		58,585		54,731
December 31, 2009	110,916		57,285		53,631
Change	+ 2,400		+1,300		+1,100

Exhibit **2.8**

Nestlé's Statement of Financial
Position

THE NESTLÉ GROUP Consolidated Statement of Financial Position (in millions of Swiss francs)		
Assets	**January 31, 2010**	**December 31, 2009**
Current assets		
Cash and cash equivalents	2,875	5,825
Short-term investments	2,585	2,585
Trade receivables	9,425	9,425
Notes receivable	3,034	2,884
Inventories	7,734	7,734
Prepayments	589	589
Other current assets	10,828	10,828
Total current assets	**37,070**	**39,870**
Non-current assets		
Property, plant and equipment	23,799	21,599
Investment in associates	11,693	8,693
Financial assets	4,162	4,162
Goodwill	27,502	27,502
Intangible assets	6,658	6,658
Other assets	2,432	2,432
Total non-current assets	**76,246**	**71,046**
Total assets	**113,316**	**110,916**
Liabilities and Equity		
Current liabilities		
Trade payables	13,033	13,033
Short-term borrowings	14,438	14,438
Income taxes payable	1,173	1,173
Accrued liabilities	2,779	2,779
Other current liabilities	4,017	4,017
Total current liabilities	**35,440**	**35,440**
Non-current liabilities		
Long-term borrowings	10,266	8,966
Deferred income tax liabilities	1,404	1,404
Provisions	3,865	3,865
Other liabilities	7,610	7,610
Total non-current liabilities	**23,145**	**21,845**
Total liabilities	**58,585**	**57,285**
Equity		
Share capital	7,548	6,248
Retained earnings	64,460	64,660
Other components	(21,993)	(21,993)
Total equity attributable to shareholders of the parent	**50,015**	**48,915**
Non-controlling interests	4,716	4,716
Total equity	**54,731**	**53,631**
Total liabilities and equity	**113,316**	**110,916**

Source: Nestlé S.A.

KEY RATIO ANALYSIS

THE DEBT-TO-EQUITY RATIO

Users of financial information compute a number of ratios in analyzing a company's past performance and financial condition as input in predicting its future potential. For example, by using the
elements and classification in the statement of financial position, creditors can assess a company's
ability to pay off its debt, or see what the company's trend is in taking on more debt. The change in

ratios over time and how they compare to the ratios of the company's competitors provide valuable information for users' decisions.

We introduce here the first of many ratios that will be presented throughout the rest of this textbook, with a final summary of ratio analysis in Chapter 13. In Chapters 2, 3, and 4, we present four ratios that provide information about management's effectiveness at managing debt and equity financing (debt-to-equity ratio), controlling revenues and expenses (net profit margin), and utilizing assets (total asset turnover ratio and return on assets), all for the purpose of enhancing returns to shareholders. The remaining chapters discuss other ratios that provide valuable information to assess a company's strategies, strengths, and areas of concern.

As we discussed earlier in the chapter, companies raise large amounts of money to acquire additional assets by issuing shares to investors and borrowing funds from creditors. These additional assets are used to generate more profit. However, since debt must be repaid, taking on increasing amounts of debt carries increased risk. The debt-to-equity ratio provides one measure for analysts to examine the company's financing strategy.

ANALYTICAL QUESTION → As an investor who must decide whether or not to buy shares, it is important to know how much of the company's assets is financed by creditors and how much is financed by owners. The *debt-to-equity ratio* is used to assess the debt capacity of a business. It is computed as follows:

$$\text{Debt-to-Equity Ratio} = \frac{\text{Total Liabilities}}{\text{Shareholders' Equity}}$$

The 2009 ratio for Nestlé is

$$\text{CHF } 57,285 \div \text{CHF } 53,631 = 1.07$$

RATIO AND COMPARISONS

Comparisons over Time			Comparisons with Competitors*	
Nestlé Group			ConAgra Foods	Kraft Foods
2007	2008	2009	2009	2009
1.11	0.93	1.07	1.34	1.57

INTERPRETATIONS

In General → The debt-to-equity ratio indicates how much debt has been used to finance the company's acquisition of assets, relative to equity financing that is supplied by shareholders. A high ratio normally suggests that a company relies heavily on funds provided by creditors. Managers use the ratio to decide whether they should finance any additional acquisitions by using debt. Creditors use this ratio to assess the risk that a company may not be able to meet its financial obligations during a business downturn. Investors use it to assess the level of financial risk associated with the expected cash flows from their investment (dividends and appreciation in the share value).

Investors look not only at ratios over time for Nestlé, but also at the debt-to-equity ratio of competitors for comparison purposes. Both ConAgra Foods and Kraft Foods have higher debt-to-equity ratios than Nestlé, suggesting that they have higher financial risk. As a result, they may not be in as good a financial position as Nestlé to generate the cash necessary to meet their financial obligations in case of a business downturn.

A Few Cautions → The debt-to-equity ratio tells only part of the story with respect to risks associated with debt. The ratio is a good indication of debt capacity, but it does not help the investor understand whether the company's operations can support the amount of debt that it has. Remember that debt carries with it the obligation to make cash payments for interest and principal. As a result, most investors would evaluate the debt-to-equity ratio within the context of the amount of cash the company is able to generate from operating activities.

*ConAgra Foods is a top food producer in the United States, offering both packaged and frozen foods. The company makes many leading brands, including Healthy Choice, Chef Boyardee, Egg Beaters, Hunt's, Orville Redenbacher's, PAM, and Banquet, among others. Kraft Foods is the second largest food company in the world behind Nestlé. It manufactures and markets packaged food products such as snacks. Its brands include Kraft cheeses and dressings, Oscar Mayer meats, Philadelphia cream cheese, Maxwell House and Jacobs coffee, Nabisco and Oreo cookies. Investors cannot always compare closest competitors. Both Nestlé and Kraft Foods are much larger companies than ConAgra Foods and market a wider variety of products.

As you can see, using the relevant financial information from financial statements to calculate a single ratio is only the first step toward understanding whether a company is healthy enough to merit your investment money. The real challenges are discovering why the ratios have changed over time, comparing the ratios with competitors' ratios, developing a keen understanding of the industry and businesses, and using all this knowledge to predict the future for a company.

SELF-STUDY **QUIZ 2-4**

Benetton Group

Benetton Group had the following balances on a recent statement of financial position (in thousands of Euros):

Liabilities—1,492,936; Shareholders' equity—1,398,937

Compute Benetton's debt-to-equity ratio:

What does this tell you about Benetton's financing strategy?

 connect   After you complete your answers, go online for the solutions.

FOCUS ON CASH FLOWS   **INVESTING AND FINANCING ACTIVITIES**

LO7

Identify investing and financing transactions and how they are reported on the statement of cash flows.

Recall from Chapter 1 that companies report cash inflows and outflows over a period in their statement of cash flows. This statement divides all transactions that affect cash into three categories: operating, investing, and financing activities. Investing and financing activities are covered in this chapter whereas operating activities are covered in Chapter 3.

The eight transactions we have analyzed for Nestlé included issuing shares, borrowing from a bank, purchasing equipment, lending to trade suppliers, purchasing shares in other companies, declaring and paying dividends, collecting cash on a note receivable, and paying down a bank loan (see Exhibit 2.9). All these transactions affected cash. Four of the eight transactions relate to investment activities and the other four relate to financing activities.

The first set includes one transaction that increased cash inflow and three transactions that decreased cash. The collection on notes receivable increased cash by 300. On the other hand, the payment of 1,500 in cash for the purchase of equipment, the short-term loan to trade suppliers for 450, and the investment in shares of other companies for 3,000 resulted in a total cash outflow of 4,950. The net change to cash from investment activities is an outflow of *4,650*.

The second set of transactions relates to financing activities and includes two transactions that increased cash and two transactions that decreased cash. The issuance of shares for 1,300 and borrowing 1,000 from the bank increased cash by 2,300. In contrast, payment of dividends of 200 and partial repayment on a bank loan of 400 decreased cash by 600 during the same period. The net change to cash from financing activities is an inflow of *1,700*.

In summary, the change in the cash balance from 5,825 at December 31, 2009, to 2,875 at January 31, 2010, can be explained as follows:

Cash from (used for) investment activities	CHF (4,650)
Cash from (used for) financing activities	1,700
Net change in cash flow	(2,950)
Cash at beginning of month	5,825
Cash at end of month	CHF 2,875

The statement of cash flows provides information that not only shows the sources and uses of cash but also helps both investors and creditors predict future cash flows for Nestlé and make appropriate financial decisions. The pattern of cash flows shown in Exhibit 2.9 (net cash outflows for investing activities and net cash flows from financing activities) is typical of Nestlé's past several annual statements of cash flows. Companies seeking to expand usually report cash outflows for investing activities.

SELF-STUDY **QUIZ 2-5**

Lance Inc. manufactures and sells snack products. Indicate whether the following transactions from a recent statement of cash flows were investing (I) or financing (F) activities, and show the direction of the effect on cash (+ means increases cash; − means decreases cash):

Transactions	Type of Activity (I or F)	Effect on Cash Flows (+ or −)
1. Paid dividends	_____	_____
2. Sold property	_____	_____
3. Sold marketable securities (investments)	_____	_____
4. Purchased vending machines	_____	_____
5. Repurchased its own shares	_____	_____

After you complete your answers, go online for the solutions.

🔲 connect

Exhibit **2.9**

Nestlé's Statement of Cash Flows

THE NESTLÉ GROUP Consolidated Statement of Cash Flows For the Month Ended January 31, 2010 (in millions of Swiss francs)	
Operating Activities	
(none in this chapter)	
Investing Activities	
Purchased equipment (c)	CHF (1,500)
Purchased long-term investments (e)	(3,000)
Lent funds to trade supplier (d)	(450)
Received payment on loans to trade supplier (g)	300
Net cash used in investing activities	**(4,650)**
Financing Activities	
Issued shares (a)	1,300
Borrowed from banks (b)	1,000
Repaid loan from bank (h)	(400)
Paid dividends (f)	(200)
Net cash provided by financing activities	**1,700**
Net decrease in cash	**(2,950)**
Cash at beginning of month	5,825
Cash at end of month	**2,875**

Items are referenced to events (a) through (h) illustrated in this chapter.

Agrees with the cash balance reported on the statement of financial position.

Some Misconceptions

Some people confuse bookkeeping with accounting. In effect, they confuse a part of accounting with the whole. Bookkeeping involves the routine, clerical part of accounting and requires only minimal knowledge of accounting. A bookkeeper may record the repetitive and uncomplicated transactions in most businesses and may maintain the simple records of a small business. In contrast, the accountant is a highly trained professional, competent in the design of information systems, analysis of complex transactions, interpretation of financial data, financial reporting, auditing, taxation, and management consulting.

Another prevalent misconception is that all transactions are subject to precise and objective measurement, and that the accounting results reported in the financial statements are exactly what happened during that period. In reality, accounting numbers are influenced by estimates, as subsequent chapters will illustrate. Some people believe that financial statements report the entity's market value (including its assets), but they do not. To understand and interpret financial statements, the user must be aware of their limitations as well as their usefulness. One should understand what the financial statements do and do not try to accomplish.

Finally, financial statements are often thought to be inflexible because of their quantitative nature. As you study accounting, you will learn that it requires considerable *professional judgment* on the part of the accountant to capture the economic essence of complex transactions. Accountants develop professional judgment after years of experience in analyzing business transactions and in applying generally accepted accounting principles in preparing and auditing financial reports. Accounting is stimulating intellectually; it is not a cut-and-dried subject. It calls on your intelligence, analytical ability, creativity, and judgment. Accounting is a communication process involving an audience (users) with a wide diversity of knowledge, interest, and capabilities; therefore, it will call on your ability as a communicator. The language of accounting uses concisely written phrases and symbols to convey information about the resource flows measured for specific organizations.

To understand financial statements, you must have a certain level of knowledge of the concepts and the measurement procedures used in the accounting process. You should learn what accounting is really like and appreciate the reasons for using certain procedures. This level of knowledge cannot be gained by reading a list of the concepts and a list of the misconceptions. Neither can a generalized discussion of the subject matter suffice. A certain amount of involvement, primarily problem solving (similar to the requirement in mathematics courses), is essential in the study of accounting focused on the needs of the user. Therefore, we provide problems aimed at the desirable knowledge level for the user as well as the preparer of financial statements.

ACCOUNTING STANDARDS
FOR PRIVATE ENTERPRISES

As noted in Chapter 1, the accounting standards applicable for the reporting of financial information by private enterprises may differ from IFRS, especially the accounting for complex transactions and the extent of detail reported in the notes to the financial statements. Differences in accounting standards may lead to different values for assets, liabilities, and equity that are reported on the statement of financial position. We will highlight such differences as we cover specific topics in future chapters. For example, when accounting for income taxes, private enterprises may use the taxes payable method, which is a simpler method than the deferred income taxes method that is required for publicly accountable enterprises. In that case, the statement of financial position would not include the account Deferred income tax liabilities. Further details on accounting for income taxes are provided in Chapter 9.

DEMONSTRATION **CASE**

On April 1, 2011, three ambitious college students started Terrific Lawn Maintenance Corporation. Completed transactions (summarized) through April 30, 2011, for Terrific Lawn Maintenance Corporation follow:

a. Issued 1,500 shares in exchange for $9,000 cash. Each investor received 500 shares.
b. Acquired rakes and other hand tools (equipment) with a list price of $690 for $600; paid the hardware store $200 cash and signed a note for the balance with the hardware store.
c. Ordered three lawn mowers and two edgers from XYZ Lawn Supply Inc. for $4,000.
d. Purchased four acres of land as a future site of a storage garage. Paid cash, $5,000.
e. Received the mowers and edgers that had been ordered, signing a note to pay XYZ Lawn Supply in full, in 30 days.
f. Sold one acre of land to the city for a park. The city paid Terrific Lawn Maintenance Corp. $1,250, the cost of the land in cash.
g. One of the owners borrowed $3,000 from a local bank for personal use.

Required:

1. Set up T-accounts for cash, equipment (for hand tools and mowing equipment), land, short-term notes payable (to equipment supply companies), and share capital. Indicate beginning balances of $0 in the T-accounts. Analyze each transaction by using the process outlined in the chapter. Prepare journal entries in chronological order. Enter the effects of the transactions in the appropriate T-accounts. Identify each amount with its letter in the preceding list.
2. Use the amounts in the T-accounts developed in (1) to prepare a classified statement of financial position for Terrific Lawn Maintenance Corporation at April 30, 2011. Show the account balances for all assets, liabilities, and shareholders' equity. Use the following transaction analysis model:

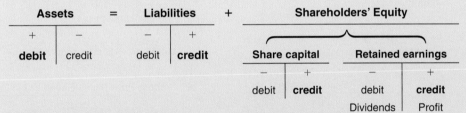

3. Prepare the investing and financing sections of the statement of cash flows.

We strongly recommend that you prepare your own answers to these requirements and then check your answers with the solution provided below.

SUGGESTED **SOLUTION**

1. Transaction analysis, journal entries, and T-accounts:

(**a**) Cash (+A)   9,000
      Share capital (+SE)   9,000

Assets		=	Liabilities	+	Shareholders' Equity	
Cash	+9,000				Share capital	+9,000

(**b**) Equipment (+A)   600
      Cash (−A)   200
      Short-term notes payable (+L)   400

Assets		=	Liabilities		+	Shareholders' Equity
Equipment	+600		Short-term notes payable	+400		
Cash	−200					

The **historical cost principle** states that assets should be recorded at the amount paid on the date of the transaction. This is $600, not the list price of $690.

(*c*) This is not a transaction; no exchange has taken place. No accounts are affected.

(*d*)   Land (+A)   5,000
       Cash (−A)   5,000

Assets		=	Liabilities	+	Shareholders' Equity
Land	+5,000				
Cash	− 5,000				

(*e*)   Equipment (+A)   4,000
       Short-term notes payable (+L)   4,000

Assets		=	Liabilities		+	Shareholders' Equity
Equipment	+4,000		Short-term notes payable	+4,000		

(*f*)   Cash (+A)   1,250
       Land (−A)   1,250

Assets		=	Liabilities	+	Shareholders' Equity
Cash	+1,250				
Land	−1,250				

(*g*) This is not a transaction that involves the company. The separate-entity assumption states that transactions of the owners are separate from transactions of the business.

Assets						=	Liabilities + Shareholders' Equity	

+ Cash (A) −

Beg. bal.	0		
(a)	9,000	(b)	200
(f)	1,250	(d)	5,000
End. bal.	5,050		

+ Equipment (A) −

Beg. bal.	0	
(b)	600	
(e)	4,000	
End. bal.	4,600	

− Short-Term Notes Payable (L) +

	Beg. bal.	0
	(b)	400
	(e)	4,000
	End. bal.	4,400

− Share Capital (SE) +

	Beg. bal.	0
	(a)	9,000
	End. bal.	9,000

+ Land (A) −

Beg. bal.	0		
(d)	5,000	(f)	1,250
End. bal.	3,750		

2. Statement of financial position:

TERRIFIC LAWN MAINTENANCE CORPORATION
Statement of Financial Position
At April 30, 2011

Assets		Liabilities	
Current Assets		*Current Liability*	
Cash	$ 5,050	Short-term notes payable	$ 4,400
Total current assets	5,050		
Equipment	4,600	**Shareholders' Equity**	
Land	3,750	Share capital	9,000
Total assets	$13,400	Total liabilities and shareholders' equity	$13,400

Notice that the statement of financial position presented earlier in the text listed assets on the top and liabilities and shareholders' equity on the bottom. It is also acceptable practice to prepare a statement of financial position with assets on the left side and liabilities and shareholders' equity on the right side, as in the preceding example.

3. Investing and financing effects of the statement of cash flows:

TERRIFIC LAWN MAINTENANCE CORPORATION
Statement of Cash Flows
For the Month Ended April 30, 2011

Operating Activities	
(none in this case)	
Investing Activities	
Purchased land (*d*)	$(5,000)
Purchased equipment (*b*)	(200)
Net cash used in investing activities	**(5,200)**
Financing Activities	
Issued shares (*a*)	9,000
Net cash provided by financing activities	9,000
Change in cash	**3,800**
Beginning cash balance	0
Ending cash balance	**$3,800**

CHAPTER **TAKE-AWAYS**

1. **Understand the objective of financial reporting and the related key accounting assumptions and principles. p. 47**
   - The primary objective of external financial reporting is to provide useful economic information about a business to help external parties, primarily investors and creditors, make sound financial decisions.
   - Key accounting assumptions and principles:
     a. Separate-entity assumption—transactions of the business are accounted for separately from transactions of the owner.
     b. Unit-of-measure assumption—financial information is reported in the national monetary unit.
     c. Continuity (going-concern) assumption—a business is expected to continue to operate into the foreseeable future.
     d. Historical cost principle—financial statement elements should be recorded at their cash-equivalent cost on the date of the transaction.

2. **Define the elements of a classified statement of financial position. p. 50**
   - Elements of the statement of financial position:
     a. Assets—probable future economic benefits owned by the entity as a result of past transactions.
     b. Liabilities—present debts or obligations of the entity as a result of past transactions, which will be paid with assets or services.
     c. Shareholders' equity—the financing provided by the owners and the operations of the business.

3. **Identify what constitutes a business transaction, and recognize common account titles used in business. p. 56**
   A transaction includes:
   - An exchange between a business and one or more external parties to a business.
   or
   - A measurable internal event such as adjustments for the use of assets in operations.
   An account is a standardized format that organizations use to accumulate the dollar effects of transactions of each financial statement item. Typical account titles include the following:
   - Assets: cash, trade receivables, inventory, prepayments, and property and equipment.
   - Liabilities: trade payables, notes payable, accrued liabilities, and taxes payable.
   - Shareholders' equity: share capital and retained earnings.

4. **Apply transaction analysis to simple business transactions in terms of the accounting model: Assets = Liabilities + Shareholders' Equity. p. 58**

   To determine the economic effect of a transaction on the entity in terms of its accounting equation, each transaction is analyzed as to the accounts (at least two) that are affected. In an exchange, the company receives something and gives something. If the accounts, direction of the effects, and amounts are correctly analyzed, the accounting equation must stay in balance. The transaction analysis model is

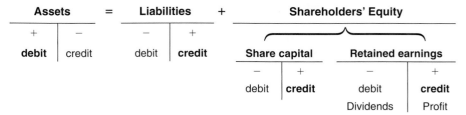

5. **Determine the impact of business transactions on the statement of financial position by using two basic tools: journal entries and T-accounts. p. 63**
   - Journal entries express the effects of a transaction on accounts by using the debit-credit framework. The accounts and amounts to be debited are listed first. Then the accounts and amounts to be credited are listed below the debits and indented, resulting in debits on the left and credits on the right. A brief description of the transaction is then included for future reference.

(date or reference)	Property, plant, and equipment	2,200	
	Cash (−A)		1,500
	Long-term borrowings (+L)		700

   - T-accounts summarize transaction effects for each account. These tools can be used to determine balances and draw inferences about a company's activities.

+	Assets	−		−	Liabilities and Shareholders' Equity	+
Beginning balance Increases		Decreases		Decreases	Beginning balance Increases	
Ending balance					Ending balance	

6. **Prepare a classified statement of financial position and analyze it by using the debt-to-equity ratio. p. 71**

   Classified statements of financial position are structured as follows:
   - Assets categorized as "current assets" (those to be used or turned into cash within the year, with inventory always considered to be a current asset) and non-current assets such as long-term investments, property and equipment, and intangible assets.
   - Liabilities categorized as "current liabilities" (those that will be paid within the next year or the operating cycle, whichever is longer) and non-current liabilities.
   - Shareholders' equity accounts are listed as share capital first, followed by retained earnings and other components. The debt-to-equity ratio (total liabilities ÷ shareholders' equity) measures the relationship between total liabilities and the shareholders' capital that finance the assets. The higher the ratio, the more debt is used to finance assets. As the ratio (and thus debt) increases, risk increases.

7. **Identify investing and financing transactions and how they are reported on the statement of cash flows. p. 74**

   A statement of cash flows reports the sources and uses of cash for the period by the type of activity that generated the cash flow: operating, investing, and financing. Investing activities are purchasing and selling long-term assets, making loans, and receiving payment from loans to others. Financing activities are borrowing and repaying loans to banks, issuing and repurchasing shares, and paying dividends.

   In this chapter, we discussed the fundamental accounting model and transaction analysis. Journal entries and T-accounts were used to record the results of transaction analysis for investing and financing decisions that affect specific accounts. In Chapter 3, we continue our detailed look at financial statements, in particular the income statement. The purpose of Chapter 3 is to build on your knowledge by discussing concepts for the measurement of revenues and expenses and by illustrating transaction analysis for operating decisions.

KEY **RATIO**

The **debt-to-equity ratio** measures the relationship between total liabilities and the shareholders' capital that finance the assets. The higher the ratio, the more debt is assumed by the company to finance assets. It is computed as follows (p. 73):

$$\text{Debt-to-Equity Ratio} = \frac{\text{Total Liabilities}}{\text{Shareholders' Equity}}$$

FINDING **FINANCIAL INFORMATION**

STATEMENT OF FINANCIAL POSITION

Current Assets	*Current Liabilities*
Cash	Bank borrowings
Trade receivables	Trade payables
Notes receivable	Notes payable
Inventory	Accrued liabilities
Prepayments	*Non-current Liabilities*
Non-current Assets	Long-term borrowings
Investments in associates	*Shareholders' Equity*
	Share capital
Property, plant, and equipment	Retained earnings
Intangibles	

INCOME STATEMENT
To be presented in Chapter 3

STATEMENT OF CASH FLOWS

Under Investing Activities
+ Sales of non-current assets for cash
− Purchases of non-current assets for cash
− Loans to others
+ Receipt of cash on loans to others

Under Financing Activities
+ Borrowing from banks
− Repayment of loans from banks
+ Issuance of shares
− Repurchase of shares
− Payment of dividends

NOTES
To be discussed in future chapters

KEY **TERMS**

Account p. 57

Assets p. 50

Continuity (Going-Concern) Assumption p. 49

Cost Principle p. 49

Credit p. 64

Current Assets p. 52

Current Liabilities p. 54

Debit p. 64

Journal Entry p. 65

Liabilities p. 53

Non-current Assets p. 53

Non-current Liabilities p. 54

Primary Objective of External Financial Reporting p. 48

Retained Earnings p. 56

Separate-Entity Assumption p. 48

Share Capital p. 55

Shareholders' Equity (Owners' Equity or Stockholders' Equity) p. 55

T-account p. 64

Transaction p. 56

Transaction Analysis p. 59

Unit-of-Measure Assumption p. 49

QUESTIONS

1. What is the primary objective of financial reporting for external users?
2. Define the following:
   - *a. Asset*   *c. Liability*   *e. Share capital*
   - *b. Current asset*   *d. Current liability*   *f. Retained earnings*
3. Explain what the following principle and assumptions mean in accounting:
   - *a.* Separate-entity assumption   *c.* Continuity assumption
   - *b.* Unit-of-measure assumption   *d.* Cost principle
4. Why is it important to have accounting assumptions?
5. How is the debt-to-equity ratio computed and how is it interpreted?
6. For accounting purposes, what is an account? Explain why accounts are used in an accounting system?
7. What are the limitations of using the historical cost principle as a basis for valuation of assets subsequent to acquisition?
8. What is the fundamental accounting model?
9. Define a business *transaction* in the broad sense and give examples of the two different kinds of transactions.
10. Explain what *debit* and *credit* mean.
11. Briefly explain what is meant by transaction analysis. What are the two steps in transaction analysis?
12. What two equalities in accounting must be maintained in transaction analysis?
13. What is a journal entry?
14. What is a T-account? What is its purpose?
15. What transactions are classified as investing activities in a statement of cash flows? What transactions are classified as financing activities?
16. What is the difference between a bookkeeper and an accountant?

EXERCISES

LO3

E2–1   Identifying Events as Accounting Transactions

Which of the following events results in an exchange transaction for O'Brien Company (Y for yes and N for no)?

_____ (1)   O'Brien purchased a machine and signed a note payable, payable in six months.
_____ (2)   Six investors in O'Brien Company sold their shares to another investor.
_____ (3)   The company lent $150,000 to a member of the board of directors.
_____ (4)   O'Brien Company ordered supplies from Office Max to be delivered next week.
_____ (5)   The founding owner, Meaghan O'Brien, purchased additional shares in another company.
_____ (6)   The company borrowed $1,000,000 from a local bank.

LO3

E2–2   Identifying Account Titles

The following are independent situations.

a. A company orders and receives 10 personal computers for office use for which it signs a note promising to pay $25,000 within three months.

b. A company purchases a new delivery truck that has a list, or sticker, price of $24,000 for $21,000 cash.

c. A women's clothing retailer orders 30 new display stands for $300 each, for future delivery.

d. A new company is formed and sells 100 shares for $12 per share to investors.

e. A manufacturing company signs a contract for the construction of a new warehouse for $500,000. At the signing, the company writes a cheque for $50,000 as a deposit on the future construction.

f. A publishing firm purchases the copyright (an intangible asset) to a manuscript for an introductory accounting text from the author for $40,000.

g. A manufacturing firm pays dividends of $100,000 to shareholders in cash.

h. A company purchases 400 shares of WestJet Airlines for $5,000 cash.

i. A company purchases a piece of land for $50,000 cash. An appraiser for the buyer valued the land at $52,500.

j. A manufacturing company purchases the patent (an intangible asset) on a new digital satellite system for television reception for $500,000 cash and a note for $400,000, payable in one year at an annual interest of 10 percent.

k. A local company is a sole proprietorship (one owner); its owner buys a car for $10,000 for personal use. Answer from the company's point of view.

l. A company signs a six-month note for a $1,000 loan on June 30, 2011, to be paid back on December 31, 2011, with 10 percent annual interest.

m. A company pays $1,500 principal on its note payable.

Required:

1. Indicate the appropriate elements on the classified statement of financial position (use account titles), if any, that are affected in each of the preceding events. Consider what is given and what is received.

2. At what amount would you record the truck in (b)? The land in (i)? What measurement principle are you applying?

3. What accounting concepts did you apply for situations (c) and (k)?

E2–3 Classifying Accounts and Their Usual Balances

LO3, 5

As described in a recent annual report, Singapore Airlines provides quality travel services to many destinations worldwide.

Singapore Airlines

Required:

For each of the following accounts from Singapore's recent statement of financial position, complete the following chart by indicating whether the account is classified as a current asset (CA), non-current asset (NCA), current liability (CL), non-current liability (NCL), or shareholders' equity (SE), and whether the account usually has a debit or credit balance.

Account	Statement of Financial Position Classification	Debit or Credit Balance
1. Investment properties		
2. Retained earnings		
3. Notes payable (due in 3 years)		
4. Prepayments		
5. Long-term investments		
6. Share capital		
7. Aircraft, spares, and spare engines		
8. Trade and other payables		
9. Short-term investments		
10. Current tax payable		
11. Trade receivables		
12. Investment in associated companies		
13. Cash and bank balances		
14. Inventories		
15. Land and buildings		
16. Deferred revenue		

E2–4 Identifying Effects on Elements of the Statement of Financial Position

LO4

Complete the following table by entering either the word *increases* or *decreases* in columns (1) and (2), and either the word *debit* or *credit* in columns (3) and (4).

	(1) Debit	(2) Credit	(3) Increases	(4) Decreases
Assets				
Liabilities				
Shareholders' equity				

LO4

E2–5 **Determining Financial Statement Effects of Several Transactions**

The following events occurred for Favata Company:

a. Received investment of $20,000 cash by organizers.

b. Borrowed cash from a bank and signed a note for $6,000.

c. Purchased $12,000 in land; paid $1,000 in cash and signed a mortgage note with a local bank for the balance (due in 15 years).

d. Loaned $300 to an employee who signed a note due in three months.

e. Paid the bank the amount borrowed in (b).

f. Purchased $8,000 of equipment, paying $1,000 in cash and signing a note due to the manufacturer.

Required:

For each of the events (a) through (f), perform transaction analysis and indicate the account, amount, and direction of the effects (+ for increase and − for decrease) on the accounting equation. Check that the accounting equation remains in balance after each transaction. Use the following headings:

Event	Assets	=	Liabilities	+	Shareholders' Equity

LO4

Nike Inc.

E2–6 **Determining Financial Statement Effects of Several Transactions**

Nike Inc., with headquarters in Beaverton, Oregon, is one of the world's leading manufacturers of athletic shoes and sports apparel. The following activities occurred during a recent year. The amounts are rounded to millions of dollars.

a. Purchased additional building for $143.5 and equipment for $70.3; paid $45 in cash and signed a long-term note for the rest.

b. Issued $21.1 in additional shares for cash.

c. Declared $110 in dividends; paid $78.8 during the year, with the rest payable in the following year.

d. Several Nike investors sold their own shares to other investors on the stock exchange for $55.

e. Repaid $30.2 in principal on long-term debt obligations.

f. Received cash for sale of investments in other companies at their cost of $1.4.

Required:

For each of these events, perform transaction analysis and indicate the account, amount, and direction of the effects on the accounting equation. Check that the accounting equation remains in balance after each transaction. Use the following headings:

Event	Assets	=	Liabilities	+	Shareholders' Equity

LO5

E2–7 **Recording Investing and Financing Activities**

Refer to E2–5.

Required:

For each of the events in E2–5, prepare journal entries, checking that debits equal credits.

LO5

Nike, Inc.

E2–8 **Recording Investing and Financing Activities**

Refer to E2–6.

Required:

1. For each of the events in E2–6, prepare journal entries, checking that debits equal credits.

2. Explain your response to E2–6 (d).

LO5

E2–9 **Analyzing the Effects of Transactions in T-Accounts**

Grady Service Company Inc. was organized by Chris Grady and five other investors. The following events occurred during the year:

a. Received $63,000 cash from the investors; each was issued 1,400 shares.

b. Purchased equipment for use in the business at a cost of $16,000; one-fourth was paid in cash, and the company signed a note for the balance, payable in six months.

c. Signed an agreement with a cleaning service to pay it $200 per week for cleaning the corporate offices.

   d. Lent $2,500 to one of the investors who signed a note due in six months.

   e. Issued shares to additional investors who contributed $6,000 in cash and a lot of land valued at $15,000.

   f. Paid the amount of the note payable in (*b*).

   g. Conor Mulkeen borrowed $10,000 for personal use from a local bank and signed a note payable in one year.

Required:

1. Prepare journal entries for each transaction. If an event does not require a journal entry, explain the reason. Use the account titles listed in (2).

2. Create T-accounts for the following accounts: cash, note receivable, equipment, land, note payable, and share capital. Beginning balances are zero. For each of the preceding transactions, record the effects of the transaction in the appropriate T-accounts. Include good referencing and totals for each T-account.

3. Using the balances in the T-accounts, fill in the following amounts for the accounting equation:

Assets $_____ = Liabilities $_____ + Shareholders' Equity $_____

E2–10 Inferring Investing and Financing Transactions, and Preparing a Statement of Financial Position   ▧ **LO4, 6**

During its first week of operations ending January 7, 2011, Cirba Sports Inc. completed seven transactions with the dollar effects indicated in the following T-accounts:

Cash		Short-Term Note Receivable		Store Fixtures	
(1) 16,000	4,000 (3)	(4) 3,000	2,000 (7)	(5) 9,000	
(2) 70,000	3,000 (4)				
(7) 2,000	9,000 (5)				
	3,000 (6)				

Land		Short-Term Note Payable		Share Capital	
(3) 12,000		(6) 3,000	70,000 (2)		16,000 (1)
			8,000 (3)		

Required:

1. Write a brief explanation of transactions 1 through 7. Explain any assumptions that you made.

2. Compute the ending balance in each account and prepare a classified statement of financial position for Cirba Sports Inc. on January 7, 2011.

E2–11 Inferring Investing and Financing Transactions, and Preparing a Statement of Financial Position   ▧ **LO5**

During its first month of operations, March 2012, Faye's Fashions Inc. completed seven transactions with the dollar effects indicated in the following T-accounts:

Cash		Short-Term Investments		Short-Term Note Receivable	
(1) 50,000	4,000 (2)	(4) 6,000	2,000 (6)	(3) 4,000	
(6) 2,000	4,000 (3)				
	6,000 (4)				
	3,000 (5)				

Computer Equipment		Delivery Truck		Long-Term Note Payable	
(7) 4,000		(2) 25,000		(5) 3,000	21,000 (2)

Share Capital	
	50,000 (1)
	4,000 (7)

Required:

1. Write a brief explanation of transactions 1 through 7. Explain any assumptions that you made.

2. Compute the ending balance in each account and prepare a classified statement of financial position for Faye's Fashions Inc. at the end of March 2012.

LO5

E2–12 **Recording Journal Entries**

BMW Group, headquartered in Munich, Germany, manufactures several automotive brands, including BMW, MINI, and Rolls-Royce. Financial information is reported in euros (€), using International Financial Reporting Standards as applicable to the European Union. The following transactions were adapted from the annual report of the BMW Group; amounts are in millions of euros.

a. Declared €532 in dividends to be paid next month.

b. Issued additional shares for €146 cash.

c. Paid €419 in dividends declared in prior months.

d. Borrowed €3,956 and signed a 12 percent note due in two years.

e. Lent €27 to trade suppliers who signed notes to repay the loans in three months.

f. Purchased equipment for €12,890, paying €9,870 in cash and signing a note for the balance.

g. Purchased investments for €2,654 cash.

Required:
Prepare journal entries for each transaction. Be sure to use good referencing and categorize each account as an asset (A), liability (L), or shareholders' equity (SE). If a transaction does not require a journal entry, explain the reason.

LO5

E2–13 **Recording Journal Entries**

Philippine Long Distance Telephone Company

Philippine Long Distance Telephone Company is the leading telecommunications provider in the Philippines. The monetary unit is the Philippine peso (₱). The following events were adapted from a recent annual report. Amounts are in millions of pesos.

a. Declared ₱37,034 in dividends to be paid next month.

b. Ordered ₱640 in equipment.

c. Paid ₱37,034 in dividends previously declared in (a).

d. Issued additional shares for ₱1,270 in cash.

e. Sold land at its cost for cash, ₱233.

f. Received the equipment ordered in transaction (b), paying ₱120 in cash and signing a note for the balance.

g. Purchased short-term investments for ₱3,457 in cash.

h. Paid ₱13,375 in principal on long-term debt.

Required:
Prepare journal entries for each transaction. Be sure to use good referencing, and categorize each account as an asset (A), liability (L), or shareholders' equity (SE). If a transaction does not require a journal entry, explain the reason.

LO5, 6

E2–14 **Analyzing the Effects of Transactions by Using T-Accounts, Preparing a Statement of Financial Position, and Interpreting the Debt-to-Equity Ratio as a Manager of the Company**

Massimo Company has been operating for one year (2010). You are a member of the management team investigating expansion ideas, all of which will require borrowing funds from banks. At the start of 2011, Massimo's T-account balances were as follows:

Assets:

Cash		Short-Term Investments		Property and Equipment	
5,000		2,000		4,000	

Liabilities:

Short-Term Notes Payable		Long-Term Notes Payable	
	2,100		6,600

Shareholders' Equity:

Share Capital		Retained Earnings	
	300		2,000

Required:

1. Using the data from these T-accounts, complete the accounting equation on January 1, 2011:

    Assets $ _____ = Liabilities $ _____ + Shareholders' Equity $ _____

2. Enter in the T-accounts the following transactions that occurred in 2011:
    (*a*) Paid one-half of the principal on the long-term note payable.
    (*b*) Sold $1,000 of the investments for $1,000 cash.
    (*c*) Paid in full the principal on the short-term notes payable.
    (*d*) Sold one-half of the property and equipment for $2,000 in cash.
    (*e*) Borrowed $2,000 from the bank and signed a note promising to pay the principal and interest at an annual rate of 10 percent in three years.
    (*f*) Paid $500 in dividends to shareholders.

3. Compute ending balances in the T-accounts to complete the statement of financial position on December 31, 2011:

    Assets $ _____ = Liabilities $ _____ + Shareholders' Equity $ _____

4. Using the ending balances in the T-accounts, prepare a classified statement of financial position at December 31, 2011, in good form.

5. Calculate the debt-to-equity ratio at December 31, 2011. If the industry average for the debt-to-equity ratio is 1.00, what does your computation suggest to you about Massimo Company? Would you support expansion by borrowing? Why or why not?

E2–15   Explaining the Effects of Transactions on Specific Accounts by Using T-Accounts   ▮ LO5
Heavey and Lovas Furniture Repair Service, a company with two shareholders, began operations on June 1, 2011. The following T-accounts indicate the activities for the month of June.

Cash (A)			
(a)	17,000	(b)	10,000
(d)	500	(c)	1,500
(f)	800	(e)	1,000

Notes Receivable (A)			
(c)	1,500	(d)	500

Tools and Equipment (A)			
(a)	3,000	(f)	800

Building (A)	
(b)	50,000

Notes Payable (L)			
(e)	1,000	(b)	40,000

Share Capital (SE)		
	(a)	20,000

Required:
Explain transactions (*a*) through (*f*), which resulted in the entries in the T-accounts. That is, what activity made the account increase or decrease?

E2–16   Inferring Typical Investing and Financing Activities in Accounts   ▮ LO5
The following T-accounts indicate the effects of normal business transactions:

Equipment		
1/1	300	
	250	?
12/13	450	

Note Receivable		
1/1	75	
	?	290
12/31	50	

Notes Payable		
	130	1/1
?	170	
	180	12/31

Required:
1. Describe the typical investing and financing transactions that affect each T-account. That is, what economic events made these accounts increase or decrease?
2. For each T-account, compute the missing amounts.

E2–17   Identifying Investing and Financing Activities Affecting Cash Flows   ▮ LO7
The Forzani Group Ltd. (FGL) is Canada's largest sporting goods retailer, with over 330 company-owned stores under the Forzani's, Sport Chek, Coast Mountain Sports, Sport Mart, National Sports, Athletes World, and Hockey Experts banners. FGL also boasts about 230 franchised stores under the Sport Experts, Atmosphere, Intersport, Nevada Bob's Golf, Fitness Source, Pegasus, S3, Econosports, and Tech Shop names. The stores sell name-brand and private-label sports equipment,

The Forzani Group Ltd.

footwear, and apparel. The following are several of FGL's investing and financing activities that were reflected in a recent annual statement of cash flows.

a. Principal repayment of long-term debt.

b. Purchase of investments.

c. Issuance of shares.

d. Addition to capital assets (property, plant, and equipment).

e. Issuance of long-term debt.

f. Repurchase of shares.

g. Disposal of other assets.

Required:
For each of these, indicate whether the activity is investing (I) or financing (F) and the direction of the effect on cash flows (+ = increases cash; − = decreases cash).

LO7

Hilton Hotels
Corporation

E2–18   **Preparing the Investing and Financing Section of the Statement of Cash Flows**
Hilton Hotels Corporation constructs, operates, and franchises domestic and international hotel and hotel-casino properties. Information from the company's recent annual statement of cash flows indicates the following investing and financing activities during that year (simplified):

Payment of debt principal	$ 24
Purchase of investments	139
Sale of property (assume sold at cost)	230
Issuance of shares	60
Purchase and renovation of properties	370
Additional borrowing from banks	992
Receipt of principal payment on a note receivable	125

Required:
Prepare the investing and financing sections of the statement of cash flows for Hilton hotels. Assume that the company's year-end is December 31, 2011.

LO3, 6, 7

E2–19   **Finding Financial Information as a Potential Investor**
You are considering investing the cash you inherited from your grandfather in various company shares. You have received the annual reports of several major companies.

Required:
For each of the following, indicate where you would locate the information in an annual report. (*Hint:* The information may be in more than one location.)

1. Total current assets.
2. Principal amount of debt repaid during the year.
3. Summary of significant accounting policies.
4. Cash received from sales of non-current assets.
5. Amount of dividends paid during the year.
6. Short-term obligations.
7. Date of the statement of financial position.

PROBLEMS

LO1, 3

Total, S.A.

P2–1   **Identifying Accounts on a Classified Statement of Financial Position and Their Normal Debit or Credit Balances** (AP2–1)
Total, S.A. is a large, international, publicly traded integrated oil and gas company that explores, produces, refines, markets, and supplies crude oil and petroleum products. It is a major actor in the chemicals business, and has operations in more than 130 countries on five continents.

The following are several of the accounts that appeared on the company's recent statement of financial position.

Account	Statement of Financial Position Classification	Debit or Credit Balance
1. Cash and cash equivalents	_____	_____
2. Deferred income tax liabilities	_____	_____
3. Retained earnings	_____	_____
4. Materials and supplies	_____	_____
5. Prepayments	_____	_____
6. Share capital	_____	_____
7. Patents (an intangible asset)	_____	_____
8. Trade and other payables	_____	_____
9. Accrued liabilities	_____	_____
10. Deferred revenue	_____	_____
11. Current financial assets	_____	_____
12. Investment in associates	_____	_____
13. Trade receivables	_____	_____
14. Crude oil products and merchandise	_____	_____
15. Land and buildings	_____	_____
16. Provisions (short-term)	_____	_____

Required:
For each account, indicate how it normally should be categorized on a classified statement of financial position. Use CA for current asset, NCA for non-current asset, CL for current liability, NCL for non-current liability, and SE for shareholders' equity. Also indicate whether the account normally has a debit or credit balance.

P2–2 **Determining Financial Statement Effects of Various Transactions** (AP2–2)   ▉ LO3, 4
Lester's Home Healthcare Services was organized on January 1, 2011, by four friends. Each organizer invested $10,000 in the company and, in turn, was issued 8,000 shares. To date, they are the only shareholders. During the first month (January 2011), the company completed the following six transactions:

a. Collected a total of $40,000 from the organizers and, in turn, issued the shares.

b. Purchased a building for $65,000, equipment for $16,000, and three acres of land for $12,000; paid $13,000 in cash, and signed a 10 percent mortgage for the balance payable to the local bank in 15 years. (*Hint:* Five different accounts are affected.)

c. One shareholder reported to the company that he sold 500 shares to another shareholder for a cash consideration of $5,000.

d. Purchased short-term investments for $3,000 cash.

e. Sold one acre of land costing $4,000 to another company for $4,000 cash.

f. Loaned one of the shareholders $5,000 for moving costs, in exchange for a signed note due in one year.

Required:
1. Was Lester's Home Healthcare Services organized as a sole proprietorship, a partnership, or a corporation? Explain the basis for your answer.

2. During the first month, the records of the company were inadequate. You were asked to prepare a summary of the preceding transactions. To develop a quick assessment of the transaction effects on Lester's Home Healthcare Services, you have decided to complete the tabulation that follows and to use plus (+) for increases and minus (−) for decreases for each account. The first transaction is used as an example.

	Assets						=	Liabilities	+	Shareholders' Equity	
Cash	Short-Term Investments	Notes Receivable	Land	Building	Equipment			Notes Payable		Share Capital	Retained Earnings
(a) +40,000							=			+40,000	

3. Did you include all the transactions in the tabulation? If not, which one did you exclude and why?

4. Based only on the completed tabulation, provide the following amounts at January 31, 2011 (show computations):

   a. Total assets

   b. Total liabilities

   c. Total shareholders' equity

   d. Cash balance

   e. Total current assets

5. Compute the debt-to-equity ratio at January 31, 2011. What does this suggest about the company?

LO6

eXcel

P2–3 **Recording Transactions in T-Accounts, Preparing a Statement of Financial Position, and Evaluating the Debt-to-Equity Ratio** (AP2–3)

Injection Plastics Company has been operating for three years. At December 31, 2011, the accounting records reflected the following:

Cash	$21,000	Intangibles	$3,000
Investments (short-term)	2,000	Trade payables	15,000
Trade receivables	3,000	Accrued liabilities	2,000
Inventories	24,000	Short-term borrowings	7,000
Notes receivable (long-term)	1,000	Notes payable (long-term)	48,000
Equipment	48,000	Share capital	90,000
Factory building	90,000	Retained earnings	30,000

During the year 2012, the following summarized transactions were completed:

a. Purchased equipment that cost $18,000; paid $6,000 cash and signed a one-year note for the balance.

b. Issued 2,000 additional shares for $12,000 cash.

c. Lent $7,000 to a supplier who signed a two-year note.

d. Purchased short-term investments for $9,000 in cash.

e. Paid $5,000 on the note in transaction (a).

f. Borrowed $12,000 cash on December 31, 2012, from a local bank and signed a note, payable June 30, 2013.

g. Purchased a patent (an intangible asset) for $3,000 cash.

h. Built an addition to the factory for $25,000; paid $9,000 in cash and signed a three-year note for the balance.

i. Hired a new president at the end of the year. The contract was for $85,000 per year plus options to purchase company shares at a set price based on company performance.

j. Returned defective equipment to the manufacturer, receiving a cash refund of $1,000.

Required:

1. Create T-accounts for each of the accounts on the statement of financial position and enter the balances at the end of 2011 as beginning balances for 2012.

2. Record each of the transactions for 2012 in T-accounts (including referencing) and determine the ending balances.

3. Explain your response to transaction (i).

4. Prepare a classified statement of financial position at December 31, 2012.

5. Compute the debt-to-equity ratio at December 31, 2012. What does this ratio suggest about Injection Plastics Company?

P2–4 **Identifying Effects of Transactions on the Statement of Cash Flows** (AP2–4)
Refer to P2–3.

Required:
Using the transactions (*a*) through (*j*) in P2–3, indicate whether each transaction is an investing (I) or financing (F) activity for the year and the direction of the effect on cash flows (+ for increase and − for decrease). If there is no effect on cash flows, write NE.

P2–5 **Recording Transactions, Preparing Journal Entries, Posting to T-Accounts, Preparing a Statement of Financial Position, and Evaluating the Debt-to-Equity Ratio** (AP2–5)
Bayer AG, with headquarters in Leverkusen, Germany, is an international, research-based group of companies active in health, agriculture, polymers, and chemicals. Popular products include Bayer Aspirin, Alka-Seltzer, and One-A-Day vitamins. The following is Bayer's (simplified) statement of financial position as at June 30, 2009:

BAYER AG Statement of Financial Position At June 30, 2009 (in millions of euros)		
ASSETS		
Current assets		
Cash and cash equivalents	€	1,834
Receivables		8,056
Inventories		6,312
Other assets		728
		16,930
Non-current assets		
Investments		415
Property, plant, and equipment		9,417
Intangible assets		21,743
Other assets		3,187
		34,762
Total assets		**€ 51,692**
LIABILITIES AND SHAREHOLDERS' EQUITY		
Current liabilities		
Trade accounts payable	€	2,013
Financial liabilities		2,304
Provisions		3,568
Other short-term liabilities		1,607
		9,492
Non-current liabilities		
Provisions		7,846
Deferred income taxes		3,568
Financial liabilities		12,279
		23,693
Shareholders' equity		
Share capital		8,284
Retained earnings		10,223
		18,507
Total liabilities and shareholders' equity		**€ 51,692**

Assume that the following transactions occurred in the second half of 2009:

a. Issued additional shares for €1,200 in cash.

b. Borrowed €3,952 from banks due in two years.

c. Declared and paid €953 in dividends to shareholders.

d. Purchased additional intangibles for €45 cash.

e. Purchased property, plant, and equipment; paid €2,647 in cash and €5,410 with additional long-term bank loans.

f. Acquired additional investments; paid €160 in cash.

g. Lent €250 to an associated company that signed a six-month note.

h. Sold investments costing €115 for the same amount in cash.

Required:

1. Prepare a journal entry for each transaction.

2. Create T-accounts for each financial statement account and include the June 30, 2009, balances. Post each journal entry to the appropriate T-accounts.

3. Prepare a statement of financial position for Bayer based on the T-account ending balances at December 31, 2009.

4. Compute Bayer's debt-to-equity ratio at December 31, 2009. What does this suggest about the company?

▇ **LO7**

Bayer AG

P2–6   **Preparing the Investing and Financing Sections of a Statement of Cash Flows** (AP2–6)
Refer to P2–5.

Required:
Based on the transactions that occurred in 2009, prepare the investing and financing sections of the statement of cash flows of Bayer for the second half of 2009.

▇ **LO6**

P2–7   **Using Financial Reports: Preparing a Classified Statement of Financial Position and Analyzing the Debt-to-Equity Ratio** (AP2–7)
The accounts below, in alphabetical order, are adapted from a recent statement of financial position for Big Burgers Inc. (amounts are in thousands of dollars):

	Current Year	Prior Year		Current Year	Prior Year
Accounts and notes receivable	$795.9	$745.5	Long-term debt	$8,937.4	$8,357.3
Accounts payable	689.4	714.3	Notes payable (short term)	544.0	—
Accrued liabilities	2,344.2	2,144.0	Other long-term liabilities	1,869.0	1,758.2
Cash and equivalents	4,260.4	1,379.8	Other non-current assets	1,245.0	1,338.4
Current maturities of long-term debt	658.7	862.2	Prepaid expenses and other current assets	646.4	585.0
Intangible assets, net	1,950.7	1,828.3	Property and equipment, net	20,108.0	20,903.1
Inventories	147.0	147.5	Retained earnings	12,331.9	11,998.9
Investments in and advances to affiliates	1,035.4	1,109.9	Share capital	2,814.2	2,202.6

Required:

1. Construct, in good form, a classified statement of financial position (with two years reported) for Big Burgers Inc.

2. Compute the company's debt-to-equity ratio at the end of the current year. How do you interpret this ratio for Big Burgers?

P2–8 **Preparing Journal Entries, Using T-Accounts, Preparing a Statement of Financial Position, and Evaluating the Debt-to-Equity Ratio over Time as a Bank Loan Officer** (AP2–8)

At the beginning of year 2012, Lee Delivery Company Inc., which was organized in 2011, applied to your bank for a $100,000 loan to expand the business. The vice-president of the bank asked you to review the information and make a recommendation on lending the funds. The following transactions occurred during year 2011 (the company's first year of operations):

a. Received cash from the organizers, $40,000.

b. Purchased land for $12,000 and signed a one-year note (at a 10 percent annual interest rate).

c. Bought two used delivery trucks for operating purposes at the start of the year at a cost of $10,000 each; paid $2,000 cash and signed a promissory note for the balance, payable over the next three years (at an annual interest rate of 11 percent).

d. Sold one-fourth of the land for $3,000 to Birkins Moving, which promised to pay in six months.

e. Paid $2,000 cash to a truck repair shop for a new motor for one of the trucks. (*Hint:* Increase the account you used to record the purchase of the trucks since the usefulness of the truck has been improved.)

f. Traded the other truck and $6,000 cash for a new one. The old truck's fair value is $10,000.

g. Shareholder Jonah Lee paid $22,000 cash for a vacant lot (land) for his personal use.

h. Collected the amount of the note due from Birkins Moving in (*d*).

i. Paid one-third of the principal of the note due for the delivery trucks in (*c*).

Required:

1. Set up appropriate T-accounts with beginning balances of $0 for cash, short-term notes receivable, land, equipment, short-term notes payable, long-term notes payable, and share capital. Using the T-accounts, record the effects of these transactions on Lee Delivery Company.

2. Prepare a classified statement of financial position for Lee Delivery Company at the end of 2011. Compute the debt-to-equity ratio at that date.

3. What recommendation would you make to the bank's vice-president about lending the money to Lee Delivery Company?

4. At the end of the next two years, Lee Delivery Company reported the following amounts on its statements of financial position:

	End of 2013	End of 2012
Assets	$120,000	$90,000
Liabilities	70,000	40,000
Shareholders' equity	50,000	50,000

Compute the company's debt-to-equity ratio for 2012 and 2013. What is the trend and what does this suggest about the company?

ALTERNATE PROBLEMS

AP2–1 **Identifying Accounts on a Classified Statement of Financial Position and Their Normal Debit or Credit Balances** (P2–1)

LO5, 6

Celestica Inc.

According to a recent annual report of Celestica Inc., the company is a "key player in the new technology-driven global economy." The company provides a broad range of services, including "design, prototyping, assembly, testing, product assurance, supply chain management, worldwide distribution, and after-sales service." The following are several of the accounts from a recent statement of financial position:

(1) Trade accounts receivable
(2) Short-term borrowings
(3) Share capital
(4) Long-term debt
(5) Prepaid expenses and other assets
(6) Intangible assets
(7) Property, plant, and equipment

(8) Retained earnings
(9) Trade accounts payable
(10) Cash and short-term investments
(11) Accrued liabilities
(12) Other long-term liabilities
(13) Inventories
(14) Income taxes payable

Required:

Indicate how each account normally should be categorized on a classified statement of financial position. Use CA for current asset, NCA for non-current asset, CL for current liability, NCL for non-current liability, and SE for shareholders' equity. Also indicate whether the account normally has a debit or credit balance.

LO3, 4

AP2–2 **Determining Financial Statement Effects of Various Transactions and Interpreting the Debt-to-Equity Ratio** (P2–2)

Kadoum Incorporated is a small manufacturing company that makes model trains to sell to toy stores. It has a small service department that repairs customers' trains for a fee. The company has been in business for five years. At the end of the most recent year, 2010, the accounting records reflected total assets of $500,000 (cash, $120,000; buildings, $310,000; equipment, $70,000) and total liabilities of $200,000 (short-term notes payable, $140,000; long-term notes payable, $60,000), and total shareholders' equity of $300,000 (share capital, $220,000; retained earnings, $80,000). During the current year, 2011, the following summarized transactions were completed:

a. Issued 10,000 shares for $100,000 cash.

b. Borrowed $120,000 cash from the bank and signed a 10-year, 12 percent note.

c. Built an addition onto the factory for $200,000 and paid cash to the contractor.

d. Purchased equipment for $30,000, paying $3,000 in cash and signing a note due in six months for the balance.

e. Purchased $85,000 in long-term investments.

f. Returned a defective piece of the equipment purchased in transaction (*d*); received a reduction of $3,000 on the note payable.

g. Paid $12,000 of the principal due on the note in (*b*).

h. Purchased a delivery truck (equipment) for $10,000; paid $5,000 cash and signed a short-term note for the remainder.

i. Loaned $2,000 cash to the company president, Zeki Kadoum, who signed a note promising to pay the amount and annual interest at the rate of 10 percent within one year.

j. A shareholder sold some of her shares in Kadoum Incorporated to her neighbour for $5,000.

k. Received $250 cash from Mr. Kadoum on the note due, transaction (*i*).

Required:

1. Prepare a summary of the preceding transactions. To develop a quick assessment of the transaction effects on Kadoum Incorporated, you have decided to complete the tabulation that follows and to use plus (+) for increases and minus (−) for decreases for each account. The first transaction is used as an example.

		Assets			=	Liabilities		+	Shareholders' Equity	
Cash	Notes Receivable	Long-Term Investments	Equipment	Building		Short-Term Notes Payable	Long-Term Notes Payable		Share Capital	Retained Earnings
(*a*) +100,000					=				+100,000	

2. Did you include all transactions in the tabulation? If not, which one did you exclude and why?

3. Based on beginning balances plus the completed tabulation, calculate the following amounts at the end of 2011 (show computations):

   a. Total assets

   b. Total liabilities

   c. Total shareholders' equity

   d. Cash balance

   e. Total current assets

4. Compute the company's debt-to-equity ratio at the end of the year. What does this ratio suggest to you about Kadoum Incorporated?

AP2–3   **Recording Transactions in T-Accounts, Preparing a Statement of Financial Position, and Evaluating the Debt-to-Equity Ratio** (P2–3)

LO5, 6

Gildan Activewear

Gildan Activewear Inc. specializes in manufacturing and selling T-shirts, sport shirts, and fleece. The following is adapted from a recent statement of financial position (assume that the fiscal year ends on December 31, 2008). Dollars are in thousands.

Cash and cash equivalents	$12,357	Accounts payable and accrued liabilities	$155,669
Accounts receivable	222,158	Other current liabilities	50,183
Inventories	316,172	Long-term debt	49,448
Prepaid expenses and other current assets	10,413	Other long-term liabilities	34,493
Property, plant, and equipment, net	436,516	Share capital	89,377
Intangible assets	59,954	Retained earnings	689,980
Other assets	44,556	Other components of equity	32,976

Assume that the following transactions occurred in the first quarter ended March 31, 2009:

a. Received $630 on sale of intangibles.

b. Paid $12,340 in principal on long-term debt.

c. Purchased $3,400 in non-current investments for cash.

d. Sold equipment at its cost for $4,020 cash.

e. Purchased additional intangibles for $2,980 cash.

f. Issued additional shares for $1,020 in cash.

g. Purchased property, plant, and equipment; paid $1,830 in cash and $9,400 with additional long-term bank loans.

h. Sold other assets at cost for $310 cash.

i. Declared and paid $300 in dividends to shareholders.

Required:

1. Create T-accounts for each of the accounts on the statement of financial position; enter the balances at December 31, 2008.
2. Record each of the transactions for the first quarter ended March 31, 2009, in the T-accounts (including referencing) and determine the ending balances.
3. Prepare a classified statement of financial position at March 31, 2009.
4. Compute the debt-to-equity ratio at March 31, 2009. What does this suggest about Gildan Activewear?

AP2–4   **Identifying Effects of Transactions on the Statement of Cash Flows** (P2–4)

Refer to AP2–3.

LO7

Gildan Activewear

Required:

Using the transactions (*a*) through (*i*) in AP2–3, indicate whether each transaction is an investing (I) or financing (F) activity for the year and the direction of the effect on cash flows (+ for increase and − for decrease). Indicate no effect on cash flows related to investing or financing with NE.

AP2–5   **Recording Transactions, Preparing Journal Entries, Posting to T-Accounts, Preparing a Statement of Financial Position, and Evaluating the Debt-to-Equity Ratio** (P2–5)

LO5, 6

Dell Inc.

Dell Inc. is a leading global provider of computer products and services for both the consumer and enterprise markets. Dell offers a full line of desktop and notebook PCs, network servers, workstations, storage systems, printers, handheld computers, digital music players, LCD and plasma televisions, and projectors. The following is Dell's (simplified) statement of financial position from a recent year:

DELL Inc.
Statement of Financial Position
At January 30, 2009
(in millions of U.S. dollars)

ASSETS

Current assets

Cash and cash equivalents	$ 8,352
Short-term investments	740
Receivables	6,443
Inventories	867
Other assets	3,749
Total current assets	20,151

Non-current assets

Property, plant, and equipment, net	2,277
Investments	454
Other assets	3,618
Total assets	$ 26,500

LIABILITIES AND SHAREHOLDERS' EQUITY

Current liabilities

Short-term borrowings	$113
Accounts payable	8,309
Deferred revenue	2,649
Accrued liabilities	3,788
Total current liabilities	14,859

Non-current liabilities

Long-term borrowings	1,898
Deferred revenue	3,000
Other liabilities	2,472
Total liabilities	22,229
Shareholders' equity	4,271
Total liabilities and shareholders' equity	$ 26,500

Assume that the following transactions (in millions of dollars) occurred in the remainder of fiscal year 2010 (ending on February 2, 2010):

a. Issued additional shares for $200 in cash.

b. Borrowed $30 from banks; due in two years.

c. Purchased additional investments for $13,000 cash; one-fifth were long term and the rest were short term.

d. Purchased property, plant, and equipment; paid $875 in cash and $1,410 with additional long-term bank loans.

e. Lent $250 to associated companies that signed a six-month note.

f. Sold short-term investments costing $10,000 for $10,000 cash.

Required:

1. Prepare a journal entry for each transaction.
2. Create T-accounts for each item on the statement of financial position and include the January 30, 2009, balances. Post each journal entry to the appropriate T-accounts.
3. Prepare a statement of financial position for Dell based on the T-account ending balances at February 2, 2010.
4. Compute Dell's debt-to-equity ratio for fiscal year 2010. What does this suggest about the company?

AP2–6 **Preparing the Investing and Financing Sections of a Statement of Cash Flows** (P2–6)
Refer to AP2–5.

Required:
Based on the transactions that occurred in fiscal year 2010, prepare the investing and financing sections of the Dell's statement of cash flows for that year.

AP2–7 **Using Financial Reports: Preparing a Classified Statement of Financial Position and Analyzing the Debt-to-Equity Ratio** (P2–7)

The accounts below, in alphabetical order, are adapted from Danier Leather Inc.'s recent statement of financial position (amounts in thousands of dollars):

	Current Year	Prior Year		Current Year	Prior Year
Accounts payable and accrued liabilities	$8,170	$9,355	Other non-current assets	$5,596	$6,399
Accounts receivable	594	626	Prepaid expenses and		
Cash	21,193	22,576	other current assets	698	1,894
Income taxes payable	-0-	952	Property and	25,314	28,891
Inventories	29,970	29,483	equipment, net		
Non-current liabilities	20,258	18,275	Retained earnings	32,214	36,902
			Share capital	22,723	24,385

Required:
1. Prepare, in good form, a classified statement of financial position (with two years reported) for Danier Leather Inc. Assume the current year ends on June 30, 2010.
2. Compute the company's debt-to-equity ratio for the current year. How do you interpret this ratio for Danier Leather?

AP2–8 **Analyzing the Effects of Transactions by Using T-Accounts, Preparing a Statement of Financial Position, and Interpreting the Debt-to-Equity Ratio as a Bank Loan Officer** (P2–8)

Chu Delivery Company Inc. was organized in 2010. The following transactions occurred during year 2010:

a. Received $40,000 cash from organizers in exchange for shares in the new company.

b. Purchased land for $12,000, signing a one-year note (ignore interest).

c. Bought two used delivery trucks for operating purposes at the start of the year at a cost of $10,000 each; paid $4,000 cash and signed a note due in three years for the rest (ignore interest).

d. Sold one-fourth of the land for $3,000 to Pablo Moving, which signed a six-month note.

e. Paid $1,000 cash to a truck repair shop for a new motor for one of the trucks. (*Hint:* Increase the account you used to record the purchase of the trucks since the productive life of the truck has been improved.)

f. Shareholder Jingbi Chu paid $27,600 from her personal savings to purchase a vacant lot (land) for her personal use.

Required:
1. Set up appropriate T-accounts with beginning balances of zero for cash, short-term note receivable, land, equipment, short-term notes payable, long-term notes payable, and share capital. Using the T-accounts, record the effects of these transactions by Chu Delivery Company.
2. Prepare a classified statement of financial position for Chu Delivery Company at December 31, 2010.
3. At the end of the next two years, Chu Delivery Company reported the following amounts on its statements of financial position:

	End of 2012	End of 2011
Assets	$120,000	$90,000
Liabilities	70,000	40,000
Shareholders' Equity	50,000	50,000

Compute the company's debt-to-equity ratio for 2011 and 2012. What is the trend and what does this suggest about the company?

4. At the beginning of year 2013, Chu Delivery Company applied to your bank for a $100,000 loan to expand the business. The vice-president of the bank asked you to review the information and make a recommendation on lending the funds based solely on the results of the debt-to-equity ratio. What recommendation would you make to the bank's vice-president about lending the money to Chu Delivery Company?

CASES AND PROJECTS

FINDING AND INTERPRETING FINANCIAL INFORMATION

LO1, 2, 3, 4, 7 CP2–1

Cadbury plc

Finding Financial Information

Refer to the financial statements and the accompanying notes of Cadbury plc, available online.

Required:

1. Is the company a corporation, a partnership, or a proprietorship? How do you know?
2. Use the company's statement of financial position to determine the amounts in the accounting equation (A = L + SE).
3. The company shows on the statement of financial position that inventories are reported at £767 million. Does this amount represent the expected selling price? Why or why not?
4. What is the company's fiscal year-end? Where did you find the exact date?
5. What are the company's non-current liabilities?
6. Compute the company's debt-to-equity ratio and explain its meaning.
7. How much cash did the company spend on purchasing property, plant, and equipment each year (capital expenditures)? Where did you find the information?

LO3, 7   CP2–2

Cadbury plc vs. the Nestlé Group

Comparing Companies

Refer to the financial statements and the accompanying notes of Cadbury plc, available online and of The Nestlé Group, given in Appendix A. Nestlé uses the Swiss franc (CHF) in preparing its financial statements, whereas Cadbury reports its financial information by using the pound sterling (£). Use the exchange rates indicated in requirements 1 and 2 below to convert the pounds sterling into Swiss francs so you can compare the specific financial statement elements for both companies.

Required:

1. Which company is larger in terms of total assets? The exchange rate between the two currencies was £1 = CHF 1.53 at December 31, 2008.
2. Compute the debt-to-equity ratio for both companies. Which company is assuming more risk? Why do you think that?
3. In the most recent year, what were the net cash flows (i.e., the increases in cash minus the decreases in cash) related to the buying and selling of investments for each company?
4. How much did each company pay in dividends for the most recent year?
5. What account title does each company use to report any land, buildings, and equipment it may have?

FINANCIAL REPORTING AND ANALYSIS CASES

LO6   CP2–3

Broadening Financial Research Skills: Locating Financial Information on the SEDAR Database

The Securities Commissions regulate companies that issue shares on the stock market. They receive financial reports from public companies electronically under a system called *SEDAR* (System for Electronic Document Analysis and Retrieval). Using the Internet, anyone may search the database for the reports that have been filed. A similar system is available for retrieval of financial information about U.S. public companies. It is known as *EDGAR* (Electronic Data Gathering and Retrieval Service).

Using your Web browser, access the SEDAR database at www.sedar.com. To search the database, select "English," then "Company Profiles"; click on the letter T to get a list of all company names that start with T. Select Thomson Reuters Corporation (TRC), and then click on "View this company's public documents" at the lower left corner of the next screen.

Required:

1. Look at SEDAR filings by clicking on the interim financial statements—English. Then locate the statement of financial position.

   a. What was the amount of TRC's total assets at the end of the most recent quarter reported?

   b. Did long-term debt increase or decrease for the quarter?

   c. Compute the debt-to-equity ratio. What does this suggest about the company?

2. Look at the "Statement of Cash Flows" in the interim report.

   a. What amount did TRC spend on capital expenditures for the most recent quarter reported?

   b. What was the total amount of cash flows from (used in) financing activities for the most recent quarter reported?

CP2–4 Interpreting the Financial Press

The December 22, 2003, edition of *Business Week* magazine includes an article titled "Is Wilbur Ross Crazy?" You can access the article online.

Required:

Read the article and then answer the following questions:

1. What is *distressed investing* according to the article?

2. Mr. Ross usually becomes a bondholder but often swaps debt with equity. Why is this riskier?

3. According to the article, what makes Mr. Ross successful (i.e., what is his approach and attitude toward investing)?

LO3, 4

CP2–5 Using Financial Reports: Evaluating the Reliability of a Statement of Financial Position

Betsey Jordan asked a local bank for a $50,000 loan to expand her small company. The bank asked Betsey to submit a financial statement of the business to supplement the loan application. Betsey prepared the following statement of financial position.

LO1, 2

Statement of Financial Position
June 30, 2011

Assets	
Cash and investments	$ 9,000
Inventory	30,000
Equipment	46,000
Personal residence (monthly payments, $2,800)	300,000
Other assets	20,000
Total assets	**$405,000**
Liabilities	
Short-term debt to suppliers	$ 62,000
Long-term debt on equipment	38,000
Total debt	100,000
Shareholders' equity	305,000
Total liabilities and shareholders' equity	**$405,000**

Required:

1. The statement of financial position has several flaws. However, there is at least one major deficiency. Identify it and explain its significance.

2. As a bank manager, would you lend the company money? Explain.

LO6

CP2–6   Using Financial Reports: Analyzing the Statement of Financial Position

Smiley Corp. and Tsang Inc. were organized in 2005. Both companies operate in the same line of business. The statements of financial position of the two companies at December 31, 2011, are as follows:

Smiley Corp. Statement of Financial Position December 31, 2011		Tsang Inc. Statement of Financial Position December 31, 2011	
Assets		**Assets**	
Cash	$ 17,000	Cash	$ 7,200
Trade receivables	30,000	Trade receivables	14,400
Inventory	16,000	Inventory	7,600
Property, plant, and equipment	117,600	Property, plant, and equipment	244,400
Total	$180,600	Total	$273,600
Liabilities and Shareholders' Equity		**Liabilities and Shareholders' Equity**	
Liabilities:		Liabilities:	
Notes payable (short-term)	$ 18,600	Notes payable (short-term)	$ 33,600
Trade payables	14,400	Trade payables	64,800
Total liabilities	33,000	Total liabilities	98,400
Shareholders' equity:		Shareholders' equity:	
Share capital	90,000	Share capital	108,000
Retained earnings	57,600	Retained earnings	67,200
Total shareholders' equity	147,600	Total shareholders' equity	175,200
Total	$180,600	Total	$273,600

Required:

1. Eric Frechette wants to invest in one of these two companies by purchasing all of its shares. As a financial adviser to Mr. Frechette, which company would you select as an investment? Provide justification for your selection.

2. Each company applied to Development Bank for a loan of $20,000, payable in four months. As a bank loan officer, would you lend each company the requested amount? Explain.

CRITICAL THINKING CASES

LO1, 2, 6

CP2–7   Making a Decision as a Financial Analyst: Preparing and Analyzing a Statement of Financial Position

Your best friend from home writes you a letter about an investment opportunity that has come her way. A company is raising money by issuing shares and wants her to invest $20,000 (her recent inheritance from her great-aunt's estate). Your friend has never invested in a company before and, knowing that you are a financial analyst, asks that you look over the statement of financial position and send her some advice. An *unaudited* statement of financial position, in only moderately good form, is enclosed with the letter:

DEWEY, CHEETUM, AND HOWE, INC. Statement of Financial Position For the Year Ending December 31, 2010	
Trade receivables	$ 8,000
Cash	1,000
Inventory	8,000
Furniture and fixtures	52,000
Delivery truck	12,000
Buildings (estimated market value)	98,000
Total assets	$179,000
Trade payables	$ 16,000
Payroll taxes payable	13,000
Long-term notes payable	15,000
Mortgage payable	50,000
Total liabilities	$ 94,000
Share capital	$ 80,000
Retained earnings	5,000
Total shareholders' equity	$ 85,000

There is only one footnote, and it states that the building was purchased for $65,000, has been amortized by $5,000 on the books, and still carries a mortgage (shown in the liability section). The footnote further states that, in the opinion of the company president, the building is "easily worth $98,000."

Required:

1. Draft a new statement of financial position for your friend, correcting any errors you note. (If any of the account balances need to be corrected, you may need to adjust the balance of retained earnings correspondingly.) If no errors or omissions exist, state so.
2. Write a letter to your friend explaining the changes you made to the statement of financial position, if any, and offer your comments on the company's apparent financial condition based only on this information. Suggest other information your friend might want to review before coming to a final decision on whether to invest.

CP2–8 Manipulating Financial Statements: Ethical Considerations

LO3

Technology N Motion is a publicly traded company that is facing financial difficulties. To survive, the company needs large new bank loans. As the chief financial officer of the company, you approached several banks, but each has asked for your audited financial statements for 2011, the most recent fiscal year. You called for a meeting with other corporate officers to discuss how the financial statements could be improved. The suggestions made by your colleagues include the following:

1. We owe $20 million to our suppliers. We could show half this amount as a liability on our statement of financial position and report the other half as share capital. This will improve our financial position.
2. We own land that is worth at least $8 million in today's market, but it cost us only $3 million when we bought it. Why not show the land at $8 million on the company's statement of financial position, which increases both the total assets and shareholders' equity by $5 million?
3. We owe FirstRate Software $2 million, due in 30 days. I can ask their chief financial officer to let us delay the payment of this debt for a year, and our company could sign him a note that pays 8 percent interest.

Required:

Evaluate each of these three proposals to improve Technology N Motion's financial statements by considering both accounting and ethical issues.

CP2–9 Evaluating an Ethical Dilemma: Analyzing Management Incentives

LO3

Nortel Networks
Corporation

Nortel Networks Corporation (Nortel), based in Brampton, Ontario, is a global supplier of networking solutions and services. In 2005, the company released the findings of an independent review as a result of continuing problems with its accounting. The review revealed that three former company executives, the chief executive officer, the chief financial officer, and the controller, used accounting practices that increased reported earnings from late 2002 to mid-2003. Through Nortel's internal investigation, several problems had become known, not the least of which was $900 million of inappropriately reported liabilities and approximately $250 million of overstated profit. This mattered to the executives who received a bonus if income before tax exceeded specific levels.

In April 2004, Nortel issued a news release announcing the appointment of its new chief executive officer (CEO) Mr. William Owens, and the termination of its previous CEO, for cause. The previous CEO resigned his position on April 28 and from the company's board of directors on May 21, 2004. Neither the chairman of the board of directors nor the new CEO would comment on the termination. A month earlier the chief financial officer and the controller had been placed on paid leave of absence and they too were fired. A day later, the U.S. Securities and Exchange Commission announced that it was investigating Nortel, and then the Ontario Securities Commission launched its own investigation. But the worst was yet to come.

In May 2004, a U.S. federal grand jury subpoenaed Nortel for accounting records and other documents prepared for the previous four years during which the previous CEO, an accountant, had served as chief financial officer. A few days later the Ontario Public Service Employees Union Pension Trust filed a class action lawsuit to recover losses arising from its investment in Nortel shares between April 2003 and 2005, based on fraudulent financial information. By August 2004, the Royal Canadian Mounted Police began a Canadian criminal investigation into the former CEO's activities. The cost to Nortel has been over $2.4 billion in cash awarded to the Ontario pension fund in April 2005 and the company sued the former CEO to recover this money from him personally. Pursuant to the independent review, 12 senior executives agreed to repay a total of $8.6 million in bonuses they received from the company in the past.

Required:

1. Describe the parties that were harmed or helped by this fraud.
2. Explain how greed may have contributed to this fraud.
3. Why do you think the independent auditors failed to catch the fraud?

FINANCIAL REPORTING AND ANALYSIS TEAM PROJECT

LO3, 7   **CP2–10**   **Team Project: Analyzing Statement of Financial Position and Ratios**

As a team, select an industry to analyze. A list of companies classified by industry can be obtained by accessing www.fpinfomart.ca and then choosing "Companies by Industry." You can also find a list of industries and companies within each industry via http://ca.finance.yahoo.com/investing. A list of industries can be obtained by clicking on "Annual Reports" under "Tools".

Each group member should acquire the annual report for a different publicly traded company in the industry. (Library files, the SEDAR service at www.sedar.com, or the company's website are good sources.)

Required:

Each team member should write a short report answering the following questions about the selected company. Discuss any patterns that you as a team observe. Then, as a team, write a short report comparing and contrasting your companies.

1. For the most recent year, what are the top three asset accounts by size? What percentage is each of total assets? (Calculated as Asset A ÷ Total Assets)
2. What are the major investing and financing activities (by dollar size) for the most recent year? (Look at the statement of cash flows.)
3. Ratio Analysis
   a. What does the debt-to-equity ratio measure in general?
   b. Compute the debt-to-equity ratio for the last three years. (You may find prior years' information in the section in the annual report called "Selected Financial Information," or search for prior years' annual reports.)
   c. What do your results suggest about the company?
   d. If available, find the industry ratio for the most recent year, compare it to your results, and discuss why you believe your company differs or is similar to the industry ratio.

Operating Decisions and the Income Statement

After studying this chapter, you should be able to do the following:

FOCUS COMPANY: **Nestlé S.A.**
OFFERING PRODUCTS TAILORED TO CLIENTS' NEEDS

Nestlé (www.nestle.com) is the leading provider worldwide of nutrition, health, and wellness products. To achieve its tremendous success, Nestlé had to produce food items and beverages that cater to the needs of a wide variety of customers with different cultural backgrounds, tastes, social status, and financial means. Nestlé's growth and enhanced performance hinge on a "4 × 4 × 4 roadmap": four competitive advantages, four growth drivers, and four strategic pillars.[1] Its four competitive advantages are an unmatched product and brand portfolio consisting of global brands, such as Nestlé and KitKat, as well as local brands sold in specific markets; an unmatched research and development capability; an unmatched geographic presence, with more than 450 factories in 84 countries; and an emphasis on people, culture, values, and openness to diversity.

Nestlé's four growth drivers comprise its focus on nutritional and health benefits across the entire product portfolio, popularly positioned products that sell predominantly in emerging markets, out-of-home foods, and premiumisation—the production and marketing of premium and luxury products that appeal to a specific class of customers.

The four competitive advantages and four growth drivers are complemented by Nestlé's four strategic pillars, which include innovation and renovation of products to provide superior quality and taste for healthier and lighter eating, operational efficiency that ensures the offering of quality products at competitive cost, consumer communication that is essential to build the company's brands and highlight the nutritional and health benefits of its products, and product ubiquity; that is, availability of Nestlé's products "whenever, wherever, however," through an extensive and diversified distribution network that includes convenience stores, gas stations, large department stores as well as the Internet.

---

[1]Nestlé's Management Report 2009 includes a detailed discussion of its 4 × 4 × 4 roadmap. It can be found on the Nestlé website, http://www.nestle.com/InvestorRelations/Reports/ManagementReports/2009.htm.

In Canada, Nestlé employs approximately 3,500 people in 21 manufacturing, sales, and distribution sites across the country, with sales exceeding 2.1 billion Canadian dollars annually.

UNDERSTANDING THE BUSINESS

To become the leading nutrition, health, and wellness company worldwide, Nestlé's executives develop strategies, plans, and measurable indicators of progress toward their goals. In developing operating and growth strategies, companies such as Nestlé plan their companywide operations in terms of the elements of the income statement (specific revenues and expenses). These strategies are most often disclosed in the management discussion and analysis section of the annual report.

Financial analysts develop their own set of expectations about Nestlé's future performance. The published income statement provides the primary basis for comparing analysts' projections to the actual results of operations. We discuss these comparisons and the stock market's reactions to Nestlé's results throughout this chapter as we learn about income recognition and measurement. To understand how business plans and the results of operations are reflected on the income statement, we need to answer the following questions:

1. How do business activities affect the income statement?

2. How are these activities recognized and measured?

3. How are these activities reported on the income statement?

In this chapter, we focus on Nestlé's operating activities, which include sales of baby foods, breakfast cereals, chocolate, coffee, dairy products, ice cream, bottled water, and pet foods to various wholesalers that distribute its products to retail outlets. The results of these activities are reported on the income statement.

ORGANIZATION OF THE CHAPTER

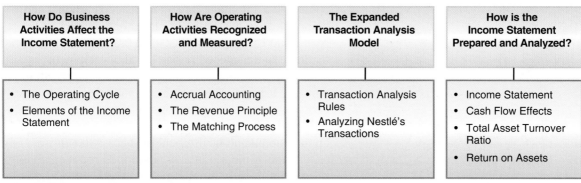

How Do Business Activities Affect the Income Statement?	How Are Operating Activities Recognized and Measured?	The Expanded Transaction Analysis Model	How is the Income Statement Prepared and Analyzed?
• The Operating Cycle • Elements of the Income Statement	• Accrual Accounting • The Revenue Principle • The Matching Process	• Transaction Analysis Rules • Analyzing Nestlé's Transactions	• Income Statement • Cash Flow Effects • Total Asset Turnover Ratio • Return on Assets

Supplemental material:
Appendix B: The Formal Recordkeeping System (online)

LO1

Describe a typical business operating cycle and explain the necessity for the periodicity assumption.

HOW DO BUSINESS ACTIVITIES AFFECT THE INCOME STATEMENT?

The Operating Cycle

The long-term objective for any business is *to turn cash into more cash*. For companies to stay in business, this excess cash must be generated from operations (i.e., from the activities for which the business was established), not from borrowing money or selling non-current assets.

Companies acquire inventory and the services of employees, and then sell inventory or services to customers. The length of time between the payment of cash to suppliers of inventory and to employees and the collection of cash from customers (known as the operating, or cash-to-cash, cycle) depends on the nature of the business.

The operating cycle for Nestlé is relatively short. It spends cash to purchase ingredients used in the preparation and packaging of its many products according to its own blends and recipes; sells these products through distribution channels that reach consumers at home, work, and play; and then collects cash from customers. In some companies, inventory is paid for well before it is sold. Toys "R" Us, for example, builds its inventory for months prior to the year-end holiday season. It borrows funds from banks to pay for the inventory and repays the loans with interest when cash is received from customers. In other companies, cash is received from customers well after a sale takes place. For example, car dealerships often sell cars over time, with monthly payments from customers due over several years. Companies attempt to shorten the operating cycle by creating incentives to encourage customers to buy sooner or pay faster in order to improve the company's cash flows.

The **OPERATING (CASH-TO-CASH) CYCLE** is the time it takes for a company to pay cash to suppliers, sell goods and services to customers, and collect cash from customers.

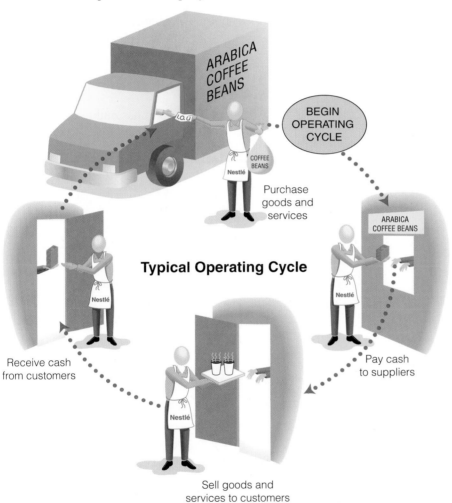

Typical Operating Cycle

BEGIN OPERATING CYCLE

Purchase goods and services

Pay cash to suppliers

Sell goods and services to customers

Receive cash from customers

SHORT-TERM DEBT FINANCING AND THE OPERATING CYCLE

FINANCIAL ANALYSIS

The timing of the cash outflows and inflows shown in the illustration above indicates that many businesses must pay suppliers and employees before they receive cash from customers, causing them to seek short-term financing. When the companies receive cash from customers, they pay off the liability. In addition, if a company plans to grow—say, to sell twice as many goods as in the prior period—it may not have collected enough cash from the prior period's customers to purchase the quantity of inventory needed in the next period. Sources of financing include suppliers and financial institutions (banks and commercial credit companies).

Managers know that reducing the time needed to turn cash into more cash (i.e., shortening the operating cycle) means higher profits and faster growth. With the excess cash, managers may purchase additional inventory or other assets for growth, repay debt, or distribute it to owners.

Until a company ceases activities, the operating cycle is repeated continuously. However, decision makers require periodic information about the financial condition and performance of a business. To measure income for a specific period of time, accountants follow the periodicity assumption, which assumes that the long life of a company can be reported in shorter time periods, such as months, quarters, and years.[2] Two types of issues arise in reporting periodic income to users:

1. Recognition issues: **When** should the effects of operating activities be recognized (recorded)?
2. Measurement issues: **What amounts** should be recognized?

Before we examine the rules accountants follow as they resolve these issues, let us review the elements of financial statements that are affected by operating activities.

The **PERIODICITY ASSUMPTION** means that the long life of a company can be reported in shorter periods.

LO2

Explain how business activities affect the elements of the income statement.

Elements of the Income Statement

Exhibit 3.1 shows a recent income statement for Nestlé. It has multiple subtotals, such as *operating profit* and *profit before interest and taxes*. This *multiple step* format is very

Exhibit **3.1**

Income Statement

Consolidated Income Statements
Years ended December 31
(in millions of Swiss francs, except for earnings per share)

	2009	2008
Sales	107,618	109,908
Cost of goods sold	(45,208)	(47,339)
Gross profit	62,410	62,569
Operating expenses		
Distribution	(8,420)	(9,084)
Marketing and administration	(36,270)	(35,832)
Research and development	(2,021)	(1,977)
	46,711	46,893
Operating profit	15,699	15,676
Other income (expenses and losses)		
Other income	509	9,426
Other expenses	(1,238)	(2,124)
Profit before interest and taxes	14,970	22,978
Finance expense	(794)	(1,247)
Finance income	179	102
Profit before taxes and associates	14,355	21,833
Income tax expense	(3,362)	(3,787)
Share of results of associates	800	1,005
Profit for the year	11,793	19,051
Profit attributable to		
Non-controlling interests	1,365	1,012
Shareholders of the parent	10,428	18,039
Earnings per share		
Basic earnings per share	2.92	4.87
Diluted earnings per share	2.91	4.84

Operating activities (central focus of business)

Subtotal of operating revenues minus operating expenses →

Peripheral activities (not the main focus of the business)

Subtotal of all income minus all expenses except taxes and results of investments in associated companies →

Allocation of the profit between the controlling shareholder or parent (Nestlé) and the non-controlling shareholders

Profit divided by weighted average number of shares outstanding →

Note: This income statement is an adaptation from Nestlé's actual consolidated income statement.

[2]In addition to the audited annual statements, most businesses prepare quarterly financial statements (also known as *interim reports* covering a three-month period) for external users. The securities commissions require publicly accountable enterprises to do so.

common. Classification of the various income statement items helps financial statement users assess the company's operating performance and predict its future profitability.

The income statement includes three major sections:

1. Results of continuing operations

2. Results of discontinued operations
   Profit (the sum of 1 and 2)

3. Earnings per share

All companies report information for sections 1 and 3, while some companies report information in section 2, depending upon their particular circumstances. The bottom line, profit, is the sum of sections 1 and 2. First, we will focus on the most common and most relevant section, continuing operations.

Continuing Operations   This section of the income statement presents the results of continuing operations. As we discuss the elements of the income statement, it is useful to refer to the conceptual framework outlined in Exhibit 2.1.

Operating Revenues   Increases in assets or settlement of liabilities from *ongoing operations* of the business are defined as revenues. Operating revenues result from the sale of goods or services. Nestlé earns revenue when it sells goods and renders services to customers. It recognizes revenue in the income statement when the significant risks and rewards of ownership have been transferred to the buyer, which is mainly upon shipment. When revenues are earned, assets, usually cash or trade receivables, often increase. Sometimes, a company receives cash in exchange for a promise to provide goods or services in the future. At that point, revenue is not earned, but a liability account, deferred revenue, is created. When the company provides the promised goods or services to the customer, revenue is recognized and the liability is settled.

> **REVENUES** are increases in assets or settlements of liabilities from ongoing operations.

Like most companies, Nestlé generates revenues from a variety of sources. Its operating activities are grouped into six main segments: powdered and liquid beverages, milk products and ice cream, prepared dishes and cooking aids, confectionary, pet care, and pharmaceutical products. The first two, Nestlé's most important segments, together account for 55 percent of its revenues.

Operating Expenses   Some students confuse the terms *expenditures* and *expenses*. An expenditure is any outflow of cash for any purpose, whether to buy equipment, pay off a bank loan, or pay employees their wages. An expense is more narrowly defined; it results when an asset, such as equipment or supplies, is *used to generate revenue during a period*, or when an amount is *incurred to generate revenues during a period*, such as using electricity, even if the amount will be paid in the future. Therefore, *not all expenditures are expenses*, and *expenses are necessary to generate revenues*. Expenses are decreases in assets or increases in liabilities from ongoing operations and are incurred to generate revenues during the period.

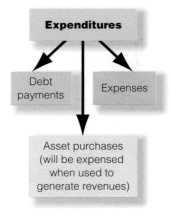

Nestlé pays employees who sell its products and provide services to clients, uses electricity to operate equipment and light facilities, advertises the goods it sells, and uses a wide variety of supplies in its production processes. Without incurring these expenses, Nestlé could not generate revenues. Although some of the expenses may result from expenditures of cash at the time they are incurred, some may be incurred after cash was paid in the past, and other expenses may be incurred before cash is paid in the future. When an expense occurs, assets such as supplies inventory decrease (are used up) *or* liabilities such as salaries payable or utilities payable increase.

> **EXPENSES** are decreases in assets or increases in liabilities to generate revenues during the period.

The following are Nestlé's primary operating expenses:

1. *Cost of goods sold* is the cost of products sold to customers. For example, when Nestlé purchases coffee beans from suppliers located in different countries, it pays for import duties, transport, and handling, in addition to the purchase price. All these costs are included in the cost of the asset "inventories." As inventories are used to produce and package the roasted and ground coffee beans, they become an

GROSS PROFIT (OR GROSS MARGIN) is net sales less cost of goods sold.

OPERATING PROFIT (profit from operations) equals net sales less cost of goods sold and other operating expenses.

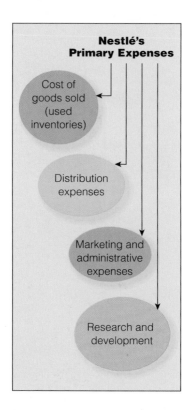

Nestlé's Primary Expenses

- Cost of goods sold (used inventories)
- Distribution expenses
- Marketing and administrative expenses
- Research and development

GAINS are increases in assets or decreases in liabilities from peripheral transactions.

LOSSES are decreases in assets or increases in liabilities from peripheral transactions.

expense, called cost of goods sold. In companies with a manufacturing or merchandising focus, the cost of goods sold (also called cost of sales) is usually the most significant expense. The cost of goods sold for Nestlé is CHF 45,208 million and represents about 42 percent of the revenues for 2009. The difference between sales revenues and cost of goods sold is known as gross profit or gross margin.

2. *Operating expenses* are the usual expenses, other than cost of goods sold, that are incurred in operating a business during a specific accounting period. The expenses reported will depend on the nature of the company's operations. International Accounting Standard 1 requires companies to classify their expenses either by function—such as marketing and promotion, distribution, and administrative—or by nature of the expense. Classification by nature includes the three main costs of production: materials, labour, and property and equipment use.

Nestlé, like most companies, classifies its expenses by function.[3] *Distribution* expenses include a variety of expenses related to the distribution of the company's products to its customers, such as the wages earned by distribution personnel and depreciation of delivery vehicles. *Marketing and administrative* expenses include, for example, the salaries of marketing personnel and those who support the sales effort such as legal counsel, accountants, and computer technicians. They may also include promotion of the company's products through various print and electronic media, rental of office space, insurance, utilities, plus other general operating expenses not directly related to production. *Research and development* expenses relate to the research and development of new products. Another subtotal, operating profit, also called profit from operations, is computed by subtracting operating expenses from gross profit.

Non-operating Items   Not all activities affecting an income statement are central to continuing operations. Any revenues, expenses, gains, or losses that result from these other activities are not included as part of operating profit, but are instead categorized as other income or expenses. For example, using excess cash to purchase shares in other companies is an investing activity for Nestlé, not a central operation. However, any interest or dividends earned on the investment is called *investment income* (or *finance income*). Likewise, borrowing money is a financing activity. However, the cost of using that money is called *interest expense*. Except for financial institutions, incurring interest expense or earning investment income are *not* the central operations of most businesses, including Nestlé. We say that these are *peripheral* (normal but not central) *transactions*.

Companies sometimes sell property, plant, and equipment occasionally and replace them with new assets to modernize their facilities. Selling land for more than the original purchase price results in a *gain*, not in revenue, because the sale of land is not a central operating focus for the business. The gain results in an increase in assets or decrease in liabilities from a peripheral transaction. Similarly, losses are decreases in assets or increases in liabilities from peripheral transactions. For example, in 2008, Nestlé sold part of its investment in other businesses, particularly Alcon, and realized a gain of CHF 9,208 million. Since the sale of this investment is not central to Nestlé's ongoing operations, the gain is reported as a component of other income on the company's income statement for fiscal year 2008. Other non-operating items include losses due to impairment of assets, restructuring costs, and litigation settlements. For Nestlé, the monetary effects of all non-operating items are reported on its 2009 income statement in four summary amounts (in millions): other income, 509; other expenses, 1,238; finance expense, 794; and finance income, 179. Note 4 to Nestlé's financial statements discloses details of the other income and other expense items.

---

[3]Further discussion of classification of expenses by nature is provided in Chapter 6.

Note 4, Net other income/(expenses)

In millions of Swiss francs	Notes	2009	2008
Profit on disposal of property, plant and equipment		26	24
Profit on disposal of businesses	24	109	47
Other		331	114
Other income		466	185
Loss on disposal of property, plant and equipment		(57)	(6)
Loss on disposal of businesses	24	(28)	(82)
Restructuring costs		(200)	(373)
Impairment of property, plant and equipment	13	(170)	(248)
Impairment of goodwill	14	(37)	(510)
Impairment of intangible assets	15	—	(1)
Other		(704)	(822)
Other expenses		(1,196)	(2,042)
Net other income/(expenses) of continuing operations		(730)	(1,857)
Net other income/(expenses) of discontinued operations		1	9,159
Total net other income/(expenses)		(729)	7,302

Source: The Nestlé Group, 2009 Consolidated Financial Statements.

The non-operating items that are subject to income taxes are added or subtracted from operating profit to obtain profit before income taxes, also called *pretax profit*.

Income Tax Expense   Income tax expense is the last expense listed on the income statement. All for-profit corporations are required to compute income taxes owed to federal, provincial, and foreign governments. Income tax expense is calculated as a percentage of profit before income taxes, reflecting the difference between income, which includes revenues and gains, and expenses and losses; it is determined by using applicable tax rates. Nestlé's effective tax rate in 2009 was 23 percent (income tax expense ÷ profit before income taxes). This indicates that for every Swiss franc of profit that Nestlé made in 2009, the company incurred a tax expense of CHF 0.23.

PROFIT BEFORE INCOME TAXES (pretax profit) equals revenues minus all expenses except income tax expense.

Discontinued Operations   Companies may dispose of a major line of business or a geographical area of operations during the accounting period, or decide to discontinue a specific operation in the near future. When the decision is made to discontinue a major component of a business, the profit or loss from that component, as well as any gain or loss on subsequent disposal, are disclosed separately on the income statement as *discontinued operations*. Because of their non-recurring nature, the financial results of discontinued operations are not useful in predicting future recurring profits; hence, they are presented separately from the results of continuing operations. In 2009, Nestlé's disposal of businesses resulted in a loss of 28, as reported in Note 4 above.

Non-controlling Interests   Nestlé has invested in many businesses by purchasing a majority, or in many cases, all of the shares issued by these companies. Purchase of all or a majority of other companies' shares allows Nestlé to control their operating, investing, and financing decisions. When Nestlé owns a majority of the shares of another company, it becomes a *controlling* shareholder. The other shareholders are then known as *non-controlling* (or minority) shareholders and entitled to a proportionate share of the profit of the company in which they invested. Hence, non-controlling interests refers to the portion of the consolidated profit that does not belong to Nestlé but to the non-controlling shareholders.[4]

---

[4]Intercorporate investment is a complex topic that is covered in advanced accounting courses.

Earnings per Share   Corporations are required to disclose earnings per share on the income statement or in the notes to the financial statements. This ratio is widely used in evaluating the operating performance and profitability of a company. To compute earnings per share, profit is divided by the weighted average number of shares outstanding during the period. The calculation of the denominator is complex and is presented in advanced accounting courses.

Nestlé's earnings per share decreased significantly from 2008 to 2009. Although this appears to be bad news, investors would want to check the historical trend of earnings per share for a period of five years. More importantly, investors need to compare Nestlé's performance to its competitors during the same period. Finally, it should be noted that overreliance on this ratio for investment decisions can lead to inadvisable decisions.

INTERNATIONAL PERSPECTIVE

DIFFERENCES IN ACCOUNTS IN FOREIGN FINANCIAL STATEMENTS

We learned in Chapters 1 and 2 that foreign companies establish their own accounting and reporting rules, with many adopting the International Financial Reporting Standards. The result is that foreign companies often use account titles different from Canadian companies. For example, the companies GlaxoSmithKline (a U.K. pharmaceutical company) and Unilever (a U.K. and Netherlands-based company supplying food, home, and personal care products such as Hellman's mayonnaise, Dove soap, and Popsicle treats) use the term "turnover" to refer to sales revenue. These two companies use IFRS for reporting purposes. On the other hand, U.S. companies, which do not follow IFRS, use "income from investments" for finance income and "interest expense" for finance expense. The key to avoiding confusion is reading the notes related to specific financial statement elements.

**CASH BASIS
Income Measurement**

Revenues (= cash receipts)
– Expenses (= cash payments)
_____
Profit

CASH BASIS ACCOUNTING records revenues when cash is received and expenses when cash is paid.

LO3

Explain the accrual basis of accounting and apply the revenue principle and matching process to measure profit.

ACCRUAL BASIS ACCOUNTING records revenues when earned and expenses when incurred, regardless of the timing of cash receipts or payments.

HOW ARE OPERATING ACTIVITIES RECOGNIZED AND MEASURED?

You probably determine your personal financial position by the balance in your bank account. Your financial performance is measured as the difference between your account balance at the end of the period and the balance at the beginning of the period (i.e., whether you end up with more or less cash). If you have a higher account balance, cash receipts exceeded cash disbursements for the period. Many local retailers, medical offices, and other small businesses use cash basis accounting, in which revenues are recorded when cash is received and expenses are recorded when cash is paid, regardless of when the revenues are earned or the expenses incurred. This basis is often quite adequate for these organizations that usually do not have to report to external users.

Accrual Accounting

Profit measured on a cash basis can be misleading. For example, a company using a cash basis can report higher profit in one period simply because (1) a customer paid cash in advance of receiving a good or service or (2) the company postponed the payment of utility bills until the next period. In the first case, the company has not performed the service or delivered the promised goods to earn revenue. In the second case, the company has already used gas, electricity, and phone service to generate revenues (creating an expense), but the expense is not recorded because payment occurs in the next period.

Financial statements created under cash basis accounting normally postpone or accelerate recognition of revenues and expenses long before or after goods and services are produced and delivered. They also do not necessarily reflect all assets and liabilities of a company on a particular date. For these reasons, cash basis financial statements are not very useful to external decision makers. Therefore, IFRS require accrual basis accounting for financial reporting purposes.

In accrual basis accounting, revenues and expenses are recognized when the transaction that causes them occurs, not necessarily when cash is received or paid. ***Revenues are recognized when they are earned and expenses when they are incurred***. The *revenue principle* and the **matching process** determine when revenues and expenses are to be recorded under accrual basis accounting.

The Revenue Principle

Companies engage in a series of events that lead to the recognition of revenue. For example, after purchasing the raw materials, such as milk, cocoa, and coffee, Nestlé places them into a production process that culminates in finished products, including Coffee-Mate, Nido, Smarties, KitKat, Nescafé, Nesquik, and many other products. The finished products are then stored in the company's warehouses and marketed to consumers through various media before they are sold to customers for either cash or on credit. Each activity (purchase of raw materials, production, promotion, sale, and collection from customers) contributes to the recognition of revenue. It is difficult, however, to estimate and recognize the value each activity adds to the amount eventually recognized as revenue. Instead, accountants attempt to identify the most critical event that leads to a flow of future benefits to Nestlé from all these activities.

To guard against identification of critical events that may favour earlier recognition of revenue, and increase in profit, the following conditions must be satisfied, as per the revenue principle, to determine the point in time when revenue from the sale of goods should be recognized[5]:

a. *The entity has transferred to the buyer the significant risks and rewards of ownership of the goods.* In most cases, the transfer of the risks and rewards of ownership coincides with the transfer of the legal title or the passing of possession to the buyer.

b. *The entity retains neither continuing managerial involvement to the degree usually associated with ownership nor effective control over the goods sold.* If the entity retains significant risks of ownership, the transaction is not a sale and revenue is not recognized. An entity may retain a significant risk of ownership in a number of ways. For example, if the buyer has the right to rescind the purchase for a reason specified in the sales contract and the entity is uncertain about the probability of return, then revenue cannot be recognized at the point of sale.

c. *The amount of revenue can be measured reliably.* There are no uncertainties as to the amount to be collected.

d. *It is probable that the economic benefits associated with the transaction will flow to the entity.* The consideration received for the sale of goods is either cash or the customer's promise to pay cash in the future. For cash sales, collection is not an issue since it is received on the date of the exchange. For sales on credit, the company reviews the customer's ability to pay. If the customer is considered creditworthy, collecting cash from the customer is reasonably likely.

e. *The costs incurred or to be incurred in respect of the transaction can be measured reliably.* Companies that provide service after sale may incur additional costs related to the sale transaction. In general, the costs to be incurred after the shipment of the goods can normally be measured reliably when the other conditions for the recognition of revenue have been satisfied. However, revenue cannot be recognized when the expenses cannot be measured reliably.

If *any* of the previous conditions is *not* met, revenue normally is *not* recognized and should not be recorded. For most businesses, these conditions are met at the point of delivery of goods or services.[6]

> **ACCRUAL BASIS**
> **Income Measurement**
>
> Revenues (= when earned)
> – Expenses (= when incurred)
> Profit

The **REVENUE PRINCIPLE** states that revenues are recognized when the significant risks and rewards are transferred to the buyer, it is probable that future economic benefits will flow to the entity, and the benefits and the costs associated with the transaction can be measured reliably.

---

[5]International Accounting Standards Board, 2009. *International Accounting Standard 18 · Revenue*, paragraph 14.
[6]Further discussion of the application of the revenue principle to special circumstances is provided in Chapter 7.

Companies usually disclose their revenue recognition practices in a note to the financial statements. The following excerpt from Nestlé's note describes how it recognizes its revenue:

REAL WORLD EXCERPT

The Nestlé Group

2009 FINANCIAL STATEMENTS

Nestlé
Notes to Consolidated Financial Statements

1. Accounting Policies

Revenue
Revenue represents amounts received and receivable from third parties for goods supplied to the customers and for services rendered. Revenue from the sales of goods is recognized in the income statement at the moment when the significant risks and rewards of ownership of the goods have been transferred to the buyer, which is mainly upon shipment. It is measured at the list price applicable to a given distribution channel after deduction of all returns, sales taxes, pricing allowances, and similar trade discounts.

Exhibit 3.2 shows excerpts from the revenue recognition policies used by other companies that offer different types of products and services. Note that the point in time when revenue should be recognized depends on the nature of the products sold and services provided by the company.

Exhibit **3.2**

Timing of Revenue Recognition

Company Name	Product or Service	Typical Timing of Revenue Recognition
Air Canada	Air transportation	Passenger and cargo revenues are recognized when the transportation is provided, except for revenue on unlimited flight passes which is recognized on a straight-line basis over the period during which the travel pass is valid. The Corporation has formed alliances with other airlines encompassing loyalty program participation, code sharing and coordination of services including reservations, baggage handling and flight schedules. Revenues are allocated based upon formulas specified in the agreements and are recognized as transportation is provided.
Thomson Reuters Corporation	Sale of intelligent information to businesses and professionals	Revenue is measured at the fair value of the consideration received or receivable, net of estimated returns and discounts, and after eliminating intercompany sales. The Company bases its estimates on historical results, taking into consideration the type of customer, the type of transaction and the specifics of each arrangement. Revenue from the rendering of services is recognized when the following criteria are met: • the amount of revenue can be measured reliably; • the stage of completion can be measured reliably; • the receipt of economic benefits is probable; and • costs incurred and to be incurred can be measured reliably. Revenue from the sale of goods is recognized when the following criteria are met: • the risks and rewards of ownership, including managerial involvement, have transferred to the buyer; • the amount of revenue can be measured reliably; • the receipt of economic benefits is probable; and • costs incurred or to be incurred can be measured reliably. In addition to the above general principles, the Company applies the following specific revenue recognition policies: *Subscription-based products, including software term licenses* Subscription revenues from sales of products and services that are delivered under a contract over a period of time are recognized on a straight-line basis over the term of the subscription. Where applicable, usage fees above a base period fee are recognized as services are delivered. Subscription revenue received or receivable in advance of the delivery of services or publications is included in deferred revenue.
Barrick Gold Corporation	Mining (production of quality precious metals)	We record revenue when the following conditions are met: persuasive evidence of an arrangement exists; delivery and transfer of title (gold revenue only) have occurred under the terms of the arrangement; the price is fixed or determinable; and collectability is reasonably assured.

Sources: Air Canada 2009 Annual Report; Thompson Reuters 2009 Annual Report; Barrick Gold 2009 Annual Report.

Although businesses expect to receive cash in exchange for their goods and services at the time of delivery, the timing of cash receipts from customers does not dictate when businesses report revenues. Instead, the key to determining when to report revenues is whether or not the business has done what it promised to do. Thus, cash can be received (1) *before* the goods or services are delivered, (2) at the *same* time as the goods or services are delivered, or (3) *after* the goods or services are delivered, as shown in Exhibit 3.3.

Exhibit **3.3**

Recording Revenues versus Cash Receipts

- If cash is received before the company delivers goods or services, the liability account Deferred revenue is recorded because the company still owes goods or services. Examples include companies that sell magazine subscriptions and companies that sell insurance. Although not corporations, colleges and universities also receive tuition revenue and sell season tickets to sporting events and plays before any revenue is earned.

- If cash is received after goods or services are delivered, the receivable account created when the revenue was recorded is reduced because the customers have paid the company what they owed.

Cash is received BEFORE revenue is earned

Company delivers

| Cash (+A) | xx | |
| Deferred revenue (+L) | | xx |

| Deferred revenue (–L) | xx | |
| Fee revenue (+R,+SE) | | xx |

Cash is received ON the date revenue is earned

Company delivers

| Cash (+A) | xx | |
| Fee revenue (+R,+SE) | | xx |

Cash is received AFTER revenue is earned

Company delivers

| Trade receivables (+A) | xx | |
| Fee revenue (+R,+SE) | | xx |

| Cash (+A) | xx | |
| Trade receivables (–A) | | xx |

SELF-STUDY **QUIZ 3-1**

This self-study quiz allows you to practise applying the revenue principle under accrual accounting. We recommend that you refer back to the *revenue recognition criteria* presented earlier as you answer each question. Complete this quiz now to make sure you can apply this principle. The following transactions are samples of typical monthly operating activities of Nestlé.

1. Indicate the account titles that are affected and the type of account for each (A for asset, L for liability, and R for revenue).

2. Identify the amount of revenue that is recognized in January, the revenue that has been earned in December, and the revenue that will be earned in future periods (deferred revenue).

3. Compute the revenue recognized in January and compare it to the amount of cash received in January.

4. Which amount—revenue recognized in January or cash received in January—is a better measure of Nestlé's operating performance? Explain.

Refer to Nestlé's income statement presented in Exhibit 3.1 on page 106 for account titles. *Note:* All amounts are in millions of Swiss francs.

Activity	Accounts Affected and Type of Account	Cash Received in January	Amount of Revenue Earned in		Deferred Revenue
			December	January	
(a) In January, Nestlé sold milk products and beverages to customers for 3,520 cash.					
(b) In January, Nestlé sold coffee products to retail outlets for 3,020, of which 2,020 was in cash and the rest was on account.					
(c) In January, Nestlé received 345 in cash from customers, of which $75 related to December sales.					
(d) In January, Nestlé signed contracts with new clients and received 500 in cash. The company provided 400 in services to these clients during January; the remainder of the services will be provided over the next three months.					
(e) In January, retail outlets paid 120 on account to Nestlé. This amount covers sales of coffee products in December.					
Totals					

  After you complete your answers, go online for the solutions.

A QUESTION OF **ACCOUNTABILITY**

MANAGEMENT'S INCENTIVES TO VIOLATE THE REVENUE PRINCIPLE

The decisions of investors in the stock market are based on expectations of future earnings. When companies announce quarterly and annual earnings information, investors evaluate how well the company met expectations and adjust their investing decisions accordingly. Companies that fail to meet expectations often experience a decline in the stock price. Thus, managers are motivated to produce earnings results that meet or exceed expectations, to bolster stock prices. Since many executives are given options to purchase company shares as part of their compensation, greed may lead some managers to make unethical accounting and reporting decisions, often involving falsifying revenues and expenses, as described in the April 1, 2002, issue of *Canadian Business*. The article includes two revenue-related frauds involving Livent Inc. and YBM Magnex International Inc.

The Company	What the Company's Management Did
Livent Inc.	Management has been accused by the Securities and Exchange Commission and the Ontario Securities Commission of using false invoices and kickbacks, filing false information, and inflating its earnings.
YBM Magnex International Inc.	The company was investigated by the Ontario Securities Commission for overstating sales by creating fictitious customer lists. At the same time, laundered money poured into the company from Russian gangsters. The company went bankrupt in 1998.

The OSC's investigation of YBM resulted in imposing penalties, totalling $1.2 million, on two brokerage firms and five company officials. The company officials were ordered to resign from their positions and were banned from holding such positions at other companies for periods of three to five years.

Livent's co-founders Garth Drabinsky and Myron Gottlieb were found guilty for fraudulent financial reporting and convicted for their white-collar crime. They were sentenced to seven and six years of prison, respectively, almost 11 years after the fraud was initially reported by the company's chief financial officer.

Sources: John Gray, "Home-grown accounting scandals," *Canadian Business*, April 1, 2002; Peter Fitzpatrick, "OSC hands down YBM penalties," *National Post*, July 3, 2003, FP1, 8; and John Gray, "Exit, stage left," *Canadian Business*, September 14, 2009.

The Matching Process

The matching process requires that when the period's revenues are properly recognized according to the revenue principle, all of the resources consumed in earning those revenues should be recorded in that same period, *a matching of costs with benefits*. Thus, expenses are recorded in the same period as the related revenues. The costs of generating revenue include expenses incurred such as the following:

The **MATCHING PROCESS** requires that expenses be recorded when incurred in earning revenue.

- Salaries to employees who *worked during the period* (salaries expense).
- Utilities for the electricity *used during the period* (utilities expense).
- Milk, cocoa, sugar, and other ingredients used to produce nutrition and health foods that are *sold during the period* (cost of goods sold).
- Facilities *rented during the period* (rent expense).
- *Use* of buildings and equipment for production purposes *during the period* (depreciation expense).

Some of these expenses are matched directly to sales revenue, such as the cost of goods sold and sales commissions. Other expenses, such as utilities, rent of facilities, insurance, and interest, may not be identifiable with specific sources of revenue but need to be incurred in order to generate revenue during the period.

As with revenues and cash receipts, expenses are recorded as incurred, *regardless of when cash is paid*. Cash may be paid before, during, or after an expense is incurred, as shown in Exhibit 3.4. An entry will be made on the date the expense is incurred and another one on the date of the cash payment, if at different times.

SELF-STUDY **QUIZ 3-2**

This self-study quiz allows you to practise applying the *matching process* under accrual accounting. It is important to complete this quiz now to make sure you can apply this process.

The following transactions are samples of typical monthly operating activities of Nestlé.

1. Indicate the account titles that are affected and the type of account for each (A for asset, L for liability, and E for expense).

2. If an expense is to be recognized in January, indicate the amount. If an expense is not to be recognized in January, indicate why.

3. Compute the amount of expenses recognized in January and compare this amount to the cash paid in January.

Refer to Nestlé's income statement presented in Exhibit 3.1 on page 109 for account titles.

Note: All amounts are in millions of Swiss francs.

Activity	Accounts Affected and Type of Account	Cash Paid in January	Amount of Expense Incurred in January OR Why an Expense Is Not Recognized
(a) In January, Nestlé paid 1,000 to suppliers on account for raw materials received in December. These raw materials were not yet used in the production process.			
(b) In January, the cost of coffee products sold to retail outlets was 1,400.			
(c) On January 5, Nestlé paid 45 for rent of warehousing facilities for January, February, and March.			
(d) In January, the cost of milk products and beverages sold to customers was 1,960. These items were produced in previous months.			
(e) In late January, Nestlé received a utility bill for 50 payable in February for electricity used in January.			
Totals			

connect   After you complete your answers, go online for the solutions.

Exhibit **3.4**

Recording Expenses versus Cash
Payments

- For example, green coffee beans and packaging supplies are acquired prior to their use. These items are recorded as inventory, an asset, when they are purchased, but are not expensed until they are used. Similarly, companies usually pay for rent in advance of using rental property and record the cash outlay in the asset account, Prepayments, representing future benefits to the company. This asset is allocated over time to Rent expense as the property is used. In addition, part of the cost of long-term assets, such as equipment used in operations, needs to be matched with the revenues generated in the period. The portion of the assets that was used up is recognized as depreciation expense.

- In some cases, resources are used to generate revenues prior to a cash outlay. Nestlé's payroll expense represents the amount earned by managers and employees who prepare the products for sale to customers. It is an expense for that period. While employees are usually paid after they provide their services, wages expense and wages payable should be recorded when the service is provided by the employees.

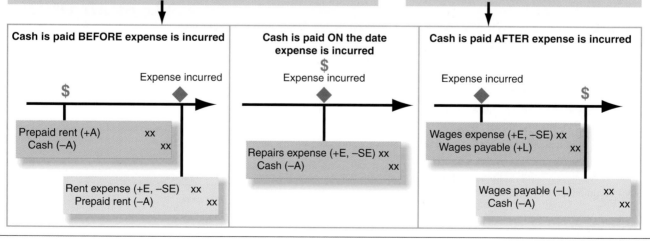

STOCK MARKET REACTIONS TO ACCOUNTING ANNOUNCEMENTS

Stock market analysts and investors use accounting information to make investment decisions. The stock market, which is based on investors' expectations about future company performance, often reacts negatively when a company does not meet previously specified operating results. A company can experience difficulty even if it does not report a loss. Any unexpected deviation of actual performance from the operating plan, such as lower than expected quarterly earnings, needs to be explained.

On February 19, 2010, Nestlé announced the results of its fiscal year 2009 ending December 31, 2009. On the day of the announcement, the price per share closed at CHF 42.70, an increase of CHF 1.25 over the closing price on the previous day.* Nestlé's annual results showed a decrease of earnings per share (EPS) from CHF 4.87 for 2008 to CHF 2.92 for 2009. Profit for 2009 included, however, a non-operating gain of CHF 9.2 billion (CHF 2.48 per share) for the sale of Nestlé's investment in Alcon. Excluding this gain, the EPS for 2008 would have been CHF 2.39. This suggests that Nestlé improved on its operating performance during 2009. The increase in share price suggests that the reported EPS figure is higher than investors' expectations.

This is a clear example of how external users reacted to the information. Accounting information has a pervasive effect on all forms of corporate decision making, as well as on the economic decisions that investors and creditors make.

*Nestlé website. June 24, 2010. http://nestle.com/InvestorRelations.

LO⁴

Apply transaction analysis to examine and record the effects of operating activities on the financial statements.

THE EXPANDED TRANSACTION ANALYSIS MODEL

Now that we have seen the variety of business activities affecting the income statement and how they are measured, we need to determine how these business activities are recorded in the accounting system and reflected in the financial statements. Chapter 2 covered investing and financing activities affecting assets, liabilities, and share capital. We now expand the transaction analysis model presented in that chapter to include operating activities.

Transaction Analysis Rules

The complete transaction model presented in Exhibit 3.5 includes all five elements: assets, liabilities, shareholders' equity, revenues, and expenses. Recall that the retained earnings account is the accumulation of all past revenues and expenses minus any profit distributed as dividends to shareholders (i.e., earnings not retained in the business). Retained earnings increase when profit is realized and decrease when a loss occurs. These relationships among financial statement elements are summarized in the upper part of Exhibit 3.5.

Before illustrating the use of the expanded transaction analysis model, we want to emphasize the following:

1. Revenues increase profit, thus increasing retained earnings and shareholders' equity, which therefore have credit balances.

2. Expenses decrease profit, thus decreasing retained earnings and shareholders' equity. Therefore, expenses have debit balances (opposite of the balance in retained earnings); that is, to increase an expense, you debit it, which decreases profit and retained earnings. You are adding to the expenses when you debit the account.

Assets

DR +	

Liabilities

	CR +

Shareholders' Equity Accounts

	CR +

Revenue and Gains

	CR +

Expenses and Losses

DR +	

Exhibit **3.5**

Expanded Transaction Analysis Model

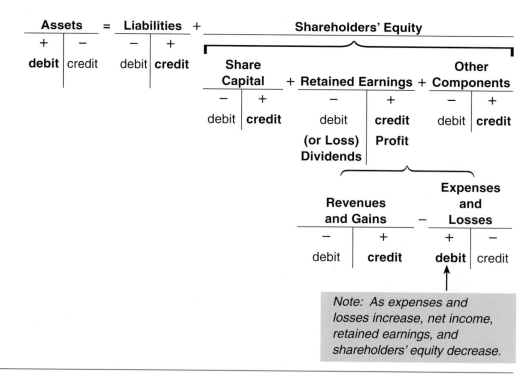

3. When revenues exceed expenses, the company reports profit, increasing retained earnings and shareholders' equity. However, when expenses exceed revenues, a loss results that decreases retained earnings and thus shareholders' equity.

When constructing and using the transaction analysis model, we maintain the direction rule and the debit-credit framework described in Chapter 2:

- All accounts can increase or decrease, although revenues and expenses tend to increase throughout a period. For accounts on the left side of the accounting equation, the increase symbol, +, is written on the left side of the T-account. For accounts on the right side of the accounting equation, the increase symbol, +, is written on the right side of the T-account.

- Debits (dr) are written on the left side of each T-account and credits (cr) are written on the right.

- Every transaction affects at least two accounts.

As indicated in Chapter 2, a systematic transaction analysis includes the following steps:

Step 1: **Identify and classify accounts and effects**.
- **Identify the accounts (by title) affected**, making sure that at least two accounts change. Ask yourself, what is received (and earned) and what is given (and incurred)?
- **Classify them by type of account**. Was each account an asset (A), a liability (L), a shareholders' equity (SE), a revenue (R), or an expense (E)?
- **Determine the direction of the effect**. Did the account increase [+] or decrease [−]?

Step 2: **Verify that the accounting equation (A = L + SE) remains in balance**.

Since revenues are defined as increases in assets or settlement of liabilities from *ongoing operations* of the business, then, by definition, the recording of revenue results in either increasing an asset or decreasing a liability. In like manner, when recording an expense, an asset is decreased or a liability is increased.

You should refer to the expanded transaction analysis model until you can construct it on your own without assistance. Study the following illustration carefully to make sure that you understand the impact of operating activities on both the statement of financial position and the income statement.

Analyzing Nestlé's Transactions

Now we build on Nestlé's statement of financial position presented at the end of Chapter 2. It included the effects of the investing and financing transactions that occurred during the accounting period. We analyze, record, and post to the T-accounts the effects of this chapter's operating activities that also occurred during the accounting cycle. In Chapter 4, we will complete the accounting cycle with the activities at the end of the period (January 31). All amounts are in millions of Swiss francs, and the effects are posted to the appropriate T-accounts at the end of the illustration.

(a) **Nestlé sold milk products and beverages to customers for 3,520 in cash. The cost of these sales was 1,960.** (*Note:* This requires two entries, one for the revenue earned and one for the expense incurred in generating the revenue.)

Cash (+A)	3,520	
Sales revenue (+R → +SE)		3,520
To record cash sales.		
Cost of goods sold (+E → −SE)	1,960	
Inventories (−A).		1,960
To record cost of goods sold.		

←——— Journal entry

Assets	=	Liabilities	+	Shareholders' Equity	
Cash	+3,520			Sales revenue	+3,520
Inventories	−1,960			Cost of goods sold	−1,960

←——— Effect on accounting equation

Notice that when the revenue is increased, we also indicate the effect on total shareholders' equity with the following notation: +R → +SE. A similar notation will be used for expenses, which decrease shareholders' equity.

These effects are posted to the appropriate T-accounts in Exhibit 3.6 on page 123 (see the shaded amounts).

Effect of adjustment on
Profit: ↑ 1,560
Cash: ↑ 3,520

Recall that revenues are recognized when Nestlé sells goods and renders services regardless of the timing of cash receipts, and expenses are recognized when incurred regardless of the timing of cash payments. To highlight the difference between accrual basis accounting and cash basis accounting, we show in the margin the net effect of each transaction on profit and on cash.

(b) **Nestlé sold coffee products to retail outlets for 3,020; 2,020 was received in cash and the rest was due from the outlets. The cost of products sold was 1,400.**

Cash (+A)	2,020	
Trade receivables (+A)	1,000	
Sales revenue (+R → +SE)		3,020
To record sales, partly for cash and the rest on account.		
Cost of goods sold (+E → −SE)	1,400	
Inventories (−A).		1,400
To record cost of goods sold.		

Effect of transaction on
Profit: ↑ 1,620
Cash: ↑ 2,020

Assets		=	Liabilities	+	Shareholders' Equity	
Cash	+2,020				Sales revenue	+3,020
Trade receivables	+1,000				Cost of goods sold	−1,400
Inventories	−1,400					

(c) **Nestlé received 345 from customers, including 75 for sales made in December and the rest from January sales.**

Effect of transaction on
Profit: ↑ 270
Cash: ↑ 345

Cash (+A) 345
   Trade receivables (−A) 75
   Sales revenue (+R → +SE) 270
To record cash sales and collection from customers.

Assets		=	Liabilities	+	Shareholders' Equity	
Cash	+345				Sales revenue	+270
Trade receivables	−75					

(d) **Nestlé signed contracts with new clients and received 500 cash. The company earned 400 immediately by performing services for these clients; the rest will be earned over the next several months.**

Effect of transaction on
Profit: ↑ 400
Cash: ↑ 500

Cash (+A) 500
   Service revenue (+R → +SE) 400
   Deferred revenue (+L) 100
To record the receipt of cash for current and future services.

Assets		=	Liabilities		+	Shareholders' Equity	
Cash	+500		Deferred revenue	+100		Sales revenue	+400

(e) **Nestlé paid 740 in advance for the following: 160 for insurance for the next four months, 450 for rent of warehousing facilities for the next three months, and 130 for advertising in February.**

Effect of transaction on
Profit: No effect
Cash: ↓ 740

Prepayments (+A) 740
   Cash (−A) 740
To record payment of cash for insurance, rent, and advertising.

Assets		=	Liabilities	+	Shareholders' Equity	
Cash	−740					
Prepayments	+740					

(f) **Nestlé paid 731 for utilities, repairs, and fuel for delivery vehicles, all considered distribution expenses.**

Effect of transaction on
Profit: ↓ 731
Cash: ↓ 731

Distribution expenses (+E → −SE) 731
   Cash (−A) 731
To record payment for various expenses.

Assets		=	Liabilities	+	Shareholders' Equity	
Cash	−731				Distribution expenses	−731

(g) **Nestlé ordered and received 2,900 in supplies inventories; 900 was paid in cash and the rest was on account with suppliers.**

Inventories (+A) 2,900
   Cash (−A) 900
   Trade payables (+L). 2,000
To record purchase of supplies with partial payment.

Assets		=	Liabilities		+	Shareholders' Equity
Cash	−900		Trade payables	+2,000		
Inventories	+2,900					

Effect of transaction on
Profit: No effect
Cash: ↓ 900

(h) **Nestlé paid 1,350 in cash to employees for work in January: 400 to personnel associated with distribution activities and 950 for employees in the corporate headquarters, considered as administrative expenses.**

Distribution expenses (+E → −SE) 400
Marketing and administrative expenses (+E → −SE) 950
   Cash (−A) 1,350
To record payment to employees.

Assets		=	Liabilities	+	Shareholders' Equity	
Cash	−1,350				Distribution expenses	−400
					Marketing and administrative expenses	−950

Effect of transaction on
Profit: ↓ 1,350
Cash: ↓ 1,350

SELF-STUDY **QUIZ 3-3**

For transactions (i) through (k), fill in the missing information. Be sure to post journal entries to the T-accounts in Exhibit 3.6.

(i) **Nestlé received 650 in cash: 50 in interest earned on notes receivable and 600 in payments made on notes receivable from customers.**

[blank box for journal entry]

Assets		=	Liabilities	+	Shareholders' Equity	
Cash	+650				Interest revenue	+50
Notes receivable	−600					

Write the journal entry, post the effects to the T-accounts, and show the effects on profit and cash

Effect of transaction on
Profit: _____
Cash: _____

(j) **Nestlé paid 1,000 on accounts owed to suppliers.**

[blank box for journal entry]

Assets	=	Liabilities	+	Shareholders' Equity

Write the journal entry; post the effects to the T-accounts

Show the effects on the accounting equation and on profit and cash

Effect of transaction on
Profit: _____
Cash: _____

Show the effects on the accounting equation and on profit and cash

(k) Nestlé sold land for 350. The cost of the land is 50.

Cash (+A) 350		
Property, plant, and equipment (−A)		50
Gain on sale of land (Gain → +SE)		300
To record sale of land at a gain.		

Assets	=	Liabilities	+	Shareholders' Equity

Effect of transaction on
   Profit: _____
   Cash: _____

≣ connect

After you complete your answers, go online for the solutions.

Exhibit 3.6 shows the T-accounts that changed during the period because of transactions (*a*) through (*k*). The balances of all other accounts remained the same. The amounts from Nestlé's statement of financial position at the end of Chapter 2 have been included as the beginning balances in Exhibit 3.6 for assets, liabilities, and shareholders' equity accounts. On the other hand, income statement accounts have zero beginning balances so that the effects of transactions affecting revenue and expense accounts can be accumulated over the period.

You can verify that you posted the entries for transactions (i) through (k) properly by adding the increase side and subtracting the decrease side, and then comparing your answer to the ending balance given in each of the T-accounts.

HOW IS THE INCOME STATEMENT PREPARED AND ANALYZED?

LO⁵

Prepare an income statement and understand the difference between profit and cash flow from operations.

Based on the January transactions that have just been posted in the T-accounts, we can now prepare an income statement reflecting the operating activities for January.

THE NESTLÉ GROUP
Consolidated Income Statement
For the Month Ended January 31, 2010
(in millions of Swiss francs)

Revenues	
Sales revenue	6,810
Service revenue	400
Total revenues	7,210
Cost of goods sold	(3,360)
Gross profit	3,850
Operating expenses	
Distribution	1,131
Marketing and administrative	950
Total operating expenses	2,081
Operating profit	1,769
Other revenues and gains (expenses and losses)	
Interest revenue	50
Gain on sale of land	300
Profit before income taxes	2,119

Exhibit **3.6**

T-Accounts

The beginning balances of financial statement accounts are taken from Exhibit 2.8.

ASSETS

+	Cash (A)			−
Beg. bal.	2,875			
a	3,520	e		740
b	2,020	f		731
c	345	g		900
d	500	h		1,350
i				
k	350	j		
End. bal.	5,539			

+	Trade Receivables (A)		−
Beg. bal.	9,425		
b	1,000	c	75
End. bal.	10,350		

+	Inventories (A)		−
Beg. bal.	7,734	a	1,960
		b	1,400
g	2,900		
End. bal.	7,274		

+	Prepayments (A)	−
Beg. bal.	589	
e	740	
End. bal.	1,329	

+	Notes Receivable (A)		−
Beg. bal.	3,034		
		i	
End. bal.	2,434		

+	Property, Plant, and Equipment, net		−
Beg. bal.	23,799	k	50
End. bal.	23,749		

LIABILITIES

−	Deferred Revenue (L)		+
		d	100
		End. bal.	100

−	Trade Payables (L)		+
		Beg. bal.	13,033
j		g	2.000
		End. bal.	14,033

REVENUES AND GAINS

−	Sales Revenue (R)		+
		a	3,520
		b	3,020
		c	270
		End. bal.	6,810

−	Service Revenue (R)		+
		d	400
		End. bal.	400

−	Interest Revenue (R)		+
		i	
		End. bal.	50

−	Gain on Sale of Land (G)		+
		k	300
		End. bal.	300

EXPENSES

+	Cost of Goods Sold (E)		−
a	1,960		
b	1,400		
End. bal.	3,360		

+	Marketing and Administrative Expenses (E)		−
f	731		
h	400		
End. bal.	1,131		

+	Distribution Expenses (E)		−
h	950		
End. bal.	950		

This income statement is not yet adjusted for all revenues earned or expenses incurred in January. For example,

- The prepayments account includes rent and insurance covering January, and future months, but the expenses are not yet recorded for the amounts used in January. This is true of the equipment used during the month as well. Until adjusted, assets are overstated and expenses are understated.

- We have not calculated income taxes for the amount incurred in January and owed within the next quarter. Thus, both expenses and liabilities are understated.

Chapter 4 will describe the adjustment process to update the accounting records. After the adjustments are made, the amount of income tax expense will be determined and the statements will reflect IFRS following accrual basis accounting.

REPORTING MORE DETAILED FINANCIAL INFORMATION IN THE NOTES

Many companies, especially very large ones, operate in more than one geographic area. These companies are often called *multinationals.* A consolidated income statement that is based on aggregated data may not prove as useful to investors seeking to assess possible risks and returns from companies operating in foreign markets. This is also true if a company operates in more than a single business. For example, a manufacturing operation in a South American country suffering from political unrest is riskier than a manufacturing facility located in Ontario. Therefore, many companies provide additional information about geographic and business segments in notes to the financial statements. An excerpt from Nestlé's 2009 financial statements provides information on its geographic segments:

Extracts from Note 3.2: Segmental Information by Product Group
(in millions of Swiss francs)

Product Group	Sales	Profit before Interest and Taxes	Assets
Powdered and liquid beverages	19,271	4,185	8,891
Water	9,066	633	8,252
Milk products and ice cream	19,557	2,345	13,258
Nutrition	9,965	1,734	15,711
Prepared dishes and cooking aids	17,205	2,226	10,127
Confectionary	11,796	1,599	6,073
Pet care	12,938	2,108	14,933
Pharmaceutical products	7,820	2,616	7,437
Unallocated items		(1,747)	818
Total segments	107,618	15,699	85,500

OPERATING ACTIVITIES

In Chapter 2, we presented Nestlé's statement of cash flows for the investing and financing activities for the month. Recall that investing activities relate primarily to transactions affecting non-current assets. Financing activities are those from bank borrowings, issuance of shares, and dividend payments to shareholders. In this chapter, we focus on cash flows from operating activities, which essentially reflects cash basis accounting. This section of the statement of cash flows reports *cash from* operating sources, primarily customers, and *cash to* suppliers and others involved in operations. The accounts most often associated with operating activities are current assets, such as trade receivables, inventories, and prepayments, and current liabilities, such as trade payables, salaries payable, and deferred revenue.

We present the cash flows from operating activities section of the statement of cash flows by using the *direct method*–cash receipts and cash disbursements. However, most companies report cash from operations by using the *indirect method* that will be discussed in Chapter 5 and later chapters.

Effect on Statement of Cash Flows

		Effect on Cash Flows
Operating activities		
Cash received:	from customers	+
	for interest and dividends on investments	+
Cash paid:	to suppliers	−
	to employees	−
	for interest on borrowings	−
	for income taxes	−
Investing activities (from Chapter 2)		
Financing activities (from Chapter 2)		

When a transaction affects cash, it is included on the statement of cash flows. When a transaction does not affect cash, such as when acquiring a building with a long-term mortgage note payable or selling goods on account to customers, it is not included on the statement. *If you see cash in a transaction, it will be reflected on the statement of cash flows.* Therefore, when preparing the cash flows from operating activities section of the statement of cash flows by using the direct method, the easiest way is to look at the activities in the cash T-account.

	+	Cash (A)		−	
	Bal.	2,875			
From customers	(a)	3,520	740	(e)	To suppliers of services
From customers	(b)	2,020	731	(f)	To suppliers of services
From customers	(c)	345	900	(g)	To trade suppliers
From customers	(d)	500	1,350	(h)	To employees
From customers	(i)	650	1,000	(j)	To trade suppliers
From investing activity	(k)	350			
	Bal.	5,539			

Operating activities contributed 2,314 in cash during January. This amount represents the increase in the cash account (5,539 − 2,875), excluding the cash received from the sale of land (350), which is an investing activity. This cash basis profit is different from the operating profit of 1,819 that is based on accrual accounting. Note that the gain of 300 on the sale of land is not included because it resulted from an investing, not an operating, transaction. The difference between these two amounts is due to the fact that revenue is recognized when earned, regardless of when cash is received, and expenses are recognized when incurred, regardless of when cash is paid.

We presented above, in the margin, the effects of each operating transaction on both profit and cash. If you compute the net effect of all transactions on profit, you will get 2,119, the same profit figure that appears in the income statement. You should not be surprised by this result because the income statement reflects the net effects of all operating transactions during a period. Similarly, the net effect of the same operating transactions on cash is 2,314, which equals the net cash flow from operating activities on the statement of cash flows.

To remain in business in the long run, companies must generate positive cash flows from operations. Cash is needed to pay suppliers and employees. When cash from operations is negative over a period of time, the only other ways to obtain the necessary funds are to (1) sell non-current assets, which reduces future productivity; (2) borrow from creditors, at increasing rates of interest as risk of default rises; or (3) issue additional shares, where investor expectations about poor future performance drives the stock price down. There are clearly limits on how many of these activities a company can undertake.

Nestlé has realized positive operating cash flows over the five-year period 2005–2009, as shown below. Furthermore, the cash flow from operations exceeded profit in four of these five years. In 2008, Nestlé's sale of investments in other businesses resulted in a gain of 9,208. If this one-time gain is ignored, then Nestlé's profit would be slightly lower than its operating cash flows for 2009. The excess of operating cash flows over profit represents a prudent way of reporting revenues and expenses that builds analysts' confidence as to the reliability of the reported profit measures.

	2005	2006	2007	2008	2009
Cash flow from operations	10,205	11,676	13,439	10,763	17,934
Profit	8,518	9,849	11,382	19,051	11,793

SELF-STUDY **QUIZ 3-4**

Canadian Tire Corporation Limited

Canadian Tire Corporation Limited is a leading hard goods retailer with more than 400 stores across Canada. The transactions below are taken from a recent annual statement of cash flows. Indicate whether the transaction affected cash flow as an operating (O), investing (I), or financing (F) activity, and indicate the direction of the effect on cash (+ for increases; − for decreases):

Transactions	Type of Activity (O, I, or F)	Effect on Cash Flows (+ or −)
1. Distribution to shareholders		
2. Receipt of cash from customers		
3. Additions to property		
4. Payment of income taxes		
5. Payment of cash to suppliers		
6. Repayment of long-term borrowings		
7. Receipt of interest on investments		
8. Long-term borrowings		
9. Issuance of shares		
10. Payment of interest on borrowings		
11. Payment of cash to employees		
12. Sale of property		

 **connect**

After you complete your answers, go online for the solutions.

KEY RATIO ANALYSIS

We now introduce two ratios to assess managers' use of assets in total to improve profits. These two ratios focus on the use of assets to generate revenue and profit, respectively. As we will see in other chapters, similar analysis on the use of specific types of assets provides additional information for decision makers.

LO6

Compute and interpret the total asset turnover ratio and the return on assets ratio.

TOTAL ASSET TURNOVER RATIO

ANALYTICAL QUESTION → How effective is management in generating sales from assets (resources)?

RATIO AND COMPARISONS → The total asset turnover ratio is useful in answering this question. It is computed as follows:

$$\text{Total Asset Turnover Ratio} = \frac{\text{Sales (or Operating) Revenues}}{\text{Average Total Assets*}}$$

*Average Total Assets = (Beginning total assets + Ending total assets) ÷ 2

The 2009 ratio for Nestlé is

$$\frac{107,618}{(106,215 + 110,916)} = 0.99$$

Comparisons over Time			Comparisons with Competitors	
Nestlé			ConAgra Foods	Kraft Foods
2007	2008	2009	2009	2009
0.99	0.99	0.99	1.03	0.62

INTERPRETATIONS

In General → The total asset turnover ratio measures the sales generated from the use of assets. A high asset turnover signifies efficient management of assets; a low asset turnover ratio signifies less efficient management. A company's products and business strategy contribute significantly to its asset turnover ratio. However, when competitors are similar, management's ability to control the firm's assets is vital in determining its success. Stronger financial performance improves the assets turnover ratio.

Creditors and security analysts use this ratio to assess a company's effectiveness at controlling current and non-current assets. In a well-run business, creditors expect the ratio to fluctuate because of seasonal upswings and downturns. For example, as inventory is built up prior to a high-sales season, companies need to borrow funds. The asset turnover ratio declines with this increase in assets. Eventually, the season's high sales provide the cash needed to repay the loans. The asset turnover ratio then rises with the increased sales.

Focus Company Analysis → Nestlé's total asset turnover ratio was stable from 2007 to 2009, suggesting that management maintained its effectiveness in using assets to generate sales. Nestlé's 2009 total asset turnover ratio is higher than Kraft Foods' ratio but on par with ConAgra's ratio. The main reason for the Kraft Foods' lower ratio is the relatively larger amount of intangible assets reported on its statement of financial position. Kraft Foods' intangible assets represent 64 percent of its total assets, whereas the intangible assets of Nestlé and ConAgra Foods represent 30 percent and 38 percent of their total assets, respectively. These intangible assets result mainly from acquisition of other businesses, and they differ from assets like equipment and inventories in terms of their contribution to generating sales for the period.

A Few Cautions → The total asset turnover ratio may decrease because of seasonal fluctuation, but a declining ratio may also be caused by changes in corporate policies leading to a rising level of assets. Examples include relaxing credit policies for new customers or reducing collection efforts in trade receivables. A detailed analysis of the changes in the key components of assets is needed to determine the causes of a change in the asset turnover ratio and thus in management's decisions. Remember that any one ratio is not sufficient as a basis for investment decisions.

SELECTED FOCUS COMPANY TOTAL ASSET TURNOVER RATIOS	
Andrew Peller Ltd.	0.95
Benetton	0.75
Nokia	1.31

RETURN ON ASSETS (ROA)

ANALYTICAL QUESTION → How well has management used the total invested capital provided by debtholders and shareholders during the period?

RATIO AND COMPARISONS → Analysts refer to the rate of return on assets (ROA) as a useful measure in addressing this issue. It is computed as follows:

$$\text{Return on Assets} = \frac{\text{Profit} + \text{Interest Expense (net of tax)}}{\text{Average Total Assets}}$$

Both the total asset turnover ratio and the return on assets measure management's effectiveness in utilizing the company's resources: the first in generating revenue during the period, the second in generating after-tax return on the use of assets.

The return on assets takes into consideration the resources contributed by both shareholders and creditors. For this reason, the return to shareholders or profit is augmented by the return to creditors, which is interest expense. Interest expense is measured net of income tax because it represents the net cost of the funds provided by the creditors to the corporation. The returns to both shareholders and creditors are measured net of tax in the numerator of this ratio.

The 2009 ratio for Nestlé is

$$\frac{11{,}793 + 622^1 \times 75\%^2}{(106{,}215 + 110{,}916) \div 2} = 0.115 \text{ (or 11.5\%)}$$

[1] As disclosed in Note 5 to Nestlé's financial statements.
[2] This illustration assumes a corporate tax rate of 25 percent.

Comparisons over Time			Comparisons with Competitors	
Nestlé			ConAgra Foods	Kraft Foods
2007	2008	2009	2009	2009
11.5%	18.0%	11.5%	8.8%	6.0%

INTERPRETATIONS

In General → ROA measures how much the firm earned from the use of its assets. It is the broadest measure of profitability and management effectiveness, independent of financing strategy. ROA allows investors to compare management's investment performance against alternative investment options. Firms with higher ROA are doing a better job of selecting new investments, all other things being equal. Company managers often compute the measure on a division-by-division basis and use it to evaluate division managers' relative performance.

Focus Company Analysis → Nestlé appears to have done well in fiscal year 2008 compared with both 2007 and 2009. Examination of the company's income statement shown in Exhibit 3.1 indicates a significant amount of other income in 2008, which includes a gain of CHF 9,208 million on the sale of its investment in Alcon. If we exclude this one-time gain from profit, then Nestlé's ROA for 2008 would drop to 9.6 percent. Nestlé achieved a higher ROA than both ConAgra Foods and Kraft Foods. Examination of the statements of financial position of ConAgra Foods and Kraft Foods indicates that their assets include a proportionally higher amount of goodwill than Nestlé. Because goodwill is not an operational asset that generates revenue and profit in the same way as food-processing equipment, its exclusion from total assets would increase the ROAs for both ConAgra Foods and Kraft Foods, bringing their ratios closer to Nestlé's.

A Few Cautions → Effective analysis of ROA requires an understanding of why ROA differs from prior levels and from the ROA of the company's competitors. Analysis of the differences in ROA over time and across companies can be facilitated by a decomposition of this ratio into two other ratios, as shown later in Chapter 13.

SELECTED FOCUS COMPANY COMPARISONS: RETURN ON ASSETS

Andrew Peller Ltd.	6.0%
Benetton	7.6%
Nokia	10.5%

SELF-STUDY **QUIZ 3-5**

Sears Canada

Sears Canada is one of the biggest Canadian retailers. It operates a large number of department stores that sell home fashions, appliances, apparel, home electronics, and garden products. It also sells merchandise online. Selected information about the company's resources and operations are presented below (amounts in millions of Canadian dollars).

	2009	2008	2007	2006	2005	2004
Total assets	$3,404.8	$3,264.7	$3,001.7	$3,093.3	$3,199	$4,262
Total revenue	5,200.6	5,733.2	6,326.4	5,932.8	6,238	6,230
Net earnings (Profit)	234.7	288.6	306.0	152.6	771	129
Interest expense	25.2	10	12.7	48	48.9	55
Tax rate	32%	31%	33%	36%	20%	32%

Required:

1. Complete the following table by computing the total asset turnover ratio and the return on assets ratio for 2006 and 2005.

	2009	2008	2007	2006	2005
Total asset turnover ratio	1.56	1.83	2.08		
Return on assets (ROA)	0.08	0.09	0.10		

2. The return on assets for 2005 is relatively high compared with those of later years. What is the most likely explanation for this high ratio?

3. What conclusion can you draw from these ratios about the company's effectiveness in managing the economic resources under its control?

After you complete your answers, go online for the solutions.

ACCOUNTING STANDARDS
FOR PRIVATE ENTERPRISES

The accounting concepts and procedures covered in this chapter are equally applicable to Canadian private enterprises.

DEMONSTRATION **CASE**

This case is a continuation of the Terrific Lawn Maintenance Corporation introduced in Chapter 2. The company was established with supplies, property, and equipment purchased ready for business. The statement of financial position at April 30, 2011, based on investing and financing activities is as follows:

TERRIFIC LAWN MAINTENANCE CORPORATION
Statement of Financial Position
As at April 30, 2011

Assets		Liabilities	
Cash	$ 4,350	Notes payable	$ 3,700
Equipment	4,600		
Land	3,750	**Shareholders' Equity**	
		Share capital	9,000
Total assets	$12,700	Total liabilities and shareholders' equity	$12,700

The following completed activities occurred during April 2011:

a. Purchased and used gasoline for mowers and edgers, paying $90 in cash at a local gas station.
b. In early April, received from the city $1,600 cash in advance for lawn maintenance service for April through July ($400 each month). The entire amount was recorded as deferred revenue.
c. In early April, purchased insurance costing $300 covering six months, April through September. The entire payment was recorded as prepayment.
d. Mowed lawns for residential customers who are billed every two weeks. A total of $5,200 of service was billed in April.
e. Residential customers paid $3,500 on their accounts.
f. Paid wages every two weeks. Total cash paid in April was $3,900.
g. Received a bill for $320 from the local gas station for additional gasoline purchased on account and used in April.
h. Paid $100 on trade payables.

Required:

1. On a separate sheet of paper, set up T-accounts for cash, trade receivables, equipment, land, prepayments, trade payables, deferred revenue, notes payable, share capital, retained earnings, mowing revenue, fuel expense, and wages expense. Beginning balances for asset, liability and equity accounts should be taken from the preceding statement of financial position. Beginning balances for operating accounts are $0. Indicate these balances on the T-accounts.

2. Analyze each transaction using the steps outlined in Chapter 2. Please refer to the expanded transaction analysis model presented in this chapter.

3. On a separate sheet of paper, prepare journal entries to record the transactions above in chronological order and indicate their effects on the accounting model (Assets = Liabilities + Shareholders' Equity) as well as their effects on profit and cash. Verify that the accounting equation is in balance.

4. Enter the effects of each transaction in the appropriate T-accounts. Identify each amount with its letter in the list of activities.

5. Compute balances in each of the T-accounts.

We strongly recommend that you prepare your own answers to these requirements and then check your answers with the following solution.

SUGGESTED **SOLUTION**

1. Journal entries, effects on accounting equation, equality checks, and T-accounts:

Effect of transaction on
  Profit: ↓ 90
  Cash: ↓ 90

(a) Fuel expense (+E → −SE)			90	
Cash (−A)				90

Assets		=	**Liabilities**	+	**Shareholders' Equity**	
Cash	−90				Fuel expense	−90

Effect of transaction on
  Profit: No effect
  Cash: ↑ 1,600

(b) Cash (+A)			1,600	
Deferred revenue (+L)				1,600

Assets		=	**Liabilities**		+	**Shareholders' Equity**
Cash	+1,600		Deferred revenue	+1,600		

Effect of transaction on
  Profit: No effect
  Cash: ↓ 300

(c) Prepayments (+A)			300	
Cash (−A)				300

Assets		=	**Liabilities**	+	**Shareholders' Equity**
Cash	−300				
Prepayments	+300				

Effect of transaction on
  Profit: ↑ 5,200
  Cash: No effect

(d) Trade receivables (+A)			5,200	
Mowing revenue (+R → +SE)				5,200

Assets		=	**Liabilities**	+	**Shareholders' Equity**	
Trade receivables	+5,200				Mowing revenue	+5,200

Effect of transaction on
  Profit: No effect
  Cash: ↑ 3,500

(e) Cash (+A)			3,500	
Trade receivables (−A)				3,500

Assets		=	**Liabilities**	+	**Shareholders' Equity**
Cash	+3,500				
Trade receivables	−3,500				

Effect of transaction on
Profit: ↓ 3,900
Cash: ↓ 3,900

(f) Wage expense (+E → −SE)................................. 3,900
        Cash (−A)   3,900

Assets		=	Liabilities	+	Shareholders' Equity	
Cash	−3,900				Wages expense	−3,900

Effect of transaction on
Profit: ↓ 320
Cash: No effect

(g) Fuel expense (+E → −SE)................................. 320
        Trade payables (+L)   320

Assets		=	Liabilities		+	Shareholders' Equity	
			Trade payables	+320		Fuel expense	−320

Effect of transaction on
Profit: No effect
Cash: ↓ 100

(h) Trade payables (−L) 100
        Cash (−A)   100

Assets		=	Liabilities		+	Shareholders' Equity	
Cash	−100		Trade payables	−100			

T-Accounts

The beginning balances of the statement of financial position accounts are taken from the solutions to the demonstration case in Chapter 2 (pp. 77–78).

ASSETS

+		Cash (A)		−
Beg. bal.	5,050			
b	1,600	a		90
e	3,500	c		300
		f		3,900
		h		100
End. bal.	5,760			

+	Trade Receivables (A)		−	
d		5,200	e	3,500
End. bal.		1,700		

+	Prepayments (A)	−
c	300	
End. bal.	300	

+	Equipment (A)	−
Beg. bal.	4,600	
End. bal.	4,600	

+	Land (A)	−
Beg. bal.	3,750	
End. bal.	3,750	

LIABILITIES

−	Trade Payables (L)		+
h	100	g	320
		End. bal.	220

−	Deferred Revenue (L)		+
		b	1,600
		End. bal.	1,600

−	Notes Payables (L)		+
		Beg. bal.	4,400
		End. bal.	4,400

SHAREHOLDERS' EQUITY

−	Share Capital (SE)		+
		Beg. bal.	9,000
		End. bal.	9,000

REVENUES

+	Mowing Revenue (R)		−
		d	5,200
		End. bal.	5,200

EXPENSES

+	Wages Expense (E)		−
f	3,900		
End. bal.	3,900		

+	Fuel Expense (E)		−
a	90		
g	320		
End. bal.	410		

CHAPTER **TAKE-AWAYS**

1. **Describe a typical business operating cycle and explain the necessity for the periodicity assumption. p. 104**
   - Operating cycle—the cash-to-cash cycle is the time it takes to purchase goods or services from suppliers, sell the goods or services to customers, and collect cash from customers.
   - Periodicity assumption—to measure and report financial information periodically, we assume that the long life of the company can be cut into shorter periods.

2. **Explain how business activities affect the elements of the income statement. p. 106**
   Elements on the classified income statement:
   a. Revenues—increases in assets or settlements of liabilities from ongoing operations.
   b. Expenses—decreases in assets or increases in liabilities from ongoing operations.
   c. Gains—increases in assets or settlements of liabilities from peripheral activities.
   d. Losses—decreases in assets or increases in liabilities from peripheral activities.

3. **Explain the accrual basis of accounting and apply the revenue principle and matching process to measure profit. p. 110**
   When applying accrual accounting concepts, revenues are recognized (recorded) when earned and expenses are recognized when incurred to generate the revenues.
   - Revenue principle—recognize revenues when the earnings process is complete or nearly complete, an exchange has taken place, and collection is probable.
   - Matching process—recognize expenses when incurred in earning revenue.

4. **Apply transaction analysis to examine and record the effects of operating activities on the financial statements. p. 117**
   The expanded transaction analysis model includes revenues and expenses:

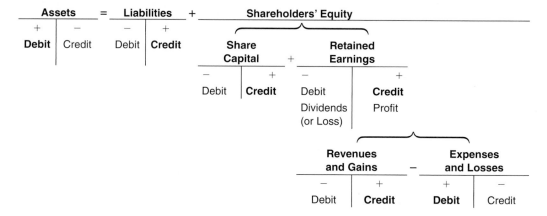

5. **Prepare an income statement and understand the difference between profit and cash flow from operations. p. 122**
   The income statement reports the revenues generated during the period and the related expenses. Profit is the difference between revenues and expenses, whereas cash flow from operations equals the difference between cash receipts and cash payments related to operations. Profit differs from cash flow from operations because the revenue principle and matching process result in the recognition of revenues and related expenses that are independent of the timing of cash receipts and payments.

6. **Compute and interpret the total asset turnover ratio and the return on assets ratio. p. 126**
   The total asset turnover ratio (Sales ÷ Average total assets) measures the sales generated from the use of assets. The higher the ratio, the more efficient the company is at managing assets. The return on assets (ROA) ratio measures how much the company earned from the use of assets. It provides information on profitability and management's effectiveness in utilizing assets. An increasing ratio over time suggests increased efficiency. ROA is computed as the sum of profit and interest expense (net of tax) divided by average total assets.

In this chapter, we discussed the operating cycle and accounting concepts relevant to income determination: periodicity assumption, definitions for the income statement elements (revenues, expenses, gains, and losses), the revenue principle, and the matching process. These accounting principles are defined in accordance with the accrual basis of accounting, which requires revenues to be recorded when earned and expenses to be recorded when incurred in generating revenues during the period. We expanded the transaction analysis model introduced in Chapter 2 by adding revenues and expenses. In Chapter 4, we discuss the activities at the end of the accounting period: adjustment process, preparation of adjusted financial statements, and closing process.

KEY **RATIOS**

The **total asset turnover ratio** measures the sales generated from the use of assets. A high ratio suggests that the company is managing its assets (resources used to generate revenues) efficiently. It is computed as follows (p. 126):

$$\text{Total Asset Turnover Ratio} = \frac{\text{Sales (or Operating) Revenues}}{\text{Average Total Assets}^*}$$

The **return on assets ratio** measures how much the company earned from the use of assets during the period. A high ratio suggests that the company is managing its assets efficiently. It is computed as follows (p. 127):

$$\text{Return on Assets (ROA)} = \frac{\text{Profit} + \text{Interest Expense (net of tax)}}{\text{Average Total Assets}^*}$$

*(Beginning Total Assets + Ending Total Assets) ÷ 2

FINDING **FINANCIAL INFORMATION**

STATEMENT OF FINANCIAL POSITION

Current Assets	*Current Liabilities*
Cash	Trade payables
Trade and notes receivable	Notes payable
	Accrued liabilities
Inventories	*Non-current Liabilities*
Prepayments	
Non-current Assets	Long-term borrowings
Long-term investments	Provisions
Property, plant, and equipment	*Shareholders' Equity*
Intangibles	Share capital
	Retained earnings

INCOME STATEMENT

Revenues
  Sales (from various operating activities)
  Investment income
Expenses
  Cost of goods sold
    Rent, wages, interest, depreciation, insurance, etc.
Pretax Profit
  Income tax expense
Profit

STATEMENT OF CASH FLOWS

Under Operating Activities
  + Cash from customers
  + Cash from interest
  − Cash to suppliers
  − Cash to employees
  − Cash for interest
  − Cash for income taxes

NOTES

Under Summary of Significant Accounting Policies
  Description of company's revenue recognition policy

KEY **TERMS**

Accrual Basis Accounting p. 110
Cash Basis Accounting p. 110
Expenses p. 107
Gains p. 108
Gross Profit (Gross Margin) p. 108
Profit before Income Taxes p. 109
Losses p. 108

Matching Process p. 115
Operating Cycle (Cash-to-Cash) p. 105
Operating Profit p. 108
Periodicity Assumption p. 106
Profit Before Income Taxes p. 109
Revenues p. 107
Revenue Principle p. 111

QUESTIONS

1. Assume that you have just opened a small gift store that specializes in gift items imported from the Far East. Explain the typical business operating cycle for your store.
2. Explain what the periodicity assumption means in accounting.
3. Indicate the income statement equation and define each element.
4. Explain the difference between
   a. revenues and gains.
   b. expenses and losses.
5. Define *accrual accounting* and contrast it with cash basis accounting.
6. What conditions normally must be met for revenue to be recognized under the accrual basis of accounting?
7. Explain the matching process.
8. Explain why shareholders' equity is increased by revenues and decreased by expenses.
9. Explain why revenues are recorded as credits and expenses as debits.
10. Complete the following matrix by entering either *debit* or *credit* in each cell:

Item	Increase	Decrease
Revenues		
Expenses		
Gains		
Losses		

11. Complete the following matrix by entering either *increase* or *decrease* in each cell:

Item	Debit	Credit
Revenues		
Expenses		
Gains		
Losses		

12. Identify whether each of the following transactions results in a cash flow effect from operating, investing, or financing activities, and indicate the effect on cash (+ for increase and − for decrease). If there is no cash flow effect, write "none":

Transaction	Operating, Investing, or Financing Effect	Direction of the Effect
Cash paid to suppliers		
Sale of goods on account		
Cash received from customers		
Purchase of investments for cash		
Cash paid for interest		
Issuance of shares for cash		

13. State the equation for the total asset turnover ratio, and explain how it is interpreted.
14. State the equation for the return on assets ratio, and explain how it is interpreted.

EXERCISES

E3–1 Inferring Income Statement Values

Supply the missing dollar amounts for the 2011 income statement of Ultimate Style Company for each of the following independent cases:

■ **LO1**

	Case A	Case B	Case C	Case D	Case E
Sales revenue	$900	$700	$410	$?	$?
Selling expense	?	150	80	400	250
Cost of goods sold	?	380	?	500	310
Income tax expense	?	30	20	40	30
Gross profit	400	?	?	?	440
Profit before income tax	200	90	?	190	?
Administrative expense	150	?	60	100	80
Profit	170	?	50	?	80

E3–2 Preparing an Income Statement

The following data were taken from the records of Village Corporation at December 31, 2011:

■ **LO2**

Sales revenue	$70,000
Gross profit	24,500
Selling (distribution) expense	8,000
Administrative expense	?
Profit before income tax	10,000
Income tax rate	30%
Number of shares outstanding	4,000

Required:

Prepare a complete income statement for the company (showing both gross profit and profit from operations). Show all computations. (*Hint:* Set up the side captions starting with sales revenue and ending with earnings per share; use the amounts and percentages given to infer missing values.)

E3–3 Reporting Cash Basis versus Accrual Basis Profit

Mostert Music Company had the following transactions in March:

■ **LO3**

a. Sold instruments to customers for $10,000; received $4,000 in cash and the rest on account.

b. Determined that the cost of the instruments sold was $7,000.

c. Purchased $4,000 of new instruments inventory; paid $2,000 in cash and the rest on account.

d. Paid $600 in wages for the month.

e. Received a $200 bill for utilities that will be paid in April.

f. Received $1,000 from customers as deposits on orders of new instruments to be sold to customers in April.

Complete the following statements:

Cash Basis Income Statement		**Accrual Basis Income Statement**	
Revenues	$	Revenues	$ . . . .
Cash sales	. . . .	Sales to customers	. . . .
Customer deposits			
Expenses		Expenses	
Inventory purchases	. . . .	Cost of sales	. . . .
Wages paid	. . . .	Wages expense	. . . .
		Utilities expense	. . . .
Profit		Profit	

Does cash basis or accrual basis of accounting provide a better indication of the operating performance of Mostert Music Company in March? Explain.

LO2, 3   **E3–4**   **Identifying Revenues**

Revenues are normally recognized when the entity has transferred to the buyer the significant risks and rewards of ownership of the goods, it retains neither continuing managerial involvement to the degree usually associated with ownership nor effective control over the goods, it is probable that future economic benefits will flow to the company, and the benefits from and costs associated with the transaction can be measured reliably. The amount recorded is the cash-equivalent sales price. The following events and transactions occurred in September 2011:

a. A customer orders and receives 10 personal computers from Gateway 2000; the customer promises to pay $20,000 within three months. Answer from Gateway's standpoint.

b. Sam Shell Dodge sells a truck with a list, or sticker, price of $24,000 for $21,000 cash.

c. The Hudson's Bay Company orders 1,000 men's shirts from Gildan Activewear Inc. at $18 each for future delivery. The terms require payment in full within 30 days of delivery. Answer from Gildan's standpoint.

d. Gildan Activewear completes production of the shirts described in (c) and delivers the order. Answer from Gildan's standpoint.

e. Gildan receives payment from the Hudson's Bay Company for the order described in (c). Answer from Gildan's standpoint.

f. A customer purchases a ticket from WestJet for $435 cash to travel the following January. Answer from WestJet's standpoint.

g. General Motors issues $26 million in new shares.

h. Hall Construction Company signs a contract with a customer for the construction of a new $500,000 warehouse. At the signing, Hall receives a cheque for $50,000 as a deposit on the future construction. Answer from Hall's standpoint.

i. On September 1, 2011, a bank lends $10,000 to a company. The loan carries a 12 percent annual interest rate, and the principal and interest are due in a lump sum on August 31, 2012. Answer from the bank's standpoint.

j. A popular ski magazine company receives a total of $1,800 from subscribers on September 30, the last day of its fiscal year. The subscriptions begin in the next fiscal year. Answer from the magazine company's standpoint.

k. Sears Canada, a retail store, sells a $100 lamp to a customer who charges the sale on his store credit card. Answer from the standpoint of Sears.

Required:

For each of the September transactions,

1. Indicate the account titles that are affected and the type of each account (A for asset, L for liability, SE for shareholders' equity, and R for revenue).

2. If revenue is to be recognized in September, indicate the amount. If revenue is not to be recognized in September, indicate which of the revenue recognition criteria are not met.

Use the following headings in structuring your solution:

Event or Transaction	Accounts Affected and Type of Account	Amount of Revenue Earned in September OR Revenue Criteria Not Met

LO2, 3   **E3–5**   **Identifying Expenses**

Revenues are normally recognized when goods or services have been provided and payment or promise of payment has been received. Expense recognition is guided by an attempt to match the costs associated with the generation of those revenues to the same time period. The following events and transactions occurred in January 2011:

a. Gateway 2000 pays its computer service technicians $85,000 in salary for the two weeks ended January 7. Answer from Gateway's standpoint.

b. Turner Construction Company pays $4,500 in workers' compensation insurance for the first three months of the year.

c. McGraw-Hill Ryerson Limited uses $1,200 worth of electricity and natural gas in its headquarters building for which it has not yet been billed.

d. Gildan Activewear Inc. completes production of 500 men's shirts ordered by Bon Ton Department Store at a cost of $9 each and delivers the order. Answer from Gildan's standpoint.

e. The campus bookstore receives 500 accounting textbooks at a cost of $70 each. The terms indicate that payment is due within 30 days of delivery.

f. During the last week of January, the campus bookstore sold 450 accounting textbooks received in (e) at a sales price of $100 each.

g. Sam Shell Dodge pays its salespeople $3,500 in commissions related to December automobile sales. Answer from Sam Shell Dodge's standpoint.

h. On January 31, Sam Shell Dodge determines that it will pay its salespeople $4,200 in commissions related to January sales. The payment will be made in early February. Answer from Sam Shell Dodge's standpoint.

i. A new grill is installed at a McDonald's restaurant. On the same day, payment of $14,000 is made in cash.

j. On January 1, 2011, Carousel Mall had janitorial supplies costing $1,000 in storage. An additional $600 worth of supplies was purchased during January. At the end of January, $900 worth of janitorial supplies remained in storage.

k. A Concordia University employee works eight hours, at $15 per hour, on January 31; however, payday is not until February 3. Answer from the university's point of view.

l. Wang Company paid $3,600 for a fire insurance policy on January 2. The policy covers the current month and the next 11 months. Answer from Wang's point of view.

m. Amber Incorporated has its delivery van repaired in January for $280 and charges the amount on account.

n. Ziegler Company, a farm equipment company, receives its phone bill at the end of January for $230 for January calls. The bill has not been paid to date.

o. Spina Company receives and pays in January a $2,100 invoice from a consulting firm for services received in January.

p. Felicetti's Taxi Company pays a $600 invoice from a consulting firm for services received and recorded in Accounts Payable in December.

Required:

For each of the January transactions,

1. Indicate the account titles that are affected and the type of each account (A for asset, L for liability, SE for shareholders' equity, and E for expense).

2. If an expense is to be recognized in January, indicate the amount. If an expense is not to be recognized in January, indicate why.

Use the following headings in structuring your solution:

Event or Transaction	Accounts Affected and Type of Account	Amount of Expense Incurred in January OR Why an Expense Is Not Recognized

E3–6 Identifying Revenues and Expenses

LO2, 3, 5

Bob's Bowling Inc. operates several bowling centres for games and equipment sales. The transactions on the following page occurred in July 2011.

Required:

1. For each transaction, indicate in the appropriate column the account titles that are affected and the type of account (A for asset, L for liability, R for revenue, and E for expense), and the amount of cash received or paid.

2. If a revenue or expense is to be recognized in July, indicate the amount. If a revenue or expense is not to be recognized in July, indicate why.

3. Explain why the difference between revenues and expenses is not equal to the net cash flow during July 2011.

Activity	Accounts Affected and Type of Account	Cash Received (Paid) in July	Amount of Revenue Earned or Expense Incurred in July OR Why a Revenue or an Expense Is Not Recognized
(a) Bob's collected $10,000 from customers for games played in July.			
(b) Bob's sold bowling equipment inventory for $5,000; received $3,000 in cash and the rest on account; cost of sales is $2,800.			
(c) Bob's received $1,000 from customers on account who purchased merchandise in June.			
(d) The bowling leagues gave Bob's a deposit of $1,500 for the upcoming fall season.			
(e) Bob's paid $2,000 for the June electricity bill and received the July bill for $2,200, which will be paid in August.			
(f) Bob's paid $4,000 to employees for work in July.			
(g) Bob's purchased and paid for $1,200 in insurance for coverage from July 1 to October 1.			
(h) Bob's paid $1,000 to plumbers for repairing a broken pipe in the restrooms.			
Totals			

LO3

E3–7 **Timing of Revenue Recognition**

Modern Equipment Corp. manufactures special-purpose machines for use in the mining industry. In late April, the company received an order from Kross Mining Company (KMC) for a special-purpose machine to be delivered in two months. The specific events related to the production of this machine are shown below.

April 29   KMC placed an order for a special-purpose machine to be manufactured and delivered in two months.
May 3   Raw materials and components are ordered so that the machine can be manufactured.
May 4   Received written confirmation of the order from KMC.
May 12   Manufacture of the machine is completed.
May 13   The machine is shipped to KMC.
May 14   KMC received the machine.
May 15   Received written confirmation that the machine was delivered to KMC.
May 16   An invoice was sent to KMC.
June 16   KMC receives free after-sales service for the machine.
June 19   A cheque received from KMC in full payment.
June 25   The cheque is cleared by the bank.

Required:
When should Modern Equipment Corp. recognize revenue from the sale of the machine? Explain.

LO4 **E3–8** **Determining the Financial Statement Effects of Operating Activities**

Bob's Bowling Inc. operates several bowling centres (for games and equipment sales). For each of the following transactions, complete the tabulation, indicating the amount and effect (+ for increase and − for decrease) of each transaction. (Remember that A = L + SE, R − E = P, and P affects SE through retained earnings.) Write NE if there is no effect. The first transaction is provided as an example.

	Statement of Financial Position			Income Statement		
Transaction	Assets	Liabilities	Shareholders' Equity	Revenues	Expenses	Profit
a. Bob's collected $10,000 from customers for games played in July.	+10,000	NE	+10,000	+10,000	NE	+10,000
b. Bob's sold $5,000 in bowling equipment inventory; received $3,000 in cash and the rest on account; cost of sales is $2,800.						
c. Bob's received $1,000 from customers on account who purchased merchandise in June.						
d. The bowling leagues gave Bob's a deposit of $1,500 for the upcoming fall season.						
e. Bob's paid $2,000 for the June electricity bill and received the July bill for $2,200 to be paid in August.						
f. Bob's paid $4,000 to employees for work in July.						
g. Bob's purchased $1,200 in insurance for coverage from July 1 to October 1.						
h. Bob's paid $1,000 to plumbers for repairing a broken pipe in the restrooms.						

E3–9 Preparing an Income Statement ▓ LO4

Refer to the transactions in E3–8 (including the example) and prepare an income statement for Bob's Bowling Inc. for the month of July 2011. Use an income tax rate of 40 percent.

E3–10 Determining Financial Statement Effects of Various Transactions ▓ LO4

The following transactions occurred during a recent year:

a. Issued shares to organizers for cash (example).

b. Borrowed cash from the local bank.

c. Purchased equipment on credit.

d. Earned revenue; collected cash.

e. Incurred expenses, on credit.

f. Earned revenue, on credit.

g. Paid cash on account.

h. Incurred expenses; paid cash.

i. Earned revenue; collected three-fourths in cash and the rest on credit.

j. Experienced theft of $100 cash.

k. Declared and paid cash dividends.

l. Collected cash from customers on account.

m. Incurred expenses; paid four-fifths in cash and the rest on credit.

n. Paid income tax expense for the period.

Required:

Complete the tabulation below for each of the transactions, indicating the effect (+ for increase and − for decrease) of each transaction. (Remember that A = L + SE, R − E = P, and P affects SE through retained earnings.) Write NE if there is no effect. The first transaction is provided as an example.

	Statement of Financial Position			Income Statement		
Transaction	Assets	Liabilities	Shareholders' Equity	Revenues	Expenses	Profit
(a) (example)	+	NE	+	NE	NE	NE

E3–11 Determining Financial Statement Effects of Various Transactions ▓ LO4

Nokia Corporation designs, develops, manufactures, markets, and sells a wide range of telecommunications software and hardware, including cell phones. Nokia also offers network security, peripherals, and service and support programs. The following transactions occurred during a recent year. Euros are in millions.

Nokia Corporation

a. Issued €53 in shares to investors (example).

b. Purchased on account €30,563 of additional inventory of raw materials used in assembling its mobile telecommunication devices.

c. Paid €34 on long-term notes.

    d. Sold €50,710 of products to customers on account; the cost of the products sold was € 33,337.

    e. Declared and paid cash dividends of €2,048.

    f. Purchased €889 of additional property, plant, and equipment for cash.

    g. Incurred €4,380 in selling expenses with two-thirds paid in cash and the rest on account.

    h. Earned €353 interest on investments; received 90 percent in cash.

    i. Incurred €185 in interest expense (not yet paid).

Required:
Complete the tabulation below for each of the transactions, indicating the effect (+ for increase and − for decrease) of each transaction. (Remember that A = L + SE, R − E = P, and P affects SE through retained earnings.) Write NE if there is no effect. The first transaction is provided as an example.

Statement of Financial Position				Income Statement		
Transaction	Assets	Liabilities	Shareholders' Equity	Revenues	Expenses	Profit
(a) (example)	+53	NE	+53	NE	NE	NE

LO4

Sysco

E3–12 **Recording Journal Entries**
Sysco, formed in 1969, is the largest U.S. marketer and distributor of food service products, serving nearly 250,000 restaurants, hotels, schools, hospitals, and other institutions. The following summarized transactions are typical of those that occurred in a recent year:

    a. Borrowed $80 million from a bank, signing a short-term note.

    b. Provided $37.5 billion in service to customers during the year, with $32.4 billion on account and the rest received in cash.

    c. Purchased plant and equipment for $515.9 million in cash.

    d. Purchased $29.2 billion inventory on account.

    e. Paid $2.3 billion in salaries during the year.

    f. Received $36.4 billion on account paid by customers.

    g. Purchased and used fuel of $637 million in delivery vehicles during the year (paid for in cash).

    h. Declared and paid $497.4 million in dividends for the year.

    i. Paid $26.2 billion cash on trade payables.

    j. Incurred $47 million in utility usage during the year; paid $30 million in cash and the rest on account.

Required:
Prepare a journal entry to record each of the transactions. Determine whether the accounting equation remains in balance and debits equal credits after each entry.

LO4

Research In Motion

E3–13 **Recording Journal Entries**
Research In Motion (RIM) designs, manufactures, and markets wireless devices to meet the communication needs of its global market. The company sells its BlackBerry products to customers in 60 countries around the world. RIM also provides communications servers to customers who need secure internal wireless communications. The following hypothetical December transactions are typical of those that occur each month (in thousands of dollars):

    a. Borrowed $600 from the bank on December 1 with a six-month note at 8 percent annual interest to finance its operations. The principal and interest are due on the maturity date.

    b. Purchased legal software for corporate use for $30 cash on December 1. The software's useful life is estimated at two years with zero residual value.

    c. Purchased and received $10,000 of raw materials for use in assembling its wireless products.

    d. Incurred $2,200 in routine selling expenses for BlackBerry.

    e. Closed a contract of $8,400 to be filled in January and received cash in full payment.

    f. Sold products in December for $100,000 in cash.

g. Sold products on account in December for $87,000.

h. Received a $2,000 deposit from a customer in Mexico for delivery of wireless products in January.

i. Paid half of the amount of the transaction in (c).

j. Received $60,000 on account from the customers in (g).

k. Paid $15,000 in wages to manufacturing employees for the month of December.

Required:

1. Prepare a journal entry to record each transaction. (Remember to check that debits equal credits and that the accounting equation is in balance after each transaction.)
2. Show the effects (direction and amount) of each transaction on profit and cash.
3. Assume that RIM had a $12,000 balance in trade receivables at the beginning of the year. Determine the ending balance in the trade receivables account. Show your work in T-account format.

E3–14 Recording Journal Entries   ▥ **LO4**

Rowland & Sons Air Transport Service Inc. has been in operation for three years. The following transactions occurred in February:

February 1   Paid $1,900 for rent of hangar space in February.
   2   Purchased fuel costing $450 on account for the next flight to Winnipeg.
   4   Received customer payment of $950 to ship several items to Montreal next month.
   7   Flew cargo from Ottawa to Edmonton; the customer paid $1,240 for the air transport.
   10   Paid pilot $4,000 in wages for flying in January.
   14   Paid $600 for an advertisement in the local paper, to run on February 19.
   18   Flew cargo for two customers from Regina to Calgary for $1,800; one customer paid $500 cash and the other asked to be billed.
   25   Purchased spare parts for the planes costing $1,350 on account.
   27   Declared a $1,300 cash dividend to be paid in March.

Required:

1. Prepare a journal entry to record each transaction. Be sure to categorize each account as an asset (A), liability (L), shareholders' equity (SE), revenue (R), or expense (E).
2. Show the effects (direction and amount) of each transaction on profit and cash.

E3–15 Analyzing the Effects of Transactions in T-Accounts, and Computing Cash Basis versus Accrual Basis Profit   ▥ **LO3, 4, 5, 6**

Sbrocchi's Piano Rebuilding Company has been operating for one year (2010). At the start of 2011, its income statement accounts had zero balances and the account balances on its statement of financial position were as follows:

Cash	$10,000	Trade payables	$16,000
Trade receivables	50,000	Deferred revenue (deposits)	6,400
Supplies	2,400	Note payable (due in three years)	80,000
Equipment	16,000	Share capital	16,000
Land	12,000	Retained earnings	36,000
Building	64,000		

Required:

1. Create T-accounts for the accounts reported on the statement of financial position and for these additional accounts: rebuilding fees revenue, rent revenue, wages expense, and utilities expense. Enter the beginning balances.
2. Enter the following January 2011 transactions in the T-accounts, using the letter of each transaction as the reference:
    a. Received a $500 deposit from a customer who wanted her piano rebuilt.
    b. Rented a part of the building to a bicycle repair shop; received $500 for rent in January.
    c. Delivered 10 rebuilt pianos to customers who paid $16,000 in cash.

    d. Received $8,000 from customers as payment on their accounts.

    e. Received an electric and gas utility bill for $420 to be paid in February.

    f. Ordered $800 in supplies.

    g. Paid $1,900 on account to suppliers.

    h. Received from the home of Ms. Sbrocchi, the major shareholder, an $850 tool (equipment) to use in the business.

    i. Paid $8,500 in wages to employees for work in January.

    j. Declared and paid a cash dividend of $3,000.

    k. Received and paid for the supplies ordered in (*f*).

3. Using the data from the T-accounts, calculate the amounts for the following on January 31, 2011:
   Revenues, $_____ − Expenses, $_____ = Profit, $_____
   Assets, $_____ = Liabilities, $_____ + Shareholders' Equity, $_____

4. Calculate the company's profit for January by using the cash basis of accounting. Why does this differ from the accrual basis profit in (3) above?

5. Calculate the return on assets ratio for January 2011. If the company had a return on assets ratio of 11 percent in December 2010 and 10 percent in November 2010, what does your computation suggest to you about Sbrocchi's Piano Rebuilding Company? What would you state in your report?

LO4

E3–16   **Analyzing the Effects of Transactions on the Statement of Cash Flows**
Refer to E3–15.

Required:
Use the following chart to identify whether each of the transactions in E3–15 results in a cash flow effect from operating (O), investing (I), or financing (F) activities, and indicate the direction and the effect on cash (+ for increase and − for decrease). If there is no cash flow effect, write "none." The first transaction is provided as an example.

Transaction	Operating, Investing, or Financing Effect	Direction and Amount of the Effect
(*a*)	O	+500

LO4

E3–17   **Preparing an Income Statement and a Partial Statement of Cash Flows**
Refer to E3–15.

Required:
1. Use the ending balances in the T-accounts in E3–15 to prepare the following:
   a. An income statement for January 2011, in good form.
   b. The operating activities section of the statement of cash flows for January 2011, in good form.
2. Explain the difference between the profit and the cash flow from operating activities computed in (1).

LO4

E3–18   **Analyzing the Effects of Transactions in T-Accounts**
Karen Gorewit and Pat Nally had been operating a catering business, Travelling Gourmet, for several years. In March 2012, the partners were planning to expand by opening a retail sales shop and decided to form the business as a corporation called Travelling Gourmet Inc. The following transactions occurred in March 2012:

a. Received $10,000 cash from each of the two shareholders to form the corporation, in addition to $2,000 in trade receivables, $5,300 in equipment, a van (equipment) appraised at a fair market value of $14,500, and $1,200 in supplies.

b. Purchased a vacant store in a good location for $60,000 with a $12,000 cash down payment and a mortgage from a local bank for the remainder.

c. Borrowed $25,000 from the local bank on a 10 percent, one-year note.

d. Purchased for cash, and used food and paper products costing $8,830.

e. Made and sold food at the retail store for $10,900 in cash.

f. Catered four parties in March for $3,200; $2,000 was billed, and the rest was received in cash.

g. Received a $320 telephone bill for March to be paid in April.

h. Paid $314 for gas to use the van in March.

i. Paid $5,080 for wages of employees who worked in March.

j. Paid a $300 dividend from the corporation to each owner.

k. Paid $15,000 to purchase equipment (refrigerated display cases, cabinets, tables, and chairs), and $9,870 to renovate and decorate the new store (added to the cost of the building).

Required:

1. Set up appropriate T-accounts for cash, trade receivables, supplies, equipment, building, trade payables, note payable, mortgage payable, share capital, retained earnings, food sales revenue, catering sales revenue, cost of food and paper products, utilities expense, wages expense, and gasoline expense.
2. Record in the T-accounts the effects of each transaction for Travelling Gourmet Inc., in March. Identify the amounts with the letters, starting with (*a*).
3. Show the effects (direction and amount) of each transaction on profit and cash.

E3–19 Analyzing the Effects of Transactions on the Statement of Cash Flows   **LO4**
Refer to E3–18.

Required:
Use the following chart to identify whether each of the transactions in E3–18 results in a cash flow effect from operating (O), investing (I), or financing (F) activities, and indicate the direction and the effect on cash (+ for increase and − for decrease). If there is no cash flow effect, write "none." The first transaction is provided as an example.

Transaction	Operating, Investing, or Financing Effect	Direction and Amount of the Effect
(*a*)	F	+20,000

E3–20 Preparing an Income Statement and a Partial Statement of Cash Flows   **LO4**
Refer to E3–18.

Required:

1. Use the ending balances in the T-accounts in E3–18 to prepare the following:
   a. An income statement for March 2012, in good form.
   b. The operating activities section of the statement of cash flows for March 2012, in good form.
2. Explain the difference between the profit and the cash flow from operating activities computed in (1).

E3–21 Inferring Operating Transactions and Preparing an Income Statement and a Statement of   **LO2, 3, 4**
Financial Position
Kiernan Kite Company (a corporation) sells and repairs kites from manufacturers around the world. Its stores are located in rented space in malls and shopping centres. During its first month of operations ended April 30, 2012, Kiernan Kite Company completed eight transactions with the dollar effects indicated in the following schedule:

Accounts	Dollar Effect of Each of the Eight Transactions								Ending Balance
	(*a*)	(*b*)	(*c*)	(*d*)	(*e*)	(*f*)	(*g*)	(*h*)	
Cash	$50,000	$(10,000)	$(5,000)	$ 7,000	$(2,000)	$(1,000)		$3,000	
Trade receivables				3,000					
Inventory			20,000	(3,000)					
Prepayments					1,500				
Store fixtures		10,000							
Trade payables			15,000				1,200		
Deferred revenue								2,000	
Share capital	50,000								
Sales revenue				10,000				1,000	
Cost of sales				3,000					
Wages expense						1,000			
Rent expense					500				
Utilities expense							1,200		

Required:

1. Write a brief explanation of transactions (*a*) through (*h*). Explain any assumptions that you made.
2. Compute the ending balance in each account and prepare an income statement for the company for April 2012 and a classified statement of financial position as at April 30, 2012.

LO6

E3–22   **Computing and Explaining the Total Asset Turnover Ratio**

The following data are from annual reports of Justin's Jewellery Company:

	2011	2010	2009
Total assets	$ 60,000	$ 50,000	$ 40,000
Total liabilities	12,000	10,000	5,000
Total shareholders' equity	48,000	40,000	35,000
Sales	154,000	144,000	130,000
Profit	5,000	3,800	25,000

Compute Justin's total asset turnover ratio and its return on assets for 2010 and 2011. What do these results suggest to you about Justin's Jewellery Company?

LO4, 6

E3–23   **Analyzing the Effects of Transactions by Using T-Accounts and Interpreting the Total Asset Turnover Ratio as a Financial Analyst**

Internet Marketing Inc. (IMI), which has been operating for three years, provides marketing consulting services worldwide for dot-com companies. You are a financial analyst assigned to report on the effectiveness of IMI's management team at managing its assets. At the start of 2011 (its fourth year), IMI's T-account balances were as follows. Dollars are in thousands.

ASSETS

Cash		Trade Receivables		Long-Term Investments	
3,000		10,000		8,000	

LIABILITIES

Trade Payables		Deferred Revenue		Long-Term Borrowings	
	3,000		6,000		2,000

SHAREHOLDERS' EQUITY

Share Capital		Retained Earnings	
	6,000		4,000

REVENUES

Consulting Fee Revenue		Investment Income	

EXPENSES

Wages Expense		Travel Expense		Utilities Expense	

Rent Expense	

Required:

1. Using the data from these T-accounts, complete the accounting equation on January 1, 2011.
   Assets, $_____ = Liabilities, $_____ + Shareholders' Equity, $_____

2. Enter the following 2011 transactions in the T-accounts:
   a. Received $7,700 cash from clients on account.
   b. Provided $70,000 in services to clients; received $50,000 in cash and the rest on account.
   c. Received $500 in income on investments.
   d. Paid $20,000 in wages, $21,800 in travel, $12,000 rent, and $2,000 on trade payables.
   e. Received a utility bill for $1,300 for the current month.
   f. Paid $600 in dividends to shareholders.
   g. Received $2,000 in cash from clients in advance of services that IMI will provide next year.

3. Compute ending balances in the T-accounts to determine the missing amounts on December 31, 2011:
   Revenues, $_____ − Expenses, $_____ = Profit, $_____
   Assets, $_____ = Liabilities, $_____ + Shareholders' Equity, $_____

4. Calculate the total asset turnover ratio for 2011. If the company had an asset turnover ratio of 2.00 in 2010 and of 1.80 in 2009, what does your computation suggest to you about IMI? What would you state in your report?

E3–24 Inferring Transactions and Computing Effects by Using T-Accounts   LO4

A recent annual report of a leading business and financial news company included the following accounts. Dollars are in millions.

Trade Receivables			Prepayments			Deferred Revenue		
1/1	313		1/1	25			240	1/1
	2,573	?		43	?	?	328	
12/31	295		12/31	26			253	

Required:

1. Describe the typical transactions that affect each T-account (i.e., the economic events that occur to make these accounts increase and decrease).

2. Compute the missing amounts for each T-account.

E3–25 Computing and Interpreting the Total Asset Turnover Ratio and the Return on Assets Ratio   LO6

Bianca Corp. and Uzma Inc. operate in the same industry. The companies' total assets, revenue, and profit for the years 2010–2013 are provided below. All amounts are in thousands of dollars.

Bianca Corp.	2013	2012	2011	2010
Total assets	$ 40,000	$ 50,000	$ 60,000	$ 65,000
Revenue	130,000	144,000	154,000	150,000
Profit	25,000	3,800	5,000	4,800
Interest expense, net of tax	1,000	800	700	800
Uzma Inc.				
Total assets	$ 65,000	$ 60,000	$ 50,000	$ 40,000
Revenue	150,000	154,000	144,000	130,000
Profit	4,800	5,000	3,800	25,000
Interest expense, net of tax	400	500	400	300

Required:

1. Compute the total asset turnover ratio and the return on assets ratio for each company for each of the years 2011, 2012, and 2013.

2. Based on the two sets of ratios that you computed, which company was more efficient in managing its assets during the 2010–2013 period? Explain.

PROBLEMS

LO4

P3–1   **Recording Non-quantitative Journal Entries** (AP3–1)

The following list includes a series of accounts for Heiss Corporation, which has been operating for three years. These accounts are listed and numbered for identification, and followed by a series of transactions. For each transaction, indicate the account(s) that should be debited and credited by entering the appropriate account number(s) to the right of each transaction. If no journal entry is needed, use number 16. The first transaction is used as an example.

Account No.	Account Title	Account No.	Account Title
1	Cash	9	Wages payable
2	Trade receivables	10	Income taxes payable
3	Supplies inventory on hand	11	Share capital
4	Prepayments	12	Retained earnings
5	Equipment	13	Service revenue
6	Patents	14	Operating expenses
7	Trade payables	15	Income tax expense
8	Short-term borrowings	16	None of the above

	Transactions	Debit	Credit
a.	Example: Purchased equipment for use in the business; paid one-third cash and signed a short-term note payable for the balance.	5	1,8
b.	Issued shares to new investors.		
c.	Paid cash for salaries and wages earned this period.		
d.	Collected cash for services performed this period.		
e.	Collected cash on trade receivables for services previously performed.		
f.	Performed services this period on credit.		
g.	Paid operating expenses incurred this period.		
h.	Paid cash on trade payables for expenses previously incurred.		
i.	Incurred operating expenses this period to be paid next period.		
j.	Purchased supplies inventory to be used later; paid cash.		
k.	Used some of the supplies inventory for operations.		
l.	Purchased a patent (an intangible asset); paid cash.		
m.	Made a payment on the equipment note in (a); the payment was part principal and part interest expense.		
n.	Paid three-fourths of the income tax expense for the year; the balance will be paid next year.		
o.	On the last day of the current period, paid cash for an insurance policy covering the next year.		

LO4

P3–2   **Recording Journal Entries** (AP3–2)

Chad Polovick organized a new company, CollegeCaps Inc. The company operates a small store in an area mall and specializes in baseball-type caps with logos printed on them. Chad, who is never without a cap, believes that his target market is college students. You have been hired to record the transactions occurring in the first two weeks of operations.

May 1   Issued 1,000 shares for $35 per share.

May 1   Borrowed $40,000 from the bank to provide additional funding to begin operations. The interest rate is 10 percent annually; principal and interest are due in 24 months.

May 1   Paid $1,200 for the current month's rent and another $1,200 for next month's rent.

May 1   Paid $1,800 for a one-year fire insurance policy (recorded as a prepaid expense).

May 3   Purchased furniture and fixtures for the store for $18,000 on account. The amount is due within 30 days.

May 4   Purchased a supply of University of Waterloo, York University, and Saint Mary's University baseball caps for the store for $2,100 cash.

May 5   Placed advertisements in local college newspapers for a total of $360 cash.

May 9   Sold caps totalling $500, half of which was charged on account. The cost of the caps sold was $250.

May 10 Made full payment for the furniture and fixtures purchased on account on May 3.

May 14 Received $100 from a customer on account.

Required:

1. Prepare a journal entry to record each of the transactions. Be sure to categorize each account as an asset (A), liability (L), shareholders' equity (SE), revenue (R), or expense (E).

2. Complete the tabulation below for each of the transactions, indicating the effect (+ for increase and − for decrease) of each transaction. Write NE if there is no effect. The first transaction is provided as an example. (Remember that A = L + SE, R − E = P, and P affects SE through retained earnings.)

	Statement of Financial Position			Income Statement		
	Assets	Liabilities	Shareholders' Equity	Revenues	Expenses	Profit
May 1	+$35,000	NE	+$35,000	NE	NE	NE

P3–3 **Analyzing the Effects of Transactions by Using T-Accounts, Preparing an Income Statement, Evaluating the Total Asset Turnover Ratio and the Return on Assets as a Manager** (AP3–3)

■ **LO4, 5**

*e**X**cel*

Paula Abboud, a connoisseur of fine chocolate, opened Paula's Passions Inc. in Collegetown on February 1, 2011. The shop specializes in a selection of gourmet chocolate candies and a line of gourmet ice cream. You have been hired as manager. Your duties include maintaining the store's financial records. The following transactions occurred in February 2011, the first month of operations:

a. Received contributions of $15,000 in total from four shareholders to form the corporation.

b. Paid store rent for three months at $800 per month (recorded as prepayment).

c. Purchased supplies for $400 cash.

d. Purchased on account and received candy for $5,000, due in 60 days.

e. Obtained a $10,000 loan at the bank and signed a note at 12 percent annual interest. The principal and interest are due in a lump sum in two years.

f. Used the money from (e) to purchase a computer for $2,000 (for recordkeeping and inventory tracking). The rest was used to buy furniture and fixtures for the store.

g. Placed a grand-opening advertisement in the local paper for $425 cash.

h. Made sales on Valentine's Day totalling $1,800; $1,525 was in cash and the rest on accounts. The cost of the candy sold was $1,000.

i. Made a $500 payment on trade payables.

j. Incurred and paid employee wages of $510.

k. Collected trade receivables of $50 from customers.

l. Made a repair on one of the display cases for $134 cash.

m. Made cash sales of $2,600 during the rest of the month. The cost of the goods sold was $1,400.

n. Incurred interest expense of $400, payable in the future.

Required:

1. Set up appropriate T-accounts for cash, trade receivables, supplies, merchandise inventory, prepaid rent, equipment, furniture and fixtures, trade payables, notes payable, interest payable, share capital, sales revenue, cost of sales, advertising expense, wages expense, repair expense, and interest expense. All accounts begin with zero balances.

2. Record in the T-accounts the effects of each transaction for Paula's Passions in February, referencing each transaction in the accounts with the transaction letter. Show the ending balances in the T-accounts.

3. Prepare an income statement for February 2011.

4. Write a short memo to Paula offering your opinion on the results of operations during the first month of business.

5. After three years in business, you are being evaluated for a promotion. One measure is how efficiently you managed the assets of the business. The following data are available:

	2013*	2012	2011
Total assets	$80,000	$45,000	$35,000
Total liabilities	45,000	20,000	15,000
Total shareholders' equity	35,000	25,000	20,000
Total sales	85,000	75,000	50,000
Profit	20,000	10,000	4,000

*At the end of 2013, Paula decided to open a second store, requiring loans and inventory purchases prior to the opening in early 2014.

Compute the total asset turnover ratio and the return on assets for 2012 and 2013 and evaluate the results. Do you think you should be promoted? Why? The company is subject to an income tax rate of 30 percent.

LO4

P3–4 **Analyzing the Effects of Transactions on the Statement of Cash Flows** (AP3–4)
Refer to P3–3.

Required:
Use the following chart to identify whether each of the transactions in P3–3 results in a cash flow effect from operating (O), investing (I), or financing (F) activities, and indicate the direction and the effect on cash (+ for increase and − for decrease). If there is no cash flow effect, write "none." The first transaction is provided as an example.

Transaction	Operating, Investing, or Financing Effect	Direction and Amount of the Effect
(a)	F	+15,000

LO4, 5

Canada Post

eXcel

P3–5 **Analyzing the Effects of Transactions by Using T-Accounts, Preparing Financial Statements, and Evaluating the Total Asset Turnover and Return on Assets Ratios** (AP3–5)
The following are several December 31, 2008, account balances (in millions of dollars) from a recent annual report of Canada Post Corporation, followed by several typical transactions. The corporation's vision is described in the annual report as follows:

Canada Post will be a world leader in providing innovative physical and electronic delivery solutions, creating value for our customers, employees, and all Canadians.

Account	Balance	Account	Balance
Non-current assets	$2,034	Equity of Canada	$1,533
Trade payables	469	Receivables	582
Prepayments	71	Other non-current assets	1,334
Accrued liabilities	509	Cash	605
Long-term borrowings	74	Investments (long-term)	965
Deferred revenues	203	Other non-current liabilities	2,803

These accounts have normal debit or credit balances, but are not necessarily in good order. The following hypothetical transactions (in millions of dollars) occurred the next month (from January 1, 2009, to January 31, 2009):

a. Provided delivery service to customers, receiving $720 in trade receivables and $60 in cash.

b. Purchased new equipment costing $816; signed a long-term note.

c. Paid $74 cash to rent equipment, with $64 for rental this month and the rest for rent for the first few days in February.

d. Spent $396 cash to maintain and repair facilities and equipment during the month.

e. Collected $652 from customers on account.

f. Borrowed $90 by signing a long-term note.

g. Paid employees $380 during the month.

h. Purchased for cash and used $49 in supplies.

i. Paid $184 on trade payable.

j. Ordered $72 in spare parts and supplies.

Required:

1. Set up T-accounts for the preceding list and enter the respective balances. (You will need additional T-accounts for income statement accounts.)

2. For each transaction, record the effects in the T-accounts. Label each by using the letter of the transaction. Compute ending balances.

3. Show the effects (direction and amount) of each transaction on profit and cash.

4. Prepare in good form an income statement for January 2009.

5. Prepare in good form a classified statement of financial position as at January 31, 2009.

6. Prepare the operating activities section of the statement of cash flows for January 2009, and explain the difference between the cash flow from operating activities and the profit computed in (4).

7. Compute the company's total asset turnover ratio and its return on assets ratio. What do these ratios suggest to you about Canada Post? Assume that the long-term note of $90 was signed on January 31, and that interest has not accrued yet.

P3–6 Determining and Interpreting the Effects of Transactions on Income Statement Categories and Return on Assets (AP3–6)

█ **LO4, 6**

Apple Computer

Apple Computer popularized both the personal computer and the easy-to-use graphic interface. Today it competes against many companies that rely on Intel microprocessors and the Windows operating system. The company's income statement for a recent year is presented below (in millions of U.S. dollars).

Net sales	$13,931
Cost of sales	9,888
Gross margin	4,043
Operating expenses:	
Research and development	534
Selling, general, and administrative	1,859
Total operating expenses	2,393
Operating income	1,650
Other income and expense:	
Interest and other income, net	165
Profit before provision for income taxes	1,815
Provision for income taxes	480
Profit	$ 1,335

Required:

Assume that the following hypothetical *additional* transactions occurred during the fiscal year. Complete the following tabulation, indicating the sign of the effect of each additional transaction (+ for increase, − for decrease, and NE for no effect). Consider each item independently and ignore income taxes.

a. Recorded sales on account of $700 and related cost of goods sold of $475.

b. Incurred additional research and development expense of $100, which was paid in cash.

c. Issued additional common shares for $350 cash.

d. Declared and paid dividends of $90.

Transaction	Gross Profit	Operating Profit (Loss)	Return on Assets
a.			
b.			
c.			
d.			

■ **LO5, 6**

Barrick Gold
West Jet Airlines
Le Groupe Jean
Coutu

P3–7 **Computing and Analyzing the Total Asset Turnover Ratio and the Return on Assets Ratio** (AP3–7)

A summary of selected historical results is presented below for three Canadian companies: Barrick Gold, WestJet Airlines, and Le Groupe Jean Coutu. Each of these companies has grown in size over time by acquiring assets and investing in other companies. (Amounts are in millions of dollars.)

	2008	2007	2006	2005	2004	2003
Barrick Gold						
Total assets	$24,161	$21,951	$21,373	$6,862	$6,287	$5,358
Total revenue	7,913	6,332	5,630	2,350	1,932	2,035
Profit	785	1,119	1,506	401	248	200
Interest expense, net of tax	16	85	95	5	14	14
Operating cash flow	2,206	1,732	2,122	726	509	519
WestJet Airlines						
Total assets	3,279	2,984	2,727	2,213	1,877	1,477
Total revenue	2,549	2,127	1,774	1,393	1,058	864
Profit (loss)	178	193	115	24	(17)	61
Interest expense, net of tax	53	57	49	39	33	18
Operating cash flow	461	541	336	247	144	192
Le Groupe Jean Coutu						
Total assets	1,949	2,337	5,591	5,695	1,344	1,723
Total revenue	1,676	13,265	11,143	9,617	3,043	4,052
Profit (loss)	(251)	163	104	104	133	164
Interest expense, net of tax	4	195	143	113	11	15
Operating cash flow	146	192	165	222	186	214

Required:

1. Complete the following table by computing the total asset turnover ratio and the return on assets ratio for each company for each of the years 2007 and 2008.

	2008	2007	2006	2005	2004
Barrick Gold					
Total asset turnover ratio			0.40	0.36	0.33
Return on assets (ROA)			0.113	0.062	0.045
WestJet Airlines					
Total asset turnover ratio			0.72	0.68	0.63
Return on assets (ROA)			0.066	0.031	0.01
Le Groupe Jean Coutu					
Total asset turnover ratio			1.98	2.73	1.98
Return on assets (ROA)			0.044	0.062	0.094

2. Based on the computed ratios, rank these companies from most successful to least successful in implementing their growth strategies and effectively utilizing their assets.

3. Which of these three companies appears to be in the best position at the end of 2008 to pay off its short-term liabilities? What additional information would help you provide a more definite answer to this requirement? Explain.

■ **LO4, 6**

Cedar Fair

P3–8 **Recording Journal Entries and Identifying Effects on the Total Assets Turnover Ratio**

Cedar Fair, L. P. (Limited Partnership), is one of the largest amusement park operators in the world, owning 11 amusement parks, five outdoor water parks, and one indoor water park. Parks in the United States include Cedar Point in Ohio; Valleyfair near Minneapolis/St. Paul; Dorney Park and Wildwater Kingdom near Allentown, Pennsylvania; Worlds of Fun/Oceans of Fun in Kansas

City; and Great America in Santa Clara, California. It also operates Canada's Wonderland, near Toronto. The following are summarized transactions similar to those that occurred in a recent year (amounts in thousands of dollars):

a. Guests at the parks paid $566,266 cash in admissions.

b. The primary operating expenses (such as employee wages, utilities, and repairs and maintenance) for the year were $418,550, with $398,574 paid in cash and the rest on account.

c. Interest paid on long-term borrowings was $129,561.

d. The parks sell food and merchandise and operate games. The cash received during the year for these combined activities was $355,917.

e. The cost of products sold during the year was $90,626.

f. Cedar Fair purchased and built additional buildings, rides, and equipment during the year, paying $83,481 in cash.

g. The most significant assets for the company are land, buildings, rides, and equipment. Therefore, a large expense for Cedar Fair is depreciation expense (related to the using of these assets to generate revenues during the year). The amount for the year was $124,500 (credit accumulated depreciation).

h. Guests may stay at accommodations owned by the company at the parks. During the year, accommodations revenue was $74,049; $73,612 was paid by the guests in cash and the rest was on account.

i. Cedar Fair paid $17,450 on notes payable.

j. The company purchased $92,326 in food and merchandise inventory for the year, paying $90,538 in cash and the rest on account.

k. The selling, general, and administrative expenses (such as the president's salary and advertising for the parks, those not classified as operating expenses) for the year were $131,882; $130,539 was paid in cash and the rest was on account.

l. Cedar Fair paid $6,452 on trade payables during the year.

Required:

1. Prepare a journal entry to record each of these transactions. Use the letter of each transaction as its reference.

2. Show the effects (direction and amount) of each transaction on profit and cash.

3. Indicate the direction of the effect (increase, decrease, or no effect) of each of the transactions *(a)* through *(l)* on the total asset turnover ratio, and provide an explanation for your answer. Cedar Fair's total asset turnover ratio was 0.56 in the previous year. For example, transaction *(a)* increases the ratio. Both sales and total assets would increase. Since the ratio is less than 1.0, the increase in sales (the numerator) is proportionally higher than the increase in total assets (the denominator).

P3–9 **Analyzing the Effects of Transactions on the Statement of Cash Flows**   ▓ **LO6**

Refer to P3–8, and use the following chart to identify whether each transaction in P3–8 results in a cash flow effect from operating (O), investing (I), or financing (F) activities, and indicate the direction and amount of the effect on cash (+ for increase and − for decrease). If there is no cash flow effect, write "none." The first transaction is provided as an example.

Transaction	Operating, Investing, or Financing Effect	Direction and Amount of the Effect
(a)	O	+566,266

ALTERNATE PROBLEMS

LO4   **AP3–1**   **Recording Non-quantitative Journal Entries** (P3–1)

The following is a series of accounts for Ortiz & Ortiz Incorporated, which has been operating for two years. The accounts are listed and numbered for identification, followed by a series of transactions. For each transaction, indicate the account(s) that should be debited and credited by entering the appropriate account number(s) to the right of each transaction. If no journal entry is needed, write "none" after the transaction. The first transaction is given as an example.

Account No.	Account Title	Account No.	Account Title
1	Cash	9	Wages payable
2	Trade receivables	10	Income taxes payable
3	Supplies inventory	11	Share capital
4	Prepayments	12	Retained earnings
5	Buildings	13	Service revenue
6	Land	14	Operating expenses
7	Trade and other payables	15	Income tax expense
8	Mortgage payable			

Transactions	Debit	Credit
a. Example: Issued shares to new investors.	1	11
b. Performed services this period on credit.		
c. Purchased (but did not use) supplies this period on credit.		
d. Prepaid a fire insurance policy this period to cover the next 12 months.		
e. Purchased a building this period with a 20 percent cash down payment and a mortgage loan for the balance.		
f. Collected cash this year for services rendered and recorded in the prior year.		
g. Paid cash this period for wages earned and recorded last period.		
h. Paid cash for operating expenses charged on trade payables in the prior period.		
i. Paid cash for operating expenses charged on trade payables in the current period.		
j. Incurred and recorded operating expenses on credit to be paid next period.		
k. Collected cash at the point of sale for services rendered.		
l. Used supplies from inventory to clean the offices.		
m. Recorded income taxes for this period to be paid at the beginning of the next period.		
n. Declared and paid a cash dividend this period.		
o. Made a payment on the building, which was part principal repayment and part interest.		
p. A shareholder sold some shares this period to another person for an amount above the original issuance price.		

LO4   **AP3–2**   **Recording Journal Entries** (P3–2)

Rhonda Bennett is the president of ServicePro Inc., a company that provides temporary employees for not-for-profit companies. ServicePro has been operating for five years; its revenues are increasing with each passing year. You have been hired to help Rhonda in analyzing the following transactions for the first two weeks of April:

April 2 Purchased office supplies for $500 on account.
   3 Received the telephone bill for $245.
   5 Billed United Way $1,950 for temporary services provided.
   8 Paid $250 for supplies purchased and recorded on account last period.
   8 Placed an advertisement in the local paper for $400 cash.
   9 Purchased a new computer for the office costing $2,300 cash.

10 Paid employee wages of $1,200. Of this amount, $200 had been earned and recorded in the prior period.

11 Received $1,000 on account from United Way.

12 Purchased land as the site of a future office for $10,000. Paid $2,000 down and signed a note payable for the balance. The note is due in five years and has an annual interest rate of 10 percent.

13 Issued 2,000 additional shares for $40 per share in anticipation of building a new office.

14 Billed Family & Children's Service $2,000 for services rendered.

Required:

1. Prepare a journal entry to record each of the transactions. Be sure to categorize each account as an asset (A), liability (L), shareholders' equity (SE), revenue (R), or expense (E).

2. Complete the tabulation below for each of the transactions, indicating the effect (+ for increase and − for decrease) of each transaction. Write NE if there is no effect. The first transaction is provided as an example. (Remember that A = L + SE, R − E = P, and P affects SE through retained earnings.)

| | Statement of Financial Position | | | Income Statement | | |
	Assets	Liabilities	Shareholders' Equity	Revenues	Expenses	Profit
April 2	+$500	+$500	NE	NE	NE	NE

AP3–3 Analyzing the Effects of Transactions by Using T-Accounts, Preparing an Income Statement, Evaluating the Total Asset Turnover Ratio and the Return on Assets as a Manager (P3–3)

LO4, 6

Green Stables Inc. was established on April 1, 2011. The company provides stables, care for animals, and grounds for riding and showing horses. You have been hired as the new assistant controller. The following transactions for April 2011 are provided for your review:

a. Received contributions from five investors of $75,000 in cash ($15,000 each), a barn valued at $100,000, and land valued at $75,000. Each investor received 5,000 shares.

b. Built a small barn for $50,000. The company paid half the amount in cash and signed a three-year note payable for the balance on April 1, 2011.

c. Provided animal care services, all on credit, for $15,260.

d. Rented stables to customers who cared for their own animals, and received cash payment of $16,300.

e. Received from a customer $1,800 to board her horse in April, May, and June (record as deferred revenue).

f. Purchased straw (a supply inventory) on account for $4,630.

g. Paid $840 in cash for water utilities expense incurred in the month.

h. Paid $1,700 on trade payables for previous purchases.

i. Received $3,000 from customers on trade receivables.

j. Paid $5,600 in wages to employees who worked during the month.

k. Purchased a one-year insurance policy for $1,800 at the end of the month.

l. Received an electric utility bill for $2,130 for usage in April; the bill will be paid next month.

m. Paid $500 cash dividend to each of the investors at the end of the month.

Required:

1. Set up appropriate T-accounts. All accounts begin with zero balances.

2. Record in the T-accounts the effects of each transaction for Green Stables in April, referencing each transaction in the accounts with the transaction letter. Show the ending balances in the T-accounts.

3. Prepare an income statement at the end of April 2011, as well as a classified statement of financial position as at April 30, 2011.

4. Write a short memo to the five owners, offering your opinion on the results of operations during the first month of business.

5. After three years in business, you are being evaluated for a promotion to chief financial officer. One measure is how efficiently you managed the assets of the business. The following data are available:

	2013*	2012	2011
Total assets	$480,000	$320,000	$300,000
Total liabilities	125,000	28,000	30,000
Total shareholders' equity	355,000	292,000	270,000
Total sales	450,000	400,000	360,000
Profit	50,000	30,000	(10,000)

*At the end of 2012, Green Stables decided to build an indoor riding arena for giving lessons year-round. The company borrowed construction funds from a local bank and the arena was opened in early 2014.

Compute the total asset turnover ratio and the return on assets for 2012 and 2013 and evaluate the results. Do you think you should be promoted? Why? Ignore interest on the long-term note related to (b).

LO4

AP3–4   **Analyzing the Effects of Transactions on the Statement of Cash Flows** (P3–4)
Refer to AP3–3.

Required:
Use the following chart to identify whether each of the transactions in AP3–3 results in a cash flow effect from operating (O), investing (I), or financing (F) activities, and indicate the direction and the effect on cash (+ for increase and − for decrease). If there is no cash flow effect, write "none." The first transaction is provided as an example.

Transaction	Operating, Investing, or Financing Effect	Direction and Amount of the Effect
(a)	F	+75,000

LO4, 5, 6

Gildan Activewear

AP3–5   **Analyzing the Effects of Transactions by Using T-Accounts, Preparing Financial Statements, and Evaluating the Total Asset Turnover and Return on Assets Ratios** (P3–5)
The following are the summary account balances from a recent statement of financial position of Gildan Activewear. The accounts are followed by a list of hypothetical transactions for the month of January 2011. The following accounts are shown in millions of dollars.

Cash	$ 635	Trade payables	$1,822
Long-term borrowings	2,229	Income tax payable	300
Trade receivables	1,503	Prepayments	16
Inventories	551	Retained earnings	4,266
Deferred income taxes (credit)	2,518	Other non-current assets	1,126
Property and equipment, net	10,759	Share capital	3,455

The accounts have normal debit or credit balances, but they are not necessarily listed in good order.

a. Purchased new equipment costing $150 million by issuing long-term debt.

b. Received $900 million on trade receivables.

c. Received and paid the telephone bills for $1 million.

d. Earned $500 million in sales to customers on account; the cost of sales was $300 million.

e. Paid employees $100 million for wages earned in January.

f. Paid half of the income taxes payable.

g. Purchased inventory for $23 million on account.

h. Prepaid rent for February for a warehouse for $12 million.

i. Paid $10 million of long-term borrowings and $1 million in interest on the debt.

j. Purchased a patent (an intangible asset) for $8 million cash.

Required:

1. Set up T-accounts for the preceding list and enter the respective balances. (You will need additional T-accounts for income statement accounts.)

2. For each transaction, record the effects in the T-accounts. Label each by using the letter of the transaction. Compute ending balances.

3. Show the effects (direction and amount) of each transaction on profit and cash.

4. Prepare in good form an income statement for the month of January 2011 and a classified statement of financial position as at January 31, 2011.

5. Prepare the operating activities section of the statement of cash flows for January 2011, and explain the difference between the cash flow from operating activities and the profit computed in (3).

6. Compute the company's total asset turnover ratio. What does this ratio suggest to you about Gildan Activewear?

AP3–6 Determining and Interpreting the Effects of Transactions on Income Statement Categories and Return on Assets (P3–6)

LO4, 6

Barnes & Noble Inc.

Barnes & Noble Inc. revolutionized bookselling by making its stores public spaces and community institutions where customers may browse, find a book, relax over a cup of coffee, talk with authors, and join discussion groups. Today it is fighting increasing competition not only from traditional sources but also from online booksellers. Presented here is a recent income statement (in millions).

Net sales	$5,121
Cost of sales	3,540
Gross margin	1,581
Operating expenses:	
Selling and administrative	1,251
Depreciation and amortization	174
Pre-opening expenses	13
Total operating expenses	1,438
Operating profit	143
Other income and expenses:	
Interest expense	2
Profit before provision for income taxes	141
Provision for income taxes	56
Profit	$ 85

Required:
Assume that the following hypothetical *additional* transactions occurred during the fiscal year: (a) recorded and received interest income of $14, (b) purchased $95 of additional inventory on open account, (c) recorded and paid additional advertising expense of $19, and (d) issued additional common shares for $90 cash.

Complete the following tabulation, indicating the sign of the effect of each *additional* transaction (+ for increase, − for decrease, and NE for no effect). Assume that the company's return on assets is less than 1 prior to these transactions. Consider each item independently and ignore income taxes.

Transaction	Operating Profit (Loss)	Profit	Return on Assets
a.			
b.			
c.			
d.			

AP3–7 Computing and Analyzing the Total Asset Turnover Ratio and the Return on Assets Ratio (P3–7)

LO5, 6

Gildan Activewear
Research In Motion
Andrew Peller

A summary of selected historical results is presented on the following page for three Canadian companies: Gildan Activewear, Research In Motion, and Andrew Peller. Each of these companies has grown in size over time by acquiring assets and investing in other companies. (Amounts are in millions of dollars.)

	2008	2007	2006	2005	2004
Gildan Activewear					
Total assets	$1,102	$875	$723	$598	$489
Total revenue	1,250	964	773	654	533
Profit	145	130	107	86	60
Interest expense, net of tax	5.8	3.9	2.5	3.7	5.1
Research In Motion					
Total assets	5,511	3,089	2,312	2,627	1,937
Total revenue	4,914	2,304	2,066	1,350	595
Profit	1,294	632	382	213	53
Interest expense, net of tax	0.3	0.2	0.3	0.3	0.2
Andrew Peller					
Total assets	260	239	222	162	146
Total revenue	237	228	212	168	156
Profit	11	9	6	8	9
Interest expense, net of tax	4	4	3	2	2

Required:

1. Complete the following table by computing the total asset turnover ratio and the return on assets ratio for each company for each of the years 2007 and 2008.

	2008	2007	2006	2005
Gildan Activewear				
Total asset turnover ratio			1.17	1.20
Return on assets (ROA)			0.166	0.165
Research In Motion				
Total asset turnover ratio			0.84	0.59
Return on assets (ROA)			0.155	0.093
Andrew Peller				
Total asset turnover ratio			1.10	1.09
Return on assets (ROA)			0.047	0.065

2. Based on the computed ratios, rank these companies from most successful to least successful in implementing their growth strategies and effectively utilizing their assets to generate revenue and profit.

3. Assume that you are interested in investing in one of these three companies, which company would you choose? Write a brief report to justify your choice.

CASES AND PROJECTS

FINDING AND INTERPRETING FINANCIAL INFORMATION

■ **LO2, 4, 6**　　**CP3–1**　**Finding Financial Information**

Cadbury

Refer to the financial statements and the accompanying notes of Cadbury plc, available online.

Required:

1. State the amount of the largest expense on the 2008 income statement and describe the transaction represented by the expense.

2. Prepare the journal entry for interest expense for the year ended December 31, 2008 (for this question, assume that the amount has not yet been paid).

3. Assuming that all net sales are on credit, how much cash did Cadbury collect from customers? (*Hint:* Use a T-account of trade receivables to infer collections.)

4. Describe and contrast the purpose of an income statement versus a statement of financial position.

5. Compute the company's total asset turnover ratio and its return on assets for 2008. Explain their meaning.

CP3–2 Comparing Companies

■ LO2, **3, 5**
Cadbury vs. Nestlé

Refer to the financial statements and the accompanying notes of the Nestlé Group given in Appendix A, and of Cadbury plc, available online.

Required:

1. What title does each company call its income statement? Explain what the term *consolidated* means.

2. Which company had higher profit at the end of its fiscal year?*

3. Compute the total asset turnover ratio and the return on assets for each company for the most recent year. Which company is utilizing assets more effectively to generate sales and profit? Explain.

4. How much cash was provided by operating activities by each company during the most recent year? What was the percentage change in operating cash flows for each company during the most recent year? (*Hint:* Percentage change = [Current year amount − Prior year amount] ÷ Prior year amount.)

5. How much did each company pay in income taxes during the last fiscal year reported in the financial statements? Where did you find this information?

6. What segments does Cadbury report in the notes? What does Nestlé report about segments?

CP3–3 Comparing a Company over Time

■ LO6
Nestlé

Refer to the annual report for the Nestlé Group in Appendix A.

Required:

1. Compute the total asset turnover ratio for fiscal years 2007 and 2008. The company had CHF 101,805 million in total assets at December 31, 2006.

2. In Chapter 2, we discussed the debt-to-equity ratio. Compute this ratio for fiscal years 2007 and 2008.

3. What do your results from the trends in the two ratios suggest to you about Nestlé?

FINANCIAL REPORTING AND ANALYSIS CASES

CP3–4 Interpreting the Financial Press

■ LO3
Business Week

The October 4, 2004, edition of *Business Week* presented an article titled "Fuzzy Numbers" on issues related to accrual accounting and its weaknesses that have led some corporate executives to manipulate estimates in their favour, sometimes fraudulently. You can access the article online.

Required:
Read the article and then answer the following questions:

1. What is accrual accounting?

2. What does the article's title "Fuzzy Numbers" mean?

3. What does the article suggest about the reforms adopted by the U.S. Congress and the SEC?

CRITICAL THINKING CASES

CP3–5 Making a Decision as a Bank Loan Officer: Analyzing and Restating Financial Statements That Have Major Deficiencies (A Challenging Case)

■ LO3, **6**

Tom Martinez started and operated a small boat repair service company during 2012. He is interested in obtaining a $100,000 loan from your bank to build a dry dock to store boats for

---

*The average exchange rate between the two currencies during 2008 was £1= CHF 1.99.

customers in the winter months. At the end of the year, he prepared the following statements based on information stored in a large filing cabinet:

MARTINEZ COMPANY
Profit for 2012

Service fees collected during 2012		$ 55,000
Cash dividends received		10,000
Total		$ 65,000
Expense for operations paid during 2012	$22,000	
Cash stolen	500	
New tools purchased during 2009 (cash paid)	1,000	
Supplies purchased for use on service jobs (cash paid)	3,200	
Total		26,700
Profit		$38,300

Assets Owned at the End of 2012

Cash in chequing account	$ 29,300
Service garage (at current market value)	32,000
Tools and equipment	18,000
Land (at current market value)	30,000
Shares in ABC Industrial	130,000
Total	$239,300

The following is a summary of completed transactions:

(*a*) Received the following contributions to the business from the owner when it was started in exchange for 1,000 shares in the new company:

Building	$21,000	Land	$20,000
Tools and equipment	17,000	Cash	1,000

(*b*) Earned service fees during 2012 of $87,000; of the cash collected, $20,000 was for deposits from customers on work to be done by Martinez during 2013.

(*c*) Received the cash dividends on shares of ABC Industrial purchased by Tom Martinez as a personal investment six years earlier.

(*d*) Incurred expenses during 2012, $61,000.

(*e*) Determined amount of supplies on hand (unused) at the end of 2012, $700.

Required:

1. Did Martinez prepare the income statement on a cash basis or an accrual basis? Explain how you can tell. Which basis should be used? Explain why.

2. Reconstruct the correct entries under accrual accounting principles and post the effects to T-accounts.

3. Prepare an accrual-based income statement for 2012 and a statement of financial position at the end of 2012. Explain (using footnotes) the reason for each change that you make to the income statement.

4. What additional information would assist you in formulating your decision regarding the loan to Mr. Martinez?

5. Based on the revised statements and additional information needed, write a letter to Mr. Martinez explaining your decision at this time regarding the loan.

LO3   **CP3–6** **Proper Measurement of Profit**
Paula Manolakos purchased La Forêt Inc., a bakery, from Gianni Fiori. The purchase agreement included a provision that required Paula to pay Gianni 25 percent of the bakery's profit in each of

the next five years. The agreement stated that the bakery's profit would be measured in a "fair and reasonable manner," but did not state that it would be measured in accordance with the applicable financial reporting standards. Neither Paula nor Gianni were familiar with accounting concepts.

In measuring profit, Paula used the following accounting policies:

(a) Revenue was recognized when cash was received from customers. Because of the nature of the business, most customers paid in cash, but a few customers purchased merchandise on account and were allowed to pay in 30 days.

(b) Paula set her annual salary at $60,000, which Gianni has agreed was reasonable. She also paid $30,000 per year to her spouse and to each of her two teenage children. These family members did not work in the business on a regular basis, but they did help during busy periods.

(c) Weekly expenditures for eggs, milk, flour, and other supplies were charged directly to supplies expense, as were the weekly groceries for Paula's family.

(d) The bakery had modern baking equipment valued at $50,000 at the time Paula purchased the company. The income statement for the first year included a $50,000 equipment expense related to these assets.

(e) Income taxes expense included the amount paid by the corporation (which was computed correctly), as well as the personal income taxes paid by various members of Paula's family on the salaries they earned for working in the business.

Gianni was disappointed, however, when Paula reported profit for the first year that was far below his expectations.

Required:

1. Discuss the fairness and reasonableness of Paula's accounting policies. Identify the accounting principle or assumption that may have been violated.

2. Do you think that the net cash flow from operations (cash receipts minus cash payments) is higher or lower than the profit reported by Paula? Explain.

3. What advice would you give Gianni to ensure that the bakery's profit would be measured properly in future years?

CP3–7 Evaluating an Ethical Dilemma

LO3

Mike Kruk is the manager of a Vancouver regional office for an insurance company. As the regional manager, his compensation package comprises a base salary, commissions, and a bonus when the region sells new policies in excess of its quota. Mike has been under enormous pressure lately, stemming largely from two factors. First, he is experiencing a mounting personal debt because of a family member's illness. Second, compounding his worries, the region's sales of new policies have dipped below the normal quota for the first time in years.

You have been working for Mike for two years, and like everyone else in the office, you consider yourself lucky to work for such a supportive boss. You also feel great sympathy for his personal problems over the last few months. In your position as accountant for the regional office, you are only too aware of the drop in new policy sales and the impact this will have on the manager's bonus. While you are working late at year-end, Mike stops by your office.

Mike asks you to change the manner in which you have accounted for a new property insurance policy for a large local business. A cheque for the premium, substantial in amount, came in the mail on December 31, the last day of the reporting year. The premium covers a period beginning on January 5. You deposited the cheque and correctly debited cash and credited a deferred *revenue* account. Mike says, "Hey, we have the money this year, so why not count the revenue this year? I never did understand why you accountants are so picky about these things anyway. I'd like you to change the way you have recorded the transaction. I want you to credit a *revenue* account. And anyway, I've done favours for you in the past, and I am asking for such a small thing in return." With that, he leaves for the day.

Required:

1. How should you handle this situation?

2. What are the ethical implications of Mike's request?

3. Who are the parties who would be helped or harmed if you complied with the request?

4. If you fail to comply with his request, how will you explain your position to him in the morning?

LO2, 3, 5, 6   CP3–8   FINANCIAL REPORTING AND ANALYSIS TEAM PROJECT

Team Project: Analyzing Income Statements and Ratios

As a team, select an industry to analyze. A list of companies classified by industry can be obtained by accessing www.fpinfomart.ca and then choosing "Companies by Industry." You can also find a list of industries and companies with each industry via http://ca.finance.yahoo.com/investing (click on "Annual Reports" under "Tools").

Each team member should acquire the annual report for a different publicly traded company in the industry. (Library files, the SEDAR service at www.sedar.com, or the company's website are good sources.)

Required:

On an individual basis, each team member should write a short report that answers the following questions about the selected company. Discuss any patterns across the companies that you as a team observe. Then, as a team, write a short report comparing and contrasting your companies.

1. For the most recent year, what is/are the major revenue account(s)? What percentage is each to total operating revenues? (Computed as Revenue A ÷ Total revenues.)

2. For the most recent year, what is/are the major expense account(s)? What percentage is each to total operating expenses? (Computed as Expense A ÷ Total expenses.)

3. Ratio Analysis

   a. What do the total asset turnover and the return on assets ratios measure in general?

   b. Compute these ratios for the last three years.

   c. What do your results suggest about the company?

   d. If available, find the industry ratio for the most recent year, compare it with your results, and discuss why you believe your company differs or is similar to the industry ratio.

4. Describe the company's revenue recognition policy, if reported. (Usually found in note 2 to the financial statements titled Significant Accounting Policies.)

5. The percentage of cash from operating activities to profit measures how liberal (i.e., speeding up revenue recognition or delaying expense recognition) or conservative (i.e., taking care not to record revenues too early or expenses too late) a company's management is in choosing among various revenue and expense recognition policies. A ratio above 1.0 suggests more conservative policies and below 1.0, more liberal policies. Compute the percentage for the last three years. What do your results suggest about the company's choice of accounting policies?

CHAPTER

Adjustments, Financial Statements, and the Quality of Earnings

4

After studying this chapter, you should be able to do the following:

FOCUS COMPANY: **Nestlé S.A.**
ESTIMATING REVENUES AND EXPENSES AT YEAR-END

The end of the accounting period is a very busy time for Nestlé (www.nestle.com). The last day of the fiscal year for Nestlé falls on December 31 of each year.[1] The financial statements, however, are not distributed to users on that day. They are released only after management and the external auditors make many critical evaluations.

- Management must ensure that the correct amounts are reported on the statement of financial position and income statement. This often requires estimations, assumptions, and judgments about the timing of revenue and expense recognition, and values for assets and liabilities.

- The auditors have to (1) assess the strength of the controls established by management to safeguard the company's assets and ensure the accuracy of the financial records, and (2) evaluate the appropriateness of estimates and accounting principles used by management in determining revenues and expenses.

Managers of most companies understand the need to present financial information fairly so as not to mislead users. However, since end-of-period adjustments are the most complex portion of the annual recordkeeping process, they are prone to error. External auditors examine the company's records on a

---

[1]A firm's fiscal year does not have to conform to the calendar year (January 1 to December 31). In a recent survey of 200 companies, 54 (27 percent) did not use a December 31 year-end in 2007, including 15 companies that chose a fiscal year-end defined as, for example, "the last Saturday of the month" or "the Sunday closest to the end of the month," which results in financial information covering 52 weeks in some years and 53 weeks in other years. Information from *Financial Reporting in Canada*. Toronto: The Canadian Institute of Chartered Accountants, accessed online on October 25, 2009.

test, or sample, basis. To maximize the chance of detecting any errors significant enough to affect users' decisions, auditors allocate more of their testing to transactions most likely to be in error.

Several accounting research studies have documented the most error-prone transactions for medium-size manufacturing companies. End-of-period adjustment errors, such as failure to provide adequate provision for product warranty, failure to include items that should be expensed, and end-of-period transactions recorded in the wrong period (called *cut-off errors*) are in the top category and thus receive much attention from the auditors.

For 2009, Nestlé's year-end estimation and auditing process took until February 18, 2010, the date on which the auditor KPMG SA completed the audit work and signed its audit opinion. At that point, the financial statements were made available to the public.

UNDERSTANDING THE BUSINESS

Managers are responsible for preparing financial statements that are useful to investors, creditors, and others. Financial information is most useful for analyzing the past and predicting the future when it is considered by users to be of *high quality*. High-quality information is relevant (i.e., important in the analysis and available in a timely manner) and faithfully represents the substance of the underlying transactions (i.e., complete, neutral, and free from material error).

Users expect revenues and expenses to be reported in the proper period, based on the revenue principle and matching process discussed in Chapter 3. Revenues must be recorded when earned, and expenses must be recorded when incurred, regardless of when cash is received or paid. Many operating activities take place over one accounting period or over several periods, such as prepaying insurance or owing salaries to employees for past work. Because recording these and similar activities daily is often very costly, most companies wait until the end of the period to record *adjustments* to revenue and expense accounts to reflect the proper amounts in the correct period. These entries update the records and are the focus of this chapter.

Analysts, creditors, and investors assess the quality of financial information by determining how *prudent* the managers' estimates and judgments are. Choices that do not overstate assets and revenues or understate liabilities and expenses are considered prudent. The users are less likely to be misled into expecting the company to have either a stronger financial position or higher earnings potential than actually exists. Thus, prudent estimates and judgments are believed to produce information of higher quality. The effects of management's choices among alternative accounting methods and the use of estimates are presented throughout the rest of this text.

In this chapter, we emphasize the use of the analytical tools introduced in Chapters 2 and 3 (journal entries and T-accounts) to help you understand how the necessary adjustments are analyzed and recorded at the end of the accounting period. Then we prepare financial statements by using adjusted account balances. Finally, we illustrate how we prepare the accounting records for the next accounting period by performing a process called "closing the books."

ORGANIZATION OF THE CHAPTER

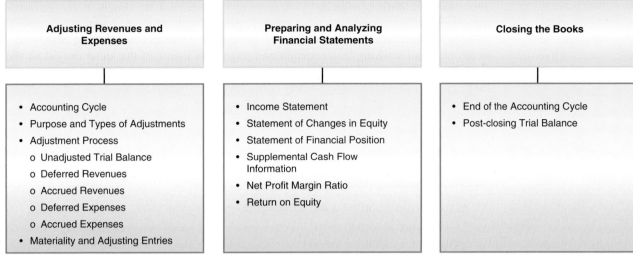

Adjusting Revenues and Expenses	Preparing and Analyzing Financial Statements	Closing the Books

• Accounting Cycle
• Purpose and Types of Adjustments
• Adjustment Process
  o Unadjusted Trial Balance
  o Deferred Revenues
  o Accrued Revenues
  o Deferred Expenses
  o Accrued Expenses
• Materiality and Adjusting Entries
	• Income Statement
	• Statement of Changes in Equity
	• Statement of Financial Position
	• Supplemental Cash Flow Information
	• Net Profit Margin Ratio
	• Return on Equity
		• End of the Accounting Cycle
		• Post-closing Trial Balance

Supplemental material:

Appendix 4A: An Operational Recordkeeping Efficiency
Appendix B: The Formal Recordkeeping System (online)

ADJUSTING REVENUES AND EXPENSES

Accounting Cycle

The accounting cycle is the process used by entities to analyze and record transactions, adjust the records at the end of the period, prepare financial statements, and prepare the records for the next cycle. *During* the accounting period, transactions that result in exchanges between the company and other external parties are analyzed and recorded in the general journal in chronological order (journal entries), and the related accounts are updated in the general ledger (T-accounts), similar to our Nestlé illustrations in Chapters 2 and 3. In this chapter, we examine the *end-of-period* steps that focus primarily on adjustments to record revenues and expenses in the proper period and to update the statement of financial position accounts for reporting purposes. Exhibit 4.1 presents the fundamental steps in the accounting cycle.

The **ACCOUNTING CYCLE** is the process used by entities to analyze and record transactions, adjust the records at the end of the period, prepare financial statements, and prepare the records for the next cycle.

Exhibit **4.1**

The Accounting Cycle

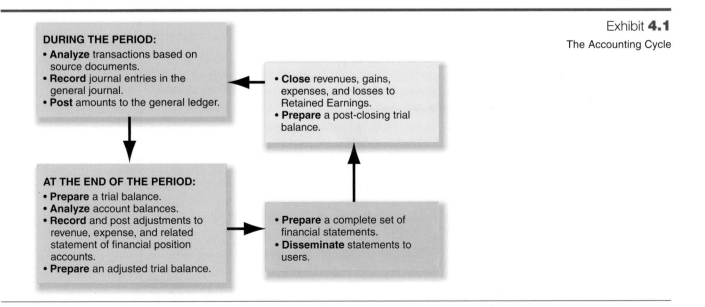

DURING THE PERIOD:
• **Analyze** transactions based on source documents.
• **Record** journal entries in the general journal.
• **Post** amounts to the general ledger.

AT THE END OF THE PERIOD:
• **Prepare** a trial balance.
• **Analyze** account balances.
• **Record** and post adjustments to revenue, expense, and related statement of financial position accounts.
• **Prepare** an adjusted trial balance.

• **Close** revenues, gains, expenses, and losses to Retained Earnings.
• **Prepare** a post-closing trial balance.

• **Prepare** a complete set of financial statements.
• **Disseminate** statements to users.

Purpose and Types of Adjustments

Purpose of Adjustments   Accounting systems are designed to record most recurring daily transactions, particularly those involving cash. As cash is received or paid, it is recorded in the accounting system. In general, this focus on cash works well, especially when cash receipts and payments occur in the same period as the activities that produce revenues and expenses. However, cash is not always received in the period in which the company earns revenue; likewise, cash is not always paid in the period in which the company incurs an expense.

How does the accounting system record revenues and expenses when one transaction is needed to record a cash receipt or payment and another transaction is needed to record revenue when it is earned or an expense when it is incurred? The solution to the problem created by such differences in timing is to record adjusting entries at the end of every accounting period, so that

- Revenues are recorded when earned (the *revenue principle*).
- Expenses are recorded when they are incurred to generate revenue during the same period (the *matching process*).
- *Assets* are reported at amounts that represent the probable future benefits remaining at the end of the period.
- *Liabilities* are reported at amounts that represent the probable future sacrifices of assets or services owed at the end of the period.

Companies wait until *the end of the accounting period* to adjust their accounts because adjusting the records daily would be very costly and time-consuming. Adjusting entries are required every time a company wants to prepare financial statements for external users. In practice, almost every account could require an adjustment. Rather than trying to memorize an endless list of specific examples, you should focus instead on learning the general types of adjustments that are needed and the process that is used to determine how to adjust the accounts.

Types of Adjustments   There are four types of adjustments divided into two categories:

LO1

Explain the purpose of adjustments and analyze the adjustments necessary at the end of the period to update statement of financial position and income statement accounts.

ADJUSTING ENTRIES are entries necessary at the end of the accounting period to identify and record all revenues and expenses of that period.

Revenues
- **Deferred Revenues** – Previously recorded liabilities that were created when cash was received in advance and that must be adjusted for the amount of revenue actually earned during the period.
- **Accrued Revenues** – Revenues that were earned but not recorded because cash was received after the services were performed or goods were delivered.

Expenses
- **Deferred Expenses** – Previously recorded assets, such as prepaid rent, supplies, and equipment, that were created when cash was paid in advance and that must be adjusted for the amount of expense actually incurred during the period through use of the asset.
- **Accrued Expenses** – Expenses that were incurred but were not recorded because cash was paid after the goods or services were used.

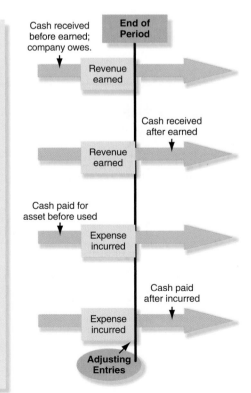

Each of these types of adjustments involves two entries:

1. One for the cash receipt of payment,
2. One for recording the revenue or expense in the proper period (through the adjusting entry).

We will illustrate the process involved in analyzing and adjusting the accounts by reviewing all the adjustments needed for Nestlé before preparing January's financial statements based on adjusted balances.

When a customer pays for goods or services before the company delivers them, the company records the amount of cash received in a deferred revenue account. The deferred revenue is a liability representing the company's promise to perform or deliver the goods or services in the future. Recognition of (recording) the revenue is deferred (postponed) until the company meets its obligation.

Sometimes companies perform services or provide goods (i.e., earn revenue) before customers pay. Because the cash that is owed for these goods has not yet been received, the revenue that was earned has not been recorded. Revenues that have been earned but have not yet been recorded at the end of the accounting period are called accrued revenues.

Exhibit 4.2 summarizes the process involved in adjusting deferred revenues and accrued revenues, using deferred fees and interest revenue as examples. The first column indicates the classification of the revenue, either deferred or accrued. The remaining columns indicate the timing and type of journal entry required. "AJE" in the exhibit refers to *adjusting journal entry*. Note that in both cases, the goal is the same—to record revenues in the proper period. Also note that adjusting entries affect one account on the statement of financial position and one account on the income statement, but *cash is never adjusted*. Cash was recorded when received prior to the end of the period, or will be recorded when collected in a future period.

Assets represent resources with probable future benefits to the company. Many assets are deferred expenses that are used over time to generate revenues, including supplies, prepaid rent, prepaid insurance, buildings, equipment, and intangible assets such as patents and copyrights. At the end of every period, an adjustment must be made to record the amount of the asset that was used during the period.

Numerous expenses are incurred in the current period without being paid for until the next period. Common examples include interest expense incurred on debt, wages expense for the wages owed to employees, and utilities expense for water, gas, and electricity used during the period for which the company has not yet received a bill. These expenses accumulate (accrue) over time but are not recognized until the end of the period in an adjusting entry to record the accrued expenses.

Exhibit 4.3 summarizes the process involved in adjusting deferred expenses and accrued expenses, using prepaid insurance and wages expense as examples. AJE refers,

DEFERRED REVENUES are previously recorded liabilities that need to be adjusted at the end of the accounting period to reflect the amount of revenues earned.

EXAMPLES:
- Deferred ticket revenue
- Deferred subscription revenue

ADJUSTING ENTRY:
↓ Liability and ↑ Revenue

ACCRUED REVENUES are previously unrecorded revenues that need to be recorded at the end of the accounting period to reflect the amount earned and its related receivable account.

EXAMPLES:
- Interest receivable
- Rent receivable

ADJUSTING ENTRY:
↑ Asset and ↑ Revenue

DEFERRED EXPENSES are previously acquired assets that need to be adjusted at the end of the accounting period to reflect the amount of expense incurred in using the assets to generate revenue.

EXAMPLES:
- Supplies
- Prepayments (e.g., rent, insurance)
- Buildings and equipment

ADJUSTING ENTRY:
↑ Expense and ↓ Asset

	During the period	End of period	Next period
	Entry when **cash is received before** the company performs (earns revenue)	**AJE** needed because the company has performed (earned a revenue) during the period	Entry when **cash is received after** the company performs (earns revenue)
Deferred Revenues	Cash (+A) Deferred fee revenue (+L)	Deferred fee revenue (−L) Fee revenue (+R, +SE)	
Accrued Revenues		Interest receivable (+A) Interest revenue (+R, +SE)	Cash (+A) Interest receivable (−A)

↑
Revenues recorded in the proper period.

Exhibit **4.2**

Illustration of Adjusting Deferred and Accrued Revenues

Exhibit **4.3**

Illustration of Adjusting Deferred and Accrued Expenses

	During the period	End of period	Next period
	Entry when **cash is paid before** the company incurs an expense	**AJE** needed because the company has incurred an expense during the period	Entry when **cash is paid after** the company incurs an expense
Deferred Expenses	Prepaid insurance (+A) 　Cash (−A)	Insurance expense (+E, −SE) 　Prepaid insurance (−A)	
Accrued Expenses		Wages expense (+E, −SE) 　Wages payable (+L)	Wages payable (−L) 　Cash (−A)

Expenses recorded
in the proper period

ACCRUED EXPENSES are previously unrecorded expenses that need to be recorded at the end of the accounting period to reflect the amount incurred and its related payable account.

EXAMPLES:
- Interest payable
- Wages payable
- Property taxes payable

ADJUSTING ENTRY:
↑ Expense and ↑ Liability

again, to *adjusting journal entry*. Note that in both cases, the goal is to record expenses in the proper period. In addition, note that the adjusting journal entry involves one account on the statement of financial position and one account on the income statement, and cash is never affected. Cash was recorded when paid prior to the end of the period or will be recorded in a future period.

Adjustment Process

Throughout the rest of the text, you will discover that nearly every account, except cash, on a company's statement of financial position will need to be adjusted, often requiring management to make judgments and estimates. In this chapter, we will illustrate common adjusting entries. In analyzing adjustments at the end of the period, there are three steps:

Step 1: **Identify the type of adjustment**. Ask "Was cash already received or paid prior to the end of the period?" or "Will cash be received or paid in the future?" If cash was received or paid, then deferred revenue and deferred expense accounts exist at the end of the period, but are overstated. On the other hand, if cash has not been received or paid, then revenues and expenses that have been accrued but have not been recorded are understated.

Step 2: **Determine the amount** of revenue that has been earned or expense that has been incurred during the period. Sometimes the amount is known, sometimes it is calculated, and sometimes it must be estimated. (This will be the amount needed in the adjusting entry for the revenue of expense account. Drawing a timeline to visualize the events that occurred during the accounting period is often very helpful.)

Step 3: **Record the adjusting journal entry** and post it to the appropriate accounts. If you have difficulty determining the accounts to use, usually name the revenue or expense account for what it is, such as interest expense or fee revenue. The related asset or liability should be similar, such as interest payable or deferred fee revenue.

A **TRIAL BALANCE** is a list of all accounts with their balances, to provide a check on the equality of the debits and credits.

What are the adjustments needed for Nestlé at the end of January 2010? We start by preparing and reviewing the unadjusted trial balance.

Unadjusted Trial Balance　　Before adjusting the accounting records, managers normally review an unadjusted trial balance produced either manually or, more often, generated by computerized software. A trial balance is a list of individual accounts in one column, usually in financial statement order, with their ending debit or credit balances in the next two columns. Debit balances are indicated in the left column and credit balances are indicated in the right column. Then the two columns are totalled to provide a check on the equality of the debits and credits. However, if wrong accounts and/or amounts are used in the journal entries, then a computer-generated trial balance will have errors even though debits equal credits.[2] Once equality is established, the accounts on the trial balance can be reviewed to determine whether any adjustments need to be recorded.

LO²

Utilize a trial balance to prepare financial statements.

A trial balance is a schedule prepared for internal purposes and is not considered to be a financial statement for external users. Exhibit 4.4 presents an unadjusted trial balance for Nestlé at January 31, 2010, based on the balances of the T-accounts illustrated in Chapters 2 and 3, plus other accounts that may be needed but currently have zero balances.

Before illustrating the adjustment process, notice that the property, plant, and equipment account is stated at original cost of 49,236 in the trial balance but was stated at 23,749 (original cost minus the portion allocated to past operations) in previous chapters. Unlike supplies that are purchased and then used over a relatively short period, property, plant, and equipment represent deferred expenses that will be used over many years. Property, plant, and equipment increase when assets are *acquired* and decrease when they are *sold*. However, these assets are also *used* over time to generate revenue. Thus, a part of their cost should be expensed in the same period (the matching process). Accountants say that these assets depreciate over time as they are used. In accounting, depreciation is an allocation of an asset's cost over its estimated useful life to the company.

To keep track of the asset's historical cost, the amount that has been used is not subtracted directly from the asset account. Instead, it is accumulated in a new kind of account called a contra account. A contra account is an account that is **directly related to another account, but has a balance on the opposite side of the T-account**. As a contra account increases, the net amount (the account balance less the contra account balance) decreases. For property, plant, and equipment, the contra account is called **accumulated depreciation**.[3] This is the first of several contra accounts you will learn throughout the text. We will designate contra accounts with an *X* in front of the type of account to which it is related (e.g., accumulated depreciation [XA] for contra asset).

A **CONTRA ACCOUNT** is an account that is an offset to, or reduction of, the primary account.

Since assets have debit balances, accumulated depreciation has a credit balance. On the statement of financial position, the amount that is reported for property, plant, and equipment is its carrying amount (also called the book value or net book value), which equals the ending balance in the property, plant, and equipment account minus the ending balance in the accumulated depreciation account. For Nestlé, accumulated depreciation has a credit balance of 25,487.

CARRYING AMOUNT (BOOK VALUE, NET BOOK VALUE) of an asset is the difference between its acquisition cost and accumulated depreciation, its related contra account.

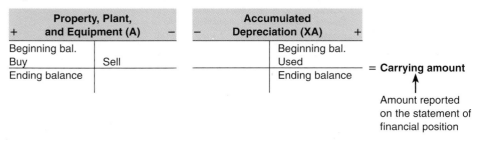

---

[2]Errors in a trial balance also may occur in a manual recordkeeping system when wrong accounts and/or amounts are posted from correct journal entries. If the two columns are not equal, errors have occurred in one or more of the following:

- In preparing journal entries when debits do not equal credits.
- In posting the correct monetary effects of transactions from the journal entry to the ledger.
- In computing ending balances in accounts.
- In copying ending balances in the ledger to the trial balance.

These errors can be traced and should be corrected before adjusting the records.

[3]Valuation of property, plant, and equipment is discussed in Chapters 6 and 9.

Exhibit **4.4**

Trial Balance for the Nestlé Group

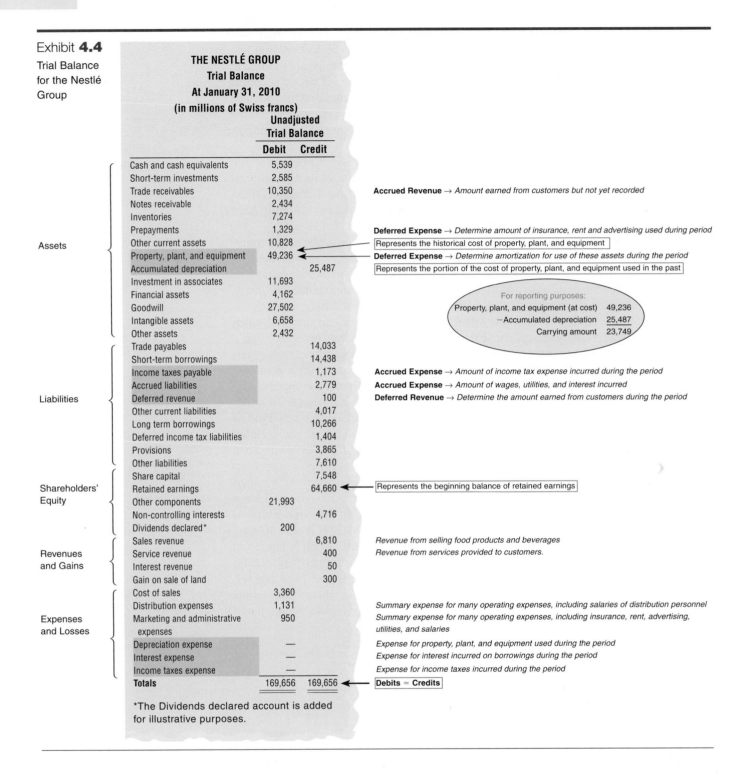

THE NESTLÉ GROUP
Trial Balance
At January 31, 2010
(in millions of Swiss francs)

	Unadjusted Trial Balance	
	Debit	**Credit**
Assets		
Cash and cash equivalents	5,539	
Short-term investments	2,585	
Trade receivables	10,350	
Notes receivable	2,434	
Inventories	7,274	
Prepayments	1,329	
Other current assets	10,828	
Property, plant, and equipment	49,236	
Accumulated depreciation		25,487
Investment in associates	11,693	
Financial assets	4,162	
Goodwill	27,502	
Intangible assets	6,658	
Other assets	2,432	
Liabilities		
Trade payables		14,033
Short-term borrowings		14,438
Income taxes payable		1,173
Accrued liabilities		2,779
Deferred revenue		100
Other current liabilities		4,017
Long term borrowings		10,266
Deferred income tax liabilities		1,404
Provisions		3,865
Other liabilities		7,610
Shareholders' Equity		
Share capital		7,548
Retained earnings		64,660
Other components	21,993	
Non-controlling interests		4,716
Dividends declared*	200	
Revenues and Gains		
Sales revenue		6,810
Service revenue		400
Interest revenue		50
Gain on sale of land		300
Expenses and Losses		
Cost of sales	3,360	
Distribution expenses	1,131	
Marketing and administrative expenses	950	
Depreciation expense	—	
Interest expense	—	
Income taxes expense	—	
Totals	**169,656**	**169,656**

*The Dividends declared account is added for illustrative purposes.

Accrued Revenue → Amount earned from customers but not yet recorded

Deferred Expense → Determine amount of insurance, rent and advertising used during period

Represents the historical cost of property, plant, and equipment

Deferred Expense → Determine amortization for use of these assets during the period

Represents the portion of the cost of property, plant, and equipment used in the past

For reporting purposes:
Property, plant, and equipment (at cost)   49,236
−Accumulated depreciation   25,487
Carrying amount   23,749

Accrued Expense → Amount of income tax expense incurred during the period
Accrued Expense → Amount of wages, utilities, and interest incurred
Deferred Revenue → Determine the amount earned from customers during the period

Represents the beginning balance of retained earnings

Revenue from selling food products and beverages
Revenue from services provided to customers.

Summary expense for many operating expenses, including salaries of distribution personnel
Summary expense for many operating expenses, including insurance, rent, advertising, utilities, and salaries

Expense for property, plant, and equipment used during the period
Expense for interest incurred on borrowings during the period
Expense for income taxes incurred during the period

Debits = Credits

Depreciation is discussed in much greater detail in Chapter 9. Now let us illustrate the adjustment process for Nestlé at the end of January.

Nestlé's trial balance in Exhibit 4.4 lists several accounts that suggest adjusting entries are necessary. Note that you can identify them as deferrals or accruals by whether cash is received or paid in the past or the future.

Account	Cash Received or Paid in the Past		Revenue Earned or Expense Incurred (during the month)		Cash to Be Received or Paid in the Future
Deferred revenue	Deferred revenue	→	All or a portion may have been earned by month-end.		
Trade receivables			Customers may owe Nestlé for merchandise delivered but not recorded.	→	Accrued revenue
Prepayments	Deferred expense	→	All or a portion of the prepaid rent, insurance, and advertising may have been used by month-end.		
Property, plant, and equipment	Deferred expense	→	These non-current assets have been used during the month to generate revenues. A portion of their historical cost is recorded as an expense.		
Accrued liabilities			Nestlé owes (1) amounts due for utilities used during the month but not yet billed and (2) wages to employees for work during the last week of January. Neither has yet been recorded as an expense.	→	Accrued expense
Borrowings			Nestlé owes interest on borrowed funds.	→	Accrued expense
Income taxes payable			Income tax expense needs to be recorded for the period.	→	Accrued expense

We will now use the adjustment process to record adjusting entries for Nestlé at the end of January.[4] Study the following illustration carefully to understand the steps in the adjustment process, paying close attention to the computation of the amounts in the adjustment and the effects on the account balances. First, we adjust the deferred revenues and accrued revenues and then the deferred expenses and accrued expenses, utilizing the three-step process previously discussed: (1) identify the original entry, if any, (2) create a timeline with relevant dates and amounts, and (3) identify the necessary adjusting entry.

Deferred Revenues

(AJE 1) Deferred Service Revenue   Nestlé provided additional services in January for 100 to new clients that had previously paid initial fees to Nestlé.

Step 1: Office services clients paid fees in cash in the past for future service, creating a *deferred revenue* account. Nestlé's earns revenue over time as it provides the services. The entry made in the past is

Cash (+A).	100	
Deferred revenue (+L)		100

Step 2: The unadjusted trial balance (Exhibit 4.4) shows that the balance in deferred revenue is 100 at January 31. This amount, 100, has been earned in January.

January	Month-end	February and beyond
	1/31	
Revenue earned = +100		To be earned = + 0

Step 3: An adjusting journal entry (AJE) is necessary to reduce the deferred revenue account by 100 and increase the service revenue account by 100.

1/31—AJE 1

Deferred revenue (−L)	100	
Service revenue (+R, → +SE)		100

Assets	=	Liabilities	+	Shareholders' Equity	
		Deferred revenue	−100	Service revenue	+100

Deferred Revenue (L)

	100 Ch. 3 bal.
*AJE 1 100	
	0 End.

Service Revenue (R)

	400 Ch. 3 bal.
	100 AJE 1
	500 End.

*AJE = adjusting journal entry

Effect of adjustment on
Profit: ↑ 100
Cash: None

---

[4]Companies can choose fiscal periods other than actual month-ends, and financial statements can cover different accounting periods (month, quarter, or year). Adjusting entries may be prepared monthly, quarterly, and/or annually to ensure that proper amounts are included on the financial reports presented to external users.

SELF-STUDY **QUIZ 4-1**

Accrued Revenues

(AJE 2) Trade Receivables   Nestlé sold merchandise on account for 900 on January 31, but the sales invoices had not been recorded yet.

Step 1: Revenue has been earned during January, but cash will be received in the future, requiring an *accrual of revenue*. No entry was made in the past.

Step 2: The timeline shows that the 900 earned in January will be collected in the future. Since no entry has yet been made, both service revenue and trade receivables are understated by 900.

January During the last week	Month-end 1/31	February and beyond
Revenue earned = 900		To be collected

Step 3: An adjusting entry is necessary to increase service revenue and trade receivables by 900. This will recognize revenue in the current period.

1/31—AJE2

Record the entry →

	Assets	=	Liabilities	+	Shareholders' Equity	
Trade receivables	+900				Sales revenue	+900

Trade Receivables (A)

Ch. 3 bal.	10,350	
Earned	☐	
End.	11,250	

Sales Revenue (R)

		6,810	Ch. 3 bal.
		☐	AJE 2
		7,710	End.

Effect of adjustment on
Profit: ↑ 900
Cash: None

 connect

After you complete your answers, go online for the solutions.

Deferred Expenses

(AJE 3) Prepayments   In January 2010, Nestlé paid a total of 740 for future expenses including insurance (160), rent (450), and advertising (130). The payment for insurance covers four months: one month has passed (January), and three months of future insurance benefits remain. The payment for rent covers three months: one month has passed, and two months of future rent benefits remain. The payment for advertising relates to February 2010 and has not been used yet. In addition to the payment of 740 in January, Nestlé has paid an amount of 589 prior to January 2010 to cover future expenses as reflected on its statement of financial position at January 1, 2010. For illustrative purposes, we assume that this amount relates entirely to prepaid advertising expenses and that 472 was used in January.

Step 1: In the past, Nestlé paid in advance for insurance, rent, and advertising, creating *deferred expense* accounts. The journal entries made in the past to record the prepayments are

Prepayments (+A)	740	
Cash (−A)		740

Step 2: As time passes, prepayments are used up. One month has expired for the prepaid insurance and prepaid rent:

Expired insurance = 160 ÷ 4 = 40
Expired rent = 450 ÷ 3 = 150

An adjusting journal entry is necessary to increase expenses by 662 (40 of expired insurance coverage, 150 of expired rent, and 472 of advertising) and reduce prepayments by 662. Until that happens, prepayments remain overstated and expenses understated.

	January	*Month-end*	*February and beyond*	
	During the month	1/31		
Insurance expense		40	Insurance to be used	120
Rent expense		150	Rent to be used	300
Advertising expense		472	Advertising to be used	247
			(130 + 589 − 472)	

Step 3: The used-up portion of the prepayments asset is an expense. The unused portion provides benefits in future periods. In this case, three expense accounts are affected by the adjustment—insurance expense, rent expense, and advertising expense—with all three expenses categorized as marketing and administrative expenses on the income statement. An adjusting entry is necessary to reduce prepayments by 662 and increase marketing and administrative expenses by the same amount.

1/31—AJE 3

Marketing and administrative expenses (+E, −SE)................. 662
   Prepayments (−A) 662

Assets	=	**Liabilities**	+	**Shareholders' Equity**	
Prepayments −662				Marketing and administrative expenses	−662

Prepayments (A)

Ch. 3 bal.	589		
Purchased	740	662	Used
End.	667		

Marketing and Administrative Expenses (E)

Ch. 3 bal.	950	
AJE 3	662	
End.	1,612	

Effect of adjustment on
Profit: ↓ 662
Cash: None

(AJE 4) Property, Plant, and Equipment As previously discussed, a contra account, accumulated depreciation, is used to accumulate the amount of the historical cost allocated to prior periods. It is directly related to the property, plant, and equipment account but has the opposite balance (a credit balance). Nestlé estimates depreciation to be 4,584 per year.

Step 1: Property, plant, and equipment were purchased in the past, creating a *deferred expense* account. The journal entry made in the past to record the purchase of these assets is

Property, plant, and equipment (+A) .... (many purchases)
   Cash (−A) [or a liability].................... (many purchases)

Step 2: As time passes, these assets are used to generate revenue for January. Thus, we need to calculate depreciation expense for only one month:
Depreciation expense per month = 4,584 ÷ 12 = 382
   The carrying amount (cost − accumulated depreciation) of Nestlé's property, plant, and equipment will be overstated until January's depreciation is recorded in the adjusting entry. In addition, expenses will be understated.

	January	*Month-end*	*February and beyond*
	One month used	1/31	
Depreciation expense = 382			
	Monthly depreciation 4,584 ÷ 12 months = 382 per month		

Step 3: An adjusting entry is necessary to recognize the use of 382 of the cost of property, plant, and equipment to generate revenue during January.

1/31—AJE 4

Depreciation expense (+E, −SE)................................ 382
   Accumulated depreciation—Property, plant, and equipment (+XA → −A) 382

Assets	=	**Liabilities**	+	**Shareholders' Equity**	
Accumulated depreciation— −382				Depreciation −382	
Property, plant, and equipment				expense	

Note that increasing the contra-asset account decreases total assets.

Accumulated Depreciation— Property, Plant, and Equipment (XA)

		25,487	Ch. 3 bal.
		382	Used
		25,869	End.

Depreciation Expense (E)

Ch. 3 bal.	0	
AJE 4	382	
End	382	

Effect of adjustment on
Profit: ↓ 382
Cash: None

Accrued Expenses

(AJE 5) Accrued Expenses (Utilities)
On January 31, Nestlé received a utility bill for 50 for use of natural gas and electricity during January. The bill will be paid in February.

Step 1: Utilities were used in January but the bill will be paid in February, requiring an *accrued expense*. No entry was made in the past.

Step 2: The timeline shows that the expense of 50 incurred in January will be paid in the future. Since using utilities was necessary for the company to generate revenues in January, this amount should be recorded as an expense for January. Until this happens, expenses on the income statement and liabilities on the statement of financial position are understated.

January During the month	Month-end 1/31	February and beyond
Expense incurred = 50		To be paid

Step 3: An adjusting journal entry is necessary to increase expenses by 50 and accrued liabilities by 50. Note that a separate liability account, utilities payable, could have been created instead of combining all accrued expenses into one liability account.

1/31—AJE 5

Marketing and administrative expenses (+E, −SE) 50
   Accrued liabilities (+L) 50

Assets	=	Liabilities	+	Shareholders' Equity	
		Accrued liabilities	+50	Marketing and administrative expenses	−50

Accrued Liabilities (L)

	2,779	Ch. 3 bal.
	50	Incurred
	2,829	End.

Marketing and Administrative Expenses (E)

Bal. from AJE 3	1,612	
AJE 5	50	
End.	1,662	

Effect of adjustment on
Profit: ↓ 50
Cash: None

(AJE 6) Accrued Expenses (Salaries)
Nestlé owed salaries to its employees for the last week in January: 150 for distribution and 160 to administrative employees working at the headquarters. The salaries will be paid during the first week in February.

Step 1: Employees worked and generated revenues during January but will be paid in February, requiring an *accrued expense*. No entry was made in the past.

Step 2: The timeline shows that the wages earned by employees in January are payable in the following period. Since the employees' work was necessary for generating revenues in January, this amount should be recorded as an expense for January. Until this is done, expenses on the income statement and liabilities on the statement of financial position are understated.

January During the last week	Month-end 1/31	February and beyond
Expenses incurred = 310		To be paid

Step 3: Since the employees worked and generated revenues during January, the amount owed to them should be recorded as a January expense. The adjusting journal entry and transaction effects are

1/31—AJE 6

Distribution expenses (+E, −SE) 150
Marketing and administrative expenses (+E, −SE) 160
   Accrued liabilities (+L) 310

Assets	=	Liabilities	+	Shareholders' Equity	
		Accrued liabilities	+310	Distribution expenses	−150
				Marketing and administrative expenses	−160

Accrued Liabilities (L)

	2,829	Bal. from AJE 5
	310	Incurred
	3,139	End.

Distribution Expenses (E)

Ch. 3 bal.	1,131	
AJE 6	150	
End.	1,281	

Marketing and Administrative Expenses (E)

Bal. from AJE 5	1,662	
AJE 6	160	
End.	1,822	

Effect of adjustment on
Profit: ↓ 310
Cash: None

(AJE 7) **Borrowings (Interest)** Nestlé has both short-term and long-term borrowings totalling 23,027. Nestlé estimates interest on these borrowings to be 115 for January.

Step 1: Interest is incurred and will be paid in the future, requiring an *accrued expense*. No entry for interest was made in the past.

Step 2: The timeline shows that the interest expense incurred in January is payable in the future.

January	Month-end	February and beyond
During the month	1/31	
Expense incurred ☐		To be paid

Step 3: Since the borrowings from banks and other creditors provided Nestlé with cash that it used for operations in order to generate revenue during January, the amount of interest owed to creditors should be recorded as a January expense. Until this is done, expenses on the income statement and liabilities on the statement of financial position are understated.

1/31—AJE 7

Record the entry →

Assets	=	Liabilities	+	Shareholders' Equity
		Accrued liabilities + ☐		Interest expense − ☐

After you complete your answers, go online for the solutions.

Accrued Liabilities (L)

	3,139 Bal. from AJE 6
	☐ Incurred
	☐ End.

Interest Expense (E)

Ch. 3 bal.	0
AJE 7	☐
End.	☐

Effect of adjustment on
Profit: _____
Cash: _____

■ connect

(AJE 8) **Income Taxes Payable** The final adjusting journal entry is to record the accrual of income taxes that will be paid in the next quarter (an unrecorded expense). This adjusting entry is recorded last because all other adjustments should be incorporated in computing profit before income taxes (i.e., balances from the unadjusted trial balance plus the effects of all the previous adjustments):

	Revenues and Gains	Expenses and Losses	
Unadjusted totals	7,560	5,441	From Exhibit 4.4
AJE 1	100		
AJE 2	900		
AJE 3		662	
AJE 4		382	
AJE 5		50	
AJE 6		310	
AJE 7		115	
	8,560 −	6,960	= **1,600 Pretax profit**

Nestlé's average income tax rate is 25 percent.

Step 1: Income taxes are computed on January's pretax profit but will be paid in the future, requiring an *accrued expense*. No entry was made in the past.

Step 2: The timeline indicates that the income tax expense for January is payable in the future. Until the 400 in income taxes are recorded as an expense in January, expenses on the income statement and liabilities on the statement of financial position are understated.

Income Taxes Payable (L)

	1,173	Ch. 3 bal.
	400	Incurred
	1,573	End.

Income Tax Expense (E)

Ch. 3 bal.	0	
AJE 8	400	
End.	400	

Effect of adjustment on
Profit: ↓ 400
Cash: None

January During the month	**Month-end** 1/31	**January and beyond**
1,600 pretax profit		
⨉ 25% tax rate		
400 tax expense incurred		To be paid

Step 3: An adjusting journal entry is necessary to increase income tax expense and income taxes payable by 400.

1/31—AJE 8
Income tax expense (+E, −SE)   400
Income taxes payable (+L)   400

Assets	=	**Liabilities**	+	**Shareholders' Equity**	
		Income taxes payable	+400	Income tax expense	−400

In all the adjustments we completed, you may have noticed that the cash account was never adjusted. The cash has already been received or paid by the end of the period or will be received or paid after the end of the period. Adjustments are required to record revenues and expenses in the proper period because the cash part of the transaction occurs at a different point in time. Now it is your turn to practise the adjustment process.

SELF-STUDY **QUIZ 4-3**

B.C. Flippers, a scuba diving and instruction business, completed its first year of operations on December 31, 2011. For each of the following adjustments, identify the type of adjustment, determine the amount of the adjustment, and record the adjusting journal entry.

AJE 1:   B.C. Flippers received $6,000 from customers on November 15, 2011, for diving trips in December and January. The $6,000 was recorded in deferred revenue on that date. By the end of December, one-third of the diving trips had been completed.

AJE 2:   On December 1, 2011, B.C. Flippers provided advanced diving instruction to 10 customers who will pay the business $800 in January. No entry was made when the instruction was provided.

AJE 3:   On September 1, 2011, B.C. Flippers paid $24,000 for insurance for the 12 months beginning on September 1. The amount was recorded as prepaid insurance on September 1.

AJE 4:   On March 1, 2011, B.C. Flippers borrowed $300,000 at 12 percent. Interest is payable each March 1.

	Type of Adjustment	Determination of Amount of Adjustment	Adjustment Journal Entry Accounts	Debit	Credit
AJE 1					
AJE 2					
AJE 3					
AJE 4					

🔲 connect   After you complete your answers, go online for the solutions.

MATERIALITY suggests that minor items that would not influence the decisions of financial statement users are to be treated in the easiest and most convenient manner.

Materiality and Adjusting Entries

The term materiality describes the relative significance of financial statement information in influencing economic decisions made by financial statement users. An item of information, or an aggregate of items, is material if it is probable that its omission or misstatement would influence or change a decision. It is a practical concept that provides scope for accountants to be cost-effective when they record the effects of transactions and prepare financial disclosure. The concept of materiality allows accountants to estimate amounts and even to ignore specific accounting principles if the results of their actions do not have a material effect on the financial statements. This concept is also of particular importance to the audit process. Auditors use professional judgment to decide whether both individual transactions and aggregated small transactions will result in a *material* misstatement of the financial position of the company.

The process of making adjusting entries can be simplified if we account for immaterial items in the easiest and most convenient manner. For example, businesses purchase many assets that provide benefits for a long period of time. Some of these assets have a very low cost, such as pencil sharpeners and wastebaskets. The proper accounting treatment for such assets is to depreciate their acquisition cost to expense over their useful lives. However, the cost of such assets can be directly charged to expense accounts rather than to asset accounts, in accordance with the materiality concept, thus eliminating the need for an adjusting entry to record periodic depreciation expense. Furthermore, adjusting entries to record accrued expenses or revenues may be ignored if the monetary amounts are immaterial.

The accountant's decision to treat a specific item as immaterial depends on a number of considerations and is a matter of professional judgment. Traditional rules of thumb in the auditing profession imply that an item is material if it exceeds 1 to 1.5 percent of total assets or sales, or 5 to 10 percent of profit. Materiality depends on the nature of the item, as well as on its monetary value. If an employee has been stealing small amounts of money systematically, these amounts should not be judged as immaterial because they indicate a weakness in the company's internal control system that should be corrected.[5] Accountants must also consider the combined effect of numerous immaterial events. While each item may be immaterial when considered by itself, the combined effect of many items may be material.

ADJUSTMENTS AND INCENTIVES

A QUESTION
OF ACCOUNTABILITY

Owners and managers of companies are most directly affected by the information presented in financial statements. If the financial performance and condition of the company appear strong, the company's share price rises. Shareholders usually receive dividends and the value of their investment increases. Managers often receive bonuses based on the strength of a company's financial performance, and many in top management are compensated with options to buy their company's shares at prices below market.* The higher the market value, the more compensation they earn. When actual performance lags behind expectations, managers and owners may be tempted to manipulate accruals and deferrals to make up part of the difference. For example, managers may record cash received in advance of being earned as revenue in the current period or may fail to accrue certain expenses at year-end.

Evidence from studies of large samples of companies indicates that some do engage in such behaviour. This research is borne out by enforcement actions of the securities commissions against companies and sometimes against their auditors. These enforcement

---

[5]In fact, a bank employee was able to accumulate a large sum of money by altering a computer program to round off amounts of exchange transactions to the nearest cent and by transferring the fractional amounts to a specific account under his control. Even though the amounts involved per transaction were very small, the volume of banking transactions resulted in the accumulation of a relatively large amount. Fortunately, the employee's fraud was detected a few years later and an appropriate penalty was imposed on him.

actions most often relate to accrual of revenue and receivables that should be deferred to future periods. In many of these cases, the firms involved, their managers, and their auditors are penalized for such actions. Furthermore, owners suffer because the company's share price is affected negatively by news of an investigation by a securities commission.

For example, in June 2004, the Ontario Securities Commission (OSC) charged four top management personnel of Atlas Cold Storage Income Trust with misleading investors after the warehouse operator restated two years of earnings. The OSC indicated that, in preparing Atlas Cold's financial statements, the four executives understated some costs and expenses and recorded some expenses in the wrong periods. These errors resulted in overstatements of profit for 2001, 2002, and the second quarter of 2003. The restatement (correction) of the company's financial results erased a total of $42.6 million of profit for 2001 and 2002, widened the loss for the third quarter of 2003, and caused suspension of payments to investors.

In September 2006, the OSC reached a settlement agreement with Ronald Perryman, the company's vice-president of Finance, who "demonstrated a lack of due diligence that contributed, in part, to the presentation of an improved picture of the financial performance of Atlas for the period including the financial years 2001, 2002, and the first two reporting periods of 2003." Perryman agreed (a) to resign all positions as an officer or director of any issuer, (b) not to become or act as a director or officer of any issuer for 10 years, (c) to be reprimanded, and (d) to pay the sum of $20,000 in respect of the costs of the investigation and hearing in this matter.**

*M. Nelson, J. Elliott, and R. Tarpley. "How Are Earnings Managed? Examples from Auditors," *Accounting Horizons*, Supplement 2003, pp. 17–35.

**In the Matter of the Securities Act, R.S.O. 1990, c. S.5, as Amended and in the Matter of Patrick Gouveia, Andrew Peters, Ronald Perryman and Paul Vickery*, Ontario Securities Commission website. Accessed January 2, 2007.

PREPARING AND ANALYZING FINANCIAL STATEMENTS

Based on the transactions that have been recorded during January and the adjustments that were recorded at January 31, 2010, we can now prepare financial statements reflecting the operating activities for January. Recall from prior chapters what the four statements are and how they relate to each other.

Statement	Relationships among Elements of the Statements
Income Statement	Revenues + Gains − Expenses − Losses = Profit
Statement of Changes in Equity (with focus on Retained Earnings)	Beginning Retained Earnings + Profit − Dividends = Ending Retained Earnings
Statement of Financial Position	Assets = Liabilities + Shareholders' Equity (Share Capital + Retained Earnings + Other Components [including Cash])
Statement of Cash Flows	Change in Cash = +/− Cash provided by or used in operating activities +/− Cash provided by or used in investing activities +/− Cash provided by or used in financing activities

As you learned in Chapter 1, these four financial statements are interrelated; that is, the numbers from one statement flow into the next statement as indicated in the coloured financial statement elements above. Thus, if a number on the income statement changes or is in error, it will affect other statements. Although shareholders' equity includes three main elements, we report changes to both share capital and retained earnings in this chapter, and discuss changes to other components of equity in future chapters.

Before we prepare a complete set of financial statements, let us update the trial balance to reflect the adjustments and provide us with adjusted balances for the statements.[6] In Exhibit 4.5, four new columns are added. Two are used to reflect the adjustments in

Exhibit **4.5**

Adjusted Trial Balance for the Nestlé Group

THE NESTLÉ GROUP
Trial Balance
At January 31, 2010
(in millions of Swiss francs)

	Unadjusted Trial Balance		Adjustments		Adjusted Trial Balance	
	Debit	**Credit**	**Debit**	**Credit**	**Debit**	**Credit**
Cash and cash equivalents	5,539				5,539	
Short-term investments	2,585				2,585	
Trade receivables	10,350		*AJE 2* 900		11,250	
Notes receivable	2,434				2,434	
Inventories	7,274				7,274	
Prepayments	1,329			*AJE 3* 662	667	
Other current assets	10,828				10,828	
Property, plant, and equipment	49,236				49,236	
Accumulated depreciation		25,487		*AJE 4* 382		25,869
Investment in associates	11,693				11,693	
Financial assets	4,162				4,162	
Goodwill	27,502				27,502	
Intangible assets	6,658				6,658	
Other assets	2,432				2,432	
Trade payables		14,033				14,033
Short-term borrowings		14,438				14,438
Income taxes payable		1,173		*AJE 8* 400		1,573
Accrued liabilities		2,779		*AJE 5* 50		3,254
				AJE 6 310		
				AJE 7 115		
Deferred revenue		100	*AJE 1* 100			
Other current liabilities		4,017				4,017
Long-term borrowings		10,266				10,266
Deferred income tax liabilities		1,404				1,404
Provisions		3,865				3,865
Other liabilities		7,610				7,610
Share capital		7,548				7,548
Retained earnings		64,660				64,660
Other components	21,993				21,993	
Non-controlling interests		4,716				4,716
Dividends declared	200				200	
Sales revenue		6,810		*AJE 2* 900		7,710
Service revenue		400		*AJE 1* 100		500
Interest revenue		50				50
Gain on sale of land		300				300
Cost of sales	3,360				3,360	
Distribution expenses	1,131		*AJE 6* 150		1,281	
Marketing and administrative expenses	950		*AJE 3* 662		1,822	
			AJE 5 50			
			AJE 6 160			
Depreciation expense	—		*AJE 4* 382		382	
Interest expense	—		*AJE 7* 115		115	
Income taxes expense	—		*AJE 8* 400		400	
Totals	169,656	169,656	2,919	2,919	171,813	171,813

Effects of the adjusting entries

To compute the adjusted balances, add or subtract across each row.

Assets

Liabilities

Shareholders' Equity

Revenues and Gains

Expenses and Losses

[6]For a discussion and illustration of the use of a worksheet for end-of-period adjustments, refer to Appendix B available online.

each of the accounts. The other two are the updated balances, determined by adding (or subtracting) across each row. Again, we note that the total debits equal the total credits in each of the columns. It is from these adjusted balances that we will prepare an income statement, a statement of changes in equity, and a statement of financial position, with supplementary cash flow information to accompany the statement of cash flows.

LO³

Prepare an income statement with earnings per share, a statement of changes in equity, a statement of financial position, and supplemental cash flow information.

Income Statement

The income statement is prepared first because profit is a component of retained earnings. The January income statement for Nestlé is based on transactions in Chapters 2 and 3 and adjustments in this chapter. Note that a few of the expense accounts have been combined into specific categories on the income statement.

You will note that the ratio earnings per share (EPS) is reported on the income statement. It is widely used in evaluating the operating performance and profitability of a company and is the only ratio required to be disclosed on the statement or in the notes to the financial statements. The actual computation of the ratio is quite complex and appropriate for advanced accounting courses. We simplify the earnings per share computation as

$$\text{Earnings per Share} = \frac{\textbf{Profit Available to the Common Shareholders}}{\textbf{Weighted-Average Number of Common Shares Outstanding during the Period}}$$

The denominator is the average number of shares outstanding (the number at the beginning of the period plus the number at the end of the period, divided by two). For Nestlé, we use 3,572 million, the average number of shares outstanding as disclosed in its 2009 annual report.

CHF 1,200 Million ÷ 3,572 Million Shares = CHF 0.34 for January

Exhibit **4.6**

Consolidated Income Statement

THE NESTLÉ GROUP Consolidated Income Statement For the Month Ended January 31, 2010 (in millions of Swiss francs)	
Revenues	
Sales revenue	7,710
Service revenue	500
Total revenues	8,210
Cost of sales	3,360
Gross profit	4,850
Operating expenses	
Distribution	1,281
Marketing and administrative	1,822
Depreciation expense	382
Total expenses	3,485
Operating profit	1,365
Other non-operating items	
Interest revenue	50
Interest expense	(115)
Gain on sale of land	300
Profit before income taxes	1,600
Income taxes expense	400
Profit for the period	1,200
Earnings per share	0.34

Statement of Changes in Equity

The final amount from the income statement, profit, is carried forward to the retained earnings column of the statement of changes in equity. Dividends declared during January 2010 are deducted to arrive at the ending balance at January 31, 2010. The issuance of additional shares (from Chapter 2) is added to the beginning balance of share capital. Other components of equity are unchanged for this illustration.

THE NESTLÉ GROUP
Statement of Changes in Equity
For the Month Ended January 31, 2010
(in millions of Swiss francs)

	Share Capital	Retained Earnings	Other Components	Shareholders' Equity
Beginning balance	6,248	64,660	(21,993)	48,915
Issuance of shares	1,300			1,300
Profit for the month		1,200		1,200
Distribution of dividends		(200)		(200)
Ending balance	7,548	65,660	(21,993)	51,215

Statement of Financial Position

The ending balances for share capital, retained earnings, and other components from the statement of changes in equity are included on the statement of financial position. You will notice that the contra-asset account, accumulated depreciation, has been subtracted from the property, plant, and equipment account to reflect its carrying amount (or net book value) at month-end for financial reporting purposes. Also, recall that assets are listed in order of liquidity, while liabilities are listed in order of time to maturity. Current assets are those used or turned into cash within one year. Current liabilities are obligations to be settled within one year.

In addition to preparing the basic financial statements, companies provide further information about specific elements of these statements in notes that follow the statements. The additional details supporting the reported numbers facilitate analysis of the company's operating performance and financial condition. A closer look at note disclosures related to financial statements is provided in Chapter 6.

DISCLOSURE

FOCUS ON CASH FLOWS

As presented in the previous chapters, the statement of cash flows explains the difference between the ending and beginning balances in the cash account during the accounting period. Put simply, the statement of cash flows is a categorized list of all transactions of the period that affected the cash account. The three categories are operating, investing, and financing activities. Since the adjustments made in this chapter did not affect cash, the components of the statement of cash flows presented in Chapters 2 and 3 have not changed.

For complete disclosure, however, companies are required to provide additional information on the statement itself or in the notes to the statements.

In General → Disclosure (on the statement or in the notes): (1) cash flows related to interest, dividends, and income taxes received and paid, and (2) a schedule of the nature and amounts of significant non-cash transactions (e.g., land exchanged for shares, acquisition of a building by signing a long-term mortgage payable).

Focus Company Analysis → For meeting the disclosure requirement using our Nestlé illustration, no significant non-cash transactions and no income taxes or interest were paid during January. In the notes to its actual 2009 financial statements, Nestlé provided the following disclosures:

Note 22.6 Interest, taxes, and dividends

	2009	2008
Interest paid	(566)	(1,138)
Interest received	97	231
Taxes paid	(2,758)	(3,207)
Dividends paid	(5,779)	(4,981)
Dividends received	400	399

THE NESTLÉ GROUP
Consolidated Statement of Financial Position
At January 31, 2010
(in millions of Swiss francs)

Assets
Current assets

Cash and cash equivalents	5,539
Short-term investments	2,585
Trade receivables	11,250
Notes receivable	2,434
Inventories	7,274
Prepayments	667
Other current assets	10,828
Total current assets	40,577
Property, plant, and equipment	23,367
Investment in associates	11,693
Financial assets	4,162
Goodwill	27,502
Intangible assets	6,658
Other assets	2,432
Total assets	**116,391**

Liabilities and Shareholders' Equity
Current liabilities

Trade payables	14,033
Short-term borrowings	14,438
Income taxes payable	1,573
Accrued liabilities	3,254
Other current liabilities	4,017
Total current liabilities	37,315
Long-term borrowings	10,266
Deferred income tax liabilities	1,404
Provisions	3,865
Other liabilities	7,610
Total liabilities	60,460

Shareholders' Equity

Share capital	7,548
Retained earnings	65,660
Other components	(21,993)
Total equity attributable to shareholders of the parent	51,215
Non-controlling interests	4,716
Total equity	55,931
Total liabilities and shareholders' equity	**116,391**

CASH FLOW FROM OPERATIONS, PROFIT, AND THE QUALITY OF EARNINGS

FINANCIAL
ANALYSIS

Many standard financial analysis texts warn analysts to look for unusual deferrals and accruals when they attempt to predict future periods' earnings. They often suggest that wide disparities between profit and cash flow from operations are a useful warning sign. For example, Wild et al. suggest that

> cash flows are often less subject to distortion than is net income. Accounting accruals determining net income rely on estimates, deferrals, allocations, and valuations. These considerations typically admit more subjectivity than factors determining cash flows. For this reason we often relate cash flows from operations to net income in assessing its quality. *Certain users consider earnings of higher quality when the ratio of cash flows from operations divided by net income is greater than 1*. This derives from a concern with revenue recognition or expense accrual criteria yielding high net income but low cash flows (emphasis added).*

The ratio of cash flow from operations to profit is illustrated and discussed in more depth in Chapter 5.

*J. Wild, K. Subramanyam, and R. Hasley, *Financial Statement Analysis*. New York, McGraw-Hill/Irwin, 2004, p. 394.

KEY RATIO
ANALYSIS

Evaluating company performance is the primary goal of financial statement analysis. Company managers, as well as competitors, use financial statements to better understand and evaluate a company's business strategy. Analysts, investors, and creditors use these same statements to evaluate performance as part of their share valuation and credit evaluation judgments. In Chapter 3, we introduced the return on assets to examine managers' effectiveness at utilizing assets to generate profit. We now discuss two other measures of profitability. The net profit margin compares profit to the revenues generated during the period, and the return on equity relates profit to shareholders' investment in the business.

NET PROFIT MARGIN RATIO

ANALYTICAL QUESTION → How effective is management at controlling revenues and expenses to generate more profit on sales?

RATIO AND COMPARISONS → The net profit margin is useful in answering this question. It is computed as follows:

$$\text{Net Profit Margin} = \frac{\text{Profit}}{\text{Net Sales}^*}$$

The 2009 ratio for Nestlé is

$$11{,}793 \,/\, 107{,}618 = 0.109 \ (10.9\%)$$

*Net sales is sales revenue less any returns from customers, and other reductions. For companies in the service industry, total operating revenues equal net sales.

LO⁴

Compute and interpret the net profit margin ratio and the return on equity ratio.

Comparisons over Time			Comparisons with Competitors	
Nestlé			**ConAgra Foods**	**Kraft Foods**
2007	**2008**	**2009**	**2009**	**2009**
10.0%	17.3%	10.9%	6.0%	7.5%

INTERPRETATIONS

In General → Net profit margin measures how much profit is earned as a percentage of revenues generated during the period. A rising net profit margin signals more efficient management of sales and expenses. Differences among industries result from the nature of the products or services provided and the intensity of competition. Differences among competitors in the same industry reflect how each company responds to changes in competition (and demand for the product or the service) and changes in managing sales volume, sales price, and costs. Financial analysts expect well-run businesses to maintain or improve their net profit margin over time.

Focus Company Analysis → Nestlé's net profit margin increased in 2008, and then dropped in 2009 to its previous, 2007, level. The increase in 2008 is due to a significant profit of 9,208 on the disposal of its investment in Alcon. Excluding this amount from the reported profit reduces the net profit margin to 8.8 percent. Compared with its competitors, Nestlé has a better performance than both ConAgra Foods and Kraft Foods. Despite the improvement in Nestlé's ratio over the past three years, its management should analyze the various expense items in an effort to better control these costs and continue to improve on its performance.

A Few Cautions → The decisions that management makes to maintain the company's net profit margin in the current period may have negative long-run implications. Analysts should perform additional analysis of the ratio to identify trends in each component of revenues and expenses. This involves dividing each line on the income statement by net sales. Statements presented with these percentages are called *common-sized income statements*. Changes in the percentages of the individual profit components provide information on shifts in management's strategies.

SELECTED FOCUS COMPANY NET PROFIT MARGINS	
BCE	9.8%
Nokia	7.9%
Benetton	5.7%

RETURN ON EQUITY

ANALYTICAL QUESTION → How well has management used shareholder investment to generate profit during the period?

RATIO AND COMPARISONS → The return on equity (ROE) helps in answering this question. It is computed as follows:

$$\text{Return on Equity} = \frac{\text{Profit}}{\text{Average Shareholders' Equity}^*}$$

*Average Shareholders' Equity = (Beginning Shareholders' Equity + Ending Shareholders' Equity) ÷ 2

The 2009 ratio for Nestlé is

$$11{,}793 / (53{,}631 + 54{,}916) \div 2 = 0.217\ (21.7\%)$$

Comparisons over Time			Comparisons with Competitors	
Nestlé			ConAgra Foods	Kraft Foods
2007	2008	2009	2009	2009
19.3%	34.7%	21.7%	12.6%	15.0%

INTERPRETATIONS

In General → ROE measures how much the firm earned as a percentage of shareholders' investment. In the long run, firms with higher ROE are expected to have higher share prices than firms with lower ROE, all other things equal. Managers, analysts, and creditors use this ratio to assess the effectiveness of the company's overall business strategy (its operating, investing, and financing strategies).

Focus Company Analysis → Nestlé's ROE increased in 2008, and then dropped in 2009 to its previous, 2007, level, which parallels the increase in its net profit margin over the same period. Nestlé's ROE is significantly higher than those of its competitors. This indicates that Nestlé's utilization of resources has generated a higher level of return on shareholders' investment than the managers of ConAgra Foods and Kraft Foods were able to achieve.

A Few Cautions → An increasing ROE can also indicate that a manufacturing company is failing to invest in research and development or in modernization of plant and equipment. While

SELECTED FOCUS COMPANY RETURN ON EQUITY RATIOS	
BCE	10.1%
Nokia	23.6%
Benetton	8.2%

such a strategy will decrease expenses and thus increase ROE in the short run, it normally results in future declines in ROE as the company's products and plant and equipment reach the end of their life cycles. As a consequence, experienced decision makers evaluate ROE in the context of a company's business strategy.

More detailed analysis of ROE and its relationship to other financial ratios are covered in Chapter 13.

SELF-STUDY **QUIZ 4-4**

Refer to Exhibit 4.5. Compute the net profit margin for Nestlé based on information disclosed in (1) the unadjusted trial balance and (2) the adjusted trial balance. Why are the two ratios different? Is the difference between the two ratios significant? Explain.

After you complete your answers, go online for the solutions.

connect

CLOSING THE BOOKS

End of the Accounting Cycle

The statement of financial position accounts are updated continuously throughout the accounting period, and the ending balance for the current period becomes the beginning account balance for the next period. The balances in these accounts, called permanent or real accounts, are not reduced to zero at the end of the accounting period. For example, the ending cash balance of one accounting period must be the beginning cash balance of the next accounting period. The only time a permanent account has a zero balance is when the item represented is no longer owned or owed.

In contrast, revenue, expense, gain, loss, and dividend accounts are used to accumulate transaction effects for the **current accounting period only**; they are called temporary or nominal accounts. At the end of each period, their balances are transferred, or closed, to the retained earnings account so that the company starts with zero balances in these accounts at the beginning of the next accounting period. This periodic clearing of the balances of the income statement accounts into retained earnings is done by recording closing entries.

The closing entries have two purposes:

1. To transfer profit or loss to retained earnings.
2. To establish a zero balance in each of the temporary accounts to start the accumulation in the next accounting period.

A special temporary (T) summary account, called Income Summary, is used to close the revenue, gain, expense, and loss accounts. Accounts with credit balances are closed by debiting the total amount to income summary, and accounts with debit balances are closed by crediting the total amount to income summary. The balance of the income summary account reflects the profit (or loss) and is then closed to retained earnings. In this way, the income statement accounts are again ready for their temporary accumulation function for the next period.

Closing entries are dated the last day of the accounting period, entered in the usual format in the journal, and immediately posted to the ledger (or T-accounts). *Temporary accounts with debit balances are credited and accounts with credit balances are debited.* We illustrate the closing process by preparing the closing entries for Nestlé at January 31, 2010, although in practice companies close their records only at the end of the fiscal year.

LO⁵

Explain the closing process at the end of the period.

PERMANENT (REAL) ACCOUNTS are the statement of financial position accounts whose ending balances are carried into the next accounting period.

TEMPORARY (NOMINAL) ACCOUNTS are income statement (and sometimes dividends declared) accounts that are closed to retained earnings at the end of the accounting period.

CLOSING ENTRIES transfer balances in temporary accounts to retained earnings and establish zero balances in temporary accounts.

INCOME SUMMARY is a temporary account used only during the closing process to facilitate closing temporary accounts.

Sales Revenue (R)

Closing	7,710	Sales in January	7,710
		End. Bal.	0

Income Summary (T)

Cost of sales in January	3,360	Sales in January	7,710
...		...	
...		...	
Closing	1,200		
		End. Bal.	0

Cost of Goods Sold (E)

Cost of sales in January	3,360	Closing	3,360
		End. Bal.	0

Dividends Declared (SE)

Dividends declared in January	200	Closing	200
		End. Bal.	0

Retained Earnings (SE)

		Ch. 3 bal.	64,660
Dividends declared	200	Profit	1,200
		End. Bal.	65,660

Sales revenue (−R)	7,710	
Service revenue (−R)	500	
Interest revenue (2R)	50	
Gain on sale of land (−R)	300	
Income summary (+T)		8,560
To close the revenue accounts to income summary.		
Income summary (−T)	7,360	
Cost of goods sold (−E)		3,360
Distribution expenses (−E)		1,281
General and administrative expenses (−E)		1,822
Depreciation expense (−E)		382
Interest expense (−E)		115
Income tax expense (−E)		400
To close the expense accounts to income summary.		
Income summary (−T)	1,200	
Retained earnings (+SE)		1,200
To close the income summary account to retained earnings.		
Retained earnings (−SE)	200	
Dividends declared (+SE)		200
To close the dividends declared account to retained earnings.		

Post-closing Trial Balance

After the closing process is complete, all of the income statement accounts have a zero balance. These accounts are then ready for recording revenues and expenses in the new accounting period. The ending balance in retained earnings now is up to date (matches the amount on the statement of financial position) and is carried forward as the beginning balance for the next period. As the last step of the accounting information processing cycle, a post-closing trial balance (Exhibit 4.7) should be prepared as a check that debits equal credits and that all temporary accounts have been closed.

FINANCIAL ANALYSIS

POST-CLOSING TRIAL BALANCE should be prepared as the last step of the accounting cycle to check that debits equal credits and all temporary accounts have been closed.

ACCRUALS AND DEFERRALS: JUDGING EARNINGS QUALITY

Most of the adjustments discussed in this chapter, such as the allocation of prepaid insurance or the determination of accrued interest revenue, involve direct calculations and require little judgment on the part of the company's management. In later chapters, we will discuss many other adjustments that involve difficult and complex estimates about the future. These include, for example, estimates of customers' ability to make payments to the company for purchases on account, the useful lives of new machines, and future amounts that a company may owe on warranties of products sold in the past. Each of these estimates and many others can have significant effects on the stream of profit that companies report over time.

When attempting to value firms based on their statement of financial position and income statement information, analysts also evaluate the estimates that form the basis for the adjustments. Those firms that make relatively pessimistic estimates that reduce current profit are judged to follow *prudent* financial reporting strategies, and their reports of performance are given more credence. The profit numbers reported by these companies are often said to be of *higher quality* because they are less influenced by management's natural optimism. Firms that consistently make optimistic estimates that result in reporting higher profit, however, are judged to be *aggressive*. Analysts judge these companies' operating performance to be of lower quality.

Exhibit **4.7**

Post-closing Trial Balance for the Nestlé Group

THE NESTLÉ GROUP
Trial Balance
At January 31, 2010
(in millions of Swiss francs)

	Adjusted Trial Balance		Post-closing Trial Balance	
	Debit	Credit	Debit	Credit
Assets				
Cash and cash equivalents	5,539		5,539	
Short-term investments	2,585		2,585	
Trade receivables	11,250		11,250	
Notes receivable	2,434		2,434	
Inventories	7,274		7,274	
Prepayments	667		667	
Other current assets	10,828		10,828	
Property, plant, and equipment	49,236		49,236	
Accumulated depreciation		25,869		25,869
Investment in associates	11,693		11,693	
Financial assets	4,162		4,162	
Goodwill	27,502		27,502	
Intangible assets	6,658		6,658	
Other assets	2,432		2,432	
Liabilities				
Trade payables		14,033		14,033
Short-term borrowings		14,438		14,438
Income taxes payable		1,573		1,573
Accrued liabilities		3,254		3,254
Deferred revenue				
Other current liabilities		10,266		10,266
Long-term borrowings		1,404		1,404
Deferred income tax liabilities		3,865		3,865
Provisions		7,610		7,610
Other liabilities		4,017		4,017
Shareholders' Equity				
Share capital		7,548		7,548
Retained earnings		64,660		65,660
Other components	21,993		21,993	
Non-controlling interests		4,716		4,716
Dividends declared	200		0	
Revenues and Gains				
Sales revenue		7,710		0
Service revenue		500		0
Interest revenue		50		0
Gain on sale of land		300		0
Expenses and Losses				
Cost of sales	3,360		0	
Distribution expenses	1,281		0	
Marketing and administrative expenses	1,822		0	
Depreciation expense	382		0	
Interest expense	115		0	
Income taxes expense	400		0	
Totals	171,813	171,813	164,253	164,253

ACCOUNTING STANDARDS
FOR PRIVATE ENTERPRISES

The accounting concepts and procedures related to adjusting and closing the appropriate accounts are equally applicable to private enterprises.

DEMONSTRATION **CASE A**

Dr. Jennifer Wong, a dentist, maintains her accounting records on an accrual basis. The following transactions occurred during the year ending December 31.

a. On September 1, the dental office loaned $2,000 to an employee for which the employee signed a note to pay the principal and interest at a 6 percent annual rate in six months.

b. On November 1, Dr. Wong paid $1,800 for six months of insurance coverage (from November 1 of this year to May 1 of next year).

c. On December 1, the dental office accepted a $2,400 payment from local businesses to provide dental care to their employees over the next three months. By December 31, Dr. Wong had provided one month of service.

d. All employees are paid a total of $3,000 biweekly, and that payment for 10 working days is made on Fridays, every two weeks. The last payment for the year was on Friday, December 27.

Required:

1. Identify deferred revenue, accrued revenue, deferred expense, and accrued expense accounts for items (a) through (d).
2. Using the process outlined in this chapter, analyze and record adjusting journal entries at December 31.

SUGGESTED **SOLUTION**

1.

Item	Account to Be Adjusted	Type of Adjustment	Explanation
a.	Accrued revenues (Interest)	Accrued revenue	Cash will be received for interest in the future.
b.	Prepayments	Deferred expense	Cash was paid for insurance prior to being used.
c.	Deferred revenues	Deferred revenue	Cash was received prior to being earned.
d.	Accrued expenses (Wages)	Accrued expense	Cash will be paid to employees in the future.

2. Analysis of deferrals and accruals, and adjusting journal entries:

a. **Accrued Revenue**

Any borrowing or lending of money involves two cash flows: one for the principal and one for the interest. Interest is the cost of borrowing money; it is an expense to the borrower and revenue to the lender. As each day passes until the principal is paid, more interest accumulates.

Step 1: When the money was loaned, the dental office increased the asset note receivable and decreased cash for $2,000. However, no entry was made at that date to recognize interest revenue because interest was not earned yet. Interest is earned over time and will be received in the future, requiring an accrued revenue.

Step 2: The interest revenue that should be recognized for this year is $40 [$2,000 × 0.06 × (4/12)]. This amount will be received on March 1 of the following year.

Year 1	**Year-end**	**Year 2**
$2,000 loaned 9/1	12/31	3/1
4 month—$40 earned	2 months $20 to be earned	$2000 + $60 to be collected

Loan period

Step 3: To recognize revenues in the period earned, an adjusting journal entry is needed. The effect is an increase in an asset and an increase in a revenue related to interest.

AJE a

Interest receivable (+A)	40	
Interest revenue (+R, +SE)		40

Assets		=	Liabilities	+	Shareholders' Equity	
Interest receivable	+40				Interest revenue	+40

Interest Receivable (A)

AJE a	40	
12/31	40	

Interest Revenue (R)

	40	AJE a
	40	12/31

Effect of adjustment on
Profit: ↑ 40
Cash: None

Since the accrued revenue has not yet been recorded until the end of the period, the adjusting entry increases a receivable account and increases a revenue account by the computed amount. When the employee pays the principal and interest on March 1 of the next period, the entry is as follows:

March 1	Cash (+A).	2,060	
	Note receivable (−A).		2,000
	Interest receivable (−A).		40
	Interest revenue (+R, +SE)		20

Assets		=	Liabilities	+	Shareholders' Equity	
Cash	+2,060				Interest revenue	+20
Note receivable	−2,000					
Interest receivable	−40					

b. Deferred Expense

On December 31, two months have passed, and two of the six months of insurance coverage have been used. To reflect incurring this expense in the current period, an adjusting entry is necessary. The process follows:

Step 1: The amount paid on November 1 represents future benefits (insurance coverage) to the dental office, creating a deferred expense account. Insurance coverage is partially used in November and December. The journal entry to record this transaction is

Prepaid insurance (+A).	1,800	
Cash (−A)		1,800

Step 2: As time passes after paying for the insurance, a portion of the asset is used during the period representing coverage received by the dentist.

Year 1	**Year-end**	**Year 2**
$1,800 received 11/1	12/31	5/1
2 months—$600 earned	4 months—$1,200 to be used (future benefits)	

Insurance coverage period

Step 3: An adjusting journal entry is necessary to increase expenses by $600 and to reduce prepaid insurance by $600. The used-up portion ($600) of the asset prepaid insurance is an expense. The remaining unused portion ($1,200) provides future benefits into next year. The adjusting entry and transaction effects follow:

AJE b

Insurance expense (+E, −SE)	600	
Prepaid insurance (−A).		600

Assets		=	Liabilities	+	Shareholders' Equity	
Prepaid Insurance	−600				Insurance expense	−600

Prepaid Insurance (A)

11/1	1,800		
		600	AJE b
12/31	1,200		

Insurance Expense (E)

11/1	0	
AJE b	600	
21/31	600	

Effect of adjustment on
Profit: ↓ 600
Cash: None

c. Deferred Revenue

Step 1: On December 1, the amount received represents an obligation to provide future service creating a deferred revenue account. The dental office earns revenue over time as it performs the services. The journal entry to record this transaction is

Cash (+A)	2,400	
Deferred dental fee revenue (+L)		2,400

Step 2: As time passes after receiving the fees, a portion of the liability ($800) is settled and revenue is earned.

Deferred Dental Fee Revenue (L)

		2,400	12/1
AJE c 800			
		1,600	12/31

	Year 1	Year-end	Year 2
	$2,400 received		
	12/1	12/31	3/1
	1 month—$800 earned	2 months—$1,600 to be earned (future obligations)	
		Service period	

Step 3: An adjusting journal entry is necessary to recognize the dental fee revenue earned this year and reduce the liability, deferred dental fee revenue. The remaining portion ($1,600) is service due in the future.

Dental Fee Revenue (R)

		0	12/1
		800	AJE c
		800	12/31

AJE c

Deferred dental fee revenue (−L)	800	
Dental fee revenue (+R, +SE)		800

Effect of adjustment on
Profit: ↑ 800
Cash: None

Assets	=	Liabilities	+	Shareholders' Equity	
		Deferred dental fee revenue	−800	Dental fee revenue	+800

d. Accrued Expense

The employees continued to work through December 31, the end of the accounting period, but they will not be paid until January 10.

Step 1: Employees worked and generated revenues during December but will be paid in January, requiring an *accrued expense*.

Step 2: The amount of wages owed to employees per day is $300 ($3,000 paid for 10 working days). By December 31, employees are owed $600 for two workdays, December 30 and December 31.

	Year 1	Year-end	Year 2
	12/27	12/31	1/10
	2 working days $600 incurred	8 working days $2,400 to be incurred	Pay $3,000
		Pay period	

Wages Payable (L)

		600	AJE d
		600	12/31

Step 3: An adjusting entry is necessary to increase wages expense and wages payable by $600.

Wages Expense (E)

AJE d	600		
12/31	600		

AJE d

Wages expense (+E, −SE)	600	
Wages payable (+L)		600

Effect of adjustment on
Profit: ↓ 400
Cash: None

Assets	=	Liabilities	+	Shareholders' Equity	
		Wages payable	+600	Wages expense	−600

To complete the analysis, consider the entry on the next payday, January 10, in the next period:

January 10	Wages expense (+E, −SE)...............	2,400	
	Wages payable (−L)......................	600	
	Cash (−A).............................		3,000

Assets		=	Liabilities		+	Shareholders' Equity	
Cash	−3,000		Wages payable	−600		Wages expense	−2,400

The $3,000 is paid, but only $2,400 relates to the expense incurred in the second period. The $600 was properly recorded as an expense in the prior period and is now paid (the liability is reduced). Because the year ended between paydays, a portion of the total paid in the second period is an expense in the first year and the rest is an expense in the second year. Thus, expenses were properly matched in the appropriate period.

DEMONSTRATION **CASE B**

We take our final look at the accounting activities of Terrific Lawn Maintenance Corporation by illustrating the activities at the end of the accounting cycle: adjustment process, financial statement preparation, and closing process. Chapter 2 presented investing and financing activities, and Chapter 3 presented operating activities. No adjustments had been made to the accounts to reflect all revenues earned and expenses incurred in April, however. The trial balance for Terrific Lawn on April 30, 2011, based on the unadjusted balances in Chapter 3, is as follows:

TERRIFIC LAWN MAINTENANCE CORPORATION
Unadjusted Trial Balance
At April 30, 2011

	Debit	Credit
Cash	5,760	
Trade receivables	1,700	
Prepayments	300	
Equipment	4,600	
Accumulated depreciation		0
Land	3,750	
Trade payables		220
Deferred revenue		1,600
Notes payable		4,400
Utilities payable		0
Wages payable		0
Interest payable		0
Income tax payable		0
Share capital		9,000
Retained earnings		0
Mowing revenue		5,200
Fuel expense	410	
Wages expense	3,900	
Insurance expense	0	
Utilities expense	0	
Depreciation expense	0	
Interest expense	0	
Income tax expense	0	
Totals	20,420	20,420

Additional Information

a. One-fourth of the $1,600 cash received from the city at the beginning of April for future mowing service has been earned in April. The $1,600 in deferred revenue represents four months of service (April through July).

b. Insurance costing $300, providing coverage for six months (April through September), was paid by Terrific Lawn at the beginning of April and has been partially used in April.

c. Mowers, edgers, rakes, and hand tools (equipment) have been used to generate revenue. They have a total cost of $4,600 and an estimated useful life of 10 years. No residual value is expected. The company uses straight-line depreciation.

d. Wages have been paid through April 29. Wages earned in April by the employees but not yet paid accrue at $130 per day.

e. An extra telephone line was installed in April at an estimated cost of $52, including hook-up and usage charges. The bill will be received and paid in May.

f. Interest accrues on the outstanding notes payable at an annual rate of 12 percent. The $4,400 in principal has been outstanding all month.

g. The estimated income tax rate for Terrific Lawn is 35 percent for both federal and provincial income taxes.

Required:

1. Using the process outlined in this chapter, (1) identify the type of adjustment related to each transaction, (2) determine the amount for the adjustment, (3) record the adjusting journal entries for April, and (4) record the effect of the adjustment on profit and cash.

2. Prepare an adjusted trial balance.

3. Prepare an income statement, a statement of changes in equity, and a statement of financial position based on the amounts in the adjusted trial balance. Include earnings per share on the income statement. The company issued 1,500 shares.

4. Prepare the closing entry for April 30, 2011.

5. Compute the company's net profit margin and the return on equity ratios for the month.

6. For each of the items (a), (b), and (c) above, indicate the effect of omitting the required adjustment on the elements of the statement of financial position and income statement. Use O for overstatement, U for understatement, and NE for no effect. Ignore the effects of income taxes on overstatements or understatements of revenues and expenses.

	Statement of Financial Position			Income Statement		
Transaction	**Assets**	**Liabilities**	**Shareholders' Equity**	**Revenues**	**Expenses**	**Profit**
a.						
b.						
c.						

We strongly recommend that you prepare your own answers to these requirements and then check your answers with the following solution.

SUGGESTED **SOLUTION**

1. Analysis of deferrals and accruals, and adjusting entries:

(a) **One fourth of the $1,600 cash received from the city at the beginning of April for future mowing service has been earned in April. The $1,600 in deferred revenues represents four months of service (April through July).**

Step 1: The city paid cash in the past for future mowing service, creating a deferred revenue account. Terrific Lawn earns revenue over time as it performs the services. The journal entry made in the past is

Cash (+A)   1,600
   Deferred revenue (+L)   1,600

Step 2: The amount of revenue that should be recognized in April is $400 ($1,600 ÷ 4 months). The remaining amount will be earned gradually in future periods.

	April	**Month-end**	**Beyond April**
$1,600 received			
	During the month	4/30	
	$400 revenue earned		$1,200 to be earned

Deferred Revenue (L)

		1,600	Bal.
AJE a	400		
		1,200	End.

Step 3: The deferred revenue account is currently overstated by $400 and mowing revenue is understated.

Mowing Revenue (R)

	5,200	Bal.
	400	AJE a
	5,600	End.

AJE a

Deferred revenue (−L) 400

   Mowing revenue (+R, +SE) 400

Effect of adjustment on

Profit: ↑ 400

Cash: None

Assets	=	**Liabilities**	+	**Shareholders' Equity**
		Deferred revenue −400		Mowing revenue +400

(b) Insurance costing $300, providing coverage for six months (April through September), was paid by Terrific Lawn at the beginning of April and has been partially used in April.

Step 1: The company paid insurance in the past, creating a deferred expense account. Insurance coverage has now been partially used. The journal entry made in the past is

Prepayments (+A). 300

   Cash (−A) 300

Step 2: The amount of insurance expense that should be recognized in April is $50 ($300 ÷ 6 months). The remaining amount, $250, will be recognized as expense gradually over the next five months.

	April	**Month-end**	**Beyond April**
$300 paid			
	During the month	4/30	
	$50 expense incurred		$250 to be incurred

Prepayments (A)

Bal.	300	50	AJE b
End.	250		

Step 3: The prepayments account is currently overstated by $50 and insurance expense is understated.

Insurance Expense (E)

Bal.	0	
AJE b	50	
End.	50	

AJE b

Insurance expense (+E, −SE) 50

   Prepayments (−A) 50

Effect of adjustment on

Profit: ↓ 50

Cash: None

Assets	=	**Liabilities**	+	**Shareholders' Equity**
Prepayments −50				Insurance expense −50

(c) Mowers, edgers, rakes, and hand tools (equipment) have been used to generate revenue. They have a total cost of $4,600 and an estimated useful life of 10 years. No residual value is expected. The company uses straight-line depreciation.

Step 1: Equipment was purchased in the past, creating a deferred expense account. It has now been used in operations during April. The journal entry made in the past is

Lawn equipment +A). 4,600

   Cash (−A) 200

   Notes payable (+L) 4,400

Step 2: The depreciation expense for April 2011 is $38 ($4,600 ÷ 120 months). The remaining amount will be recognized in future periods as the equipment is used.

Accumulated Depreciation (XA)

		0	Bal.
		38	AJE c
		38	End.

Depreciation Expense (E)

Bal.	0		
AJE c	38		
End.	38		

Effect of adjustment on
Profit: ↑ 400
Cash: None

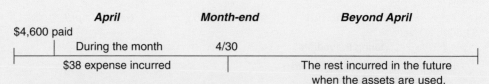

April	Month-end	Beyond April

$4,600 paid

During the month	4/30	
$38 expense incurred		The rest incurred in the future when the assets are used.

Step 3: Depreciation expense is understated by $38 while the carrying amount of equipment is overstated.

AJE c

Depreciation expense (+E, −SE)................................ 38
    Accumulated depreciation (+XA → −A)......................   38

Assets	=	Liabilities	+	Shareholders' Equity	
Accumulated depreciation −38				Depreciation expense −38	

(d) **Wages have been paid through April 29. Wages earned in April by the employees but not yet paid accrue at $130 per day.**

Step 1: Employees worked and generated revenue during April but will be paid in May, requiring an accrued expense. No entry was made in the past.

Step 2: The amount of wages expense incurred in April will be paid in the next accounting period.

April	Month-end	Beyond April
1 day worked	4/30	
$130 expense incurred		To be paid

Wages Payable (L)

		0	Bal.
		130	AJE d
		130	End.

Wages Expense (E)

Bal.	3,900		
AJE d	130		
End.	4,030		

Effect of adjustment on
Profit: ↓ 130
Cash: None

Step 3: Both wages expense and wages payable are currently understated by $130.

AJE d

Wages expense (+E, −SE)................................ 130
    Wages payable (+L).....................................   130

Assets	=	Liabilities	+	Shareholders' Equity	
		Wages payable +130		Wages expense −130	

(e) **An extra telephone line was installed in April at an estimated cost of $52, including hook-up and usage charges. The bill will be received and paid in May.**

Step 1: Utilities were installed and used in April, but the bill will be paid in May, requiring an accrued expense. No entry was made in the past.

Step 2: The amount of the telephone bill should be recognized in April and will be paid in May.

Utilities Payable (L)

		0	Bal.
		52	AJE e
		52	End.

April	Month-end	Beyond April
During the month	4/30	
$52 expense incurred		To be paid

Step 3: Both utilities expense and utilities payable are understated by $52.

Utilities Expense (E)

Bal.	0		
AJE e	52		
End.	52		

Effect of adjustment on
Profit: ↓ 52
Cash: None

AJE e

Utilities expense (+E, −SE)................................ 52
    Utilities payable (+L)...................................   52

Assets	=	Liabilities	+	Shareholders' Equity	
		Utilities payable +52		Utilities expense −52	

(f) **Interest accrued on the outstanding notes payable at an annual rate of 12 percent. The $4,400 in principal has been outstanding all month.**

Step 1: The notes payable were recorded when signed. Interest is incurred and will be paid in the future, requiring an accrued expense.

Step 2: The interest expense that should be recognized in April is $44 [$4,400 $\times$ 0.12 $\times$ (1/12)]. This amount is payable in a future period.

April	Month-end	Beyond April
During the month	4/30	
$44 expense incurred		To be paid

Step 3: Both interest expense and interest payable are understated by $44.

AJE f

Interest expense (+E, −SE)	44	
Interest payable (+L)		44

Assets	=	Liabilities	+	Shareholders' Equity	
		Interest payable	+44	Interest expense	−44

Interest Payable (L)

	0	Bal.
	44	AJE f
	44	End.

Interest Expense (E)

Bal.	0	
AJE f	44	
End.	44	

Effect of adjustment on
Profit: ↓ 44
Cash: None

(g) **The estimated income tax rate for Terrific Lawn is 35 percent for both federal and provincial income taxes.**

Step 1: Income taxes are computed on April's pretax profit but will be paid in the future, requiring an accrued expense. No entry was made in the past.

Step 2: The income tax expense that should be recognized in April is $342, calculated as follows:

	Revenues	Expenses	
Unadjusted totals	5,200	$4,310	From trial balance
a	400		
b		50	
c		38	
d		130	
e		52	
f		44	
	5,600	− 4,624	= **976 Pretax profit**

Income tax expense = Pretax profit (976) × Income tax rate (0.35) = $342 (rounded).

April	Month-end	Beyond April
	4/30	
$342 expense incurred		To be paid

Step 3: Both income tax expense and income taxes payable are currently understated by $342. The adjusting journal entry to record the income tax expense follows:

AJE g

Income tax expense (+E, −SE)	342	
Income taxes payable (+L)		342

Assets	=	Liabilities	+	Shareholders' Equity	
		Income taxes payable	+342	Income tax expense	−342

Income Taxes Payable (L)

	0	Bal.
	342	AJE g
	342	End.

Income Tax Expense (E)

Bal.	0	
AJE g	342	
End.	342	

Effect of adjustment on
Profit: ↓ 342
Cash: None

Note that all the adjustments affected profit because the revenue and expense accounts had to be increased to record all the revenues earned and the expenses incurred during the period. These adjustments affected specific asset and liability accounts, but none of the adjustments affected the Cash account, because adjustments are internal transactions that do not involve an exchange with an outside party.

2. Adjusted trial balance:

TERRIFIC LAWN MAINTENANCE CORPORATION
Trial Balance
At April 30, 2011
(in thousands of dollars)

	Unadjusted Trial Balance Debit	Unadjusted Trial Balance Credit	Adjustments Debit		Adjustments Credit		Adjusted Trial Balance Debit	Adjusted Trial Balance Credit
Cash	5,760						5,760	
Trade receivables	1,700						1,700	
Prepayments	300				(b)	50	250	
Equipment	4,600						4,600	
Accumulated depreciation		0			(c)	38		38
Land	3,750						3,750	
Trade payables		220						220
Deferred revenue		1,600	(a)	400				1,200
Notes payable		4,400						4,400
Utilities payable		0			(e)	52		52
Wages payable		0			(d)	130		130
Interest payable		0			(f)	44		44
Income taxes payable		0			(g)	342		342
Share capital		9,000						9,000
Retained earnings		0						0
Mowing revenue		5,200			(a)	400		5,600
Fuel expense	410						410	
Wages expense	3,900		(d)	130			4,030	
Insurance expense	0		(b)	50			50	
Utilities expense	0		(e)	52			52	
Depreciation expense	0		(c)	38			38	
Interest expense	0		(f)	44			44	
Income tax expense	0		(g)	342			342	
Totals	20,420	20,420	1,056		1,056		21,026	21,026

3. Financial statements:

TERRIFIC LAWN MAINTENANCE CORPORATION
Income Statement
For the Period Ended April 30, 2011

Revenues:		
Mowing revenue	$5,600	
Total revenues	5,600	
Expenses:		
Fuel	410	
Wages	4,030	
Insurance	50	
Utilities	52	
Depreciation	38	
Interest	44	
Total expenses	4,624	
Profit before income taxes	976	
Income tax expense	342	
Profit	$ 634	
Earnings per share	$0.423	← $634 Profit ÷ 1,500 shares outstanding

TERRIFIC LAWN MAINTENANCE CORPORATION
Statement of Changes in Equity
For the Period Ended April 30, 2011

	Share Capital	Retained Earnings	Total
Balance, April 1, 2011	$ 0	$ 0	$ 0
Issuance of shares	9,000		9,000
Profit		634	634
Dividends			0
Balance, April 30, 2011	$9,000	$634	$9,634

TERRIFIC LAWN MAINTENANCE CORPORATION
Statement of Financial Position
At April 30, 2011

Assets			Liabilities		
Current Assets:			**Current Liabilities:**		
Cash		$ 5,760	Trade payables		$ 220
Trade receivables		1,700	Deferred revenue		1,200
Prepayments		250	Wages payable		130
Total current assets		7,710	Utilities payable		52
Equipment	$4,600		Interest payable		44
Less: Accumulated depreciation	38	4,562	Income taxes payable		342
Land		3,750	Notes payable		4,400
			Total current liabilities		6,388
			Shareholders' Equity		
			Share capital		9,000
			Retained earnings		634
			Total shareholders' equity		9,634
Total assets		$16,022	Total liabilities and shareholders' equity		$16,022

4. Closing entries:

Mowing revenue (−R)	5,600	
Income summary (+T)		5,600
Income summary (−T)	4,966	
Fuel expense (−E)		410
Wages expense (−E)		4,030
Insurance expense (−E)		50
Utilities expense (−E)		52
Depreciation expense (−E)...		38
Interest expense (−E)...		44
Income tax expense (−E)...		342
Income summary (−T)	634	
Retained earnings (+SE)		634

5. Net profit margin for April:

$$\frac{\text{Profit}}{\text{Net Sales}} = \$634 \div \$5,600 = 0.1132 \text{ or } 11.32\%$$

Return on equity for April:

$$\frac{\text{Profit}}{\text{Average Shareholders' Equity}} = \frac{\$634}{(\$9,000 + \$9,634) \div 2} = 0.0680 \text{ or } 6.80\%$$

6.

	Statement of Financial Position			Income Statement		
Transaction	**Assets**	**Liabilities**	**Shareholders' Equity**	**Revenues**	**Expenses**	**Profit**
a.	NE	O, $400	U, $400	U, $400	NE	U, $400
b.	O, $50	NE	O, $50	NE	U, $50	O, $50
c.	O, $38	NE	O, $38	NE	U, $38	O, $38

Appendix 4A

An Optional Recordkeeping Efficiency

In Demonstration Case A, cash received or paid prior to revenue or expense recognition was recorded in a statement of financial position account. This approach is consistent with accrual accounting since, on the cash exchange date, either an asset or a liability exists. Payments or receipts are often recorded, however, as expenses or revenues on the transaction date. This is done to simplify recordkeeping since revenues or expenses are frequently earned or incurred by the end of the accounting period. When the full amount is not completely incurred or earned, an adjustment is necessary in these cases also. Note that, regardless of how the original entry is recorded, the same correct ending balances in the deferred dental fee revenue and dental fee revenue accounts result after the adjustment. The adjusting entry is different, however, in each case.

For example, for the December 1 illustration, the original entry could have been recorded in a revenue account and adjusted as follows:

Step 1: On December 1, the amount received could have been recorded as revenue.

Cash (+A)...	2,400	
Dental fee revenue (+R, +SE)		2,400

Step 2: As time passes after receiving the fees, only a portion of the fees are earned and the rest is due as service in the future.

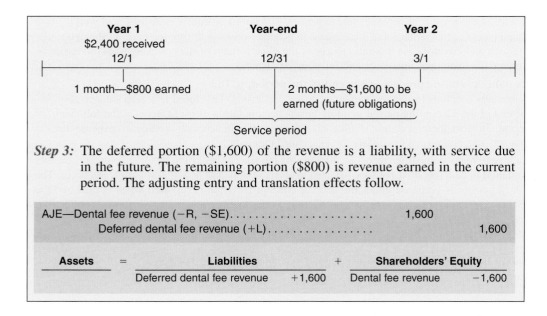

Step 3: The deferred portion ($1,600) of the revenue is a liability, with service due in the future. The remaining portion ($800) is revenue earned in the current period. The adjusting entry and translation effects follow.

AJE—Dental fee revenue (−R, −SE)...................... 1,600
      Deferred dental fee revenue (+L)................   1,600

Assets	=	Liabilities		+	Shareholders' Equity	
		Deferred dental fee revenue	+1,600		Dental fee revenue	−1,600

CHAPTER **TAKE-AWAYS**

1. **Explain the purpose of adjustments and analyze the adjustments necessary at the end of the period to update statement of financial position and income statement accounts. p. 164**
   Adjusting entries are necessary at the end of the accounting period to measure income properly and provide for appropriate amounts for financial statement accounts. The analysis involves
   Step 1: Identify the type of adjustments:
   > Deferred revenues—previously recorded liabilities created when cash was received in advance. They must be adjusted for the amount of revenue earned during the period.
   > Accrued revenues—revenues that were earned during the period but were not yet recorded (cash will be received in the future).
   > Deferred expenses—previously recorded assets (prepaid rent, supplies, and equipment) that must be adjusted for the amount of expense incurred during the period.
   > Accrued expenses—expenses that were incurred during the period but were not yet recorded (cash will be paid in the future).
   Step 2: Determine the amount of the earned revenue or incurred expense.
   Step 3: Record the adjusting entry needed to obtain the appropriate ending balances in the accounts, and post the effects to the respective T-accounts.
   Recording adjusting entries has no effect on the Cash account.

2. **Utilize a trial balance to prepare financial statements. p. 167**
   A trial balance is a list of all accounts with their debit or credit balances indicated in the appropriate column to provide a check on the equality of the debits and credits. The trial balance may be
   • Unadjusted—before adjustments are made.
   • Adjusted—after adjustments are made.
   • Post-closing—after revenues, expenses, gains, and losses are closed to retained earnings.

3. **Prepare an income statement with earnings per share, a statement of changes in equity, a statement of financial position, and supplemental cash flow information. p. 178**
   Adjusted account balances are used in preparing the following financial statements:
   • Income statement: Revenues − Expenses = Profit (including earnings per share computed as profit divided by the weighted-average number of common shares outstanding during the period).
   • Statement of changes in equity (Beginning share capital + issuance of shares − repurchase of shares) + (Beginning retained earnings + profit − dividends) = Ending shareholders' equity.
   • Statement of financial position: Assets = Liabilities + Shareholders' equity.
   • Supplemental cash flow information—Interest received and paid, dividends received and paid, income taxes paid, and significant non-cash transactions.

4. **Compute and interpret the net profit margin ratio and the return on equity ratio. p. 181**
   The net profit margin ratio (profit ÷ net sales) measures how much profit is earned as a percentage of revenues generated during the period. A rising net profit margin signals more

efficient management of revenues and expenses. The return on equity measures how well management used shareholders' investment to generate revenue during the period. Managers, analysts, and creditors use this ratio to assess the effectiveness of the company's overall business strategy (its operating, investing, and financing strategies).

5. **Explain the closing process at the end of the period. p. 183**
   Temporary accounts (revenues, expenses, gains, and losses) are closed to a zero balance at the end of the accounting period to allow for the accumulation of profit items in the following period. To close these accounts, debit each revenue and gain account, credit each expense and loss account, and record the difference to retained earnings.

   Each year, many companies report healthy profits but file for bankruptcy. Some investors consider this situation to be a paradox, but sophisticated analysts understand how this situation can occur. The income statement is prepared under the accrual concept (revenue is reported when earned and the related expense is reported when incurred). The income statement does not report cash collections and cash payments. Troubled companies usually file for bankruptcy because they cannot meet their cash obligations (e.g., they cannot pay their suppliers or meet their required interest payments). The income statement does not help analysts assess the cash flows of a company. The statement of cash flows discussed in Chapter 5 is designed to help statement users evaluate a company's cash inflows and outflows.

KEY **RATIOS**

Net profit margin measures how much profit each sales dollar generated during the period. A high or rising ratio suggests that the company is managing its sales and expenses efficiently. It is computed as follows (p. 181):

$$\text{Net Profit Margin} = \frac{\text{Profit}}{\text{Net Sales}}$$

Return on equity measures how much the firm earned for each dollar of shareholders' investment. It is computed as follows (p. 182):

$$\text{Return on Equity} = \frac{\text{Profit}}{\text{Average Shareholders' Equity}}$$

FINDING **FINANCIAL INFORMATION**

STATEMENT OF FINANCIAL POSITION

Current Assets
  Accruals include
    Interest receivable
    Rent receivable
  Deferrals include
    Inventory
    Prepayments
Non-current Assets
Deferrals include
  Property and equipment
  Intangibles

Current Liabilities
  Accruals include
    Interest payable
    Wages payable
    Utilities payable
    Income tax payable
  Deferrals include
    Deferred revenue

INCOME STATEMENT

Revenues
  Include end-of-period adjustments
Expenses
  Include end-of-period adjustments
Profit before Income Taxes
  Income tax expense
Profit

STATEMENT OF CASH FLOWS

Adjusting Entries Do not Affect Cash
  Supplemental Disclosure
    Interest paid
    Interest and dividends received
    Income taxes paid
    Significant non-cash transactions

NOTES

In Various Notes, if not on the Financial Statements
  Details of accrued liabilities
  Interest paid, interest and dividends
    received, income taxes paid, significant
    non-cash transactions (if not reported on
    the statement of cash flows)

KEY TERMS

Accounting Cycle p. 163
Accrued Expenses p. 166
Accrued Revenues p. 165
Adjusting Entries p. 164
Carrying Amount (Book Value, Net Book Value) p. 167
Closing Entries p. 183
Contra Account p. 167

Deferred Expenses p. 165
Deferred Revenues p. 165
Income Summary p. 183
Materiality p. 174
Permanent (Real) Accounts p. 183
Post-closing Trial Balance p. 184
Temporary (Nominal) Accounts p. 183
Trial Balance p. 166

QUESTIONS

1. Explain the accounting information processing cycle.
2. Identify, in sequence, the phases of the accounting information processing cycle.
3. Briefly explain adjusting entries. List the four types of adjusting entries, and give an example of each type.
4. What is a trial balance? What is its purpose?
5. What is a contra asset? Give an example of one.
6. Explain why adjusting entries are entered in the journal on the last day of the accounting period and then are posted to the ledger.
7. Explain how the financial statements relate to each other.
8. What is the equation for each of the following: (a) income statement, (b) the retained earnings component of the statement of changes in equity, (c) statement of financial position, and (d) statement of cash flows?
9. Explain the effect of adjusting entries on cash.
10. How is earnings per share computed and interpreted?
11. Contrast an unadjusted trial balance with an adjusted trial balance. What is the purpose of each?
12. Why does profit differ from cash flow from operations? Explain.
13. What is the practical importance of the concept of materiality to preparers, auditors, and users of financial statements?
14. What is meant by the "quality of earnings"?
15. What is the purpose of closing entries? Why are they recorded in the journal and posted to the ledger?
16. Differentiate among (a) permanent, (b) temporary, (c) real, and (d) nominal accounts.
17. Why are the income statement accounts closed, but the statement of financial position accounts are not?
18. What is a post-closing trial balance? Is it a useful part of the accounting information processing cycle? Explain.
19. How is the net profit margin ratio computed and interpreted?
20. How is the return on equity computed and interpreted?

EXERCISES

E4–1 Preparing a Trial Balance

LO2

Swanson Company has the following adjusted accounts and balances at year-end (June 30, 2011):

Trade payables	200	Cash	120	Land	200
Trade receivables	400	Cost of sales	820	Long-term borrowings	1,300
Accrued expenses		Income taxes		Prepayments	40
Payable	150	expense	110	Rent expense	400
Accumulated	250	Income taxes		Retained earnings	170
depreciation		payable	30	Salaries expense	660
Depreciation expense	110	Interest expense	80	Sales revenue	2,400
Buildings and		Interest income	50	Share capital	300
equipment	1,400	Inventories	610	Unearned fees	100

All these accounts have normal debit or credit balances.

Required:

Prepare an adjusted trial balance in good form for the Swanson Company at June 30, 2011.

LO1

E4–2   **Identifying Adjusting Entries from an Unadjusted Trial Balance**

As stated in its annual report, Unik Computer Corporation is an information technology company, developing and marketing hardware, software, solutions, and services. The following hypothetical trial balance lists accounts that Unik uses. Assume that the balances are unadjusted at the end of a recent fiscal year ended December 31.

UNIK COMPUTER CORPORATION
Unadjusted Trial Balance
At December 31, 2010
(millions of dollars)

	Debit	Credit
Cash	4,091	
Trade receivables	6,998	
Inventories	2,005	
Prepayments	624	
Property, plant, and equipment	5,223	
Accumulated depreciation		$ 2,321
Intangible assets	3,641	
Other assets	3,414	
Trade payables		4,237
Accrued liabilities		1,110
Income taxes payable		282
Pension obligations		545
Other liabilities		5,104
Share capital		7,270
Retained earnings		8,633
Product revenue		27,372
Services revenue		3,797
Cost of products sold	21,383	
Cost of services sold	2,597	
Marketing and administrative expenses	4,978	
Research and development costs	1,353	
Other operating expenses	4,283	
Income tax expense	81	
	60,671	60,671

Required:

1. Based on the information in the unadjusted trial balance, list the deferred accounts that may need to be adjusted at December 31 and the related income statement account in each case (no computations are necessary).

2. Based on the information in the unadjusted trial balance, list the accrual accounts that may need to be recorded at December 31 and the related income statement account in each case (no computations are necessary).

3. Which accounts should be closed at the end of the year? Why?

LO1

E4–3   **Recording Adjusting Entries and Determining Financial Statement Effects (Deferral Accounts)**

Consider the following transactions for Liner Company:

a. Collected $1,500 rent for the period December 1, 2011, to March 1, 2012, which was credited to deferred rent revenue on December 1, 2011.

b. Paid $1,800 for a one-year insurance premium on July 1, 2011; debited prepaid insurance for that amount.

c. Purchased a machine for $10,000 cash on January 1, 2010; estimated a useful life of five years with a residual value of $2,000.

Required:

1. Prepare the adjusting entries required for the year ended December 31, 2011, using the process illustrated in the chapter.

2. For each of the transactions above, indicate the amounts and direction of effects of the adjusting entry on the elements of the statement of financial position and income statement. Use the following format: + for increase, − for decrease, and NE for no effect.

	Statement of Financial Position			Income Statement		
Transaction	Assets	Liabilities	Shareholders' Equity	Revenues	Expenses	Profit
a.						
b.						
c.						

E4–4 Recording Adjusting Entries and Determining Financial Statement Effects (Accrual Accounts)   ▪ **LO1**

Consider the following transactions for Liner Company:

a. Received a $220 utility bill for electricity usage in December to be paid in January 2012.

b. Owed wages to 10 employees who worked three days at $150 each per day at the end of December 2011. The company will pay employees at the end of the first week of January 2012.

c. On September 1, 2011, loaned $3,000 to an officer who will repay the loan in one year at an annual interest rate of 12 percent.

Required:

1. Prepare the adjusting entries required for the year ended December 31, 2011, using the process illustrated in the chapter.

2. For each of the transactions above, indicate the amounts and direction of effects of the adjusting entry on the elements of the statement of financial position and income statement. Use the following format: + for increase, − for decrease, and NE for no effect.

	Statement of Financial Position			Income Statement		
Transaction	Assets	Liabilities	Shareholders' Equity	Revenues	Expenses	Profit
a.						
b.						
c.						

E4–5 Recording Adjusting Entries   ▪ **LO1**

Evans Company completed its first year of operations on December 31, 2011. All of the 2011 entries have been recorded, except for the following:

a. At year-end, employees earned wages of $6,000, which will be paid on the next payroll date, January 6, 2012.

b. At year-end, the company had earned interest revenue of $3,000. The cash will be collected March 1, 2012.

Required:

1. What is the annual reporting period for this company?

2. Identify whether each transaction above is a deferral or an accrual. Using the process illustrated in the chapter, prepare the required adjusting entry for transactions (*a*) and (*b*). Include appropriate dates and write a brief explanation of each entry.

3. Why are these adjustments made?

LO1

E4–6   Recording Adjusting Entries and Reporting Balances in Financial Statements

Dion Ltée is making adjusting entries for the year ended December 31, 2012. In developing information for the adjusting entries, the accountant learned the following:

a. Paid a one-year insurance premium of $3,000 on September 1, 2012, for coverage beginning on that date.

b. At December 31, 2012, obtained the following data relating to shipping supplies. The company uses a large amount of shipping supplies that are purchased in volume, stored, and used as needed.

Shipping supplies on hand, January 1, 2012	$14,000
Purchases of shipping supplies during 2012	72,000
Shipping supplies on hand, per inventory December 31, 2012	11,000

Required:

1. What amount should be reported on the 2012 income statement for insurance expense? for shipping supplies expense?

2. What amount should be reported on the December 31, 2012, statement of financial position for prepaid insurance? for shipping supplies inventory?

3. Using the process illustrated in the chapter, record the adjusting entry for insurance at December 31, 2012, assuming that the bookkeeper debited the full amount paid on September 1, 2012, to prepaid insurance.

4. Using the process illustrated in the chapter, record the adjusting entry for shipping supplies at December 31, 2012, assuming that the purchases of shipping supplies were debited in full to shipping supplies inventory.

LO1

E4–7   Recording Seven Typical Adjusting Entries

Crawford's Department Store is completing the accounting process for the year just ended, December 31, 2011. The transactions during 2011 have been journalized and posted. The following data with respect to adjusting entries are available:

a. Office supplies inventory at January 1, 2011, was $350. Office supplies purchased and debited to office supplies inventory during the year amounted to $900. The year-end inventory showed $200 of supplies on hand.

b. Wages earned during December 2011, unpaid and unrecorded at December 31, 2011, amounted to $2,700. The last payroll date was December 28; the next pay date will be January 6, 2012.

c. Three-fourths of the basement of the store is rented for $1,200 per month to another merchant, M. Riesman. Riesman sells compatible, but not competitive, merchandise. On November 1, 2011, the store collected six months' rent in the amount of $7,200 in advance from Riesman and credited the amount to deferred rent revenue.

d. The remaining basement space is rented to Rita's Specialty Shop for $500 per month, payable monthly. On December 31, 2011, the rent for November and December 2011 was neither collected nor recorded. Collection is expected on January 10, 2012.

e. The store used delivery equipment that cost $30,000 and was estimated to have a useful life of four years and a residual value of $4,000 at the end of the four years. Assume depreciation for a full year for 2011. The asset will be depreciated evenly over its useful life.

f. On July 1, 2011, a one-year insurance premium amounting to $1,800 was paid in cash and debited to prepaid insurance. Coverage began on July 1, 2011.

g. Crawford's operates an alteration shop to meet its own needs. The shop also does alterations for M. Riesman. At the end of December 31, 2011, Riesman had not paid for alterations completed, amounting to $750. This amount has not yet been recorded as alteration shop revenue. Collection is expected during January 2012.

Required:

1. Identify each of these transactions as a deferred revenue, deferred expense, accrued revenue, or accrued expense.

2. Using the process illustrated in the chapter, prepare for each situation the adjusting entry that should be recorded for Crawford's at December 31, 2011.

E4–8 Determining Financial Statement Effects of Seven Typical Adjusting Entries   LO1, 3
Refer to E4–7.

Required:

For each of the transactions in E4–7, indicate the amount and direction of effects of the adjusting entry on the elements of the statement of financial position and income statement. Use the following format: + for increase, − for decrease, and NE for no effect.

	Statement of Financial Position			Income Statement		
Transaction	Assets	Liabilities	Shareholders' Equity	Revenues	Expenses	Profit
a.						
b.						
c.						
etc.						

E4–9 Recording Seven Typical Adjusting Entries   LO1

Keanu's Boat Yard Inc. is completing the accounting process for the year just ended, November 30, 2012. The transactions during 2012 have been journalized and posted. The following data with respect to adjusting entries are available:

a. Keanu cleaned and covered three boats for customers at the end of November, but did not bill the customers $2,100 for the service until December.

b. The Tonga family paid Keanu $2,400 on November 1, 2012, to store their sailboat for the winter until May 1, 2013. Keanu credited the full amount to deferred storage revenue on November 1.

c. Wages earned by employees during November 2012, unpaid and unrecorded at November 30, 2012, amounted to $2,900. The next payroll date will be December 5, 2012.

d. On October 1, 2012, Keanu paid $600 to the local newspaper for an advertisement to run every Thursday for 12 weeks. All ads have been run, except for three Thursdays in December, to complete the 12-week contract.

e. Keanu used boat-lifting equipment that cost $230,000; the estimated depreciation for fiscal year 2012 is $23,000.

f. Boat repair supplies on hand at December 1, 2011 totalled $15,600. Repair supplies purchased and debited to supplies inventory during the year amounted to $47,500. The year-end inventory showed $12,200 of the supplies remaining on hand.

g. On April 1, 2012, Keanu borrowed $150,000 at an annual interest rate of 10 percent to expand boat storage facility. The loan requires Keanu to pay interest quarterly until the note is repaid in three years. Keanu paid quarterly interest on July 1 and October 1, 2012.

Required:

1. Identify each of these transactions as a deferred revenue, deferred expense, accrued revenue, or accrued expense.

2. Using the process illustrated in the chapter, prepare for each situation the adjusting entry that should be recorded for Keanu's at November 30, 2012.

E4–10 Determining Financial Statement Effects of Seven Typical Adjusting Entries   LO1, 3
Refer to E4–9.

Required:

For each of the transactions in E4–9, indicate the amount and direction of effects of the adjusting entry on the elements of the statement of financial position and income statement. Use the following format: + for increase, − for decrease, and NE for no effect.

	Statement of Financial Position			Income Statement		
Transaction	Assets	Liabilities	Shareholders' Equity	Revenues	Expenses	Profit
a.						
b.						
c.						
etc.						

LO1, 3

E4–11 **Determining Financial Statement Effects of Three Adjusting Entries**

Kwan Corp. started operations on January 1, 2011. It is now December 31, 2011: the end of the fiscal year. The part-time bookkeeper needs your help to analyze the following three transactions:

a. On January 1, 2011, the company purchased a special machine for a cash cost of $15,000. The machine has an estimated useful life of 10 years and no residual value.

b. During 2011, the company purchased office supplies that cost $1,800. At the end of 2011, office supplies worth $400 remained on hand.

c. On July 1, 2011, the company paid cash of $900 for a one-year premium on an insurance policy on the machine. Coverage began on July 1, 2011.

Required:

Complete the following schedule of the amounts that should be reported for 2011:

Selected Statement of Financial Position Amounts at December 31, 2011	Amount to Be Reported
Assets	
Equipment	$ _____
Accumulated depreciation	_____
Carrying amount of equipment	_____
Office supplies inventory	_____
Prepaid insurance	_____
Selected Income Statement Amounts for the Year Ended December 31, 2011	
Expenses	
Depreciation expense	$ _____
Office supplies expense	_____
Insurance expense	_____

LO1

Deere & Company

E4–12 **Inferring Transactions**

Deere & Company is the world's leading producer of agricultural equipment; a leading supplier of a broad range of industrial equipment for construction, forestry, and public works; a producer and marketer of a broad line of lawn and grounds care equipment; and a provider of credit, managed health care plans, and insurance products for businesses and the general public. The following information is taken from an annual report (in millions of dollars):

Income Taxes Payable				Dividends Payable				Interest Payable			
		Beg. bal.	71			Beg. bal.	43			Beg. bal.	45
(a)	?	(b)	332	(c)	?	(d)	176	(e)	297	(f)	?
		End. bal.	80			End. bal.	48			End. bal.	51

Required:

1. Identify the nature of each of the transactions (*a*) through (*f*). Specifically, what activities cause the accounts to increase and decrease?

2. Compute the amounts of transactions (*a*), (*c*), and (*f*).

E4–13   Analyzing the Effects of Errors on Financial Statement Items   LO1

Scarletti and Long Inc., publishers of movie and song trivia books, made the following errors in adjusting the accounts at year-end (December 31):

a. Did not record depreciation on equipment costing $130,000 with a residual value of $30,000 and a 10-year useful life.

b. Failed to adjust the deferred revenue account to reflect that $2,000 was earned by the end of the year.

c. Recorded a full year of accrued interest expense on an $18,000, 10 percent note payable that has been outstanding since November 1 of the current year.

d. Failed to adjust insurance expense to reflect that $400 relates to future insurance coverage.

e. Did not accrue $800 owed to the company by another company renting part of the building as a storage facility.

Required:

1. For each error, prepare (a) the adjusting journal entry that was made, if any, (b) the entry that should have been made at year-end, and (c) the entry to correct the error.

2. Using the following headings, indicate the effect of each error and the amount of the effect (i.e., the difference between the entry that was or was not made and the entry that should have been made). Use O if the effect overstates the item, U if the effect understates the item, and NE if there is no effect.

	Statement of Financial Position			Income Statement		
Transaction	Assets	Liabilities	Shareholders' Equity	Revenues	Expenses	Profit
a.						
b.						
c.						
etc.						

3. Explain the concept of materiality and how it might affect the adjusting entries you prepared in (1).

E4–14   Analyzing the Effects of Adjusting Entries on the Income Statement and Statement of   LO1, 3
Financial Position

On December 31, 2010, Cohen and Company prepared an income statement and a statement of financial position but failed to take into account four adjusting entries. The income statement, prepared on this incorrect basis, reflected pretax profit of $30,000. The statement of financial position (before the effect of income taxes) reflected total assets, $90,000; total liabilities, $40,000; and shareholders' equity, $50,000. The data for the four adjusting entries follow:

a. Depreciation for the year on equipment that cost $75,000 was not recorded. The equipment's useful life is 10 years and its residual value is $5,000.

b. Wages amounting to $17,000 for the last three days of December 2010 were not paid and not recorded (the next pay date is January 10, 2011).

c. An amount of $4,500 was collected on December 1, 2010, for rental of office space for the period December 1, 2010, to February 28, 2011. The $4,500 was credited in full to deferred rent revenue when collected.

d. Income taxes were not recorded. The income tax rate for the company is 30 percent.

Required:

Complete the following tabulation to correct the financial statements for the effects of the four errors (indicate deductions with parentheses):

Items	Profit	Total Assets	Total Liabilities	Shareholders' Equity
Balances reported	$30,000	$90,000	$40,000	$50,000
Effect of depreciation	_____	_____	_____	_____
Effect of wages	_____	_____	_____	_____
Effect of rent revenue	_____	_____	_____	_____
Adjusted balances	_____	_____	_____	_____
Effect of income taxes	_____	_____	_____	_____
Correct balances	_____	_____	_____	_____

LO1, 3, 4   **E4–15**   **Reporting a Correct Income Statement with Earnings per Share to Include the Effects of Adjusting Entries and Evaluating the Net Profit Margin as an Auditor**

Barton Inc. completed its first year of operations on December 31, 2011. Because this is the end of the fiscal year, the company bookkeeper prepared the following tentative income statement:

Income Statement, 2011		
Rental revenue		$114,000
Expenses:		
Salaries and wages expense	$28,500	
Maintenance expense	12,000	
Rent expense (on location)	9,000	
Utilities expense	4,000	
Gas and oil expense	3,000	
Miscellaneous expenses (items not listed elsewhere)	1,000	
Total expenses		57,500
Profit		$ 56,500

You are an independent accountant hired by the company to audit its accounting systems and review its financial statements. In your audit, you developed additional data as follows:

a. Unpaid wages for the last three days of December amounting to $310 were not recorded.

b. The unpaid $400 telephone bill for December 2011 has not been recorded.

c. Depreciation on rental cars, amounting to $23,000 for 2011, was not recorded.

d. Interest on a $20,000, one-year, 10 percent note payable dated October 1, 2011, was not recorded. The full amount of interest is payable on the maturity date of the note.

e. The deferred rental revenue account has a balance of $4,000 as at December 31, 2011, which represents rental revenue for the month of January 2012.

f. Maintenance expense includes $1,000, which is the cost of maintenance supplies still on hand at December 31, 2011. These supplies will be used in 2012.

g. The income tax expense is $7,000. Payment of income tax will be made in 2012.

Required:

1. For each item (*a*) through (*g*) what adjusting entry, if any, do you recommend that Barton should record at December 31, 2011? If none is required, explain why.

2. Prepare a correct income statement for 2011 in good form, including earnings per share, assuming that 7,000 shares are outstanding. Show computations.

3. Compute net profit margin based on the corrected information. What does this ratio suggest? If the industry average for net profit margin is 18 percent, what might you infer about Barton?

LO3   **E4–16**   **Evaluating the Effect of Adjusting Deferred Subscriptions on Cash Flows and Performance as a Manager**

You are the regional sales manager for Weld News Company. Weld is making adjusting entries for the year ended March 31, 2012. On September 1, 2011, $12,000 cash was received from customers in your region for two-year magazine subscriptions beginning on that date. The magazines are published and mailed to customers monthly. These were the only subscription sales in your region during the year.

Required:

1. What amount should be reported as cash from operations on the 2012 statement of cash flows?

2. What amount should be reported on the 2012 income statement for subscriptions revenue?

3. What amount should be reported on the March 31, 2012, statement of financial position for deferred subscriptions revenue?

4. Prepare the adjusting entry at March 31, 2012, assuming that the subscriptions received on September 1, 2011, were recorded for the full amount in deferred subscriptions revenue.

5. The company expects your region's annual revenue target to be $4,000.

   a. Evaluate your region's performance, assuming that the revenue target is based on cash sales.

   b. Evaluate your region's performance, assuming that the revenue target is based on accrual accounting.

E4–17 **Recording Adjusting Entries, Completing a Trial Balance, Preparing Financial Statements, and Recording Closing Entries** LO1, 3, 5

Cayuga Ltd. prepared the following trial balance at the end of its first year of operations ending December 31, 2012. To simplify the case, the amounts given are in thousands of dollars. Other data not yet recorded at December 31, 2012:

a. Insurance expired during 2012, $4.

b. Depreciation expense for 2012, $4.

c. Wages payable, $8.

d. Income tax expense, $9.

	Unadjusted		Adjustments		Adjusted	
Account Titles	**Debit**	**Credit**	**Debit**	**Credit**	**Debit**	**Credit**
Cash	38					
Trade receivables	9					
Prepaid insurance	6					
Machinery (20-year life, no residual value)	80					
Accumulated depreciation		8				
Trade payables		9				
Wages payable						
Income taxes payable						
Share capital (4,000 shares)		68				
Retained earnings (deficit)	4					
Revenues (not detailed)		84				
Expenses (not detailed)	32					
Totals	169	169				

Required:

1. Prepare the adjusting entries for 2012.

2. Show the effects (direction and amount) of the adjusting entries on profit and cash.

3. Complete the trial balance Adjustments and Adjusted columns.

4. Using the adjusted balances, prepare an income statement, a statement of changes in equity, and a statement of financial position.

5. What is the purpose of "closing the books" at the end of the accounting period?

6. Using the adjusted balances, prepare the closing entries for 2012.

LO3, 4   **E4–18**   **Preparing Financial Statements, Closing Entries, and Analyzing Net Profit Margin and Return on Equity**

Liner Company has the following adjusted trial balance at December 31, 2011. No dividends were declared; however, 400 additional shares were issued during the year for $2,000:

	Debit	Credit
Cash	$ 2,700	
Trade receivables	3,000	
Interest receivable	120	
Prepayments	600	
Notes receivable	3,000	
Equipment	12,000	
Accumulated depreciation		$ 2,000
Trade payables		1,600
Accrued liabilities		3,820
Income taxes payable		2,900
Deferred rent revenue		600
Share capital (500 shares)		2,400
Retained earnings		1,000
Sales revenue		45,000
Interest revenue		120
Rent revenue		300
Wages expense	20,600	
Depreciation expense	2,000	
Utilities expense	1,220	
Insurance expense	600	
Rent expense	10,000	
Income tax expense	3,900	
Total	$59,740	$59,740

Required:

1. Prepare an income statement in good form for 2011. Include earnings per share.
2. Prepare closing entries and post the effects to the appropriate ledger accounts.
3. Prepare a statement of financial position in good form at December 31, 2011.
4. Compute Liner Company's net profit margin for the year. What does this ratio mean?
5. Compute Liner Company's return on equity for the year. What does this ratio mean?

LO4   **E4–19**   **Analyzing and Evaluating Return on Equity from a Security Analyst's Perspective**

Papa John's

Papa John's is one of the fastest-growing pizza delivery and carry-out restaurant chains. Selected income statement and statement of financial position amounts (in thousands) for two recent years are presented below.

	Current Year	Prior Year
Profit	$ 36,796	$ 32,735
Average shareholders' equity	128,445	136,536

Required:

1. Compute the return on equity for the current and prior years and explain the meaning of the change.
2. Would security analysts more likely increase or decrease their estimates of share value on the basis of this change? Explain.

LO4   **E4–20**   **Evaluating Profitability by Using Net Profit Margin and Return on Equity**

Sears Canada

Sears Canada is one of the biggest Canadian department store retailers. It operates a large number of department stores that sell home fashions, appliances, apparel, home electronics, and garden products. It also sells merchandise online. Selected information about the company's resources and operations are presented on the following page (amounts in millions of dollars).

	2008	2007	2006	2005	2004
Total shareholders' equity	$1,508	$1,093	$ 785	$ 645	$1,877
Total revenue	5,733	6,326	5,933	6,238	6,230
Net earnings (Profit)	289	306	153	771	129

Required:

1. Compute the net profit margin and the return on equity for 2005 to 2008.

2. Both ratios are relatively high in 2005 compared to later years. What are the most likely reasons for the significant increase in both ratios? (*Hint:* Think about the reasons for an increase in profit and a decrease in shareholders' equity.)

3. As a potential investor, how do you interpret these ratios?

4. What additional information would you require before deciding whether or not to invest in Sears' shares?

E4–21 (Appendix 4A) Recording Adjusting Entries

LO1

Consider each of the following independent cases and prepare the adjusting journal entry at year-end.

1. On June 30, 2011, Able Ltd. paid $18,000 for a two-year insurance policy. Insurance coverage started on July 1, 2011. The company's bookkeeper debited insurance expense and credited cash, $18,000. Able's fiscal year ends on January 31, 2012.

2. On August 1, 2011, Landlord Inc. received $6,400 from a tenant representing payment of rent in advance for eight months (including August). Landlord's bookkeeper debited cash and credited rent expense for $6,400. Landlord's fiscal year ends on December 31, 2011.

3. The accountant for Jung Corp. computed the income tax expense for the year 2011 to be $12,200. Before recording the journal entry, she noticed that the unadjusted trial balance at December 31, 2011, (the company's fiscal year-end) included prepaid income taxes of $3,400 and a zero balance for income tax expense.

4. On June 1, 2012, the supplies inventory account for Katz Ltd. showed a debit balance of $4,400. During June 2012 miscellaneous supplies totalling $1,800 were purchased on account and recorded as follows:

Supplies expense	1,800	
Trade payables		1,800

A physical count of supplies available at June 30, 2012, showed that $2,600 of supplies were still on hand. Katz's fiscal year ends on June 30, 2012.

PROBLEMS

P4–1 Preparing a Trial Balance (AP4–1)

LO2

Geox S.p.A. is an Italy-based company active in the footwear and apparel manufacturing industry, which includes classic, casual, and sports footwear, as well as apparel for men, women, and children. The company's products are sold in more than 70 countries worldwide through a widespread distribution network. The following is a list of accounts and amounts reported in the company's financial statements for 2008. The accounts have normal debit or credit balances and their balances are rounded to the nearest thousand. Geox's fiscal year ends on December 31.

Geox S.p.A.

Accounts payable	$149,206	Income tax expense	52,900	Property, plant, and	
Accounts receivable	124,594	Income taxes payable	17,246	equipment	78,020
Advertising and		Intangibles	78,231	Provisions for liabilities and	
promotion expense	66,917	Inventories	228,764	charges	7,214
Cash	68,672	Long-term loans	27,410	Retained earnings	?
Cost of sales	424,461	Other assets	60,171	Sales revenue	892,513
Financial assets	18,643	Other current liabilities	23,427	Selling and distribution	
General and		Other non-current liabilities	5,122	expenses	43,248
administrative expenses	187,397			Share capital	25,920

Required:

Prepare an adjusted trial balance at December 31, 2008. How did you determine the amount for retained earnings?

■ **LO1, 3**   **P4–2**   **Recording Adjusting Entries** (AP4–2)

McGraw Company's fiscal year ends on December 31. It is December 31, 2012, and all of the 2012 entries have been made, except the following adjusting entries.

a. On September 1, 2012, McGraw collected six months' rent of $7,200 on storage space. At that date, McGraw debited cash and credited deferred rent revenue for $7,200.

b. The company earned service revenue of $2,000 on a special job that was completed December 29, 2012. Collection will be made during January 2013; no entry has been recorded.

c. On November 1, 2012, McGraw paid a premium of $4,200 for a one-year property insurance policy, for coverage starting on that date. Cash was credited and prepaid insurance was debited for this amount.

d. At December 31, 2012, wages earned by employees totalled $14,300. The employees will be paid on the next payroll date, January 15, 2013.

e. Depreciation must be recognized on a service truck that cost $12,000 on July 1, 2012 (estimated useful life is six years with no residual value).

f. Cash of $2,400 was collected on November 1, 2012, for services to be rendered evenly over the next year beginning on November 1 (deferred service revenue was credited).

g. On December 27, 2012, the company received a tax bill of $450 from the city for property taxes on land for 2012. The amount is payable during January 2013.

h. On October 1, 2012, the company borrowed $20,000 from a local bank and signed an 8 percent note for that amount. The principal and interest are payable on September 30, 2013.

Required:

1. Indicate whether each transaction relates to a deferred revenue, deferred expense, accrued revenue, or accrued expense.

2. Prepare the adjusting entry required for each transaction at December 31, 2012.

3. Show the effects (direction and amount) of the adjusting entries on profit and cash.

■ **LO1, 3**   **P4–3**   **Recording Adjusting Entries and Determining Their Financial Statement Effects** (AP4–3)

Handy Haulers Company is at the end of its fiscal year, December 31, 2011. The following data were developed from the company's records and related documents:

a. On July 1, 2011, a one-year insurance premium on equipment in the amount of $1,200 was paid and debited to prepaid insurance. Coverage began on July 1.

b. During 2011, office supplies amounting to $800 were purchased for cash and debited in full to supplies inventory. At the end of 2010, the inventory of supplies remaining on hand (unused) amounted to $200. The inventory of supplies on hand at December 31, 2011, showed $300.

c. On December 31, 2011, Bert's Garage completed repairs on one of the company's trucks at a cost of $800; the amount is not yet recorded and by agreement will be paid during January 2012.

d. In December 2011, a tax bill for $2,000 on land owned during 2011 was received from the city. The taxes, which have not been recorded, are due on February 15, 2012.

e. On December 31, 2011, the company completed a contract for another company. The bill was for $8,000 payable within 30 days. No journal entry has been made for this transaction.

f. On July 1, 2011, the company purchased a new hauling van at a cash cost of $23,600. The estimated useful life of the van was 10 years, with an estimated residual value of $1,100. No depreciation has been recorded for 2011 (compute depreciation for six months in 2011).

g. On October 1, 2011, the company borrowed $10,000 from the local bank on a one-year, 9 percent note payable. The principal plus interest is payable on September 30, 2012.

h. The profit before any of the adjustments or income taxes was $30,000. The company's income tax rate is 30 percent. Compute the adjusted profit after considering the effects of Transactions (a) through (g) to determine the income tax expense for 2011.

Required:

1. Indicate whether each transaction relates to a deferred revenue, deferred expense, accrued revenue, or accrued expense.

2. Prepare the adjusting entry required for each transaction at December 31, 2011.

3. Using the following headings, indicate the effect of each adjusting entry and the amount of each. Use + for increase, − for decrease, and NE for no effect.

	Statement of Financial Position			Income Statement		
Transaction	**Assets**	**Liabilities**	**Shareholders' Equity**	**Revenues**	**Expenses**	**Profit**
a.						
b.						
c.						
etc.						

P4–4 Computing Amounts on Financial Statements and Finding Financial Information (AP4–4) ■ **LO3**
The following transactions and events are provided by the records of South Hill Apartments (a corporation) at the end of its fiscal year, December 31, 2011:

Revenue

a. Rent revenue collected in cash during 2011 for occupancy in 2011 .... $512,000

b. Rent revenue earned for occupancy in December 2011; not collected until 2012 16,000

c. Rent collected in December 2011 in advance of occupancy in January 2012 12,000

Salaries

d. Cash payment in January 2011 for employee salaries earned in December 2010 4,000

e. Salaries incurred and paid during 2011 62,000

f. Salaries earned by employees during December 2011 that will be paid in January 2012 3,000

g. Cash advance to employees in December 2011 for salaries that will be earned in January 2012 1,500

Supplies

h. Maintenance supplies inventory on January 1, 2011 (balance on hand) 3,000

i. Maintenance supplies purchased for cash during 2011 8,000

j. Maintenance supplies inventory on December 31, 2011 1,700

Required:
For each of the following accounts, compute the balance that should be reported in South Hill's 2011 financial statements, indicate on which financial statement the item will be reported, and the effect (direction and amount) on cash flows (+ for increase, − for decrease, and NE for no effect). (*Hint:* Create T-accounts to determine account balances.)

Account	2011 Balance	Financial Statement	Effect on Cash Flows
1. Rent revenue			
2. Salary expense			
3. Maintenance supplies expense			
4. Rent receivable			
5. Receivables from employees			
6. Maintenance supplies inventory			
7. Deferred rent revenue			
8. Salaries payable			

P4–5 Inferring Year-End Adjustments, Computing Earnings per Share and Net Profit Margin, and Recording Closing Entry (AP4–5) ■ **LO1, 2, 4, 5**
Willenborg Company is completing the information processing cycle at its fiscal year-end, December 31, 2012. Following are the correct account balances at December 31, 2012, both before and after the adjusting entries for 2012.

| | Trial Balance, December 31, 2012 | | | | | | |
| | Before Adjusting Entries | | Adjustments | | After Adjusting Entries | | |
Items	Debit	Credit	Debit	Credit	Debit	Credit
a. Cash	$ 9,000				$ 9,000	
b. Service revenue receivable					400	
c. Prepaid insurance	600				400	
d. Equipment	120,200				120,200	
e. Accumulated depreciation, equipment		$31,500				$ 40,000
f. Accrued advertising payable						4,700
g. Share capital		80,000				80,000
h. Retained earnings, January 1, 2012		14,000				14,000
i. Service revenue		46,000				46,400
j. Salary expense	41,700				41,700	
k. Depreciation expense					8,500	
l. Insurance expense					200	
m. Advertising expense					4,700	
	$171,500	$171,500			$185,100	$185,100

Required:

1. Compare the amounts in the columns before and after the adjusting entries to reconstruct the adjusting entries made in 2012. Provide an explanation for each adjustment.
2. Compute the amount of profit, assuming that it is based on the amounts (a) before adjusting entries and (b) after adjusting entries. Which profit amount is correct? Explain.
3. Compute the earnings per share, assuming that 4,000 shares are outstanding.
4. Compute the net profit margin. What does this suggest to you about the company?
5. Compute the return on equity, assuming that share capital did not change during the year. What does the computed ratio suggest to you about the company?
6. Prepare the closing entries at December 31, 2012.

■ LO1, 2, 3, 5   **P4–6**   **Recording Adjusting and Closing Entries and Preparing a Statement of Financial Position and an Income Statement Including Earnings per Share** (AP4–6)

Mostert Inc. a small service company, keeps its records without the help of an accountant. After much effort, an outside accountant prepared the following unadjusted trial balance as at the end of the company's fiscal year, December 31, 2011.

Data not yet recorded at December 31, 2011, included:

a. The supplies inventory on December 31, 2011, reflected $200 remaining on hand.
b. Insurance expired during 2011, $400.
c. Depreciation expense for 2011, $4,000.
d. Wages earned by employees not yet paid on December 31, 2011, $1,100.
e. Income tax expense of $7,350.

Account Titles	Debit	Credit
Cash	60,000	
Trade receivables	13,000	
Service supplies inventory	800	
Prepaid insurance	1,000	
Service trucks (5-year life, no residual value)	20,000	
Accumulated depreciation, service trucks		12,000
Other assets	11,200	
Trade payables		3,000
Note payable (3 years; 10% each December 31)		20,000
Share capital (5,000 shares outstanding)		28,200
Retained earnings		7,500
Service revenue		77,000
Other expenses, excluding income tax	41,700	
Totals	147,700	147,700

Required:

1. Prepare the adjusting entries at December 31, 2011.

2. Show the effects (direction and amount) of the adjusting entries on profit and cash.

3. Prepare an income statement for 2011 and a statement of financial position at December 31, 2011, including the effects of the preceding five transactions.

4. Assume that you forgot to adjust the balance of the service supplies inventory account. How would this error affect the amount of profit for the year? Does this error lead to a material effect on profit? Explain.

5. Prepare the closing entries at December 31, 2011.

P4–7 **Preparing Both an Income Statement and a Statement of Financial Position from a Trial Balance and Closing Entries** (AP4–7)   ▌**LO3, 4, 5**

Juan Real Estate Company (organized as a corporation on April 1, 2010) has completed the accounting cycle for the second year, ended March 31, 2012. Juan also has completed a correct trial balance as follows:

JUAN Real Estate Company
Adjusted Trial Balance
At March 31, 2012

Account Titles	Debit	Credit
Cash	$ 53,000	
Trade receivables	44,800	
Office supplies inventory	300	
Automobiles (company cars)	30,000	
Accumulated depreciation, automobiles		$ 10,000
Office equipment	3,000	
Accumulated depreciation, office equipment		1,000
Trade payables		20,250
Salaries and commissions payable		1,500
Note payable, long term		30,000
Share capital (30,000 shares)		35,000
Retained earnings (on April 1, 2007)		7,350
Dividends declared	8,000	
Sales commissions earned		77,000
Management fees earned		13,000
Operating expenses (detail omitted to conserve your time)	48,000	
Depreciation expense (including $500 on office equipment)	5,500	
Interest expense	2,500	
Totals	$195,100	$195,100

Required:

1. Prepare an income statement for the reporting year ended March 31, 2012. Include income tax expense, assuming a 30 percent tax rate. Use the following major captions: revenues, expenses, profit before income taxes, income tax, profit, and earnings per share (list each item under these captions as appropriate).

2. Prepare the journal entry to record income taxes for the year (not yet paid).

3. Prepare a statement of financial position at the end of the reporting year, March 31, 2012. Use the following captions (list each item under these captions as appropriate).

Assets

Current assets
Non-current assets

Liabilities

Current liabilities
Non-current liabilities

Shareholders' Equity

Share capital
Retained earnings

4. Compute the net profit margin and the return on equity. What do these ratios suggest?

5. Prepare the closing entries at March 31, 2012.

LO1, 2, 3, 4, 5 P4–8

eXcel

Comprehensive Review Problem: From Recording Transactions (Including Adjusting and Closing Entries) to Preparing a Complete Set of Financial Statements and Performing Ratio Analysis (See Chapters 2, 3, and 4) (AP4–8)

Brothers Hadi and Hamid Gaber began operations of their tool and die shop (H & H Tool Inc.) on January 1, 2010. The company's fiscal year ends on December 31. The trial balance on January 1, 2011, was as follows (the amounts are rounded to thousands of dollars):

Account No.	Account Titles	Debit	Credit
01	Cash	3	
02	Trade receivables	5	
03	Service supplies inventory	12	
04	Land		
05	Equipment	60	
06	Accumulated depreciation (equipment)		6
07	Other assets (not detailed to simplify)	4	
11	Trade payables		5
12	Notes payable		
13	Wages payable		
14	Interest payable		
15	Income taxes payable		
21	Share capital (65,000 shares)		65
31	Retained earnings		8
35	Service revenue		
40	Depreciation expense		
41	Income tax expense		
42	Interest expense		
43	Other expenses		
	Totals	84	84

Transactions and events during 2011 (summarized in thousands of dollars) follow:

a. Borrowed $10 cash on a 12 percent note payable, dated March 1, 2011.

b. Purchased land for future building site, paid cash, $9.

c. Earned revenues for 2011 of $160, including $50 on credit.

d. Sold 3,000 additional shares for $1 cash per share (show dollars in thousands).

e. Recognized other expenses for 2011; $85, including $20 on credit.

f. Collected trade receivables, $24.

g. Purchased additional assets, $10 cash (debit other assets account).

h. Paid trade payables, $13.

i. Purchased service supplies on account, $18 (debit to Account No. 03).

j. Signed a $25 service contract to start February 1, 2012.

k. Declared and paid cash dividend, $15.

Data for adjusting entries:

l. Service supplies inventory on hand at December 31, 2011, $12 (debit other expenses account).

m. The equipment's useful life is 10 years; no residual value.

n. Accrued interest on notes payable (to be computed).

o. Wages earned since the December 24 pay date but not yet paid, $15.

p. Income tax expense payable in 2012, $8.

Required:

1. Set up T-accounts for the accounts on the trial balance and enter their beginning balances.

2. Record transactions (*a*) through (*k*) and post them to the T-accounts.

3. Record and post the adjusting entries (*l*) through (*p*).

4. Prepare an income statement (including earnings per share), a statement of changes in equity for 2011, and a statement of financial position at December 31, 2011.

5. Record and post the closing entries.

6. Prepare a post-closing trial balance.

7. Compute the following ratios for 2011 and explain what they mean:
   a. debt-to-equity
   b. total asset turnover
   c. net profit margin
   d. return on equity

P4–9 Using Financial Reports: Evaluating Profitability by Using Net Profit Margin and Return on Equity Ratios (AP4–9)

A summary of selected historical results is presented below for three Canadian companies: Barrick Gold, WestJet Airlines, and Le Groupe Jean Coutu. Each of these companies has grown in size over time by acquiring assets and investing in other companies. (Amounts are in millions of dollars.)

■ **LO4**

Barrick Gold
WestJet Airlines
Le Groupe Jean Coutu

	2008	2007	2006	2005	2004	2003
Barrick Gold						
Total shareholders' equity	$15,277	$15,256	$14,199	$3,850	$3,574	$3,481
Total revenue	7,913	6,332	5,630	2,350	1,932	1,035
Profit	785	1,119	1,506	401	248	200
Operating cash flow	2,206	1,732	2,122	726	509	519
WestJet Airlines						
Total shareholders' equity	1,086	950	806	670	590	581
Total revenue	2,549	2,127	1,774	1,393	1,058	864
Profit (Loss)	178	193	115	24	(17)	61
Operating cash flow	461	541	336	247	144	192
Le Groupe Jean Coutu						
Total shareholders' equity	753	1,223	1,906	1,412	853	1,020
Total revenue	1,676	13,265	11,143	9,617	3,043	4,052
Profit (Loss)	(251)	163	104	104	133	164
Operating cash flow	146	192	165	222	186	214

Required:

1. Compute the net profit margin and the return on equity ratios for each company for each of the years 2006–2008 using the table below.

	2008	2007	2006	2005	2004
Barrick Gold					
Net profit margin				17.06%	12.84%
Return on equity (ROE)				10.80%	7.03%
Quality of earnings				1.81	2.05
WestJet Airlines					
Net profit margin				1.72%	−1.61%
Return on equity (ROE)				3.81%	−2.90%
Quality of earnings				10.29	NA
Le Groupe Jean Coutu					
Net profit margin				1.08%	4.37%
Return on equity (ROE)				9.18%	14.20%
Quality of earnings				2.13	1.40

2. Based on the computed ratios, rank these companies from most successful to least successful in generating income for shareholders.

3. Assume that you are interested in investing in one of these three companies, which company would you choose? Write a brief report to justify your choice.

4. Analysts examine both profit and cash flow from operating activities in evaluating a company. One measure that relates these two numbers is the quality of earnings ratio, which equals cash flow from operations divided by profit. The higher the ratio, the higher the quality of earnings. Compute this ratio for 2006–2008, and rank the three companies from highest to lowest, based on the quality of their earnings.

LO1

P4–10   **Recording Journal Entries and Inferring Adjustments**

Stay'N Shape was started by Jennifer Long several years ago to provide physical fitness services to its customers. The following balances were extracted from the company's general ledger as at the following dates:

	May 31, 2011	April 30, 2011
Deferred revenue	$ 4,500	$ 3,000
Trade receivables	44,000	59,000
Prepaid rent	?	4,900
Prepaid insurance	?	1,200
Notes payable	20,000	20,000
Supplies inventory	?	7,200
Supplies expense	17,200	

Additional information about several transactions that occurred in May is provided below:

a. Some customers pay for services in advance. The remaining customers are sent invoices for services used and are allowed one month to pay their invoices. During May, the company received from customers a total of $62,000 in cash, including an amount of $7,000 which was paid by customers in advance.

b. At the end of April, the company had paid rent for the next five months and recorded the amount as prepaid rent.

c. The balance of prepaid insurance at April 30 represents the cost of insuring the company's premises and equipment for one month. In May, the company received an invoice from the insurance company for a renewal of the company's insurance policy for one year. The insurance premium was increased by 10 percent over the amount of the premium of the previous year because the company filed a few insurance claims. The company paid the one-year insurance premium.

d. The note payable carries interest at 6 percent and is due on June 30, 2011, along with accrued interest. The company recognizes interest expense on a monthly basis.

e. An invoice for $780 pertaining to advertising work done during May was received on May 2.

f. Supplies amounting to $17,200 were purchased on account during May and debited to the supplies expense account. A physical count of supplies on hand on May 31 valued the inventory at $11,500.

Required:

Prepare journal entries to record the following transactions and events:

1. The receipt of cash from customers and the recognition of all revenues earned in May.

2. Rent expense for May.

3. Payment of the premium for the new insurance policy.

4. Interest expense that accrued in May.

5. The invoice for advertising work, received on May 2.

6. The adjustment to the supplies inventory account.

LO1, 2, 4

P4–11   **Inferring Adjusting Entries and Information Used in Computations and Recording Closing Entries**

The T-accounts of Longhorn Company at the end of the third year of operations, December 31, 2012, follow. The adjusting entries at December 31 are identified by letters.

Cash	
Bal. 20,000	

Note Payable 8%	
	1/1/2011 10,000

Share Capital (8,000 shares)	
	Bal. 56,000

Inventory, Maintenance Supplies	
Bal. 500	(a) 300

Interest Payable	
	(b) 800

Retained Earnings	
	Bal. 9,000

Service Equipment	
1/1/2010 90,000	

Income Taxes Payable	
	(f) 13,020

Service Revenue	
(c) 6,000	Bal. 220,000

Accumulated Depreciation, Service Equipment	
	Bal. 18,000
	(d) 9,000

Wages Payable	
	(e) 500

Expenses	
Bal. 160,000	
(a) 300	
(b) 800	
(d) 9,000	
(e) 500	
(f) 13,020	

Other Assets	
Bal. 42,500	

Deferred Revenue	
	(c) 6,000

Required:

1. Develop three trial balances of Longhorn Company at December 31, 2012, using the following format:

	Unadjusted Trial Balance		Adjusted Trial Balance		Post-closing Trial Balance	
Account	**Debit**	**Credit**	**Debit**	**Credit**	**Debit**	**Credit**

2. Write an explanation for each adjusting entry for 2012.
3. Prepare the closing journal entries.
4. What was the apparent useful life of the service equipment? What assumptions must you make to answer this question?
5. What was the average income tax rate for 2012?
6. What was the average issue (sale) price per share of the share capital?

ALTERNATE PROBLEMS

AP4–1 Preparing a Trial Balance (P4–1)

LO2

Starbucks Corporation

Starbucks Corporation purchases and roasts high-quality, whole-bean coffees and sells them along with fresh-brewed coffees, Italian-style espresso beverages, a variety of pastries and confections, coffee-related accessories and equipment, and a line of premium teas. In addition to sales through its company-operated retail stores, Starbucks also sells coffee and tea products through other distribution channels. The following is a simplified list of accounts and amounts reported in financial statements. The accounts have normal debit or credit balances and the dollars are rounded to the nearest million. Assume the year ended on September 28, 2008.

Accrued liabilities	$ 783	Interest expense	53	Property, plant, and	
Cash and cash equivalents	270	Interest revenue	123	equipment, net	2,956
Cost of sales	4,645	Inventories	693	Retained earnings	?
Depreciation and		Long-term investments	374	Share capital	88
amortization expense	549	Long-term liabilities	992	Short-term borrowings	713
Deferred revenue	368	Net sales revenues	10,383	Short-term investments	53
General and administrative		Other assets	328	Store operating expenses	3,745
expenses	723	Other operating expenses	330	Trade payables	325
Goodwill	266	Prepayments	403	Trade receivables	329
Income tax expense	144				

Required:

Prepare an adjusted trial balance at September 28, 2008. How did you determine the amount for retained earnings?

LO1, 3   AP4–2   Recording Adjusting Entries and Determining Their Financial Statement Effects (P4–2)

eXcel

Chandra Company's fiscal year ends on June 30. It is June 30, 2012, and all of the 2012 entries have been made, except the following adjusting entries:

a. On March 30, 2012, Chandra paid $3,200 for a six-month premium for property insurance starting on that date. Cash was credited and prepaid insurance was debited for this amount.

b. At June 30, 2012, wages of $900 were earned by employees but not yet paid. The employees will be paid on the next pay date, July 15, 2012.

c. On June 1, 2012, Chandra collected maintenance fees of $450 for two months. At that date, Chandra debited cash and credited deferred maintenance revenue for $450.

d. Depreciation must be recognized on a service truck that cost $19,000 on July 1, 2011. The truck's estimated useful life is four years with a $3,000 residual value.

e. Cash of $4,200 was collected on May 1, 2012, for services to be rendered evenly over the next year, beginning on May 1 (deferred service revenue was credited).

f. On February 1, 2012, the company borrowed $16,000 from a local bank and signed a 9 percent note for that amount. The principal and interest are payable on January 31, 2013.

g. On June 15, 2012, the company received from the city a tax bill for $500, covering property taxes on land for the first half of 2012. The amount is payable during July 2012.

h. The company earned service revenue of $2,000 on a special job that was completed on June 29, 2012. Collection will be made during July 2013; no entry has been recorded.

Required:

1. Indicate whether each transaction relates to a deferred revenue, deferred expense, accrued revenue, or accrued expense.

2. Prepare the adjusting entry required for each transaction at June 30, 2012.

3. Show the effects (direction and amount) of the adjusting entries on profit and cash.

LO1, 3   AP4–3   Recording Adjusting Entries and Determining Their Financial Statement Effects (P4–3)

Sophie's Catering Company is at its fiscal year-end, December 31, 2011. The following data were developed from the company's records and related documents:

a. During 2011, office supplies amounting to $1,200 were purchased for cash and debited to supplies inventory. At the beginning of 2011, the inventory of supplies on hand (unused) amounted to $350. The inventory of supplies on hand at December 31, 2011, was $400.

b. On December 31, 2011, the company catered an evening gala for a local celebrity. The $7,500 bill was payable by the end of January 2012. No cash has been collected, and no journal entry has been made for this transaction. (Ignore cost of goods sold.)

c. On December 15, 2011, repairs on one of the company's delivery vans were completed at a cost of $600; the amount is not yet recorded and will be paid at the beginning of January 2012.

d. On October 1, 2011, a one-year insurance premium on equipment in the amount of $1,200 was paid and debited to prepaid insurance. Coverage began on November 1.

e. In November 2011, Sophie's signed a lease for a new retail location, providing a down payment of $2,100 for the first three months. The amount was debited to prepaid rent. The lease began on December 1, 2011.

f. On July 1, 2011, the company purchased new refrigerated display counters at a cash cost of $18,000. The estimated useful life of the equipment is five years, with an estimated residual value of $3,000. No depreciation has been recorded for 2011 (compute depreciation for six months in 2011).

g. On November 1, 2011, the company loaned $6,000 to one of its employees who signed a one-year, 10 percent note. The principal and interest are payable on October 31, 2012.

h. Profit before any of the adjustments or income taxes was $22,400. The company's income tax rate is 30 percent. Compute the adjusted profit, taking into consideration transactions (a) through (g) to determine the income tax expense for 2011.

Required:

1. Indicate whether each transaction relates to a deferred revenue, deferred expense, accrued revenue, or accrued expense.

2. Prepare the adjusting entry required for each transaction at December 31, 2011.

3. Using the following headings, indicate the effect of each adjusting entry and the amount of each. Use + for increase, − for decrease, and NE for no effect.

	Statement of Financial Position			Income Statement		
Transaction	**Assets**	**Liabilities**	**Shareholders' Equity**	**Revenues**	**Expenses**	**Profit**
a.						
b.						
c.						
etc.						

AP4–4 **Computing Amounts on Financial Statements and Finding Financial Information** (P4–4) ▪ **LO3**

The following transactions and events are provided by the records of Deerfield Cleaning (a corporation) at the end of its fiscal year, December 31, 2012:

Cash Receipts and Revenue

a. Collected cash in January 2012 for the only cleaning contracts completed in past years that were not yet paid by customers	$ 11,000
b. Service revenue collected in cash during 2012 for cleaning contracts in 2012	213,000
c. Service revenue earned for contracts in December 2012 but not collected until 2013	14,000
d. Amount collected in advance in December 2012 for service to be provided in January 2013	19,000

Salaries

e. Cash payment made in January 2012 for employee salaries earned in 2011; no other amounts were due to employees for past periods	1,500
f. Salaries incurred and paid during 2012	78,000
g. Salaries earned by employees during December 2012 that will be paid in January 2013	1,900

Supplies

h. Cleaning supplies inventory on January 1, 2012	1,800
i. Cleaning supplies purchased for cash during 2012	14,500
j. Cleaning supplies inventory on December 31, 2012	2,700

Required:

For each of the following accounts, compute the balance that should be reported in Deerfield's 2012 financial statements, indicate on which financial statement the item will be reported, and report the effect (direction and amount) on cash flows (+ for increase, − for decrease, and NE for no effect). (*Hint:* Create T-accounts to determine account balances.)

Account	2012 Balance	Financial Statement	Effect on Cash Flows
1. Service revenue			
2. Cleaning supplies expense			
3. Trade receivables			
4. Wages expense			
5. Cleaning supplies inventory			
6. Deferred revenue			
7. Wages payable			

AP4–5 **Inferring Year-End Adjustments, Computing Earnings per Share and Net Profit Margin, and Recording Closing Entries** (P4–5) ▪ **LO1, 2, 4, 5**

Gilca Ltd. is completing the information processing cycle at the end of its fiscal year, December 31, 2011. The correct account balances at December 31, 2011, both before and after the adjusting entries for 2011, are shown on the following page.

	Trial Balance, December 31, 2011					
	Before Adjusting Entries		Adjustments		After Adjusting Entries	
Items	**Debit**	**Credit**	**Debit**	**Credit**	**Debit**	**Credit**
a. Cash	$ 18,000				$ 18,000	
b. Service revenue receivable					1,500	
c. Prepayments	1,200				800	
d. Property, plant, and equipment	210,000				210,000	
e. Accumulated depreciation, PP&E		$52,500				$ 70,000
f. Income taxes payable						6,500
g. Deferred revenue		16,000				8,000
h. Share capital		110,000				110,000
i. Retained earnings, January 1, 2011		21,700				21,700
j. Service revenue		83,000				92,500
k. Salary expense	54,000				54,000	
l. Depreciation expense					17,500	
m. Rent expense					400	
n. Income tax expense					6,500	
	$283,200	$283,200			$308,700	$308,700

Required:

1. Compare the amounts in the columns before and after the adjusting entries to reconstruct the adjusting entries made in 2011. Provide an explanation for each adjustment.

2. Compute the profit for 2011, assuming that it is based on the amounts (a) before adjusting entries and (b) after adjusting entries. Which profit amount is correct? Explain.

3. Compute the earnings per share, assuming that 5,000 shares are outstanding.

4. Compute the net profit margin. What does this suggest to you about the company?

5. Compute the return on equity, assuming that share capital did not change during the year. What does the computed ratio suggest to you about the company?

6. Prepare the closing entries at December 31, 2011.

■ **LO1, 2, 3, 5**   **AP4–6**   **Recording Adjusting and Closing Entries and Preparing a Statement of Financial Position and an Income Statement Including Earnings per Share** (P4–6)

Vialdi Co., a small service repair company, keeps its records without the help of an accountant. After much effort, an outside accountant prepared the following unadjusted trial balance as at the end of the company's fiscal year, December 31, 2012:

Account Titles	Debit	Credit
Cash	$19,600	
Trade receivables	7,000	
Supplies inventory	1,300	
Prepaid insurance	900	
Equipment (5-year life, no residual value)	27,000	
Accumulated depreciation, equipment		$12,000
Other assets	5,100	
Trade payables		2,500
Note payable (2 years; 12% each December 31)		5,000
Share capital (4,000 shares outstanding)		16,000
Retained earnings		10,300
Service revenue		48,000
Other expenses, excluding income tax	32,900	
Totals	$93,800	$93,800

Data not yet recorded at December 31, 2012, include

a. Depreciation expense for 2012, $3,000.

b. Insurance expired during 2012, $450.

c. Wages earned by employees not yet paid on December 31, 2012, $1,100.

d. The supplies inventory on December 31, 2012, reflected $600 remaining on hand.

e. Income tax expense was $2,950.

Required:

1. Prepare the adjusting entries at December 31, 2012.

2. Show the effects (direction and amount) of the adjusting entries on profit and cash.

3. Prepare an income statement for 2012 and a statement of financial position at December 31, 2012. Include the effects of the preceding five transactions.

4. Compute the profit for the year assuming that you did not make an adjustment to the balance of the supplies inventory account. Does this error cause a material change to profit? Explain.

5. Prepare the closing entries at December 31, 2012.

AP4–7 Preparing Both an Income Statement and a Statement of Financial Position from a Trial Balance (P4–7)

LO3, 4, 5

ACME Pest Control Services (organized as a corporation on September 1, 2009) has completed the accounting cycle for the second year, ended August 31, 2011. ACME Pest Control also has completed a correct trial balance as follows:

ACME PEST CONTROL SERVICES
Trial Balance
At August 31, 2011

Account Titles	Debit	Credit
Cash	$ 26,000	
Trade receivables	30,800	
Supplies inventory	1,300	
Service vehicles (company vans)	60,000	
Accumulated depreciation, automobiles		$ 20,000
Equipment	14,000	
Accumulated depreciation, equipment		4,000
Trade payables		16,700
Salaries payable		1,100
Note payable, long term		34,000
Share capital (10,000 shares)		40,000
Retained earnings (on September 1, 2007)		4,300
Dividends declared	2,000	
Sales revenue		38,000
Maintenance contract revenue		17,000
Operating expenses (detail omitted to conserve your time)	27,000	
Depreciation expense (including $2,000 on equipment)	12,000	
Interest expense	2,000	
Totals	$175,100	$175,100

Required:

1. Prepare an income statement for the reporting year ended August 31, 2011. Include income tax expense, assuming a 30 percent tax rate. Use the following major captions: revenues, expenses, profit before income tax, income tax, profit, and earnings per share (list each item under these captions as appropriate).

2. Prepare the journal entry to record income taxes for the year (not yet paid).

3. Prepare a statement of financial position at the end of the reporting year, August 31, 2011. Use the following captions (list each item under these captions as appropriate).

Assets
Current assets
Non-current assets

Liabilities
Current liabilities
Non-current liabilities

Shareholders' Equity
Share capital
Retained earnings

4. Compute the net profit margin and the return on equity ratios. What do these ratios suggest?

5. Prepare the closing entries at August 31, 2011.

LO1, 2, 3, 4, 5 AP4–8 **Comprehensive Review Problem: From Recording Transactions (Including Adjusting and Closing Entries) to Preparing a Complete Set of Financial Statements and Performing Ratio Analysis (See Chapters 2, 3, and 4)** (P4–8)

Serena and Bill Davis began operations of their furniture repair shop, Rumours Furniture Inc., on January 1, 2010. The company's fiscal year ends December 31. The trial balance on January 1, 2011, was as follows (the amounts are rounded to thousands of dollars):

Account No.	Account Titles	Debit	Credit
01	Cash	5	
02	Trade receivables	4	
03	Supplies inventory	2	
04	Small tools inventory	6	
05	Equipment		
06	Accumulated depreciation (equipment)		
07	Other assets (not detailed to simplify)	9	
11	Trade payables		7
12	Notes payable		
13	Wages payable		
14	Interest payable		
15	Income taxes payable		
16	Deferred revenue		
21	Share capital (15,000 shares)		15
31	Retained earnings		4
35	Service revenue		
40	Depreciation expense		
41	Income tax expense		
42	Interest expense		
43	Other expenses		
	Totals	26	26

Transactions during 2011 (summarized in thousands of dollars) follow:

a. Borrowed $25 cash on an 8 percent note payable, dated July 1, 2011.

b. Purchased equipment for $18 cash on July 1, 2011.

c. Sold 5,000 additional shares for $1 cash per share (show dollars in thousands).

d. Earned revenues for 2011, $74, including $15 on credit.

e. Recognized other expenses for 2011, $35, including $9 on credit.

f. Purchased additional small tools inventory, $3 cash.

g. Collected trade receivables, $8.

h. Paid trade payables, $11.

i. Purchased supplies on account, $10 (debit to Account No. 03).

j. Received a $3 deposit on work to start January 15, 2012.

k. Declared and paid cash dividend, $12.

Data for adjusting entries:

l. Service supplies inventory of $4 and small tools inventory of $9 were on hand at December 31, 2011 (debit other expenses account).

m. The equipment's useful life is four years and its residual value is $2.

n. Accrued interest on notes payable (to be computed).

o. Wages earned since the December 24 pay date but not yet paid, $4.

p. Income tax expense payable in 2012, $4.

Required:

1. Set up T-accounts for the accounts on the trial balance and enter their beginning balances.
2. Record transactions (*a*) through (*k*) and post them to the T-accounts.
3. Record and post the adjusting entries (*l*) through (*p*).
4. Prepare an income statement (including earnings per share) for 2011, a statement of changes in equity for 2011, and a statement of financial position at December 31, 2011.
5. Record and post the closing entries.
6. Prepare a post-closing trial balance.
7. Compute the following ratios for 2011 and explain what they mean:
   a. debt-to-equity
   b. total asset turnover
   c. net profit margin
   d. return on equity

AP4–9 Using Financial Reports: Evaluating Profitability by Using Net Profit Margin and Return on Equity Ratios (P4–9)

A summary of selected historical results is presented below for three Canadian companies: Gildan Activewear, Research In Motion, and Andrew Peller. Each of these companies has grown in size over time by acquiring assets and investing in other companies. (Amounts are in millions of dollars.)

■ **LO4**

Gildan Activewear
Research In Motion
Andrew Peller

	2008	2007	2006	2005	2004
Gildan Activewear					
Total shareholders' equity	812	664	531	421	328
Total revenue	1,250	964	773	654	533
Profit	145	130	107	86	60
Cash flow from operations	239	91	95	93	59
Research In Motion					
Total shareholders' equity	3,934	2,484	1,999	1,984	1,716
Total revenue	4,914	2,304	2,066	1,350	595
Profit	1,294	632	382	213	53
Cash flow from operations	1,577	736	150	278	64
Andrew Peller					
Total shareholders' equity	97	103	96	90	87
Total revenue	237	228	212	168	156
Profit	11	9	6	8	9
Cash flow from operations	14	10	5	19	7

Required:

1. Compute the net profit margin and the return on equity ratios for each company for each of the years 2007 and 2008 by using the table on the following page.

	2008	2007	2006	2005
Gildan Activewear				
Net profit margin			13.8%	13.1%
Return on equity (ROE)			22.5%	23.0%
Quality of earnings			0.89	1.08
Research In Motion				
Net profit margin			18.5%	15.8%
Return on equity (ROE)			19.2%	11.5%
Quality of earnings			0.39	1.31
Andrew Peller				
Net profit margin			2.83%	4.76%
Return on equity (ROE)			6.45%	8.99%
Quality of earnings			0.83	2.38

2. Based on the computed ratios, rank these companies from most successful to least successful in generating profit for shareholders.

3. Assume that you are interested in investing in one of these three companies, which company would you choose? Write a brief report to justify your choice.

4. Analysts examine both the profit and the cash flow from operating activities in evaluating a company. One measure that relates these two numbers is the quality of earnings ratio, which equals cash flow from operations divided by profit. The higher the ratio, the higher the quality of earnings. Compute this ratio for 2007 and 2008, and rank the three companies from highest to lowest based on the quality of their earnings.

CASES AND PROJECTS

FINDING AND INTERPRETING FINANCIAL INFORMATION

LO1, 3, 4, 5   CP4–1

Cadbury, plc.

Finding Financial Information
Go online for the financial statements of Cadbury, plc.

Required:

1. How much did the company pay in interest for the 2008 fiscal year? Where did you find this information?

2. To what account is accumulated depreciation related?

3. What company accounts would not appear on a post-closing trial balance?

4. Prepare the closing entry for prepayments.

5. What is the company's basic earnings per share for the two years reported?

6. Compute the company's net profit margin ratio for the six years 2003 to 2008 based on information reported on the income statement. Annual reports for years prior to 2008 are available on the company's website (**http://www.cadburyinvestors.com/cadbury_ir/report/**). What does the trend suggest to you about Cadbury?

LO2, 5   CP4–2

Cadbury, plc
vs. the Nestlé Group

Comparing Companies over Time
Go online for the financial statements of Cadbury, plc. and to Appendix A for the financial statements of the Nestlé Group.

Required:

1. What was the cost of goods sold for each company's most recent fiscal year? Where did you find the information?

2. Compute the percentage of cost of goods sold to sales for each company if possible. Compute the same ratios for the previous two fiscal years. Access the company's annual reports for previous years for information that is not available in the annual report for 2008.

3. Compute each company's net profit margin ratio for the years shown in its annual report. What do your results suggest about each company over the two-year period?

4. Compute each company's return on equity ratio for the most recent year. Which company is more profitable? Explain.

FINANCIAL REPORTING AND ANALYSIS CASES

CP4–3 Interpreting the Financial Press

LO1, 2, 4

A March 8, 2004, article in *The Wall Street Journal* discusses the underlying cause of accounting scandals and offers a suggestion for improved reporting.* You can access the article online.

Required:

Read the brief article and answer the following questions:

1. What did the author suggest as the root cause of accounting scandals?

2. What are the uncertainties referred to in the article and why does the author believe these are problems in current financial reporting?

CP4–4 Analyzing the Effects of Adjustments

LO1

Seneca Land Company, a closely held corporation, invests in commercial rental properties. Seneca's fiscal year ends on December 31. At the end of each year, numerous adjusting entries must be made because many transactions completed during the current and prior years have economic effects on the financial statements of the current and future years. Assume that the current year is 2011.

Required:

This case concerns four transactions that have been selected for your analysis. Answer the questions for each.

TRANSACTION (*a*): On July 1, 2010, the company purchased office equipment costing $14,000 for use in the business. The company estimates that the equipment will have a useful life of 10 years and no residual value.

1. Over how many accounting periods will this transaction directly affect Seneca's financial statements? Explain.

2. Assuming straight-line depreciation, how much depreciation expense was reported on the 2010 and 2011 income statements?

3. How should the office equipment be reported on the statement of financial position at December 31, 2012?

4. Would Seneca make an adjusting entry at the end of each year during the life of the equipment? Explain your answer.

TRANSACTION (*b*): On September 1, 2011, Seneca collected $24,000 for rent of office space. This amount represented rent for a six-month period, September 1, 2011, through February 28, 2012. Deferred rent revenue was increased (credited), and cash was increased (debited) for $24,000.

1. Over how many accounting periods will this transaction affect Seneca's financial statements? Explain.

2. How much rent revenue on this office space should Seneca report on the 2011 income statement? Explain.

3. Did this transaction create a liability for Seneca as of the end of 2011? Explain. If yes, how much?

4. Should Seneca make an adjusting entry on December 31, 2011? Explain. If your answer is yes, prepare the adjusting entry.

TRANSACTION (*c*): On December 31, 2011, Seneca owed employees wages of $7,500 because the employees worked the last three days in December 2011. The next payroll date is January 5, 2012.

1. Over how many accounting periods does this transaction affect Seneca's financial statements? Explain.

2. How would this $7,500 amount affect Seneca's income statement for 2011 and the statement of financial position at December 31, 2011?

3. Should Seneca make an adjusting entry on December 31, 2011? Explain. If your answer is yes, prepare the adjusting entry.

---

*Alfred Rappaport, "Shareholder Scoreboard (A Special Report): The Best & Worst Performers of the WSJ 1000—Beyond Quarterly Earnings: How to Improve Financial Reporting," *The Wall Street Journal*, March 8, 2004.

TRANSACTION (*d*): On January 1, 2011, Seneca agreed to supervise the planning and subdivision of a large tract of land for a customer, J. Ray. This service job that Seneca will perform involves four separate phases. By December 31, 2011, three phases had been completed to Ray's satisfaction. The remaining phase will be done during 2012. The total price for the four phases (agreed on in advance by both parties) was $60,000. Each phase involves about the same amount of services. On December 31, 2011, Seneca had not collected any cash for the services already performed.

1. Should Seneca record any service revenue on this job for 2011? Explain. If yes, prepare the adjusting entry to record the revenue.

2. What entry will Seneca make when it completes the last phase, assuming that the full contract price is collected on the completion date, February 15, 2012?

LO1, 2, 4, 5   **CP4–5**   **Using Financial Reports: Inferring Adjusting and Closing Entries and Answering Analytical Questions**

Rowland Company was organized on January 1, 2010. At the end of the first year of operations, December 31, 2010, the bookkeeper prepared the following trial balances (amounts in thousands of dollars):

Account No.	Account Titles	Unadjusted Trial Balance Debit	Unadjusted Trial Balance Credit	Adjustments		Adjusted Trial Balance Debit	Adjusted Trial Balance Credit
11	Cash	40				40	
12	Trade receivables	17				17	
13	Prepaid insurance	2				1	
14	Rent receivable					2	
15	Property, plant, and equipment	46				46	
16	Accumulated depreciation						11
17	Other assets	6				6	
18	Trade payables		27				27
19	Wages payable						3
20	Income taxes payable						5
21	Deferred rent revenue						4
22	Note payable (10%; dated January 1, 2010)		20				20
23	Share capital (1,000 shares)		30				30
24	Retained earnings	3				3	
25	Revenues (total)		105				103
26	Expenses (total including interest)	68				83	
27	Income tax expense					5	
	Totals	182	182			203	203

Required:

1. Based on inspection of the two trial balances, prepare the 2010 adjusting entries recorded by the bookkeeper (provide brief explanations).

2. Based on these data, prepare the 2010 closing entries with brief explanations.

3. Answer the following questions (show computations):
   a. How many shares were outstanding at year-end?
   b. What was the amount of interest expense included in the total expenses?
   c. What was the balance of retained earnings on December 31, 2010?
   d. What was the average income tax rate?
   e. How would these two accounts, rent receivable and deferred rent revenue, be reported on the statement of financial position?
   f. Explain why cash increased by $40,000 during the year even though profit was comparatively very low.
   g. What was the amount of earnings per share for 2010?
   h. What was the average selling price of the shares?
   i. When was the insurance premium paid and over what period of time did the coverage extend?
   j. What was the net profit margin ratio for the year?
   k. What was the return on equity ratio for the year?

CP4–6 Using Financial Reports: Analyzing Financial Information in a Sale of a Business—A Challenging Case

LO1, 3

Robert Brissette, a local massage therapist, decided to sell his practice and retire. He has had discussions with a therapist from another province who wants to relocate. The discussions are at the complex stage of agreeing on a price. The financial statements of Brissette's practice, Brissette Stress Reduction, played an important role in this process. Brissette's secretary, Kelsey, maintained the records, under his direction. Each year, Kelsey developed a statement of profit on a cash basis from the records she maintained but she did not prepare a statement of financial position. Upon request, Brissette provided the other therapist with the following statements for 2012 prepared by Kelsey:

BRISSETTE STRESS REDUCTION Statement of Profit 2012		
Therapy fees collected		$130,000
Expenses paid:		
Rent for office space	$19,500	
Utilities expense	360	
Telephone expense	2,200	
Office salaries expense	22,500	
Office supplies expense	900	
Miscellaneous expenses	2,400	
Total expenses		47,860
Profit for the year		$ 82,140

Upon agreement of the parties, you have been asked to examine the financial figures for 2012. The other therapist said, "I question the figures because, among other things, they appear to be on a 100 percent cash basis." Your investigations revealed the following additional data at December 31, 2012:

a. Of the $130,000 in therapy fees collected in 2012, $30,000 was for services performed prior to 2012.

b. At the end of 2012, therapy fees of $6,000 for services performed during the year were uncollected.

c. Office equipment owned and used by Brissette cost $8,000 and had an estimated useful life of 10 years, with no salvage value.

d. An inventory of office supplies at December 31, 2012, reflected $400 worth of items purchased during the year that were still on hand. Also, the records for 2011 indicate that the supplies on hand at the end of that year were about $250.

e. At the end of 2012, the secretary whose salary is $24,000 per year had not been paid for December because of a long trip that extended to January 15, 2013.

f. The $140 phone bill for December 2012 was not paid until January 11, 2013.

g. The payment for office rent was for 13 months, including January 2013.

Required:

1. Prepare a correct income statement for 2012 based on the information above. Show your computations for any amounts changed from those in the statement prepared by Brissette's secretary. (Suggested solution format—use four-column headings: Items; Cash Basis per Brissette's Statement, $; Explanation of Changes; and Corrected Basis, $.)

2. Write a memo to support your schedule prepared in (1). The purpose should be to explain the reasons for your changes and to suggest other important items that should be considered in the pricing decision.

CP4–7 Using Financial Reports: Preparing Income Statements for Different Periods

LO1, 3

Wong's Insurance Agency adjusts its accounts at the end of each month. The adjusted balances of the revenue and expense accounts at two different dates of the year appear on the following page. The company's fiscal year starts on July 1.

	March 31, 2012	December 31, 2011
Commissions earned	$72,000	$45,000
Salaries expense	18,000	12,000
Rent expense	11,250	7,500
Depreciation expense	1,350	900
Advertising expense	14,000	7,500

The company is subject to an income tax rate of 40 percent.

Required:
Prepare income statements for two separate time periods: the quarter ending March 31, 2012, and the nine-month period ending March 31, 2012. Explain how you determined the amounts for each time period and show supporting computations.

LO1, 3   **CP4–8**   **Using Financial Reports: Analyzing Financial Information from Real Financial Statements**

WestJet Airlines

The current liabilities of WestJet Airlines include the account advance ticket sales. The company's recent annual reports show the following trend in the balance of this account over a three-year period.

	2009	2008	2007
Advance ticket sales (in thousands)	286,361	251,354	194,929

The first note to the company's financial statements, titled *Significant accounting policies*, includes the following disclosure about revenue recognition:

> Guest revenues, including the air component of vacation packages, are recognized when air transportation is provided. Tickets sold but not yet used are included in the consolidated balance sheet as advance ticket sales.

Required:
1. What does the balance in the advance ticket sales account represent?
2. Why does WestJet recognize guest revenue when transportation is provided, rather than when cash is received?
3. How does WestJet Airlines normally settle this liability?
4. Should WestJet recognize flight expenses, such as jet fuel, salaries of flight crew, and cost of food and beverage, in the period when the flights occur or during the period when tickets are sold? Explain.
5. Explain the most probable reason for the increase in the amount of this liability from 2007 to 2009.
6. Based on the trend in the amount of this liability, would you expect the annual amounts of guest revenue to increase, decrease, or remain stable over the three-year period? Explain.

LO1, 3   **CP4–9**   **Using Financial Reports: Analyzing Financial Information from Real Financial Statements**

Andrew Peller

Andrew Peller Ltd. is a leading producer and marketer of quality wines in Canada. Selected information from the company's financial statements for the year ended March 31, 2010, are provided below (in thousands of dollars).

	March 31, 2010	March 31, 2009
Statement of Financial Position		
Trade receivables	22,902	21,044
Prepayments	2,429	2,309
Income taxes recoverable (receivable)	1,327	6,318
Accrued liabilities	8,229	10,563
Dividends payable	1,197	1,088
Income taxes payable		
Long-term debt	47,633	71,549
Other information		
Sales for fiscal year 2010	263,151	
Income taxes paid during the year	640	

Required:

1. Compute the amount of cash collected from customers during the year. Assume that all sales for fiscal year 2010 were on credit.

2. Prepayments represent the net amount of a number of accounts, including prepaid insurance. The company had $935 in prepaid insurance at March 31, 2009, and $1,180 at March 31, 2010. It also paid $2,345 in June 2009 to renew its insurance policies. Prepare the adjusting journal entry on March 31, 2010, to record the amount of insurance expense for fiscal year 2010. The payment of $2,345 was debited to the insurance expense account.

3. Explain the nature of the account accrued liabilities. What would have caused the account balance to increase during the year?

4. The company's board of directors declared dividends of $4,787 during the year. Prepare a summary journal entry to record the amount of dividends paid during the year.

5. The company is required to pay income taxes in advance on a quarterly basis even though the exact amount of income taxes expense is not calculated until the end of the fiscal year. For this reason, the company may overpay the amount of taxes due to taxation authorities. Compute the amount of income taxes expense for 2010 and prepare the related adjusting journal entry at March 31, 2010.

6. The company's long-term debt includes a long-term bank loan for $6,000. The company signed for this loan on October 31, 2009, to be repaid on October 31, 2013. Interest on the loan, at an annual rate 8 percent, is payable each year on October 31. Prepare the adjusting journal entry that should be made on March 31, 2010 to recognize interest expense for fiscal year 2010.

7. Assume that the company's accountant did not record the journal entry you prepared for (6) above, what would be the effect of this error (overstatement, understatement, no effect) on the following:

   a. total assets at March 31, 2010,

   b. profit for the year 2010, assuming that the company is subject to an income tax rate of 40%,

   c. current liabilities at March 31, 2010.

CRITICAL THINKING CASES

CP4–10 **Using Financial Reports: Evaluating Financial Information as a Bank Loan Officer**

  LO1, 3, 4

 eXcel

Magliochetti Moving Corp. has been in operation since January 1, 2011. It is now December 31, 2011, the end of the company's fiscal year. The company has not done well financially during the first year, although revenue has been fairly good. The three shareholders manage the company, but they have not given much attention to recordkeeping. In view of a serious cash shortage, they have applied to your bank for a $20,000 loan. You requested a complete set of financial statements. The following annual financial statements for 2011 were prepared by a clerk and then were given to the bank.

MAGLIOCHETTI MOVING CORP.

Income Statement		Statement of Financial Position	
For the Period Ended December 31, 2011		**At December 31, 2011**	
Transportation revenue	$85,000	**Assets**	
Expenses:		Cash	$ 2,000
Salaries expense	17,000	Receivables	3,000
Maintenance expense	12,000	Inventory of maintenance supplies	6,000
Other expenses	18,000	Equipment	40,000
Total expenses	$47,000	Prepayments	4,000
Profit	$38,000	Other assets	27,000
		Total assets	$82,000
		Liabilities	
		Trade payables	$ 9,000
		Shareholders' Equity	
		Share capital (10,000 shares outstanding)	35,000
		Retained earnings	38,000
		Total liabilities and shareholders' equity	$82,000

After briefly reviewing the statements and looking into the situation, you requested that the statements be redone (with some expert help) to "incorporate depreciation, accruals, inventory counts, income taxes, and so on." As a result of a review of the records and supporting documents, the following additional information was developed:

a. The inventory of maintenance supplies of $6,000 shown on the statement of financial position has not been adjusted for supplies used during 2011. An inventory count of the maintenance supplies on hand (unused) on December 31, 2011, showed $1,800. Supplies used should be debited to maintenance expense.

b. The insurance premium paid in 2011 was for years 2011 and 2012; therefore, the prepaid insurance at December 31, 2011, amounted to $2,000. The total insurance premium was debited to prepaid insurance when paid in 2011.

c. The equipment cost $40,000 when purchased January 1, 2011. It had an estimated useful life of five years (no residual value). No depreciation has been recorded for 2011.

d. Unpaid (and unrecorded) salaries at December 31, 2011, amounted to $2,200.

e. At December 31, 2011, transportation revenue collected in advance amounted to $7,000. This amount was credited to transportation revenue when the cash was collected.

f. The company is subject to an income tax rate of 30 percent.

Required:

1. Record the six adjusting entries required on December 31, 2011, based on the preceding additional information.

2. Recast the preceding statements after taking into account the adjusting entries. Use the following format for the solution:

Items	Amounts Reported	Changes Plus	Minus	Correct Amounts
(List here each item from the two statements)				

3. Omission of the adjusting entries caused the following:
   a. Profit to be overstated or understated (select one) by $_____.
   b. Total assets to be overstated or understated (select one) by $_____.
   c. Total liabilities to be overstated or understated (select one) by $_____.

4. Use both the unadjusted and adjusted balances to calculate the following ratios for the company: (a) earnings per share, (b) net profit margin, and (c) return on equity. Explain the causes of the differences and the impact of the changes on financial analysis.

5. Write a letter to the company explaining the results of the adjustments, your analysis, and your decision regarding the loan.

LO1, 3   **CP4–11**   **Making a Decision as an Auditor: Effects of Errors on Income, Assets, and Liabilities**

Megan Company (not a corporation) was careless about its financial records during its first year of operations, 2010. It is December 31, 2010, the end of the company's fiscal year. An external auditor examined the records and discovered numerous errors, all of which are described on the following page. Assume that each error is independent of the others.

| | Effect on | | | | | |
| Independent Errors | Profit | | Assets | | Liabilities | |
	2010	2011	2010	2011	2010	2011
1. Depreciation expense for 2010, not recorded in 2010, $950.	O $950	NE	O $950	O $950	NE	NE
2. Wages earned by employees during 2010 not recorded in 2010 but will be paid in 2011, $500.						
3. Revenue earned during 2010 but not collected or recorded until 2011, $600; will be collected in 2011.						
4. Amount paid in 2010 and recorded as expense in 2010, but it is not an expense until 2011, $200.						
5. Revenue collected in 2010 and recorded as revenue in 2010, but it is not earned until 2011, $900.						
6. Sale of services for cash in 2010. Recorded as a debit to cash and as a credit to trade receivables, $300.						
7. On December 31, 2010, bought land on credit for $8,000, but did not record the transaction until payment was made on February 1, 2011.						

Required:

Analyze each error and indicate its effect on 2010 and 2011 profit, assets, and liabilities if not corrected. Do not assume any other errors. Use these codes to indicate the effect of each dollar amount: O = overstated, U = understated, and NE = no effect. Write an explanation of your analysis of each transaction to support your response. (The answer for the first item is given as an example.) A sample explanation of analysis of errors that are not corrected is provided below, using the first error as an example:

1. Failure to record depreciation in 2010 caused depreciation expense to be too low; therefore, profit was overstated by $950. Accumulated depreciation also is too low by $950, which causes assets to be overstated by $950 until the error is corrected.

CP4–12   Making Decisions as a Manager: Evaluating the Effects of Business Strategy on Return on Equity   ■ **LO4**

Sony is a world leader in the manufacture of consumer and commercial electronics as well as the entertainment and insurance industries.

Sony

Required:

Using the table below, indicate the most likely effect of each of the following changes in business strategy on Sony's return on equity for the current period and future periods (+ for increase, − for decrease, and NE for no effect), assuming all other things are unchanged. Explain your answer for each. Treat each item independently.

a. Sony decreases its investment in research and development aimed at products to be brought to market in more than one year.

b. Sony begins a new advertising campaign for a movie to be released during the next year.

c. Sony issues additional shares for cash, the proceeds to be used to acquire other high-technology companies in future periods.

Strategy Change	Current Period ROE	Future Periods' ROE
a.		
b.		
c.		

FINANCIAL REPORTING AND ANALYSIS TEAM PROJECT

CP4–13   Team Project: Analyzing Accruals, Earnings per Share, Net Profit Margin, and Return on Equity   ■ **LO1, 3, 4**

As a team, select an industry to analyze. A list of companies classified by industry can be obtained by accessing www.fpinfomart.ca and then choosing "Companies by Industry." You can also find a list of industries and companies with each industry via **http://ca.finance.yahoo.com/investing** (click on "Annual Reports" under "Tools"). Using a Web browser, each team member should then use the Internet to obtain the annual report for one Canadian publicly traded company in the industry, with each member selecting a different company.

Required:

On an individual basis, each team member should write a short report answering the following questions about the selected company. Discuss any patterns across the companies that you as a team observe. Then, as a team, write a short report comparing and contrasting your companies.

1. From the income statement, what is the company's earnings per share for the last three years?

2. Ratio analysis
   a. What does the net profit margin ratio measure in general?
   b. What does the return on equity ratio measure in general?
   c. Compute these ratios for the last three years.
   d. What do your results suggest about the company? (You may refer to the Management Discussion and Analysis section of the annual report to learn about the company's stated reasons for any change over time.)
   e. If available, find the industry ratio for the most recent year, compare it to your results, and discuss why you believe the ratio for your company differs or is similar to the industry ratio.

3. List the accounts and amounts of accrued liabilities on the most recent statement of financial position. (You may find the detail in the notes to the statements.) What is the ratio of the total accrued liabilities to total liabilities?

Reporting and Interpreting Cash Flows

After studying this chapter, you should be able to do the following:

FOCUS COMPANY: **Andrew Peller Limited**

MANAGING PRODUCTION AND CASH FLOWS IN A SEASONAL BUSINESS

A ndrew Peller, who immigrated to Canada from Hungary in 1927, founded Andrés Wines Ltd. (**www.andrewpeller.com**) in 1961 to produce wine, using grapes from the fertile Okanagan Valley in British Columbia. Thirty years later, in 1991, the company established Peller Estates as the pre-eminent premium wine label in Canada, offering a variety of white and red wines produced in the Niagara Peninsula. Over the next 17 years, the company continued to grow and expand its business and markets to become Canada's second largest producer and marketer of wines. By 2008, the company's sales exceeded $237 million. In 2006, its name was changed to Andrew Peller Limited, in honour of its founder.

Although it may be puzzling, growing profitable operations does not always ensure positive cash flow. Also, seasonal fluctuations in sales, purchases of inventory, and advertising expenditures may bring *high profits* and *net cash outflows* in some quarters and losses and *net cash inflows* in others. As we have seen in earlier chapters, this occurs because the timing of revenues and expenses does not always match cash inflows and outflows. As a consequence, Andrew Peller Limited (APL) must carefully manage cash flows as well as profits. For the same reasons, financial analysts must consider the information provided in APL's statement of cash flows in addition to information reported on its statement of financial position and its income statement.

UNDERSTANDING THE BUSINESS

Clearly, profit is an important indicator of performance, but cash flow is also critical to a company's success. Cash flow permits a company to expand its operations, replace worn assets, take advantage of new investment opportunities, and pay dividends to its owners. Some financial analysts go as far as saying that "cash flow is king." Both managers and analysts need to understand the various sources and uses of cash that are associated with business activity.

The statement of cash flows focuses attention on a firm's ability to generate cash internally, its management of current assets and current liabilities, and the details of its investments and external financing. It is designed to help both managers and analysts answer important cash-related questions such as these:

- Will the company have enough cash to pay its short-term debts to suppliers, employees, taxation authorities, and other creditors without additional borrowing?
- Is the company adequately managing its trade receivables, inventory, and other current assets?
- Has the company made necessary investments in new productive capacity?
- Did the company generate enough cash flow internally to finance necessary investments, or did it rely on external financing?
- Is the company changing the proportion of debt and equity in its capital structure?

Andrew Peller Limited is a particularly good example to illustrate the importance of the statement of cash flows. Like all companies in its industry, APL's wine production, inventory purchases, and sales vary with the seasons. This seasonal variation has surprising effects on cash flows and profit.

We begin our discussion with an overview of the statement of cash flows. We then use APL's statement of cash flows for the second quarter of fiscal year 2009 to provide detailed coverage of the preparation, reporting, and interpretation of information in the statement of cash flows.

ORGANIZATION OF THE CHAPTER

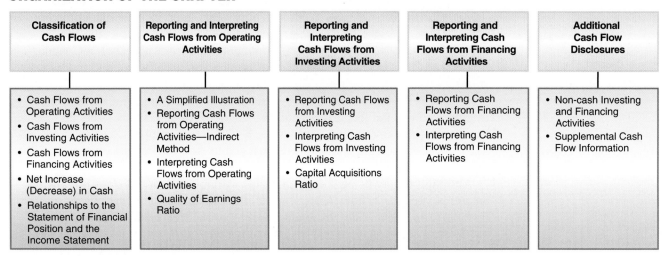

Supplemental material:

Appendix 5A: Adjustment for Gains and Losses—Indirect Method

Appendix 5B: Reporting Cash Flows from Operating Activities—Direct Method

Appendix 5C: Spreadsheet Approach—Statement of Cash Flows: Indirect Method (online)

CLASSIFICATION OF CASH FLOWS

A **CASH EQUIVALENT** is a short-term, highly liquid investment with an original maturity of less than three months.

Basically, the statement of cash flows explains how the cash balance at the beginning of the period changed to another cash balance at the end of the period. For purposes of this statement, the definition of cash includes cash and cash equivalents. Cash equivalents are short-term, highly liquid investments that are both

1. readily convertible to known amounts of cash.
2. so near their maturity that there is little risk that their value will change if interest rates change.

Generally, an investment qualifies as a cash equivalent only when it has an original maturity of three months or less from the date of acquisition. Examples of cash equivalents are treasury bills (a form of short-term government debt), money market funds, and commercial paper (short-term notes payable issued by large corporations).

As you can see in Exhibit 5.1, the statement of cash flows reports cash inflows and outflows based on three broad categories: (1) operating activities, (2) investing activities, and (3) financing activities. To improve comparability, International Accounting Standard 7 – Statement of Cash Flows defines each category included in the required statement. These definitions (with explanations) are presented in the following sections.

LO1

Classify cash flow items into cash flows from operating, investing, and financing activities.

Exhibit **5.1**

Consolidated Statement of Cash Flows

REAL WORLD EXCERPT

Andrew Peller Limited

QUARTERLY REPORT

ANDREW PELLER LIMITED
Consolidated Statements of Cash Flows—Unaudited
As at September 30, 2008
(in thousands of dollars)

	Three Months Ended September 30, 2008
Cash provided by (used in)	
Operating activities	
Net earnings/Profit	3,517
Items not affecting cash:	
Depreciation of plant and equipment	2,126
Deferred income taxes	(1,562)
Changes in non-cash operating working capital items related to operations	(3,354)*
	727
Investing activities	
Purchase of property and equipment	(3,006)
Proceeds from long-term investments	58
	(2,948)
Financing activities	
Repayment of long-term debt	(464)
Increase in bank borrowings	3,882
Payment of dividends	(1,197)
	2,221
Net cash flow and cash balance, end of period	-0-**

The balances of certain accounts have been adjusted to simplify the presentation.

*Changes in non-cash operating working capital items:	
Increase in trade receivables	$(5,509)
Increase in inventories	(1,382)
Increase in prepayments	(1,006)
Increase in trade payables	5,708
Decrease in accrued liabilities	(1,165)
	$(3,354)

**Normally, the net cash flow is not equal to zero, and the cash balances at the beginning and end of the period are different from zero. In this specific case, APL did not have any cash either at the beginning or at the end of the period as shown on its statement of financial position in Exhibit 5.3. In fact, it borrowed from the bank to cover the shortfall in cash.

Cash Flows from Operating Activities

CASH FLOWS FROM OPERATING ACTIVITIES are cash inflows and outflows directly related to earnings from normal operations.

Cash flows from operating activities (cash flows from operations) are the cash inflows and cash outflows that directly relate to revenues and expenses reported on the income statement. These cash flows are not affected by accruals, deferrals, and allocations that result from the timing of revenue and expense recognition. There are two alternative approaches for presenting the operating activities section of the statement:

1. The direct method reports the components of cash flows from operating activities listed as gross receipts and gross payments.

The **DIRECT METHOD** of presenting the operating activities section of the statement of cash flows reports components of cash flows from operating activities as gross receipts and gross payments.

Inflows	Outflows
Cash received from	*Cash paid for*
Customers	Purchase of goods for resale
Dividends and interest on investments	and services (electricity, etc.)
	Salaries and wages
	Income taxes
	Interest on borrowings

The difference between the inflows and outflows is called the ***net cash inflow (outflow) from operating activities***. APL experienced a net cash inflow of $727 from its operations for the second quarter of fiscal year 2009.[1] Although IAS 7 encourages companies to report cash flows from operating activities by using the direct method, it is rarely seen in practice.[2] Many financial executives have reported that they do not use it because it is more expensive to implement than the indirect method.

2. The indirect method starts with profit for the period and then eliminates non-cash items to arrive at net cash inflow (outflow) from operating activities.

The **INDIRECT METHOD** of presenting the operating activities section of the statement of cash flows adjusts profit to compute cash flows from operating activities.

> Profit
> +/−Adjustments for non-cash items
> Net cash inflow (outflow) from operating activities

Notice in Exhibit 5.1 that in the second quarter of 2009, APL reported profit of $3,517 but generated positive cash flows from operating activities of $727. Why do profit and cash flows from operating activities differ? Recall that the income statement is prepared under the accrual concept, whereby revenues are recorded when earned without regard to when the related cash is collected. Similarly, expenses are recorded in the same period as the revenues without regard to when the related cash payments are made.

For now, the most important thing to remember about the two methods is that they are simply alternative ways to compute the same amount. The total amount of **cash flows from operating activities is *always the same*** (an inflow of $727 in APL's case), **whether it is computed by using the direct or indirect method.**

Cash Flows from Investing Activities

CASH FLOWS FROM INVESTING ACTIVITIES are cash inflows and outflows related to the acquisition or sale of productive facilities and investments in the securities of other companies.

Cash flows from investing activities are cash inflows and outflows related to the purchase and disposal of long-term productive assets and investments in the

---

[1] APL's fiscal year starts on April 1 and ends on March 31 instead of the calendar year (January 1–December 31) that is used by most companies. As a result, APL's first quarter starts on April 1 and ends on June 30, and its second quarter starts on July 1 and ends on September 30.

[2] A recent survey of 200 companies revealed that only one company used the direct method in its 2007 annual report. Financial Reporting in Canada, Toronto: The Canadian Institute of Chartered Accountants, accessed online on October 31, 2009.

securities of other companies. Typical cash flows from investing activities include the following:

Inflows	Outflows
Cash received from	*Cash paid for*
Sale or disposal of property, plant, and equipment	Purchase of property, plant, and equipment
Sale or maturity of investments in securities	Purchase of investments in securities

The difference between these cash inflows and outflows is called ***net cash inflow (outflow) from investing activities.***

For APL, this amount was an outflow of $2,948 for the second quarter of 2009. The investing activities section of the statement shows APL's long-term investment strategy. The management discussion and analysis (MD&A) section of the report indicates that the company was continuing to invest in expanding its production facilities.

Cash Flows from Financing Activities

Cash flows from financing activities include exchanges of cash with external sources (owners and creditors) to finance the enterprise and its operations. Usual cash flows from financing activities include these:

CASH FLOWS FROM FINANCING ACTIVITIES are cash inflows and outflows related to external sources of financing (owners and creditors) for the enterprise.

Inflows	Outflows
Cash received from	*Cash paid for*
Borrowing on notes, mortgages, bonds, etc., from creditors	Repayment of principal to creditors
Issuing shares to shareholders	Interest on borrowings if it is classified as a financing activity
	Repurchasing shares from owners
	Dividends to shareholders

The difference between these cash inflows and outflows is called ***net cash inflow (outflow) from financing activities.***

For APL, this amount was an inflow of $2,221 for the second quarter of 2009. The financing activities section of the statement shows that APL repaid $464 to its creditors during the period, increased its borrowings from banks by $3,882, and paid $1,197 in dividends to shareholders.

Net Increase (Decrease) in Cash

The combination of the net cash flows from operating activities, investing activities, and financing activities must equal the net increase (decrease) in cash for the reporting period. For the second quarter of 2009, APL reported a net change of zero in cash. In fact, APL did not report any cash on its statements of financial position at June 30, 2008, and September 30, 2008. The cash it generated from operations was not sufficient to pay for the acquisition of property and equipment, and to repay long-term debt, which led APL to borrow from banks to cover the shortfall in cash. Note that significant cash transactions took place during the quarter even though the cash balances were zero at both the beginning and end of this quarter.

	(in thousands)
Net cash provided by operating activities	$ 727
Net cash used in investing activities	(2,948)
Net cash from financing activities	2,221
Net increase in cash and cash equivalents	0
Cash and cash equivalents at beginning of period	0
Cash and cash equivalents at end of period	$ 0

SELF-STUDY **QUIZ 5-1**

Canadian Tire Corporation

Canadian Tire Corporation is a network of businesses engaged in retail, financial services, and petroleum. A listing of some of its cash flows follows. Indicate whether each item is disclosed in the operating activities (O), investing activities (I), or financing activities (F) sections of the statement. (Refer to Exhibit 5.1 as a guide.)

_____ a. Purchase of short-term investments	_____ f. Change in inventories
_____ b. Profit	_____ g. Change in accrued liabilities
_____ c. Change in trade receivables	_____ h. Depreciation and amortization
_____ d. Additions to property and equipment	_____ i. Issuance of common shares
_____ e. Change in prepayments and other current assets	_____ j. Change in trade payables

▥ connect

After you complete your answers, go online for the solutions.

To give you a better understanding of the statement of cash flows, we now discuss in more detail APL's statement and the way that it relates to the statement of financial position and the income statement. Then we examine the way that each section of the statement describes a set of important decisions that APL's management made. We also discuss the way financial analysts use each section to evaluate the company's performance.

Relationships to the Statement of Financial Position and the Income Statement

Preparing and interpreting the statement of cash flows require analyzing the accounts that are reported on the statement of financial position and the income statement. As we discussed in previous chapters, accountants record transactions as journal entries that are posted to specific ledger accounts. The accounts' balances are then used to prepare the income statement and the statement of financial position. Companies cannot prepare the statement of cash flows by using amounts recorded in the specific accounts because these amounts are based on accrual accounting. Instead, accountants must analyze the amounts recorded under the accrual basis and adjust them to a cash basis. To prepare the statement of cash flows, they need the following data:

1. **Comparative statements of financial position** that are used in computing the cash flows from all activities (operating, investing, and financing).

2. A **complete income statement**, which is used primarily in identifying cash flows from operating activities.

3. **Additional details** concerning selected accounts that reflect different types of transactions and events. Analysis of individual accounts is necessary because often the net change in an account balance during the year does not reveal the underlying nature of the cash flows.

Our approach to preparing and understanding the statement of cash flows focuses on the changes in the accounts that are reported on the statement of financial position. It relies on a simple algebraic manipulation of the accounting equation

$$\textbf{Assets = Liabilities + Shareholders' Equity}$$

First, assets can be split into cash and non-cash assets:

$$\textbf{Cash + Non-cash Assets = Liabilities + Shareholders' Equity}$$

If we move the non-cash assets to the right side of the equation, then

$$\textbf{Cash = Liabilities + Shareholders' Equity − Non-cash Assets}$$

Category	Transaction	Effect on Cash	Other Account Affected
Operating	Collect trade receivables	+Cash	−Trade receivables (A)
	Pay trade payables	−Cash	−Trade payables (L)
	Prepay rent	−Cash	+Prepaid rent (A)
	Pay interest	−Cash	−Retained earnings (SE)
	Sell for cash	+Cash	+Retained earnings (SE)
Investing	Purchase equipment for cash	−Cash	+Equipment (A)
	Sell investment securities for cash	+Cash	−Investments
Financing	Pay back debt to bank	−Cash	−Notes payable—Bank (L)
	Issue shares for cash	+Cash	+Share capital (SE)

Exhibit **5.2**

Selected Cash Transactions and Their Effects on Other Statement of Financial Position Accounts

Given this relationship, the change in cash (Δ) between the beginning and end of the period must equal the changes (Δ) in the amounts on the right side of the equation during the same period:

$$\Delta \text{ Cash} = \Delta \text{ Liabilities} + \Delta \text{ Shareholders' Equity} - \Delta \text{ Non-cash Assets}$$

Thus, **any transaction that changes cash must be accompanied by a change in liabilities, shareholders' equity, or non-cash assets.**

In general increases in cash are associated with decreases in non-cash asset accounts and increases in liability and shareholders' equity accounts. In contrast, cash decreases when non-cash assets increase, and when liabilities or shareholders' equity decrease. Exhibit 5.2 illustrates this concept along with a sample of cash transactions that affect different asset, liability, and equity accounts.

Decrease in Non-cash Assets
Increase in Liabilities and Shareholders' Equity → **Cash Inflow**

Increase in Non-cash Assets
Decrease in Liabilities and Shareholders' Equity → **Cash Outflow**

Next, we will compute the change in each account on the statement of financial position (ending balance − beginning balance) and classify each change as relating to operating (O), investing (I), or financing (F) activities, based on APL's quarterly financial statements.

Exhibit 5.3 shows APL's comparative statements of financial position at the end of the first and second quarters of 2009, and its income statement for the second quarter of 2009. **The financial position accounts related to earning income (operating items) should be marked with an O**. These accounts include the following:

- most current assets (other than short-term investments which relate to investing activities).[3]

- most current liabilities (other than amounts owed to investors and financial institutions,[4] all of which relate to financing activities).

- retained earnings because it increases by the amount of profit, which is the starting point of the operating section. (Retained earnings also decreases by the amount of dividends declared and paid, which is a financing outflow noted by an F.)

In Exhibit 5.3, all of the relevant current assets and liabilities have been marked with an O. These items include trade receivables, inventories, prepayments, trade payables, and accrued liabilities. As we have noted, retained earnings is also relevant to operations.

---

[3]Certain non-current assets such as long-term receivables from customers and non-current liabilities such as post-retirement obligations to employees are considered to be operating items. These items are covered in advanced accounting courses.

[4]Examples of the accounts excluded are dividends payable, short-term borrowing (or bank indebtedness), and current portion of long-term debt (representing long-term debt with an original term longer than one year that is due within one year of the statement date).

Exhibit **5.3**

Andrew Peller Limited: Comparative Statements of Financial Position and Current Income Statement

Related Cash Flow Section	ANDREW PELLER LIMITED Consolidated Statements of Financial Position—Unaudited (in thousands of dollars)	Sept. 30, 2008	June 30, 2008	Change
	Assets			**Change**
	Current assets			
O	Trade receivables	$ 29,721	$ 24,212	5,509
O	Inventories	94,715	93,333	1,382
O	Prepayments	7,849	6,843	1,006
	Total current assets	132,285	124,388	
I*	Property, plant, and equipment (net)	101,354	100,474	880
I	Long-term investments	7,399	7,457	−58
I	Goodwill	44,499	44,499	0
	Total assets	$285,537	$276,818	
	Liabilities			
	Current liabilities			
F	Bank borrowings	$ 51,046	$ 47,164	3,882
O	Trade payables	24,423	18,715	5,708
O	Accrued liabilities	9,875	11,040	−1,165
F	Dividends payable	1,197	1,197	0
F	Current portion of long-term borrowings	6,158	6,184	−26
	Total current liabilities	92,699	84,300	
F	Long-term borrowings	74,767	75,205	−438
O	Deferred income taxes	12,682	14,244	−1,562
	Total liabilities	180,148	173,749	
	Shareholders' Equity			
F	Share capital	7,375	7,375	0
O and F	Retained earnings	98,014	95,694	2,320
	Total shareholders' equity	105,389	103,069	
	Total liabilities and shareholders' equity	$285,537	$276,818	

The balances of certain accounts have been adjusted to simplify the presentation.
*The accumulated depreciation account is also related to operations because depreciation expense is added back to profit.

ANDREW PELLER LIMITED
Consolidated Statement of Earnings—Unaudited
(in thousands of dollars)

	Quarter ended Sept. 30, 2008
Net sales	$69,356
Cost of sales	40,254
Gross margin	29,102
Selling, general, and administrative	20,808
Depreciation of plant and equipment	2,126
Operating profit	6,168
Interest expense	1,505
Profit before income taxes	4,663
Provision for income taxes	1,146
Profit	$ 3,517

The financial position accounts related to investing activities should be marked with an I. These include all of the remaining assets on the statement of financial position. In Exhibit 5.3, these are property, plant and equipment, long-term investments, and goodwill.

The financial position accounts related to financing activities should be marked with an F. These include all of the remaining liability and shareholders' equity accounts on the statement of financial position. In Exhibit 5.3, these are share capital and retained earnings (for decreases resulting from dividends declared and paid).

In the next sections of this chapter, we use this information to prepare the statement of cash flows.

REPORTING AND INTERPRETING CASH FLOWS FROM OPERATING ACTIVITIES

The operating activities section can be prepared in one of two formats: the direct method and the indirect method. The next section presents a comparison of the direct and indirect methods by using a simplified illustration. We then reconstruct the operating activities section of APL's statement of cash flows by using the indirect method.

A Simplified Illustration

LO²

Report and interpret cash flows from operating activities by using the indirect method.

The simplified example below illustrates the difference between the computation of cash flows from operating activities by using both the *direct* and *indirect* methods. We first show the effects of a series of summary transactions on the accounting equation and the statement of cash flows. We then show how the transaction effects on operating activities can be grouped to prepare the operating activities section of the statement of cash flows.

Sample Corporation reported the following account balances at December 31, 2010:

SAMPLE CORPORATION
Statement of Financial Position
At December 31, 2010

Assets

Cash		$ 19,200
Trade receivables		22,000
Merchandise inventory		75,000
Prepayments		15,000
Property, plant, and equipment	$113,500	
Less: Accumulated depreciation	20,000	93,500
Total assets		$224,700

Liabilities and Shareholders' Equity

Liabilities

Trade payables		$ 14,000
Salaries payable		1,500
Income tax payable		4,500
Long-term borrowings		54,000
Total liabilities		$ 74,000

Shareholders' equity

Common shares	$126,000	
Retained earnings	24,700	150,700
Total liabilities and shareholders' equity		$224,700

The following summary transactions occurred during 2011:

1. Purchased merchandise for $62,000 on account, and paid $59,000 to various suppliers.

2. Sold merchandise on account for $140,000, and collected $145,000 in cash from customers. The cost of merchandise sold was $69,000.

3. Salaries expense totalled $28,000, but only $27,000 was paid to employees during the year.

4. Interest expense of $5,000 was paid in full.

5. Other operating expenses totalled $15,800, including expenses of $5,000 that were prepaid, and $10,800 that were paid during the year.

6. Purchased a new building for $20,000 and issued common shares in full payment.

7. Declared and paid cash dividend of $6,000.

8. Depreciation expense was $7,000 for the year.

9. The income tax expense for 2011 totalled $9,000; the company paid $10,500 to the tax authorities.

The effects of these transactions on the accounting equation and cash flows are shown in Exhibit 5.4. Note that some of the accounts we use, such as prepayments, property, plant and equipment, accrued liabilities, and retained earnings, are groupings of many accounts. The main ideas that we present in this illustration do not change with the addition of more detailed accounts.

The detailed transaction effects in Exhibit 5.4 can be used to prepare the operating activities section of the statement of cash flows by listing the cash receipts and cash payments related to operations.

SAMPLE CORPORATION
Statement of Cash Flows (Partial)
For the Year Ended December 31, 2011
(Direct Method)

Operating Activities		
Collections from customers		$145,000
Payments:		
to suppliers	$59,000	
to employees	27,000	
for interest	5,000	
for other operating expenses	10,800	
for income taxes	10,500	
Total payments		112,300
Net cash flows from operating activities		$ 32,700

Let us now turn our attention to the reporting of cash flow from operations under the indirect method. The starting point of the computation is profit, which is the difference between revenues (including gains) and expenses (including losses). We know that the revenues earned by the company in 2011 do not necessarily result in an equal amount of cash collections from customers during the year. In fact, the amount of cash received from customers during the year could be equal to, lower, or higher than the amount of revenues. Similarly, the amount of expenses incurred during the year may not coincide with the amount of cash payments for these expenses. Given that revenues and expenses include both cash and non-cash components, we need to remove the non-cash revenues and non-cash expenses from profit in order to obtain the cash components. Exhibit 5.5 shows how we can decompose the revenues and expenses into cash and non-cash components.

The amounts in column A are taken from the retained earnings column in Exhibit 5.4, and the amounts in column B are the corresponding cash receipts or payments that appear in the operating activities column of the same exhibit. The profit, $6,200, comprises a cash component of $32,700 and a non-cash component of $26,500.

Exhibit 5.4

Effects of Summary Transactions on the Accounting Equation

Transaction	Cash	Trade Receivables	Merchandise Inventory	Prepaid Expenses	Property, Plant, and Equipment (net)	Trade Payables	Salaries payable	Income Tax Payable	Long-Term Borrowings	Common Shares	Retained Earnings	Description of Item	Operating Activities	Investing Activities	Financing Activities
						=				+					
			Assets				Liabilities				Shareholders' Equity			Effect on Cash Flows	
Balance, Jan. 1, 2011	19,200	22,000	75,000	15,000	93,500	14,000	1,500	4,500	54,000	126,000	24,700				
1a. Purchase of merchandise			62,000			62,000									
1b. Payment to suppliers	(59,000)					(59,000)							(59,000)		
2a. Credit sales		140,000									140,000	Sales			
2b. Cost of sales			(69,000)								(69,000)	Costs of sales			
2c. Collection from customers	145,000	(145,000)											145,000		
3a. Salaries expense							28,000				(28,000)	Salaries			
3b. Payment to employees	(27,000)						(27,000)						(27,000)		
4. Payment of interest	(5,000)										(5,000)	Interest	(5,000)		
5. Other operating expenses	(10,800)			(5,000)							(15,800)	Other expenses	(10,800)		
6. Purchase of building					20,000					20,000					
7. Payment of dividends	(6,000)										(6,000)	Dividends			(6,000)
8. Depreciation expense					(7,000)						(7,000)	Depreciation			
9a. Income tax expense								9,000			(9,000)	Income tax			
9b. Payment of income taxes	(10,500)							(10,500)					(10,500)		
Balance, Dec. 31, 2011	45,900	17,000	68,000	10,000	106,500	17,000	2,500	3,000	54,000	146,000	24,900		32,700	–	(6,000)

Exhibit **5.5**

Decomposition of Revenues and Expenses into Cash and Non-cash Components

Transaction	A Operating Revenue or Expense (Accrual Amount)	−	B Cash Component	=	C Difference (Non-cash Component)
Sales	$140,000		$145,000		$ (5,000)
Cost of sales	(69,000)		(59,000)		(10,000)
Salaries expense	(28,000)		(27,000)		(1,000)
Interest expense	(5,000)		(5,000)		-0-
Other operating expenses	(15,800)		(10,800)		(5,000)
Depreciation expense	(7,000)		-0-		(7,000)
Income tax expense	(9,000)		(10,500)		1,500
Cash/Accrual profit from operations	$ 6,200		$ 32,700		$(26,500)

As indicated previously, the direct method focuses on the cash elements of profit by computing cash receipts and cash payments for operating purposes, and reports the details found in column B of Exhibit 5.5 to arrive at net cash flows from operating activities. In contrast, the indirect method starts with profit and eliminates the non-cash elements reported in column C of Exhibit 5.5 to arrive at the same result. In general,

Profit = Cash elements +/− Non-cash elements
Cash elements = Profit +/− Non-cash elements

Hence, the net cash flows from operating activities can be computed indirectly as

Net cash flows from operating activities = $6,200 + $26,500 = $32,700

The decomposition of profit into cash and non-cash components, as presented in Exhibit 5.5, requires a reconstruction of all the transactions that occurred during the year. Such details are not publicly available. But, because transactions that affect revenue or expense accounts also affect primarily the current asset or current liability accounts, we can use the changes in the statement of financial position accounts to compute the non-cash components of profit, which are identified in column C of Exhibit 5.5. This process, which is explained in detail in the next section, leads to an alternative way of computing and reporting the net cash flows from operating activities.

SAMPLE CORPORATION
Statement of Cash Flows (Partial)
For the Year Ended December 31, 2011
(Indirect Method)

Operating Activities

Profit from operations		$ 6,200
Add (deduct) items not affecting cash:		
Depreciation expense	$ 7,000	
Decrease in trade receivables	5,000	
Decrease in merchandise inventory	7,000	
Decrease in prepayments	5,000	
Increase in trade payables	3,000	
Increase in salaries payable	1,000	
Decrease in income tax payable	(1,500)	
Net adjustments		26,500
Net cash flows from operating activities		$32,700

Notice that the adjustments listed above are the same amounts that appear in column C in Exhibit 5.5, except for showing the non-cash component of the cost of sales ($10,000) as the result of a decrease in merchandise inventory by $7,000, and an increase in trade payables by $3,000.

Before proceeding further, remember that

1. Cash flows from operating activities is always the same regardless of whether it is computed by using the direct or indirect method.

2. The investing and financing sections are always presented in the same manner, regardless of the format of the operating section.

Reporting Cash Flows from Operating Activities— Indirect Method

The indirect method of reporting cash flows from operating activities starts with profit and eliminates the non-cash components of revenues and expenses. The general structure of the operating activities section is

```
Operating Activities
Profit
Add/Subtract items not affecting cash:
 + Depreciation expense
 + Decreases in non-cash current assets
 − Increases in non-cash current assets
 + Increases in current liabilities
 − Decreases in current liabilities
   Net Cash Flows from Operating Activities
```

To keep track of all the additions and subtractions made to convert profit to cash flows from operating activities, it is helpful to set up a schedule to record the computations. We construct such a schedule for APL in Exhibit 5.6.

We begin our schedule presented in Exhibit 5.6 with profit of $3,517, taken from APL's income statement (Exhibit 5.3). Completing the operating section by using the indirect method involves two steps:

Step 1: Adjust profit for the effect of depreciation expense. Recording depreciation expense does not affect the cash account (or any other current asset or liability). It affects a non-current asset (such as Equipment, net). **Since depreciation expense is subtracted in computing profit, but does not affect cash, we always add it back** to convert profit to cash flows from operating activities.[5] In the case of APL, we need to remove the effect of depreciation expense by adding back $2,126 to profit (see Exhibit 5.6).[6]

Step 2: Adjust profit for changes in current assets and current liabilities marked as operating (O). Each **change** in current assets and current liabilities (other than cash and cash equivalents) causes a difference between profit and cash flows from operating activities.[7] When converting profit to cash flows from operating activities, apply the following general rules:

- Add the change when a current asset decreases or current liability increases.

- Subtract the change when a current asset increases or current liability decreases.

Understanding what makes these current assets and current liabilities increase and decrease is the key to understanding the logic of these additions and subtractions.

---

[5]The adding back of depreciation and amortization to profit does not mean that this expense is a source of cash. In fact, depreciation and amortization are the result of a process of allocating the cost of assets over time regardless of the timing of payment for the assets.

[6]Gains and losses on sales of equipment and investments are dealt with in a similar manner and are discussed in Appendix 5A. Other similar additions and subtractions are discussed in more advanced accounting courses.

[7]Certain non-current assets such as long-term receivables from customers and non-current liabilities, such as post-retirement obligations to employees, are considered to be operating items. These items are covered in advanced accounting courses.

Exhibit **5.6**

Andrew Peller Limited: Schedule for Net Cash Flows from Operating Activities, Indirect Method (in thousands)

Conversion of profit to net cash flows from operating activities:

Items	Amount	Explanation
Profit, accrual basis	$ 3,517	From income statement.
Add (subtract) to convert to cash basis:		
Depreciation and amortization expense	+2,126	Add because depreciation and amortization expense is a non-cash expense.
Deferred income taxes	−1,562	Subtract because deferred income taxes do not affect cash.
Increase in trade receivables	−5,509	Subtract because cash collected from customers is less than accrual basis revenues.
Increase in inventories	−1,382	Subtract because cost of sales is less than purchases.
Increase in prepayments	−1,006	Subtract because accrual basis expenses are less than cash prepayments for expenses.
Increase in trade payables	+5,708	Add because purchases on account (due to suppliers) are more than cash payments to suppliers.
Decrease in accrued liabilities	−1,165	Subtract because the cash payments for expenses are more than accrual basis expenses.
Net cash inflow from operating activities	$ 727	Reported on the statement of cash flows.

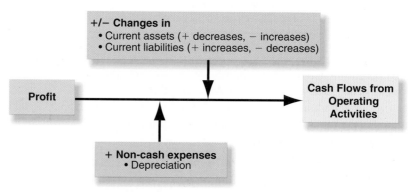

Change in Trade Receivables   We illustrate this logic with the first operating item (O) listed on APL's statement of financial position (Exhibit 5.3), trade receivables. Remember that the income statement reflects sales revenue, but the statement of cash flows must reflect cash collections from customers. As the following trade receivables T-account illustrates, when sales revenues are recorded, trade receivables increase, and when cash is collected from customers, trade receivables decrease.

Trade Receivables (A)

Change +5,509 {	Beginning balance	24,212		
	Sales revenue (on account)	69,356	Collections from customers	63,847
	Ending balance	29,721		

In the APL example, sales revenue on account reported on the income statement is larger than cash collections from customers by $69,356 − $63,847 = $5,509.[8] Since less money was collected from customers, this amount must be subtracted from profit to convert to cash flows from operating activities. Note that this amount is also the same as the **change** in the trade receivables account shown:

Ending balance	$29,721
Beginning balance	24,212
Change	$ 5,509

---

[8]The amount of cash collected from customers is the same, regardless of the mix of cash sales and credit sales. To make sure, assume that sales are 20 percent cash and 80 percent on account, and calculate the amount of cash collected from customers during the period.

This same underlying logic is used to determine adjustments for the other current assets and liabilities.

To summarize, the income statement reflects revenues of the period, but cash flows from operating activities must reflect cash collections from customers. Sales on account increase the balance in trade receivables, and collections from customers decrease the balance.

Trade Receivables (A)

Beg. bal.	24,212	
Increase	5,509	
End. bal.	29,721	

The statement of financial position for APL indicates an **increase** in trade receivables of $5,509 for the period, which means cash collected from customers is lower than revenue. To convert to cash flows from operating activities, the amount of the increase must be **subtracted** from profit in Exhibit 5.6. (A decrease is added to profit.)

Change in Inventory The income statement reflects merchandise sold for the period, whereas cash flows from operating activities must reflect cash purchases.

Both the change in inventory and the change in trade payables (borrowing from suppliers) determine the magnitude of this difference. It is easiest to think about the change in inventory in terms of the simple case in which the company pays cash to trade suppliers. We address the added complexity involved when purchases are made on account when we discuss the adjustment for the change in trade payables.

As shown in the T-account on the left, purchases of goods increase the balance in inventory and recording the cost of sales decreases the balance in inventory. Therefore, the change in inventory is the difference between purchases and cost of sales.

Inventories (A)

Beg. bal.		
Purchases	Cost of sales	
End. bal.		

Inventories (A)

Beg. bal.	93,333	
Increase	1,382	
End. bal.	94,715	

APL's statement of financial position indicates that inventory **increased** by $1,382, which means that the cost of purchases is larger than the cost of merchandise sold. The increase must be **subtracted** from profit to convert to cash flows from operating activities in Exhibit 5.6. (A decrease is added to profit.)

Change in Prepayments The income statement reflects expenses of the period, but cash flows from operating activities must reflect the cash payments. Cash paid in advance increases the prepayments balance, and expenses recognized during the period decrease the balance.

Prepayments (A)

Beg. bal.		
Purchases	Services used (expense)	
End. bal.		

Prepayments (A)

Beg. bal.	6,843	
Increase	1,006	
End. bal.	7,849	

APL's statement of financial position indicates that prepayments **increased** by $1,006 during the quarter, which means that the amount of expenses is smaller than new cash prepayments. The increase (the extra payments) must be **subtracted** from profit in Exhibit 5.6. (A decrease is added to profit.)

Change in Trade Payables Cash flow from operations must reflect cash purchases, but not all purchases are for cash. Purchases on account increase trade payables, and cash paid to suppliers decreases trade payables.

Trade Payables (L)			Trade Payables (L)	
	Beg. bal.		Beg. bal.	18,715
Cash payments	Purchases on account		Increase	5,708
	End. bal.		End. bal.	24,423

APL's trade payables **increased** by $5,708, indicating that cash payments were smaller than purchases on account, and this increase (the lower payments) must be **added** to profit in Exhibit 5.6. (A decrease is subtracted from profit.)

Change in Accrued Liabilities The income statement reflects all accrued expenses, but the statement of cash flows must reflect actual payments for those expenses. Recording accrued expenses increases the accrued liabilities balance, and cash payments for the expenses decrease it.

Accrued Liabilities (L)			Accrued Liabilities (L)	
	Beg. bal.		Beg. bal.	11,040
Payment of accruals	Accrued expenses	Decrease 1,165		
	End. bal.		End. bal.	9,875

APL's accrued liabilities **decreased** by $1,165, which indicates that accrual-basis expenses are smaller than cash paid for the expenses. The decrease must be **subtracted** from profit in Exhibit 5.6. (An increase is added to profit.)

Summary We can summarize the typical additions and subtractions that are required to reconcile profit with cash flows from operating activities as follows:

Item	Additions and Subtractions to Reconcile Profit to Cash Flows from Operating Activities	
	When Item Increases	When Item Decreases
Depreciation and amortization	+	NA
Trade receivables	−	+
Inventory	−	+
Prepayments	−	+
Trade payables	+	−
Accrued liabilities	+	−

Notice in this table that an increase in a current asset or a decrease in a current liability is always subtracted to reconcile profit to cash flows from operating activities. A decrease in a current asset or an increase in a current liability is always added to reconcile profit to cash flows from operating activities. The statement of cash flows for APL (Exhibit 5.1) shows the same additions and subtractions to reconcile profit to cash flows from operating activities described in Exhibit 5.6.

It is important to note again that the net cash inflow or outflow is the same regardless of whether the direct or indirect method of presentation is used (in this case, an inflow of $727). The two methods differ only in terms of the details reported on the statement. We show in Appendix 5B how cash flows from operations can be computed by using the direct method.

AUSTRALIAN PRACTICES

Foster's Brewing is the first name in Australian beer and a major player in world beverage markets. Following Australian GAAP, which require use of the direct method of presentation, Foster's cash flow from operations is presented as follows:

REAL WORLD EXCERPT

Foster's Brewing
ANNUAL REPORT

STATEMENT OF CASH FLOWS
For the Year Ended 30 June 2009
(in millions of Australian dollars)

Cash Flows from Operating Activities	
Receipts from customers	7,532.1
Payments to suppliers, governments, and employees	(6,233.4)
Dividends received	1.2
Interest received	17.4
Borrowing costs	(172.4)
Income taxes paid	(260.0)
Net cash flows from operating activities	884.9

Note that Foster's combines payments to suppliers, governments, and employees, but other companies report these items separately. Like Canadian companies that choose the direct method, Foster's reports the indirect presentation in a note to the financial statements.

SELF-STUDY **QUIZ 5-2**

Indicate which of the following items taken from Canadian Tire Corporation's statement of cash flows would be added (+), subtracted (−), or not included (0) in the reconciliation of profit to cash flow from operations.

_____ *a.* Increase in inventories.

_____ *b.* Net borrowings from bank.

_____ *c.* Depreciation and amortization expense.

_____ *d.* Decrease in trade receivables.

_____ *e.* Increase in trade payables and accrued expenses.

_____ *f.* Increase in prepayments and other current assets.

After you complete your answers, go online for the solutions.

Canadian Tire Corporation

■ connect

Interpreting Cash Flows from Operating Activities

The operating activities section of the statement of cash flows focuses attention on the firm's ability to generate cash internally through operations and its management of working capital (current assets minus current liabilities). Many analysts regard this as the most important section of the statement because, in the long run, operations are the only sustainable source of cash. Investors should not invest in a company if they believe that it will not be able to pay them dividends or make reinvestments with cash generated from operations. Similarly, creditors should not lend money if they believe that cash generated from operations will not be available to pay back the loan. For example, many Internet-based companies crashed when investors lost faith in their ability to turn business ideas into cash from operations.

A common rule followed by financial and credit analysts is to avoid firms with rising profit but falling cash flow from operations. Rapidly rising inventories require the use of cash until goods are sold. Similarly, rapidly rising trade receivables reflect a delay in the collection of cash. Rising inventories and trade receivables often predict a future slump in profit as revenues fall. This increases the need for external financing as overall cash inflows from operations decline. A true understanding of the meaning of the difference between profit and cash flow from operations requires a detailed understanding of its causes.

In the second quarter of fiscal year 2009, APL reported that profit was higher than cash flow from operations. What caused this relationship? To answer these questions, we must carefully analyze how APL's operating activities are reported in the statement of cash flows. To properly interpret this information, we also must learn more about the wine industry.

Analyzing Changes in Trade Receivables   Managers sometimes attempt to boost declining sales by extending credit terms (e.g., from 30 to 60 days) or by lowering credit standards (i.e., lending to riskier customers). The resulting increase in trade receivables can cause profit to outpace cash flow from operations. As a consequence, many analysts view this pattern as a warning sign.

Analysts who cover the wine industry know that APL normally sees an increase in receivables from normal seasonal fluctuations in wine sales to distributors. They recognize that wine sales are low in the months of April to June (the first quarter for APL), and that sales are higher during the second quarter (July to September) in anticipation of the fall season. The higher sales volume in the second quarter requires a buildup of inventories over time to meet demand in the fall months, which leads to cash payments to suppliers and employees exceeding cash collections from customers. The imbalance in cash inflows and outflows increases the need for external financing. However, the use of cash for operations during the first quarter is followed by a net cash inflow from operations in the second quarter, when sales and collections from customers increase. This normal seasonal fluctuation in sales is clearly not a sign of problems for APL.

Analyzing Inventory Changes   An unexpected increase in inventory can be another cause for profit to outpace cash flow from operations. Such inventory growth can be a sign that planned sales growth did not materialize. Alternatively, a decline in inventory can be a sign that the company is anticipating lower sales in the next quarter. In the case of APL, an increase in inventory at the end of the second quarter results from the normal inventory buildup in anticipation of higher sales in fall. Many analysts compute the quality of earnings ratio as a general warning sign of these and similar problems.

KEY RATIO ANALYSIS

QUALITY OF EARNINGS RATIO

LO3

Analyze and interpret the quality of earnings ratio.

ANALYTICAL QUESTION → How much cash does each dollar of profit generate?

RATIO AND COMPARISONS → The quality of earnings ratio is useful in answering this question. It is computed as follows:

$$\text{Quality of Earnings Ratio} = \frac{\text{Cash Flows from Operating Activities}}{\text{Profit}}$$

APL's ratio for the year* 2009 is

$$\$7,156 \ / \ \$13,705 = 0.52$$

Comparisons over Time			Comparisons with Competitors	
Andrew Peller (annual)			Constellation Brands	Foster's Group
2007	2008	2009	2009	2009
0.77	0.48	0.52	−1.68	2.02

*We use the ratio for the annual period to eliminate the effects of seasonality.

SELECTED FOCUS COMPANY COMPARISONS

Nestlé	Gildan	Benetton
1.52	1.77	2.51

INTERPRETATIONS

In General → The quality of earnings ratio measures the portion of earnings that was generated in cash. All other things being equal, a higher quality of earnings ratio indicates a greater ability to finance operating and other cash needs from operating cash inflows.[9] A higher ratio also indicates that it is less likely that the company is using aggressive revenue recognition policies to increase profit. When this ratio does not equal 1.0, analysts must establish the source of the difference to determine the significance of the findings. There are four potential causes of any difference:

1. *The corporate life cycle (growth or decline in sales).* When sales are increasing, receivables and inventory normally increase faster than trade payables. This often reduces operating cash flows below the reported profit, which, in turn, reduces the ratio. When sales are declining, the opposite occurs and the ratio increases.

2. *Seasonality.* As was the case for APL, seasonal variations in sales and purchases of inventory can cause the ratio to deviate from 1.0.

3. *Changes in revenue and expense recognition.* Aggressive revenue recognition or failure to accrue appropriate expenses will inflate profit and reduce the ratio.

4. *Changes in management of operating assets and liabilities.* Inefficient management will increase operating assets and decrease liabilities, which will reduce operating cash flows and reduce the ratio. More efficient management will have the opposite effect.

Focus Company Analysis → APL's quality of earnings ratio has decreased from 0.77 to 0.52 during the last three years. As we noted earlier, the difference between profit and cash flow from operations in the case of APL for the second quarter of 2009 was not a cause for alarm. It was due to normal seasonal changes in sales and receivables. In comparison with APL, Constellation Brands has a negative ratio because it reported a net loss for fiscal year 2009 but it generated cash from its operations. Foster's Group has a positive ratio that exceeds 2.0. Both companies have done better than APL in terms of generating cash flow from their operations in excess of the reported profit or loss.

A Few Cautions → The quality of earnings ratio can be interpreted only based on an understanding of the company's business operations and strategy. For example, a low ratio can be due simply to normal seasonal changes. However, it also can indicate obsolete inventory, slowing sales, or failed expansion plans. To test for these possibilities, analysts often analyze this ratio in tandem with the trade receivables turnover and inventory turnover ratios.

FRAUD AND CASH FLOWS FROM OPERATIONS

A QUESTION OF ACCOUNTABILITY

The statement of cash flows often gives outsiders the first hint that financial statements may contain errors and irregularities. The importance of this indicator as a predictor is receiving more attention following corporate scandals. For example, *Investors Chronicle* reported on an accounting fraud at a commercial credit company, suggesting that

> ... a look at Versailles's cash flow statement—an invaluable tool in spotting creative accounting—should have triggered misgivings. In the company's last filed accounts ... Versailles reported operating profits of ... $25 million but a cash outflow from operating activities of $24 million ... such figures should ... have served as a warning. After all, what use is a company to anyone if it reports only accounting profits which are never translated into cash?*

As noted in earlier chapters, unethical managers sometimes attempt to reach earnings targets by manipulating accruals and deferrals of revenues and expenses to inflate profit. Since

---

[9]When a loss is reported, a more negative ratio indicates greater ability to finance the company from operations.

these adjustments do not affect the cash account, they have no effect on the statement of cash flows. As a consequence, a growing difference between profit and cash flow from operations can be a sign of such manipulations. This early warning sign has been evident before some famous bankruptcies, such as that of W. T. Grant. This company had inflated profit by failing to make adequate accruals of expenses for uncollectible trade receivables and obsolete inventory. The growing difference between profit and cash flow from operations was noted by the more astute analysts who recommended selling the stock long before the bankruptcy.

Source: James Chapman, "Creative Accounting: Exposed!" *Investor's Chronicle*, February 3, 2001.

REPORTING AND INTERPRETING CASH FLOWS FROM INVESTING ACTIVITIES

Reporting Cash Flows from Investing Activities

Preparing this section of the statement of cash flows requires analyzing the accounts related to property, plant, and equipment; intangible assets; and investments in the securities of other companies. Normally, the relevant statement of financial position accounts include short-term investments and non-current asset accounts such as long-term investments and property, plant, and equipment. The following relationships are the ones that you will encounter most frequently:

LO⁴

Report and interpret cash flows from investing activities.

Investing Activity	Related Statement of Financial Position Account(s)	Cash Flow Effect
Purchase of property, plant, and equipment or intangible assets for cash	Property, plant, and equipment and intangible assets (e.g., patents)	Outflow
Sale of property, plant, and equipment or intangible assets for cash		Inflow
Purchase of investment securities for cash	Short- or long-term investments in shares and bonds issued by other companies	Outflow
Sale (maturity) of investment securities for cash		Inflow

Typical investing activities include the following:

1. Cash expenditures that include the acquisition of tangible productive assets such as buildings and equipment or intangible assets such as trademarks and patents. **Only purchases paid for with cash or cash equivalents are included.**

2. Cash proceeds from the sale of productive assets or intangible assets. This is the amount of cash that was received from the sale of assets, regardless of whether the assets were sold at a gain or a loss.

3. Purchase of short- or long-term investments for cash. These investments can include shares or bonds issued by other companies, guaranteed investment certificates, or government securities with maturities of more than three months. (Remember that securities with maturities of three months or less are cash equivalents.)

4. Cash proceeds from the sale or maturity of short- or long-term investments. Again, this is the amount of cash that was received from the sale, regardless of whether the assets were sold at a gain or a loss.

In the case of APL, the analysis of changes in the statement of financial position (shown in Exhibit 5.3) indicates that two non-current assets (noted with "I") have changed during the period: property, plant, and equipment (net), and long-term investments. To determine the causes of changes in these assets, accountants need to search the related company records.

Property, Plant, and Equipment (net) The company's property, plant, and equipment (PPE) account increased by an amount of $880, net of accumulated depreciation. Typically, the net change in PPE is the result of three main changes: (1) purchase of new assets, (2) disposal of old assets, and (3) periodic depreciation of these assets. The purchase of assets increases the balance of PPE, the disposal of assets decreases the balance by the carrying amount (original cost − accumulated depreciation) of the assets disposed of, and the periodic depreciation increases the accumulated depreciation, which in turn reduces the balance of PPE.

During the second quarter of 2009, APL purchased new property, plant, and equipment for cash in the amount of $3,006, which is a cash outflow. This amount less the depreciation expense of $2,126, which is added to the profit in the operations section of the statement of cash flows, explains the net increase in PPE of $880.

Property, Plant, and Equipment (net)

Beg. bal.	100,474	Depreciation	2,126
Purchases	3,006		
End. bal.	101,354		

Cash purchases and sales of plant and equipment are listed separately on the statement of cash flows.

Long-Term Investments APL's records indicate that it sold long-term investments at its carrying amount during the quarter and received $58 in cash. This transaction explains the decrease in the account balance.

Long-Term Investments (A)

Beg.	7,457	Sale	58
End.	7,399		

These investing items are listed in the schedule of investing activities in Exhibit 5.7 and result in a cash outflow of $2,948.

Interpreting Cash Flows from Investing Activities

Two common ways of assessing a company's ability to finance its expansion needs from internal sources are the capital acquisitions ratio and free cash flow.

Items from Statement of Financial Position and Account Analysis	Cash Inflow (Outflows)	Explanation
Additions to property, plant, and equipment	($3,006)	Payment in cash for buildings and equipment.
Proceeds from long-term investments	58	Receipt of cash for sale of investments.
Net cash inflow (outflow) from investing activities	($2,948)	Reported on the statement of cash flows.

Exhibit **5.7**

Andrew Peller Limited: Schedule for Net Cash Flow from Investing Activities (in thousands of dollars)

KEY RATIO
ANALYSIS

CAPITAL ACQUISITIONS RATIO

LO5

Analyze and interpret the capital acquisitions ratio.

ANALYTICAL QUESTION → To what degree was the company able to finance purchases of property, plant, and equipment with cash provided by operating activities?

RATIO AND COMPARISONS → Since capital expenditures for plant and equipment often vary greatly from year to year, this ratio is often computed over longer periods of time than one year, such as the three-year period used here. It is computed as follows:

$$\text{Capital Acquisitions Ratio} = \frac{\text{Cash Flow from Operating Activities}}{\text{Cash Paid for Property, Plant, and Equipment}}$$

The 2007 through 2009 ratio for APL is

$$\$28,200/\$34,320 = 0.82$$

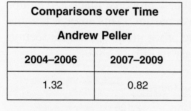

**SELECTED FOCUS
COMPANY COMPARISONS**

Nestlé 2.91

Gildan 3.76

Benetton 1.07

Comparisons over Time		Comparisons with Competitors	
Andrew Peller		Constellation Brands	Foster's Group
2004–2006	2007–2009	2007–2009	2007–2009
1.32	0.82	2.89	4.70

INTERPRETATIONS

In General → The capital acquisitions ratio reflects the portion of purchases of property, plant, and equipment financed from operating activities without the need for outside debt or equity financing or the sale of other investments or property, plant, and equipment. A high ratio indicates less need for outside financing for current and future expansion. This provides the company with opportunities for strategic acquisitions, avoids the cost of additional debt, and reduces the risks of bankruptcy that come with additional leverage (see Chapter 11).

Focus Company Analysis → APL's ratio decreased from 1.32 to 0.82 in recent years and is significantly lower than the ratios of its competitors. To many, the tangible nature of plant and equipment may suggest that it is a low-risk investment. When companies in an industry build more productive capacity than is necessary to meet customer demand, however, the costs of maintaining and financing an idle plant can drive a company to ruin. While APL produces and markets its own wine and premium beer, both Constellation Brands and Foster's Group market wine, beer, and other alcoholic beverages produced by other companies, in addition to marketing their own brands. By marketing other brands, these two companies reduce their need to invest in additional productive capacity to expand their operations. These differences in operating strategies are reflected in the companies' capital acquisitions ratio.

A Few Cautions → Since the needs for investment in plant and equipment differ dramatically across industries (e.g., airlines versus pizza delivery restaurants), a particular firm's ratio should be compared only with its prior years' figures or with other firms in the same industry. Also, a high ratio may indicate a failure to update plant and equipment, which can limit a company's ability to compete in the future.

FINANCIAL
ANALYSIS

FREE CASH FLOW

FREE CASH FLOW =
Cash Flows from Operating Activities − Dividends − Capital Expenditures

Managers and analysts also often calculate free cash flow as a measure of the firm's ability to pursue long-term investment opportunities. It is normally calculated as follows:

**Free Cash Flow = Cash Flows from Operating Activities −
Dividends − Capital Expenditures**

Any positive free cash flow is available for additional capital expenditures, investments in other companies, and mergers and acquisitions, without the need for external financing. While free cash flow is considered a positive sign of financial flexibility, it also can represent a hidden cost to shareholders. Sometimes managers use free cash flow to pursue unprofitable investments just for the sake of growth or for perquisites for management use (such as fancy offices and corporate jets). In these cases, the shareholders would be better off if free cash flow were paid as additional dividends or used to repurchase the company's shares in the open market.

REPORTING AND INTERPRETING CASH FLOWS FROM FINANCING ACTIVITIES

Reporting Cash Flows from Financing Activities

Financing activities are associated with generating capital from creditors and owners. This section reflects changes in two current liabilities, *notes payable to financial institutions* (often called *short-term borrowings*), and *current portion of long-term borrowings*, as well as changes in *non-current liabilities and shareholders' equity accounts*. These statement of financial position accounts relate to the issuance and retirement of debt, repurchase of shares, and the payment of dividends. The following relationships are the ones that you will encounter most frequently:

LO6

Report and interpret cash flows from financing activities.

Related Statement of Financial Position Account(s)	Cash Flow Financing Activity	Effect
Short-term borrowings	Borrowing cash from bank or other financial institution	Inflow
	Repayment of loan principal	Outflow
Long-term borrowings	Long-term borrowings for cash	Inflow
	Repayment of principal on long-term borrowings	Outflow
Share capital	Issuance of shares for cash	Inflow
	Repurchase (retirement) of shares with cash	Outflow
Retained earnings	Payment of cash dividends	Outflow

Financing activities are associated with generating capital from creditors and owners. Typical financing activities include the following:

1. *Proceeds from issuance of short- and long-term borrowings.* This represents cash received from borrowing from banks and other financial institutions, and issuance of long-term debt (e.g., notes) to the public. **If the debt is issued for other than cash** (e.g., issued directly to a supplier of equipment to pay for a purchase), **it is not included in the statement.**

2. *Principal payments on short- and long-term borrowings.* Cash outflows associated with debt include the periodic repayment of principal as well as interest payments. Cash repayments of principal are listed as cash flows from financing activities.

3. *Proceeds from the issuance of shares.* This represents cash received from the sale of shares to investors. **If the shares are issued for other than cash** (for e.g., issued directly to an employee as part of salary), **the amount is not included in the statement.**

4. *Purchase of shares for retirement.* This cash outflow includes cash payments for repurchase of the company's own shares from shareholders.

5. *Interest and dividends.* Cash flows from interest and dividends received and paid should be classified in a consistent manner from period to period as operating, investing, or financing activities. Cash dividends are usually reported as a financing activity because they are payments to shareholders. Alternatively, dividends paid may be classified as a component of cash flows from operating activities in order to assist users to determine the ability of an entity to pay dividends out of operating cash flows.

Dividends received may be classified as investing cash flows because they represent returns on investments. Alternatively, they may be classified as operating cash flows because they enter into the determination of profit or loss.

Interest paid and interest received may be classified as financing cash flows because they are costs of obtaining financial resources or returns on investments. Alternatively, they may be classified operating cash flows because they enter into the determination of profit or loss.

To compute cash flows from financing activities, you should review changes in debt and shareholders' equity accounts. In the case of APL, analysis of changes in the account balances on the statement of financial position indicates that bank borrowings, long-term borrowings, and retained earnings changed during the period (noted with an F).

Short-Term Borrowings   Company records indicate that the change in bank borrowings resulted from additional borrowing of $3,882 in cash. This item is listed in Exhibit 5.6.

Bank Borrowings (L)

		Beg. bal.	47,164
Payment		Additional loans	3,882
		End. Bal.	51,046

Long-Term Borrowings   The company's long-term borrowings, including the current portion, decreased from $81,389 to $80,925. Therefore, APL repaid $464 of its long-term borrowings during the second quarter of 2009, as shown in Exhibit 5.8.

Long-Term Borrowings (L)

		Beg. bal.	80,925
Payment	464		
		End. bal.	81,389

Retained Earnings   The change in retained earnings resulted from the addition of profit and the declaration of dividends.

Retained Earnings (SE)

		Beg. bal.	95,694
Dividends declared	1,197	Profit	3,517
		End. bal.	98,014

Exhibit **5.8**

Andrew Peller Limited: Schedule for Net Cash Flow from Financing Activities (in thousands)

Items from Statement of Financial Position and Account Analysis	Cash Inflow (Outflows)	Explanation
Increase in bank borrowings	$3,882	Additional borrowing from banks
Long-term borrowings—principal repayments	(464)	Repayment of the principal amount of long-term debt, including the current portion
Payment of dividends	(1,197)	Payment of cash dividends to shareholders
Net cash inflow from financing activities	$2,221	Reported on the statement of cash flows

Dividends Payable The dividends payable at June 30, 2009, were paid during the quarter ended September 30, 2009.

		Dividends Payable (L)	
		Beg. bal.	1,197
Payment	1,197	Dividends declared	1,197
		End. bal.	1,197

Interpreting Cash Flows from Financing Activities

The long-term growth of a company is normally financed from three sources: internally generated funds (cash from operating activities), the issuance of shares, and money borrowed on a long-term basis. As we discuss in Chapter 11, companies can adopt a number of different capital structures (the balance of debt and equity). The financing sources that management uses to fund growth will have an important impact on the firm's risk and return characteristics. The statement of cash flows shows how management has elected to fund its growth. This information is used by analysts who wish to evaluate the capital structure and growth potential of a business.

INTERPRETATION OF CASH FLOW PATTERNS

FINANCIAL
ANALYSIS

The statement of cash flows depicts the relationships among the operating, investing, and financing activities. Throughout this chapter, we have illustrated the reporting and interpretation of APL's cash flows for the second quarter of 2009. These cash flows are specific to one company for a specified time period. To generalize, the table below shows the eight possible patterns of cash flows generated from (used for) operating, investing, and financing activities. A general explanation for each observed pattern is also provided.

TABLE 1
Analysis of Cash Flow Patterns

	1	2	3	4	5	6	7	8
Cash Flow from Operating	+	+	+	+	−	−	−	−
Cash Flow from Investing	+	−	+	−	+	−	+	−
Cash Flow from Financing	+	−	−	+	+	+	−	−

A general explanation of each pattern follows:

1. The company is using cash generated from operations, from the sale of non-current assets, and from financing to build its cash reserves. This is a very liquid company, possibly looking for acquisitions. This pattern is very unusual.

2. The company is using cash generated from operations to buy non-current assets and to reduce its debt or distribute cash dividends to shareholders. This pattern reflects a mature, successful firm.

3. The company is using cash from operations and from the sale of non-current assets to reduce its debt or distribute cash dividends to shareholders. It is actually downsizing its operations.

4. The company is using cash from operations and from borrowing (or from equity investment) to expand. This pattern is typical of many growing companies.

5. The company's operating cash flow problems are covered by the sale of non-current assets and by borrowing or shareholder contributions. The company is selling its non-current assets to stay in business, and the fact that investors are willing to supply the financing indicates that they apparently expect a turnaround in operating cash flows.

6. The company experiences a shortfall in cash flow from operations and from investing activities. The deficiency in cash is financed by long-term borrowings or investments by shareholders. This pattern is most typical of a young, fast-growing company.

7. The company is financing operating cash flow shortages, paying its debtholders and/or its shareholders via the sale of non-current assets. The company is actually shrinking.

8. The company is using cash reserves to finance operations, pay long-term creditors and/ or investors, and acquire new non-current assets. This unusual scenario is possible only if cash previously accumulated is being used to meet these cash outflows.

Source: Adapted from M. T. Dugan, B. E. Gup, and W. D. Samson, "Teaching the Statement of Cash Flows," *Journal of Accounting Education*, Vol. 9, 1991, pp. 33–52.

SELF-STUDY QUIZ 5-3

American International Group, Inc.

American International Group Inc. (AIG) is a leading international insurance organization with operations in more than 130 countries and jurisdictions. Its statement of cash flows for the year 2009 included the following summary:

Years Ended December 31,
(in millions of US dollars)

	2009	2008	2007
Net cash provided by (used in) operating activities	$ 18,584	$ (122)	$ 32,792
Net cash provided by (used in) investing activities	5,778	47,176	(67,241)
Net cash provided by (used in) financing activities	(28,997)	(40,734)	35,093

What conclusions can you derive by examining the pattern of the company's cash flows during these three years?

■ connect

After you complete your answers, go online for the solutions.

LO7

Explain the effect of additional cash flow disclosures.

ADDITIONAL CASH FLOW DISCLOSURES

Refer to the formal statement of cash flows for APL that is shown in Exhibit 5.1. As you can see, it is a simple matter to construct the statement after the detailed analysis of the accounts and transactions has been completed (shown in Exhibits 5.7, 5.8, and 5.9). Companies that use the direct method for computing cash flow from operations usually present a reconciliation of profit to cash flow from operations (the indirect method as presented in Exhibit 5.7) as a supplemental schedule. Companies also must provide two other disclosures related to the statement of cash flows.

Non-cash Investing and Financing Activities

NON-CASH INVESTING AND FINANCING ACTIVITIES are transactions that do not have direct cash flow effects; they are reported as a supplement to the statement of cash flows in narrative or schedule form.

Certain transactions are important investing and financing activities but have no cash flow effects. These are called non-cash investing and financing activities. For example, the purchase of a $100,000 building with a $100,000 mortgage given by the former owner does not cause either an inflow or an outflow of cash. As a result, these non-cash activities are not listed in the three main sections of the statement of cash flows. International Accounting Standard 7 requires supplemental disclosure of these transactions in either narrative or schedule form. APL's statement of cash flows does not list any non-cash investing and financing activities. The following excerpt from the 2009 annual report of Gildan Activewear Inc. provides examples of these non-cash transactions.

Supplemental cash flow disclosure (in thousands of US dollars)

	2009	2008	2007
Non-cash transactions			
Additions to property, plant, and equipment included in trade payables and accrued liabilities	627	1,720	566
Proceeds on disposal of long-lived assets in trade receivables	456	—	1,050

Supplemental Cash Flow Information

Companies that use the indirect method of presenting cash flows from operations also must also disclose the amounts of interest and dividends received and paid during the period as well as cash paid for income taxes. These are normally listed at the bottom of the statement or in the notes.

ACCOUNTING STANDARDS
FOR PRIVATE ENTERPRISE

The requirements for the reporting of cash flow information by Canadian private enterprises (Section 1540 of the *CICA Handbook*) are practically the same as the requirements for Canadian publicly accountable enterprises (IAS 7). One notable difference is the classification of interest and dividends received and paid. For private enterprises, cash flows from interest and dividends are classified as cash flows from operating activities if they are included in the determination of profit. If not, then interest and dividends are classified as either investing or financing activities according to their nature. In contrast, IAS 7 provides more flexibility. Cash flows from interest and dividends received and paid are classified in a consistent manner as operating, investing, or financing activities, as noted on page 256.

DEMONSTRATION **CASE**

Old Style Brewery

During the year ended December 31, 2011, Old Style Brewery, a craft brewer, reported profit of $3,182 (all numbers in thousands), and cash and cash equivalents of $472 at the beginning and $24,676 at the end of the year. It also engaged in the following activities:

a. Paid $18,752 in principal on long-term borrowings.
b. Received $46,202 in cash from initial public offering of common shares.
c. Incurred other non-current accrued operating expenses of $857.
d. Paid $18,193 in cash for purchase of property and equipment.
e. Trade receivables increased by $881.
f. Borrowed $16,789 from various lenders.
g. Refundable deposits payable increased by $457.
h. Inventories increased by $574.
i. Made cash deposits on equipment of $5,830.
j. Income tax refund receivable decreased by $326.
k. Sold (issued) shares to employees for $13 in cash.
l. Trade payables decreased by $391.
m. Received $4 from other investing activities.

n. Accrued liabilities increased by $241.
o. Prepayments increased by $565.
p. Recorded depreciation of $1,324.
q. Paid $5 cash for other financing activities.

Required:
Based on this information, prepare the statement of cash flows for the year ended December 31, 2011. Use the indirect method to compute the cash flows from operating activities.

We strongly recommend that you prepare your own answer to this requirement and then check it with the solution below.

SUGGESTED **SOLUTION**

OLD STYLE BREWERY
Statement of Cash Flows
For the Year Ended December 31, 2011
(in thousands)

Operating activities	
Profit	$ 3,182
Add (deduct) items not affecting cash:	
Depreciation	1,324
Other non-current accrued expenses	857
Increase in trade receivables	(881)
Increase in inventories	(574)
Decrease in income taxes receivable	326
Increase in prepayments	(565)
Decrease in trade payables	(391)
Increase in accrued liabilities	241
Increase in refundable deposits payable	457
Net cash flows from operating activities	3,976
Investing activities	
Expenditures for property and equipment	(18,193)
Deposits on equipment	(5,830)
Other	4
Net cash flow from investing activities	(24,019)
Financing activities	
Proceeds from debt	16,789
Repayment of debt	(18,752)
Proceeds from sale of shares (IPO)	46,202
Proceeds from sale of shares (options)	13
Other	(5)
Net cash flow from financing activities	44,247
Increase in cash and cash equivalents	24,204
Cash and cash equivalents:	
Beginning of year	472
End of year	$24,676

Appendix 5A

Adjustment for Gains and Losses—Indirect Method

The operating activities section of the statement of cash flows may include an adjustment for gains and losses reported on the income statement. The transactions that cause gains and losses should be classified on the statement of cash flows as operating, investing, or financing activities, depending on their dominant characteristics. For example, if the sale of a productive asset (e.g., a delivery truck) produced a gain, it would be classified as an investing activity.

An adjustment must be made in the operating activities section to avoid double counting of the gain or the loss. To illustrate, consider the following entry for Andrew Peller Limited to record the sale of a delivery truck:[10]

Cash (+A)...	8,000	
Accumulated depreciation (−XA, +A)	4,000	
Property, plant, and equipment (−A).....................................		10,000
Gain on sale of assets (+Gain, +SE).....................................		2,000

Assets		=	Liabilities	+	Shareholders' Equity	
Cash	+8,000				Gain on sale of assets	+2,000
Accumulated depreciation	+4,000					
Property, plant, and equipment	−10,000					

The $8,000 inflow of cash is an investing cash inflow, but the gain of $2,000 is also reported on the income statement. Because the gain is included in the computation of profit, it is necessary to remove (subtract) the $2,000 gain from the operating activities section of the statement to avoid double counting.

When a loss is reported on the income statement, it also must be removed from cash flows from operating activities. Consider the following entry to record the sale of assets:

Cash (+A)...	41,000	
Accumulated depreciation (−XA, +A)	15,000	
Loss on sale of assets (−Loss, −SE).....................................	12,000	
Property, plant, and equipment (−A).....................................		68,000

Assets		=	Liabilities	+	Shareholders' Equity	
Cash	+41,000				Loss on sale of assets	−12,000
Accumulated depreciation	+15,000					
Property, plant, and equipment	−68,000					

On the statement of cash flows, the loss of $12,000 must be removed (added to profit) in the computation of cash flows from operating activities, and the total cash collected of $41,000 must be shown in the investing activities section of the statement.

Appendix 5B

Reporting Cash Flows from Operating Activities—Direct Method

Exhibit 5.3 shows APL's comparative statements of financial position at the end of the first and second quarters of 2009, and its income statement for the second quarter

---

[10] The disposal of assets and the resulting gains or losses are discussed in detail in Chapter 9.

of 2009. Recall that the direct method reports gross cash receipts and gross cash payments related to operating activities. It presents a summary of all operating transactions that resulted in either a debit or a credit to cash.

Cash Flows from Operating Activities

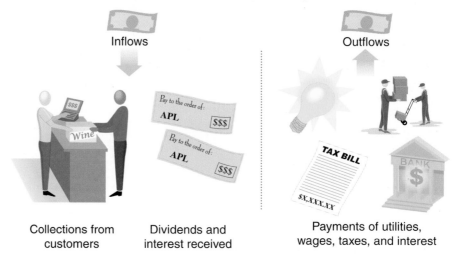

| Collections from customers | Dividends and interest received | Payments of utilities, wages, taxes, and interest |

The computation of cash receipts and payments requires adjusting each item on the income statement from an accrual basis to a cash basis. To facilitate this process, the asset, liability, and equity accounts in Exhibit 5.3 that relate to operating activities have been marked with an O. These items include trade receivables, inventories, prepayments, trade payables, accrued liabilities, deferred income taxes, and retained earnings.

Converting Revenue and Expense Items from an Accrual Basis to a Cash Basis   The computation of cash receipts and payments requires adjusting each item on the income statement from an accrual basis. To facilitate this process, we analyze the change in the balances of each current asset and current liability account by examining the type of transactions that affect the account. This process helps us determine the amount of cash received or paid during the accounting period.

We will use the following relation to analyze the changes in each current asset and liability account:

Converting Revenues to Cash Inflows   When sales are recorded, trade receivables increase, and when cash is collected, trade receivables decrease. Hence, the change from the beginning balance of trade receivables to the ending balance can be represented as follows:

In general	APL's example
Trade receivables, beginning (known)	$24,212
+ Sales revenue (known)	69,356
− Cash collections from customers (computed)	A
= Trade receivables, ending (known)	$29,721

The beginning and ending balances of trade receivables are reported on the statement of financial position, and sales revenue is reported on the income statement.

However, the amount collected from customers is not reported on either statement, but can be derived from the relation on the previous page.

The beginning balance of trade receivables increases the cash received from customers on the assumption that all amounts owed to the company at the beginning of the period are collected during the period. In contrast, the ending balance of trade receivables is deducted from sales revenue because these receivables have already been included in sales revenue but have not yet been collected from customers.

Using information from APL's income statement and statement of financial position presented in Exhibit 5.3, we can compute the cash collected from customers as follows:

Trade Receivables

Beg. bal.	24,212		
Sales	69,356	Collections	**63,847**
End. bal.	29,721		

$$\text{Cash collections} = \$24{,}212 + \$69{,}356 - \$29{,}721 = \$63{,}847^{[11]}$$

Converting Cost of Sales to Cash Paid to Suppliers The cost of sales during the accounting period may be greater or smaller than the amount of cash paid to suppliers of merchandise during the period. The computation of the cash paid to suppliers is a two-stage process. First, we analyze the change in the inventories account to determine the amount of merchandise purchases during the period, and then we analyze the change in the trade payables account to compute the amount of cash payments to suppliers by using the following relations:

In general	APL's example
Inventories, beginning (known)	$93,333
+ Merchandise purchases (computed)	+ A
− Cost of sales (known)	− 40,254
= Inventories, ending (known)	=$94,715

In general	APL's example
Trade payables, beginning (known)	$18,715
+ Merchandise purchases (computed)	+ A
− Cash payments to suppliers (computed)	− B
= Trade payables, ending (known)	=$24,423

The beginning and ending balances of inventory and trade payables are reported on the statement of financial position, and the cost of sales is reported on the income statement. However, the amount of merchandise purchases and the payments to suppliers are not reported on either statement, but can be derived from the relations above.

The ending balance of inventory is added to cost of sales to determine the cost of goods that were available for sale during the period. Given that part of the merchandise was available at the beginning of the period, it is deducted from the goods available to determine the amount of purchases during the period.

Using information from APL's income statement and statement of financial position presented in Exhibit 5.3, we can compute the cash paid to suppliers in two steps as follows:

Inventories

Beg. bal.	93,333	Cost	40,254
		of sales	
Purchases	**41,636**		
End. bal.	94,715		

$$\text{Merchandise purchases} = \$40{,}254 + \$94{,}715 - \$93{,}333 = \$41{,}636$$

The beginning balance of trade payables is added to merchandise purchases to determine the total amount payable to suppliers. The ending balance of trade payables

---

[11]We assume that all sales are made on account. However, the amount of cash collected from customers is the same regardless of the mix of cash and credit sales. To be sure, assume that sales are 20 percent cash and 80 percent on account, and compute the amount of cash collected from customers during the period. You can use other percentages as well.

is then deducted from that total because this amount has not been paid to suppliers yet.

Trade Payables			
Cash payments	**35,928**	Beg. bal.	18,715
		Purchases	**41,636**
		End. bal.	24,423

$$\text{Cash payments to suppliers} = \$41,636 + \$18,715 - \$24,423 = \$35,928^{12}$$

Converting Other Operating Expenses to a Cash Outflow   The total amount of any operating expense on the income statement may differ from the cash payment for that expense during the accounting period. Some expenses are paid before they are recognized as expenses (e.g., prepaid rent). When prepayments are made, the balance in the asset account prepayments increases; when prepayments are used up and recognized as expenses for the period, the account balance decreases. Other expenses are paid for after they are recognized in the same or previous periods. In this case, when expenses are recorded, the balance in the accrued liabilities account increases; when payments are made, the account balance decreases. The computation of the cash paid for operating expenses is therefore a two-stage process. First, we analyze the change in the prepayments account to determine the amount of cash paid during the period, and then we analyze the change in the accrued liabilities account to compute the amount of cash that was paid during the period for various other expenses, as shown in the following relations:

In general	APL's example
Prepayments, beginning (known)	$6,843
+ Cash payments for future (deferred) expenses (unknown)	+ A
− Prepayments that were used up during the period (unknown)	− B
= Prepayments, ending (known)	=$7,849

In general	APL's example
Accrued liabilities, beginning (known)	$11,040
+ Expenses accrued during the period (unknown)	+ C
− Cash payments for accrued expenses (unknown)	− D
= Accrued liabilities, ending (known)	=$ 9,875

The beginning and ending balances of prepayments and accrued liabilities are reported on the statement of financial position. But, the prepayments (B) that were used up during the period are not reported separately on the income statement. Hence, we cannot compute the amount of cash (A) paid for future expenses. Similarly, the expenses (C) that accrued during the period are not reported separately on the income statement, which makes it difficult to compute the amount of cash (D) paid during the period to settle accrued expenses. However, the amounts B and C are reported together on the income statement as operating expenses (or selling, general, and administrative expenses). By combining the two relations, we can then compute the sum of A and D, which represents the payments made for other expenses.

---

[12]We assume that all purchases are made on account. However, the amount of cash paid to suppliers is the same regardless of the mix of cash and credit purchases. To be sure, assume that purchases are 10 percent cash and 90 percent on account, and compute the amount of cash paid to suppliers during the period. You can use other percentages as well.

Using information from APL's income statement and statement of financial position presented in Exhibit 5.3, we can compute the cash paid for other expenses as follows:

Cash paid for other expenses = $20,808 (general, selling, and administrative expenses, reflecting prepayments that expired during the quarter and accrued expenses)

+ 7,849 (prepayments, end of quarter)

– 6,843 (prepayments, beginning of quarter)

+11,040 (accrued liabilities, beginning of quarter)

– 9,875 (accrued liabilities, end of quarter)

= $22,979

Prepayments

Beg. bal.	6,843	Prepayments that expired	unknown
Cash payments	unknown		
End. bal.	7,849		

Accrued Liabilities

Cash payments	unknown	Beg. bal.	11,040
		Unpaid expenses	unknown
		End. bal.	9,875

Similar analysis can be applied to computing the cash payments for interest and income taxes. APL reports interest expense of $1,505. Since there is no interest payable balance, interest paid must be equal to interest expense.

APL's income tax expense equals $1,146. This expense usually consists of two components: an amount that is currently payable to the federal and provincial taxation authorities and another amount labelled deferred income taxes. Deferred income taxes result from temporary differences that exist between amounts reported on the financial statements in accordance with international financial reporting standards and amounts included in tax reports in conformity with tax rules that must be used by corporations. These differences relate to the timing of recognition of revenues and expenses for financial reporting (that is based on accrual accounting) compared to taxation rules that essentially use a cash basis of accounting.

The computation of cash paid for income taxes should take into consideration changes in two accounts: income taxes payable and deferred income taxes. We show the general computation of tax payments even though there are no beginning and ending balances in the income taxes payable account:

Income tax expense	$1,146
+ Income taxes payable, beginning	0
– Income taxes payable, ending	0
	1,146
+ Decrease in deferred income tax liability	1,562
Cash payments for income taxes	$2,708

The operating cash inflows and outflows are accumulated in Exhibit 5.9.

Cash flows from operating activities		
Cash collected from customers		$63,847
Cash payments		
–to suppliers	$35,928	
–for other operating expenses	22,979	
–for interest	1,505	
–for income taxes	2,708	63,120
Net cash provided by operating activities		$ 727

Exhibit **5.9**

Andrew Peller Limited: Schedule of Net Cash Flows from Operating Activities, Direct Method (in thousands of dollars)

To summarize, the following adjustments must commonly be made to convert income statement items to the related operating cash flow amounts:

Income Statement Account	+/− Change in Statement of Financial Position Account(s)	= Operating Cash Flow
Sales revenue	+ Beginning trade receivables − Ending trade receivables	= Collections from customers
Cost of sales	− Beginning inventory + Ending inventory + Beginning trade payables − Ending trade payables	= Payments to suppliers of inventory
Other operating expenses	− Beginning prepayments + Ending prepayments + Beginning accrued liabilities − Ending accrued liabilities	= Payments to suppliers of services (e.g., rent, utilities, wages)
Interest expense	+ Beginning interest payable − Ending interest payable	= Payments for interest
Income tax expense	+ Beginning income taxes payable − Ending income taxes payable +/− Changes in deferred incomes tax assets and liabilities	= Payments for income taxes

SELF-STUDY **QUIZ 5-4**

Indicate which of the following items taken from the statement of cash flows would be added (+), subtracted (−), or not included (0) in the cash flow from operations section when the direct method is used.

_____ *a.* Increase in inventories.

_____ *b.* Payment of dividends to shareholders.

_____ *c.* Cash collections from customers.

_____ *d.* Purchase of plant and equipment for cash.

_____ *e.* Payment of interest to debtholders.

_____ *f.* Payment of taxes to the taxation authorities.

connect

After you complete your answers, go online for the solutions.

Appendix 5C: Spreadsheet Approach—Statement of Cash Flows: Indirect Method (online)

CHAPTER **TAKE-AWAYS**

1. **Classify cash flow items into cash flows from operating, investing, and financing activities.**
   p. 235
   The statement has three main sections: cash flows from operating activities, which are related to earning revenue from normal operations; cash flows from investing activities, which are related to the acquisition and sale of productive assets; and cash flows from financing activities, which are related to external financing of the enterprise. The net cash inflow or outflow for the year is the same amount as the increase or decrease in cash and cash equivalents for the year. Cash equivalents are highly liquid investments with original maturities of less than three months.

2. **Report and interpret cash flows from operating activities by using the indirect method.**
   p. 241
   The indirect method for reporting cash flows from operating activities presents a conversion of profit to net cash flows from operating activities. The conversion involves additions and subtractions for (1) non-current accruals, including expenses (such as depreciation expense) and revenues that do not affect current assets or current liabilities, and (2) changes in each of the individual current assets (other than cash and short-term investments) and current liabilities

(other than short-term borrowings from financial institutions and current portion of long-term borrowings, which relate to financing) that reflect differences in the timing of accrual basis profit and cash flows.

3. **Analyze and interpret the quality of earnings ratio. p. 250**
The quality of earnings ratio (Cash flows from operating activities ÷ Profit) measures the portion of profit that was generated in cash. A higher quality of earnings ratio indicates greater ability to finance operating and other cash needs from operating cash inflows. A higher ratio also indicates that it is less likely that the company is using aggressive revenue recognition policies to increase profit.

4. **Report and interpret cash flows from investing activities. p. 252**
Investing activities reported on the statement of cash flows include cash payments to acquire property, plant, and equipment, and short- and long-term investments. They also include cash proceeds from the sale of these assets.

5. **Analyze and interpret the capital acquisitions ratio. p. 254**
The capital acquisitions ratio (Cash flows from operating activities ÷ Cash paid for property, plant, and equipment) reflects the portion of purchases of property, plant, and equipment financed from operating activities without the need for outside debt or equity financing or the sale of other investments or other non-current assets. A high ratio is beneficial because it provides the company with opportunities for strategic acquisitions.

6. **Report and interpret cash flows from financing activities. p. 255**
Cash inflows from financing activities include cash proceeds from issuance of short- and long-term borrowings and share capital. Cash outflows include principal payments on short- and long-term borrowings, cash paid for the repurchase of the company's shares, and dividend payments. Cash payments associated with interest relate to operating activities.

7. **Explain the effect of additional cash flow disclosures. p. 258**
Non-cash investing and financing activities are investing and financing activities that do not involve cash. They include, for example, purchases of non-current assets with long-term borrowings or shares, exchanges of non-current assets, and exchanges of debt for shares. These transactions are disclosed only as supplemental disclosures to the statement of cash flows along with cash paid for taxes and interest under the indirect method.

The previous five chapters discussed the important steps in the accounting process that lead to the preparation of the four basic financial statements. This end to the internal portions of the accounting process, however, is just the beginning of the process of communicating accounting information to external users.

In the next chapter, we discuss the important players in this communication process, the many statement format choices available, the additional note disclosures required for publicly accountable enterprises, and the process, manner, and timing of the transmission of this information to users. At the same time, we discuss common uses of the information in investment analysis, debt contracts, and management compensation decisions. These discussions will help you consolidate much of what you have learned about the financial reporting process from previous chapters. It will also preview many of the important issues we will address later in the book.

KEY **RATIOS**

The **quality of earnings ratio** indicates what portion of profit was generated in cash. It is computed as follows (p. 250):

$$\text{Quality of Earnings Ratio} = \frac{\text{Cash Flows from Operating Activities}}{\text{Profit}}$$

The **capital acquisitions ratio** measures the ability to finance purchases of property, plant, and equipment from operations. It is computed as follows (p. 254):

$$\text{Capital Acquisitions Ratio} = \frac{\text{Cash Flows from Operating Activities}}{\text{Cash Paid for Property, Plant, and Equipment}}$$

FINDING **FINANCIAL INFORMATION**

STATEMENT OF FINANCIAL POSITION
Changes in Assets, Liabilities, and Shareholders' Equity

INCOME STATEMENT
Profit and Accruals

STATEMENT OF CASH FLOWS
Cash Flows from Operating Activities
Cash Flows from Investing Activities
Cash Flows from Financing Activities
Separate Schedule (or note):
   Non-cash investing and financing
     activities
   Interest and taxes paid
   Interest, dividends, and taxes received

NOTES
Under Summary of Significant Accounting Policies
   Definition of cash equivalents
Under Separate Note:
   If not listed on statement of cash flows
   Non-cash investing and financing activities
   Interest and taxes paid
   Interest, dividends, and taxes received

KEY **TERMS**

Cash Equivalent p. 234
Cash Flows from Financing Activities p. 237
Cash Flows from Investing Activities p. 236
Cash Flows from Operating Activities p. 236

Direct Method p. 236
Free Cash Flow p. 254
Indirect Method p. 236
Non-cash Investing and Financing Activities p. 258

QUESTIONS

1. Compare the purposes of the income statement, the statement of financial position, and the statement of cash flows.
2. What information does the statement of cash flows report that is not reported on the other required financial statements? How do investors and creditors use that information?
3. What are cash equivalents? How are purchases and sales of cash equivalents reported on the statement of cash flows?
4. What are the major categories of business activities reported on the statement of cash flows? Define each of these activities.
5. What are the typical cash inflows from operating activities? What are the typical cash outflows for operating activities?
6. Under the indirect method, depreciation expense is added to profit to compute cash flows from operating activities. Does depreciation cause an inflow of cash?
7. Explain why cash paid during the period for purchases and for salaries is not specifically reported as cash outflows on the statement of cash flows under the indirect method.
8. Explain why a $50,000 increase in inventory during the year must be included in developing cash flows for operating activities under the indirect method.
9. Compare the two methods of reporting cash flows from operating activities in the statement of cash flows.
10. What are the typical cash inflows from investing activities? What are the typical cash outflows for investing activities?
11. What are the typical cash inflows from financing activities? What are the typical cash outflows for financing activities?

12. What are non-cash investing and financing activities? Give two examples. How are they reported on the statement of cash flows?
13. A company used cash for both operating and investing activities, but had positive cash flow from financing activities. What does this cash flow pattern suggest about this company?

EXERCISES

E5–1 Determining Effects of Transactions on Statement of Cash Flows

Leon's Furniture Limited is an Ontario-based retailer of home furnishings. For each of the following first-quarter transactions, indicate whether *net cash inflows (outflows)* from operating activities (O), investing activities (I), or financing activities (F) are affected and whether the effect is an inflow (+) or outflow (−), or (NE) if the transaction has no effect on cash. (*Hint:* Determine the journal entry recorded for the transaction. The transaction affects net cash flows if, and only if, the cash account is affected.)

▪ **LO1**

Leon's Furniture

____ 1   Paid cash to purchase new equipment.
____ 2. Purchased raw materials inventory on account.
____ 3. Collected cash from customers.
____ 4. Recorded an adjusting entry to record an accrued salaries expense.
____ 5. Recorded and paid interest on notes payable.
____ 6. Repaid principal on credit loan from the bank.
____ 7. Paid rent for the following period.
____ 8. Sold used equipment for cash at its carrying amount.
____ 9. Made payment to suppliers.
____ 10. Declared and paid cash dividends to shareholders.

E5–2 Determining Effects of Transactions on Statement of Cash Flows

Dell Inc. is a leading manufacturer of personal computers and servers for the business and home markets. For each of the following transactions, indicate whether net cash inflows (outflows) from operating activities (O), investing activities (I), or financing activities (F) are affected and whether the effect is an inflow (+) or outflow (−), or (NE) if the transaction has no effect on cash. (*Hint:* Determine the journal entry recorded for the transaction. The transaction affects net cash flows if, and only if, the cash account is affected.)

▪ **LO1**

Dell Inc.

____ 1. Recorded and paid income taxes to the federal government.
____ 2. Issued common shares for cash.
____ 3. Paid rent for the following period.
____ 4. Recorded an adjusting entry for expiration of a prepayment.
____ 5. Paid cash to purchase new equipment.
____ 6. Borrowed cash and signed notes payable in five years.
____ 7. Collected cash from customers.
____ 8. Purchased raw materials inventory on account.
____ 9. Recorded and paid salaries to employees.
____ 10. Purchased new equipment by signing a three-year note.

E5–3 Interpreting Depreciation Expense from a Management Perspective

▪ **LO2**

QuickServe, a chain of convenience stores, was experiencing some serious cash flow difficulties because of rapid growth. The company did not generate sufficient cash from operating activities to finance its new stores, and creditors were not willing to lend money because the company had not produced any profit for the previous three years. The new controller for QuickServe proposed a reduction in the estimated life of store equipment to increase depreciation expense; thus, "We can improve cash flows from operating activities because depreciation expense is added back on the statement of cash flows." Other executives were not sure that this was a good idea because the increase in depreciation would make it more difficult to have positive earnings: "Without profit, the bank will never lend us money."

Required:
What action would you recommend for QuickServe? Why?

LO2

E5–4 **Reporting and Interpreting Cash Flows from Operating Activities from an Analyst's Perspective (Direct and Indirect Method)**

Kane Company completed its income statement and statement of financial position for 2012 and provided the following information:

Service revenue		$52,000
Expenses		
Salaries	$42,000	
Depreciation	7,300	
Utilities	7,000	
Other	1,700	58,000
Loss		($ 6,000)
Decrease in trade receivables	$12,000	
Purchase of a small service machine	5,000	
Increase in salaries payable	9,000	
Decrease in deferred service revenue	4,000	

Required:

1. Prepare the operating activities section of the statement of cash flows for Kane Company by using the indirect method.

2. What were the major reasons that caused Kane to report a loss but positive cash flow from operations? Why are the reasons for the difference between cash flow from operations and profit important to financial analysts?

LO2

Coolbrands
International Inc.

E5–5 **Reporting and Interpreting Cash Flows from Operating Activities from an Analyst's Perspective (Indirect Method)**

Coolbrands International Inc. manufactures and distributes ice cream, sorbet, frozen yogurt, and other frozen dairy-based snacks. The following information is available from the company's annual report for a recent year (in thousands):

	2005
Loss	$(74,070)
Depreciation and amortization	60,567
Decrease in receivables	13,815
Decrease in inventories	4,500
Increase in prepayments	2,207
Increase in trade payables	5,842
Increase in accrued liabilities	8,744
Increase in income taxes payable	4,935
Reduction of long-term borrowings	4,007
Additions to equipment	12,409

Required:

1. Based on this information, compute the cash flows from operating activities by using the indirect method.

2. What were the major reasons that caused Coolbrands to report a loss but positive cash flow from operations? Why are the reasons for the difference between cash flow from operations and profit important to financial analysts?

LO2

E5–6 **Inferring Statement of Financial Position Changes from the Statement of Cash Flows**

A statement of cash flows for Colgate-Palmolive reported the following information (in millions of U.S. dollars):

Operating Activities	Current Year
Profit	$1,957.2
Depreciation and amortization	347.6
Cash effect of changes in	
Receivables	(69.8)
Inventories	(134.7)
Payables	125.2
Other current assets	12.8
Net cash provided by operations	$2,238.3

Required:

Based on the information reported on the statement of cash flows for Colgate-Palmolive, determine whether the following accounts increased or decreased during the year: receivables, inventories, payables, and other current assets.

E5–7 **Inferring Changes in Statement of Financial Position from the Statement of Cash Flows**

A statement of cash flows for Apple Computer contained the following information (in millions of U.S. dollars):

LO2

Apple Computer

Operations	Current Year
Profit	$ 8,329
Depreciation and amortization	3,356
Changes in assets and liabilities	
Trade receivables	(261)
Inventories	89
Trade payables	1,630
Income taxes payable	(43)
Other adjustments	1,491
Cash generated by operations	$14,591

Required:

For each of the asset and liability accounts listed on the statement of cash flows, determine whether the account balances increased or decreased during the current year.

E5–8 **Analyzing Cash Flows from Operating Activities; Interpreting the Quality of Earnings Ratio**

An annual report for PepsiCo contained the following information (in millions of U.S. dollars):

LO3

PepsiCo

Profit	$5,142
Depreciation and amortization	1,543
Decrease in trade receivables	549
Decrease in inventories	345
Decrease in prepayments	68
Increase in trade payables	718
Decrease in taxes payable	180
Decrease in other current liabilities	367
Cash dividends paid	2,541
Repurchase of shares	4,726

Required:

1. Compute the cash flows from operating activities for PepsiCo by using the indirect method.
2. Compute the quality of earnings ratio.
3. What were the major reasons why Pepsi's quality of earnings ratio did not equal 1.0?

LO4, 6

Pan American Silver
Corp.

E5–9   **Reporting Cash Flows from Investing and Financing Activities**

Pan American Silver Corp. is a mining company based in British Columbia. In a recent quarter, it reported the following activities:

Profit	$ 24,602
Purchase of property, plant, and equipment	243,800
Shares issued for cash	50,843
Dividends paid	2,626
Cash collection from customers	317,425
Depreciation and amortization	46,349
Income taxes paid	27,577
Payments for products and services	209,032
Proceeds from sale of short-term investments	62,779

Required:

Based on this information, present the Investing and Financing Activities sections of the statement of cash flows.

LO4, 6

Sobeys

E5–10   **Reporting and Interpreting Cash Flows from Investing and Financing Activities with Discussion of Management Strategy**

Sobeys Inc. is one of Canada's two national retail grocery and food distributors. The company owns or franchises more than 1,300 corporate and franchised stores in all 10 provinces under retail banners that include Sobeys, Garden Market IGA, IGA, IGA Extra, and Price Chopper. In a recent year, it reported the following activities (in millions):

Profit	$265.7
Purchases of property and equipment	431.0
Increase in trade payables and accrued liabilities	138.7
Issue of shares	129.1
Depreciation and amortization	324.8
Proceeds from sale of discontinued operations	78.0
Repayment of long-term borrowings	307.7
Increase in trade receivables	27.6
Payment of dividends	46.1

Required:

1. Based on this information, prepare the investing and financing activities sections of the statement of cash flows.

2. What do you think was management's plan for the use of the cash generated by the sale of discontinued operations?

LO5

Boston Beer

E5–11   **Analyzing and Interpreting the Capital Acquisitions Ratio**

A recent annual report for Boston Beer Company contained the following data for the three most recent years (in millions of U.S. dollars):

	2008	2007	2006
Cash flow from operating activities	$39.8	$53.8	$28.8
Cash flow from investing activities	(104.5)	(37.1)	(9.0)
Cash flow from financing activities	59.3	(0.5)	1.7

Assume that all investing activities involved acquisition of new plant and equipment.

Required:

1. Compute the capital acquisitions ratio for the three-year period in total.

2. What portion of Boston Beer's investing activities was financed from external sources or preexisting cash balances during the three-year period?

3. What do you think is the likely explanation for the large amount of cash flow from financing activities during 2008?

E5–12 Reporting Non-cash Transactions on the Statement of Cash Flows; Interpreting the Effect on the Capital Acquisitions Ratio   ▇ LO7

An analysis of Martin Corporation's operational asset accounts provided the following information:

a. Acquired a large machine that cost $26,000, paying for it by signing a $15,000, 12 percent interest-bearing note due at the end of two years, and issuing 500 common shares with a market value of $22 per share.

b. Acquired a small machine that cost $8,700. Full payment was made by transferring a tract of land that had a carrying amount of $8,700.

Required:

1. Show how this information should be reported on the statement of cash flows.

2. What would be the effect of these transactions on the capital acquisitions ratio? How might these transactions distort interpretation of the ratio?

E5–13 (Appendix 5B) Matching Items Reported on the Statement of Cash Flows to Specific Categories (Direct Method)   ▇ LO7

BHP Billiton

The Australian company BHP Billiton is one of the world's biggest mining companies. Some of the items included in its annual consolidated statement of cash flows, presented using the *direct method*, are listed below.

Indicate whether each item is disclosed in the operating activities (O), investing activities (I), or financing activities (F) section of the statement or (NA) if the item does not appear on the statement.

_____ 1. Dividends paid

_____ 2. Income taxes paid

_____ 3. Interest received

_____ 4. Profit

_____ 5. Payments for property, plant, and equipment

_____ 6. Payments in the course of operations

_____ 7. Proceeds from ordinary share issues

_____ 8. Proceeds from the sale of property, plant, and equipment

_____ 9. Receipts from customers

_____ 10. Repayment of loans

E5–14 (Appendix 5B) Comparing the Direct and Indirect Methods

To compare the computation of cash flow from operations under the direct and indirect methods, enter check marks to indicate which items are used with each method.

Cash Flows (and Related Changes)	Method of Computing Cash Flows from Operations	
	Direct	Indirect
1. Collections from customers		
2. Increase or decrease in trade receivables		
3. Payments to suppliers		
4. Increase or decrease in inventory		
5. Increase or decrease in trade payables		
6. Payments to employees		
7. Increase or decrease in wages payable		
8. Depreciation expense		

E5–15   **(Appendix 5B) Reporting Cash Flows from Operating Activities (Direct Method)**

The following information pertains to Day Company:

Sales		$80,000
Expenses		
Cost of sales	$50,000	
Depreciation	7,000	
Salaries	11,000	68,000
Profit		$12,000
Increase in trade receivables	$ 4,000	
Decrease in merchandise inventory	8,000	
Increase in salaries payable	500	

Required:

Prepare the operating activities section of the statement of cash flows for Day Company by using the direct method.

PROBLEMS

LO1, 2, 4, 6, 7   **P5–1**   **Preparing the Statement of Cash Flows (Indirect Method)** (AP5–1)

Selected financial information for Frank Corporation is presented below.

Selected 2011 Transactions:

a. Purchased investment securities for $5,000 cash.

b. Borrowed $15,000 on a two-year, 8 percent interest-bearing note.

c. During 2011, sold machinery for its carrying amount; received $11,000 in cash.

d. Purchased machinery for $50,000; paid $9,000 in cash and signed a four-year note payable to the dealer for $41,000.

e. Declared and paid a cash dividend of $10,000 on December 31, 2011.

Selected account balances at December 31, 2010 and 2011 are as follows:

	December 31	
	2011	**2010**
Cash	$76,000	$21,000
Trade receivables	17,000	12,000
Inventory	52,000	60,000
Trade payables	7,000	10,000
Accrued wages payable	800	1,000
Income taxes payable	5,000	3,000

One-fourth of the sales and one-third of the purchases were made on credit.

FRANK CORPORATION
Income Statement
For the Year Ended December 31, 2011

Sales revenue		$400,000
Cost of sales		268,000
Gross profit		132,000
Expenses		
Salaries and wages	$51,000	
Depreciation	9,200	
Rent (no accruals)	5,800	
Interest (no accruals)	12,200	
Income tax	$11,800	
Total expenses		90,000
Profit		$ 42,000

Required:

1. Prepare a statement of cash flows for the year ended December 31, 2011. Use the indirect method to compute the cash flows from operating activities. Include any additional required note disclosures.

2. Compute and explain the quality of earnings ratio and the capital acquisitions ratio.

P5–2 Preparing Statement of Cash Flows (Indirect Method)   ▄ LO2

The comparative statement of financial positions of Mikos Inc. as at December 31, 2011 and 2012, and its income statement for the year ended December 31, 2012, are presented below.

MIKOS INC.
Comparative Statements of Financial Position
December 31

	2012	2011
Assets		
Cash	$ 9,000	$ 17,000
Short-term investments	45,000	20,000
Trade receivables	68,000	26,000
Inventories, at cost	54,000	40,000
Prepayments	4,000	6,000
Land	45,000	70,000
Buildings and equipment, net	280,000	179,000
Intangible assets	24,000	28,000
	$529,000	$386,000
Liabilities and Shareholders' Equity		
Trade payables	$ 17,000	$ 40,000
Income tax payable	6,000	1,000
Accrued liabilities	10,000	-0-
Long-term notes payable	110,000	150,000
Share capital	200,000	60,000
Retained earnings	186,000	135,000
	$529,000	$386,000

MIKOS INC.
Income Statement
For the Year Ended December 31, 2012

Sales		$850,000
Cost of sales	$430,000	
Amortization expense—intangible assets	4,000	
Depreciation expense—buildings and equipment	33,000	
Operating expenses	221,000	
Interest expense	12,000	700,000
Profit before income taxes		150,000
Income tax expense		45,000
Profit		$105,000

Additional information:

a. Land was sold for cash at its carrying amount.

b. The short-term investments will mature in February 2013.

c. Cash dividends were declared and paid in 2012.

d. New equipment with a cost of $166,000 was purchased for cash, and old equipment was sold at its carrying amount.

e. Long-term notes of $10,000 were paid in cash, and notes of $30,000 were converted to shares.

Required:

1. Prepare a statement of cash flows for Mikos Inc. for the year ended December 31, 2012. Use the indirect method to report cash flows from operating activities.

2. Assume the role of a bank loan officer who is evaluating this company's cash flow situation. Analyze the statement of cash flows you prepared in (1).

3. What additional information does the statement of cash flows provide that is not available on either the statement of financial position or the income statement? Explain.

LO2

P5–3   **Comparing Cash Flows from Operating Activities (Indirect Method)** (AP5–2)

Beta Company's accountants just completed the financial statements for the year and have provided the following information (in thousands):

Income Statement for 2011

Sales revenue		$20,600
Expenses and losses:		
Cost of sales	$9,000	
Depreciation	2,000	
Salaries	5,000	
Rent	2,500	
Insurance	800	
Utilities	700	
Interest	600	20,600
Profit		$ 0

Selected Statement of Financial Position Accounts

	2011	2010
Merchandise inventory	$ 82	$ 60
Trade receivables	380	450
Trade payables	240	210
Salaries payable	29	20
Rent payable	2	6
Prepaid rent	2	7
Prepaid insurance	14	5

Other data:

The company signed long-term notes for $20,000 during the year.

Required:

1. Prepare the operating activities section of the statement of cash flows for 2011 by using the indirect method.

2. As a financial analyst, would you prefer to see the cash flow from operations reported using the direct method or the indirect method? Justify your answer.

3. As the accountant who prepares the company's statement of cash flows, would you prefer to use the direct or the indirect method to report the cash flow from operations? Explain.

LO2, 3, 5

P5–4   **(Appendix 5A) Preparing the Statement of Cash Flows with Sale of Equipment (Indirect Method)** (AP5–3)

McGregor Corp.'s accountants prepared the statements of financial position and income statement to be reported in the company's annual report for 2012, and you have been asked to prepare the company's statement of cash flows for 2012 based on the following financial information.

McGREGOR CORP.
Statements of Financial Position
As at December 31

	2012	2011
Assets		
Cash	$ 16,000	$ 4,000
Trade receivables	40,000	27,000
Merchandise inventory	28,000	20,000
Prepayments	9,000	5,000
Equipment, at cost	60,000	24,000
Less: Accumulated depreciation	(10,000)	(7,000)
Total Assets	$143,000	$73,000
Liabilities and Shareholders' Equity		
Trade payables	$ 10,000	$ 8,000
Income taxes payable	2,000	5,000
Wages payable	-0-	15,000
Long-term notes payable	60,000	43,000
Common shares	7,000	1,000
Retained earnings	64,000	1,000
Total Liabilities and Shareholders' Equity	$143,000	$73,000

McGREGOR CORP.
Income Statement
For the Year Ended December 31, 2012

Sales revenues		$762,000
Cost of sales	$410,000	
Wages expense	122,000	
General expenses	24,000	
Depreciation expense	4,000	
Interest expense	5,000	
Gain on sale of equipment	(3,000)	562,000
Profit before income taxes		200,000
Income tax expense		60,000
Profit		$140,000

Note: Equipment which originally cost $7,000 was sold for $9,000 cash during 2012. It had a carrying amount of $6,000 at the date of sale.

Required:

1. Prepare a statement of cash flows for McGregor Corp. for the year ended December 31, 2012. Use the indirect method to report cash flows from operating activities.

2. Using the statement of cash flows you prepared in (1), compute and explain each of the following: (a) quality of earnings ratio, (b) capital acquisitions ratio, and (c) free cash flow.

P5–5 (Appendices 5A and 5B) Preparing the Statement of Cash Flows with Sale of Equipment (Direct Method) (AP5–4)

Refer to the information for McGregor Corp. in P5–4.

Required:

1. Compute the following amounts:
   a. Cash collected from customers
   b. Cash paid to suppliers of merchandise
   c. Cash paid for general expenses

2. Prepare a statement of cash flows for McGregor Corp. for the year ended December 31, 2012. Use the direct method to report cash flows from operating activities.

3. What additional information does the statement of cash flows provide that is not available on either the statement of financial position or the income statement?

P5–6   **(Appendix 5B) Preparing a Statement of Cash Flows (Direct Method)** (AP5–5)
Refer to the information for Frank Corporation in P5–1.

Required:

1. Prepare a statement of cash flows for the year ended December 31, 2011. Use the direct method to compute the cash flows from operating activities. Include any additional required note disclosures.

2. Is the direct method of reporting cash flows from operating activities easier to prepare than the indirect method? Explain.

3. Is the direct method of reporting cash flows from operating activities easier to understand than the indirect method? Explain.

ALTERNATE PROBLEMS

LO1, 2, 4, 6, 7 AP5–1   **Preparing the Statement of Cash Flows (Indirect Method)** (P5–1)
Stonewall Company was organized on January 1, 2012. During the year ended December 31, 2012, the company provided the following data:

Income Statement	
Sales revenue	$ 80,000
Cost of sales	(35,000)
Depreciation expense	(4,000)
Other expenses	(32,000)
Profit	$ 9,000
Statement of Financial Position	
Cash	$ 48,000
Trade receivables	18,000
Merchandise inventory	15,000
Machinery (net)	25,000
Total assets	$106,000
Trade payables	$ 10,000
Accrued liabilities	21,000
Dividends payable	2,000
Note payable, short term	15,000
Share capital	54,000
Retained earnings	4,000
Total liabilities and shareholders' equity	$106,000

Analysis of selected accounts and transactions:

a. Issued 3,000 common shares for cash, at $18 per share.

b. Borrowed $15,000 on a one-year, 8 percent interest-bearing note; the note was dated June 1, 2012.

c. Paid $29,000 to purchase machinery.

d. Purchased merchandise for resale at a cost of $50,000; paid $40,000 cash and the balance on account. The company uses a perpetual inventory system.

e. Exchanged plant machinery with a carrying amount of $2,000 for office machines with a market value of $2,000.

f. Declared a cash dividend of $5,000 on December 15, 2012, payable to shareholders on January 15, 2013.

g. Because this is the first year of operations, all account balances are zero at the beginning of the year; therefore, the changes in the account balances are equal to the ending balances.

Required:

1. Prepare a statement of cash flows for the year ended December 31, 2012. Use the indirect method to report cash flows from operating activities.

2. Compute and explain the quality of earnings ratio and the capital acquisitions ratio.

AP5–2   Comparing Cash Flows from Operating Activities (Indirect Method) (P5–3)

The accountants of Pan American Silver Corp. completed the statement of financial position at June 30, 2009, and the income statement for the quarter ended on that date and have provided the following information (in thousands):

■ **LO2**

Pan American Silver Corp.

Amounts to be updated

Income Statement		
Sales revenue		$111,392
Gain on sale of assets		2,479
		113,871
Expenses		
Cost of sales	$66,046	
Depreciation and amortization	21,856	
Reclamation	754	
Exploration	2,161	
General and administration	2,498	
Bad debts	4,375	
Interest and financing	2,190	
Income tax	2,694	102,574
Profit		$ 11,297

Selected Statement of Financial Position Accounts		
	June 30, 2009	March 31, 2009
Short-term investments	$75,120	$78,081
Trade receivables	51,382	63,663
Inventories	83,623	83,445
Prepayments	3,464	3,462
Trade payables	17,834	21,564
Accrued liabilities	40,018	26,297
Income taxes payable	884	4,711

Required:

1. Prepare the operating activities section of the statement of cash flows by using the indirect method.

2. Companies that use the direct method to report cash flows from operations are also required to disclose in the notes a reconciliation of profit to cash flows from operating activities. What additional information does this disclosure requirement provide to users of financial statements? Explain.

AP5–3   (Appendix 5A) Preparing the Statement of Cash Flows with Sale of Equipment (Indirect Method) (P5–4)

Steven Cheng, the sole shareholder and manager of Musical Instruments Ltd. (MIL), has approached you and asked you to prepare a statement of cash flows for his company. MIL sells different types of flutes and wind instruments to bands, orchestras, and music stores. Steven is presently worried about the meeting that he has scheduled in two weeks with a lending officer of his bank. It is time for a review of the bank loan. This also involves a review of MIL's profitability and financial position.

■ **LO2, 3, 5**

Steven provided you with the following condensed financial statements for the fiscal years ended December 31, 2010 and 2011. He assures you that the financial statements are free of any omissions or misstatements, and that they conform to IFRS.

MUSICAL INSTRUMENTS LTD.
Statements of Financial Position as at December 31
(In thousands of dollars)

	2011	2010
Assets		
Current assets		
Cash	$ 500	$ 1,700
Short-term investments	1,000	4,000
Trade receivables	28,150	5,300
Inventories	5,000	15,000
Total current assets	34,650	26,000
Non-current assets		
Furniture and fixtures, at cost	29,500	13,000
Less: accumulated depreciation	(12,000)	(6,000)
Investments	1,000	1,500
Total non-current assets	18,500	8,500
Total assets	$53,150	$34,500
Liabilities and Shareholders' Equity		
Current liabilities		
Bank loan	$ 9,000	$ 4,000
Trade payables	8,500	6,550
Dividends payable	-0-	300
Total current liabilities	17,500	10,850
Non-current liabilities		
Mortgage notes payable	14,000	-0-
Total liabilities	31,500	10,850
Shareholders' equity		
Share capital	12,000	11,000
Retained earnings	9,650	12,650
Total shareholders' equity	21,650	23,650
Total liabilities and shareholders' equity	$53,150	$34,500

MUSICAL INSTRUMENTS LTD.
Income Statements
For the Years Ended December 31

	2011	2010
Sales revenue	$245,000	$220,000
Cost of sales	(160,000)	(140,000)
Gross profit	85,000	80,000
Operating expenses:		
Depreciation	(6,600)	(3,000)
Selling and general	(71,900)	(72,000)
Operating profit	6,500	5,000
Interest expense	(2,400)	(800)
Loss on sale of furniture	(300)	-0-
Gain on sale of investments	200	-0-
Profit before income taxes	4,000	4,200
Income tax expense (@25%)	(1,000)	(1,050)
Profit	$ 3,000	$ 3,150

Additional information:

a. In 2011, MIL sold older obsolete furniture with an original cost of $1,000 and accumulated depreciation of $600 up to the date of sale.

b. During 2011, one of the non-current investments that had cost $500 was sold at a gain of $200.

c. The company considers short-term investments as cash equivalents.

Required:

1. Prepare a statement of cash flows for MIL for the year ended December 31, 2012. Use the indirect method to report cash flows from operating activities.

2. Using the statement of cash flows you prepared in (1), compute and explain each of the following: (a) quality of earnings ratio, (b) capital acquisitions ratio, and (c) free cash flow.

3. In an effort to improve the company's financial performance, Steven Cheng proposed that the furniture and fixtures be amortized over a longer period. This change will decrease depreciation expense by $1,000 in 2010 and by $2,000 in 2011. As a professional accountant, would this proposed change be acceptable to you? Explain.

AP5–4 **(Appendices 5A and 5B) Preparing the Statement of Cash Flows with Sale of Equipment (Direct Method)** (P5–5)
Refer to the information for Musical Instruments Ltd. (MIL) in AP5–3.

Required:

1. Compute the following amounts:
   a. Cash collected from customers
   b. Cash paid to suppliers of merchandise
   c. Cash received for sale of obsolete furniture
   d. Cash received for sale of non-current investments

2. Prepare a statement of cash flows for MIL for the year ended December 31, 2012. Use the direct method to report cash flows from operating activities.

3. Discuss the importance of the statement of cash flows to users of financial statements. What additional information does it provide that is not reported in the other financial statements? Explain by referring to the statement that you prepared in (2) above.

AP5–5 **(Appendix 5B) Preparing a Statement of Cash Flows (Direct Method)** (P5–6)
Refer to the information for Stonewall Company in AP5–1.

Required:

1. Prepare a statement of cash flows for the year ended December 31, 2011. Use the direct method to compute the cash flows from operating activities. Include any additional required note disclosures.

2. Is the direct method of reporting cash flows from operating activities easier to prepare than the indirect method? Explain.

3. Is the direct method of reporting cash flows from operating activities easier to understand than the indirect method? Explain.

CASES AND PROJECTS

FINDING AND INTERPRETING FINANCIAL INFORMATION

CP5–1 **Finding Financial Information**
Refer to the financial statements of the Nestlé Group and related notes given in Appendix A of this book.

LO2, 4, 6

The Nestlé Group

Required:

1. Which of the two basic reporting approaches for the cash flows from operating activities did the company adopt?

2. What amount of cash did the company pay for taxes during the current year?

3. Explain why the depreciation of property, plant, and equipment was added in the reconciliation of profit to net cash provided by operating activities.

4. What was the amount of free cash flow for the year ended December 31, 2011?

5. Has the company paid cash dividends during the last two years? How did you know?

LO2, 4, 6 **CP5–2** **Finding Financial Information**

Cadbury plc

Go to Connect online for the financial statements of Cadbury plc and related notes.

Required:

1. What were the three largest adjustments to reconcile profit from operations to the net cash provided by operating activities? Refer to Note 34 of the financial statements. Explain the direction of the effect of each adjustment in the reconciliation.

2. What have been Cadbury plc's major uses of cash over the past two years? What have been its major sources of cash for these activities?

3. What was the amount of free cash flow for the year ended December 31, 2008? What does this imply about the company's financial flexibility?

LO3, 5 **CP5–3** **Comparing Companies**

The Nestlé Group

Go to Connect online for the financial statements of Cadbury plc and to Appendix A of this book for the financial statements of the Nestlé Group.

Required:

1. Compute the quality of earnings ratio for both companies for the current year. How might the difference in their sales growth rates explain the difference in the ratio? Sales growth rate = (Current year's sales − Prior year's sales) ÷ Prior year's sales.

2. Compute the capital acquisitions ratio for both companies for the current year. Compare their abilities to finance purchases of property, plant, and equipment with cash provided by operating activities.

FINANCIAL REPORTING AND ANALYSIS CASES

LO2, 3, 4, 5, 6 CP5–4 **Using Financial Reports: Analyzing the Nestlé Group's Statement of Cash Flows**

The Nestlé Group

The Nestlé Group is the world's leading nutrition, health, and wellness company. Its statement of cash flows for fiscal years 2009 and 2008 and the related notes are shown below.

Consolidated Cash Flow Statement For the Year Ended 31 December 2009		
In millions of CHF	2009	2008
Operating activities		
Profit for the year	11,793	19,051
Non-cash items of income and expense	3,478	(6,157)
Decrease/(increase) in working capital	2,442	(1,787)
Variation of other operating assets and liabilities	221	(344)
Operating cash flow	17,934	10,763
Investing activities		
Capital expenditure	(4,641)	(4,869)
Expenditure on intangible assets	(400)	(585)
Sale of property, plant, and equipment	111	122
Acquisition of businesses	(796)	(937)
Disposal of businesses	242	10,999
Cash flows with associates	195	266
Other investing cash flows	(110)	(297)
Cash flow from investing activities	(5,399)	4,699
Financing activities		
Dividend paid to shareholders of the parent	(5,047)	(4,573)
Purchase of treasury shares	(7,013)	(8,696)
Sale of treasury shares and options exercised	292	639

Consolidated Cash Flow Statement
For the Year Ended 31 December 2009

In millions of CHF	2009	2008
Cash flows with non-controlling interests	(720)	(367)
Bonds issued	3,957	2,803
Bonds repaid	(1,744)	(2,244)
Inflows from other non-current financial liabilities	294	374
Outflows from other non-current financial liabilities	(175)	(168)
Inflows/(outflows) from current financial liabilities	(446)	(6,100)
Inflows/(outflows) from short-term investments	(1,759)	1,448
Cash flow from financing activities	(12,361)	(16,884)
Currency retranslations	(184)	663
Increase/(decrease) in cash and cash equivalents	(10)	(759)
Cash and cash equivalents at beginning of year	5,835	6,594
Cash and cash equivalents at end of year	5,825	5,835

22. Cash flow statement

22.1 Non-cash items of income and expense

In millions of CHF	2009	2008
Share of results of associates	(800)	(1,005)
Depreciation of property, plant, and equipment	2,713	2,625
Impairment of property, plant, and equipment	170	248
Impairment of goodwill	57	561
Amortisation of intangible assets	656	624
Impairment of intangible assets	–	1
Net result on disposal of businesses	(105)	(9,252)
Net result on disposal of assets	(71)	186
Non-cash items in financial assets and liabilities	315	(759)
Deferred taxes	229	(1,090)
Taxes in other comprehensive income and equity	82	1,454
Equity compensation plans	232	250
	3,478	(6,157)

22.2 Decrease/(increase) in working capital

In millions of CHF	2009	2008
Inventories	1,099	(1,523)
Trade receivables	(83)	13
Trade payables	444	78
Other current assets	(487)	(870)
Other current liabilities	1,469	515
	2,442	(1,787)

Required:

1. The cash flows from operating activities show that "depreciation of property, plant, and equipment" in Note 22.1 is added to "profit." Is depreciation (or amortization) a source of cash? Explain.

2. Was the cash collected from customers during fiscal year 2009 higher or lower than the Nestlé Group's sales revenue for that year? Explain.

3. Explain why the Nestlé Group's cash flow from operations increased in 2009 compared to 2008, while its profit decreased during the same year?

4. Did the Nestlé Group expand during 2008 and 2009? If so, how did the company pay for its expansion? Explain.

5. Compute and analyze the Nestlé Group's quality of earnings ratio, capital acquisitions ratio, and free cash flow for both years.

LO2, 3, 4, 5, 6

Research In Motion

CP5–5   **Using Financial Reports: Analyzing Research In Motion's Statement of Cash Flows**

Research In Motion (RIM) is a leading designer, manufacturer, and marketer of innovative wireless solutions for the worldwide mobile communications market. Its products are used around the world and include the BlackBerry® wireless platform, software development tools, and software/hardware licensing agreements. RIM's statement of cash flows for fiscal years 2010, 2009, and 2008 are shown below.

RESEARCH IN MOTION LIMITED
Consolidated Statements of Cash Flows
(United States dollars, in thousands)

	For the Year Ended		
	February 27, 2010	February 28, 2009	March 1, 2008
Cash flows from operating activities			
Net income	$2,457,144	$1,892,616	$1,293,867
Adjustments to reconcile net income to net cash provided by operating activities:			
Amortization	615,621	327,896	177,366
Deferred income taxes	51,363	(36,623)	(67,244)
Income taxes payable	4,611	(6,897)	4,973
Stock-based compensation	58,038	38,100	33,700
Other	8,806	5,867	3,303
Net changes in working capital items	(160,709)	(769,114)	130,794
Net cash provided by operating activities	3,034,874	1,451,845	1,576,759
Cash flows from investing activities			
Acquisition of long-term investments	(862,977)	(507,082)	(757,656)
Proceeds on sale or maturity of long-term investments	473,476	431,713	260,393
Acquisition of property, plant, and equipment	(1,009,416)	(833,521)	(351,914)
Acquisition of intangible assets	(421,400)	(687,913)	(374,128)
Business acquisitions, net of cash acquired	(143,375)	(48,425)	(6,200)
Acquisition of short-term investments	(476,956)	(917,316)	(1,249,919)
Proceeds on sale or maturity of short-term investments	970,521	739,021	1,325,487
Net cash used in investing activities	(1,470,127)	(1,823,523)	(1,153,937)
Cash flows from financing activities			
Issuance of common shares	30,246	27,024	62,889
Additional paid-in capital	—	—	9,626
Excess tax benefits from stock-based compensation	1,943	12,648	8,185
Purchase of treasury stock (note 11)	(94,463)	—	—
Common shares repurchased	(775,008)	—	—
Repayment of debt	(6,099)	(14,305)	(302)
Net cash provided by (used in) financing activities	(843,381)	25,367	80,398
Effect of foreign exchange gain (loss) on cash and cash equivalents	(6,051)	(2,541)	4,034
Net increase (decrease) in cash and cash equivalents for the year	715,315	(348,852)	507,254
Cash and cash equivalents, beginning of year	835,546	1,184,398	677,144
Cash and cash equivalents, end of year	$1,550,861	$ 835,546	$1,184,398

See notes to consolidated financial statements

SUPPLEMENTAL INFORMATION

(a) Cash flows resulting from net changes in working capital items are as follows:

	For the year ended		
	February 27, 2010	February 28, 2009	March 1, 2008
Accounts receivable	$ (480,610)	$(936,514)	$ (602,055)
Other receivables	(44,719)	(83,039)	(34,515)
Inventories	60,789	(286,133)	(140,360)
Other current assets	(52,737)	(50,280)	(26,161)
Accounts payable	167,281	177,263	140,806
Accrued liabilities	442,065	506,859	383,020
Income taxes payable	(266,517)	(113,868)	401,270
Deferred revenue	13,739	16,598	8,789
	$ (160,709)	$(769,114)	$ 130,794

(b) Certain statement of cash flow information related to interest and income taxes paid is summarized as follows:

Interest paid during the year	$ —	$ 502	$ 518
Income taxes paid during the year	$1,081,720	$ 946,237	$ 216,095

Required:

1. Have RIM's accounts receivable increased or decreased during fiscal year 2010? By how much have its accounts receivable changed during the past three years? Explain.

2. How does the change in inventory during fiscal year 2010 affect cash? Explain.

3. Explain why RIM shows a decrease in cash flow from operations from fiscal year 2008 to 2009 while it reported an increase in net income for the same period.

4. How did the company finance the acquisition of non-current assets during fiscal years 2008 and 2009? Explain.

5. What additional information does the statement of cash flows provide that is not available on either the statement of financial position or the income statement?

CP5–6 Using Financial Reports: Analyzing Celestica's Statement of Cash Flows

LO2, 3, 4, 5, 6

Celestica Inc.

Celestica Inc. is a world leader in providing electronics manufacturing services to original equipment manufacturers, communications, and other industries. Celestica provides a wide variety of products and services to its customers, including complex printed circuit board assemblies such as PC motherboards and communication and networking cards. These assemblies end up in servers, workstations, personal computers, peripherals, and communications devices. Celestica also offers supply chain management, as well as design, global distribution, and post-sales repair services. Celestica operates facilities in the Americas, Europe, and Asia. Its statement of cash flows for the years 2007, 2008, and 2009 are shown on the following page.

Required:

1. The cash flows from operating activities show that "depreciation and amortization" is added to net earnings for 2009. Are depreciation and amortization sources of cash? Explain.

2. How does the change in inventory during 2009 affect cash? Explain.

3. Compare the changes in non-cash working capital items across the three years. What conclusions can you draw from this comparison?

4. Compute and analyze Celestica's capital acquisitions ratio and free cash flow for the three years.

5. Has Celestica become more or less risky during 2009? What other financial statement might include information that would help you confirm your answer? Explain.

6. Analyze the company's pattern of cash flows from operating, investing, and financing activities over the three years. What conclusion can you draw from the changing pattern of cash flows? Explain.

7. Obtain a copy of Celestica's statement of cash flows for the year 2010 through the company's website (www.celestica.com) or the SEDAR service (www.sedar.com). Did the company's cash flow situation in 2010 improve or deteriorate relative to previous years? Explain.

8. As a potential investor in Celestica's shares, what additional information would you need before making your decision as to whether or not to invest in this company's shares?

CELESTICA INC.
Consolidated Statements of Cash Flows
(in millions of U.S. dollars)

	Year ended December 31		
	2007	2008	2009
Cash provided by (used in):			
Operations:			
Net earnings (loss)	$ (13.7)	$ (720.5)	$ 55.0
Items not affecting cash:		—	—
Depreciation and amortization	130.8	109.2	100.4
Deferred income taxes (recovery) (note 11)	6.4	(13.4)	(28.2)
Stock-based compensation (note 8(d) and (e))	13.2	23.4	28.0
Restructuring charges (note 10)	5.1	1.1	3.8
Other charges (note 10)	14.0	850.3	9.5
Other	11.8	(0.2)	(4.0)
Changes in non-cash working capital items:			
Accounts receivable	32.0	(132.8)	244.9
Inventories	406.0	4.5	110.2
Prepaid and other assets	(6.8)	22.5	21.7
Income taxes recoverable	11.4	5.7	(7.1)
Accounts payable and accrued liabilities	(237.6)	58.9	(265.2)
Income taxes payable	(21.2)	(0.5)	24.5
Non-cash working capital changes	183.8	(41.7)	129.0
Cash provided by operations	351.4	208.2	293.5
Investing:			
Purchase of property, plant and equipment	(63.7)	(88.8)	(77.3)
Proceeds from sale of operations or assets	27.0	7.7	10.0
Other	(0.2)	0.3	1.0
Cash used in investing activities	(36.9)	(80.8)	(66.3)
Financing:			
Repurchase of Senior Subordinate Notes (note 7(d))	—	(30.4)	(495.8)
Proceeds from termination of swap agreements (note 7(d))	—	—	14.7
Repayment of capital lease obligations	(0.6)	(0.4)	(1.0)
Financing costs	(1.4)	(0.5)	(2.8)
Issuance of share capital	3.5	2.1	2.7
Other	(3.0)	(13.9)	(8.3)
Cash used in financing activities	(1.5)	(43.1)	(490.5)
Increase (decrease) in cash	313.0	84.3	(263.3)
Cash and cash equivalents, beginning of year	803.7	1,116.7	1,201.0
Cash and cash equivalents, end of year	$1,116.7	$1,201.0	$ 937.7

Supplemental cash flow information (note 19).

CP5–7 Using Financial Reports: Analyzing Ryanair's Statement of Cash Flows

Ryanair is a European discount airline, offering low-fare, no-frills air transportation. Its airplanes fly to about 150 destinations in more than 25 countries in Europe. Ryanair prepares its financial statements in accordance with International Financial Reporting Standards. Its statement of cash flows for fiscal years 2007, 2008, and 2009 are shown below.

LO1, 2

Ryanair

RYANAIR
Consolidated Cash Flow Statement

	Year ended March 31, 2009	Year ended March 31, 2008	Year ended March 31, 2007
	€000	€000	€000
Operating activities			
(Loss)/profit before tax	(180,487)	438,927	451,037
Adjustments to reconcile (loss)/profit before tax to net cash provided by operating activities			
Depreciation	256,117	175,949	143,503
(Increase)/decrease in inventories	(78)	423	1,002
(Increase)/decrease in trade receivables	(7,613)	(10,766)	6,497
Decrease/(increase) in other current assets	73,757	(35,899)	(51,386)
Increase in trade payables	3,382	2,046	27,039
Increase in accrued expenses	13,323	80,629	233,839
Increase/(decrease) in other creditors	6,619	(5,267)	75,351
Increase in maintenance provisions	19,017	14,071	11,997
(Gain) on disposal of property, plant and equipment	–	(12,153)	(91)
Loss on impairment of available-for-sale financial asset	222,537	91,569	–
Decrease/(increase) in interest receivable	4,770	(985)	48
(Increase)/decrease in interest payable	(3,457)	1,235	2,671
Retirement costs	(265)	432	588
Share based payments	3,757	10,925	3,935
Income tax refunded/(paid)	1,755	(47,234)	(5,194)
Net cash provided by operating activities	413,134	703,902	900,836
Investing activities			
Capital expenditure (purchase of property, plant and equipment)	(702,017)	(937,115)	(525,956)
Proceeds from sale of property, plant and equipment	314,205	150,042	495
Purchase of equities classified as available-for-sale	(4,225)	(58,114)	(344,917)
Decrease/(increase) in restricted cash	830	(33,623)	(54,768)
Decrease/(increase) in financial assets: cash > 3 months	2,873	186,500	(263,847)
Net cash used in investing activities	(388,334)	(692,310)	(1,188,993)
Financing activities			
Shares purchased under share buy-back programme	(46,015)	(299,994)	–
Net proceeds from shares issued	1,615	8,403	11,234
Proceeds from long term borrowings	459,000	646,392	339,409
Repayments of long term borrowings	(327,055)	(241,963)	(155,071)
Net cash provided by financing activities	87,545	112,838	195,572
Increase/(decrease) in cash and cash equivalents	112,345	124,430	(92,585)
Cash and cash equivalents at beginning of year	1,470,849	1,346,419	1,439,004
Cash and cash equivalents at end of year	1,583,194	1,470,849	1,346,419

The accompanying notes are an integral part of the financial information.

Required:

1. The cash flows from operating activities show that "depreciation" is added to profit or loss before tax. Is depreciation a source of cash? Explain.
2. Ryanair reported operating revenues of €2,941,965 during fiscal year 2009. Compute the amount of cash collected from customers during the year, assuming all sales are on account.
3. How does the change in trade payables during 2009 affect cash?

4. Did Ryanair expand during 2007, 2008, and 2009? If so, how did the company pay for its expansion? Explain.

5. Compute and analyze Ryanair's quality of earnings ratio, capital acquisitions ratio, and free cash flow for the three years.

6. As a potential investor in Ryanair's shares, what additional information would you need before making your decision as to whether or not to invest in the company's shares?

CP5–8   **(Appendices 5A and 5B) Using Financial Reports: Analyzing Operating Cash Flows of Foster's Group**

Foster's Group

Foster's Group is a global multi-beverage Australian company that produces and markets a variety of beer, wine, spirits, cider, and non-alcoholic beverages. Foster's reports its cash flows from operating activities by using the direct method. Its statement of cash flows for 2009 included the following information (in millions of Australian dollars):

CASH FLOW STATEMENTS
Foster's Group Limited and Its Controlled Entities

	NOTE	FGL		Consolidated	
		2009	2008	2009	2008
		$m	$m	$m	$m
		Inflows/ (Outflows)	Inflows/ (Outflows)	Inflows/ (Outflows)	Inflows/ (Outflows)
Cash flow statements for the financial year ended 30 June					
Cash flows from operating activities					
Receipts from customers				7,532.1	6,418.2
Payments to suppliers, governments and employees		(46.1)	(45.0)	(6,233.4)	(5,202.3)
Dividends received		500.0	350.0	1.2	–
Interest received		–	0.6	17.4	21.3
Borrowing costs		(1.0)	(1.4)	(172.4)	(174.7)
Income taxes paid		(237.6)	(159.5)	(260.0)	(392.6)
Net cash flows on behalf of controlled entities		(500.0)	(350.0)		
Net cash flows from operating activities	31	(284.7)	(205.3)	884.9	669.9

Foster's also presents a reconciliation of profit to cash flows from operating activities in a note to its financial statements. A condensed version of this reconciliation, which is essentially the indirect method of reporting cash flows from operations, is presented below.

	FGL		Consolidated	
	2009	2008	2009	2008
	$m	$m	$m	$m
Reconciliation of net cash flows from operating activities to profit after income tax				
Profit for the year	437.3	331.0	442.7	117.5
Depreciation and amortisation	6.0	6.8	180.1	169.6
Contributions from partnerships			(15.6)	(11.5)
(Profit)/loss on disposal of non-current assets	–	(0.5)	10.9	(33.7)
(Profit)/loss on disposal of investments and other assets			–	0.8
(Profit)/loss on disposal of controlled entities			(7.1)	(1.3)
Valuation decrement on grapes and vines			21.9	22.9
Recoverable amount write downs	–	(0.2)	274.6	702.9
Provisions charged	28.1	8.4	137.6	57.6
Movement in unrealised foreign exchange	(0.7)	0.3	1.3	(11.4)
Net cash provided by operating activities before change in assets and liabilities	470.7	345.8	1,046.4	1,013.4

	FGL		Consolidated	
	2009	**2008**	**2009**	**2008**
	$m	$m	$m	$m
Change in working capital, net of effects from acquisition/disposal of controlled entities				
– receivables	(504.9)	(344.1)	169.6	61.3
– inventories	–	0.1	(79.5)	(101.6)
– other assets	4.2	(0.3)	7.1	20.2
– payables	23.3	(33.9)	(21.0)	(28.1)
– net tax balances	(266.7)	(160.4)	(103.6)	(238.7)
– provisions	(11.3)	(12.5)	(134.1)	(56.6)
Net cash flows from operating activities	(284.7)	(205.3)	884.9	669.9

Required:

1. As a user of financial statements, would you prefer to see the cash flows from operating activities reported using the direct method or the indirect method? Explain.

2. Did Foster's sales to its customers exceed the amount it collected from them during fiscal year 2009? Can you determine Foster's sales during fiscal year 2009? Show computations.

3. Assume, for simplicity, that Foster's purchases its inventories from trade suppliers. Did Foster's pay its trade suppliers for all the purchases it made during fiscal year 2009? Explain.

4. Compute and interpret the quality of earnings ratios for both years 2008 and 2009.

5. What additional information is reported under the indirect method but is not reported under the direct method.

CRITICAL THINKING CASE

CP5–9   Making a Decision as a Financial Analyst: Analyzing Cash Flow for a New Company

Carlyle Golf Inc. was formed in September of last year. The company designs, contracts for the manufacture of, and markets a line of men's golf apparel. A portion of the statement of cash flows for Carlyle follows:

■ **LO2**

Carlyle Golf Inc.

	Current Year
Cash flows from operating activities	
Profit	$(460,089)
Depreciation	3,554
Non-cash compensation (stock)	254,464
Deposits with suppliers	(404,934)
Increase in prepayments	(42,260)
Increase in trade payables	81,765
Increase in accrued liabilities	24,495
Net cash flows	$(543,005)

Management expects a solid increase in sales in the near future. To support the increase in sales, it plans to add $2.2 million to inventory. The company did not disclose a sales forecast. At the end of the current year, Carlyle had less than $1,000 in cash. It is not unusual for a new company to experience a loss and negative cash flows during its start-up phase.

Required:

As a financial analyst recently hired by a major investment bank, you have been asked to write a short memo to your supervisor evaluating the problems facing Carlyle. Emphasize typical sources of financing that may or may not be available to support the expansion.

FINANCIAL REPORTING AND ANALYSIS TEAM PROJECT

LO1, 2, 3, 4, 5, 6   **CP5–10**   **Team Project: Analyzing Cash Flows**

As a team, select an industry to analyze. A list of companies classified by industry can be obtained by accessing **www.fpinfomart.ca** and then choosing "Companies by Industry." You can also find a list of industries and companies with each industry via **http://ca.finance.yahoo.com/investing** (click on "Annual Reports" under "Tools"). Using a Web browser, each team member should acquire the annual report for one publicly traded company in the industry, with each member selecting a different company.

Required:

On an individual basis, each team member should write a short report answering the following questions about the selected company. Discuss any patterns across the three companies that your team observes. Then, as a team, write a short report comparing and contrasting your companies.

1. Which of the two basic reporting approaches for cash flows from operating activities did the company adopt?
2. What is the quality of earnings ratio for the most current year? What were the major causes of differences between profit and cash flow from operations?
3. What is the capital acquisitions ratio for the three-year period presented in total? How is the company financing its capital acquisitions?
4. What portion of the cash from operations in the current year is being paid to shareholders in the form of dividends?

Communicating and Interpreting Accounting Information

After studying this chapter, you should be able to do the following:

LO1 Recognize the people involved in the accounting communication process (regulators, managers, board of directors, auditors, information intermediaries, and users), their roles in the process, and the guidance they receive from legal and professional standards. p. 294

LO2 Identify the steps in the accounting communication process, including the issuance of press releases, annual reports, quarterly reports, and documents filed with securities commissions, as well as the guiding principles in communicating useful information. p. 300

LO3 Recognize and apply the different financial statement and disclosure formats used by companies in practice. p. 307

FOCUS COMPANY: **Thomson Reuters Corporation**

COMMUNICATING FINANCIAL INFORMATION AND CORPORATE STRATEGY

Thomson Reuters Corporation (**thomsonreuters. com**) is the result of the combination in 2008 of two companies —The Thompson Corporation and Reuters Group plc. The Thompson Corporation originated in 1934 when Roy Thomson acquired his first newspaper in Canada, *The Timmins Press* in Ontario. Reuters Group plc dates back to 1850 when Paul Julius Reuter started a business that transmitted news and stock price information between Aachen, Germany, and Belgium, using a combination of carrier pigeons and telegraph cables. These two companies grew from their early beginnings to become the world's leading source of intelligent information for businesses and professionals.

The growth of Thomson Reuters was the result of numerous acquisitions of other businesses over the years. The offering of shares to the public allowed both The Thomson Corporation and Reuters Group plc to access the capital markets which provided them with the necessary funds to expand further by acquiring other businesses.[1] The company combines industry expertise with innovative technology to deliver essential information to leading decision makers in the financial, legal, tax and accounting, science, healthcare, and media areas, in many languages.

As a publicly traded company, Thomson Reuters is required to provide detailed information in regular filings with the Ontario Securities Commission. As the certifying officers of the company, Thomas H. Glocer, the chief executive officer, and Robert D. Daleo, executive vice-president and chief financial officer, are responsible for the accuracy of the filings. The board of directors

---

[1]A brief history of both companies is available on the company's website: http://thomsonreuters.com/about/company_history.

and auditors monitor the integrity of the system that produces the disclosures. Integrity in communicating with investors and other users of financial statements is a key to maintaining relationships with providers of capital. Furthermore, clear and timely communication of the company's financial situation enables Thomson Reuters to comply with exchange rules and regulations of securities commissions. It also informs the company's customers, investors, creditors, and other users of financial statements of the company's success in implementing its business strategy.

UNDERSTANDING THE BUSINESS

Thomson Reuters Corporation provides information for decision makers and professionals throughout the world. The company is a leading provider of solutions for accounting, tax, and corporate finance professionals. It also provides information solutions for financial market professionals, critical information for healthcare delivery and management, as well as legal, compliance, and intellectual property solutions. It also dispenses news and information for media and business professionals. The company's operations are influenced by external, market-driven factors such as demand for information in specific sectors of the economy, and competition from other companies. These external factors influence both management decisions concerning the breadth of the products and services offered and its plans for acquisition of additional companies to help grow the business.

Successful companies such as Thomson Reuters learn to match their financial reporting to their business strategies. Marketing and communication are fundamental to both. As Thomson Reuters strives to maintain its leading position in the industry, it continues to look for opportunities to innovate in response to its customers' needs. Thomson Reuters's investments in new businesses, the results of operating, investing, and financing activities, and the company's financial condition are communicated to shareholders, creditors, and other interested parties through press releases, conference calls with shareholders, financial analysts together with the media, and periodic reporting of financial information.

Thomson Reuters knows that when investors lose faith in the truthfulness of a firm's accounting numbers, they also normally punish the company's stock. Disclosure of an accounting fraud causes, on average, a 20 percent drop in the price of a company's shares.[2] The accounting scandals that occurred in recent years at large corporations such as Nortel Networks Corporation, Livent Inc., and Parmalat S.p.A. caused these companies' shares to become worthless.

CORPORATE GOVERNANCE refers to the procedures designed to ensure that the company is managed in the interests of the shareholders.

Thomson Reuters also invests in corporate governance, the procedures designed to ensure that the company is managed in the interests of the shareholders. Much of its corporate governance system consists of practices required by the Ontario Securities Commission and the Toronto Stock Exchange that aim at ensuring integrity in the financial reporting process. Good corporate governance eases the company's access to capital, lowering both the cost of borrowing (interest rates) and the perceived riskiness of investment in its shares.

In an attempt to restore investor confidence following the scandals at Enron and WorldCom, the U.S. Congress passed the *Public Accounting Reform and Investor Protection Act* (the *Sarbanes-Oxley Act*), which strengthens financial reporting and corporate governance for public companies. Compliance with the provisions of this Act has also affected Canadian companies that are publicly traded on U.S. stock exchanges. In light of the U.S. experience, the Canadian Securities Administrators,

---

[2]Z. Palmrose, V. Richardson, and S. Scholz, "Determinants of Market Reactions to Restatement Announcements," *Journal of Accounting and Economics*, 2004, pp. 59–90.

which coordinates and harmonizes regulation of the Canadian capital markets among the 13 securities regulators of Canada's provinces and territories, has imposed new requirements on all publicly traded companies to bolster investors' confidence in financial reporting by Canadian companies. Even with these added safeguards, the wisdom of famed analyst Jack Ciesielski's warning to financial statement users is still evident:

> One usual answer to the question "why does accounting matter?" is that it helps to avoid "blow-ups": the unpleasant outcome when a stock crashes because the firm's management engaged in accounting chicanery that subsequently becomes visible.... the analyst who understands accounting matters will know precisely where the "soft spots" are in financial reporting, the ones that can be manipulated in order to meet an expected earnings target or avoid breaking a loan covenant.
>
> *Source:* Analyst's Accounting Observer, *Accounting Observer*, August 2000.

Chapters 2 through 5 focused on the mechanics of preparing the statement of financial position, income statement, statement of changes in equity, and statement of cash flows. In these chapters, we explained the importance of International Financial Reporting Standards (e.g., historical cost and revenue recognition) in generating the information disclosed in these statements. We also learned to compute and interpret some financial ratios to analyze and understand how creditors and investors use the information that accountants report to justify financial investment decisions.

In this chapter, we will take a more detailed look at the people involved in the regulations that govern the process that conveys accounting information to statement users in the Internet age. We will also take a look at disclosures provided in financial reports to help you learn how to find relevant information.

ORGANIZATION OF THE CHAPTER

Players in the Accounting Communication Process	The Disclosure Process	A Closer Look at Financial Statements and Notes
• Regulators (CSA, AcSB, AASB, Stock Exchanges) • Managers (CEO, CFO, and Accounting Staff) • Board of Directors (Audit Committee) • Auditors • Information Intermediaries: Analysts and Information Services • Users: Institutional and Private Investors, Creditors, and Others	• Press Releases • Annual Reports • Quarterly Reports • Reports to Securities Commissions • Guiding Principles for Communicating Useful Information • Constraints of Accounting Measurement	• Overview of Thomson Reuters's Financial Statements • Classified Statement of Financial Position • Classified Income Statement • Profit Measurement • Statement of Comprehensive Income • Statement of Changes in Equity • Statement of Cash Flows • Notes to Financial Statements • Voluntary Disclosures

Supplemental material:

Appendix 6A: Canadian Capital Markets (online)

PLAYERS IN THE ACCOUNTING COMMUNICATION PROCESS

LO¹

Recognize the people involved in the accounting communication process (regulators, managers, board of directors, auditors, information intermediaries, and users), their roles in the process, and the guidance they receive from legal and professional standards.

Exhibit 6.1 summarizes the major actors involved in the integrity of the financial reporting process.

Regulators (CSA, AcSB, AASB, Stock Exchanges)

The financial information reported by Canadian companies is subject to strict regulations and standards issued by government regulators and private standard-setting organizations. Canadian publicly traded corporations must comply with provincial securities regulations that are coordinated by the Canadian Securities Administrators (CSA). The CSA is a forum for the 13 securities regulators of Canada's provinces and territories that was established to harmonize regulation of the Canadian capital markets. The CSA's mission is to protect investors from unfair, improper, or fraudulent practices and to foster fair, efficient, and vibrant capital markets. However, provincial or territorial regulators handle all complaints regarding securities violations in their respective jurisdictions and have legal authority to enforce provincial regulations concerning the timeliness and quality of financial disclosure.[3]

Securities regulators work closely with the Accounting Standards Board (AcSB) that is responsible for establishing standards of accounting and reporting by Canadian companies. External auditors ensure that companies prepare their financial reports in accordance with these standards, and their audit work is guided by International Standards on Auditing, which have been adopted by the Canadian Auditing and Assurance Standards Board as Canadian Auditing Standards.

Stock exchanges also provide an essential quality assurance service to listed companies by undertaking ongoing surveillance of their reporting and trading activities. When they suspect non-compliance with accounting standards, the stock exchanges undertake independent investigations and share information with securities commissions; Canada Revenue Agency, which collects income taxes from corporations; and other law enforcement agencies such as the Royal Canadian Mounted Police (RCMP). As intermediaries, the stock exchanges may also enforce their rules through penalties ranging from temporary cease trade orders to fines and delisting of companies.

Exhibit **6.1**

Ensuring the Integrity of Financial Position

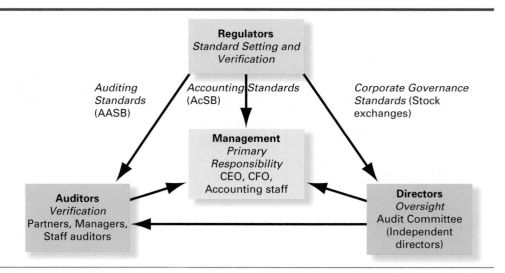

---

[3]The most prominent of these regulators is the Ontario Securities Commission (OSC). The OSC staff review company reports for compliance with their standards, investigate irregularities, and punish violators. Many OSC investigations are reported in the business press such as the *National Post* or *The Globe and Mail*. The OSC also publishes this information online each month at www.oscbulletin.carswell.com.

Managers (CEO, CFO, and Accounting Staff)

As noted in Chapter 1, the primary responsibility for the information in Thomson Reuters's financial statements and related disclosures lies with management as represented by the highest officer in the company, often called the *chief executive officer* (CEO), and the highest officer associated with the financial and accounting side of the business, often called the *chief financial officer* (CFO). These two officers must sign the statement of management responsibility that is included in the annual report. At Thomson Reuters and all publicly accountable enterprises, these two officers must personally certify that

- Each report filed with the provincial securities commission does not contain any untrue material statement or omit a material fact and fairly presents in all material respects the financial condition, results of operations, and cash flows of the company.
- There are no significant deficiencies and material weaknesses in the internal controls over financial reporting.
- They have disclosed to the auditors and audit committee of the board any weaknesses in internal controls or any fraud involving management or other employees who have a significant role in financial reporting.

The members of the *accounting staff* who actually prepare the details of the reports also have professional responsibility for the accuracy of this information, although their legal responsibility is smaller. Indeed, their future professional success depends heavily on their reputations for honesty and competence. Accounting managers responsible for financial statements with material errors are routinely dismissed—subject to professional review and sanction, which may include permanent curtailment of their licence to practice—and often have difficulty finding other employment.[4]

Board of Directors (Audit Committee)

As Thomson Reuters's corporate governance policy indicates, the board of directors (elected by the shareholders) is responsible for ensuring that processes are in place for maintaining the integrity of the company's accounting, financial statement preparation, and financial reporting. The audit committee of the board, which must be composed of non-management (independent) directors with financial knowledge, is responsible for hiring the company's independent auditors. They also meet separately with the auditors to discuss management's compliance with their financial reporting responsibilities.

The **BOARD OF DIRECTORS**, elected by the shareholders to represent their interests, is responsible for maintaining the integrity of the company's financial reports.

Recent changes to securities regulations have increased the burden of responsibility for accurate financial disclosure on company executives and external auditors. If any company listed on a stock exchange is found guilty of knowingly violating any disclosure regulation, not only the company but also members of its board of directors and audit committee can be sued. If experts such as accountants or financial analysts who relied on the company's financial reports also issued disclosure that misrepresented the company, they too may be individually sued by users who seek to recover some or all of their financial losses, which may have resulted from relying on such misleading information.

Auditors

The provincial securities commissions require publicly traded companies to have their statements audited by professional independent accountants following International Standards on Auditing. Many privately owned companies also have their statements

---

[4]H. Desai, C. E. Hogan, and M. S. Wilkins, "The Reputational Penalty for Aggressive Accounting: Earnings Restatements and Management Turnover." *The Accounting Review*, 2006, pp. 83–113.

UNQUALIFIED (CLEAN) AUDIT OPINION Auditors' statement that the financial statements are fair presentations in all material respects in conformity with Canadian Auditing Standards.

audited. By signing an unqualified (or clean) audit opinion, the audit firm assumes part of the financial responsibility for the fairness of the financial statements and related presentations. This opinion, which adds credibility to the statements, is also often required by agreements with lenders and private investors.[5] Subjecting the company's statements to independent verification reduces the risk that the company's condition is misrepresented in the statements. As a consequence, rational investors and lenders should lower the rate of return (interest) they charge for providing capital.[6]

PricewaterhouseCoopers is currently Thomson Reuters's auditor. KPMG, Deloitte & Touche, Ernst & Young, and PricewaterhouseCoopers are the largest audit firms, employing thousands of professional accountants practicing in offices throughout the world. They audit the great majority of publicly traded companies and many privately held companies. Some public companies and most private companies are audited by audit firms of smaller size. A list of well-known companies and their auditors at the time this chapter was written follows.

Company	Industry	Auditor
Nestlé, S.A.(Switzerland)	Health and nutrition	KPMG
Singapore Airlines (Singapore)	Airline	Ernst & Young
Tim Hortons (Canada)	Fast food	PricewaterhouseCoopers
Royal Bank of Canada	Financial services	Deloitte & Touche

Companies often hire financial managers from their audit firms because of their broad financial experience as well as their specific company knowledge gained during prior years' audits.

A QUESTION OF ACCOUNTABILITY WHERE WERE THE AUDITORS?

Most professional accountants act in an honest and ethical manner, abiding by the codes of ethics developed by the professional accounting organizations. Nevertheless, a few accountants act in their own interest and disregard ethical conduct. They even become accomplices in spectacular fraud cases and subsequent company bankruptcies. For example, Enron Corp., a U.S. energy trading company, intentionally inflated its net earnings by hiding assets and related debts from 1997 to 2001. Throughout this period, the auditors of Arthur Andersen LLP, a global accounting services company with revenues in excess of $500 million, should have known that the financial statements issued by Enron's management were fraudulent.[7]

The collapse of Enron, the largest unexpected bankruptcy in U.S. history at that time, caused tremendous losses to the company's shareholders, creditors, employees, and other

---

[5]In some cases, the auditor may not be satisfied that the company's financial statements are in compliance with IFRS. A qualified opinion would then be issued if the company's management is not willing to modify the financial reports as per the auditor's recommendation. If the exceptions to IFRS are very serious, then the auditor may issue an adverse opinion if the company's management cannot be persuaded to rectify the problems to avoid such an opinion. In extreme cases, the auditor may deny the issuance of an opinion if insufficient information is available to express an opinion. These latter types of opinions are rarely issued by auditors.

[6]Examples of accounting research that examine this relationship are P. Hribar and N. Jenkins, "The Effect of Accounting Restatements on Earnings Revisions and the Estimated Cost of Capital," *Review of Accounting Studies*, 2004, pp. 337–356, and C. A. Botosan and M. A. Plumlee, "A Re-Examination of Disclosure Level and the Expected Cost of Equity Capital," *Journal of Accounting Research*, March 2002, pp. 21–40.

[7]An overview of the financial and reporting environment in the United States and the specific situation faced by Enron's executives and Arthur Andersen's auditors is provided by G. Cunningham and J. Harris, "Enron and Arthur Andersen: The Case of the Crooked E and the Fallen A," *Global Perspectives on Accounting Education*, Vol. 3, 2006, pp. 27–48.

stakeholders. Furthermore, Enron's bankruptcy in December 2001 caused the collapse of Arthur Andersen. More than 300 clients left the firm within 90 days, taking $250 million of potential revenue with them to other audit firms. This audit failure led to calls for improved accountability by managers and auditors. This generated considerable discussion among securities regulators, financial analysts, investors, and creditors for stricter regulation of the accounting profession.

The *Sarbanes-Oxley Act* (*SOX*) approved by the U.S. Congress in July 2002 was a direct response to the Enron scandal and others that occurred in the United States. This law has set higher standards of responsibility on the officers and directors of publicly listed companies as well as on auditors. Canadian companies that are listed on U.S. stock exchanges must also comply with the *SOX* requirements.

Information Intermediaries: Analysts and Information Services

Students often view the communication process between companies and financial statement users as a simple process of mailing the report to individual shareholders who read the report and then make investment decisions based on what they have learned. This simple picture is far from today's reality. Now most investors rely on sophisticated financial analysts and information services to gather and analyze information. Exhibit 6.2 summarizes this process.

Financial Analysts   Financial analysts receive accounting reports and other information about the company from electronic information services. They also gather information through conversations with company executives and visits to company facilities and competitors. The results of their analyses are combined into analysts' reports.

Analysts' reports normally include forecasts of share price and future quarterly and annual earnings per share; a buy, sell, or hold recommendation for the company shares; and explanations for these judgments. In making these earnings forecasts, the analysts rely heavily on their knowledge of how the accounting system translates business events into the numbers on a company's financial statements, which is the subject matter of this text. Individual analysts often specialize in particular industries (such as sporting goods or energy companies). Analysts are regularly evaluated based on the accuracy of their forecasts, as well as the profitability of their stock picks.[8]

EARNINGS FORECASTS are predictions of earnings for future accounting periods.

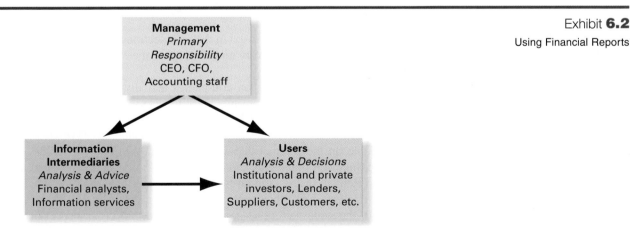

Exhibit **6.2**

Using Financial Reports

[8]See M. B. Mikhail, B. R. Walther, and R. H. Willis, "Does Forecast Accuracy Matter to Security Analysts?" *The Accounting Review*, April 1999, pp. 185–200, and R. A. McEwen and J.E. Hunton, "Is Analyst Forecast Accuracy Associated with Accounting Information Use?" *Accounting Horizons*, March 1999, pp. 1–16.

Analysts often work in the research departments of brokerage and investment banking houses such as RBC Dominion Securities, mutual fund companies such as the Investors Group, and investment advisory services such as Standard & Poor's, which sell their advice to others. Through their reports and recommendations, analysts transfer their knowledge of accounting, the company, and the industry to others who lack this expertise. Many believe that decisions that are based on analysts' advice cause stock market prices to react quickly to information in financial statements. A quick, unbiased reaction to information is called *market efficiency* in finance. It is highly unlikely that unsophisticated investors can glean more information from financial statements than the sophisticated analysts have already learned. Careful analysis does not lead all analysts to the same conclusions, however. These differences of opinion are reflected in the following earnings (per share) forecasts for Thomson Reuters Corporation and stock recommendations made by a number of analysts at the time of writing this chapter.

REAL WORLD EXCERPT

Reuters.com

THOMSON REUTERS CORPORATION
Earnings Forecasts

	For fiscal 2010	For fiscal 2011
Average forecast	$ 1.76	$2.38
Lowest forecast	1.67	2.15
Highest forecast	1.89	2.66
Number of analysts	15	16

Reprinted with permission of Thomson Reuters.

Analysts make recommendations to buy, hold, or sell a company's shares based on their earnings forecasts. In the case of Thomson Reuters, the analysts' recommendations at the time of writing this chapter were "buy" (3 analysts), "outperform" (4 analysts), "hold" (8 analysts), "underperform" (2 analysts), and "sell" (1 analyst).

In general, financial analysts tend to make optimistic earnings forecasts in order to maintain a good relationship with the company's management. The reason is that managers provide analysts with vital information for their analysis. Optimistic earnings forecasts, however, put additional pressure on management to meet and even exceed analysts' forecasts to please investors. The drive to meet analysts' earnings expectations has led the management of some companies to adopt accounting policies that result in either premature recognition of revenue or deferral of expenses, or both, to increase reported earnings.

The information services discussed in the next section allow investors to gather their own information about the company and to monitor the recommendations of analysts.

Information Services Canadian companies actually file financial statements and other securities-related forms electronically with *SEDAR* (*System for Electronic Document Analysis and Retrieval*), which is the official site for the filing of documents by public companies as required by securities laws in Canada.[9] *SEDAR* is currently a free service available on the Internet at www.sedar.com.[10] Many companies also provide access to their financial statements and other information over the Internet. You can contact Thomson Reuters by clicking on Investor Relations at www.thomsonreuters.com.

Financial analysts and other sophisticated users obtain much of the information they use from the wide variety of commercial online information services. Services

---

[9]Canadian companies that have shares traded on U.S. stock exchanges can file SEC forms electronically with EDGAR (Electronic Data Gathering and Retrieval) sponsored by the SEC.

[10]To look at SEDAR, just type the address on your Web browser. Select French or English, depending on your preference, and then select Company Profiles, followed by the letter of the alphabet that corresponds to the first letter of the company's name. You will then see a list of companies that includes the selected company. Many of the financial statement examples used in this book were downloaded from this website.

such as *Lexis-Nexis* (lexisnexis.com), *Compustat* (compustat.com), *Thomson Research* (research.thomsonib.com), and *CanWest Interactive Inc.* (fpinfomart.ca) provide broad access to financial statements and related news information. They also allow users to search the database by keywords, including various financial statement terms.

More general information services include *Factiva* (factiva.com), *Bloomberg* (bloomberg.com), as well as the financial sections of national newspapers such as *The Globe and Mail* and *National Post. Factiva* provides access to news stories about companies and company press releases, including the initial announcements of annual and quarterly financial results. The *Bloomberg* service also provides the ability to combine these sources of information in sophisticated analyses.

A growing number of other resources offer a mixture of free and fee-based information on many companies on the Internet. These include reuters.com, hoovers.com, finance.yahoo.com, and moneycentral.msn.com.

INFORMATION SERVICES AND JOB SEARCHES

FINANCIAL ANALYSIS

Information services have become the primary tool for professional analysts who use them. Information services are an important source of information for job seekers. Potential employers expect top job applicants to demonstrate knowledge about their companies during an interview, and electronic information services are an excellent source of company information. The best place to learn about your potential employers is their websites. Be sure to read the material in the employment section and the investor relations section of the site. To learn more about electronic information services, contact the business or reference librarian at your college or university library or explore some of the websites mentioned earlier.

Users: Institutional and Private Investors, Creditors, and Others

Institutional investors include private pension funds (associated with unions and employees of specific companies); public pension funds (for provincial and municipal employees); mutual funds; and endowment, charitable foundation, and trust funds (such as the endowment of your college or university). These institutional shareholders usually employ their own analysts who also rely on the information intermediaries just discussed. Institutional shareholders control the majority of publicly traded shares of Canadian companies. For example, at the time of writing this book, institutional investors owned approximately 34 percent of Thomson Reuters's outstanding shares.

Private investors include large individual investors such as Thomas Glocer, the company's chief executive officer, and some of the company's directors, as well as small retail investors who, like most individuals, buy a relatively small number of shares of publicly traded companies through brokers such as BMO Nesbitt Burns. Retail investors normally lack the expertise to understand financial statements and the resources to gather data efficiently. As a consequence, they often rely on the advice of information intermediaries or turn their money over to the management of mutual and pension funds (institutional investors).

Lenders, or creditors, include suppliers, banks, commercial credit companies, and other financial institutions that lend money to companies. Lending officers and financial analysts in these organizations use these same public sources of information. In addition, when companies borrow money from financial institutions, they often agree to provide additional financial information (e.g., monthly statements) as part of the lending contract. Lenders are often the primary external user group for financial statements of private companies. Institutional and private investors also become creditors when they buy a company's publicly traded bonds and debentures.[11]

INSTITUTIONAL INVESTORS are managers of pension funds, mutual funds, endowment funds, and other funds that invest on behalf of others.

PRIVATE INVESTORS include individuals who purchase shares in companies.

LENDERS (CREDITORS) include suppliers and financial institutions that lend money to companies.

---

[11]Debentures are debt securities that are not secured with specific collateral (no specific assets are pledged as security for the debt). Bonds normally are secured by specific collateral such as investments in shares of other companies. Chapter 11 provides more details about bonds and debentures.

Financial statements play an important role in the relationships between customers and suppliers. Customers evaluate the financial health of suppliers to determine whether they will be reliable, up-to-date sources of supply. Suppliers evaluate their customers to estimate their future needs and ability to pay debts. Competitors also attempt to learn useful information about a company from its statements. The potential loss of competitive advantage is one of the costs to the preparer of public financial disclosures. Accounting regulators consider these costs as well as the direct costs of preparation when they require new disclosures.

THE DISCLOSURE PROCESS

LO²

Identify the steps in the accounting communication process, including the issuance of press releases, annual reports, quarterly reports, and documents filed with securities commissions, as well as the guiding principles in communicating useful information.

As noted in our discussion of information services and information intermediaries, the accounting communication process includes more steps and participants than one would envision in a world in which annual and quarterly reports are simply mailed to shareholders.

Press Releases

A **PRESS RELEASE** is a written public news announcement normally distributed to major news services.

To provide timely information to external users and to limit the possibility of selective leakage of information, Thomson Reuters and most public companies announce quarterly and annual earnings through a press release as soon as the audited annual figures (or reviewed quarterly figures) are available. Thomson Reuters normally issues its earnings press releases within five weeks of the end of the accounting period. The announcements are sent electronically to the major print and electronic news services, including *Thomson Reuters* and *Bloomberg*, which make them immediately available to subscribers. Exhibit 6.3 shows an excerpt of a typical quarterly press release for Thomson Reuters that includes key financial figures and an invitation to interested parties to access a live webcast concerning the company's quarterly results. The press release also includes condensed unaudited financial statements that form part of the formal quarterly report to shareholders, distributed after the press release.

Many companies, including Thomson Reuters, follow these press releases with a conference call at which senior managers answer questions from analysts about the quarterly results. These calls are open to the investing public. Listening to these recordings is a good way to learn about a company's business strategy and its expectations for the future, as well as key factors that analysts consider when they evaluate a company.

FINANCIAL ANALYSIS

HOW DOES THE STOCK MARKET REACT TO EARNINGS ANNOUNCEMENTS?

For actively traded shares such as those of Thomson Reuters, most of the stock market reaction (share price increases and decreases from investor trading) to the news in the press release usually occurs quickly. Recall that a number of analysts follow Thomson Reuters and regularly predict the company's earnings. When the actual earnings are published, the market reacts *not* to the amount of earnings but to the difference between actual earnings and expected earnings. This amount is called *unexpected earnings*. For example, Thomson Reuters's share price decreased slightly from $32.35 to $32.15 on the day of the press release, which implies that earnings per share for the third quarter of fiscal year 2009 did not meet analysts' expectations.

Companies such as Thomson Reuters issue press releases concerning other important events including announcements of new services or acquisition of new companies. Press releases related to annual earnings and quarterly earnings often precede the issuance of the quarterly or annual report by 15 to 45 days. This time is necessary to prepare the additional detail and to print and distribute those reports.

Exhibit **6.3**
Earnings Press Release for
Thomson Reuters Corporation

REAL WORLD EXCERPT

Thomson Reuters
Corporation
PRESS RELEASE

THOMSON REUTERS REPORTS THIRD-QUARTER 2009 RESULTS

NEW YORK, NY, November 5, 2009 – Thomson Reuters (TSX / NYSE: TRI), the world's leading source of intelligent information for businesses and professionals, today reported results for the third quarter ended September 30, 2009. While net sales began to improve in the third quarter, revenue flow-through from weaker year-to-date net sales in Legal and Markets overshadowed strong performances in Tax & Accounting and Healthcare & Science. Underlying operating profit margin improvement was driven by the benefit of currency, continuing progress on the integration program and strong cost management.

. . .

- Revenues from ongoing businesses were $3.2 billion, a decrease of 2% before currency and 4% after currency. IFRS revenues were down 4% after currency against the prior year period.
- Underlying operating profit was up 3% to $711 million, with the related margin up 140 basis points, driven by the benefit of currency, integration-related savings and a continued commitment to strong cost management.
- Adjusted earnings per share were $0.43 compared with $0.47 in the third quarter of 2008. The decline was due to higher integration-related spending, which is included in adjusted earnings but not underlying operating profit.
- Free cash flow remained strong in the third quarter, with net cash flow provided by operations of $513 million and reported free cash flow of $260 million, down versus the prior period reflecting planned integration and interest costs.
- During the quarter, the company further strengthened its capital structure with the redemption of $600 million of outstanding debt, financed through cash-on-hand and the issuance of $500 million of 4.70% notes, due 2019. Year-to-date, the company has refinanced $1.1 billion of long-term debt, reflecting its continued ability to access and take advantage of favorable capital markets.

. . .

Thomson Reuters will webcast a discussion of its third-quarter results today beginning at 8:30 a.m. U.S. Eastern Standard Time (EST). You can access the webcast by visiting www.thomsonreuters.com and clicking on "Investor Relations" at the top of the page and then "Thomson Reuters Reports Third-Quarter 2009 Results" on the right side of the page. An archive of the webcast will be available in the "Investor Relations" section of the Thomson Reuters website.

Source: www.thomsonreuters.com.

Annual Reports

For privately held companies, *annual reports* are relatively simple documents photocopied on white paper. They normally include the following:

1. Basic financial statements: income statement, statement of financial position, statement of changes in equity, and statement of cash flows.
2. Related notes.
3. Report of independent accountants (auditor's opinion).

The annual reports of public companies are significantly more elaborate, both because of additional reporting requirements imposed on these companies by securities commissions and because many companies use their annual reports as public relations tools to communicate non-accounting information to shareholders, customers, the press, and others.

The annual reports of public companies are normally split into two sections. The first, "non-financial," section usually includes a letter to shareholders from the chairperson and CEO, along with descriptions of the company's management philosophy, products, successes (and occasionally its failures), and exciting prospects and challenges for the future. Beautiful photographs of products, facilities, and personnel often are included. The second, "financial," section includes the core of the report. Securities regulators set minimum disclosure standards for the financial section of the annual reports of public companies. The principal components of the financial section follow:

1. Summarized financial data for a 5- or 10-year period.
2. Management's Discussion and Analysis, covering financial condition and results of operations.
3. The basic financial statements.
4. Notes (Footnotes).
5. Report of Independent Accountants (Auditor's Opinion) and the Management Certification.
6. Recent stock price information.
7. Summaries of the unaudited quarterly financial data (described later).
8. Lists of directors and officers of the company and relevant addresses.

The order of these components varies.

Most of these components, except for Management's Discussion and Analysis (MD&A), have been discussed in earlier chapters. This component includes management's discussion and explanation of key figures in the financial statements and risks the company faces in the future. The MD&A section contains important non-financial and strategic information to help users interpret the financial statements. Many companies devote a sizeable portion of their annual reports to the MD&A section, For example, Thomson Reuters devoted 50 pages of its 2009 annual report to a detailed analysis of the company's results of operations and its various business segments. Thomson Reuters's MD&A section also includes a review of the company's liquidity, capital resources, and contractual obligations. The complete annual report of Thomson Reuters for 2009, which includes all of these sections, is available on the company's website.

Quarterly Reports

Quarterly reports normally begin with a short letter to shareholders. This is followed by a condensed income statement for the quarter, which often shows less detail than the annual income statement, and a condensed statement of financial position dated at the end of the quarter (e.g., March 31 for the first quarter). These condensed financial statements are not audited and so are marked *unaudited*. Often, the statement of cash flows, statement of changes in equity, and some notes to the financial statements are omitted. Private companies also normally prepare quarterly reports for lenders. Companies issue their quarterly reports about five weeks after the end of each quarter.

Reports to Securities Commissions

Public companies must also file periodic reports with the OSC and other provincial securities commissions. These reports include the annual report, quarterly reports, an annual information form, and an information circular.

The annual information form provides a more detailed description of the business, including such items as the company's corporate structure, the industry in which it operates, the products and services it offers, product and project development, sales and marketing, manufacturing, and competition. The form also lists the properties owned and leased by the company, and significant contracts that the company has signed.

The information circular is a legal document that is forwarded to the company's shareholders prior to the annual general or special meeting of shareholders. It provides information about the items that the shareholders will be asked to consider and vote on during the meeting, including election of new directors, appointment of independent auditors, and other matters of a legal nature. The circular also provides details of the monetary compensation of key management personnel.

In addition to these periodic reports, companies file other types of reports as the need arises. These include a short-form prospectus that provides details of the equity and/or debt securities that they plan to issue to investors, and press releases concerning new developments. The *SEDAR* website, www.sedar.com, lists all of the reports, documents, and news items that Thomson Reuters and other corporations have filed.[12]

Guiding Principles for Communicating Useful Information

Information presented in financial reports is useful if it makes a difference in the context of making a decision. Several qualitative characteristics determine the usefulness of accounting information for decision making.[13] These were introduced in Chapter 2 (Exhibit 2.1) and are presented in more detail in Exhibit 6.4.

A number of qualitative characteristics of accounting information have been included in conceptual frameworks developed by the FASB and the IASB, and adopted by other standard-setting organizations. The desirable qualities of accounting information are part of a joint IASB/FASB project to revisit the conceptual framework for financial reporting. This first phase of the conceptual framework identifies relevance and faithful representation as the two fundamental qualitative characteristics, supported by four enhancing qualitative characteristics: comparability, verifiability, timeliness, and understandability.[14] These six characteristics are discussed below along with important constraints on accounting measurement.

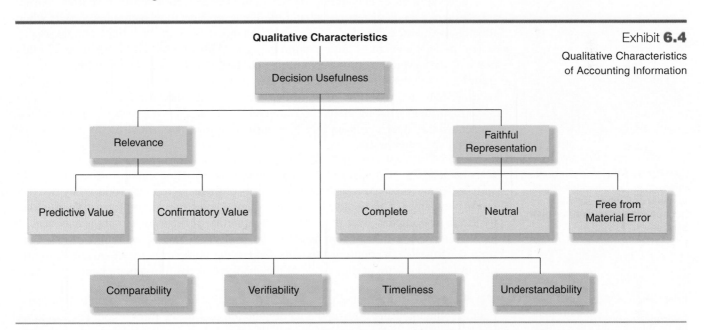

Qualitative Characteristics

Exhibit **6.4**

Qualitative Characteristics of Accounting Information

---

[12]U.S., Canadian, and international companies that have shares trading on U.S. securities exchange markets are required to file a number of reports with the SEC. These include Form 10-K, which provides a detailed description of the business, and more detailed schedules concerning various figures reported in the annual financial statements, and Form 10-Q, which is essentially a quarterly report to shareholders.

[13]These qualitative characteristics are discussed in Chapter 3, Qualitative Characteristics of Useful Financial Information of *The Conceptual Framework for Financial Reporting 2010*, IASB, September 2010. This Framework has been incorporated in Part I of the CICA Handbook – Accounting.

[14]International Financial Standards Board. 2010. *The Conceptual Framework for Financial Reporting 2010*, September, London: IASB.

RELEVANT INFORMATION can influence a decision; it has predictive and/or confirmatory value.

Relevance Information disclosed in financial statements is relevant if it can influence users' decisions by helping them assess the economic effect of past activities and/or predict future events. For example, the various elements of an income statement have predictive value if they help users predict future levels of profit or its subcomponents, such as operating profit. The *predictive value* of the income statement is enhanced if non-recurring items are presented separately on a multiple-step income statement, because these items are transient in nature. Similarly, information presented on the income statement has *confirmatory value* if it confirms or changes prior expectations based on previous evaluations.

While all transactions affecting an entity must be accounted for, items and amounts that are of low significance do not have to conform precisely to specified accounting guidelines or be separately reported if they would not influence reasonable decisions. Accountants usually designate such items and amounts as *immaterial.* Determining material amounts is often very subjective and is viewed as an *entity-specific aspect of relevance.*[15]

MATERIAL AMOUNTS are amounts that are large enough to influence a user's decision.

FAITHFUL REPRESENTATION suggests that information provided in financial statements must reflect the substance of the underlying transactions.

Faithful Representation To be useful for decision making, information provided in financial statements must be a faithful representation of the economic phenomena it is supposed to represent, thus reflecting the substance of the underlying transactions. The information must be complete, neutral, and free from material error. For instance, the inventory account of a company that sells computer equipment would include items that are held for sale to customers. If inventory included also desktop and laptop computers used by employees in their daily work, then the inventory balance is not a faithful representation of the cost of goods available for sale. Similarly, deferred revenue that is recognized prematurely as revenue for the period overstates the amount of revenue reported on the income statement, causing a lack of faithful representation of current period revenues.

The usefulness of accounting information is enhanced when it is neutral; that is, free from bias in its measurement and presentation. Bias in measurement occurs when the item being measured is consistently understated or overstated. For example, a consistent understatement of amortization expense leads to a biased higher profit. In this context, the development of accounting standards for measurement and reporting of transaction effects should not result in favouring one group of users over others. The measurement and reporting of liabilities, for example, should not result in consistent underreporting of liabilities on the statement of financial position because this would favour owners over creditors and may influence investment and credit decisions of financial statement users.

COMPARABILITY of accounting information across businesses is enhanced when similar accounting methods have been applied.

Comparability Comparability of accounting information enables users to identify similarities and discrepancies between two sets of financial reports produced by two different companies. This quality is also important when comparing information provided by the same company over time. The comparability of financial reports is enhanced if there is consistent information available by using the same accounting methods over time. Changes in accounting methods reduce the comparability of information and necessitate disclosure of the effects of the change in order to maintain comparability.

Information is VERIFIABLE if independent accountants can agree on the nature and amount of the transaction.

Verifiability Information presented in financial statements is verifiable if independent accountants can agree on the nature and amount of the transaction. For example, the historical cost of a piece of land that is reported on Thomson Reuters's statement of financial position on December 31, 2009, is usually highly verifiable. The cost of acquisition is based on the purchase price and related costs that result from actual exchanges with external parties. However, the appraised market value of the land at that date is a subjective estimate that reflects the appraiser's past experience. It is

---

[15]An alternative view is to consider materiality as a constraint of accounting measurement. For further clarification, refer to Agenda paper 6: *Conceptual Framework - Measurement: Objective and qualitative characteristics: Sweep issues from the ballot draft*, International Accounting Standards Board, May 17, 2010.

not verifiable because it is not based on an actual exchange transaction. However, if Thomson Reuters is considering the sale of land, its market value would be relevant for that decision even though it is less verifiable than the land's historical cost.[16]

Timeliness   Information that is not available to users in a timely manner loses its relevance because it would not be considered in making decisions. Timeliness of accounting information enhances both its predictive and confirmatory values. The relevance of accounting information for decision making declines as time passes. For this reason, companies produce quarterly reports and issue press releases to convey timely information to investors, creditors, and other user groups.

TIMELY information enhances both its predictive and confirmatory values.

Understandability   Information cannot be useful if it is not properly understood. It is assumed that users of accounting information have a reasonable understanding of business and economic activities and accounting and that they are willing to study the information with reasonable diligence.[17] Clear and concise classification and presentation of information enhances its understandability.

UNDERSTANDABILITY is the quality of information that enables users to comprehend its meaning.

Constraints of Accounting Measurement

Accurate interpretation of financial statements requires that the statements' reader be aware of important constraints of accounting measurement.

Cost   Companies produce and disseminate accounting information to users with the expectation that the benefits to users from using such information exceed the cost of producing it. The perceived benefits of new information relate to its usefulness in decision making. Such benefits may be difficult to measure, but the costs of producing additional information can be estimated with reasonable accuracy. When standards setters, such as the Accounting Standards Board of Canada, require companies to disclose specific information, known as *mandatory* disclosure, they would have determined implicitly that the benefits to users exceed the costs the company will incur to produce the information. For example, a recently introduced regulation by the Canadian Securities Administrators concerning internal control over financial reporting imposed additional costs on companies to evaluate the effectiveness of internal control procedures put in place to discourage corporate fraud by managers.[18] These additional expenditures are expected to lead to improvements in internal control procedures that would curb the misappropriation of assets by managers and other employees. The perceived benefits of this new regulation include increased verifiability and decision usefulness of the accounting information disclosed in financial statements. While the cost of improving internal control procedures can be estimated, the related benefits to users of financial statements may be difficult to measure.

The **COST CONSTRAINT** suggests that information should be produced only if the perceived benefits of increased decision usefulness exceed the expected costs of providing that information.

In other cases, the company's managers may decide that *voluntary* disclosure of information about specific aspects of the company's operations would be beneficial to users. In such cases, the costs of disclosure should not exceed the expected benefits. In this context, the cost constraint plays an important role in determining whether new information should be produced and communicated to users.

---

[16]In the original conceptual frameworks produced by the FASB and the IASB, verifiability was considered a component of reliability, which also encompassed accuracy and freedom from bias. In the revised conceptual framework, reliability has been replaced with faithful representation as the second fundamental qualitative characteristic. A review of the primary qualitative characteristics and their relative significance for performance evaluation and investment and credit decisions is provided in Patricia O'Brien, "Changing the Concepts to Justify the Standards," *Accounting Perspectives*, Vol. 8, No. 4, 2009, pp. 263–275.

[17]To help users better understand the contents of its financial reports, IBM includes on its website (**www.ibm.com/investor/tools/financials.phtml**) a glossary of terms and provides basic explanations of the information contained in financial statements.

[18]Status of Proposed MI52-111 *Reporting on Internal Control over Financial Reporting* and Proposed Amended and Restated MI52-109 *Certification of Disclosure in Issuers' Annual and Interim Filings*, Canadian Securities Administrators, Notice 52-313, March 10, 2006, as posted on CSA's website: **www.csa-acvm.ca**, accessed on October 19, 2010.

PRUDENCE suggests that care should be taken not to overstate assets and revenues or understate liabilities and expenses.

Prudence   Prudence requires that special care be taken to avoid (1) overstating assets and revenues and (2) understating liabilities and expenses. Users of financial statements often want to know about possible sources of trouble for the company. For example, creditors need to know how secure their investments will be if the company's fortunes deteriorate, but they may not be interested in whether the company might do exceptionally well. They care more about the downside risk than the upside potential. For this reason, financial statements that show assets at historical cost, but reduce these amounts when current values are significantly lower, help satisfy the needs of creditors. This lower-of-cost-or-market guideline attempts to offset managers' natural optimism about their business operations, which sometimes creeps into the financial reports that they prepare. More companies have perished through excessive optimism than through excessive caution. It should be noted that prudence is not considered as a desirable quality of accounting information, because the prudent reporting of accounting information contradicts the concept of neutrality and is likely to result in bias in the values reported on financial statements.

INTERNATIONAL PERSPECTIVE

GLOBAL DIFFERENCES IN ACCOUNTING STANDARDS

Financial accounting standards and disclosure requirements are set by national regulatory agencies and standard-setting bodies. Many countries have already adopted international financial reporting standards (IFRS) issued by the International Accounting Standards Board (IASB). However, the Financial Standard Accounting Board (FASB) and the U.S.'s Securities and Exchange Commission (SEC) are still considering when and how U.S. companies should prepare their financial statements using accounting standards that are based on IFRS. Despite efforts by the IASB and the FASB to harmonize U.S. accounting standards with IFRS, there are still several important differences. A partial list of the differences at the time of writing this chapter is presented below, along with the chapter in which these issues are addressed:

Difference*	U.S. GAAP	IFRS	Chapter
Extraordinary items	Permitted	Prohibited	3
Last-in, first-out method for inventory	Permitted	Prohibited	8
Reversal of inventory write-downs	Prohibited	Permitted	8
Basis of property, plant, and equipment	Historical cost	Fair value or historical cost	9

*Source: Deloitte *IAS Plus*, July 2010.

SELF-STUDY **QUIZ 6-1**

Match the players involved in the accounting communication process with their roles or the guiding principles for communicating information with their definitions.

1. Relevant information
2. CEO and CFO
3. Financial analyst
4. External auditor
5. Cost constraint

    a. Management primarily responsible for accounting information.
    b. An independent party that provides an opinion that financial statements are presented fairly in accordance to IFRS.
    c. Information that influences users' decisions.
    d. Only information that provides benefits in excess of costs should be reported.
    e. An individual who analyzes financial information and provides advice.

After you complete your answers, go online for the solutions.

A CLOSER LOOK AT FINANCIAL STATEMENTS AND NOTES

To make financial statements more useful to investors, creditors, and analysts, specific *classifications* of information are included in the statements. Various classifications are used in practice. You should not be confused when you notice different formats used by different companies. You will find that each format is consistent with the principles discussed in this text.

LO3

Recognize and apply the different financial statement and disclosure formats used by companies in practice.

Overview of Thomson Reuters's Financial Statements

Exhibits 6.5 to 6.9 show the financial statements of Thomson Reuters for the fiscal year 2009.

THOMSON REUTERS CORPORATION				
Consolidated Statement of Financial Position				
(millions of U.S. dollars)	Notes	December 31, 2009	December 31, 2008	January 1, 2008
ASSETS				
Cash and cash equivalents	13	**1,111**	841	7,497
Trade and other receivables	14	**1,742**	1,818	1,581
Other financial assets	20	**76**	261	70
Prepaid expenses and other current assets	15	**734**	766	426
Current assets		**3,663**	3,686	9,574
Computer hardware and other property, net	16	**1,546**	1,556	731
Computer software, net	17	**1,495**	1,299	721
Other identifiable intangible assets, net	18	**8,694**	8,702	3,440
Goodwill	19	**18,130**	18,324	6,939
Other financial assets	20	**383**	286	511
Other non-current assets	21	**649**	627	488
Deferred tax	24	**13**	109	74
Total assets		**34,573**	34,589	22,478
LIABILITIES AND EQUITY				
Liabilities				
Current indebtedness	20	**782**	688	595
Payables, accruals and provisions	22	**2,651**	2,704	1,505
Deferred revenue		**1,187**	1,193	1,105
Other financial liabilities	20	**92**	60	29
Current liabilities		**4,712**	4,645	3,234
Long-term indebtedness	20	**6,821**	6,783	4,224
Provisions and other non-current liabilities	23	**1,878**	1,798	851
Other financial liabilities	20	**42**	222	—
Deferred tax	24	**1,785**	2,653	856
Total liabilities		**15,238**	16,101	9,165
Equity				
Capital	25	**10,177**	10,034	2,836
Retained earnings		**10,561**	10,650	10,476
Accumulated other comprehensive (loss) income		**(1,471)**	(2,268)	1
Total shareholders' equity		**19,267**	18,416	13,313
Non-controlling interests	31	**68**	72	—
Total equity		**19,335**	18,488	13,313
Total liabilities and equity		**34,573**	34,589	22,478

Contingencies (note 30)
The related notes form an integral part of these consolidated financial statements.
These financial statements were approved by the Company's board of directors on March 2, 2010.
Reprinted with permission of Thomson Reuters.
Source: Thomson Reuters Annual Report 2009.

Exhibit **6.5**
Thomson Reuters Consolidated Statement of Financial Position

REAL WORLD EXCERPT

Thomson Reuters Corporation
ANNUAL REPORT

Classified Statement of Financial Position

Exhibit 6.5 shows the December 31, 2009, statement of financial position for Thomson Reuters. This statement looks very similar to the structure of the statements of financial position for the Nestlé Group and Andrew Peller Limited presented in previous chapters. Assets are listed by order of liquidity, with current assets preceding non-current assets. Liabilities are listed by order of time to maturity, with current liabilities reported before non-current liabilities. Finally, the equity section lists contributed capital, retained earnings, and other components.

Alternatively, assets may be reported by increasing order of liquidity, starting with the least liquid asset and ending with the most liquid asset. On the financing side, the equity section would be presented before liabilities, with non-current liabilities listed before current liabilities. This presentation format has been adopted by many European companies and is consistent with IFRS.

Classified Income Statement

As we have seen in previous chapters, the income statement includes a number of sections and subtotals to aid the user in identifying the company's operating profit for the year and to highlight the effect of other items on the net profit.

Most manufacturing and merchandising companies use the following basic structure:

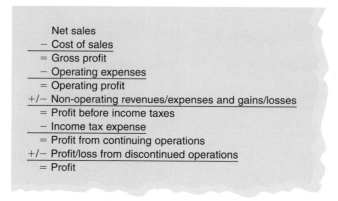

The operating expenses consist mainly of distribution costs, administrative expenses, and other operating expenses.[19] When a corporation controls less than 100 percent of the voting shares of other corporations, the profit for the period is allocated between the company's shareholders that hold a controlling interest and other shareholders that have a non-controlling interest.

Thomson Reuters is a service company. Consequently, its income statement does not include the subtotal "gross profit." In addition, the company reports the depreciation and amortization expense separately from other operating expenses.

---

[19]The expenses that are deducted from revenue to obtain operating profit can alternatively be classified in accordance with the main elements of the costs of production and sale, namely the cost of raw materials and consumables used, changes in inventories of finished products and work in progress, employee benefit costs, and depreciation and amortization expenses. For example, the Danish company ECCO Sko A/S that produces and markets footwear products worldwide classifies its operating expenses by nature (see, for example, its 2009 annual report, page 43, accessible at **www.ecco.com/downloads/ ECCO_Annual_Report_2009.pdf**).

Exhibit **6.6**

Income Statement of Thomson Reuters Corporation

REAL WORLD EXCERPT

Thomson Reuters Corporation

ANNUAL REPORT

THOMSON REUTERS CORPORATION
Consolidated Income Statement

(millions of U.S. dollars, expect per share amounts)	Notes	Year ended December 31, 2009	2008
Revenues		**12,997**	11,707
Operating expenses	5	**(9,875)**	(8,700)
Depreciation		**(509)**	(414)
Amortization of computer software		**(548)**	(482)
Amortization of other intangible assets		**(499)**	(425)
Impairment of assets held for sale	6	**—**	(86)
Other operating gains, net	7	**9**	68
Operating profit		**1,575**	1,668
Finance costs, net:			
Net interest expense	8	**(410)**	(224)
Other finance (costs) income	8	**(242)**	231
Other non-operating charge	9	**(385)**	—
Income before tax and equity method investees		**538**	1,675
Share of post tax earnings (loss) in equity method investees		**7**	(5)
Tax benefit (expense)	10	**299**	(350)
Earnings from continuing operations		**844**	1,320
Earnings from discontinued operations, net of tax	11	**23**	1
Net earnings		**867**	1,321
Earnings attributable to:			
Common shareholders[1]		**844**	1,307
Non-controlling interests	31	**23**	14
Earnings per share	12		
Basic earnings per share:			
From continuing operations		**$0.99**	$1.69
From discontinued operations		**0.02**	—
Basic earnings per share		**$1.01**	$1.69
Diluted earnings per share:			
From continuing operations		**$0.99**	$1.68
From discontinued operations		**0.02**	—
Diluted earnings per share		**$1.01**	$1.68

[1]On September 10, 2009, all Thomson Reuters PLC ordinary shares were exchanged for an equivalent number of Thomson Reuters Corporation common shares in connection with unification of the dual listed company structure.

The related notes form an integral part of these consolidated financial statements.
Reprinted with permission of Thomson Reuters.
Source: Thomson Reuters Annual Report 2009.

DIFFERENT EARNINGS FOR DIFFERENT PURPOSES

FINANCIAL ANALYSIS

In recent years, many companies reported different measures of earnings in addition to profit, as determined by IFRS. When companies report non-IFRS measures of earnings, they divert investors' attention away from the financial results of continuing operations.

For example, in discussing its annual and quarterly results of operations, Thomson Reuters's management focuses investors' and analysts' attention on revenues, operating profit from ongoing businesses, and underlying operating profit, which they define as operating profit excluding amortization of other intangible assets, impairment charges, fair value adjustments, integration program costs, other operating gains and losses, and the results of disposals.

Comparison of the revenue, operating profit, and underlying operating profit for the years 2007–2009 shows clearly why investors and analysts should be cautious about interpreting non-IFRS measures of profit (amounts in millions of dollars).

	2009	2008	2007
Revenue	$12,997	$13,441	$12,442
Operating profit	1,575	1,942	1,571
Underlying operating profit	2,754	2,778	2,337

For comparison purposes, the amounts for 2008 and 2007 are based on the assumption that Reuters was acquired on January 1, 2007, instead of April 17, 2008.

Both revenue and operating profit increased from 2007 to 2008, but declined in 2009. In contrast, underlying operating profit decreased only marginally in 2009, which explains why management of Thomson Reuters wants to draw analysts' and users' attention to this alternative measure of profit.

Profit Measurement

The measurement of profit continues to be a subject of debate. Accountants have attempted over the years to estimate the true profit that an entity achieves during a specific period. Until recently, the dominant approach to profit measurement has focused on measurement of revenues and expenses. The principles of revenue recognition, matching, and historical cost were predominant in measuring revenues, expenses, gains, and losses that are reported on the income statement. Consequently, the values of assets and liabilities reported on the statement of financial position did not necessarily reflect their current values but the values that resulted from the application of these accounting principles. For example, depreciation of property and equipment reflects an allocation of historical acquisition costs instead of a decline in the current value of these assets over time.

More recently, the desire to provide more relevant information for decision-making purposes has focused the attention of accounting standard setters toward measuring the current values of assets and liabilities. While the measurement of assets and liabilities at their current values is consistent with economic theory and leads to an estimation of economic profit, the actual determination of current value is not a simple task. Different measures of current value have been proposed over time and are currently used in determining the values reported on the statement of financial position. Ideally, companies should measure their assets and liabilities at fair value or exit value, which is defined as "the price that would be received to sell an asset or paid to transfer a liability in an orderly transaction between market participants at the measurement date."[20] Because of practical difficulties in determining a price for an asset or liability in the absence of an active market, accounting standard setters have provided guidance to accountants for the measurement of fair value under different circumstances.

The lack of active markets for many assets and liabilities has resulted in the use of different valuation approaches, ranging from historical cost to exit value. The following table summarizes the valuation bases that are currently permitted by IFRS for the reporting of asset and liability values on the statement of financial position.

Asset or Liability Group	Valuation Basis
Financial assets (e.g., investment in shares of other corporations, trade receivables, notes receivable)	Amortized cost or fair value
Inventories	Lower of cost and net realizable value
Property, plant, and equipment	Depreciated cost or recoverable amount
Investment properties (e.g., commercial real estate properties)	Depreciated cost or fair value
Intangible assets	Amortized cost or fair value
Financial liabilities	Amortized cost or fair value

---

[20]International Accounting Standards Board, "Fair Value Measurement," Exposure Draft, May 2009, p. 13.

Because end-of-period valuations are not based on actual exchange transactions between the company and outside parties, the gains and losses that result from such valuations are usually reported separately in a statement of comprehensive income and distinguished from gains and losses that have been realized through actual transactions. This also led to the preparation of a statement of changes in equity that reconciles the values reported on the statement of financial position to those reported on the statement of comprehensive income. The effects of the various asset and liability valuation methods on the values reported on financial statements are discussed in later chapters.[21]

Statement of Comprehensive Income

The income statement includes the results of operations for a specific accounting period as well as the effects of discontinued operations. Over the years, accounting academics and standard setters have debated whether the income statement should include additional elements reflecting unrealized changes in the values of specific assets and liabilities. Hence, publicly accountable enterprises are now required to disclose additional information in a "Statement of Comprehensive Income." The additional components of income reflect the financial effect of events that cause changes in shareholders' equity other than investments by shareholders or distributions to shareholders. Specifically, the elements of comprehensive income would include the following items, among others:

- Profit, as reported on the income statement.
- Unrealized gains or losses on translating the financial statements of companies that have operations in other countries but are controlled by the Canadian reporting entity.
- Unrealized gains or losses on financial assets that are classified as available for sale.
- Gains or losses on derivatives transactions that are designated as cash flow hedges.[22]
- Actuarial gains (losses) on defined benefit pension plans.

The statement of comprehensive income for Thomson Reuters for the year ended December 31, 2009, (Exhibit 6.7) includes most of these items. Measurement of the various components of other comprehensive income (loss) is rather complex, and is covered in advanced accounting courses.

Statement of Changes in Equity

The statement of changes in equity shows a summary of the changes to the various components of equity that occurred during the period because of transactions with shareholders (issuance of additional shares, repurchase of shares, declaration of dividends); the profit or loss that the company realized from its operating, investing, and financing activities; and the adjustments to asset and liability values that are not reflected in the profit or loss for the year. This statement reconciles the beginning and ending values for each component of equity and indicates the nature of the changes that occurred to each of these components. For example, the decrease in retained earnings from $10,650 to $10,561 has resulted from an addition of $840, based on the statement of comprehensive income, and reduction of $2 and $927 for dividends declared on preferred and common shares, respectively.

---

[21]An excellent review of fair value accounting of financial assets and liabilities, and its role in the 2007–2009 financial crisis is provided in M. Magnan, "Fair Value Accounting and the Financial Crisis: Messenger or Contributor?" *Accounting Perspectives*, 2009, Vol.8, No. 3, pp. 189–213.

[22]A derivative is a legal contract between two or more parties that fixes both the future date and price at which some specified transaction will occur. It is called a derivative because the value of a derivative contract is always based on or derived from the value of some underlying asset or liability. The transaction defined in a derivative contract may be a purchase or sale of a commodity, such as oil, or a trade, such as an interest rate swap. A derivative provides one way for corporations to hedge or limit their exposure to one financial risk by taking on an offsetting financial risk. It is similar to other debt contracts because it fixes the terms of payment between two parties. However, where most debt contracts assure the transfer of money from one party to another, a derivative either transfers or spreads the risk of the loss of cash from one party to other parties.

Exhibit **6.7**

Thomson Reuters Consolidated Statement of Comprehensive Income

THOMSON REUTERS CORPORATION
Consolidated Statement of Comprehensive Income

(millions of U.S. dollars)	Notes	Year ended December 31	
		2009	2008
Net earnings		867	1,321
Other comprehensive income (loss):			
Net gain (loss) on cash flow hedges		296	(313)
Net (gain) loss on cash flow hedges transferred to earnings		(350)	333
Foreign currency translation adjustments to equity		678	(2,143)
Foreign currency translation adjustments to earnings		173	(146)
Actuarial losses on defined benefit pension plans, net of tax[1]		(4)	(389)
Other comprehensive income (loss)		793	(2,658)
Total comprehensive income (loss)		1,660	(1,337)
Comprehensive income (loss) for the period attributable to:			
Common shareholders[2]		1,637	(1,351)
Non-controlling interests	31	23	14

[1]The related tax benefit was $7 million and $177 million for the years ended December 31, 2009 and 2008, respectively.

[2]On September 10, 2009, all Thomson Reuters PLC ordinary shares were exchanged for an equivalent number of Thomson Reuters Corporation common shares in connection with unification of the dual listed company structure.

The related notes form an integral part of these consolidated financial statements.
Source: Thomson Reuters Annual Report 2009.

Exhibit **6.8**

Thomson Reuters Consolidated Statement of Changes in Equity

THOMSON REUTERS CORPORATION
Consolidated Statement of Changes in Equity

(millions of U.S. dollars)	Stated share capital[1]	Contributed surplus	Total capital	Retained earnings	Unrecognized gain (loss) on cash flow hedges	Foreign currency translation adjustments	Total accumulated other comprehensive (loss) income ("AOCI")	Non-controlling interests	Total
Balance, December 31, 2008	3,050	6,984	10,034	10,650	21	(2,289)	(2,268)	72	18,488
Comprehensive income (loss)[2]	–	–	–	840	(54)	851	797	23	1,660
Distributions to non-controlling interest	–	–	–	–	–	–	–	(27)	(27)
DLC unification[1]	6,828	(6,828)	–	–	–	–	–	–	–
Dividends declared on preference shares	–	–	–	(2)	–	–	–	–	(2)
Dividends declared on common shares[1]	–	–	–	(927)	–	–	–	–	(927)
Shares issued under Dividend Reinvestment Plan ("DRIP")	22	–	22	–	–	–	–	–	22
Effect of stock compensation plans	57	64	121	–	–	–	–	–	121
Balance, December 31, 2009	9,957	220	10,177	10,561	(33)	(1,438)	(1,471)	68	19,335

[1]On September 10, 2009 all Thomas Reuters PLC ordinary shares were exchanged for an equivalent number of Thomson Reuters Corporation common shares in connection with unification of the dual listed company structure. Following unification, stated share capital includes common and preference share capital.

[2]Retained earnings for the year ended December 31, 2009 includes actuarial losses of $4 million, net of tax.

[3]Retained earnings for the year ended December 31, 2008 includes actuarial losses of $389 million, net of tax.

The related notes form an integral part of these consolidated financial statements.
Source: Thomson Reuters Annual Report 2009.

Exhibit **6.9**

Statement of Cash Flows of the
Thomson Reuters Corporation

REAL WORLD EXCERPT

Thomson Reuters Corporation

ANNUAL REPORT

THOMSON REUTERS CORPORATION
Consolidated Statement of Cash Flows

(million of U.S. dollars)	Notes	Year ended December 31 2009	Year ended December 31 2008
Cash provided by (used in):			
Operating Activities			
Net earnings		**867**	1,321
Adjustments for:			
Depreciation		**509**	414
Amortization of computer software		**548**	482
Amortization of other intangible assets		**499**	425
Impairment of assets held for sale	6	**—**	86
Deferred tax	24	**(544)**	31
Embedded derivatives fair value adjustments	20	**147**	(124)
Net losses (gains) on foreign exchange and derivative financial instruments		**182**	(257)
Other non-operating charge	9	**385**	—
Other	28	**290**	104
Changes in working capital and other items	28	**(219)**	299
Operating cash flows from continuing operations		**2,664**	2,781
Operating cash flows from discontinued operations	11	**2**	(20)
Net cash provided by operating activities		**2,666**	2,761
Investing Activities			
Acquisitions, less cash acquired	29	**(349)**	(8,502)
Proceeds from other disposals, net of taxes paid		**56**	244
Capital expenditures, less proceeds from disposals		**(1,097)**	(939)
Other investing activities		**3**	7
Investing cash flows from continuing operations		**(1,387)**	(9,190)
Investing cash flows from discontinued operations	11	**22**	(72)
Net cash used in investing activities		**(1,365)**	(9,262)
Financing Activities			
Proceeds from debt	20	**1,107**	7,600
Repayments of debt	20	**(1,249)**	(5,487)
Net borrowings (repayments) under short-term loan facilities		**4**	(1,065)
Share repurchases	25	**—**	(522)
Dividends paid on preference shares		**(2)**	(5)
Dividends paid on common shares[1]	25	**(905)**	(596)
Dividends payable assumed from Reuters Group PLC	25	**—**	(246)
Other financing activities		**(6)**	207
Net cash used in financing activities		**(1,051)**	(114)
Translation adjustments on cash and cash equivalents		**20**	(41)
Increase (decrease) in cash and cash equivalents		**270**	(6,656)
Cash and cash equivalents at beginning of period		**841**	7,497
Cash and cash equivalents at end of period		**1,111**	841
Supplemental cash flow information is provided in note 28			
Interest paid		**(425)**	(297)
Interest received		**8**	165
Income taxes paid		**(200)**	(299)

[1]On September 10, 2009, all Thomson Reuters PLC ordinary shares were exchanged for an equivalent number of Thomson Reuters Corporation common shares in connection with unification of the dual listed company structure.

Amounts paid and received for interest were reflected as operating cash flows in the consolidated statement of cash flows. Interest paid is net of debt related hedges.
Amounts paid for income taxes were reflected as either operating cash flows or investing cash flows in the consolidated statement of cash flows depending upon the nature of the underlying transaction.
The related notes form an integral part of these consolidated financial statements.
Source: Thomson Reuters Annual Report 2009.

Statement of Cash Flows

Lastly, Thomson Reuters's statement of cash flows shows the sources and uses of cash that resulted from its operating, investing, and financing activities during the years ended December 31, 2008 and 2009. Such a classification of the cash flows is important, especially those resulting from operating activities. Companies cannot survive for a long time without generating positive cash flows from their operations.

The cash flows from operating activities can be reported by using either the **direct** or **indirect** method, as illustrated in Chapter 5. For Thomson Reuters, the first section is reported by using the indirect method, which presents a reconciliation of profit (net earnings) on an accrual basis to cash flows from operations.

 **FOCUS ON CASH FLOWS**

OPERATING ACTIVITIES (INDIRECT METHOD)

The operating activities section prepared by using the indirect method helps the analyst understand the **causes of differences** between a company's profit and cash flows. Profit and cash flows from operating activities can be quite different. Remember that the income statement is prepared under the accrual concept. Revenues are recorded when earned, without regard to when the related cash flow occurs. Likewise, expenses are recorded when incurred in the same period, without regard to when the related cash flows occur.

In the indirect method, the operating activities section starts with profit computed under the accrual concept and then eliminates non-cash items, leaving cash flows from operating activities:

$$\begin{array}{r} \text{Profit} \\ +/- \text{ Adjustment for non-cash items} \\ \hline = \text{Cash provided by operating activities} \end{array}$$

The items listed between profit and cash flow from operations identify the sources of the difference. For example, since no cash is paid during the current period for Thomson Reuters's depreciation expense of $509, this amount is added back to profit (net earnings) in the conversion process. Similarly, increases and decreases in certain current assets and liabilities (also known as non-cash elements of working capital) also account for some of the difference between profit and cash flow from operations. As we cover different portions of the income statement and the statement of financial position in more detail in Chapters 7 to 12, we will also review the relevant sections of the statement of cash flows that are covered in Chapter 5.

Notes to Financial Statements

While the amounts reported on the various financial statements provide important information, users require additional details to facilitate their analysis. Standards-setting organizations, such as the Accounting Standard Board of Canada, and securities commissions, such as the Ontario Securities Commission, require public companies to provide a minimum set of detailed information to assist the users of financial statements in making informed investment and credit decisions. In addition, companies may provide other information voluntarily if management believes that such information will reflect positively on the company. In general, management refrains from disclosing information that may have a negative effect on the company's future profitability and financial condition—hence the need for a minimum set of disclosures that are typically provided in notes to financial statements. Thomson Reuters included 34 notes to its financial statements for the year 2009, covering both mandatory and voluntary disclosures.

Notes to financial statements include three types of information:

1. Description of the key accounting policies (rules) applied to the company's statements.

2. Additional details supporting reported amounts in the financial statements.

3. Relevant financial information not disclosed in the statements.

Excerpts from Thomson Reuters's notes are illustrated below, along with our discussion of selected elements of the company's financial statements.

Accounting Policies Applied in the Company's Statements   The first or second note is typically a summary of significant accounting policies. As you will see in your study of subsequent chapters, IFRS permit companies to select from alternative methods for measuring the effects of transactions. The summary of significant accounting policies tells the user which accounting methods the company has adopted. For example, Thomson Reuters's accounting policy for computer hardware and other property is as follows:

NOTES TO CONSOLIDATED FINANCIAL STATEMENTS

Note 1: Summary of Business and Significant Accounting Policies

Computer hardware and other property
Computer hardware and other property are recorded at cost and depreciated on a straight-line basis over their estimated useful lives as follows:

Computer hardware	3–5 years
Buildings and building improvements	5–40 years
Furniture, fixtures and equipment	3–10 years

Residual values and useful lives are reviewed at the end of each reporting period and adjusted if appropriate.

Without an understanding of the various accounting methods used, it is impossible to analyze a company's financial results effectively.

ALTERNATIVE ACCOUNTING METHODS AND IFRS

FINANCIAL ANALYSIS

Many people mistakenly believe that IFRS permit only one accounting method to be used to compute each value in the financial statements (e.g., inventories). Actually, IFRS often allow selection of an accounting method from a menu of acceptable methods. This permits a company to choose the methods that most closely reflect its particular economic circumstances. This flexibility complicates the financial statement users' task. Users must understand how the company's choice of accounting methods affects its financial statement presentations.

For example, before analyzing two companies' statements prepared by using different accounting methods, one company's statements must be converted to the other's methods to make them comparable. Otherwise, the reader is in a situation similar to comparing distances in kilometres and miles without conversion to a common scale. In Chapters 8 and 9, we discuss alternative accounting methods and their effects on financial statements.

Additional Detail Supporting Reported Amounts   The second category of notes provides supplemental information concerning the data shown in the financial statements. Among other information, these notes may show revenues broken down by geographic region of business segments, describe unusual transactions, or offer expanded detail on a specific classification. For example, in Note 5 on the next page, Thomson Reuters indicates the make-up of its operating expenses for 2009. It lists the different types of expenses that make up the total amount of operating expenses reported on the income statement. Details indicate that staff costs and expenses related to professional fees, consulting service and contractors, among others, make up about 75 percent of the operating expenses.

REAL WORLD EXCERPT

Thomson Reuters Corporation

ANNUAL REPORT

NOTES TO CONSOLIDATED FINANCIAL STATEMENTS

Note 5: Operating Expenses

The components of operating expenses include the following

	Year ended December 31	
	2009	**2008**
Salaries, commission and allowances	**4,668**	4,252
Share-based payments	**105**	80
Post-employment benefits	**209**	163
Total staff costs	**4,982**	4,495
Goods and services[1]	**2,567**	2,481
Data	**1,047**	985
Telecommunications	**634**	455
Real estate	**475**	403
Fair value adjustments[2]	**170**	(119)
Total operating expenses	**9,875**	8,700

[1]Goods and services include professional fees, consulting services, contractors, technology-related expenses, selling and marketing, and other general and administrative costs.
[2]Fair value adjustments primarily represent the impact from embedded derivatives.

Source: Thomson Reuters Annual Report 2009.

Relevant Financial Information Not Disclosed on the Statements The final category of notes includes information that impacts the company financially but is not shown on the financial statements. Examples include information on legal matters and any material event that occurred subsequent to year-end but before the financial statements are published. In Note 30, Thomson Reuters disclosed information related to lawsuits and legal claims.

REAL WORLD EXCERPT

Thomson Reuters Corporation

ANNUAL REPORT

NOTES TO CONSOLIDATED FINANCIAL STATEMENTS

Note 30: Contingencies, Commitments and Guarantees

Lawsuits and legal claims

In November 2009, the European Commission initiated an investigation relating to the use of the Company's Reuters Instrument Codes ("RIC symbols"), which is at a preliminary stage. RIC symbols help financial professionals retrieve news and information on financial instruments (such as prices and other data on stocks, bonds, currencies and commodities). The Company has responded to the Commission's questionnaire and is fully cooperating with the investigation. The Company does not believe that it has engaged in any anti-competitive activity related to RICs.

In February 2008, a purported class action complaint alleging violations of U.S. federal antitrust laws was filed in the United States District Court for the Central District of California against West Publishing Corporation, d/b/a BAR/BRI and Kaplan Inc.

In April 2008, this case was dismissed with prejudice. The plaintiffs have appealed this dismissal.

In addition to the matters described above, the Company is engaged in various legal proceedings and claims that have arisen in the ordinary course of business. The outcome of all of the proceedings and claims against the Company, including those described above, is subject to future resolution, including the uncertainties of litigation. Based on information currently known to the Company and after consultation with outside legal counsel, management believes that the probable ultimate resolution of any such proceedings and claims, individually or in the aggregate, will not have a material adverse effect on the financial condition of the Company, taken as a whole.

Source: Thomson Reuters Annual Report 2009.

Voluntary Disclosures

IFRS and securities regulations set only a minimum level of required financial disclosures. Many companies, including Thomson Reuters, provide important disclosures beyond those required. Such voluntary disclosures may appear in the annual report, in documents filed with securities commissions, in press releases, or on the company's website.

ACCOUNTING AND SUSTAINABLE DEVELOPMENT

A QUESTION OF ACCOUNTABILITY

REAL WORLD EXCERPT

CFO Magazine

A growing area of voluntary disclosures in North America is sustainability reporting as described by *CFO Magazine*:

> The idea that a company should conduct its business in ways that benefit not just shareholders but the environment and society, too, is called sustainability, or sustainable development. It's an idea championed by a small but growing number of companies around the globe. One business group, the World Business Council for Sustainable Development, lists some 170 international members, including more than 30 Fortune 500 companies. According to the council's website, these companies share the belief that "the pursuit of sustainable development is good for business and business is good for sustainable development."
>
> To tell stakeholders about that pursuit, companies are issuing sustainability reports. Many, like Suncor, are doing so following the strict guidelines of the Global Reporting Initiative (GRI), an independent institution founded in 1997, to develop a common framework for sustainability reporting. Enter the words "sustainability reporting" into your favorite search engine and you'll find such well-known company names as Alcoa, Alcan, Bristol-Myers Squibb, General Motors, Baxter International and FedEx Kinko's. In all, some 500 organizations publish sustainability reports according to GRI guidelines. Some countries, such as France, South Africa, and the Netherlands, now mandate environmental or social sustainability reporting as a condition to being listed on their stock exchanges.

Such reports are voluntary disclosures in Canada. However, many believe that managing a company in the interests of a wider group of stakeholders and reporting on these efforts is an ethical imperative.

Source: CFO Magazine, November 2004, pp. 97–100.

ACCOUNTING STANDARDS
FOR PRIVATE ENTERPRISES

Accounting standard setting is a long process of consultation among the users, the preparers, and the standard-setting boards. The Accounting Standards Board of Canada, after careful consideration of the information provided by preparers and users, decided to proceed with a set of accounting standards for private enterprises that are simpler than the IFRS applicable to publicly accountable enterprises.

While IFRS and the accounting standards for private enterprises are based on the same conceptual framework, the main differences relate to the extent of disclosures required for the two types on enterprises. For private enterprises, shareholders have access to the entity's financial information; hence, the disclosures are intended primarily for the other user groups. In contrast, shareholders of publicly accountable enterprises do not generally have direct access to the entity's financial information, which require disclosure of the necessary information that would assist financial statement users to make informed decisions.

DEMONSTRATION **CASE**

Canadian Tire Corporation is an interrelated network of businesses across Canada that sell home, car, sports, and leisure products, as well as work clothes and casual attire. In addition, Canadian Tire is the country's largest independent gasoline retailer through its Canadian Tire Petroleum subsidiary, which sells fuel and related products at many outlets in most provinces. Canadian Tire's financial statements for the years 2008 and 2009 are shown below.

CANADIAN TIRE CORPORATION
Consolidated Statements of Financial Position

As at (Dollars in millions)	January 2, 2010	January 3, 2009
Assets		
Current assets		
Cash and cash equivalents (Note 15)	$ 786.0	$ 429.0
Short-term investments (Note 15)	64.0	—
Trade receivables	835.9	824.1
Loans receivable (Note 2)	2,274.8	1,683.4
Merchandise inventories (Note 3)	933.6	917.5
Income taxes recoverable	94.7	64.6
Prepaid expenses and deposits	40.7	40.2
Future income taxes (Note 14)	82.8	20.2
Total current assets	5,112.5	3,979.0
Long-term receivables and other assets (Note 4)	110.6	262.1
Other long-term investments, net	48.8	25.2
Goodwill (Note 5)	71.8	70.7
Intangible assets (Note 6)	265.4	247.9
Property and equipment, net (Note 7)	3,180.4	3,198.9
Total assets	$ 8,789.5	$ 7,783.8
Liabilities		
Current liabilities		
Deposits (Note 8)	$ 863.4	$ 540.7
Trade payables and other	1,391.4	1,444.2
Current portion of long-term debt (Note 9)	309.3	14.8
Total current liabilities	2,564.1	1,999.7
Long-term debt (Note 9)	1,101.9	1,373.5
Future income taxes (Note 14)	49.8	44.7

(continued)

Long-term deposits (Note 8)	1,196.9	598.7
Other non-current liabilities (Note 10)	188.9	202.2
Total liabilities	5,101.6	4,218.8
Shareholders' Equity		
Share capital (Note 12)	720.4	715.4
Contributed surplus	0.2	—
Accumulated other comprehensive income (loss)	(46.4)	97.2
Retained earnings	3,013.7	2,752.4
Total shareholders' equity	3,687.9	3,565.0
Total liabilities and shareholders' equity	$ 8,789.5	$ 7,783.8

(Signed)   (Signed)

Maureen J. Sabia   **Graham W. Savage**

Director   Director

Consolidated Statements of Earnings

For the years ended (Dollars in millions except per share amounts)	January 2, 2010	January 3, 2009
Gross operating revenue	$ 8,686.5	$ 9,121.3
Operating expenses		
Cost of merchandise sold and all other operating expenses except for the undernoted items (Note 3)	7,788.5	8,200.5
Interest		
Long-term debt	130.0	117.9
Short-term debt	17.0	4.7
Depreciation and amortization	247.5	226.2
Employee profit sharing plan (Note 13)	24.7	29.0
Total operating expenses	8,207.7	8,578.3
Earnings before income taxes	479.2	543.0
Income taxes (Note 14)		
Current	135.2	209.1
Future	9.0	(41.5)
Total income taxes	144.2	167.6
Net earnings	$ 335.0	$ 375.4
Basic and diluted earnings per share	$ 4.10	$ 4.60
Weighted average number of Common and Class A Non-voting shares outstanding (Note 12)	81,678,775	81,517,702

Consolidated Statements of Cash Flows

For the years ended (Dollars in millions)	January 2, 2010	January 3, 2009
Cash generated from (used for):		
Operating activities		
Net earnings	$ 335.0	$ 375.4
Items not affecting cash		
Depreciation	193.7	168.6
Net provision for loans receivable (Note 2)	181.2	87.3
Amortization of intangible assets	53.8	57.6
Future income taxes	9.0	(41.5)

(continued)

Employee future benefits expense (Note 11)	**6.0**	6.4
Other	**4.0**	7.9
Impairments on property and equipment (Note 7)	**1.9**	2.5
Loss on disposal of mortgage portfolio	**0.6**	—
Impairment of other long-term investments	**1.1**	2.0
Gain on disposals of property and equipment	**(1.6)**	(7.8)
Changes in fair value of derivative instruments	**(11.4)**	55.6
Gain on sales of loans receivable (Note 2)	**(39.2)**	(73.7)
Securitization loans receivable	**(39.4)**	(51.9)
	694.7	588.4
Changes in other working capital components (Note 15)	**(275.9)**	(406.9)
Cash generated from operating activities	**418.8**	181.5
Investing activities		
Net securitization of loans receivable	**(532.3)**	(31.7)
Additions to property and equipment	**(220.0)**	(359.5)
Investment in loans receivable, net	**(208.5)**	(140.5)
Purchases of stores	**(6.1)**	(36.5)
Additions to intangible assets	**(67.8)**	(76.5)
Other long-term investments	**(50.7)**	(19.6)
Short-term investments	**(38.0)**	—
Other	**(7.7)**	(3.6)
Long-term receivables and other assets	**(3.1)**	(27.2)
Proceeds on disposition of property and equipment	**27.8**	239.5
Proceeds on disposal of mortgage portfolio (Note 2)	**162.2**	—
Cash used for investing activities	**(944.2)**	(455.6)
Financing activities		
Net change in deposits	**917.3**	1,024.1
Issuance of long-term debt (Note 9)	**200.1**	0.2
Class A Non-Voting Share transactions (Note 12)	**(0.9)**	7.0
Repayment of long-term debt (Note 9)	**(165.4)**	(156.3)
Dividends	**(68.7)**	(66.4)
Cash generated from (used for) financing activities	**882.4**	808.6
Cash generated in the year	**357.0**	534.5
Cash and cash equivalents, beginning of year	**429.0**	(105.5)
Cash and cash equivalents, end of the year (Note 15)	**$ 786.0**	$ 429.0

Required:

1. Examine Canadian Tire's statements of financial position. Identify the six largest changes in the carrying amount of assets, liabilities, and shareholders' equity between the statement dates. Based on what you have learned so far, what type of transactions could have caused the changes in the carrying amount of these items?

2. Access Note 7 to the financial statements from the company's website (www.canadiantire.ca), and identify the specific changes to the property and equipment account.

3. Compute the following ratios for fiscal years 2008 and 2009: debt-to-equity, total asset turnover, return on assets, return on equity, and net profit margin. Use the results of your computations to comment on the company's financial situation and profitability of its operations in both years. Canadian Tire's total assets and shareholders' equity at the beginning of fiscal year 2008 amounted to $7,788.1 million and $3,568.1 million, respectively.

4. Canadian Tire's operations generated significant amounts of cash during both the fiscal years 2008 and 2009. The company also made significant investments in long-term assets in fiscal year 2009. How did the company finance the investment in these assets?

5. Compute and interpret the quality of earnings ratio and the capital acquisitions ratio for both fiscal years 2008 and 2009.

6. Access fpinfomart.ca through your university's library and search for Canadian Tire Corporation under "Company snapshots." Click on FP Investor Reports under the heading FP INVESTOR COVERAGE and then choose *I/B/E/S* Forecasts. What is the consensus analysts' estimate of Canadian Tire's earnings per share (EPS) for the next two fiscal years? Do analysts expect Canadian Tire's EPS to increase or decrease in the future? What information did the analysts take into consideration in computing their EPS estimates for the next two years?

SUGGESTED **SOLUTION**

1. The six statements of financial position items that had the largest changes in their carrying amounts on the statements of financial position, and the typical reasons for these changes are summarized below (amounts in $ millions):

Statement of Financial Position Item	Change	Typical Reasons for Change
Cash and cash equivalents	$357.0	Increase in investments in highly liquid assets such as certificates of deposit and commercial paper.
Loans receivable	591.4	Increase in the amount of loans to customers, net of collections.
Deposits (both long term and short term)	920.9	Increase in deposits made by customers for future delivery of merchandise and service.
Current portion of long-term debt	294.5	Increase in the long-term borrowings that are payable within a year.
Long-term debt	−271.6	Decrease in the long-term borrowings; a portion has been reclassified as current portion of long-term debt.
Retained earnings	261.3	Profit for the year minus dividends declared during the year.

2. Note 7 to the financial statements shows that Canadian Tire's property and equipment includes land, buildings, fixtures and equipment, leasehold improvements, computer software, assets under capital lease, and construction in progress. The cost of these assets increased by $110.9 million during 2009. At the same time, accumulated depreciation and amortization of the buildings, fixtures and equipment, leasehold improvements, computer software, and assets under capital lease increased by $129.4 million during the year, which reduced the carrying amounts of these assets.

3.

Ratio	2009	2008
Debt to equity = Total liabilities ÷ Total shareholders' equity	1.38	1.18
Total asset turnover = Net sales ÷ Average total assets	1.05	1.17
Return on assets = $\dfrac{\text{Profit + Interest expense, net of tax}}{\text{Average total assets}}$	5.3%	5.9%
Return on equity = Profit ÷ Average shareholders' equity	9.2%	10.5%
Net profit margin = Profit ÷ Net sales	3.9%	4.1%

Computations:

2009
D/E = $5,101.6 ÷ $3,687.9 = 1.38
TAT/O = $8,686.5 ÷ [($7,783.8 + $8,789.5)/2] = 1.05
ROA = [$335.0 + 147.0 × (1 − 0.30*)] ÷ [($7,783.8 + $8,789.5)/2] = 0.053
ROE = $335.0 ÷ [($3,565.0 + 3,687.9)/2] = 0.092
NPM = $335.0 ÷ $8,686.5 = 0.039

*Tax rate = $144.2 / $479.2 = 0.30

2008
D/E = $4,218.8 ÷ $3,565.0 = 1.18
TAT/O = $9,121.3 ÷ [($7,788.1 + $7,783.8)/2] = 1.17
ROA = [$375.4 + 122.6 × (1 − 0.31**)] ÷ [($7,788.1 + $7,783.8)/2] = 0.059
ROE = $375.4 ÷ [($3,568.1 + $3,565.0)/2] = 0.105
NPM = $375.4 ÷ $9,121.3 = 0.041

**Tax rate = $167.6 / $543.0 = 0.31

The debt-to-equity ratio increased from 1.18 to 1.38, suggesting a relative increase in liabilities and an increase in the company's financial risk. The total asset turnover ratio decreased by 10 percent, suggesting deterioration in the utilization of the company's assets to generate revenue. The three profitability ratios—return on assets, return on equity, and net profit margin—decreased as well because of the lower asset turnover and the increase in interest expense that reduced the profit for 2009. This suggests that management needs to improve on its use of the company's resources to generate higher profit in the future.

4. Canadian Tire's statement of cash flows shows that the company used a net amount of $944.2 on investing activities during 2009. This amount was partially financed by $418.8 of cash generated from operations, and the rest was financed by deposits received from customers.

5. Quality of earnings ratio = Cash flow from operating activities ÷ Profit

    2008: $181.5 ÷ $375.4 = 0.48

    2009: $418.8 ÷ $335.0 = 1.25

The ratios indicate that the quality of the company's earnings was not good in 2008, but it improved significantly in 2009. The quality of earnings for previous years should also be examined to determine if the low ratio in 2008 is an unusual occurrence.

$$\text{Capital Acquisitions Ratio} = \frac{\text{Cash Flow from Operating Activities}}{\text{Cash Paid for Property and Equipment}}$$

    2008: $181.5 ÷ $359.5 = 0.50

    2009: $418.8 ÷ $220.0 = 1.90

In 2008, the company did not generate enough cash from its operations to cover the payments needed for the additional investments in property and equipment, but the situation changed in 2009 as the company generated more cash from operations and reduced the amount of its investments in property and equipment.

6. The average analyst's estimate of Canadian Tire's EPS for fiscal year 2010 is $4.69 and $5.61 for fiscal year 2011, at the time of writing this text. These average EPS estimates are based on individual estimates of 11 analysts.

    Canadian Tire's basic EPS for fiscal year 2009 is $4.10, as disclosed in its income statement. Analysts expect the company to improve on its performance in the next two years.

    Analysts use a variety of information sources to arrive at their EPS estimates. First, they need to develop a very good understanding of the industry and Canadian Tire's role in it. Their information sources would include examination of the company's financial statements, analysis of population trends and expectations of future demand for the company's products, analysis of the company's strategies and future plans, conversations with company executives, and information about the company's competitors.

Appendix 6A: Canadian Capital Markets (online)

CHAPTER TAKE-AWAYS

1. **Recognize the people involved in the accounting communication process (regulators, managers, board of directors, auditors, information intermediaries, and users), their roles in the process, and the guidance they receive from legal and professional standards. p. 294**
   Management of the reporting company must decide on the appropriate format (categories) and level of detail to present in its financial reports. Independent audits increase the credibility of the information. Financial statement announcements from public companies usually are first transmitted to users through electronic information services. The securities commission staff reviews public reports for compliance with legal and professional standards, investigates irregularities, and punishes violators. Analysts play a major role in making financial statements and other information available to average investors through their stock recommendations and earnings forecasts.

2. **Identify the steps in the accounting communication process, including the issuance of press releases, annual reports, quarterly reports, and documents filed with securities commissions, as well as the guiding principles in communicating useful information. p. 300**
   Earnings are first made public in press releases. Companies follow these announcements with annual and quarterly reports containing statements, notes, and additional information. Public companies must also file additional reports with the securities commissions (e.g., OSC, SEC), which contain more details about the company.

3. **Recognize and apply the different financial statement and disclosure formats used by companies in practice. p. 307**

Most statements are classified and include subtotals that are relevant to analysis. On the statement of financial position, the most important distinctions are between current and non-current assets and liabilities. On the income statement and statement of cash flows, the separation of operating and non-operating items is most important. The notes to the statements provide descriptions of the accounting rules applied and more information about items disclosed in the statements, as well as information about economic events not disclosed in the statements.

In Chapter 7 we begin our in-depth discussion of financial statements. We will begin with two of the most liquid assets, cash and trade receivables, and transactions that involve revenues and certain selling expenses. Accuracy in revenue recognition and the related recognition of cost of sales (discussed in Chapter 8) are the most important determinants of the accuracy—and, thus, the usefulness—of financial statement presentations. We will also introduce concepts related to the management and control of cash and receivables, which is a critical business function. A detailed understanding of these topics is crucial to future managers, accountants, and financial analysts.

FINDING **FINANCIAL INFORMATION**

STATEMENT OF FINANCIAL POSITION
Key Classifications
Current and non-current assets and liabilities
Contributed capital and retained earnings

INCOME STATEMENT
Key Subtotals
Gross profit
Profit from operations
Profit
Earnings per share

STATEMENT OF CASH FLOWS
Under Operating Activities (indirect method)
Profit
± Items not affecting cash
= Cash provided by operating activities

NOTES
Key Classifications
Descriptions of accounting rules applied in the statements
Additional detail supporting reported numbers
Relevant financial information not disclosed on the statements

KEY **TERMS**

Board of Directors p. 295
Comparability p. 304
Corporate Governance p. 292
Cost Constraint p. 305
Earnings Forecasts p. 297
Faithful Representation p. 304
Institutional Investors p. 299
Lenders (Creditors) p. 299
Material Amounts p. 304

Press Release p. 300
Private Investors p. 299
Prudence p. 306
Relevant Information p. 304
Timely p. 305
Understandability p. 305
Unqualified (Clean) Audit Opinion p. 296
Verifiable p. 304

QUESTIONS

1. Describe the roles and responsibilities of management, the board of directors, and independent auditors in the financial reporting process.
2. Define the following three users of financial accounting disclosures and the relationships among them: *financial analysts, private investors,* and *institutional investors.*
3. Briefly describe the role of information services in the communication of financial information.
4. Explain why information must be relevant and representationally faithful to be useful.
5. Identify the constraints of accounting measurement and their role in the reporting of accounting information.

6. What basis of accounting (accrual or cash) does IFRS require on the (a) income statement, (b) statement of financial position, and (c) statement of cash flows?

7. Briefly explain the normal sequence and form of financial reports produced by private companies in a typical year.

8. Briefly explain the normal sequence and form of financial reports produced by public companies in a typical year.

9. What are the major subtotals on the income statement, and what purpose do they serve?

10. List the six major classifications reported on a statement of financial position.

11. What are the three major classifications on a statement of cash flows?

12. What are the three major categories of notes or footnotes presented in annual reports? Cite an example of each.

EXERCISES

LO2

E6–1   Finding Financial Information: Matching Information Items to Financial Reports

Following are information items included in various financial reports. Match each information item with the report(s) where it would most likely be found by entering the appropriate letter(s) in the space provided.

Information Item	Report
_____ (1) Summarized financial data for 5- or 10-year period.	A. Annual report
_____ (2) Initial announcement of quarterly earnings.	B. Annual information form
_____ (3) Complete quarterly income statement, statement of financial position, and statement of cash flows.	C. Press release
_____ (4) Basic financial statements for the year.	D. Quarterly report
_____ (5) Detailed discussion of the company's competition.	E. None of the above
_____ (6) Notes to financial statements.	
_____ (7) Identification of those responsible for the financial statements.	
_____ (8) Initial announcement of hiring of new vice-president of sales.	

LO2

The Forzani Group

E6–2   Understanding the Disclosure Process through The Forzani Group Ltd. Website

Using your Web browser, visit The Forzani Group at **www.forzanigroup.com**. Examine the most recent quarterly earnings press release and the related interim report.

Required:
Based on the information provided on the site, answer the following questions:

1. What were the release dates of the quarterly earnings press release and the interim report?

2. What additional information was provided in the interim report that was not reported in the earnings press release?

LO2, 3

Canadian Tire
Corporation

E6–3   Researching Information Provided on Company Websites

Using your Web browser, visit Canadian Tire Corporation at **www.canadiantire.com**.

Required:
Based on the information provided on the site, answer the following questions:

1. Which document(s) provided the most recent information on quarterly earnings?

2. For the most recent quarter, what was the change in sales revenue compared with the same quarter one year earlier? What was management's explanation for the change (if any)?

3. What was the annual earnings per share, stock price per share, and price-to-earnings ratio (see Chapter 1) on the day of the most recent fourth-quarter earnings press release?

LO1

E6–4   Understanding Earnings per Share and Stock Prices

The following news story appeared in **Finance.yahoo.com** on February 2, 2010, after Suncor Energy Inc. released its results of operations for the fourth quarter of fiscal year 2009.

REAL WORLD EXCERPT

Finance.yahoo. com

Suncor quarterly earnings fall below expectations

Tue Feb 2, 9:21 AM

TORONTO (Reuters) - Suncor Energy Inc, Canada's largest energy company, reported fourth-quarter earnings below Wall Street expectations on Tuesday, due to weaker than expected results from its natural gas unit and its international operations.

Suncor, which bulked up last year with its C$22.7 billion ($21.4 billion) purchase of Petro-Canada, posted net income of C$457 million, or 29 Canadian cents per share, compared with a year-earlier loss of C$215 million, or 24 Canadian cents a share.

Earnings before special items were 21 Canadian cents per share. On that basis, analysts were expecting 41 Canadian cents, according to Thomson Reuters I/B/E/S.

In a note to clients, UBS analyst Andrew Potter attributed the earnings miss in part to operating costs, capital expenditures and royalties that were higher than forecast.

Shares of the Suncor were down 2 cents at $32.71 in trading before the morning bell on the New York Stock Exchange.

Source: ca.news.finance.yahoo.com. Accessed February 3, 2010.

Required:

The earnings of Suncor Energy Inc. increased from a loss of 0.24 cents per share to a profit of 0.29 cents per share, but its share price dropped by 0.02 cents. Explain why the price per share decreased even though the company announced an increase in its earnings per share.

E6–5 **Understanding Earnings per Share and Share Prices**   ▊ **LO1**

Reuters reported the following news story on July 17, 2008, after Nexen Inc. released its results of operations for the second quarter of 2008.

REAL WORLD EXCERPT

Reuters

UPDATE 4—Nexen profit inches up, shares plunge

Thu Jul 17, 2008 4:57pm EDT

By Scott Haggett

(Reuters) - Nexen Inc. (NXY.TO)'s quarterly profit rose a disappointing 3.3 percent as its one-time charges and trading losses nearly wiped out the benefits of record oil prices, the Canadian oil company said on Thursday, sending its shares down 11 percent.

...

Canada's No. 4 independent oil explorer and producer said its second-quarter oil production was nearly unchanged from the year-earlier quarter, to 254,000 barrels of oil equivalent a day before royalties. That reflected a two-day strike at a Scottish refinery that shut down a pipeline serving its massive Buzzard oil field in the North Sea.

...

Net income rose a scant 3.3 percent to C$380 million, or 70 Canadian cents a share, in the quarter, from C$368 million, or 68 Canadian cents, for the same period last year. Revenue rose 48 percent to C$2.07 billion.

...

The company also recorded a C$240 million after-tax charge for stock-based compensation, while poor trading results at its marketing arm cut cash flow by C$164 million as bets on natural gas price disparities went awry. "We were a little surprised," said Chris Feltin, an analyst

(continued)

at Tristone Capital. "We were caught offside by the larger-than-expected stock compensation charges and the marketing loss."

...

Without the charge, earnings per share would have come in at C$1.15, below analysts' average operating profit estimate of C$1.33 a share, according to Reuters Estimates.

...

Nexen shares fell C$4.01 or 11 percent, to C$32.95 on the after the release of its results. The shares have dropped 4.5 percent over the past 12 months. ($1=$1.01 Canadian) (Additional reporting by Scott Anderson; editing by Janet Guttsman)

Source: **www.reuters.com/article/idUSN1726055820080717.** Accessed February 4, 2010.

Required:

1. Identify the direction and amount of the change in earnings per share for the second quarter of 2008 compared with the same quarter of 2007.
2. Identify the direction and amount of the change in Nexen's share price after the release of the second-quarter results.
3. Explain why Nexen's share price changed in the opposite direction from the change in its earnings.

LO2   **E6–6**   **Guiding Principles for Communicating Useful Information**

Match each qualitative characteristic of useful accounting information with the related definition by entering the appropriate letter in the space provided.

Qualitative Characteristics	Definitions
_____ (1) Relevance	A. Application of the same accounting methods over time.
_____ (2) Timeliness	B. Agreement between what really happened and the disclosed information.
_____ (3) Predictive value	C. The information is available prior to the decision.
_____ (4) Confirmatory value	D. The accounting information does not favour a particular group.
_____ (5) Verifiability	E. The information helps reduce the uncertainty in the future.
_____ (6) Faithful representation	F. The information provides input to evaluate previous expectations.
_____ (7) Neutrality	G. The information allows the evaluation of one alternative against another alternative.
_____ (8) Comparability	H. The information has a bearing on a specific decision.
_____ (9) Consistency	I. The information can be depended upon.
	J. Implies that qualified persons working independently arrive at similar conclusions.

LO2   **E6–7**   **Assessing the Relevance and Faithful Representation of Information**

Paula Romanov is the credit manager of Pinnacle Inc. She is considering whether to extend credit to Mak Inc., a new customer. Pinnacle sells most of its goods on credit, but is very careful in extending credit to new customers. Tim Mak, the owner of Mak Inc., provided the following documents to Paula to assist her in her evaluation:

1. A detailed analysis of the sales revenue and profit that Mak Inc. expects to achieve within the next 12 months.
2. Projections of the company's sales during the next five years.
3. The company's monthly bank statements for the past three years.
4. A report of the company's credit history prepared by Mak's employees.
5. A letter signed by all four company officers indicating that they are prepared to personally guarantee the amount of credit that Pinnacle approves.
6. Brief resumés of the four company officers along with descriptions of the functions they perform in the company.
7. Eight letters of reference from close friends and relatives of the four company officers.

Required:

Analyze each of the items above with respect to the characteristics of relevance (predictive value and confirmatory value) and faithful representation (complete, neutral, and free from material error). Explain whether or not each item possesses these characteristics.

E6–8 **Finding Financial Information: Matching Financial Statements with the Elements of Financial Statements**

LO3

Match each financial statement with the items presented in it by entering the appropriate letter in the space provided.

Elements of Financial Statements	Financial Statements
_____ (1) Liabilities	A. Income statement
_____ (2) Cash from operating activities	B. Statement of financial position
_____ (3) Losses	C. Statement of cash flows
_____ (4) Assets	D. None of the above
_____ (5) Revenues	
_____ (6) Cash from financing activities	
_____ (7) Shareholders' equity	
_____ (8) Expenses	
_____ (9) Assets owned by a shareholder	

E6–9 **Ordering the Classifications on a Typical Statement of Financial Position**

LO3

A list of classifications on the statement of financial position is shown below. Number the classifications in the order in which they normally appear on a statement of financial position.

No.	Title
_____	Current liabilities
_____	Non-current liabilities
_____	Long-term investments
_____	Intangible assets
_____	Property, plant, and equipment
_____	Current assets
_____	Retained earnings
_____	Share capital
_____	Other non-current assets

E6–10 **Finding Financial Information as a Potential Investor**

LO3

You are considering investing the cash gifts you received for graduation in shares of various companies. You visit the websites of major companies, searching for relevant information.

Required:

For each of the following, indicate where you would locate the information in an annual report (*Hint:* The information may be in more than one location):

1. The detail on major classifications of non-current assets.
2. The accounting method(s) used for financial reporting purposes.
3. Whether the company has had any capital expenditures for the year.
4. Net amount of property, plant, and equipment.
5. Policies on amortizing intangibles.
6. Depreciation expense.
7. Any significant gains or losses on disposals of property, plant, and equipment.
8. Accumulated depreciation of property, plant, and equipment at the end of the last fiscal year.

E6–11 **Inferring Share Issuances and Cash Dividends from Changes in Shareholders' Equity**

LO3

Power Corporation recently reported the following December 31 balances in its shareholders' equity accounts (in millions):

Power Corporation

	Current Year	Prior Year
Share capital	$1,300	$ 1,269
Contributed surplus	103	78
Retained earnings	8,612	8,304
Accumulated other comprehensive income (loss)	(258)	386
Total shareholders' equity	$9,757	$10,037

During the current year, Power Corp. reported profit of $868 million. Assume that the only other transactions that affected share capital and retained earnings during the current year were the issuance of shares and the declaration and payment of cash dividends.

Required:
Recreate the two journal entries reflecting the issuance of shares and the declaration and payment of dividends.

PROBLEMS

LO1, 2   **P6–1**   **Matching Transactions with Concepts**

The concepts of accounting covered in Chapters 2 through 6 are shown below. Match each transaction with its related concept by entering the appropriate letter in the space provided. Use only one letter for each blank space.

Concepts	Transactions
Concepts	**Transactions**
_____ (1) Users of financial statements	A. Recorded a $1,000 sale of merchandise on credit.
_____ (2) Objective of financial statements	B. Counted (inventoried) the unsold items at the end of the period and valued them in dollars.
Qualitative Characteristics	C. Acquired a vehicle for use in operating the business.
_____ (3) Relevance	D. Reported the amount of depreciation expense because it likely will affect important decisions of statement users.
_____ (4) Verifiability	E. Identified as the investors, creditors, and others interested in the business.
_____ (5) Materiality	F. Used special accounting approaches because of the uniqueness of the industry.
Assumptions	G. Issued notes payable of $1 million.
_____ (6) Separate entity	H. Paid a contractor for an addition to the building with $10,000 cash and $20,000 market value of the company's shares ($30,000 was deemed to be the cash equivalent price).
_____ (7) Continuity	
_____ (8) Unit of measure	I. Engaged an outside independent accountant to audit the financial statements.
_____ (9) Periodicity	J. Sold merchandise and rendered services for cash and on credit during the year; then determined the cost of those goods sold and the cost of rendering those services.
Elements of Financial Statements	
_____ (10) Revenues	K. Established an accounting policy that sales revenue shall be recognized only when ownership of the goods sold passes to the customer.
_____ (11) Expenses	
_____ (12) Gains	L. To design and prepare the financial statements to assist the users in making decisions.
_____ (13) Losses	
_____ (14) Assets	M. Established a policy not to include in the financial statements the personal financial affairs of the owners of the business.
_____ (15) Liabilities	
_____ (16) Accounting equation	N. Sold an asset at a loss that was a peripheral or incidental transaction.
Principles and Related Concepts	O. The value to users of a special financial report exceeds the cost of preparing it.
_____ (17) Cost	P. Valued an asset, such as inventory, at lower than its purchase cost because its market value is lower.
_____ (18) Revenue recognition	
_____ (19) Matching	Q. Dated the income statement "For the Year Ended December 31, 2011."
_____ (20) Full disclosure	R. Used services from outsiders—paid cash for some and the remainder on credit.
Constraints of Accounting	S. Acquired an asset (a pencil sharpener that will have a useful life of five years) and recorded it as an expense when purchased for $2.99.
_____ (21) Cost	
_____ (22) Prudence	T. Disclosed in the financial statements all relevant financial information about the business; necessitated the use of notes to the financial statements.
_____ (23) Industry peculiarities	
	U. Sold an asset at a gain that was a peripheral or incidental transaction.
	V. Assets of $500,000 − Liabilities of $300,000 = Shareholders' equity of $200,000.
	W. Accounting and reporting assume a "going concern."

P6–2 Matching Definitions with Statement of Financial Position—Related Terms ▪ LO3

Selected terms related to the statement of financial position, which were discussed in Chapters 2 through 5, are listed below. Match each definition with its related term by entering the appropriate letter in the space provided.

Terms

_____ (1) Retained earnings

_____ (2) Current liabilities

_____ (3) Liquidity

_____ (4) Contra-asset account

_____ (5) Accumulated depreciation

_____ (6) Intangible assets

_____ (7) Other assets

_____ (8) Shares outstanding

_____ (9) Normal operating cycle

_____ (10) Carrying amount

_____ (11) Contributed surplus

_____ (12) Liabilities

_____ (13) Non-current assets

_____ (14) Shareholders' equity

_____ (15) Current assets

_____ (16) Assets

_____ (17) Non-current liabilities

Definitions

A. A miscellaneous category of assets.

B. Amount of contributed capital for which shares were not issued.

C. Total assets minus total liabilities.

D. Nearness of assets to cash (in time).

E. Assets expected to be collected in cash within one year or the operating cycle, if longer.

F. Same as book value; cost less accumulated depreciation to date.

G. Accumulated earnings minus accumulated dividends.

H. Asset offset account (subtracted from asset).

I. Balance of the common shares account divided by the issue price per share.

J. Assets that do not have physical substance.

K. Probable future economic benefits owned by the entity from past transactions.

L. Liabilities expected to be paid out of current assets, normally within the next year.

M. The average cash-to-cash time involved in the operations of the business.

N. Sum of the annual depreciation expense on an asset from the date of its acquisition to the current date.

O. All liabilities not classified as current liabilities.

P. Property, plant, and equipment.

Q. Debts or obligations from past transactions to be paid with assets or services.

R. None of the above.

P6–3 Preparing a Statement of Financial Position and Analyzing Some of Its Parts (AP6–1) ▪ LO3

Gold Jewellers Inc. is developing its annual financial statements for 2012. The following amounts were correct at December 31, 2012: cash, $58,000; trade receivables, $71,000; merchandise inventory, $154,000; prepaid insurance, $1,000; investment in shares of Z Corporation (long term), $36,000; store equipment, $67,000; used store equipment held for disposal, $9,000; accumulated depreciation, store equipment, $13,000; trade payables, $58,000; long-term note payable, $42,000; income taxes payable, $9,000; retained earnings, $164,000; and common shares, 100,000 shares outstanding (originally issued at $1.10 per share).

Required:

1. Based on these data, prepare the company's statement of financial position at December 31, 2012. Use the following major captions (list the individual items under these captions):

   a. Assets: current assets; long-term investments; property, plant, and equipment; and other assets.

   b. Liabilities: current liabilities and non-current liabilities.

   c. Shareholders' equity: share capital and retained earnings.

2. What is the carrying amount of store equipment? Explain what this value means.

LO2, 3

WestJet Airlines

P6–4

Using Financial Reports: Interpreting Financial Statement Information, Analyzing and Interpreting Ratios (AP6–2)

WestJet Airlines Ltd. was founded in 1996 by four Calgary entrepreneurs and has grown from serving western Canadian destinations to being Canada's largest coast-to-coast low-fare airline. WestJet's financial statements for 2009 and 2008 and excerpts from selected notes to its financial statements are shown below.

CONSOLIDATED STATEMENTS OF FINANCIAL POSITION
WestJet Airlines Ltd.
December 31, 2009 and 2008
(Stated in thousands of Canadian dollars)

	2009	2008
Assets		
Current assets:		
Cash and cash equivalents (Note 4)	$1,005,181	$ 820,214
Trade receivables	27,654	16,837
Future income tax (Note 9)	2,560	8,459
Prepaid expenses, deposits, and other [Note 14(a)]	56,239	53,283
Inventory	26,048	17,054
	1,117,682	915,847
Property and equipment (Note 5)	2,307,566	2,269,790
Intangible assets (Note 6)	14,087	12,060
Other assets [Note 12(a)]	54,367	71,005
	$3,493,702	$3,268,702
Liabilities and Shareholders' Equity		
Current liabilities:		
Trade payable and accrued liabilities	$ 231,401	$ 249,354
Advance ticket sales	286,361	251,354
Non-refundable guest credits	64,506	73,020
Current portion of long-term debt (Note 7)	171,223	165,721
Current portion of obligations under capital lease (Note 8)	744	395
	754,235	739,844
Long-term debt (Note 7)	1,048,554	1,186,182
Obligations under capital leases (Note 8)	3,358	713
Other liabilities [Note 14(a)]	19,628	24,233
Future income tax (Note 9)	278,999	241,740
	2,104,774	2,192,712
Shareholders' equity:		
Share capital [Note 10(b)]	633,075	452,885
Contributed surplus	71,503	60,193
Accumulated other comprehensive loss [Note 14(c)]	(14,852)	(38,112)
Retained earnings	699,202	601,024
	1,388,928	1,075,990
Commitments and contingencies (Note 10)		
	$3,493,702	$3,268,702

The accompanying notes are an integral part of the consolidated financial statements.

Source: WestJet Annual Report 2009.

On behalf of the Board:

[signature]   [signature]

Sean Durly, Director   **Hugh Bolton, Director**

CONSOLIDATED STATEMENTS OF EARNINGS
WestJet Airlines Ltd.
Years Ended December 31, 2009 and 2008
(Stated in thousands of Canadian dollars, except per share amounts)

	2009	2008
Revenues:		
Guest revenues	$2,067,860	$2,301,301
Charter and other revenues	213,260	248,205
	2,281,120	2,549,506
Expenses:		
Aircraft fuel	570,569	803,293
Airport operations	352,333	342,922
Flight operations and navigational charges	298,762	280,920
Marketing, general and administration	208,316	211,979
Sales and distribution	172,326	170,693
Depreciation and amortization	141,303	136,485
Inflight	112,054	105,849
Aircraft leasing	103,954	86,050
Maintenance	96,272	85,093
Employee profit share	14,675	33,435
	2,070,564	2,256,719
Earnings from operations	210,556	292,787
Non-operating income (expense):		
Interest income	5,601	25,485
Interest expense	(67,706)	(76,078)
Gain (loss) on foreign exchange	(12,306)	30,587
Loss on disposal of property and equipment	(1,177)	(701)
Gain (loss) on derivatives [Note 13(b)]	1,828	(17,331)
	(73,760)	(38,038)
Earnings before income taxes	136,796	254,749
Income tax expense: (Note 9)		
Current	2,690	2,549
Future	35,928	73,694
	38,618	76,243
Net earnings	$ 98,178	$ 178,506
Earnings per share: [Note 10(c)]		
Basic	$ 0.74	$ 1,39
Diluted	$ 0.74	$ 1,37

The accompanying notes are an integral part of the consolidated financial statements.

Source: WestJet Annual Report 2009.

CONSOLIDATED STATEMENTS OF CASH FLOWS
WestJet Airlines Ltd.
Years Ended December 31, 2009 and 2008
(Stated in thousands of Canadian dollars)

	2009	2008
Operating activities		
Net earnings	$98,178	$178,506
Items not involving cash:		
Depreciation and amortization	141,303	136,485
Amortization of other liabilities	(7,595)	(937)
Amortization of hedge settlements	1,400	1,400
Unrealized (gain) loss on derivative instruments	(2,406)	6,725
Issuance of shares pursuant to employee share purchase plan	11,071	—
Loss on disposal of property, equipment, and aircraft parts	1,504	1,809
Stock-based compensation expense	13,440	13,485
Income tax credit receivable	(1,952)	—
Future income tax expense	35,928	73,694
Unrealized foreign exchange loss (gain)	8,440	(34,823)
Change in non-cash working capital [Note 14(b)]	19,350	84,242
	318,661	460,586
Financing activities		
Increase in long-term debt	33,855	101,782
Repayment of long-term debt	(165,757)	(179,397)
Decrease in obligations under capital leases	(406)	(375)
Issuance of shares	172,463	227
Share issue costs	(7,468)	—
Shares repurchased	—	(29,420)
Decrease (increase) in other assets	3,427	(4,135)
Change in non-cash working capital	(1,463)	(4,111)
	34,651	(115,429)
Investing activities		
Aircraft additions	(118,686)	(114,470)
Aircraft disposals	27	84
Other property and equipment and intangible additions	(48,155)	(90,663)
Other property and equipment and intangible disposals	134	172
Change in non-cash working capital	—	5,147
	(166,680)	(199,730)
Cash flow from operating, financing and investing activities	186,632	145,427
Effect of foreign exchange on cash and cash equivalents	(1,665)	21,229
Net change in cash and cash equivalents	184,967	166,656
Cash and cash equivalents, beginning of year	820,214	653,558
Cash and cash equivalents, end of year	$1,005,181	$ 820,214
Cash interest paid	$ 67,973	$ 76,604
Cash taxes paid	$ 3,369	$ 2,305

The accompanying notes are an integral part of the consolidated financial statements.

Source: WestJet Annual Report 2009.

NOTES TO CONSOLIDATED FINANCIAL STATEMENTS

1. Significant accounting policies:

. . .

(*d*) *Revenue recognition*

    (i) Guest revenue, including the air component of vacation packages, are recognized when air transportation is provided. Tickets sold but not yet used are reported in the consolidated statement of financial position as advance ticket sales.

. . .

Required:

1. Examine WestJet's statements of financial position. The company's assets increased in 2009. Which asset shows the largest increase?

2. Compute and interpret the debt-to-equity ratios for 2008 and 2009.

3. WestJet's current liabilities include the advanced ticket sales account with a balance of $286,361. What does this account represent, and what type of transactions would cause an increase or a decrease in the account balance? Explain.

4. Compute the total asset turnover ratio, return on assets, return on equity, and net profit margin for both years 2008 and 2009. Comment on the profitability of WestJet's operations in both years. WestJet's total assets and shareholders' equity at December 31, 2007, amounted to $2,984,222 and $949,908, respectively.

5. WestJet's operations generated significant amounts of cash during both the years 2008 and 2009. The company also made significant investments in new aircraft in 2009. How did the company finance the acquisition of additional aircraft?

6. Compute and interpret the quality of earnings ratio and the capital acquisitions ratio for both 2008 and 2009. (*Note:* Include property and equipment, and intangible assets in your computation of the ratio.)

7. Access one of the online information services listed in the chapter, search for WestJet Airlines Ltd. (WJA.TO) and look for earnings estimates. What is the average analysts' estimate of WestJet's earnings per share (EPS) for the next two fiscal years? Do analysts expect WestJet's EPS to increase or decrease in the future? What information did the analysts take into consideration in computing their EPS estimates for the next two years?

P6–5 **Using Financial Reports: Interpreting Financial Statement Information, Analyzing and Interpreting Ratios** (AP6–3)

Danier Leather Inc. (DL) is one of the largest publicly traded specialty leather apparel retailers in the world. It designs, manufactures, and sells high-quality fashionable leather clothing and accessories to customers. Its products are sold in stores at shopping malls, through its corporate sales division, and online through its website, **www.danier.com**. Since entering the retail business in 1974, the company has produced a strong, long-term track record of growth and profits from continuing operations. DL's financial statements for 2008 and 2009 are shown on the next few pages.

■ **LO2, 3**

Danier Leather

Required:

1. Examine DL's statements of financial position. Identify the four largest changes in the carrying amount of assets, liabilities, and shareholders' equity between the statement of financial position dates. What type of transactions could have caused the changes in the carrying amounts of these items?

2. The carrying amounts of the assets and liabilities reported on the company's statement of financial position reflect a mix of historical acquisition costs, amortized costs, and fair values. Refer to the notes to the company's financial statements for fiscal year 2009 that are available on the company's website (**http://cnrp.marketwire.com/client/danier/ annualReports.jsp**) and identify the valuation bases used by the company for financial reporting purposes.

3. Using information from the company's statements of financial position and income statement for 2009, can you determine the amount of cash flow generated from operations? If not, where can one find such information?

4. Compute the following ratios for fiscal years 2008 and 2009: debt-to-equity, total asset turnover, return on assets, return on equity, and net profit margin. Use the results of your computations to comment on the company's financial situation and profitability of its operations in both years. DL's total assets and shareholders' equity at June 24, 2007, amounted to $81,746 and $48,709, respectively.

5. Suppose that you are evaluating DL's financial statements for a potential investment in the company's shares. To what extent is the information contained in these financial statements relevant for your decision? What additional information would you require before making your decision?

Danier Leather Inc.
Consolidated Statements of Financial Position
(thousands of dollars)

	June 27, 2009	June 28, 2008
Assets		
Current Assets		
Cash	$ 24,628	$ 19,882
Trade receivables	351	755
Income taxes recoverable	631	8
Inventories (Note 4)	21,045	27,404
Prepaid expenses	1,156	1,242
Future income tax asset (Note 11)	245	562
	48,056	49,853
Other Assets		
Property and equipment (Note 5)	19,339	21,312
Goodwill (Note 6)	—	342
Future income tax asset (Note 11)	1,657	1,556
	$ 69,052	$ 73,063
Liabilities		
Current Liabilities		
Trade payable and accrued liabilities	$ 10,601	$ 9,845
Current portion of capital lease obligation	—	858
Future income tax liability (Note 11)	366	502
	10,967	11,205
Deferred lease inducements and rent liability	1,389	1,675
Future income tax liability (Note 11)	—	50
	12,356	12,930
Shareholders' Equity		
Share capital (Note 8)	19,853	21,409
Contributed surplus	823	548
Retained earnings	36,020	38,176
	56,696	60,133
	$ 69,052	$ 73,063

See accompanying notes to the consolidated financial statements.

Approved by the Board

(signature)   (signature)

Edwin F. Hawken, Director   **Jeffrey Wortsman, Director**

Source: Danier Leather Annual Report 2009.

Danier Leather Inc.
Consolidated Statements of Earnings (Loss) and Comprehensive Earnings (Loss)
(thousands of dollars, except per share amounts)

	For the Years Ended	
	June 27, 2009	June 28, 2009
Revenue	$162,106	$ 163,550
Cost of sales (Note 9)	88,589	87,365
Gross profit	73,517	76,185
Selling, general and administrative expenses (Note 9)	74,726	78,582
Interest expense (income) – net	104	81
Loss before undernoted items and income taxes	(1,313)	(2,478)
Restructuring costs (Note 10)	1,466	—
Goodwill impairment charge (Note 6)	342	—
Litigation provision (recovery) and related expenses (Note 12)	—	(20,016)
Earnings (loss) before income taxes	(3,121)	17,538
Provision for (recovery of) income taxes (Note 11)		
Current	(842)	192
Future	30	4,454
Net earnings (loss) and comprehensive earnings (loss)	**($2,309)**	**$ 12,892**
Net earnings (loss) per share:		
Basic	($0.37)	$2.04
Diluted	($0.37)	$2.03

See accompanying notes to the consolidated financial statements.

Source: Danier Leather Annual Report 2009.

ALTERNATE PROBLEMS

AP6–1 Preparing a Statement of Financial Position and Analyzing Some of Its Parts (P6–3)   ■ LO3

The Java House is developing its annual financial statements for 2011. The following amounts were
correct at December 31, 2011: cash, $58,800; investment in shares of PAX Corporation (long term),
$36,400; store equipment, $67,200; trade receivables, $71,820; carpet inventory, $154,000;
prepaid rent, $1,120; used store equipment held for disposal, $9,800; accumulated depreciation,
store equipment, $13,440; income taxes payable, $9,800; long-term note payable, $42,000; trade
payables, $58,800; retained earnings, $165,100; and common shares, (100,000 shares outstanding,
originally sold and issued at $1.10 per share).

Required:

1. Based on these data, prepare the company's statement of financial position at December 31,
   2011. Use the following major captions (list the individual items under these captions):

   a. Assets: current assets; long-term investments; property, plant, and equipment; and other
   assets.

   b. Liabilities: current liabilities and long-term liabilities.

   c. Shareholders' equity: share capital and retained earnings.

2. What is the carrying amount of the store equipment? Explain what this value means.

**AP6–2 Using Financial Reports: Interpreting Financial Statement Information, Analyzing and
Interpreting Ratios** (P6–4)   ■ LO2, 3

RONA Inc. (**www.rona.ca**), founded in 1939, is Canada's leading distributor and retailer of
hardware, home improvement, and gardening products. It has a network that exceeds 600 stores
across Canada. Its sales grew from $478 million in 1993 to $4,677 million in 2009. Its financial
statements for 2008 and 2009 are shown on the next few pages.

RONA Inc.

Required:

1. Examine RONA's balance sheets. Why did the company's assets increase significantly in 2009? Which sections of the annual reports would include information that helps the reader answer this question? Which assets show the largest increases, and how did the company finance the increase in these assets?

2. Compute and interpret the debt-to-equity ratios for 2008 and 2009.

3. RONA's current assets include a Prepaid expenses account with a balance of $18,114. What does this account represent, and what type of transactions would cause an increase or a decrease in the account balance? Explain.

4. RONA's income statement does not include information related to cost of sales and general, selling, and administrative expenses. Why did the company exclude such details from its income statement? Explain.

5. Compute the total asset turnover ratio, return on assets, return on equity, and net profit margin for both years 2008 and 2009. Comment on the profitability of RONA's operations in both years. RONA's total assets and shareholders' equity at December 31, 2007, amounted to $2,482,446 and $1,325,206, respectively.

6. RONA's operations generated significant amounts of cash during both the years 2008 and 2009. The company also made significant investments in 2009. How did the company finance these investments?

7. Compute and interpret the quality of earnings ratio for both 2008 and 2009.

8. Access one of the online information services listed in the chapter, search for RONA Inc. (RON.TO) and look for analyst estimates. What is the average analysts' estimate of RONA's earnings per share (EPS) for the next two years? Do analysts expect RONA's EPS to increase or decrease in the future? What information did the analysts take into consideration in computing their EPS estimates for the next two years?

RONA Inc.
Consolidated Balance Sheets
December 28, 2009 and December 30, 2008
(in thousands of dollars)

	2009	2008
Assets		
Current assets		
Cash	$ 239,257	$ 12,345
Trade receivables (Note 10)	250,845	234,027
Income taxes receivable	2,436	6,475
Inventory (Note 5)	726,262	763,239
Prepaid expenses	18,114	11,202
Derivative financial instruments (Note 23)	801	1,089
Future income taxes (Note 7)	15,914	19,274
	1,253,629	1,047,651
Investments (Note 11)	11,978	10,186
Fixed assets (Note 12)	868,359	822,375
Fixed assets held for sale (Note 13)	13,242	34,870
Goodwill	455,572	454,889
Intangible assets (Note 14)	89,828	57,056
Other assets (Note 15)	29,682	27,210
Future income taxes (Note 7)	27,593	24,681
	$2,749,883	$ 2,478,918
Liabilities		
Current liabilities		
Bank loans (Note 16)	$ 5,211	$ 8,468
Trade payable and accrued liabilities	427,817	422,318
Derivative financial instruments (Note 23)	776	2,180
Future income taxes (Note 7)	4,900	4,461
Installments on long-term debt (Note 17)	9,996	15,696
	448,700	453,123

(continued)

Long-term debt (Note 17)	430,524	478,475
Other long-term liabilities (Note 18)	31,317	28,571
Future income taxes (Note 7)	27,542	21,304
Non-controlling interest	32,761	29,220
	970,844	1,010,693
Shareholders' equity		
Capital stock (Note 20)	603,756	426,786
Retained earnings	1,161,808	1,028,876
Contributed surplus	13,475	12,563
	1,779,039	1,468,225
	$2,749,883	$ 2,478,918

The accompanying notes are an integral part of the consolidated financial statements.

On behalf of the Board,

J. Spencer Lanthier

Jean Gaulin

Chairman of the Audit Committee

Chairman of the Board of Directors

Source: RONA Annual Report 2009.

RONA Inc.
Consolidated Statement of Earnings
Years ended December 28, 2009 and December 30, 2008
(in thousands of dollars, except earnings per share)

	2009	2008
Sales	$ 4,677,359	$4,891,122
Earnings before the following items (Note 6)	332,994	364,729
Interest on long-term debt	20,951	28,106
Interest on bank loans	2,586	2,134
Depreciation and amortization (Notes 12, 14, 15)	103,160	100,958
	126,697	131,198
Earnings before income taxes and non-controlling interest	206,297	233,531
Income taxes (Note 7)	62,714	71,928
Earnings before non-controlling interest	143,583	161,603
Non-controlling interest	5,331	5,152
Net earnings and comprehensive income	$ 138,252	$156,451
Net earnings per share (Note 27)		
Basic	$ 1.12	$ 1.35
Diluted	$ 1.11	$ 1.34

The accompanying notes are an integral part of the consolidated financial statements.

Source: RONA Annual Report 2009.

RONA Inc.
Consolidated Statements of Cash Flows
Years Ended December 28, 2009 and December 30, 2008
(in thousands of dollars)

	2009	2008
Operating activities		
Net earnings	$138,252	$ 156,451
Non-cash items		
Depreciation and amortization	103,160	100,958
Derivative financial instruments	(1,116)	1,192
Future income taxes	9,225	(2,917)
Net gain on disposal of assets	(2,358)	(2,796)
Impairment charge on fixed assets held for sale	2,050	—
Compensation cost relating to stock option plans	946	1,518
Compensation cost relating to share unit plans	2,557	1,091
Non-controlling interest	5,331	5,152
Other items	1,975	3,465
	260,022	264,114
Changes in working capital items (Note 8)	22,752	83,373
Cash flows from operating activities	282,774	347,487
Investing activities		
Business acquisitions (Note 9)	(3,734)	(4,824)
Advances to joint ventures and other advances	5	8,139
Other investments	(3,995)	(3,155)
Fixed assets	(115,713)	(161,869)
Intangible assets	(46,186)	(34,276)
Other assets	(4,837)	(10,565)
Disposal of assets	6,291	11,686
Disposal of investments	2,422	10,618
Cash flows from investing activities	(165,747)	(184,246)
Financing activities		
Bank loans and revolving credit	(43,046)	(131,518)
Other long-term debt	646	8,560
Repayment of other long-term debt and redemption of preferred shares	(15,819)	(33,946)
Issue of common shares	176,936	5,592
Cash dividends paid by a subsidiary to non-controlling interest	(1,470)	(2,450)
Expenses relating to the issue of common shares	(7,362)	–
Cash flows from financing activities	109,885	(153,762)
Net increase in cash	226,912	9,479
Cash, beginning of year	12,345	2,866
Cash, end of year	$239,257	$ 12,345
Supplementary information		
Interest paid	$ 25,493	$ 33,165
Income taxes paid	$ 49,450	$ 75,508

The accompanying notes are an integral part of the consolidated financial statements.

Source: RONA Annual Report 2009.

 LO2, 3

Sun-Rype Products Ltd.

AP6–3   **Using Financial Reports: Interpreting Financial Statement Information, Analyzing and Interpreting Ratios** (P6-5)

Sun-Rype Products Ltd. is a Canadian juice and fruit snack company based in Kelowna, British Columbia. Its sales grew from $73 million when it became a public company in 1996 to $125 million in 2009. Sun-Rype's financial statements for 2008 and 2009 are shown on the next few pages.

Required:

1. Examine Sun-Rype's statements of financial position. Identify the four largest changes in the carrying amount of assets, liabilities, and shareholders' equity between the statement of financial position dates. What type of transactions could have caused the changes in the carrying amount of these items?

2. The carrying amounts of the assets and liabilities reported on the company's statement of financial position reflect a mix of historical acquisition costs, amortized costs and fair values. Refer to the notes to the company's financial statements for fiscal year 2009 that are available on the company's website (http://ir.sunrype.com) and identify the valuation bases used by the company for financial reporting purposes.

3. Using information from the company's statements of financial position and income statement for 2009, can you determine the amount of cash flow generated from operations? If not, where can one find such information?

4. Compute the following ratios for fiscal years 2008 and 2009: debt-to-equity, total asset turnover, return on assets, return on equity, and net profit margin. Use the results of your computations to comment on the company's financial situation and profitability of its operations in both years. Sun-Rype's total assets and shareholders' equity at December 31, 2007, amounted to $56,884 and $41,023, respectively.

5. Suppose that you are evaluating Sun-Rype's financial statements for a potential investment in the company's shares. To what extent is the information contained in these financial statements relevant for your decision? What additional information would you require before making your decision?

SUN-RYPE PRODUCTS LTD.
Statements of Financial Position
(thousands of dollars)

	Dec. 31, 2009	Dec. 31, 2008
Assets		
Current		
Cash	$ 2,411	$ 625
Trade receivables	14,811	11,830
Unrealized foreign exchange gain on currency contracts	—	718
Income taxes recoverable	—	6,987
Inventories (Note 3)	21,614	27,778
Prepaid expenses	594	554
	39,430	48,492
Property, plant, and equipment (Note 4)	21,556	25,130
	$60,986	$73,622
Liabilities and Shareholders' Equity		
Current		
Bank operating loan (Note 5)	$ —	$12,554
Promissory note payable (Note 6)	—	400
Trade payable and accrued liabilities	15,809	15,229
Unrealized foreign exchange loss on currency contracts	10	—
Income taxes payable	2,808	—
Future income taxes (Note 7)	77	11
Current portion, obligation under capital leases (Note 8)	101	97
Current portion, long-term obligations (Note 9)	—	220
Current portion, long-term debt (Note 10)	1,500	1,500
	20,305	30,011
Obligation under capital leases (Note 8)	294	395
Long-term obligations (Note 9)	—	145
Long-term debt (Note 10)	3,250	12,750
Future income taxes (Note 7)	1,392	1,343
	25,241	44,644
Shareholders' Equity		
Share capital and contributed surplus (Note 11)	18,698	18,698
Retained earnings	17,047	10,280
	35,745	28,978
	$60,986	$73,622

Commitments, guarantees and contingencies (Note 17)

Approved by the Board

(signature)   (signature)

D. Selman, Director   **M. J. Korenberg, Director**

See accompanying notes to financial statements.

SUN-RYPE PRODUCTS LTD.
Statements of Operations and Comprehensive Income
(thousands of dollars, except per share amounts)

	For the Years Ended	
	Dec. 31, 2009	Dec. 31, 2008
Net sales (Note 12)	$147,696	$125,368
Cost of sales (Note 13)	110,826	112,995
Gross profit	36,870	12,373
Expenses		
Selling, general, and administrative	25,742	29,053
Amortization	539	570
Interest	528	879
Foreign exchange loss	111	–
Loss on disposal of property, plant, and equipment	9	–
	26,929	30,502
Income (loss) before income taxes	9,941	(18,129)
Income tax expense (recovery) (Note 7)	3,174	(6,456)
Net income (loss) and comprehensive income (loss)	6,767	(11,673)
Retained earnings, beginning of year	10,280	22,386
Dividends paid	—	(433)
Retained earnings, end of year	$ 17,047	$ 10,280
Earnings (loss) per share		
Basic and diluted (Note 11)	$ 0.62	$ (1.08)

See accompanying notes to financial statements.

Source: Sun-Rype Annual Report 2009.

CASES AND PROJECTS

FINDING AND INTERPRETING FINANCIAL INFORMATION

LO2, 3

The Nestlé Group

CP6–1   **Finding Financial Information**

Refer to the financial statements of the Nestlé Group given in Appendix A at the end of this book. The following questions illustrate the types of information that you can find in the financial statements and accompanying notes.

Required:

1. What items were included as non-current assets on the statement of financial position (balance sheet)?
2. What is the carrying amount of machinery and equipment the company owned at the end of the most recent reporting year?
3. The company spent CHF 4,869 million on capital expenditures in 2008. Were operating activities or financing activities the major source of cash for these expenditures?
4. What was the company's largest asset (net) at December 31, 2008?
5. What was the amount of interest expense for 2008?

LO2, 3

Cadbury, plc.

CP6–2   **Finding Financial Information**

Go to Connect online for the financial statements of Cadbury, plc. The following questions illustrate the types of information that you can find in the financial statements and accompanying notes. (*Hint:* Use the notes.)

Required:

1. What subtotals does the company report in its income statement?
2. What was the highest stock price for the company during 2008?

3. Over what useful life are buildings depreciated?

4. What portion of gross property, plant, and equipment is composed of land and buildings?

5. The company reported cash flow from operating activities of £469 million. However, its cash and cash equivalents decreased during 2008. Explain how that happened.

FINANCIAL REPORTING AND ANALYSIS CASES

CP6–3 Interpreting the Financial Press

The Committee of Sponsoring Organizations (COSO) published a research study that examined financial statement fraud occurrences between 1987 and 1997. A summary of the findings by M. S. Beasley, J. V. Carcello, and D. R. Hermanson, "Fraudulent Financial Reporting: 1987–1997: An Analysis of U.S. Public Companies," *The Auditor's Report*, Summer 1999, pp. 15–17, is available online. Read the article and then write a short memo outlining the following:

■ **LO3**

The Auditor's Report

1. The size of the companies involved.

2. The extent of top management involvement.

3. The specific accounting fraud techniques involved.

4. What might lead managers to introduce misstatements into the income statement near the end of the accounting period.

*Copyright © 1999 by American Accounting Association. Reprinted with permission.

CP6–4 Using Financial Reports: Financial Statement Inferences

The following amounts were selected from the annual financial statements for Genesis Corporation at December 31, 2012 (end of the third year of operations):

■ **LO2, 3**

From the 2012 income statement:	
Sales revenue	$275,000
Cost of sales	(170,000)
All other expenses (including income tax)	(95,000)
Profit	$ 10,000
From the December 31, 2012, statement of financial position:	
Current assets	$ 90,000
All other assets	212,000
Total assets	302,000
Current liabilities	40,000
Non-current liabilities	66,000
Common shares*	100,000
Contributed surplus	16,000
Retained earnings	80,000
Total liabilities and shareholders' equity	$302,000
*10,000 shares issued and outstanding throughout the year.	

Required:

Analyze the data on the 2012 financial statements of Genesis by answering the questions that follow. Show computations.

1. What was the gross margin on sales?

2. What was the amount of earnings per share?

3. If the income tax rate was 25 percent, what was the amount of pretax profit?

4. What was the average issuance price per common share?

5. Assuming that no dividends were declared or paid during 2012, what was the beginning balance (January 1, 2012) of retained earnings?

CRITICAL THINKING CASES

LO2

CP6–5   Assessing the Relevance and Verifiability of Information

Intrawest is a world leader in destination resorts and leisure travel. The company's success formula starts with a resort and then builds an animated village with shops, hotels, conventions facilities, and restaurants. Intrawest's development of real estate properties has resulted in a significant portfolio of real estate holdings.

By June 30, 2005, Intrawest's assets included resort properties with a carrying amount of US$791.8 million, representing the costs incurred by the company to acquire land and build its resort properties. In contrast, financial analysts estimated the market value of these properties at amounts ranging from US$1.12 billion to US$1.70 billion. In fact, analyst Michael Smith of National Bank Financial estimated the market value of Intrawest's real estate at US$1.12 billion compared to an estimate of US$1.45 billion by Pirate Capital. However, both of these estimates were lower than a third estimate by Mark Hill of JMP Securities, who values these properties at US$1.70 billion.

Required:

1. Assume the role of an auditor of Intrawest's financial statements. Which of these four values would you advise the company's management to report on its statement of financial position at June 30, 2005? Justify your reasoning.

2. Assume the role of an investment broker who is advising a client about the purchase of Intrawest's resort properties. Which value would you use as a basis for your recommendation to your client and why?

LO1, 3

Royal Ahold

CP6–6   Evaluating an Ethical Dilemma: Management Incentives and Fraudulent Financial Statements

Netherlands-based Royal Ahold ranks among the world's three largest food retailers. In the United States it operates the Stop & Shop and Giant supermarket chains. Dutch and U.S. regulators and prosecutors have brought criminal and civil charges against the company and its executives for overstating earnings by more than US$1 billion. The nature of the fraud is described in the following excerpt:

TWO FORMER EXECS OF AHOLD SUBSIDIARY PLEAD NOT GUILTY TO FRAUD

NEW YORK (AP)—Two former executives pleaded not guilty Wednesday to devising a scheme to inflate the earnings of U.S. Foodservice Inc., a subsidiary of Dutch supermarket giant Royal Ahold NV.

Former chief financial officer Michael Resnick and former chief marketing officer Mark Kaiser entered their pleas in a Manhattan federal court, a day after prosecutors announced fraud and conspiracy charges against them.

The government contends they worked together to boost the company's earnings by $800 million from 2000 to 2003 by reporting fake rebates from suppliers—and sweetened their own bonuses in the process. Two other defendants have already pleaded guilty in the alleged scheme: Timothy Lee, a former executive vice-president, and William Carter, a former vice-president. Both are set for sentencing in January.

Netherlands-based Ahold's U.S. properties include the Stop & Shop and Giant supermarket chains. U.S. Foodservice is one of the largest distributors of food products in the country, providing to restaurants and cafeterias.

Ahold said last year it had overstated its earnings by more than $1 billion, mostly because of the fraud at U.S. Foodservice. Its stock lost 60 percent of its value, and about $6 billion in market value evaporated.

Source: Associated Press Newswires. 28 July 2004.

Required:

Using more recent news reports (*Wall Street Journal Index*, *Factiva*, and *Bloomberg Business News* are good sources), answer the following questions.

1. Whom did the courts and regulatory authorities hold responsible for the misstated financial statements?

2. Did the company co-operate with investigations into the fraud? How did this affect the penalties imposed against the company?

3. How might executive compensation plans that tied bonuses to accounting earnings motivate unethical conduct in this case?

FINANCIAL REPORTING AND ANALYSIS TEAM PROJECT

CP6–7 Team Project: Analyzing the Accounting Communication Process

LO2, 3

As a team, select an industry to analyze. A list of companies classified by industry can be obtained by accessing **www.fpinformat.ca** and then choosing "Companies by Industry." You can also find a list of industries and companies with each industry via **http://ca.finance.yahoo.com/investing** (click on "Annual Reports" under "Tools"). Using a Web browser, each team member should acquire the annual report for one publicly traded company in the industry, with each member selecting a different company.

Required:

On an individual basis, each team member should write a short report answering the following questions about the selected company. Discuss any patterns across the companies that you as a team observe. Then, as a team, write a short report comparing and contrasting your companies.

1. What formats are used to present the

   a. Statements of financial position?

   b. Income statements?

   c. Operating activities section of the statement of cash flows?

2. Find a footnote for each of the following and describe its contents in brief:

   a. An accounting rule applied in the company's statements.

   b. Additional detail about a reported financial statement number.

   c. Relevant financial information but without numbers reported in the financial statements.

3. Using electronic sources, find one article reporting the company's annual earnings announcement. When is it dated and how does that date compare to the statement of financial position date?

4. Using electronic sources, find two analysts' reports for your company.

   a. Give the date, name of the analyst, and his or her recommendation from each report.

   b. Discuss why the recommendations are similar or different. Look at the analysts' reasoning for their respective recommendations.

Reporting and Interpreting Sales Revenue, Receivables, and Cash

After studying this chapter, you should be able to do the following:

FOCUS COMPANY: **Gildan Activewear Inc.**

BUILDING BRANDS TO BUILD GROSS PROFIT: MANAGING PRODUCT DEVELOPMENT, PRODUCTION, AND WORKING CAPITAL

Over the past several years, casual wear has become increasingly acceptable in the workplace as employers adopt flexible dress codes. Gildan Activewear Inc. (**www.gildan. com**), which is based in Montréal, Québec, took advantage of this trend and became a significant producer and marketer of high-quality casual wear, including T-shirts, sports shirts, and sweatshirts. In 2006, Gildan expanded its product line to include underwear and basic athletic socks. Its core market is high volume, basic, frequently replenished non-fashion apparel, which is distributed primarily in North America and Europe, with growing market share in the Asia-Pacific region. Its products can be purchased in retail stores, as well at corporate, tourist, entertainment, and sports events.

Gildan started as a family operation, and grew to become a publicly traded company in both Canada and the United States. Gildan is successful in part because it specialized in 100 percent cotton or blends of cotton and synthetic fibres that are manufactured at low cost in developing countries located in Central America and the Caribbean basin. Its cotton is harvested and spun in the states of Georgia and North Carolina in the United States. With control over every important element in its supply chain, Gildan effectively profits from reliable and on-time delivery of consistent quality products at a low cost.

Gildan's sales grew from US$224 million for fiscal year 1999 to US$1,038.8 million for its fiscal year ended October 4, 2009.[1] Such a growth in sales

---

[1] Gildan uses the U.S. dollar as a reporting currency because a significant portion of its revenues, expenses, assets, and liabilities are denominated in U.S. dollars.

could not happen if the company did not pursue specific business strategies to produce quality products and market them effectively to targeted customers. The company's focus on low-cost manufacturing of premium-quality casual wear and its marketing philosophy of controlled distribution have been important factors in its success. The company's management recognized that its dedication to being the lowest-cost producer and leading marketer of branded basic casual wear to wholesale channels of distribution required the adoption of a set of objectives and principles such as (1) nurturing and strengthening the Gildan Activewear brand, (2) remaining price-competitive by constantly reinvesting in state-of-the-art facilities, and (3) maintaining strong relationships with the distributors of the company's products. These objectives and related action plans are aimed at increasing net sales and/or decreasing the cost of sales, thereby increasing gross profit.

UNDERSTANDING THE BUSINESS

The success of each element of Gildan's strategy can be seen in the information presented in the income statement excerpt in Exhibit 7.1. Net sales (revenue) is reported first, and cost of sales (cost of goods sold, cost of products sold) is set out separately from the remaining expenses. The income statement then reports *gross profit* (*gross margin*), which is net sales minus cost of sales.

Planning Gildan's growth strategy requires careful coordination of sales and production activities, as well as cash collection from customers. Much of this coordination involves judicious use of credit card and sales discounts as well as prudent management of sales returns and bad debts. These activities affect both *net sales revenue* on the income statement and *cash* and *trade receivables* on the statement of financial position, which are the focus of this chapter. We will introduce the gross profit percentage ratio as a basis for evaluating changes in gross profit, as well as the receivables turnover ratio as a measure of the efficiency of credit-granting and collection activities. But the cash collected from customers is a tempting target for fraud and embezzlement, therefore we will discuss some common controls integral to most accounting systems to minimize these misdeeds.

Lenders, shareholders, and analysts carefully monitor net sales and receivables because of their importance as predictors of the future success of companies. Their importance is supported by the fact that the majority of shareholder lawsuits and enforcement actions by securities regulators against companies for misleading financial statements relate to these accounts.

Exhibit **7.1**

Net Sales and Gross Profit on the Income Statement

REAL WORLD EXCERPT

Gildan Activewear

ANNUAL REPORT

CONSOLIDATED STATEMENTS OF EARNINGS AND COMPREHENSIVE INCOME
Years ended October 4, 2009, October 5, 2008, and September 30, 2007
(in thousands of U.S. dollars)

	2009	2008	2007
Net sales	$1,038,319	$1,249,711	$964,429
Cost of sales	807,986	911,242	705,546
Gross profit	230,333	338,469	258,883

Source: Gildan Activewear Annual Report 2009.

ORGANIZATION OF THE CHAPTER

Accounting for Sales Revenue	Measuring and Reporting Receivables	Reporting and Safeguarding Cash
• Sales to Consumers • Sales Discounts to Businesses • Sales Returns and Allowances • Reporting Net Sales • Gross Profit Percentage	• Classifying Receivables • Accounting for Bad Debts • Reporting Trade Receivables • Estimating Bad Debts • Receivables Turnover Ratio • Internal Control and Management Responsibility • Control over Trade Receivables	• Cash and Cash Equivalents Defined • Cash Management • Internal Control of Cash • Reconciliation of the Cash Accounts and the Bank Statements

Supplemental material:

Appendix 7A: Applying the Revenue Principle in Special Circumstances
Appendix 7B: Recording Discounts and Returns
Appendix 7C: Accounting for Passive Investments in Securities (online)

ACCOUNTING FOR SALES REVENUE

LO¹

Apply the revenue principle to determine the accepted time to record sales revenue for typical retailers, wholesalers, manufacturers, and service companies.

As indicated in Chapter 3, the *revenue principle* requires that revenues be recorded when the following conditions are met: (1) the entity has transferred to the buyer the significant risks and rewards of ownership of the goods, (2) the entity retains neither continuing managerial involvement to the degree usually associated with ownership nor effective control over the goods sold, (3) the amount of revenue can be measured reliably, (4) it is probable that the economic benefits associated with the transaction will flow to the entity, and (5) the costs incurred or to be incurred in respect of the transaction can be measured reliably. For sellers of goods, these criteria are most often met and sales revenue is recorded when title and risks of ownership pass to the buyer. The point at which title (ownership) changes hands is determined by the shipping terms in the sales contract. When goods are shipped *FOB (free on board) shipping point*, title changes hands at shipment, and the buyer normally pays for shipment. When they are shipped *FOB destination point*, title changes hands on delivery, and the seller normally pays for shipment. Revenues from goods sold FOB shipping point are normally recognized at shipment. Revenues from goods sold FOB destination point are normally recognized at delivery.

Service companies most often record sales revenue when they have provided services to the buyer. Companies disclose the specific revenue recognition rules they follow in the note to their financial statements titled Significant Accounting Policies. Gildan reported the following in its accounting policies:

REAL WORLD EXCERPT

Gildan Activewear

ANNUAL REPORT

NOTES TO CONSOLIDATED FINANCIAL STATEMENTS

1. Significant Accounting Policies

(l) *Revenue recognition:*

Revenue is recognized upon shipment of products to customers, since title passes upon shipment, and when the selling price is fixed or determinable. At the time of sale, estimates are made for customer price discounts and volume rebates based on the terms of existing programs. Accruals required for new programs, which relate to prior sales, are recorded at the time the new program is introduced. Sales are recorded net of these program costs and a provision for estimated sales returns, which is based on historical experience, current trends and other known factors, and exclude sales taxes.

Like Gildan, many manufacturers, wholesalers, and retailers recognize revenue at shipment. This is when the title and risks of ownership pass to the buyer. Auditors expend a lot of effort to ensure that revenue recognition rules are applied consistently and revenues are recognized in the proper period.

The appropriate *amount* of revenue to record is the *cash equivalent sales price*. Sales practices differ depending on whether sales are made to businesses or consumers. Gildan sells its products primarily through wholesale distributors, a strategy that enables the company to use a small sales force. Gildan sells its products to a network of distributors in Canada, the United States, Mexico, Europe, and Asia, which in turn resell the products to retailers and garment decorators. Consumers ultimately purchase the company's products in such venues as sports, entertainment, and corporate events as well as travel and tourism destinations. In 2005, Gildan decided to enter the retail market and began selling its product line of activewear, underwear, and athletic socks to Canadian and U.S. retailers.

For some companies, delivery of the product is bundled with a longer-term service contract. Some companies such as Xerox Corporation chose to recognize 100 percent of the service revenue upon delivery of the product, which is contrary to accepted accounting standards. Revenue from long-term service contracts is recognized most often by using the percentage of completion method, discussed in Appendix A.

ACCELERATED REVENUE RECOGNITION IS FRAUD

A QUESTION OF ACCOUNTABILITY

In 2002, the U.S. regulatory enforcement agency, the Securities and Exchange Commission (SEC), negotiated a settlement pursuant to its two-year investigation of fraud at Xerox Corporation. A variety of accounting irregularities were alleged, resulting in an overstatement of profit by US$1.5 billion over a period extending from 1997 to 2000. The premature recognition of all revenue from long-term leasing contracts amounted to US$3 billion during that period. In fact, the lease revenue should have been recognized month by month. The company also failed to disclose special obligations to provide extraordinary repairs or replacement and failed to properly disclose uncollectible amounts of receivables.

While the corporation's auditor, KPMG, challenged management's choice of accounting methods, it did not refuse to attest to the quality of disclosure provided by Xerox's management. Neither the corporation, its auditor KPMG, nor the six executives who were defendants admitted or denied any wrongdoing. In early April 2002, Xerox agreed to the appointment of a board of directors comprised entirely of external members to review its internal control system. The company also agreed to restate its financial statements from 1997 to 2000, and to pay a penalty of US$10 million. The two auditors of KMPG who personally oversaw the auditing process agreed to pay US$150,000 each, and another partner, who resigned from the firm, agreed to pay US$100,000. All three auditors were suspended from professional practice for one to three years. In total, the six defendants at Xerox agreed to personally pay in excess of US$22 million plus disgorgement of any interest accumulated on the money. The funds were intended by the SEC to be distributed to those who were victims of the alleged fraud.

Gildan uses a variety of methods to motivate its customers, both businesses and consumers, to buy its products and make payment for their purchases. The principal methods include (1) allowing all customers to use credit cards to pay for purchases, (2) providing business customers direct credit and discounts for early payment, and (3) allowing returns from all customers under specific circumstances. These methods, in turn, affect the way we compute *net sales revenue*.

LO²

Analyze the impact of credit card sales, sales discounts, and sales returns on the amounts reported as net sales.

Sales to Consumers

Sales to consumers are for cash or credit card (mainly Visa, MasterCard, and American Express). The seller accepts credit cards as payment for a variety of reasons:

1. Increasing customer traffic at its stores.
2. Avoiding the costs of providing credit directly to customers, including for record-keeping and bad debts (discussed later).
3. Lowering losses due to bad cheques.
4. Avoiding losses from fraudulent credit card sales. (Normally, the credit card company absorbs any losses if the seller follows the credit card company's verification procedure.)
5. Faster receipt of its money. (Since credit card receipts can be directly deposited in its bank account, the seller receives cash payments faster than it would if it provided credit directly to consumers.)

A **CREDIT CARD DISCOUNT** is the fee charged by the credit card company for services.

The credit card company charges a fee for the service it provides. For example, when a seller processes the credit card payment, it might receive credit for an amount equal to only 97 percent of the sales price. The credit card company is charging a 3 percent fee (the credit card discount) for its service. If daily credit card sales were $3,000, Gildan would report the following:[2]

Sales revenue	$3,000
Less: Credit card discounts (0.03 × $3,000)	90
Net sales (reported on the income statement)	$2,910

Sales Discounts to Businesses

Most of Gildan's sales to businesses are credit sales on open account; that is, there is no formal written promissory note indicating the amount owed to Gildan by the customer. When Gildan sells T-shirts to wholesalers on credit, credit terms are printed on each sales document and invoice (bill) sent to the customer. Often credit terms are abbreviated, using symbols. For example, if the full amount of the invoice is due within 30 days of the invoice date, the credit terms would be noted as **n/30**. Here, the **n** means the sales amount **net** of, or less, any sales returns.

Early Payment Incentive

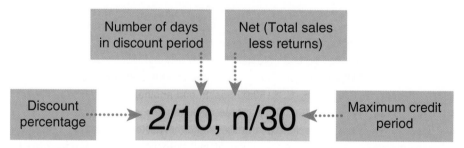

A **SALES (OR CASH) DISCOUNT** is a cash discount offered to encourage prompt payment of an account receivable.

In most cases, a sales discount (often called a *cash discount*) is granted to the purchaser to encourage early payment.[3] For example, Gildan may offer standard credit

---

[2]Some retail businesses, such as Canadian Tire (CT), issue their own cards and avoid credit card discounts when customers use CT's credit card to pay for their purchases.

[3]It is important not to confuse a cash discount with a trade discount. Vendors sometimes use a trade discount for quoting sales prices; the sales price is the list or printed catalogue price less the trade discount. For example, an item may be quoted at $10 per unit, subject to a 20 percent trade discount, on orders of 100 units or more; thus, the price for the large order is $8 per unit. Similarly, the price on a slow-moving product line can be lowered simply by increasing the trade discount. Sales revenue should always be recorded net of trade discounts. Manufacturers also offer discounts for early order and shipment to help manage production flows.

terms of 2/10, n/30, which means that the customer may deduct 2 percent from the invoice amount if cash payment is made within 10 days from the date of sale. If cash payment is not made within the 10-day discount period, the full invoice amount (less any returns) is due within a maximum of 30 days.

Gildan offers this sales discount to encourage customers to pay more quickly. This provides two benefits to Gildan:

1. Prompt receipt of cash from customers reduces the necessity to borrow money to meet operating needs.
2. Since customers tend to pay invoices providing discounts first, a sales discount also decreases the likelihood that the customer will run out of funds before Gildan's invoice is paid.

Companies commonly record sales discounts taken by subtracting the discount from sales if payment is made within the discount period (the usual case).[4] For example, if credit sales are recorded with terms 2/10, n/30 and payment of $980 (= 1,000 × 0.98) is made within the discount period, net sales of the following amount would be reported:

Sales revenue	$1,000
Less: Sales discounts (0.02 × $1,000)	20
Net sales (reported on the income statement)	$980

If the payment is made after the discount period, the full $1,000 would be reported as net sales.

Note that both the purpose of and the accounting for both sales discounts and credit card discounts are similar. Both sales discounts and credit card discounts provide an attractive service to customers and promote faster receipt of cash, thereby reducing recordkeeping costs and minimizing bad debts. Accounting for sales discounts is discussed in more detail in Appendix 7B.

TO TAKE OR NOT TO TAKE THE DISCOUNT, THAT IS THE QUESTION

FINANCIAL ANALYSIS

Customers usually pay within the discount period because the savings are substantial. With terms 2/10, n/30, 2 percent is saved by paying 20 days early (the 10th day instead of the 30th), which is equivalent to an annual interest rate of 37 percent. This annual interest rate is obtained by first computing the interest rate for the discount period. When the 2 percent discount is taken, the customer pays only 98 percent of the gross sales amount. For example, on a $100 sale with terms 2/10, n/30, $2 would be saved and $98 would be paid 20 days early. The interest rate for the 20 day discount period is

(Amount saved ÷ Amount paid) = Interest rate for 20 days

($2 ÷ $98) = 2.04% for 20 days or 0.102% per day

Given that there are 365 days in a year, the annual interest rate is then computed in the following manner:

Annual interest rate = 0.102% × 365 days = 37.23%

Credit customers would save a lot of money even if they had to borrow cash from a bank at a high rate such as 15 percent to take advantage of cash discounts. Normally, the bank's interest rate is less than the high interest rate associated with failing to take cash discounts.

---

[4]We use the gross method in all examples in this textbook. Some companies use the alternative net method, which records sales revenue after deducting the amount of the cash discount. Since the choice of method has little effect on the financial statements, discussion of this method is left for an advanced course.

A QUESTION
OF ACCOUNTABILITY   **STRETCHING OUT THE PAYABLES**

Hoffa Shoes has been incurring significant interest charges (12 percent) on short-term borrowing from its bank.* Hoffa normally purchases shoes from suppliers on terms 1/10, n/30.
The annual rate of interest earned by taking the discount is 18.43 percent computed as
follows:

(Amount saved ÷ Amount paid) = Interest rate for 20 days

($1 ÷ $99) = 1.01% for 20 days or 0.0505 per day

Annual interest rate = 0.0505% × 365 days = 18.43%

Hoffa's policy had been to take all purchase discounts even if it had to borrow at 12 percent
to make the early payment. Management reasoned that the company earned 6.43 percent
more than it paid in interest (18.43 percent – 12 percent).

A new employee suggested a new plan. Records indicated that, even though the terms of
Hoffa's agreement with its suppliers (1/10, n/30) required payment of the full amount within a
maximum of 30 days, the suppliers would not complain as long as payment was made within
55 days of the purchase date, since they normally did not send out a second bill until 60 days
after the purchase date. She reasoned that Hoffa would be better off forgoing the discount
and paying on the 55th day after the purchase date. She argued that, since Hoffa would now
be paying in 55 days instead of 10 days of the purchase, not taking the discount would be
borrowing for 45 days, not the 20 days used in the former analysis. The analysis supporting
the proposal is as follows:

(Amount saved ÷ Amount paid) = Interest rate for 45 days

($1 ÷ $99) = 1.01% for 45 days or 0.02244%

Annual interest rate = 0.02244% × 365 days = 8.19%

In effect, her plan allows Hoffa to borrow from suppliers at 8.19 percent instead of the
bank's rate of 12 percent, saving 3.81 percent. When she presented this plan to the management for discussion, the purchasing manager agreed with the arithmetic presented but
objected nonetheless. Since the plan violated its agreement with suppliers, the purchasing
manager thought it was unethical. Many ethical dilemmas in business involve trade-offs
between monetary benefits and potential violations of moral values.

*Hoffa Shoes is a fictitious company, but most companies face this dilemma.

Sales Returns and Allowances

For Gildan, prompt delivery of exactly what the customer ordered is a key to maintaining good relations with the customers to whom it sells. Delivery of incorrect or
damaged merchandise may cost the customer sales and can destroy these relationships.
When this occurs, the customers have a right to return unsatisfactory or damaged merchandise and receive a refund or an adjustment to their bill.

Such returns are often accumulated in a separate account called "Sales Returns
and Allowances," and must be deducted from gross sales revenue in determining
net sales. This account informs Gildan's management of the volume of returns and
allowances, providing an important measure of the quality of customer service.
Assume, for example, that a customer bought 40-dozen T-shirts from Gildan for
$2,000 on account. Before paying for the T-shirts, the customer discovered that

**SALES RETURNS AND
ALLOWANCES** is a reduction
of gross sales revenues for
return of or allowances for
unsatisfactory goods.

10-dozen T-shirts were not the colour ordered and returned them to Gildan.[5] Gildan would compute net sales as follows:

Sales revenue	$2,000
Less: Sales returns (0.25 × $2,000)	500
Net sales (reported on the income statement)	$1,500

The cost of sales related to the 10-dozen T-shirts would also be reduced.

Based on past experience, Gildan's management knows that some customers that purchased socks, underwear, and activewear products during the current year may return the purchased merchandise or be granted an allowance for potentially defective products in the following year. Because the expected product returns relate to sales made during the current year, Gildan estimates the potential sales returns for the year and establishes a provision for sales returns, as indicated in the following excerpt from its annual report.

REAL WORLD EXCERPT

Gildan Activewear

ANNUAL REPORT

MANAGEMENT'S DISCUSSION AND ANALYSIS

Critical Accounting Estimates

Sales Promotional Programs

In the normal course of business, certain incentives are granted to our customers including discounts and rebates. At the time of sale, estimates are made for customer price discounts and rebates based on the terms of existing programs. Accruals required for new programs, which relate to prior sales, are recorded at the time the new program is introduced. Sales are recorded net of these program costs and a provision for estimated sales returns, which is based on historical experience, current trends and other known factors. If actual price discounts, rebates or returns differ from estimates, significant adjustments to net sales could be required in future periods.

Source: Gildan Activewear Annual Report 2009.

Reporting Net Sales

On the company's books, credit card discounts, sales discounts, and sales returns and allowances are accounted for separately to allow managers to monitor the costs of credit card use, sales discounts, and returns. Using the numbers in the preceding examples, the amount of net sales reported on the income statement is computed in the following manner:[6]

Sales revenue	$6,000
Less: Credit card discounts (a contra revenue)	90
Sales discounts (a contra revenue)	20
Sales returns and allowances (a contra revenue)	500
Net sales (reported on the income statement)	$5,390

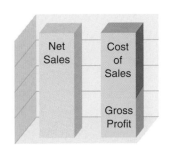

Gildan indicates in its revenue recognition note that its revenues are reported net of returns, discounts, and allowances. Companies rarely disclose the determinants of net

---

[5]Alternatively, Gildan might offer the customer a $200 allowance to keep the wrong-colour T-shirts. If the customer accepts the offer, Gildan would report $200 as sales returns and allowances.

[6]Sales and credit card discounts may also be reported as expenses on the income statement.

sales in the annual report, so it often is difficult to determine the effects of these items, even for well-educated external users. As we noted earlier, net sales less cost of sales equals the subtotal *gross profit* or *gross margin*. Analysts often examine gross profit as a percentage of net sales, called the *gross profit* or *gross margin percentage*.

KEY RATIO ANALYSIS

GROSS PROFIT PERCENTAGE

ANALYTICAL QUESTION →How effective is management in selling goods and services for more than the costs to purchase or produce them?

RATIO AND COMPARISONS →The gross profit percentage is helpful in answering this question. It is computed as follows:

$$\text{Gross Profit Percentage} = \frac{\text{Gross Profit}}{\text{Net Sales}}$$

LO3

Compute and interpret the gross profit percentage.

The 2009 ratio for Gildan is

$$\$230{,}333 \div \$1{,}038{,}319 = 0.221\,(22.1\%)$$

Comparisons over Time			Comparisons with Competitors	
Gildan			Hanesbrands Inc.	Delta Apparel
2007	2008	2009	2009	2009
26.8%	27.1%	22.1%	32.5%	21.5%

INTERPRETATIONS

In General → The gross profit percentage measures how much gross profit is generated from every sales dollar. It reflects the ability to charge premium prices and produce goods and services at low cost. All other things being equal, a higher gross profit results in higher profit.

Business strategy, as well as competition, affects the gross profit percentage. Companies pursuing a product-differentiation strategy use research and development and product promotion activities to convince customers of the superiority or distinctiveness of the company's products. This allows them to charge premium prices, producing higher gross profit percentages. Companies following a low-cost strategy rely on more efficient management of production to reduce costs and increase the gross profit percentage. Managers, analysts, and creditors use this ratio to assess the effectiveness of the company's product development, marketing, and production strategy.

Focus Company Analysis →Gildan's gross profit percentage decreased significantly in 2009 compared with the previous two years because of the global economic downturn. Gildan's ratio slightly surpassed the ratio for Delta Apparel, but it fell significantly below the ratio achieved by Hanesbrands. At the beginning of the chapter, we discussed key elements of Gildan's business strategy that focused on vertical integration and low-cost manufacturing of premium-quality products in Central America and the Carribean basin, its marketing philosophy, and its distribution strategy. According to Gildan's annual report for fiscal year 2009, the deterioration in the gross profit percentage occurred because the company's cost of sales increased at a faster rate than the increase in net sales. While net revenue has decreased by 17 percent from 2008 to 2009, Gildan could reduce its cost of sales only by 11 percent.

A Few Cautions → To assess the company's ability to sustain its gross margins, you must understand the sources of any change in its gross profit percentage. For example, an increase in margin resulting from increases in seasonal sales of high-margin products is less likely to be sustainable than one resulting from introducing new products. Also, higher prices must often be sustained with higher research and development and advertising expenses, which may reduce the operating and net profit substantially. This is why, if operating expenses do not decrease too, a small decrease in gross profit percentage can lead to a large decrease in net profit.

SELECTED FOCUS COMPANY COMPARISONS

Nokia 34.3%

Andrew Peller 40.0%

Nestlé 56.9%

SELF-STUDY **QUIZ 7-1**

1. Assume that Sportswear Inc. sold $30,000 worth of T-shirts to various retailers with terms 1/10, n/30, and half of that amount was paid within the discount period. Gross sales at company-owned stores were $5,000 for the same period, 80 percent being paid using credit cards with a 3 percent discount and the rest in cash. Compute net sales for the period.

_____

_____

2. During the first quarter of fiscal year 2011, the company's net sales were $150,000 and cost of sales was $110,000. Verify that its gross profit percentage was 26.66 percent.

_____

_____

After you complete your answers, go online for the solutions.

connect

MEASURING AND REPORTING RECEIVABLES

Classifying Receivables

Receivables may be classified in three common ways. First, receivables may be classified as trade or non-trade receivables. A trade receivable is created in the normal course of business when there is a sale of merchandise or services on credit. A *non-trade receivable* arises from transactions other than the normal sale of merchandise or services. For example, if Gildan loaned money to key employees to assist them in financing the purchase of their first homes, the loans would be classified as non-trade receivables.

TRADE RECEIVABLES are open accounts owed to the business by trade customers.

Second, the receivable may be either an account receivable or a note receivable. An **account receivable** is created when there is a sale of products and services on open account to customers or when a company expects to receive payments from other parties, such as collection from an insurance company following an unfortunate accident. A note receivable is a written promise made by another party (e.g., a customer) to pay the company (1) a specified amount of money, called the *principal*, at a definite future date, known as the *maturity date*, and (2) a specified amount of interest at one or more future dates. Interest is the amount charged for use of the principal. A note receivable is also classified as a financial asset, reflecting the contractual right to receive cash from debtors in the future. We discuss the computation of interest when we discuss notes payable in another chapter.

NOTES RECEIVABLE are written promises that require another party to pay the business under specific conditions (amount, time, interest).

Third, in a classified statement of financial position, receivables also are classified as either *current* or *non-current* (short-term or long-term), depending on when the cash is expected to be collected.

FOREIGN CURRENCY RECEIVABLES

INTERNATIONAL **PERSPECTIVE**

Export (international) sales are a growing part of the Canadian economy. For example, international sales amounted to 97 percent of Gildan's revenues in 2009, particularly sales to the U.S. market. As is the case with domestic sales to other businesses, most export sales to businesses are on credit. When the buyer has agreed to pay in its local currency instead of Canadian dollars, Gildan cannot add these trade receivables, which are denominated in foreign currency, directly to its Canadian-dollar denominated trade receivables*.

*Gildan has reported its financial statements in U.S. dollars since 2004. The use of Canadian dollars here is for illustrative purposes only.

Selected Foreign Currency Exchange Rates (in CDN$)

Mexican Peso $0.08

American Dollar $1.05

Euro $1.43

Gildan's accountants must first convert them into Canadian dollars by using the end-of-period exchange rate between the two currencies. For example, if a European distributor purchased goods from Gildan for €20,000 on August 31, 2009, and each euro was worth CDN$1.58 on that date, Gildan would add $31,600 to its trade receivables on that date. If Gildan has not collected the €20,000 by October 4, 2009, the end of its fiscal year, then the receivable should be adjusted for the change in the value of the euro, and an exchange gain or loss would be reported on the income statement.

Accounting for Bad Debts

LO⁴

Estimate, report, and evaluate the effects of uncollectible trade receivables (bad debts) on financial statements.

As we noted before in the discussion of sales discounts and allowances, Gildan allows its customers (wholesalers and retailers) to purchase goods on open account because it believes that providing this service will increase sales, but it also has a cost. Gildan must pay to maintain a credit-granting and collection system because some customers may not pay their debts. Credit policies should be based on the *trade-off* between profit on additional sales and any additional bad debts. If the credit policy is too restrictive, it will result in a low rate of bad debts, but the company will turn away many good credit customers, causing a loss of sales revenue. On the other hand, if Gildan's credit policy is too liberal, then net sales would increase, but bad debts will likely increase as well because more customers are likely to default on their payments, causing a write-off of trade receivables.

For billing and collection purposes, Gildan keeps a separate trade receivables account (called a **subsidiary account**) for each of the retailers and wholesalers that buys its products. The trade receivables amount on the statement of financial position represents the total of these individual customer accounts. When Gildan extends credit to its customers, it knows that a certain amount of credit sales may not be collected in the future. The matching process requires the recording of bad debt expense in the *same* accounting period in which the related sales are made. This presents an important accounting problem. Gildan may not learn which particular customers will not pay until the *next* accounting period. So, at the end of the period of sale, it normally does not know which customers' trade receivables are bad debts.

The **ALLOWANCE METHOD** bases bad debt expense on an estimate of uncollectible accounts.

Gildan resolves this problem by using the allowance method to estimate the expected amount of bad debts. There are two primary steps in applying the allowance method: (1) estimating and recording of bad debts expense and (2) writing off specific accounts determined to be uncollectible during the period. The estimation of bad debts is an example of prudence, whereby Gildan deducts the estimated amount of bad debts from the ending balance of trade receivables and reports the net realizable value of trade receivables on the statement of financial position.

BAD DEBT EXPENSE (DOUBTFUL ACCOUNTS EXPENSE) is the expense associated with estimated uncollectible trade receivables.

Recording Bad Debt Expense Estimates   Bad debt expense (also called *doubtful accounts expense, uncollectible accounts expense*) is the expense associated with estimated uncollectible trade receivables. It is recorded through an **adjusting journal entry at the end of the accounting period**. For the year ended October 4, 2009, Gildan estimated bad debt expense to be $6,000 and made the following adjusting entry:

Bad debt expense (E) 6,000
    Allowance for doubtful accounts (XA)   6,000

Assets		=	Liabilities	+	Shareholders' Equity	
Allowance for doubtful accounts	−6,000				Bad debt expense	−6,000

Gildan includes the bad debt expense in the category "selling, general and administrative" expenses on the income statement. It decreases profit and shareholders' equity.

Trade receivables could not be credited in the journal entry, because it is difficult to know at that date which customers may not pay in the future. The credit is made, instead, to a contra-asset account called *Allowance for Doubtful Accounts* (also called *Allowance for Doubtful Receivables* or *Allowance for Doubtful Debts*). As a contra asset, the balance in allowance for doubtful accounts is always subtracted from the balance of the asset trade receivables. Thus, the entry decreases the net realizable value of trade receivables and total assets.

ALLOWANCE FOR DOUBTFUL ACCOUNTS (ALLOWANCE FOR DOUBTFUL RECEIVABLES, ALLOWANCE FOR DOUBTFUL DEBTS) is a contra-asset account containing the estimated uncollectible trade receivables.

Impaired Receivables—Writing Off Specific Uncollectible Accounts
Throughout the year, when it is determined that a customer will not pay its debt (e.g., due to bankruptcy), the receivable is considered impaired. The write-off of that individual receivable is recorded through a journal entry. When a specific trade receivable has been identified as uncollectible, it must be removed from the appropriate trade receivables account. At the same time, the previously established allowance for such a doubtful receivable is no longer needed and should be removed from the allowance for doubtful accounts.

The following journal entry summarizes the write-offs of $2,800 in trade receivables during the year:

Allowance for doubtful accounts (XA)	2,800	
Trade receivables (A)		2,800

Assets		=	Liabilities	+	Shareholders' Equity
Allowance for doubtful accounts	−2,800				
Trade receivables	−2,800				

Notice that this journal entry *did not affect any income statement accounts.* The estimated bad debt expense was already recorded with an adjusting entry in the period of sale. Also, the entry *did not change the carrying amount of trade receivables,* since the decrease in the asset account (trade receivables) was offset by an equal decrease in the contra-asset account (allowance for doubtful accounts). Thus, it did not affect total assets.

Recovery of Accounts Previously Written Off When a customer makes a payment on an account previously written off, the initial journal entry to write off the account is reversed for the amount that is collected, and another journal entry is made to record the collection of cash. Assume that of the $2,800 of receivables that were written off during the fiscal year 2009, $200 was recovered from a customer that faced financial difficulties but was able to arrange for long-term financing to restart the business. The journal entries and transaction effects related to the recovery of bad debts are shown below:

Trade receivables (A)	200	
Allowance for doubtful accounts (XA)		200
Cash (A)	200	
Trade receivables (A)		200

Assets		=	Liabilities	+	Shareholders' Equity
Trade receivables	+200				
Allowance for doubtful accounts	−200				
Cash	+200				
Trade receivables	−200				

Notice that the net effect of the recovered amount on trade receivables is zero. The recovered amount is first recorded in trade receivables to show that the customer has honoured its previous commitment to pay Gildan $200.

Summary of the Accounting Process It is important to remember that accounting for bad debts is a two-step process:

Step	Timing	Accounts Affected		Financial Statement Effects	
1. Record estimated bad debts adjustment	End of period in which sales are made	Bad debt expense (E) ↑		Profit	↓
		Allowance for doubtful accounts (XA) ↑		Assets (trade receivables, net)	↓
2. Identify and write off actual bad debts	Throughout period as bad debts become known	Trade receivables (A) ↓		Profit	No effect
		Allowance for doubtful accounts (XA) ↓		Assets (trade receivables, net)	

Gildan's complete 2009 process for bad debts can now be summarized in terms of the changes in trade receivables (gross) and the allowance for doubtful accounts:[7]

Trade Receivables (gross) (A)

Beginning balance	209,100	Collections on account	1,079,019
Sales on account	1,038,319	Write-offs	2,800
Ending balance	165,600		

Allowance for Doubtful Accounts (XA)

Write-offs	2,800	Beginning balance	2,800
		Bad debt expense adjustment	6,000
		Ending balance	6,000

Trade receivables (gross) includes the total trade receivables, both collectible and uncollectible. The balance in the allowance for doubtful accounts is the portion of the trade receivables balance the company estimates to be uncollectible. Trade receivables (net) reported on the statement of financial position is the portion of the accounts the company expects to collect (or its estimated net realizable value). These details are useful to external users of financial statements for assessing the quality of the company's receivables.

Reporting Trade Receivables

Analysts who want information on Gildan's receivables will find accounts receivable, net of allowance for doubtful accounts (the *carrying amount*), of $166,762 and $215,833 for fiscal years 2009 and 2008, respectively, reported on the statement of financial position (Exhibit 7.2). These amounts include trade receivables of $159,600

Exhibit **7.2**

Accounts Receivable on the Statement of Financial Position

REAL WORLD EXCERPT

Gildan Activewear

ANNUAL REPORT

CONSOLIDATED STATEMENT OF FINANCIAL POSITION
October 4, 2009, and October 5, 2008
(in thousands of dollars)

	2009	2008
Assets		
Current assets:		
Cash and cash equivalents	$ 99,732	$ 12,357
Accounts receivable	166,762	215,833
Inventories	301,867	316,172
Prepaid expenses and deposits	11,604	10,413

Source: Gildan Activewear Annual Report 2009.

[7]This assumes that all sales are on account.

and $206,300 for fiscal years 2009 and 2008, respectively as reported in Exhibit 7.4. The remaining amounts relate to non-trade receivables.

Gildan disclosed the amounts of bad debt expense and trade receivables written off for the period in the Management Discussion and Analysis section of its annual report.[8]

REAL WORLD EXCERPT

Gildan Activewear

ANNUAL REPORT

The movement in the allowance for doubtful accounts in respect of trade receivables was as follows:

(in $ thousands)*	October 4, 2009	October 5, 2008
Balance, beginning of year	$2,800	2,000
Bad debt expense	6,000	4,500
Write-off of accounts receivable	(2,800)	(4,000)
Increase due to acquisition of Prewett	—	300
Balance, end of year	6,000	2,800

*Original amounts are reported in millions, but have been changed to thousands so that the amounts above are consistent with those reported in the related T-accounts shown.

Source: Gildan Activewear Annual Report 2009.

The allowance for doubtful accounts had a balance of $2,800 at the beginning of fiscal year 2009, which was augmented by an additional amount of $6,000 based on the company's credit sales during the year. Write-offs of uncollectible accounts caused a reduction of $2,800, leading to an ending balance of $6,000 at October 4, 2009.

SELF-STUDY **QUIZ 7-2**

In a recent year, Delta Apparel Inc., a Gildan competitor, had a beginning credit balance in the allowance for doubtful accounts of $1,290 (all numbers in thousands of dollars). It wrote off trade receivables totalling $1,160 during the year and made a bad debt expense adjustment of $1,230 for the year.

1. Prepare the adjusting journal entry that Delta made to record bad debt expense at the end of the year.

2. Prepare the journal entry summarizing Delta's total write-offs of bad debts during the year.

3. Compute the balance in the allowance for doubtful accounts at the end of the year.

After you complete your answers, go online for the solutions.

▤ connect

Estimating Bad Debts

The bad debt expense recorded in the end-of-period adjusting entry often is estimated based on an aging of trade receivables. Alternatively, it can be estimated as a percentage of the total credit sales for the period. The aging method is generally more accurate, but the percentage of credit sales method is simpler to apply. Many companies use the simpler method on a weekly or monthly basis and use the more accurate method on a monthly or quarterly basis to check the accuracy of the earlier estimates.

Aging of Trade Receivables Method Many companies estimate bad debt expense by examining the age of trade receivables that are outstanding. The aging of

---

[8]Prior to the adoption of IFRS by Canadian publicly accountable enterprises, Canadian companies seldom reported the detailed changes in their allowance for doubtful accounts. Following the adoption of IFRS, publicly accountable enterprises have disclosed more details about their trade receivables and the related allowance account.

AGING OF TRADE RECEIVABLES METHOD estimates uncollectible accounts based on the age of each trade receivable.

trade receivables method relies on the fact that, as trade receivables become older and overdue, they usually are less likely to be collectible. For example, a receivable that is due in 30 days but has not been paid after 60 days is more likely to be collected, on average, than a similar receivable that still remains unpaid after 120 days. Based on its prior experience, the company could estimate the percentage of receivables of different ages that may not be paid.

Suppose that Amer and Ciero (a hypothetical company) split its receivables into five age categories, as presented in Exhibit 7.3. Management of the company might then *estimate* the following probable bad debt rates: 1 percent of receivables not yet due, 3 percent of receivables that are past due by 1 to 30 days, 6 percent of receivables that are past due by 31 to 60 days, and so on. The total of the amounts estimated to be uncollectible under the aging method is the balance that *should be* in the allowance for doubtful accounts at the end of the period. This is called the *estimated ending balance*. From this, the adjustment to record bad debt expense (and an increase in the allowance for doubtful accounts) for 2011 would be computed.

This computation also can be illustrated in T-account form. The current credit balance in the allowance account, before the end-of-period adjustment, is $188. We insert the new ending balance from the aging schedule and then solve for the current amount of bad debt expense.

Allowance for Doubtful Accounts (XA)

		2011 Beginning balance	1,455
Write-offs (throughout the year)	1,267		
		Unadjusted balance	188
Step 2: Adjustment inferred ⟶		2011 Bad debt expense (adjustment)	1,344
Step 1: Ending balance estimated ⟶ from aging of trade receivables		2011 Ending balance	1,532

The end-of-period adjusting entry to bad debt expense and allowance for doubtful accounts is made on December 31 for $1,344.

The amount written off throughout the year may sometimes exceed the beginning balance of the allowance in doubtful accounts, which indicates that the company underestimated the amount that is potentially uncollectible. If the total amount written off equals $1,567, the allowance account will have an unadjusted *debit* balance of $112, and the bad debt expense would equal $1,644.

Gildan disclosed the aging of its trade receivables in the Management's Discussion and Analysis section of its annual report, as shown in Exhibit 7.4. If these receivables were due within 30 days, then the longer the receivable remains uncollected, the lower the likelihood it will be collected. Beyond 90 days, collectability is very

Exhibit **7.3**

Aging Analysis of Trade Receivables

AMER AND CIERO
Analysis of Aged Trade Receivables
December 31, 2011

Customer	Not Yet Due	1–30 Days Past Due	31–60 Days Past Due	61–90 Days Past Due	Over 90 Days Past Due	Total
Adams, Inc.	$ 600					$ 600
Baker Stores	300	$ 900	$ 100			1,300
Cox Co.			400	$ 900	$ 100	1,400
Zoe Stores	2,000		1,000			3,000
Total	$17,200	$12,000	$8,000	$1,200	$1,600	$40,000
Estimated % uncollectable	1%	3%	6%	10%	25%	
Estimated uncollectable accounts	$ 172	$ 360	$ 480	$ 120	$ 400	$ 1,532

The aging of trade receivable balances was as follows as at

(in $ millions)	October 4, 2009	October 5, 2008
Not past due	144.5	186.0
Past due 0–30 days	14.9	15.7
Past due 31–60 days	3.5	3.2
Past due 61–120 days	1.2	1.9
Past due over 121 days	1.5	2.3
Trade receivables	165.6	209.1
Less allowance for doubtful accounts	(6.0)	(2.8)
Total trade receivables	159.6	206.3

Source: Gildan Activewear Annual Report 2009.

doubtful. The percentage of receivables past due increased from 11 percent in 2008 to 13 percent in 2009, which is not an encouraging signal. The increase in the allowance for doubtful accounts from $2.8 million for 2008 to $6.0 million for 2009 reflects management's increased concern that additional customers may default on their debt to Gildan because of the economic downturn during that period. These details help shareholders, lenders, and analysts estimate future impairments of trade receivables.

Percentage of Credit Sales Method As an alternative to the aging of trade receivables, many companies make their estimates by using the percentage of credit sales method, which bases bad debt expense on the historical percentage of credit sales that result in bad debts. The average percentage of credit sales that result in bad debts can be computed by dividing total bad debts by total *credit* sales. A company that has been operating for some years has sufficient experience to estimate probable future bad debts. For example, assume that Amer and Ciero had experienced the following in three recent years:

PERCENTAGE OF CREDIT SALES METHOD bases bad debt expense on the historical perspective of credit sales that result in bad debts.

Year	Bad Debts	Credit Sales
2009	$ 900	$190,000
2010	1,200	220,000
2011	1,400	290,000
Total	$3,500	$700,000

The average bad debt rate equals 0.005 ($3,500 ÷ $700,000) or 0.5% for the three-year period 2009–2011.

If net credit sales for the year 2011 were approximately $268,000 and the company used this method, then the bad debt expense is $1,340, computed as follows:

$$\textbf{Bad debt expense} = \textbf{Credit sales} \times \textbf{Bad debt rate}$$
$$= \textbf{\$268,000} \times \textbf{0.5\%} = \textbf{\$1,340}$$

This amount is directly recorded as bad debt expense for 2011, with a corresponding increase in the allowance for doubtful accounts. New companies often rely on the experience of similar companies that have been operating for a number of years. A company usually adjusts the historical average bad debt rate to reflect future expectations. For example, if retail sales were rising, the company might decrease its rate to 0.4 percent, reasoning that fewer of its business customers (retailers) will become bankrupt. In difficult economic times, the company might increase its rate because more customers are likely to face financial difficulties.

Allowance for Doubtful Accounts (XA)

		Beginning balance	1,455
Write-offs (throughout the year)	1,267		
		Unadjusted balance	188
		Bad debt expense (adjustment)	1,340
		Ending balance	1,528

Based on percentage of credit sales

Notice that the bad debt expense, $1,340, differs slightly from the amount, $1,344, computed under the aging of trade receivables method. Because the two methods are different, one should not expect that they produce the same bad debt expense.

Comparison of the Two Methods   Students often fail to recognize that the approach of recording bad debt expense by using the aging of trade receivables method is different from that of the percentage of credit sales method:

Aging of trade receivables. Compute the *final ending balance* in the allowance for doubtful accounts. Thus, the amount of bad debt expense for the period is the *difference* between the estimated uncollectible accounts (just calculated) and the balance of the allowance for doubtful accounts at the end of the period *before the adjusting entry* has been made.

Percentage of credit sales. Directly compute the amount to be recorded in the journal entry as *bad debt expense* and reported on the *income statement* for the period.

The computation of bad debt expense under the two methods are contrasted below, where the computed amounts are highlighted.

Aging of Trade Receivables	Percentage of Credit Sales
Beginning balance of Allowance account	Beginning balance of Allowance account
− Write-offs throughout the year	− Write-offs throughout the year
+ Bad debt expense (inferred)	**+ Bad debt expense (computed)**
= Ending balance of Allowance account (computed)	= Ending balance of Allowance account (inferred)

Actual Write-Offs Compared with Estimates   The amount of uncollectible accounts actually written off seldom equals the estimated amount previously recorded. This error in estimating bad debts is taken into consideration in determining the bad

FINANCIAL ANALYSIS

SALES VERSUS COLLECTIONS: THE MARKETING–FINANCIAL MANAGEMENT CONFLICT

Company managers often forget that while extending credit increases sales volume, it may also increase the volume of bad debts if proper credit checks of the customers are not made or if the company relaxes its credit policy too much. Marketing-oriented companies that emphasize sales without monitoring the collection of credit sales will soon find much of their current assets tied up in trade receivables. On the other hand, the absence of bad debts may be the result of a very tight credit policy that reduces both sales and profit.

In the last decade, the leading domestic automotive companies, such as General Motors and DaimlerChrysler, contributed to sales growth by providing short- and medium-term financing to their dealers and distributors in order to encourage them to purchase their products. Financing of sales by the seller, called *vendor financing*, had become common industry practice until the risks of vendor financing came to light when demand for automobiles and auto parts weakened. Dealers and distributors started to default on their debts, and vendors were forced to absorb credit losses and increase their allowances for doubtful accounts.

When credit losses are relatively high because of vendor financing, financial analysts should be cautious in their analysis of companies' sales growth.

debt expense at the end of the next accounting period. *When estimates are found to be incorrect, financial statement values for prior annual accounting periods are not corrected.*

Prudence in the Valuation of Trade Receivables   Creditors and analysts prefer that companies follow *prudent* financial strategies that result in reporting lower amounts for profit and assets, and higher amounts for liabilities. Accountants and auditors are also cautious about reporting optimistic values that overstate the company's operating performance and its financial position. For trade receivables, the amount reported on the statement of financial position should reflect the amount expected to be collected from customers. In this context, prudence suggests that the allowance for doubtful accounts be commensurate with the creditworthiness of the company's customers. A prudent measure of trade receivables means a larger amount of bad debt expense and a larger allowance for doubtful accounts. It is better to err on the side of having a larger allowance than having a smaller one that may not be adequate to cover future bad debts.

TRADE RECEIVABLES

FOCUS ON
CASH FLOWS

The change in trade receivables can be a major determinant of a company's cash flow from operations. The income statement reflects the revenues earned during the period, whereas the cash flow from operating activities reflects the cash collections from customers for the same period. Since sales on account increase the balance in trade receivables, and cash collections from customers decrease the balance in trade receivables, the change in trade receivables from the beginning to the end of the period is the difference between sales and cash collections.

EFFECT ON STATEMENT OF CASH FLOWS

In General → When a net *decrease in trade receivables* for the period occurs, the amount of cash collected from customers exceeds revenue; thus, the decrease must be *added* to revenue or to profit (since revenue is a component of profit) in computing cash flows from operations. When a net *increase in trade receivables* occurs, cash collected from customers is less than revenue; thus, the increase must be *subtracted* from profit in computing cash flows from operations.

	Effect on Cash Flows
Operating activities (indirect method)	
Profit	$xxx
Adjusted for	
Decrease in trade receivables	+
or	
Increase in trade receivables	−

Focus Company Analysis → Exhibit 7.5 is the operating activities section of Gildan's statement of cash flows. Sales decline during 2009 has resulted in a decrease in Gildan's balance in trade receivables. This decrease is added back to profit (net earnings) in the computation of Gildan's cash flow from operations, because revenues are lower than cash collected from customers during 2009. When trade receivables increase, the amount of the increase is subtracted from profit in determining the cash flow from operating activities, because cash collected from customers is lower than revenues.

To assess the effectiveness of overall credit granting and collection activities, managers and analysts often compute the receivables turnover ratio.

Exhibit **7.5**

Receivables on the Statement of
Cash Flows

REAL WORLD EXCERPT

Gildan Activewear

ANNUAL REPORT

GILDAN ACTIVEWEAR INC.
Consolidated Statements of Cash Flows
Years ended October 4, 2009, October 5, 2008, and September 30, 2007
(in thousands of U.S. dollars)

	2009	2008	2007
Cash flows from (used in) operating activities:			
Net earnings	$ 95,329	$ 146,350	$ 129,062
Adjustments for:			
Depreciation and amortization (note 17(b))	65,407	57,135	37,268
Variation of depreciation included in inventories (note (b))	(2,437)	(957)	(1,837)
Restructuring charges related to assets held for sale and property, plant and equipment (note 16)	976	2,174	5,523
Loss on disposal of property, plant and equipment	561	1,369	332
Stock-based compensation costs	3,007	2,965	1,814
Future income taxes (note 14)	(2,434)	(15,885)	(8,919)
Non-controlling interest	110	230	1,278
Unrealized net (gain) loss on foreign exchange and financial derivatives	(1,012)	(2,222)	3,226
	159,507	191,159	167,747
Changes in non-cash working capital balances:			
Accounts receivable	48,351	10,263	(34,919)
Inventories	16,742	(31,178)	(37,473)
Prepaid expenses and deposits	(1,191)	(881)	(2,202)
Accounts payable and accrued liabilities	(22,731)	25,700	(4,800)
Income taxes payable	(31,499)	43,802	343
	169,179	238,865	88,696

Source: Gildan Activewear Annual Report 2009.

KEY RATIO
ANALYSIS

RECEIVABLES TURNOVER RATIO

LO5

Compute and interpret the
receivables turnover ratio
and the effects of trade
receivables on cash flows.

ANALYTICAL QUESTION → How effective are credit-granting and collection activities?
RATIO AND COMPARISONS → An answer to this question is provided by the receivables
turnover ratio, which is computed as follows:

$$\text{Receivables Turnover} = \frac{\text{Net Sales*}}{\text{Average Net Trade Receivables**}}$$

*Since the amount of net credit sales is normally not reported separately, most analysts use net sales in this
equation.
**Average net trade receivables = (Beginning net trade receivables + Ending net trade receivables) ÷ 2

The 2009 ratio for Gildan is

$$\frac{\$1,038,319}{(\$209,100 + \$165,600) \div 2} = 5.54$$

This ratio can be stated in a more intuitive manner by dividing the average trade receivables by the
average credit sales per day:

$$\text{Average Collection Period} = \frac{\text{Average Net Trade Receivables}}{\text{Net Sales} / 365}$$

The 2009 average collection period for Gildan is

$$\text{Average Collection Period} = \frac{\$187,350}{\$1,038,319 / 365} = 65.9 \text{ days}$$

An equivalent computation is

$$\text{Average Collection Period} = \frac{365}{\text{Receivables Turnover}} = \frac{365}{5.54} = 65.9 \text{ days}$$

Comparisons over Time			Comparisons with Competitors	
Gildan			Hanesbrands Inc.	Delta Apparel
2007	2008	2009	2009	2009
5.64	6.31	5.54	9.10	6.08

INTERPRETATIONS

In General → The receivables turnover ratio reflects how many times average trade receivables were recorded and collected during the period. The higher the ratio, the faster the collection of receivables. A higher ratio benefits the company because it can invest the cash collected to earn interest income or reduce borrowings to reduce interest expense. Overly generous payment schedules and ineffective collection methods keep the receivables turnover low. Analysts and creditors watch this ratio because a sudden decline may mean that a company is extending payment deadlines in an attempt to prop up lagging sales, or even recording sales that will later be returned by customers. Many managers and analysts compute the *average collection period*, which indicates the average time it takes a customer to pay the amounts due.

Focus Company Analysis → Gildan's receivables turnover increased from 5.64 in 2007 to 6.31 in 2008 and then decreased to 5.54 in 2009. Its ratio is lower than both Hanesbrands's and Delta Apparel's. Gildan's customers are slower in paying their bills than the customers of its competitors. Alternatively, Gildan may have a less effective collections practice or different receivables contracts with longer credit terms.

A Few Cautions → Since differences across industries and between firms in the manner in which customer purchases are financed can cause dramatic differences in the ratio, a particular firm's ratio should be compared only with its own prior years' figures or with other firms in the same industry following the same financing practices.

> **Selected Industry Comparisons: Receivables Turnover Ratio**
>
> Retailing 143.74
>
> Food and Beverages 18.47
>
> Paper and Forest Products 11.87

SELF-STUDY QUIZ 7-3

1. Assume that Kleer Company reported beginning and ending balances in the allowance for doubtful accounts of $723 and $904, respectively. It also reported that write-offs of bad debts amounted to $648 (all numbers in thousands). Assuming that the company did not collect any amounts that were written off previously, what amount did the company record as bad debt expense for the period? (*Hint:* Use the allowance for doubtful accounts T-account to solve for the missing value.)

Allowance for Doubtful Accounts (XA)

2. Kleer Company reported an increase in trade receivables for the period. Was that increase added to or subtracted from profit in the computation of cash flow from operations? Explain your answer.

3. Explain whether **granting longer payment deadlines** (e.g., 60 days instead of 30 days) will most likely **increase** or **decrease** the trade receivables turnover ratio.

After you complete your answers, go online for the solutions.

connect

Internal Control and Management Responsibility

The term *internal control* refers to the process by which a company's board of directors, audit committee, management, and other personnel provide reasonable assurance that the accounting system minimizes the risk of material misstatement of reported financial information.[9] In addition, the system must assure compliance with all laws and regulations, and ensure the efficiency and effectiveness of operations. A well-designed

> **INTERNAL CONTROLS** are the processes by which the company's board of directors, management, and other personnel provide reasonable assurance regarding the reliability of the company's financial reporting, the effectiveness and efficiency of its operations, and its compliance with applicable laws and regulations.

---

[9] Internal control is defined as the "process designed, implemented and maintained by those charged with governance, management and other personnel to provide reasonable assurance about the achievement of an entity's objectives with regard to reliability of financial reporting, effectiveness and efficiency of operations, and compliance with applicable laws and regulations." *CICA Assurance Handbook*, Part 1, Glossary of Terms.

system of internal controls prevents inadvertent errors and removes opportunities for individuals to steal, misrepresent, defraud, or embezzle assets from a company. New Canadian legislation prevents top executives and members of the board of directors from ignoring their management responsibility to design, supervise, and implement appropriate internal control systems.

Recent Canadian scandals such as Nortel Networks Corp. and Livent Inc. led the Canadian Securities Administrators to enact new regulations regarding internal control systems. In August 2008, the Canadian Securities Administrators issued National Instrument (NI) 52-109, which requires the corporation's chief executive officer and chief financial officer to sign form 52-109F1 (certification of annual filings), a legal document that certifies the quality of the internal control system.[10] In particular for corporations listed on the Toronto Stock Exchange, the two officers certify the reliability of financial reporting in accordance with applicable accounting standards. Executives must also attest to the effectiveness of the internal control and financial reporting system. The annual report must disclose any deficiencies in the disclosure controls and procedures, the related risks, and any plans to remedy these deficiencies. No audit is necessary but auditors would find it unusual if an executive certified a deficient system. Auditors must correct or refuse to attest to all audited disclosure, including false claims made on form 52-109F1.

A QUESTION OF ACCOUNTABILITY   ETHICS AND THE NEED FOR INTERNAL CONTROL

Some people are bothered by the recommendation that all well-run companies should have strong internal control procedures. These people believe that control procedures suggest that the company's management does not trust its employees. Although the vast majority of employees are trustworthy, employee theft costs businesses billions of dollars each year. Interviews with convicted felons indicate that, in many cases, they stole from their employers because they thought that it was easy and that no one cared (internal control procedures were not present).

A recent survey of global economic crime (which includes asset misappropriations, accounting fraud, bribery, money laundering, and illegal insider trading) revealed that these activities continue to be serious issues affecting many organizations in many countries. This is particularly true during difficult economic times when the reduction of the workforce also affects accounting staff that are responsible for internal control of operations. The survey indicated that asset misappropriation, accounting fraud, and corruption and bribery are the most prevalent types of economic crime, with a significant increase in accounting fraud over time. It also revealed that internal controls were not effective in detecting the fraud. In fact, internal audit procedures were identified as the primary source of fraud detection in fewer than 20 percent of the cases.[11] This explains the continued emphasis by securities regulators on the validation of internal controls over financial reporting.

Many companies have a formal code of ethics that requires high standards of behaviour in dealing with customers, suppliers, fellow employees, and the company's assets. Although each employee is ultimately responsible for his or her own ethical behaviour, internal control procedures can be thought of as important value statements from management. Preventing theft through strong internal controls prevents people from destroying their lives if they steal and are subsequently caught and penalized for their unethical behaviour.

---

[10]Canadian Securities Administrators, "National Instrument 52-109, Certification of Disclosure in Issuers' Annual and Interim Filings," August 2008.

[11]PricewaterhouseCoopers, "The Global Economics Crimes Survey." November 2009. The report is accessible through PwC's website, **www.pwc.com/gx/en/economic-crime-survey/index.jhtml**. Interested readers may also wish to consult two other reports on occupational fraud: Association of Certified Fraud Examiners (ACFE), "The 2008 Report to the Nation on Occupational Fraud and Abuse." Austin: USA (available at **www.acfe.com/documents/2008-rttn.pdf**) and Association of Certified Fraud Examiners and Dominic Peltier-Rivest, "Detecting Occupational Fraud in Canada: A Study of Its Victims and Perpetrators (available at **www.acfe.com/documents/rttn-canadian.pdf**).

Control over Trade Receivables

The internal control system must respond to different sets of activities with different types of control. Controlling and protecting cash to prevent embezzlement, for example, will be different from controlling the security and accuracy of the information system. Many managers forget that although extending credit will increase sales volume, the related receivables do not increase profit unless they are collected. Companies that emphasize sales without monitoring the collection of credit sales will soon find much of their current assets tied up in trade receivables. To guard against extending credit to non-worthy customers, the following practices can help minimize bad debts:

1. Require approval of customers' credit history by a person independent of the sales and collection functions.

2. Monitor the age of trade receivables periodically, and contact customers with overdue payments.

3. Reward both sales and collection personnel for speedy collections so that they work as a team.

REPORTING AND SAFEGUARDING CASH

Cash and Cash Equivalents Defined

Cash is defined as money or any instrument that banks will accept for deposit and immediate credit to the company's account, such as a cheque, money order, or bank draft. Cash usually is divided into three categories: cash on hand, cash deposited in banks, and other instruments that meet the definition of cash.

International Accounting Standard 7 – Statement of Cash Flows defines cash equivalents as short-term, highly liquid investments that are readily convertible to known amounts of cash and that are subject to an insignificant risk of change in value. Typical instruments included as cash equivalents are bank certificates of deposit and treasury bills issued by the government to finance its activities.

Even though a company may have several bank accounts and several types of cash equivalents, all cash accounts and cash equivalents are usually combined as one amount for financial reporting purposes. Gildan reports a single account, cash and cash equivalents, with a balance of $99.7 million at October 4, 2009. The company clearly specifies cash equivalents as all liquid investments with maturities of three months or less from the date of acquisition.

Cash Management

Many businesses receive a large amount of cash, cheques, and credit card receipts from their customers each day. Anyone can spend cash, so management must develop procedures to safeguard the cash it uses in the business. Effective cash management involves more than protecting cash from theft, fraud, or loss through carelessness. Other cash management responsibilities include the following:

1. Accurate accounting so that reports of cash flows and balances may be prepared.

2. Controls to ensure that enough cash is on hand to meet (a) current operating needs, (b) maturing liabilities, and (c) unexpected emergencies.

3. Prevention of the accumulation of excess amounts of idle cash. Idle cash earns no revenue; therefore, it is often invested in securities to earn revenue (return) until it is needed for operations.

Internal Control of Cash

Because cash is the asset most vulnerable to theft and fraud, a significant number of internal control procedures should focus on cash. You have already observed internal control procedures for cash, although you may not have known it at the time. At most movie theatres, one employee sells tickets and another employee collects them. It would be less expensive to have one employee do both jobs, but it would also be easier

LO6

Report, control, and safeguard cash.

CASH is money or any instrument that banks will accept for deposit and immediate credit to the company's account, such as a cheque, money order, or bank draft.

CASH EQUIVALENTS are short-term, highly liquid investments that are readily convertible to known amounts of cash and which are subject to an insignificant risk of change in value.

for that single employee to steal cash and admit a patron without issuing a ticket. If different employees perform the tasks, a successful theft requires participation of both.

Effective internal control of cash should include the following:

1. **Separation of duties related to cash handling and recordkeeping:**

    a. Complete separation of the tasks of receiving cash and disbursing cash ensures that the individual responsible for depositing cash has no authority to sign cheques.

    b. Complete separation of the procedures of accounting for cash receipts and cash disbursements ensures, for example, that those handling sales returns do not create fictitious returns to conceal cash shortages.

    c. Complete separation of the physical handling of cash and all phases of the accounting function ensures that those either receiving or paying cash have no authority to make accounting entries.

The following diagram illustrates how the separation of duties contributes to strong internal control:

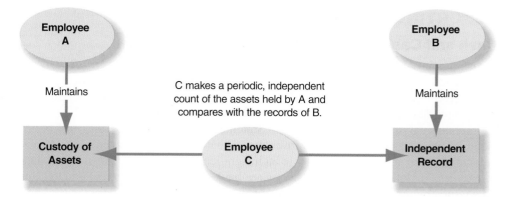

The separation of individual responsibilities deters theft because the collusion of two or more persons is needed to steal cash and then conceal the theft in the accounting records.

2. **Prescribed policies and procedures.**

    Specific policies and procedures should be established so that the work done by one individual is compared with the results reported by other individuals. Exhibit 7.6 provides a summary of typical policies and procedures to control cash.

Exhibit **7.6**

Typical Internal Controls for Cash

Internal Control Component	Prescribed Policies or Procedures
Cash budget	Prepare a monthly forecast of cash receipts, disbursements, and balances for the year, and require that managers document and justify any deviations from the budget each month.
Cash receipts	Prepare a listing of cash receipts on a daily basis. In practice, this often takes the form of cash register receipts or a descriptive list of incoming cheques. Require that all cash receipts be deposited in a bank daily. Keep any cash on hand under strict control.
Cash payments	Require separate approval of the purchases and other expenditures and separate approval of the actual cash payments. Assign the cash payment approval and the actual cheque-signing responsibilities to different individuals. Use pre-numbered cheques and pay special attention to payments by electronic funds transfers, since the bank does not process controlled documents (cheques).
Independent internal verification	Require comparison, by an independent supervisor, of cash receipts to bank deposits and cheques issued to invoices. Require monthly reconciliation of bank accounts with the cash accounts on the company's books (discussed in detail in the next section).
Rotation of duties	Require that employees take vacations, and rotate their duties.

When procedures similar to those described in Exhibit 7.6 are followed, concealing a fraudulent cash disbursement is difficult without the collusion of two or more persons. Reconciliation of cash accounts with bank statements provides an additional control on disbursements. The level of internal control, which is reviewed by the outside independent auditor, increases the reliability of the financial statements of the business.

LO7

Reconcile cash accounts and bank statements.

Reconciliation of the Cash Accounts and the Bank Statements

Content of a Bank Statement Proper use of the bank accounts of a business can be an important internal control procedure for cash. Each month, the bank provides the company (the depositor) with a bank statement that lists (1) each deposit recorded by the bank during the period, (2) each cheque cleared by the bank during the period, and (3) the balance in the company's account. The bank statement also shows the bank charges or deductions (such as service charges) made directly to the company's account by the bank. A typical bank statement is shown in Exhibit 7.7.

Exhibit 7.7 lists four items that need explanation. Notice that the payment of salaries on June 3 is coded *EFT*.[12] This is the code for electronic funds transfer. Gildan pays salaries to its employees by using electronic chequing, depositing electronic payments directly into the employees' bank accounts instead of issuing paper cheques. When Gildan orders the electronic payments, it records this item on the company's books in the same manner as a paper cheque, so no additional entry is needed. Gildan's customers can pay their bills electronically as well. Electronic funds transfer has become commonplace among companies and individuals as they use this form of payments for hydro, telecommunication, insurance, and other recurring expenses.

A **BANK STATEMENT** is a monthly report from a bank that shows deposits recorded, cheques cleared, other debits and credits, and a running bank balance.

Exhibit **7.7**

Example of a Bank Statement

	Canadian Bank		STATEMENT OF ACCOUNT			
CB	123 Bank Street Anytown, ON L5Z 2M7					

DATE	BRANCH NUMBER	ACCOUNT TYPE	ACCOUNT NUMBER	PAGE NO.
30 06 2010	1379	Chequing	79253	1 OF 2

J. Doe Company
10945 Long Road
Anytown, ON
L5X 3L5

Date	Code	Description	Debits	Credits	Balance
		Balance Forward			7,762.40
1-6	CK	Cheque No. 53	500.00		7,262.40
1-6	CK	Cheque No. 48	153.49		7,108.91
3-6	EFT	Payment of salaries	2,572.50		4,536.41
5-6	MD	Deposit		3,000.00	7,536.41
5-6	CK	Cheque No. 55	56.00		7,480.41
9-6	CK	Cheque No. 49	682.27		6,797.14
11-6	CK	Cheque No. 54	400.00		6,397.14
12-6	MD	Deposit		1,000.00	7,397.14
14-6	CK	Cheque No. 50	289.50		7,107.64
16-6	CK	Cheque No. 56	735.00		6,372.64
20-6	NSF	Cheque returned—not sufficient funds	204.76		6,167.88
20-6	SC	Service charge—cheque returned	10.00		6,157.88
21-6	MD	Deposit		1,500.00	7,657.88
22-6	CK	Cheque No. 58	1,583.00		6,074.88
24-6	CK	Cheque No. 61	79.50		5,995.38
24-6	CK	Cheque No. 57	192.25		5,803.13
26-6	CK	Cheque No. 62	573.00		5,230.13
29-6	MD	Deposit		4,500.00	9,730.13
30-6	CK	Cheque No. 59	936.00		8,794.13
30-6	INT	Interest earned		25.37	8,819.50

Code:
CK—Cheque
INT—Interest
EFT—Electronic funds transfer
MD—Merchant deposit
NSF—Not sufficient funds
SC—Service charge

Please check this statement and report any errors or omissions within 30 days of its delivery.
Please notify your branch of any change of address.

---

[12]These codes vary among banks.

Notice that on June 20, listed under debits, there is a deduction for $204.76 coded *NSF*. A cheque for $204.76 was received from a customer, R. Smith, and deposited by J. Doe Company with its bank, the Canadian Bank. The bank processed the cheque through banking channels to Smith's bank. Smith's account did not have sufficient funds to cover it; therefore, Smith's bank returned it to the Canadian Bank, which then charged it back to J. Doe Company. This type of cheque is often called an *NSF cheque* (not sufficient funds). The company needs to collect the amount of the cheque again from the customer. The NSF cheque is now a receivable; consequently, J. Doe Company must make an entry to debit receivables (R. Smith) and credit cash for the $204.76.

Notice the $10 listed under debits on June 20 and coded *SC*. This is the code for bank service charges. The bank statement included a memo by the bank explaining this service charge (which was not documented by a cheque). J. Doe Company must make an entry to reflect the $10 decrease in the bank balance as a debit to a relevant expense account, such as bank service expense, and a credit to cash.

Notice the $25.37 listed on June 30 under credits and the code *INT* for interest earned. The bank pays interest on chequing account balances, which increased J. Doe Company's account for interest earned during the period. The company must record the interest by making an entry to debit cash and credit interest revenue for the $25.37.

A **BANK RECONCILIATION** is the process of verifying the accuracy of both the bank statement and the cash accounts of a business.

Need for Reconciliation   A bank reconciliation is the process of comparing (reconciling) the ending cash balance in the company's records and the ending cash balance reported by the bank on the monthly bank statement. A bank reconciliation should be completed for each separate chequing account (i.e., for each bank statement received from each bank) at the end of each month.

Usually, the ending cash balance as shown on the bank statement does not agree with the ending cash balance shown by the related cash ledger account on the books of the company. For example, the cash ledger account of J. Doe Company showed the following at the end of June (Doe has only one chequing account):

Cash

June 1 balance	6,637.14	Cheques written in June	8,714.45
June deposits	11,800.00		
Ending balance	9,722.69		

The $8,819.50 ending cash balance shown on the bank statement (Exhibit 7.7) is different from the $9,722.69 ending balance of cash shown on the books of J. Doe Company. This difference exists because (1) some transactions affecting cash were recorded in the books of J. Doe Company but were not shown on the bank statement, (2) some transactions were shown on the bank statement but had not been recorded in the books of the J. Doe Company, and (3) errors occurred in recording transactions.

The flow of documents that have not reached either the company or the bank by the end of the accounting period is illustrated below:

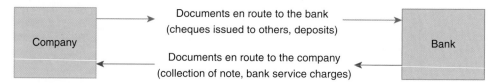

The most common causes of differences between the ending bank balance and the ending book balance of cash are as follows:

1. **Outstanding cheques.** These are cheques written by the company and recorded in the company's ledger as credits to the cash account that have not cleared the bank (they are not shown on the bank statement as a deduction from the bank balance). The outstanding cheques are identified by comparing the cancelled cheques that

the bank returned with the record of cheques (such as cheque stubs or a journal) maintained by the company.

2. **Deposits in transit.** These are deposits sent to the bank by the company and recorded in the company's ledger as debits to the cash account. The bank has not recorded these deposits (they are not shown on the bank statement as an increase in the bank balance). Deposits in transit usually happen when deposits are made one or two days before the close of the period covered by the bank statement. Deposits in transit are determined by comparing the deposits listed on the bank statement with the copies of the deposit slips retained by the company or other company records.

3. **Bank service charges.** An expense for bank services listed on the bank statement. This expense is not recorded on the company's books.

4. **NSF cheques.** A "bad cheque" or "bounced cheque" that was deposited but must be deducted from the company's cash account and recorded as an account receivable.

5. **Interest.** The interest paid by the bank to the company on its bank balance.

6. **Errors.** Both the bank and the company may make errors, especially when the volume of cash transactions is large.

Bank Reconciliation Illustrated   The company should make a bank reconciliation immediately after receiving each bank statement. The general format for the bank reconciliation follows:

Ending cash balance per books	$xxx	Ending cash balance per bank statement	$xxx
+ Collections by bank	xx	+ Deposits in transit	xx
− NSF cheques/Service charges	xx	− Outstanding cheques	xx
± Company errors	xx	± Bank errors	xx
Ending correct cash balances	$xxx	Ending correct cash balance	$xxx

Exhibit 7.8 shows the bank reconciliation prepared by J. Doe Company for the month of June to reconcile the ending bank balance ($8,819.50) with the ending book balance ($9,722.69). On the completed reconciliation, the correct cash balance is $9,542.30. This balance is different from both the reported bank and book balances before the reconciliation with the bank statement. This correct balance is the amount that should be shown in the cash account after the reconciliation. In this example, it is also the correct amount of cash that should be reported on the statement of financial position (J. Doe Company has only one chequing account and no cash on hand). J. Doe Company followed these steps in preparing the bank reconciliation:

Exhibit 7.8

Bank Reconciliation Illustrated

J. DOE COMPANY
Bank Reconciliation
June 30, 2010

Company's Books		Bank Statement	
Ending cash balance per books	$9,722.69	Ending cash balance per bank statement	$8,819.50
Additions		Additions	
Interest earned	25.37	Deposit in transit	1,800.00
Error in recording			
cheque No. 55	9.00		10,619.50
	9,757.06	Deductions	
Deductions		Outstanding cheques	1,077.20
NSF cheque of R. Smith	204.76		
Bank service charges	10.00	Ending correct cash balance	$9,542.30
Ending correct cash balance	$9,542.30		

1. **Identify the outstanding cheques.** A comparison of the cancelled cheques returned by the bank with the company's records of all cheques drawn showed the following cheques still outstanding (not cleared) at the end of June:

Cheque No.	Amount
60	$ 145.00
63	815.00
64	117.20
Total	$1,077.20

This total was entered on the reconciliation as a deduction from the bank account. These cheques will be deducted by the bank when they clear the bank.

2. **Identify the deposits in transit.** A comparison of the deposit slips on hand with those listed on the bank statement revealed that a deposit of $1,800 made on June 30 was not listed on the bank statement. This amount was entered on the reconciliation as an addition to the bank account. It will be added by the bank when it records the deposit.

3. **Record bank charges and credits.**

   a. Interest received from the bank, $25.37—entered on the bank reconciliation as an addition to the book balance; it already has been included in the bank balance.

   b. NSF cheque of R. Smith, $204.76—entered on the bank reconciliation as a deduction from the book balance; it has been deducted from the bank statement balance.

   c. Bank service charges, $10—entered on the bank reconciliation as a deduction from the book balance; it has been deducted from the bank balance.

4. **Determine the impact of errors.** At this point, J. Doe Company found that the reconciliation did not balance by $9. Because this amount is divisible by 9, a transposition of numbers was suspected. (A transposition, such as writing 27 for 72, always will cause an error that is exactly divisible by 9.) Upon checking the journal entries made during the month, a cheque written for $56 to pay a trade payable was found. The cheque was recorded in the company's accounts as $65. The incorrect entry made was a debit to trade payables and a credit to cash for $65 (instead of $56). Therefore, $9 (i.e., $65 − $56) must be added to the book cash balance on the reconciliation; the bank cleared the cheque for the correct amount, $56.

Note that in Exhibit 7.8, the two sections of the bank reconciliation now show a correct cash balance of $9,542.30. This amount will be reported as cash on a statement of financial position prepared at June 30, 2010.

A bank reconciliation as shown in Exhibit 7.8 accomplishes two major objectives:

1. Checks the accuracy of the bank balance and the company cash records, which involves developing the correct cash balance. The correct cash balance (plus cash on hand, if any) is the amount of cash that is reported on the statement of financial position.

2. Identifies any previously unrecorded transactions or changes that are necessary to cause the company's cash account(s) to show the correct cash balance. Any transactions or changes on the **company's books side** of the bank reconciliation need journal entries. Therefore, the following journal entries based on the company's books side of the bank reconciliation must be entered into the company's records.

Accounts of J. Doe Company

(a) Cash (A)		25.37	
Interest revenue (R)			25.37
To record interest from bank.			
(b) Trade receivables (A)		204.76	
Cash (A)			204.76
To record NSF cheque.			
(c) Bank service expense (E)		10.00	
Cash (A)			10.00
To record service fees charged by bank.			
(d) Cash (A)		9.00	
Trade payables (L)			9.00
To correct error made in recording a cheque payable to a creditor.			

Assets		=	Liabilities	+	Shareholders' Equity	
Cash (+ 25.37 − 204.76 − 10.00 + 9.00)	−180.39		Trade payables	+9.00	Bank service expense	−10.00
Trade receivables	+204.76				Interest earned	+25.37

Cash Account of J. Doe Company

The cash account prior to reconciliation was given earlier in this chapter. After the preceding journal entries are posted, the cash account is as follows:

Cash

June 1	Balance	6,637.14	June	Cheques written	8,714.45
June	Deposits	11,800.00	June 30	NSF cheque*	204.76
June 30	Interest earned*	25.37	June 30	Bank service charge*	10.00
June 30	Correcting entry*	9.00			
	Correct cash balance	9,542.30			

*Based on the bank reconciliation.

Notice that all of the additions and deductions on the company's books side of the reconciliation need journal entries to update the cash account. The additions and deductions on the bank statement side do not need journal entries because they will work out automatically when they clear the bank.

ACCOUNTING STANDARDS
FOR PRIVATE ENTERPRISES

This chapter covered the revenue recognition criteria that are applicable mainly to the sale of merchandise. We discuss in Appendix 7A the revenue recognition methods that are applicable for companies involved in long-term contracts extending beyond one accounting period. Accounting standard setters require companies to use the percentage of completion method to recognize both revenue and expenses on long-term contracts on a gradual basis over the duration of the contract. When this method cannot be used, Canadian private enterprises are required to use the completed contract method, which recognizes revenue and the related expenses in the period of completion of the contract, but not in prior periods. In contrast, Canadian publicly accountable enterprises are required to use the zero profit method. Both methods are discussed in more detail in Appendix 7A.

DEMONSTRATION CASE A

Wholesale Warehouse Stores sold $950,000 in merchandise during 2011, $400,000 of which was on credit with terms 2/10, n/30 (75 percent of these amounts were paid within the discount period), $500,000 was paid with credit cards (there was a 3 percent credit card discount), and the rest was paid in cash. On December 31, 2011, the trade receivables balance was $80,000, and the allowance for doubtful accounts was $3,000 (credit balance).

Required:

1. Compute net sales for 2011, assuming that sales and credit card discounts are treated as contra revenue accounts.
2. Assume that Wholesale uses the aging of trade receivables method and that it estimates that $10,000 worth of current accounts are uncollectible. Record bad debt expense for 2011.
3. Assume that Wholesale uses the percentage of credit sales method for estimating bad debt expense and that it estimates that 2 percent of credit sales will produce bad debts. Record bad debt expense for 2011.

We strongly recommend that you prepare your own answers to these requirements and then check your answers with the following suggested solution.

SUGGESTED **SOLUTION**

1. Both sales discounts and credit card discounts should be subtracted from sales revenues in the computation of net sales.

Sales revenue	$950,000
Less: Sales discounts (0.02 × 0.75 × $400,000)	6,000
Credit card discounts (0.03 × $500,000)	15,000
Net sales	$929,000

2. The entry made when using the aging of trade receivables method is the estimated balance minus the unadjusted balance.

Bad debt expense (E) ($10,000 − $3,000)	7,000	
Allowance for doubtful accounts (XA)		7,000

Assets		=	Liabilities	+	Shareholders' Equity	
Allowance for doubtful accounts	−7,000				Bad debt expense	−7,000

3. The percentage estimate of bad debts should be applied to credit sales. Cash sales never produce bad debts.

Bad debt expense (E) (0.02 × $400,000)	8,000	
Allowance for doubtful accounts (XA)		8,000

Assets		=	Liabilities	+	Shareholders' Equity	
Allowance for doubtful accounts	−8,000				Bad debt expense	−8,000

DEMONSTRATION **CASE B**

Heather Ann Long, a first-year university student, has just received her first chequing account statement. This was her first chance to attempt a bank reconciliation. She had the following information to work with:

Bank balance, September 1	$1,150
Deposits during September	650
Cheques cleared during September	900
Bank service charge	5
Bank balance, October 1	895

Heather was surprised that the deposit of $50 she made on September 29 had not been posted to her account and was pleased that her rent cheque of $200 had not cleared her account. Her chequebook balance was $750.

Required:

1. Complete Heather's bank reconciliation.
2. Why is it important for individuals such as Heather and businesses to do a bank reconciliation each month?

We strongly recommend that you prepare your own answers to these requirements and then check your answers with the following suggested solution.

SUGGESTED **SOLUTION**

1. Heather's bank reconciliation:

Heather's Books		Bank Statement	
October 1 cash balance	$750	October 1 cash balance	$895
Additions		Additions	
None		Deposit in transit	50
Deductions		Deductions	
Bank service charge	(5)	Outstanding cheque	(200)
Correct cash balance	$745	Correct cash balance	$745

2. Bank statements, whether personal or business, should be reconciled each month. This process helps ensure that a correct balance is reflected in the customer's books. Failure to reconcile a bank statement increases the chance that an error will not be discovered and may result in bad cheques being written. Businesses must reconcile their bank statements for an additional reason: the correct balance that is calculated during reconciliation is reported on the statement of financial position. A bank reconciliation is an important internal control measure.

Appendix 7A

Applying the Revenue Principle in Special Circumstances

The revenue principle was introduced in Chapter 3. As noted earlier, application of this principle in the case of Gildan and similar companies was fairly straightforward. Such companies record revenue according to their sales contract, which specifies the point at which transfer of ownership occurs. We now expand our discussion of the revenue principle and see how it is applied in business practice by companies other than typical manufacturers, wholesalers, and retailers.

DELAYED REVENUE RECOGNITION: INSTALMENT METHOD

Recall that to record revenue the following conditions must be met: (1) the entity has transferred to the buyer the significant risks and rewards of ownership of the goods, (2) the entity retains neither continuing managerial involvement to the degree usually associated with ownership nor effective control over the goods sold, (3) the amount of revenue can be measured reliably, (4) it is probable that the economic benefits associated with the transaction will flow to the entity, and (5) the costs incurred or to be incurred in respect of the transaction can be measured reliably. Failure to meet the fourth revenue recognition criterion (collection must be probable) requires that revenue recognition be delayed until after an initial exchange. When a high level of uncertainty concerning the collectability of the sales price exists, revenue recognition is postponed until *cash is collected from the customer*. This revenue recognition method, called the *instalment method*, is considered to be a prudent method since it

The **INSTALMENT METHOD** recognizes revenue on the basis of cash collection after the delivery of goods.

postpones revenue recognition, sometimes until long after goods have been delivered. The most common applications are in certain types of *retail* and *real estate transactions* in which payment is made over a multi-year period and a large proportion of customers stop making payments long before the final payment is due. Certain types of expensive equipment, such as supercomputers, are sometimes sold under contracts calling for payment to be made over a multi-year period and giving the customers the right to return the equipment and cease making payments if they are dissatisfied. The instalment method is also applicable for such cases. Application of this specialized revenue recognition method is discussed in intermediate accounting courses.

REVENUE RECOGNITION BEFORE THE EARNINGS PROCESS IS COMPLETE: LONG-TERM CONSTRUCTION CONTRACTS

An important exception to the usual criteria for revenue recognition exists for companies involved in long-term construction projects such as building an office complex for a large corporation. These projects may take a number of years to complete. As a result, if the company recorded no revenue or expenses directly related to the project during the years that it worked on the project and then recorded massive amounts of revenue and related expenses in the year that it delivered the product to the customer, the financial statements would not accurately represent the company's economic activities during the period of construction. This method of accounting is often referred to as the *completed contract method.*

The **PERCENTAGE OF COMPLETION METHOD** records revenue based on a reliable measure of the percentage of work completed during the accounting period.

To deal with this unique problem for long-term construction projects, many companies use the percentage of completion method, which records revenue based on the percentage of work completed during the accounting period, instead of the completed contract method, which records revenue when the completed product is delivered to the customer.

Under the percentage of completion method, contract revenue and contract costs are recognized periodically as revenue and expenses during each period, based on the stage of completion of the contract activity at the end of the reporting period, provided that the outcome of the construction contract can be estimated reliably.[13] Typically, the amount of work accomplished each year is measured by the *percentage of total cost* that was incurred during the year.[14] For example, assume that the total contract price for building a bridge was $50 million and the total cost for construction was $40 million. In 2010, the construction company spent $10 million, which was 25 percent of the contract cost ($10 million ÷ $40 million).[15] This percentage of completion is then multiplied by the total contract revenue to determine the amount of revenue to be reported in 2010 (25% × $50 million = $12.5 million). The amount of expense reported in 2010 is the actual cost incurred, $10 million, and the profit is $2.5 million, the difference between revenue and expense ($12.5 million − $10 million).

The **COMPLETED CONTRACT METHOD** records revenue when the completed product is delivered to the customer.

Notice that the percentage of completion method does not completely satisfy the first revenue recognition criterion because revenue is reported before the significant risks and rewards of ownership are transferred to the customer. It is an acceptable method, however, because it reflects the economic substance of a company's construction activity throughout the contract period.

The **ZERO PROFIT METHOD** records revenue that is equals to the actual costs incurred during the accounting period.

When the outcome of a construction contract cannot be estimated reliably, the amount of revenue that shall be recognized each period is limited to the contract costs that have been incurred in that period, assuming that they are recoverable from the customer. The contract costs shall be recognized as an expense in that period. This cost recovery, or zero profit, method is more prudent than the percentage of completion

---

[13]International Accounting Standards Board, "International Accounting Standard 11—Construction Contracts" para. 22 (IASB).

[14]Other measures of completion include surveys of work performed or completion of a physical proportion of the contract work. See IAS 11, para. 30.

[15]The difference between the expected cost and the actual cost of construction, which did not occur in this simple example, creates additional accounting problems.

method because the amount of revenue that can be recognized is equal to the actual expenses incurred in the same accounting period. In the previous example, the revenue that can be recognized is exactly equal to the costs incurred in the first year of the contract. Therefore, the revenue and expenses recognized in 2010 will both equal $10 million, resulting in zero profit in that year.

REVENUE RECOGNITION FOR SERVICE CONTRACTS

Companies that provide services over more than one accounting period often follow revenue recognition policies similar to those followed for long-term construction contracts.[16] They may record revenue after all services have been provided (after the contract is completed) or may recognize revenue from the completed portion of the services. Since the individual size of the contracts involved often is small (compared to construction contracts) and companies often are engaged in many service contracts with different beginning and ending dates, the distortion caused by the completed contract method is usually smaller than that of long-term construction contracts. Yet many service companies, such as Federal Express, which provides air delivery service, employ the percentage of completion revenue recognition policy as indicated in the following note:

FEDERAL EXPRESS CORPORATION AND SUBSIDIARIES

Note 1. Summary of Significant Accounting Policies

Notes to Consolidated Financial Statements

Revenue Recognition. We recognize revenue upon delivery of shipments for our transportation businesses and upon completion of services for our business services, logistics and trade services businesses.... For shipments in transit, revenue is recorded based on the percentage of service completed at the balance sheet date.

For the services in progress at the end of the accounting period, Federal Express uses the percentage of completion method for revenue recognition, recognizing only a percentage of the revenues and related costs of providing the services based on the degree of completion of the service. This method is also called the *proportional performance* method. This form of revenue recognition is very similar to Shaw Communications Inc.'s accounting for its cable and Internet contracts and SNC-Lavalin's accounting for its construction contracts. Each company recognizes revenues and expenses related to the *completed portion* of its contract with the customer. The major difference is that Shaw Communications is paid for the cable and Internet subscriptions in advance, SNC-Lavalin receives progress payments throughout the contract period, and Federal Express receives payment from its business customers after it provides the service.

In some situations, neither the percentage of completion nor the zero profit methods provide reliable estimates of the stage of completion of the contract. This most often occurs when there are many projects and services bundled together in a single contract. Service obligations such as project management, for example, may require an indeterminate number of actions that must be separated from the actual construction project. If the actual costs incurred for actions undertaken in the reporting period are not a reliable basis for revenue allocation over time, then revenue is recognized on a straight-line basis, whereby the total service revenue is spread uniformly over the contract period.

The **STRAIGHT-LINE METHOD** allocates the total contract revenue uniformly over the contract period.

---

[16]International Accounting Standards Board, "International Accounting Standard 18—Revenue," para. 20 and 26 (IASB).

REVENUE RECOGNITION AND FINANCIAL STATEMENT ANALYSIS

Financial analysts cannot evaluate the profit earned by a company if they do not understand how it applied the revenue recognition criteria. As a result, all companies disclose any special revenue recognition issues in the notes to their financial statements. For example, Nokia Corporation the world's leading maker of cell phones, states the following in its annual report:

REAL WORLD EXCERPT

Nokia Corporation

ANNUAL REPORT

NOTES TO THE CONSOLIDATED FINANCIAL STATEMENTS

1. Accounting Policies

Revenue recognition

… Service revenue is generally recognized on a straight line basis over the service period unless there is evidence that some other method better represents the stage of completion.

. . .

In addition, sales and cost of sales from contracts involving solutions achieved through modification of complex telecommunications equipment are recognized using the percentage of completion method when the outcome of the contract can be estimated reliably. A contract's outcome can be estimated reliably when total contract revenue and the costs to complete the contract can be estimated reliably, it is probable that the economic benefits associated with the contract will flow to the Group and the stage of contract completion can be measured reliably. When the Group is not able to meet those conditions, the policy is to recognize revenues only equal to costs incurred to date, to the extent that such costs are expected to be recovered.

Progress towards completion is measured by reference to cost incurred to date as a percentage of estimated total project costs, the cost-to-cost method.

The percentage of completion method relies on estimates of total expected contract revenue and costs, as well as dependable measurement of the progress made towards completing a particular project. Recognized revenues and profits are subject to revisions during the project in the event that the assumptions regarding the overall project outcome are revised. The cumulative impact of a revision in estimates is recorded in the period such revisions become likely and estimable. Losses on projects in progress are recognized in the period they become probable and estimable.

Source: Nokia Corporation Annual Report 2009.

This succinct explanation of the percentage of completion method is adequate for someone who has read this chapter, but it is doubtful that someone who has not studied accounting would understand its meaning. Shareholders, lenders, and analysts must examine the company's accounting policy choices for recognition of long-term contract revenue. This will assist them in understanding whether or not reported net revenues are comparable among companies operating in the same industry. Long-term contract revenue recognition is covered in detail in advanced accounting courses.

DEMONSTRATION **CASE C**

Assume that Landevco Inc., a major land development company, decided to subdivide a large lot of land and develop it into a commercial and residential complex. Landevco contracted with Construk Corp. for the construction of this complex that will take three years to complete and cost Landevco $400 million, payable in three instalments of $100, $150, and $150 million at the end of years 1, 2, and 3, respectively. Construk expects to incur $300 million in total costs of construction over the three years. Construk is confident that Landevco will make the promised progress payments on time. The actual costs incurred totalled $90, $120, and $90 million for years 1, 2, and 3, respectively.

Required:

1. Assume that all the criteria for use of the percentage of completion method are met. Determine the amount that Construk should recognize as profit each year.
2. Assume that the costs of constructing this project could not be estimated reliably prior to starting the construction. Use the completed contract method to determine the amount of profit that would be recognized each year.
3. Assume also that the costs of constructing this project could not be estimated reliably. Use the zero profit method to determine the amount of revenue and profit recognized by Construk each year.
4. Compare the three revenue recognition methods with respect to the recognition of profit each year and for the three-year period as a whole.

We strongly recommend that you prepare your own answers to these requirements and then check your answers with the suggested solution below.

SUGGESTED **SOLUTION**

1., 2., and 3.

	Year 1	Year 2	Year 3	Three-year Period
Actual costs incurred per year	$90	$120	$90	$300
Percentage of completion method				
Percentage of work completed (= annual cost ÷ total costs)	30%	40%	30%	
Revenue (= contract price × percentage of work completed)	$120	$160	$120	400
Profit (= revenue − actual costs)	30	40	30	100
Completed contract method				
Revenue	0	0	$400	400
Expenses*	0	0	300	300
Profit (= revenue − expenses)	0	0	100	100
Zero profit method				
Revenue (= actual costs)	90	120	190	400
Expenses	90	120	90	300
Profit (= revenue − actual costs)	0	0	100	100

*The costs incurred each year are accumulated in an asset account until the project is completed. They are recognized as expenses in the year of the completion of the project.

4. The percentage of completion method recognizes each year a proportion of the overall profit based on the percentage of work completed. Both the completed contract and zero profit methods do not recognize profit during the first two years of the contract period but recognize the total amount of profit during the third year. These two methods differ, however, with respect to the amounts of revenue and expense recognized each year. All three methods show the same amount of profit, $100 million, over the three-year period.

Appendix 7B

Recording Discounts and Returns

In the chapter, both *credit card discounts* and *cash discounts* have been recorded as contra revenues. For example, if the credit card company is charging a 3 percent fee for its service, and credit card sales were $3,000 at a factory store for January 2, the sales transaction is recorded as follows:

```
Cash (A) ....................................  2,910
Credit card discount (XR or E) ...............    90
    Sales revenue (R) ........................         3,000
```

Assets		=	Liabilities	+	Shareholders' Equity	
Cash	+2,910				Sales revenue	+3,000
					Credit card discount	−90

Similarly, if credit sales are recorded with terms 2/10, n/30 ($1,000 × 0.98 = $980), and payment is made within the discount period, the selling company would record the following:

```
Trade receivables (A) ........................  1,000
    Sales revenue (R) ........................         1,000
```

Assets		=	Liabilities	+	Shareholders' Equity	
Trade receivables	+1,000				Sales revenue	+1,000

```
Cash (A) ....................................   980
Sales discount (XR or E) .....................    20
    Trade receivables (A) ....................         1,000
```

Assets		=	Liabilities	+	Shareholders' Equity	
Cash	+980				Sales discount	−20
Trade receivables	−1,000					

Sales returns and allowances should always be treated as a contra revenue account. Assume that the T-shirt Company bought 1,000 T-shirts for $6,000 on account. On the date of sale, the selling company makes the following journal entry:

```
Trade receivables (A) ........................  6,000
    Sales revenue (R) ........................         6,000
```

Assets		=	Liabilities	+	Shareholders' Equity	
Trade receivables	+6,000				Sales revenue	+6,000

Before paying for the T-shirts, the T-shirt Company discovered that 50 T-shirts were not the colour ordered and returned them to the seller. On that date, the seller records the following:

```
Sales returns and allowances (XR) ............   300
    Trade receivables (A) ....................         300
```

Assets		=	Liabilities	+	Shareholders' Equity	
Trade receivables	−300				Sales returns and allowances	+300

In addition, the related cost of sales entry for the 50 T-shirts would be reversed, and the T-shirts returned to inventory. If the returned merchandise is defective, then it would have to be reworked before it can be restored to inventory. Accounting for returned merchandise that is either defective or damaged is discussed in other accounting courses.

Appendix 7C: Accounting for Passive Investments in Securities (online)

CHAPTER TAKE-AWAYS

1. **Apply the revenue principle to determine the accepted time to record sales revenue for typical retailers, wholesalers, manufacturers, and service companies. p. 346**
   Revenue recognition policies are widely recognized as one of the most important determinants of the fair presentation of financial statements. For most merchandisers and manufacturers, the required revenue recognition point is the time of shipment or delivery of goods. For service companies, it is the time at which services are provided.

2. **Analyze the impact of credit card sales, sales discounts, and sales returns on the amounts reported as net sales. p. 348**
   Both credit card discounts and cash discounts can be recorded either as contra revenues or as expenses. When recorded as contra revenues, they reduce net sales. Sales returns and allowances, which should always be treated as contra revenues, also reduce net sales.

3. **Compute and interpret the gross profit percentage. p. 352**
   The gross profit percentage measures the ability to charge premium prices and produce goods and services at lower cost. Managers, analysts, and creditors use this ratio to assess the effectiveness of the company's product development, marketing, and production strategy.

4. **Estimate, report, and evaluate the effects of uncollectible trade receivables (bad debts) on financial statements. p. 354**
   When receivables are material, companies must employ the allowance method to account for uncollectibles. The steps in the process are
   1. Preparing the end-of-period adjusting entry to record an estimate of bad debt expense.
   2. Writing off specific accounts determined to be uncollectible during the period, and recovery of amounts written off.

   The adjusting entry reduces profit as well as net trade receivables. The write-off of trade receivables affects neither.

5. **Compute and interpret the trade receivables turnover ratio and the effects of trade receivables on cash flows. p. 362**
   Trade receivables turnover ratio—Measures the effectiveness of credit granting and collection activities. It reflects how many times average trade receivables were recorded and collected during the period. Analysts and creditors watch this ratio because a sudden decline in it may mean that a company is extending collection deadlines in an attempt to prop up lagging sales or even is recording sales that later will be returned by customers. Alternatively, the average age of receivables indicates the average number of days it takes to collect from customers.

   Effects on cash flows—When a net decrease in trade receivables for the period occurs, cash collected from customers exceeds revenue and cash flows from operations increase. When a net increase in trade receivables occurs, cash collected from customers is less than revenue; thus, the cash flow from operations declines.

6. **Report, control, and safeguard cash. p. 365**
   Cash is the most liquid of all assets, flowing continually into and out of a business. As a result, a number of critical control procedures, including the reconciliation of bank accounts, should be applied. Also, management of cash may be critically important to decision makers who must have cash available to meet current needs yet must avoid excess amounts of idle cash that produce no revenue.

7. **Reconcile cash accounts and bank statements. p. 367**
   A bank reconciliation compares (reconciles) the ending cash balance in the company's records to the ending cash balance reported by the bank on the monthly bank statement. It also identifies the accounts that must be adjusted as a result of this process.

Closely related to recording revenue is recording the cost of what was sold. Chapter 8 will focus on transactions related to inventory and cost of sales. This topic is important because cost of sales has a major impact on a company's gross profit and net profit, which are watched closely by investors, analysts, and other users of financial statements. Increasing emphasis on quality, productivity, and costs has further focused production managers' attention on cost of sales and inventory. Since inventory cost figures play a major role in product introduction and pricing decisions, they also are important to marketing and general managers. Finally, since inventory accounting has a major effect on many companies' tax liabilities, this is an important place to introduce the effect of taxation on management decision making and financial reporting.

KEY **RATIOS**

The **gross profit percentage ratio** measures the excess of sales prices over the costs to purchase or produce the goods or services sold, as a percentage. It is computed as follows (p. 352):

$$\text{Gross Profit Percentage} = \frac{\text{Gross Profit}}{\text{Net Sales}}$$

The **receivables turnover ratio** measures the effectiveness of credit-granting and collection activities. It is computed as follows (p. 362):

$$\text{Receivables Turnover} = \frac{\text{Net Sales}}{\text{Average Net Trade Receivables}}$$

FINDING **FINANCIAL INFORMATION**

STATEMENT OF FINANCIAL POSITION
Under Current Assets
 Trade receivables (net of allowance for doubtful accounts)

INCOME STATEMENT
Revenues
 Net sales (sales revenue less discounts, if treated as contra revenues, and sales returns and allowances)
Expenses
 Selling expenses (including bad debt expense and discounts if treated as expenses)

STATEMENT OF CASH FLOWS
Under Operating Activities (indirect method)
 Profit
 + decrease in trade and other receivables (net)
 − increase in trade and other receivables (net)

NOTES
Under Summary of Significant Accounting Policies
 Revenue recognition policy

KEY **TERMS**

Aging of Trade Receivables Method p. 358

Allowance for Doubtful Accounts (Allowance for Doubtful Receivables or Allowance for Doubtful Debts) p. 355

Allowance Method p. 354

Bad Debt Expense (Doubtful Accounts Expense) p. 354

Bank Reconciliation p. 368

Bank Statement p. 367

Cash p. 365

Cash Equivalents p. 365

Completed Contract Method p. 374

Credit Card Discount p. 348

Instalment Method p. 373

Internal Controls p. 363

Notes Receivable p. 353

Percentage of Completion Method p. 374

Percentage of Credit Sales Method p. 359

Sales (or Cash) Discount p. 348

Sales Returns and Allowances p. 350

Straight-line Method p. 375

Trade Receivables p. 353

Zero Profit Method p. 374

QUESTIONS

1. Explain the difference between sales revenue and net sales.
2. What is gross profit or gross margin on sales? How is the gross profit ratio computed? In your explanation, assume that net sales revenue is $100,000 and cost of sales is $60,000.
3. What is a credit card discount? How does it affect amounts reported on the income statement?
4. What is a sales discount? Use credit terms 1/10, n/30 in your explanation.
5. What is the distinction between sales allowances and sales discounts?
6. Differentiate trade receivables from notes receivable.
7. Which basic accounting concept is satisfied by using the allowance method of accounting for bad debts?
8. Using the allowance method, is bad debt expense recognized in (a) the period in which sales related to the uncollectible amounts were made or (b) the period in which the seller learns that the customer is unable to pay?
9. What is the effect of the write-off of bad debts (using the allowance method) on (a) profit and (b) net trade receivables?
10. Does an increase in the receivables turnover ratio generally indicate faster or slower collection of receivables? Explain.
11. Define cash and cash equivalents in the context of accounting. Indicate the types of items that should be included.
12. Summarize the primary characteristics of an effective internal control system for cash.
13. Trade receivables are typically collected within three months from the date of sale. Can they be considered cash equivalents? Explain.
14. Why should cash-handling and cash-recording activities be separated? How is this separation accomplished?
15. What are the purposes of bank reconciliation? What balances are reconciled?
16. Briefly explain how the total amount of cash reported on the statement of financial position is computed.
17. (Appendix 7A) When is it acceptable to use the percentage of completion method?
18. (Appendix 7B) Under the gross method of recording sales discounts, is the amount of sales discount taken recorded (a) at the time the sale is recorded or (b) at the time the collection of the account is recorded?

EXERCISES

E7–1 Interpreting the Revenue Principle

LO1

Identify the most likely point in time when sales revenue should be recorded for each of the listed transactions.

Transaction	Point A	Point B
a. Airline tickets sold by an airline on a credit card	____ Point of sale	____ Completion of flight
b. Computer sold by mail-order company on a credit card	____ Shipment	____ Delivery to customer
c. Sale of inventory to a business customer on open account	____ Shipment	____ Collection from customers

E7–2 Reporting Net Sales with Credit Sales and Sales Discounts

LO2

During the months of January and February, Silver Corporation sold goods to three customers on open account with credit terms of 2/10, net/30. The sequence of events was as follows:

Jan. 6 Sold goods for $4,000 to S. Green.
     9 Sold goods to M. Munoz for $800.
    14 Collected cash due from S. Green.
Feb. 8 Collected cash due from M. Munoz.
    28 Sold goods for $2,000 to R. Reynolds.

Required:

1. Assuming that sales discounts are treated as contra revenues, compute net sales for the two months ended February 28.
2. Prepare the journal entries to record the transactions that occurred on January 6 and 14.

LO2

E7–3 Reporting Net Sales with Credit Sales, Sales Discounts, and Credit Card Sales

The following transactions were selected from the records of Evergreen Company:

July	12	Sold merchandise to Rami, who charged the $1,000 purchase on his Visa credit card. Visa charges Evergreen a 2 percent credit card fee.
	15	Sold merchandise to Steven at an invoice price of $6,000; terms 2/10, n/30.
	20	Sold merchandise to Tania at an invoice price of $2,000; terms 2/10, n/30.
	23	Collected payment from Steven from July 15 sale.
Aug.	25	Collected payment from Tania from July 20 sale.

Required:

1. Assuming that sales discounts are treated as contra revenues, compute net sales for the two months ended August 31.

2. Prepare the journal entries to record the transactions that occurred on July 12, 15, and 23.

LO2

E7–4 Reporting Net Sales with Credit Sales, Sales Discounts, Sales Returns, and Credit Card Sales

The following transactions were selected from among those completed by Gunzo Wholesalers in 2011:

Nov.	20	Sold two items of merchandise to Brigitte, who charged the $800 sales amount on her Visa credit card. Visa charges Gunzo a 2 percent credit card fee.
	25	Sold 20 items of merchandise to Clara for $5,000; terms 2/10, n/30.
	28	Sold 10 identical items of merchandise to David for $6,000; terms 2/10, n/30.
	30	David returned one of the items purchased on the 28th; the item was defective, and credit was given to the customer.
Dec.	6	David paid the account balance in full.
	30	Clara paid in full the amount due for the purchase on November 25, 2011.

Required:

1. Assume that sales discounts and credit card discounts are treated as contra revenues; compute net sales for the two months ended December 31, 2011.

2. Prepare the journal entries to record the transactions that occurred on November 20, 25, and December 30.

LO2

E7–5 Determining the Effects of Credit Sales, Sales Discounts, Credit Card Sales, and Sales Returns and Allowances on Income Statement Categories

Rockland Shoe Company records sales returns and allowances as contra revenues, and sales discounts and credit card discounts as selling expenses. Complete the following tabulation, indicating the effect (+ for increase, − for decrease, and NE for no effect) of each transaction. Do not record the related cost of sales.

July	12	Sold merchandise to Rosa, who charged the $400 purchase on her American Express card. American Express charges a 3 percent credit card fee.
	15	Sold merchandise to Thomas for $6,000; terms 2/10, n/30.
	20	Collected the amount due from Thomas.
	21	Lee returned shoes with an invoice price of $1,000, before paying for them.

Transaction	Net Sales	Gross Profit	Profit from Operations
July 12			
July 15			
July 20			
July 21			

LO2

E7–6 Evaluating the Effects of Sales Returns and Allowances on Sales

Teen World Inc. sells a wide selection of clothing items for teenage girls. The company imports merchandise from various international suppliers and distributes its merchandise to retail stores in major shopping areas. The company sells merchandise on credit, allows retailers to return incorrect or damaged merchandise within a period of two months, and grants sales allowances under certain circumstances. The company is currently reviewing its sales returns policy and provided you with the following information for the past six quarters:

Quarter	Gross Sales	Cost of Sales	Sales Returns and Allowances
Jan. 1–March 31, 2011	$1,346,300	$ 942,400	$ 53,852
April 1–June 30, 2011	1,474,500	1,042,100	76,674
July 1–Sept. 30, 2011	1,529,100	1,080,300	94,804
Oct. 1–Dec. 31, 2011	1,671,400	1,101,200	140,397
Jan. 1–March 31, 2012	1,708,800	1,103,600	153,792
April 1–June 30, 2012	1,992,700	1,317,500	219,197

Required:

1. Compute the following percentages for each of the six quarters: (a) cost of sales to net sales and (b) sales return and allowances to gross sales.

2. Comment on the ratios computed in (1) and identify possible reasons for the increase in the amount of sales returns and allowances, and give your recommendations for controlling the amount of sales returns and allowances.

E7–7 Analyzing Gross Profit Percentage on the Basis of a Multiple-Step Income Statement
The following summarized data were provided by the records of Slate Inc. for the year ended December 31, 2011:

LO3

Sales of merchandise for cash	$220,000
Sales of merchandise on credit	32,000
Cost of sales	147,000
Selling expenses	40,200
Administrative expenses	19,000
Sales returns and allowances	7,000
Items not included in the above amounts:	
Estimated bad debt, 2.5% of credit sales	
Average income tax rate, 30%	
Number of common shares outstanding, 5,000	

Required:

1. Based on these data, prepare a multiple-step income statement (showing both gross profit and income from operations).

2. What was the amount of gross profit? What was the gross profit percentage? Explain what these two numbers mean.

E7–8 Analyzing Gross Profit Percentage on the Basis of a Multiple-Step Income Statement and Within-Industry Comparison
Brown Shoe Company Inc. and Payless Shoesource Inc. are two leading footwear companies in the United States and Canada. The following data were taken from the 2008 annual reports of both companies (amounts in millions of U.S. dollars):

LO3

Brown Shoe
Payless Shoesource

	Brown	Payless
Sales of merchandise	$2,276.4	$3,442.0
Income taxes	(53.8)	(48.0)
Cash dividends declared	9.1	–
Selling and administrative expense	851.9	1,007.2
Cost of products sold	1,394.1	2,344.6
Interest expense	17.1	77.1
Other expenses	204.6	130.4
Number of common shares outstanding	41.5	62.9

Required:

1. Based on these data, prepare a multiple-step income statement for each company for the year ending December 31, 2008 (showing both gross profit and profit from operations).

2. Compute the gross profit and the gross profit percentage for each company. Explain what these two numbers mean. What do you believe accounts for the difference between the gross profit percentages of both companies?

LO4

E7–9 **Comparing Two Methods of Estimating Bad Debts**

Kwan Ltd. earned $328,000 in net credit sales during its first year of operation. At year-end, it had $79,630 in trade receivables and estimated that 10 percent of this amount may not be collectible in the future.

Required:

1. Compute the balance of the allowance for doubtful accounts at year-end, and prepare the adjusting journal entry to record bad debt expense.

2. Assume that the company estimated the uncollectible amount as 2.5 percent of its net credit sales. Prepare the adjusting journal entry to record bad debt expense, and compute the balance of the allowance for doubtful accounts at year-end.

3. What are the main differences between the two methods of estimating bad debt expense?

LO4

E7–10 **Recording and Determining the Effects of Bad Debt Transactions on Income Statement Categories by Using the Percentage of Credit Sales Method**

During 2012, Choi and Goldstein Furniture recorded credit sales of $500,000. Based on prior experience, the company estimates that the bad debt rate is 2 percent of credit sales.

Required:

1. Prepare journal entries to record the following transactions:

   a. The appropriate bad debt expense adjustment that was recorded for the year 2012.

   b. On December 31, 2012, an account receivable for $1,600 from a prior year was determined to be uncollectible and was written off.

2. Complete the following tabulation, indicating the amount and effect (+ for increase, − for decrease, and NE for no effect) of each transaction.

Transaction	Net Sales	Gross Profit	Profit from Operations
a.			
b.			

LO4

E7–11 **Computing Bad Debt Expense by Using Aging Analysis**

Brown Cow Dairy uses the aging approach to estimate bad debt expense. The balance of each account receivable is aged on the basis of three time periods as follows: (1) not yet due, $25,000; (2) up to 120 days past due, $10,000; and (3) more than 120 days past due, $5,000. Experience has shown that, for each age group, the average bad debt rates on the receivables at year-end due to uncollectability are (1) 2 percent, (2) 10 percent, and (3) 30 percent, respectively. At December 31, 2011 (end of the current year), the allowance for doubtful accounts balance was $600 (credit) before the end-of-period adjusting entry is made.

Required:

What amount should be recorded as bad debt expense for the current year?

LO4

E7–12 **Computing Bad Debt Expense by Using Aging Analysis and Reporting Trade Receivables**

The Nestlé Group disclosed the following analysis of its trade receivables at December 31, 2009 (amounts in millions of Swiss francs, CHF):

Aged Trade Receivable	Amount
Not past due	$10,554
Past due 1–30 days	916
Past due 31–60 days	341
Past due 61–90 days	130
Past due 91–120 days	134
Past due more than 120 days	685
	$12,760

Assume that the estimated percentages of uncollectible accounts were determined as 1 percent, 5 percent, 10 percent, 20 percent, 30 percent, and 40 percent for the six aged groups, respectively. At January 1, 2009, the allowance for doubtful accounts had a balance of CHF450, and a total of CHF396 were written off as uncollectible during 2009. The company recovered CHF40 from a major customer whose account was written off in 2008.

Required:

1. Prepare the journal entries to record the receivables that were written off in 2009, the recovery of receivables written off in 2008, and the bad debt expense for 2009.

2. Show how the information related to trade receivables is presented on the company's statement of financial position as at December 31, 2009.

E7–13 **Recording, Reporting, and Evaluating a Bad Debt Estimate**   ▓ **LO4**

During 2012, Gauthier's Camera Shop had sales revenue of $190,000, of which $95,000 was on credit. At the start of 2012, Trade receivables showed a $10,000 debit balance, and the allowance for doubtful accounts showed a credit balance of $800. Collections of trade receivables during 2012 amounted to $68,000. On December 31, 2012, a trade receivable (J. Doe) of $1,500 from a prior year was determined to be uncollectible; therefore, it was written off immediately as a bad debt. On the basis of experience, a decision was made to continue the accounting policy of basing estimated bad debt at 2 percent of credit sales for the year.

Required:

1. Prepare the required journal entries on December 31, 2012 (end of the accounting period).

2. Show how the amounts related to bad debt expense and trade receivables would be reported on the income statement for 2012 and the statement of financial position at December 31, 2012. Disregard income tax considerations.

3. On the basis of the data available, does the 2 percent rate appear to be reasonable? Explain.

4. There are two alternative methods that can be used to determine the amount of bad debt expense for the year. Do you have a preference for either of these methods? Explain.

E7–14 **Interpreting Bad Debt Disclosures**   ▓ **LO4**

Daimler AG is a globally leading producer of premium passenger cars and the largest manufacturer of commercial vehicles in the world. Its group of businesses includes Mercedes-Benz Cars, Daimler Trucks, Daimler Financial Services, Mercedes-Benz Vans, and Daimler Buses. In a recent annual report, it disclosed the following information concerning its allowance for doubtful accounts:

Daimler AG

Allowances. Changes in the allowance account for receivables from financial service were as follows:			
in millions of €	2009	2008	2007
Balance at January 1	934	594	924
Charged to costs and expenses	850	712	457
Amounts written off	(446)	(237)	(321)
Reversals	(165)	(131)	(153)
Disposal of Chrysler activities	–	–	(310)
Currency translation and other changes	(5)	(4)	(3)
Balance at December 31	1,168	934	594
Source: Daimler AG Annual Report 2009.			

Required:

1. Record summary journal entries related to bad debts for the current year. Ignore the currency translations and other changes.

2. If Daimler had written off an additional €10 million of trade receivables during the period, how would net receivables and profit have been affected? Explain.

E7–15 **Inferring Bad Debt Write-Offs and Cash Collections from Customers**   ▓ **LO4**

Microsoft develops, produces, and markets a wide range of computer software, including the Windows operating system. In a recent annual report, Microsoft reported the following information about trade receivables and net sales revenue.

Microsoft

	Year 2	Year 1
Trade receivable, net of allowances of $451 and $153	$11,192	$13,589
Net revenues	58,437	60,420

According to its annual report, Microsoft recorded bad debt expense of $360 and did not reinstate any previously written-off accounts during year 2.

Required:

1. What amount of bad debts was written off during year 2?

2. Assuming that all of Microsoft's sales during the period were on open account, compute the amount of cash collected from customers for year 2.

LO4

Bombardier

E7–16   **Determining the Impact of Uncollectible Accounts on Profit and Working Capital**

An annual report for Bombardier Inc. contained the following information at the end of its fiscal year (in millions of dollars):

	Year 2	Year 1
Credit card receivables	$2,051	2,073
Allowance for uncollectible accounts	(70)	(75)
	1,981	1,998

A footnote to the financial statements disclosed that uncollectible accounts of $29 million and $12 million were written off as bad during years 1 and 2, respectively. Assume that the tax rate for Bombardier was 30 percent.

Required:

1. Determine the bad debt expense for year 2 based on the preceding facts.

2. Working capital is defined as current assets minus current liabilities. How was Bombardier's working capital affected by the write-off of $12 million in uncollectible accounts during year 2? What impact did the recording of bad debt expense have on working capital in year 2?

3. How was profit affected by the $12 million write-off during year 2? What impact did recording bad debt expense have on profit for year 2?

LO5

The Benetton Group

E7–17   **Analyzing and Interpreting the Receivables Turnover Ratio**

The Benetton Group is one of the world's largest manufacturers of casual knitwear and sportswear for men, women, and children. Its annual reports include the following details reported in thousands of euro:

Year	2009	2008	2007	2006	2005	2004
Net sales	€2,049,259	€2,127,941	€2,085,272	€1,910,975	€1,765,073	€1,704,124
Net trade receivables	786,476	781,458	680,741	610,741	655,386	657,584

Required:

1. Determine the trade receivables turnover ratio and average age of receivables for the past five years.

2. Explain the meaning of the numbers that you calculated in (1).

LO5

Aer Lingus
WestJet Airlines

E7–18   **Comparing Receivables Turnover Ratios of Two Companies**

Aer Lingus provides passenger and cargo transportation services from Ireland to markets in the United Kingdom, continental Europe, and the United States. It uses the euro as the monetary unit for financial reporting purposes. WestJet Airlines is a Canadian airline that serves more than 65 destinations, mainly in Canada but also in the United States, the Caribbean, and Mexico. The net sales and average balances of trade receivables for Aer Lingus and WestJet Airlines for a recent fiscal year are shown below.

	Aer Lingus		WestJet Airlines	
	2009	2008	2009	2008
Net revenues	€1,205,739	€1,357,356	$2,281,120	$2,549,506
Trade receivables (net)	32,022	33,049	27,654	16,837

Required:

1. Compute the following for each company:

   a. The receivable turnover ratio.

   b. The average collection period.

2. Based on your computations for (1), which company's trade receivables appear to be the more "liquid" asset? Explain.

3. Both companies use different currencies to prepare their financial statements. Does the use of different currencies affect the interpretation of the turnover ratio and the average collection period? Explain.

E7–19 Interpreting the Effects of Sales Growth and Changes in Receivables on Cash Flow from Operations

LO5

Apple

Apple Computer Inc. is best known for its iMac, iPod, and iPad product lines. Three recent years produced a combination of dramatic increases in sales revenue and profit. Cash flows from operations declined during the period, however. Contributing to that declining cash flow was the change in trade receivables. The current and prior year statements of financial position reported the following:

	(in millions)	
	Current Year	**Previous Year**
Trade receivables, less allowance for doubtful accounts	$2,422	$1,637

Required:

1. How would the change in trade receivables affect cash flow from operations for the current year? Explain why it would have this effect.

2. Explain how increasing sales revenue often leads to (a) increasing trade receivables and (b) an excess of sales revenue over collections from customers.

3. The company reported $32,479 million in net sales for the current year. Compute the trade receivables turnover ratio and the average collection period for the current year. Are the computed numbers useful to an investor? Explain.

E7–20 Identifying Strengths and Weaknesses of Internal Control

LO6

You have been engaged to review the internal control procedures used by Data Flow Inc. During the course of your review, you note the following practices:

a. The credit manager maintains the trade receivables records and handles all collections from customers, because the accounting department personnel are not authorized to handle cash receipts.

b. All cash received from customers is deposited daily in the company's bank account.

c. Employees who handle cash receipts are not permitted to write off trade receivables as uncollectible.

d. Invoices that require payment are first verified by the accounting personnel for accuracy. An accounting clerk stamps them "paid" if they are cleared for payment and sends them to the treasurer who issues and signs the cheques.

e. The cheques issued by the company treasurer are not pre-numbered.

f. After preparing the bank reconciliation, any difference between the adjusted cash balance per the company's books and the adjusted balance per the bank statement is debited (or credited) to the cash account.

Required:

Indicate whether each of these six practices reflects a strength or a weakness of the internal control system. Provide justification for your answer.

E7–21 Internal Control over Cash

LO6

Organic Growers Inc. is a successful grower of summer fruits and vegetables. The company has a seasonal business that starts in June and ends in October. The owners use a vast agricultural terrain to grow a variety of vegetables and fruits. They employ four workers to help during the planting season and to pick the vegetables and fruits as they become ready for consumption. To save on the cost of harvesting the produce, the owners allow customers to pick the produce they like from the field and then collect the cash for the goods sold. They also have a small store where they keep small quantities of produce for sale to customers who do not wish to pick the produce themselves. Receipts for the purchased goods are given only to those who ask for them. During the summer, the owners accumulate enough cash to pay for farm supplies at the time they are delivered. They do so to avoid wasting time preparing cheques and balancing the chequebook.

Required:

How can Organic Growers strengthen its internal control over cash and improve on its overall cash management?

LO6 **E7–22** **Reporting Cash and Cash Equivalents When There Are Several Bank Accounts**
Singh Corporation has manufacturing facilities in several cities and has cash on hand at several locations, as well as in several bank accounts. The general ledger at the end of 2011 showed the following accounts:

Cash on hand—Home Office	$ 700	Cash on hand—Location C	$ 200
City Bank—Home Office	58,600	National Bank—Location C	965
Cash on Hand—Location A	100	Petty cash fund	300
National Bank—Location A	3,350	Credit Suisse—3-month Certificate of Deposit	5,800
Cash on hand—Location B	200	FransaBank—6-month Certificate of Deposit	4,500
National Bank—Location B	785		

The bank balances given represent the current cash balances as reflected on the bank reconciliations.

Required:
What amount of cash and cash equivalents should be reported on the company's 2011 statement of financial position? Explain the basis for your decisions on any questionable items.

LO7 **E7–23** **Preparing Bank Reconciliation, Entries, and Reporting**
The June 30, 2012, bank statement for Zoltan Company and the June ledger accounts for cash are summarized below:

Bank Statement	Cheques	Deposits	Balance
Balance, June 1, 2012			$ 7,200
Deposits during June		$17,000	24,200
Cheques cleared through June	$18,100		6,100
Bank service charges	50		6,050
Balance, June 30, 2012			6,050

Cash in Bank			
June 1 Balance	6,800	June Cheques written	18,400
June Deposits	19,000		

Cash on Hand	
June 30 Balance	300

Required:
1. Reconcile the bank balance to the book balance at June 30, 2012. A comparison of the cheques written with the cheques that have cleared the bank shows outstanding cheques of $700. Some of the cheques that cleared in June were written prior to June. No deposits in transit were carried over from May, but a deposit is in transit at the end of June.
2. Prepare any journal entries that should be made as a result of the bank reconciliation.
3. What is the balance in the cash in bank account after the reconciliation entries?
4. What is the total amount of cash that should be reported on the statement of financial position at June 30, 2012?

LO7 **E7–24** **Preparing Bank Reconciliation, Entries, and Reporting**
The September 30, 2011, bank statement for Russell Company and the September ledger accounts for cash are summarized here:

Bank Statement	Cheques	Deposits	Balance
Balance, September 1, 2011			$ 6,300
Deposits recorded during September		$27,000	33,300
Cheques cleared during September	$28,500		4,800
NSF cheque—Betty Brown	150		4,650
Bank service charges	50		4,600
Balance, September 30, 2011			4,600

Cash in Bank

Sept 1	Balance	6,300	Sept.	Cheques written	28,600
Sept.	Deposits	28,000			

Cash on Hand

Sept 30	Balance	400	

No outstanding cheques and no deposits in transit were carried over from August; however, there are deposits in transit and cheques outstanding at the end of September.

Required:

1. Reconcile the balance in the bank account with the cash balance in the books at September 30, 2011.

2. Prepare any journal entries that should be made as a result of the bank reconciliation.

3. What should be the balance in the cash in bank account after the reconciliation entries?

4. What total amount of cash should the company report on the statement of financial position at September 30, 2011?

E7–25 Preparing Bank Reconciliation, Entries, and Reporting   ▦ **LO7**

The bank statement for the Mini Mart Corporation shows a balance of $1,330 on June 30, but the company's "cash in bank" account had a balance of $499 on the same date. Comparison of the amounts reported on the bank statement with the company's records indicates (a) deposits of $160, representing cash receipts of June 30, that did not appear on the bank statement; (b) outstanding cheques totalling $240; (c) bank service charges for June amounting to $9; (d) collection of a note receivable by the bank on behalf of the company for $800 plus $40 in interest revenue; and (e) a cheque for $80 from a customer that was returned with the bank statement and marked NSF.

Required:

1. Prepare a bank reconciliation statement for Mini Mart Corporation as at June 30.

2. Prepare any journal entries that should be made as a result of the bank reconciliation.

3. Why is it important to reconcile the balance in the bank statement with the cash balance in the company's records?

4. What is the amount of cash that the company should report on its statement of financial position at June 30?

E7–26 (Appendix 7A) Determining Profit for a Construction Contract

Blanchard Construction Company entered into a long-term construction contract with the government to build a special landing strip at an Air Force base in Saint Hubert, Québec. The project took three years and cost the government $12 million. Blanchard spent the following amounts each year: 2011, $2 million; 2012, $5 million; and 2013, $3 million. The company uses the percentage of completion method. Cost estimates equalled actual costs.

Required:

1. Determine the amount of profit that Blanchard can report each year for this project. Ignore income taxes.

2. Assume that the costs of this project could not be estimated reliably. What amount of profit should the company recognize in each of the three years? Explain.

E7–27 (Appendix 7B) Recording Credit Sales, Sales Discounts, Sales Returns, and Credit Card Sales

The following transactions were selected from among those completed by Hailey Retailers in 2011:

Nov. 20   Sold two items of merchandise to Baja, who charged the $400 sales amount on her Visa credit card. Visa charges Hailey a 2 percent credit card fee.

      25   Sold 20 items of merchandise to Christine for $4,000; terms 2/10, n/30.

      28   Sold 10 identical items of merchandise to Daoud for $6,000; terms 2/10, n/30.

      30   Daoud returned one of the items purchased on the 28th; the item was defective, and credit was given to the customer.

Dec.   6   Daoud paid the account balance in full.

      30   Christine paid in full the amount due for the purchase on November 25, 2011.

Required:

Prepare the appropriate journal entry for each of these transactions, assuming the company uses the gross method to record sales revenue. Do not record the cost of sales.

PROBLEMS

LO1

P7–1   Applying the Revenue Principle (AP7–1)

At what point should revenue be recognized in each of the following independent cases? Explain your answers.

Case A. For December holiday gifts, a fast-food restaurant sells coupon books for $10. Each of the $1 coupons in a book may be used in the restaurant at any time during the following 12 months. The customer must pay cash when purchasing the coupon book.

Case B. Howard Land Development Corporation sold a lot to Quality Builders to construct a new home. The price of the lot was $50,000. Quality made a down payment of $10,000 and agreed to pay the balance in six months. After making the sale, Howard learned that Quality Builders often entered into these agreements but refused to pay the balance if it did not find a customer who wanted a house built on the lot.

Case C. Driscoll Corporation has always recorded revenue at the point of sale of its refrigerators. Recently, it has extended its warranties to cover all repairs for a period of seven years. One young accountant with the company now questions whether Driscoll has completed its earning process when it sells the refrigerators. She suggests that the warranty obligation for seven years means that a significant amount of additional work must be performed in the future.

LO2, 4

P7–2   Reporting Net Sales and Expenses with Discounts, Returns, and Bad Debts (AP7–2)
The following data were selected from the records of Tunga Company for the year ended December 31, 2012.

Balances January 1, 2012	
Trade receivables (various customers)	$110,000
Allowance for doubtful accounts	5,000

The company sells merchandise for cash and on open account with credit terms 2/10, n/30. Assume a unit sales price of $500 in all transactions, and use the gross method to record sales revenue.

Transactions during 2012:

a. Sold merchandise for cash, $236,000.

b. Sold merchandise to R. Agostino on open account for $11,000.

c. Sold merchandise to K. Black on open account for $30,000.

d. Two days after purchase, R. Agostino returned one of the units purchased in (b) and received account credit.

e. Sold merchandise to B. Assaf on open account for $22,000.

f. R. Agostino paid his account in full within the discount period.

g. Collected $98,000 cash from customers for credit sales made in 2012, all within the discount periods.

h. K. Black paid the invoice in (c) within the discount period.

i. Sold merchandise to R. Fong on open account for $17,000.

j. Three days after paying the account in full, K. Black returned seven defective units and received a cash refund.

k. Collected $8,000 cash on a trade receivable for sales made in 2011. The amount was received after the discount period.

l. Wrote off an old account of $2,900 after deciding that the amount would never be collected.

m. The estimated bad debt rate used by the company was 1 percent of net credit sales.

Required:

1. Using the following categories, indicate the dollar effect (+ for increase, − for decrease, and NE for no effect) of each listed transaction, including the write-off of the uncollectible account and the adjusting entry for estimated bad debts (ignore cost of sales). The effects of the first transaction are shown as an example:

Sales Revenue	Sales Discounts (taken)	Sales Returns and Allowances	Bad Debt Expense
a. $236,000	NE	NE	NE

2. Show how the accounts related to the preceding sale and collection activities should be reported on the income statement for 2012. (Treat sales discounts as contra revenues.)

P7–3   **Understanding the Income Statement Based on the Gross Profit Percentage** (AP7–3)

■ LO3

The following data were taken from the year-end records of Nomura Export Company.

Income Statement Items	Year 1	Year 2
Gross sales revenue	$160,000	$232,000
Sales returns and allowances	?	18,000
Net sales revenue	?	?
Cost of sales	68%	?
Gross profit	?	30%
Operating expenses	18,000	?
Profit before income taxes	?	20,000
Income tax expense (20%)	?	?
Profit	?	?
Earnings per share (10,000 shares outstanding)	2.40	?

Required:
Fill in all of the missing amounts. Show computations.

P7–4   **Interpreting Disclosure of Allowance for Doubtful Accounts** (AP7–4)

■ LO4

Peet's Coffee and Tea Inc. is a specialty coffee roaster and marketer of branded fresh whole-bean coffee. It recently disclosed the following information concerning the allowance for doubtful accounts in its annual report (dollars in thousands).

Peet's Coffee and Tea

Allowances for Doubtful Accounts	Balance at Beginning of Period	Additions (Charges) to Expense	Write-Offs	Balance at End of Period
Year 1	$61	$?	$ 15	$69
Year 2	69	30	?	58
Year 3	58	162	145	75

Required:

1. Record summary journal entries related to bad debts for year 3.

2. Supply the missing dollar amounts for year 1 and year 2.

P7–5   **Determining Bad Debt Expense Based on Aging Analysis** (AP7–5)

■ LO4

Green Pastures Equipment Company uses the aging approach to estimate bad debt expense at the end of each accounting year. Credit sales occur frequently on terms n/60. The balance of each trade receivable is aged on the basis of three time periods as follows: (1) not yet due, (2) up to one year past due, and (3) more than one year past due. Experience has shown that for each age group, the average bad debt rate on the amounts receivable at year-end due to uncollectibility are (1) 1 percent, (2) 5 percent, and (3) 30 percent, respectively.

At December 31, 2011 (end of the current accounting year), the trade receivables balance was $45,000, and the unadjusted balance of the allowance for doubtful accounts was $1,020 (credit). To simplify, the accounts of only five customers are used; the details of each follow:

B. Brown—Trade Receivable				
Date	**Explanation**	**Debit**	**Credit**	**Balance**
3/11/2010	Sale	$13,000		$13,000
6/30/2010	Collection		$4,000	9,000
1/31/2011	Collection		3,000	6,000
D. Di Lella— Trade Receivable				
2/28/2011	Sale	22,000		22,000
4/15/2011	Collection		10,000	12,000
11/30/2011	Collection		7,000	5,000
N. Gidda— Trade Receivable				
11/30/2011	Sale	9,000		9,000
12/15/2011	Collection		2,000	7,000
S. Kavouris— Trade Receivable				
3/2/2009	Sale	5,000		5,000
4/15/2009	Collection		5,000	0
9/1/2010	Sale	10,000		10,000
10/15/2010	Collection		8,000	2,000
2/1/2011	Sale	19,000		21,000
3/1/2011	Collection		5,000	16,000
12/31/2011	Sale	4,000		20,000
T. Patel—Trade Receivable				
12/30/2011	Sale	7,000		7,000

Required:

1. Prepare an aging analysis schedule and complete it.

2. Compute the estimated uncollectible amount for each age category and in total.

3. Prepare the adjusting entry for bad debt expense at December 31, 2011.

4. Show how the amounts related to trade receivables should be presented on the income statement for 2011 and the statement of financial position at December 31, 2011.

LO4

P7–6   **Determining Bad Debts and Reporting Trade Receivables** (AP7–6)

The bookkeeper of Vital Inc. has asked you to assist him with the preparation of information about the company's trade receivables for presentation in the statement of financial position at December 31, 2012, the end of the company's fiscal year. The following details have been extracted from the company's files.

	Debit	**Credit**
Trade receivables, January 1, 2012	$500,000	
Allowance for doubtful accounts, January 1, 2012		$25,000

Sales for 2012 totalled $1,300,000; $300,000 were in cash and the rest on account. The company collected $1,100,000 from credit customers during 2012, and wrote off $30,000 of trade receivables as uncollectible.

Required:

1. Determine the balance of trade receivables at December 31, 2012.

2. Vital estimates that 6 percent of the ending balance of its trade receivables may not be collected in the future. Prepare the journal entries to record the write-off of trade receivables and the bad debt expense for 2012.

3. Show how the information related to trade receivables is presented on the company's statement of financial position as at December 31, 2012.

4. After you finished helping the bookkeeper with the journal entries and the statement of financial position presentation, he said, "These calculations seem to be complicated. Would it not be simpler to treat the $30,000 as bad debt expense when the company is certain that the customers are not able to pay the amount owed? That way, you record the exact amount of bad debt when it happens, and you do not have to estimate an amount of doubtful accounts and risk being incorrect." Prepare a response to the bookkeeper.

P7–7 **Preparing a Multiple-Step Income Statement and Computing the Gross Profit Percentage with Discounts, Returns, and Bad Debts** (AP7–7)

Builders Company Inc. sells heavy-construction equipment. It has 10,000 common shares outstanding and its fiscal year ends on December 31. The adjusted trial balance was taken from the general ledger on December 31, 2011.

Account Titles	Debit	Credit
Cash	$ 33,600	
Trade receivables (net)	14,400	
Inventory, ending	52,000	
Property, plant, and equipment	40,000	
Accumulated depreciation		$ 16,800
Liabilities		24,000
Common shares		72,000
Retained earnings, January 1, 2011		9,280
Sales revenue		145,600
Sales returns and allowances	5,600	
Cost of sales	78,400	
Selling expenses	13,600	
Administrative expenses	14,400	
Bad debt expense	1,600	
Sales discounts	6,400	
Income tax expense	7,680	
Totals	$267,680	$267,680

Required:

1. Beginning with net sales, prepare a multiple-step income statement (showing both gross profit and profit from operations). Treat sales discounts as contra revenues.

2. The beginning balance of trade receivables (net) was $16,000. Compute the gross profit percentage and trade receivables turnover ratio and explain their meaning.

P7–8 **Evaluating Internal Controls** (AP7–8)

Cripple Creek Company has one trusted employee who, as the owner said, "handles all of the bookkeeping and paperwork for the company." This employee is responsible for counting, verifying, and recording cash receipts and payments, making the weekly bank deposit, preparing cheques for major expenditures (signed by the owner), making small expenditures from the cash register for daily expenses, and collecting trade receivables. The owner asked the local bank for a $20,000 loan. The bank asked that an audit be performed covering the year just ended. The independent auditor, in a private conference with the owner, presented some evidence of the following activities of the trusted employee during the past year:

a. Cash sales sometimes were not entered in the cash register, and the trusted employee pocketed approximately $50 per month.

b. Cash taken from the cash register (and pocketed by the trusted employee) was replaced with expense memos with fictitious signatures (approximately $12 per day). Cripple Creek is open five days per week throughout the year.

c. A $300 collection on a trade receivable of a valued out-of-town customer was pocketed by the trusted employee and was covered by making a $300 entry as a debit to sales returns and a credit to trade receivables.

d. An $800 collection on a trade receivable from a local customer was pocketed by the trusted employee and was covered by making an $800 entry as a debit to allowance for doubtful accounts and a credit to trade receivables.

Required:

1. What was the approximate amount stolen during the past year?

2. What would be your recommendations to the owner about the company's internal controls?

P7–9 **Preparing a Bank Reconciliation** (AP7–9)

Sergio Lucas worked long hours during the summer and saved enough money to pay his tuition and living expenses to continue his studies at the local university. On September 1, he downloaded from the bank's website his bank statement for August to make sure that the bank has not made any errors related to his bank account. Sergio has developed a habit of verifying all the entries in his bank account ever since he discovered that the bank had charged him a service fee for a transaction that was unrelated to his account. After comparing the bank statement with the entries he has made in his chequebook, Sergio found that the bank statement showed a balance of $12,506.60 but his chequebook showed a balance of $12,651.65 on August 31, a difference of $145.05. He decided to compare the entries in his chequebook with those in the bank statement, hoping that the bank owes him this difference.

Sergio's review of the bank statement showed the following:

a. Three cheques (#124, #125, and #126) that he made in late August have not been withdrawn from his bank account yet. They totalled $619.35.

b. An automatic deduction of $44.10 was made to pay the hydro bill for August.

c. Another automatic deduction of $55.30 was made to pay for telecommunication services from Telus Corp.

d. He forgot to record in his chequebook two withdrawals from instant teller machines totalling $300.

e. A cheque for $385 that he deposited in the bank the night of August 31 did not appear on the bank statement.

f. Sergio discovered that he recorded cheque #123 as $96.25 but the correct amount that cleared his bank account was $69.25.

g. The bank charged him a service fee of $7 for August transactions.

Required:

1. Assume the role of Sergio and prepare a bank reconciliation at August 31.

2. Which amounts should Sergio enter into his chequebook to avoid making any errors in reconciling his chequebook with the bank statement for September?

 LO7

 e**X**cel

P7–10 **Preparing a Bank Reconciliation and Related Journal Entries** (AP7–10)
The bookkeeper at Hopkins Company has not reconciled the bank statement with the cash account, saying, "I don't have time." You have been asked to prepare a reconciliation and review the procedures with the bookkeeper.

The April 30, 2012, bank statement and the April ledger accounts for cash showed the following (summarized):

Bank Statement			
	Cheques	**Deposits**	**Balance**
Balance, April 1, 2012			$31,000
Deposits during April		$36,100	67,100
Notes collected for company			
(including $70 interest)		1,180	68,280
Cheques cleared during April	$44,500		23,780
NSF cheque—A. B. Wright	160		23,620
Bank service charges	70		23,550
Balance, April 30, 2012			23,550

Cash in Bank					
Apr. 1	Balance	23,500	Apr.	Cheques written	41,100
Apr.	Deposits	41,500			

Cash on Hand		
Apr. 30	Balance	100

A comparison of cheques written before and during April with the cheques cleared through the bank showed that cheques of $4,100 are still outstanding at April 30. No deposits in transit were carried over from March, but a deposit was in transit at April 30.

Required:

1. Prepare a detailed bank reconciliation at April 30, 2012.

2. Prepare any required journal entries as a result of the reconciliation. Why are they necessary?

3. What were the balances in the cash accounts in the ledger on May 1, 2012?

4. What total amount of cash should be reported on the statement of financial position at April 30, 2012?

P7-11 (Appendix 7B) Recording Sales, Returns, and Bad Debts

Use the data presented in P7-2, which was selected from the records of Tunga Company for the year ended December 31, 2012.

Required:

Prepare the journal entries for these transactions, including the write-off of the uncollectible account and the adjusting entry for estimated bad debts. Do not record the cost of sales. Show computations for each entry.

ALTERNATE PROBLEMS

AP7-1 Applying the Revenue Principle (P7–1)   ▇ **LO1**

Review the revenue recognition practices of the following companies, and indicate at what point in time revenue should be recognized in each of these independent cases. Explain your answer.

Case A. The sales representatives of Computec Corporation are under intense pressure to achieve very high sales levels. To achieve their specific objectives, the sales representatives ask customers to order computer equipment in advance, with payment to be made later. In many cases, the company records sales on the basis of customers' orders, even though the ordered equipment may have not been manufactured yet.

Case B. Scenic Trails Inc. is a campground operator that sells annual memberships to interested campers. Members are allowed to pay the annual memberships fees over a period of six months. The company records revenue from membership fees as soon as a new member signs the membership agreement. Members are allowed 10 days to cancel their memberships, and many members cancel their memberships within days of signing.

Case C. Educational Toys Inc. sells a wide variety of toys to distributors and allows them to return unsold merchandise within a period of three months. The company's policy encourages distributors to buy products and keep them for three months, knowing they could return any unsold merchandise during this period. The company recognizes revenue as soon as it delivers its products to distributors.

AP7-2 Reporting Net Sales and Expenses with Discounts, Returns, and Bad Debts (P7–2)   ▇ **LO2, 4**

The following data were selected from the records of Fluwars Company for the year ended December 31, 2011.

Balances January 1, 2011:	
Trade receivables (various customers)	$103,000
Allowance for doubtful accounts	6,000

The company sold merchandise for cash and on open account with credit terms 1/10, n/30. Assume a unit sales price of $400 in all transactions and use the gross method to record sales revenue.

Transactions during 2011:

a. Sold merchandise for cash, $128,000.

b. Sold merchandise to Abbey Corp; invoice amount, $7,600.

c. Sold merchandise to Brown Company; invoice amount, $14,000.

d. Abbey paid the invoice in (b) within the discount period.

e. Sold merchandise to Cavendish Inc.; invoice amount, $9,200.

f. Two days after paying the account in full, Abbey returned four defective units and received a cash refund.

g. Collected $99,000 cash from customers for credit sales made in 2011, all within the discount periods.

h. Three days after the purchase date, Brown returned three of the units purchased in (c) and received account credit.

i. Brown paid its account in full within the discount period.

j. Sold merchandise to Decca Corporation; invoice amount, $7,000.

k. Cavendish paid its account in full after the discount period.

l. Wrote off an old account of $1,400 after deciding that the amount would never be collected.

m. The estimated bad debt rate used by the company was 2 percent of net credit sales.

Required:

1. Using the following categories, indicate the dollar effect (+ for increase, − for decrease, and NE for no effect) of each listed transaction, including the write-off of the uncollectible account and the adjusting entry for estimated bad debts (ignore the cost of sales). The effects of the first transaction are shown as an example.

Sales Revenue	Sales Discounts (taken)	Sales Returns and Allowances	Bad Debt Expense
a. $128,000	NE	NE	NE

2. Show how the accounts related to the preceding sale and collection activities should be reported on the income statement for 2011. (Treat sales discounts as contra revenues.)

LO3

AP7–3 **Understanding the Income Statement Based on the Gross Profit Percentage** (P7–3)

The following data were taken from the year-end records of Glare Import Company.

Income Statement Items	Year 1	Year 2
Gross sales revenue	$210,000	$255,000
Sales discounts	?	5,000
Net sales revenue	207,000	?
Cost of sales	?	60%
Gross profit	40%	?
Operating expenses	42,800	?
Profit before income taxes	?	70,000
Income tax expense (30%)	?	?
Profit before discontinued operations	?	?
Discontinued operations, net of tax	10,000 (loss)	2,500 (gain)
Profit	?	?
Earnings per share (8,000 shares outstanding)	?	?

Required:

Fill in all of the missing amounts. Show computations.

LO4

Dell Inc.

AP7–4 **Interpreting Disclosure of Allowance for Doubtful Accounts** (P7–4)

Dell Inc. sells computer systems and accessories and provides services for customers to build their information technology and Internet infrastructures. Dell recently disclosed the following information concerning the allowance for doubtful accounts in its annual report:

Provision for Doubtful Accounts	Balance at Beginning of Period	Charged to Bad Debt Expense	Write-Offs Charged to Allowance	Balance at End of Period
Year 3	$84	$31	$37	?
Year 2	71	?	35	$84
Year 1	68	39	?	71

Required:

1. Record summary journal entries related to bad debts for year 1.
2. Supply the missing dollar amounts for year 1, year 2, and year 3.

LO4

AP7–5 **Determining Bad Debt Expense Based on Aging Analysis** (P7–5)

Briggs & Stratton Engines Inc. uses the aging approach to estimate bad debt expense at the end of each fiscal year. Credit sales occur frequently on terms n/45. The balance of each trade receivable is aged on the basis of four time periods as follows: (1) not yet due, (2) up to 6 months past due, (3) 6 to 12 months past due, and (4) more than one year past due. Experience has shown that for each age group, the average bad debt rate on the amounts receivable at year-end due to uncollectibility is (1) 1 percent, (2) 5 percent, (3) 20 percent, and (4) 50 percent, respectively.

At December 31, 2011 (end of the current fiscal year), the trade receivables balance was $39,500, and the allowance for doubtful accounts balance was $1,550 (debit). To simplify, the accounts of only five customers are used; the details of each follow:

Date	Explanation	Debit	Credit	Balance
		R. Aouad—Trade Receivable		
3/13/2011	Sale	$19,000		$19,000
5/12/2011	Collection		$10,000	9,000
9/30/2011	Collection		7,000	2,000
		C. Chronis—Trade Receivable		
06/01/2010	Sale	31,000		31,000
11/01/2010	Collection		20,000	11,000
12/01/2011	Collection		5,000	6,000
		D. McClain—Trade Receivable		
10/31/2011	Sale	12,000		12,000
12/10/2011	Collection		8,000	4,000
		T. Skibinski—Trade Receivable		
05/02/2011	Sale	15,000		15,000
06/01/2011	Sale	10,000		25,000
06/15/2011	Collection		15,000	10,000
07/15/2011	Collection		10,000	0
10/01/2011	Sale	26,000		26,000
11/15/2011	Collection		16,000	10,000
12/15/2011	Sale	4,500		14,500
		H. Wu—Trade Receivable		
12/30/2011	Sale	13,000		13,000

Required:

1. Set up an aging analysis schedule and complete it.

2. Compute the estimated uncollectible amount for each age category and in total.

3. Prepare the adjusting entry for bad debt expense at December 31, 2011.

4. Show how the amounts related to trade receivables should be presented on the income statement for 2011 and the statement of financial position at December 31, 2011.

AP7–6 Determining Bad Debts and Reporting Trade Receivables (P7–6)   ■ **LO4**

Modern Kitchens Inc. (MKI) is a Montréal-based company that sells imported fancy kitchenware to retailers. Selected account balances as at September 30, 2011, are shown below.

	Debit	Credit
Trade receivables	$119,000	
Allowance for doubtful accounts		$3,000

During October 2011, the following transactions occurred:

a. The company sold merchandise on account to various retailers for a total amount of $76,000, terms 2/10, n/30. A few retailers who purchased merchandise for a gross amount of $40,000 paid the amount due within 10 days. A total of $16,000 of the October sales remained unpaid at October 31, 2011.

b. Customers paid the company $50,000 for merchandise they purchased prior to September 30, 2011. These customers did not pay within the discount period.

c. Two of MKI's customers owed the company a total of $5,000 and were facing financial difficulties during October due to increased competition. They were forced to close their businesses before the end October 2011. MKI does not expect to receive any money from these two customers and considered their accounts uncollectible.

d. The company received new kitchenware from a Korean supplier, Kim & Sons Ltd., for $40,000. The invoice indicated that the supplier would allow a cash discount of 1 percent if the invoice were paid before the end of October 2011. MKI paid the supplier on November 10, 2011.

MKI estimates that 4 percent of its trade receivables at October 31, 2011 will not be collected in the future.

Required:

1. Prepare the journal entries to record the transactions that occurred in October 2011, and any related adjusting journal entries at October 31, 2011, the end of MKI's fiscal year.

2. Show how the information related to trade receivables is presented on the company's statement of financial position at October 31, 2011.

3. The major shareholder of MKI, Michel Beauregard, was reading through the company's statement of financial position and noticed the account allowance for doubtful accounts. He called Carol, MKI's accountant, and made the following statement: "Carol, I don't think we need to make a provision for doubtful accounts as it will reduce the amount of trade receivables unnecessarily. I think we should wait until we are certain that we cannot collect from our customers before showing a reduction in the trade receivables on the statement of financial position. This way, the trade receivables balance will be more accurate. I would like you to make the necessary change to the financial statements before they are distributed to the other shareholders." Assume the role of Carol and prepare a response to Mr. Beauregard.

4. MKI had an opportunity to get a loan from the Bank of International Trade (BIT) to pay the amount due to Kim & Sons Ltd. The loan would have cost MKI $300 in interest charges. Should MKI have obtained the loan from BIT to pay its debt to Kim & Sons Ltd. before October 31, 2011?

LO2, 3, 4   **AP7–7**   **Preparing a Multiple-Step Income Statement and Computing the Gross Profit Percentage with Discounts, Returns, and Bad Debts** (P7–7)

Big Tommy Corporation is a local grocery store organized seven years ago as a corporation. At that time, 6,000 common shares were issued to the three organizers. The store is in an excellent location, and sales have increased each year. At the end of 2012, the bookkeeper prepared the following statement (assume that all amounts are correct; note the incorrect terminology and format):

BIG TOMMY CORPORATION
Profit and Loss
December 31, 2012

	Debit	Credit
Sales		$210,000
Cost of sales	$139,500	
Sales returns and allowances	4,000	
Selling expenses	29,000	
Administrative and general expenses	8,000	
Bad debt expense	1,500	
Sales discounts	3,000	
Income tax expense	7,500	
Net profit	17,500	
Totals	$210,000	$210,000

Required:

1. Beginning with net sales, prepare a multiple-step income statement (showing both gross profit and profit from operations). Treat sales discounts as an expense.

2. The beginning and ending balances of trade receivables were $19,000 and $21,000, respectively. Compute the gross profit percentage and receivables turnover ratio and explain their meaning.

LO6   **AP7–8**   **Evaluating Internal Controls**

Cory Magnum has been working for Matrix Products Inc. for five years and has gained the respect of his peers for his exemplary behaviour and work ethic. His job includes receiving cash and cheques from customers, depositing the cash receipts in the company's account at the local bank, and recording the transactions in the company's computerized accounting program. Cory was faced with personal financial problems and decided to make use of $2,000 of the company's available cash to solve them. He planned to return the money as soon as his financial situation improved. The $2,000 he took was part of the total cash sales to customers during the previous two business days. At the same time, Cory had received a cheque for $2,000 from PLC Ltd. as a partial payment on its trade receivables.

To hide his theft, Cory deposited the cheque instead of the cash into the company's bank account and made the following journal entry:

Cash in bank	2,000	
Cash on hand		2,000

In addition, he recorded the following journal entry to credit the account of PLC Ltd. to avoid any questions from that company in the future.

Sales returns and allowances	2,000	
Trade receivables—PLC Ltd.		2,000

Required:

1. Assume that Matrix Products prepares financial statements on a monthly basis. Would any items on the income statement or the statement of financial position be incorrect? Explain.

2. Identify the weaknesses that exist in the company's internal control system. What changes should be made to strengthen internal control over cash receipts?

AP7–9 Preparing a Bank Reconciliation and Related Journal Entries (P7–9)   ▢ **LO7**

The president of Kostas Fashions Ltd., Joan Kostas, has just received the monthly bank statement for June, which shows a balance of $10,517. She remembers seeing a different balance for cash at June 30 when the company accountant, Peter Wong, presented to her the monthly statement of financial position. She checks the statement of financial position and finds a cash balance of $6,518. She is not sure which amount is correct. She calls Peter and asks him why the two amounts are different. Peter takes the bank statement and related documents and promises to provide his boss with an explanation within a few hours. He then proceeds to prepare a bank reconciliation report for the month of June.

A review of the documents that accompanied the bank statement shows the following:

a. A credit memorandum for the collection of a note for $2,080, including $80 of interest on the note. The bank charged the company a collection fee of $25.

b. A debit memorandum for an NSF cheque for $286 from customer Rami Cossette.

c. Total service charges for June amounting to $39.

When comparing the bank statement with the company's records, Peter discovers the following discrepancies:

d. A deposit of $1,145 was not recorded on the bank statement.

e. Three cheques had not been presented to the bank for payment yet. The amounts of these cheques are $1,573, $679, and $1,252.

f. A deposit of $2,340 was recorded incorrectly in the books at $2,430.

Required:

1. Explain to Joan Kostas why the two balances for cash are not equal, and why it is important to prepare a bank reconciliation statement.

2. Prepare a bank reconciliation statement at June 30 and the related journal entries.

AP7–10 Computing Outstanding Cheques and Deposits in Transit and Preparing a Bank Reconciliation and Journal Entries (P7–10)   ▢ **LO7**

The August 2011 bank statement for Martha Company and the August 2011 ledger accounts for cash follow:

PB Provincial Bank
594 Water Street
Faubourg, ON
L2G 4S6

STATEMENT OF ACCOUNT

Martha Company
2784, 7th Avenue
Faubourg, ON
L3G 3B5

DATE	BRANCH NUMBER	ACCOUNT TYPE	ACCOUNT NUMBER	PAGE NO.
31 08 2011	815	Chequing	85157	1 OF 1

Date	Description	Debits	Credits	Balance
Aug. 1	Balance Forward			17,470
2	Cheque No. 103	300		17,170
3	Deposit		12,000	29,170
4	Cheque No. 101	400		28,770
5	Cheque No. 105	250		28,520
9	Cheque No. 102	900		27,620
10	Cheque No. 104	300		27,320
15	Deposit		4,000	31,320
21	Cheque No. 106	400		30,920
24	Cheque No. 108	21,000		9,920
25	Deposit		7,000	16,920
30	Cheque No. 109	800		16,120
30	Collection of note		2,180	18,300
30	Service charge	10		18,290
31	Interest earned		80	18,370

The amount collected on August 30 includes interest of $180.

Cash in Bank

Aug.	1 Balance	16,520	Cheques written		
	Deposits		Aug.	2	300
Aug.	2	12,000		4	900
	12	4,000		15	290
	24	7,000		17	550
	31	5,000		18	800
				20	400
				23	21,000

Cash on Hand

Aug. 31	Balance	200

Outstanding cheques at the end of July were for $250, $400, and $300. No deposits were in transit at the end of July.

Required:

1. Compute the amount of deposits in transit at August 31, 2011.
2. Compute the amount of outstanding cheques at August 31, 2011.
3. Prepare a bank reconciliation at August 31, 2011.
4. Prepare any journal entries that the company should make as a result of the bank reconciliation. Why are they necessary?
5. After the reconciliation journal entries are posted, what balances would be reflected in the cash accounts in the ledger?
6. What total amount of cash should be reported on the August 31, 2011, statement of financial position?

CASES AND PROJECTS

FINDING AND INTERPRETING FINANCIAL INFORMATION

LO1, 3, 4, 6   **CP7–1**   **Finding Financial Information**

The Nestlé Group

Refer to the financial statements of the Nestlé Group in Appendix A of this book.

Required:

1. Does the company disclose its revenue recognition policy? What point in time does it use to recognize revenue?
2. Compute the company's gross profit percentage for the most recent two years. Has it risen or fallen? Explain the meaning of the change.
3. Does the company report an allowance for doubtful accounts in the notes to its financial statements? If so, review the details disclosed by the company and explain what they mean.
4. Compute Nestlé's trade receivables turnover for the year 2008. Is it significantly different from the ratio computed for Gildan in the Key Ratio Analysis section in the chapter? If so, what are some possible reasons for the difference?
5. What does the company include in "cash and cash equivalents"? How close do you think the disclosed amount is to the actual fair market value of these assets?

LO2, 5, 6   **CP7–2**   **Finding Financial Information**

Cadbury plc

Go to Connect online for the financial statements of Cadbury, plc.

Required:

1. The company distributes its products through wholesalers. What items would you expect to be subtracted from sales revenue in the computation of net sales?
2. What expenses does Cadbury subtract from net sales in the computation of profit before income taxes? How does this differ from Nestlé's practice?
3. Compute Cadbury's trade receivables turnover ratio for the year ended December 31, 2008. What characteristics of its business might cause it to be so high?
4. What was the change in trade receivables and how did it affect the cash provided by operating activities for 2008?

CP7–3 Comparing Companies

Go to Connect online for the financial statements of Cadbury plc and to Appendix A for the financial statements of the Nestlé Group.

Required:

1. Compute the gross profit percentage for both companies for the current year and the previous year. What do the changes in the ratios suggest?

2. Compute the trade receivables turnover ratio for both companies for fiscal years 2007 and 2008. The Nestlé Group had 11,240 Swiss francs in trade receivables (net) at December 31, 2006, and Cadbury had £932 in trade receivables (net) at the same date. What accounts for the change in these ratios?

FINANCIAL REPORTING AND ANALYSIS CASES

CP7–4 Using Financial Reports: International Bad Debt Disclosure

Foster's Group Limited is an Australian company that sells beer, wine, pre-mixed spirits, cider, and non-alcoholic drinks, worldwide, The company prepares its financial statements in conformity with Australian accounting standards and International Financial Reporting Standards. In the footnotes to a recent annual report, it discloses information on receivables (all numbers are reported in millions of Australian dollars).

Foster's Group Limited

Note 10: Receivables	Year 2	Year 1
Current		
Trade debtors	637.9	757.3
Provision for doubtful debts	(7.4)	(9.2)
Other debtors	309.9	313.0
Provision for doubtful debts	(1.5)	(1.5)
Non-current		
Other debtors	8.1	13.5
Note 2: Revenue, Income and Expenses	**Year 2**	**Year 1**
Amounts to provisions for		
Doubtful debts—trade debtors	(0.2)	(2.3)

Required:

1. The account titles used by Foster's are different from those normally used by Canadian companies. What account titles does it use in place of allowance for doubtful accounts and bad debt expense?

2. Sales on account for year 2 were $4,684.5. Compute the trade receivables (trade debtors) turnover ratio for year 2 (ignore uncollectible accounts).

3. Compute the provision for doubtful debts as a percentage of current receivables separately for receivables from trade debtors and receivables from others. Explain why these percentages might be different.

4. What was the total amount of receivables written off in year 2, net of recoveries?

CP7–5 Canadian Banks

The global economic downturn that started in 2007 affected most sectors in the Canadian economy, particularly the financial sector, including the banking industry. For example, the common shares of Toronto Dominion Bank decreased from $68.12 per share on January 2, 2008, to $32.80 per share on February 23, 2009, before they started climbing up in March 2009 onward. Because banks lend money to individuals and companies, one would expect the banks to experience some difficulty in collecting money from their customers during an economic downturn.

Using your Web browser, contact the websites and consult the annual reports of three of the following banks: Bank of Montreal, Scotiabank, Canadian Imperial Bank of Commerce, National Bank of Canada, Royal Bank of Canada, and TD Canada Trust for fiscal year 2009.

Required:

1. What is the amount of the "provision for credit losses" that each bank reported on its income statement for both years 2008 and 2009?

2. Compute the following percentage: Provision for credit losses/Net interest income, for both years 2008 and 2009. Did the ratio increase from 2008 to 2009 for each of these banks? If so, what could have caused the increase? Explain.

3. What is the amount of the "allowance for loan losses" that each bank reported on its statement of financial position (balance sheet) at the end of its 2009 fiscal year?

4. Compute the following ratio: Allowance for loan losses/Total loans receivable, for both years 2008 and 2009, and comment on the changes in the ratio from 2008 to 2009.

CRITICAL THINKING CASES

LO6   **CP7–6**   **Making Decisions as an Independent Accountant**

Lane Manufacturing Company is a relatively small local business that specializes in the repair and renovation of antique furniture. The owner is an expert craftsperson. Although a number of skilled workers are employed, there is always a large backlog of work to be done. A long-time employee who serves as clerk-bookkeeper handles cash receipts, keeps the records, and writes cheques for disbursements. The owner signs the cheques. The clerk-bookkeeper pays small amounts in cash, subject to a month-end review by the owner. Approximately 80 regular customers are extended credit that typically amounts to less than $1,000. Although credit losses are small, in recent years the bookkeeper had established an allowance for doubtful accounts, and all write-offs were made at year-end. During January 2011 (the current year), the owner decided to start as soon as possible the construction of a building for the business that would provide many advantages over the currently rented space and would allow space to expand facilities. As a part of the considerations in financing, the financing institution asked for 2010 audited financial statements. The company statements had never been audited. Early in the audit, the independent accountant found numerous errors and one combination of amounts, in particular, that caused concern.

There was some evidence that a $2,500 job completed by Lane had been recorded as a receivable (from a new customer) on July 15, 2010. The receivable was credited for a $2,500 cash collection a few days later. The new account was never active again. The auditor also observed that shortly thereafter, three write-offs of trade receivables balances had been made to allowance for doubtful accounts as follows: Jones, $800; Blake, $750; and Sellers, $950—all of whom were known as regular customers. These write-offs drew the attention of the auditor.

Required:

1. Explain what caused the auditor to be concerned. Should the auditor report the suspicions to the owner?

2. What recommendations would you make with respect to internal control procedures for this company?

LO1   **CP7–7**   **Evaluating an Ethical Dilemma: Management Incentives, Revenue Recognition, and Sales with the Right of Return**

Symbol Technologies

Symbol Technologies Inc. was a fast-growing maker of bar-code scanners. According to the federal charges, Symbol's CEO, Tomo Razmilovic, was obsessed with meeting the stock market's expectation for continued growth. His executive team responded by improperly recording revenue and allowances for returns, manipulating inventory levels and trade receivables data to conceal the adverse side effects of the revenue recognition schemes, as well as a variety of other tricks, to overstate revenues by $230 million and pretax earnings by $530 million. What makes this nearly unique is that virtually the whole senior management team is charged with participating in the six-year fraud. At the time this case was written, the former CEO has fled the United States to avoid prosecution, and six other former Symbol executives pleaded guilty to various charges.

The exact nature of the fraud is described in the following excerpt dealing with the guilty plea of the former vice-president of finance:

Ex-Official at Symbol Pleads Guilty
By Kara Scannel
26 March 2003

The Wall Street Journal

A former finance executive at Symbol Technologies Inc. pleaded guilty to participating in a vast accounting fraud that inflated revenue at the maker of bar-code scanners by roughly 10%, or $100 million a year, from 1999 to 2001.

. . .

The criminal information and civil complaint filed yesterday accuse Mr. Asti and other high-level executives of stuffing the firm's distribution channel with phony orders at the end of each quarter to meet revenue and earnings targets. Under generally accepted accounting practices, revenue can be booked only when the products are shipped to a customer. Symbol's customers include delivery services and grocery stores.

Investigators alleged that Mr. Asti and others engaged in "candy" deals, where Symbol bribed resellers with a 1% fee to "buy" products from a distributor at the end of a quarter, which Symbol would later buy back. Symbol would then allegedly convince the distributor to order more products from the company to satisfy the newly created inventory void. The SEC said the inflated inventory figures helped boost Symbol's stock price, as well as enriching Mr. Asti. He allegedly sold thousands of shares of Symbol stock, which he received from exercising stock options, when the stock was trading at inflated prices.

Copyright 2003, Dow Jones & Company Inc.

Required:

1. What facts, if any, presented in the article suggest that Symbol violated the revenue principle?
2. Assuming that Symbol did recognize revenue when goods were shipped, how could it have properly accounted for the fact that customers had a right to cancel the contracts (make an analogy with accounting for bad debts)?
3. What do you think may have motivated management to falsify the statements? Why was management concerned with reporting continued growth in profit?
4. Explain who was hurt by management's unethical conduct.
5. Assume that you are the auditor for other firms. After reading about the fraud, to what types of transactions would you pay special attention in the audit of your clients in this industry? What ratio might provide warnings about channel stuffing?

CP7–8 Evaluating the Effects of Credit Policy Changes on the Receivables Turnover Ratio and Cash Flows from Operating Activities

■ **LO5**

V. R. Rao and Company has been operating for five years as a software consulting firm specializing in the installation of industry standard products. During this period, it has experienced rapid growth in sales revenue and trade receivables. Ms. Rao and her associates all have computer science backgrounds. This year, the company hired you as its first corporate controller. You have put into place new credit-granting and collection procedures that are expected to reduce receivables by approximately one-third by year-end. You have gathered the following data related to the changes:

	(in thousands)	
	Beginning of Year	**End of Year (projected)**
Trade receivables	$1,000,608	$660,495
Less: Allowance for doubtful accounts	36,800	10,225
Net trade receivables	$ 963,808	$650,270
		Current Year (projected)
Net sales (assume all on credit)		$7,015,069

Required:

1. Compute the trade receivables turnover ratio based on two different assumptions:

    a. Those presented in the preceding table (a decrease in the balance in trade receivables, net).

    b. No change in the balance of net trade receivables; the balance was $963,808 at year-end.

2. Compute the effect (sign and amount) of the projected change in net trade receivables on cash flow from operating activities for the year.

3. On the basis of your findings in (1) and (2), write a brief memo explaining how an increase in the trade receivables turnover ratio can result in an increase in cash flow from operating activities. Also explain how this increase can benefit the company.

FINANCIAL REPORTING AND ANALYSIS TEAM PROJECT

LO1, 4, 5   **CP7–9**   **Team Project: Analyzing Revenues and Receivables**

As a team, select an industry to analyze. A list of companies classified by industry can be obtained by accessing **www.fpinfomart.ca** and then choosing "Companies by Industry." You can also find a list of industries and companies within each industry via **http://ca.finance.yahoo.com/investing** (click on "Annual Reports" under "Tools"). Using a Web browser, each team member should acquire the annual report for one publicly traded company in the industry, with each member selecting a different company.

Required:

On an individual basis, each team member should write a short report answering the following questions about the selected company. Discuss any patterns across the companies that you as a team observe. Then, as a group, write a short report comparing and contrasting your companies.

1. If your company lists receivables on its statement of financial position, what percentage is this asset of total assets for each of the last three years? If your company does not list receivables, discuss why this is so.

2. Ratio analysis:

    a. What does the trade receivables turnover ratio measure in general?

    b. If your company lists receivables, compute the ratio for the last three years.

    c. What do your results suggest about the company?

    d. If available, find the industry ratio for the most recent year, compare it to your results, and discuss why you believe your company differs from or is similar to the industry ratio.

3. If your company lists receivables, determine what additional disclosure is available concerning the allowance for doubtful accounts. If the necessary information is provided, what is bad debt expense as a percentage of sales for the last three years?

4. What is the effect of the change in trade receivables on cash flows from operations for the most recent year—that is, did the change increase or decrease operating cash flows? Explain your answer.

Reporting and Interpreting Cost of Sales and Inventory

After studying this chapter, you should be able to do the following:

LO1 Apply the cost principle to identify the amounts that should be included in inventory and determine the cost of sales for typical retailers, wholesalers, and manufacturers. p. 407

LO2 Compare methods for controlling and keeping track of inventory, and analyze the effects of inventory errors on financial statements. p. 411

LO3 Report inventory and cost of sales by using three inventory costing methods. p. 415

LO4 Decide when the use of different inventory costing methods is beneficial to a company. p. 424

LO5 Report inventory at the lower of cost and net realizable value (NRV). p. 427

LO6 Evaluate inventory management by using the inventory turnover ratio and the effects of inventory on cash flows. p. 429

FOCUS COMPANY: **Nokia Corporation**

DEVELOPING AND PROVIDING WORLD-CLASS TELECOMMUNICATION SOLUTIONS

If you shopped for a cell phone recently, you probably considered buying one of the well-known brand names such as iPhone, Nokia, or Sony Ericsson. You made your choice when you subscribed to a mobile telecommunications provider such as Rogers, TELUS, or Bell. Nokia designs, develops, manufactures, markets, and sells a wide range of telecommunications software and hardware, but we will focus our attention on Nokia's cell phones. The company sells its cell phones directly to large mobile telecommunications providers such as Rogers, TELUS, and Bell and to retailers such as Future Shop and Best Buy.

Nokia incurs inventory costs associated with the production and distribution of its cell phones through wholesale and retail channels. To remain a leader in this rapidly changing technological market, Nokia must continually introduce new and improved products. It must also control the quality and cost of its inventory to enhance the profitability of its operations. Nokia accomplishes this not only by establishing mutually beneficial relationships with its suppliers, but also by developing accounting information systems that provide real-time inventory information. Furthermore, Nokia's choice of accounting methods to value and report inventory can affect the amount paid in income taxes.

UNDERSTANDING THE BUSINESS

Concerns about the cost and quality of inventory face all modern manufacturers and merchandisers and turn a reader's attention to *cost of sales* (cost of goods sold, cost of products sold) on the income statement (or profit and loss accounts) and *inventory* on the statement of financial position (or balance sheet). Exhibit 8.1 presents the relevant excerpts from Nokia's financial statements that include these accounts. The cost of sales is subtracted from net sales to produce gross profit on Nokia's income statement.

Exhibit **8.1**

Excerpts from Income Statement and Statement of Financial Position

REAL WORLD EXCERPT

Nokia Corporation

ANNUAL REPORT

NOKIA CORPORATION
Consolidated Profit and Loss Accounts (Partial)
(in millions of euro)

	Financial year ended December 31		
	2009	**2008**	**2007**
Net sales	40,984	50,710	51,058
Cost of sales	27,720	33,337	33,781
Gross profit	13,264	17,373	17,277

NOKIA CORPORATION
Consolidated Balance Sheets (Partial)
(in millions of euro)

	December 31	
	2009	**2008**
ASSETS		
Current assets:		
Inventories	1,865	2,533
Accounts receivable, net of allowances for doubtful accounts	7,981	9,444
Prepaid expenses and accrued income	4,551	4,538
Current portion of long-term loans receivable	14	101
Other financial assets	329	1,034
Investments at fair value	580	0
Available-for-sale investments, liquid assets	2,367	1,272
Available-for-sale investments, cash equivalents	4,784	3,842
Cash and bank	1,142	1,706
Total current assets	23,613	24,470

Inventory is a current asset on the statement of financial position; it is the first item reported in the current assets section because it is least liquid of all the current assets.[1]

Nokia's successful management of both inventory and cost of sales requires a combined effort by human resource managers, engineers, production managers, marketing managers, and accounting and financial managers. It is truly a multidisciplinary task. The primary goals of inventory management are to have sufficient quantities of high-quality inventory available to serve customers' needs while minimizing the costs of carrying inventory (production, storage, obsolescence, and financing). Low quality leads to customer dissatisfaction, returns, and a decline in future sales. Also, purchasing or producing too few units of a hot-selling item causes stock-outs which mean lost sales revenue and potential customer dissatisfaction. Conversely, purchasing or producing too many units of a slow-selling item increases the storage costs and interest costs on short-term borrowings to finance the production or purchases. It may even lead to losses if the merchandise cannot be sold at normal prices.

To meet its inventory management goals, the multidisciplinary team will forecast expected customer demand for different mobile devices and related software. It will also provide feedback on actual outcomes so that adjustments to production or purchasing schedules can be made to control the cost of sales and improve gross profit. Both cost of sales and inventory are such important determinants of a company's success, that managers, investors, and financial analysts pay close attention to these financial statement items.

---

[1]As explained in Chapter 1, assets may be listed on the statement of financial position by either increasing or decreasing order of their convertibility to cash. Some companies list their assets beginning with the most liquid asset, cash, and ending with the least liquid assets, such as patents. In contrast, other companies, such as Nokia, list their least liquid assets first and most liquid assets last.

The accounting system plays three roles in the inventory management process. First, the system must provide accurate information necessary for preparation of periodic financial statements and reports to tax authorities.[2] Second, it must provide up-to-date information on inventory quantities and costs to facilitate ordering and manufacturing decisions. Third, because inventories are subject to theft and other forms of misuse, the system also must provide the information necessary to help protect and control these important assets.

First we discuss the components of inventory costs, the important choices management must make in the financial and tax reporting process, and how these choices affect the financial statements and taxes paid. Then we will briefly discuss how accounting systems are organized to keep track of inventory quantities and costs for decision making and control. This topic will be the principal subject matter of your managerial accounting course. Finally, we discuss how managers, investors, and financial analysts evaluate management's effectiveness at inventory management.

ORGANIZATION OF THE CHAPTER

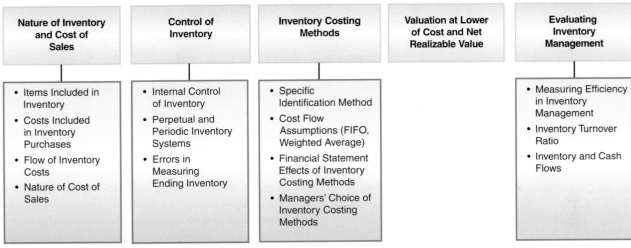

Nature of Inventory and Cost of Sales	Control of Inventory	Inventory Costing Methods	Valuation at Lower of Cost and Net Realizable Value	Evaluating Inventory Management
• Items Included in Inventory • Costs Included in Inventory Purchases • Flow of Inventory Costs • Nature of Cost of Sales	• Internal Control of Inventory • Perpetual and Periodic Inventory Systems • Errors in Measuring Ending Inventory	• Specific Identification Method • Cost Flow Assumptions (FIFO, Weighted Average) • Financial Statement Effects of Inventory Costing Methods • Managers' Choice of Inventory Costing Methods		• Measuring Efficiency in Inventory Management • Inventory Turnover Ratio • Inventory and Cash Flows

Supplemental material:

Appendix 8A: Additional Issues in Measuring Purchases
Appendix 8B: Last-in, First-out Method (online)

NATURE OF INVENTORY AND COST OF SALES

Items Included in Inventory

Inventory is tangible property that is either (1) held for sale in the normal course of business or (2) used to produce goods or services for sale. Inventory is reported on the statement of financial position as a current asset because it normally is used or converted into cash within one year or within the next operating cycle of the business, whichever is longer. The types of inventory normally held depend on the characteristics of the business.

Companies that do not manufacture the products they sell, but simply purchase those products then sell them to customers, are called *merchandisers*. Wholesale merchandisers distribute products to retail merchandisers for resale to customers through retail stores.

Merchandisers (wholesale or retail businesses) hold the following:

Merchandise inventory. Goods (or merchandise) held for resale in the normal course of business. The goods usually are acquired in a finished condition and are ready for sale without further processing. Nokia's cell phones are sold to consumers through most mobile telecommunications providers. Nokia's cell phones represent merchandise inventory for the telecommunications companies that sell them.

LO1

Apply the cost principle to identify the amounts that should be included in inventory and determine the cost of sales for typical retailers, wholesalers, and manufacturers.

INVENTORY is tangible property held for sale in the normal course of business or used in producing goods or services for sale.

MERCHANDISE INVENTORY includes goods held for resale in the ordinary course of business.

---

[2]Tax reports often differ from the statements prepared for shareholders and other external users.

Manufacturing businesses hold the following types of inventory:

Raw materials inventory. Items acquired by purchase, growth (such as food products), or extraction (natural resources) for processing into finished goods. Such items are included in raw materials inventory until used, at which point they become part of work-in-process inventory.

Work-in-process inventory. Goods in the process of being manufactured but not yet complete. When complete, work-in-process inventory becomes finished goods inventory.

Finished goods inventory. Manufactured goods that are complete and available for sale.

Inventories related to Nokia's manufacturing operations are recorded in these accounts. Nokia's note on inventories reports the following:

REAL WORLD EXCERPT

Nokia Corporation

ANNUAL REPORT

Inventories	(in millions of euro)	
	2009	2008
17.		
Raw materials, supplies and other	409	519
Work in progress	681	744
Finished goods	775	1,270
	1,865	2,533

Costs Included in Inventory Purchases

Goods in inventory are recorded in conformity with the *cost principle*. The primary basis of accounting for inventory is cash equivalent cost, which is either the price paid or consideration given to acquire an asset. Inventory cost includes, in principle, the sum of the applicable expenditures and charges directly or indirectly incurred in bringing an article to a usable or saleable condition and location.

When Nokia purchases raw materials (e.g., microprocessor chips) for use in the manufacturing of cell phones, the amount recorded should include the invoice price and indirect expenditures related to the purchase, such as import duties; freight charges if the items are purchased FOB shipping point, as explained in Chapter 7; as well as inspection and preparation costs. In general, the company should cease accumulating purchase costs when the raw materials are either *ready for use* or when the merchandise inventory is *ready for shipment* to customers. Any additional costs related to selling the merchandise inventory to customers, such as salaries of marketing personnel, should be included in selling and marketing expenses of the period of sale since they are incurred after the inventory is ready for sale. Direct sales to customers, by telephone or through the Internet, have reduced the need to stock inventory for long periods and help reduce inventory storage costs and the cost of obsolescence.

FINANCIAL ANALYSIS

APPLYING THE MATERIALITY CONCEPT IN PRACTICE

Incidental costs such as inspection and preparation costs often are not very large relative to other costs (see the discussion of materiality in Chapter 4) and do not have to be assigned to the inventory cost. Thus, for practical reasons, many companies use the invoice price, less returns and discounts, to assign a unit cost to raw materials or merchandise and record other indirect expenditures as separate costs that are reported as expenses.

Flow of Inventory Costs

The flow of inventory costs for merchandisers (wholesalers and retailers) is relatively simple, as shown in Exhibit 8.2A. When merchandise is purchased, the merchandise inventory account is increased. When the goods are sold, the merchandise inventory is decreased and the cost of sales is increased.

The flow of inventory costs in a manufacturing environment is more complex, as diagrammed in Exhibit 8.2B. First *raw materials* (also called *direct materials*) must be purchased. For Nokia, these raw materials include memory chips and liquid crystal displays, among others. As materials are used in production, their cost is removed from the raw materials inventory and added to the cost of the work-in-process inventory.

Two other components of manufacturing costs, direct labour and factory overhead, are also added to the work-in-process inventory when incurred in the manufacturing process. Direct labour cost represents the earnings of employees who work directly on the products being manufactured. Factory overhead costs include all other *manufacturing* costs. For example, the salary of the factory supervisor and the cost of utilities, security, and material handling are included in factory overhead. When the cell phones are completed and ready for sale, the related amounts in work-in-process inventory are transferred to finished goods inventory. When the finished goods are sold, cost of sales increases and the costs in the finished goods inventory decreases.

As Exhibit 8.2 indicates, there are three stages to inventory cost flows for both merchandisers and manufacturers. The first involves purchasing and/or production activities. In the second, these activities result in additions to inventory accounts on the statement of financial position. At the third stage, the inventory items are sold and the amounts become cost of sales on the income statement. Since the flow of inventory costs for both merchandise inventory and finished goods into cost of sales are very similar, we will focus the rest of our discussion on merchandising inventory.

DIRECT LABOUR refers to the earnings of employees who work directly on the products being manufactured.

FACTORY OVERHEAD comprises manufacturing costs that are not raw material or direct labour costs.

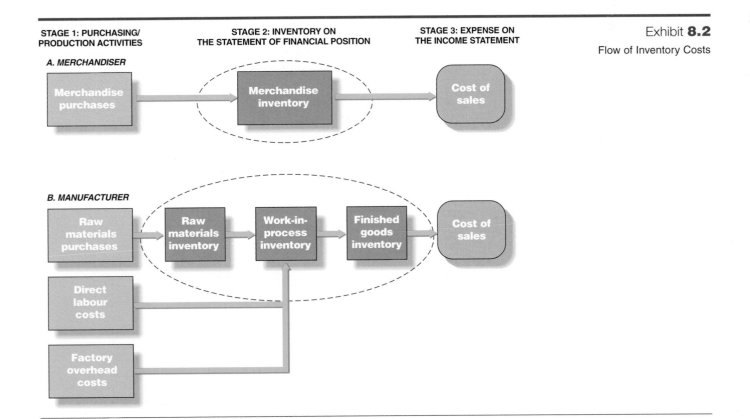

| STAGE 1: PURCHASING/ PRODUCTION ACTIVITIES | STAGE 2: INVENTORY ON THE STATEMENT OF FINANCIAL POSITION | STAGE 3: EXPENSE ON THE INCOME STATEMENT |

Exhibit **8.2**

Flow of Inventory Costs

FINANCIAL ANALYSIS

MODERN MANUFACTURING TECHNIQUES AND INVENTORY COSTS

The flows of inventory costs diagrammed in Exhibit 8.2B represent the keys to manufacturing cost and quality control. The company must pay to finance the purchase and storage of raw materials and purchased parts. This means that minimizing the quantities of these inventories and more closely matching them with projected manufacturing demand is the first key to an effective process of cost control. Nokia must work closely with its suppliers in design, production, and delivery of raw materials and/or manufactured parts. (This approach to inventory management is called *just-in-time* or *JIT*.) To reduce the costs of work-in-process and finished goods, companies redesign and simplify manufacturing processes and retrain their manufacturing personnel to minimize both direct labour and factory overhead costs. Simplified product design and production processes often lead to higher product quality and reduced scrap and rework costs.

Nokia's management accounting system is designed to monitor the success of these changes and provide information to allow continuous improvements in manufacturing. The design of such systems is the subject matter of management accounting and cost accounting courses.

Nature of Cost of Sales

Cost of sales (COS) is directly related to sales revenue. The amount of sales revenue during an accounting period is the number of units sold multiplied by the sales price. Cost of sales is the same number of units multiplied by their unit costs; it includes all costs of the merchandise purchased or the finished goods sold during the period.

Let us examine the relationship between cost of sales on the income statement and inventory on the statement of financial position. Nokia starts each accounting period with a stock of finished goods inventory called *beginning inventory* (BI). During the accounting period, new *purchases* (P) are added to inventory. The sum of the cost of beginning inventory and the cost of purchases (or additions to finished goods) is the cost of goods available for sale during that period. What remains unsold at the end of the period becomes *ending inventory* (EI) of finished goods on the statement of financial position. The portion of the cost of goods available for sale that are actually sold becomes *cost of sales* on the income statement. The ending inventory for one accounting period then becomes the beginning inventory for the next period. The relationships between these various amounts are brought together in the cost of sales equation.

The **COST OF GOODS AVAILABLE FOR SALE** refers to the sum of the cost of beginning inventory and the cost of purchases (or additions to finished goods) for the period.

COST OF SALES EQUATION: BI + P − EI = COS

Although Nokia manufactures its cell phones, we assume, for illustrative purposes only, that it subcontracts the production of touchscreen cell phone model N97 to another manufacturer and purchases the finished product at specific prices. To illustrate the relationships represented by the cost of sales equation, assume that Nokia began the period with €1 million of cell phones in beginning inventory, purchased additional cell phones during the period for €9 million, and had €2 million in inventory at the end of the period. These amounts are combined as follows to compute the cost of sales of €8 million:

Beginning inventory	€ 1 million
Add: Purchases of merchandise during the year	9 million
Cost of goods available for sale	10 million
Deduct: Ending inventory	−2 million
Cost of sales	€ 8 million

These same relationships are illustrated in Exhibit 8.3 and can be represented in the merchandise inventory T-account as follows (amounts in millions):

Merchandise Inventory (A)

Beginning inventory	1		
Purchases of inventory	9	Cost of sales	8
Ending inventory	2		

If three of these four amounts are known, either the cost of sales equation or the inventory T-account can be used to solve for the fourth amount.

SELF-STUDY **QUIZ 8-1**

Assume the following facts for cell phone model N97 that Nokia purchased and sold to customers during the year:

Beginning inventory: 5,000 units at unit cost of €200.

Ending inventory: 10,000 units at unit cost of €200.

Sales: 40,000 units at a sales price of €300 (cost per unit €200).

1. Using the cost of sales equation, compute the cost of purchases of cell phone model N97 for the period.

2. Prepare the first three lines of an income statement (showing gross profit) for cell phone model N97 for the year.

After you complete your answers, go online for the solutions.

▓ connect™

CONTROL OF INVENTORY

Internal Control of Inventory

LO2

Compare methods of controlling and keeping track of inventory, and analyze the effects of inventory errors on financial statements.

After cash, inventory is the asset second-most vulnerable to theft. Efficient management of inventory to avoid cost of stock-outs and overstock situations is also crucial to the profitability of most companies. Consequently, a number of control features focus on safeguarding inventories and providing up-to-date information for management decisions. The following are the most important control features:

1. Separation of responsibilities for inventory accounting and physical handling of inventory.

2. Storage of inventory in a manner that protects it from theft and damage.

Exhibit **8.3**

Nature of Cost of Sales for Merchandise Inventory

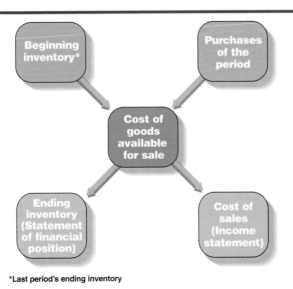

*Last period's ending inventory

3. Limiting access to inventory to authorized employees.
4. Maintaining perpetual inventory records (described below).
5. Comparing perpetual records to periodic physical counts of inventory.

Perpetual and Periodic Inventory Systems

To compute cost of sales, three amounts must be known: (1) beginning inventory; (2) purchases of merchandise, or additions to finished goods, during the period; and (3) ending inventory. The amount of purchases for the period is always accumulated in the accounting system. The amounts of cost of sales and ending inventory can be determined by using one of two different inventory systems: perpetual or periodic. To simplify the discussion of how accounting systems keep track of these amounts, we focus this discussion on cell phone model N97 that Nokia sells. Although the same general principles apply, the more complex details of manufacturing accounting systems are discussed in management accounting courses.

In a **PERPETUAL INVENTORY SYSTEM**, a detailed inventory record is maintained, recording each purchase and sale during the accounting period.

Perpetual Inventory System   In a perpetual inventory system, a detailed record is maintained for each type of merchandise stocked, showing (1) units and cost of the beginning inventory, (2) units and cost of each purchase, (3) units and cost of the goods for each sale, and (4) the units and cost of the goods on hand at any point in time. This up-to-date record is maintained on a transaction-by-transaction basis throughout the period. In a complete perpetual inventory system, the inventory record gives both the cost of ending inventory and the cost of sales at any point in time. Under this system, a physical count must be performed from time to time to ensure that records are accurate in case errors or theft of inventory occur.

All journal entries for purchase and sale transactions discussed in the text so far have been recorded by using a perpetual inventory system. In a perpetual inventory system, purchase transactions are directly recorded in an inventory account. Simultaneously, when each sale is recorded, a companion cost of sales entry is made, decreasing inventory and recording cost of sales. As a result, information on cost of sales and ending inventory is available on a continuous (perpetual) basis.

Whether the accounting system is manual or electronic, the rules for recording and reporting accounting data are the same. The maintenance of a separate inventory record for each type of good stocked on a transaction-by-transaction basis usually is necessary for purchasing, manufacturing, and distribution decisions. Most companies rely heavily on this system and may even share some of this information electronically with their suppliers or customers.[3]

In a **PERIODIC INVENTORY SYSTEM**, ending inventory and cost of sales are determined at the end of the accounting period based on a physical count.

Periodic Inventory System   Under the periodic inventory system, companies do *not* maintain an ongoing record of inventory during the year. An actual physical count of the goods remaining on hand is required at the *end of each period*. The number of units of each type of merchandise on hand is multiplied by their unit cost to compute the total cost of the ending inventory. Cost of sales is calculated by using the cost of sales equation.

Because the amount of inventory is not known until the end of the period when the physical inventory count is taken, the cost of sales cannot be determined reliably until the inventory count is completed. Inventory purchases are debited to a temporary account called *purchases*. Revenues are recorded at the time of each sale. However, the cost of sales is not recorded until after the inventory count is completed. At all other times, companies using a periodic system must estimate the value of inventory on hand. We briefly discuss the estimation of inventory amounts later in the chapter.

---

[3]Many companies, such as Gildan Activewear Inc., provide product information to their current and potential customers. The website **www.gildanfinder.com** allows Gildan's customers to find out how many units of each product are available at each location that distributes its products in Canada, the United States, Mexico, Europe, or the Asia-Pacific region.

Before affordable computers and bar code readers were available, the primary reason for using the periodic inventory system was its low cost. The primary disadvantage of a periodic inventory system is the lack of timely inventory information. Managers do not receive information quickly about either low stock or overstocked situations. Most modern companies could not survive without this information. As noted at the beginning of the chapter, cost and quality pressures from increasing competition, combined with dramatic declines in the cost of computers, have made sophisticated perpetual inventory systems a minimum requirement at all but the smallest companies.

A perpetual inventory system provides more timely information about inventory quantities and costs. As explained in Chapter 6, timeliness of accounting information enhances its relevance for decision-making purposes. Accordingly, a perpetual inventory system is preferable to a periodic system because it provides more relevant information for inventory management decisions. A perpetual inventory system is also preferred over a periodic system because internal control procedures have gained more importance in the past few years with recent legislation requiring chief executive officers (CEOs) and chief financial officers (CFOs) of all companies listed on Canadian stock exchanges to certify the quality of internal control systems, as explained in Chapter 7.

Perpetual Inventory Records in Practice   The decision to use a perpetual versus a periodic inventory system is based primarily on management's need for timely information for use in operating decisions and on the cost of the perpetual system. Further, the specific manner in which the perpetual system is designed will also be determined with these trade-offs in mind. Many inventory ordering and production decisions require accurate information on inventory quantities but not costs. Quantities on hand provide the information necessary for efficient management of inventory, providing delivery information to dealers, and quality control.

METHODS FOR ESTIMATING INVENTORY

FINANCIAL
ANALYSIS

When a periodic inventory system is used and detailed perpetual inventory records are not kept, the cost of sales and the amount of ending inventory can be directly computed only when a physical inventory count is taken. Because taking a physical inventory count is expensive, it is normally done only once each year. In these circumstances, managers who wish to prepare monthly or quarterly financial statements for internal use often estimate the cost of sales and cost of ending inventory by using the *gross profit method.* The gross profit method uses the historical gross profit percentage (introduced in Chapter 7) to estimate cost of sales.

For example, if Nokia's historical gross profit percentage on cell phone model N97 is 30 percent and €500,000 worth of this model were sold in January, it would estimate the cost of sales to be €350,000 (€500,000 × [100% − 30%]) for the month. If Nokia keeps track of purchases and other additions to inventory, it could then use the cost of sales equation to solve for an estimate of ending inventory. Retailers often take their physical inventory counts based on the retail price instead of cost and then use a similar method (called the *retail method*) to estimate cost. Methods for estimating inventory and cost of sales are discussed in detail in intermediate accounting courses.

Errors in Measuring Ending Inventory

As the cost of sales equation indicates, a direct relationship exists between the cost of ending inventory and cost of sales because items not in the ending inventory are assumed to have been sold. Thus, the measurement of ending inventory quantities and costs affects both the statement of financial position (assets) and the income statement (cost of sales, gross profit, and profit). The measurement of ending inventory affects not only the profit for that period but also the profit for the next accounting period. This two-period effect occurs because the ending inventory for one accounting period is the beginning inventory for the next.

Greeting card maker Gibson Greetings had overstated its current year profit by 20 percent because one division had overstated ending inventory for the year. You can compute the effects of the error on both the current year's and next year's profit before taxes by using the cost of sales equation. Assume that the ending inventory was inadvertently overstated by $10,000 because of a clerical error that was not discovered. This error would have the following effects in the current year and next year:

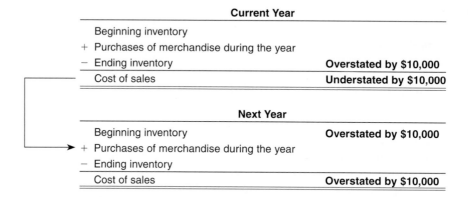

Current Year	
Beginning inventory	
+ Purchases of merchandise during the year	
− Ending inventory	**Overstated by $10,000**
Cost of sales	**Understated by $10,000**

Next Year	
Beginning inventory	**Overstated by $10,000**
+ Purchases of merchandise during the year	
− Ending inventory	
Cost of sales	**Overstated by $10,000**

Because the cost of sales was understated, *profit before taxes would be overstated* by $10,000 in the *current year.* Consequently, income tax expense, income tax payable, and profit would be overstated. In addition, since the current year's ending inventory becomes next year's beginning inventory, it would have the following effects: cost of sales would be overstated and *profit before taxes would be understated* by the same amount in the *next year.* Furthermore, income tax expense, income tax payable, and profit would be understated. Accountants often refer to this as the iron law of accruals, because if there are no other changes, an overstatement during one time period will reverse to an identical understatement in the next.

Each of these errors would flow into retained earnings so that, at the end of the current year, retained earnings would be overstated by $10,000 (less the related income tax expense). This error would be offset in the next year, and retained earnings and inventory at the end of next year would be correct.

Exhibit 8.4 shows how an error that understates the cost of ending inventory affects other elements of financial statements during the year of the error and the following year.

An error that overstates ending inventory would have exactly the opposite effects on the financial statement items shown in Exhibit 8.4.

Exhibit **8.4**

Effect of Understatement in Ending Inventory on Selected Financial Statement Items

ERROR: UNDERSTATEMENT OF ENDING INVENTORY

	Year of the Error	Following Year
Beginning inventory	NE*	U
Ending inventory	U	NE
Cost of sales	O	U
Gross profit	U	O
Profit before income tax	U	O
Income tax expense	U	O
Profit	U	O
Retained earnings, end of year	U	NE

*U = Understated; O = Overstated; NE = No Effect

Sarlos Ltd. provided the following summary income statements for fiscal years 2011 and 2012. Assume that an error in the inventory count at December 31, 2011, resulted in an overstatement of ending inventory by $10,000.

SARLOS LTD. Income Statements For the Years Ended December 31				
	With inventory error		**Without inventory error**	
	2012	**2011**	**2012**	**2011**
Sales	$600,000	$500,000	$600,000	$500,000
Cost of sales	350,000	300,000	?	?
Gross profit	250,000	200,000	?	?
Selling, general, and administrative expenses	120,000	100,000	?	?
Profit before income tax	130,000	100,000	?	?
Income tax expense (at 40%)	52,000	40,000	?	?
Profit	$ 78,000	$ 60,000	?	?

1. Complete the income statements above for 2011 and 2012, assuming that the inventory error was discovered at the end of 2012.

2. Compute the combined profit for both years 2011 and 2012. Would the inventory error at December 31, 2011, affect the financial statements for year 2013? Explain.

After you complete your answers, go online for the solutions.

INVENTORY COSTING METHODS

LO3

Report inventory and cost of sales by using three inventory costing methods.

In the Nokia example presented earlier, the cost of all units of model N97 was the same: €200. If inventory costs do not change, this would be the end of our discussion. As we are all aware, the prices of most goods do change. In recent years, the costs of many manufactured items such as automobiles and motorcycles have risen gradually. In other high-technology industries, such as the computer industry, however, costs of production have dropped dramatically, along with retail prices.

When inventory costs change, the determination of the cost of sales and the cost of ending inventory can turn profits into losses (and vice versa) and cause companies to pay or save millions in taxes. A simple example will illustrate these dramatic effects. Do not let the simplicity of our example mislead you. It applies broadly to actual company practices.

The example is based on the following data for Nokia during the first quarter of the current year, assuming for simplicity that Nokia purchases and sells only model N97.

Date	Transaction or Event	Number of N97 Cell Phones	Number of Cell Phones on Hand	Cost per Cell Phone	Sale Price per Cell Phone
January 1	Beginning inventory	800	800	€200	
January 31	Sale to customers	(600)	200		€279
February 5	Purchase	800	1,000	210	
February 28	Sale to customers	(900)	100		295
March 10	Purchase	900	1,000	220	
March 31	Sale to customers	(200)	800		299

Total number of cell phones sold = 600 + 900 + 200 = 1,700

Ending inventory = 800 cell phones

Note that the cost per cell phone increased between January and March. On March 31, 200 units are sold for €299 each and revenues of €198,000 are recorded. What amount would the accountant record as cost of sales? *The answer depends on which specific goods we assume are sold.* Three generally accepted inventory costing methods are available to determine the cost of sales:[4]

1. Specific identification

2. First-in, first-out (FIFO)

3. Weighted average

The three inventory costing methods are alternative ways to assign the total cost of goods available for sale between (1) ending inventory and (2) cost of sales. International Accounting Standard 2 requires only that the inventory costing method used be rational and systematic. The selected inventory costing method should be the one that provides the best correspondence between expenses and revenues. The first method identifies individual items that remain in inventory or are sold. The remaining two methods assume that inventory items follow a certain physical flow.

Specific Identification Method

The **SPECIFIC IDENTIFICATION METHOD** identifies the cost of the specific item that was sold.

When the specific identification method is used, the cost of each item sold is individually identified and recorded as cost of sales. Without electronic tracking, the method may be manipulated when the units are identical, because one can affect the cost of sales and the ending inventory accounts by picking and choosing from among the several available unit costs. For this reason, International Financial Reporting Standards prohibit the use of this method when there are large numbers of inventory items that are interchangeable, such as cell phones.

The specific identification method is impractical when large quantities of similar items are kept in stock. It is appropriate, however, when dealing with very expensive items such as broadband telecommunications systems, aircraft, yachts, fine art objects, buildings, luxury cars, or fine jewellery because each item tends to differ from the other items. This method requires keeping track of the purchase cost of each item. This is done by either (1) coding the purchase cost on each unit before placing it in stock or (2) keeping a separate record of the unit and identifying it with a serial number.

The technology of bar code scanning and radio frequency identification is a simple and cost-effective method to keep track of inventory items at all times, even for items with low unit costs. The scanner transmits cost and quantity information to a company's central database, thereby creating a perpetual record of inventory costs. This affects the computation of the cost of sales and the cost of ending inventory. To compute the cost of sales, the bar code identifies the specific unit that is sold and matches it to the recorded cost through the scanning process. The recorded cost of all units that remain unsold at March 31 represents the cost of ending inventory.

Cost Flow Assumptions

Most inventory items are accounted for by using one of two cost flow assumptions. The *choice of an inventory costing method is NOT based on the physical flow of goods* on and off the shelves. That is why the methods are called *cost flow assumptions.* A useful visual learning tool for representing inventory cost flows is a stack of inventory units such as cell phones. The different inventory costing methods then can be visualized as flows of inventory in and out of the stack. We use this concept to illustrate inventory cost flow throughout the following sections. We assume first that Nokia uses a periodic

---

[4]A fourth method—last-in, first-out (LIFO)—is accepted in the United States but is prohibited under International Accounting Standard 2 – Inventories.

inventory system, where the costs of sales and ending inventory are determined at the end of the accounting period.[5] Next, we illustrate the computation of cost of sales and ending inventory with the more widely used perpetual inventory system.

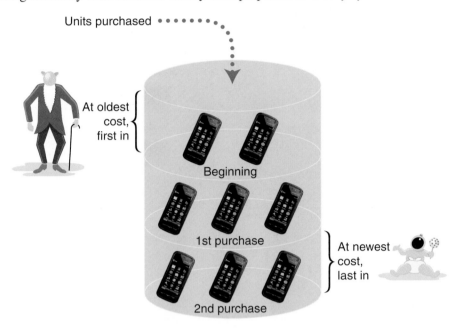

The oldest cell phones are placed at the top of the stack because they are typically sold first.

First-In, First-Out Method

The first-in, first-out method, frequently called *FIFO*, assumes that the earliest goods purchased (the first ones in) are the first units sold (the first ones out) and the last goods purchased remain in ending inventory. First, each purchase is treated as if it were added to the stack in sequence (800 cell phones of beginning inventory at €200 each, followed by a first purchase on February 5 of 800 cell phones at €210 each, and a second purchase on March 10 of 900 cell phones at €220 each). Each of the 1,700 cell phones sold is then removed from the stack in the same sequence it was added (800 units at €200, 800 units at €210, and 100 units at €220); *first in is first out.* FIFO allocates the *oldest* unit costs to *cost of sales* and the *newest* unit costs to *ending inventory.* We assume that physical inventory is taken at March 31, the end of the first quarter, to determine the number of cell phones unsold, and that the number of cell phones in stock is the same under both inventory control systems without any shrinkage or impairment in inventory value.

The **FIRST-IN, FIRST-OUT (FIFO) METHOD** assumes that the oldest units (the first costs in) are the first units sold.

Periodic Inventory System   When a periodic inventory system is used, the cost of sales and the cost of ending inventory are computed at the end of the account-ing period. Exhibit 8.5 summarizes the flow of goods. The table at the bottom of Exhibit 8.5 shows the flow of units and costs during the period. Notice that purchases are accumulated until the end of the period when the physical inventory count is taken and the cost of ending inventory is determined. The cost of sales is calculated at that time as the difference between the cost of goods available for sale (beginning inven-tory plus purchases) and the cost of ending inventory.

---

[5]This assumption, though unrealistic, allows us to focus our attention on the fundamental differences between the two inventory costing methods.

Exhibit **8.5**

FIFO Inventory Flows—Periodic
Inventory System

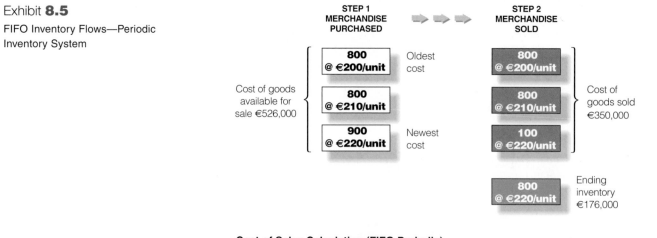

Cost of Sales Calculation (FIFO Periodic)

Cost of cell phones purchased and sold

Date			Units		Cost		Total	
January 1	Beginning inventory	**Oldest cost**	800	×	€ 200	=	€ 160,000	
February 5	Purchase		800	×	€ 210		168,000	
March 10	Purchase	**Newest cost**	900	×	€ 220		198,000	
	Number of units available for sale:		2,500				€ 526,000	**Cost of goods available for sale**
	Number of units in ending inventory:		800	×	€ 220	=	€ 176,000	**Cost of ending inventory**
	Number of units sold:		1,700				€ 350,000	**Cost of sales**

Perpetual Inventory System Would the computation of cost of sales and ending inventory change if Nokia used a FIFO perpetual inventory system? The answer is no. The only difference is that when a perpetual inventory system is used, the inventory records are updated after every purchase and each sale transaction. When using the perpetual inventory system, Nokia must compute the cost of sales for each sales transaction to continuously update its inventory records. But under FIFO, the order of costs in and out of inventory is identical for both the perpetual and the periodic systems. Therefore, the cost of sales will be the same under both systems. The same applies to the cost of ending inventory.

In Exhibit 8.6, the cost of sales is computed after each sales transaction. The graphic depicts the same purchase and sale transactions to help you visualize how the cost of sales is computed under this system. The 600 cell phones sold on January 31 are taken from the beginning inventory of 800 cell phones at a cost of €200 per cell phone. When Nokia sold 900 cell phones on February 28, the company shipped to customers the remaining 200 cell phones at a cost of €200 each, plus 700 cell phones from the 800 units purchased on February 5 at a cost of €210 each. The remaining 100 cell phones were then sold to customers on March 31 along with an additional 100 cell phones taken from the 900 cell phones purchased on March 10 at a cost of €220 each. This leaves 800 cell phones in ending inventory. The total cost of sales under both systems is €350,000, the same amount computed under the periodic inventory system. This is not surprising because the old units that are in inventory at any date are assumed to be sold first before the new units are sold. Under both the perpetual and periodic systems, the 800 units in beginning inventory, the 800 units purchased on February 5, and 100 of the 900 units purchased on March 10 are assumed to be sold.

Comparison of Perpetual and Periodic Systems The differences between the perpetual and periodic inventory systems are highlighted in italics in Exhibit 8.7.

The recording of the purchases and sales transactions under both inventory control systems are presented in Exhibit 8.8, assuming that all transactions are on account.

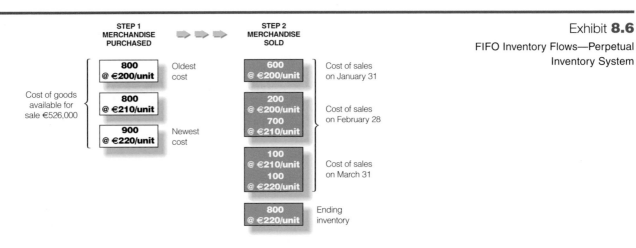

Exhibit **8.6**

FIFO Inventory Flows—Perpetual Inventory System

Cost of cell phones purchased and sold

Date			Units		Cost		Total
January 1	Beginning inventory	**Oldest cost**	800	×	€ 200	=	€ 160,000
January 31	Cost of sales		(600)	×	€ 200		(120,000)
	Cost of remaining inventory		200	×	€ 200	=	40,000
February 5	Purchases		800	×	€ 210	=	168,000
	Cost of goods available for sale		1,000				208,000
February 28	Cost of sales (900 units)		(200)	×	€ 200		(40,000)
			(700)	×	€ 210		(147,000)
	Cost of remaining inventory		100	×	€ 210	=	21,000
March 10	Purchases	**Newest cost**	900	×	€ 220	=	198,000
	Cost of goods available for sale		1,000				219,000
March 31	Cost of sales (200 units)		(100)	×	€ 210	=	(21,000)
			(100)	×	€ 220	=	(22,000)
	Ending inventory		800	×	€ 220	=	€ 176,000
	Cost of sales						€ 350,000

Weighted-Average Cost Method

The weighted-average cost method requires computation of the weighted-average unit cost of the goods available for sale.

Periodic Inventory System   When a periodic inventory system is used, the cost of goods and ending inventory are computed at the end of the accounting period. The cost of sales and cost of ending inventory would be different than if FIFO was used because the cost of the ending inventory is based on an average cost instead of the newest costs.

The **WEIGHTED-AVERAGE COST METHOD** uses the weighted-average unit cost of the goods available for sale for both cost of sales and ending inventory.

Exhibit **8.7**

Comparison of Perpetual and Periodic Inventory Systems

Perpetual	Periodic
Beginning inventory (carried over from prior period)	Beginning inventory (carried over from prior period)
+ Purchases for the period (accumulated in an *Inventory* account	+ Purchases for the period (accumulated in *Purchases* account)
= Cost of goods available for sale	= Cost of goods available for sale
− *Cost of sales (measured at every sale, based on perpetual record)*	− *Ending inventory (measured at end of period, based on physical inventory count)*
= *Ending inventory (perpetual record updated at every sale)*	= *Cost of sales (computed as a residual amount)*

Exhibit **8.8**

Comparison of Journal Entries under Both the
Perpetual and Periodic Inventory Systems

Perpetual Records (FIFO Costing Method)	**Periodic Records (FIFO Costing Method)**
1. Record all transactions in chronological order. Purchases should be recorded in the *inventory* account and in a detailed perpetual inventory record. Sales should be recorded in sales revenue and the cost of sales should be recognized on the date of sale.	1. Record all transactions in chronological order. Record all purchases in the *purchases* account, and all sales in the sales revenue account.

January 31:

Trade receivables (A)	167,400	
Sales revenue (R) (600 units × €279)		167,400
Cost of sales (E)	120,000	
Inventory (A) (600 units × €200)		120,000

February 5:

Inventory (A) (800 units × €210)	168,000	
Trade payables (L)		168,000

February 28:

Trade receivables (A)	265,500	
Sales revenue (R) (900 units × €295)		265,500
Cost of sales (E)	187,000	
Inventory (A)		187,000
(200 units × €200 + 700 units × €210)		

March 10:

Inventory (A) (900 units × €220)	198,000	
Trade payables (L)		198,000

March 31:

Trade receivables (A)	59,800	
Sales revenue (R) (200 units × €299)		59,800
Cost of sales (E)	43,000	
Inventory (A)		43,000
(100 units × €210 + 100 units × €220)		

2. At March 31, end of period:
   Use the cost of sales and inventory amounts. It is not necessary to compute the cost of sales because, under the perpetual inventory system, the cost of sales account is up to date. The balance in the cost of sales account is reported on the income statement. Also, the inventory account shows the ending inventory amount reported on the statement of financial position. A physical inventory count is still necessary to assess the accuracy of the perpetual records and to assess theft and other forms of misuse (called *shrinkage*).

March 31:
No entry

Periodic Records (FIFO Costing Method) column:

January 31:

Trade receivables (A)	167,400	
Sales revenue (R) (600 units × €279)		167,400

February 5:

Purchases* (T) (800 units × €210)	168,000	
Trade payables (L)		168,000

*Purchases is a temporary account (T) closed to cost of sales at the end of the period

February 28:

Trade receivables (A)	265,500	
Sales revenue (R) (900 units × €295)		265,500

March 10:

Purchases (T) (900 units × €220)	198,000	
Trade payables (L)		198,000

March 31:

Trade receivables (A)	59,800	
Sales revenue (R) (200 units × €299)		59,800

2. At March 31, end of period:
   a. Count the number of units on hand.
   b. Compute the cost of the ending inventory.
   c. Compute and record the cost of sales.

Beginning inventory (last period's ending inventory)	€160,000
Add purchases (balance in the Purchases account)	*366,000*
Cost of goods available for sale	526,000
Deduct ending inventory (physical count—800 units at €220)	176,000
Cost of sales	€350,000

March 31:

Transfer beginning inventory and purchases to the cost of sales account:

Cost of sales (E)	526,000	
Inventory (A) (beginning)		160,000
Purchases (T)		366,000

Transfer the ending inventory amount from the cost of sales account to determine the cost of sales and establish the ending inventory balance:

Inventory (A) (ending)	176,000	
Cost of sales (E)		176,000

The average cost is calculated by dividing the cost of goods available for sale by the total units available for sale. For our example, the weighted-average unit cost for the quarter is computed as indicated in Exhibit 8.9.

In these circumstances, the cost of sales and the ending inventory are assigned the same weighted-average cost of €210.40 per cell phone. The cost of the ending inventory is €168,320 (800 cell phones at €210.40 each) and the cost of sales is €357,680 (1,700 cell phones at €210.40 each).

Perpetual Inventory System Would the computation of cost of sales and ending inventory change if Nokia used a perpetual inventory system instead of a periodic system? As indicated before, when a perpetual inventory system is used, the inventory records are updated after every purchase and sale transaction in order to keep track of the number of inventory items on hand.

The 600 cell phones sold on January 31 are taken from the beginning inventory of 800 cell phones at a cost of €200 per unit, for a total cost of €120,000. The cost of the remaining 200 cell phones is then added to the cost of the 800 cell phones purchased on February 5 to compute a new weighted-average unit cost of €208 per cell phone, as shown in Exhibit 8.10.

This average cost is then used to compute the cost of the 900 cell phones sold on February 28; that is, 900 × €208, or €187,200. The cost of the remaining 100 cell phones is then added to the cost of the 900 cell phones purchased on March 10 to compute a third weighted-average cost of €218.80 per cell phone. This average cost is then used to compute the cost of the 200 cell phones sold on March 31; that is, 200 × €218.80, or €43,760. Since the average cost changed three times, this method is called the *moving weighted-average cost* method.

The total cost of sales during the quarter is €350,960 (€120,000 + €187,200 + €43,760) compared to €357,680 under the periodic inventory system. The periodic average cost is always higher than the perpetual average cost in a period of rising prices because the periodic average cost per unit includes the cost of all units available for sale during the accounting period, whereas the perpetual average cost method considers only the cost of units available for sale at different dates in the accounting period.

Exhibit **8.9**

Weighted-Average Inventory
Flows—Periodic Inventory System

Cost of Sales Calculation (Weighted-Average Periodic)

Cost of cell phones purchased and sold

Date		Units		Cost		Total	
January 1	Beginning inventory	800	×	€ 200	=	€ 160,000	
February 5	Purchase	800	×	€ 210		168,000	
March 10	Purchase	900	×	€ 220		198,000	
Number of units available for sale (NUAS):		2,500				€ 526,000	= **Cost of goods available for sale (COGAS)**
Number of units in ending inventory:		800	×	€ 210.4	=	168,320	**Cost of ending inventory**
Number of units sold:		1,700	×	€ 210.4	=	€ 357,680	**Cost of sales**

$$\text{Weighted-average cost per unit} = \frac{\text{COGAS}}{\text{NUAS}} = \frac{€\,526,000}{2,500} = €\,210.40^{6}$$

---

[6]Notice that the simple average of the unit costs is $210 [($200 + $210 + $220)/3], but the weighted average is $210.40 because the latter considers the number of units purchased at each unit cost. Beware of using a simple average.

Exhibit **8.10**

Weighted-Average Inventory
Flows—Perpetual Inventory
System

Cost of Sales Calculation (Weighted-Average Perpetual)

Cost of cell phones purchased and sold

Date	Transaction	Units		Cost		Total	
January 1	Beginning inventory	800	×	€ 200	=	€ 160,000	
January 31	Sale	(600)	×	€ 200		(120,000)	
		200	×	€ 200		40,000	
February 5	Purchase	800	×	€ 210		168,000	
	Number of units available for sale (NUAS) =	1,000				€ 208,000	Cost of goods available for sale (COGAS)
February 28	Sale	(900)	×	€ 208		(187,200)	
		100	×	€ 208		20,800	
March 10	Purchase	900	×	€ 220		198,000	
	Number of units available for sale (NUAS) =	1,000				€ 218,800	Cost of goods available for sale (COGAS)
March 31	Sale	(200)	×	€ 218.8 =		(43,760)	
		800		€ 218.8 =		175,040	

$$\text{First weighted-average cost per unit} = \frac{\text{COGAS}}{\text{NUAS}} = \frac{€\,208{,}000}{1{,}000} = €\,208$$

$$\text{Second weighted-average cost per unit} = \frac{\text{COGAS}}{\text{NUAS}} = \frac{€\,218{,}800}{1{,}000} = €\,218.8$$

The process of recording the purchase and sale transactions during the three-month period and the adjustments at the end of March 31 are similar to those that are presented in Exhibit 8.8, except for the differences in the cost of sales amounts.

Financial Statement Effects of Inventory Costing Methods

Each of the three alternative inventory costing methods is in conformity with IFRS. To understand why managers choose different methods in different circumstances, we must first understand their effects on the income statement and statement of financial position. Exhibit 8.11 summarizes the financial statement effects of FIFO and weighted-average methods using either the periodic or perpetual inventory system. Remember that the methods differ only in the portion of goods available for sale allocated to cost of sales versus ending inventory. For that reason, the method that gives the highest ending inventory amount also gives the lowest cost of sales and the highest gross profit, income tax expense, and profit amounts, and vice versa.

Notice in Exhibit 8.11 that the cost of sales under FIFO is the same whether Nokia uses either a periodic or a perpetual inventory system, as previously illustrated. Furthermore, the weighted-average cost of sales is closer to FIFO cost when a perpetual inventory system is used, because the moving average cost increased with each new purchase of units, thus approaching FIFO cost. In the comparison in Exhibit 8.11, unit costs were increasing. *When unit costs are rising, the weighted-average cost method produces lower profit and a lower inventory valuation than FIFO. When unit costs are declining, the weighted-average cost method produces*

	Periodic Inventory System		Perpetual Inventory System	
	FIFO	Weighted Average	FIFO	Weighted Average
Cost of Sales Calculation				
Beginning inventory	€160,000	€160,000	€160,000	€160,000
Add: Purchases	366,000	366,000	366,000	366,000
Cost of goods available for sale	526,000	526,000	526,000	526,000
Deduct: Ending inventory (to statement of financial position)	176,000	168,320	176,000	175,040
Cost of sales (to income statement)	€350,000	€357,680	€350,000	€350,960
Effect on the income statement Sales	€492,700*	€492,700	€492,700	€492,700
Cost of sales	350,000	357,680	350,000	350,960
Gross profit	€142,700	€135,020	€142,700	€141,740
Effect on the statement of financial position				
Inventory	€176,000	€168,320	€176,000	€175,040

*(600 × €279) + (900 × €295) + (200 × €299)

Exhibit **8.11**

Financial Statement Effects of Inventory Costing Methods

higher profit and a higher inventory valuation than FIFO. These effects are summarized in the following table:

	Normal Financial Statement Effects of			
	Rising Costs		Declining Costs	
	FIFO	Weighted Average	FIFO	Weighted Average
Cost of sales	Lower	Higher	Higher	Lower
Gross profit	Higher	Lower	Lower	Higher
Profit	Higher	Lower	Lower	Higher
Ending inventory	Higher	Lower	Lower	Higher

These effects occur because the weighted-average cost method causes the newer unit costs to be reflected in cost of sales on the income statement; FIFO causes the older unit costs to be reflected in cost of sales on the income statement. In contrast, on the statement of financial position, the ending inventory amount under the weighted-average cost method reflects a mix of unit costs, which may be an unrealistic valuation, whereas FIFO ending inventory is based on the newest costs, thus assisting the user in predicting the amount of cash needed to replace the inventory.

DIFFERENT INVENTORY COSTING METHODS AND INTERNATIONAL COMPARISONS

INTERNATIONAL **PERSPECTIVE**

While most countries have or will shortly harmonize their accounting standards to IFRS, the United States has delayed its harmonization process. The Financial Accounting Standards Board (FASB) in the United States permits a fourth last-in, first-out (LIFO) method. LIFO assumes that the most recently purchased items (the last ones in) are sold first and the oldest items are left in inventory. LIFO allocates the *newest* unit costs to *cost of sales* and the *oldest* unit costs to *ending inventory*. Because, in general, prices rise rather than fall, the effect is to increase cost of sales and therefore decrease taxable income. Reducing income tax payable retains more cash in a corporation to finance future growth or payout to existing debtors and shareholders.

The use of LIFO by U.S. companies for some or all of their inventories creates comparability problems when one attempts to compare companies across international borders. For example, Nissan Motor Company (of Japan) uses FIFO for all inventories, while General Motors uses LIFO to value most of its U.S. inventories, and either average cost or FIFO for non-U.S. inventories. Managers, investors, and financial analysts who read audited financial statements must also carefully read the significant accounting policies that companies use in preparing their financial statements and related note disclosures.

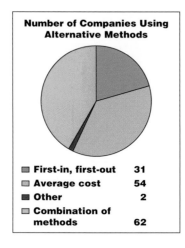

Number of Companies Using Alternative Methods

■ First-in, first-out	31
▢ Average cost	54
■ Other	2
▢ Combination of methods	62

Consistency in Use of Inventory Costing Methods It is important to remember that regardless of the physical flow of goods, a company can use either the weighted-average or FIFO inventory costing methods. Companies are expected to select the most representationally faithful inventory costing method. Therefore, a company is not required to use the same inventory costing method for all inventory items. The justification arises from the pervasive principle of economic substance over form. Each component of inventory value is supposed to reflect most accurately the anticipated benefit that will eventually be realized from either the use or sale of the inventory. *Financial Reporting in Canada* shows that 29 of the 200 companies surveyed used different inventory costing methods for different inventory items.[7] For example, Telestra Corporation uses FIFO for valuation of raw materials and weighted average for other inventory items.

To enhance comparability, accounting rules require companies to apply their accounting methods on a consistent basis. A company is not permitted to use FIFO one period, weighted average the next, and then go back to FIFO. A change in method is allowed only if the change will improve the measurement of financial results and better report the financial position. Changing from one inventory costing method to another is a significant event. Such a change requires full disclosure about the reason for the change and the accounting effects.

Managers' Choice of Inventory Costing Methods

LO⁴

Decide when the use of different inventory costing methods is beneficial to a company.

Financial Reporting in Canada reported that the methods of cost determination varied, with 54 of the 200 surveyed companies using only weighted-average cost in 2008, compared to 31 companies that used only FIFO. This raises one important question: what motivates companies to choose different inventory costing methods? Our discussion in Chapter 6 suggests that management should choose the method that best reflects its economic circumstances for financial reporting purposes. Management must also make a second choice of inventory costing method to use on its tax return (for tax purposes). In general, the choice from among the acceptable methods for use on the company's tax return differs from accounting principles. In general the best choice should be the one that allows payment of the least amount of taxes, as late as possible—the "least-latest rule."

The income tax effects associated with FIFO and weighted average for companies facing rising costs can be illustrated by continuing our simple Nokia example. Using the data from Exhibit 8.11 and assuming expenses other than cost of sales are €42,700 and a tax rate of 25 percent, the following differences in taxes result:

[7]Canadian Institute of Chartered Accountants, *Financial Reporting in Canada 2008*. Chapter 7, Inventories, Significant Accounting Policies. Toronto, Canada: 2008.

	Periodic Inventory System		Perpetual Inventory System	
	FIFO	Weighted Average	FIFO	Weighted Average
Sales	€492,700*	€492,700	€492,700	€492,700
Cost of sales	350,000	357,680	350,000	350,960
Gross profit	142,700	135,020	142,700	141,740
Other expenses	42,700	42,700	42,700	42,700
Profit before income taxes	100,000	92,320	100,000	99,040
Income tax expense (at 25%)	25,000	23,080	25,000	24,760
Profit	€ 75,000	€ 69,240	€ 75,000	€ 74,280

*(600 × €279) + (900 × €295) + (200 × €299)

For this illustration, the use of weighted average produces a lower amount of income taxes than FIFO but the difference in income taxes under the perpetual inventory system are not material. While the lowest amount of income taxes results from the use of weighted average and a periodic inventory system, other important considerations should be taken into account when choosing between a periodic and a perpetual inventory system, such as the cost savings that may result from better control of the inventory flows throughout the year.

Many high-technology companies enjoy declining costs for basic commodities such as computer chips. In such circumstances, the FIFO method—in which the oldest, most expensive goods become cost of sales—produces the largest cost of sales, the lowest gross profit, and thus the lowest income tax liability.

Most Canadian companies use the perpetual inventory system and either FIFO or weighted moving average for inventory costing. The choice of either method affects both the reported value on the statement of financial position as well as profit and cash flows. The reported amounts also affect the calculation of several financial ratios. When prices are rising, companies that wish to minimize their income taxes would logically choose weighted-average cost rather than FIFO because the weighted-average cost method produces lower profit before income taxes. The lower profit reduces profitability and other ratios. However, management may be interested in maximizing profit and the reported inventory value to satisfy restrictions imposed by creditors in lending agreements. While companies are expected to adopt the inventory costing method that provides the best representation of the flow of costs during the period, the choice of a specific accounting method is influenced, in some cases, by management's objectives and the effects of the chosen method on the reported results.

INVENTORY COSTING AND CONFLICTS BETWEEN MANAGERS' AND OWNERS' INTERESTS

A QUESTION
OF ACCOUNTABILITY

We have seen that the selection of an inventory method can have significant effects on financial statements. Company managers may have an incentive to select a particular method that may not be consistent with the objectives of the owners. For example, the use of weighted-average cost during a period of rising prices may be in the best interests of the owners because the weighted-average cost method often reduces the company's tax liability. If managers' compensation is tied to reported profit, they may prefer FIFO, which typically results in higher profit.

A well-designed compensation plan should reward managers for acting in the best interests of the owners, but unfortunately, this is not always the case. Clearly, a manager who selects an accounting method that is not optimal for the company, solely to increase his or her compensation, has engaged in questionable ethical behaviour.[8]

SELF-STUDY **QUIZ 8-3**

Assume that a company began operations this year. Its purchases for the year included

January	10 units @ $10 each
May	5 units @ $11 each
November	5 units @ $13 each

During the year, 15 units were sold for $20 each and other operating expenses totalled $100.

1. Compute cost of sales and pretax profit for the year under FIFO and weighted-average cost methods, assuming the use of a periodic inventory system.
2. Which method would you recommend that the company adopt? Why?

 After you complete your answers, go online for the solutions.

FINANCIAL ANALYSIS

INVENTORY COSTING METHODS AND FINANCIAL STATEMENT ANALYSIS

Critics of multiple inventory valuation methods argue that the existence of alternatives is inconsistent with the *comparability* characteristic of useful information. This quality is needed so that managers, investors, and financial analysts can compare information for a company with that of other companies for the same period. These types of comparisons are more difficult when companies use different accounting methods. Often it is impossible to convert, for example, a FIFO-based inventory value to a weighted-average cost of inventory because the data needed for the conversion is unavailable. In reality, however, a particular method may result in a better representation of the economic substance of inventory transactions than their legal form might. Absolute standardization based on one inventory costing method could readily result in formal comparability that fails to inform users of the best estimate of either cost of sales or inventory value.

Users of financial statements must be certain that their decisions are based on real differences, not artificial differences created by alternative accounting methods. For this reason, users must be knowledgeable about alternative accounting methods and how they affect financial statements. This is why accounting standards require companies to inform external users when the method of inventory valuation has changed and to restate the prior year's information: not only must a change in method be communicated, but also the reasons why the alternative now in place provides an improved reflection of economic substance.

---

[8]As indicated in Chapter 6, corporate governance is no longer at the discretion of managers if an important corporate goal is to retain the company's listing on a stock exchange such as the TSX. Corporate governance is a matter of full compliance with the laws and the regulations of the country in which companies have listed their shares. Companies such as Nokia are listed on both the London Stock Exchange (LSE) and the New York Stock Exchange (NYSE). In the United States, Nokia's internal control system and quality of financial disclosure must comply with *Sarbanes-Oxley* sections 303 (similar to Canada's NI 52-209) and 404, requiring that Nokia have a third-party audit of the design and implementation of its internal control system. The penalties for non-compliance, however, can be in the millions of dollars for both companies and their executives. The reward to managers who act in the best interests of the shareholders is not only a reputation for ethical behaviour but also avoidance of significant financial penalties, and sometimes of jail.

VALUATION AT LOWER OF COST AND NET REALIZABLE VALUE

Inventories should be measured at their acquisition cost, in conformity with the cost principle. However, the cost of inventories may not be recoverable if their selling prices have declined, they are damaged, or they have become obsolete. When the market value of ending inventory drops below cost, the lower amount should be used as the inventory valuation. This is consistent with prudence, which suggests that care should be taken not to overstate inventory values. For the purpose of inventory valuation, market value refers to the net realizable value of the inventory, which is essentially an estimate of the amount that a company expects to receive for selling its inventory in the ordinary course of business, net of estimated selling expenses. This valuation rule is known as measuring inventories at the lower of cost and net realizable value (LCNRV).

NET REALIZABLE VALUE is the expected sales price less estimated selling costs (e.g., repair and disposal costs).

LOWER OF COST AND NET REALIZABLE VALUE (LCNRV) is a valuation method departing from the cost principle; it serves to recognize a loss when the net realizable value drops below cost.

This departure from the cost principle is particularly important for two types of companies: (1) high-technology companies such as Nokia that manufacture goods for which the cost of production and the selling price are declining and (2) companies such as The Gap that sell seasonal goods such as clothing, the value of which drops dramatically at the end of each selling season (fall or spring).

Nokia's industry thrives on innovation that delights its customers. The global companies in this industry are continuously engaged in research and development to improve existing products and bring new products to market. For example, one of Nokia's innovations at the time of writing this text is a bendable cell phone called a Morph. The advantage of being first to market such a new product is the opportunity to capture customers from competitors. One possible result would be that sales of cell phones by Nokia's competitors will be lower than previously expected and may be permanently reduced if demand for their products decreases. Consequently, the costs incurred by Nokia's competitors to produce or purchase their inventories of cell phones may not be recovered from future sales, causing them to write down their inventories to net realizable values.

Under LCNRV, companies recognize a loss in the period in which the net realizable value of an item drops rather than in the period in which the item is sold. The loss is the difference between the purchase cost and the net realizable value, and is added to the cost of sales of the period. To illustrate, assume that Nokia had the following items in the current period's ending inventory:

Item	Quantity	Cost per Item	Net Realizable Value (NRV) per Item	Lower of Cost and NRV per Item	Total Lower of Cost and NRV
N97 cell phone	1,000	€220	€200	€200	1,000 × €200 = €200,000
Smartphones	400	100	210	100	400 × €100 = 40,000

The 1,000 N97 cell phones should be recorded in the ending inventory at the net realizable value (€200), which is lower than the cost (€220). Nokia makes the following journal entry to record the write-down:[9]

Cost of sales (E) (1,000 × €20)	20,000	
Allowance for excess and obsolete inventory (XA)		20,000

Assets	=	Liabilities	+	Shareholders' Equity	
Allowance for excess and obsolete inventory	−20,000			Cost of sales	−20,000

---

[9]The loss could be debited to a separate account, such as loss due to write-down of inventory, which is closed to cost of sales at the end of the accounting period.

Nokia uses an allowance account to record the decline in the value of its inventory, similar to using an allowance for doubtful accounts to record the estimated doubtful accounts. Alternatively, the inventory account could have been directly reduced by €20,000.

Since the net realizable value of the smartphones (€210) is higher than the original cost (€100), no write-down is necessary. The smartphones remain on the books at their cost of €100 per unit (€40,000 in total). Recognition of holding gains on inventory is not permitted by IFRS.

The write-down of the inventory of N97 cell phones to net realizable value produces the following financial statement effects:

Effects of LCNRV Write-Down	Current Period	Period of Sale
Cost of sales	Increase €20,000	Decrease €20,000
Pretax profit	Decrease €20,000	Increase €20,000
Ending inventory on statement of financial position	Decrease €20,000	Unaffected

The LCNRV rule accounts for the added expense in the current period, not in the period of sale. Consequently, pretax profit is reduced by €20,000 in the period in which the net realizable value drops, rather than in the next period when the cell phones are sold. Since the cost of sales for the current period *increases* by €20,000 and the cost of sales for the next period *decreases* by €20,000, the total cost of sales (and profit before taxes) for the two periods combined does not change. On the statement of financial position, the €20,000 loss in the current period reduces the amount of inventory reported at year-end.

If the net realizable value of the inventory items that were written down increases in a subsequent accounting period because of changed economic circumstances, then the amount of the write-down is reversed up to the original cost, so that the new carrying amount of the inventory is the lower of the cost and the revised net realizable value. Normally, a reversal of a previous write-down occurs when an inventory item that is carried at net realizable value is still on hand in a subsequent period when its selling price has increased.

Under IFRS, the LCNRV rule must be applied to all inventories, regardless of the inventory costing methods that a company uses. For example, in the excerpt below, Nokia reports the use of the lower of cost (FIFO) and NRV rule for financial statement purposes.

REAL WORLD EXCERPT

Nokia Corporation

ANNUAL REPORT

NOKIA CORPORATION
NOTE 1 TO THE CONSOLIDATED FINANCIAL STATEMENTS

1. Accounting Policies

Inventories

Inventories are stated at the lower of cost or net realizable value. Cost is determined using standard cost, which approximates actual cost on a FIFO (First-in First-out) basis. Net realizable value is the amount that can be realized from the sale of the inventory in the normal course of business after allowing for the costs of realization.

In addition to the cost of materials and direct labor, an appropriate proportion of production overhead is included in the inventory values.

An allowance is recorded for excess inventory and obsolescence based on the lower of cost or net realizable value.

Inventory-related allowances

The Group periodically reviews inventory for excess amounts, obsolescence and declines in market value below cost and records an allowance against the inventory balance for any such declines. These reviews require management to estimate future demand for products. Possible changes in these estimates could result in revisions to the valuation of inventory in future periods.

Source: Nokia Corporation Annual Report 2009.

Nokia also reports changes in the balance of its allowance for excess and obsolete inventory account in Note 19 below. These details inform the financial statement users that €221 million was recovered during the year 2009, but an additional allowance or loss of €151 million was made at the end of the year. The balance of the allowance account at December 31, 2009, €361 million, represents almost 19.4 percent of the carrying value of inventories on that date.

REAL WORLD EXCERPT

Nokia Corporation

ANNUAL REPORT

Notes to the consolidated financial statements					
19. Valuation and qualifying accounts					
EURm					
Allowances on assets to which they apply:	**Balance at beginning of year**	**Charged to cost and expenses**	**Deductions[1]**	**Acquisitions**	**Balance at end of year**
2009					
Allowance for doubtful accounts	415	155	−179	—	391
Excess and obsolete inventory	348	192	−179	—	361
2008					
Allowance for doubtful accounts	332	224	−141	—	415
Excess and obsolete inventory	417	151	−221	1	348
2007					
Allowance for doubtful accounts	212	38	−72	154	332
Excess and obsolete inventory	218	145	−202	256	417

[1] Deductions include utilization and releases of the allowances

Source: Nokia Corporation Annual Report 2009.

EVALUATING INVENTORY MANAGEMENT

Measuring Efficiency in Inventory Management

As noted at the beginning of the chapter, the primary goals of inventory management are to have sufficient quantities of high-quality inventory available to serve customers' needs, while minimizing the costs of carrying inventory (production, storage, obsolescence, and financing). The inventory turnover ratio is an important measure of the company's success in balancing these conflicting goals.

LO6

Evaluate inventory management by using the inventory turnover ratio and the effects of inventory on cash flows.

INVENTORY TURNOVER RATIO

KEY RATIO
ANALYSIS

ANALYTICAL QUESTION → How efficient are inventory management activities?

RATIO AND COMPARISONS → The answer to this question is facilitated by the computation of the inventory turnover ratio as follows:

$$\text{Inventory Turnover} = \frac{\text{Cost of Sales}}{\text{Average Inventory}^*}$$

*Average Inventory − (Beginning Inventory + Ending Inventory) ÷ 2

The 2009 inventory turnover ratio for Nokia is

€27,720 / (€1,865 + €2,533) / 2 = 12.61

Comparisons over Time				Comparisons with Competitors	
Nokia				Ericsson	Telestra
2007	2008	2009		2009	2009
15.24	12.33	12.61		5.39	7.98

INTERPRETATIONS

In General → The inventory turnover ratio reflects how many times the average inventory was produced and sold during the period. A higher ratio indicates that inventory moves more quickly through the production process to the ultimate customer, reducing storage and obsolescence costs. Because less money is tied up in inventory, the excess can be invested to earn interest income or to reduce borrowings, which reduces interest expense. More efficient purchasing and production techniques such as just-in-time inventory, as well as high product demand, cause this ratio to be high. Inefficient purchasing and production techniques and declining product demand cause this ratio to be low. Analysts and creditors watch this ratio because a sudden decline may mean that a company is facing an unexpected decline in demand for its products or is becoming sloppy in its production management. Many managers and analysts compute the related number of average days to sell inventory, which is equal to average inventory ÷ (cost of sales ÷ 365 days), or 28.9 days for Nokia. It indicates the average time it takes the company to produce and deliver inventory to customers.

Focus Company Analysis → Nokia's inventory turnover ratio has decreased during the period 2007–2009. Nokia's inventory turnover is much higher than those of its competitors, Sony Ericsson and Telestra, Each company reports in a different currency, Nokia in euro, Sony Ericsson in Swedish kroner, and Telestra in Australian dollars. But each company reports according to IFRS and, therefore, their ratios can be readily compared by external users.

A Few Cautions → Differences across industries in purchasing, production, and sales processes cause dramatic differences in the ratio. For example, restaurants such as Pizza Hut, which must turn over their perishable inventory very quickly, tend to have much higher inventory turnover than automakers such as Toyota. A particular firm's ratio should be compared only with its prior years' figures or with other firms in the same industry. Financial statement users need to interpret the ratios carefully, because while all three companies report the value of raw materials inventory on a FIFO basis, Telestra reports other inventories on a weighted average basis.

SELECTED FOCUS COMPANY INVENTORY TURNOVER	
Andrew Peller	1.7
Home Depot	4.2
Nestlé	5.1

Inventory and Cash Flows

When companies expand production to meet increases in demand, this increases the amount of inventory reported on the statement of financial position. However, when companies overestimate demand for a product, they usually produce too many units of the slow-moving item. This increases storage costs as well as the interest costs on short-term borrowings that finance the inventory. It may even lead to losses if the excess inventory cannot be sold at normal prices. The statement of cash flows often provides the first sign of such problems.

FOCUS ON CASH FLOWS   INVENTORY

As with the change in trade receivables, the change in inventories can be a major determinant of a company's cash flow from operations. The income statement reflects the cost of sales during the period, whereas the statement of cash flows should reflect the cash payments to suppliers for the same period. Cost of sales may be more or less than the amount of cash paid to suppliers during the period. Since most inventory is purchased on open credit (borrowing from suppliers is normally called *trade payables*), reconciling cost of sales with cash paid to suppliers requires consideration of the changes in both the inventory and trade payables accounts.

The simplest way to think about the effects of changes in inventory is that buying (increasing) inventory eventually decreases cash, and selling (decreasing) inventory eventually increases cash. Similarly, borrowing from suppliers, which increases trade payables, increases cash; paying suppliers, which decreases trade payables, decreases cash.

Effect on Statement of Cash Flows

In General → A *decrease in inventory* for the period indicates that the cost of sales exceeded the cost of goods purchased; thus, the decrease in inventory must be *added* to profit to reflect the cost of goods purchased.

An *increase in inventory* for the period indicates that the cost of goods purchased exceeded the cost of sales; thus, the increase in inventory must be *subtracted* from profit to reflect the cost of goods purchased.

A *decrease in trade payables* for the period indicates that the payments to suppliers exceeded the cost of goods purchased; thus, the decrease in trade payables must be *subtracted* from profit in computing cash flows from operations.

An *increase in trade payables* for the period indicates that the cost of goods purchased exceeded the payments to suppliers; thus, the increase in trade payables must be *added* to profit in computing cash flows from operations.

Effect on Cash Flows

Operating activities (indirect method)
Profit	$xxx
Adjusted for	
Add inventory *decrease*	+
or	
Subtract inventory *increase*	−
Add trade payables *increase*	+
or	
Subtract trade payables *decrease*	−

Focus Company Analysis → Exhibit 8.12 is the Operating Activities section of Nokia's statement of cash flows. When the inventory balance decreases during the period, as was the case at Nokia for the years ended December 31, 2008, and 2009, the company has sold more inventory than it purchased or produced during the period. Thus, the decrease in inventory is added to profit in the computation of cash flow from operations. Conversely, when the inventory balance increases during the period, the company has sold more inventory than it purchased or produced. When the trade payables balance decreases during the period, as was the case at Nokia during 2008 and 2009, the company has paid more to its suppliers than it purchased on credit. Thus, the decrease is subtracted from profit in the computation of cash flow from operations.* The highlighted section of Exhibit 8.12 indicates that Nokia's payment of interest-free short-term liabilities, including trade payables, more than offset the positive adjustment to profit that resulted from the decrease in inventories.

*For companies with foreign currency or business acquisitions/dispositions, the amount of the change reported on the statement of cash flows will not equal the change in the accounts reported on the statement of financial position.

Consolidated statements of cash flows

		Financial year ended December 31		
	Notes	**2009 EURm**	**2008 EURm**	**2007 EURm**
Cash flow from operating activities				
Profit attributable to equity holders of the parent		891	3,988	7,205
Adjustments, total	31	3,390	3,024	1,159
Change in net working capital	31	140	−2,546	605
Cash generated from operations		4,421	4,466	8,969
Interest received		125	416	362
Interest paid		−256	−155	−59
Other financial income and expenses, net		−128	250	67
Income taxes paid, net		−915	−1,780	−1,457
Net cash from operating activities		3,247	3,197	7,882

(*continued*)

Exhibit **8.12**

Inventories on the Statement of Cash Flows

REAL WORLD EXCERPT

Nokia Corporation

ANNUAL REPORT

31. Notes to cash flow statements

EURm	2009	2008	2007
Adjustments for:			
Depreciation and amortization (Note 9)	1,784	1,617	1,206
Profit (−)/loss (+) on sale of property, plant and equipment and available-for-sale investments	−111	−11	−1,864
Income taxes (Note 11)	702	1,081	1,522
Share of results of associated companies (Note 14)	−30	−6	−44
Minority interest	−631	−99	−459
Financial income and expenses (Note 10)	265	2	−239
Transfer from hedging reserve to sales and cost of sales (Note 20)	44	−445	−110
Impairment charges (Note 7)	1,009	149	63
Asset retirements (Note 8, 12)	35	186	—
Share-based compensation (Note 23)	16	74	228
Restructuring charges	307	448	856
Finnish pension settlement (Note 5)	—	152	—
Other income and expenses	—	−124	—
Adjustments, total	3,390	3,024	1,159
Change in net working capital			
Decrease (+)/increase (−) in short-term receivables	1,145	−534	−2,146
Decrease (+)/increase (−) in inventories	640	321	−245
Decrease (−)/increase (+) in interest-free short-term borrowings	−1,698	−2,333	2,996
Loans made to customers	53	—	—
Change in net working capital	140	−2,546	605

Source: Nokia Corporation Annual Report 2009.

SELF-STUDY **QUIZ 8-4**

Nokia model N97 is a cell phone that offers multiple services: mobile phone, email device, Web browser, and organizer. It has a touchscreen and full keyboard to compete against both the iPhone and the BlackBerry. Sales increased significantly over time, which is reflected in the following cost of sales and ending inventory for a recent seven-year period (amounts in millions of euro).

Year	2009	2008	2007	2006	2005	2004	2003
Cost of sales	€27,720	€33,337	€33,754	€27,742	€22,209	€18,179	€17,325
Ending inventory	1,865	2,533	2,876	1,554	1,668	1,305	1,169

1. Compute the inventory turnover ratios for 2004 through 2009. Is Nokia managing its inventory efficiently?

2. If Nokia had been able to manage its inventory more efficiently and *decreased* purchases and ending inventory by €100 in 2009, would its inventory turnover ratio for 2009 increase or decrease? Explain.

3. If Nokia had been able to manage its inventory more efficiently and *decreased* ending inventory, would its cash flow from operations increase or decrease?

After you complete your answers, go online for the solutions.

ACCOUNTING STANDARDS
FOR PRIVATE ENTERPRISES

The accounting standards related to measuring and reporting of inventories by Canadian private enterprises are very similar to those included in IAS 2 – Inventories, which Canadian publicly accountable enterprises must use.

DEMONSTRATION **CASE A**

This case reviews the application of the inventory costing methods and the inventory turnover ratio.

Balent Appliances distributes a number of high-cost household appliances. One product, microwave ovens, has been selected for case purposes. Assume that the following summarized transactions were completed during the accounting period in the order given:

	Units	Unit Cost
a. Beginning inventory	11	$200
b. Inventory purchases	9	220
c. Sales (at $420 per unit)	8	?
d. Inventory purchases	10	210
e. Sales (at $420 per unit)	11	?

Required:

1. Compute the following amounts in accordance with each of the inventory costing methods, assuming that a periodic inventory system is used.

	Ending Inventory		Cost of Sales	
	Units	Dollars	Units	Dollars
a. FIFO				
b. Weighted Average				

2. Compute the inventory turnover ratio for the current period by using each of the inventory costing methods. What does this ratio mean? Which inventory costing method provides the higher ratio? Is this true in all situations? Explain.

3. Will the choice of inventory costing method affect cash flow from operations? Explain.

We strongly recommend that you prepare your own answers to these requirements and then check your answers with the suggested solution.

SUGGESTED **SOLUTION**

1.

	Ending Inventory		Cost of Sales	
	Units	Dollars	Units	Dollars
a. FIFO	11	$2,320	19	$3,960
b. Weighted Average	11	2,303	19	3,977

Computations

Cost of goods available for sale = Beginning inventory + Purchases

$\qquad$ = (11 units × $200) + (9 units × $220 + 10 units × $210)

$\qquad$ = $6,280

FIFO Cost

$\quad$ Ending inventory = (10 units × $210 + 1 unit × $220) = $2,320

$\quad$ Cost of sales $\quad$ = $6,280 − $2,320 = $3,960

Weighted-Average Cost

$\quad$ Average cost $\quad$ = $6,280/30 units $\quad$ = $209.33

$\quad$ Ending inventory = 11 units × $209.33 = $2,303

$\quad$ Cost of sales $\quad$ = $6,280 − $2,303 $\quad$ = $3,977

2. Inventory turnover ratio = Cost of sales ÷ Average inventory
   FIFO $3,960 ÷ [($2,200 + $2,320) ÷ 2] = 1.75
   Weighted Average $3,977 ÷ [($2,200 + $2,303) ÷ 2] = 1.77

The inventory turnover ratio reflects how many times the average inventory was purchased and sold during the period. Thus, Balent Appliances purchased and sold its average inventory less than two times during the period.

The weighted-average costing method provides the higher inventory turnover ratio. This is generally true when the prices of inventory items increase over time, because the cost of sales reflects more recent, higher prices and ending inventory includes older, lower prices, than FIFO.

3. The choice of an inventory costing method does not affect the total amount of purchases and the amount paid to suppliers. It simply allocates the purchases differently between cost of sales and ending inventory. However, the method chosen affects the computation of cost of sales, gross profit, and profit before income taxes. Hence, the amount of income taxes payable is affected by the inventory costing method.

DEMONSTRATION CASE B

Metal Products Inc. has been operating for three years as a distributor of a line of metal products. It is now the end of 2010, and for the first time, the company will undergo an audit by an external auditor. The company uses a *periodic* inventory system. The annual income statements prepared by the company are as follows:

	For the Year Ended December 31			
	2011		**2010**	
Sales revenue		$800,000		$750,000
Cost of sales				
Beginning inventory	$ 40,000		$ 45,000	
Add purchases	484,000		460,000	
Cost of goods available for sale	524,000		505,000	
Less ending inventory	60,000		40,000	
Cost of sales		464,000		465,000
Gross margin on sales		336,000		285,000
Operating expenses		306,000		275,000
Pretax profit		30,000		10,000
Income tax expense (20%)		6,000		2,000
Profit		$ 24,000		$ 8,000

During the early stages of the audit, the external auditor discovered that the ending inventory for 2010 was understated by $15,000.

Required:

1. Based on the preceding income statement amounts, compute the gross profit percentage on sales for each year. Do the results suggest an inventory error? Explain.
2. Correct and reconstruct the two income statements.
3. Answer the following questions:
   a. What are the correct gross profit percentages?
   b. What effect did the $15,000 understatement of the ending inventory have on the pretax profit for 2010? Explain.
   c. What effect did the inventory error have on the pretax income for 2011? Explain.
   d. How did the inventory error affect the income tax expense?

We strongly recommend that you prepare your own answers to these requirements and then check your answers with the suggested solution.

SUGGESTED **SOLUTION**

1. The gross profit percentages as reported are

    2010: $285,000 ÷ $750,000 = 0.38
    2011: $336,000 ÷ $800,000 = 0.42

    The change in the gross profit percentage from 0.38 to 0.42 suggests the possibility of an inventory error in the absence of any other explanation.

2. The corrected income statements follow:

	For the Year Ended December 31			
	2011		**2010**	
Sales revenue		$800,000		$750,000
Cost of sales				
Beginning inventory	$ 55,000*		$ 45,000	
Add purchases	484,000		460,000	
Cost of goods available for sale	539,000		505,000	
Less ending inventory	60,000		55,000*	
Cost of sales		479,000		450,000
Gross margin on sales		321,000		300,000
Operating expenses		306,000		275,000
Pretax profit		15,000		25,000
Income tax expense (20%)		3,000		5,000
Profit		$ 12,000		$ 20,000

*Increased by $15,000.

3. *a.* The correct gross profit percentages are

    2010: $300,000 ÷ $750,000 = 0.400
    2011: $321,000 ÷ $800,000 = 0.401

    The inventory error of $15,000 was responsible for the difference in the gross profit percentages reflected in (1). The error in the 2010 ending inventory affected the gross margin for both 2010 and 2011 by the same amount, $15,000, but in the opposite direction.

   b. Effect on pretax profit in 2010: The *understatement* ($15,000) of ending inventory caused an *understatement* of pretax profit by the same amount.

   c. Effect on pretax profit in 2011: The *understatement* of beginning inventory (by the same $15,000 since the inventory amount is carried over from the prior period) caused an *overstatement* of pretax profit by the same amount.

   d. The total income tax expense for 2010 and 2011 combined was the same ($8,000) regardless of the error. However, there was a shift of $3,000 ($15,000 × 20%) in income tax expense from 2010 to 2011.

OBSERVATION An ending inventory error in one year affects pretax profit by the amount of the error and in the same direction. It affects pretax profit again in the following year by the same amount but in the opposite direction.

Appendix 8A

Additional Issues in Measuring Purchases

PURCHASE RETURNS AND ALLOWANCES

Goods purchased may be returned to the vendor if they do not meet specifications, arrive in damaged condition, or are otherwise unsatisfactory. When the goods are returned or when the vendor makes an allowance because of the circumstances, the effect on the cost of purchases must be measured. The purchaser normally receives a cash refund or a reduction in the liability to the vendor. Assume that Nokia returned unsatisfactory software that cost €1,000 to a supplier. The return would be recorded by Nokia as follows:

Trade payables (L) (or Cash)	1,000	
Inventory* (A)		1,000

Assets		=	Liabilities		+	Shareholders' Equity
Inventory	−1,000		Trade payables	−1,000		

*Purchase returns and allowances (T) may be credited when the periodic inventory system is used. It is subtracted in the calculation of cost of sales.

PURCHASE RETURNS AND ALLOWANCES are a reduction in the cost of purchases associated with unsatisfactory goods.

Purchase returns and allowances are treated as a reduction in the cost of inventory purchases associated with unsatisfactory goods.

PURCHASE DISCOUNTS

A **PURCHASE DISCOUNT** is a cash discount received for prompt payment of an account.

Cash discounts must be accounted for by both the seller and the buyer (accounting by the seller was discussed in Chapter 7). When merchandise is bought on credit, terms such as 2/10, n/30 are sometimes specified. This means that, if payment is made within 10 days from date of purchase, a 2 percent cash discount known as the purchase discount is granted. If payment is not made within the discount period, the full invoice cost is due 30 days after the date of purchase. Assume that on January 17, Nokia bought goods that had a €1,000 invoice price with terms 2/10, n/30. Assuming that the company uses the *gross method*, the purchase should be recorded as follows:

Date of Purchase:

Jan. 17	Inventory* (A)	1,000	
	Trade payables (L)		1,000

Assets		=	Liabilities		+	Shareholders' Equity
Inventory	+1,000		Trade payables	+1,000		

*Purchases (T) is debited when a periodic inventory system is used.

Date of Payment, within the Discount Period:

Jan. 26	Trade payables (L)	1,000	
	Inventory* (A)		20
	Cash		980

Assets		=	Liabilities		+	Shareholders' Equity
Inventory	−20		Trade payables	−1,000		
Cash	−980					

*Purchase Discounts (T) is credited when a periodic inventory system is used. Purchase discounts would be reported as a deduction from the cost of purchases in the calculation of cost of sales.

If for any reason Nokia did not pay within the 10-day discount period, the following entry would be needed:

Feb. 1	Trade payables (L)	1,000	
	Cash (A)		1,000

Assets		=	Liabilities		+	Shareholders' Equity
Cash	−1,000		Trade payables	−1,000		

If Nokia used the net method instead of the gross method, then the debit to inventory on January 17 would be €980. If payment is made after January 26, then a Discount lost account is debited for €20, the difference between the cash paid (€1,000) and the amount that Nokia owed the supplier if it were paid within 10 days. The balance of the Discount lost account highlights the potential savings from early payments to suppliers that Nokia has forgone.

Appendix 8B: Last-In, First-Out Method (online)

CHAPTER TAKE-AWAYS

1. **Apply the cost principle to identify the amounts that should be included in inventory and determine the cost of sales for typical retailers, wholesalers, and manufacturers. p. 407**
   Inventory should include all of the items held for resale that the entity owns. Costs flow into inventory when goods are purchased or manufactured, and they flow out (as an expense) when the goods are sold or otherwise disposed of. In conformity with the matching process, the total cost of sales during the period must be related to the sales revenue earned during the period.

2. **Compare methods for controlling and keeping track of inventory, and analyze the effects of inventory errors on financial statements. p. 411**
   A company can keep track of the ending inventory and cost of sales for the period using (1) the perpetual inventory system, which is based on the maintenance of detailed and continuous inventory records for each kind of inventory stocked, and (2) the periodic inventory system, which is based on a physical inventory count of ending inventory and the costing of those goods to determine the proper amounts for cost of sales and ending inventory. An error in the measurement of ending inventory affects the cost of sales on the current period's income statement and ending inventory on the statement of financial position. It also affects the cost of sales in the following period by the same amount, but in the opposite direction, because this year's ending inventory becomes next year's beginning inventory. These relationships can be seen through the cost of sales equation, ($BI + P - EI = COS$).

3. **Report inventory and cost of sales by using three inventory costing methods. p. 415**
   The chapter discussed three different inventory costing methods and their applications in different economic circumstances. The methods discussed were specific identification, FIFO, and weighted-average cost. Each of the inventory costing methods is in conformity with IFRS. Remember that the cost flow assumption need not match the physical flow of inventory.

4. **Decide when the use of different inventory costing methods is beneficial to a company. p. 424**
   The selection of a method of inventory costing is important because it will affect reported profit, income tax expense (and, hence, cash flow), and the inventory valuation reported on the statement of financial position. In a period of rising prices, FIFO results in a higher income than does weighted-average cost; in a period of falling prices, the opposite result occurs.

5. **Report inventory at the lower of cost and net realizable value (NRV). p. 427**
   Ending inventory should be measured based on the lower of actual cost or net realizable value (LCNRV basis). This practice can have a major effect on the statements of companies facing declining costs. Damaged, obsolete, and out-of-season inventory also should be written down to their current estimated net realizable value if that is below cost. The LCNRV adjustment increases cost of sales, decreases profit, and decreases reported inventory.

6. **Evaluate inventory management by using the inventory turnover ratio and the effects of inventory on cash flows. p. 429**
   The inventory turnover ratio measures the efficiency of inventory management. It reflects how many times the average inventory was produced and sold during the period. Analysts and creditors watch this ratio because a sudden decline in this ratio may mean that a company is facing an unexpected decline in demand for its products or is becoming sloppy in its production management. When a net *decrease in inventory* for the period occurs, sales are more than purchases; thus, the decrease must be *added* to profit in computing cash flows from operations. When a net *increase in inventory* for the period occurs, sales are less than purchases; thus, the increase must be *subtracted* from profit in computing cash flows from operations.

   In this and previous chapters, we discussed the current assets of a business. These assets are critical for the operations of a business, but in general they produce value only when they are sold. In

Chapter 9, we will discuss the property, plant, and equipment; natural resources; and intangibles that are the elements of productive capacity. Many of the capital assets produce value, such as a factory that manufactures cars. These assets present some interesting accounting problems because they benefit a number of accounting periods.

KEY **RATIOS**

Inventory turnover ratio measures the efficiency of inventory management. It reflects how many times the average inventory was produced and sold during the period (p. 429):

$$\text{Inventory Turnover} = \frac{\text{Cost of Sales}}{\text{Average Inventory}}$$

FINDING **FINANCIAL INFORMATION**

STATEMENT OF FINANCIAL POSITION
Under Current Assets
  Inventory

INCOME STATEMENT
Expenses
  Cost of sales

STATEMENT OF CASH FLOWS
Under Operating Activities (indirect method):
  + decrease in inventory
  − increase in inventory
  + increase in trade payables
  − decrease in trade payables

NOTES
Under Summary of Significant Accounting Policies:
  Description of management's choice of inventory accounting policy (FIFO, weighted-average cost, LCNRV, etc.)
Under a Separate Note
  If not listed on the statement of financial position, components of inventory (merchandise, raw materials, work-in-process, finished goods)

KEY **TERMS**

Cost of Goods Available for Sale p. 410
Cost of Sales Equation p. 410
Direct Labour p. 409
Factory Overhead p. 409
Finished Goods Inventory p. 408
First-in, First-out (FIFO) Method p. 417
Inventory p. 407
Lower of Cost and Net Realizable Value (LCNRV) p. 427
Merchandise Inventory p. 407

Net Realizable Value p. 427
Periodic Inventory System p. 412
Perpetual Inventory System p. 412
Purchase Discount p. 436
Purchase Returns and Allowances p. 436
Raw Materials Inventory p. 408
Specific Identification Method p. 416
Weighted-Average Cost Method p. 419
Work-in-Process Inventory p. 408

QUESTIONS

1. Why is inventory an important item to both internal (management) and external users of financial statements?
2. What are the general guidelines for deciding which items should be included in inventory?

3. Explain the application of the cost principle to an item in the ending inventory.
4. Define *cost of goods available for sale.* How does it differ from cost of sales?
5. Define *beginning inventory* and *ending inventory.*
6. When a perpetual inventory system is used, unit costs of the items sold are known at the date of each sale. In contrast, when a periodic inventory system is used, unit costs are known only at the end of the accounting period. Why are these statements correct?
7. The periodic inventory calculation is BI + P − EI = COS. The perpetual inventory calculation is BI + P − COS = EI. Explain the significance of the difference between these two calculations.
8. The chapter discussed three inventory costing methods. List the three methods and briefly explain each.
9. Explain how profit can be manipulated when the specific identification inventory costing method is used.
10. Contrast the effects of weighted average versus FIFO on reported assets (i.e., the ending inventory) when (a) prices are rising and (b) prices are falling.
11. Contrast the income statement effect of weighted average versus FIFO (i.e., on profit before income taxes) when (a) prices are rising and (b) prices are falling.
12. Contrast the effects of weighted average versus FIFO on cash outflow and inflow.
13. Explain briefly the application of the LCNRV concept to the ending inventory and its effect on the income statement and statement of financial position when the net realizable value of inventory is lower than its cost.
14. Explain the difference between a reversal of a write-down and a holding gain.

EXERCISES

E8–1   Recording the Cost of Purchases for a Merchandiser   ▮ LO1
Elite Apparel purchased 80 new shirts for cash and recorded a total cost of $2,620, determined as follows:

Invoice amount	$2,180
Shipping charges	175
Import taxes and duties	145
Interest paid in advance on loan to finance the purchase	120
	$2,620

Required:
Make the needed corrections in this calculation. Prepare the journal entry(ies) to record this purchase in the correct amount, assuming a perpetual inventory system. Show computations.

E8–2   Analyzing Items to Be Included in Inventory   ▮ LO1
Boilard Inc. planned to report inventory of $50,000 based on its physical count of inventory in its warehouse at year-end, December 31, 2010. During the audit, the auditor developed the following additional information:

a. Goods from a supplier costing $300 are in transit with Canada Post on December 31, 2010. The terms are F.O.B. shipping point (explained on the following page). Because these goods had not arrived, they were excluded from the physical inventory count.

b. Boilard delivered samples costing $400 to a customer on December 27, 2010, with the understanding that they would be returned to Boilard on January 18, 2011. Because these goods were not on hand, they were excluded from the physical inventory count.

c. On December 31, 2010, goods in transit to customers, with terms F.O.B. shipping point, amounted to $2,000 (the expected delivery date was January 10, 2011). Because the goods had been shipped, they were excluded from the physical inventory count.

d. On December 31, 2010, goods in transit to a customer, F.O.B. destination, amounted to $1,000 and are not expected to arrive at their destination before January 10, 2011. Because the goods had been shipped, they were not included in the physical inventory count.

Required:

Boilard's accounting policy requires including in inventory all goods for which it has title. Note that the point where title (ownership) changes hands is determined by the shipping terms in the sales contract. When goods are shipped "F.O.B. shipping point," title changes hands at shipment and the buyer normally pays for shipping. When they are shipped "F.O.B. destination," title changes hands on delivery, and the seller normally pays for shipping. Begin with the $50,000 inventory amount, and compute the correct amount for the ending inventory. Explain the basis for your treatment of each of the preceding items. (*Hint:* Set up three columns: item, amount, and explanation.)

LO1

E8–3 Inferring Missing Amounts Based on Income Statement Relationships

Supply the missing dollar amounts for the 2011 income statement of Laurin Retailers for each of the following independent cases:

Cases	Sales Revenue	Beginning Inventory	Purchases	Total Available	Ending Inventory	Cost of Sales	Gross Profit	Operating Expenses	Pretax Profit or (Loss)
A	$ 650	$100	$700	$?	$500	$?	$?	$200	$?
B	900	200	800	?	?	?	?	150	0
C	?	150	?	?	300	200	400	100	?
D	800	?	600	?	250	?	?	250	100
E	1,000	?	900	1,100	?	?	500	?	(50)

LO1

E8–4 Inferring Missing Amounts Based on Income Statement Relationships

Supply the missing dollar amounts for the 2011 income statement of Kwan Company for each of the following independent cases:

	Case A	Case B	Case C
Sales revenue	$ 8,000	$ 6,000	$?
Sales returns and allowances	150	?	275
Net sales revenue	?	?	5,920
Beginning inventory	11,000	6,500	4,000
Purchases	5,000	?	9,420
Transportation-in	?	120	170
Purchase returns	350	600	?
Cost of goods available for sale	?	14,790	13,370
Ending inventory	10,000	10,740	?
Cost of sales	?	?	5,400
Gross profit	?	1,450	?
Expenses (operating)	1,300	?	520
Pretax profit (loss)	$ 800	$ (500)	$ 0

LO1

The Gap Inc.

E8–5 Inferring Merchandise Purchases

The Gap Inc. is a specialty retailer that operates stores selling clothes under the trade names Gap, GapKids, BabyGap, and Banana Republic. Assume that you are employed as a stock analyst and your boss has just completed a review of the new Gap annual report. She provided you with her notes, but they are missing some information that you need. Her notes show that the ending inventory for Gap in the current year was $1,506 million and in the previous year was $1,575 million. Net sales for the current year were $14,256 million. Gross profit was $5,447 million; profit was $967 million. For your analysis, you determine that you need to know the amount of purchases and the cost of sales for the year.

Required:

Do you need to ask your boss for her copy of the annual report, or can you develop the information from her notes? Explain and show calculations.

LO2

E8–6 Analyzing the Effects of an Error in Recording Purchases

Garraway Ski Company mistakenly recorded purchases of inventory on account received during the last week of December 2011 as purchases during January of 2012 (this is called a *purchases cut-off error*). Garraway uses a periodic inventory system, and ending inventory was correctly counted and reported each year. Assuming that no correction was made in 2011 or 2012, indicate whether each of the following financial statement amounts will be understated, overstated, or correct.

1. Profit for 2011.
2. Profit for 2012.
3. Retained earnings at December 31, 2011.
4. Retained earnings at December 31, 2012.

E8–7 **Recording Purchases and Sales by Using a Perpetual and Periodic Inventory System**

LO2

Demski Company reported beginning inventory of 100 units at a unit cost of $20. It engaged in the following purchase and sale transactions during 2010:

Jan. 14 Sold 20 units at unit sales price of $40 on open account.
April 9 Purchased 15 additional units at unit cost of $20 on open account.
Sept. 2 Sold 45 units at sales price of $50 on open account.

At the end of the 2010, a physical count showed that Demski Company had 50 units of inventory still on hand.

Required:

Record each transaction, assuming that Demski Company uses (a) a perpetual inventory system and (b) a periodic inventory system (including any necessary entries at December 31, the end of the accounting period). Demski Company uses the FIFO inventory costing method.

E8–8 **Analyzing the Effect of an Inventory Error Disclosed in an Actual Note to a Financial Statement**

LO2

Gibson Greeting Cards

Several years ago, the financial statements of Gibson Greeting Cards contained the following note:

> On July 1, the Company announced that it had determined that the ending inventory ... had been overstated ... The overstatement of inventory ... was $8,806,000.

Gibson reported an incorrect profit of $25,852,000 for the year in which the error occurred and the income tax rate was 39.3 percent.

Required:

1. Compute the amount of profit that Gibson reported after correcting the inventory error. Show computations.
2. Assume that the inventory error was not discovered. Identify the financial statement accounts that would have been incorrect for the year the error occurred and for the subsequent year. State whether each account was understated or overstated.

E8–9 **Analyzing and Interpreting the Impact of an Inventory Error**

LO2

Dalez Corporation prepared the following two income statements (simplified for illustrative purposes):

	First Quarter 2011		Second Quarter 2011	
Sales revenue		$11,000		$18,000
Cost of sales				
Beginning inventory	$4,000		$3,800	
Purchases	3,000		13,000	
Cost of goods available for sale	7,000		16,800	
Ending inventory	3,800		9,000	
Cost of sales		3,200		7,800
Gross profit		7,800		10,200
Expenses (operating)		5,000		6,000
Pretax profit		$ 2,800		$ 4,200

During the third quarter, it was discovered that the ending inventory for the first quarter should have been $4,200.

Required:

1. What effect did this error have on the combined pretax profit of the two quarters? Explain.

2. Did this error affect the earnings per share amounts for each quarter? (See the discussion of earnings per share in Chapter 6.) Explain.

3. Prepare corrected income statements for each quarter.

4. Set up a schedule with the following headings to reflect the comparative effects of the correct and incorrect amounts on the income statement:

	1st Quarter			2nd Quarter		
	Incorrect	**Correct**	**Error**	**Incorrect**	**Correct**	**Error**
Income Statement Item		Amount	(if any)	Amount	Amount	(if any)

LO2

E8–10 **Calculating Ending Inventory and Cost of Sales Under FIFO and Weighted-Average Cost Methods**

Clor Company uses a periodic inventory system. At December 31, 2011, the accounting records provided the following information for Product 1:

	Units	Unit Cost
Inventory, December 31, 2010	3,000	$8
For the year 2011:		
Purchases, March 31	5,000	9
Purchases, August 1	2,000	7
Inventory, December 31, 2011	4,000	

Required:

Compute the cost of sales and the ending inventory under the FIFO and weighted-average costing methods. (*Hint:* Set adjacent columns for each case.)

LO2

E8–11 **Analyzing and Interpreting the Financial Statement Effects of FIFO and Weighted-Average Cost Methods**

Lunar Company uses a periodic inventory system. The company's accounting records provided the following information for Product 2:

Transactions	Units	Unit Cost
a. Inventory, December 31, 2010	3,000	$12
For the year 2011:		
b. Purchase, April 11	9,000	10
c. Sale, May 1 ($30 each)	5,000	
d. Purchase, June 1	8,000	13
e. Sale, July 3 ($30 each)	6,000	
f. Operating expenses (excluding income tax expense), $85,000		

Required:

1. Prepare an income statement for 2011, through pretax profit, showing the detailed computation of cost of sales for two cases:

   a. Case A—FIFO

   b. Case B—Weighted average

   For each case, show the computation of the ending inventory. (*Hint:* Set up adjacent columns, one for each case.)

2. Compare the pretax profit and the ending inventory amounts between the two cases. Explain the similarities and differences.

3. Which inventory costing method may be preferred for income tax purposes? Explain.

4. Prepare journal entries to record transactions (b) through (e), as well as the cost of sales at December 31, 2011, assuming that Lunar uses FIFO for inventory costing.

E8–12 Analyzing and Interpreting the Financial Statement Effects of FIFO and Weighted-Average Cost Methods   ▮ **LO3**

Scoresby Inc. uses a perpetual inventory system. At December 31, 2012, the company's accounting records provided the following information for Product B:

Transactions	Units	Unit Cost
a. Inventory, December 31, 2011	7,000	$ 8
For the year 2012:		
b. Purchase, March 5	19,000	9
c. Sale, June 15 ($29 each)	10,000	
d. Purchase, September 19	8,000	11
e. Sale, November 20 ($31 each)	16,000	
f. Operating expenses (excluding income tax expense), $500,000		

Required:

1. Prepare an income statement for 2012 through pretax profit, showing the detailed computation of cost of sales for two cases:

   a. Case A—FIFO

   b. Case B—Weighted average

   For each case, show the computation of the ending inventory. (*Hint:* Set up adjacent columns, one for each case.)

2. Compare the two cases with regard to the pretax profit and the ending inventory amounts. Explain the similarities and differences.

3. Which inventory costing method may be preferred for income tax purposes? Explain.

4. Prepare journal entries to record transactions (b) through (e), assuming that Scoresby uses FIFO for inventory costing.

E8–13 Evaluating the Choice between Two Alternative Inventory Costing Methods Based on Cash Flow and Profit Effects   ▮ **LO3, 4**

Courtney Company uses a periodic inventory system. Data for 2011: beginning merchandise inventory (December 31, 2010), 3,000 units at $35; purchases, 12,000 units at $38; operating expenses (excluding income taxes), $213,000; ending inventory per physical count at December 31, 2011, 2,700 units; sales price per unit, $70; and average income tax rate, 30 percent.

Required:

1. Prepare income statements under the FIFO and weighted-average costing methods. Use a format similar to the following:

		Inventory Costing Method	
Income Statement	Units	FIFO	Weighted Average
Sales revenue	_____	$_____	$_____
Cost of sales			
Beginning inventory	_____	_____	_____
Purchases	_____	_____	_____
Cost of goods available for sale	_____	_____	_____
Ending inventory	_____	_____	_____
Cost of sales	_____	_____	_____
Gross profit		_____	_____
Expenses (operating)		_____	_____
Pretax profit		_____	_____
Income tax expense		_____	_____
Profit		_____	_____

2. Which method, FIFO or weighted-average cost, is preferable in terms of (a) profit and (b) cash flow? Explain.

3. What would be your answer to (2), assuming that prices were falling? Explain.

LO3, 4

E8–14 **Evaluating the Choice between Two Alternative Inventory Costing Methods Based on Cash Flow Effects**

Following is partial information for the income statement of Timber Company under two different inventory costing methods, assuming the use of a periodic inventory system:

	FIFO	Weighted Average
Unit sales price, $50		
Cost of sales		
Beginning inventory (330 units)	$11,220	$11,220
Purchases (475 units)	17,100	17,100
Cost of goods available for sale		
Ending inventory (510 units)		
Cost of sales		
Operating expenses, $1,600		

Required:

1. Compute the cost of sales under the FIFO and weighted-average inventory costing methods.

2. Prepare an income statement through pretax profit for each method.

3. Rank the two methods with regard to favourable cash flow and explain the basis for your ranking.

LO5

E8–15 **Reporting Inventory at Lower of Cost and Net Realizable Value**

Peterson Company is preparing the annual financial statements dated December 31, 2011. Ending inventory information about the five major items stocked for regular sale follows:

	Ending Inventory		
Item	Quantity on Hand	Unit Cost When Acquired (FIFO)	Net Realizable Value at Year-End
A	50	$15	$12
B	80	30	40
C	10	45	52
D	30	25	30
E	350	10	5

Required:

1. Compute the value of the 2011 ending inventory by using the LCNRV rule applied on an item-by-item basis. (*Hint:* Set up columns for item, quantity, total cost, total net realizable value, and LCNRV valuation.)

2. What will be the effect of the write-down of inventory to lower of cost and net realizable value on cost of sales for the year 2011?

3. Assume that 20 units of item E had not been sold by December 31, 2012, and that the net realizable value of that item increased to $7.50 per unit. How would this information be reflected in Peterson's income statement for 2012 and its statement of financial position at year-end? Explain.

LO5

E8–16 **Reporting Inventory at Lower of Cost and Net Realizable Value**

Research In Motion Inc. (RIM), which is best known for its wireless communication product, the BlackBerry, disclosed the following information in Note 5 to its annual report:

Inventory is made up of the following:

	February 28, 2009
Raw materials	$464,497
Work in process	250,728
Finished goods	35,264
Provision for excess and obsolete inventory	(68,089)
	$682,400

The provision for excess and obsolete inventory is essentially a write-down of specific inventory items to their net realizable values.

Required:

1. Assume that the write-down relates to the values of specific items of raw materials. Prepare the journal entry to record the write-down of inventory costs. RIM uses a perpetual inventory system.

2. Assume that some of the raw materials that were written down on February 28, 2009, were not used for production purposes by February 27, 2010, the end of its 2010 fiscal year. The inventory items that were written down had an original cost of $9,347 and their net realizable value was $7,634. Changes in market conditions increased the net realizable values of these items to $9,563, which exceeded their original cost. How would this information be reflected in RIM's income statement for fiscal 2010 and its statement of financial position at February 27, 2010? Explain.

E8–17   Analyzing and Interpreting the Inventory Turnover Ratio

■ **LO6**

Sony Ericsson competes with Nokia Corporation in manufacturing and selling cell phones directly to mobile telecommunications service suppliers. The company reported the following amounts for 2008 (in millions of Swedish krona).

Sony Ericsson

Net sales revenue	208,930
Cost of sales	134,661
Beginning inventory	22,475
Ending inventory	27,836

Required:

1. Determine the inventory turnover ratio and the average days to sell inventory for the current year.

2. Explain the meaning of each of the amounts computed in (1).

E8–18   Analyzing and Interpreting the Effects of the FIFO/Weighted Average Choice on Inventory Turnover Ratio

■ **LO6**

The records at the end of January 2011 for All Star Company showed the following for a particular kind of merchandise:

Inventory, December 31, 2010, at FIFO: 19 units @ $12 = $228
Inventory, December 31, 2010, at weighted average: 19 units @ $10 = $190

Transactions	Units	Unit Cost	Total Cost
Purchase, January 9, 2011	25	15	$375
Purchase, January 20, 2011	50	16	800
Sale, January 11, 2011 (at $38 per unit)	40		
Sale, January 27, 2011 (at $39 per unit)	28		

Required:

Compute the inventory turnover ratio under the FIFO and weighted-average inventory costing methods and a perpetual inventory system (show computations and round to the nearest dollar). Explain which method you believe is the better indicator of the efficiency of inventory management.

E8–19   Interpreting the Effect of Changes in Inventories and Trade Payables on Cash Flow from Operations

■ **LO6**

First Team Sports Inc.

First Team Sports Inc. is engaged in the manufacture (through independent contractors) and distribution of in-line roller skates, ice skates, street hockey equipment, and related accessory products. Its recent annual report included the following on its statement of financial position:

CONSOLIDATED STATEMENTS OF FINANCIAL POSITION		
	Current Year	Previous Year
. . . .		
Inventory (Note 3)	22,813,850	20,838,171
. . . .		
Trade payables	9,462,883	9,015,376

Required:
Explain the effects of the changes in inventory and trade payables on cash flow from operating activities for the current year.

E8–20 **(Appendix 8A) Recording Sales and Purchases with Cash Discounts**

A. The Cycle Shop sells merchandise on credit terms of 2/10, n/30. Merchandise that cost $900 was sold to Claudette Labelle on February 1, 2011, at $1,600. The company uses the gross method of recording sales discounts.

Required:

1. Prepare the journal entry to record the credit sale. Assume that the company uses the perpetual inventory system.

2. Prepare the journal entry to record the collection of cash from C. Labelle. Assume that the cash was received on (a) February 9, 2011, and (b) March 2, 2011.

B. On March 4, 2011, the Cycle Shop purchased bicycles and accessories from a supplier on credit for $8,000; the terms were 1/15, n/30. The company uses the net method to record purchases.

Required:

3. Prepare the journal entry to record the purchase on credit. Assume that the company uses the perpetual inventory system.

4. Prepare the journal entry to record the payment of the invoice, assuming that the cash was paid on (a) March 12, 2011, and (b) March 28, 2011.

PROBLEMS

LO1

P8–1 **Analyzing Items to Be Included in Inventory**

Reggie Company has just completed a physical inventory count at year-end, December 31, 2011. Only the items on the shelves, in storage, and in the receiving area were counted and costed on a FIFO basis. The inventory amounted to $65,000. During the audit, the auditor developed the following additional information:

a. Goods costing $750 were being used by a customer on a trial basis and were excluded from the inventory count at December 31, 2011.

b. Goods costing $900 were in transit to Reggie on December 31, 2011, with terms F.O.B. destination. Because these goods had not arrived, they were excluded from the physical inventory count.

c. On December 31, 2011, goods in transit to customers, with terms F.O.B. shipping point, amounted to $1,300 (the expected delivery date was January 10, 2012). Because the goods had been shipped, they were excluded from the physical inventory count.

d. On December 28, 2011, a customer purchased goods for $2,650 cash and left them "for pick-up on January 3, 2012." The cost of sales totalled $1,590 and was included in the physical inventory count because the goods were still on hand.

e. On the date of the inventory count, the company received notice from a supplier that goods ordered earlier at a cost of $2,550 had been delivered to the transportation company on December 27, 2011; the terms were F.O.B. shipping point. Because the shipment had not arrived by December 31, 2011, it was excluded from the physical inventory count.

f. On December 31, 2011, the company shipped goods to a customer, F.O.B. destination. The goods, which cost $850, are not expected to arrive at their destination before January 8, 2012. Because the goods were not on hand, they were not included in the physical inventory count.

g. One of the items sold by the company has such a low volume that the management planned to drop it last year. To induce Reggie Company to continue carrying the item, the manufacturer-supplier provided the item on a "consignment basis." This means that the manufacturer-supplier retains ownership of the item, and Reggie Company (the consignee) has no responsibility to pay for the items until they are sold to customers. Each month, Reggie Company sends a report to the manufacturer on the number sold and remits cash for the cost. At the end of December 2011, Reggie Company had five of these items on hand; therefore, they were included in the physical inventory count at $950 each.

Required:

Assume that Reggie's accounting policy requires including in inventory all goods for which it has title. Note that the point where title (ownership) changes hands is determined by the shipping terms in the sales contract. When goods are shipped "F.O.B. shipping point," title changes hands at shipment and the buyer normally pays for shipping. When they are shipped "F.O.B. destination," title changes hands on delivery, and the seller normally pays for shipping. Begin with the $65,000 inventory amount and compute the correct amount for the ending inventory. Explain the basis for your treatment of each of the preceding items. (*Hint:* Set up three columns: item, amount, and explanation.)

P8–2   Analyzing and Interpreting the Effects of Inventory Errors (AP8–1)

■ LO2

The income statements for four consecutive years for Clement Company reflected the following summarized amounts:

e**X**cel

	2013	2012	2011	2010
Sales revenue	$58,000	$62,000	$51,000	$50,000
Cost of sales	37,000	43,000	35,000	32,500
Gross profit	21,000	19,000	16,000	17,500
Operating expenses	12,000	14,000	12,000	10,000
Pretax profit	$ 9,000	$ 5,000	$ 4,000	$ 7,500

Subsequent to the development of these amounts, it has been determined that the physical inventory taken on December 31, 2011, was understated by $3,000.

Required:

1. Revise the income statements to reflect the correct amounts, taking into consideration the inventory error.

2. Compute the gross profit percentage for each year (a) before the correction and (b) after the correction. Do the results lend confidence to your corrected amounts? Explain.

3. What effect would the error have had on the income tax expense, assuming an average tax rate of 30 percent?

P8–3   Analyzing the Effects of Three Alternative Inventory Methods (AP8–2)

■ LO3

Allsigns Company uses a periodic inventory system. The company's accounting records for the most popular item in inventory showed the following details:

Transactions	Units	Unit Cost
Beginning inventory, January 1, 2012	400	$30
Transactions during 2012:		
a. Purchase, February 20	600	32
b. Sale, April 1 ($46 each)	(700)	
c. Purchase, June 30	500	36
d. Sale, August 1 ($46 each)	(100)	
e. Sales return August 5 (relating to Transaction [d])	20	

Required:

Compute (a) the cost of goods available for sale during 2012, (b) the cost of ending inventory at December 31, 2012, and (c) the cost of sales for 2012, under each of the following inventory costing methods (show computations and round to the nearest dollar):

1. Weighted-average cost.

2. First-in, first-out.

3. Specific identification, assuming that the company is permitted to use it and that two-fifths of the units sold on April 1, 2012, were selected from the beginning inventory and three-fifths were taken from the purchase of February 20, 2012. Assume that the sale of August 1, 2011, was selected from the purchase of June 30, 2012.

As a shareholder, which of these three methods would you prefer?

P8–4 **Evaluating Three Alternative Inventory Methods Based on Profit and Cash Flow**

At the end of January 2012, the records of Regina Company showed the following for a particular item that sold at $18 per unit:

Transactions	Units	Amount
Inventory, January 1, 2012	500	$2,500
Sale, January 10	(400)	
Purchase, January 12	600	3,600
Sale, January 17	(300)	
Purchase, January 26	160	1,280

Required:

1. Assuming the use of a perpetual inventory system, prepare a summarized statement through gross profit on sales under each of the following inventory costing methods: (a) weighted-average cost, (b) FIFO, and (c) specific identification, assuming that the company is permitted to use this method. For specific identification, assume that the first sale was out of the beginning inventory and the second sale was out of the January 12 purchase. Show the inventory computations in detail.

2. Which method would result in

   a. the highest pretax profit?

   b. the lowest income tax expense?

   c. the more favourable cash flow? Explain.

3. Prepare journal entries to record the transactions that occurred in January 2012, assuming that FIFO is used for inventory costing.

P8–5 **Evaluating the FIFO/Weighted Average Choice When Costs Are Rising and Falling**

Profit is to be evaluated under four different situations as follows:

  i. Prices are rising:

    Situation A—FIFO is used.   Situation B—Weighted average is used.

  ii. Prices are falling:

    Situation C—FIFO is used.   Situation D—Weighted average is used.

    The basic data common to all four situations are sales, 500 units for $12,000; beginning inventory, 300 units; purchases, 400 units; ending inventory, 200 units; and operating expenses, $4,000. The following tabulated income statements for each situation have been set up for analytical purposes:

| | Prices Rising | | Prices Falling | |
	Situation A FIFO	Situation B Weighted Average	Situation C FIFO	Situation D Weighted Average
Sales revenue	$12,000	$12,000	$12,000	$12,000
Cost of sales				
Beginning inventory	3,300	?	?	?
Purchases	4,800	?	?	?
Cost of goods available				
for sale	8,100	?	?	?
Ending inventory	2,400	?	?	?
Cost of sales	5,700	?	?	?
Gross profit	6,300	?	?	?
Operating expenses	4,000	4,000	4,000	4,000
Pretax profit	2,300	?	?	?
Income tax expense (30%)	690			
Profit	$ 1,610	?	?	?

Required:

1. Complete the preceding tabulation for each situation. In Situations A and B (prices rising), assume the following: beginning inventory, 300 units at $11 = $3,300; purchases, 400 units at $12 = $4,800. In Situations C and D (prices falling), assume the opposite; that is, beginning inventory, 300 units at $12 = $3,600; purchases, 400 units at $11 = $4,400. Use periodic inventory procedures.

2. Analyze and discuss the relative effects on pretax profit and on profit as demonstrated by (1) when prices are rising and when prices are falling.

3. Discuss the relative effects, if any, on the cash position for each situation.

4. Would you recommend FIFO or weighted average? Explain.

P8–6 Evaluating the Effects of Inventory Costing Methods on Financial Statement Elements (AP8–3)   ▨ **LO4**
Neverstop Corporation sells item A as part of its product line. Information about the beginning inventory, purchases, and sales of item A are given in the following table for the first six months of 2011. The company uses a perpetual inventory system.

	Purchases		Sales	
Date	Number of Units	Unit Cost	Number of Units	Sales Price
January 1 (beginning inventory)	500	$2.50		
January 24			300	$4.00
February 8	600	$2.60		
March 16			560	$4.20
June 11	300	$2.75		

Required:

1. Compute the cost of ending inventory by using the weighted-average costing method.

2. Compute the gross profit for the first six months of 2011 by using the FIFO costing method.

3. Would the gross profit be higher, lower, or the same if Neverstop used the weighted-average costing method rather than the FIFO method? Explain. No calculations are required.

4. Prepare journal entries to record the purchase and sale transactions, as well as the cost of sales, assuming that the weighted-average method is used.

5. Assume that because of a clerical error, the ending inventory is reported to be 440 units rather than the actual number of units (540) on hand. If FIFO is used, calculate the amount of the understatement or overstatement in

   a. the cost of sales for the first six months of 2011.

   b. the current assets at June 30, 2011.

P8–7 Evaluating the Income Statement and Cash Flow Effects of Lower of Cost and Net Realizable Value   ▨ **LO5**
Smart Company prepared its annual financial statements dated December 31, 2010. The company applies the FIFO inventory costing method; however, the company neglected to apply the LCNRV valuation to the ending inventory. The preliminary 2010 income statement follows:

Sales revenue		$280,000
Cost of sales		
Beginning inventory	$31,000	
Purchases	184,000	
Cost of goods available for sale	215,000	
Ending inventory (FIFO cost)	46,500	
Cost of sales		168,500
Gross profit		111,500
Operating expenses		62,000
Pretax profit		49,500
Income tax expense (30%)		14,850
Profit		$ 34,650

Assume that you have been asked to restate the 2010 financial statements to incorporate the LCNRV inventory valuation rule. You have developed the following data relating to the ending inventory at December 31, 2010:

Item	Quantity	Acquisition Cost Unit	Acquisition Cost Total	Net Realizable Value (Market)
A	3,050	$3	$ 9,150	$4
B	1,500	5	7,500	3.5
C	7,100	1.5	10,650	3.5
D	3,200	6	19,200	4
			$46,500	

Required:

1. Restate the income statement to reflect the valuation of the ending inventory on December 31, 2010, at the lower of cost and net realizable value. Apply the LCNRV rule on an item-by-item basis and show computations.

2. Compare and explain the LCNRV effect on each amount that was changed in (1).

3. What is the conceptual basis for applying LCNRV to merchandise inventories?

4. What effect (increase, decrease, no effect) did the LCNRV rule have on the cash flow for 2010? What will be the long-term effect on cash flow (increase, decrease, no effect)? Computations are not necessary.

LO5

P8–8 **Evaluating the Effects of Manufacturing Changes on Inventory Turnover Ratio and Cash Flows from Operating Activities** (AP8–4)

H. T. Tan and Company has been operating for five years as an electronics component manufacturer specializing in cell phone components. During this period, it has experienced rapid growth in sales revenue and inventory. Mr. Tan and his associates have hired you as the company's first corporate controller. You have put into place new purchasing and manufacturing procedures that are expected to reduce inventories by approximately one-third by year-end. You have gathered the following data related to the changes:

	(in thousands)	
	Beginning of Year	End of Year (projected)
Inventory	$495,700	$304,310
		Current Year (projected)
Cost of sales		$7,008,984

Required:

1. Compute the inventory turnover ratio based on two different assumptions:
   a. Those presented in the preceding table (a decrease in the balance in inventory).
   b. No change from the beginning of the year in the inventory balance.

2. Compute the effect of the projected change in the balance in inventory on cash flow from operating activities for the year (show the sign and amount of the effect).

3. On the basis of the preceding analysis, write a brief memo explaining how an increase in inventory turnover can result in an increase in cash flow from operating activities. Also explain how this increase can benefit the company.

P8–9 **(Appendix 8A) Recording Sales and Purchases with Cash Discounts and Returns** (AP8–5)

Campus Stop Inc. is a student co-op. On January 1, 2011, the beginning inventory was $150,000, the trade receivables balance was $4,000, and the allowance for doubtful accounts had a credit balance of $800. Campus Stop uses a perpetual inventory system and records inventory purchases by using the gross method.

The following transactions (summarized) occurred during 2011:

a. Sold merchandise for $275,000 cash; the cost of sales is $137,500

b. Received merchandise returned by customers as unsatisfactory and paid a cash refund of $1,600; the returned merchandise had cost $800

c. Purchased merchandise from vendors on credit; terms 3/10, n/30 as follows:

    i. August Supply Company, invoice price, $5,000

    ii. Other vendors, invoice price, $120,000

d. Purchased equipment for use in store for cash, $2,200

e. Purchased office supplies for future use in the store; paid cash, $700

f. Paid freight on merchandise purchased, $400 cash

g. Paid trade payables in full during the period as follows:

    i. Paid August Supply Company after the discount period, $5,000

    ii. Paid other vendors within the discount period, $116,400

Required:
Prepare journal entries for each of the preceding transactions.

ALTERNATE PROBLEMS

AP8–1 Analyzing and Interpreting the Effects of Inventory Errors (P8–2) LO2
The income statements for Sherwood Company summarized for a four-year period shows the following:

eXcel

	2012	2011	2010	2009
Sales revenue	$2,025,000	$2,450,000	$2,700,000	$2,975,000
Cost of sales	1,505,000	1,627,000	1,782,000	2,113,000
Gross profit	520,000	823,000	918,000	862,000
Operating expenses	490,000	513,000	538,000	542,000
Pretax profit	30,000	310,000	380,000	320,000
Income tax expense (30%)	9,000	93,000	114,000	96,000
Profit	$ 21,000	$ 217,000	$ 166,000	$ 224,000

An audit revealed that in determining these amounts, the ending inventory for 2010 was overstated by $22,000. The company uses a periodic inventory system.

Required:

1. Revise these income statements to reflect the correct amounts.
2. Did the error affect the cumulative profit for the four-year period? Explain.
3. What effect did the error have on the income tax expense for years 2010 and 2011?

AP8–2 Analyzing the Effects of Four Alternative Inventory Methods (P8–3) LO3
Yared Company uses a periodic inventory system. The company's accounting records for the most popular item in inventory showed the following details:

Transactions	Units	Unit Cost
Beginning Inventory, January 1, 2012	1,800	$2.50
Transactions during 2012:		
a. Purchase, January 30	2,500	3.10
b. Sale, March 14 ($5 each)	(1,450)	
c. Purchase, May 1	1,200	4.00
d. Sale, August 31 ($5 each)	(1,900)	

Required:

Compute (a) the cost of goods available for sale during 2012, (b) the cost of ending inventory at December 31, 2012, and (c) the cost of sales for 2012, under each of the following inventory costing methods (show computations and round to the nearest dollar):

1. Weighted-average cost.

2. First-in, first-out.

3. Specific identification, assuming that the company is permitted to use it and that two-fifths of the units sold on March 14, 2012, were selected from the beginning inventory and three-fifths from the purchase of January 30, 2012. Assume that the sale of August 31, 2012, was selected from the remainder of the beginning inventory, with the balance from the purchase of May 1, 2012.

4. As a shareholder, which of these three methods would you prefer?

LO4   **AP8–3**   **Evaluating the Effects of Inventory Costing Methods on Financial Statement Elements** (P8–6)

The Sportex Company, a diversified distribution outlet for sporting goods, purchases cartons of tennis balls from the Ball Corporation and markets the balls under the Sportex name. Purchases and sales data for January 2013, the first month of operations, are provided below.

	Date	Number of Cartons	Total Cost	Amount of Invoice
Purchases:	January 2	800	$16,000	
	January 19	600	13,200	
	January 29	500	11,000	
Sales:	January 5	500		$20,000
	January 21	700		29,200

Sportex uses a perpetual inventory system.

Required:

1. Compute the cost of sales in January 2013 by using the FIFO method.

2. Compute the cost of ending inventory at January 31, 2013, assuming that Sportex uses the weighted-average cost method. (Round your calculation of the average cost to the nearest cent.)

3. Would the computation you made in (1) and (2) change if the company used a periodic inventory system? Explain.

LO6   **AP8–4**   **Evaluating the Effects of Failed Expansion Plans on Inventory Turnover Ratio and Cash Flows from Operating Activities** (P8–8)

Arctic Cat

Arctic Cat Inc. was the world's second-largest manufacturer of snowmobiles and had experienced exceptional growth in recent years. It planned for a major increase in sales in the following period by increasing production dramatically. Unfortunately, North America experienced less snow that year than in any of the preceding 25 years. As a consequence, sales remained flat, and Arctic reported a loss of $9.5 million. However, its inventory balance increased by $6 million. Based on the following information, answer the questions that follow:

	(in thousands)	
	Beginning of Year	End of Year
Inventory	$120,804	$126,981
		Current Year
Cost of sales		$480,441

Required:

1. Compute the inventory turnover ratio based on two different assumptions:
    a. Those presented in the preceding table.
    b. No change from the beginning of the year in the inventory balance.

2. Compute the effect of the change in the balance in inventory on cash flow from operating activities for the year (show the sign and amount of the effect).

3. On the basis of your analysis, write a brief memo explaining how a decrease in inventory turnover can result in a decrease in cash flow from operating activities.

AP8–5   (Appendix 8A) Recording Sales and Purchases with Cash Discounts and Returns (P8–9)

The following transactions were selected from those occurring during the month of January 2011 for Dan's Store Inc. A wide variety of goods is offered for sale. Credit sales are extended to a few select customers; the usual credit terms are n/EOM (end of the month). The cost of sales is always one-half of the gross sales price.

a. Sales to customers:
Cash, $228,000
Credit, $72,000

b. Unsatisfactory merchandise returned by customers:
Cash, $3,000
Credit, $2,000

c. Purchased merchandise from vendors on credit; terms 2/10, n/30:

   i. Amount billed by Amy Supply Company, $4,000

   ii. Amount billed by other vendors, $68,000

d. Paid freight on merchandise purchased, $1,500 cash

e. Collections on trade receivables, $36,000

f. Paid trade payables in full during the period as follows:

   i. Amy Supply Company after the discount period, $4,000

   ii. Paid other vendors within the discount period, $66,640

g. Paid $1,000 for two new typewriters for the office

Required:
Prepare journal entries for these transactions, assuming that a perpetual inventory system is used. Record inventory purchases by using the gross method.

CASES AND PROJECTS

FINDING AND INTERPRETING FINANCIAL INFORMATION

CP8–1   Finding Financial Information

Go to Connect online for the financial statements of Cadbury plc.

1. How much inventory does the company own at the end of the current year?
2. Estimate the amount of inventory that the company purchased and produced during the current year. (*Hint:* Use the cost of sales equation.)
3. What method does the company use to determine the cost of its inventory?
4. Compute the inventory turnover ratio for the current year. What does an inventory turnover ratio tell you?
5. What was the change in inventory? How did it affect net cash provided by operating activities for the current year?

■ **LO1, 3**

Cadbury plc

CP8–2   Finding Financial Information

Refer to the financial statements of the Nestlé Group given in Appendix A at the end of this book.

1. What method does the company use to determine the cost of its inventory?
2. What are the components of the company's inventory balance? What aspects of its operations might determine why finished goods is the largest component?
3. Compute Nestlé's inventory turnover ratio for the year ended December 31, 2008.
4. If the company overstated ending inventory by 10 million Swiss francs for the year ended December 31, 2008, what would be the correct value for "profit before income taxes and associates"?

■ **LO1, 3, 6**

The Nestlé Group

■ **LO6**

The Nestlé Group vs. Cadbury

CP8–3   Comparing Companies

Go to Connect online for the financial statements of Cadbury, plc., and to Appendix A of this book for the financial statements of the Nestlé Group.

Required:

1. Compute the inventory turnover ratio for both companies for the current year. What would you infer from the difference?

2. Both companies measure inventory at the lower of cost or net realizable value. However, one of the companies determines cost of inventory by using the weighted-average cost method while the other uses both FIFO and the weighted-average cost methods for different types of inventory. Would you expect the different methods to cause a large difference in cost of sales? Why?

FINANCIAL REPORTING AND ANALYSIS CASES

CP8–4   **Review of Business Operations and Preparation of a Correct Income Statement: A Comprehensive and Challenging Case**[*]

It is July 15, 2011. You, a junior accountant at a small accounting firm, go over your notes from your afternoon meeting with Marco Douga. Marco came to your office looking for help with his business, Marco's Professional Print Shop Ltd. (MPP). Marco is the owner-manager of MPP, a copy and print shop located in Newville. He recently approached a bank for a loan.

At his last meeting with the bank, the bank manager indicated that the loan is almost approved and told Marco that he needed to examine MPP's 2010 financial statements. In your file, you have the following information:

Exhibit I: Summary notes of the discussion with Marco Douga
Exhibit II: Income statement for the year ended December 31, 2010, and 2009, prepared by the client

Your supervisor is eager to see a draft income statement for the year ended December 31, 2010, based on the information you have thus far.

Required:

1. Identify any areas of concern that you may have about the operation of the business, particularly the proper accounting for revenue and expenses, and the control of operations.

2. Prepare a revised income statement based on the information that you gathered during your meeting with Marco.

3. Identify the weaknesses in MPP's internal control of operations. What changes would you recommend? Explain.

EXHIBIT I

Summary Notes of the Discussion with Marco Douga

MPP provides copying and small print job services from a single location close to a university. The business was organized in January 2009 to meet the needs of companies, the university, and students in the area. At the time, there were no copying businesses in the area, and Marco saw this as an opportunity to become his own boss after many years of working as a mechanic for the local bus company.

Marco remortgaged his home for $55,000. This money was invested in the share capital of MPP. He also borrowed money from relatives to get the business started. With the money, Marco was able to purchase the computers, printers, copiers, and scanners needed to provide the full range of quality services that he thought his customers would need. Most of the equipment he purchased was used, which greatly reduced start-up costs. He also purchased the furniture and fixtures needed to set up a functional and attractive place for the business. As of December 31, 2010, MPP still owed Marco's relatives $100,000. Marco personally paid $3,800 interest for each of the last two years on the additional mortgage on his home. MPP now needs a loan for two reasons. First, some of Marco's relatives want their loans repaid. Since the business is now on its way, Marco thinks MPP can repay some of the money it owes. Second, Marco would like to upgrade some of MPP's equipment and obtain some additional pieces of equipment.

In addition to providing copying and printing services, MPP sells a variety of stationery and office products, and provides assistance in designing documents and other printed materials. MPP operates long hours to provide high-quality customer service as well as to

---

[*]Adapted with permission from *Filling the GAAP to IFRS: Teaching Supplements for Canada's Accounting Academics,* CD3–Questions and Answers Pack, Canadian Institute of Chartered Accountants: Toronto, 2008. Any changes to the original material are the sole responsibility of the author and have not been reviewed or endorsed by the CICA.

complete customer orders. More than one person has to be on duty at all times to ensure that production can be done while customers are being served, and so that pick-ups from and deliveries to customers can be made. Marco tries to be in the store as much as possible, but he is not able to be there all the time. His wife, Carla, works in the store about 15 hours per week. The store is operated by employees only (when neither Marco nor his wife are present) for about 25 hours per week, mostly at non-peak times.

Marco spends a lot of time trying to attract new customers. He regularly visits businesses in the area to meet the decision makers, often treating them to an evening out or a meal. About 40 percent of the advertising and promotion budget goes toward this type of activity. The remaining money is spent on advertising in community newspapers, sponsorship of various community activities, and printing and delivering flyers to businesses in the vicinity.

Marco is satisfied with the performance of his business. He thinks that it has grown nicely since its inception and anticipates that it will be profitable soon. Carla performs MPP's accounting and prepares a yearly income statement, but she has little training in accounting.

Customers can pay by cash or credit card, or MPP will provide credit to any customers who ask. About 25 percent of MPP's business is for cash, 25 percent is on credit cards, and the remainder is on credit offered by MPP. MPP asks customers to pay within 10 days, but often they do not. When a sale is completed, it is rung up on the cash register. When Marco and Carla are in the store, they are the only ones who operate the register. Marco admits that, because he is in too much of a hurry, he sometimes puts the cash in his pocket rather than take the time to ring up the sale. Having cash in hand allows him to pay his babysitter and other personal expenses. Though it was hard for him to be certain, Marco estimated that transactions worth about $10,000 each year have been handled in this way. When Marco and Carla are out of the store, the cash is controlled by one of the employees. That employee is required to lock up for the day, count the cash in the register, and then lock the cash in a drawer in Marco's office. Marco has a lot of confidence in his employees, most of whom are students attending university and working part-time to make money.

Carla records the revenue by adding up the deposits made to the company's bank account during the year. Amounts owed by customers are recorded at the time of delivery on a specially designated sheet of paper kept by the cash register. As cash is received, the related balance on the list is reduced. The accounts receivable balance on December 31 is the total amount on the list on that date. On December 31, 2010, there was $16,200 on the list and on December 31, 2009, the amount was $11,505. When Carla prepared the income statement, she included a bad debt expense of $1,955 in 2009 and $2,754 in 2010, the amounts being estimated at 17 percent of the accounts receivable balance.

Marco obtained a corporate credit card on which he makes MPP's purchases. Items purchased on the credit card are expensed in the year as long as a statement is received from the credit card company before Carla prepares the year-end income statement. If the statement comes in after that time, the expenses will get picked up the following year. Marco sometimes makes personal purchases on the corporate credit card if he thinks he is too close to his credit limit on his personal credit card. Marco estimates that he charged about $4,000 of personal expenses to the corporate credit card in each of the last two years. In addition, Marco has taken about $25,000 in cash each year from the business for personal reasons. Carla included these amounts in the payments to employees item on the income statement.

MPP maintains supplies of paper, toner, bindings, and other materials used to meet customers printing and photocopying needs. In addition, there is an inventory of merchandise that MPP sells to customers. Marco determines what he needs for inventory by doing a visual check of the storeroom every few days. When he needs particular items, he calls the suppliers who are usually able to deliver the goods within a few days. On occasion, Marco has to go to a large business supply store because he has run out of needed stock before the supplier can deliver the goods, and he pays for these purchases with the corporate credit card. Carla determines the cost of merchandise sold during a year by adding up the amounts on the invoices received from the suppliers.

The amount of inventory on hand at the end of each year is counted so that Marco can get a clear idea of what he has on hand. Marco was told that we needed the inventory value on December 31, 2010, and 2009. He determined the value of the inventory by using the list of what was in the stockroom on December 31 and by applying prices from the most recent supplier price lists. On December 31, 2010, MPP had inventory of $12,222 and on December 31, 2009, the balance was $8,200.

Marco pays suppliers' invoices in full as soon as they are received. Marco explained that he is afraid to miss a payment because suppliers may stop supplying. He figures that paying the bills as soon as they are received is the best way of avoiding the problem.

Employees are paid minimum wage. Since it is easier for Carla, employees are paid their gross earnings by cheque at the end of each week.

EXHIBIT II

Income statement supplied by the client

MARCO'S PROFESSIONAL PRINT SHOP LTD.
INCOME STATEMENT
For the year ended December 31

	2010	2009
Sales	$ 360,547	$ 260,034
Cost of merchandise sold	124,984	96,212
Selling, general and administrative	42,204	35,249
Payments to employees	90,099	83,740
Computers, printers, copiers and scanners	10,000	85,000
Furniture and fixtures	—	15,000
Advertising and promotion	34,727	29,503
Utilities	18,300	17,900
Interest on loans from relatives	5,000	5,000
Bank charges	2,000	1,500
Rent	22,000	22,000
Bad debt expense	2,754	1,955
Other expenses	16,618	12,444
	368,686	405,503
Net loss	$ (8,139)	$ (145,469)

LO2, 3, 6   **CP8–5**   **Using Financial Reports: Analyzing Reported Information**

Alimentation
Couche-Tard

Alimentation Couche-Tard is the third-largest convenience store operator in North America. It has more than 5,000 outlets: Couche-Tard in eastern Canada; Mac's in central and western Canada; and Circle K in the United States. The following table includes selected information from its financial statements (amounts in millions of U.S. dollars).

	Year Ended April 26, 2009	Year Ended April 27, 2008	Year Ended April 29, 2007
Revenues	15,781.1	15,370.0	12,087.4
Cost of sales	13,334.5	13,146.5	10,082.9
Earnings before income taxes	368.6	257.5	310.3
Income tax expense	114.7	68.2	113.9
Trade receivables	209.2	235.3	199.0
Inventories	400.3	444.5	382.1
Trade payables	510.3	618.0	537.0

Required:

1. Compute the following amounts for each of the fiscal years 2008 and 2009:
   a. Collections from customers.
   b. Purchases of merchandise from suppliers.
   c. Payments to suppliers.
   d. The trade receivables turnover ratio and the average collection period.
   e. The inventory turnover ratio and the average period to sell inventory.
   f. The average period for conversion of inventories into cash.

2. The company uses the indirect method to report its cash flows from operations. How would the changes in trade receivables, inventory, and trade payables be reported in the operating activities section of its statement of cash flows for 2009?

3. In the notes to its financial statements, the company states that the cost of merchandise is determined according to the first-in, first-out method. Would you expect the company's profit to increase or decrease if it used the weighted-average costing method instead of FIFO? Explain.

4. Assume that the company purchased canned products from a local supplier on April 26, 2009, with terms F.O.B. shipping point. The merchandise, at a cost of $1,400, had not arrived at the company's warehouse until April 28, and was not included in the inventory count at year-end. What effect would this error have on the company's profit for 2009? Show calculations.

CP8–6   Using Financial Reports: Analyzing Reported Information

■ **LO**2, 3, 6

Geox S.p.A.

Geox S.p.A. is an Italy-based company active in the footwear and apparel manufacturing industry, which includes classic, casual, and sports footwear, as well as apparel for men, women, and children. The company's products are sold in more than 70 countries worldwide through a widespread distribution network. Geox prepares its financial statements in accordance with the International Financial Reporting Standards. The following table includes selected information from its financial statements (amounts in millions of euro).

	2008	2007	2006
Net sales	892.5	770.2	612.3
Cost of sales	424.5	358.3	302.0
Profit before income taxes	170.5	179.7	133.9
Income tax expense	48.6	55.4	36.7
Trade receivables	124.6	108.0	84.2
Inventories	228.8	187.1	131.0
Trade payables	149.2	127.6	96.9

Required:

1. Compute the following amounts for each of the fiscal years 2007 and 2008:
   a. Collections from customers.
   b. Purchases of merchandise from suppliers. Assume for simplicity that the company buys its products from other manufacturers.
   c. Payments to suppliers.
   d. Trade receivables turnover ratio and the average collection period.
   e. Inventory turnover ratio and the average period to sell inventory.
   f. Average period for conversion of inventories into cash.

2. The company uses the indirect method to report its cash flows from operations. How would the changes in trade receivables, inventory, and trade payables be reported in the operating activities section of its statement of cash flows for 2008?

3. In the notes to its financial statements, the company states that the cost of merchandise is determined by using the weighted-average costing method. Would you expect the company's profit to increase or decrease if it used FIFO instead of weighted-average cost? Explain.

4. Assume that the company purchased goods from a supplier in the Far East with terms F.O.B. destination. These goods, which cost €1.2 million, were shipped on December 24, 2008, but had not arrived by December 31. The company's accountant included the cost of these goods in inventory at year-end. Is that an error? If so, what effect would this error have on the company's profit for 2008? Show calculations.

CP8–7   Analyzing and Interpreting the Inventory Turnover Ratio

■ **LO**6

Loblaw Companies
Shoppers Drug Mart

Loblaw Companies Ltd. and Shoppers Drug Mart Corporation are two companies operating in the same industry. Starting in 2004, Loblaw expanded the scope of the goods it sold from primarily food to include pharmaceutical items, cosmetics, appliances, home entertainment products, and items for use at home. At the same time, Shoppers expanded the scope of the goods it sold from primarily items for use at home, pharmaceutical products, and electronic goods such as digital cameras to include food items, excluding fresh fruit and vegetables. These changes affected the type of inventory items carried by both companies.

Selected financial statement information over the five-year period 2004–2008 is presented below:

	2008	2007	2006	2005	2004
Loblaw Companies Ltd.					
Sales	$30,802	$29,384	$28,640	$27,801	$26,209
Cost of sales, selling and administrative expenses	29,172	27,838	26,917	25,716	24,084
Inventory	2,188	2,032	2,037	2,020	1,821
Shoppers Drug Mart Corp.					
Revenue	9,423	8,478	7,786	7,151	6,566
Cost of sales and other operating expenses	8,335	7,520	6,958	6,431	5,928
Inventory	1,743	1,545	1,372	1,217	1,136

Neither company disclosed its cost of sales separately. However, the industry average indicates that the cost of sales represents 77 percent of revenue, on average.

Required:

1. Compute the inventory turnover ratio and the average number of days to sell inventory for each company for the years 2005–2008.

2. In your opinion, which of these two companies was more efficient in managing its inventory subsequent to the change in the lines of products they sell? Explain.

CRITICAL THINKING CASES

LO2

CP8–8   **Evaluating the Use of a Perpetual Inventory System to Control Theft**

The president of National Wholesalers suspected that employees are stealing several items of merchandise, particularly items that are small enough to hide in clothing. The president's suspicions resulted from complaints made in April by several retailers who claimed that shortages were frequently found when orders of financial and programmable calculators were inspected upon receipt.

The assistant controller was asked to provide whatever information might prove helpful in identifying the extent of any problem that might have developed since the end of the previous fiscal year on December 31. The following report was submitted on May 1.

	Financial Calculators	Programmable Calculators
Number of units in inventory on December 31, per physical count	19,600	7,600
Cost per unit	$ 8.40	$ 29.25
Number of units purchased since January 1:		
January	4,200	1,400
February	3,600	3,100
March	5,100	2,700
April	2,700	1,800
Total	15,600	9,000
Average cost per unit of purchases since January 1	$ 8.40	$30.00
Average gross profit percentage on merchandise billed to retailers	30%	25%
Sales recorded from January 1 to April 30	$343,200	$496,400
Number of units physically counted in the warehouse on April 30	6,400	3,900

Required:

1. Compute the number of units of each type of merchandise that are unaccounted for on May 1. The company uses a periodic inventory system and the weighted-average inventory costing method.

2. Determine the monetary value of the apparent loss.

3. Assuming that the apparent loss realized during the period January 1–April 30 is representative of the loss that might be realized on these two items during an entire year, would you recommend that (a) a new inventory system be installed in the warehouse at an annual cost of $4,000 to maintain perpetual inventory records of these two items of merchandise and (b) a quarterly physical inventory count of these items be implemented at an additional cost of $1,000 per quarterly count? Show supporting computations.

CP8–9 Evaluating an Ethical Dilemma: Earnings, Inventory Purchases, and Management Bonuses

■ **LO2**

Micro Warehouse is a computer software and hardware online and catalogue sales company. A *Wall Street Journal* article disclosed the following:

Micro Warehouse

MICRO WAREHOUSE IS REORGANIZING TOP MANAGEMENT

Micro Warehouse Inc. announced a "significant reorganization" of its management, including the resignation of three senior executives.

The move comes just a few weeks after the Norwalk, Conn., computer catalogue sales company said it overstated earnings by $28 million since 1992 as a result of accounting irregularities. That previous disclosure prompted a flurry of shareholder lawsuits against the company. In addition, Micro Warehouse said it is cooperating with an "informal inquiry" by the Securities and Exchange Commission.

Source: Stephan E. Frank, *The Wall Street Journal*, November 21, 1996, p. B2.

Its quarterly report filed with the Securities and Exchange Commission two days before indicated that inaccuracies involving understatement of purchases and trade payable in current and prior periods amounted to $47.3 million. It also indicated that, as a result, $2.2 million of executive bonuses for 1995 would be cancelled. Micro Warehouse's effective tax rate is approximately 40.4 percent. Both cost of sales and executive bonuses are fully deductible for tax purposes.

Required:

As a new staff member at Micro Warehouse's auditing firm, you are assigned to write a memo outlining the effects of the understatement of purchases and the cancellation of the bonuses. In your report, be sure to include the following:

1. The total effect on pretax and after-tax earnings of the understatement of purchases.

2. The total effect on pretax and after-tax earnings of the cancellation of the bonuses.

3. An estimate of the percentage of after-tax earnings that management is receiving in bonuses.

4. A discussion of why Micro Warehouse's board of directors may have decided to tie managers' compensation to reported earnings and the possible relationship between this type of bonus scheme and the accounting errors.

FINANCIAL REPORTING AND ANALYSIS TEAM PROJECT

CP8–10 Team Project: Analyzing Inventories

■ **LO4**

As a team, select an industry to analyze. A list of companies classified by industry can be obtained by accessing **www.fpinfomart.ca** and then choosing "Companies by Industry." You can also find a list of industries and companies with each industry via **http://ca.finance.yahoo.com/investing** (click on "Annual Reports" under "Tools"). Each team member should acquire the annual report for one publicly traded company in the industry, with each member selecting a different company. (Library files, the SEDAR service at **www.sedar.com**, or the company websites are good sources.)

Required:

On an individual basis, each team member should then write a short report answering the following questions about the selected company. Discuss any patterns across the companies that you as a team observe. Then, as a group, write a short report comparing and contrasting your companies.

1. If your company lists inventories on its statement of financial position, what percentage is this asset of total assets for each of the last three years? If your company does not list inventories, discuss why this is so.

2. If your company lists inventories, what inventory costing method does it use? What do you think motivated this choice?

3. Ratio analysis:

   a. What does the inventory turnover ratio measure in general?

   b. If your company reports inventories, compute the ratio for the last three years.

   c. What do your results suggest about the company?

   d. If available, find the industry ratio for the most recent year, compare it to your results, and discuss why you believe your company differs or is similar to the industry ratio.

4. What is the effect of the change in inventories on cash flows from operations for the most recent year; that is, did the change increase or decrease operating cash flows? Explain your answer.

Reporting and Interpreting Property, Plant, and Equipment; Natural Resources; and Intangibles

After studying this chapter, you should be able to do the following:

FOCUS COMPANY: **WestJet Airlines**

MANAGING PROFITS THROUGH CONTROL OF PRODUCTIVE CAPACITY

WestJet Airlines (www.westjet.com), Canada's second largest airline, has provided low-fare, friendly service to customers since its first flight took off in 1996. Clive Beddoe, along with a small team of Calgary entrepreneurs, started up WestJet with three Boeing 737-200 aircraft. In 1999, the company completed its initial public offering on the Toronto Stock Exchange. In 2009, the company employed 7,600 people and flew to 69 global destinations. By the end of 2009, the company's fleet had grown to 86 aircraft, including 10 new Next Generation 737s. This investment in new aircraft allows WestJet to operate one of the youngest and most fuel efficient fleets of any large North American commercial airline, and illustrates one way of responding to environmental concerns.

WestJet is a capital-intensive company, with more than $2.3 billion in property and equipment reported on its statement of financial position at December 31, 2009, representing over 66 percent of its total assets. In fiscal years 2007, 2008, and 2009, WestJet spent over $500 million dollars on aircraft and other flight equipment as it replaced old aircraft with newer, quieter, more fuel-efficient Boeing 737 aircraft. WestJet's expansion plan is part of a long-term strategy of controlled growth, financed by a combination of debt, equity, and cash generated from its operations.

Since the demand for air travel is seasonal, with peak demand occurring during the summer months, planning for optimal productive capacity in the airline industry is very difficult. WestJet's managers must determine how many aircraft are needed in which cities at what points in time to fill all seats demanded. Otherwise, the company loses revenue (not enough seats to meet demand) or has higher costs (too many seats unfilled and unpaid for).

UNDERSTANDING THE BUSINESS

Running a business such as an airline, a resource extraction and processing organization, or a pharmaceuticals company, means acquiring adequate property, plant facilities, and equipment that will provide the capacity to serve the customers' current and future needs. Capital intensive companies must pay large sums for their capacity, with the expectation of regaining that money over time, plus all operating costs and a reasonable profit. This explains why property, plant, and equipment of this type are referred to as long-lived assets and often as fixed assets. For any airline, aircraft, spare engines and parts, hangars, flight simulators, buildings, and equipment are all fixed assets. In comparison, resource extraction, processing, and distribution companies require the property to extract raw resources from, the plant facilities to process raw materials into refined products, and a distribution system to bring the refined products to the point of sale.

In contrast, pharmaceutical and biotechnology companies require the property, plant, and equipment to conduct research and manufacture their products, but more importantly, they require the know-how to discover and apply scientific information. Technology companies are similar in that the capacity to invent, develop, and successfully install communication systems relies heavily on intellectual capital. In these two industries, patents provide evidence that knowledge expected to provide long-term benefit to the company has legal protection for a limited period of time. The most prominent assets on the statements of financial position of companies in these industries are usually intangible assets such as licences, brand names, and patents. The most valuable knowledge, however, may not be patented because of the legal time limit to the protection provided, but kept secret from competitors indefinitely through strong confidentiality agreements.

One of the major challenges facing managers of most businesses is forecasting the level of long-lived productive capacity it will need to produce forecasted revenue streams. If managers underestimate the level of capacity needed in the future, the company will not be able to produce goods or services that are in demand and will miss the opportunity to earn revenue. On the other hand, if managers overestimate the productive capacity needed, the company will incur excessive costs that will reduce its profitability.

The airline industry provides an outstanding example of the difficulty associated with planning for and analyzing the capacity to produce service revenue. If an aircraft destined for Toronto takes off from Calgary with empty seats, the economic value associated with these seats is lost for that flight. There is obviously no way to sell the seat to a customer after the aircraft has left the gate. Unlike a manufacturer, an airline cannot place seats in inventory for use on future flights.

Likewise, if a large number of people want to board a flight, the airline must turn away some customers if seats are not available. You might be willing to buy a television set from Future Shop even if you are told that it is out of stock and there will be a one-week delay in delivery. But you probably won't fly home for a holiday on an airline that would have you wait one week because no seats were available on its flights when you wanted to fly. You would simply pick another airline or choose a different mode of transportation.

The battle for passengers in the airline industry is fought in terms of property, plant, and equipment. Passengers want convenient schedules (which require a large number of aircraft), and they want to fly in new, modern aircraft. Because airlines have such a large investment in equipment with no opportunity to hold unused seats in inventory, they work hard to fill aircraft to capacity for each flight. Airlines in North America measure their capacity as available seat miles (ASM).[1] A passenger in a seat transforms it from an ASM into a revenue passenger mile (RPM). The importance of filling aircraft with passengers is highlighted in the following excerpt from WestJet's annual report for 2009.

---

[1] An available seat mile is the number of miles a seat travels in a given period of time, regardless of whether or not it contains a passenger.

Management's Discussion and Analysis of Financial Results

Our load factor[2] was down slightly by 1.4 points to 78.7 per cent in 2009, from 80.1 per cent in 2008. Despite the decline, our load factor for 2009 remained within our optimal operating range of 78 per cent to 82 per cent.

Source: WestJet Annual Report 2009.

While each flight generates revenue, it also creates wear and tear on the equipment, no matter how many seats are filled. Conceptually, WestJet's managers understand that this wear and tear means the cash flow from using this aircraft in future time periods will be lower than the cash flow currently experienced. In pricing an airline ticket for a specific flight, WestJet's management includes an amount to cover this daily wear and tear that is part of the cost of operating an aircraft. The wear and tear is estimated and recorded as annual depreciation expense. WestJet estimates that the lifetime of an aircraft is between 30,000 and 50,000 flights, during which the company expects to recover the acquisition cost of the aircraft; to recover the related maintenance, operating, and financing costs; and to turn a profit.

In summary, issues related to property, plant, and equipment have a pervasive impact on a company in terms of strategy, pricing decisions, and profitability. Business managers devote considerable time planning optimal levels of productive capacity adequate to meet expected future demand. Accountants estimate and report the cost of using these assets throughout their productive lives, taking into consideration applicable income tax laws and regulations, and financial analysts closely review financial statements to determine the impact of management decisions on the company's profitability and financial condition.

This chapter is organized according to the life cycle of long-lived assets—acquisition, use, and disposal. First we will discuss the measuring and reporting issues related to land, buildings, and equipment. Then we will discuss the measurement and reporting issues for natural resources and intangible assets. Among the issues we will discuss are maintaining, using, and disposing of property and equipment over time and measuring and reporting assets considered impaired in their ability to generate future cash flows.

ORGANIZATION OF THE CHAPTER

Acquisition and Maintenance of Plant and Equipment	Use, Impairment, and Disposal of Plant and Equipment	Natural Resources and Intangible Assets
• Classification of Long-Lived Assets • Fixed Asset Turnover Ratio • Measuring and Recording Acquisition Cost • Various Acquisition Methods • Repairs, Maintenance, and Betterments	• Depreciation Concepts • Alternative Depreciation Methods • Changes in Depreciation Estimates • Managers' Selection among Accounting Alternatives • Measuring Asset Impairment • Disposal of Property, Plant, and Equipment	• Acquisition and Depletion of Natural Resources • Acquisition and Depreciation of Intangible Assets • Examples of Intangible Assets

---

[2]The load factor is a measure of total capacity utilization, calculated as the proportion of total available seats occupied by revenue passengers, or RPM/ASM.

LO¹

Define, classify, and explain the nature of long-lived assets and interpret the fixed asset turnover ratio.

Property, Plant, and Equipment as a Percentage of Total Assets for Selected Focus Companies

Nokia 13.8%

Nestlé 19.5%

Benetton 35.6%

LONG-LIVED (OR LONG-TERM OR CAPITAL) ASSETS are tangible or intangible resources owned by a business and used in its operations to produce benefits over several years.

TANGIBLE ASSETS have physical substance.

ACQUISITION AND MAINTENANCE OF PLANT AND EQUIPMENT

Exhibit 9.1 shows the asset section of WestJet's statement of financial position at December 31, 2009. Nearly two-thirds of WestJet's total assets are property and equipment. The company's annual report contains additional information about the acquisition cost of property, plant, and equipment owned or controlled by WestJet, and related depreciation; the amount of new investment in equipment during the year; and the amount of equipment that was sold or retired, as well as details of other long-lived assets with probable long-lived benefits. Let us begin by classifying these long-lived assets.

Classification of Long-Lived Assets

Accountants use the terms long-lived assets, long-term assets, or capital assets to identify property, plant, equipment, and intangible properties held for production, rental to others, or administrative purposes, as well as the development, construction, maintenance, or repair of other assets. Long-lived assets are acquired, constructed, or developed for use on a continuing basis. They are not normally sold to generate revenue, although the normal course of business for real estate companies is the purchase and sale of long-lived assets such as land and buildings. Long-lived assets can be tangible or intangible, and have the following characteristics:

1. Tangible assets (or fixed assets) can be touched because they have physical substance. This classification is most often called *property, plant, and equipment*. The three kinds of tangible assets held for use in operations are as follows:

   a. *Land*, which is reported on the statement of financial position as a separate item if it has a material value. Unlike aircraft or patents on pharmaceutical products, land does not become obsolete; therefore, it is never depreciated. It may, however, be impaired in value.

   b. *Buildings, fixtures, and equipment*, which are reported as a separate item on the statement of financial position or in the notes. WestJet reports the details of such

Exhibit **9.1**

WestJet Airlines Asset Section of the Statement of Financial Position

REAL WORLD EXCERPT

WestJet Airlines

ANNUAL REPORT

WESTJET AIRLINES LTD.
Consolidated Balance Sheets
December 31, 2009, and 2008
(in thousands of dollars)

	2009	2008
Assets		
Current assets:		
Cash and cash equivalents (Note 4)	$1,005,181	$ 820,214
Accounts receivable	27,654	16,837
Future income tax (Note 9)	2,560	8,459
Prepaid expenses and deposits (Note 14[a])	56,239	53,283
Inventory	26,048	17,054
	1,117,682	915,847
Property and equipment (Note 6)	2,307,566	2,269,790
Intangible assets (Note 6)	14,087	12,060
Other assets (Note 14[a])	54,367	71,005
	$3,493,702	$3,268,702

Source: Westjet Annual Report 2009.

assets in Note 5, separating aircraft, spare engines, buildings, ground property and equipment, leasehold improvements, and assets under capital lease.

c. *Natural resources*, which include mineral deposits such as gold or iron ore, oil wells and reserves, and timber tracts. Corporations such as Barrick Gold, Royal Dutch Shell, and Anglo American extract natural resources.

2. Intangible assets have no physical substance. Historically, they were called "*intangibles and other nothings*." WestJet's intangible assets include its name, logo, slogans, computer software, and landing rights—which give the airline the exclusive right for departure or landing at specific time periods. Often, intangible assets arise from intellectual effort and are known as *intellectual property*. Examples include copyrights, patents, licences, trademarks, software, franchises, and subscription lists.

INTANGIBLE ASSETS have property ownership rights but not physical substance.

FIXED ASSET TURNOVER RATIO

KEY RATIO ANALYSIS

ANALYTICAL QUESTION → How effectively is management utilizing its property, plant, and equipment to generate revenues?

RATIO AND COMPARISONS → The fixed asset turnover ratio is useful in answering this question. It is computed as follows:

$$\text{Fixed Asset Turnover} = \frac{\text{Net Sales (or operating revenues)}}{\text{Average Net Fixed Assets*}}$$

*[Beginning + Ending Balances of Property, Plant, and Equipment (net of accumulated depreciation)] ÷ 2

The 2009 ratio for WestJet is

$$\$2,281,120 \div [(\$2,269,790 + \$2,307,566) \div 2] = 1.00 \text{ time}$$

Comparisons over Time			Comparisons with Competitors	
WestJet Airlines			Southwest	Ryanair
2007	2008	2009	2009	2009
0.96	1.10	1.00	0.93	1.23

INTERPRETATIONS

In General → The fixed asset turnover ratio measures the sales dollars generated by each dollar of fixed assets used. A high rate normally suggests effective management. An increasing rate over time signals more efficient fixed asset use. Creditors and security analysts use this ratio to assess a company's effectiveness in generating sales from its long-lived assets.

Focus Company Analysis → WestJet's fixed asset turnover ratio has decreased through the economic downturn in 2009, suggesting that there has been deterioration in the efficiency of using long-lived assets. The fleet renewal at WestJet is expected to help the company improve on its service to passengers and increase its net sales. When compared to two other companies in the industry, WestJet appears to be more efficient in utilizing its fixed assets than Southwest Airlines but less efficient than Ryanair. WestJet can further improve on its ratio by continuing to dispose of older aircraft and by increasing its revenues from flights, either by increasing the number of flights, by increasing the number of paying passengers for existing flights, or by increasing its RPMs.

A Few Cautions → A lower or declining rate may indicate that a company is expanding (by acquiring additional productive assets) in anticipation of higher sales in the future. An increasing ratio could also signal that a firm has cut back on capital expenditures because it anticipates a downturn in business. As a consequence, appropriate interpretation of the fixed asset turnover ratio requires an investigation of related activities.

SELECTED FOCUS COMPANIES' FIXED ASSET TURNOVER RATIOS FOR 2009

Gildan 2.44

Nokia 4.33

Nestlé 5.09

Measuring and Recording Acquisition Cost

The *cost principle* requires that all reasonable and necessary costs incurred in acquiring a long-lived asset, placing it in its operational setting, and preparing it for use should be recorded in a designated asset account. We say that the costs are *capitalized* when they are recorded as assets instead of as expenses in the current period. These costs, including any sales taxes, legal fees, transportation costs, and installation costs are added to the purchase price of the asset. Special discounts and interest charges associated with the purchase should not, however, be included in the cost of the asset. Interest charges should be reported as interest expense.

In addition to purchasing buildings and equipment, a company may acquire undeveloped land, typically with the intent to build a new factory or office building. When a company purchases land, all of the incidental costs paid by the purchaser, such as title fees, sales commissions, legal fees, title insurance, delinquent taxes, and surveying fees, should be included in its cost. Because land is not subject to depreciation, it must be recorded as a separate asset.

Sometimes a company purchases an old building or used machinery for use in its business operations. Renovation and repair costs incurred by the purchaser prior to the asset's use should be included as a part of its cost. The statement of cash flows of WestJet for fiscal year 2009 shows that WestJet acquired additional aircraft for approximately $119 million. However, details of these purchases are not publicly available.

Assume that WestJet purchased one new 737-800 aircraft from Boeing on January 1, 2011 (the beginning of WestJet's 2011 fiscal year), for a list price of $79 million. Also assume that Boeing offered WestJet a discount of $2.5 million for signing the purchase agreement. This means that the price of a new airplane to WestJet is $76.5 million. In addition, WestJet paid $500,000 to have the airplane delivered and $1,000,000 to prepare the airplane for use. The amount recorded for the purchase, called the *acquisition cost*, is the net cash amount paid or, when non-cash assets are used up as payment, the fair market value of the asset given or asset received, whichever can be more clearly determined (called the **cash equivalent price**). WestJet would calculate the acquisition cost of the aircraft as follows:

The **ACQUISITION COST** is the net cash equivalent amount paid or to be paid for the asset.

Invoice price	$79,000,000
Less: Discount from Boeing	2,500,000
Net cash invoice price	76,500,000
Add: Transportation charges paid by WestJet	500,000
Preparation costs paid by WestJet	1,000,000
Cost of the aircraft (added to the asset account)	$78,000,000

Various Acquisition Methods

For Cash   Assuming that WestJet paid cash for the aircraft and related transportation and preparation costs, the transaction is recorded as follows:

Aircraft (A)	78,000,000	
Cash (A)		78,000,000

Assets		=	Liabilities	+	Shareholders' Equity
Aircraft	+78,000,000				
Cash	−78,000,000				

It might seem unusual for WestJet to pay cash to purchase new assets that cost $78 million, but this is often the case. When it acquires productive assets, a company may pay with cash that was either generated from operations or cash that was recently borrowed. Notice that WestJet's cash balance at December 31, 2009, exceeds $1 billion. It also is possible for the seller to finance the purchase on credit.

For Debt Now let us assume that WestJet signed a note payable for the aircraft and paid cash for the transportation and preparation costs. WestJet would record the following journal entry:

Aircraft (A)	78,000,000	
Cash (A)		1,500,000
Note payable (L)		76,500,000

Assets		=	Liabilities		+	Shareholders' Equity
Aircraft	+78,000,000		Note payable	+76,500,000		
Cash	−1,500,000					

For Equity (or Other Non-cash Consideration) Any non-cash consideration, such as a company's common shares or a right given by the company to the seller to purchase the company's goods or services at a special price, might be part of the transaction. When a non-cash consideration is included in the purchase of an asset, the cash-equivalent cost (fair market value of the asset given or received) is determined.

Assume that WestJet gave Boeing 5,000,000 of its common shares, with a market value of $13.50 per share (the approximate stock price on the date of the transaction), and paid the balance in cash, including cash for the transportation and preparation costs. The journal entry and transaction effects follow:

Aircraft (A)	78,000,000	
Cash (A)		10,500,000
Common shares (SE)		67,500,000

Assets		=	Liabilities	+	Shareholders' Equity	
Aircraft	+78,000,000				Common shares	+67,500,000
Cash	−10,500,000					

By Construction In some cases, a company may construct an asset for use instead of buying it from a manufacturer. For example, a mining company such as Barrick Gold must construct the extraction facilities on a mining site. The acquisition cost of this self-constructed asset will comprise all direct and indirect costs of construction, including interest on any loans obtained to construct the asset. As soon as the asset is available for use, the accumulated construction costs will be depreciated over its productive life. The amount of interest that is included in the cost of the construction is called *capitalized interest*, which reduces the company's total interest expense every year until the facility is ready for use. Once the construction of the facility is completed, any interest costs on construction loans, however, must now be expensed. The complex computation of interest capitalization is discussed in other accounting courses.

For example, in 2009, WestJet completed the construction of its new head office in Calgary, which the company refers to as its Campus facility. Because the company had the asset built for its own use, the cost includes necessary costs of construction such as labour and materials, as well as overhead costs directly attributable to the construction activity. The costs also include the interest expense incurred during the construction period, based on the amount of funds invested in the construction of the hangar. WestJet added the interest incurred to the other construction costs of the new building until it was ready for use in operations. The amount of interest that is included in the cost of the building is called capitalized interest, which reduces the company's total interest expense every year until the building is in use. The complex computation of interest capitalization is discussed in other accounting courses.

CAPITALIZED INTEREST represents interest on borrowed funds directly attributable to construction until the asset is ready for is intended use.

Capitalizing labour, materials, and a portion of interest expense increases assets, decreases expenses, and increases profit. Let us assume the new hangar cost WestJet $600,000 in labour costs, $1,300,000 in materials and supplies, as well as interest expense of $100,000 incurred during the construction project:

| Building (A) | .... | 2,000,000 | |
| Cash (A) | .... | | 2,000,000 |

Assets		=	Liabilities	+	Shareholders' Equity
Building	+2,000,000				
Cash	−2,000,000				

WestJet described its policy on capitalized interest in Note 1 to its financial statements:

NOTES TO CONSOLIDATED FINANCIAL STATEMENTS

1. Summary of Significant Accounting Policies

. . .

(o) Capitalized costs

Costs associated with assets under development, which have probable future economic benefit, can be clearly defined and measured, and are incurred for the development of new products or technologies, are capitalized. These costs are not amortized until the asset is substantially complete and ready for its intended use, at which time, they are amortized over the life of the underlying asset. Interest attributable to funds used to finance property and equipment is capitalized to the related asset until the point of commercial use.

Source: WestJet Annual Report 2009.

In 2008, WestJet recorded $2,132,000 of interest related to aircraft financing, but it did not capitalize any interest in 2009.

BASKET PURCHASE is an acquisition of two or more assets in a single transaction for a single lump sum.

As a Basket Purchase of Assets   When several long-lived assets, such as land, building, and equipment, are acquired in a single transaction and for a single lump sum, known as a basket purchase, the cost of each asset must be measured and recorded separately. This is true because land is not depreciated but buildings and equipment are, although at different rates. The purchase price must be apportioned among the land, the building, and the equipment, on a rational basis.

Accountants use current market values of the acquired assets on the date of acquisition to apportion the single lump sum to the various assets in the basket. Assume that WestJet paid $300,000 cash to purchase a building and the land on which the building is located. As the current market values of the building and land were not known, a professional appraisal was obtained. This appraisal, totalling $315,000, indicated the following estimated market values: $189,000 for the building and $126,000 for the land. The total purchase price is then apportioned on the basis of relative market values as follows:

Building	Land
$\dfrac{\text{Market value}}{\text{Total market value}} = \dfrac{\$189,000}{\$315,000} = 60\%$	$\dfrac{\text{Market value}}{\text{Total market value}} = \dfrac{\$126,000}{\$315,000} = 40\%$
$60\% \times \$300,000 \text{ Total cost} = \$180,000$	$40\% \times \$300,000 \text{ Total cost} = \$120,000$

The cost of the building is determined by multiplying the total cost of $300,000 by the ratio of the market value of the building to the total market value ($189,000 ÷ $315,000 = 60 percent). Similarly, the cost of the land is determined by multiplying the total cost by the ratio of the market value of the land to the total market value ($126,000 ÷ $315,000 = 40 percent). Assuming that WestJet purchases the assets with cash, the journal entry and effects are as follows:

Land (A)..	120,000	
Building (A)	180,000	
Cash (A)		300,000

Assets		=	Liabilities	+	Shareholders' Equity
Land	+120,000				
Building	+180,000				
Cash	−300,000				

SELF-STUDY **QUIZ 9-1**

McDonald's Corporation

In a recent year, McDonald's Corporation purchased property, plant, and equipment priced at $1.8 billion. Assume that the company also paid $70 million for sales tax; $8 million for transportation costs; $1.3 million for installation and preparation of the property, plant, and equipment before use; and $100,000 in maintenance contracts to cover repairs to the property, plant, and equipment during use.

1. Compute the acquisition cost for the buildings and equipment.

2. For each situation below, indicate the effects of this acquisition on the following financial statement categories. Use "+" for increase and "−" for decrease, and indicate the accounts and amounts:

	Assets	Liabilities	Shareholders' Equity
a. Paid 30% in cash and signed a note payable for the balance.			
b. Issued 10 million shares at a market price of $45 per share and paid the balance in cash.			

After you complete your answers, go online for the solutions.

connect

Repairs, Maintenance, and Betterments

Most assets require substantial expenditures during their useful lives to maintain or enhance their productive capacity. These expenditures include cash outlays for ordinary repairs and maintenance, major repairs, replacements, and additions. Remember that the terms *expenditure* and *expense* are not synonymous. An expenditure is the payment of money to acquire goods or services. These goods and services may be recorded as either assets or expenses, depending on whether they benefit future periods or only the current period. Expenditures that are made *after* an asset is acquired are classified as follows:

1. Ordinary repairs and maintenance—expenditures that maintain the productive capacity of the asset during the current accounting period only. These cash outlays are recorded as **expenses** in the current period. Ordinary repairs and maintenance, also called *revenue expenditures*, are expenditures for the normal maintenance and

ORDINARY REPAIRS AND MAINTENANCE are expenditures for normal operating upkeep of long-lived assets.

REVENUE EXPENDITURES maintain the productive capacity of the asset during the current accounting period only and are recorded as expenses.

upkeep of long-lived assets. These expenditures are recurring in nature, involve relatively small amounts at each occurrence, and do not directly lengthen the useful life of the asset.

In the case of WestJet, examples of ordinary repairs include changing oil in aircraft engines, replacing the lights in the control panels, and fixing torn fabric on passenger seats. Although the cost of individual ordinary repairs is relatively small, in the aggregate these expenditures can be substantial. In the year 2009, WestJet incurred more than $96.2 million for aircraft maintenance and repairs. This amount was reported as an expense on its income statement.

EXTRAORDINARY REPAIRS are infrequent expenditures that increase the asset's economic usefulness in the future.

BETTERMENTS are costs incurred to enhance the productive or service potential of a long-lived asset.

CAPITAL EXPENDITURES increase the productive life, operating efficiency, or capacity of the asset and are recorded as increases in asset accounts, not as expenses.

2. Extraordinary repairs and betterments—expenditures that increase the productive life, operating efficiency, or capacity of the asset. These capital expenditures, which provide benefits to the company over a number of accounting periods, are added to the appropriate *asset* accounts. They occur infrequently, involve large amounts of money, and increase an asset's economic usefulness in the future through either increased efficiency or longer life. Examples include additions, complete reconditioning, and major overhauls and replacements, such as the complete replacement of an engine on an aircraft.

An example of an extraordinary repair has also arisen in the airline industry from a change in Transport Canada's regulation to reduce the acceptable level of engine noise. WestJet had to undertake an unplanned, very expensive, one-time repair that extended the economic life of its aircraft. It installed hushkits on all of its old aircraft engines that did not meet new noise-abatement regulations. Without hushkits, WestJet would not have been able to fly these planes. This extraordinary repair is a one-time cost that certainly increased the aircraft's future economic usefulness.

An example of a betterment is WestJet's installation of blended winglets on its aircraft to improve the aerodynamic performance and handling design of the 737-800s. From a maintenance perspective, winglets help aircraft achieve better climb performance that allows lower thrust settings, which extends engine life and reduces costs. The aircraft itself uses less fuel, helping WestJet implement its greener air strategy.

In many cases, no clear line distinguishes capital expenditures (assets) from revenue expenditures (expenses). In these situations, accountants must exercise professional judgment and make subjective decisions. Many managers prefer to classify an item as a capital expenditure for financial reporting because it reduces expenses and increases profit for the period. Of course, most managers prefer to classify the expenditure as a deductible expense on the income tax return, to pay lower taxes in the current period. Because the decision to capitalize or expense is subjective, auditors closely review the items reported as capital and revenue expenditures.

To avoid spending too much time on classifying capital and revenue expenditures, some companies develop simple policies that govern the accounting for these expenditures. For example, one large computer company expenses all individual items that cost less than $1,000. These policies are acceptable because immaterial (relatively small dollar) amounts will not affect users' decisions when analyzing financial statements.

FINANCIAL ANALYSIS   **LIVENT: HIDING HUNDREDS OF MILLIONS IN EXPENSES THROUGH CAPITALIZATION**

When expenditures that should be recorded as current period expenses are improperly capitalized as part of the cost of an asset, the effects on the financial statements can be enormous. In one of the largest Canadian accounting frauds in history, Livent inflated its profit and cash flows from operations by hundreds of millions of dollars in just such a scheme. This fraud turned Livent's actual losses into profits. For example, in 1997 an actual $8 million loss was reported as a $4.3 million profit. Charges were initially brought in 1999 in the United States after the former chief financial officer informed a new manager of the fraud. The founders, Myron Gottlieb and

Garth Drabinsky were finally convicted and sentenced for forgery and fraud in February 2009. The company's auditor, Deloitte & Touche, is also facing a civil suit filed by Livent Inc. against it. The Institute of Chartered Accountants of Ontario (ICAO) has fined Deloitte & Touche in excess of CDN$1.5 million for professional misconduct.

The forgery pertained primarily to invoices of an engineering firm, which actually did fulfill its contractual obligations to construct the sets for Livent's productions. In essence, Livent reported expenses incurred to prepare for the production of its musicals on Broadway as if they were long-lived assets. These false additions to long-lived assets were then depreciated and a fraction of their total cost reported on the income statement as depreciation expense, instead of their full cost. In combination, the accounting statements were materially misleading and overstated the financial health of Livent. At present, over $233 million in claims have been filed against Livent, which in turn has sued Gottlieb, Drabinsky, and Deloitte & Touche for $550 million.

SELF-STUDY **QUIZ 9-2**

A building that originally cost $400,000 has been used over the past 10 years and needs continuous maintenance and repairs. For each of the following expenditures, indicate whether it should be expensed in the current period or capitalized as part of the cost of the asset.

	EXPENSE OR CAPITALIZE?
1. Replacing electrical wiring throughout the building.	_____
2. Repairs to the front door of the building.	_____
3. Annual cleaning of the filters on the building's air conditioning system.	_____
4. Significant repairs due to damage from an unusual and infrequent flood.	_____

After you complete your answers, go online for the solutions.

▦ connect™

USE, IMPAIRMENT, AND DISPOSAL OF PLANT AND EQUIPMENT

Depreciation Concepts

All long-lived assets, such as aircraft purchased by WestJet, have limited useful lives, except land. Long-lived assets represent the prepaid cost of a bundle of future services or benefits. A portion of an asset's acquisition cost must be allocated as an expense to the periods in which revenue is earned as a result of its use. WestJet earns revenue when it provides air travel service and incurs an expense when using its aircraft to generate the revenue.

The term used to identify and allocate the acquisition cost of using buildings and equipment that generate revenue over time is *depreciation*. The term *depletion* most often refers to the allocation of the acquisition cost of natural resources, while the term *amortization* is often used in reference to the allocation of the acquisition cost of intangible assets.

> Depreciation: The process of *allocating the acquisition cost* of property, plant, and equipment other than land over their productive lives by using a systematic and rational method. Depreciation is sometimes referred to as amortization.

Students are often confused about the concept of depreciation as accountants define it. In accounting, depreciation is a process of *cost allocation*, not a process of determining an asset's current market value or worth. Depreciation is not a cash expense but a distribution of the acquisition cost over the same time period in which the asset is expected to generate revenue. When an asset is depreciated, the amount remaining on the statement of financial position *does not represent its current market value*. Under the cost principle, the cost of a long-lived asset is recorded at its current market value

LO3

Apply various depreciation methods as assets are held and used over time.

DEPRECIATION is the process of allocating the acquisition cost of property, plant, and equipment (but not land) over their useful lives by using a systematic and rational method.

only on the acquisition date. At subsequent dates, the undepreciated cost is not measured on a market value basis. WestJet reported in its income statement a depreciation and amortization expense of $141,303,000 for the year 2009. The journal entry and transaction effects, including the contra-asset account (XA) follow:

| Depreciation expense (E) .... | 141,303,000 | |
| Accumulated depreciation (XA) .... | | 141,303,000 |

Assets	=	Liabilities	+	Shareholders' Equity
Accumulated depreciation (XA) −141,303,000				Depreciation expense (E) −141,303,000

The periodic depreciation expenses throughout the asset's useful life are accumulated in the contra-asset account, accumulated depreciation, and deducted from the related asset's acquisition cost. The acquisition cost minus accumulated depreciation and any write downs in asset value is called *carrying amount* or *book value* and appears on the statement of financial position. In addition, companies like WestJet disclose information about the long-lived assets they own or control, and the related accumulated depreciation, in a note to the financial statements.

CARRYING AMOUNT (OR BOOK VALUE) is the acquisition cost of an asset less accumulated depreciation and any write downs in asset value.

REAL WORLD EXCERPT

Westjet Airlines

ANNUAL REPORT

NOTES TO CONSOLIDATED FINANCIAL STATEMENTS

5. Property and Equipment

2009	Cost	Accumulated Depreciation	Net Book Value
Aircraft	$2,456,988	$513,521	$1,943,467
Ground property and equipment	120,031	52,804	67,227
Spare engines and parts	100,567	24,360	76,207
Buildings	136,228	9,843	126,385
Leasehold improvements	9,910	2,877	7,033
Assets under capital leases	5,882	2,210	3,672
	2,829,606	605,615	2,223,991
Deposits on aircraft	83,489	—	83,489
Assets under development	86	—	86
	$2,913,181	$605,615	$2,307,566

Source: WestJet Annual Report 2009.

FINANCIAL ANALYSIS

CARRYING AMOUNT AS AN APPROXIMATION OF REMAINING LIFE

Some analysts compare the carrying amount of assets to their original cost as an approximation of their remaining life. If the carrying amount of an asset is 100 percent of its cost, it is a new asset; if the carrying amount is 25 percent of its cost, the asset has about 25 percent of its estimated life remaining. In WestJet's case, the carrying amount of its aircraft is 79 percent of the original cost. This compares with 72 percent for Southwest Airlines and 84 percent for Ryanair. This comparison suggests that the aircraft used by WestJet have more estimated life remaining than those of Southwest Airlines.

Based on the information WestJet provided in its Note 1 (k) and Note 5, the carrying amount can be used to estimate the asset's remaining useful life. You simply calculate the ratio of

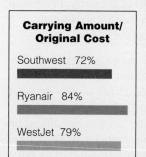

Carrying Amount/ Original Cost

Southwest 72%

Ryanair 84%

WestJet 79%

carrying amount to acquisition cost, and multiply this by the asset's estimated useful life. Consider, for example, WestJet's spare engines and parts.

$$\frac{\text{Carrying amount}}{\text{Acquisition cost}} \times \text{Estimated useful life} = \frac{\$76,207,000}{\$100,567} \times 20 = 15.2 \text{ years}$$

The useful life of WestJet's important assets can be analyzed in this manner and comparisons can be made to other companies in the industry. This is, however, only a rough approximation because the carrying amount of long-lived assets depends on the estimates of useful life and residual value, as well as the specific depreciation method used.

The calculation of depreciation expense requires three amounts for each depreciable asset:

1. Acquisition cost.
2. *Estimated* useful life to the company.
3. *Estimated* residual (or salvage) value at the end of the asset's useful life to the company.

Two of these three amounts are estimates. Therefore, ***depreciation expense is an estimate***.

Estimated useful life represents management's estimate of the asset's useful *economic life* to the company rather than of its total economic life to all potential users. The asset's expected physical life is often longer than the company intends to use the asset. Economic life may be expressed in terms of years or units of capacity, such as the number of hours a machine is expected to operate or units it can produce. WestJet's aircraft is expected to fly between 30,000 and 50,000 flights whereas its buildings are expected to last for 40 years. The subsequent owner of the aircraft would use an estimated useful life based on its own policies.

The determination of estimated useful life of a long-lived asset must conform to the *continuity assumption*. This assumption holds that the business will continue to pursue its commercial objectives and will not liquidate in the foreseeable future. In Note 1 to its financial statements, WestJet, as do other companies, discloses the useful lives of its long-lived assets and the methods used to depreciate them. We will use the same estimates in our illustrations, where appropriate.

ESTIMATED USEFUL LIFE is the expected service life of an asset to the present owner.

REAL WORLD EXCERPT

Westjet Airlines

ANNUAL REPORT

NOTES TO CONSOLIDATED FINANCIAL STATEMENTS

1. Summary of Significant Accounting Policies

(k) Property and equipment:

Property and equipment is stated at cost and depreciated to its estimated residual value. Assets under capital lease are initially recorded at the present value of minimum lease payments at the inception of the lease.

Asset Class	Basis	Rate
Aircraft, net of estimated residual value	Cycles[3]	Cycles flown
Live satellite television included in aircraft	Straight-line	10 years/lease term
Ground property and equipment	Straight-line	3 to 25 years
Spare engines and parts, net of estimated residual value	Straight-line	20 years
Buildings	Straight-line	40 years
Leasehold improvements	Straight-line	Term of lease
Assets under capital lease	Straight-line	Term of lease

Aircraft are amortized over a range of 30,000 to 50,000 cycles. Estimated residual values of the Corporation's aircraft range between $4,000,000 and $6,000,000.

Source: WestJet Annual Report 2009.

---

[3]WestJet defines a cycle as one flight, counted by the aircraft leaving the ground and landing.

RESIDUAL (OR SALVAGE) VALUE is the estimated amount to be recovered, less disposal costs, at the end of the estimated useful life of an asset.

Residual (or salvage) value represents management's estimate of the amount the company expects to recover upon disposal of the asset at the end of its estimated useful life. The residual value may be the estimated value of the asset if sold to another user. Salvage or scrap value is usually negligible but is also a residual value.

Residual value is the estimated amount to be recovered, less any estimated costs of dismantling, disposal, and sale. In many cases, disposal costs may approximately equal the gross residual value. Therefore, many depreciable assets are assumed to have no residual value. In the case of aircraft owned by WestJet, the company uses third-party industry market valuations, recommendations from Boeing, and actual experience to estimate useful life and expected residual value. WestJet explains that revisions will arise from changes to both market prices of used aircraft and utilization of the aircraft. In contrast, Delta Air Lines has increased the estimated useful life and changed the residual value of its much older fleet four times in the last 30 years.

FINANCIAL
ANALYSIS

DIFFERENCES IN ESTIMATED LIVES WITHIN A SINGLE INDUSTRY

Notes to actual financial statements of companies in the airline industry reveal the following estimates for lives of flight equipment:

Company	Estimated Life (in years)	Residual Value
Delta Air Lines	21–30	5–10 percent of cost
Singapore Airlines	15	15 percent of cost
JetBlue Airways	25	20 percent of cost
Southwest Airlines	23–25	10–15 percent of cost

The differences in estimated lives may be attributable to a number of factors, such as type of aircraft used by each company, equipment replacement plans, differences in operations, and the degree of management prudence in setting its accounting policies. In addition, given the same type of aircraft, companies that plan to use the equipment over fewer years may estimate higher residual values than do companies that plan to use the equipment longer. For example, Singapore Airlines uses a residual value of 15 percent of cost over a relatively short useful life of 15 years, as compared with a minimum of 5 percent for Delta Air Lines over a useful life that could extend to 30 years.

Differences in estimated lives and residual values of assets used by specific companies can have a significant impact on the comparison of the profitability of the companies. Analysts must be certain that they identify the causes for the differences in depreciable lives.

Alternative Depreciation Methods

Accountants agree that there is no single, best method of depreciation, because the cost of using long-lived assets to generate revenue differs significantly among companies. Thus, managers may choose from different acceptable depreciation methods. Their decision should reflect the anticipated reduction in future cash flow as a result of the wear and tear from using the asset over time. Once selected, the depreciation method should be applied consistently over time to enhance comparability of financial information to users. We will discuss the three most common depreciation methods:

1. Straight-line
2. Units-of-production
3. Declining (or diminishing) balance

WESTJET AIRLINES		
Acquisition cost of aircraft, purchased on January 1, 2011		$78,000,000
Estimated useful life (in years)		20
Estimated residual value		$6,000,000
Estimated life in flights		40,000 flights
Actual flights in	Year: 2011 2,100 flights	
	Year: 2012 1,950 flights	
	Year: 2013 2,050 flights	

Exhibit **9.2**

Illustrative Data for Computing Depreciation under Alternative Methods

The facts shown in Exhibit 9.2 will be used to illustrate each of the three methods of calculating depreciation expense for one 737-800 aircraft purchased on January 1, 2011.[4]

Straight-Line Method More companies, including WestJet, use straight-line depreciation in their financial statements than all other methods combined. Under the straight-line method, an equal portion of an asset's depreciable cost is allocated to each accounting period over its estimated useful life. The formula to estimate annual depreciation expense follows:

STRAIGHT-LINE DEPRECIATION is the method that allocates the cost of an asset in equal periodic amounts over its useful life.

Straight-Line Formula

Depreciable Cost | Straight-Line Rate

(Cost − Residual Value) × 1/Useful Life = Depreciation Expense

In this formula, "cost minus residual value" is the amount to be depreciated, also called *depreciable cost*. The term "1 ÷ useful life" is the straight-line rate. Using the data provided in Exhibit 9.2, the depreciation expense is computed as follows:

$$(\$78,000,000 - \$6,000,000) \times 1/20 = \$3,600,000$$

Amount for the adjusting entry: reported on the Income Statement (closed at year-end)

Balance in the contra-asset account after the adjusting entry

Cost less accumulated depreciation: reported on the Statement of Financial Position

Straight-Line Method

Year	Computation (Cost − Residual value) × 1/Useful Life	Depreciation Expense	Accumulated Depreciation	Carrying Amount
At acquisition:				
2011	($78,000,000 − $6,000,000) × 1/20	$ 3,600,000	$ 3,600,000	74,400,000
2012	($78,000,000 − $6,000,000) × 1/20	3,600,000	7,200,000	70,800,000
2013	($78,000,000 − $6,000,000) × 1/20	3,600,000	10,800,000	67,200,000
	Total	$10,800,000		

---

[4]Most of the examples that we discuss in this chapter assume that assets were acquired on the first day of the year and depreciated for the entire year. In practice, assets are purchased at various times during the year. Most companies adopt a policy to cover partial-year depreciation, such as "to the nearest full month" or "half year in the year of acquisition."

Notice that

- Depreciation expense is a constant amount for each year.
- Accumulated depreciation increases by an equal amount each year.
- Carrying amount decreases by the same amount each year until it equals the estimated residual value.

This is the reason for the name ***straight-line method***. Notice, too, that the adjusting entry can be prepared from this schedule, and the effects on the income statement and ending balance on the statement of financial position are known. WestJet uses the straight-line method for all of its long-lived assets, except for aircraft. Most companies in the airline industry use the straight-line method. Depreciation expense, accumulated depreciation, and carrying amount decrease systematically from period to period at a constant rate each year. The depreciation expense is said to be a *fixed expense* because it is constant each year, irrespective of the actual air miles flown by the aircraft.

UNITS-OF-PRODUCTION DEPRECIATION is a method to allocate the cost of an asset over its useful life based on the relation of its periodic output to its total estimated output.

Units-of-Production (Activity) Method   Assume WestJet uses the units-of-production depreciation method to relate depreciable cost to the total estimated productive output. The formula to estimate annual depreciation expense under this method follows:

Units-of-Production Formula

Depreciation rate per unit

$$\overbrace{\frac{(\text{Cost} - \text{Residual Value})}{\text{Estimated Total Production}}} \times \frac{\text{Actual}}{\text{Production}} = \text{Depreciation Expense}$$

Dividing the depreciable amount by the estimated total production yields the depreciation rate per unit of production (or activity), which is then multiplied by the actual annual production (or activity) to determine depreciation expense. Using the information in Exhibit 9.2, the computation of the depreciation rate per unit follows:

$$\frac{\$78,000,000 - \$6,000,000}{40,000 \text{ flights}} = \$1,800 \text{ per flight}$$

For every flight, WestJet would record depreciation expense of $1,800. The depreciation schedule for the years 2009, 2010, and 2011 under the units-of-production method follows:

Units-of-Production Method				
Year	Computations	Depreciation Expense	Accumulated Depreciation	Carrying Amount
At acquisition				$78,000,000
2011	$1,800 × 2,100 flights	$ 3,780,000	$ 3,780,000	74,220,000
2012	1,800 × 1,950 flights	3,510,000	7,290,000	70,710,000
2013	1,800 × 2,050 flights	3,690,000	10,980,000	67,020,000
	Total	$10,980,000		

When the units-of-production method is used, depreciation expense is said to be a *variable expense* because it varies directly with production or use. The carrying amount and the amount of accumulated amortization will also fluctuate from year to year.

You might wonder what happens if the total estimated productive output differs from actual output. Remember that the estimate is management's best guess of total output. If any difference occurs at the end of the asset's life, the final adjusting entry to depreciation expense should be for the amount needed to bring the asset's carrying amount to equal the asset's estimated residual value.

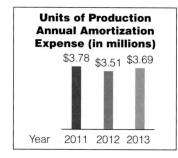

Units of Production Annual Amortization Expense (in millions)

$3.78 $3.51 $3.69

Year   2011 2012 2013

The units-of-production method is based on an estimate of an asset's total productive capacity or output that is difficult to determine.

Declining-Balance Method   If the asset is considered to be more efficient or productive in its earliest years, with a levelling off in later years, managers might choose the declining-balance depreciation method to reflect a sharper reduction in the economic benefits (cash flow) expected to be derived from the asset in the earlier rather than later years. This is called *accelerated depreciation*. Special equipment acquired to produce a patented drug is an example. The drug faces little or no competition in its early years. Therefore, the producer can demand a higher price and derive more benefits from the equipment. In later years, as products mimicking the benefits of the drug are developed and brought to market, the asset's economic benefits will drop because of competition. Finally, when the drug is no longer protected by the patent, manufacturers of generic products can flood the market at very low prices. While the therapeutic benefits of the drug will not change, the economic benefits to the pharmaceutical company will be relatively low. Hence, a declining-balance method is used to better reflect the decline of economic benefits over time.

The relationship between accelerated depreciation expense, repair expense, and the total expense of using the asset is shown in Exhibit 9.3. Although accelerated methods are seldom used for financial reporting purposes, the method that is used more frequently than others is the declining-balance method.

Declining-balance depreciation is based on multiplying the asset's carrying amount by a fixed rate that exceeds the straight-line (SL) rate. The rate is often double (two times) the SL rate and is called the ***double-declining-balance rate***. For example, if the estimated useful life of an asset is 10 years and the SL rate is 10 percent (1 ÷ 10), then the declining-balance rate is 20 percent (2 × the SL rate of 10 percent). Other typical acceleration rates are 1.5 times and 1.75 times. The double-declining-balance (DDB) rate is adopted most frequently by companies utilizing the accelerated method, and will be used in our illustration.

To calculate depreciation expense under the double-declining-balance method, the carrying amount of the asset is multiplied by the DDB rate as follows:

> **DECLINING-BALANCE DEPRECIATION** is the method that allocates the cost of an asset over its useful life based on a multiple of the straight-line rate (often two times).

Double-Declining-Balance Formula

Carrying Amount	**Declining-Balance Rate**	

(Cost − Accumulated Depreciation) × 2/Useful Life = Depreciation Expense

---

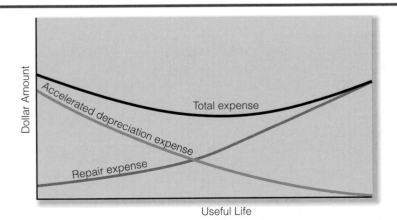

Exhibit **9.3**

The Relationship among Depreciation Expense, Repair Expense, and Total Expense

There are two important differences between this method and the others described previously:

- Notice that accumulated depreciation, not residual value, is included in the formula. Since accumulated depreciation increases each year, carrying amount (cost − accumulated depreciation) decreases. The DDB rate is applied to a lower carrying amount each year, resulting in a decline in depreciation expense over time.

- An asset's carrying amount cannot be depreciated below residual value. Therefore, if the annual computation reduces carrying amount below residual value, a lower amount of depreciation expense must be recorded so that carrying amount equals residual value. No additional depreciation expense is computed in subsequent years.

Computation of DDB depreciation expense is illustrated using the data given in Exhibit 9.2 (amounts in thousands of dollars):

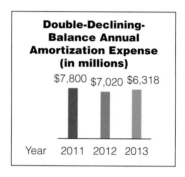

Double-Declining- Balance Annual Amortization Expense (in millions)

$7,800 $7,020 $6,318

Year   2011 2012 2013

	Double-Declining-Balance Method			
Year	Computation (Cost − Residual Value) × 1/Useful Life	Depreciation Expense	Accumulated Depreciation	Carrying Amount
At acquisition:				$78,000,000
2011	($78,000,000 − $0) × 2/20	$ 7,800,000	$ 7,800,000	70,200,000
2012	($78,000,000 − $7,800,000) × 2/20	7,020,000	14,820,000	63,180,000
2013	($78,000,000 − $14,820,000) × 2/20	6,318,000	21,138,000	56,862,000
	Total	$21,138,000		

The calculated depreciation expense for this asset differs depending upon the depreciation method used. Using the straight-line method, the annual expense is $3,600,000 each year of the aircraft's 20-year useful life. Using the units-of-production method, annual depreciation expense varies each year from a low of $3,510,000 in 2012 to a high of $3,780,000 in 2011. Finally, using the double-declining-balance method, depreciation expense declines every year from $7,800,000 in 2011 to $6,318,000 in 2013. This, in part, explains why an analyst must be careful when using the carrying amount to estimate the remaining useful life of an asset. Using our example, we obtain different estimates for the remaining useful life for the same aircraft after three years, depending on the depreciation method used:

Depreciation Method	Estimated Remaining Useful Life
Straight-line	($67,200,000/$78,000,000) × 20 = 17.23 years or approximately 17 years
Units-of-production	($67,020,000/$78,000,000) × 20 = 17.18 years or approximately 17 years
Double-declining-balance	($56,862,000/$78,000,000) × 20 = 14.58 years or approximately 15 years

This example illustrates why care must be taken to read the notes to the financial statements of any company and identify the accounting policies it uses before comparing its financial results to those of other companies.

The depreciation method that is selected by management informs external users of management's expectation of the pattern of economic benefits that the company will derive from the asset over time. Companies will use different depreciation methods for different types of assets. For example, WestJet uses the units-of-production method to depreciate its aircraft rather than the straight-line method. For a company such as

Sony that operates in an industry where electronic systems and equipment rapidly become obsolete, managers have chosen the declining-balance method for this type of equipment:

REAL WORLD EXCERPT

Sony

ANNUAL REPORT

2. Summary of significant accounting policies:

Property, plant, and equipment and depreciation

Property, plant, and equipment are stated at cost. Depreciation of property, plant, and equipment is primarily computed on the declining-balance method for Sony Corporation and Japanese subsidiaries except for certain semiconductor manufacturing facilities and buildings whose depreciation is computed on the straight-line method over the estimated useful lives of the assets.... Useful lives for depreciation range from 2 to 60 years for buildings and from one to 25 years for machinery and equipment.

Source: Sony Annual Report 2009.

As this note indicates, companies may use different depreciation methods for different classes of assets. Under the consistency principle, they are expected to apply the same methods to those assets over time.

In the previous illustration, we assumed that the aircraft was purchased at the beginning of the year. In reality, however, companies purchase assets at any date during the year, which complicates the computation of depreciation expense for the first year of acquisition. For practical purposes, acquisitions made during the year are depreciated in a convenient manner during the asset's first year of operation. Depreciation expense can be computed for the number of months the asset is actually in use, or it can be computed for half a year using the half-year convention.

For example, if WestJet acquired the aircraft on September 1, 2011, instead of April 1, 2011, the annual straight-line depreciation expense could be pro-rated by determining the monthly depreciation expense and multiplying the monthly depreciation by the number of months WestJet flew this aircraft during 2011 (seven months in this case):

$$\text{Depreciation expense} = (\$3,600,000 \div 12) \times 7 \text{ months} = \$2,100,000$$

Alternatively, companies that acquire many long-lived assets during the year may use the half-year rule, which implies that similar long-lived assets, such as office equipment, that are acquired at different dates throughout the year can be assumed to have been purchased around the middle of the year. Thus, all the office equipment acquired during the fiscal year is depreciated for half a year at the end of the year of acquisition. This practical rule is acceptable as long as the amount of depreciation expense for the year is not materially misstated.

In Summary The following table summarizes the three depreciation methods and computations for each method. Exhibit 9.4 shows graphically the differences in depreciation expense over time for each method.

Method	Computation	Depreciation Expense
Straight-line	(Cost − Residual value) × 1/Useful life	Equal amounts each year
Units-of-production	(Cost − Residual value)/Estimated total production × Annual production	Varying amounts based on production level
Double-declining-balance	(Cost − Accumulated depreciation) × 2/Useful life	Declining amounts over time

Exhibit **9.4**

Differences in Depreciation
Methods over Time

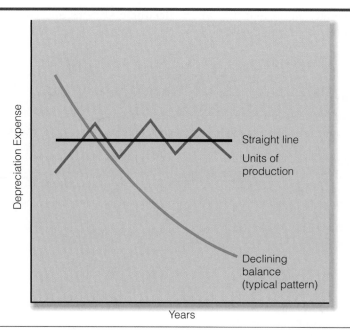

FINANCIAL
ANALYSIS

IMPACT OF ALTERNATIVE DEPRECIATION METHODS

Assume that you are analyzing two companies that are identical except that one uses accelerated depreciation and the other uses the straight-line method. Which company would you expect to report higher profit? Actually, the question is tricky; you cannot say for certain which company's profit would be higher.

The accelerated methods report higher depreciation expense and, therefore, lower profit during the early years of the life of an asset. In later years, this effect reverses. Therefore, companies that use accelerated amortization report lower amortization expense and higher profit during the later years of an asset's life compared to those using the straight-line method. The graph shows the pattern of depreciation over the life of an asset for the straight-line and declining-balance methods discussed in this chapter. When the curve for the accelerated method falls below the curve for the straight-line method, the accelerated method produces a higher profit than the straight-line method. The total depreciation of the asset over its useful life should be the same for each method.

Users of financial statements must understand the impact of alternative depreciation methods over time. What is important is that the method chosen be consistent with the decline in the ability of the asset to generate economic benefits in the future. Differences in depreciation methods rather than real economic differences can cause significant variations in reported profit. For example, Norbord Inc., a Canadian manufacturer of a specific type of wood substitute used in housing construction, changed its depreciation method from straight-line to units-of-production for its production assets, because this latter method is more appropriate in periods of fluctuating production levels. This change reduced depreciation expense by $4 million in the second quarter of 2009 and a further $6 million in the third quarter of that year.

Changes in Depreciation Estimates

Depreciation is based on two estimates—useful life and residual value. These estimates are made at the time a depreciable asset is acquired. As experience with the asset accumulates, one or both of these initial estimates may have to be revised to more faithfully represent the economic effect of using the asset in operations. In addition, extraordinary repairs and betterments may be added to the original acquisition cost at some time during the asset's use. When it is clear that either estimate should be revised to a material degree or the asset's cost has been changed, the undepreciated asset balance (less any residual value at that date) should be apportioned over the remaining estimated life from the current year into the future. This is called a *change in estimate*.

To compute the new depreciation expense because of a change in estimate for any of the depreciation methods described in this chapter, substitute the carrying amount for the original acquisition cost, the new residual value for the original amount, and the estimated remaining life in place of the original estimated life. As an illustration, the computation using the straight-line method is as follows.

Assume the following for an aircraft owned by WestJet:

Cost of aircraft when acquired	$78,000,000
Estimated useful life	20 years
Estimated residual value	$6,000,000
Accumulated depreciation through year 5	
($78,000,000 − $6,000,000) × 1/20 = $3,600,000 per year	
× 5 years	
= $18,000,000	

Shortly after the start of year 6, WestJet changed the initial estimated life to 25 years and lowered the estimated residual value to $4,000,000. At the end of year 6, the computation of the new amount for depreciation expense is as follows:

Acquisition cost	$78,000,000
Less: Accumulated depreciation (years 1–5)	18,000,000
Carrying amount	$60,000,000
Less: New residual value	4,000,000
New depreciable amount	$56,000,000
Annual depreciation based on remaining life:	
$56,000,000 ÷ 20 years (25 − 5 years) =	$ 2,800,000 per year

Companies may also change depreciation methods (e.g., from declining-balance to straight-line), although such change requires significantly more disclosure since the consistency principle is violated. Changes in accounting estimates and depreciation methods should be made only when the new estimate or accounting method "better measures" the periodic profit of the business.

SELF-STUDY **QUIZ 9-4**

Assume that WestJet Airlines owned a service truck that originally cost $100,000. When purchased, the truck had an estimated useful life of 10 years, with no residual value. After operating the truck for five years, WestJet determined that the remaining life was only two more years. Based on this change in estimate, what amount of annual depreciation should be recorded over the remaining life of the asset? WestJet uses the straight-line method.

▦ connect

After you complete your answers, go online for the solutions.

Managers' Selection among Accounting Alternatives

Financial Reporting   For financial reporting purposes, corporate managers must select the depreciation method that provides the best matching of revenues and expenses for any given asset. If the asset is expected to provide benefits evenly over time, then the straight-line method is preferred. Managers also find this method easy to use and explain. If no other method is more systematic or rational, then the straight-line method is selected. Also, during the early years of an asset's life, the straight-line method reports higher profit than the accelerated methods do. For these reasons, the straight-line method is by far the most common.

On the other hand, certain assets produce more revenue in their early lives because they are more efficient then than in later years. In this case, managers select an accelerated method to allocate cost. In addition, as the asset ages, repair costs are likely to increase. Thus, the total of the depreciation expense and repair expense for any given period is likely to provide a nearly constant amount of expenses each period.

Tax Reporting   WestJet Airlines, like most public companies, must prepare two sets of reports. One set is prepared under IFRS for reporting to shareholders. The other set is prepared to determine the company's tax obligation and is computed in conformity with the tax rules enacted by the tax authorities of the country where the company has been legally established. Canadian corporations must compute their tax obligations in accordance with the *Income Tax Act*. The reason that the two sets of rules are different is simple: the objectives of financial reporting and tax reporting differ.

Financial Reporting (IFRS)	Tax Reporting
The primary objective of financial reporting is to provide economic information about a business that is useful in projecting the future cash flows of that business. Financial accounting rules follow international financial reporting standards.	The objective of the *Income Tax Act* is to raise sufficient revenues to pay for the expenditures of the federal government, with many provisions designed to encourage certain behaviours that are thought to benefit society (e.g., contributions to charities are tax-deductible to encourage people to support worthy programs).

It is easy to understand why two sets of accounting reports are permitted, but perhaps the more interesting aspect concerns the reason why managers incur the extra cost of preparing two sets of reports. In some cases, differences between the *Income Tax Act* and IFRS leave the manager no choice but to have separate reports. In other cases, the explanation is an economic one, called the ***least and the latest rule***. In general, taxpayers want to pay the lowest amount of tax that is legally permitted at the latest possible date. If you had the choice of paying $100,000 to the federal government at the end of this year or at the end of next year, you would choose the end of next year. By doing so, you would be able to invest the money for an extra year and earn a return on the investment.

By complying with the requirements of the *Income Tax Act*, corporations can defer (delay) paying millions and sometimes billions of dollars in taxes. The following companies, which prepare their financial statements in compliance with IFRS, reported significant gross deferred tax obligations in a recent year. The deferral of payment of income tax to future years was in large part due to differences between the depreciation methods used for financial reporting versus tax reporting:

Company	Deferred Tax Liabilities Due to Applying Different Depreciation Methods
WestJet Airlines	$279 million
Cadbury	$181 million
Royal Dutch Shell	$12,518 million

The depreciation methods discussed in the previous section are not acceptable for federal income tax reporting. One objective of domestic tax law is to provide an incentive for existing Canadian companies to invest in modern property, plant, and equipment in order to retain their global competitiveness. Governments around the world also compete to attract production facilities by using their tax laws to support their domestic economic growth. More production usually means more employment for Canadians, and economic growth.

Corporations that are subject to taxation in Canada must apply capital cost allowance (CCA) to tangible assets, as determined by the schedules provided by the tax authorities. The CCA schedules must be used to calculate the maximum annual expense used in computing taxable income according to the tax rules and regulations. These schedules classify capital assets into different classes and stipulate the maximum CCA rate (a declining-balance rate) for each class. For example, aircraft is currently Class 9, with a CCA rate of 25 percent per year.

CCA does not attempt to match the cost of an asset with the revenue it produces over its useful life, in conformity with the matching process. Instead, CCA provides for accelerated depreciation of an asset over a period that is usually much shorter than the asset's estimated useful life. Because CCA is based on an accelerated method, the high expense reported under CCA reduces a corporation's taxable profit more in the early years of a long-lived asset than in later years.

TWO SETS OF REPORTS

A QUESTION
OF ACCOUNTABILITY

When they first learn that companies prepare two sets of reports, some people question the ethics or the legality of the practice. In reality, *it is both legal and ethical to prepare separate reports for tax and financial reporting purposes. However, these records must reflect the same transactions.* Understating revenues or overstating expenses on a tax return can result in financial penalties and/or imprisonment. Accountants who aid tax evaders can also be fined or imprisoned, and lose their professional licences.

DEPRECIATION METHODS IN OTHER COUNTRIES

INTERNATIONAL
PERSPECTIVE

With the severe and extreme economic contraction in 2008 and 2009, many countries, worldwide, relaxed either their accounting or tax regulations in an effort to stimulate their domestic economies. Austria, for example, has permitted accelerated depreciation up to 30 percent of either acquisition or construction costs for property, plant, and equipment, such as aircraft, for assets acquired in 2009 and 2010. The Netherlands has proposed a similar change with acceleration in the year of acquisition of up to 50 percent, while the United States enacted the *American Recovery and Reinvestment Act of 2009*, extending a 50 percent acceleration provision to include properties placed into service in 2009 as well as those already available for 2008.

While accounting methods have remain unchanged, tax regulations in some countries have changed to reduce the cash burden of tax payments on capital intensive industries and stimulate investment in new long-lived assets. The economic goal is to sustain economic growth and retain jobs. When users of financial statements for airlines compare reported profit for companies operating in these three countries, knowing the income tax regimes are comparable is as important as knowing the accounting methods are comparable as well.

Measuring Asset Impairment

Canadian corporations are required to review the carrying amount of their tangible and intangible assets for possible impairment. Assets can have different values that are used for different purposes. Historical acquisition costs are essential for verifiability of past transactions. These costs are then adjusted for systematic depreciation over their useful lives. However, adjusted historical costs are not relevant for investment decisions that rely on expectations of future cash flows. Consequently, investors and creditors may be interested in the asset's *fair value*, which reflects the amount at which an asset can be bought or sold between two knowledgeable, willing parties in an arm's length transaction. On the other hand, companies usually acquire long-lived assets for use in their production processes, and not for resale to others. Therefore, a long-lived asset has *value in use*, which is measured as the present value (or current cash equivalent) of future cash flows expected to be derived from use of the asset over time.

Subsequent to acquisition, the economic benefits or future cash flows associated with assets do change for a variety of reasons. Adverse changes to future benefits may be triggered, for example, by reduced market price for the asset, contraction in the economy, ongoing evidence of operating cash flow losses, and technological obsolescence. Consequently, assets should then be assessed for possible impairment.

Impairment occurs when events or changed circumstances cause the carrying amount of these assets to exceed their recoverable amount, which is the higher of its value in use or its fair value less costs to sell.

If Carrying amount > Recoverable amount, then the asset is impaired

A simple illustration will help in understanding how this concept is applied. Assume that WestJet had an old aircraft that is still in good working condition. This aircraft has a carrying amount of $15 million. Because of an economic downturn, its current market price dropped to $13 million, and the company will incur $0.5 million in costs to sell this aircraft to an interested buyer. At the same time, the value in use of the aircraft or current cash equivalent of future net cash flows expected to be derived from using it is $14 million. In this case, the test for impairment indicates that this aircraft is impaired by $1 million, which is determined as follows:

Fair value less costs to sell	$12.5 million
Value in use	14 million
Recoverable amount (= Value in use)	14 million
Carrying amount	15 million

Since the carrying amount exceeds the recoverable amount, the aircraft is impaired by $1 million, the difference between these two values. If the aircraft's value in use was greater than $15 million, then the aircraft is not impaired and there would be no need, in this case, to determine the aircraft's fair value less costs to sell.

Fair values can be determined based on quoted market prices. If there is no current market price, then fair values can be based on prices of similar assets for which a recent transaction occurred, on an arm's length appraisal value, or by using specific valuation techniques.

In the previous example, the recoverable amount was determined for one asset—an aircraft. Sometimes, however, an asset does not generate cash inflows that are largely independent from other assets or groups of assets. In this case, the asset would be grouped with other assets that would form a cash-generating unit. The recoverable amount would then be determined for the cash-generating unit as a whole instead of the individual assets to which they belong.

Although WestJet reported no impairment losses to its property, plant, and equipment, let us assume that a review of WestJet's aircraft indicated that an asset group of aircraft has a carrying amount of $132 million. The value in use of this asset group was estimated at $120 million, and fair value less costs to sell was estimated at $125 million by using published sources of market prices of used aircraft as well as third-party bids. These aircraft are therefore impaired because their recoverable amount, $125 million, is lower than their carrying amount. The following journal entry would be recorded:

Loss due to impairment of assets (SE)	7,000,000	
Aircraft (A)		7,000,000

Assets		=	Liabilities	+	Shareholders' Equity	
Aircraft	−7,000,000				Loss due to impairment	−7,000,000

An impairment loss recognized in a prior period can be reversed in the future if there has been a change in the estimates used to determine the asset's recoverable amount since the impairment loss was recognized. In this case, the increased carrying amount of the asset shall not exceed the carrying amount that would have been determined (net of depreciation) had no impairment loss been recognized for the asset in prior years.

Companies that recognize impairment losses or reversal of prior impairment losses are required to disclose in the notes to their financial statements specific details about each material impairment loss recognized or reversed during the period, either for an individual asset or for a cash-generating unit. The disclosures include the nature of the asset or the cash-generating unit, the events and circumstances that led to the recognition or reversal of the impairment loss, the amount of the impairment loss recognized or reversed, as well as the methods used to determine the recoverable amount.

For example, in the year 2007, Anglo American reported in great detail the sources of restructuring and impairment charges, including impairment of $434 million on specific reserves of diamonds relating to its two Canadian mines, Snap Lake and Victor. In 2008, Anglo American took an impairment loss of $1,131 million against several of its base and precious metal mining reserves.

US$ Million	Note	Before Special Items and Remeasurements 2008	Special Items and Remeasurements (Note 7) 2008	2008
Group revenue	2	26,311	–	26,311
Total operating costs		(18,330)	(1,131)	(19,461)
Operating profit from subsidiaries and joint ventures	2, 4	7,981	(1,131)	6,850

7. Special items and remeasurements continued

Following structural review of the Industrial Minerals business by management and as a result of trading conditions in the building industry, restructuring and impairment charges totalling $91 million have been recorded. The impairment brings the carrying value in line with fair value (less costs to sell).

Impairments have been recorded at Black Mountain and Lisheen resulting from a reduction in the near term zinc and lead prices. These charges were based on a value in use assessment of recoverable amount using a pre-tax, risk free discount rate which equated to a post tax rate of 6%.

Source: Anglo American Annual Report 2008.

The complex nature of testing for asset impairment is covered in advanced accounting courses.

Disposal of Property, Plant, and Equipment

LO⁵

Analyze the disposal of property, plant, and equipment.

In some cases, a business may *voluntarily* decide not to hold a long-lived asset for its entire life. The company may drop a product from its line and no longer need the equipment that was used to produce the product, or managers may want to replace a machine with a more efficient one. These disposals include sale, trade-in, or retirement. When WestJet disposes of an old aircraft, it may sell it to a cargo airline or regional airline. A business may also dispose of an asset *involuntarily* as a result of a casualty, such as a storm, fire, or accident.

Disposals of long-lived assets seldom occur on the last day of the accounting period. Therefore, depreciation must be updated to the date of disposal. The disposal of a depreciable asset usually requires two entries:

1. An adjusting entry to update the depreciation expense and accumulated depreciation accounts.

2. An entry to record the disposal. The cost of the asset and any accumulated depreciation at the date of disposal must be removed from the accounts. The difference between any resources received on disposal of an asset and its carrying amount at the date of disposal is a gain or loss on disposal of the asset. This gain (or loss) is revenue (or expense) from "peripheral or incidental" activities rather than from normal operations. Gains and losses from disposals are usually shown separately on the income statement after profit from operations.

Assume that at the end of 2009 WestJet sold an aircraft that was no longer needed because of the elimination of service to a small city. The original cost of the aircraft was $2.6 million, with an estimated useful life of 35,000 flights and no residual value. The unrecorded amortization expense for the year was $71,000.[5] The aircraft

---

[5]Sale of the aircraft during the year requires updating the accumulated depreciation account to the date of sale by computing depreciation for a fraction of the year. The depreciation expense could be based on the number of months of depreciation or 50 percent of the annual depreciation if the company uses the half-year rule.

was sold for $1.9 million in cash and had accumulated amortization of $224,000 at the beginning of 2009. The loss on the sale of this aircraft is $405,000, calculated as follows:

Cash received		$1,900,000
Original cost	$2,600,000	
Less: Accumulated amortization	295,000	
Carrying amount		2,305,000
Loss on disposal		$ (405,000)

The entries and effects of the transaction on the date of the sale are as follows:

1. Amortization expense (E)	71,000	
Accumulated amortization—Aircraft (XA)		71,000
2. Cash (A)	1,900,000	
Accumulated amortization—Aircraft (XA)	295,000	
Loss on sale of asset (SE)	405,000	
Aircraft (A)		2,600,000

Assets		= Liabilities +	Shareholders' Equity	
1. Accumulated amortization	−71,000		1. Amortization expense	−71,000
2. Cash	+1,900,000		2. Loss on sale of asset	−405,000
Accumulated amortization	+ 295,000			
Aircraft	−2,600,000			

A gain or loss on disposal occurs because (1) depreciation expense is based on estimates that may differ from actual experience and (2) depreciation is based on original cost, not current market value. Because the gain or loss on disposal is not part of the continuing operating activities of a company, it usually is shown as a separate line item on the income statement. In 2009, for example, WestJet sold property and equipment and reported a net loss of $1,177,000 as a separate item on its income statement.

SELF-STUDY **QUIZ 9-5**

Now let us assume the same facts as above, except that the aircraft was sold for $2,500,000 cash. Prepare the two entries on the date of the sale.

1. Update the depreciation expense for the year.

2. Record the sale.

After you complete your answers, go online for the solutions.

connect

Companies may also trade in an old asset in exchange for a new asset and pay cash to cover the difference in the assets' values. Let us assume that an old vehicle, originally acquired at $20,000 with $16,000 of accumulated depreciation, has a fair market value of $3,000. The company exchanges this vehicle in partial payment for computer hardware, and pays an additional amount of $1,600 in cash. This trade-in transaction includes a non-cash consideration. Hence, the computer hardware is recorded at its fair market value, unless the fair market value of the old vehicle is more objectively determinable. Notice that the carrying amount of the vehicle is $4,000 and the total payment for the computer hardware is $4,600, which is equal to the fair market value of the vehicle plus the cash consideration. Assuming that the fair market value of the vehicle is more objectively determinable, the journal entry and effects of the trade-in transaction would be as follows:[6]

Computer hardware (A)	4,600	
Accumulated depreciation—Vehicle (XA)	16,000	
Loss on disposal of assets (SE)	1,000	
Vehicle (A)		20,000
Cash (A)		1,600

In certain situations, the company may dispose of an old, unusable asset if it cannot sell it to another party. The abandonment or retirement of an asset results in a loss that is equal to the asset's carrying amount. The journal entry to record the retirement of an asset is similar to the case of a sale or a trade-in, except that the cash account is not affected.

NATURAL RESOURCES AND INTANGIBLE ASSETS

Acquisition and Depletion of Natural Resources

You may be familiar with some large companies that develop raw materials and products from natural resources, such as oil, diamonds, gold, or iron ore (e.g., Royal Dutch Shell, Anglo American, Barrick Gold). These resources are often called *wasting assets* because they are depleted (i.e., physically used up). Companies that develop natural resources are critical to the economy because they produce such essential items as lumber for construction and fuel for heating and transportation. Such companies attract considerable public attention because of the significant effect they can have on the environment.

It may surprise you to know that, in Canada, natural resource companies do not own the land from which they extract oil or minerals. They acquire mineral rights from the government to explore, develop, and extract minerals from the land, but they do not own the land itself. When the rights to explore and develop natural resources are acquired, they are recorded in conformity with the *cost principle*. The land remains the common property of Canadians. This is one reason why concerned citizens often read financial statements from companies involved in mineral exploration, development, and extraction to determine the amount of money spent to protect and remediate any damage done to the environment.

Through exploration, the company estimates the value of the resources extracted and sold throughout their productive lives. The quantity of resources in the reserve is carefully surveyed by using sophisticated geological engineering methods. The initial reserve value is then allocated or depleted on a reasonable basis to match the expected revenue generated from the sale of the resources.[7]

Often these companies keep the reserve value separate from other property, plant, and equipment values incurred, because the companies may have to construct special roads and erect housing, buildings, and facilities in remote locations to extract the resources. When the site is put into production, these accumulated costs will be depreciated over the productive life of the site. Thus, natural resource companies amortize the acquisition costs of intangible mineral rights, deplete their reserve values, and depreciate exploration and development costs as well as self-constructed extraction facilities.

Royal Dutch Shell, for example, is a global company identified as an integrated petroleum explorer, developer, and refiner. The company depletes the acquisition cost

LO6

Apply measurement and reporting concepts for natural resources and intangible assets.

NATURAL RESOURCES are assets that occur in nature, such as mineral deposits, timber, oil, and gas.

DEPLETION is the systematic and rational allocation of the cost of a natural resource over the period of exploitation.

---

[6]The same analysis applies when a company exchanges an old asset for a new asset of the same kind, such as an old vehicle for a newer model.

[7]Consistent with the procedure for recording depreciation, an accumulated depletion account may be used. In practice, most companies credit the asset account directly for the periodic depletion. This procedure is also typically used for intangible assets, which are discussed in the next section.

of oil and gas reserves by using the units-of-production method. The company values the barrels of oil and cubic feet of natural gas in the reserves by using an estimate of proved, proved developed, and undeveloped reserves.

DEPRECIATION, DEPLETION AND AMORTISATION

[B] Depreciation, depletion and amortisation

Property, plant and equipment related to hydrocarbon production activities are depreciated on a unit-of-production basis over the proved developed reserves of the field concerned (proven and probable minable reserves in respect of oil sands extraction facilities), except in the case of assets whose useful life is shorter than the lifetime of the field, in which case the straight-line method is applied. Rights and concessions are depleted on the unit-of-production basis over the total proved reserves of the relevant area. Where individually insignificant, unproved properties may be grouped and amortised based on factors such as average concession term and past experience of recognising proved reserves. Other property, plant and equipment are generally depreciated on a straight-line basis.

Estimation of Oil and Gas Reserves

Proved oil and gas reserves are the estimated quantities of crude oil, natural gas and natural gas liquids that geological and engineering data demonstrate with reasonable certainty to be recoverable in future years from known reservoirs under existing economic and operating conditions, i.e., prices and costs as of the date the estimate is made. Proved developed reserves are reserves that can be expected to be recovered through existing wells with existing equipment and operating methods. Estimates of oil and gas reserves are inherently imprecise, require the application of judgement and are subject to future revision.

...

Proved reserves are estimated by reference to available reservoir and well information, including production and pressure trends for producing reservoirs and, in some cases, subject to definitional limits, to similar data from other producing reservoirs. Proved reserves estimates are attributed to future development projects only where there is a significant commitment to project funding and execution and for which applicable governmental and regulatory approvals have been secured or are reasonably certain to be secured. Furthermore, estimates of proved reserves only include volumes for which access to market is assured with reasonable certainty.

...

Assume that the depletion of one of Royal Dutch Shell's proved and proved developed oil reserves is $6,000,000 for the current year. The journal entry to record the depletion of reserves and the transaction effects are:

Oil inventory (A)...................................	6,000,000	
Oil reserves (A)................................		6,000,000
(or Accumulated depletion XA)		

Assets		=	Liabilities	+	Shareholders' Equity
Oil inventory	+6,000,000				
Oil reserves	−6,000,000				
(or Accumulated depletion)					

Note that the amount of the natural resource that is depleted is capitalized as inventory, not expensed. When the inventory is sold, the cost of sales is then included as an expense on the income statement.

A ***depletion rate*** is computed by dividing the total acquisition and development cost (less any estimated residual value, which is rare) by the estimated units that can be withdrawn economically from the resource. The depletion rate is multiplied each period by the actual number of units withdrawn during the accounting period. This procedure is the same as the units-of-production method of calculating depreciation.

When buildings and similar improvements are acquired for the development and exploitation of a natural resource, they should be recorded in separate asset accounts and depreciated—not depleted. Their estimated useful lives cannot be longer than the time needed to exploit the natural resource, unless they have a significant use after the source is depleted.

Acquisition and Depreciation of Intangible Assets

Intangible assets are increasingly important resources for organizations. An intangible asset has value because of certain rights and privileges conferred by law on its owner. An intangible asset has no material or physical substance. Examples include mineral rights to explore and develop land, landing rights for timeslots at airports, patents, trademarks, and licences. Most intangible assets usually are evidenced by a legal document. The growth in the importance of intangible assets has resulted from the tremendous expansion in computer information systems and Web technologies. In fact, many lawyers specialize in finding potential targets for patent infringement lawsuits for their clients.

Intangible assets are recorded *at historical cost only if they are purchased*. If an intangible asset is developed internally, the cost of development normally is recorded as an expense. Upon acquisition of intangible assets, managers determine whether the separate intangibles have definite or indefinite lives.

Definite Life: The cost of an intangible with a definite life is allocated on a straight-line basis each period over its useful life in a process called *amortization* that is similar to depreciation and depletion. However, most companies do not estimate a residual value for their intangible assets. Let us assume a company purchases a patent for $800,000 and intends to uses it for 20 years. The adjusting entry to record $40,000 in patent amortization expense ($800,000 ÷ 20 years) is as follows:

Patent amortization expense (E)	40,000	
Patent (A) (or Accumulated amortization XA)		40,000

Amortization expense is included on the income statement each period, and the intangible assets are reported at cost less accumulated amortization on the statement of financial position.

Indefinite Life: Intangible assets with indefinite lives are *not amortized*. Instead, these assets are to be tested at least annually for possible impairment, and the asset's carrying amount is written down (decreased) to its recoverable amount if impaired. The two-step process is similar to that used for other long-lived assets, including intangibles with definite lives.

Let us assume a company purchases for $120,000 cash a copyright that is expected to have an indefinite life. At the end of the current year, management determines that the fair value of the copyright is $90,000. The $30,000 loss ($120,000 carrying amount less $90,000 fair value) is recorded as follows:

Loss due to impairment (SE).	30,000	
Copyright (A)		30,000

Examples of Intangible Assets

Many Canadian companies disclose information about goodwill and other intangible assets in their annual reports. These intangibles include broadcast rights, publishing rights, trademarks, patents, licences, customer lists, franchises, and purchased research and development. For example, WestJet provided the following details on its intangible assets in the notes to its 2009 annual report:

REAL WORLD EXCERPT

Westjet Airlines

ANNUAL REPORT

NOTES TO CONSOLIDATED FINANCIAL STATEMENTS

6. Intangible assets

	Cost	Accumulated Depreciation	Net Book Value
2009			
Software	$40,392	$26,305	$14,087
2008			
Software	$41,835	$29,775	$12,060

All of the Corporation's software is acquired separately. Included in the totals for software is $4,085 [2008 – $1,591] for acquired software that is being developed and is not yet being amortized. For the year ended December 31, 2009, the Corporation recognized $5,601 [2008 – $4,675] of depreciation expense related to software.

Source: Westjet Annual Report 2009.

Goodwill By far, the most frequently reported intangible asset is **goodwill**. The term goodwill, as used by most business people, means the favourable reputation that a company has with its customers. Goodwill arises from factors such as customer confidence, reputation for good service and quality products, and financial standing. For example, WestJet's promise to deliver no-frills, friendly, reliable transportation combines factors that produce customer loyalty and repeated travel. From its first day of operations, a successful business continually builds its own goodwill through a combination of factors that cannot be sold separately. In this context, goodwill is said to be *internally generated* and is not reported as an asset.

The only way to report goodwill as an asset is to purchase another business. Often, the purchase price of a business exceeds the fair market value of all of the identifiable assets owned by the business minus all of the identifiable liabilities owed to others. Why would a company pay more to acquire a business as a whole than it would pay if it bought the assets individually? The answer is to obtain the acquired company's goodwill. It may be easy for the acquiring company to buy a fleet of aircraft, but a new business would not generate the same level of revenue flying the same routes as if it acquired WestJet's goodwill.

For accounting purposes, goodwill is defined as the difference between the purchase price of a company as a whole and the fair market value of its net assets (all identifiable assets minus all identifiable liabilities).

For accounting purposes, GOODWILL is the excess of the purchase price of a business over the market value of its identifiable assets and liabilities.

> Purchase price
> −Fair market value of identifiable assets and liabilities
> Goodwill to be reported

Both parties to the sale estimate an acceptable amount for the goodwill of the company and add it to the appraised fair value of the company's assets and liabilities. Then the sale price of the business is negotiated. The resulting amount of goodwill is recorded as an intangible asset only when it actually is purchased at a measurable cost, in conformity with the *cost principle*.

Companies that reported goodwill related to acquisitions prior to July 1, 2001, were required to amortize it over an estimated useful life (not to exceed 40 years) by using the straight-line method. IFRS standards consider goodwill to have an indefinite life, but any subsequent impairment in its value should be written down. This leads to the recognition of a loss that is reported as a separate item on the income statement in the year the impairment occurs.

A **TRADEMARK** is an exclusive legal right to use a special name, image, or slogan.

Trademarks   A trademark is a special name, image, or slogan identified with a product or a company. For example, banks such as the Bank of Montreal, auto manufacturers such as Toyota and General Motors, and fast-food restaurant chains such as Pizza Hut have familiar trademarks. Trademarks are protected by law when they are registered at the Canadian Intellectual Property Office of Industry Canada. The protection of a trademark provides the registered holder with exclusive rights to the trademark and can be renewed every 15 years throughout its life. Trademarks are often some of the most valuable assets that a company can own, but they are rarely seen on statements of financial position. The reason is simple: intangible assets are not recorded unless they are purchased. Companies often spend millions of dollars developing trademarks, but these expenditures are recorded as expenses and not capitalized. Purchased trademarks that have definite lives are amortized on a straight-line basis over their estimated useful life, up to a maximum period of 40 years.

A **PATENT** is granted by the federal government for an invention; it is an exclusive right given to the owner to use, manufacture, and sell the subject of the patent.

Patents   A patent is an exclusive right granted by the Canadian Intellectual Property Office of Industry Canada for a period of 20 years. It is typically granted to a person who invents a new product or discovers a new process. The patent enables the owner to use, manufacture, and sell both the subject of the patent and the patent itself. Without the protection of a patent, inventors likely would be unwilling to develop new products. The patent prevents a competitor from simply copying a new invention or discovery until the inventor has had a period of time to earn an economic return on the new product.

A patent that is *purchased* is recorded at cost. An ***internally developed*** patent is recorded at only its registration and legal cost because IFRS require the immediate expensing of research and development costs. In conformity with the matching process, the cost of a patent must be amortized over the shorter of its economic life or its remaining legal life.

A **COPYRIGHT** is the exclusive right to publish, use, and sell a literary, musical, or artistic work.

Copyrights   Copyright protection also is granted by the Canadian Intellectual Property Office. It gives the owner the exclusive right to publish, use, and sell a literary, musical, or artistic piece of work for a period not exceeding 50 years after the author's death. The book that you are reading has a copyright to protect the publisher and the authors. It is **illegal**, for example, for an instructor to copy several chapters from this book and hand them out in class. The same principles, guidelines, and procedures used in accounting for the cost of patents also are used for copyrights.

A **FRANCHISE** is a contractual right to sell certain products or services, use certain trademarks, or perform activties in a geographical region.

Franchises   Franchises may be granted by either the government or other businesses for a specified period and purpose. A city may grant one company a franchise to distribute gas to homes for heating purposes, or a company may sell franchises, such as the right for a local outlet to operate a Mike's restaurant. Franchise agreements are contracts that can have a variety of provisions. They usually require an investment by the franchisee; therefore, they should be accounted for as intangible assets. The life of the franchise agreement depends on the contract. It may be for a single year or an indefinite period. Tim Hortons, for example, had nearly 3,000 restaurants at December 31, 2008. The company's franchisees operate under several types of license agreements. A typical franchise term for a standard restaurant is 10 years, with possible renewal periods. In Canada, franchisees who lease land and/or buildings from the company are required to pay a royalty of 3.0 percent of the weekly gross sales of the restaurant.

TECHNOLOGY includes costs for computer software and Web development.

Technology   The number of companies reporting a technology intangible asset has increased significantly in recent years. Computer software and Web development costs are becoming increasingly significant as companies modernize their processes and make greater use of advances in information and communication technology. In 2009, CGI Group Inc. reported a carrying amount of $124 million in *Business Solutions* in a note to its statement of financial position and disclosed the following in its accounting policies:

REAL WORLD EXCERPT

CGI Group

ANNUAL REPORT

NOTES TO THE CONSOLIDATED FINANCIAL STATEMENTS

2. Summary of Significant Accounting Policies

Other intangible assets

Other intangible assets consist mainly of internal-use software, business solutions, software licenses and client relationships. Internal-use software, business solutions and software licenses are recorded at cost. Business solutions developed internally and marketed for distribution are capitalized when they meet specific capitalization criteria related to technical, market and financial feasibility. Business solutions and software licenses acquired through a business combination are initially recorded at fair value based on the estimated net future income producing capabilities of the software products.

Source: CGI Group Annual Report 2009.

Licences and Operating Rights Licences and operating rights are typically obtained through agreements with governmental units or agencies and permit the holders to use public property in performing their services. For airline companies, the operating rights are authorized landing slots that are regulated by the government and are in limited supply at many airports. They are intangible assets that can be bought and sold by the airlines. Other types of licences that grant permission to companies include air waves for radio and television broadcasts, and land for cable and telephone lines.

LICENCES AND OPERATING RIGHTS, obtained through agreements with governmental units and agencies, permit owners to use public property in performing their services.

Research and Development Expense—Not an Intangible Asset If an intangible asset is developed internally, the cost of development normally is recorded as research and development expense. Nokia Corporation has grown through acquisition of other companies with technology complementary to Nokia's, and it has recognized the value of its intangible assets, including goodwill. This industry can often attribute research and development expense to specific projects that are commercialized and successfully put into production. If Nokia can demonstrate that adequate resources are available or can be obtained to complete the project, and that future benefits are reasonably certain, then research and development costs can be deferred and amortized over the lifetime of the commercialized product as disclosed in the following note:

REAL WORLD EXCERPT

Nokia Corporation

ANNUAL REPORT

NOTES TO THE CONSOLIDATED FINANCIAL STATEMENTS

1. Accounting Principles

Research and development

Research and development costs are expensed as they are incurred, except for certain development costs, which are capitalized when it is probable that a development project will generate future economic benefits, and certain criteria, including commercial and technological feasibility, have been met.

Capitalized development costs, comprising direct labor and related overhead, are amortized on a systematic basis over their expected useful lives between two and five years. Capitalized development costs are subject to regular assessments of recoverability based on anticipated future revenues, including the impact of changes in technology. Unamortized capitalized development costs determined to be in excess of their recoverable amounts are expensed immediately.

. . .

Source: Nokia Corporation Annual Report 2009.

LEASEHOLDS are rights granted to a lessee under a lease contract.

Leaseholds   A leasehold is the right granted in a contract called a *lease* to use a specific asset. Leasing is a common type of business contract. For a consideration called *rent*, the owner (lessor) extends to another party (lessee) certain rights to use specified property. Leases may vary from simple arrangements, such as the month-to-month (*operating*) lease of an office or the daily rental of an automobile, to long-lived (*capital*) leases having complex contractual arrangements.

Lessees sometimes make significant improvements to a leased property when they enter into a long-term lease agreement. A company that agrees to lease office space on a 15-year lease may install new fixtures or move walls to make the space more useful. These improvements are called **leasehold improvements** and are recorded as an asset by the lessee despite the fact that the lessor usually owns the leasehold improvements at the end of the lease term. The cost of leasehold improvements should be amortized over the estimated useful life of the related improvements or the remaining life of the lease, whichever is shorter.

FOCUS ON CASH FLOWS

EFFECT ON STATEMENT OF CASH FLOWS

The indirect method for preparing the operating activities section of the statement of cash flows involves reconciling profit (reported on the income statement) to cash flows from operations. This means that, among other adjustments, (1) revenues and expenses that do not affect cash and (2) gains and losses that relate to investing or financing activities (not operations) should be eliminated. When depreciation is recorded, no cash payment is made (i.e., there is no credit to Cash). Since depreciation expense (a non-cash expense) is subtracted from revenues in calculating profit, it must be added back to profit to eliminate its effect.

Gains and losses on disposal of long-lived assets represent the difference between cash proceeds and the carrying amount of the assets disposed of. Hence, gains and losses are non-cash amounts that do not relate to operating activities, but they are included in the computation of profit. Therefore, gains are subtracted from profit and losses are added to profit in the computation of cash flow from operations.

LO7

Explain the impact on cash flows of the acquisition, use, and disposal of long-lived assets.

EFFECT ON STATEMENT OF CASH FLOWS

IN GENERAL → Acquiring, selling, and depreciating long-lived assets affect a company's cash flows as indicated in the following table:

	Effect on Cash Flows
Operating activities (indirect method)	
Profit	$xxx
Adjusted for:	
Depreciation expense	+
Gains on disposal of long-lived assets	−
Losses on disposal of long-lived assets	+
Losses due to asset impairment write downs	+
Investing activities	
Purchase of long-lived assets	−
Sale of long-lived assets	+

SELECTED FOCUS COMPANY COMPARISONS: PERCENTAGE OF DEPRECIATION TO CASH FLOWS FROM OPERATIONS

WestJet Airlines	44.3%
Nestlé	24.4%
Thompson Reuters	45.0%

FOCUS COMPANY ANALYSIS → Exhibit 9.5 shows a condensed version of WestJet's statement of cash flows prepared by using the indirect method. Buying and selling long-lived assets are investing activities. In 2009, WestJet used $119 million in cash to purchase aircraft and other property and equipment. WestJet sold old aircraft during 2009 and received $27,000 in cash. Since selling long-lived assets is not an operating activity, any gains (losses) on sale of long-lived assets that are included in profit are deducted from (added to) profit in the operating activities section to eliminate the effect of the sale. Unless they are large, these

(Amounts in thousands)	2009	2008
Cash provided by (used in):		
Operating activities:		
Net earnings	$ 98,178	$178,506
Items not involving cash:		
Depreciation, amortization and other liabilities	141,303	136,485
Amortization of other liabilities	(7,595)	(937)
Loss on disposal of property and equipment	1,504	1,809
Other (gains) or losses, net	6,034	24,480
Other (summarized)	79,237	120,243
	318,661	**460,586**
Investing activities:		
Aircraft additions	(118,686)	(114,470)
Aircraft disposals	27	84
Other property and equipment and intangible additions	(48,155)	(90,663)
Other property and equipment and intangible disposals	134	172
Change in non-cash working capital	—	5,147
	$(166,680)	**$(199,730)**

Exhibit **9.5**
WestJet Statement of Cash Flows

REAL WORLD EXCERPT

WestJet Airlines
ANNUAL REPORT

gain and loss adjustments are normally not specifically highlighted on the statement of cash flows. WestJet reports a gain of $1,504,000 in its statement of cash flows for 2009.

Finally, in capital-intensive industries such as airlines, depreciation is a significant non-cash expense included in profit. In WestJet's case, depreciation expense is the single largest adjustment to profit in determining cash flows from operations. It was 39 percent of operating cash flows in 2008 and has reached 44 percent in 2009.

A MISINTERPRETATION

FINANCIAL
ANALYSIS

Some analysts misinterpret the meaning of a non-cash expense and often say that "cash is provided by depreciation." Although depreciation is added in the operating section of the statement of cash flows, **depreciation is not a source of cash**. Cash from operations can be provided only by selling goods and services. A company with a large amount of depreciation expense does not generate more cash compared with a company that reports a small amount of depreciation expense, assuming that they are exactly the same in every other respect. Depreciation expense reduces the amount of reported profit for a company, but it does not reduce the amount of cash generated by the company, because it is a non-cash expense. Remember that the effects of recording depreciation are a reduction in shareholders' equity and in long-lived assets, not in cash. That is why, on the statement of cash flows, depreciation expense is added back to profit (on an accrual basis) to compute cash flows from operations (profit on a cash basis).

Although depreciation is a non-cash expense, the **depreciation method used for tax purposes can affect a company's cash flows**. Depreciation, in the form of capital cost allowance (CCA), is a deductible expense for income tax purposes. The higher the amount of CCA reported by a company for tax purposes, the lower the taxable profit and the taxes it must pay. Because taxes must be paid in cash, a reduction in the tax obligation of a company reduces the company's cash outflows.

The maximum deduction for CCA for each class of assets is based on rates specified by Canada Revenue Agency, but corporations may choose to deduct lower amounts for CCA during periods of losses or low profit before taxes, and postpone CCA deductions to future years to minimize their tax obligations.

ACCOUNTING STANDARDS
FOR PRIVATE ENTERPRISES

Accounting standards for private enterprises differ from IFRS in two main areas: valuation of long-lived assets at market value and measurement of impairment losses.

Under IFRS, Canadian publicly accountable enterprises may report their property, plant, and equipment by using either the cost model or the revaluation model that uses the fair value of these assets as a basis for measurement. However, most companies choose the cost model. In contrast, the accounting standards for Canadian private enterprises do not permit the use of fair value as a basis for valuation of property, plant, and equipment.

The second area of difference relates to the measurement of impairment of long-lived assets. As a first step, the undiscounted future cash flows expected to be generated from an asset, not the present value of the future cash flows, are compared with the asset's carrying amount. If the asset's carrying amount exceeds the undiscounted future cash flows, then the asset's carrying amount is compared with its net realizable value. When the asset's net realizable value is less than its carrying amount, then the asset is impaired and should be written down to its net realizable value. The write down of the asset would not be reversed in the future if its net realizable value improves. In contrast, write downs of property, plant, and equipment of Canadian publicly accountable enterprises can be reversed if the asset's recoverable amount increases in the future.

DEMONSTRATION **CASE**

Diversified Industries has been operating for a number of years. It started as a residential construction company. In recent years, it expanded into heavy construction, ready-mix concrete, sand and gravel, construction supplies, and earth-moving services.

The following transactions were selected from those completed during year 2011. They focus on the primary issues discussed in this chapter. Amounts have been simplified for case purposes.

2011

Jan. 1   The management decided to buy a building that was about 10-years old. The location was excellent, and there was adequate parking space. The company bought the building and the land on which it was situated for $305,000. It paid $100,000 in cash and signed a mortgage note payable for the rest. A reliable appraiser provided the following market values: land, $132,300, and building, $182,700.

Jan. 12   Paid renovation costs on the building of $38,100, prior to use.

June 19   Bought a third location for a gravel pit (designated No. 3) for $50,000 cash. The location had been carefully surveyed. It was estimated that 100,000 cubic metres of gravel could be removed from the deposit.

July 10   Paid $1,200 for ordinary repairs on the building.

Aug. 1   Paid $10,000 for costs of preparing the new gravel pit for exploitation.

Dec. 31   Year-end adjustments:

    a. The building will be depreciated on a straight-line basis over an estimated useful life of 30 years. The estimated residual value is $35,000.

    b. During 2011, 12,000 cubic metres of gravel were removed from gravel pit No. 3 and sold.

    c. The company owns a patent right that is used in operations. On January 1, 2011, the patent account had a balance of $3,300. The patent has an estimated remaining useful life of six years (including 2011).

    d. At the beginning of the year, the company owned equipment with a cost of $650,000 and a carrying amount of $500,000. The equipment is being depreciated by using the double-declining-balance method, with a useful life of 20 years with no residual value.

    e. At year-end, the company identified a piece of old excavation equipment with a cost of $156,000 and remaining carrying amount of $120,000. Due to its smaller size and lack of safety features, the old equipment has limited use. The company reviewed the asset for possible impairment of value. The equipment has a fair value of $40,000.

Required:

1. Indicate the accounts affected and the amount and direction (+ for increase and − for decrease) of the effect for each of the preceding events on the basic accounting equation. Use the following headings:

Date	Assets	=	Liabilities	+	Shareholders' Equity

2. Record the adjusting journal entries based on the information for December 31([a] and [b] only).
3. Show the December 31, 2011, statement of financial position classifications and amount for each of the following items:

> Property, plant, and equipment —land, building, equipment, and gravel pit
> Intangible asset—patent

4. Assuming that the company had sales of $1,000,000 for the year and a carrying amount of $500,000 for property, plant, and equipment at the beginning of the year, compute the fixed asset turnover ratio. Explain its meaning.

We strongly recommend that you attempt to answer the requirements on your own and then check your answers with the suggested solution.

SUGGESTED **SOLUTION**

Date	Assets		Liabilities		Shareholders' Equity	
Jan. 1 (1)	Cash	−100,000	Note payable	+205,000		
	Land	+128,100				
	Building	+176,900				
Jan. 12 (2)	Cash	−38,100				
	Building	+38,100				
June 19 (3)	Cash	−50,000				
	Gravel pit No. 3	+50,000				
July 10 (4)	Cash	−1,200			Repairs expense	−1,200
Aug. 1 (5)	Cash	−10,000				
	Gravel pit No. 3	+10,000				
Dec. 31 a (6)	Accumulated depreciation	−6,000			Depreciation expense	−6,000
Dec. 31 b (7)	Gravel pit No. 3	−7,200				
	Gravel inventory	+7,200				
Dec. 31 c (8)	Patent	−550			Amortization expense	−550
Dec. 31 d (9)	Accumulated depreciation	−50,000			Depreciation expense	−50,000
Dec. 31 e (10)	Accumulated depreciation	−80,000			Loss due to asset impairment	−80,000

(1)

	Land		Building		Total
Market	$132,300	+	$182,700	=	$315,000
Percentage of total	42%	+	58%	=	100%
Cost	$128,100	+	$176,900	=	$305,000

(2) Capitalize the expenditure of $38,100 because it is necessary to prepare the asset for use.

(3) This is a natural resource.

(4) This is an ordinary repair (revenue expenditure) that should be expensed.

(5) Capitalize the expenditure of $10,000 because it is necessary to prepare the asset for use.

(6) **Cost of building**

Initial payment	$176,900
Repairs prior to use	38,100
Acquisition cost	$215,000

Straight-line depreciation

Depreciation = ($215,000 − $35,000)/30 years
= $6,000 annually

(7) **Cost of gravel pit**

Initial payment	$50,000
Preparation costs	10,000
Acquisition cost	$60,000

Units-of-production depletion

Depletion rate = $60,000/100,000
= $0.60 per cubic metre
Depletion amount = $12,000 × $0.60 = $7,200

(8) **Straight-line depreciation**

Unamortized cost of patent	$3,300
Remaining useful life	÷ 6 years
	$ 550

(9) **Double-declining-balance depreciation**

Annual depreciation = $500,000 (carrying amount) × 2/20 = $50,000

(10) **Asset impairment**

Carrying amount of old equipment	$120,000
Fair value	− 40,000
Loss due to impairment	$ 80,000

2. Adjusting entries Dec. 31, 2011:

a.	Depreciation expense, building (E)	6,000	
	Accumulated depreciation (XA)		6,000
b.	Gravel inventory (A)	7,200	
	Gravel pit No. 3 (A)		7,200

3. Statement of financial position, December 31, 2011:

Assets		
Property, plant, and equipment		
Land		$128,100
Building	$215,000	
Less: Accumulated depreciation	6,000	209,000
Equipment	650,000	
Less: Accumulated depreciation ($150,000 + 50,000 + 80,000)	280,000	370,000
Gravel pit		52,800
Total		$759,900
Intangible asset		
Patent ($3,300 − $550)		$ 2,750

4. Fixed asset turnover ratio:

$$\frac{\text{Net Sales}}{\text{Average Net Fixed Assets}} = \frac{\$1,000,000}{(\$500,000 + \$759,900) \div 2} = 1.59$$

This construction company is capital-intensive. The fixed asset turnover ratio measures the company's efficiency at using its investment in property, plant, and equipment to generate sales.

CHAPTER TAKE-AWAYS

1. **Define, classify, and explain the nature of long-lived assets and interpret the fixed asset turnover ratio. p. 464**
   a. Noncurrent assets are those that a business retains for long periods of time, for use in the course of normal operations rather than for sale. They may be divided into tangible assets (land, buildings, equipment, natural resources) and intangible assets (including goodwill, patents, and franchises).
   b. The cost allocation method utilized affects the amount of net property, plant, and equipment that is used in the computation of the fixed asset turnover ratio. Accelerated methods reduce book value and increase the turnover ratio.

2. **Apply the cost principle to measure the acquisition and maintenance of property, plant, and equipment. p. 466**
   Acquisition cost of property, plant, and equipment is the cash-equivalent purchase price plus all reasonable and necessary expenditures made to acquire and prepare the asset for its intended use. These assets may be acquired by using cash, debt, or equity, or through

self-construction. Expenditures made after the asset is in use are either capital expenditures or revenue expenditures:

a. Capital expenditures provide benefits for one or more accounting periods beyond the current period. Amounts are debited to the appropriate asset accounts and depreciated or depleted over their useful lives.

b. Revenue expenditures provide benefits during the current accounting period only. Amounts are debited to appropriate current expense accounts when the expenses are incurred.

3. **Apply various depreciation methods as assets are held and used over time. p. 471**
Cost allocation methods: In conformity with the matching process, cost (less any estimated residual value) is allocated to periodic expense over the periods benefited. Because of depreciation, the carrying amount of an asset declines over time and profit is reduced by the amount of the expense. Common depreciation methods include straight-line (a constant amount over time), units-of-production (a variable amount over time), and double-declining-balance (a decreasing amount over time).
   - Depreciation—buildings and equipment.
   - Depletion—natural resources.
   - Amortization—intangibles.

4. **Explain the effect of asset impairment on the financial statements. p. 484**
When events or changes in circumstances reduce the estimated future cash flows of long-lived assets below their carrying amounts, the carrying amounts should be written down (by recording a loss) to the fair value of the assets.

5. **Analyze the disposal of property, plant, and equipment. p. 486**
When assets are disposed of through sale or abandonment,
   - Record additional depreciation since the last adjustment was made.
   - Remove the cost of the old asset and its related accumulated depreciation or depletion.
   - Recognize the cash proceeds.
   - Recognize any gains or losses when the asset's carrying amount is not equal to the cash received.

6. **Apply measurement and reporting concepts for natural resources and intangible assets. p. 488**
The cost principle should be applied in recording the acquisition of natural resources and intangible assets. Natural resources should be depleted (usually by the units-of-production method) usually with the amount of the depletion expense capitalized to an inventory account. Intangibles with definite useful lives are amortized by using the straight-line method. Intangibles with indefinite useful lives, including goodwill, are not amortized, but are reviewed at least annually for impairment. Intangibles are reported at their carrying amount on the statement of financial position.

7. **Explain the impact on cash flows of the acquisition, use, and disposal of long-lived assets. p. 494**
Depreciation expense is a non-cash expense that has no effect on cash. It is added back to profit on the statement of cash flows to determine cash from operations. Acquiring and disposing of long-lived assets are investing activities.

In the previous chapters, we discussed business and accounting issues related to the assets a company holds. In Chapters 10, 11, and 12, we shift our focus to the other side of the statement of financial position to see how managers finance the operations of their business and the acquisition of productive assets. We discuss various types of liabilities in Chapters 10 and 11 and examine owners' equity in Chapter 12.

KEY **RATIO**

The **fixed asset turnover ratio** measures how efficiently a company utilizes its investment in property, plant, and equipment over time. Its ratio can be compared to the ratio of its competitors. It is computed as follows (p. 465):

$$\text{Fixed Asset Turnover} = \frac{\text{Net Sales (or operating revenues)}}{\text{Average Net Fixed Assets}}$$

FINDING **FINANCIAL INFORMATION**

STATEMENT OF FINANCIAL POSITION
Under Long-Lived Assets
Property, plant, and equipment (net of accumulated depreciation)
Natural resources (net of accumulated depletion)
Intangibles (net of accumulated amortization)

INCOME STATEMENT
Under Operating Expenses
Depreciation and depletion expense or as part of
Selling, general, and administrative expenses and
Cost of sales (with the amount of depreciation expense disclosed in a note)

STATEMENT OF CASH FLOWS
Under Operating Activities (indirect method)
Profit
+ Depreciation expense
− Gains on sales of assets
+ Losses on sales of assets
Under Investing Activities
+ Sales of assets for cash
− Purchases of assets for cash

NOTES
Under Summary of Significant Accounting Policies
Description of management's choice for depreciation methods, including useful lives, and the amount of annual depreciation expense, if not listed on the income statement.
Under a Separate Footnote
If not specified on the statement of financial position, a listing of the major classifications of long-lived assets at cost and the balance in accumulated depreciation and depletion.

KEY **TERMS**

Acquisition Cost p. 466
Basket Purchase p. 468
Betterments p. 470
Capital Expenditures p. 470
Capitalized Interest p. 467
Carrying Amount (or Book Value) p. 472
Copyright p. 492
Declining-Balance Depreciation p. 477
Depletion p. 488
Depreciation p. 471
Estimated Useful Life p. 473
Extraordinary Repairs p. 470
Franchise p. 492
Goodwill p. 491
Intangible Assets p. 465

Leaseholds p. 494
Licences and Operating Rights p. 493
Long-Lived (or Long-Term or Capital) Assets p. 464
Natural Resources p. 488
Ordinary Repairs and Maintenance p. 469
Patent p. 492
Residual (or Salvage) Value p. 474
Revenue Expenditures p. 469
Straight-Line Depreciation p. 475
Tangible Assets p. 464
Technology p. 492
Trademark p. 492
Units-of-Production Depreciation p. 476

QUESTIONS

1. Define *long-lived assets*. Why are they considered a "bundle of future services"?
2. How is the fixed asset turnover ratio computed? Explain its meaning.
3. What are the classifications of long-lived assets? Explain each.

4. Relate the cost principle to accounting for long-lived assets. Under the cost principle, what amounts usually should be included in the acquisition cost of a long-lived asset?

5. Describe the relationship between the matching process and accounting for long-lived assets.

6. What is a basket purchase? What measurement problem does it pose?

7. Distinguish between
   a. Capital expenditures and revenue expenditures. How is each accounted for?
   b. Ordinary and extraordinary repairs. How is each accounted for?

8. Distinguish between depreciation and depletion.

9. In computing depreciation, three values must be known or estimated; identify and explain the nature of each.

10. Estimated useful life and residual value of a long-lived asset relate to the current owner or user rather than all potential users. Explain this statement.

11. What type of depreciation expense pattern is provided under each of the following methods? When is the use of each method appropriate?
    a. Straight-line
    b. Units-of-production
    c. Double-declining-balance

12. Over what period should an addition to an existing long-lived asset be depreciated? Explain.

13. What is an asset impairment? How is it accounted for?

14. Define *intangible asset*. What period should be used to amortize an intangible asset?

15. Define *goodwill*. When is it appropriate to record goodwill as an intangible asset?

16. Distinguish between a leasehold and a leasehold improvement. Over what period should a leasehold improvement be amortized? Explain.

17. Why is depreciation expense added to profit on the statement of cash flows when using the indirect method of reporting cash flow from operations?

EXERCISES

E9–1 Classifying Long-Lived Assets and Related Cost Allocation Concepts   LO1
For each of the following long-lived assets, indicate its nature and related cost allocation concept. Use the following symbols:

Nature		Cost Allocation Concept	
L	Land	DP	Depletion
B	Building	A	Amortization
E	Equipment	D	Depreciation
NR	Natural resource	NO	No cost allocation
I	Intangible	O	Other

Asset	Nature	Cost Allocation	Asset	Nature	Cost Allocation
(1) Copyright	___	___	(6) Operating licence	___	___
(2) Land held for use	___	___	(7) Land held for sale	___	___
(3) Warehouse	___	___	(8) Delivery vans	___	___
(4) Oil well	___	___	(9) Timber tract	___	___
(5) New engine for old machine	___	___	(10) Production plant	___	___

LO1

Ballard Power
Systems Inc.

E9–2   **Preparing a Partial Classified Statement of Financial Position**

The following is a list of account titles and amounts (in thousands) reported by Ballard Power Systems Inc., a leading developer and manufacturer of fuel cells, an alternative power source for automobiles:

Raw materials	$ 6,632	Work in progress	$ 1,891
Leasehold improvements	10,659	Accumulated amortization—Intangibles	46,075
Prepaid expenses	1,434	Fuel cell technology	49,801
Accounts receivable	18,856	Cash and cash equivalents	54,086
Finished goods	1,879	Computer equipment	17,874
Furniture and fixtures	5,342	Building	13,574
Land	4,803	Short-term investments	31,313
Long-term investments	1,765	Production and test equipment	65,877
Goodwill	48,106	Accumulated depreciation—	
		Property, plant, and equipment	79,374

Required:

Prepare the asset section of the statement of financial position for Ballard Power Systems Inc., classifying the assets into current assets and noncurrent assets.

LO2

E9–3   **Identifying Capital and Revenue Expenditures**

For each of the following items, enter the correct letter to the left to show the type of expenditure. Use the following:

Type of Expenditure

C Capital expenditure   **R** Revenue expenditure   **N** Neither

Transactions

_____ (1) Paid $400 for ordinary repairs.
_____ (2) Paid $6,000 for extraordinary repairs.
_____ (3) Paid cash, $20,000, for addition to old building.
_____ (4) Paid for routine maintenance, $200, on credit.
_____ (5) Purchased a machine, $7,000; signed a long-term note.
_____ (6) Paid $2,000 for organization costs.
_____ (7) Paid one-year insurance premium in advance, $900.
_____ (8) Purchased a patent, $4,300 cash.
_____ (9) Paid $10,000 for monthly salaries.
_____ (10) Paid cash dividends, $20,000.

LO1

E9–4   **Computing and Evaluating the Fixed Asset Turnover Ratio**

The following information was reported by Cutter's Air Cargo Service for 2009:

Net fixed assets (beginning of year)	$1,500,000
Net fixed assets (end of year)	2,300,000
Net sales	3,300,000
Profit	1,600,000

Compute the company's fixed asset turnover ratio for the year. What can you say about Cutter's ratio when compared with WestJet's ratio for 2009, as computed in the chapter?

LO1

QLT Inc.

E9–5   **Computing and Interpreting the Fixed Asset Turnover Ratio from a Financial Analyst's Perspective**

The following data were disclosed in the annual reports of QLT Inc., a Canadian biotechnology company that produces Visudyne, a product to treat macular degeneration of the eyes. If left untreated, this medical condition causes blindness.

(in thousands of dollars)	2008	2007	2006	2005	2004
Net sales	$124,140	$127,606	$175,090	$241,973	$186,072
Net property, plant, and equipment	3,184	10,017	50,497	75,497	81,674

Required:

1. Compute QLT's fixed asset turnover ratio for the four years 2005 through 2008.

2. How might a financial analyst interpret the results?

E9–6 Determining Financial Statement Effects of Acquisition of Several Assets in a Basket Purchase   ▇ LO2

Kline Corporation acquired additional land and a building that included several pieces of equipment for $600,000. The acquisition was settled as follows: cash, $120,000; issuance of Kline's common shares, $120,000; and signing a long-term note, $360,000. An appraiser estimated the market values to be $200,000 for the land, $500,000 for the building, and $100,000 for the equipment. Indicate the accounts affected and the amount and direction (+ for increase and − for decrease) of the effect of this acquisition on the accounting equation. Use the following headings:

Assets	=	Liabilities	+	Shareholders' Equity

E9–7 Computing and Recording Cost and Depreciation of Assets in a Basket Purchase (Straight-Line Depreciation)   ▇ LO2, 3

Zeidler Company bought a building and the land on which the building is located for a total cash price of $178,000. The company paid transfer costs of $2,000. Renovation costs on the building were $23,000. An independent appraiser provided market values for the land, $50,000, and building, $150,000 before renovation.

Required:

1. Apportion the cost of the property on the basis of the appraised values. Show computations.

2. Prepare the journal entry to record the purchase of the building and land, including all expenditures. Assume that all transactions were for cash and that all purchases occurred at the start of the year.

3. Compute depreciation of the building at the end of one year, using the straight-line method. Assume an estimated useful life of 12 years and an estimated residual value of $14,000.

4. What would be the carrying amount of the property (building and land) at the end of year 2?

E9–8 Determining Financial Statement Effects of an Asset Acquisition and Depreciation (Straight-Line Depreciation)   ▇ LO2, 3

Vicario Company purchased a machine on March 1, 2012, at an invoice price of $10,000. On the date of delivery, March 2, 2012, the company paid $8,000 on the machine, and signed a note for the balance at 12 percent interest. On March 3, 2012, it paid $250 for freight on the machine. On March 5, Vicario paid installation costs of $475 relating to the machine. On October 1, 2012, the company paid the balance due on the machine plus the interest. On December 31, 2012 (the end of the accounting period), Vicario recorded straight-line depreciation on the machine based on an estimated useful life of 10 years and an estimated residual value of $1,725.

Required (round all amounts to the nearest dollar):

1. Indicate the accounts affected and the amount and direction (+ for increase and − for decrease) of the effect of each transaction (March 1, 2, 3, 5, and October 1) on the accounting equation. Use the following headings:

Date	Assets	=	Liabilities	+	Shareholders' Equity

2. Compute the acquisition cost of the machine.

3. Compute the depreciation expense to be reported for 2012.

4. What is the impact on the cost of the machine of the interest paid on the 12 percent note? Under what circumstances can interest expense be included in an asset's cost?

5. What would be the carrying amount of the machine at the end of 2013?

LO1, 2

ACE Aviation
Holdings

E9–9   **Evaluating the Impact of Capitalized Interest on Cash Flows and Fixed Asset Turnover from an Analyst's Perspective**

You are a financial analyst charged with evaluating the asset efficiency of companies in the airline industry. The financial statements for ACE Aviation Holdings Inc. include the following note:

> **(I) Interest Capitalized**
>
> Interest on funds used to finance the acquisition of new flight equipment and other property and equipment is capitalized for periods preceding the dates the assets are available for service.

Required:

1. Assume that ACE Aviation followed this policy for a major construction project this year. What is the direction of the effect of ACE Aviation's policy on the following? Use + for increase, − for decrease, and NE for no effect.

   a. Cash flows

   b. Fixed asset turnover ratio

2. Normally, how would your answer to (1*b*) affect your evaluation of ACE Aviation's effectiveness in utilizing property, plant, and equipment?

3. If the fixed asset turnover ratio changes because of interest capitalization, does this change indicate a real change in efficiency? Why or why not?

LO3

E9–10   **Recording Depreciation and Repairs (Straight-Line Depreciation) and Determining Financial Statement Effects**

Stacey Company operates a small manufacturing facility as a supplement to its regular service activities. At the beginning of 2012, an asset account for the company showed the following balances:

Manufacturing equipment	$80,000
Accumulated depreciation through 2011	55,000

In early January 2012, the following expenditures were incurred for repairs and maintenance:

Routine maintenance and repairs on the equipment	$ 850
Major overhaul of the equipment	10,500

The equipment is being depreciated on a straight-line basis over an estimated life of 15 years, with a $5,000 estimated residual value. The company's fiscal year ends on December 31.

Required:

1. Prepare the adjusting entry to record the depreciation of the manufacturing equipment on December 31, 2011.

2. Prepare the journal entries to record the two expenditures that occurred during 2012.

3. Prepare the adjusting entry at December 31, 2012, to record the depreciation of the manufacturing equipment, assuming no change in the estimated life or residual value of the equipment. Show computations.

4. Indicate the accounts affected, amount, and direction (+ for increase and − for decrease) of the effects of the journal entries you prepared for (1) to (3) on the accounting question. Use the following headings:

Date	Assets	=	Liabilities	+	Shareholders' Equity

LO3

E9–11   **Computing Depreciation under Alternative Methods**

Rita's Pita Company bought a new dough machine at the beginning of the year at a cost of $7,600. The estimated useful life was four years, and the residual value was $800. Assume that the estimated productive life of the machine is 10,000 hours. Annual usage was 3,600 hours in year 1; 3,200 hours in year 2; 2,200 hours in year 3; and 1,200 hours in year 4.

Required:

1. Complete a separate depreciation schedule for each of the alternative methods. Round your computations to the nearest dollar.
   a. Straight-line
   b. Units-of-production
   c. Double-declining-balance

Method: _____		Depreciation Expense	Accumulated Depreciation	Carrying Amount
Year	Computation			
At acquisition				
1				
2				
Etc.				

2. Assuming that the machine was used directly in the production of one of the products that the company manufactures and sells, what factors might management consider in selecting a preferable depreciation method in conformity with the matching process?

E9–12 Computing Depreciation under Alternative Methods   ▓ **LO3**

Alexa Plastics Company purchased a new stamping machine at the beginning of the year at a cost of $125,000. The estimated residual value was $15,000. Assume that the estimated useful life was five years and the estimated productive life of the machine was 250,000 units. Actual annual production was as follows:

Year	1	2	3	4	5
Units	75,000	60,000	40,000	45,000	30,000

Required:

1. Complete a separate depreciation schedule for each of the alternative methods. Round your computations to the nearest dollar.
   a. Straight-line
   b. Units-of-production
   c. Double-declining-balance

Method: _____		Depreciation Expense	Accumulated Depreciation	Carrying Amount
Year	Computation			
At acquisition				
1				
2				
Etc.				

2. Assuming that the machine was used directly in the production of one of the products that the company manufactures and sells, what factors might management consider in selecting a preferable depreciation method in conformity with the matching process?

E9–13 Explaining Depreciation Policy   ▓ **LO3**

An annual report for Ford Motor Company contained the following note:

Ford Motor Company

Significant Accounting Policies

Depreciation of Property, Plant, and Equipment. Property and equipment are stated at cost and depreciated primarily using the straight-line method over the estimated useful life of the asset. Useful lives range from 3 years to 36 years. The estimated useful lives generally are 14.5 years for machinery and equipment and 30 years for buildings and land improvements. Special tools placed in service beginning in 1999 are depreciated using the units-of-production method over the expected vehicle model cycle life. Maintenance, repairs, and rearrangement costs are expensed as incurred.

Required:

Why do you think the company changed its depreciation method for special tools acquired in 1999 and subsequent years? What impact did the change have on profit?

LO3

Federal Express

E9–14 **Interpreting Management's Choice of Different Depreciation Methods for Tax and Financial Reporting**

An annual report for Federal Express Corporation included the following information:

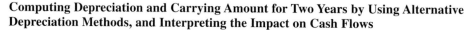

For financial reporting purposes, depreciation of property and equipment is provided on a straight-line basis over the asset's service life. For income tax purposes, depreciation is generally computed using accelerated methods.

Required:

Explain why Federal Express uses different methods of depreciation for financial reporting and tax purposes.

LO3, 7

E9–15 **Computing Depreciation and Carrying Amount for Two Years by Using Alternative Depreciation Methods, and Interpreting the Impact on Cash Flows**

Silk Company bought a machine for $65,000 cash. The estimated useful life was five years, and the estimated residual value was $5,000. Assume that the estimated useful life is 150,000 units. Units actually produced were 45,000 in year 1 and 40,000 in year 2.

Required:

1. Determine the appropriate amounts to complete the following schedule. Show computations, and round to the nearest dollar.

Method of Depreciation	Depreciation Expense for Year 1	Year 2	Carrying Amount at the End of Year 1	Year 2
Straight-line				
Units-of-production				
Double-declining-balance				

2. Which method would result in the lowest earnings per share for year 1? For year 2?
3. Which method would result in the highest amount of cash outflows in year 1? Why?
4. Indicate the effects of (a) acquiring the machine and (b) recording annual depreciation on the operating and investing activities on the statement of cash flows for year 1. Assume that straight-line depreciation is used.

LO4

E9–16 **Identifying Asset Impairment**

For each of the following scenarios, indicate whether an asset has been impaired (Y for yes and N for no) and, if so, the amount of loss that should be recorded.

	Carrying Amount	Value in Use	Fair Value Less Costs to Sell	Is Asset Impaired?	If So, Amount of Loss
a. Machine	$ 15,500	$ 10,000	$ 8,500		
b. Copyright	31,000	41,000	39,900		
c. Factory building	58,000	26,000	29,000		
d. Building	227,000	237,000	210,000		

LO4

Orca Exploration Group Inc.

E9–17 **Inferring Asset Impairment and Disposal of Assets**

Orca Exploration Group Inc. explores for and develops natural gas properties in Tanzania, Africa. The following note and information were reported in a recent annual report:

Note 1—SUMMARY OF SIGNIFICANT ACCOUNTING POLICIES

Impairment of exploration and evaluation assets, property, plant, and equipment

At each balance sheet date, the Company reviews the carrying amounts of its property, plant, and equipment and intangible assets to determine whether there is any indication that those assets have suffered an impairment loss. Individual assets are grouped together as a cash-generating unit for impairment assessment purposes at the lowest level at which there are identifiable cash flows that are independent from other group assets. In the case of exploration and evaluation assets, this will normally be at the Company's field level. If any such indication of impairment exists, the Company makes an estimate of its recoverable amount. The recoverable amount is the higher of fair value less costs to sell and value in use. Where the carrying amount of a cash-generating unit exceeds its recoverable amount, the cash-generating unit is considered impaired and is written down to its recoverable amount. In assessing the value in use, the estimated future cash flows are adjusted for the risks specific to the cash-generating unit and are discounted to their present value with a discount rate that reflects the current market indicators. Where an impairment loss subsequently reverses, the carrying amount of the asset cash-generating unit is increased to the revised estimate of its recoverable amount, but so that the increased carrying amount does not exceed the carrying amount that would have been determined had no impairment loss been recognized for the cash-generating unit in prior years. A reversal of an impairment loss is recognized as income immediately.

	Dollars in millions
Cost of property, plant, and equipment (beginning of year)	$68,682
Cost of property, plant, and equipment (end of year)	70,763
Capital expenditures during the year	4,453
Accumulated depreciation (beginning of year)	7,705
Accumulated depreciation (end of year)	12,380
Depreciation expense during the year	4,792
Cost of equipment sold during the year	207
Accumulated depreciation on equipment sold	117
Cash received on equipment sold	110

Required:

1. Reconstruct the journal entry for the disposal of equipment during the year.

2. Compute the amount of property, plant, and equipment that Orca Exploration Group wrote off as impaired during the year. (*Hint:* Set up T-accounts.)

E9–18 Inferring Asset Impairment and Disposal of Assets

easyJet plc

Low-fare airline, easyJet plc, is based in London, England. Its destinations include popular vacation spots and business centres throughout Europe, North Africa, and the Middle East. The following note and information were reported in a recent annual report:

Note 1—ACCOUNTING POLICIES

Impairment of noncurrent assets

An impairment loss is recognised to the extent that the carrying value exceeds the higher of the asset's fair value less cost to sell and its value in use. Impairment losses recognised on assets other than goodwill are only reversed where changes in the estimates used result in an increase in recoverable amount. Impairment losses recognised on goodwill are not reversed.

	Dollars in millions
Cost of property, plant, and equipment (beginning of year)	£1,216.9
Cost of property, plant, and equipment (end of year)	1,636.3
Capital expenditures during the year	515.0
Accumulated depreciation (beginning of year)	114.3
Accumulated depreciation (end of year)	177.5
Depreciation expense during the year	55.4
Cost of property and equipment sold during the year	10.1
Accumulated depreciation on property and equipment sold	5.2
Gain on disposal of property and equipment sold	7.5

During the year, easyJet wrote down certain buildings, machinery, and equipment to their fair value. The impairment loss was included in the reported depreciation expense for the year.

Required:

1. Reconstruct the journal entry for the disposal of property and equipment during the year.

2. Compute the amount of property and equipment that easyJet wrote off as impaired during the year. (*Hint:* Set up T-accounts.)

LO5

Sears Canada Inc.

E9–19 **Recording the Disposal of an Asset and Financial Statement Effects**

Sears Canada Inc. has developed a consolidated distribution network in Vaughan, Ontario, and in Calgary, Alberta. As part of its distribution service, Sears trucks transport inventory to its various department, furniture, appliance, automotive, and outlet stores, as well as to individual customers. Assume that Sears sold a small delivery truck that had been used in the business for three years. The records of the company reflect the following:

Delivery truck	$28,000
Accumulated depreciation	24,000

Required:

1. Prepare the journal entry to record the disposal of the truck and the related transaction effects, assuming that the sales price was (a) $4,000, (b) $4,600, or (c) $3,600.

2. Based on the three preceding situations, explain the effects of the disposal of an asset on financial statements.

LO5

E9–20 **Inferring Asset Age and Recording Accidental Loss on a Long-Lived Asset (Straight-Line Depreciation)**

On January 1, 2012, the records of Smita Corporation showed the following:

Truck (estimated residual value, $6,000)	$36,000
Accumulated depreciation (straight line, two years)	12,000

On September 30, 2012, the delivery truck was a total loss as a result of an accident. As the truck was insured, the company collected $11,200 cash from the insurance company on October 5, 2012.

Required:

1. Based on the data given, compute the estimated useful life of the truck.

2. Prepare all journal entries to record the events that occurred on September 30 and October 5, 2012, and the related adjustments to the accounts. Show computations.

LO6

Freeport-McMoRan
Copper & Gold Inc.

E9–21 **Computing the Acquisition and Depletion of a Natural Resource**

Freeport-McMoRan Copper & Gold Inc. is a natural resources company involved in the exploration, development, and extraction of natural resources with the majority of its resources in Indonesia. Annual revenues exceed $18 billion. Assume that in February 2011, Freeport-McMoRan paid $680,000 for a mineral deposit in Bali. During March, it spent $85,000 in preparing the deposit for exploitation. It was estimated that 900 million pounds could be extracted economically. During 2011, 70 million pounds were extracted and sold. During January 2012, the company spent another $6,000 for additional developmental work. After conclusion of the latest work, the estimated remaining recovery was increased to 1,200 million pounds over the remaining life. During 2012, 60 million pounds were extracted.

Required:

1. Compute the acquisition cost of the deposit in 2011.

2. Compute the depletion expense for 2011.

3. Compute the carrying amount of the deposit after payment of the January 2012 developmental costs.

4. Compute the depletion expense for 2012.

5. Prepare the journal entries to record the acquisition of the deposit in 2011 and the depletion expense for 2011.

E9–22 Computing Goodwill and Patents

LO6

Elizabeth Pie Company has been in business for 30 years and has developed a large group of loyal restaurant customers. Vaclav's Foods made an offer to buy Elizabeth Pie Company for $5,000,000. The carrying amount of Elizabeth Pie's recorded assets and liabilities on the date of the offer is $4,400,000, with a market value of $4,600,000. Elizabeth Pie holds a patent for a pie crust–fluting machine that the company invented (the patent, with a market value of $200,000, was never recorded by Elizabeth Pie because it was developed internally). The company estimates goodwill from loyal customers to be $300,000 (also never recorded by the company). Should Elizabeth Pie Company management accept Vaclav's Foods' offer of $5,000,000? If so, compute the amount of goodwill that Vaclav's Foods should record on the date of the purchase.

E9–23 Computing and Reporting the Acquisition and Amortization of Three Different Intangible Assets

LO6

Wyatt Company had three intangible assets at the end of 2012 (end of the fiscal year):

a. A patent purchased from R. Jay on January 1, 2012, for a cash cost of $7,670. Jay had registered the patent with the Canadian Intellectual Property Office seven years earlier on January 1, 2005. The cost of the patent is amortized over its legal life.

b. A franchise acquired from the local community to provide certain services for five years starting January 1, 2012. The franchise cost $25,000 cash.

c. A lease on some property for a five-year term beginning January 1, 2012. The company immediately spent $7,800 cash for long-lived improvements (estimated useful life, eight years; no residual value). At the termination of the lease, there will be no recovery of these improvements.

d. A trademark that was purchased for $16,000. Management decided that the trademark has an indefinite life.

Required:

1. What is the acquisition cost of each intangible asset?

2. Compute the amortization of each intangible asset at December 31, 2012. The company does not use contra accounts.

3. Show how these assets and any related expenses should be reported on the statement of financial position at December 31, 2012, and on the income statement for 2012.

E9–24 Recording Rent Paid in Advance, Leasehold Improvements, Periodic Rent, and Related Amortization

LO6

Starbucks Coffee Company

Starbucks Coffee Company is a leading retailer of specialty coffee with more than 16,000 coffee shops worldwide. Assume that Starbucks planned to open a new store on St. George Street near the University of Toronto and obtained a 15-year lease starting January 1, 2012. Although a serviceable building was on the property, the company had to build an additional structure for storage. The 15-year lease required an $18,000 cash advance payment plus cash payments of $5,000 per month during occupancy. During January 2012, the company spent $90,000 cash building the structure. The new structure has an estimated life of 18 years with no residual value.

Required:

1. Prepare the journal entries for the company to record the payment of the $18,000 advance on January 1, 2012, and the first monthly rental.

2. Prepare the journal entry to record the construction of the new structure.

3. Prepare any adjusting entries required at December 31, 2012, the end of the company's fiscal year, with respect to (a) the advance payment and (b) the new structure. Assume that straight-line depreciation is used. Show computations.

4. Compute the total expense resulting from the lease for 2012.

LO1-7

E9–25 Finding Financial Information as a Potential Investor

You are considering investing the cash gifts you received for graduation in shares of various companies. You visit the websites of major companies, searching for relevant information.

Required:

For each of the following, indicate where you would locate the information in an annual report (*Hint:* The information may be in more than one location):

1. The detail on major classifications of long-lived assets.

2. The accounting method(s) used for financial reporting purposes.

3. Whether the company has had any capital expenditures for the year.

4. Net amount of property, plant, and equipment.

5. Policies on amortizing intangibles.

6. Depreciation expense.

7. Any significant gains or losses on disposals of long-lived assets.

8. Accumulated depreciation of property, plant, and equipment at the end of the last fiscal year.

9. The amount of assets written off as impaired during the year.

LO2

E9–26 Recording and Explaining Depreciation, Extraordinary Repairs, and Changes in Estimated Useful Life and Residual Value (Straight-Line Depreciation)

The records of Luci Company reflected the following details for Machine A at December 31, 2012, the end of the company's fiscal year.

Cost when acquired	$28,000
Accumulated depreciation	10,000

During January 2013, the machine was renovated at a cost of $11,000. As a result, the estimated life increased from five years to eight years and the residual value increased from $3,000 to $5,000. The company uses straight-line depreciation.

Required:

1. Prepare the journal entry to record the renovation.

2. How old was the machine at the end of 2012?

3. Prepare the adjusting entry at the end of 2013 to record straight-line depreciation for the year.

4. Explain the rationale for your entries in (1) and (3).

LO3

E9–27 Computing the Effect of a Change in Useful Life and Residual Value on Financial Statements and Cash Flows (Straight-Line Depreciation)

Dustin Company owns the office building occupied by its administrative office. The office building was reflected in the accounts at the end of last year as follows:

Acquisition cost	$225,000
Accumulated depreciation (based on straight-line depreciation, an	
estimated life of 30 years, and residual value of $15,000)	98,000

Following a careful study, management decided in January of this year that the total estimated useful life should be changed to 25 years (instead of 30) and the residual value reduced to $11,500 (from $15,000). The depreciation method will not change.

Required:

1. Compute the annual depreciation expense prior to the change in estimates.

2. Compute the annual depreciation expense after the change in estimates.

3. What will be the net effect of changing the estimates on the statement of financial position, profit, and cash flows for the year?

PROBLEMS

P9–1 **Understanding the Nature of Depreciation**　　　　　　　　　　　　　　　　　　**LO3, 5**

At the beginning of his first year at university, Georgio Labos bought a used combination colour television and stereo system for $960. He estimates that these two items will be almost worthless by the time he graduates in four years and plans to abandon them then.

Required:

1. Assume that Georgio expects to receive four years of entertainment services for the $960. What is the book value of these items after one year? Use straight-line depreciation with no residual value.

2. The university's academic year lasts a total of 30 weeks, from early September to late April. Georgio does not take the TV and stereo system with him on vacations. During the academic year, he participates in many activities, so he averages three hours per week of watching television and listening to music. What is the average cost per hour of use? (Ignore costs of electricity and repairs.)

3. Georgio is disturbed by the answer to (2). He complains to a friend that this amount exceeds the hourly cost of going to the movies on specific days of the week. His friend suggests that he could lower the average cost by leaving the TV set on whenever he goes to class. Georgio attends classes for 12 hours per week. Comment on this suggestion.

4. After owning the TV set and stereo system for one year, Georgio became curious about the price he could get for selling these items. He discovered that the most he could receive is $600. He does not plan to sell them but the information distresses him. What amount should he associate with the TV set and stereo system after one year? Explain.

P9–2 **Determining the Acquisition Cost and the Financial Statement Effects of Depreciation,**　　**LO1, 2, 3, 5**
Extraordinary Repairs, and Asset Disposal (AP9–1)

On January 2, 2009, Athol Company bought a machine for use in operations. The machine has an estimated useful life of eight years and an estimated residual value of $1,500. The company provided the following information:

a. Invoice price of the machine, $70,000.

b. Freight paid by the vendor per sales agreement, $800.

c. Installation costs, $2,000 cash.

d. Cost of cleaning up the supplies, boxes and other garbage that remained after the installation of the machine, $100 cash.

e. Payment of the machine's price was made as follows:

January 2:

- Issued 1,000 common shares of Athol Company at $5 per share.
- Signed a $40,000 note payable due April 16, 2009, plus 12 percent interest.
- Balance of the invoice price to be paid in cash. The invoice allows for a 2 percent cash discount if the cash payment is made by January 11.

　　January 15:　Paid the balance of the invoice price in cash.
　　April 16:　　Paid the note payable and interest in cash.

f. On June 30, 2011, the company completed the replacement of a major part of the machine that cost $12,375. This expenditure is expected to reduce the machine's operating costs, increase its estimated useful life by two years, and its estimated residual value to $2,000.

g. Assume that on October 1, 2016, the company decided to replace the machine with a newer, more efficient model. It then sold the machine to Sako Ltd. on that date for $17,000 cash.

Required:

1. Compute the acquisition cost of the machine, and explain the basis for including certain costs in the determination of the machine's acquisition cost.

2. Indicate the accounts affected, amounts and direction (+ for increase and – for decrease) of the effects of the purchase and subsequent cash payments on the accounting equation. Use the following headings:

Date	Assets	=	Liabilities	+	Shareholders' Equity

3. Prepare the journal entries to record the purchase of the machine and subsequent cash payments on January 15 and April 16, 2009.

4. Compute the depreciation expense for each of the years 2009, 2010, and 2011, assuming the company's fiscal year ends on December 31. Use the straight-line depreciation method.

5. Prepare the journal entry to record the sale of the machine on October 1, 2016. (*Hint:* First determine the balance of the accumulated depreciation account on that date.)

LO2, 3

Sears Canada Inc.

P9–3   **Analyzing the Effects of Repairs, a Betterment, and Depreciation** (AP9–2)

Assume that Sears Canada Inc. made extensive repairs on an existing office building and added a new wing. The existing building originally cost $75 million when it was purchased at the beginning of 1992, and was depreciated on a straight-line basis over a 40-year useful life, with no residual value. During the year 2011, the following expenditures related to the building were made:

a. Ordinary repairs and maintenance expenditures for the year, $585,000 paid in cash.

b. Extensive and major repairs to the roof of the building, $850,000 paid in cash. These repairs were completed on December 31, 2011.

c. The new wing, completed on December 31, 2011, at a cost of $26 million, has an estimated useful life of 20 years and no residual value.

Required:

1. Applying the policies of Sears Canada Inc., complete the following schedule, indicating the effects of the preceding expenditures. If there is no effect on an account, write NE on the line (amounts in thousands):

	Building	Accumulated Depreciation	Depreciation Expense	Repairs Expense	Cash
Balance January 1, 2011	$75,000	$35,625			
Depreciation for 2011		____	____		____
Balance prior to expenditures	75,000	____	____		
Expenditure a	____	____	____	____	____
Expenditure b	____	____	____	____	____
Expenditure c	____	____	____	____	____
Balance December 31, 2011	____	____	____	____	____

2. What was the carrying amount of the building at December 31, 2011?

3. Compute the depreciation expense for 2012, assuming no additional capital expenditures on this building in 2012.

4. Explain the effect of depreciation on cash flows.

LO2, 3

e**X**cel

P9–4   **Computing a Basket Purchase Allocation and Recording Depreciation under Three Alternative Methods** (AP9–3)

At the beginning of the year, Wong's Martial Arts Centre bought three used fitness machines from Hangar Inc. for a total cash price of $38,000. Transportation costs on the machines were $2,000. The machines immediately were overhauled, installed, and started operating. The machines were different; therefore, each had to be recorded separately in the accounts. An appraiser was requested to estimate their market value at the date of purchase (prior to the overhaul and installation). The carrying amounts shown on Hangar's books also are available. The carrying amounts, appraisal results, installation costs, and renovation expenditures follow:

	Machine A	Machine B	Machine C
Carrying amount—Hangar	$8,000	$12,000	$6,000
Appraisal value	9,500	32,000	8,500
Installation costs	300	500	200
Renovation costs prior to use	2,000	400	600

By the end of the first year, each machine had been operating 8,000 hours.

Required:

1. Compute the cost of each machine by making a supportable allocation of the total cost to the three machines. Explain the rationale for the allocation basis used.

2. Prepare the entry to record depreciation expense at the end of year 1, assuming the following:

| Machine | Estimates | | Depreciation Method |
	Life	Residual Value	
A	5	$1,500	Straight-line
B	40,000 hours	900	Units-of-production
C	4	2,000	Double-declining-balance

P9–5 **Inferring Depreciation Amounts and Determining the Effects of a Depreciation Error on Key Ratios** (AP9–4)

REX Stores Corporation

REX Stores Corporation, headquartered in Dayton, Ohio, is one of the leading consumer electronics retailers in the United States, operating more than 200 stores in 37 states. The following is a note from a recent annual report:

(1) SUMMARY OF SIGNIFICANT ACCOUNTING POLICIES

Property and Equipment—Property and equipment is recorded at cost. Depreciation is computed using the straight-line method. Estimated useful lives are 15 to 40 years for buildings and improvements and 3 to 12 years for fixtures and equipment. Leasehold improvements are depreciated over the initial lease term and one renewal term when exercise of the renewal term is assured. The components of property and equipment at January 31, 2009 and 2008, are as follows:

	2009	2008
	(in thousands)	
Land	$ 38,519	$ 38,567
Buildings and improvements	101,448	99,448
Fixtures and equipment	18,567	18,471
Leasehold improvements	9,797	9,882
Construction in progress		1,251
	168,331	167,619
Less: Accumulated depreciation	(36,922)	(33,056)
	$131,409	$134,563

Required:

1. Assuming that REX Stores did not sell any property, plant, and equipment in 2009, what was the amount of depreciation expense recorded in 2009?

2. Assume that REX Stores failed to record depreciation in 2009. Indicate the effect of the error (i.e., overstated or understated) on the following ratios: (*a*) earnings per share, (*b*) fixed asset turnover, and (*c*) return on equity. Computations are not required.

P9–6 **Evaluating the Effect of Alternative Depreciation Methods on Key Ratios from an Analyst's Perspective**

Bombardier

eXcel

Bombardier Inc. is one of the largest manufacturers of planes and trains in the world. The company's assets exceed $20 billion. As a result, depreciation is a significant item on Bombardier's income statement. You are a financial analyst for Bombardier and have been asked to determine the impact of alternative depreciation methods. For your analysis, you have been asked to compare methods based on a machine that cost $90,225. The estimated useful life is 10 years, and the estimated residual value is $2,225. The machine has an estimated useful life in productive output of 88,000 units. Actual output was 10,000 in year 1 and 8,000 in year 2.

Required:

1. For years 1 and 2 only, prepare a separate depreciation schedule for each of the following alternative methods. Round your computations to the nearest dollar.

   a. Straight-line

   b. Units-of-production

   c. Double-declining-balance

Method: _____				
Year	Computation	Depreciation Expense	Accumulated Depreciation	Carrying Amount
At acquisition				
1				
2				

2. Evaluate each method in terms of its effect on cash flow, fixed asset turnover, and earnings per share (EPS). Assuming that Bombardier is most interested in reducing taxes and maintaining a high EPS for year 1, which method of depreciation would you recommend to management? Would your recommendation change for year 2? Why or why not?

LO5, 7

Mattel Inc.

P9–7 **Inferring Asset Age and Determining Financial Statement Effects of a Long-Lived Asset Disposal (Challenging)** (AP9–5)

Mattel Inc. is the leading toy maker in the world. The company's revenues exceed $6 billion. In the toy business, it is very difficult to determine the life expectancy of a product. Products that children love one year may sit on the shelf the following year. As a result, companies in the toy business often sell productive assets that are no longer needed. Assume that on December 31, 2011, the end of the company's fiscal year, Mattel's records showed the following data about a machine that was no longer needed to make a toy that was popular last year:

Machine, original cost	$104,000
Accumulated depreciation	55,000*

*Based on an estimated useful life of eight years, a residual value of $16,000, and straight-line depreciation.

On April 1, 2012, the machine was sold for $52,000 cash.

Required:

1. How old was the machine on January 1, 2012? Show computations.

2. Indicate the effect (i.e., the amount and direction—increase or decrease) of the sale of the machine on April 1, 2012, on

   a. Total assets

   b. Profit

   c. Cash flows (by each section of the statement: operating, investing, and financing activities)

LO5, 7

Singapore Airlines

P9–8 **Inferring Activities Affecting Fixed Assets from Notes to the Financial Statements and Analyzing the Impact of Depreciation on Cash Flows** (AP9–6)

Singapore Airlines reported the following information in the notes to a recent annual report (in Singapore dollars):

SINGAPORE AIRLINES
Notes to the Accounts
19. Property, plant, and equipment (in $ million)

	Beginning of Year	Additions	Disposals/ Transfers	End of Year
Cost				
Aircraft	$18,180.1	$2,257.2	$1,730.3	$18,707.0
Other property, plant, and equipment (summarized)	6,659.1	2,160.8	2,399.0	6,420.9
Accumulated depreciation				
Aircraft	5,634.2	1,468.5	843.9	6,258.8
Other fixed assets (summarized)	2,730.9	376.2	230.4	2,876.7

Singapore Airlines also reported the following cash flow details:

Cash Flow from Operating Activities (in $ million)

	The Company	
	Current Year	Prior Year
Operating profit	$ 903.6	$2,124.5
Adjustments for:		
Depreciation of property, plant, and equipment	1,844.7	1,488.8
Gain on disposal of property, plant, and equipment	(62.7)	(49.1)
Other adjustments (summarized)	(1.240.2)	641.3
Net cash provided by operating activities	1,445.4	4,205.5

Required:

1. Reconstruct the information in Note 19 into T-accounts for property, plant, and equipment and accumulated depreciation:

Fixed Assets		**Accumulated Depreciation**	
Beg. balance			Beg. Balance
Acquisitions	Disposals/transfers	Disposals/transfers	Depreciation expense
End. balance			End. Balance

2. Compute the amount of cash the company received for disposals and transfers. Show computations.

3. Compute the percentage of depreciation expense to cash flows from operations. How do you interpret this percentage?

P9–9 Recording and Interpreting the Disposal of Three Long-Lived Assets (AP9–7)   ▩ **LO5**
During 2012, Côté Company disposed of three different assets. On January 1, 2012, prior to the disposal of the assets, the accounts reflected the following:

Asset	Original Cost	Residual Value	Estimated Life	Accumulated Depreciation (straight line)
Machine A	$20,000	$3,000	8 years	$12,750 (6 years)
Machine B	42,600	4,000	20 years	15,440 (8 years)
Machine C	76,200	4,200	15 years	57,600 (12 years)

The machines were disposed of in the following ways:

a. Machine A: Sold on January 1, 2012, for $8,200 cash.

b. Machine B: Sold on April 1, 2012, for $27,000; received cash, $23,000, and a $4,000 interest-bearing (12%) note receivable due at the end of 12 months.

c. Machine C: Suffered irreparable damage from an accident on July 2, 2012. On July 10, 2012, a salvage company removed the machine immediately at no cost. The machine was insured, and $18,000 cash was collected from the insurance company.

Required:

1. Prepare all journal entries related to the disposal of each machine in 2012.

2. Explain the accounting rationale for the way that you recorded each disposal.

LO6

P9–10 **Determining Financial Statement Effects of Activities Related to Various Long-Lived Assets** (AP9–8)

During the 2013 fiscal year, Boyd Company completed the following transactions:

a. On January 10, 2013, paid $7,000 for a complete reconditioning of each of the following machines acquired on January 1, 2009 (total cost, $14,000). Although the reconditioning of the machines was necessary, it did not extend their useful lives.

    i. Machine A: Original cost, $26,000; accumulated depreciation (straight line) to December 31, 2012, $18,400 (residual value, $3,000).

    ii. Machine B: Original cost, $32,000; accumulated depreciation (straight line) to December 31, 2012, $13,000 (residual value, $6,000).

b. On July 1, 2013, purchased a patent for $19,600 cash (estimated useful life, seven years).

c. On January 1, 2013, purchased another business for cash $160,000, including $46,000 for goodwill. The company assumed no liabilities.

d. On September 1, 2013, constructed a storage shed on land leased from A. Kumar. The cost was $10,800, paid in cash; the estimated useful life was five years with no residual value. The company uses straight-line depreciation. The lease will expire in three years.

e. Total expenditures during 2013 for ordinary repairs and maintenance were $6,800.

f. On July 1, 2013, sold Machine A for $6,500 cash.

Required:

1. Indicate the accounts affected, amounts, and direction of the effects (+ for increase, – for decrease, and NE for no effect) of each transaction on the accounting equation. Use the following structure:

Date	Assets	=	Liabilities	+	Shareholders' Equity

2. For each of the long-lived assets, compute the depreciation expense for 2013 to the nearest month.

LO6

RONA Inc.

P9–11 **Computing Goodwill from the Purchase of a Business and Related Amortization** (AP9–9)

RONA is the largest Canadian distributor and retailer of hardware, home renovation, and gardening products. RONA operates a large network of franchised, affiliated, and corporate stores of various sizes and formats. The notes to the company's financial statements for the year 2005 indicate that it acquired the outstanding shares of TOTEM Building Supplies Ltd. (TOTEM) on April 1, 2005. The purchase price was $96,400,000 and the fair market value of identifiable assets acquired and liabilities assumed are as follows (in thousands of dollars):

Current assets	$ 55,547
Property, plant, and equipment	22,910
Current liabilities	(43,448)
Deferred income tax liability	(657)
Long-term debt	(15,109)

Required:

1. Compute the amount of goodwill resulting from the purchase.

2. Compute the adjustments that RONA would make at the end of its fiscal year, December 31, 2005, for depreciation or amortization of all long-lived assets (straight line), assuming an estimated remaining useful life of 10 years and no residual value. The company does not amortize goodwill.

P9–12 **Determining the Financial Statement Effects of the Acquisition and Amortization of Intangibles**

LO6

Figg Company, with a fiscal year ending December 31, acquired three intangible assets during 2012. For each of the following transactions, indicate the accounts affected, amounts and direction of the effect (+ for increase, − for decrease, and NE for no effect) on the accounting equation. Use the following headings:

Date	Assets	=	Liabilities	+	Shareholders' Equity

a. On January 1, 2012, the company purchased a patent from Ullrich Ltd. for $6,000 cash. Ullrich had developed the patent and registered it with the Canadian Intellectual Property Office on January 1, 2007.

b. On January 1, 2012, the company purchased a copyright for a total cash cost of $12,000; the remaining legal life was 25 years. Company executives estimated that the copyright would have no value by the end of 20 years.

c. The company purchased another company in January 2012 at a cash cost of $130,000. Included in the purchase price was $30,000 for goodwill; the balance was for plant, equipment, and fixtures (no liabilities were assumed).

d. On December 31, 2012, amortized the patent over its remaining legal life.

e. On December 31, 2012, amortized the copyright over the appropriate period.

P9–13 **Computing Amortization, Carrying Amount, and Asset Impairment Related to Different Intangible Assets** (AP9–10)

LO4, 6

Havel Company has five different intangible assets to be accounted for and reported on the financial statements. The management is concerned about the amortization of the cost of each of these intangibles. Facts about each intangible follow:

a. *Patent.* The company purchased a patent at a cash cost of $54,600 on January 1, 2011. The patent had a legal life of 20 years from the date of registration with the Canadian Intellectual Property Office, which was January 1, 2007. It is amortized over its remaining legal life.

b. *Copyright.* On January 1, 2011, the company purchased a copyright for $22,500 cash. The legal life remaining from that date is 30 years. It is estimated that the copyrighted item will have no value by the end of 25 years.

c. *Franchise.* The company obtained a franchise from McKerma Company to make and distribute a special item. It obtained the franchise on January 1, 2011, at a cash cost of $14,400 for a 12-year period.

d. *Licence.* On January 1, 2010, the company secured a licence from the city to operate a special service for a period of five years. Total cash expended to obtain the licence was $14,000.

e. *Goodwill.* The company started business in January 2009 by purchasing another business for a cash lump sum of $400,000. Included in the purchase price was $60,000 for goodwill. Company executives stated that "the goodwill is an important long-lived asset to us." It has an indefinite life.

Required:

1. Compute the amount of amortization that should be recorded for each intangible asset at the end of the fiscal year, December 31, 2011.

2. Compute the carrying amount of each intangible asset on December 31, 2012.

3. Assume that on January 2, 2013, the copyrighted item was impaired in its ability to continue to produce strong revenues. The other intangible assets were not affected. Havel estimated that the

copyright will be able to produce future cash flows of $18,000. The fair value of the copyright is determined to be $16,000. Compute the amount, if any, of the impairment loss to be recorded.

LO3

eXcel

P9–14 **Analyzing and Recording Entries Related to a Change in Estimated Life and Residual Value**

Rungano Corporation is a global publisher of magazines, books, and music and video collections, and it is one of the world's leading direct-mail marketers. Many direct-mail marketers use high-speed Didde press equipment to print their advertisements. These presses can cost more than $1 million. Assume that Rungano owns a Didde press acquired at an original cost of $1,200,000. It is being depreciated on a straight-line basis over a 20-year estimated useful life and has a $150,000 estimated residual value. At the end of 2012, the press had been depreciated for eight years. In January 2013, a decision was made, on the basis of improved maintenance procedures, that a total estimated useful life of 25 years and a residual value of $219,000 would be more realistic. The fiscal year ends December 31.

Required:

1. Compute (a) the amount of depreciation expense recorded in 2012 and (b) the carrying amount of the printing press at the end of 2012.

2. Compute the amount of depreciation that should be recorded in 2013. Show computations.

3. Prepare the adjusting entry to record depreciation expense at December 31, 2013.

ALTERNATE PROBLEMS

LO1, 2, 3, 5 **AP9–1** **Explaining the Nature of a Long-Lived Asset and Determining the Financial Statement Effects of Its Purchase** (P9–2)

On July 1, 2009, the Fitzgerald Corp. bought a machine for use in operations. The machine has an estimated useful life of six years and an estimated residual value of $2,500. The company provided the following information:

a. Invoice price of the machine, $60,000.

b. Freight paid by the vendor per sales agreement, $650.

c. Installation costs, $2,500 cash.

d. Payment of the machine's price was made as follows:

July 1:

- Fitzgerald Corp. issued 2,000 common shares at $5 per share.
- Signed an interest-bearing note for the balance of the invoice price, payable on September 1, 2009, plus 9 percent interest.

October 1: Paid the note payable and related interest in cash.

e. On June 30, 2012, the company completed the replacement of a major part of the machine that cost $11,500. This expenditure is expected to reduce the machine's operating costs and increase its estimated useful life by two years. At the same time, the machine's estimated residual value was reduced to $2,000.

f. Assume that on July 1, 2016, the company decided to dispose of the machine by selling it to Ayad Inc. on that date for $16,000 cash.

Required:

1. Compute the acquisition cost of the machine, and explain the basis for including certain costs in the determination of the machine's acquisition cost.

2. Indicate the accounts affected and the amounts and direction (+ for increase and – for decrease) of the effects of the purchase and subsequent cash payment on the accounting equation. Use the following headings:

Date	Assets	=	Liabilities	+	Shareholders' Equity

3. Prepare the journal entries to record the purchase of the machine and subsequent cash payments on October 1, 2009.

4. Compute the depreciation expense for each of the years 2009 and 2012, assuming the company's fiscal year ends on December 31. Use the straight-line depreciation method.

5. Prepare the journal entry to record the sale of the machine on July 1, 2016. (*Hint:* First determine the balance of the account Accumulated Depreciation on that date.)

AP9–2 **Analyzing the Effects of Repairs, a Betterment, and Depreciation** (AP9–3)

A recent annual report for AMERCO, the holding company for U-Haul International Inc. included the following note:

LO2, 3

AMERCO

Property, Plant, and Equipment

Property, plant, and equipment are stated at cost. Interest costs incurred during the initial construction of buildings or rental equipment are considered part of the cost. Depreciation is computed for financial reporting purposes principally using the straight-line method over the following estimated useful lives: rental equipment 2–20 years, building and non-rental equipment 3–55 years. Major overhauls to rental equipment are capitalized and are depreciated over the estimated period benefited. Routine maintenance costs are charged to operating expense as they are incurred.

AMERCO subsidiaries own property, plant, and equipment that provide offices for U-Haul and that are utilized in the manufacture, repair, and rental of U-Haul equipment. Assume that AMERCO made extensive repairs on an existing building and added a new wing. The building is a garage and repair facility for rental trucks that serve the Seattle area. The existing building originally cost $460,000, and by the end of 2011 (5 years), it was one-quarter depreciated on the basis of a 20-year estimated useful life and no residual value. Assume straight-line depreciation, computed to the nearest month. During 2012, the following expenditures related to the building were made:

a. Ordinary repairs and maintenance expenditures for the year, $10,000 paid in cash.

b. Extensive and major repairs to the roof of the building, $34,000 paid in cash. These repairs were completed on June 30, 2012.

c. The new wing was completed on June 30, 2012, at a cash cost of $173,000. By itself, the wing had an estimated useful life of 15 years and no residual value. The company intends to sell the building and wing at the end of the building's useful life (in $14\frac{1}{2}$ years from June 30, 2012).

Required:

1. Applying the policies of AMERCO, complete the following schedule, indicating the effects of the preceding expenditures. If there is no effect on an account, write NE on the line:

	Building	Accumulated Depreciation	Depreciation Expense	Repairs Expense	Cash
Balance, January 1, 2012	$460,000	$115,000			
Depreciation Jan. 1–June 30		_____	_____		_____
Balance prior to expenditures	460,000	_____	_____		
Expenditure a	_____	_____	_____	_____	_____
Expenditure b	_____	_____	_____	_____	_____
Expenditure c	_____	_____	_____	_____	_____
Depreciation July 1–December 31:					
Existing building		_____	_____	_____	_____
Major repairs and betterments		_____	_____	_____	_____
Balance, December 31, 2012	_____	_____	_____	_____	_____

2. What was the carrying amount of the building on December 31, 2012?

3. Explain the effect of depreciation on cash flows.

AP9–3 **Computing a Basket Purchase Allocation, and Recording Depreciation under Three Alternative Methods** (P9–4)

LO2, 3

At the beginning of the year, Labinski Inc. bought three used machines from Dumas Corporation, for a total cash price of $62,000. Transportation costs on the machines were $3,000. The machines immediately were overhauled, installed, and started operating. The machines were different; therefore, each had to be recorded separately in the accounts. An appraiser was requested to estimate their market value at the date of purchase (prior to the overhaul and installation). The carrying amounts shown on Dumas's books also are available. The carrying amounts, appraisal results, installation costs, and renovation expenditures follow:

	Machine A	Machine B	Machine C
Carrying amount—Dumas	$10,500	$22,000	$16,000
Appraisal value	11,500	32,000	28,500
Installation costs	800	1,100	1,100
Renovation costs prior to use	600	1,400	1,600

By the end of the first year, each machine had been operating 7,000 hours.

Required:

1. Compute the cost of each machine by making a supportable allocation of the total cost to the three machines (round your calculations to two decimal places). Explain the rationale for the allocation basis used.

2. Prepare the entry to record depreciation expense at the end of year 1, assuming the following:

Machine	Estimates		Depreciation Method
	Life	Residual Value	
A	4	$1,000	Straight-line
B	35,000 hours	2,000	Units-of-production
C	5	1,500	Double-declining-balance

LO1,3   **AP9–4**

The Forzani Group Ltd.

Inferring Depreciation Amounts and Determining the Effects of a Depreciation Error on Key Ratios (P9–5)

The Forzani Group Ltd. (FGL) franchises several specialty sports retail clothing and sports equipment stores. Its stores include SportChek, Coast Mountain Sports, Sport Mart, and National Sports. Its franchises are Intersport, RnR, Atmosphere, and Sports Experts. As at February 1, 2009, its fiscal year-end, the company operated 337 corporate stores and sold merchandise to 227 franchises. The following is a note from a recent annual report:

1. Significant Accounting Policies

(c) Capital Assets

Capital assets are recorded at cost and are depreciated using the following methods and ratios:

Building	Declining-balance	—4%
Building on leased land	Straight-line	—Lesser of the time of the lease or estimated useful life.
Furniture, fixtures, equipment, software, and automotive	Straight-line	—3–8 years
Leasehold improvements	Straight-line	—Lesser of the time of the lease or estimated useful life.

Capital assets at February 1, 2009, and February 3, 2008, are as follows (in thousands of dollars):

	2009	2008
Land	$ 3,173	$ 3,173
Building	20,928	20,928
Building on leased land	4,583	4,583
Furniture, fixtures, equipment, software, and automotive	243,564	217,365
Leasehold improvements	260,030	239,439
Construction in progress	14,029	6,054
	546,307	491,542
Less accumulated depreciation	349,542	302,021
Carrying amount	$196,765	$189,521

Required:

1. Assuming that FGL did not have any asset impairment losses and did not sell any property, plant, and equipment in fiscal year 2009, what was the amount of depreciation expense recorded in 2009?

2. Assume that FGL failed to record depreciation in 2009. Indicate the effect of the error (i.e., overstated or understated) on the following ratios: (*a*) earnings per share, (*b*) fixed asset turnover, and (*c*) return on equity. Computations are not required.

AP9–5 **Inferring Asset Age and Determining Financial Statement Effects of a Long-Lived Asset Disposal (Challenging)** (P9–7)

■ **LO5, 7**

Hasbro Inc.

Hasbro Inc. designs, manufactures, and markets high-quality toys, games, and infant products. The company's revenues exceed $4.0 billion. In the toy business, it is very difficult to determine the life expectancy of a product. Products that children love one year may sit on the shelf the following year. As a result, companies in the toy business often sell productive assets that are no longer needed. Assume that on December 31, 2011, the end of the company's fiscal year, Hasbro's records showed the following data about a machine that was no longer needed to make a toy that was popular last year:

Machine, original cost	$214,000
Accumulated depreciation	128,000*

*Based on an estimated useful life of six years, a residual value of $22,000, and straight-line depreciation.

On July 1, 2012, the machine was sold for $76,000 cash.

Required:

1. How old was the machine on January 1, 2012? Show computations.
2. Indicate the effect (i.e., the amount and direction—increase or decrease) of the sale of the machine on July 1, 2012, on
   a. Total assets
   b. Profit
   c. Cash flows (for each section of the statement: operating, investing, and financing activities)

AP9–6 **Inferring Activities Affecting Property, Plant, and Equipment from Notes to the Financial Statements and Analyzing the Impact of Depreciation on Cash Flows** (P9–8)

■ **LO5, 7**

Cathay Pacific Airways

Cathay Pacific Airways reported the following information in the notes to a recent annual report (in Hong Kong dollars):

CATHAY PACIFIC AIRWAYS
Notes to the Accounts
11. Fixed Assets (in millions of HK dollars)

	Acquisition Cost	Accumulated Depreciation
Balance, beginning of year	$107,454	$45,066
Additional acquisitions	9,202	
Depreciation expense		5,169
Disposals	(3,376)	(2,994)
Balance, end of year	$113,280	$47,241

Cathay Pacific also reported the following cash flow details:

Cash Flow from Operating Activities (in millions of HK dollars)

	2008	2007
Operating (loss)/Profit	$(7,929)	$7,739
Adjustments for:		
Depreciation of fixed assets	5,169	4,831
Loss on disposal of fixed assets	245	70
Other adjustments (summarized)	6,397	3,461
Cash generated from operations	$3,882	$16,101

Required:

1. Reconstruct the information in Note 11 into T-accounts for fixed assets and accumulated depreciation:

Fixed Assets			Accumulated Depreciation		
Beg. balance				Beg. Balance	
Acquisitions	Disposals		Disposals	Depreciation expense	
End. balance				End. Balance	

2. Compute the amount of cash the company received for disposals during 2008. Show computations.

3. Compute the percentage of depreciation expense to cash flows from operations for 2008. How do you interpret this percentage?

▓ **LO5**   **AP9–7**   **Recording and Interpreting the Disposal of Three Long-Lived Assets** (P9–9)

During 2012, Callaway Company disposed of three different assets. On January 1, 2012, prior to the disposal of the assets, the accounts reflected the following:

Asset	Original Cost	Residual Value	Estimated Life	Accumulated Depreciation (straight line)
Machine A	$24,000	$2,000	5 years	$17,600 (4 years)
Machine B	16,500	5,000	10 years	8,050 (7 years)
Machine C	59,200	3,200	14 years	48,000 (12 years)

The machines were disposed of in the following ways:

a. Machine A: Sold on January 1, 2012, for $6,250 cash.

b. Machine B: Sold on July 1, 2012, for $9,500; received cash, $4,500, and a $5,000 interest-bearing (10 percent) note receivable due at the end of 12 months.

c. Machine C: Suffered irreparable damage from an accident on October 2, 2012. On October 10, 2012, a salvage company removed the machine immediately at a cost of $500. The machine was insured, and $11,500 cash was collected from the insurance company.

Required:

1. Prepare all journal entries related to the disposal of each machine.

2. Explain the accounting rationale for the way that you recorded each disposal.

▓ **LO6**   **AP9–8**   **Determining Financial Statement Effects of Activities Related to Various Long-Lived Assets** (P9–10)

During the 2013 fiscal year, Zhou Corporation completed the following transactions:

a. On January 1, 2013, paid $8,000 for a complete reconditioning of each of the following machines acquired on January 1, 2010 (total cost, $16,000). Although the reconditioning of the machines was necessary, it did not extend their useful lives.

    i. Machine A: Original cost, $21,500; accumulated depreciation (straight-line) to December 31, 2012, $13,500 (residual value, $3,500).

    ii. Machine B: Original cost, $18,000; accumulated depreciation (straight-line) to December 31, 2012, $10,200 (residual value, $1,000).

b. On July 1, 2013, purchased a licence for $6,300 cash (estimated useful life, three years).

c. On July 1, 2013, purchased another business for cash $120,000, including $29,000 for goodwill. The company assumed $24,000 of liabilities from the other business. The company does not amortize goodwill.

d. On July 1, 2013, sold Machine A for $11,000 cash.

e. On October 1, 2013, repaved the parking lot of the building leased from J. Caldwell. The cost was $7,800, paid in cash; the estimated useful life was five years with no residual value. The company uses straight-line depreciation. The lease will expire on December 31, 2016.

f. Total expenditures during 2013 for ordinary repairs and maintenance were $6,700.

Required:

1. For each of these transactions, indicate the accounts affected, amounts, and direction of the effects (+ for increase and − for decrease) on the accounting equation. Use the following structure:

Date	Assets	=	Liabilities	+	Shareholders' Equity

2. For each of the long-lived assets, compute the depreciation expense for 2013 to the nearest dollar.

AP9–9   Computing Goodwill from the Purchase of a Business and Related Depreciation (P9–11)   ▓ **LO6**

The notes to a recent annual report from Weebok Corporation included the following:

> **Business Acquisitions**
>
> During the current year, the company acquired the assets of Sport Shoes Inc.

Assume that Weebok acquired Sport Shoes on January 2, 2011. Weebok acquired the name of the company and all of its assets, except cash, for $450,000 cash. Weebok did not assume the liabilities. On January 2, 2011, the statement of financial position of Sport Shoes reflected the following book values and an independent appraiser estimated the following market values for the assets:

January 2, 2011	Carrying Amount	Market Value
Trade receivables, net	$ 45,000	$ 45,000
Inventory	220,000	210,000
Property, plant, and equipment, net	32,000	60,000
Other assets	3,000	10,000
Total assets	$300,000	
Liabilities	$ 60,000	
Shareholders' equity	240,000	
Total liabilities and shareholders' equity	$300,000	

Required:

1. Compute the amount of goodwill resulting from the purchase. (*Hint:* Assets are purchased at market value, which is their cost at the date of acquisition.)

2. Compute the adjustments that Weebok would make at the end of its fiscal year, December 31, 2011, for depreciation of all long-lived assets (straight line), assuming an estimated remaining useful life of 15 years and no residual value. The company does not amortize goodwill.

AP9–10   Computing Amortization, Carrying Amount, and Asset Impairment Related to Different Intangible Assets (P9–13)   ▓ **LO4, 6**

Theriault Corporation has five different intangible assets to be accounted for and reported on the financial statements. The management is concerned about the amortization of the cost of each of these intangibles. Facts about each intangible follow:

a. *Patent.* The company purchased a patent at a cash cost of $18,600 on January 1, 2012. The patent had a legal life of 20 years from the date of registration with the Canadian Intellectual Property Office, which was January 1, 2010. It is amortized over its remaining legal life.

b. *Copyright.* On January 1, 2012, the company purchased a copyright for $24,750 cash. The legal life remaining from that date is 30 years. It is estimated that the copyrighted item will have no value by the end of 15 years.

c. *Franchise.* The company obtained a franchise from Farrell Company to make and distribute a special item. It obtained the franchise on January 1, 2012, at a cash cost of $19,200 for a 12-year period.

d. *Licence.* On January 1, 2011, the company secured a licence from the city to operate a special service for a period of seven years. Total cash expended to obtain the licence was $21,000.

e. *Goodwill.* The company started business in January 2010 by purchasing another business for a cash lump sum of $650,000. The purchase price included $75,000 for goodwill. Company executives stated that "the goodwill is an important long-lived asset to us." It has an indefinite life.

Required:

1. Compute the amount of amortization expense that should be recorded for each intangible asset at the end of the fiscal year, December 31, 2012.

2. Compute the carrying amount of each intangible asset on January 1, 2015.

3. Assume that on January 2, 2015, the franchise was impaired in its ability to continue to produce strong revenues. The other intangible assets were not affected. Theriault estimated that the franchise will be able to produce future cash flows of $16,500, with a fair value of $15,000. Compute the amount, if any, of the impairment loss to be recorded.

CASES AND PROJECTS

FINDING AND INTERPRETING FINANCIAL INFORMATION

LO1, 3   **CP9–1**

The Nestlé Group

Finding Financial Information
Refer to the financial statements and accompanying notes of The Nestlé Group given in Appendix A at the end of this book.

Required:

1. What method(s) of depreciation and amortization does the company use?

2. What is the amount of accumulated depreciation and amortization at the end of the current year?

3. For depreciation purposes, what is the estimated useful life of the buildings?

4. What amount of depreciation and amortization was reported as expense for the current year?

5. What is the fixed asset turnover ratio for the current year? What does it suggest?

6. For each of the preceding questions, where did you locate the information?

LO1, 3   **CP9–2**

WestJet Airlines vs.
Southwest Airlines

Comparing Companies within an Industry
Southwest Airlines is an exuberant, no-frills airline that was started more than 30 years ago. WestJet Airlines has followed Southwest's successful corporate strategy, which is based on "keeping airplanes in the air." Selected data from Southwest's annual reports appear below (in millions of dollars):

	December 31	
	2009	**2008**
Property and equipment, at cost	$15,888	$15,871
Less allowance for depreciation	5,254	4,831
	10,634	11,040
Total assets	14,629	14,068
Total operating revenues for the year	10,350	11,023
Southwest uses the straight-line depreciation method.		

Similar data for WestJet Airlines for fiscal year 2009 were provided earlier in this chapter.

Required:

1. Compute the percentage of property and equipment, net to total assets, for both companies each year. Why might the two ratios differ?

2. Compute the percentage of the property and equipment that has been depreciated for each company for the most recent year. Why do you think the percentages differ?

3. Compute the fixed asset turnover ratio for the most recent year presented for both companies. Which has the higher efficiency in using assets? Why?

4. Would you expect Southwest's ratios to increase or decrease over time? Why? What about WestJet's ratios?

FINANCIAL REPORTING AND ANALYSIS CASES

CP9–3

Broadening Financial Research Skills: Identifying Competitors in an Industry
Reuters provides lists of industries and the competitors in each at **www.reuters.com**.

Required:

Using your Web browser, contact Reuters and identify three competitors for the following industries:

1. Airline
2. Consumer electronics
3. Food processing
4. Footwear

CP9–4 Using Financial Reports: Analyzing the Age of Assets

Papa John's International is a major pizza chain with about 3,500 pizzerias across the United States and in many other countries, including 35 restaurants in Canada. A note to a recent annual report for Papa John's International contained the following information (in thousands of dollars):

	Current Year	Previous Year
Land	$ 32,876	$ 31,450
Buildings and improvements	83,765	79,586
Leasehold improvements	89,272	82,319
Equipment and other	199,993	190,913
Construction in progress	6,331	3,812
	412,237	388,080
Less accumulated depreciation and amortization	(217,995)	(198,088)
Next property and equipment	$194,242	$189,992

Source: Papa John's International Annual Report 2009, Form 10-K.

Depreciation and amortization expense (in thousands of dollars) charged to operations was $32,756 in the current year and $32,846 in the previous year. Depreciation generally is computed by using the straight-line method for financial reporting purposes.

Required:

1. What is your best estimate of the average expected life for Papa John's depreciable assets?
2. What is your best estimate of the average age of Papa John's depreciable assets?

LO3

Papa John's
International

CP9–5 Using Financial Reports: Analyzing Fixed Asset Turnover Ratio and Cash Flows

CanWest Global Communications Corp., with headquarters in Winnipeg, Manitoba, is one of Canada's largest media conglomerates and the owner of many Canadian newspapers, television stations, and cable channels, as well as several stations in Australia, Ireland, and New Zealand. Selected data from a recent annual report are as follows (in thousands of dollars):

LO1, 3, 6, 7

CanWest Global
Communications
Corp.

Property and equipment, and intangibles	Current Year	Prior Year
From the consolidated statement of financial position and notes		
Property and equipment, net	$ 692,698	$ 705,339
Intangible assets with indefinite lives	1,096,655	1,054,037
Intangible assets with finite lives, net	77,301	88,081
From the consolidated income statement		
Revenue	2,878,625	3,032,485
From the consolidated statement of cash flows		
Net earnings for the year	178,672	10,205
Adjustments:		
Depreciation of property, plant, and equipment	94,171	90,943
Amortization of intangible assets	12,423	20,341
Other adjustments, net	(168,332)	415,319
Cash provided by operations	$116,934	$536,808
From the notes to the financial statements		
Accumulated depreciation on property and equipment	$600,737	$536,702

Required:

1. Compute the cost of the property and equipment at the end of the current year. Explain your answer.

2. What is your best estimate of the average expected life of CanWest's property and equipment? What was the approximate age of the property and equipment at the end of the current year? Assume that CanWest uses straight-line depreciation.

3. Compute the fixed asset turnover ratio for the current year. Explain your results.

4. Compute an estimate of the amortization expense of intangible assets with finite lives for the next year.

5. On the consolidated statement of cash flows, why are the depreciation and amortization amounts added to net earnings for the year?

LO5   **CP9–6**   **Using Financial Reports: Inferring the Sale of Assets**

Eastman Kodak

An annual report for Eastman Kodak reported that the balance of property, plant, and equipment at the end of the current year was $6,805 million. At the end of the previous year, it had been $7,327 million. During the current year, the company bought $254 million worth of new equipment. The balance of accumulated depreciation at the end of the current year was $5,254 million and $5,516 million at the end of the previous year. Depreciation expense for the current year was $500 million. The annual report did not disclose any gain or loss on the disposition of property, plant, and equipment, so you may assume that the amount was zero.

Required:
What amount of proceeds did Eastman Kodak receive when it sold property, plant, and equipment during the current year? (*Hint:* Set up T-accounts.)

CRITICAL THINKING CASES

LO3   **CP9–7**   **Making a Decision as a Financial Analyst: Interpreting the Impact of the Capitalization of Interest on an Accounting Ratio**

WestJet Airlines

The capitalization of interest associated with self-constructed assets was discussed in this chapter. A recent annual report for WestJet Airlines disclosed the following information concerning capitalization of interest:

> **1. Significant accounting policies (continued):**
>
> (o) Capitalized interest costs:
>
> Costs associated with assets under development, which have probable future economic benefit, can be clearly defined and measured, and are incurred for the development of new products or technologies, are capitalized. These costs are not amortized until the asset is substantially complete and ready for its intended use, at which time they are amortized over the life of the underlying asset. Interest attributable to funds used to finance property and equipment is capitalized to the related asset until the point of commercial use. Costs of new route development are expensed as incurred.

Assume that WestJet capitalized interest in the amount of $500,000 and disclosed $2.2 million of interest expense in its income statement for the year. One useful accounting ratio is the interest coverage ratio (Profit before interest and taxes divided by Interest expense).

Required:

1. Explain why an analyst would calculate this ratio.

2. Did WestJet include the $500,000 in the reported interest expense of $2.2 million? If not, should an analyst include it when calculating the interest coverage ratio? Explain.

CP9–8 Evaluating an Ethical Dilemma: Analyzing an Accounting Change

The interim report for the fourth quarter of 2009 for Norbord Inc. included the following information:

LO3, 7

Norbord Inc.

Note 2. Changes In Accounting Policies and Significant Accounting Estimates

Property, Plant, and Equipment

In accordance with *Canadian Institute of Chartered Accountants* (CICA) *Handbook* Section 3061, "Property, Plant and Equipment," depreciation methods should be reviewed on a regular basis and significant events may indicate a need to revise depreciation methods. The Company had utilized the straight line method of depreciation for production equipment, which allocates cost equally to each period. In a period of fluctuating production levels, the straight line depreciation method does not result in rational allocation of the cost of equipment to production. Consequently, effective March 29, 2009, the Company changed to the unit of production depreciation method for its production assets. This method allocates the equipment costs to the actual units produced based on estimated annual capacity over the remaining useful life of the assets. The impact of this change has been applied prospectively as a change in an estimate, and it resulted in a $12 million reduction in depreciation expense in 2009.

Required:

1. What was the stated reason for the change in depreciation method? What other factors do you think management considered when it decided to make this accounting change?

2. Do you think this is an ethical decision?

3. Who were affected by the change, and how were they benefited or harmed?

4. What impact did this change have on cash flows for Norbord?

5. As an investor, how would you react to the fact that Norbord's depreciation expense will decrease by $12 million?

FINANCIAL REPORTING AND ANALYSIS TEAM PROJECT

CP9–9 Team Project: Analyzing of Long-Lived Assets

LO3, 7

As a team, select an industry to analyze. A list of companies classified by industry can be obtained by accessing **www.fpinfomart.ca** and then choosing "Companies by Industry." You can also find a list of industries and companies within each industry via **http://ca.finance.yahoo.com/investing** (click on "Annual Reports" under "Tools"). Using a Web browser, each team member should acquire the annual report for one publicly traded company in the industry, with each member selecting a different company.

Required:

On an individual basis, each team member should then write a short report answering the following questions about the selected company. Discuss any patterns across the companies that you as a team observe. Then, as a group, write a short report comparing and contrasting your companies.

1. List the accounts and amounts of the company's long-lived assets (land, buildings, equipment, intangible assets, natural resources, and other).
   a. What is the percentage of each to total assets?
   b. What do the results of your analysis suggest about the strategy your company has followed with respect to investing in long-lived assets?

2. What cost allocation method(s) and estimates does the company use for each type of long-lived asset?

3. Compute the approximate average remaining life of property, plant, and equipment overall.

4. What does the company disclose regarding asset impairment? What was its impairment loss, if any, in the most recent year?

5. Ratio analysis:

   a. What does the fixed asset turnover ratio measure in general?

   b. Compute the ratio for the last three years.

   c. What do your results suggest about the company?

   d. If available, find the industry ratio for the most recent year, compare it to your results, and discuss why you believe your company differs or is similar to the industry ratio.

6. What was the effect of depreciation expense on cash flows from operating activities? Compute the percentage of depreciation expense to cash flows from operating activities for each of the past three years.

7. Refer to the statement of cash flows and identify the capital expenditures that the company made over the last three years. Did the company sell any long-lived assets?

Reporting and Interpreting Current Liabilities

After studying this chapter, you should be able to do the following:

LEARNING OBJECTIVES

LO1 Define, measure, and report current liabilities. p. 531

LO2 Compute and interpret the current ratio. p. 532

LO3 Compute and interpret the trade payables turnover ratio. p. 535

LO4 Report notes payable and explain the time value of money. p. 539

LO5 Report contingent liabilities and commitments. p. 545

LO6 Explain the impact of changes in current liabilities on cash flows. p. 548

FOCUS COMPANY: **Benetton Group**
MANAGING CAPITAL STRUCTURE

The Benetton Group (http://investors.benettongroup.com) was founded in Treviso, Italy, in 1965. The company comprises two segments: textile manufacturing and the production, marketing, and distribution of finished garments and fashionable accessories. Benetton Group owns 54 retail stores in Canada and the United States. Outlets are typically located in commercial or historic centres and carry a full selection of brands for mothers-to-be, infants, toddlers, young children, and adults.

Benetton Group comprises the brands United Colors of Benetton (UCB), Undercolors, Sisley, Sisley Young, Playlife, and Killer Loop. Producing over 150 million garments each year, the Benetton Group retails through more than 6,200 global outlets. Approximately 50 percent of revenue arises from sales of the UCB products, 18 percent from Sisley, and the remainder from UCB Kid and Playlife. Sales for 2009 totalled €2 billion, mostly to wholesalers (78 percent) and the remainder to retailers.

The textiles and garments are manufactured in Italy and other Mediterranean countries such as Tunisia, in Eastern European countries such as Romania and Croatia, as well as in Asian and South American countries. The tailoring, finishing, and ironing are labour-intensive and completed by small and medium-sized enterprises. The dyeing, weaving, and quality control is, however, highly automated and controlled centrally.

One important reason for Benetton's success as a manufacturer, distributor, and seller of garments and accessories is its commitment to new systems and equipment to control its industrial logistics. At its operations in Castrette, Italy, its automated sorting system packs and transports garments to an automated distribution centre. The centre's capacity is 800,000 boxes. The centre can handle 80,000 boxes of throughput per day, yet only 26 people work there. Benetton Group augments this central hub with others in Hong Kong, Taiwan, and Shanghai. A centralized information technology system ensures those managing this huge global company receive accurate and up-to-date information regarding what brands and accessories are shipped to which of the 6,200 outlets.

In addition to operating activities, management must focus on a number of critical financing activities to ensure that the company remains profitable and is able to generate sufficient resources to eventually meet its goals. The financing activities for Benetton Group generate funds to serve two important purposes: (1) to finance the current operating activities of the business and (2) to acquire long-lived assets that permit the company to grow in the future.

UNDERSTANDING THE BUSINESS

CAPITAL STRUCTURE is the mixture of debt and equity that finances the short- and long-term operating requirements of a company.

Businesses finance the acquisition of their assets from two sources: funds supplied by creditors (debt) and funds provided by owners (equity). The mixture of debt and equity used by a business is called its *capital structure*. In addition to selecting a capital structure, management can select from a variety of sources when borrowing money, as illustrated in the liabilities section of the statement of financial position of Benetton Group in Exhibit 10.1.

In deciding how best to finance its projects, Benetton Group's management must consider two key factors: the financial risk associated with the source of financing and the return to shareholders on their investment in the company. From the firm's perspective, debt capital is riskier than equity because interest and principal payments on debt are legal obligations that must be paid. If a company cannot meet a required debt payment because of a temporary cash shortage, creditors may force the company into bankruptcy. Creditors may require the sale of assets to satisfy the debt obligations.

In contrast, dividend payments to shareholders are not legal obligations until declared by the board of directors. Therefore, equity offers lower financial risk to the issuing corporation. While companies may suspend or reduce the amount of

Exhibit **10.1**
Benetton Group's Liabilities

REAL WORLD EXCERPT

Benetton Group

ANNUAL REPORT

BENETTON GROUP S.P.A.
Consolidated Statements of Financial Position (Partial)
(in thousands of euro)

	Dec. 31, 2009	Dec. 31, 2008
Liabilities		
Non-current liabilities		
Medium/long-term loans	401,095	400,310
Other medium/long-term payables	21,597	17,525
Lease financing	668	464
Retirement benefit obligations	47,357	49,178
Other medium/long-term provisions and liabilities	31,386	28,175
	502,103	495,652
Current liabilities		
Trade payables	403,911	415,594
Other payables, accrued expenses and deferred income	137,639	166,535
Current income tax liabilities	9,570	8,569
Other current provisions and liabilities	6,474	5,967
Current portion of lease financing	411	1,828
Current portion of medium/long-term loans	238	71
Financial payables and bank loans	311,621	460,585
	869,864	1,059,149
Total liabilities	1,371,967	1,554,801

Source: Benetton Group Annual Report 2009.

dividends during periods of financial difficulty, they may not suspend the payment of principal and interest owed to creditors without negative consequences. As with any business transaction, borrowers and lenders attempt to negotiate the most favourable terms possible. Managers devote considerable effort to analyzing alternative funding arrangements.

Companies that include debt in their capital structure also must make strategic decisions concerning the proper balance between short-term and long-term debt. To evaluate a company's capital structure, financial analysts calculate a number of accounting ratios. In this chapter, we primarily discuss current (short-term) liabilities as well as some important accounting ratios. In the next chapter, we discuss non-current liabilities, including a special category of long-term debt, bonds payable.

ORGANIZATION OF THE CHAPTER

Supplemental material:
Appendix 10A: Deferred Income Tax Assets and Liabilities

LIABILITIES DEFINED AND CLASSIFIED

Most people have a reasonable understanding of the definition of the word *liability*. Accountants formally define liabilities as debts or obligations arising from an entity's past transactions that will be paid with assets or services. As Exhibit 10.1 shows, Benetton Group reported current and non-current liabilities of €1,372 million at December 31, 2009. Benetton Group has borrowed money in the past from creditors and purchased goods and services on credit (past transactions), promising its creditors to pay cash (an asset) at some point in the future, based on the terms of its debt agreements.

When a liability is first recorded, it is measured in terms of its current cash equivalent, which is the cash amount that a creditor would accept to settle the liability immediately. Although Benetton Group had short-term and medium/long-term loans of €772.1 million as at December 31, 2009, it will repay much more than that because the company must also pay interest on the debt. Interest payable in the future is not included in the amount of the liability because it accrues and becomes a liability with the passage of time. For fiscal year 2009, the company reported €34.7 million of interest expense in the notes to its financial statements.

Like most businesses, Benetton Group has several kinds of liabilities and a wide range of creditors. The list of liabilities on the statement of financial position differs from one company to the next because different operating activities result in different types of liabilities. The liability section of Benetton Group's statement of financial position begins with the caption "Non-current liabilities" followed by "Current

LO1

Define, measure, and report current liabilities.

LIABILITIES are debts or obligations arising from past transactions that will be paid with assets or services.

CURRENT LIABILITIES are short-term obligations that will be paid within the normal operating cycle or one year, whichever is longer.

liabilities." We discuss current liabilities in this chapter and non-current liabilities in the next chapter.

Current liabilities are defined as short-term obligations that will be paid within the current operating cycle of the business or within one year of the statement of financial position date, whichever is longer. Because most companies have an operating cycle that is shorter than one year, normally, current liabilities can be defined simply as liabilities that are due within one year. Non-current liabilities include all other liabilities.

LIQUIDITY is the ability to pay current obligations.

Information about current liabilities is very important to managers and analysts because these obligations must be paid in the near future. Analysts say that a company has liquidity if it has the ability to pay its current obligations. Companies that do not settle their current obligations in a timely manner quickly find that suppliers of goods and services may not be prepared to grant them credit for their purchases, and may be forced to seek short-term financing through banks. A number of financial ratios, including the current ratio, are useful in evaluating liquidity.

 KEY RATIO **ANALYSIS**

CURRENT RATIO

LO²

Compute and interpret the current ratio.

ANALYTICAL QUESTION → Does the company currently have the resources to pay its short-term debt?

RATIO AND COMPARISONS → Analysts use the *current ratio* as an indicator of the amount of current assets available to satisfy current liabilities. It is computed as follows:

Current Ratio = Current Assets ÷ Current Liabilities

The 2009 ratio for Benetton Group is

€1,334,809 ÷ €869,864 = 1.53

Comparisons over Time				Comparisons with Competitors	
Benetton Group				Burberry*	Guess*
2007	2008	2009		2009	2009
1.74	1.34	1.53		1. 52	3.20

* The fiscal years of Burberry and Guess end on March 31 and January 31, respectively.

INTERPRETATIONS

In General → A high ratio normally suggests good liquidity, but too high a ratio suggests inefficient use of resources. An old guideline was that companies should have a current ratio between 1 and 2. Today, many strong companies use sophisticated management techniques to minimize funds invested in current assets, and, as a result, have current ratios below 1.

Focus Company Analysis → Benetton Group's current ratio for 2009 indicates that the company has €1.53 to pay each €1.00 in current liabilities. The decrease in the current ratio from 2007 to 2009 may indicate improved efficiencies in managing financial resources. In comparison to Benetton Group's ratio, Burberry's ratio is very similar and Guess's is much higher.

A Few Cautions → The current ratio may be a misleading measure of liquidity if significant funds are tied up in assets that will not be easily converted into cash. A company with a high current ratio might still have liquidity problems if the majority of its current assets are slow-moving inventory. This is most certainly an issue for these three apparel companies whose ability to generate sales depends on the availability of up-to-the-moment fashionable garments. Analysts recognize that managers can manipulate the current ratio by engaging in particular types of transactions just before the close of the fiscal year. For example, the current ratio can be improved by paying creditors immediately prior to the preparation of financial statements.

FINANCIAL POSITION RATIOS AND DEBT CONTRACTS

When firms borrow money, they agree to make specific payments of interest and principal in the future. To provide protection for the creditors, they also often agree to other restrictions on their activities. For example, Benetton Group's bank loans are subject to certain conditions or covenants such as a ratio of net financial position to equity that must not exceed 1.0, where net financial position represents the difference between financial liabilities and financial assets. Lenders impose these conditions to ensure that the borrower does not increase debt relative to equity, which increases the borrower's financial risk and reduces its ability to make timely debt payments. Other types of debt contracts require companies to maintain a minimum specified current ratio and a maximum debt-to-equity ratio. Maintaining a specified level of the current ratio assures creditors that the company has sufficient *liquidity* to pay its current debts.

SELF-STUDY **QUIZ 10-1**

Benetton Group reported the following amounts in its financial statements (in thousands):

	Dec. 31, 2009	Dec. 31, 2008
Current assets	1,334,809	1,420,248
Shareholders' equity	1,436,826	1,391,753
Net financial position	574,730	688,972

Assume that the debt contracts require Benetton Group to maintain a minimum current ratio of 1.50 and a maximum net financial-position-to-equity ratio of 1.00.

1. Compute the current ratio and the net financial-position-to-equity ratio at December 31, 2009, and December 31, 2008, to verify whether Benetton Group violated these conditions of its lending agreement.

2. Should the company's management be concerned about the level of these two ratios? Explain.

After you complete your answers, go online for the solutions.

The current ratio relates current assets to current liabilities, which are also related through another concept called *working capital*, defined as the difference between current assets and current liabilities. It is important to both managers and financial analysts because it has a significant impact on the health and profitability of a company.

The working capital accounts are actively managed to achieve a balance between costs and benefits. If a business has too little working capital, it runs the risk of not being able to meet its obligations to creditors. On the other hand, too much working capital may tie up resources in unproductive assets and incur additional costs. Excess inventory, for example, ties up funds that could be invested more profitably elsewhere in the business and incur additional costs associated with storage and deterioration.

The current ratio and working capital are measures of a company's liquidity. Benetton Group's positive working capital of €464.9 million confirms that if all current liabilities had to be repaid immediately, the company would have excess cash of €464.9 million, assuming that all current assets can be readily converted into cash at their carrying amounts.

WORKING CAPITAL is the difference between current assets and current liabilities.

SELF-STUDY **QUIZ 10-2**

The current ratio for Benetton Group is 1.53 at December 31, 2009. For each of the following events, indicate whether the current ratio and working capital will increase or decrease:

1. Benetton Group signs a note, payable in six months, in exchange for new equipment that cost €250,000.

2. The company borrows €1,000,000 in long-term debt.

3. The company pays taxes payable in the amount of €750,000.

4. The company finances a new building with long-term debt.

connect

After you complete your answers, go online for the solutions.

Liabilities are very important from an analytical perspective because they affect a company's future cash flows and risk characteristics. Current liabilities are usually grouped according to type of creditor, separating liabilities owed to suppliers and other trade creditors (trade and other payables) from those owed to banks (short-term borrowings), providers of services (accrued liabilities), governments (taxes payable), and others. For many types of liabilities, the amount of the debt is determined based on contractual agreements between the company and suppliers of goods, services, or funds. Most of these liabilities are recorded as they occur during the accounting period, as in the case of trade payables for merchandise purchases, loans from banks, and notes payable to creditors. However, specific liabilities that can be determined with accuracy, such as salaries payable and interest payable, require accrual through adjusting entries at the end of the accounting period prior to the preparation of financial statements.

For other types of liabilities, the exact amount will not be known with certainty until a future event, but they must be estimated and recorded if they relate to transactions that occurred during the accounting period. For example, a liability for product warranty will not be known until the repair work is carried out in the future. But the matching process requires that warranty costs be recognized in the period of sale. As these costs and the related liability are not known, they must be estimated based on past experience or some reasonable basis and recorded through adjusting entries. Most often, the estimate of future warranty costs is based on a percentage of net sales.

In particular cases, it may not be possible to provide a reasonable estimate of a potential future liability that is contingent on a future event. Relevant information about contingent liabilities must therefore be disclosed in notes to the financial statements.

CURRENT LIABILITIES

Many current liabilities have a direct relationship to the operating activities of a business. In other words, specific operating activities are financed, in part, by a related current liability. By understanding the relationship between operating activities and current liabilities, an analyst can easily explain changes in the various current liability accounts.

We will now discuss the current liability accounts that are found on most statements of financial position.

Trade Payables

Most companies do not produce all the goods and services they use in their basic operations. Instead, they purchase goods and services from other businesses.

Typically, these transactions are made on credit, with cash payments occurring after the goods and services have been provided. As a result, these transactions create *trade payables*.

For many companies, trade credit is a relatively inexpensive way to finance the purchase of inventory, because interest does not normally accrue on trade payables. As an incentive to encourage more sales, some vendors may offer very generous credit terms that may allow the buyer to resell merchandise and collect cash before payment must be made to the original vendor. For example, Dell Inc. maintains an efficient cash management system, as it collects cash from its credit customers before it pays its trade suppliers. In fiscal year 2010, Dell collected cash from customers within 38 days, on average, but paid its trade suppliers 82 days after the date of purchase.

Some managers may be tempted to delay payment to suppliers for as long as possible to conserve cash. Normally, this strategy is not advisable. Most successful companies develop positive working relationships with their suppliers to ensure that they receive quality goods and services. Managers can destroy good supplier relationships if they are slow to pay. In addition, financial analysts become concerned if a business does not meet its obligations to trade creditors on a timely basis, because delayed payment often indicates that the company is experiencing financial difficulties. Both managers and analysts use the trade payables turnover ratio to evaluate effectiveness in managing payables.

TRADE PAYABLES TURNOVER RATIO

**KEY RATIO
ANALYSIS**

ANALYTICAL QUESTION → How efficient is management in meeting its obligations to suppliers?

RATIO AND COMPARISONS → The *trade payables turnover ratio* is a measure of how quickly management is paying trade creditors. Analysts use this ratio as a measure of liquidity. It is computed as follows:

Trade Payables Turnover = Cost of Sales ÷ Average Net Trade Payables

The 2009 ratio for Benetton Group is

€1,106,639 ÷ €409,752.5* = 2.70

*(€415,594 + €403,911) ÷ 2 = €409,752.5

In reality, the numerator of this ratio should be net credit purchases, not cost of sales. Because credit purchases are not usually reported in financial statements, we use total purchases of merchandise inventory as a rough approximation, assuming that all purchases are made on credit. For merchandising companies, we compute purchases by adjusting the cost of sales for the change in inventory during the period as follows[1]:

Purchases = Cost of Sales + Ending Inventory − Beginning Inventory

For Benetton Group, the trade payables turnover ratio for 2009 would have decreased to 2.67 if purchases was substituted for cost of sales in the numerator. The decrease in the ratio from 2.70 to 2.67 is immaterial, because inventories did not change significantly during the year. For most companies, inventories do not change significantly over time; hence, the cost of sales can be used instead of purchases in computing this ratio.

LO3

Compute and interpret the trade payables turnover ratio.

---

[1] For manufacturing companies, the purchases consist primarily of raw materials used in the production of finished goods. The computation of raw materials purchased is discussed in cost accounting courses.

Comparisons over Time			Comparisons with Competitors	
Benetton Group			Burberry	Guess
2007	2008	2009	2009	2009
2.89	2.86	2.70	8.14	6.13

INTERPRETATIONS

In General → A high ratio normally suggests that a company is paying its suppliers in a timely manner. The ratio can be stated in a more intuitive manner by dividing average trade payables by the cost of sales per day:

Average Age of Payables = Average Trade Payables ÷ (Cost of Sales ÷ 365)

The 2009 ratio for Benetton is

€409,752.5 ÷ (€1,106,639 ÷ 365) = 135.1 days

Alternatively, the average age of payables can be computed by dividing the trade payables turnover into 365 (365 ÷ 2.70 = 135.1 days).

Focus Company Analysis → The trade payables turnover for Benetton has decreased over the past three years, from 2.89 in 2007 to 2.70 in 2009. Benetton Group's 2009 ratio is much lower than those of its competitors, which may indicate that Benetton Group is more aggressive than both Burberry and Guess in its cash management policy. By conserving cash (with slower payments to suppliers), the company is able to minimize the amount of money it must borrow and pay back with interest.

A Few Cautions → The trade payables turnover ratio is an average associated with all trade payables. The ratio might not reflect reality if a company pays some creditors on time but is late with others. The ratio is also subject to manipulation. Managers could be late with payments to creditors during the entire year but catch up at year-end so that the ratio is at an acceptable level. As our focus company analysis indicates, a low ratio can indicate either liquidity problems (i.e., the company is not able to generate sufficient cash to meet its obligations) or aggressive cash management (i.e., the company maintains only the minimum amount of cash necessary to support its operating activities). The first is a problem; the second is a strength. Analysts would have to study other factors, such as the current ratio and the amount of cash flows generated from operating activities, to determine which is the case.

ACCRUED LIABILITIES are expenses that have been incurred but have not been paid at the end of the accounting period.

Accrued Liabilities

In many situations, a business incurs an expense in one accounting period and makes cash payment for the expense in a subsequent period. Accrued liabilities are expenses that have been incurred before the end of an accounting period but have not yet been paid. These expenses include such items as employee salaries and wages, rent, interest, and income taxes. They are recorded as adjusting entries at year-end.

Income Taxes Payable   Like individuals, corporations must pay tax at the appropriate federal and provincial rates on income from active business operations, property income, and capital gains arising from the sale of assets. Federal income tax rates change over time because of changes in governmental tax policies, and provincial income tax rates vary across Canadian provinces. In general, the combined corporate income tax rate is in the range of 30 to 35 percent.

Benetton Group reported an income tax expense of €67.71 million for the year 2009, as shown in the following excerpt from its consolidated statement of income.

BENETTON GROUP
Consolidated Statement of Income
For the Years Ended December 31,

(in thousands of Euro)	2009	2008
Income before taxes	185,567	212,286
Income taxes	(67,715)	(56,210)
Net income from continuing operations	117,852	156,076
Excerpt from Note 11 - Income Taxes		
Current	60,341	60,265
Deferred	7,374	(4,055)
Income taxes reported on the income statement	67,715	56,210

Source: Benetton Group Annual Report 2009.

Notice that the income tax expense for each year has two components: a current portion and a deferred portion. The current portion is payable within prescribed time limits, but the deferred portion arises because of differences between the accounting rules used for financial reporting and the tax rules corporations must use to determine their taxable income, as explained in Chapter 9.[2] Differences between financial reporting and tax rules, over time, have resulted in a balance of €156,869 thousands in deferred tax assets on the statement of financial position for Benetton Group at December 31, 2009. The company also reported a balance of €9,570 thousand in current income tax liabilities, representing the portion of current income tax that has been deferred as of that date.

Taxes Other than Income Taxes   In addition to paying taxes on income, companies are often required to pay other types of taxes and fees, depending on the specific industry and geographical location in which they operate. These taxes add to the cost of producing and selling goods and services and are eventually passed on to customers through higher sales prices.[3] Companies serve as agents of the federal and provincial governments in collecting taxes charged to customers for their purchases of goods and services. Sales of most goods and services in Canada are subject to sales taxes at both the federal and provincial levels. Typically, the prices of goods and services are increased by the federal Goods and Services Tax (GST), currently set at 5 percent, and a Provincial Sales Tax (PST) that varies between zero and 10 percent, depending on the province, or a combined federal and provincial sales tax called *Harmonized Sales Tax*.[4]

The GST and PST amounts are added to the sales price, collected from customers, and then remitted to the federal and provincial governments. In this respect, the seller acts as an intermediary between the customer and the government and facilitates the collection of sales taxes from customers. When a company sells goods and services,

---

[2]Appendix 10A provides further details on the current and deferred components of income tax expense.
[3]To highlight the relative significance of the taxes and fees imposed on the airlines industry, WestJet Airlines offered to sell one-way tickets for $3 on flights between Calgary and Edmonton on June 30, 2002. However, the price of a $6 return ticket quickly rose to $89.27 when all of the applicable fees and taxes were added! See P. Fitzpatrick, "WestJet Launches $3 Ticket Protest." *National Post* (*Financial Post*), June 21, 2002, p. FP1.
[4]The provinces of British Columbia, New Brunswick, Newfoundland and Labrador, Nova Scotia, and Ontario have harmonized sales taxes. The provinces of Manitoba, Prince Edward Island, Quebec, and Saskatchewan have separate provincial sales taxes. The province of Alberta, and the three territories—Northwest Territories, Nunavut, and Yukon—do not have provincial sales taxes. At the time of writing this text, sales taxes ranged from the low of a combined GST/PST rate of 10 percent in Saskatchewan to an HST rate of 15 percent in Prince Edward Island.

the applicable sales taxes, if any, are added to the sales price, but they are not revenue for the seller. The sales taxes collected from customers represent liabilities that are remitted periodically (monthly or quarterly) to the respective governments. For example, when a Benetton retail outlet in Montreal sells apparel to a customer for $40, the total cash paid by the customer would include a GST of $2 ($40 × 5%) and a PST of $3.15 [($40 + $2) × 7.5%]. In Quebec, the PST is applied to the GST as well as the sales amount. The journal entry to record this transaction and the transaction effects would be as follows:

Cash (A)	45.15	
Sales revenue (R)		40.00
GST payable (L)		2.00
PST payable (L).		3.15

Assets		=	Liabilities		+	Shareholders' Equity	
Cash	+45.15		GST payable	+2.00		Sales revenue	+40.00
			PST payable	+3.15			

All of the GST and PST collected from customers are accumulated in these two liability accounts. The balance of the account GST payable is reduced by the amount of GST that the company pays on its own purchases of goods and services, and the net amount is then remitted to the federal government. Provincial governments follow different practices for collecting provincial sales taxes from companies and for reimbursing them for the PST they pay on their purchases. The unpaid amounts at year-end are included in current liabilities.

In Europe this consumption tax is called a *value-added tax*, or *VAT*.

SELF-STUDY **QUIZ 10-3**

Assume that the sale of apparel for $40 was made in a Benetton store located in Toronto, where sales of apparel are subject to a harmonized sales tax of 13 percent. Prepare the journal entry to record the sale transaction.

≣ connect   After you complete your answers, go online for the solutions.

Payroll Liabilities   At the end of each accounting period, employees usually will have earned salaries that have not been paid. Unpaid salaries may be reported as a separate item or as part of accrued liabilities, as is the case with Benetton Group. In addition to reporting salaries that have been earned but are unpaid, companies also must report the cost of unpaid benefits, which include retirement programs, vacation time, employment insurance, health insurance, and many others. Employers must also remit income tax and other social benefit contributions on behalf of their employees to the appropriate government agencies.

Employee Deductions   Employee income tax is usually the largest amount withheld from wages and salaries by the employer. Federal and provincial laws require the employer to deduct an appropriate amount of income tax each period from the gross earnings of each employee. The amount of income tax withheld from the employee's salary is recorded by the employer as a current liability between the date of deduction and the date on which the amount held is remitted to the government. If you have been employed and received a paycheque, you would have noticed that additional amounts were deducted from your gross earnings for employment insurance (EI), contributions to the Canada Pension Plan (CPP) for future retirement benefits, health insurance, and other contributions that you and your employer must remit to the appropriate agencies.

In general, employers match the employee's CPP remittance, but pay $1.40 for every $1.00 remitted by the employee for employment insurance. Other deductions, such as union dues and workers' compensation, depend on the terms of employment and will result in a future obligation for the employer to remit these amounts to the legal recipient. In total, the employer's share of contributions remitted by a corporation on behalf of its employees to other parties can add up to 20 percent of the employee's gross earnings. This is one reason why corporations prefer to have existing employees work overtime rather than hire new ones.

Compensation expense for employee services includes all funds earned by the employee as well as funds that must be paid to others on behalf of employees (i.e., benefits). To illustrate, let us assume that Benetton Group's Canadian operations accumulated the following information in its detailed payroll records for the first two weeks of January 2011:

Salaries and wages earned	$1,800,000
Income taxes withheld	450,000
CPP contributions	71,000
EI contributions	35,000

The employer must also contribute an equal amount of CPP contributions and 1.40 times the employees' contributions to employment insurance. As a result, the total liability associated with CPP and EI contributions is $226,000 ($71,000 + $71,000 + $35,000 + $49,000). The entry to record the payroll and employee deductions, and the related transaction effects, follows:

Compensation expense (E)	1,920,000	
Liability for income taxes withheld (L)		450,000
CPP payable (L)		142,000
EL payable (L)		84,000
Cash (A)		1,244,000

Assets	=	Liabilities	+	Shareholders' Equity
Cash −1,244,000		Liability for income taxes withheld +450,000		Compensation expense −1,920,000
		CPP payable +142,000		
		EI payable +84,000		

The compensation expense ($1,800,000 + $120,000) includes salaries and wages earned, as well as the employer's share of CPP and EI contributions because these are fringe benefits earned by the employees. The cash paid to employees ($1,244,000) is less than the total amount earned ($1,800,000) because the employer must withhold both income taxes ($450,000) and the employees' share of CPP and EI contributions ($106,000). The CPP and EI payable reflect both the employees' share and the employer's share.

Notes Payable

Most companies need to borrow money to finance their operations. When a company borrows money, a formal written contract is usually prepared. Obligations supported by these written notes are typically called *notes payable*. A note payable specifies the amount borrowed, the date by which it must be paid, and the interest rate associated with the borrowing.

Creditors are willing to lend cash because they will earn interest as compensation for giving up the use of their money for a period. This simple concept is called the *time value of money.*[5] The longer the borrowed money is held, the larger is the amount

LO4

Report notes payable and explain the time value of money.

The **TIME VALUE OF MONEY** is interest that is associated with the use of money over time.

---

[5]The present value concept that relates to the valuation of future cash flows is discussed in detail in Chapter 11 (Appendix 11A).

of interest expense. Interest at a given interest rate on a two-year loan is more than interest on a one-year loan. To the *borrower*, interest is an expense; to the *creditor*, interest is revenue.

To calculate interest, three variables must be considered: (1) the principal (i.e., the cash that was borrowed), (2) the annual interest rate, and (3) the time period for the loan. The interest formula is

$$\textbf{Interest} = \textbf{Principal} \times \textbf{Annual interest rate} \times \textbf{Time}$$

To illustrate the accounting for a note payable, assume that on November 1, 2011, Benetton Group borrowed €100,000 cash on a one-year, 6 percent note payable. The interest is payable on April 30, 2012, and October 31, 2012. The principal is payable at the maturity date of the note, October 31, 2012. The note is recorded in the accounts as follows:

Cash (A) 100,000
    Note payable, short term (L)   100,000

Assets		=	Liabilities		+	Shareholders' Equity
Cash	+100,000		Notes payable	+100,000		

Interest on this note is incurred as long as the debt is outstanding. Interest expense is recorded when it is incurred rather than when the cash actually is paid. Because the company uses the money for two months during 2011, it records interest expense in 2011 for two months, even though cash is not paid until April 30.

The computation of interest expense for 2011 is as follows:

$$\textbf{Interest} = \textbf{Principal} \times \textbf{Annual interest rate} \times \textbf{Time}$$

$$\textbf{Interest} = €100{,}000 \times 6\% \times 2/12 = €1{,}000$$

Note that interest expense is calculated for a specific accounting period, which varies from one month up to one year. The entry to record interest expense on December 31, 2011, is

Interest expense (E) 1,000
    Interest payable (L)   1,000

Assets	=	Liabilities		+	Shareholders' Equity	
		Interest payable	+1,000		Interest expense	−1,000

On April 30, 2012, Benetton Group would pay €3,000 in interest, which includes the €1,000 accrued and reported in 2011, plus the €2,000 interest accrued in the first four months of 2012. The following journal entry would be made:

Interest expense (E) 2,000
Interest payable (L) 1,000
    Cash (A)   3,000

Assets		=	Liabilities		+	Shareholders' Equity	
Cash	−3,000		Interest payable	−1,000		Interest expense	−2,000

In the previous example, we assumed that the €100,000 note payable by Benetton Group required payment of interest on April 30 and October 31. Assume that the note required payment of interest on January 31 and July 31.

1. What adjusting entry should Benetton Group make at December 31, 2011, the end of its fiscal year?

2. What entry should the company make on January 31, 2012?

3. What entry should the company make on July 31, 2012?

After you complete your answers, go online for the solutions.

connect

Current Portion of Long-Term Debt

The distinction between current and long-term debt is important for both managers and analysts. Because current debt must be paid within the next year, companies must have sufficient cash to repay currently maturing debt. To provide accurate information concerning current liabilities, a company must reclassify long-term debt within a year of its maturity date as a current liability. Assume that Benetton Group signed a note payable of €5 million on June 1, 2010. Repayment is required on December 1, 2013. The statements of financial position at December 31, 2011 and 2012, would report the following:

December 31, 2011

Non-current liabilities	
Note payable	€5,000,000

December 31, 2012

Current liabilities	
Current portion of long-term note	€5,000,000

An example of this type of disclosure can be seen in Exhibit 10.1. Notice that Benetton Group reported €238 thousand as the current portion of medium/long-term loans at December 31, 2009. This portion is payable in full during 2010. In some cases, companies will refinance debt when it comes due rather than pay out cash currently on hand.

FINANCIAL ANALYSIS

REFINANCED DEBT: CURRENT OR NON-CURRENT?

Instead of repaying a debt from current cash, a company may refinance it either by negotiating a new loan agreement with a new maturity date or by borrowing money from a new creditor and repaying the original creditor. If a company expects to refinance a currently maturing debt and has the ability to do so, should the debt be classified as a current or long-term liability? Remember that analysts are interested in a company's current liabilities because those liabilities will require cash outflows in the next accounting period. If a liability will not require a cash outflow in the next accounting period, it should not be classified as current.

Deferred Revenues

In most business transactions, cash is paid after the product or service has been delivered. In some cases, cash is paid before delivery. You have probably paid for magazines that you will receive at some time in the future. The publisher collects money for your subscription in advance, before publishing the magazine. When a company

DEFERRED REVENUES are revenues that have been collected but not earned; they are liabilities until the goods or services are provided.

collects cash before the related revenue has been earned, the cash received represents deferred revenue or deferred income.

For example, Dell Inc., which sells computer products, also sells extended warranty services on the products it sells, a common practice in the electronics industry. Should the product break down, Dell will provide repair services within its contractual obligations. More frequently, however, the product will function properly and no service is required. Dell initially defers revenue from selling extended warranties. Revenue from the sale of extended warranties is recognized gradually over the duration of the contracts or when the service is completed. Dell included the following details in a recent annual report.

REAL WORLD EXCERPT

Dell Inc.

ANNUAL REPORT

NOTES TO CONSOLIDATED FINANCIAL STATEMENTS

Note 7 — Warranty and Deferred Extended Warranty Revenue

... Revenue from the sale of extended warranties is recognized over the term of the contract or when the service is completed, and the costs associated with these contracts are recognized as incurred. Deferred extended warranty revenue is included in deferred services revenue on Dell's Consolidated Statements of Financial Position. Changes in Dell's ... deferred services revenue related to extended warranties are presented in the following tables:

	Fiscal Year Ended		
	Jan. 29, 2010	Jan. 30, 2009	Feb. 1, 2008
Deferred extended warranty revenue (in millions of U.S. dollars):			
Deferred extended warranty revenue at beginning of period	5,587	5,233	4,194
Revenue deferred for new extended warranties	3,481	3,470	3,806
Revenue recognized	(3,158)	(3,116)	(2,767)
Deferred extended warranty revenue at end of period	5,910	5,587	5,233
Current portion	2,906	2,601	2,459
Non-current portion	3,004	2,986	2,774

Source: Dell Annual Report 2009, Form 10K.

Deferred revenues are reported as a liability because cash has been collected but the related revenue has not been earned by the end of the accounting period. The obligation to provide the services or goods in the future still exists. These obligations are classified as current or long-term, depending on when they must be settled.

The journal entry to record the deferred extended warranty revenue for new contracts signed in fiscal year 2010, and related transaction effects, follow:

```
Cash (A) ...................................................  3,481
    Deferred extended warranty revenue (L)....................        3,481
```

Assets		=	Liabilities		+	Shareholders' Equity
Cash	+3,481		Deferred extended warranty revenue	+3,481		

As time passes, Dell earns a portion of the deferred revenue on the new contracts as well as part of the deferred revenue recorded in previous accounting periods. The entry to record the recognition of revenue earned during fiscal year 2010 would be

Deferred extended warranty revenue (L)	3,158	
Revenue from extended warranties (R).		3,158

The current liabilities of Benetton Group include €137.6 million in other payables, accrued expenses, and deferred income. The various items that make up this amount are disclosed in Note 34 to the company's financial statements for 2009.

REAL WORLD EXCERPT

Benetton Group
ANNUAL REPORT

Explanatory Notes

[34] Other payables, occrued expenses and deferred income

(thousands of Euro)	12.31.2009	12.31.2008
Other payables:		
– other payables due to holding and replaced companies	25,828	60,158
– payables for the purchase of fixed assets	21,818	35,449
– other payables due to third parties	21,713	22,728
– VAT	21,011	3,079
– other payables due to employees	18,631	18,868
– payables due to social security and welfare institutions	9,503	9,742
– other payables due to tax authorities	9.033	8,317
Total other payables	127,537	158,341
Accrued expenses:		
– lease installments	6,971	5,340
– other expenses	262	322
– consulting and other fees	57	120
Total accrued expenses	7,290	5,782
Deferred income:		
– rental income	1,121	780
– revenue from concession of rights	336	437
– other income	1,355	1,195
Total deferred income	2,812	2,412
Total	137,639	166,535

Source: Benetton Group Annual Report 2009.

Provisions Reported on the Statement of Financial Position

The liabilities discussed so far reflect specific amounts to be paid to identifiable parties by certain dates. When either the amount or the timing of the liability is uncertain, it is referred to as a provision. A provision must be recognized when the following conditions are met: (1) an entity has a present obligation as a result of a past event, (2) it is probable that cash or other assets will be required to settle the obligation, and (3) a reliable estimate can be made of the amount of the obligation. For example, an estimated liability is created when a company offers a warranty with the products it sells. The cost of providing repair work must be estimated and recorded as a liability

A **PROVISION** is a liability of uncertain timing or amount.

(and expense) in the period in which the product is sold. Most companies quickly refund money for any defective products that they sell. The following disclosures from a recent Dell Inc. annual report illustrate this:

NOTES TO CONSOLIDATED FINANCIAL STATEMENTS

Note 7 — Warranty and Deferred Extended Warranty Revenue

Dell records liabilities for its standard limited warranties at the time of sale for the estimated costs that may be incurred. The liability for standard warranties is included in accrued and other current and other non-current liabilities on Dell's Consolidated Statements of Financial Position. ... Changes in Dell's liabilities for standard limited warranties ... are presented in the following table:

	Fiscal Year Ended		
	Jan. 29, 2010	Jan. 30, 2009	Feb. 1, 2008
Warranty liability (in millions of U.S. dollars):			
Warranty liability at beginning of period	1,035	929	958
Costs accrued for new warranty contracts and changes in estimates for pre-existing warranties	987	1,180	1,176
Service obligations honored	(1,110)	(1,074)	(1,205)
Warranty liability at end of period	912	1,035	929
Current portion	593	721	690
Non-current portion	319	314	239

Dell determines its warranty liability based on number of units sold, historical and anticipated rates of warranty claims on those units, and cost per claim to satisfy Dell's warranty obligation. Assuming that Dell's costs of new warranties is $900 million, the journal entry to record the estimated liability at year-end follows:

Warranty expense (E)	900	
Provision for product warranty (L)		900

Assets	=	Liabilities	+	Shareholders' Equity
		Provision for product warranty +900		Warranty expense −900

When the company receives units that require repair under the warranty, its computer technicians repair the defective product, replace component parts as needed, and return the units to customers. If repairs during the year total $1,110 million, the entry to record the repairs would be

Provision for product warranty (L)	1,110	
Inventories (A), Wages payable (L)		1,110

The cost of repairs affects two accounts: inventories for the cost of parts replaced, and wages payable for the cost of labour needed to replace or repair the defective products. If Dell paid cash to satisfy the warranty, then the cash account would be credited instead of inventories. The warranty expense is not affected by the costs incurred under the warranty because the warranty expense is recognized separately, based on the volume of sales made during the accounting period.

In addition to estimated liabilities for warranties, provisions are usually made for legal and tax disputes that arise in the ordinary course of business, closing of stores or specific operations, and restructuring of the production, sales, or administrative structures. Benetton Group reported a total of €6,474 thousand in current provisions as indicated in Note 36 to its financial statements for 2009. The company also reports medium and long-term provisions for a total of €31,386 thousand. Information on provisions for items such as store closures will help potential and existing creditors, investors, and analysts to understand the implications of these liabilities.

REAL WORLD EXCERPT

Benetton Group

ANNUAL REPORT

Explanatory Notes

[36] Other current provisions and liabilities

(thousands of Euro)	Provision for legal and tax risks	Other provisions	Total
Balance at 01.01.2009	4,403	1,564	5,967
Additions to provisions	1,168	2,637	3,805
Releases to income	(797)	(285)	(1,082)
Uses and other changes	(1,055)	(1,161)	(2,216)
Balance at 12.31.2009	3,719	2,755	6,474

Source: Benetton Group Annual Report 2009.

OVERSTATEMENT OF LIABILITIES AND MANAGEMENT INCENTIVES

A QUESTION OF ACCOUNTABILITY

The amount of liabilities that companies are expected to pay in the future is not always known with certainty. As we indicated above, estimates of potential liabilities are often made when companies accrue expenses associated with specific accounting periods. The methods of estimating such expenses and liabilities often lead to imprecise amounts of future payments. The imprecise nature of the estimation process leads to either an overstatement or an understatement of the correct amount of the liability. An overstatement of expenses leads to an understatement of profit in the estimation period, and a subsequent overstatement of profit in the next accounting period. Occasionally, managers may rely on the inaccurate nature of estimated liabilities to manipulate profit in ways that serve their self-interests. For example, the key executives of Nortel, which was one of the top global makers of telecommunication equipment in North America, overstated accrued liabilities during the years 2000 to 2002. In the first quarter of 2003, Nortel's executives reduced the overstated accrued liabilities, which had the effect of turning a loss for that quarter into a profit figure. Since the compensation of key executives was related to the company's financial performance, the key executives, who decided to reduce the balance of accrued liabilities in order to increase profit, received bonus payments from the company because the reported profit was sufficiently large to cause a distribution of bonuses to key management personnel. When such an action was later uncovered by auditors, the company's board of directors fired the three top executives who were responsible for this manipulation of the company's profit.

CONTINGENT LIABILITIES AND COMMITMENTS

Each of the liabilities that we have discussed is reported on the statement of financial position with a specific monetary value because each involves the *probable* future sacrifice of economic benefits. Some transactions or events create only a possible (but not probable) future sacrifice of economic benefits. These situations create contingent liabilities, which are possible liabilities that arise from past events and whose existence will be confirmed only by the occurrence or non-occurrence of one or more uncertain future events not entirely under the control of the company. In some cases, it is not probable that cash of other assets will be required to settle the

LO⁵

Report contingent liabilities and commitments.

A **CONTINGENT LIABILITY** is a possible liability that is created as a result of a past event; it is not an effective liability until some future event occurs.

obligation, or the amount of the obligation cannot be measured with sufficient reliability.[6] A contingent liability may or may not become a recorded liability depending on future events.

Contingent Liability Examples

Lawsuits   Environmental problems   Tax disputes

Whether a situation produces a provision or a contingent liability depends on two factors: the probability of the future economic sacrifice and the ability of management to estimate the amount of the liability reliably. The following table illustrates the various possibilities when a past event has resulted in a present obligation, or a possible obligation that depends on whether specific future events occur or not.

Level of certainty of the present or possible obligation	Should a liability be recognized?	Disclosure requirements
There is a present obligation that probably requires an outflow of resources.	A provision must be recognized.	Disclosure of the provision is required.
There is a present obligation or a possible obligation that may, but probably will not, require an outflow of resources.	There is no need to recognize a provision.	Disclosure is required for the contingency.
There is a present obligation or a possible obligation where the likelihood of an outflow of resources is remote.	There is no need to recognize a provision.	Disclosure is not required.

The notes to Benetton Group's financial statements include an extensive note on contingent liabilities that relate mostly to tax disputes. The company believes that it is unlikely that any liability will materialize once the disputes are resolved.

REAL WORLD EXCERPT

Benetton Group

ANNUAL REPORT

Contingent liabilities

The Group has an estimated €27.9 million in contingent liabilities associated with ongoing legal disputes, against which it has made no provision, believing the likelihood of any outlay to be remote. Following the bankruptcy of Lehman Brothers Commercial Corporation (LBCC), the Group concentrated all its debtor and creditor positions with LBCC in a single subsidiary, Benetton International S.A. This process has produced a net creditor balance of around €0.9 million, which was written down in full in 2008. In September, Benetton International S.A. tendered proof of its creditor position as part of LBCC's liabilities. However, as part of the Chapter 11 proceedings, it is possible that the above offsetting could be contested by the official receivers, meaning that a liability of around €2 million to LBCC might re-emerge along with a receivable for an equal amount. The Group believes such an event is unlikely and so has not made any provision against this liability in its financial statements.

---

[6]International Accounting Standards Board, International Accounting Standard 37 – Provisions, Contingent Liabilities and Contingent Assets, para. 10 (IASB).

The subsidiary Bencom S.r.l. had a partial tax inspection at the end of 2007 by the Venice Tax Police for tax periods 2004–2005–2006 in relation to IRES (Italian corporate income tax), IRAP (Italian regional business tax) and VAT. The related report, received on October 18, 2007, raised issues regarding the alleged evasive nature of permanent establishments set up abroad upon the introduction of the "Tremonti" reform and the partial deductibility of sponsorship paid to amateur sports associations.

On May 25, 2009, the Venice Tax Police sent Bencom S.r.l. another notice for tax periods 2004–2005–2006–2007 in relation to VAT, IRES, and IRAP. The related report disputes the tax deductibility of certain costs; i) commissions paid to agents resident in tax havens (from 2004 to 2007); ii) sponsorship costs incurred in respect of amateur sports associations; iii) costs associated with tax avoidance involved in the setting up of permanent establishments abroad (2007).

The reports dated October 18, 2007, and May 25, 2009, quantify the extra tax payable by Bencom S.r.l. as €89.3 million.

At the end of December 2009, the Revenue Office sent the company a notice of assessment for IRES and IRAP relating to tax period 2004, which quantified the extra tax payable at around €20.5 million, plus penalties and interest.

Source: Benetton Group Annual Report 2009.

The Benetton Group reported not only its contingent liabilities, but also its guarantees and commitments to pay specific amounts in the future. Commitments reflect contractual agreements to enter into transactions with other parties. Commitments to buy or sell goods and services or to make specific payments are not normally recorded in the accounting system, as long as there is no exchange transaction. Commitments to pay or receive cash are relevant to financial statement users and help them in predicting the company's future cash flows.

REAL WORLD EXCERPT

Benetton Group

ANNUAL REPORT

EXPLANATORY NOTES

Other Information

Guarantees given, commitments and other contingent liabilities

(thousands of Euro)	12.31.2008
Unsecured guarantees given:	
- sureties	250,362
Commitments:	
- purchase commitments	19,831
- sale commitments	1,480
Total	271,673

The sureties mostly refer to payment obligations given to guarantee VAT credits offset within the Group.

Source: Benetton Group Annual Report 2009.

Financial Reporting in Canada surveyed the financial statements of 200 companies and found that 80 percent of the surveyed companies disclosed contingent liabilities in their 2007 financial statements. The most common contingent liabilities disclosed pertain to lawsuits.[7]

---

[7]Canadian Institute of Chartered Accountants, *Financial Reporting in Canada 2008*. Toronto: 2008, Chapter 10, Contractual Obligations and Contingencies. Online version.

FOCUS ON CASH FLOWS

CURRENT LIABILITIES AND CASH FLOWS

LO6

Explain the impact of changes in current liabilities on cash flows.

The changes in current liabilities can be a major determinant of a company's cash flow from operations. While the income statement reflects the expenses of the period, the cash flow from operating activities reflects cash payments to suppliers of goods and services.

EFFECT ON THE STATEMENT OF CASH FLOWS

IN GENERAL → When there is a net *increase in a current liability* for the period, cash paid to suppliers is less than the expense reported on the income statement; thus, the increase must be added to profit in computing cash flow from operations.

When there is a net *decrease in a current liability* for the period, cash paid to suppliers is more than the related expense; thus, the decrease must be *subtracted* from profit in computing cash flow from operations.

	Effect on Cash Flows
Operating activities (indirect method)	
Profit	$xxx
Adjusted for:	
Add increase in any current liability	+
Subtract decrease in any current liability	−

FOCUS COMPANY ANALYSIS → A segment of Benetton Group's statement of cash flows for 2009 and related note follow.

REAL WORLD EXCERPT

Benetton Group

ANNUAL REPORT

BENETTON GROUP
CONSOLIDATED STATEMENT OF CASH FLOWS
(thousands of euro)
For the Years Ended December 31

(thousands of Euro)	2009	2008
Operating activities		
Net income for the year attributable to the Group and minority interests	117,852	156,076
Net income from discontinued operations	—	1,107
Income taxes expense	67,715	56,210
Income before taxes	185,567	213,393
Adjustments for:		
– depreciation and amortization	103,671	99,680
– net capital (gains)/losses and non-monetary items	16,729	(5,762)
– net provisions charged to statement of income	32,792	25,710
– use of provisions	(9,664)	(8,540)
– share of (income)/losses of associated companies	(2,262)	(229)
– net financial expenses/(income) and exchange differences	22,497	42,212
Cash flow from operating activities before changes in working capital	349,330	366,464
Cash flow provided/(used) by changes in working capital	53,405	(114,815)
Payment of taxes	(84,084)	(52,231)
Net interest paid and exchange differences	(23,136)	(39,278)
Cash flow provided by operating activities	295,515	160,140

Source: Benetton Group Annual Report 2009.

Recall from our previous discussions of the statement of cash flows that revenues and expenses reported on the income statement include both cash and non-cash components, and that changes in working capital accounts (other than cash and cash equivalents) reflect non-cash revenues and expenses during the accounting period. The disclosed information shows that changes in non-cash working capital items increased cash flows from operating activities by €53,405 thousand. In a commentary on the statement of cash flows, Benetton Group indicated that the increase in working capital was partially due to a decrease in both inventories and trade payables (due to extensions of average payment terms), and to a decrease in the value-added tax (VAT) owed by Italian subsidiaries. The level of detailed information shown in the excerpt below helps users evaluate how well Benetton Group is managing the sources and uses of its operating cash flows.

Note also that, instead of adjusting profit (net income) for the non-cash components of income tax expense and interest expense, both the income tax expense and net financial expenses (financial expenses − financial income) are added back to profit, and then the amounts paid for taxes and interest are deducted from profit while interest received is added to profit.

REAL WORLD EXCERPT

Benetton Group

ANNUAL REPORT

Commentary on the cash flow statement

Cash flow from operating activities before changes in working capital amounted to €349,330 thousand in the year, compared with €366,464 thousand in 2008, reflecting the slight deterioration in EBITDA. Changes in working capital provided €53,405 thousand in cash flow (€114,815 thousand used in 2008), mostly reflecting

- an increase in net trade receivables, despite slightly lower revenues, due to the growth in business in emerging countries, combined with a slight worsening of receivables turnover for current collections and higher receivables for the new commercial initiatives in the textile segment.
- a reduction in inventories, thanks to actions under the reorganization plan in terms of production sources and supply chain efficiency.
- a decrease in trade payables, which, despite fewer purchases in fourth quarter 2009, benefited from the actions taken to extend average payment terms.
- an increase in net other payables, mainly because of higher balances owed by Italian subsidiaries to the tax authorities for VAT.

Source: Benetton Group Annual Report 2009.

ACCOUNTING STANDARDS FOR PRIVATE ENTERPRISES

Accounting standards for private enterprises do not differ much from IFRS in reporting the common types of current liabilities. Two notable differences in the standards relate to reporting contingent liabilities and accounting for income taxes.

Under IFRS, distinction is made between provisions and contingent liabilities. Provisions are estimated liabilities that are reported on the statement of financial position, whereas contingent liabilities are not recognized as liabilities because of the uncertainty of the amount and timing of future payments. In contrast, Canadian private enterprises are required to report contingent losses and related liabilities if it is likely that a future event will confirm that a liability has been incurred at the date of the financial statements, and the amount of the loss can be reasonably estimated.

The second area of difference relates to accounting for income taxes. We noted in the chapter that the income tax expense usually differs from the income tax payable because of differences between financial reporting standards and income tax rules. Users of the financial statements of Canadian private enterprises remain unconvinced of the incremental value of information conveyed by deferred income taxes. For this reason, Canadian private enterprises may report an income tax expense that simply equals the income tax payable.

Appendix 10A

Deferred Income Tax Assets and Liabilities

In previous chapters, we made simplifying assumptions concerning income tax expense. We often provided the amount of income tax expense (e.g., $100,000) and prepared a journal entry similar to the following:

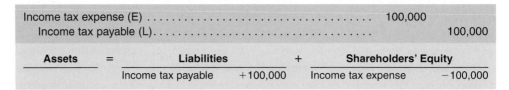

| Income tax expense (E) .... | 100,000 | |
| Income tax payable (L).. | | 100,000 |

Assets	=	Liabilities		+	Shareholders' Equity	
		Income tax payable	+100,000		Income tax expense	−100,000

However, separate rules govern the preparation of financial statements (IFRS) and tax returns (*Income Tax Act*). Specifically, some types of revenue are exempt from tax while other types of expenses are not deductible in computing taxable income. These ***permanent differences*** do not cause much complication in accounting for income taxes. However, ***temporary differences*** of the following types result in complex accounting:

1. Revenue that is recognized in financial statements (e.g., rent revenue) when the goods are sold or the services are rendered, but is taxable only when the cash is received.

2. Product warranty costs that are recognized as a liability and an expense for financial reporting purposes when the related products are sold, but are deductible for tax purposes only when payments under the warranty are made.

3. Long-lived assets, including development costs, that are usually depreciated by using the straight-line method for financial reporting purposes, but are depreciated on an accelerated basis (Capital Cost Allowance) for tax purposes.

The differences between depreciation expense and CCA are by far the most common source of temporary differences, which disappear over the long run. Assuming the corporation is a going concern, a specific long-lived asset will eventually be unable to generate further benefits to the corporation and will be fully amortized. Similarly, the cost of this asset would have been deducted over the years as CCA for tax purposes. So the main issue is timing of the recognition of revenues and expenses for financial reporting versus tax purposes. These temporary differences cause the income tax expense (which is based on profit before taxes reported on the income statement) to be different from the income tax payable (which is based on taxable income computed on the income tax return).

This difference creates an interesting accounting problem: should the tax liability reported on the statement of financial position be the amount of income taxes currently payable based on the tax return, or should the liability include deferred tax effects that exist because of differences between IFRS and the income tax rules? Accountants have resolved this issue by recording the "economic" liability, which includes income taxes currently payable, adjusted for the effects of temporary differences between IFRS and the income tax rules.

The difference between the amounts of income tax expense and income taxes payable is called ***deferred income tax***. Deferred income tax items exist because of temporary differences caused by reporting revenues and expenses on a company's income statement in conformity with IFRS, and on the tax return in accordance with the *Income Tax Act*. In practice, deferred income taxes can be either assets (such as taxes related to cash collected from a customer, which is taxable before it is reported as a revenue on the income statement) or liabilities (such as taxes related to depreciation and amortization, reported on the tax return on an accelerated basis and on the income statement on a straight-line basis).

To illustrate, let us consider one item that gives rise to deferred income taxes. Assume that a Canadian company uses straight-line depreciation for its financial statements and capital cost allowance (CCA) for its tax return. As a result, it reports lower income on its tax return than on its income statement, because CCA reported on the tax return exceeds depreciation expense reported on the income statement. Assume that the company computed income taxes payable of $8,000,000 based on the numbers reported on the tax return, and reported income tax expense of $10,000,000 on its income statement. The company records its tax obligation as follows:

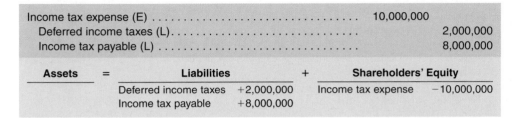

Income tax expense (E)	10,000,000	
Deferred income taxes (L)		2,000,000
Income tax payable (L)		8,000,000

Assets	=	Liabilities		+	Shareholders' Equity	
		Deferred income taxes	+2,000,000		Income tax expense	−10,000,000
		Income tax payable	+8,000,000			

The deferred income tax amount is settled when the difference between CCA and depreciation expense "reverses" in the future. This happens when the CCA recorded on the tax return becomes lower than the straight-line depreciation reported on the income statement (remember from Chapter 9 that declining depreciation, such as CCA, causes higher depreciation expense than straight-line depreciation in the early years of an asset's life and lower depreciation in the later years). When a temporary difference reverses, the deferred income tax amount is reduced.

In reality, although temporary differences reverse in theory, new temporary differences are created as companies purchase new long-lived assets, offsetting the reversing differences. Consequently, the deferred income tax liabilities reported by most companies may not result in significant cash outflows in the foreseeable future.

As indicated earlier, the deferred income tax liability arises primarily from differences between depreciation expense and CCA. What if companies used CCA for reporting purposes instead of straight-line depreciation? In this case, most of the temporary differences would disappear and the deferred income tax asset or liability would be reduced to a relatively small amount, thus reducing the significance of this item on the statements of financial position of most companies. However, the use of CCA for financial reporting purposes increases the depreciation expense, thus reducing profit. Managers may not favour this outcome if it affects their remuneration and the market value of the company's shares, even though the use of CCA instead of straight-line depreciation does not affect cash outflows for income tax purposes.

The Benetton Group, which is based in Italy, computes its current income tax payable in conformity with Italian tax rules and uses IFRS to report its profit. The following excerpts from the company's financial statement notes illustrate its tax-related disclosures.

REAL WORLD EXCERPT

Benetton Group
ANNUAL REPORT

Explanatory Notes

Income taxes. Current income taxes are calculated on the basis of taxable income, in accordance with applicable local regulations.

...

Deferred tax assets are recorded for all temporary differences to the extent it is probable that taxable income will be available against which the deductible temporary difference can be utilized. The same principle is applied to the recognition of deferred tax assets on the carryforward of unused tax losses.

...

Deferred tax assets and liabilities are calculated using tax rates which are expected to apply in the period when the asset is realized or the liability settled, using the tax rates and tax regulations which are in force at the balance sheet date.

...

Exhibit **10.2**

Disclosure Made by Benetton Group

REAL WORLD EXCERPT

Benetton Group

ANNUAL REPORT

Explanatory Notes

[11] Income taxes

The balance includes current taxes and deferred tax income and expenses:

(thousands of Euro)	2009	2008
Current taxes	60,341	60,265
Deferred tax income:		
- reversal of intercompany profits	2,852	(1,636)
- additions uses and releases from provisions for risks and other charges	1,590	(1,510)
- taxes on a different depreciable/amortizable base for property. plant and equipment and intangible assets		(2,500)
- carried forward tax losses	2,027	1,200
- fair value of derivatives	(1,630)	837
- other	1,791	3,552
Total deferred tax income	6,630	(57)
Deferred tax expenses:		
- reversal of excess depreciation and the application of finance lease accounting	798	(4,371)
- capital gains	(68)	1,049
- distributable earnings/reserves of subsidiaries	948	487
- tax effect of business combination	(741)	(1,189)
- other	(193)	26
Total deferred tax expenses	744	(3,998)
Total	67,715	56,210

The tax charge amounts to Euro 67,715 thousand compared with Euro 56,210 thousand in 2008: the tax rate is 36.5%, up from 26.5% in 2008, mainly reflecting increased operating losses by certain foreign subsidiaries and higher impairment of property, plant and equipment and intangible assets recognized in 2009.

Source: Benetton Group Annual Report 2009.

Exhibit 10.2 shows the disclosures made by Benetton Group in the notes to its financial statements for 2009. The disclosures include a detailed account of the components of the income tax expense for 2009, as well as a listing of the items that caused temporary differences between financial reporting and income tax reporting. Note that the different amounts used for depreciation of property, plant, and equipment and amortization of intangible assets for financial reporting versus income tax reporting, resulted in a significant effect on the deferred income tax assets reported on Benetton Group's statement of financial position.

Note also that the €156.9 million balance of deferred tax assets at December 31, 2009, is largely due to the different bases that are used to compute depreciation and amortization for tax versus financial reporting purposes. The computation of deferred income taxes involves some complexities that are discussed in advanced accounting courses.

Deferred Assets

[19] Deferred tax assets

The following table provides a breakdown of net deferred tax assets:

(thousands of Euro)	12.31.2008	Increases	Decreases	Translation differences and other movements	12.31.2009
Tax effect of eliminating intercompany profits	7,756	4,904	(7,756)	—	4,904
Tax effect of provisions, costs and revenues relating to future periods for fiscal purposes	31,622	11,924	(13,482)	602	30,666
Deferred taxes on reversal of excess depreciation and application of finance lease accounting	(5,381)	(5,014)	4,217	23	(6,155)
Deferred taxes on capital gains taxable over a number of accounting periods	(3,935)	(1,914)	1,982	(140)	(4,007)
Different basis for depreciation/ amortization	129,223	7,400	(7,400)	—	129,223
Benefit on carried forward tax losses	20,178	497	(2,524)	(734)	17,417
Deferred taxes on distributable earnings/reserves	(8,065)	(948)	—	—	(9,013)
Tax effect of business combination	(6,908)	—	741	1	(6,166)
Total	164,490	16,849	(24,222)	(248)	156,869

The Group offsets deferred tax assets against deferred tax liabilities for Italian companies that have made the group tax election and for foreign subsidiaries to the extent legally allowed in their country of origin. This balance is mostly attributable to taxes paid in advance as a result of differences in calculating the depreciable/amortizable base of assets. The associated deferred tax assets have been recognized on the basis of the Group's future expected profitability following its reorganization in 2003. The balance also includes deferred tax assets recognized on provisions and costs already reported in the financial statements that will become deductible for tax in future periods. The potential tax benefit associated with carried forward tax losses of Group companies is Euro 243 million (about Euro 237 million in 2008) but has been adjusted by Euro 226 million for amounts that are currently unlikely to be fully recovered.

Source: Benetton Group Annual Report 2009.

CHAPTER **TAKE-AWAYS**

1. **Define, measure, and report current liabilities. p. 531**
   Strictly speaking, accountants define liabilities as obligations arising from past transactions that will be settled in the future by some transfer or use of assets or provision of services. They are classified on the statement of financial position as either current or non-current. Current liabilities are short-term obligations that will be paid within the normal operating cycle of the business or within one year of the statement of financial position date, whichever is longer. Non-current liabilities are all obligations not classified as current.

2. **Compute and interpret the current ratio. p. 532**
   The current ratio is a comparison of current assets to current liabilities. Analysts use this ratio to assess the liquidity of a company.

3. **Compute and interpret the trade payables turnover ratio. p. 535**
   This ratio is computed by dividing cost of sales by average trade payables. It shows how quickly management is paying its trade creditors and is considered to be a measure of liquidity.

4. **Report notes payable and explain the time value of money. p. 539**
   A note payable specifies the amount borrowed, when it must be repaid, and the interest rate associated with the debt. Accountants must report the debt and the interest as it accrues. The time value of money refers to the fact that interest accrues on borrowed money with the passage of time.

5. **Report contingent liabilities and commitments. p. 545**
   A contingency is a possible liability that has arisen as a result of a past event. Such contingencies are disclosed in a note if it is not probable that cash of other assets will be required to settle

the obligation, or if the amount of the obligation cannot be measured with sufficient reliability. A commitment is a contractual agreement to enter into a transaction with another party in the future.

6. **Explain the impact of changes in current liabilities on cash flows. p. 548**
Changes in trade payables and accrued liabilities affect cash flows from operating activities. Cash flows are increased when trade payables and accrued liabilities increase, and vice versa.

In this chapter, we focused on current liabilities. In the next chapter, we will discuss non-current liabilities in the context of the capital structure of the company, and use present value concepts to measure long-term debt.

KEY **RATIOS**

Current ratio measures the ability of a company to pay its current obligations. It is computed as follows (p. 532):

$$\text{Current Ratio} = \frac{\text{Current Assets}}{\text{Current Liabilities}}$$

Trade payables turnover and its companion **average age of payables** are measures of how quickly a company pays its creditors. They are computed as follows (p. 535):

$$\text{Trade Payables Turnover} = \frac{\text{Cost of Sales}}{\text{Average Net Trade Payables}}$$

$$\text{Average Age of Payables} = \frac{\text{Average Net Trade Payables}}{\text{Cost of Sales} \div 365}$$

FINDING FINANCIAL INFORMATION

STATEMENT OF FINANCIAL POSITION
Under Current Liabilities
Liabilities listed by account title, such as
Trade payables
Accrued liabilities
Notes payable
Deferred income taxes
Under Non-current Liabilities
Liabilities listed by account title, such as
Long-term debt
Deferred income taxes

INCOME STATEMENT
Liabilities are shown only on the statement of financial position, never on the income statement. Transactions affecting liabilities often affect an income statement account. For example, accrued salary compensation affects an income statement account (compensation expense) and a statement of financial position account (salaries payable).

STATEMENT OF CASH FLOWS
Under Operating Activities (indirect method)
Profit
+ Increases in most current liabilities
− Decreases in most current liabilities
Under Financing Activities
+ Increases in non-current liabilities
− Decreases in non-current liabilities

NOTES
Under Summary of Significant Accounting Policies
Description of pertinent information concerning the accounting treatment of liabilities. Normally, there is minimal information.
Under a Separate Note
If not listed on the statement of financial position, a listing of the major classifications of liabilities with information about maturities and interest rates appears in a note. Information about contingent liabilities is reported in the notes.

KEY **TERMS**

Accrued Liabilities p. 536

Capital Structure p. 530

Contingent Liability p. 546

Current Liabilities p. 532

Deferred Revenues p. 542

Liabilities p. 531

Liquidity p. 532

Provision p. 543

Time Value of Money p. 539

Working Capital p. 533

QUESTIONS

1. Define *liability*. Differentiate between a current liability and a non-current liability.
2. How can external parties be informed about the liabilities of a business?
3. Liabilities are measured and reported at their current cash equivalent amount. Explain.
4. A *liability* is a known obligation of either a definite or an estimated amount. Explain.
5. Define *working capital*. How is it computed?
6. What is the current ratio? How is it related to the classification of liabilities?
7. Define *accrued liability*. What type of entry usually reflects an accrued liability?
8. Define *deferred revenue*. Why is it a liability?
9. Define *note payable*. What other liability is associated with a note payable? Explain.
10. Define *provisions*. How do they differ from other liabilities?
11. What is a contingent liability? How is a contingent liability reported?
12. Compute interest expense for the following note: face value, $4,000; 12 percent interest; date of note, April 1, 2011. Assume that the fiscal year ends on December 31, 2011.
13. Explain the concept of the time value of money.

EXERCISES

E10–1 Identifying Current Liabilities   ☐ **LO1**

A current liability is a short-term obligation that is normally expected to be settled within one year. For each of the following events and transactions that occurred in November 2011 indicate the title of the current liability account that is affected and the amount that would be reported on a statement of financial position prepared on December 31, 2011. If an event does not result in a current liability, explain why.

a. A customer purchases a ticket from WestJet Airlines for $470 cash to travel in January 2012. Answer from WestJet's standpoint.

b. Hall Construction Company signs a contract with a customer for the construction of a new $500,000 warehouse. At the signing, Hall receives a cheque for $50,000 as a deposit on the future construction. Answer from Hall's standpoint.

c. On November 1, 2011, a bank lends $10,000 to a company. The loan carries a 9 percent annual interest rate, and the principal and interest are due in a lump sum on October 31, 2012. Answer from the company's standpoint.

d. A popular ski magazine company receives a total of $1,800 from subscribers on December 31, the last day of its fiscal year. The subscriptions begin in the next fiscal year. Answer from the magazine company's standpoint.

e. On November 20, the campus bookstore receives 500 accounting textbooks at a cost of $70 each. The terms indicate that payment is due within 30 days of delivery. Answer from the bookstore's standpoint.

f. Ziegler Company, a farm equipment company, receives its phone bill at the end of January 2012 for $230 for January calls. The bill has not been paid to date.

■ **LO1, 2**

E10–2 **Computing Shareholders' Equity and Working Capital; Explaining the Current Ratio and Working Capital**

Flair Corporation is preparing its 2011 statement of financial position. The company records show the following related amounts at the end of the fiscal year, December 31, 2011:

Total assets	$530,000
Total non-current assets	362,000
Notes payable (8%, due in 5 years)	15,000
Trade payables	56,000
Income taxes payable	14,000
Liability for withholding taxes	3,000
Deferred rent revenue	7,000
Bonds payable (due in 15 years)	90,000
Wages payable	7,000
Property taxes payable	3,000
Note payable (10%; due in 6 months)	12,000
Interest payable	400
Shareholders' equity	100,000

Required:

1. Compute (a) the amount of working capital and (b) the current ratio (show computations). Why is working capital important to management? How do financial analysts use the current ratio?

2. Would your computations be different if the company reported $250,000 worth of contingent liabilities in the notes to its financial statements? Explain.

■ **LO2**

E10–3 **Analyzing the Impact of Transactions on Liquidity**

API Ltd. has a current ratio of 2.0 and working capital in the amount of $1,240,000. For each of the following transactions, determine whether the current ratio and working capital will increase, decrease, or remain the same.

a. Paid trade payables in the amount of $50,000.

b. Recorded accrued salaries in the amount of $100,000.

c. Borrowed $250,000 from a local bank, to be repaid in 90 days.

d. Purchased $20,000 of new inventory on credit.

■ **LO1**

E10–4 **Recording Payroll Costs with Discussion**

Matyas Company completed the salary and wage payroll for March 2011. The payroll provided the following details:

Salaries and wages earned	$224,000
Employee income taxes withheld	46,000
Union dues withheld	3,000
Insurance premiums withheld	1,000
CPP contributions*	16,445
EI contributions†	9,611

*$16,445 each for employer and employees.
†Employment insurance, employees' share.

Required:

1. Prepare the journal entry to record the payroll for March, including employee deductions.

2. Prepare the journal entry to record the employer's additional payroll expenses.

3. Prepare a combined journal entry to show the payment of amounts owed to governmental agencies and other organizations.

4. What was the total compensation expense for the company? Explain. What percentage of the payroll was take-home pay? From the employers' perspective, does an economic difference between the cost of salaries and the cost of benefits exist? From the employees' perspective, does a difference exist?

E10–5 Computing Payroll Costs; Discussion of Labour Costs

Town Lake Company has completed the payroll for January 2012, reflecting the following data:

Salaries and wages earned	$69,000
Employee income taxes withheld	16,900
Union dues withheld	1,200
CPP contributions*	6,013
EI contributions†	3,514

*$6,013 each for employer and employee.
†Employment insurance, employees' share.

■ LO1

Required:

1. What amount of additional compensation expense must be paid by the company? What was the amount of the employees' take-home pay?

2. List the liabilities that are reported on the company's statement of financial position at January 31, 2012. The employees' take-home pay was paid on that day.

3. Would employers react differently to a 10 percent increase in the employer's share of CPP than to a 10 percent increase in the basic level of salaries? Would financial analysts react differently?

E10–6 Recording a Note Payable through Its Time to Maturity with Discussion of Management Strategy

Many businesses borrow money during periods of increased business activity to finance inventory and trade receivables. Sears Canada Inc. is one of Canada's largest general merchandise retailers. Each year, Sears Canada builds up its inventory to meet the needs of December holiday shoppers. A large portion of these holiday sales are on credit. As a result, Sears Canada often collects cash from the sales several months after the December holidays. Assume that on November 1, 2011, Sears Canada borrowed $4.5 million cash from Provincial Bank for working capital purposes and signed an interest-bearing note due in six months. The interest rate was 8 percent per annum, payable at maturity. Assume that the fiscal year of Sears Canada ends on December 31.

LO1, 4

Sears Canada

Required:

1. Prepare the journal entry to record the note on November 1, 2011.

2. Prepare any adjusting entry required at December 31, 2011.

3. Prepare the journal entry to record payment of the note and interest on the maturity date, April 30, 2012.

4. If Sears Canada needs extra cash for every December holiday season, should management borrow money on a long-term basis to avoid the necessity of negotiating a new short-term loan each year?

E10–7 Determining Financial Statement Effects of Transactions Involving Notes Payable

Refer to the previous exercise.

LO1, 4

Sears Canada

Required:

Determine the financial statement effects for each of the following transactions: (a) issuance of the note on November 1, 2011, (b) impact of the adjusting entry at December 31, 2011, and (c) the payment of the note and interest on April 30, 2012. Indicate the accounts affected, amounts, and direction of the effects (+ for increases and − for decreases) on the accounting equation. Use the following headings:

Date	Assets	Liabilities	Shareholders' Equity

E10–8 Reporting Short-Term Borrowings

PepsiCo Inc. engages in a number of businesses that include Pepsi-Cola, Slice, Mountain Dew, and Fritos. The company's annual revenues exceed $45 billion. A recent PepsiCo annual report contained the following information:

LO1

PepsiCo Inc.

At the end of the current year, we have reclassified $1.4 billion of short-term debt to long-term based on our intent and ability to refinance on a long-term basis.

Required:

As an analyst, comment on the company's classification of short-term debt as long-term debt. What conditions should exist to permit a company to make this type of classification?

LO1 **E10–9** **Reporting Warranty Liability**

Gonzales Co. provides warranties for many of its products. Its estimated warranty liability account had a balance of $70,400 at January 1, 2011. Based on an analysis of warranty claims during the past several years, the warranty expense for 2011 was established at 0.4 percent of sales. During 2011, the actual cost of servicing products under warranty was $32,200, and sales were $7,200,000.

Required:

1. Compute the warranty expense that should appear on the company's income statement for the year ended December 31, 2011.

2. What amount will be reported in the estimated warranty liability account on the statement of financial position as at December 31, 2011?

LO1 **E10–10** **Reporting Warranty Liabilities**

Amster Corp. produces and sells a single product that requires considerable servicing and adjustment during the first two years after sale. The company offers a warranty for two years covering most service requirements. The product's price ranges from $900 to $1,200, depending on the particular model produced. Warranty work costs $100 per product, regardless of the model. This amount has been quite stable for several years. Most of the warranty work occurs between the 6th and the 18th months after sale. The company's sales have been expanding, from approximately 9,000 units in 2006 to approximately 12,000 units in 2011.

Required:

How should Amber Corp. account for warranty costs, and how should the information be reported on its financial statements?

LO1, 2, 6 **E10–11** **Determining the Impact of Transactions, Including Analysis of Cash Flows**

Mawani Company sells a wide range of goods through two retail stores operating in adjoining cities. Most purchases of goods for resale are on account. Occasionally, a short-term note payable is used to obtain cash for current use. The following transactions were selected from those occurring during 2012:

a. On January 10, 2012, purchased merchandise on credit, $36,000; the company uses a perpetual inventory system.

b. On March 1, 2012, borrowed $200,000 cash from Local Bank and signed an interest-bearing note payable at the end of one year, with an annual interest rate of 6 percent payable at maturity.

c. On April 5, 2012, sold merchandise on credit, $67,800; this amount included GST of $3,000 and PST of $4,800. The cost of sales represents 70 percent of the sales invoice.

Required:

1. Describe the financial statement effects of these transactions. Indicate the accounts affected, amounts, and direction of the effects (+ for increases and − for decreases) on the accounting equation. Use the following headings:

Date	Assets	Liabilities	Shareholders' Equity

2. What amount of cash is paid on the maturity date of the note?

3. Discuss the impact of each transaction on Mawani's cash flows.

4. Discuss the impact of each transaction on the current ratio. Assume that the current ratio is greater than 1.0 before considering each transaction.

LO5 **E10–12** **Reporting Contingent Liabilities**

Buzz Coffee Shops is famous for its large servings of hot coffee. After a famous case involving McDonald's, the lawyer for Buzz warned management (during 2008) that it could be sued if someone were to spill hot coffee and be burned: "With the temperature of your coffee, I can guarantee it's just a matter of time before you're sued for $1,000,000." Unfortunately, in 2010, the prediction came true when a customer filed suit. The case went to trial in 2011, and the jury awarded the customer $400,000 in damages, which the company immediately appealed. During 2012, the customer and the company settled their dispute for $150,000. What is the proper reporting each year of the events related to this liability?

E10–13 **(Appendix 10A) Computing Deferred Income Tax: One Temporary Difference, with Discussion**   LO1
The comparative income statements of Martin Corporation for fiscal years 2011 and 2012 showed the following summarized pretax data:

	Year 2011	Year 2012
Sales revenue	$55,000	$63,000
Expenses (excluding income tax)	39,000	43,000
Pretax income	$16,000	$20,000

The expenses in 2011 included an amount of $4,000 that was deductible for tax purposes in 2012. The average income tax rate was 32 percent. Taxable income from the income tax returns was $20,000 for 2011 and $16,000 for 2012.

Required:

1. For each year, compute (a) the income taxes payable and (b) the deferred income tax. Is the deferred income tax a liability or an asset? Explain.

2. Show what amounts related to income taxes should be reported each year on the income statement and the statement of financial position. Assume that the income tax is paid on March 1 of the next year.

3. Explain why tax expense is not simply the amount of cash paid during the year.

E10–14 **(Appendix 10A) Recording Deferred Income Tax: One Temporary Difference; Discussion of Management Strategy**   LO1
The comparative income statement for Chung Corporation for fiscal years 2010 and 2011 provided the following summarized pretax data:

	Year 2010	Year 2011
Revenue	$75,000	$82,000
Expenses (excluding income tax)	54,000	58,000
Pretax profit	$21,000	$24,000

The expenses for 2011 included an amount of $3,000 that was deductible only in the 2010 income tax return. The average income tax rate was 30 percent. Taxable income shown in the tax returns was $18,000 for 2010 and $27,000 for 2011.

Required:

1. For each year, compute (a) the income taxes payable and (b) the deferred income tax. Is the deferred income tax a liability or an asset? Explain.

2. Prepare the journal entry for each year to record the income taxes payable, the deferred income tax, and the income tax expense.

3. Show the tax-related amounts that should be reported each year on the income statement and the statement of financial position. Assume that income tax is paid on March 1 of the next year.

4. Why would management want to incur the cost of preparing separate tax and financial accounting reports to defer the payment of taxes?

E10–15 **(Appendix 10A) Computing and Reporting Deferred Income Tax: Depreciation**   LO1
Amber Corporation reported the following summarized pretax data at the end of each year:

Income Statement for the Year	2010	2011	2012
Revenues	$170,000	$182,000	$195,000
Expenses (including depreciation)*	122,000	126,000	130,000
Pretax profit	$ 48,000	$ 56,000	$ 65,000

*Straight-line depreciation expense on a machine purchased January 1, 2010, for $75,000. The machine has a three-year estimated life and no residual value. The company used capital cost allowance on the income tax return as follows: 2010, $37,500; 2011, $25,000; and 2012, $12,500. The average income tax rate is 28 percent for each of the three years.

Taxable income from the income tax return was as follows: 2010, $32,000; 2011, $56,000; and 2012, $85,000.

Required:

1. For each year, compute (a) the income taxes payable and (b) the deferred income tax. Is the deferred income tax a liability or an asset? Explain.

2. Show the tax-related amounts that should be reported each year on the income statement and the statement of financial position.

PROBLEMS

LO1   **P10–1**   **Recording and Reporting Current Liabilities**

Valdir Company completed the following transactions during 2011. The company's fiscal year ends on December 31.

Jan.	15	Purchased and paid for merchandise for resale at an invoice cost of $13,580; assume a periodic inventory system.
April	1	Borrowed $500,000 from Summit Bank for general use; signed an 11-month, 8 percent interest-bearing note.
June	14	Received a deposit of $10,000 from customer Marina Malek for services to be performed in the future.
July	15	Performed services to Marina Malek for $2,500.
Dec.	12	Received electricity bill for $540. The company will pay it in early January 2012.
	31	Determined that wages of $12,000 were earned but not yet paid on December 31 (disregard payroll taxes).

Required:

1. Prepare journal entries for each of these transactions.

2. Prepare all adjusting entries required on December 31, 2011.

3. What is the effect of each transaction on working capital and on the current ratio (increase, decrease, no effect)? Assume that the current ratio is 1.40 at January 1, 2011.

LO1, 2   **P10–2**   **Recording and Reporting Current Liabilities with Discussion of Effects on Current Ratio** (AP10–1)

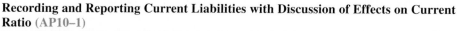

Uzma Company completed the following transactions during 2012. The company's fiscal year ends on December 31, 2012.

Jan.	8	Purchased merchandise for resale at a cost of $12,420. The company uses a periodic inventory system.
	17	Paid the invoice received on January 8.
Mar.	10	Sold merchandise on credit for a total amount of $22,600, which included GST at 5 percent and PST at 8 percent of the sales amount.
Apr.	1	Borrowed $40,000 from National Bank for general use; signed a 12-month, 8 percent interest-bearing note.
June	3	Purchased merchandise for resale at a cost of $17,820.
July	5	Paid the invoice received on June 3.
Aug.	1	Rented a small office in a building owned by the company and collected $6,000 for six months' rent in advance. Ignore sales taxes. (Record the collection in a way that will not require an adjusting entry at year-end.)
Dec.	20	Received a $100 deposit from a customer as a guarantee to return a large trailer "borrowed" for 30 days.
	31	Determined that wages earned but not yet paid on December 31 amounted to $7,200. Ignore payroll taxes.

Required:

1. Prepare journal entries for each of these transactions.

2. Prepare the adjusting entry (entries) required on December 31, 2012.

3. Show how all of the liabilities arising from these transactions are reported on the statement of financial position at December 31, 2012.

4. For each transaction and related adjusting entry, state whether the current ratio is increased, decreased, or remains the same. Assume that the current ratio is greater than 1.0 before considering each transaction.

P10–3 **Determining Financial Effects of Transactions Affecting Current Liabilities with Discussion of Cash Flow Effects** (AP10–2)

LO1, 6

Refer to the previous problem.

Required:

1. For each transaction (including adjusting entries) listed in the previous problem, indicate the accounts affected, amounts, and direction of the effects (+ for increases and − for decreases) on the accounting equation. Use the following headings:

Date	Assets	Liabilities	Shareholders' Equity

2. For each transaction and related adjusting entry, state whether cash flow from operating activities is increased, decreased, or remains unchanged.

P10–4 **Recording and Reporting Accrued Liabilities and Deferred Revenue and Financial Statement Effects with Discussion**

LO1

During 2012, Riverside Company completed the following two transactions. The company's fiscal year ends on December 31.

a. Paid and recorded wages of $260,000 during 2012; however, at the end of December 2012, wages of $10,200 for three days are unpaid and unrecorded because the next weekly pay day is January 6, 2013.

b. Rented office space to another party and collected $6,000 on December 10, 2012. The rent collected was for 30 days from December 12, 2012, through January 10, 2013, and was credited in full to rent revenue.

Required:

1. Prepare (a) the adjusting entry required on December 31, 2012, and (b) the journal entry on January 6, 2013, to record the payment of any unpaid wages from December 2012.

2. Prepare (a) the journal entry for the collection of rent on December 10, 2012, and (b) the adjusting entry on December 31, 2012.

3. Determine the financial statement effects for each of the journal entries you prepared in (1) and (2). Indicate the accounts affected, amounts, and direction of the effects (+ for increases and − for decreases) on the accounting equation. Use the following headings:

Date	Assets	Liabilities	Shareholders' Equity

4. Show how the liabilities related to these transactions should be reported on the company's statement of financial position at December 31, 2012.

5. Explain why the accrual method of accounting provides more relevant information to financial analysts than the cash method.

P10–5 **Determining Financial Statement Effects of Various Liabilities** (AP10–3)

LO1, 4

Dell Inc.

1. Dell Inc. is a leading technology company that offers a broad range of product categories, including mobility products, desktop PCs, software and peripherals, servers and networking, and storage. Its annual report contained the following note:

> *Warranty* — We record warranty liabilities at the time of sale for the estimated costs that may be incurred under the terms of the limited warranty. The specific warranty terms and conditions vary depending upon the product sold and the country in which we do business, but generally include technical support, parts, and labour over a period ranging from one to three years. Factors that affect our warranty liability include the number of installed units currently under warranty, historical and anticipated rates of warranty claims on those units, and cost per claim to satisfy our warranty obligation.

Required:

Assume that estimated warranty costs for 2010 were $1 billion and that the warranty work was performed during 2011. Describe the financial statement effects for each year.

Walt Disney   2. Walt Disney is a well-recognized brand in the entertainment industry, with products ranging from broadcast media to parks and resorts. The following note is from its annual report:

> **Walt Disney**
>
> **Revenue Recognition**
>
> Revenues from advance theme park ticket sales are recognized when the tickets are used. For non-expiring, multi-year tickets, we recognize revenue over a three-year time period based on estimated usage, which is derived from historical usage patterns.

Required:

Assume that Disney collected $100 million in 2010 multi-year tickets that will be used in future years. For 2011, the company estimates that 60 percent of the tickets will be used. Describe the financial statement effects for each year.

Brunswick   3. Brunswick Corporation is a multinational company that manufactures and sells marine and
Corporation   recreational products. Its annual report contained the following information:

> **Litigation**
>
> A jury awarded $44.4 million in damages in a suit brought by Independent Boat Builders Inc., a buying group of boat manufacturers and its 22 members. Under the antitrust laws, the damage award has been tripled, and the plaintiffs will be entitled to their attorney's fees and interest.
>
> The Company has filed an appeal contending the verdict was erroneous as a matter of law, both as to liability and damages.

Required:

How should Brunswick report this litigation in its financial statements?

The Coca-Cola   4. A recent annual report for the Coca-Cola Company reported current assets of $12,176 million
Company   and current liabilities of $12,988 million. Based on the current ratio, do you think that Coca-Cola is experiencing financial difficulty?

Alcoa   5. Alcoa is involved in the mining and manufacturing of aluminum. Its products can become an advanced alloy for the wing of a Boeing 767 or a common, recyclable Coca-Cola can. The annual report for Alcoa stated the following:

> **Environmental Expenditures**
>
> Liabilities are recorded when remedial efforts are probable and the costs can be reasonably estimated.

Required:

In your own words, explain Alcoa's accounting policy for environmental expenditures. What is the justification for this policy?

LO1   **P10–6**   **Recording and Reporting Product Warranties** (AP10–4)

Bombardier Inc. specializes in manufacturing transportation products (aircraft, railway equipment, snowmobiles, and watercraft). The company offers warranties on all of its products. Note 12 to Bombardier's financial statements for fiscal year 2010 stated the following:

Product warranties typically range from one to five years, except for aircraft structural warranties that extend up to 20 years.

Selected information from Bombardier's annual reports follows (amounts in millions of U.S. dollars).

	2010	2009	2008
Revenues	19,366	19,721	17,506
Estimated warranty liability at year-end	1,040	931	1,041

During fiscal year 2010, Bombardier paid $400 million to customers in exchange for returned products under the warranty.

Required:

1. Compute the amount of warranty expense for fiscal year 2010.

2. Prepare journal entries to record both the warranty expense for the year and the payments made under the warranty.

3. Compute the ratio of the warranty liability to revenues for the three years. Has the ratio increased or decreased during the three-year period?

4. Based on the limited information available about the warranty expense and payments in 2010, should Bombardier increase the balance of the warranty liability in future years? Explain.

P10–7 **Determining Financial Statement Effects of Deferred Revenues**   ▪ **LO1**

A. Deferred revenues—customer deposits

Eastern Brewing Company (EBC) distributes its products in an aluminium keg. Customers are charged a deposit of $25 per keg, and deposits received from customers are recorded in the keg deposits account.

Required:

1. Where on the statement of financial position will the keg deposits account be found? Explain.

2. A production specialist who works for EBC estimates that 50 kegs for which deposits were received during the year will never be returned. How would the deposits related to these 50 kegs be reflected in the company's financial statements?

B. Deferred revenues—rent

On September 1, 2011, Noreen Ltd. collected $72,000 in cash from its tenant as an advance rent payment on its store location. The six-month lease period ends on February 28, 2012, at which time the lease contract may be renewed. Noreen's fiscal year ends on December 31.

Required:

1. Prepare journal entries to record the collection of rent on September 1, 2011, and the related adjustment for the amount of rent earned during 2011.

2. If the amount received on September 1, 2011, had covered a period of 18 months, how should Noreen report the deferred rent amount on its statement of financial position as at December 31, 2011?

C. Deferred revenues—subscription fees

Tremblay Inc. publishes a monthly newsletter for retail marketing managers and requires its subscribers to pay $60 in advance for a one-year subscription. During the month of April 2012, Tremblay Inc. sold 150 one-year subscriptions and received payments in advance from all new subscribers. Only 90 of the new subscribers paid their fees in time to receive the April newsletter. The other subscribers received the newsletter in May.

Required:

Prepare journal entries to record the subscription fees received in advance during April 2012, and the related adjusting entry to recognize the subscription revenue earned during April 2012.

LO2

PepsiCo Inc.

P10–8 **Analyzing the Reclassification of Debt** (AP10–5)

PepsiCo Inc. is a leading company in the beverage, snack food, and restaurant businesses. Note 9 to the company's financial statement included the following:

> At the end of the current year, we have reclassified $1.3 billion of short-term debt to long-term based on our intent and ability to refinance on a long-term basis.

As a result of this reclassification, PepsiCo's total current liabilities changed to $8.8 billion. Its total current assets were $10.8 billion. What was the current ratio before the reclassification? What is the current ratio after the reclassification? Do you think the reclassification was appropriate? Why do you think management made the reclassification? As a financial analyst, would you use the current ratio before the reclassification or after the reclassification to evaluate PepsiCo's liquidity?

LO1

CHC Helicopter

P10–9 **Defining and Analyzing Changes in Current Liabilities** (AP10–6)

CHC Helicopter Corporation is the world's largest provider of helicopter services to the global offshore oil and gas industry, with aircraft operating in more than 30 countries around the world. The company reported the following items in its statement of financial position dated April 30, 2008 (in thousands of Canadian dollars):

	April 30, 2008	April 30, 2007
Current liabilities		
Payables and accruals	$394,221	$340,912
Deferred revenue	10,541	2,057
Dividends payable	11,412	11,241
Income taxes payable	18,392	9,637
Deferred income tax liabilities	8,969	9,813
Current portion of debt obligations	67,182	333,728

Required:

1. Define each of the current liabilities and identify the type of transactions that cause each liability to change (increase, decrease).

2. The company reported that $15,473 of deferred revenue was earned during fiscal year 2008. Determine the amount that was collected in advance from customers during 2008 and prepare the related journal entry.

3. The company's board of directors declared dividends of $22,891 during 2008. Prepare the journal entries to record the declaration and payment of dividends during 2008.

LO1, 5

P10–10 **Making a Decision as Chief Financial Officer: Contingent Liabilities**

For each of the following situations, determine whether the company should (a) report a liability on the statement of financial position, (b) disclose a contingent liability, or (c) not report the situation. Justify and explain your conclusions.

1. An automobile company introduces a new car. Past experience demonstrates that lawsuits will be filed as soon as the new model is involved in any accidents. The company can be certain that at least one jury will award damages to people injured in an accident.

2. A research scientist determines that your company's bestselling product may infringe on another company's patent. If the other company discovers the infringement and files a lawsuit, your company could lose millions of dollars.

3. As part of land development for a new housing project, your company has polluted a natural lake. Under provincial law, you must clean up the lake once you complete the development. The development project will take five to eight years to complete. Current estimates indicate that it will cost $2 to $3 million to clean up the lake.

4. Your company has just been notified that it lost a product liability lawsuit for $1 million that it plans to appeal. Management is confident that the company will win on appeal, but the lawyers believe that it will lose.

5. A key customer is unhappy with the quality of a major construction project. The company believes that the customer is being unreasonable but, to maintain goodwill, has decided to do $250,000 in repairs next year.

P10–11 **Analyzing and Interpreting the Current Ratio and the Trade Payables Turnover Ratio** (AP10–7)

■ **LO2, 3**

Burberry Group plc

 e**X**cel

Burberry Group plc is a U.K.-based retail and wholesale business that owns 400-plus stores and concessions in high-end department stores worldwide and sells men's, women's, and children's designer apparel and accessories under the Prorsum and Burberry London names. Selected financial statement information for the company over the six-year period 2004–2009 is presented below (amounts in £ millions).

	2009	2008	2007	2006	2005	2004
Current assets	742.4	588.4	423.7	348.9	387.7	374.4
Current liabilities	546.8	436.2	330.4	255.8	180.5	471.9
Cost of sales	535.7	377.7	329.0	296.8	291.3	284.2
Trade payables	54.5	62.5	196.2	154.6	152.5	148.1

Required:

1. Compute the current ratio for each of the six years, and comment on the six-year trend of the ratio.

2. Compute the trade payables turnover ratio and the average age of payables for the years 2005–2009. Did the company's management of its trade payables improve over time? Explain.

P10–12 **Determining Cash Flow Effects** (AP10–8)

■ **LO6**

For each of the following transactions, determine whether cash flows from operating activities will increase, decrease, or remain the same:

a. Purchased merchandise on credit.

b. Paid a trade payable.

c. Accrued payroll for the month but did not pay it.

d. Borrowed money from the bank. The term of the note is 90 days.

e. Reclassified a long-term note as a current liability.

f. Paid accrued interest expense.

g. Recorded a liability based on a pending lawsuit.

h. Paid back the bank for money borrowed in (*d*), along with related interest.

i. Collected cash from a customer for services that will be performed in the next accounting period.

j. Paid GST to the federal government. The amount was previously collected from customers.

P10–13 **(Appendix 10A) Recording and Reporting Deferred Income Tax: Depreciation** (AP10–9)

■ **LO1, 5**

At December 31, 2011, the records of Pearson Corporation provided the following information:

Income statement	
Revenues	$160,000
Depreciation expense (straight line)	(11,000)
Other expenses (excluding income tax)	(90,000)
Profit before income taxes	$ 59,000

Additional information:

a. Revenues include $20,000 interest on tax-free municipal bonds.

b. Depreciation expense relates to equipment acquired on January 1, 2011, at a cost of $44,000, with no salvage value and an estimated useful life of four years.

c. The accelerated depreciation (capital cost allowance) used on the tax return is as follows: 2011, $17,600; 2012, $13,200; 2013, $8,800; and 2014, $4,400.

d. The company is subject to an income tax rate of 30 percent. Assume that 85 percent of the income tax liability is paid in the year incurred.

e. The income tax return for 2011 shows a taxable income of $32,400.

Required:

1. Compute the income taxes payable and the deferred income tax for 2011. Is the deferred income tax a liability or an asset? Explain.

2. Prepare the journal entry to record income taxes for 2011.

3. Show how the tax-related amounts should be reported on the income statement for 2011 and the statement of financial position at December 31, 2011.

ALTERNATE PROBLEMS

LO1, 6

AP10–1   **Recording and Reporting Current Liabilities, with Discussion of Effects on the Current Ratio** (P10–2)

Fontaine Company completed the following transactions during 2012. The company's fiscal year ends on December 31, 2012.

Jan.	2	Paid accrued interest in the amount of $52,000.
Apr.	30	Borrowed $550,000 from Commerce Bank; signed a 12-month, 6 percent interest-bearing note.
May	20	Sold merchandise for $6,000 cash plus harmonized sales tax at 14 percent.
June	3	Purchased merchandise for resale at a cost of $75,800, terms 2/10, n/30.
July	5	Paid the invoice received on June 3.
Aug.	31	Signed a contract to provide security service to a small apartment complex and collected $6,000 of fees for six months in advance. (Record the collection in a way that will not require an adjusting entry at year-end.)
Dec.	31	Reclassified a long-term debt in the amount of $100,000 to a current liability.
	31	Determined that salary and wages earned but not yet paid on December 31 totalled $85,000. Ignore payroll taxes.
	31	Recorded income tax expense for the year in the amount of $125,000. The current income taxes payable were $93,000.

Required:

1. Prepare journal entries to record each of these transactions.

2. Prepare all adjusting and reclassification entries required on December 31, 2012.

3. Show how all of the current liabilities arising from these transactions are reported on the statement of financial position at December 31, 2012.

4. For each transaction and entry, state whether the current ratio is increased, decreased, or remains unchanged. Assume that the current ratio is less than 1.0 prior to each transaction.

LO1, 6

AP10–2   **Determining Financial Effects of Transactions Affecting Current Liabilities, with Discussion of Cash Flow Effects** (P10–3)

Refer to the previous problem.

Required:

1. For each transaction (including adjusting and reclassification entries), indicate the accounts affected, amounts, and direction of the effects (+ for increases and − for decreases) on the accounting equation. Use the following headings:

Date	Assets	Liabilities	Shareholders' Equity

2. For each transaction, state whether cash flow from operating activities is increased, decreased, or remains unchanged.

LO1, 4

Ford

AP10–3   **Determining Financial Statement Effects of Various Liabilities** (P10–5)

1. Ford Motor Company is one of the world's largest companies, with annual sales of cars and trucks in excess of $120 billion. Its annual report contained the following note:

Warranties

Estimated warranty costs are accrued for at the time the vehicle is sold to a dealer. Estimates for warranty costs are made based primarily on historical warranty claim experience.

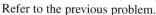

Required:

This year, Ford reported claims amounting to $4.0 billion and accrued expenses for warranties in the amount of $3.9 billion. Describe the financial statement effects for this year.

2. Carnival Cruise Lines operates cruise ships in Alaska, the Caribbean, the South Pacific, and the Mediterranean. Some cruises are brief; others can last for several weeks. The company does more than $1 billion in cruise business each year. The following note is from its annual report:

Carnival Cruise Lines

Revenues

Customer cruise deposits, which represent deferred revenue, are included in the statement of financial position when received and are recognized as cruise revenue upon completion of voyages of a duration of 10 days or less and on a pro rata basis computed using the number of days completed for voyages in excess of 10 days.

Required:

In your own words, explain how deferred revenue is reported on the statement of financial position for Carnival. Assume that Carnival collected $19 million in 2011 for cruises that will be completed in the following year. Of that amount, $4 million was related to cruises of 10 or fewer days that were not complete; $8 million to cruises of more than 10 days that, on average, were 60 percent complete; and $7 million was related to cruises that had not yet begun. What is the amount of unearned revenue that should be reported on the 2011 statement of financial position?

3. Sunbeam Corporation is a consumer products company that manufactures and markets a number of familiar brands, including Mr. Coffee, Osterizer, First Alert, and Coleman. Annual revenues for the company exceed $2 billion. Its annual report contained the following information:

Sunbeam

Litigation

The Company and its subsidiaries are involved in various lawsuits, arising from time to time, that the Company considers to be ordinary routine litigation incidental to its business. In the opinion of the Company, the resolution of these routine matters will not have a material adverse effect upon the financial position, results of operations, or cash flows of the Company. At the end of the current year, the Company had established accruals for litigation matters of $31.2 million.

The Company recorded a $12.0 million charge related to a case for which an adverse development arose. In the fourth quarter of this year, the case was favourably resolved and, as a result, $8.1 million of the charge was reversed into profit.

Required:

Explain the meaning of this note in your own words. Describe how litigation has affected the financial statements for Sunbeam.

4. An annual report for Exxon reported a current ratio of 0.90. For the previous year, the ratio was 1.08. Based on this information, do you think that Exxon is experiencing financial difficulty? What other information would you want to consider in making this evaluation?

Exxon

5. Brunswick Corporation is a multinational company that manufactures and sells marine and recreational products. Its annual report contained the following information:

Brunswick

Legal and Environmental

The company is involved in numerous environmental remediation and clean-up projects with an aggregate estimated exposure of approximately $21 million to $42 million. The Company accrues for environmental remediation-related activities for which commitments or clean-up plans have been developed and for which costs can be reasonably estimated.

Required:

In your own words, explain Brunswick's accounting policy for environmental expenditures. What is the justification for this policy?

LO1

IBM

AP10–4 **Recording and Reporting Warranty Liabilities** (P10–6)

International Business Machines (IBM) is a leading provider of computer products and services. The company is known for its hardware products but has focused on providing information technology services in recent years. IBM provides standard warranties with the sale of its products. The company's note on significant accounting policies states:

> The company offers warranties for its hardware products that range up to three years, with the majority being either one or three years. Estimated costs for warranty terms standard to the deliverable are recognized when revenue is recorded for the related deliverable. The company estimates its warranty costs standard to the deliverable, based on historical warranty claim experience, and applies this estimate to the revenue stream for products under warranty.

In addition, IBM offers its customers an option to purchase extended warranties. Revenue from extended warranty contracts, for which the company is obligated to perform, is recorded as deferred revenue income and subsequently recognized on a straight-line basis over the delivery period.

Selected information related to warranties provided by IBM follows (in millions of U.S. dollars):

	2009	2008	2007
Net revenues	$95,758	$103,630	$98,786
Standard warranty liability, end of year	316	358	412
Settlements made during the year	406	460	607
Extended warranty deferred revenue, end of year	665	589	409
Additions to extended warranty deferred revenue during the year	283	335	331

Required:

1. Compute the amount of warranty expense for 2008 and 2009.

2. Prepare journal entries to record both the warranty expense for 2009 and the payments made under the warranty during the year.

3. Compute the ratio of the warranty expense to net revenues for the three years. Assume that the warranty expense is $466 for 2007. Has the ratio increased or decreased during the three-year period? Provide possible reasons for the changes in the ratio.

4. Based on the limited information available about the warranty expense and settlements during these three years, should IBM reduce the ratio of the warranty expense to net sales in future years? Explain.

5. Compute the extended warranty revenue recognized during 2008 and 2009, and prepare the journal entry to record the revenue recognized in 2009.

LO2

General Mills

AP10–5 **Analyzing the Reclassification of Debt** (P10–8)

General Mills is a multi-billion dollar company that makes and sells products used in the kitchens of most homes. The company's annual report included the following note:

> We have a revolving credit agreement, expiring in two years, that provides for a credit line (which permits us to borrow money when needed). This agreement provides us with the opportunity to refinance short-term borrowings on a long-term basis.

Should General Mills classify the short-term borrowings as current or non-current debt based on this ability to borrow money to refinance the debt if needed? Explain what you would want to do, and why, if you were a member of the management team. If you were a financial analyst, would your answer be different?

AP10–6   Defining and Analyzing Changes in Current Liabilities (P10–9)

■ **LO1**

Leon's Furniture

Leon's Furniture is one of Canada's largest retailers of home furnishings. The company reported the following items in its statement of financial position dated December 31, 2009 (in thousands of Canadian dollars):

	Dec. 31, 2009	Dec. 31, 2008
Current liabilities		
Trade payables and accrued liabilities	$83,880	$95,247
Customers' deposits	15,362	14,119
Dividends payable	4,938	4,952
Deferred warranty plan revenue	16,150	15,267
Income taxes payable	1,958	—

The company's annual report included the following information:

Warranty revenues are deferred and taken into income on a straight-line basis over the life of the warranty period. Warranty revenues included in sales for fiscal year 2009 are $15,900,000 compared to $14,541,000 in 2008. Warranty expenses deducted through cost of sales for the year 2009 are $6,666,000 compared to $5,548,000 in 2008.

Required:

1. Define each of the current liabilities and identify the type of transactions that cause each liability to change (increase, decrease).

2. Determine the amount that the company received from customers to purchase deferred warranty plans during fiscal year 2009, and prepare the related journal entries to record the transactions that affected this account.

3. The company's board of directors declared dividends of $33,951 during 2009. Prepare the journal entries to record the declaration and payment of dividends during the year.

AP10–7   Analyzing and Interpreting the Current Ratio and the Trade Payables Turnover Ratio (P10–11)

■ **LO2, 3**

Guess

 eXcel

Guess Inc. is a competitor of Benetton Group. Selected financial statement information for this company over the most recent six-year period is shown below.

	2009	2008	2007	2006	2005	2004
Current assets	€ 894,189	€814,739	€563,467	€558,892	€410,777	€271,023
Current liabilities	335,884	382,156	279,529	283,896	217,226	132,799
Cost of sales	1,170,762	957,147	690,315	665,805	555,223	455,278
Trade payables	192,168	210,258	258,725	249,539	182,175	71,588

Required:

1. Compute the current ratio for each of the six years, and comment on the six-year trend of the ratio.

2. Compute the trade payables turnover ratio and the average age of payables for the years 2005–2009. Did the company improve on its management of trade payables? Explain.

AP10–8   Determining Cash Flow Effects (P10–12)

■ **LO4**

For each of the following transactions, determine whether cash flows from operating activities will increase, decrease, or remain the same:

a. Purchased merchandise for cash.

b. Paid salaries and wages for the last month of the previous accounting period.

c. Paid PST to the provincial government, based on collections from customers.

d. Borrowed money from the bank. The term of the note is two years.

e. Withheld CPP contributions from employees' paycheques and immediately paid these to the government.

f. Recorded accrued interest expense.

g. Paid cash as a result of losing a lawsuit. A liability had been recorded.

h. Paid salaries and wages for the current month.

i. Performed services for a customer who had paid for them in the previous accounting period.

LO1, 5   **AP10–9**   **(Appendix 10A) Recording and Reporting Deferred Income Taxes: Two Temporary Differences (P10–13)**

The records of Calib Corporation provided the following summarized data for 2011 and 2012:

Year-End December 31		
	2011	**2012**
Income statement		
Revenues	$210,000	$218,000
Expenses (excluding income tax)	130,000	133,000
Profit before income taxes	$ 80,000	$ 85,000

a. Calib is subject to an income tax rate of 35 percent. Assume that 80 percent of the income taxes payable are paid in the current year and 20 percent on February 28 of the next year.

b. The temporary differences resulted from the following:

    i. The 2012 expenses include an amount of $8,000 that must be deducted only in the 2011 tax return.

    ii. The 2012 revenues include an amount of $6,000 that was taxable only in 2013.

c. The taxable income shown in the tax returns was $72,000 for 2011 and $87,000 for 2012.

Required:

1. For each year compute (a) the income taxes payable and (b) the deferred income taxes. Identify whether the deferred income tax amounts are assets or liabilities. Explain.

2. Prepare the journal entry for each year to record income taxes payable, deferred income taxes, and income tax expense.

3. Show the tax-related amounts that should be reported each year on the income statement and the statement of financial position.

4. As a financial analyst, would you evaluate differently a deferred income tax liability compared with income taxes currently payable?

CASES AND PROJECTS

FINDING AND INTERPRETING FINANCIAL INFORMATION

LO1, 3, 4   **CP10–1**   **Finding Financial Information**

The Nestlé Group

Refer to the financial statements of the Nestlé Group in Appendix A of this book.

Required:

1. Does Nestlé report income taxes payable as a separate account on its statement of financial position at the end of the current year? If not, where would this account be included on Nestlé's statement of financial position?

2. How did changes in trade payables affect cash flows from operating activities in the current year?

3. What is the amount of non-current financial liabilities at the end of the current year?

4. What amounts of deferred income tax assets and liabilities are reported on the statement of financial position at the end of the current year?

5. Does the company disclose information on contingent liabilities?

LO1, 4   **CP10–2**   **Finding Financial Information**

Cadbury plc

Go to Connect online for the financial statements of Cadbury plc.

Required:

1. What is the amount of trade and other payables at the end of the current year?
2. How did changes in trade payables affect cash flows from operating activities in the current year?
3. What is the amount of non-current borrowings at the end of the current year?
4. Does the company have any contingent liabilities?

CP10–3 Comparing Companies within an Industry

Go to Connect online for the financial statements of Cadbury and to Appendix A of this book for the financial statements of the Nestlé Group.

LO2, 3

The Nestlé Group vs. Cadbury

Required:

1. Compute the current ratio for each company for each year shown in the financial statements.
2. Compute the trade payables turnover ratio for each company for each year.
3. Using this information and any other data from the annual report, write a brief assessment of the liquidity of the two companies.

FINANCIAL REPORTING AND ANALYSIS CASES

CP10–4 Explaining a Note: Accrued Liability for a Frequent Flyer Program

Most major airlines have frequent flyer programs that permit passengers to earn free tickets based on the number of reward miles they have flown. A Southwest Airlines annual report contained the following note:

LO1

Southwest Airlines

> **Frequent Flyer Awards**
>
> The Company accrues the estimated incremental cost to provide transportation for travel awards when earned under its Company Club frequent flyer program.

The phrase *incremental cost* refers to additional expense associated with an extra passenger taking the flight (e.g., the cost of a soft drink and a snack).

Required:

1. What cost measures other than incremental cost could Southwest use?
2. What account should Southwest debit when it accrues this liability?

CP10–5 Using Financial Reports: Evaluating Cash Management

The Nestlé Group is the world's leading nutrition, health, and wellness company. Selected financial information is presented below for the period 2004–2009 (amounts are in millions of Swiss francs):

LO2, 3

The Nestlé Group

	2009	2008	2007	2006	2005	2004
Net Sales	107,618	109,908	107,552	98,458	91,115	86,769
Trade receivables	9,425	10,552	12,025	11,693	11,461	9,587
Inventories	7,734	9,342	9,272	8,029	8,162	7,025
Cost of sales	43,467	47,339	45,037	40,713	37,946	36,146
Trade payables	10,033	12,608	14,179	12,572	11,117	9,107

Required:

1. Compute the following ratios for each of the years 2005–2009:
   a. Trade payables turnover
   b. Inventory turnover
   c. Trade receivables turnover
2. One of the measures of a company's effectiveness in utilizing cash resources is the cash conversion cycle, which is the difference between the average number of days needed to convert inventory to cash and the average number of days to pay trade suppliers. Compute the cash conversion cycle for each of the years 2005–2009. Did Nestlé improve on its management of cash? Explain.

■ **LO5**

Research In Motion

CP10–6   **Interpreting Contingent Liabilities: Litigation**

Research In Motion (RIM) is a leading designer, manufacturer, and marketer of innovative wireless solutions for the worldwide mobile communications market. RIM's products include the BlackBerry wireless platform, software development tools, and software/hardware licensing agreements.

The following excerpt from the company's statement of financial position as at February 26, 2005, shows Accrued litigation and related expenses for US$455,610,000. Note 15 to the company's financial statements provides an explanation for the nature of this liability.

Consolidated Balance Sheets

As at	March 4, 2006	February 26, 2005
	(in thousands of U.S. dollars)	
Liabilities		
Current		
Trade payables	$ 94,954	$ 68,464
Accrued liabilities (Notes 13 and 18[c])	144,912	87,133
Accrued litigation and related expenses (Note 15)	—	455,610
Income taxes payable (Note 9)	17,584	3,149
Deferred revenue	20,968	16,235
Current portion of long-term debt (Note 10)	262	223
	278,680	630,814
Long-term debt (Note 10)	6,851	6,504
	$285,531	$637,318

Source: Research In Motion Annual Report 2006.

Required:

1. Review Note 15 to RIM's financial statements and identify the main reason for the reported liability as well as the specific amounts that the company recorded as liabilities during each of the fiscal years 2003–2006.

2. Reconstruct the journal entry to record the payment of $612.5 million in settlement of the NTP lawsuit, as disclosed in Note 15 to RIM's financial statements.

3. Does the company's annual report include information about other litigation during the past few years? If so, has the company provided an estimate of the liabilities that it may have to pay in the future? Explain.

CRITICAL THINKING CASES

■ **LO1, 2**

CP10–7   **Making Decisions as a Manager: Liquidity**

In some cases, a manager can engage in transactions that improve the appearance of financial reports without affecting the underlying economic reality. In this chapter, we discussed the importance of liquidity as measured by the current ratio and working capital. For each of the following transactions, (a) determine whether reported liquidity, as measured by the current ratio and working capital, is improved and (b) state whether you believe that the fundamental liquidity of the company has been improved. Assume that the company has positive working capital and a current ratio of 2.0 immediately prior to each transaction.

a. Borrowed $1 million from the bank, payable in 90 days.

b. Borrowed $10 million with a long-term note, payable in five years.

c. Reclassified the current portion of long-term debt as long term as a result of a new agreement with the bank that guarantees the company's ability to refinance the debt when it matures.

d. Paid $100,000 of the company's trade payables.

e. Entered into a borrowing agreement that allows the company to borrow up to $10 million when needed.

f. Required all employees to take accrued vacation to reduce its liability for vacation compensation.

CP10–8 Evaluating an Ethical Dilemma: Managing Reported Results

The president of a regional wholesale distribution company planned to borrow a significant amount of money from a local bank at the beginning of the next fiscal year. He knew that the bank placed a heavy emphasis on the liquidity of potential borrowers. To improve the company's current ratio, the president told his employees to stop shipping new merchandise to customers and to stop accepting merchandise from suppliers for the last three weeks of the fiscal year. Is this behaviour ethical? Would your answer be different if the president had been concerned about reported profits and asked all of the employees to work overtime to ship out merchandise that had been ordered at the end of the year?

CP10–9 Making a Decision as a Financial Analyst: Cash Flows

LO2

As a young analyst at a large mutual fund, you have found two companies that meet the basic investment criteria of the fund. One company has a very high current ratio but a relatively low amount of cash flow from operating activities reported on the statement of cash flows. The other company has a very low current ratio but very significant cash flows from operating activities. Which company would you prefer?

FINANCIAL REPORTING AND ANALYSIS TEAM PROJECT

CP10–10 Team Project: Examining an Annual Report

LO1, 2, 3, 4

As a team, select an industry to analyze. A list of companies classified by industry can be obtained by accessing www.fpinfomart.ca and then choosing "Companies by Industry." You can also find a list of industries and companies within each industry via http://ca.finance.yahoo.com/investing (click on "Annual Reports" under "Tools"). Using a Web browser, each team member should acquire the annual report for one publicly traded company in the industry, with each member selecting a different company.

Required:

On an individual basis, each team member should then write a short report answering the following questions about the selected company. Discuss any patterns across the companies that you as a team observe. Then, as a group, write a short report comparing and contrasting your companies.

1. List the accounts and amounts of the company's current liabilities for the last three years.
   a. What is the percentage of each to the respective year's total liabilities?
   b. What do the results of your analysis suggest about the strategy your company has followed with respect to borrowed funds overall and over time?

2. What, if any, contingent liabilities are reported by the company for the most recent year and what is your assessment of the risk of each after reading the note(s)?

3. Ratio analysis:
   a. What does the current ratio measure in general?
   b. Compute the ratio for the last three years.
   c. What do your results suggest about the company?
   d. If available, find the industry ratio for the most recent year, compare it to your results, and discuss why you believe the ratio for your company differs or is similar to the industry ratio.

4. Ratio analysis:
   a. What does the trade payables turnover ratio measure in general?
   b. Compute the ratio for the last three years.
   c. What do your results suggest about the company?
   d. If available, find the industry ratio for the most recent year, compare it to your results, and discuss why you believe the ratio for your company differs from or is similar to the industry ratio.

5. What is the effect of the change in trade payables on cash flows from operating activities for the most recent year; that is, did the change increase or decrease operating cash flows? Explain your answer.

Reporting and Interpreting Non-current Liabilities

After studying this chapter, you should be able to do the following:

FOCUS COMPANY: **Nestlé S.A.**

FINANCING GROWTH WITH LONG-TERM DEBT

Nestlé (www.nestle.com) produces and sells "wellness" products. In 2010, it was ranked by *Fortune* magazine as number one in the consumer foods industry and number 37 of the 50 most admired companies in all industries. The ranking was based on survey results received from executives, directors, and analysts, worldwide.

Nestlé's strategic objective is to become the recognized world leader in health and wellness products. It has the largest private nutrition research capacity in the world, employing over 5,000 people in 26 research and technology centres working to improve the nutritional quality of the food products it sells. From increasing the yields of raw cocoa beans in Mexico to fortifying food with micronutrients such as iodine to combat disease, Nestlé's motto is "Good Nutrition, Good Life."

It takes considerable financial strength and solid growth in revenue and profit to maintain an investment in research and development as wide-ranging as Nestlé's. The company also manufactures its products in 19 African, 25 South American, and 10 Middle Eastern countries as well as in China, Japan, the United States, Canada, the United Kingdom, Russia, and 32 other European countries. Nestlé's growth is often through acquisition of other corporations. In 2009, Nestlé acquired companies valued at approximately 856 million Swiss francs (CHF). This level of long-term investment requires new capital. Some of this capital was borrowed from creditors through long-term notes and bonds. For example, in 2009, Nestlé issued approximately CHF 3.9 billion in bonds and will likely finance its investment program in the future by selling additional long-term notes and bonds. By December 31, 2009, Nestlé had raised almost CHF 9.4 billion of funds through bonds.

UNDERSTANDING THE BUSINESS

Non-current liabilities include all of the entity's obligations that are not classified as current liabilities, such as long-term notes and bonds payable. Typically, a non-current liability will require payment more than one year in the future. These obligations may be created by borrowing money, or they may result from other activities.

Nestlé reports its non-current liabilities on the statement of financial position, after current liabilities, as shown in Exhibit 11.1. Details of the financial liabilities, employee benefits liabilities, provisions, deferred tax liabilities, and other payables accounts are disclosed separately and explained in the notes.

In Chapter 10, we introduced the term *capital structure*, the mix of debt and equity that is used to finance a company's growth. Almost all companies employ some debt in their capital structure. In this chapter, we focus on long-term debt, which simply reflects a contractual obligation whereby the borrower receives cash or other assets in exchange for a promise to pay the lender a fixed or determinable amount of money at a specific date in the future.

The use of long-term debt offers significant advantages to companies such as Nestlé:

1. *Shareholders maintain control.* Debt does not dilute ownership and control of the company, because debtholders participate neither in the management of operations nor in the eventual distribution of retained earnings to shareholders.

2. *Interest expense is tax deductible.* The deductibility of interest for tax purposes reduces the net cost of borrowing. This is an advantage compared to dividends paid on shares that are not tax deductible.

3. *The impact on earnings is positive.* Money can often be borrowed at a low interest rate and invested at a higher rate. Assume that Nutrition Plus Inc. owns a store selling special food products. The company has shareholders' equity of $100,000 invested in the store and earns $40,000 in profit before interest and taxes per year. Management plans to open a new store that will also cost $100,000 and earn

NON-CURRENT LIABILITIES are all of the entity's obligations not classified as current liabilities.

CONSOLIDATED BALANCE SHEET as at 31 December 2009			
In millions of CHF	Notes	2009	2008
Current liabilities			
Financial liabilities	19	14,438	15,383
Trade and other payables	19	13,033	12,608
Accruals and deferred income		2,779	2,931
Provisions	18	643	417
Derivative liabilities	11/19	1,127	1,477
Current income tax liabilities	19	1,173	824
Liabilities directly associated with assets held for sale	25	2,890	—
Total current liabilities		36,083	33,640
Non-current liabilities			
Financial liabilities	19	8,966	6,344
Employee benefits liabilities	16	6,249	5,464
Provisions	18	3,222	3,246
Deferred tax liabilities	7	1,404	1,341
Other payables		1,361	1,264
Total non-current liabilities		21,202	17,659
Total liabilities		57,285	51,299

Source: Nestlé Group Annual Report 2009.

Exhibit **11.1**

Non-current Liabilities

REAL WORLD EXCERPT

The Nestlé Group

ANNUAL REPORT

$40,000 in profit before interest and taxes per year. Should management issue new shares or borrow the money at an interest rate of 8 percent? The following analysis shows that the use of debt will increase the return to the owners:

	Option 1 Equity	Option 2 Debt
Profit before interest and income taxes	$40,000	$40,000
Interest expense	0	8,000
	40,000	32,000
Income tax expense (at 35%)	14,000	11,200
Profit	$ 26,000	$ 20,800
Owners' equity	$200,000	$100,000
Return on equity (Profit/Owners' equity)	13%	20.8%

FINANCIAL LEVERAGE is the use of borrowed funds to increase the rate of return on owners' equity; it occurs when the after-tax interest rate on debt is lower than the rate of return on total assets.

It is evident from this simplified illustration that borrowing reduces profit but the deductibility of interest expense for tax purposes increases the return on the owners' investment. This example also illustrates the use of positive financial leverage, whereby a company borrows funds at a specified interest rate and invests them in productive assets. Shareholders benefit from borrowing when the rate of return on assets exceeds the after-tax interest rate on the debt.

Unfortunately, long-term debt carries higher risk than equity. The following are the major disadvantages associated with issuing long-term debt:

1. *Risk of bankruptcy.* Interest payments to the debtholders must be made each period whether the corporation earns profit or incurs a loss.

2. *Negative impact on cash flows.* Debt must be repaid at a specific time in the future. Management must be able to generate sufficient cash to repay the debt or have the ability to refinance it.

Sound business practice requires maintaining an appropriate balance between debt and equity capital.

In this chapter, we examine Nestlé's issuance of bonds and study the accounting rules governing the recording and reporting of bonds payable. We also describe other typical non-current liabilities, considering the reasons that management raises money through long-term debt, and examine how the reported debt and supplementary disclosures are used by analysts to make informed judgments about investment and/or credit risk.

ORGANIZATION OF THE CHAPTER

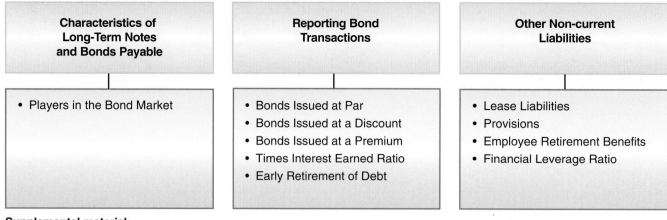

Characteristics of Long-Term Notes and Bonds Payable	Reporting Bond Transactions	Other Non-current Liabilities
• Players in the Bond Market	• Bonds Issued at Par • Bonds Issued at a Discount • Bonds Issued at a Premium • Times Interest Earned Ratio • Early Retirement of Debt	• Lease Liabilities • Provisions • Employee Retirement Benefits • Financial Leverage Ratio

Supplemental material:
Appendix 11A: Present Value Concepts
Appendix 11B: Present Value Tables
Appendix 11C: Reporting Interest Expense on Bonds by Using the Straight-Line Amortization Method
Appendix 11D: Present Value Computations Using Excel (online)
Appendix 11E: Future Value Concepts (online)

CHARACTERISTICS OF LONG-TERM NOTES AND BONDS PAYABLE

Companies can raise long-term debt directly from a number of financial service organizations, including banks, insurance companies, and pension fund companies. Raising debt from one of these organizations is known as *private placement*. This type of debt often is called a *note payable*, which is a written promise to pay a stated sum of money at one or more specified future dates, called the *maturity date(s)*.

In many cases, a company's need for debt capital exceeds the financial capability of any single creditor. In these situations, the company may issue publicly traded debt called *bonds*. The bonds can be traded in established markets that provide bondholders with liquidity (i.e., the ability to sell the bond and receive cash quickly). Nestlé borrows billions of Swiss francs or other currencies in long-term debt to develop, produce, and distribute more nutritional and tasty foods to its customers. In exchange for the borrowed money, Nestlé signs debt agreements in the form of loans, notes, or mortgage notes with banks and other institutional lenders. Loans and notes are often for terms of five years or less, while mortgage terms can exceed 25 years.

Lenders often protect their interests by requesting that the debt be secured rather than unsecured. If you have a credit card, a student loan, or perhaps an automobile loan, you may have read the terms of the debt contract, which indicate whether or not the debt is secured. In the case of a personal credit card, the debt is unsecured, which means that if a debtor fails to make the required payment, or *defaults*, the lender cannot repossess any specific asset of the cardholder. In the case of a large, personal long-term loan such as an automobile loan, lenders will insist on the right to repossess the automobile in the event of default. Repossession allows the lender to sell the automobile and recover all or part of the unpaid loan.

Corporations such as Nestlé can secure their notes and bonds payable by using revenue, inventory, property, equipment, and buildings. Secured debt provides the creditor with the right to foreclose on the debt and repossess the assets, or collateral, pledged by the company as security should the company violate the terms of its debt contract. Nestlé has disclosed information concerning its bonds, as shown in Exhibit 11.2. The note lists the different types of bonds that the company has issued in the past—with denominations in different currencies. After studying this chapter, you will understand the terms used in the note, particularly the accounting and financial issues associated with bonds.

A bond usually requires the payment of interest over its life, with the repayment of principal on the maturity date. The bond principal is (1) the amount payable at the maturity date and (2) the basis for computing periodic cash interest payments. The principal also is called the *par value, face amount*, and *maturity value*. All bonds have a par value, which is the amount that will be paid when the bond matures. For most Canadian bonds, the par value is $1,000, but it can be any amount.

A bond always specifies a stated rate of interest and the timing of periodic cash interest payments, usually annually or semi-annually. Each periodic interest payment is equal to the principal times the stated interest rate. The selling price of a bond does not affect the periodic cash payment of interest. For example, a $1,000, 8 percent bond always pays cash interest of $80 on an annual basis or $40 on a semi-annual basis.

Different types of bonds have different characteristics, for good economic reasons; different types of creditors have different types of risk and return preferences. A retired person, for example, may be willing to receive a lower interest rate in return for greater security. This type of creditor might want a mortgage bond that pledges a specific asset as security if the company is unable to repay the bond. Another creditor might be willing to accept higher risk with a low interest rate and an unsecured status if the company provides the opportunity to convert the bond into common shares at some

LO¹

Describe the characteristics of long-term notes and bonds payable.

The **BOND PRINCIPAL** is the amount payable at the maturity of the bond. It is also the basis for computing periodic cash interest payments.

PAR VALUE and **FACE AMOUNT** are other names for bond principal or the maturity value of a bond.

The **STATED RATE** is the rate of interest per period specified in the bond contract.

Exhibit **11.2**

Note from Nestlé's
Annual Report

REAL WORLD EXCERPT

The Nestlé Group

ANNUAL REPORT

19.4 Bonds

In millions of CHF   2009   2008

Issuer	Face value in millions	Coupon	Effective interest rate	Year of issue/ maturity	Comments	Carrying amount 2009	2008
Nestlé Holdings, Inc., USA	EUR 250	2.13%	2.97%	2005–2009		—	367
	AUD 300	5.50%	5.68%	2005–2009		—	223
	GBP 200	5.13%	5.38%	2006–2009		—	313
	USD 300	4.38%	4.49%	2005–2009		—	321
	AUD 300	6.00%	6.36%	2006–2010	(a)(b)	277	225
	CHF 625	2.75%	2.69%	2007–2010	(c)	626	620
	HUF 10,000	6.88%	7.20%	2007–2010	(a)	54	53
	NOK 1,500	4.75%	5.16%	2007–2010	(a)(d)	267	230
	NZD 100	8.25%	8.53%	2008–2010	(a)	75	62
	AUD 600	7.25%	7.63%	2008–2011	(e)	560	451
	CHF 300	2.25%	2.30%	2008–2011	(f)	299	296
	NOK 1,000	5.00%	5.55%	2008–2011	(f)	178	152
	USD 750	4.00%	3.87%	2008–2011	(a)	799	822
	USD 500	4.75%	4.90%	2007–2011	(a)	533	537
	CHF 675	3.00%	2.86%	2007–2012	(g)	701	700
	AUD 350	6.00%	6.24%	2009–2013	(f)	321	—
	CHF 450	2.50%	2.57%	2006–2013	(a)	468	454
	USD 275	2.00%	2.26%	2009–2013	(h)	282	—
	CHF 250	2.63%	2.66%	2007–2018	(a)	259	245
Nestlé Purina PetCare Company, USA	USD 83	9.25%	5.90%	1989–2009		—	90
	USD 48	7.75%	6.25%	1995–2015		53	54
	USD 63	9.30%	6.46%	1991–2021		80	83
	USD 79	8.63%	6.46%	1992–2022		96	99
	USD 44	8.13%	6.47%	1993–2023		52	53
	USD 51	7.88%	6.45%	1995–2025		60	62
Nestlé Finance International Ltd, Luxembourg (formerly Nestlé Finance-France S.A., France)	HUF 25,000	7.00%	7.00%	2004–2009		—	138
	EUR 100	3.50%	3.52%	2006–2009		—	149
	CHF 1,075	1.25%	1.40%	2009–2012	(i)	1,077	—
	CHF 1,200	2.00%	2.04%	2009–2013	(j)	1,198	—
	CHF 425	2.00%	2.03%	2009–2014	(j)	424	—
	CHF 275	2.13%	2.13%	2009–2014	(j)	275	—
	CHF 350	2.13%	2.20%	2009–2015	(j)	349	—
Other bonds						9	19
Total						**9,372**	**6,818**
of which due within one year						1,300	1,607
of which due after one year						8,072	5,211

Source: Nestlé Group Annual Report 2009.

point in the future. Companies design bond features that are attractive to different groups of creditors, just as automobile manufacturers try to design cars that appeal to different groups of consumers. Important types of bonds are shown on the following page.

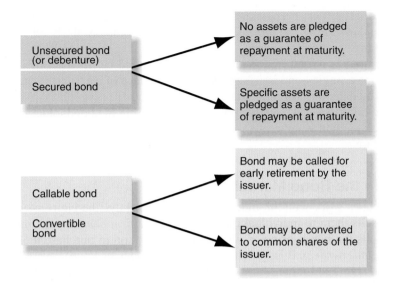

A **DEBENTURE** is an unsecured bond; no assets are specifically pledged to guarantee repayment.

CALLABLE BONDS may be called for early retirement at the option of the issuer.

CONVERTIBLE BONDS may be converted to other securities of the issuer (usually common shares).

Companies such as Nestlé often need to build research and production facilities to develop and manufacture consumer foods. One possibility is for Nestlé to finance the project by issuing bonds that are secured by the assets that will be in place once the project is finished. Another possibility is to issue bonds secured by the amount of revenues expected from the completed project. The company could also issue debentures that are unsecured, depending on how much risk the debenture holders are willing to take.

When a company decides to issue new bonds, it prepares a bond indenture (bond contract) that specifies the legal provisions of the bonds. These provisions include the maturity date, rate of interest to be paid, date of each interest payment, and any conversion privileges. The indenture also contains covenants designed to protect the creditors. Typical covenants include limitations on new debt that the company might issue in the future, limitations on the payment of dividends, and required minimum levels of certain accounting ratios, such as the current ratio. Managers prefer covenants that are less restrictive because they may limit the company's future actions. Creditors, however, prefer more restrictive covenants that reduce the risk of losing their investment. As with any business transaction, the final result is achieved through a process of negotiation.

An **INDENTURE** is a bond contract that specifies the legal provisions of a bond issue.

Bond covenants are usually reported in the notes to the financial statements. For example, ConAgra Foods Inc., a competitor of Nestlé, included the following disclosure to its 2009 financial statements.

NOTES TO THE CONSOLIDATED FINANCIAL STATEMENTS

11. Senior Long-Term Debt...

. . .

Our most restrictive note agreements (the revolving credit facility and certain privately placed long-term debt) require that our consolidated funded debt not exceed 65% of our consolidated capital base, and that our fixed charges coverage ratio be greater than 1.75 to 1.0. At May 31, 2009, we were in compliance with our debt covenants.[1]

---

[1]The fixed charges coverage ratio or times interest earned ratio is explained later in this chapter.

A **BOND CERTIFICATE** is the bond document that each bondholder receives.

A **TRUSTEE** is an independent party appointed to represent the bondholders.

The bond issuer also prepares a prospectus, which is a legal document given to potential bond investors. The prospectus describes the company, the bond, and how the proceeds of the bond will be used.[2]

When a bond is issued, the investor receives a bond certificate. All of the bond certificates for a single bond issue are identical. The face of each certificate shows the same maturity date, interest rate, interest dates, and other provisions. An independent party, called the *trustee*, is usually appointed to represent the bondholders. A trustee's duties are to ascertain whether the issuing company fulfills all of the provisions of the bond indenture.

Players in the Bond Market

Most companies work with an underwriter that either buys the entire issue of bonds and then resells them to individual creditors (called a *firm commitment underwriter*), or simply sells the bonds or notes without any obligation to purchase them (called a *best efforts underwriter*). It is not uncommon for companies to use several underwriters to sell a large bond issue. For example, Nestlé deals with underwriters located in Switzerland, the European Union, and North America. Canadian underwriters that help companies sell bond issues include CIBC World Markets Inc., Scotia Capital Inc., TD Securities Inc., RBC Dominion Securities Inc., and National Bank Financial Inc., among others.

Bond dealers sell bonds, typically, to institutional investors such as banks, insurance companies, and mutual and pension funds. They also create a secondary market for bonds by trading them for their own account in response to supply and demand by institutional investors. Almost all trades occur by telephone, known as an over-the-counter (OTC) market, not through a formal bond exchange. The market for bonds exceeds, by far, the value of stocks traded on a typical day because of the high value of each trade. A bond trade of $200 million would not be unusual in this market.[3]

Because of the complexities associated with bonds, several agencies exist to evaluate the probability that a bond issuer will not be able to meet the requirements specified in the indenture. This risk is called ***default risk***. In general, the higher the risk of default, the higher will be the interest rate required to successfully persuade investors to purchase the bond, and the more restrictive will be the covenants protecting the bondholder. Dominion Bond Rating Service (DBRS), Moody's Investor Services Inc. (Moody's), Fitch Inc., and Standard and Poor's Rating Services (S&P) each assess the default risk for every issue of corporate debentures and bonds.[4] Their ratings range from investment grade to extremely speculative junk bonds. If it becomes apparent that there has been a change in default risk for any debt already issued, each rating service will issue a public bulletin that upgrades or downgrades the credit rating, along with reasons for the change.[5]

Bond prices change for two main reasons: changes in creditworthiness of the bond issuer and changes in interest rates. The company's creditworthiness depends on the operating, investing, and financing decisions made by management. However, interest rates are not within the control of corporations but depend on the supply and demand for money. The most important interest rate is the rate at which the federal government can borrow money for the long term. This is the benchmark, risk-free rate of return on bonds because purchasers believe that the federal government will never fail to repay,

---

[2]An example of a prospectus issued by Shaw Communications Inc. is available on the *SEDAR* system (www.sedar.com). Access the website, search for Shaw Communications Inc. under the letter S, view the documents filed by the company, and select "Prospectus supplement – English," dated November 4, 2009.

[3]Further details about the bond market are available at www.investinginbonds.com.

[4]Standard & Poor's (S&P) has a useful website at www.standardandpoors.com for those interested in learning about the credit ratings used by this credit rating agency.

[5]The details of how default risk is rated vary slightly from one agency to another. You can view a sample of these descriptions in detail at www.dbrs.com.

or default, on its debts. The interest rates of all other debt instruments are established relative to this risk-free rate. The difference between the interest rate on debt instruments and the risk-free rate is called the *spread*. The size of the spread depends upon the perceived additional risk that the company will default on either its interest or principal payments on the debt.

REPORTING BOND TRANSACTIONS

Exhibit 11.2 shows that the Nestlé Group has issued bonds for a total face value of CHF 9.372 billion as at December 31, 2009. Each bond indenture specifies two types of cash payments:

1. ***Principal***. This is usually a single payment made when the bond matures. It is also called the ***par*** or ***face value***.

2. ***Cash interest payments***. These payments are computed by multiplying the principal amount times the interest rate, called the *contract, stated*, or *coupon rate* of interest stated in the bond contract. The bond contract specifies whether these payments are made quarterly, semi-annually, or annually.

Neither the company nor the underwriter determines the price at which the bonds sell. Instead, the market determines the current cash equivalent of future interest and principal payments by using present value concepts.[6] To determine the present value of the bond, you compute the present value of the principal (a single payment) and the present value of the interest payments (an annuity) and add the two amounts.

Creditors demand a certain rate of interest to compensate them for the risks related to bonds, called the *market interest rate* (also known as the *yield*, or *effective interest rate*). Because the market rate is the interest rate on a debt when it is incurred, it should be used in computing the present value of the bond.

The present value of a bond may be the same as par, above par (bond premium), or below par (bond discount). If the stated and the market interest rates are the same, a bond sells at par. If a bond pays a stated interest rate that is lower than the market rate that creditors demand, they will not buy it unless its price is reduced (i.e., a discount must be provided). If a bond pays a stated rate that is higher than the market rate that creditors demand, they will be willing to pay a premium to buy it.

This relationship can be shown graphically as follows:[7]

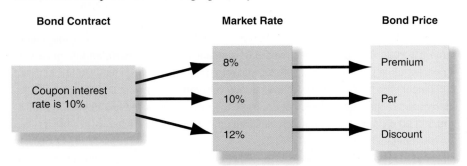

Basically, corporations and creditors are indifferent to whether a bond is issued at par, at a discount, or at a premium because bonds are always priced to provide the market rate of interest. To illustrate, consider a corporation that issues three separate

---

LO²

Report bonds payable and interest expense for bonds sold at par, at a discount, or at a premium.

The **COUPON RATE** is the stated rate of interest on bonds.

MARKET INTEREST RATE is the current rate of interest on a debt when incurred; also called the **YIELD**, or **EFFECTIVE INTEREST RATE**.

BOND PREMIUM is the difference between the selling price and par when the bond is sold for more than par.

BOND DISCOUNT is the difference between the selling price and par when the bond is sold for less than par.

[6]Students who have not been exposed to present value concepts in previous courses are strongly advised to read Appendix 11A before continuing with the rest of this chapter.

[7]The difference between the coupon interest rate and the market interest rate is often very small, usually a fraction of 1 percent, when the bonds are sold. Companies try to sell their bonds at prices close to their par value. However, the market rate of interest continually changes as a result of such factors as inflation expectations and the level of business activity. It is therefore virtually impossible to issue a bond at a point when the coupon rate and the market rate are exactly the same.

bonds on the same day. The bonds are exactly the same except that one has a stated interest rate of 6 percent, another 7 percent, and a third 8 percent. If the market rate of interest was 7 percent, the first would be issued at a discount, the second at par, and the third at a premium, but a creditor who bought any one of the bonds would earn the market interest rate of 7 percent.

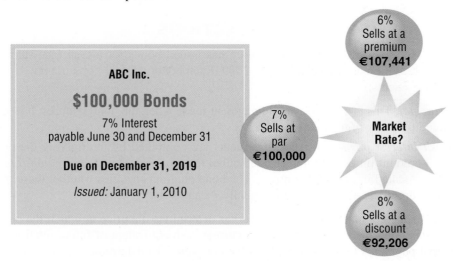

 **FINANCIAL ANALYSIS**

BOND INFORMATION FROM THE BUSINESS PRESS

Bond prices are reported each day in the business press based on transactions that occurred in the market on the previous trading day. The following is typical of the information you will find:

Bond	Coupon	Mat. Date	April 5, 2010		April 6, 2010	
			Bid $	Yld	Bid $	Yld
TransCanada Corp.	5.60	March 31, 2034	99.82	5.61	99.90	5.605
Domtar Corp.	10.75	June 1, 2017	125.00	8.60	126.00	8.532

TransCanada's bond, highlighted above, has a coupon rate of 5.6 percent and will mature on March 31, 2034. The bond's yield was 5.61 percent on April 5, 2010, and its price was 99.82 percent of its par value, or $998.20. Market conditions caused the yield to decrease to 5.605 percent the following day, but the coupon rate remains fixed at 5.60 percent. As the yield decreased relative to the fixed coupon rate, the price increased from $99.82 on April 5, 2010, to $99.90 on April 6, 2010, which illustrates the inverse relationship between the yield and the bond price.

TransCanada's bond sold on April 5, 2010, at a discount because the market rate demanded by buyers is slightly higher than the coupon rate offered by the company. In comparison, Domtar's bond sold at a premium of 25 percent of its face value on the same date because it offers a coupon rate of 10.75 percent that exceeded by far the market interest rate of 8.60 percent.

Changes in the daily bond prices do not affect the company's financial statements. For financial reporting purposes, the company uses the interest rates that existed when the bonds were first sold to the public. Subsequent changes do not affect the company's accounting for the bonds.

Bonds Issued at Par

Bonds sell at their par value when buyers are willing to invest in them at the interest rate stated on the bond. To illustrate, let us assume that on January 1, 2010, Nesca Corp., a hypothetical Canadian company, issued 10 percent bonds with a par value of $400,000 and received $400,000 in cash (which means that the bonds sold at par). The bonds were dated to start interest on January 1, 2010, and will pay interest each June 30 and December 31. The bonds mature in 10 years, on December 31, 2019.

The amount of money a corporation receives when it sells bonds is the present value of the future cash flows associated with them. When Nesca issued its bonds, it agreed to make two types of payments in the future: a single payment of $400,000 when the bond matures in 10 years and an annuity of $20,000 payable twice each year for 10 years. The bond payments can be shown graphically as follows:

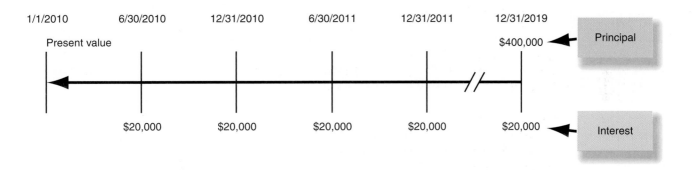

The present value of the bond payments can be computed with the tables contained in Appendix 11B by using the factor for 20 periods and an interest rate of 5 percent (10 percent ÷ 2):

	Present Value
a. Single payment: $400,000 × 0.3769	$150,760
b. Annuity: $20,000 × 12.4622	249,240*
Issue price of Nesca's bonds	$400,000
*Rounded	

When the effective rate of interest equals the stated rate of interest, the present value of the future cash flows associated with a bond always equals the bond's par value. Remember that a bond's selling price is determined by the present value of its future cash flows, not the par value. On the date of issue, bond liabilities are recorded at the present value of future cash flows as follows:

| Cash (A) .... | 400,000 | |
| Bonds payable (L) .... | | 400,000 |

Assets		=	**Liabilities**	+	**Shareholders' Equity**
Cash	+400,000		Bonds payable	+400,000	

Reporting Interest Expense on Bonds Issued at Par The creditors who bought the bonds did so with the expectation that they would earn interest over the life of the bond. Nesca will pay interest at 5 percent (i.e., 10 percent per year) on the par value of the bonds each June 30 and December 31 until the bond's maturity date. The amount of interest each period will be $20,000 (5% × $400,000). The entry to record the interest payments follows:

| Bond interest expense (E) .... | 20,000 | |
| Cash (A) .... | | 20,000 |

Assets		=	**Liabilities**	+	**Shareholders' Equity**	
Cash	−20,000				Bond interest expense	−20,000

Bond interest payment dates rarely coincide with the last day of a company's fiscal year. Interest expense incurred but not paid must be accrued with an adjusting entry. If Nesca's fiscal year ended on May 31, the company would accrue interest for five months and record interest expense and interest payable.

SELF-STUDY **QUIZ 11-2**

Assume that Nesca issued $100,000 bonds that will mature in 10 years. The bonds pay interest at the end of each year at an annual rate of 9 percent. They were sold when the market rate was 9 percent. Determine the selling price of the bonds.

connect

After you complete your answers, go online for the solutions.

Bonds Issued at a Discount

Bonds sell at a discount when the market rate of interest demanded by the buyers is higher than the stated interest rate offered by the issuer. Assume that the market rate of interest was 12 percent when Nesca sold its bonds (which have a par value of $400,000). The bonds have a stated rate of 10 percent, payable semi-annually, which is less than the market rate on that date. Therefore, the bonds sold at a *discount*. This usually occurs when the market rate of interest increases after the company determines the coupon rate on the bonds.

To compute the issue price of the bonds, we need to compute the present value of the future cash flows specified on the bond. As in the previous example, the number of periods is 20, but we must use an interest rate of 6 percent (12 percent ÷ 2), which is the market rate of interest. Thus, the issue price of Nesca's bonds is computed as follows:

	Present Value
a. Principal: $400,000 × 0.3118	$124,720
b. Interest: $20,000 × 11.4699	229,398
Issue (sale) price of Nesca's bonds	$354,118*
*Discount: $400,000 − $354,118 − $45,882.	

The cash price of the bonds issued by Nesca is $354,118. Some people refer to this price as 88.5, which means that the bonds were sold at 88.5 percent of their par value ($354,118 ÷ $400,000).

When a bond is sold at a discount, the bonds payable account is credited for the par value, and the discount is recorded as a debit to discount on bonds payable. The issuance of Nesca's bonds at a discount is recorded as follows:

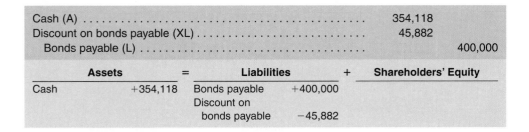

Cash (A)	354,118	
Discount on bonds payable (XL)	45,882	
Bonds payable (L)		400,000

Assets		=	Liabilities		+	Shareholders' Equity
Cash	+354,118		Bonds payable	+400,000		
			Discount on bonds payable	−45,882		

Note that the discount is recorded in a separate contra-liability account (discount on bonds payable) as a debit. The statement of financial position reports the bonds payable at their carrying amount, which is their maturity amount less any unamortized discount. Nesca, like most companies, does not separately disclose the amount of unamortized discount (or premium) when the amount is small relative to other amounts reported on the statement of financial position.

Although Nesca received only $354,118 when it sold the bonds, it must repay $400,000 when the bonds mature. This extra cash that must be paid is an adjustment to the interest payments, ensuring that creditors earn the market rate of interest on the bonds. To compute the interest expense, the borrower apportions or amortizes the bond discount to each semi-annual interest period as an increase to the interest payment. Therefore, the amortization of bond discount is an increase in bond interest expense. Canadian publicly accountable enterprises are required to use the effective interest method to amortize bond discount or premium. An alternative method, straight-line amortization, which may be used by Canadian private enterprises, is discussed in Appendix 11C.

Reporting Interest Expense on Bonds Issued at a Discount by Using Effective Interest Amortization Under the effective interest method, interest expense for a bond is computed by multiplying the current unpaid balance (i.e., the amount that was actually borrowed) times the market rate of interest that existed on the date the bonds were sold. The periodic amortization of a bond discount or premium is then calculated as the difference between interest expense and the amount of cash paid or accrued. This process can be summarized as follows:

The **EFFECTIVE INTEREST METHOD** amortizes a bond discount or premium on the basis of the effective interest rate.

Step 1: Compute interest expense.

Unpaid balance × Effective interest rate × *n*/12
_n_ = Number of months in each interest period

Step 2: Compute amortization amount.

Amortization of bond discount = Interest expense − Interest paid (or accrued)

The first interest payment on Nesca's bonds is on June 30, 2010. Interest expense at the end of the first six months is calculated by multiplying the unpaid balance of the debt by the market rate of interest for six months ($354,118 × 12% × 6/12 = $21,247). This represents the amount of interest revenue that bondholders expected to earn on their investment during this six-month period when they decided to purchase the bonds. The amount of cash paid is calculated by multiplying the principal by the stated rate of interest for six months ($400,000 × 10% × 6/12 = $20,000). The difference between the interest expense and the cash paid (or accrued) is the amount of discount that has been amortized ($21,247 − $20,000 = $1,247).

The journal entry to record the periodic interest expense is as follows:

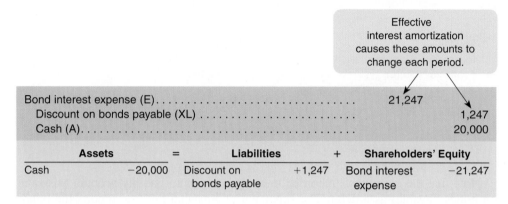

Effective interest amortization causes these amounts to change each period.

Bond interest expense (E)........................	21,247	
Discount on bonds payable (XL)		1,247
Cash (A)........................		20,000

Assets		=	Liabilities	+	Shareholders' Equity	
Cash	−20,000		Discount on bonds payable	+1,247	Bond interest expense	−21,247

Each period, the amortization of the bond discount increases the bond's carrying amount (or unpaid balance). The amortization of bond discount can be thought of as interest that was earned by the bondholders but not paid to them. During the first six months of 2010, the bondholders earned interest of $21,247 but received only $20,000 in cash. The additional $1,247 was added to the principal of the bond and will be paid when the bond matures.

Interest expense for the second half of 2010 is calculated by multiplying the unpaid balance on June 30, 2010, by the market rate of interest for six months ($355,365 × 12% × 6/12 = $21,322). The amortization of the bond discount in the second period is $1,322.

Bond interest expense (E)........................	21,322	
Discount on bonds payable (XL)		1,322
Cash (A)........................		20,000

Assets		=	Liabilities	+	Shareholders' Equity	
Cash	−20,000		Discount on bonds payable	+1,322	Bond interest expense	−21,322

Notice that interest expense for the second half of 2010 is greater than the amount for the first six months of 2010. This is logical because Nesca effectively borrowed more money during the second half of the year (i.e., the $1,247 unpaid interest). Interest expense increases each year during the life of the bond because the amortized bond discount reflects unpaid interest on an increasing amount. This process can be illustrated with the amortization schedule at the top of page 587 for the first two years and the last year of the bond's life.

Interest expense (column b) is computed by multiplying the market rate of interest by the carrying amount at the beginning of the period (column d). Amortization is computed by subtracting interest paid (column a) from interest expense (column b). The carrying amount (column d) is computed by adding amortization of bond discount (column c) to the carrying amount at the beginning of the period.

Bonds payable are reported on the statement of financial position at their carrying amount—that is, the maturity amount less any unamortized bond discount (or plus any unamortized bond premium). The carrying amount reflects the present value of remaining payments using the effective interest rate at the date of issue. It increases over time as the amortized bond discount is added to the initial bond issue price. At the maturity date of the bonds, the unamortized discount (i.e., the balance in the discount on bonds payable account) is zero. At that time, the maturity value of the bonds and the carrying amount are the same (i.e., $400,000).

Amortization Schedule: Bond Discount (effective interest)			
Date	**(a)** **Interest to Be Paid** **[$400,000 × 5%]**	**(b)** **Interest Expense** **[6% × (d) Carrying Amount,** **Beginning of Period]**	**(c)** **Amortization** **[(b) − (a)]**	**(d)** **Carrying Amount** **[Beginning** **Carrying** **Amount + (c)]**
1/1/2010				$354,118
6/30/2010	$20,000	$21,247	$1,247	355,365
12/31/2010	20,000	21,322	1,322	356,687
6/30/2011	20,000	21,401	1,401	358,088
12/31/2011	20,000	21,485	1,485	359,573
.	.	.	.	.
.	.	.	.	.
6/30/2019	20,000	23,560	3,560	396,226
12/31/2019	20,000	23,774	3,774	400,000

SELF-STUDY **QUIZ 11-3**

Assume that Nesca issued $100,000 bonds that will mature in 10 years. The bonds pay interest twice each year at an annual rate of 7 percent. They were sold when the market rate was 8 percent.

1. What amount of interest expense would be reported at the end of the first year?

2. What is the carrying amount of the bonds at the end of the first year?

After you complete your answers, go online for the solutions.

Bonds are recorded at the present value of their future cash flows using an interest rate determined by the market on the date the bonds were sold. The accounting for the bonds is not affected by subsequent changes in the market rate of interest. This interest rate is based on the terms of the debt issue and the risk characteristics of the debt.[8]

REAL WORLD EXCERPT

The Nestlé Group

ANNUAL REPORT

NOTES

1. Accounting Policies

Financial liabilities at amortized cost

Financial liabilities are initially recognized at the fair value of consideration received less directly attributable transaction costs.

Subsequent to initial measurement, financial liabilities are recognized at amortized cost unless they are part of a fair value hedge relationship (refer to fair value hedges). The difference between the initial carrying amount of the financial liabilities and their redemption value is recognized in the income statement over the contractual terms using the effective interest rate method. This category includes the following classes of financial liabilities: trade, tax and other payables; commercial paper; bonds and other financial liabilities.

Financial liabilities at amortized cost are further classified as current and non-current depending whether these will fall due within twelve months after the balance sheet date or beyond.

Source: Nestlé Group Annual Report 2009.

---

[8]While most companies issue bonds that pay interest on a semi-annual basis, certain bond issues do not pay interest on a regular basis. These bonds are often called *zero coupon bonds* because the coupon interest rate is zero. Why would an investor buy a bond that does not pay interest? Our discussion of bond discounts has probably given you a good idea of the right answer. The coupon interest rate on a bond can be virtually any amount and the price of the bond will be adjusted so that investors earn the market rate of interest. A bond with a zero coupon interest rate is a *deep discount bond* that will sell for substantially less than its maturity value.

Nestlé records all its financial liabilities as disclosed in its accounting policies and uses the effective interest method to amortize any discount or premium its bonds.

Exhibit 11.2 lists all the outstanding bonds issued by the Nestlé Group, showing the face value of each bond, its coupon or stated interest rate, the effective interest rate on the date of issuance, and the carrying value of the bond at year-end. Some of these bonds were sold at a discount while other bonds were sold at a premium.

Bonds Issued at a Premium

Bonds sell at a premium when the market rate of interest is lower than the stated interest rate. Assume that the market rate of interest was 8 percent while Nesca's bonds paid interest of 10 percent. In this case, the bonds sell at a premium. The issue price for Nesca's bonds is computed as follows:

	Present Value
a. Principal: $400,000 × 0.4564	$182,560
b. Interest: $20,000 × 13,5903	271,806
Issue (sale) price of Nesca's bonds	$454,366

When a bond is sold at a premium, the bonds payable account is credited for the par value, and the premium is recorded as a credit to premium on bonds payable, an adjunct-liability account. The issuance of Nesca's bonds at a premium is recorded as follows:

Cash (A)	454,366	
Premium on bonds payable (L)		54,366
Bonds payable (L)		400,000

Assets		=	Liabilities		+	Shareholders' Equity
Cash	+454,366		Premium on bonds payable	+54,366		
			Bonds payable	+400,000		

The carrying amount of the bond is the sum of the balances of the two accounts, premium on bonds payable and bonds payable, or $454,366.

Reporting Interest Expense on Bonds Issued at a Premium by Using Effective Interest Amortization   The effective interest method is basically the same for a discount or a premium. In either case, interest expense for a bond is computed by multiplying the carrying amount (i.e., the unpaid balance) by the market rate of interest on the date the bonds were sold. The periodic amortization of a bond premium or discount is then calculated as the difference between interest expense and the amount of cash paid or accrued.

The first interest payment on Nesca's bonds is made on June 30, 2010. The interest expense at the end of the first six months is calculated by multiplying the unpaid balance of the debt by the market rate of interest for six months ($454,366 × 8% × 6/12 = $18,175). It also represents the interest revenue that bondholders expected to earn on their investment during this six-month period when they decided to purchase the bonds. The amount of cash paid is calculated by multiplying the principal by the stated rate of interest for six months ($400,000 × 10% × 6/12 = $20,000). The difference between the interest expense and the cash paid (or accrued) is the amount of premium that has been amortized ($20,000 − $18,175 = $1,825). Thus, the amount of cash paid to bondholders includes two components: interest expense of $18,175, reflecting interest revenue to the bondholders for the first six-month period, and an amortized premium of $1,825, representing a partial payment of the premium that bondholders paid initially when they purchased the bonds.

The payment of interest on the bonds is recorded as follows:

Bond interest expense (E).............................	18,175	
Premium on bonds payable (L)	1,825	
Cash (A).....................................		20,000

Assets		=	Liabilities		+	Shareholders' Equity	
Cash	−20,000		Premium on bonds payable	−1,825		Bond interest expense	−18,175

The basic difference between effective interest amortization of a bond discount and a bond premium is that the amortization of a discount *increases* the carrying amount of the liability and the amortization of a premium *reduces* it. The following schedule illustrates amortization of the bond premium for the first two years and the last year of the bond's life.

Amortization Schedule: Bond Premium (effective interest)			
Date	(a) Interest to Be Paid [$400,000 × 5%]	(b) Interest Expense [4% × (d) Carrying Amount, Beginning of Period]	(c) Amortization [(a) − (b)]	(d) Carrying Amount [Beginning Carrying Amount − (c)]
---	---	---	---	---
1/1/2010				$454,366
6/30/2010	$20,000	$18,175	$1,825	452,541
12/31/2010	20,000	18,102	1,898	450,643
6/30/2011	20,000	18,026	1,974	448,669
12/31/2011	20,000	17,947	2,053	446,616
.	.	.	.	.
.	.	.	.	.
6/30/2019	20,000	16,444	3,556	403,846
12/31/2019	20,000	16,154	3,846	400,000

Interest expense (column b) is computed by multiplying the market rate of interest by the carrying amount at the beginning of the period (column d). Amortization is computed by subtracting interest expense (column b) from interest paid (column a). The carrying amount (column d) is computed by subtracting amortization of bond premium (column c) from the carrying amount at the beginning of the period.

In summary, interest expense changes each accounting period as the effective amount of the liability changes. As in the case of a bond discount, the carrying amount of the bonds reflects the present value of remaining payments using the effective interest rate at the date of issue.

SELF-STUDY **QUIZ 11-4**

Refer to the amortization schedule above and answer the following requirements:

1. Complete the schedule for three additional semi-annual payments of interest until June 30, 2013.

2. Compute the unpaid balance of the bonds at June 30, 2013. Can you think of another way of computing this balance? If so, show your computations.

After you complete your answers, go online for the solutions.

■ connect

Interest expense is reported on the income statement. Because interest is related to financing activities rather than operating activities, it is normally not included in operating expenses on the income statement. Instead, interest expense is reported as a

Exhibit **11.3**

Consolidated Income Statement

REAL WORLD EXCERPT

The Nestlé Group

ANNUAL REPORT

Consolidated Income Statement
For the Year Ended 31 December 2009

In millions of CHF	Notes	Continuing operations	Discontinued operations	Total
				2009
Profit before interest and taxes		**12,492**	**2,478**	**14,970**
Financial income	5	123	56	179
Financial expense	5	(777)	(17)	(794)
Profit before taxes and associates		**11,838**	**2,517**	**14,355**
Taxes	7	(3,087)	(275)	(3,362)
Share of results of associates	8	800	—	800
Profit for the year		**9,551**	**2,242**	**11,793**

Source: Nestlé Group Annual Report 2009.

deduction from "profit from operations." Nestlé reports a financial expense of CHF 794 million on its income statement as the last item among its expenses before tax, as shown in Exhibit 11.3. This amount includes interest expense of CHF 745 million as disclosed in Note 5 to the financial statements.

Interest payments are legal obligations for the borrower and, therefore, financial analysts, investors, and creditors want to be certain that a business is generating sufficient resources to meet its obligations. The times interest earned ratio is useful when making this assessment.

KEY RATIO
ANALYSIS

TIMES INTEREST EARNED RATIO

LO³

Compute and interpret the times interest earned ratio.

ANALYTICAL QUESTION → Is the company generating sufficient resources (added value) from its profit-making activities to meet its current obligations associated with debt?

RATIO AND COMPARISONS → The times interest earned ratio is helpful in answering this question. It is computed as follows:

$$\text{Times Interest Earned Ratio} = \frac{\text{Profit before Interest and Taxes}}{\text{Interest Expense}}$$

The 2009 ratio for the Nestlé Group (in millions of CHF) is

14,970 ÷ 745 = 20.1[9]

Comparisons over Time			Comparisons with Competitors	
Nestlé			ConAgra Foods	Kraft Foods
2007	2008	2009	2009	2009
9.7	20.9	20.1	4.58	4.38

INTERPRETATIONS

In General → A high ratio is viewed more favourably than a low ratio. Basically, the ratio shows the amount of profit before interest and income tax that is generated relative to interest

---

[9]The Nestlé Group reported financial income of CHF 179. This amount is also available to cover interest expense. If it is added to the profit before interest and taxes, the ratio would increase to 20.3, which is not significantly different from 20.1.

expense. A high ratio shows an extra margin of protection in case profitability deteriorates. Analysts are particularly interested in a company's ability to meet its required interest payments because failure to do so could result in bankruptcy.

Focus Company Analysis → In 2009, Nestlé's profit-making activities generated in 2009 20.1 Swiss francs for each Swiss franc of interest expense. Nestlé's profit could fall substantially before the company would appear to have trouble meeting its interest obligations with resources generated by normal operations. Nestlé's ability to repay its creditors has strengthened since 2007, and is much better than that of its competitors.

A Few Cautions → The times interest earned ratio is often misleading for new or rapidly growing companies that tend to invest considerable resources to build capacity for future operations. In such cases, the times interest earned ratio will reflect significant amounts of interest expense associated with the new capacity but not the profit that will be earned with the new capacity. Analysts should consider the company's long-term strategy when using this ratio. While this ratio is widely used, some analysts prefer to compare interest expense to the amount of cash that a company can generate, because creditors cannot be paid with "profit" that is generated. The cash coverage ratio addresses this concern and is discussed in Chapter 13.

Early Retirement of Debt

Bonds are normally issued for long periods, such as 20 or 30 years. As mentioned earlier, bondholders who need cash prior to the maturity date can simply sell the bonds to another investor. This transaction does not affect the books of the company that issued the bonds.

As mentioned earlier, each bond issue has characteristics specified in the bond indenture. The issuing company often adds special characteristics to a bond to make it more attractive to investors, who normally have a large number of investment alternatives from which to select.

Bonds sometimes offer different features with respect to early retirement. Callable (redeemable) bonds may be called for early retirement at the option of the issuer. Retractable bonds may be turned in for early retirement at the option of the bondholder. Convertible bonds may be converted to other securities of the issuer (usually common shares) at the option of the bondholder. These features are normally present for debt issues that are marketable.

Assume that Nesca's bonds are redeemable. Typically, the bond indenture would include a call premium for redeemable bonds.

Assume that the $400,000 face-value bonds that were issued by Nesca on January 1, 2010, were sold for $354,118 as shown on page 584, and that the company called the bonds on December 31, 2015, at 102 percent of par, four years before their maturity. The company's decision to call these bonds is typically made when the market rate of interest decreases to the point where the market value of the bonds exceeds the call price. Nesca would issue new bonds that pay a lower interest rate than the outstanding bonds, thus saving on interest payments.

If the market rate of interest drops to 8 percent, then Nesca can issue new bonds that pay interest of 8 percent instead of 10 percent. Semi-annual interest payments would then be reduced from $20,000 to $16,000 ($400,000 × 0.04). The cash savings of $4,000 every six months are equivalent to $26,930.80 ($4,000 × 6.7327) at December 31, 2015. Redemption of the bonds requires Nesca to pay a premium of $8,000 ($400,000 × 0.02), but it saves the company $26,930.80. It is therefore a sound economic decision.

However, the early retirement of these bonds would result in an accounting loss that equals the difference between the redemption amount and the carrying amount of the bonds. At December 31, 2015, the carrying amount of the bond is $375,156, representing the present value of the remaining future principal and interest payments.[10]

LO4

Report the early retirement of bonds.

RETRACTABLE BONDS may be turned in for early retirement at the option of the bondholder.

---

[10]The carrying amount is the present value of the remaining cash payments (eight interest payments and the principal amount), which equals $400,000 × 6.2098 + $20,000 × 0.2674 or $375,156.

This amount is then compared to the redemption amount of $408,000 ($400,000 × 1.02), resulting in a loss of $32,844. The company's accountants would make the following journal entry to record the bond redemption:

Bonds payable (L)	400,000	
Loss on redemption of bonds (SE)	32,844	
Discount on bonds payable (XL)		24,844
Cash (A).		408,000

Assets		=	Liabilities		+	Shareholders' Equity	
Cash	−408.000		Bonds payable	−400,000		Loss on redemption of bonds	−32,844
			Discount on bonds payable	+24,844			

The bond redemption results in an economic gain but also in an accounting loss, because the carrying amount of the bonds is not adjusted over time to reflect changes in the market value of these bonds.

In some cases, a company may elect to retire debt early by purchasing it on the open market, just as an investor would. This approach is necessary when the bonds do not have a call feature. It might also be an attractive approach if the price of the bonds fell after the date of issue. What could cause the price of a bond to fall? The most common cause is a rise in interest rates. As you may have noticed during our discussion of present value concepts, bond prices move in the opposite direction of interest rates. If interest rates go up, bond prices fall, and vice versa. When interest rates go up, a company wanting to retire a bond before maturity may find that buying the bond on the open market is less expensive than paying a call premium.

When interest rates increase, the market value of the bonds decrease, and the redemption or repurchase of the bonds in the open market results in a gain. The gain increases the company's profit, which reflects positively on the performance of management. However, if the company needs to reissue bonds at a higher interest rate, then the gain on redemption or repurchase of the bonds is misleading, because the company will need to make higher interest payments on the refinanced debt. In contrast, when interest rates decrease, the refinancing of long-term debt by retiring old debt and issuing new debt will result in a loss on debt retirement, but it will reduce the amount of periodic interest payments. Hence, management may be inclined to retire debt prematurely in order to show improved financial performance, but this decision may affect cash flows negatively in the future.

INTERNATIONAL PERSPECTIVE
BORROWING IN FOREIGN CURRENCIES

Many corporations with foreign operations elect to finance those operations with foreign debt to lessen the exchange rate risk. This type of risk exists because the relative value of each nation's currency varies virtually on a daily basis due to various economic factors. As this book is being written, the euro is worth approximately $1.40. A year earlier, it was worth $1.70. A Canadian company that owed debt denominated in euro would experience a gain from this decrease in the value of the euro relative to the value of the Canadian dollar.

A Canadian corporation that conducts business operations in Europe might decide to borrow money in euro to finance its operations. The cash flows from the business will be in euro, which can be used to pay off the debt, which is in euro. If the business generated cash flows in euro but paid off debt in Canadian dollars, it would be exposed to exchange rate risk because the value of the Canadian dollar fluctuates relative to the euro.

As indicated in Exhibit 11.2, the Nestlé Group issued bonds denominated in different currencies as follows:

American Dollar	USD	2,193 million
Australian Dollar	AUD	1,550 million
Euro	EUR	350 million
Hungary Forint	HUF	35,000 million
New Zealand Dollar	NZD	100 million
Norway Kroner	NOK	2,500 million
Switzerland Francs	CHF	5,625 million

The bonds denominated in the various currencies had to be translated to Swiss francs at exchange rates in effect on December 31, 2009, before the amounts could be added together and reported on the statement of financial position at that date.

For reporting purposes, accountants must convert, or translate, foreign debt into a single currency. Conversion rates for all major currencies are published in most newspapers and on the Internet. To illustrate foreign currency translation, assume that Nestlé borrowed USD 1 million. For reporting purposes, the accountant must use the conversion rate at December 31, 2009, which was USD 1 = CHF 1.031. The equivalent of the USD 1,000,000 debt is CHF 1,031,000 (USD1,000,000 × 1.031). As you can see, the CHF equivalent of foreign debt may change if the conversion rate changes, even when no additional borrowings or repayments occur. Changes in conversion rates result in foreign exchange gains or losses that are covered in advanced accounting courses.

Borrowing in foreign currencies gives rise to foreign exchange risk whereby a decrease in the value of domestic currency relative to foreign currency would require a larger amount of the domestic currency to settle the foreign debt. The reverse is true if the domestic currency appreciates relative to foreign currency. A variety of risk reduction techniques can be undertaken by Nestlé to limit the potential increase in Swiss francs it may have to pay. These include currency forwards, futures, swaps and options, which are different types of financial instruments. Accounting for financial instruments is taught in advanced accounting courses.

OTHER NON-CURRENT LIABILITIES

In addition to long-term debt, companies report a number of other non-current liabilities that result from their operating, investing, and financing activities. Typical non-current liabilities include lease obligations, asset retirement obligations, accrued retirement benefits liability, and deferred income taxes (covered in Appendix 10A).

LO5

Describe other non-current liabilities.

Lease Liabilities

Companies often lease rather than purchase assets. For example, renting extra delivery trucks during a busy period is more economical than owning them if they are not needed during the rest of the year. When a company leases an asset on a short-term basis, the agreement is called an *operating lease*. No liability is recorded when an operating lease is created. Instead, a company records rent expense as it uses the asset. Assume that on December 15, 2011, Nestlé signed an operating lease contract to rent five large trucks during January 2012. No liability is recorded in 2011. Rent expense is recorded during January 2012 as the trucks are actually used.

For a number of reasons, a company may prefer to lease an asset on a long-term basis rather than purchase it. If control of the leased asset has been transferred to

An **OPERATING LEASE** does not transfer substantially all the risks and rewards of ownership from the lessor to the lessee.

A **FINANCE LEASE** transfers substantially all the risks and rewards of ownership from the lessor to the lessee.

the lessee along with the risks and rewards of ownership, then the lease is called a *finance lease*, irrespective of the contractual form of the obligation the two parties signed. In essence, a finance lease contract represents the purchase and financing of an asset even though it is legally a lease agreement. Unlike an operating lease, finance leases are accounted for as if an asset has been purchased, by recording an asset and a liability.

Because of the significant differences in accounting for operating and finance leases, guidelines have been established to distinguish between both types of leases. A finance lease would normally satisfy one or more of the following situations:[11]

- Ownership of the asset is transferred to the lessee at the end of the lease term.
- The lease contract permits the lessee to purchase the asset at a price that is expected to be sufficiently lower than its fair market value.
- The lease term is for the major part of the asset's economic life.
- The present value of the minimum lease payments is substantially all of the fair value of the leased asset when the lease is signed.
- The leased assets are of such a specialized nature that only the lessee can use them without major modifications.

The accounting for leases as finance leases reflects the economic substance of the transaction, which is in essence a purchase of an asset with long-term financing, rather than the legal form of the commitment to make specific payments in the future. If managers have a choice of recording a lease as either operating or finance, most would prefer to record it as an operating lease. By doing so, the company is able to report less debt on its statement of financial position.

In contrast, the accounting for finance leases requires reporting a non-current liability, thereby increasing the debt-to-equity ratio. Furthermore, the current portion of the lease liability increases current liabilities, reduces working capital, and lowers the current ratio. Companies would avoid these undesirable consequences if finance leases are accounted for as operating leases. It is important to note, however, that the cash outflows would not be affected by the classification of leases. Many financial analysts are concerned that companies can avoid reporting debt associated with finance leases by structuring the lease agreement in a manner that meets the requirements for recording it as an operating lease.

To record a finance lease, it is necessary to determine the current cash equivalent of the required lease payments. Assume that Nestlé signs a lease for new delivery trucks. The accountant has determined that the lease is a finance lease with a current cash equivalent of CHF 250,000. Once the lease is signed, the transaction would be recorded in a manner similar to the actual purchase of delivery trucks:

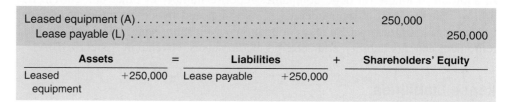

| Leased equipment (A) | 250,000 | |
| Lease payable (L) | | 250,000 |

Assets	=	Liabilities	+	Shareholders' Equity
Leased equipment +250,000		Lease payable +250,000		

The Nestlé Group leases assets for use in its operations. Some of the lease contracts qualify as finance leases, but most are accounted for as operating leases, as disclosed in the following excerpts from the notes to the financial statements.

[11]International Accounting Standards Board. International Accounting Standard 17, *Leases,* para. 10 (IASB, 2009).

NOTES

1. Accounting Policies

Leased assets

Assets acquired under finance leases are capitalized and depreciated in accordance with the Group's policy on property, plant, and equipment unless the lease term is shorter. Land and building leases are recognized separately, provided an allocation of the lease payments between these categories is reliable. The associated obligations are included under financial liabilities.

Rentals payable under operating leases are expensed.

The costs of the agreements that do not take the legal form of a lease but convey the right to use an asset are separated into lease payments and other payments if the entity has the control of the use or of the access to the asset or takes essentially all the output of the asset. Then the entity determines whether the lease component of the agreement is a finance or an operating lease.

Source: Nestlé Group Annual Report 2009.

NOTES

26. Lease commitments

26.1 Operating leases

Lease commitments refer mainly to buildings, industrial equipment, vehicles and IT equipment.

In millions of CHF	2009	2008
	Minimum lease payments	
	Future value	
Within one year	583	609
In the second year	460	487
In the third to the fifth year inclusive	834	918
After the fifth year	575	524
	2,452	2,538

26.2 Finance leases

In millions of CHF	2009		2008	
	Minimum lease payments			
	Present value	Future value	Present value	Future value
Within one year	71	75	65	67
In the second year	58	68	54	64
In the third to the fifth year inclusive	120	169	101	139
After the fifth year	80	182	74	181
	329	494	294	451

The difference between the future value of the minimum lease payments and their present value represents the discount on the lease obligations.

Source: Nestlé Group Annual Report 2009.

Provisions

In Chapter 10, we indicated that companies establish provisions when either the amount or the timing of the liability is uncertain. In many cases, companies make investing or operating decisions resulting in future obligations that may not be determinable with accuracy, particularly if the amount of the obligation is dependent on the timing of future events. Examples include restructuring of the company's operations; legal disputes; and the dismantlement, removal, and restoration of property, plant, and equipment. In the next section, we focus on obligations that result from the impact of companies' operations on the environment.

Asset Retirement Obligations In recent years, concern about the adverse impact of business activities on the environment and the effects of environmental obligations on companies' financial positions and profitability led to new accounting standards that require the reporting of such obligations. These reporting requirements are particularly important for companies operating in industries that result in environmental pollution, such as the chemical and petrochemical industries. Companies in these industry sectors incur significant obligations associated with the environmental impact of their operations.

For example, if Suncor Energy Inc., which explores for and develops oil and gas products, completes construction of and places into service an offshore oil platform in June 2011, it would be legally required to dismantle and remove the platform at the end of its useful life. Suncor should then recognize a liability for an asset retirement obligation, and capitalize an amount for an asset retirement cost. The fair value of the asset retirement obligation is determined by using the present value concept. In this regard, Suncor's liabilities include an asset retirement obligation of $3,200 million as at December 31, 2009, representing 9 percent of its long-term liabilities. This liability reflects legal obligations to retire long-lived assets and restore sites, such as producing well sites, offshore production platforms, and natural gas–processing plants and marketing sites.

Liabilities associated with future service obligations are often based on estimates that are very difficult to develop accurately. For example, the future cost of cleaning up pollution depends on a number of factors, including changing technology and legal standards. Many companies have faced bankruptcy because they underestimated the cost of environmental regulations. Managers and analysts must be very cautious in evaluating potential costs associated with activities that impact the environment.

Employee Retirement Benefits

Most employers provide retirement programs for their employees. In a ***defined contribution*** program, the employer makes cash payments to an investment fund. When employees retire, they are entitled to a portion of the fund. If the investment strategy of the fund is successful, the retirement income for the employees will be larger. If the strategy is not successful, it will be lower. In other words, the employees bear the risk associated with the investments in the plan. The employer's only obligation is to make the required annual payments to the fund, which are recorded as pension expense.

Other employers offer ***defined benefit*** programs. Under these programs, an employee's retirement benefits are based on a percentage of his or her pay at retirement or a certain amount of money for each year of employment. In these cases, the amount of pension expense that must be accrued each year is the change in the current cash value of the employee's retirement package. The current cash value changes each year for a variety of reasons. For example, it changes (1) as employees get closer to receiving benefits, (2) as employees' retirement benefits increase because of higher pay or longer service,

REAL WORLD EXCERPT

Suncor Enegry Inc.

ANNUAL REPORT

Notes to Consolidated Financial Statements

(a) Asset Retirement obligations (ARO)

The following table presents the reconciliation of the beginning and ending aggregate carrying amount of the total obligations associated with the retirement of property, plant and equipment.

($ millions)	2009	2008
Asset retirement obligations, beginning of year	1,600	1,072
Liabilities incurred	253	38
Petro-Canada liabilities acquired during the year (note 2)[1]	1,605	—
Changes in estimates	(145)	560
Liabilities settled	(248)	(134)
Accretion of asset retirement obligations	155	64
Foreign exchange	(20)	—
Asset retirement obligations, end of year	3,200	1,600
Less: Current portion	(312)	(156)
	2,888	1,444

[1] The majority of the asset retirement obligation liability acquired as a result of the merger with Petro-Canada was discounted at August 1, 2009 using the company's long-term credit-adjusted risk-free rate at that time of 6.5%.

The total undiscounted amount of estimated future cash flows required to settle the obligations at December 31, 2009, was approximately $8.3 billion (2008–$3.5 billion). Substantially all of the liability recognized in 2009 was discounted using the company's long-term credit-adjusted risk-free rate at 6.2% (2008–9.0%). The credit-adjusted risk-free rate used reflects the expected timeframe of the related liability. Payments to settle the ARO occur on an ongoing basis and will continue over the lives of the operating assets, which can exceed fifty years. The current portion of asset retirement obligations is included in accounts payable and accrued liabilities.

A significant portion of the company's assets, including the upgrading facilities at the oil sands operation and the downstream refineries, have retirement obligations for which the fair value cannot be reasonably determined because the assets currently have an indeterminate life. The asset retirement obligation for these assets will be recorded in the first period in which the lives of the assets are determinable.

Source: Suncor Annual Report 2009.

or (3) if the employees' life expectancies change. The company must report a pension liability based on any portion of the current cash value of the retirement program that has not actually been funded. For example, if the company transferred $8 million to the pension fund manager but the current cash value of the pension program was $10 million, the company would report a $2-million pension liability on its statement of financial position.

For many corporations, especially those with unionized workforces, the financial obligation associated with defined benefit retirement programs can be very large because the risk associated with investments in the pension plan is borne by the employer, which must cover any shortfall between the investment earnings and the payments to retirees. For this reason, companies are moving away from defined benefit pension plans in favour of defined contribution pension plans.

Nestlé has set up both defined benefit pension plans and defined contribution pension plans for its eligible employees. In addition, Nestlé provides post-retirement benefits, including certain health and life insurance benefits for its retired employees and eligible surviving dependants.

NOTES

16. Employee benefits

Pensions and retirement benefits
The majority of Group employees are eligible for retirement benefits under defined benefit schemes based on pensionable remuneration and length of service.

Post-employment medical benefits and other employee benefits
Group companies, principally in the Americas, maintain medical benefits plans, which cover eligible retired employees. The obligations for other employee benefits consist mainly of end of service indemnities, which do not have the character of pensions.

Source: Nestlé Group Annual Report 2009.

Nestlé's obligations under these various plans totalled CHF 25,610 million as at December 31, 2009. The company has set aside funds that had a fair value of CHF 19,545 million at that date. The shortfall of CHF 6,065 million is important to analysts who forecast Nestlé's future cash flows and to employees who may be concerned about the availability of money in the pension fund to pay them cash during their retirement. However, Nestlé reported an amount of CHF 6,249 million in employee benefit liabilities on its statement of financial position at December 31, 2009. The difference of CHF 184 million reflects additional adjustments that resulted from complying with the applicable accounting standards. The computation of employee benefit liabilities is complex and covered in advanced accounting courses.

In recent years, employer-provided healthcare benefits have been the subject of much discussion. These have often been referred to in the financial press as legacy costs. As more people retire and live longer, these legacy costs will increase. Moreover, large companies pay for a portion of their employees' post-retirement health insurance costs. The issue arises because these potential future payments are recorded as an expense in the current accounting period. These potential future costs have come sharply into focus during the recent deep economic recession when, worldwide, companies suffered from sharply reduced revenue. Bankrupt companies cannot pay these future obligations to either those already retired or those who would have been contractually entitled to them.

The cost of these future benefits must be estimated and recorded as an expense in the periods when the employees perform services. The recording of future healthcare costs for retired employees is an excellent example of the use of estimates in accounting. Imagine the difficulty of estimating future healthcare costs when you do not know how long employees will live, how healthy they will be during their lives, and how much doctors and hospitals will charge for their services in the future.

Accounting for retirement benefits is a complex topic that is discussed in detail in subsequent accounting courses. We introduce the topic at this point as another example of the application of the matching process, which requires that expenses be recorded in the year in which the benefit is received. The benefit in this case is the work performed by the employees, and all costs incurred to compensate employees for their work must be recorded regardless of the timing of pension payments. This accounting procedure also avoids creating improper incentives for managers. If the future cost of retirement benefits was not included in the period in which work was performed, managers might have the incentive to offer employees increases in their retirement benefits instead of increases in their salaries. In this manner, managers could understate the true cost of employee services and make their companies appear more profitable.

FINANCIAL LEVERAGE RATIO

ANALYTICAL QUESTION → How is management using debt to increase the amount of assets the company employs to earn profit for shareholders?

RATIO AND COMPARISONS → The financial leverage ratio is useful in addressing this issue. It is computed as follows:

$$\text{Financial Leverage Ratio} = \frac{\text{Average Total Assets}}{\text{Average Shareholders' Equity}}$$

The 2009 ratio for Nestlé Group (in CHF) is

$$\frac{(110{,}916 + 106{,}215)/2}{(53{,}631 + 54{,}916)/2} = 2.00$$

Comparisons over Time		
Nestlé		
2007	2008	2009
2.02	2.02	2.00

Comparisons with Competitors	
ConAgra Foods	Kraft Foods
2009	2009
2.46	2.69

INTERPRETATIONS

In General → The financial leverage ratio measures the relationship between total assets and shareholders' equity that finances the assets. As noted, companies finance their assets with shareholders' equity and debt. The higher the proportion of assets financed by debt, the higher the financial leverage ratio. Conversely, the higher the proportion of assets financed with shareholders' equity, the lower the ratio. Increasing debt (and the leverage ratio) increases the amount of assets the company employs to earn profit for shareholders, which increases the chances of earning higher profit. However, it also increases *risk*. Debt financing is riskier than financing with shareholders' equity because the interest payments on debt must be made every period (they are legal obligations), whereas dividends on shares can be postponed. An increasing ratio over time signals more reliance on debt financing and more risk.

Creditors and security analysts use this ratio to assess a company's risk level, while managers use the ratio in deciding whether to expand by adding debt. As long as the interest on borrowing is less than the additional profit generated, utilizing debt will enhance shareholders' profit.

Focus Company Analysis → Nestlé's financial leverage was relatively stable during the three-year period 2007–2009. For every CHF 1.00 of equity, the company had CHF 1.00 of debt during 2009. The company's financial leverage for 2009 is lower than those of its competitors. This suggests that Nestlé is following a slightly more prudent financing strategy than are other companies in the same industry. Nestlé's use of debt has been beneficial to its shareholders as the company's return on equity for both 2008 and 2009 exceeded 17 percent.

A Few Cautions → A financial leverage ratio near 1:1 indicates a company that is choosing not to utilize debt to expand. This suggests the company has lower risk but is not enhancing the return to shareholders. When comparing competitors, the ratio may be influenced by differences in business strategies, such as whether the company rents or buys facilities.

SELECTED FOCUS COMPANY LEVERAGE RATIOS	
WestJet	2.74
Nokia	2.41
Benetton	2.03

FINANCING ACTIVITIES ON THE STATEMENT OF CASH FLOWS

BONDS PAYABLE

The financing activities section of the statement of cash flows reports both cash inflows and outflows that relate to how cash was obtained from owners and creditors to finance the enterprise and its operations, and repaid to them. The issuance of long-term debt is reported as a

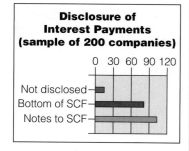

Disclosure of Interest Payments (sample of 200 companies)

cash inflow from financing activities. The repayment of principal is reported as an outflow from financing activities. Many students are surprised to learn that the payment of interest may *not* be reported in the financing activities section of the statement of cash flows. As noted in Chapter 5, interest paid may be classified as an operating cash flow because interest expense is directly related to the determination of profit or loss and is therefore reported in the cash flows from operating activities section of the statement.

EFFECT ON STATEMENT OF CASH FLOWS

In General → As we saw in Chapter 10, transactions involving short-term creditors (e.g., trade payables) affect working capital and are, therefore, reported in the operating activities section of the statement of cash flows. Cash received from long-term creditors is reported as an inflow from financing activities. Cash payments made to long-term creditors are reported as outflows from financing activities. Examples are shown in the following table:

	Effect on Cash Flows
Financing activities	
Issuance of bonds	+
Debt retirement	−
Repayment of bond principal upon maturity	−

> **SELECTED FOCUS COMPANY COMPARISONS: CASH FLOWS FROM FINANCING ACTIVITIES (IN MILLIONS OF DOLLARS)**
>
> | | |
> |---|---|
> | WestJet | 34.6 |
> | Gildan | −47.7 |
> | BCE | −4,044 |

Focus Company Analysis → A segment of Nestlé's statements of cash flows for the years 2008 and 2009 follows.

In 2009, the company raised a substantial amount of long-term debt (CHF 3,957 million) to finance its operating and investing activities. It also reduced its long-term debt by CHF 1,744 million. Repayments of long-term debt are made when the debt matures or when a company decides to redeem the outstanding debt prematurely in order to take advantage of lower interest rates. In addition, cash transactions related to non-current financial liabilities resulted in a net inflow of CHF 119 million.

Analysts are particularly interested in the financing activities section of the statement of cash flows because it provides important insights about the future capital structure for the company. Rapidly growing companies typically report significant amounts of funds in this section of the statement.

REAL WORLD EXCERPT

The Nestlé Group

ANNUAL REPORT

Consolidated cash flow statement for the year ended 31 December 2009		
In millions of CHF	**2009**	**2008**
Financing activities		
Dividend paid to shareholders of the parent	(5,047)	(4,573)
Purchase of treasury shares	(7,013)	(8,696)
Sale of treasury shares and options exercised	292	639
Cash flows with non-controlling interests	(720)	(367)
Bonds issued	3,957	2,803
Bonds repaid	(1,744)	(2,244)
Inflows from other non-current financial liabilities	294	374
Outflows from other non-current financial liabilities	(175)	(168)
Inflows/(outflows) from current financial liabilities	(446)	(6,100)
Inflows/(outflows) from short-term investments	(1,759)	1,448
Cash flow from financing activities	(12,361)	(16,884)

Source: Nestlé Group Annual Report 2009.

ACCOUNTING STANDARDS
FOR PRIVATE ENTERPRISES

The accounting standards for private enterprises differ from IFRS in reporting specific types of non-current liabilities.

- As noted in the chapter, Canadian publicly accountable enterprises are required to use the effective interest method to amortize bond discount or premium. Canadian private enterprises, however, may use the simpler straight-line method of amortization, particularly as the two methods do not usually produce significant differences in the carrying amounts of long-term debt.

- The Canadian accounting standard for leases provides quantitative guidelines for the classification of leases into either finance or operating leases. In contrast, IFRS provides more room for professional judgment in classifying leases.

- The Canadian accounting standard for reporting asset retirement obligations is not as onerous as the international accounting standard that Canadian publicly accountable enterprises must comply with. Again, the primary consideration in simplifying the reporting requirements for Canadian private enterprises is the cost of measuring these obligations compared with the benefits that users of financial statements may derive from such measures.

- The accounting and reporting standards for pension and other post-retirement benefits also differ between publicly accountable enterprises and private enterprises. Details of the differences in reporting requirements are covered in advanced accounting courses.

DEMONSTRATION **CASE**

To raise funds to build a new plant, Reed Company management issued bonds. The bond indenture specified the following:

> Par value of the bonds ($1,000 bonds): $600,000.
> Date of issue: February 1, 2011; due in 10 years on January 31, 2021.
> Stated interest rate: 10.5 percent per annum, payable semi-annually on July 31 and January 31.

The market interest rate was 10 percent when the bonds were sold on February 1, 2011. The fiscal year for Reed Company ends on December 31.

Required:

1. How much cash did Reed Company receive from the sale of the bonds on February 1, 2011? Show your computations.
2. Prepare the journal entry on February 1, 2011, to record the sale and issuance of the bonds payable.
3. Prepare the journal entry for the payment of interest and amortization of the premium for the first interest payment on July 31, 2011. The company uses the effective interest method.
4. Prepare the adjusting entry required on December 31, 2011, the end of the fiscal year.
5. Prepare the journal entry to record the second interest payment and the amortization of the premium on January 31, 2012.
6. Show how bond interest expense and bonds payable are reported on the financial statements at December 31, 2011.

We highly recommend that you attempt to answer the requirements on your own before consulting the following suggested solution.

SUGGESTED **SOLUTION**

1. The sale price of the bonds is the present value of future payments:

Principal: $600,000 × 0.3769 (Table A.2, *n* = 20, *i* = 5) = $226,140
Interest: ($600,000 × 10.5% × ½) × 12.4622 (Table A.1, *n* = 20, *i* = 5) =   392,560
                                                                        $618,700

2. February 1, 2011 (issuance date):

Cash (A)	618,700	
Premium on bonds payable (L)		18,700
Bonds payable (L)		600,000
To record sale of bonds payable.		

3. July 31, 2011 (first interest payment date):

Bond interest expense (E) ($618,700 x 5%)	30,935	
Premium on bonds payable (L)	565	
Cash (A) ($600,000 × 5.25%)		31,500
To record payment of semi-annual interest.		

4. December 31, 2011 (end of the accounting period):

Bond interest expense (E) [($618,700 − $565) × 10% × 5/12]	25,756	
Premium on bonds payable (L)	494	
Bond interest payable (L) ($600,000 × 10.5% × 5/12)		26,250
Adjusting entry for five months' interest accrued plus amortization of the premium, August 1 to December 31, 2011.		

5. January 31, 2012 (second interest date):

Bond interest payable (L).....................................	26,250	
Bond interest expense (E) [($618,700 − $565) × 5%] − $25,756	5,151	
Premium on bonds payable (L)	99	
Cash (A)		31,500
To record payment of semi-annual interest.		

6. Interest expense reported on the 2011 income statement should be for 11 months, February 1 through December 31. Interest expense, per these entries, is $30,935 + $25,756 = $56,691.

> **Income Statement for 2011:**
>
> | | |
> |---|---:|
> | Interest expense | $ 56,691 |
>
> **Statement of Financial Position, December 31, 2011:**
> Non-current liabilities:
>
> | | |
> |---|---:|
> | Bonds payable, 10% (due January 31, 2021) | 600,000 |
> | Add unamortized premium* | 17,681 |
> | | $617,681 |
>
> *$18,740 − ($565 + $494) = $17,681.

Appendix 11A

Present Value Concepts

PRESENT VALUE is the current cash equivalent of an amount to be received in the future; a future amount discounted for compound interest.

The concept of present value (PV) is based on the time value of money. It provides a foundation for measuring and reporting long-term notes and bonds. Quite simply, money received today is worth more than money to be received one year from today (or at any other future date) because it can be used to earn interest. If you invest $1,000 today at 10 percent, you will have $1,100 in one year. In contrast, if you receive $1,000 one year from today, you will lose the opportunity to earn the $100 interest revenue. The difference between the $1,000 and the $1,100 is interest that can be earned during the year.

In one of your mathematics courses, you have probably already solved some problems involving the time value of money. In the typical problem, you were told a certain dollar amount had been deposited in a savings account earning a specific rate of interest. You were asked to determine the dollar amount that would be in the savings account after a certain number of years. In this appendix, we will show you how to solve problems that are the opposite of the ones you have worked with. In present value problems, you are told a dollar amount to be received in the future (such as the balance of a savings account after five years) and asked to determine the present value of the amount (the amount that must be deposited in the savings account today).

The value of money changes over time because money can earn interest. With a present value problem, you know the dollar amount of a cash flow that will occur in the future and need to determine its value now. The opposite situation occurs when you know the dollar amount of a cash flow that occurs today and need to determine its value at some point in the future. These problems are called *future value* problems. The following illustrates the basic difference between present value and future value problems:

> **FUTURE VALUE** is the sum to which an amount will increase as a result of compound interest.

	Now	Future
Present value	?	$1,000
Future value	$1,000	?

Present and future value problems may involve two types of cash flow: a single payment or an annuity (a series of cash payments).[12] Thus, four different situations are related to the time value of money:

1. Present value of a single payment
2. Future value of a single payment
3. Present value of an annuity
4. Future value of an annuity

Present value problems involving single amounts and annuities are discussed below. Future value problems are covered in an online appendix to this chapter.

PRESENT VALUE OF A SINGLE AMOUNT

The present value of a single amount is the amount of cash you are willing to accept today in lieu of a cash receipt at some date in the future. You might be offered the opportunity to invest in a debt instrument paying you $10,000 in 10 years. Before you decided whether to invest, you would want to determine the present value of the instrument. Graphically, the present value of $1 due at the end of the third period with an interest rate of 10 percent can be represented as follows:

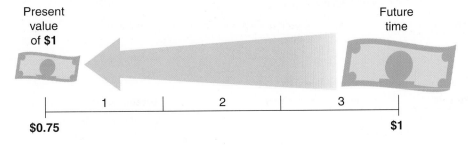

Present value of $1 ... Future time

| 1 | 2 | 3 |

$0.75 ... $1

---

[12]Present value and future value problems involve cash flows. The basic concepts are the same for cash inflows (receipts) and cash outflows (payments). No fundamental differences exist between present value and future value calculations for cash payments versus cash receipts.

To compute the present value of an amount to be received in the future, we subtract interest that is earned over time from the amount to be received in the future. For example, if you place $100 in a savings account that earns 5 percent, you will have $105 at the end of a year. In a present value problem, you are told that you have $105 at the end of the year and must compute the amount to be deposited at the beginning of the year. To solve this type of problem, you must discount the amount to be received in the future at interest rate i for n periods. The formula to compute the present value of a single amount is

$$\text{Present Value} = \frac{1}{(1+i)^n} \times \text{Amount}$$

The formula is not difficult to use, but most analysts use calculators, Excel, or present value tables for computations. We will illustrate how to use present value tables. Assume that today is January 1, 2011, and you have the opportunity to receive $1,000 cash on December 31, 2013. At an interest rate of 10 percent per year, how much is the $1,000 payment worth to you on January 1, 2011? You could discount the amount year by year,[13] but it is easier to use Table A.1 in Appendix 11B, "Present Value of $1." For $i = 10\%$, $n = 3$, we find that the present value of $1 is 0.7513. The present value of $1,000 to be received at the end of three years can be computed as follows:

$$\textbf{\$1,000} \times \textbf{0.7513} = \textbf{\$751.30}$$

From Table A.1,
$i = 10\%$
$n = 3$

Learning how to compute a present value amount is not difficult, but it is more important that you understand what it means. The $751.30 is the amount that you would pay to have the right to receive $1,000 at the end of three years, assuming an interest rate of 10 percent. Conceptually, you would be indifferent about having $751.30 today and receiving $1,000 in three years, because you can use financial institutions to convert dollars from the present to the future and vice versa. If you had $751.30 today but preferred $1,000 in three years, you could simply deposit the money into a savings account that paid annual interest at 10 percent and it would grow to $1,000 in three years. Alternatively, if you had a contract that promised you $1,000 in three years, you could sell it to an investor for $751.30 cash today because it would permit the investor to earn the difference in interest.

SELF-STUDY QUIZ 11-5

1. If the interest rate in a present value problem increases from 10 percent to 11 percent, will the present value increase or decrease? Explain.

2. What is the present value of $10,000 to be received 10 years from now if the interest rate is 5 percent compounded annually?

connect   After you complete your work, check your answer with the solution in footnote 14.

---

[13]The detailed discounting is as follows:

Periods	Interest for the Year	Present Value*
1	$1,000 − ($1,000 × 1/1.10) = $90.91	$1,000 − $90.91 = $909.09
2	$909.09 − ($909.09 × 1/1.10) = $82.65	$909.09 − $82.65 = $826.44
3	$826.44 − ($826.44 × 1/1.10) = $75.14†	$826.44 − $75.14 = $751.30

*Verifiable in Table A.1. †Adjusted for rounding.

[14]1. The present value will decrease. With a higher interest rate, more interest will accumulate over time, so the initial amount needed at the start would be smaller because the interest component will be larger.

2. $10,000 × 0.6139 = $6,139.

PRESENT VALUE OF AN ANNUITY

Many business problems involve multiple cash payments over a number of periods instead of a single payment. An **annuity** is a series of consecutive payments characterized by

An **ANNUITY** is a series of equal amounts of cash that are paid or received at equally distant points in time.

1. An equal dollar amount each interest period.

2. Interest periods of equal length (year, semi-annual, quarter, or month).

3. An equal interest rate each interest period.

Examples of annuities include monthly payments on an automobile or a home loan, annual contributions to a savings account, and monthly retirement benefits.

The present value of an annuity is the value now of a series of equal amounts to be received (or paid) each period for some specified number of periods in the future. It is computed by discounting each of the equal periodic amounts. A good example of this type of problem is a retirement program that offers the retiree a monthly income after retirement. The present value of an annuity of $1 for three periods at 10 percent may be represented graphically as follows:

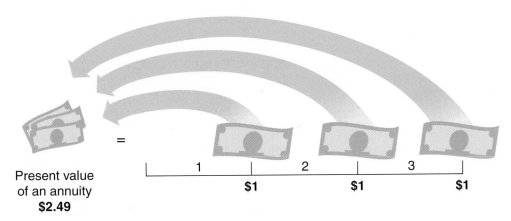

Present value
of an annuity
$2.49

Assume you are to receive $1,000 cash on each December 31, 2011, 2012, and 2013. How much would the sum of these three $1,000 future amounts be worth on January 1, 2011, assuming an interest rate of 10 percent per year? We could use Table A.1 in Appendix 11B to calculate the present value as follows:

		Factor from Table A.1		
Year	Amount		Appendix 11B, i = 10%	Present Value
1	$1,000	×	0.9091 (n = 1)	=	$ 909.10
2	$1,000	×	0.8264 (n = 2)	=	826.40
3	$1,000	×	0.7513 (n = 3)	=	751.30
			Total present value	=	$2,486.80

We can compute the present value of this annuity more easily, however, by using Table A.2, Appendix 11B, as follows:

$$\mathbf{\$1{,}000 \times 2.4869 = \$2{,}487 \text{ (rounded)}}$$

From Table A.2,
i = 10%
n = 3

Exhibit 11.5 provides a graphical illustration of the present value computations discussed above.

Exhibit **11.5**

Overview of Present Value
Computations

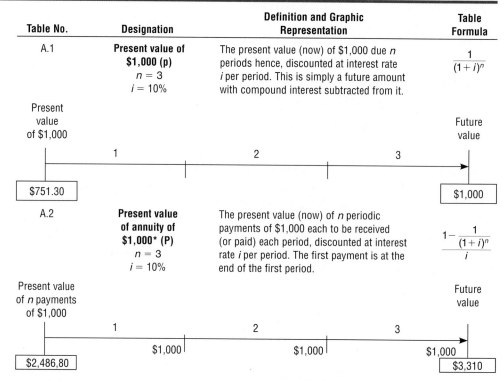

Table No.	Designation	Definition and Graphic Representation	Table Formula
A.1	**Present value of $1,000 (p)** $n = 3$ $i = 10\%$	The present value (now) of $1,000 due n periods hence, discounted at interest rate i per period. This is simply a future amount with compound interest subtracted from it.	$\dfrac{1}{(1+i)^n}$

Present
value
of $1,000   Future
value

                   1   2   3

$751.30 $1,000

Table No.	Designation	Definition and Graphic Representation	Table Formula
A.2	**Present value of annuity of $1,000* (P)** $n = 3$ $i = 10\%$	The present value (now) of n periodic payments of $1,000 each to be received (or paid) each period, discounted at interest rate i per period. The first payment is at the end of the first period.	$\dfrac{1 - \dfrac{1}{(1+i)^n}}{i}$

Present value
of n payments
of $1,000   Future
value

          1   2   3

          $1,000 $1,000 $1,000

$2,486,80 $3,310

*Notice that these are ordinary annuities; that is, they are often called *end-of-period annuities*. Thus, the table values for P, the present value, are at the beginning of the period of the first payment. Annuities due assume the opposite; that is, they are *beginning-of-period annuities*. Ordinary annuity values can be converted into annuities due simply by multiplication of $(1 + i)$.

Interest Rates and Interest Periods   The preceding illustrations assumed annual periods for compounding and discounting. Although interest rates almost always are quoted on an annual basis, most interest-compounding periods encountered in business are less than one year (semi-annually or quarterly). When interest periods are less than a year, the values of n and i must be restated to be consistent with the length of the interest period.

To illustrate, 12 percent interest compounded annually for five years requires use of $n = 5$ and $i = 12\%$. If compounding is quarterly, the interest period is one-quarter of a year (i.e., four periods per year), and the quarterly interest rate is one-quarter of the annual rate (i.e., 3 percent per quarter). Therefore, 12 percent interest compounded quarterly for five years requires use of $n = 20$ and $i = 3\%$.

A QUESTION
OF ACCOUNTABILITY   **TRUTH IN ADVERTISING**

A number of advertisements in newspapers, in magazines, on television, and on the Internet easily can be misinterpreted if the consumer does not understand present value concepts. We discuss two examples.

Most car companies offer seasonal promotions with special financing incentives. A car dealer may advertise 1.9 percent interest on car loans when banks are charging 10 percent. Typically, the lower interest rate is not a special incentive because the dealer simply charges a higher price for cars that the dealership finances. It may be better to borrow from the bank and "pay cash" at the dealership to negotiate a lower price. Customers should use the present value concepts illustrated in this chapter to compare financing alternatives.

Another misleading advertisement is one that promises a chance to become an instant millionaire. The fine print discloses that the winner will receive $25,000 for 40 years, which is $1,000,000 (40 × $25,000), but the present value of this annuity at 8 percent is only $298,000. Most winners are happy to get the money, but they are not really millionaires.

Some consumer advocates criticize businesses that use these types of advertisements. They argue that consumers should not have to study present value concepts to understand advertisements. Some of these criticisms may be valid, but the quality of information contained in advertisements that include interest rates has improved during the past few years.

ACCOUNTING APPLICATIONS OF PRESENT VALUES

Many business transactions require the use of present value concepts. We illustrate two such cases so that you can test your understanding of these concepts:

Case A   On January 1, 2011, Nesca Corp. bought some new equipment. The company signed a note and agreed to pay $200,000 for the equipment on December 31, 2012. The market interest rate for this note was 12 percent. The $200,000 represents the cash equivalent price of the equipment and the interest that will be earned for two years.

1. How should the accountant record the purchase?

Answer: This case requires application of the present value of a single amount. In conformity with the cost principle, the cost of the equipment is its current cash equivalent price, which is the present value of the future payment. The problem can be shown graphically as follows:

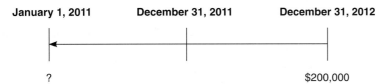

January 1, 2011	December 31, 2011	December 31, 2012
?		$200,000

The present value of the $200,000 is computed as follows:

$$\$200{,}000 \times 0.7972 = \$159{,}440$$

From Table A.1,
$i = 12\%$
$n = 2$

Therefore, the journal entry is as follows:

Equipment (A)	159,440	
Note payable (L).		159,440

Assets		=	Liabilities		+	Shareholders' Equity
Equipment	+159,440		Note payable	+159,440		

Some companies prefer to record the following journal entry:

Equipment (A)	159,440	
Discount on notes payable (XL)	40,560	
Note payable (L).		200,000

Assets		=	Liabilities		+	Shareholders' Equity
Equipment	+159,440		Note payable	+200,000		
			Discount	−40,560		

The discount account is a contra-liability account that represents the interest that will accrue on the note over its life.

2. What journal entry should be made at the end of the first and second years for interest expense?

Answer: The following schedule shows the computation of interest expense for the two years.

Date	Interest Expense Unpaid Balance × 12%	Unpaid Balance of Note Payable
January 1, 2011		$159,440
December 31, 2011	$159,440 × 12% = $19,132	178,572
December 31, 2012	178,573 × 12% = 21,428	200,000

Each year's interest expense is recorded in an adjusting entry as follows:

Dec. 31, 2011   Interest expense (E)   19,132
                   Note payable (L)........................   19,132

Assets	=	Liabilities	+	Shareholders' Equity	
		Note payable	+19,132	Interest Expense	−19,132

Dec. 31, 2012   Interest expense (E)   21,428
                   Note payable (L)........................   21,428

Assets	=	Liabilities	+	Shareholders' Equity	
		Note payable	+21,428	Interest Expense	−21,428

Notice that interest of $19,132 accrued during 2011 but was not paid. It is therefore added to the balance of the note payable account. This interest amount has itself earned interest during 2012.

3. What journal entry should be made on December 31, 2012, to record the payment of the debt?

Answer: At this date, the amount to be paid is the note payable balance, which is the same as the maturity amount on the due date. The journal entry to record full payment of the debt follows:

Note payable (L)   200,000
   Cash (A)...   200,000

Assets		=	Liabilities		+	Shareholders' Equity
Cash	−200,000		Note payable	−200,000		

Case B   On January 1, 2011, Nesca bought new research equipment. The company elected to finance the purchase with a note payable to be paid in three equal annual instalments of $163,686. Each instalment includes principal plus interest on the unpaid balance at 11 percent per year. The annual instalments are due on December 31, 2011, 2012, and 2013. This problem can be shown graphically as follows:

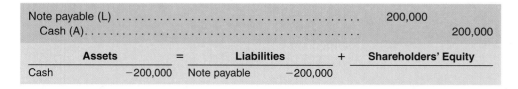

January 1, 2011	December 31, 2011	December 31, 2012	December 31, 2013
?	$163,686	$163,686	$163,686

1. What is the amount of the note?
Answer: The note is the present value of each instalment payment, $i = 11\%$ and $n = 3$. This is an annuity because payment is made in three equal instalments. The amount of the note is computed as follows:

$$\textbf{\$163,686} \times \textbf{2.4437} = \textbf{\$400,000}$$

From Table A.2,
$i = 11\%$
$n = 3$

The acquisition is recorded as follows:

Research equipment (A)	400,000		
Note payable (L)		400,000	

Assets		=	Liabilities		+	Shareholders' Equity
Research equipment	+400,000		Note payable	+400,000		

2. What was the total amount of interest expense in dollars?

Answer:

$$\$163{,}686 \times 3 - \$400{,}000 = \$91{,}058$$

3. Prepare a debt payment schedule that shows the entry for each payment and the effect on interest expense and the unpaid amount of principal each period.

Answer:

	Debt Payment Schedule			
Date	Cash Payment (Credit)	Interest Expense (Unpaid Principal × 11%) (Debit)	Decrease in Principal (Debit)	Unpaid Principal
1/1/2011				$400,000
12/31/2011	$163,686	$400,000 × 11% = $44,000	$119,686[a]	280,314[b]
12/31/2012	163,686	280,314 × 11% = $30,835	132,851	147,463
12/31/2013	163,686	147,463 × 11% = $16,223*	147,463	0
Total	$491,058	$91,058*	$400,000	

*To accommodate rounding error.
Computations: [a]$163,686 − $44,000 = $119,686   [b]$400,000 − $119,686 = $280,314

Notice in the debt payment schedule that for each successive payment, the payment on principal increases and interest expense decreases. This effect occurs because the interest each period is based on a lower amount of the unpaid principal. When an annuity is involved, schedules such as this one often are useful analytical tools.

4. What journal entry should be made at the end of each year to record the payments on this note?

Answer:

Dec. 31, 2011	Note payable (L)	119,686	
	Interest expense (E)	44,000	
	Cash (A)		163,686

Assets		=	Liabilities		+	Shareholders' Equity	
Cash	−163,686		Note payable	−119,686		Interest expense	−44,000

Dec. 31, 2012	Note payable (L)	132,851	
	Interest expense (E)	30,835	
	Cash (A)		163,686

Assets		=	Liabilities		+	Shareholders' Equity	
Cash	−163,686		Note payable	−132,851		Interest expense	−30,835

Dec. 31, 2013	Note payable (L)	147,463	
	Interest expense (E)	16,223	
	Cash (A)		163,686

Assets		=	Liabilities		+	Shareholders' Equity	
Cash	−163,686		Note payable	−147,463		Interest expense	−16,223

Appendix 11B

Present Value Tables

Table **A.1**

Present Value of $1,
$p = 1/(1 + i)^n$

Periods	2%	3%	3.75%	4%	4.25%	5%	6%	7%	8%
1	0.9804	0.9709	0.9639	0.9615	0.9592	0.9524	0.9434	0.9346	0.9259
2	0.9612	0.9426	0.9290	0.9246	0.9201	0.9070	0.8900	0.8734	0.8573
3	0.9423	0.9151	0.8954	0.8890	0.8826	0.8638	0.8396	0.8163	0.7938
4	0.9238	0.8885	0.8631	0.8548	0.8466	0.8227	0.7921	0.7629	0.7350
5	0.9057	0.8626	0.8319	0.8219	0.8121	0.7835	0.7473	0.7130	0.6806
6	0.8880	0.8375	0.8018	0.7903	0.7790	0.7462	0.7050	0.6663	0.6302
7	0.8706	0.8131	0.7728	0.7599	0.7473	0.7107	0.6651	0.6227	0.5835
8	0.8535	0.7894	0.7449	0.7307	0.7168	0.6768	0.6274	0.5820	0.5403
9	0.8368	0.7664	0.7180	0.7026	0.6876	0.6446	0.5919	0.5439	0.5002
10	0.8203	0.7441	0.6920	0.6756	0.6595	0.6139	0.5584	0.5083	0.4632
20	0.6730	0.5537	0.4789	0.4564	0.4350	0.3769	0.3118	0.2584	0.2145

Periods	9%	10%	11%	12%	13%	14%	15%	20%	25%
1	0.9174	0.9091	0.9009	0.8929	0.8850	0.8772	0.8696	0.8333	0.8000
2	0.8417	0.8264	0.8116	0.7972	0.7831	0.7695	0.7561	0.6944	0.6400
3	0.7722	0.7513	0.7312	0.7118	0.6931	0.6750	0.6575	0.5787	0.5120
4	0.7084	0.6830	0.6587	0.6355	0.6133	0.5921	0.5718	0.4823	0.4096
5	0.6499	0.6209	0.5935	0.5674	0.5428	0.5194	0.4972	0.4019	0.3277
6	0.5963	0.5645	0.5346	0.5066	0.4803	0.4556	0.4323	0.3349	0.2621
7	0.5470	0.5132	0.4817	0.4523	0.4251	0.3996	0.3759	0.2791	0.2097
8	0.5019	0.4665	0.4339	0.4039	0.3762	0.3506	0.3269	0.2326	0.1678
9	0.4604	0.4241	0.3909	0.3606	0.3329	0.3075	0.2843	0.1938	0.1342
10	0.4224	0.3855	0.3522	0.3220	0.2946	0.2697	0.2472	0.1615	0.1074
20	0.1784	0.1486	0.1240	0.1037	0.0868	0.0728	0.0611	0.0261	0.0115

Table **A.2**

Present Value of Annuity of
$1, $p = [1 - 1/(1 + i)^n]/i$

Periods*	2%	3%	3.75%	4%	4.25%	5%	6%	7%	8%
1	0.9804	0.9709	0.9639	0.9615	0.9592	0.9524	0.9434	0.9346	0.9259
2	1.9416	1.9135	1.8929	1.8861	1.8794	1.8594	1.8334	1.8080	1.7833
3	2.8839	2.8286	2.7883	2.7751	2.7620	2.7232	2.6730	2.6243	2.5771
4	3.8077	3.7171	3.6514	3.6299	3.6086	3.5460	3.4651	3.3872	3.3121
5	4.7135	4.5797	4.4833	4.4518	4.4207	4.3295	4.2124	4.1002	3.9927
6	5.6014	5.4172	5.2851	5.2421	5.1997	5.0757	4.9173	4.7665	4.6229
7	6.4720	6.2303	6.0579	6.0021	5.9470	5.7864	5.5824	5.3893	5.2064
8	7.3255	7.0197	6.8028	6.7327	6.6638	6.4632	6.2098	5.9713	5.7466
9	8.1622	7.7861	7.5208	7.4353	7.3513	7.1078	6.8017	6.5152	6.2469
10	8.9826	8.5302	8.2128	8.1109	8.0109	7.7217	7.3601	7.0236	6.7101
20	16.3514	14.8775	13.8962	13.5903	13.2944	12.4622	11.4699	10.5940	9.8181

Periods*	9%	10%	11%	12%	13%	14%	15%	20%	25%
1	0.9174	0.9091	0.9009	0.8929	0.8550	0.8772	0.8696	0.8333	0.8000
2	1.7591	1.7355	1.7125	1.6901	1.6681	1.6467	1.6257	1.5278	1.4400
3	2.5313	2.4869	2.4437	2.4018	2.3612	2.3216	2.2832	2.1065	1.9520
4	3.2397	3.1699	3.1024	3.0373	2.9745	2.9137	2.8550	2.5887	2.3616
5	3.8897	3.7908	3.6959	3.6048	3.5172	3.4331	3.3522	2.9906	2.6893
6	4.4859	4.3553	4.2305	4.1114	3.9975	3.8887	3.7845	3.3255	2.9514
7	5.0330	4.8684	4.7122	4.5638	4.4226	4.2883	4.1604	3.6046	3.1611
8	5.5348	5.3349	5.1461	4.9676	4.7988	4.6389	4.4873	3.8372	3.3289
9	5.9952	5.7590	5.5370	5.3282	4.1317	4.9464	4.7716	4.0310	3.4631
10	6.4177	6.1446	5.8892	5.6502	5.4262	5.2161	5.0188	4.1925	3.5705
20	9.1285	8.5136	7.9633	7.4694	7.0248	6.6231	6.2593	4.8696	3.9539

*There is one payment each period.

Appendix 11C

Reporting Interest Expense on Bonds by Using the Straight-Line Amortization Method

While the effective interest method is the preferred method to amortize bond discount or premium, Canadian private enterprises may use the straight-line amortization method because it is relatively easy to compute the required numbers. You may wonder why private enterprises are permitted to use a method that is not conceptually correct. The answer is *materiality*. Private enterprises are permitted to use the straight-line method because the amortized discounts or premiums that result from the two methods are normally not materially different. We use the examples in the chapter to illustrate the amortization of a bond discount as well as of a bond premium.

Bonds Issued at a Discount Refer to the illustration on page 584 whereby Nesca's $400,000 bond issue was sold at a discount of $45,882. To amortize the bond discount over the life of Nesca's bonds by using straight-line amortization, an equal amount is allocated to each interest period. Nesca's bonds have 20 six-month interest periods. Therefore, the amount amortized on each semi-annual interest date is $2,294 ($45,882 ÷ 20 periods). This amount is added to the interest paid ($20,000) to compute interest expense for the period ($22,294).

STRAIGHT-LINE AMORTIZATION of a bond discount or premium is a simplified method that allocates an equal amount to each interest period.

The journal entry to record the interest payment each period is as follows:

Bond interest expense (E)	22,294	
Discount on bonds payable (XL)		2,294
Cash (A)		20,000

Assets		=	Liabilities	+	Shareholders' Equity	
Cash	−20,000		Discount on bonds payable	+2,294	Bond interest expense	−22,294

Bonds payable are reported on the statement of financial position at their carrying amount—that is, the maturity amount less any unamortized bond discount (or plus any unamortized bond premium). At June 30, 2010, the carrying amount of Nesca's bonds is more than the original issue price. The carrying amount increases to $356,412 ($354,118 + $2,294) because of the amortization of the discount. In each interest period, the carrying amount of the bonds increases by $2,294 because the unamortized discount decreases by $2,294. At the maturity date of the bonds, the unamortized discount (i.e., the balance in the discount on bonds payable account) is zero. At that time, the maturity amount of the bonds and the carrying amount are the same (i.e., $400,000). The process can be seen in the following amortization schedule, which shows the first two years and the last year of the bond's life. Compare it to the amortization schedule based on the effective interest method page 587.

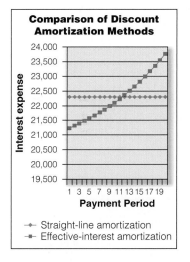

Comparison of Discount Amortization Methods

Interest expense / Payment Period

- Straight-line amortization
- Effective-interest amortization

Amortization Schedule: Bond Discount (straight line)				
Date	(a) Interest to Be Paid [$400,000 × 5%]	(b) Interest Expense [(a) + (c)]	(c) Amortization [$45,882 ÷ 20 periods]	(d) Carrying Amount [Beginning Carrying Amount + (c)]
1/1/2010				$354,118
6/30/2010	$20,000	$22,294	$2,294	356,412
12/31/2010	20,000	22,294	2,294	358,706
6/30/2011	20,000	22,294	2,294	361,000
12/31/2011	20,000	22,294	2,294	363,294
.	.	.	.	.
6/30/2019	20,000	22,294	2,294	397,706
12/31/2019	20,000	22,294	2,294	400,000

Under the straight-line method, interest expense remains constant over the life of the bond, but it increases when the effective interest method is used. The graph in the margin illustrates these differences. However, both methods amortize the same historic discount and do not reflect current market values.

SELF-STUDY **QUIZ 11-6**

Assume that Nesca issued $100,000 bonds that will mature in 10 years. The bonds pay interest twice each year at an annual rate of 7 percent. They were sold when the market rate was 8 percent.

1. Determine the selling price of the bonds.

2. What amount of interest was paid at the end of the first year?

3. What amount of interest expense would be reported at the end of the first year using straight-line amortization of bond discount?

After you complete your work, check your answer with the solution in footnote 15.

Bonds Issued at a Premium   Refer to the illustration on page 588 whereby Nesca's $400,000 bond issue was sold at a premium of $54,366. The premium recorded by Nesca must be apportioned to each of the 20 interest periods. Using the straight-line method, the premium that is amortized in each semi-annual interest period is $2,718 ($54,366 ÷ 20 periods). This amount is subtracted from the interest payment ($20,000) to calculate the interest expense ($17,282). Thus, amortization of the bond premium decreases interest expense.

The payment of interest on the bonds is recorded as follows:

Bond interest expense (E).................................	17,282	
Premium on bonds payable (L)............................	2,718	
Cash (A)...		20,000

Assets		=	Liabilities		+	Shareholders' Equity	
Cash	−20,000		Premium on bonds payable	−2,718		Bond interest expense	−17,282

Notice that the $20,000 cash paid each period includes $17,282 interest expense and $2,718 premium amortization. Thus, the cash payment to the investors includes the current interest they have earned, plus a return of part of the premium they paid when they bought the bonds.

The carrying amount of the bonds is the amount in the bonds payable account plus any unamortized premium. On June 30, 2010, the carrying amount of the bonds is $451,648 ($400,000 + $54,366 − $2,718). A partial amortization schedule follows:

	(a) Interest to Be Paid [$400,000 × 5%]	(b) Interest Expense [(a) − (c)]	(c) Amortization [$54,366 ÷ 20 periods]	(d) Carrying Amount [Beginning Carrying Amount − (c)]
Date				
1/1/2010				$454,336
6/30/2010	$20,000	$17,282	$2,718	451,618
12/31/2010	20,000	17,282	2,718	448,900
6/30/2011	20,000	17,282	2,718	446,182
12/31/2011	20,000	17,282	2,718	443,464
.	.	.	.	.
.	.	.	.	.
6/30/2019	20,000	17,282	2,718	402,718
12/31/2019	20,000	17,282	2,718	400,000

Amortization Schedule: Bond Premium (straight line)

----

[15]1. Principal: $100,000 × 0.4565 = $45,650
   Interest: $3,500 × 13.5903 = 47,566
                                   $93,216

2. Interest paid   = $100,000 × 0.07 = $7,000
3. Interest expense = Interest payment + Amortization of bond discount
                    = $7,000 + $6,784/10 = $7,678.40

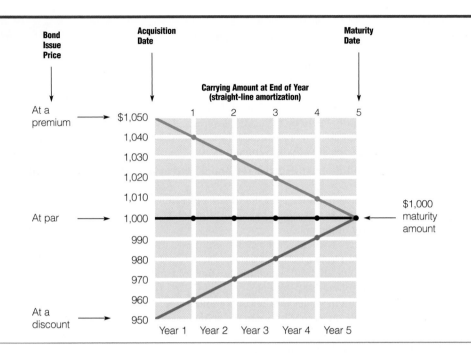

Exhibit **11.6**

Amortization of Bond Discount and Premium Compared—Straight-Line Amortization

At the maturity date, after the last interest payment, the bond premium is fully amortized, and the maturity amount equals the carrying amount of the bonds. When the bonds are paid off in full, the same entry will be made whether the bond was originally sold at par, at a discount, or at a premium. Exhibit 11.6 compares the effects of the amortization of bond discount and bond premium on a $1,000 bond.

Under the straight-line method, interest expense remains constant over the life of the bond, but it decreases when the effective interest method is used. The graph in the margin illustrates these differences.

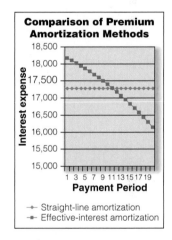

Comparison of Premium Amortization Methods

→ Straight-line amortization
→ Effective-interest amortization

SELF-STUDY **QUIZ 11-7**

Assume that Nesca issued $100,000 bonds that will mature in 10 years. The bonds pay interest twice each year at an annual rate of 9 percent. They were sold when the market rate was 8 percent.

1. Determine the selling price of the bonds.
2. What amount of interest was paid at the end of the first year?
3. What amount of interest expense would be reported at the end of the first year using straight-line amortization?

After you complete your work, check your answer with the solution in footnote 16.

Appendix 11D: Present Value Computations Using Excel (online)
Appendix 11E: Future Value Concepts (online)

---

[16]1. Principal: $100,000 × 0.4565 = $45,650
   Interest: $4,500 × 13.5903 = $\underline{61,156}$
   $\overline{\underline{$106,806}}$

2. Interest paid   = $100,000 × 0.09 = $9,000
3. Interest expense = Interest payment − Amortization of bond premium
              = $9,000 − $6,806/10 = $8,319.40

CHAPTER **TAKE-AWAYS**

1. **Describe the characteristics of long-term notes and bonds payable. p. 577**
   Long-term notes and bonds payable have a number of characteristics designed to meet the needs of the issuing corporation and the creditor.

   Corporations use debt to raise long-term capital. Long-term debt offers a number of advantages compared to equity, including financial leverage, the tax deductibility of interest, and the fact that control of the company is not diluted. Long-term debt carries additional risk because interest and principal payments are not discretionary.

2. **Report bonds payable and interest expense for bonds sold at par, at a discount, or at a premium. p. 581**
   Three types of events must be recorded over the life of a typical bond: (1) the receipt of cash when the bond is first sold, (2) the periodic payment of interest, and (3) the repayment of principal upon the maturity of the bond.

   Bonds are sold at a discount whenever the coupon interest rate is less than the market rate of interest. A discount is the difference between the par value of the bond and its selling price. The discount is recorded as a contra liability when the bond is sold and is amortized over the life of the bond as an adjustment to interest payment.

   Bonds are sold at a premium whenever the coupon interest rate is higher than the market rate of interest. A premium is the difference between the selling price of the bond and its par value. The premium is recorded as a liability when the bond is sold and is amortized over the life of the bond as an adjustment to interest payment.

3. **Compute and interpret the times interest earned ratio. p. 590**
   This ratio measures the ability of a company to meet its interest obligations with resources from its profit-making activities. The ratio is computed by comparing interest expense to profit before interest expense and income taxes.

4. **Report the early retirement of bonds. p. 591**
   A corporation may retire bonds before their maturity date. The difference between the carrying amount and the amount paid to retire the bonds is reported as a gain or a loss, depending on the circumstances.

5. **Describe other non-current liabilities. p. 593**
   In addition to long-term debt, companies report a number of other non-current liabilities that result from their operating, investing, and financing activities. Typical non-current liabilities include lease obligations, asset retirement obligations, accrued retirement benefits liability, and deferred income taxes.

6. **Compute and interpret the financial leverage ratio. p. 599**
   The financial leverage ratio compares the amount of capital supplied by creditors to the amount supplied by owners. It is a measure of a company's debt capacity. It is an important ratio because high risk is associated with debt capital due to obligatory payments.

7. **Explain how financing activities are reported on the statement of cash flows. p. 599**
   Cash flows associated with transactions involving long-term creditors are reported in the financing activities section of the statement of cash flows. Interest paid may be reported either in the operating activities section or the financing activities section.

   The capital structure of a business is made up of funds supplied by both the creditors and the owners. In this chapter, we discussed the role of bonds payable in the capital structure of a business. In the next chapter, we will discuss shareholders' equity.

KEY **RATIOS**

Times interest earned ratio measures a company's ability to generate resources from current operations to meet its interest obligations. The computation of this ratio follows (p. 590):

$$\text{Times Interest Earned} = \frac{\text{Profit before Interest and Taxes}}{\text{Interest Expense}}$$

The **financial leverage ratio** measures the relationship between total assets and the shareholders' equity that finances the assets. The ratio is computed as follows (p. 599):

$$\text{Financial Leverage} = \frac{\text{Average Total Assets}}{\text{Average Shareholders' Equity}}$$

FINDING **FINANCIAL INFORMATION**

STATEMENT OF FINANCIAL POSITION

Under Current Liabilities

Notes, bonds, and debentures are normally listed as non-current liabilities. An exception occurs when these liabilities are within one year of maturity. Such debts are reported as current liabilities with the following title:

Current portion of long-term debt

Under Non-current Liabilities

Notes, bonds, and debentures are listed under a variety of titles, depending on the characteristics of the debt. Titles include

Notes payable

Bonds payable

Debentures

Financial liabilities

INCOME STATEMENT

Interest expense associated with long-term debt is reported on the income statement. Most companies report interest expense in a separate category on the income statement.

STATEMENT OF CASH FLOWS

Under Financing Activities

+ Cash inflows from long-term creditors

− Cash outflows to long-term creditors (including interest paid)

Under Operating Activities

Interest paid if classified as an operating activity.

NOTES

Under Summary of Significant Accounting Policies

Description of pertinent information concerning accounting treatment of liabilities. Normally, there is minimal information. Some companies report the method used to amortize bond discounts and premiums.

Under a Separate Note

Most companies include a separate note called "Long-Term Debt" that reports information about each major debt issue, including amount and interest rate. The note may also provide detail concerning debt characteristics and covenants.

KEY **TERMS**

Effective Interest Rate p. 581
Face Amount p. 577
Finance Lease p. 594
Financial Leverage p. 576
Future Value p. 603
Indenture p. 579
Market Interest Rate p. 581
Non-current Liabilities p. 575
Operating Lease p. 593

Par Value p. 577
Present Value p. 602
Retractable Bonds p. 591
Stated Rate p. 577
Straight-Line Amortization p. 611
Trustee p. 580
Yield p. 581

QUESTIONS

1. What are the primary characteristics of a bond? For what purposes are bonds usually issued?
2. What is the difference between a bond indenture and a bond certificate?
3. Differentiate secured debt from unsecured debt.
4. Differentiate among redeemable, retractable, and convertible bonds.
5. From the perspective of the issuer, what are some advantages of using debt instead of issuing shares?
6. As the tax rate increases, the net cost of borrowing money decreases. Explain.
7. Explain financial leverage. Can it be negative?
8. At the date of issuance, bonds are recorded at their current cash equivalent amount. Explain.
9. What is the nature of the discount and premium on bonds payable? Explain.
10. What is the difference between the stated interest rate and the effective interest rate on a bond?
11. Differentiate between the stated and effective rates of interest on a bond sold (a) at par, (b) at a discount, and (c) at a premium.
12. What is the carrying amount of a bond payable?
13. If a company issues a bond at a discount, will interest expense each period be more or less than the cash payment for interest? If another company issues a bond at a premium, will interest expense be more or less than the cash payment for interest? Is your answer to either question affected by the method used to amortize the discount or premium?
14. (Appendix 11A) Explain the basic difference between future value and present value.
15. (Appendix 11A) What does an annuity mean?
16. (Appendix 11C) Explain the basic difference between the straight-line and effective interest methods of amortizing bond discount or premium. Explain when the straight-line method may be used.

EXERCISES

LO1   **E11–1**   **Bond Terminology: Fill in the Blanks**

1. The _____ is the amount (a) payable at the maturity of the bond and (b) on which the periodic cash interest payments are computed.

2. _____ is another name for bond principal, or the maturity amount for a bond.

3. The _____ is the rate of cash interest per period stated in the bond contract.

4. A _____ is an unsecured bond; no assets are specifically pledged to guarantee repayment.

5. _____ may be called for early retirement at the option of the issuer.

6. _____ may be converted to other securities of the issuer (usually common shares).

E11–2 **Determining Financial Statement Effects for Long-Term Note and First Interest Payment, with Premium**

Grocery Corporation sold $500,000, 11 percent notes on January 1, 2011, at a market rate of 8 percent. The notes were dated January 1, 2011, with interest to be paid each December 31; they mature 10 years from January 1, 2011. Use effective interest amortization.

Required:

1. How are the financial statements affected by the issuance of the notes? Describe the impact on the financial leverage and times interest earned ratios, if any.

2. How are the financial statements affected by the payment of interest on December 31? Describe the impact on the financial leverage and times interest earned ratios, if any.

3. Show how the interest expense, interest payment, and the notes payable should be reported on the financial statements for 2011.

E11–3 **Explaining Why Debt Is Sold at a Discount**

The annual report of Shaw Communications Inc. contained the following note:

> **9. LONG-TERM DEBT**
>
> On March 27, 2009, the Company issued $600,000,000 of senior notes at a rate of 6.50%. The senior notes were issued at a discount and the effective interest rate is 6.56%.

After reading this note, one student asked why Shaw didn't simply sell the notes for an effective yield of 6.5 percent and avoid having to account for a very small discount over the life of the notes. Prepare a written response to this question.

E11–4 **Explaining Bond Features**

Carnival Corporation is a global cruise company and one of the largest vacation companies in the world. The notes to its financial statements for 2009 include the following:

> **CONVERTIBLE NOTES**
>
> At November 30, 2009, Carnival Corporation's 2% convertible notes ("2% Notes") are convertible into 15.2 million shares of Carnival Corporation common stock. The 2% Notes are convertible at a conversion price of $39.14 per share, subject to adjustment, during any fiscal quarter for which the closing price of the Carnival Corporation common stock is greater than $43.05 per share for a defined duration of time in the preceding fiscal quarter. The conditions for conversion of the 2% Notes were not satisfied during 2009 and 2008. Only a nominal amount of our 2% Notes have been converted since their issuance in 2000.
>
> On April 15, 2011, the 2% noteholders may require us to repurchase all or a portion of the 2% Notes at their face values plus any unpaid accrued interest. In addition, we currently may redeem all or a portion of the outstanding 2% Notes at their face value plus any unpaid accrued interest, subject to the noteholders' right to convert. Upon conversion, redemption or repurchase of the 2% Notes, we may choose to deliver Carnival Corporation common stock, cash or a combination of cash and common stock with a total value equal to the value of the consideration otherwise deliverable.
>
> *Source:* Carnival Corporation Annual Report 2009.

Required:

1. Explain the various features of these notes.
2. When the notes were issued, interest rates were much higher than the 2 percent offered by the company. Why would an investor accept such a low interest rate?

LO1, 2

LO1

Shaw
Communications

LO2

Carnival Corporation

LO1

Walmart Stores Inc.

E11–5 **Interpreting Information Reported in the Business Press**

The business press reported the following information concerning a bond issued by Walmart Stores Inc.:

Bonds	Coupon	Maturity	Bid	Yield
Walmart	3.20	May 15/2014	104.59	3.06

Required:

1. Explain the meaning of the reported information. If you bought Walmart Stores bonds with $10,000 face value, how much would you pay (based on the information reported above)?
2. Assume that the bond was originally sold at par. What impact would the increase in value have on the financial statements for Walmart Stores?

LO1

PepsiCo Inc.

The Walt Disney Company

E11–6 **Evaluating Bond Features**

You are a personal financial planner working with a married couple in their early 40s who have decided to invest $100,000 in corporate bonds. You have found two bonds that you think will interest your clients. One is a zero coupon bond issued by PepsiCo with an effective interest rate of 9 percent and a maturity date of 2015. It is callable at par. The other is a Walt Disney bond that matures in 2093. It has an effective interest rate of 9.5 percent and is callable at 105 percent of par. Which bond would you recommend and why? Would your answer be different if you expected interest rates to fall significantly over the next few years? Would you prefer a different bond if the couple's ages were in the late 60s and they were retired?

LO1, 2

The Walt Disney Company

E11–7 **Explaining an International Transaction**

A Walt Disney annual report contained the following note:

> The Company issued yen 100 billion (approximately $920 million) of Japanese yen bonds through a public offering in Japan. The bonds are senior, unsecured debt obligations of the Company, which mature in June 2019. Interest on the bonds is payable semi-annually at a fixed interest rate of 5% per year through maturity. The bonds provide for principal payments in dollars and interest payment in Japanese yen.

Required:

1. Describe how this bond would be reported on the statement of financial position.
2. Explain why you think management borrowed money in this manner.

LO1, 3, 6

E11–8 **Analyzing Financial Ratios**

You have just started your first job as a financial analyst for a large investment company. Your boss, a senior analyst, has finished a detailed report evaluating bonds issued by two different companies. She stopped by your desk and asked for help: "I have compared two ratios for the companies and found something interesting." She went on to explain that the financial leverage ratio for Applied Technologies Inc. is much lower than the industry average and that the one for Innovative Solutions Inc. is much higher. On the other hand, the times interest earned ratio for Applied Technologies is much higher than the industry average, and the ratio for Innovative Solutions is much lower. Your boss then asked you to think about what the ratios indicate about the two companies so that she could include the explanation in her report. How would you respond to your boss?

LO2

E11–9 **Computing the Issue Price of a Note Payable**

On January 1, 2011, Kaizen Corporation issued a $500 million note that matures in 10 years. The note has a stated interest rate of 6 percent. When the note was issued, the market rate was 6 percent. The note pays interest twice per year on June 30 and December 31. At what price was the note issued?

LO2, 7

E11–10 **Computing the Issue Price of a Bond with Analysis of Profit and Cash Flow Effects**

Imai Company issued a $1-million bond that matures in five years. The bond has a 9 percent coupon rate. When the bond was issued, the market rate was 8 percent. The bond pays interest twice per year on June 30 and December 31. Record the issuance of the bond on June 30. Was the bond issued at a discount or at a premium? How will the discount or premium affect future profit and future cash flows?

E11–11 Computing Issue Prices of Bonds for Three Cases   ■ LO2

Thompson Corporation is planning to issue $100,000, five-year, 6 percent bonds. Interest is payable semi-annually each June 30 and December 31. All of the bonds will be sold on July 1, 2011; they mature on June 30, 2016.

Required:

Compute the issue (sale) price on July 1, 2011, if the yield is (a) 6 percent, (b) 5 percent, and (c) 7 percent. Show computations.

E11–12 Recording Bond Issue and First Interest Payment with Premium (Effective Interest   ■ LO2
Amortization)

On January 1, 2012, Bochini Corporation sold a $10 million, 8.25 percent bond issue. The bonds were dated January 1, 2012, had a yield of 8 percent, pay interest each December 31, and mature 10 years from that date.

Required:

1. Prepare the journal entry to record the issuance of the bonds.

2. Prepare the journal entry to record the interest payment on December 31, 2012. Use effective interest amortization.

3. Show how the bond interest expense and the bonds payable should be reported on the annual financial statements for 2012.

E11–13 Determining Financial Statement Balance with the Effective Interest Amortization of a Bond   ■ LO3
Discount

Eagle Corporation issued $10,000,000, 6.5 percent bonds dated April 1, 2012. The market rate of interest was 7 percent, with interest paid each March 31. The bonds mature in three years, on March 31, 2015. Eagle's fiscal year ends on December 31.

Required:

1. What was the issue price of these bonds?

2. Compute the bond interest expense for fiscal year 2012. The company uses the effective interest method of amortization.

3. Show how the bonds should be reported on the statement of financial position at December 31, 2012.

4. What amount of interest expense will be recorded on March 31, 2013? Is this amount different from the amount of cash that is paid? If so, why?

E11–14 Analyzing a Bond Amortization Schedule: Reporting Bonds Payable   ■ LO2

Stein Corporation issued a $1,000 bond on January 1, 2011. The bond specified an interest rate of 9 percent payable at the end of each year. The bond matures at the end of 2013. It was sold at a market rate of 11 percent per year. The following schedule was completed:

	Cash Paid	Interest Expense	Amortization	Carrying Amount
January 1, 2011 (issuance)				$ 951
End of year 2011	?	$105	$15	966
End of year 2012	?	106	16	982
End of year 2013	?	108	18	1,000

Required:

1. What was the bond's issue price?

2. Did the bond sell at a discount or a premium? How much was the premium or discount?

3. What amount of cash was paid each year for bond interest?

4. What amount of interest expense should be shown each year on the income statement?

5. What amount(s) should be shown on the statement of financial position for bonds payable at each year-end? (For year 2013, show the balance just before repayment of the bond.)

6. What method of amortization was used?

7. Show how the following amounts were computed for year 2012: (a) $106, (b) $16, and (c) $982.

8. Is the method of amortization that was used preferable? Explain why.

LO2   **E11–15**   **Preparing a Debt Payment Schedule with Effective Interest Method of Amortization and Determining Reported Amounts**

Shuttle Company issued $1,000,000, three-year 10 percent bonds on January 1, 2010. The bond interest is paid each December 31. The bond was sold to yield 9 percent.

Required:

1. Complete a bond payment schedule. Use the effective interest method.

2. What amounts will be reported on the financial statements (statement of financial position, income statement, and statement of cash flows) for the years 2010, 2011, and 2012?

LO4   **E11–16**   **Reporting the Retirement of a Bond with Discount**

The Nair Company issued a $5 million bond at a discount five years ago. The current carrying amount of the bond is $4.75 million. The company now has excess cash and decides to retire the bond. The bond is callable at 101 percent of its face value.

Required:

Prepare the journal entry to record the retirement of the bond.

LO7   **E11–17**   **Determining Effects on the Statement of Cash Flows**

The effects of specific events that occur over the life of a bond are reported on the statement of cash flows. Determine whether each of the following events affects the statement of cash flows. If so, describe the impact and specify where the effect is reported on the statement.

1. A $1,000,000 bond is issued at a discount in 2010. The carrying amount of the bond reported on the statement of financial position on that date is $985,000, before any amortization of bond discount.

2. At year-end, accrued interest amounted to $50,000 and $1,000 of the bond discount is amortized by using the effective interest method.

3. Early in 2011, the accrued interest is paid. At the same time, $8,000 of interest that accrued in 2011 is paid.

LO5   **E11–18**   **Evaluating Lease Alternatives**

As the new vice-president for consumer products at Acme Manufacturing, you are attending a meeting to discuss a serious problem associated with delivering merchandise to customers. Bob Vargas, director of logistics, summarized the problem, saying, "It's easy to understand, we just don't have enough delivery trucks given our recent growth." Barb Belini from the accounting department responded, "Maybe it's easy to understand, but it's impossible to do anything. Because of Bay Street's concern about the amount of debt on our statement of financial position, we're under a freeze and can't borrow money to acquire new assets. There's nothing we can do."

On the way back to your office after the meeting, your assistant offers a suggestion, "Why don't we just lease the trucks we need? That way we can get the assets we want without having to record a liability on the statement of financial position."

How would you respond to this suggestion?

LO5   **E11–19**   **Reporting a Liability**

McDonald's Corporation

McDonald's Corporation is one of the world's most popular fast-food restaurants, offering good food at convenient locations. Effective management of its properties is a key to its success. McDonald's both owns and leases property, as the following note in its current annual report indicates:

> The Company owns and leases real estate primarily in connection with its restaurant business. The Company identifies and develops sites that offer convenience to customers and long-term sales and profit potential to the Company. The Company generally owns the land and building or secures long-term leases for restaurant sites, which ensures long-term occupancy rights and helps control related costs.

Required:

Should McDonald's report finance leases on its statement of financial position? Explain. If the obligation should be reported as a liability, how should the amount be measured?

E11–20 **Reporting Retirement Benefits and Effect on Financial Leverage Ratio**

LO5, 6

Sears Canada

Sears Canada Inc. offers Canadian consumers a diverse array of shopping options, with department and specialty stores, a comprehensive website, and a broad range of home-related services. At December 31, 2009, Sears had approximately 35,000 associates (or employees) helping customers through their personal shopping and catalogue ordering. The company's annual report for 2009 included the following information:

NOTES TO CONSOLIDATED FINANCIAL STATEMENTS

11. Associate Future Benefits

In July 2008, the Company amended its pension plan and introduced a defined contribution component. The defined benefit component continues to accrue benefits related to future compensation increases although no further service credit is earned....

The Company currently maintains a defined benefit registered pension plan and a defined contribution registered pension plan, which covers some of its regular full-time associates as well as some of its part-time associates.

The defined benefit plan provides pensions based on length of service and final average earnings....

Source: Sears Canada Annual Report 2009.

The company's statements of financial position at December 31, 2009 and 2008, include the following information (in millions of dollars):

	2009	2008
Total assets	$3,404.8	$3,237.3
Shareholders' equity	1,657.5	1,483.2
Accrued benefit asset (liability)	167.7	158.5

In addition, a note to the company's financial statements shows that Sears had unfunded benefit obligations of $223.4 million at December 31, 2009, and a funding surplus of $107.2 million at December 31, 2008.

Required:

1. Compare and contrast defined benefit and defined contribution pension plans.

2. What change did Sears introduce to its employee retirement program? What is the main reason for this change? Explain.

3. Compute and interpret the financial leverage ratio for 2009.

4. Assume that the unfunded benefit obligation at December 31, 2009, was reported on Sears's statement of financial position as a non-current liability with an equal decrease in shareholders' equity, and the surplus funding at December 31, 2008, was reported as a non-current asset with an equal increase in shareholders' equity. Compute the financial leverage ratio by using the adjusted statement of financial position amounts. Do you think Sears's management would favour the reporting of the unfunded benefit obligation on the company's statement of financial position? Explain.

E11–21 **Reporting a Liability, with Discussion**

An annual report for ACE Aviation Holdings Inc. contained the following information:

ACE Aviation Holdings

9. PENSION AND OTHER BENEFIT LIABILITIES

Air Canada maintains several defined benefit and defined contribution plans providing pension, other retirement and post-employment benefits to its employees....

The other employee benefits consist of health, life, and disability [insurance]. These benefits consist of both post-employment and post-retirement benefits. The post-employment benefits relate to disability benefits available to eligible active employees, while the post-retirement benefits are comprised of health care and life insurance benefits available to eligible retired employees.

Required:

Should ACE Aviation report a liability for these benefits on its statement of financial position? Explain.

E11–22   **(Appendix 11A) Computing Value of an Asset Based on Present Value**
Quetario Company is considering purchasing a machine that would save the company $13,500 in cash per year for six years, at the end of which the machine would be retired with no residual value. The firm wishes to earn a minimum return of 12 percent, compounded annually, on any such investment. Assume that the cash savings occur at year-end, and ignore income taxes.

Required:

1. What is the maximum amount that the firm should be willing to pay for this machine? Show your computations.
2. Would the maximum amount be different if the machine is expected to have a residual value of $4,000 at the end of six years? Explain.
3. As an alternative to the scenario in (2), the company could buy a machine that had no residual value and offered no cost savings for the first five years, but this machine would offer cost savings of $113,561 at the end of the sixth year. If the company can buy only one machine, which one should it be? Defend your answer.

E11–23   **(Appendix 11A) Reporting a Mortgage Note**
On January 1, 2012, Wong Corporation signed a mortgage note for $5,000,000 at 8 percent for a term of 5 years. Mortgage payments are made semi-annually on June 30 and on December 31. Each mortgage payment is a blend of interest on the unpaid amount and a partial repayment of the principal loan.

Required:

1. Compute the amount of each mortgage payment.
2. Record the mortgage payments on June 30, 2012, and December 31, 2012.
3. What is the current portion of the mortgage at December 31, 2012? What portion of the mortgage would appear as long-term debt on the statement of financial position at that same date?

LO1, 2

E11–24   **(Appendix 11C) Computing the Issue Price of a Bond, with Discussion**
Charger Corporation issued a $250,000 bond that matures in five years. The bond has a stated interest rate of 8 percent and pays interest on February 1, May 1, August 1, and November 1. When the bond was issued, the market rate of interest was 12 percent. Record the issuance of the bond on February 1. Also record the payment of interest on May 1 and August 1. Use the straight-line method for amortization of any discount or premium. Explain why someone would buy a bond that did not pay the market rate of interest.

LO2   **E11–25**   **(Appendix 11C) Recording Bond Issue and First Interest Payment with Discount (Straight-Line Amortization)**
On January 1, 2012, Seton Corporation sold a $10,000,000, 5.5 percent bond issue. The bonds were dated January 1, 2012, had a yield of 6 percent, pay interest each December 31, and mature 10 years from January 1, 2012.

Required:

1. Prepare the journal entry to record the issuance of the bonds.
2. Prepare the journal entry to record the interest payment on December 31, 2012. Use straight-line amortization.
3. Show how the bond interest expense and the bonds payable should be reported on the financial statements for 2012.

LO2   **E11–26**   **(Appendix 11C) Recording Bond Issue: Entries for Issuance and Interest**
Northland Corporation had $400,000, 10-year bonds outstanding on December 31, 2011 (end of the fiscal year). Interest is payable each December 31. The bonds were issued (sold) on January 1, 2011. The 2011 annual financial statements showed the following:

Income statement	
Bond interest expense (straight-line amortization)	$ 33,200
Statement of financial position	
Bonds payable (net liability)	389,200

Required (show computations):

1. What was the issue price of the bonds? Prepare the journal entry to record the issuance of the bonds on January 1, 2011.

2. What was the coupon rate on the bonds? Prepare the entry to record interest expense for 2011.

E11–27 **(Appendix 11C) Determining Financial Statement Effects of Long-Term Debt and Related Interest** **LO2, 3, 6**

Chamandy Corporation issued a $25,000,000, 7 percent note on July 1, 2011, at a market rate of 6 percent. The note was dated July 1, 2011, with interest to be paid each June 30. The note matures in 10 years. The company's fiscal year ends on December 31.

Required:

1. How are the financial statements affected by the issuance of the note? Describe the impact on the financial leverage and the times interest earned ratios, if any.

2. How are the financial statements affected by the payment of interest on June 30, 2012? Describe the impact on the financial leverage and the times interest earned ratios, if any.

3. Show how the interest expense and the note payable should be reported on the December 31, 2012, annual financial statements. Use the straight-line method to amortize any discount or premium.

PROBLEMS

P11–1 **Recording Issuance of Note and Computation of Interest** (AP11–1) **LO1, 2**

Rogers Communications Inc. is a diversified Canadian communications and media company engaged in wireless, cable, and media communications. On November 1, 2009, Rogers sold notes with the following specifications:

Principal amount:	$500 million
Maturity date:	November 1, 2019
Issue price:	99.931% of principal amount
Coupon rate:	5.38%
Interest payment dates:	May 1 and November 1

The underwriters (Scotia Capital Inc., RBC Dominion Securities Inc., BMO Nesbitt Burns Inc., TD Securities Inc., and CIBC World Markets Inc.), which sold these notes to investors, received an underwriting fee of $2,000,000 and remitted to the company the net proceeds of $497,655,000 from the sale of these notes. The effective interest rate on these notes is 5.389 percent.

Required:

1. Prepare a journal entry to record the sale of these notes on November 1, 2009.

2. Compute the interest expense that accrued from November 1, 2009, to December 31, 2009, the end of Rogers' fiscal year, and prepare the adjusting journal entry on December 31, 2009, to record interest expense and amortization of the discount on the notes. The company uses the effective interest method of amortization.

3. Prepare the journal entry to record the payment of interest and amortization of the discount on May 1, 2010.

4. Show the amounts that should be reported on Rogers' financial statements for the year 2009.

5. Compute the total amount of interest expense over the life of the notes.

6. After looking at the issue price, a student asked why Rogers did not simply sell the notes at 100 percent of the principal amount instead of selling them at a discount. How would you respond to this question?

P11–2 **Recording Bond Issuance and Interest Payment with Explanation of Bond Premium and Discussion of Management Strategy** (AP11–2) **LO2, 3, 6**

On March 1, 2011, Catalin Corporation issued $40 million in bonds that mature in 10 years. The bonds have a stated interest rate of 5.8 percent and pay interest on March 1 and September 1. When the bonds were sold, the market rate of interest was 6 percent. Catalin uses the effective interest method. By December 31, 2011, the market interest rate had increased to 6.5 percent.

Required:

1. Record the issuance of the bond on March 1, 2011.

2. Compute the present value of the difference between the interest paid each six months ($40 million × 5.8% × 6/12 = $1.16 million) and the interest demanded by the market ($40 million × 6% × 6/12 = $1.2 million). Use the market rate of interest and the 10-year life of the bond in your present value computation. What does this amount represent? Explain.

3. Record the payment of interest on September 1, 2011.

4. Record the adjusting entry for accrued interest on December 31, 2011.

5. Why does interest expense change each year when the effective interest method is used?

6. Compute the present value of the Catalin's bonds, assuming that they had a 7-year life instead of a 10-year life. Compare this amount to the carrying amount of the bond at March 1, 2014. What does this comparison demonstrate?

7. Determine the impact of these transactions at year-end on the financial leverage ratio and the times interest earned ratio.

P11–3   **Recording Bond Issuance and Interest Payments (Effective Interest Method)** (AP11–3)
Nordic Company issued bonds with the following provisions:

Maturity value: $60,000,000.
Interest: 7.9 percent per annum payable semi-annually each June 30 and December 31.
Terms: Bonds dated January 1, 2011, due five years from that date.

The company's fiscal year ends on December 31. The bonds were sold on January 1, 2011, at a yield of 8 percent.

Required:

1. Compute the issue (sale) price of the bonds (show computations).

2. Prepare the journal entry to record the issuance of the bonds.

3. Prepare the journal entries at the following dates: June 30, 2011; December 31, 2011; and June 30, 2012. Use the effective interest method to amortize bond discount or premium.

4. How much interest expense would be reported on the income statement for 2011? Show how the liability related to the bonds should be reported on the statement of financial position at December 31, 2011.

P11–4   **Completing an Amortization Schedule (Effective Interest Amortization)**
Berj Corporation issued bonds and received cash in full for the issue price. The bonds were dated and issued on January 1, 2010. The coupon rate was payable at the end of each year. The bonds mature at the end of four years. The following schedule has been partially completed (amounts in thousands):

Date	Cash Paid	Interest Expense	Amortization	Carrying Amount
January 1, 2010				$6,101
End of year 2010	$450	$427	$23	6,078
End of year 2011	450	?	?	6,053
End of year 2012	450	?	?	?
End of year 2013	450	?	?	6,000

Required:

1. Complete the amortization schedule.

2. What was the maturity amount of the bonds?

3. How much cash was received at the date of issuance (sale) of the bonds?

4. What was the amount of discount or premium on the bond?

5. How much cash will be disbursed for interest each period and in total for the full life of the bond issue?

6. What method of amortization is being used? Explain.

7. What is the coupon rate of interest?

8. What is the effective rate of interest?

9. What amount of interest expense should be reported on the income statement each year?

10. Show how the bonds should be reported on the statement of financial position at the end of each year (show the last year immediately before repayment of the bonds).

P11–5 Understanding the Early Retirement of Debt (AP11–4)

LO4

AMC Entertainment Inc. owns and operates movie theatres. The company sold 11 7/8 percent bonds for $52,750,000 and used the cash proceeds to retire bonds with a face value of $50,000,000 with a coupon rate of 13.6 percent. At that time, the old bonds had a carrying amount of $49,547,000.

Required:

1. Why did the company issue new bonds to retire the old bonds?

2. Prepare the journal entries to record the issuance of the new bonds and the early retirement of the old bonds.

3. How should AMC report the gain or loss on retirement of the old bonds?

P11–6 (Appendix 11A) Comparing Options by Using Present Value Concepts (AP11–5)

After hearing a knock at your front door, you are surprised to see the Prize Patrol from a large, well-known magazine subscription company. It has arrived with the good news that you are the big winner, having won $20 million. Later, after consulting with a lawyer, you discover that you have three options: (1) you can receive $1 million per year for the next 20 years (starting one year from now), (2) you can have $8 million today, or (3) you can have $2 million today and receive $700,000 for each of the next 20 years. Your investment adviser tells you that it is reasonable to expect to earn 10 percent compound interest on investments. Which option do you prefer? What factors influenced your decision?

P11–7 (Appendix 11A) Computing Equal Periodic Debt Payments and Completing a Schedule (AP11–6)

eXcel

On January 1, 2011, you bought a new Toyota automobile for $30,000. You made a $5,000 cash down payment and signed a $25,000 note, payable in four equal instalments on each December 31, the first payment to be made on December 31, 2011. The interest rate is 8 percent per year on the unpaid balance. Each payment will include payment on principal plus the interest.

Required:

1. Compute the amount of the equal payments that you must make.

2. What is the total amount of interest that you will pay during the four years?

3. Complete the following schedule:

		Debt Payment Schedule		
Date	Cash Payment	Interest Expense	Decrease in Principal	Unpaid Principal
1/1/2011				
12/31/2011				
12/31/2012				
12/31/2013				
12/31/2014				
Totals				

4. Explain why the amount of interest expense decreases each year.

5. To reduce the total amount of interest paid on this note, you considered the possibility of making equal payments every three months (four payments per year). Compute the amount of the equal payments that you must make, and the amount of interest that will be saved over the life of the note.

P11–8 (Appendix 11A) Computing Amounts for a Debt Fund with Journal Entries

eXcel

On December 31, 2010, Post Company decided to invest a sufficient amount of cash to pay the principal amount of a $160,000 debt due on December 31, 2013. The company will make four equal annual deposits on December 31 of the years 2010 through 2013. The fund will earn 7 percent compound annual interest, which will be added to the balance at each year-end. The fund trustee will pay the loan principal (to the creditor) upon receipt of the last fund deposit. The company's fiscal year ends on December 31. The four annual deposits have a present value of $122,064 on December 31, 2010.

Required (show computations and round to the nearest dollar):

1. How much cash must be deposited each December 31?

2. What amount of interest will be earned on the four deposits until December 31, 2013?

3. How much interest revenue will the fund earn each year?

4. Prepare journal entries for the company to record the following transactions:

     a. The first deposit on December 31, 2010.

     b. The deposit at December 31, 2011, and interest revenue for 2011.

     c. The payment of the debt on December 31, 2013.

5. Show how the effect of the fund will be reported on the income statement for 2011 and the statement of financial position at December 31, 2011.

LO1, 2

P11–9   **(Appendix 11C) Comparing Bonds Issued at Par, Discount, and Premium**

Sikes Corporation, whose fiscal year ends on December 31, issued the following bonds:

Date of bonds: January 1, 2012
Maturity amount and date: $10 million due in 10 years (December 31, 2021)
Interest: 10 percent per annum payable each December 31
Date of sale: January 1, 2012

Required:

1. Provide the following amounts to be reported on the 2012 financial statements (use straight-line amortization and show amounts in thousands):

	Issued at Par	at 96	at 102
	Case A	Case B	Case C
a. Interest expense	$	$	$
b. Bonds payable			
c. Unamortized premium or discount			
d. Carrying amount of bonds			
e. Stated rate of interest			
f. Cash paid for interest			

2. Explain why items (*a*) and (*f*) in (1) are different for cases B and C.

3. Assume that you are an investment adviser and a retired person has written to you asking, "Why should I buy a bond at a premium when I can find one at a discount? Isn't that stupid? It's like paying the list price for a car instead of negotiating a discount." Write a brief letter in response to the question.

LO2

e**X**cel

P11–10   **(Appendix 11C) Completing Schedule Comparing Bonds Issued at Par, Discount, and Premium** (AP11–7)

Quartz Corporation sold a $50 million, 7 percent bond issue on January 1, 2012. The bonds pay interest each December 31 and mature 10 years from January 1, 2012. For comparative study and analysis, assume three independent selling scenarios: Case A, bonds sold at par; Case B, bonds sold at 98; Case C, bonds sold at 102. Use straight-line amortization and disregard income tax unless specifically required.

Required:

1. Complete the following schedule to analyze the differences among the three cases.

	Case A (Par)	Case B (at 98)	Case C (at 102)
a. Cash inflow at the date of issue (sale).			
b. Total cash outflow through the maturity date.			
c. Net cash outflow = total interest expense over the life of the bonds.			
d. Total interest expense, net of income tax (25 percent).			
Income statement for 2012			
e. Bond interest expense.			
Statement of financial position at December 31, 2012, non-current liabilities			
f. Bonds payable, 7 percent.			
g. Unamortized discount.			
h. Unamortized premium.			
i. Net liability.			

2. For each case, explain why the amounts in items (*c*), (*d*), and (*e*) of (1) are the same or different.

P11–11 (Appendix 11C) Computing Amounts for Bond Issue and Comparing Amortization Methods (AP11–8) ▉ **LO2**

Dektronik Corporation manufactures electrical test equipment. The company's board of directors authorized a bond issue on January 1, 2010, with the following terms:

Maturity (par) value: $800,000
Interest: 7.5 percent per annum payable each December 31
Maturity date: December 31, 2014
Effective interest rate when sold: 8 percent

Required:

1. Compute the bond issue price. Explain why both the stated and effective interest rates are used in this computation.

2. Assume that the company used the straight-line method to amortize the discount or premium on the bond issue. Compute the following amounts for each year (2010–2014):

   a. Cash payment for bond interest.

   b. Amortization of bond discount or premium.

   c. Bond interest expense.

   d. Carrying amount of the bond.

   e. Interest expense as a percentage of carrying amount (item [*c*] ÷ item [*d*]).

   The straight-line method is theoretically deficient when interest expense is related to the carrying amount of the debt. Explain.

3. Assume instead that the company used the effective interest method to amortize the discount or premium. Prepare an effective interest bond amortization schedule similar to the one in the text (see p. 587). The effective interest method provides a constant interest rate when interest expense is related to the carrying amount (unpaid balance). Explain by referring to the bond amortization schedule.

4. Which method should the company use to amortize the bond discount or premium? As a financial analyst, would you prefer one method over the other? If so, why?

ALTERNATE PROBLEMS

LO1, 2   **AP11–1**   **Recording Issuance of Note and Computation of Interest** (P11–1)

Shaw Communications Inc. is a diversified Canadian communications company that provides cable television, Internet, digital phone, telecommunications, and satellite direct-to-home services to more than 3 million customers. On October 1, 2009, the company sold long-term notes with the following specifications:

Principal amount:	$1,250 million
Maturity date:	October 1, 2019
Issue price:	99.683% of principal amount
Coupon rate:	5.65%
Interest payment dates:	April 1 and October 1

The underwriters (TD Securities Inc., RBC Dominion Securities Inc., CIBC World Markets Inc., Scotia Capital Inc., and National Bank Financial Inc.) that sold these notes to investors received an underwriting fee of $5 million and remitted to the company the net proceeds of $1,241,037,500 from the sale of these notes. The effective interest rate on these notes is 5.692 percent.

Required:

1. Prepare the journal entries to record the sales of the notes on October 1, 2009.
2. Compute the interest expense that accrued from October 1, 2009, to December 31, 2009, the end of Shaw's fiscal year, and prepare the adjusting journal entries on December 31, 2009, to record interest expense and amortization of the discount on the notes. The company uses the effective interest method to amortize the discount.
3. Prepare the journal entry to record the payment of interest and amortization of the discount on April 1, 2010.
4. Show the amounts that should be reported on Shaw's financial statements for the year 2009.
5. Compute the total amount of interest expense over the life of the notes.
6. After looking at the issue price, a student asked why the management of Shaw Communications did not simply sell the notes at 100 percent of the principal amount instead of selling them at a discount. How would you respond to this question?

LO2   **AP11–2**   **Using the Effective Interest Method with Explanation of Bond Premium and Discussion of Management Strategy** (P11–2)

On March 1, 2012, Carter Corporation issued $15,000,000 in bonds that mature in 10 years. The bonds have a coupon rate of 6.3 percent and pay interest on March 1 and September 1. When the bonds were sold, the market rate of interest was 6 percent. Carter uses the effective interest method to amortize bond discount or premium. By December 31, 2012, the market interest rate of interest had increased to 7 percent.

Required:

1. Record the issuance of the bond on March 1, 2012.
2. Compute the present value of the difference between the interest paid each six months ($472,500) and the interest demanded by the market ($15 million × 6% × 6/12 = $450,000). Use the market rate of interest and the 10-year life of the bond in your present value computation. What does this amount represent? Explain.
3. Record the payment of interest on September 1, 2012.
4. Record the adjusting entry for accrued interest on December 31, 2012.
5. Why does interest expense change each year when the effective interest method is used?
6. Compute the present value of the Carter's bonds, assuming that they had a 7-year life instead of 10-year life. Compare this amount to the carrying amount of the bond at March 1, 2015. What does this comparison demonstrate?
7. Determine the impact of the transactions at year-end on the financial leverage ratio and the times interest earned ratio.

AP11–3 **Computing Issue Price of Bonds and Recording Issuance and Interest Payments** (P11–3)

LO2

eXcel

Jaymar Company issued bonds with the following provisions:

Maturity value: $100,000,000
Interest: 8.1 percent per annum payable semi-annually each June 30 and December 31
Terms: Bonds dated January 1, 2012, due 10 years from that date

The company's fiscal year ends on December 31. The bonds were sold on January 1, 2012, at a yield of 8 percent.

Required:

1. Compute the issue (sale) price of the bonds. Show computations.

2. Prepare the journal entry to record the issuance of the bonds.

3. Prepare the journal entries at the following dates: June 30, 2012; December 31, 2012; and June 30, 2013. Use the effective interest method to amortize bond discount or premium.

4. How much interest expense would be reported on the income statement for 2012? Show how the liability related to the bonds should be reported on the statement of financial position at December 31, 2012.

AP11–4 **Understanding the Difference between Carrying Amount and Market Value** (P11–5)

LO1, 4

Thomson Reuters is the world's leading source of electronic information and services to businesses and professionals in various fields such as the media, financial services, tax and accounting, and healthcare and science. The company's annual report for 2009 indicates that the carrying amount of long-term debt is $7,603 million, but its fair value is $8,153 million. The fair value of debt is estimated based on either quoted market prices for similar issues or current rates offered to the company for debt of the same maturity.

Required:

What is meant by "fair value"? Explain why there is a difference between the carrying amount and the fair value of the long-term debt for Thomson Reuters. Assume that Thomson Reuters decided to retire all of its long-term debt for cash (a very unlikely event). Prepare the journal entry to record the transaction.

AP11–5 **(Appendix 11A) Comparing Options by Using Present Value Concepts** (P11–6)

After completing a long and successful career as senior vice-president for a large bank, you are preparing for retirement. After visiting the human resources office, you have found that you have several retirement options: (1) you can receive an immediate cash payment of $600,000, (2) you can receive $60,000 per year for life (you have a life expectancy of 20 years), or (3) you can receive $50,000 per year for 10 years and then $70,000 per year for life (this option is intended to give you some protection against inflation). You have determined that you can earn 8 percent compounded annually on your investments. Which option do you prefer and why?

AP11–6 **(Appendix 11A) Computing Equal Periodic Debt Payments and Completing a Schedule with Journal Entries** (P11–7)

On January 1, 2011, Ontario Company sold a new machine to Canada Company for $70,000. Canada Company made a cash down payment of $20,000 and signed a $50,000, 8 percent note for the balance due. The note is payable in three equal instalments due on December 31, 2011, 2012, and 2013. Each payment includes principal plus interest on the unpaid balance. Canada Company recorded the purchase as follows:

Jan.1, 2011

Machinery	70,000	
Cash		20,000
Note payable		50,000

Required (show computations and round to the nearest dollar):

1. What is the amount of the equal annual payments that Canada Company must make?

2. What is the total interest on the note over the three years?

3. Complete the following debt payment schedule:

		Debt Payment Schedule		
Date	**Cash Payment**	**Interest Expense**	**Decrease in Principal**	**Unpaid Principal**
1/1/2011				
12/31/2011				
12/31/2012				
12/31/2013				
Total				

4. Prepare the journal entries for each of the three payments.

5. Explain why interest expense decreased in amount each year.

LO2, 7   **AP11–7**   **(Appendix 11C) Completing a Schedule That Involves a Comprehensive Review of the Issuance of Bonds at Par, Discount, and Premium, Including Cash Flows** (P11–10)

eXcel

On January 1, 2010, Ontec Corporation sold and issued $100 million, five-year, 10 percent bonds. The bond interest is payable annually each December 31. Assume three separate and independent selling scenarios: Case A, bonds sold at par; Case B, bonds sold at 90; and Case C, bonds sold at 110.

Required:

1. Complete a schedule similar to the following for each separate case, assuming straight-line amortization of discount and premium. Disregard income tax. Show all dollar amounts in millions.

						At End of 2014	
	At Start of 2010	**At End of 2010**	**At End of 2011**	**At End of 2012**	**At End of 2013**	**Prior to Payment of Principal**	**Payment of Principal**
Case A: sold at par (100)	$	$	$	$	$	$	$
Cash inflow							
Cash outflow							
Interest expense on income statement							
Carrying amount on statement of financial position							
Case B: sold at a discount (90)							
Cash inflow							
Cash outflow							
Interest expense on income statement							
Carrying amount on statement of financial position							
Case C: sold at a premium (110)							
Cash inflow							
Cash outflow							
Interest expense on income statement							
Carrying amount on statement of financial position							

2. For each separate case, calculate the following:
   a. Total cash outflow.
   b. Total cash inflow.
   c. Net cash outflow.
   d. Total interest expense over the life of the bonds.

3. a. Explain why the net cash outflows differ among the three cases.
   b. For each case, explain why the net cash outflow is the same as total interest expense.

AP11–8 (Appendix 11C) Straight-Line versus Effective Interest Methods of Amortizing Bond Discount, with Discussion (P11–11)

LO2

Canadian Products Corporation manufactures office equipment and supplies. The company authorized a bond issue on January 1, 2010, with the following terms:

Maturity (par) value: $120,000,000
Interest: 7.9 percent per annum payable each December 31
Maturity date: December 31, 2014
Effective interest rate when sold: 8 percent

Required:

1. Compute the bond issue price. Explain why both the stated and effective interest rates are used in this computation.

2. Prepare the entry to record this bond issue.

3. Assume that the company used the straight-line method to amortize the discount or premium on the bond issue. Compute the following amounts for each year (2010–2014):

   a. Interest paid.

   b. Amortization of bond discount or premium.

   c. Bond interest expense.

   d. Carrying amount of the bond.

   e. Interest expense as a percentage of the carrying amount (item [*c*] ÷ item [*d*]).

   The straight-line method is theoretically deficient when interest expense is related to the carrying amount of the debt. Explain.

4. Assume instead that the company used the effective interest method to amortize the discount or premium. Prepare an effective interest bond amortization schedule similar to the one in the text (see p. 589). The effective interest method provides a constant interest rate when interest expense is related to the net liability. Explain by referring to the bond amortization schedule.

5. Which method should the company use to amortize the bond discount or premium? As a financial analyst, would you prefer one method over the other? If so, why?

CASES AND PROJECTS

FINDING AND INTERPRETING FINANCIAL INFORMATION

CP11–1 Finding Financial Information

Refer to the financial statements of the Nestlé Group given in Appendix A of this book.

LO2, 7

The Nestlé Group

Required:

1. How much cash was paid for interest during year ended December 31, 2008?

2. Review the company's note on bonds and explain the rates and amounts reported for the first two issues of bonds denominated in Australian dollars.

3. Does the company report other non-current liabilities? If so, identify these liabilities.

CP11–2 Finding Financial Information

Go to Connect online for the financial statements of Cadbury plc.

LO2, 7

Cadbury, plc

Required:

1. How much cash was paid for interest during the year ended December 31, 2008?

2. Review the company's note on borrowings. Does the company provide details about its debt issues? If so, identify the characteristics of one of the debt issues.

3. Describe the company's established arrangements, if any, that permit it to borrow money if needed.

4. Does the company report other non-current liabilities? If so, identify these liabilities.

■ **LO1, 3, 6**   **CP11–3**   **Comparing Companies**

The Nestlé Group vs.
Cadbury plc

Go to Connect online for the financial statements of Cadbury plc and to Appendix A of this textbook for the financial statements of the Nestlé Group.

Required:

1. Examine the statements of cash flows for both companies. What are the primary sources of cash flows for both companies?

2. Two financial ratios (the financial leverage ratio and the times interest earned ratio) are discussed in this chapter. Compute these ratios for both companies for the most recent year. Are they relevant for these companies? Explain.

FINANCIAL REPORTING AND ANALYSIS CASES

■ **LO1**   **CP11–4**   **Analyzing Financial Leverage**

Cricket Corporation's financial statements for 2011 showed the following:

Income Statement	
Revenues	$300,000
Expenses	(198,000)
Interest expense	(2,000)
Pretax profit	100,000
Income tax (30%)	(30,000)
Profit	$ 70,000

Statement of Financial Position	
Assets	$300,000
Liabilities (average interest rate, 10%)	$ 20,000
Share capital	200,000
Retained earnings	80,000
	$300,000

Notice that the company had a debt of only $20,000 compared with share capital of $200,000. A consultant recommended the following: debt, $100,000 (at 10 percent) instead of $20,000 and share capital of $120,000 (12,000 shares) instead of $200,000 (20,000 shares). That is, the company should finance the business with more debt and less owner contribution.

Required (round to nearest percent):

1. You have been asked to develop a comparison between (a) the actual results and (b) the results based on the consultant's recommendation. To do this, you decided to develop the following schedule:

Item	Actual Results for 2011	Results with an $80,000 Increase in Debt and an $80,000 Decrease in Equity
a. Total debt		
b. Total assets		
c. Total shareholders' equity		
d. Interest expense		
e. Profit		
f. Return on total assets		
g. Earnings available to shareholders:		
(1) Amount		
(2) Per share		
(3) Return on shareholders' equity		

2. Based on the completed schedule in (1), provide a comparative analysis and interpretation of the actual results and the consultant's recommendation.

CP11–5 **Analyzing Zero Coupon Bonds from an Actual Company**

LO1

Shaw Communications Inc.

In July 2001, Shaw Communications issued a convertible zero coupon debt and raised $790 million. The debt is called a *liquid yield option note* or *LYON*. The LYONs were issued at $639.23 per $1,000 and the maturity date is May 1, 2021. The yield to maturity is 2.25 percent over 20 years. The LYONs are both redeemable after May 1, 2007, and convertible by the holders at any time into 8.82988 common shares per LYON. When this debt was issued, the yield ranged between 6 and 7 percent. A magazine article has noted, "It's easy to see why corporations like to issue debt that does not pay interest. But why would anybody want to buy that kind of paper?"

Required:
Explain why an investor would buy a LYON with a zero interest rate.

CP11–6 **International Financing**

LO1

Access the website of Bombardier Inc. at **www.bombardier.ca** and retrieve the most recent annual report. The note related to long-term debt discloses that Bombardier has borrowed money in a currency other than the Canadian dollar. Write a brief memo explaining why the company borrowed money in a foreign currency.

CRITICAL THINKING CASES

CP11–7 **Making a Decision as a Financial Analyst**

LO1

You are working for a large mutual fund company as a financial analyst. You have been asked to review two competitive companies in the same industry. Both have similar cash flows and profit, but one has no debt in its capital structure while the other has a financial leverage ratio of 3.2. Based on this limited information, which company would you prefer? Justify your conclusion. Would your preference be influenced by the companies' industry?

CP11–8 **Evaluating an Ethical Dilemma**

LO1

You work for a small company considering investing in a new Internet business. Financial projections suggest that the company will be able to earn in excess of $40 million per year on an investment of $100 million. The company president suggests borrowing the money by issuing bonds that will carry a 7 percent interest rate. He says, "This is better than printing money! We won't have to invest a penny of our own money, and we get to keep $33 million per year after we pay interest to the bondholders." As you think about the proposed transaction, you feel a little uncomfortable about taking advantage of the creditors in this fashion. You feel that it must be wrong to earn such a high return by using money that belongs to other people. Is this an ethical business transaction?

CP11–9 **Evaluating an Ethical Dilemma**

LO1

Many retired people invest a significant portion of their money in bonds of corporations because of the relatively low level of risk. During the 1980s, significant inflation caused some interest rates to rise to as high as 15 percent. Retired people who bought bonds that paid only 6 percent continued to earn at the lower rate. During the 1990s, inflation subsided and interest rates declined. Many corporations took advantage of call options on bonds and refinanced high interest rate debt with low interest rate debt. In your judgment, is it ethical for corporations to continue paying low interest rates when rates increase but to call bonds when rates decrease?

CP11–10 **Evaluating an Ethical Dilemma**

LO1

Assume that you are a portfolio manager for a large insurance company. The majority of the money you manage is from retired school teachers who depend on the income you earn on their investments. You have invested a significant amount of money in the bonds of a large corporation and have just received a call from the company's president explaining that it is unable to meet its current interest obligations because of deteriorating business operations related to increased international competition. The president has a recovery plan that will take at least two years. During that time, the company will not be able to pay interest on the bonds and, she admits, if the plan does not work, bondholders will probably lose more than half of their money. As a creditor, you can force the company into immediate bankruptcy and probably get back at least 90 percent of the bondholders' money. You also know that your decision will cause at least 10,000 people to lose their jobs if the company ceases operations. Given only these two options, what should you do?

■ **LO1**

Suncor Energy Inc.

CP11–11   **(Appendix 11A) Computing the Present Value of Lease Obligations**

The 2009 annual report for Suncor Energy Inc. indicated that the company has made the following commitments in relation to its operating leases during the next five years:

Years	Minimum Payments (in millions of dollars)
2010	376
2011	212
2012	160
2013	114
2014	101

You are a lending officer for a large commercial bank and for comparative purposes want to compute the present values of these leases.

Required:
Determine the present value of the lease payments shown as of December 31, 2010. You may assume an interest rate of 4 percent.

CP11–12   **(Appendix 11A) Evaluating an Ethical Dilemma: Fair Advertising**

The New York State Lottery Commission ran the following advertisement in a number of New York newspapers:

> The Lotto jackpot for Wednesday, August 25, will be $3 million, including interest earned over a 20-year payment period. Constant payments will be made each year.

Explain the meaning of this advertisement in your own words. Evaluate the "fairness" of this advertisement. Could anyone be misled? Do you agree that the lottery winner has won $3 million? If not, what amount is more accurate? State any assumptions that you make.

FINANCIAL REPORTING AND ANALYSIS TEAM PROJECT

LO1,2,3,6,7 CP11–13   **Team Project: Examining an Annual Report**

As a team, select an industry to analyze. A list of companies classified by industry can be obtained by accessing www.fpinfomart.ca and then choosing "Companies by Industry." You can also find a list of industries and companies within each industry via http://ca.finance.yahoo.com/investing (click on "Annual Reports" under "Tools"). Using a Web browser, each group member should acquire the annual report for one publicly traded company in the industry, with each member selecting a different company.

Required:
On an individual basis, each team member should then write a short report answering the following questions about the selected company. Discuss any patterns across the companies that you, as a team, observe. Then, as a group, write a short report comparing and contrasting your companies.

1. Has your company issued any long-term bonds or notes? If so, read the related note and list any unusual features (e.g., callable, convertible, secured by specific collateral).

2. If your company issued any bonds, were they issued at either a premium or a discount? If so, does the company use the straight-line or effective interest amortization method?

3. Ratio analysis:

   a. What does the times interest earned ratio measure, in general?

   b. Compute the ratio for the last three years.

   c. What do your results suggest about the company?

   d. If available, find the industry ratio for the most recent year, compare it with your results, and discuss why you believe your company differs from or is similar to the industry ratio.

4. Ratio analysis:

   a. What does the financial leverage ratio measure, in general?

   b. Compute the ratio for the last three years.

   c. What do your results suggest about the company?

   d. If available, find the industry ratio for the most recent year, compare it with your results, and discuss why you believe your company differs or is similar to the industry ratio.

5. During the recent year, how much cash did the company receive on issuing debt? How much did it pay on debt principal? What does management suggest were the reasons for issuing and/or repaying debt during the year?

Reporting and Interpreting Owners' Equity

After studying this chapter, you should be able to do the following:

FOCUS COMPANY: **BCE Inc.**

FINANCING CORPORATE GROWTH WITH CAPITAL SUPPLIED BY OWNERS

Bell Canada Enterprises Inc. (BCE) (www.bce.ca) is Canada's largest communications company. It provides voice, data, and image communications services to millions of global customers. BCE has achieved its current size and profitability through investments in and acquisitions of companies such as CTV and The Globe and Mail. But the business has changed rapidly in the last five years, and economic conditions have been extremely difficult. The company's focus has shifted to improving its mobile communications network. BCE now boasts the fastest and most comprehensive network in Canada, with roaming service to more than 200 other countries. Its recent acquisitions include full ownership of Virgin Mobile Canada, a minority investment in the Montréal Canadiens Hockey Club, and The Source with its 750 retail outlets.

In order to continue to thrive and grow, BCE has announced its intention of improving household service, investing in the most reliable and highest speed communications technology, and improving cost efficiency. The company closely manages its statement of financial position and, in particular, its capital structure—that is, the proportion of debt and equity used to finance its growth. BCE wants to ensure a strong credit profile in order to encourage both new investment and increase the dividends paid to its shareholders.

In Chapters 10 and 11, we discussed the role of liabilities in the capital structure of a company. In this chapter, we study both the role that shareholders' equity plays in building a successful business and strategies that managers use to maximize shareholders' wealth.

UNDERSTANDING THE BUSINESS

To some people, the words *corporation* and *business* are almost synonymous. You have probably heard friends refer to a career in business as "the corporate world." Equating business and corporations is understandable, because corporations are the dominant form of business organization in terms of volume of operations. If you were to write the names of 50 familiar companies on a piece of paper, probably all of them would be corporations.

The popularity of the corporate form can be attributed to a critical advantage that corporations have over sole proprietorships and partnerships. They can raise large amounts of capital because both large and small investors can easily participate in their ownership. This ease of participation is related to three important factors:

- Shares can be purchased in small amounts. You could buy a single share of BCE for approximately $34 and become one of the owners of this company.

- Ownership interest can easily be transferred through the sale of shares on established markets, such as the Toronto Stock Exchange.

- Stock ownership provides investors with limited liability.[1]

Many Canadians own shares, either directly or indirectly through a mutual fund or pension program. Share ownership offers them the opportunity to earn higher returns than they otherwise could on deposits to bank accounts or investments in corporate bonds. Unfortunately, share ownership also involves higher risk of loss of the investment in shares. The proper balance between risk and the expected return on an investment depends on individual preferences.

BCE's statement of financial position at December 31, 2009, reports total equity of $16,974 million, as indicated in Exhibit 12.1. For most corporations, shareholders' equity includes two primary sources:

1. *Contributed capital*, which reflects the amount invested by shareholders. Contributed capital has two distinct components: (a) amounts initially received from the sale of shares and (b) contributed surplus that reflects contributions made by shareholders in excess of the amounts credited to share capital accounts. The contributed capital accounts for BCE are preferred shares, common shares, and contributed surplus.

2. *Retained earnings* generated by the profit-making activities of the company. This is the *cumulative* amount of profit earned since the corporation's organization, less the cumulative amount of dividends paid by the corporation since organization.[2]

Most companies generate a significant portion of their shareholders' equity from retained earnings rather than from capital raised through the sale of shares. In the case of BCE, Exhibit 12.1 shows a negative amount, a deficit, which suggests that BCE has not been a profitable company. We will address this interesting issue as well as other details in Exhibit 12.1 later in this chapter.

SELECTED FOCUS COMPANY COMPARISONS: RETAINED EARNINGS AS A PERCENTAGE OF SHAREHOLDERS' EQUITY	
WestJet Airlines	99.3%
Home Depot	68.2%
Andrew Peller	92.4%

[1] If a corporation becomes insolvent, creditors have recourse for their claims only to the corporation's assets. Thus, shareholders stand to lose only their equity in the corporation. In the case of a partnership or sole proprietorship, creditors have recourse to the owners' personal assets if the assets of the business are insufficient to meet its debts.

[2] Publicly accountable enterprises are required to report a third component of equity called *accumulated other comprehensive income (loss)*. We discuss this component briefly later in this chapter.

Exhibit **12.1**

Shareholders' Equity Sections of Consolidated Statements of Financial Position and Related Notes

REAL WORLD EXCERPT

BCE Inc.

ANNUAL REPORT

CONSOLIDATED STATEMENTS OF FINANCIAL POSITION
SHAREHOLDERS' EQUITY
At December 31

(in millions of Canadian dollars)	2009	2008
Preferred shares	2,770	2,770
Common shareholders' equity		
Common shares	12,921	13,525
Treasury stock	—	(86)
Contributed surplus	2,490	2,531
Retained earnings (deficit)	(1,299)	(1,468)
Accumulated other comprehensive income (loss), net of taxes	92	39
Total common shareholders' equity	14,204	14,541
Total shareholders' equity	16,974	17,311

	2009	2008
Preferred shares		
Balance, beginning of year	2,770	2,770
Balance, end of year	2,770	2,770
Common shares		
Balance, beginning of year	13,525	13,536
Shares issued under employee stock option plan	2	56
Shares repurchased and cancelled	(606)	(67)
Balance, end of year	**12,921**	**13,525**
Contributed Surplus		
Balance, beginning of year	2,531	2,537
Repurchase of common shares	(44)	(5)
Other	3	(1)
Balance, end of year	**2,490**	**2,531**
Deficit		
Balance, beginning of year	(1,468)	(1,679)
Profit	1,738	943
Dividends declared on preferred shares	(107)	(124)
Dividends declared on common shares	(1,218)	(588)
Excess of purchase price over stated capital of cancelled common shares and related contributed surplus	(244)	(20)
Balance, end of year	**(1,299)**	**(1,468)**
Accumulated other comprehensive income (loss), net of taxes		
Balance, beginning of year	39	68
Other comprehensive income (loss)	53	(29)
Balance, end of year	**92**	**39**
Accumulated other comprehensive income (loss), net of taxes		
Balance, end of year, consists of:		
Unrealized gains (losses) on available-for-sale assets	123	41
Unrealized gains (losses) on derivatives designated as cash flow hedges	(29)	—
Unrealized foreign currency translation gains (losses)	(2)	(2)
Balance, end of year	**92**	**39**

This excerpt is adapted from the company's actual financial statements and related notes.

ORGANIZATION OF THE CHAPTER

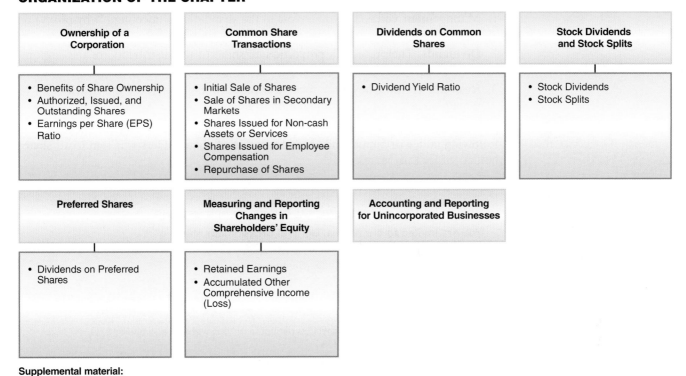

Supplemental material:

Appendix 12A: Accounting for Owners' Equity for Sole Proprietorships and Partnerships

OWNERSHIP OF A CORPORATION

The corporation is the only business form that the law recognizes as a separate entity. As a distinct entity, the corporation enjoys a continuous existence, separate and apart from its owners. It may own assets, incur liabilities, expand and contract in size, sue others, be sued, and enter into contracts independently of the shareholders.

To protect everyone's rights, both the creation and governance of corporations are tightly regulated by law. Corporations are created by making application to the federal government or a specific provincial government. The *Canada Business Corporations Act* (*CBCA*) outlines all of the legal requirements of federal incorporation (**www.laws. justice.gc.ca**).

To create a corporation, an application for a charter must be submitted to the appropriate government authorities. The application must specify the name of the corporation, the purpose (type of business), the types and number of shares authorized, and a minimum amount of capital that the owners must invest at the date of organization. Upon approval of the application, the government issues a charter, sometimes called the *articles of incorporation*. Each corporation is governed by a board of directors elected by the shareholders.

Benefits of Share Ownership

When you invest in a corporation, you are known as a *shareholder* or *stockholder*. As a shareholder, you receive shares that you can subsequently sell on established stock exchanges without affecting the corporation.

LO1

Explain the role of share capital in the capital structure of a corporation.

Owners of common shares receive the following benefits:

1. **Management voice.** They may vote at the shareholders' meeting (or by proxy) on major issues concerning management of the corporation.[3]

2. **Dividends.** They receive a proportionate share of the distribution of the corporation's profits.

3. **Residual claim.** They may receive a proportionate share of the distribution of remaining assets upon the liquidation of the company.

Owners, unlike creditors, are able to vote at the annual shareholders' meeting. The following notice of annual and special meeting of shareholders was sent to all shareholders of BCE in March 2010.

NOTICE OF 2010 ANNUAL GENERAL SHAREHOLDER MEETING

You are invited to our Annual General Shareholder Meeting

When
Thursday, May 6, 2010, 9:30 a.m. (Eastern time)

Where
Palais des Congrès, 1001 Place Jean-Paul-Riopelle, Montréal, Québec, in room 511

Webcast
A live webcast of the meeting will be available on our website at www.bce.ca.

What the meeting is about
We will be covering four items at the meeting:

1. receiving the financial statements for the year ended December 31, 2009, including the auditors' report
2. electing directors who will serve until the end of the next annual shareholder meeting
3. appointing the auditors who will serve until the end of the next annual shareholder meeting
4. considering an advisory (non-binding) resolution on executive compensation

The meeting may also consider other business that properly comes before it.

You have the right to vote
You are entitled to receive notice of and vote at our annual general shareholder meeting, or any adjournment, if you are a holder of common shares of the Corporation on March 19, 2010.

You have the right to vote your shares on items 2 to 4 listed above and any other items that may properly come before the meeting or any adjournment.

Your vote is important
As a shareholder, it is very important that you read this material carefully and then vote your shares, either by proxy or in person at the meeting.

The following pages tell you more about how to exercise your right to vote your shares.

Admission to meeting
You will need an admission ticket to enter the meeting. Your ticket is provided with your form of proxy.

By order of the Board,
(s) Alain F. Dussault
Corporate Secretary

Montréal, Québec
March 11, 2010

Source: Notice of 2010 Annual General Shareholder Meeting and Management Proxy Circular.

---

[3]A voting proxy is written authority given by a shareholder that gives another party the right to vote the shareholder's shares in the annual meeting of the shareholders. Typically, proxies are solicited by, and given to, the president of the corporation.

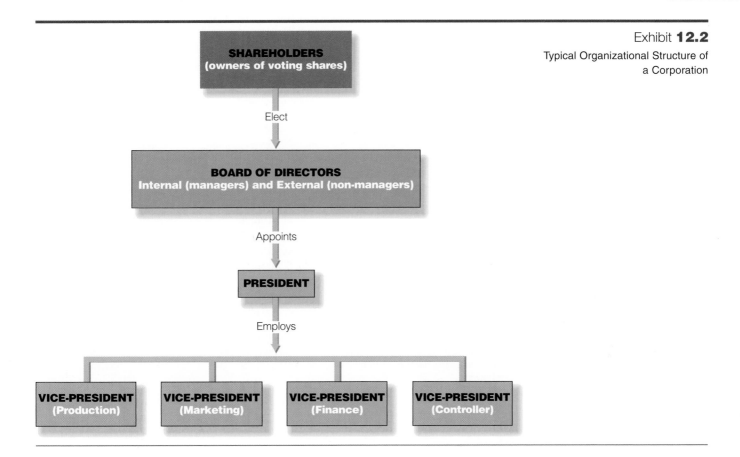

Exhibit **12.2**

Typical Organizational Structure of
a Corporation

The notice of the annual meeting was accompanied by a *management information (or proxy) circular* that contained several pages of information concerning the people who were nominated to be members of the board of directors. Since most owners do not actually attend the annual meeting, the notice included a proxy card, which is similar to an absentee ballot. Each owner may complete the proxy and mail it to the company, which will include it in the votes at the annual meeting.

Shareholders have ultimate authority in a corporation, as shown in Exhibit 12.2. The board of directors and, indirectly, all the employees are accountable to the shareholders. The organizational structure shown in Exhibit 12.2 is typical of most corporations, but the specific structure depends on the nature of the company's business.

Authorized, Issued, and Outstanding Shares

When a corporation is created, its corporate charter specifies the type and maximum number of shares that it can sell to the public. This maximum is called the authorized number of shares. Typically, the corporate charter authorizes a larger number of shares than the corporation expects to issue initially. This strategy provides future flexibility for the issuance of additional shares without the need to amend the charter. In the case of BCE, the number of authorized common shares is unlimited.

The number of issued shares and the number of outstanding shares are determined by the corporation's equity transactions. For BCE, the numbers of issued shares and outstanding shares are the same; at December 31, 2009, this number was 767.2 million. The number of issued shares may differ from the number of outstanding shares if the company has bought back some of its shares from shareholders. If a corporation needs to sell more shares than its charter authorizes, it must seek permission from the current shareholders to modify the charter.

Exhibit 12.3 defines and illustrates the terms usually used in relation to corporate shares.

The **AUTHORIZED NUMBER OF SHARES** is the maximum number of shares that a corporation can issue, as specified in the charter.

The term **ISSUED SHARES** refers to the number of shares that have been issued.

The term **OUTSTANDING SHARES** refers to the total number of shares that are owned by shareholders on any particular date.

Exhibit **12.3**

Authorized, Issued, and Outstanding Shares

Definitions	Illustrations	
Authorized number of shares: The maximum number of shares that can be issued, as specified in the charter of the corporation.	The charter specifies "an unlimited number of common shares."	
Issued number of shares: The total number of shares that the corporation has issued to date.	To date, XYZ Corporation has sold and issued 30,000 common shares.	
Unissued number of shares: The number of authorized shares that have never been issued to date.	Authorized shares	100,000
	Issued shares	30,000
	Unissued shares	70,000
Treasury shares:* Shares that have been issued to investors and then reacquired by the issuing corporation.	To date, XYZ Corporation has repurchased 1,000 previously issued shares.	
Outstanding number of shares: The number of shares currently owned by shareholders—that is, the number of shares authorized, minus the total number of unissued shares, and minus the number of treasury shares.	Authorized shares	100,000
	Treasury shares	(1,000)
	Unissued shares	(70,000)
	Outstanding shares	29,000

*Notice that when treasury shares are held, the number of shares issued and the number outstanding differ by the number of treasury shares held (treasury shares are included in "issued" but not in "outstanding").

KEY RATIO ANALYSIS

EARNINGS PER SHARE RATIO

LO²

Analyze the earnings per share ratio.

ANALYTICAL QUESTION → How profitable is a company?

RATIO AND COMPARISONS → The *earnings per share* is a measure of the return on investment that is based on the number of shares outstanding instead of the dollar amounts reported on the statement of financial position. In simple situations, it is computed as follows:

$$\text{Earnings per Share} = \frac{\text{Profit Available to Common Shareholders}}{\text{Average Number of Common Shares Outstanding}}$$

The 2009 ratio for BCE is

$$\$1,631 \div 772.9 = \$2.11$$

Comparisons over Time			Comparisons with Competitors	
BCE			Rogers Communications	TELUS
2007	2008	2009	2009	2009
$4.88	$1.02	$2.11	$2.38	$3.14

INTERPRETATIONS

In General → All analysts and investors are interested in a company's earnings. You have probably seen newspaper headlines announcing a company's earnings. Notice that those news stories normally report earnings on a per share (EPS) basis. The reason is simple. Numbers are much easier to compare on a per share basis. For example, in 2009, BCE earned profit of $1,738 million compared to $3,959 million in 2007. If we make that comparison on a per share basis, EPS decreased from $4.88 to $2.11, a decrease of 56.8 percent that takes into consideration the change in the number of common shares outstanding during the two-year period.

Focus Company Analysis → BCE's EPS had increased from $2.04 in 2005 to $4.88 in 2007, and then decreased significantly to $1.02 in 2008 because of the financial crisis that affected the global economy. It has subsequently increased in 2009 to $2.11. BCE's EPS is lower that the EPS figures of its competitors. However, comparison of the EPS figures for the three companies may not be very informative as a measure of profitability of shareholders' investments in these companies. The reason is simple: shares of different companies are likely to have different prices, which makes EPS comparisons less meaningful than other measures of profitability.

A Few Cautions → While EPS is an effective and widely used measure of profitability, it can be misleading if there are significant differences in the market values of the shares being compared. Two companies earning $1.50 per share might appear to be comparable, but if shares in one company cost $10 while shares of the other cost $175, they are not comparable. Obviously, investors expect a large EPS number for companies with higher stock prices.

COMMON SHARE TRANSACTIONS

Corporations issue two types of shares: common shares and preferred shares. All corporations issue common shares, while only some issue preferred shares, which grant preferences that the common shares do not have. In this section, we discuss common shares, and in a subsequent section we discuss preferred shares.

Common shares are the basic voting shares issued by a corporation. They are often called the *residual equity* because they rank after the preferred shares for dividend and asset distribution upon liquidation of the corporation. The dividend rate for common shares is determined by the board of directors based on the company's profitability, unlike the dividend rate on preferred shares that is determined by contract. When the company is not profitable, the board may cut or eliminate dividends on common shares, but in most cases it cannot reduce preferred dividends.

No Par Value and Par Value Shares

Par value is the nominal value per share established in the charter of a corporation. It has no relationship to the market value per share. The *Canada Business Corporations Act* (*CBCA*) and most provincial corporation acts prohibit the issuance of par value shares. The few Canadian companies that still have par value shares outstanding issued them before the *CBCA* was amended in 1985. For this reason, the remainder of this chapter focuses on no par value shares, which do not have an amount per share specified in the corporate charter. In contrast, most U.S. corporations issue par value shares.

The original purpose of requiring corporations to specify a par value per share was to establish a minimum permanent amount of capital that the owners could not withdraw as long as the corporation existed. Thus, owners could not withdraw all of their capital in anticipation of a bankruptcy, which would leave creditors with an empty corporate shell. This permanent amount of capital is called legal capital. The requirement that shares not be issued for less than their par value often resulted in par values that were too small to be effectively meaningful. This notion of legal capital has lost its significance over time because the par values of shares have been set at very low amounts by issuing corporations. In contrast, when a corporation issues no par value shares, the legal capital is the initial amount received from shareholders.

BCE's corporate charter authorizes the issue of no par value common shares. However, its preferred shares have a stated value upon which the dividend payments are based. This stated value has no relationship to the market value of the preferred shares.

LO3

Describe the characteristics of common shares and analyze transactions affecting common shares.

COMMON SHARES are the basic voting shares issued by a corporation; called *residual equity* because they rank after preferred shares for dividend and liquidation distributions.

PAR VALUE is the nominal value per share specified in the charter; it serves as the basis for legal capital.

NO PAR VALUE SHARES are shares that have no par value specified in the corporate charter.

LEGAL CAPITAL is the permanent amount of capital, defined by law, that must remain invested in the business; it serves as a cushion for creditors.

Initial Sale of Shares

Two names are applied to transactions involving the initial sale of a company's shares to the public. An *initial public offering*, or *IPO*, involves the very first sale of a company's shares to the public (i.e., when the company first "goes public"). You have probably heard stories of Internet companies that had their shares increase dramatically in value on the day of their IPO. While investors sometimes earn significant returns on IPOs, they also take significant risks. Once the shares of a company are traded on established markets, additional sales of new shares to the public are called *seasoned new issues* or *secondary share offerings*.

As was the case with debt (discussed in Chapter 11), most companies use an underwriter to assist in the sale of shares. The underwriter is usually an investment bank that acts as an intermediary between the corporation and the investors. The underwriter advises the corporation on matters concerning the sale and is directly involved in the sale of shares to the public.

Most sales of shares to the public are cash transactions. To illustrate accounting for an initial sale of shares, assume that BCE sold 100,000 common shares for $22 per share. The company records the following journal entry:

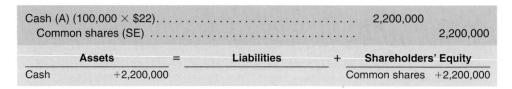

| Cash (A) (100,000 × $22) | 2,200,000 | |
| Common shares (SE) | | 2,200,000 |

Assets		=	Liabilities	+	Shareholders' Equity	
Cash	+2,200,000				Common shares	+2,200,000

In 2009, BCE issued new shares for $2 million as shown in Exhibit 12.1. These shares were issued on exercise of stock options as explained on page 647.

Sale of Shares in Secondary Markets

When a company sells shares to the public, the transaction is between the issuing corporation and the buyer. Subsequent to the initial sale, investors can sell shares to other investors without directly affecting the corporation. For example, if investor Jon Drago sold 1,000 of BCE's common shares to Jennifer Lea, BCE does not record a journal entry on its books. Mr. Drago received cash for the shares he sold, and Ms. Lea received shares for the cash she paid. BCE itself did not receive or pay anything because of this transaction.

Each business day, the financial information service providers, such as bloomberg. com, reuters.com, finance.yahoo.com, and moneycentral.msn.com report the results of thousands of transactions between investors in the secondary markets, where trading of shares takes place. These markets include the Toronto Stock Exchange (TSX) and TSX Venture Exchange (in Canada), New York Stock Exchange, American Stock Exchange, and NASDAQ (in the United States), as well as similar markets in other countries.

Managers of corporations follow very closely the movements in the price of their company's shares. Shareholders expect to earn money on their investment from both dividends and increases in the share (or stock) price. In many instances, senior management has been replaced because of poor performance of the shares in the secondary markets. Although managers watch the share price on a daily basis, it is important to remember that the transactions between investors do not directly affect the company's financial statements.

GOING PUBLIC

As noted earlier, an initial public offering (IPO) is the first sale of shares to the public. Prior to that sale, the company is a private company. A company might want to go public for two common reasons. For it to grow and meet consumer demand, it must expand its productive capacity. The need for new capital may be beyond the capability of the private owners. By going public, the company can raise the funds needed to expand.

In some cases, the company may not need significant funds, but the current owners may want to create a market for its shares. Often, selling shares is difficult if the company is not listed on a major stock exchange. By going public, a company can increase the marketability of its shares.

Initial public offerings often create a lot of interest among investors. Some good opportunities are available to earn excellent returns by investing in growing companies. Substantial risk also is associated with many IPOs.

In recent years, much interest has surrounded Internet companies that have gone public. Virtually any company with ".com" in its name has received significant attention from investors. For example, Google Inc., which operates one of the most popular search engines, had an IPO of its shares at an initial price of $85. Since the IPO in August 2004, Google's share price increased significantly, reaching $573 by April 2009 because of investors' expectations of the company's future profitability.

There are countless stories of people in their twenties and thirties who have become instant millionaires after the IPO of a new Internet company. Less well publicized, however, are the stories of individuals who have lost money investing in shares of new and unproven businesses.

Shares Issued for Non-cash Assets or Services

Small companies are playing an increasingly important role in the North American economy. Often they are private enterprises that account for a large percentage of the new jobs that have been created in the past decade. Many of today's corporate giants were small start-up companies just a few years ago. Companies such as Dell, Microsoft, Amazon.com, and Google Inc. began, literally, as basement operations in the homes of their founders.

One feature common to all start-up companies is a shortage of cash. Because these companies often cannot afford to pay cash for needed assets and services, they sometimes issue shares to people who can supply these assets and services. Many executives, for instance, will join start-up companies for very low salaries because they also earn compensation in the form of common shares. An executive who was granted Google shares during its early days would be very wealthy today.

When a company issues shares to acquire assets or services, the acquired items are recorded at the *market value* of the shares issued at the date of the transaction in accordance with the *cost principle*. If the market value of the shares issued cannot be determined, the market value of the consideration received should be used.

To illustrate, assume that during its early years of operation, BCE was unable to pay cash for needed legal services. The company issued 10,000 shares to a law firm when a share was selling for $15. At that time, the company recorded the following journal entry:

Legal fees (E)	150,000	
Common shares (SE)		150,000

Assets	=	Liabilities	+	Shareholders' Equity	
				Legal fees	−150,000
				Common shares	+150,000

Notice that the value of the legal services received is assumed to be the same as the value of the shares that were issued. This assumption is reasonable because two independent parties usually keep negotiating a deal until the value of what is given up equals the value of what is received.

Shares Issued for Employee Compensation

One of the advantages of the corporate form is the possibility to separate the management of a business from its ownership. This separation can also be a disadvantage because some managers may not act in the best interests of shareholders. This problem can be overcome in a number of ways. Compensation packages can be developed to reward managers for meeting goals that are important to shareholders. Another strategy is to offer managers *stock options*, which permit them to buy shares at a fixed price.

The holder of a stock option has an interest in a company's performance in the same manner as a shareholder. Stock option plans have become an increasingly common form of compensation over the past years. However, the excessive use of stock options as a form of compensating key executives led the executives of some companies to manipulate reported financial information in an effort to increase the share price, allowing them to benefit by buying shares at a fixed price and selling them at a higher price for a profit.

The BCE annual report provides the following disclosures with respect to its future contractual obligations related to stock options:

REAL WORLD EXCERPT

BCE Inc.

ANNUAL REPORT

NOTES TO CONSOLIDATED FINANCIAL STATEMENTS

Note 21. Stock-based compensation plans

The following table provides additional information about BCE Inc.'s stock option plans at December 31, 2009.

Range of Exercise Prices	Stock Options Exercisable			Stock Options Outstanding		
	Number	Weighted Average Remaining Life	Weighted Average Exercise Price ($)	Number	Weighted Average Remaining Life	Weighted Average Exercise Price ($)
$20–$29	2,285,790	3.0	$28	3,075,790	3.5	$26
$30–$39	4,181,286	2.4	$33	5,891,286	2.6	$32
$40 or more	2,331,163	0.8	$41	2,331,163	0.8	$41
	8,798,239	2.1	$34	11,298,239	2.5	$32

Source: BCE Annual Report 2009.

The options issued by BCE specify that shares could be bought at a predetermined exercise price. Granting a stock option is a form of compensation even if the exercise price and the current share price are the same. BCE estimated the average fair value of the stock options granted to its employees to be between $4.00 and $6.00 per share.

Stock options are a widely used form of executive compensation. Most companies offer them with an exercise price equal to the current market price per share. For example, assume that BCE granted a key employee options to purchase a total of 10,000 common shares in the future at an average price of $30, which equals the market price per share on the date of the grant. The option holder would benefit from the stock option in a few years if the market price per share exceeds $30, presumably because the increase in BCE's market value is partially attributed to the employee's managerial skills. Undoubtedly, the difference between the increased market price and the exercise price of $30 is a form of compensation to the employee. Exhibit 12.1 shows that BCE issued common shares for $2 million on exercise of stock options during 2009, compared to $56 million in 2008. The decrease in the number and value of shares issued reflects the decrease in share price relative to the exercise price following the economic downturn that started in 2007.

When the options are exercised, BCE receives $30 per common share, while it could obtain a higher price if it sold the same shares in the market to other investors. Clearly, the exercise of employee stock options entails a cost to BCE that should be measured and reported. The more interesting issue, however, is whether BCE incurs a cost at the time of granting the options. In general, a fair value of the options can be estimated by using specific valuation methods and then compared with the exercise price to determine the additional compensation expense for the period.

The measurement and reporting of the cost of stock options has been hotly debated by accounting standard setters and company executives. Many companies rely on stock options to compensate their employees and key executives, especially in the technology, energy, and gold mining sectors. Companies in these sectors have lobbied against reporting the cost of stock options as an expense on the income statement because it would lower their profit, and may even turn profit into losses.

Canadian companies must estimate and report compensation expense associated with stock options. BCE reported a compensation expense of $3 million in Note 21 to its financial statements for 2009. The specific procedures to compute the compensation expense are covered in intermediate accounting courses.

Repurchase of Shares

A corporation may want to purchase its own shares from existing shareholders for a number of reasons. One common reason is to increase the market price per share and the earnings per share that result from the reduction in the number of outstanding shares.

Most Canadian companies cancel their shares when they buy them back from shareholders. When shares are cancelled, the appropriate share capital account is reduced by an amount that reflects the average issuance price per share. If the purchase price is less than the average issuance price, the difference is credited to contributed surplus. For example, if BCE purchased 50,000 common shares in the open market at $30 per share and the average price of the previously issued common shares is $34[4], the journal entry and the transaction effects would be as follows:

Common shares (SE) (50,000 × $34)	1,700,000	
Cash (A).		1,500,000
Contributed surplus (SE)		200,000

Assets	=	Liabilities	+	Shareholders' Equity	
Cash −1,500,000				Common shares	−1,700,000
				Contributed surplus	+200,000

---

[4]The average issue price per share equals the balance of the common shares account divided by the number of common shares outstanding.

Repurchases of shares at prices lower than the average issue price do not result in profit for the issuing company because they are capital transactions, not operating transactions. Companies profit from buying and selling shares issued by other companies, but not their own shares.[5]

Assume further that BCE subsequently purchased 50,000 of its own common shares when the price per share was $40. In this case, the excess of the purchase price over the issuance price is $6 per share for a total of $300,000. This difference is debited first to contributed surplus to the extent of $200,000 (the account balance) and the remaining amount, $100,000, is debited to retained earnings. The retained earnings account is reduced because the excess of the purchase price over the contribution made previously by shareholders reflects the company's profitable operations, which resulted in profit and caused an increase in share price. Hence, the $100,000 is viewed as a distribution of accumulated profit or retained earnings to shareholders who sold their shares to the company. The journal entry and the transaction effects follow:

Common shares (SE) (50,000 × $34)	1,700,000
Contributed surplus (SE)	200,000
Retained earnings (SE)	100,000
Cash (A)	2,000,000

Assets		=	Liabilities	+	Shareholders' Equity	
Cash	−2,000,000				Common shares	−1,700,000
					Contributed surplus	−200,000
					Retained earnings	−100,000

Contributed surplus related to one class of shares, such as common shares, can be used only for share transactions involving the same class of shares. The change in contributed surplus reported by BCE during 2009 is primarily related to repurchases of common shares.

The disclosures in Exhibit 12.1 show that BCE repurchased and cancelled common shares in both 2008 and 2009. The repurchased shares had book values of $67 million and $606 million, respectively. Exhibit 12.1 also shows that the repurchase price of these shares exceeded their average issuance price and related contributed surplus by $20 million in 2008 and $244 million in 2009.

SELF-STUDY **QUIZ 12-1**

BCE Inc. purchased 32.5 million of its common shares for $894 million cash during 2009.

1. Use the information reported in Exhibit 12.1 to reconstruct the journal entry to record the repurchase transaction.

2. Compute the average issuance price of BCE's common shares prior to the repurchase transaction.

 After you complete your answers, go online for the solutions.

LO⁴

Discuss dividends and analyze related transactions.

DIVIDENDS ON COMMON SHARES

Investors buy common shares because they expect a return on their investment. This return can come in two forms: appreciation of the share price and dividends. Some investors prefer to buy shares that pay little or no dividends because companies that

---

[5]Assume that a company issues shares at $10 per share then buys them back from some shareholders at $9 per share. If the difference of $1 is treated as profit, then the company will have to pay income tax, causing a reduction in cash. If it continues with similar transactions, then it will pay income taxes on profit that did not result from operating transactions. The decrease in cash causes a decrease in the company's assets, which depresses the company's market value, and causes further deterioration in the share price. No one would want to invest in such a company. Profit is generated from operating activities, not capital transactions.

reinvest the majority of their earnings tend to increase their future earnings potential, along with their stock price. Wealthy investors in high tax brackets prefer to receive their return on equity investments in the form of higher stock prices because capital gains may be taxed at a lower rate than dividend income. Other investors, such as retired people who need a steady income, prefer to receive their return on an investment in the form of dividends. These people often seek shares that will pay very high dividends, such as shares of utility companies.

A corporation does not have a legal obligation to pay dividends. While creditors can force a company into bankruptcy if it does not meet required interest payments on debt, shareholders do not have a similar right if a corporation is unable to pay dividends. Although a corporation does not have a legal obligation to pay a dividend, a liability is created when the board of directors approves (i.e., declares) a dividend.

Without a qualifier, the term *dividend* means a cash dividend, but dividends can also be paid in assets other than cash or by issuing additional shares. The most common type of dividend is a cash dividend.

A dividend declaration by BCE's board of directors includes three important dates:

1. Declaration date is the date on which the board of directors officially approved the dividend. As soon as it makes the declaration, it creates a dividend liability.

2. Date of record follows the declaration; it is the date on which the corporation prepares the list of current shareholders, based on its shareholder records. The dividend is payable only to those names listed on the record date. No journal entry is made on this date.

3. Payment date is the date on which the cash is disbursed to pay the dividend liability. It follows the date of record as specified in the dividend announcement.

BCE pays cash dividends on its outstanding common shares on a quarterly basis. The company provides details of the quarterly dividends on its preferred and common shares on its website. For example, details related to the cash dividends on common shares declared during 2010 are as follows:

The **DECLARATION DATE** is the date on which the board of directors officially approves a dividend.

The **DATE OF RECORD** is the date on which the corporation prepares the list of current shareholders as shown on its records; dividends can be paid only to the shareholders who own shares on that date.

The **PAYMENT DATE** is the date on which a cash dividend is paid to the shareholders of record.

REAL WORLD EXCERPT

BCE Inc.

DIVIDEND INFORMATION

Date of Declaration	Date of Record	Date of Payment	Amount of Dividend
February 3, 2010	March 15, 2010	April 15, 2010	$0.4350
May 5, 2010	June 15, 2010	July 15, 2010	0.4350
August 4, 2010	September 15, 2010	October 15, 2010	0.4575
November 3, 2010	December 15, 2010	January 15, 2011	0.4575

For instructional purposes, the time lag between the date of declaration and the date of payment may be ignored because it does not pose any substantive issues. When all three dates fall in the same accounting period, a single entry on the date of payment may be made in practice, for purely practical reasons.

Assume, for simplicity, that BCE had 767 million common shares outstanding on November 3, 2010. The total amount of cash dividends to be paid on January 15, 2011, is therefore $350,902,500.

The declaration of dividends creates a liability on November 3, 2010, that is recorded as follows:

Dividends declared—Common (SE) 350,902,500
    Dividend payable—Common (L) 350,902,500

Assets	=	Liabilities	+	Shareholders' Equity
		Dividends payable—		Dividends declared—
		Common +350,902,500		Common −350,902,500

The payment of the dividends on common shares on January 15, 2011, is recorded as follows:

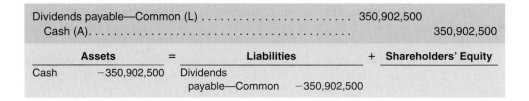

| Dividends payable—Common (L) . . . . 350,902,500 | | | |
| Cash (A). . . . . 350,902,500 | | | |

	Assets	=	Liabilities	+	Shareholders' Equity
Cash	−350,902,500	Dividends			
		payable—Common	−350,902,500		

Notice that the declaration and payment of a cash dividend have two impacts: they reduce assets (cash) and shareholders' equity (retained earnings) by the same amount. This observation explains the two fundamental requirements for the payment of a cash dividend:

1. ***Sufficient retained earnings.*** The corporation must have accumulated a sufficient amount of retained earnings to cover the amount of the dividend. Incorporation laws often limit cash dividends to the balance in the retained earnings account. BCE reports a deficit instead of retained earnings in its statement of financial position as shown in Exhibit 12.1, yet it has declared cash dividends to its shareholders during 2009. How it that possible? According to section 42 of the *CBCA*, a corporation may declare and pay dividends if payment of the dividend does not place the company into a position which would prevent it from paying its liabilities as they become due. BCE's statement of financial position at December 31, 2009, shows that the book value of its assets far exceeds the book value of its liabilities. In addition, BCE's statement of cash flows shows that the company generated $4.9 billion from operating activities in 2009. BCE's liquidity position allowed its board of directors to declare and pay dividends even though its retained earnings account has a debit balance.[6]

2. ***Sufficient cash.*** The corporation must have access to sufficient cash to pay the dividend and to meet the operating needs of the business. The mere fact that the retained earnings account has a large credit balance does not mean that the board of directors can declare and pay a cash dividend. The cash generated in the past by earnings represented in the retained earnings account may have been expended to acquire inventory, buy operational assets, and pay liabilities. Consequently, no necessary relationship exists between the balance of retained earnings and the balance of cash on any particular date. Quite simply, retained earnings are not cash.

Exhibit 12.1 indicates that BCE declared dividends on common shares for a total amount of $1,218 million in 2009, which is less than the profit applicable to common shares.

The company has established a dividend reinvestment plan that allows shareholders to receive additional common shares instead of cash dividends. It also encourages its employees to purchase BCE common shares through an employee savings plan, whereby employees can use a percentage of their salaries to buy BCE common shares through regular payroll deductions.

---

[6]BCE's deficit dates back to 2003 when the company wrote off goodwill and other intangibles by $8.18 billion because of its investment in Teleglobe, Bell Globalmedia Inc., and BCE Emergis. Despite this massive write-off of assets, BCE continued to report profit each year and declare dividends to shareholders. The excess of its profits over dividends declared has resulted in reducing the deficit from $5,830 million in 2003 to $1,299 in 2009.

IMPACT OF DIVIDENDS ON SHARE PRICE

When a company declares a dividend, it is important to establish which shareholders receive the dividend. For this reason, the stock exchanges set an *ex-dividend date*, which is normally two business days before the date of record, to make certain that dividend cheques are sent to the right people. If you buy shares before the ex-dividend date, you receive the dividend. If you buy the shares on the ex-dividend date or later, the previous shareholder receives the dividend. While this date is important in understanding dividends, it has no accounting implications.

If you follow share prices, you will notice that the price of a company's common share often falls on the ex-dividend date. The reason is simple. On that date, the share is worth less because it no longer includes the right to receive the next dividend.

SELF-STUDY **QUIZ 12-2**

The board of directors of BCE Inc. announced on February 3, 2010, a quarterly dividend of $0.435 per common share, payable on April 15, 2010, to shareholders of record on March 15, 2010. Assume that BCE had 750 million common shares outstanding on the declaration date. Answer the following questions concerning this dividend:

1. On which date is a liability created?
2. On which date does a cash outflow occur?
3. Prepare the journal entry to record the payment of the dividend.
4. What are the three fundamental requirements for the payment of a dividend?

After you complete your answers, go online for the solutions.

≣ connect

Because of the importance of dividends to many investors, analysts often compute the dividend yield ratio to evaluate a corporation's dividend policy.

DIVIDEND YIELD RATIO

ANALYTICAL QUESTION → Investors in common shares expect to earn a return on their investment. A portion of this return comes in the form of dividends. How much do investors earn on their investment based on dividends?

RATIO AND COMPARISONS → The *dividend yield ratio* is a measure of the percentage return that shareholders earn from the dividends they receive. Potential investors often use this ratio to help select from alternative investment opportunities. In 2009, BCE declared two quarterly dividends of $0.385 each and two quarterly dividends of $0.405 per share, for a total of $1.58 per share. The ratio is computed as follows:

LO5

Analyze the dividend yield ratio.

$$\text{Dividend Yield Ratio} = \frac{\text{Dividends per Share}}{\text{Market Price per Share}}$$

The 2009 ratio for BCE is

$$\$1.58 \div \$29.00 = 5.4\%$$

Comparisons over Time				Comparisons with Competitors	
BCE				**Rogers Communications**	**TELUS**
2007	**2008**	**2009**		**2009**	**2009**
3.6%	2.9%	5.4%		3.5%	5.6%

INTERPRETATIONS

In General → Investors in common shares earn a return from dividends and capital appreciation (increases in the market price of the shares they own). Growth-oriented companies often pay out very small amounts of dividends and rely on increases in their market price to provide a return to investors. Others pay out large dividends but have more stable market prices. Each type of share appeals to different types of investors with different risk and return preferences.

Focus Company Analysis → During the three years 2007 through 2009, BCE distributed annual dividends of $1.44, $0.73, and $1.58 per share, respectively. Its share price was $39.65, $25.31, and $29.00 on December 31, 2007, 2008, and 2009, respectively. The economic downturn that started in 2007 affected the company's investments portfolio and resulted in lower profit in 2008, prompting its board of directors to reduce the dividend per share for 2008, which explains the decrease in the dividend yield for that year. BCE's dividend yield is similar to that of TELUS, but higher than that of Rogers Communications, which distributed a low dividend per share relative to its share price; hence, the lower dividend yield.

A Few Cautions → Remember that the dividend yield ratio tells only part of the return on investment story. Often, potential capital appreciation is a much more important consideration. When analyzing changes in the ratio, it is important to understand the cause. For example, a company might pay out $2 per share in dividends each year. If the market price of its shares is $100 per share, the yield is 2 percent. If the market price per share falls to $25 the following year and the company continues to pay out $2 per share in dividends, the dividend yield ratio will "improve" to 8 percent. Most analysts would not interpret this change as being favourable.

LO⁶

Discuss the purpose of stock dividends, stock splits, and report transactions.

A **STOCK DIVIDEND** is a distribution of additional shares of a corporation's own equity.

STOCK DIVIDENDS AND STOCK SPLITS

Stock Dividends

A stock dividend is a distribution of additional shares of a corporation's own share capital to its shareholders on a pro rata basis, at no cost to the shareholder. Stock dividends usually consist of additional common shares issued to the holders of common shares. The phrase *pro rata basis* means that each shareholder receives additional shares equal to the percentage of shares already held. A shareholder with 10 percent of the outstanding shares receives 10 percent of any additional shares issued as a stock dividend.

The term *stock dividend* is sometimes misused in annual reports and news articles. A recent *Wall Street Journal* headline announced that a particular company had just declared a "stock dividend." A close reading of the article revealed that the company had declared a cash dividend on the shares.

The value of a stock dividend is the subject of much debate. In reality, a stock dividend has no economic value. All shareholders receive a pro rata distribution of shares, which means that each shareholder owns exactly the same portion of the company as before. The value of an investment is determined by the percentage of the company that is owned, not the number of shares that are held. If you get change for a dollar, you are not wealthier because you hold *four* quarters instead of only *one* dollar. Similarly, if you own 10 percent of a company, you are not wealthier simply because the company declares a stock dividend and gives you (and all other shareholders) more shares.

At this point, you may still wonder why having extra shares does not make an investor wealthier. The reason is simple: the stock market reacts immediately when a stock dividend is issued, and the share price falls proportionally. Theoretically, if the share price was $60 before a stock dividend, normally (in the absence of events affecting the company) the price will fall to $30 if the number of shares is doubled. Thus, an investor could own 100 shares worth $6,000 before the stock dividend (100 × $60) and 200 shares worth $6,000 after the stock dividend (200 × $30).

In reality, the fall in price is not exactly proportional to the number of new shares that are issued. In some cases, the stock dividend makes the stock more attractive to new investors. Many investors prefer to buy shares in round lots, which are multiples of 100 shares. An investor with $10,000 might not buy a share selling for $150 because she cannot afford to buy 100 shares. She might buy the share, however, if the price is less than $100 as a result of a stock dividend. In other cases, stock dividends are accompanied by an announcement of increases in cash dividends, which are attractive to some investors.

When a common stock dividend occurs, the company must transfer from retained earnings an additional amount into the common shares account to reflect the additional shares that have been issued. The amount transferred should reflect the fair market value per share at the declaration date, as recommended in the *CBCA*.

For small stock dividends that are less than 20–25 percent of the outstanding shares, the amount transferred from the retained earnings account to the common shares account is based on the market price per share at the date of declaration. If the company declared a cash dividend instead of a stock dividend, and the shareholders used the cash they receive to buy additional shares, the shareholders would be paying the market price to acquire additional shares. This assumption is valid if the stock dividend is relatively small, so that it will not cause a significant change in the market price. For larger stock dividends, the market price per share will drop significantly, so it will not be an appropriate basis for transferring an amount from retained earnings to common shares. In this case, the amount transferred is based on the average issue price per share. In either situation, the stock dividend does not change total shareholders' equity. It changes only the balances of specific shareholders' equity accounts.

Let us assume that a company declared on July 25, 2011, a 10 percent stock dividend on common shares to be issued on August 25, 2011, to shareholders of record on August 10, 2011. The company had 100,000 shares outstanding and the market price per share was $20 on the date of declaration. The declaration of the stock dividend requires the following journal entry on July 25, 2011:

| Dividends declared—Common (SE) (100,000 × 10% × $20) .... | 200,000 | |
| Stock dividend to be issued (SE)......................... | | 200,000 |

Assets	=	Liabilities	+	Shareholders' Equity	
				Dividends declared— Common	−200,000
				Stock dividend to be issued	+200,000

The equity account, stock dividend to be issued, is credited, instead of the common shares account, until the shares are issued. The issuance and distribution of the additional shares on August 25, 2011, is recorded as follows:

| Stock dividend to be issued (SE) .... | 200,000 | |
| Common shares (SE) .... | | 200,000 |

Assets	=	Liabilities	+	Shareholders' Equity	
				Stock dividend to be issued	−200,000
				Common shares	+200,000

If the company had declared a 50 percent stock dividend, the average price received for issuing all of the common shares would be used instead of the market price per share as a basis for the reduction of retained earnings. If the average issue price per share is $15, the dividends declared—common account would be reduced by $750,000 (100,000 × 50% × $15) and the common shares account would be increased by the same amount.

Stock Splits

A **STOCK SPLIT** is an increase in the total number of authorized shares by a specified ratio; it does not decrease retained earnings.

Stock splits are *not* dividends. They are similar to a stock dividend but are quite different in terms of their impact on the shareholders' equity accounts. In a stock split, the *total* number of authorized shares is increased by a specified number, such as a 2-for-1 split. In this instance, each share held is called in, and two new shares are issued in its place.

BCE has had three stock splits over the years. A 4-for-1 split occurred on October 4, 1948, followed by a 3-for-1 split on April 26, 1979. The last split was a 2-for-1, executed on May 14, 1997. In summary, a common share issued prior to October 4, 1948, has already split into 24 shares. If these stock splits did not occur, BCE's share price would have been $792 at the time of writing this book.

In both a stock dividend and a stock split, the shareholder receives more shares but does not pay to acquire the additional shares. A stock dividend requires a journal entry; a stock split does not require one but is disclosed in the notes to the financial statements. The comparative effects of a stock dividend versus a stock split may be summarized as follows:

Shareholders' Equity	Before	After a 100% Stock Dividend	After a Two-for-One Stock Split
Contributed capital			
Number of shares outstanding	30,000	60,000	60,000
Issue price per share	$ 10	$ 10	$ 5
Common shares	300,000	600,000	300,000
Retained earnings	650,000	350,000	650,000
Total shareholders' equity	$950,000	$950,000	$950,000

SELF-STUDY **QUIZ 12-3**

Barton Corporation issued 100,000 new common shares as a result of a stock dividend when the market value was $30 per share. The average issue price is $10 per share.

1. Record this transaction, assuming that it was a small stock dividend.
2. Record this transaction, assuming that it was a large stock dividend.
3. What journal entry is required if the transaction is a stock split?

 connect

After you complete your answers, go online for the solutions.

LO7

Describe the characteristics of preferred shares and analyze transactions affecting preferred shares.

PREFERRED SHARES

PREFERRED SHARES are shares that have specified rights over common shares.

In addition to common shares, some corporations issue preferred shares. Preferred shares differ from common shares because of a number of rights granted to the preferred shareholders. The most significant differences are as follows:

- **Preferred shares do not grant voting rights.** As a result, they do not appeal to investors who want some control over the operations of the corporation. Indeed, this is one of the main reasons why some corporations issue preferred shares to raise equity capital. Preferred shares permit them to raise funds without diluting common shareholders' control of the company.

- **Preferred shares are less risky than common shares.** Preferred shareholders have a priority over common shareholders for the receipt of dividends and in the distribution of assets if the corporation goes out of business. Usually a specified amount per share must be paid to preferred shareholders upon dissolution before any remaining assets can be distributed to the common shareholders.

- **Preferred shares typically have a fixed dividend rate.** Preferred shares typically have no par value but, unlike common shares, they often carry a nominal value called the *stated value*. BCE's preferred shares have a stated value of $25 per share. Most preferred shares have fixed dividend rates or amounts per share. The fixed dividend is attractive to certain investors who want a stable income from their investment.

Special Features of Preferred Shares

Some corporations issue convertible preferred shares, which provide preferred shareholders the option to exchange their preferred shares for a different series of preferred shares or common shares of the corporation. The terms of the conversion specify the conversion dates and a conversion ratio.

The classification of preferred shares as equity or debt depends upon the terms of the preferred equity issue. Preferred shares may be *redeemable* or *callable* at some future date at the option of the issuing corporation. Corporations are unlikely to redeem preferred shares if conditions are financially unfavourable to the company. Such redeemable shares are classified as equity because the issuing corporation can choose to not redeem the shares. However, preferred shares that have fixed redemption dates are classified as debt because the issuing corporation has a future financial liability. Moreover, dividends on these shares are treated as expenses, much like the interest expense related to long-term debt.

Some preferred share issues are *retractable* at the option of the shareholder. In that case, preferred shareholders have the right to receive the redemption price from the corporation at a specific future date. Thus, retractable preferred shares represent a contractual obligation to deliver cash or another financial asset at a future date under conditions that may be unfavourable to the issuing corporation. Consequently, retractable preferred shares are classified as debt.

The notes to BCE's consolidated financial statements for the year 2009 provide a considerable amount of detail regarding its preferred shares.

CONVERTIBLE PREFERRED SHARES are preferred shares that are convertible to common shares at the option of the holder.

REAL WORLD EXCERPT

BCE Inc.

ANNUAL REPORT

NOTE 20: SHARE CAPITAL

Preferred Shares

BCE Inc.'s article of amalgamation provide for an unlimited number of First Preferred Shares and Second Preferred Shares. The terms set out in the articles authorize BCE Inc.'s directors to issue the shares in one or more series and to set the number of shares and conditions for each series.

The following table is a summary of the principal terms of BCE Inc.'s First Preferred Shares. There were no Second Preferred Shares issued and outstanding at December 31, 2009. BCE Inc.'s articles of amalgamation, as amended, describe the terms and conditions of these shares in detail.

Series	Annual Dividend Rate	Convertible Into	Conversion Date	Redemption Date	Redemption Price	Number of Shares Authorized	Number of Shares Issued and Outstanding	Stated Capital At December 31 2009	2008	2007
Q	floating	Series R	December 1, 2015	At any time	$25.50	8,000,000	—	—	—	—
R	4.54%	Series Q	December 1, 2010	December 1, 2010	$25.00	8,000,000	8,000,000	200	200	200
S	floating	Series T	November 1, 2011	At any time	$25.50	8,000,000	2,279,791	57	57	57
T	4.502%	Series S	November 1, 2011	November 1, 2011	$25.00	8,000,000	5,720,209	143	143	143
Y	floating	Series Z	December 1, 2012	At any time	$25.50	10,000,000	8,126,330	203	203	203
Z	4.331%	Series Y	December 1, 2012	December 1, 2012	$25.00	10,000,000	1,873,670	47	47	47
AA	4.80%	Series AB	September 1, 2012	September 1, 2012	$25.00	20,000,000	10,081,586	257	257	257
AB	floating	Series AA	September 1, 2012	At any time	$25.50	20,000,000	9,918,414	253	253	253
AC	4.60%	Series AD	March 1, 2013	March 1, 2013	$25.00	20,000,000	9,244,555	236	236	510
AD	floating	Series AC	March 1, 2013	At any time	$25.50	20,000,000	10,755,445	274	274	—
AE	floating	Series AF	February 1, 2010	At any time	$25.50	24,000,000	1,914,218	48	48	48
AF	4.40%	Series AE	February 1, 2010	February 1, 2010	$25.00	24,000,000	14,085,782	352	352	352
AG	4.35%	Series AH	May 1, 2011	May 1, 2011	$25.00	22,000,000	10,051,751	251	251	251
AH	floating	Series AG	May 1, 2011	At any time	$25.50	22,000,000	3,948,249	99	99	99
AI	4.65%	Series AJ	August 1, 2011	August 1, 2011	$25.00	22,000,000	14,000,000	350	350	350
AJ	floating	Series AI	August 1, 2016	At any time	$25.50	22,000,000	—	—	—	—
								2,770	2,770	2,770

Source: BCE Annual Report 2009.

BCE has also disclosed details of the specific features of each series of preferred shares. All of its outstanding preferred shares at December 31, 2009, are nonvoting, except under special circumstances, when the holders are entitled to one vote per share. Holders of Series R, T, Z, AA, AC, AF, AG, and AI shares are entitled to fixed cumulative quarterly dividends, which is reset every five years, whereas holders of Series S, Y, AB, AD, AE, and AH shares are entitled to floating adjustable cumulative monthly dividends with a floating dividend rate that is calculated every month. All these preferred shares are convertible at the holder's option into another associated series of preferred shares on a one-for-one basis. In addition, BCE may redeem each of the preferred shares in the first series above at $25.00 per share on the applicable redemption date and every five years after that date, whereas each preferred share in the second series may be redeemed at any time at $25.50 per share.[7]

SELF-STUDY **QUIZ 12-4**

Refer to the previous table showing a summary of BCE's preferred shares, and answer the following questions related to Preferred Shares, Series AC.

1. What is the total amount of dividends payable on Series AC per year?

2. What is meant by redemption date?

3. What is the earliest date when BCE can redeem its Series AC shares?

connect   After you complete your answers, go online for the solutions.

Dividends on Preferred Shares

Investors who purchase preferred shares give up certain advantages that are available to investors in common shares. Generally, preferred shareholders do not have the right to vote at the annual meeting, nor do they share in increased earnings if the company becomes more profitable. To compensate these investors, preferred shares offer a dividend preference. The two most common dividend preferences are

1. Current dividend preference.
2. Cumulative dividend preference.

CURRENT DIVIDEND PREFERENCE is the feature of preferred shares that grants preferred shareholders priority for dividends over common shareholders.

Current Dividend Preference   Preferred shares always carry a current dividend preference, which requires that the current preferred dividend be paid before any dividends are paid on the common shares. When the current dividend preference has been met and there are no other preferences, dividends can then be paid to the common shareholders.

Declared dividends must be allocated between the preferred and common shares. First, dividends are allocated to the preferred shares, and then the remainder of the total dividend is allocated to the common shares. Exhibit 12.4 illustrates the allocation of the current dividend preference under three different assumptions concerning the total amount of dividends to be paid.

CUMULATIVE DIVIDEND PREFERENCE is the feature of preferred shares that requires specified current dividends not paid in full to accumulate for every year in which they are not paid. These cumulative preferred dividends must be paid before any common dividends can be paid.

DIVIDENDS IN ARREARS are dividends on cumulative preferred shares that have not been declared in prior years.

Cumulative Dividend Preference   The cumulative dividend preference states that if all or a part of the current dividend is not paid in full, the unpaid amount, known as *dividends in arrears*, must be paid before any common dividends can be paid. Of course, if the preferred shares are non-cumulative, dividends cannot be in arrears; any dividends that are not declared are lost permanently by the preferred shareholders. Because preferred shareholders are not willing to accept this unfavourable feature, preferred shares are usually cumulative.

---

[7]Further details about each series of BCE's preferred shares are available on its website at www.bce.ca/en/investors/preferredshares/bce/.

Preferred shares outstanding, $1.20; 2,000 shares.

Common shares outstanding, 5,000 shares.

Allocation of dividends between preferred and common shares assuming current dividend preference only:

Assumptions	Total Dividends Paid	$1.20 Preferred Shares (2,000 shares)*	Common Shares (5,000 shares)
No. 1	$ 2,000	$2,000	0
No. 2	3,000	2,400	$ 600
No. 3	18,000	2,400	15,600

*Preferred dividends = 2,000 × $1.20 = $2,400.

Preferred shares outstanding, $1.20; 2,000 shares.

Common shares outstanding, 5,000 shares.

Dividends are in arrears for the two preceding years.

Allocation of dividends between preferred and common shares, assuming cumulative preference:

Assumptions (dividends in arrears, 2 years)	Total Dividends Paid	$1.20 Preferred Shares (2,000 shares)*	Common Shares (5,000 shares)
No. 1	$ 2,400	$2,400	0
No. 2	7,200	7,200	0
No. 3	8,000	7,200	$ 800
No. 4	30,000	7,200	22,800

*Current dividend preference, 2,000 × $1.20 = $2,400; dividends in arrears preference, $2,400 × 2 years = $4,800; and current dividend preference plus dividends in arrears × $7,200.

The allocation of dividends between cumulative preferred shares and common shares is illustrated in Exhibit 12.5 under four different assumptions concerning the total amount of dividends to be paid. Notice that the dividends in arrears are paid first, then the current dividend preference is paid, and, finally, the remainder is paid to the common shareholders.

In 2009, BCE declared a total amount of $107 million in dividends on preferred shares, as disclosed in Exhibit 12.1.

MEASURING AND REPORTING CHANGES IN SHAREHOLDERS' EQUITY

LO⁸

Measure and report changes in shareholders' equity.

Exhibit 12.1 discloses the balances of the various components of BCE's shareholders' equity at December 31, 2008 and 2009, as well as the changes that occurred to each component over these two years. While we provided explanations for most of the changes that occurred in 2009, two components of shareholders' equity deserve further discussion: retained earnings and accumulated other comprehensive income (loss).

Retained Earnings

Retained earnings represent profit that has been earned less dividends that have been declared since the first day of the company's operations. Most companies report retained earnings on their statements of financial position. In BCE's case, its retained earnings turned into a deficit in 2003 after a massive write-off of the value of BCE's investments in other companies. Its deficit of $5,830 million on December 31, 2003, has been reduced each year and reached $1,299 by December 31, 2009. The gradual reduction of this deficit will allow BCE to report retained earnings in future years.

Under rare circumstances, you may see a statement that includes an adjustment to the beginning balance of retained earnings resulting from a correction of a material accounting error that occurred in the financial statements of a prior period.

If an accounting error from a previous period is corrected by making an adjustment to the current income statement, profit for the current period would be improperly measured. To avoid this problem, the financial statements of the prior period in which the error occurred are restated to reflect the correction of the error. The nature of the prior period error should be disclosed along with the effect of the correction on each financial statement item that is affected by the error. To the extent that prior period errors affect income statement items, retained earnings of the prior period will also be affected.

Adjustments to the financial statements of prior periods should also be made if the entity changes its accounting policies, such as a change from the FIFO method of inventory valuation to the weighted-average cost method, or when companies are required to adopt new accounting standards. In these cases, the entity adjusts the opening balance of each affected component of equity, including retained earnings. For example, Norbord Inc. made the following disclosure in its annual report for 2009:

REAL WORLD EXCERPT

Norbord Inc.

ANNUAL REPORT 2009

Years ended December 31 (US $ millions)	2009	2008
Retained Earnings		
Balance, beginning of year	$24	$204
Adoption of new accounting standards (*note* 2)	2	1
Adjusted balance, beginning of year	26	205

Note 2. Changes in Accounting Policies and Significant Accounting Estimates

. . .

Goodwill and Intangible Assets

In February 2008, the CICA issued Handbook Section 3064, Goodwill and Intangible Assets and replaced Handbook Sections 3062, Goodwill and Other Intangible Assets; Section 3450, Research and Development Costs; and Emerging Issues Committee (EIC) Abstract 27, Revenues and Expenditures during the Pre-Operating Period. Section 3064 establishes standards for the recognition, measurement, presentation, and disclosure of goodwill subsequent to its initial recognition and of intangible assets by profit-oriented enterprises. This new standard became effective January 1, 2009. The impact of adopting this new standard was a $6 million increase in property, plant, and equipment, a $4 million decrease in other assets, a $1 million increase in opening retained earnings, and a $1 million increase in future income tax liability as at January 1, 2008.

Source: Norbond Annual Report 2009.

Accumulated Other Comprehensive Income (Loss)

International Financial Reporting Standards require Canadian publicly accountable enterprises to report accumulated other comprehensive income (loss). As explained in Chapter 6, this equity item reflects the financial effect of events that cause changes in shareholders' equity, other than investments by shareholders or distributions to shareholders. Such changes in equity result from unrealized gains or losses because of the valuation of specific assets and liabilities at fair value. For BCE, these changes, shown in Exhibit 12.1, include such items as unrealized gains or losses on available-for-sale assets, unrealized gains or losses on derivatives transactions that are designated as cash flow hedges, and unrealized gains or losses on translating the financial statements of companies that have operations in other countries but are controlled by the Canadian reporting entity. The gains and losses resulting from these changes are not reported on the income statement because they have not been realized yet. Measurement of the unrealized gains and losses related to these and similar items is fairly complex and is covered in intermediate and advanced accounting courses.

RESTRICTIONS ON THE PAYMENT OF DIVIDENDS

FINANCIAL ANALYSIS

Two common constraints on the ability of a corporation to pay dividends are the existence of loan covenants and preferred stock dividends in arrears. For additional security, some creditors include a loan covenant that limits the amount of dividends a corporation can pay. These debt covenants often include a limit on borrowing and require a minimum balance of cash or working capital. If debt covenants are violated, the creditor can demand immediate repayment of the debt. The full-disclosure principle requires the disclosure of loan covenants, typically in a separate note to the financial statements.

The existence of dividends in arrears on preferred shares can also limit a company's ability to pay dividends to its common shareholders and can affect a company's future cash flows. Dividends are never an actual liability until the board of directors declares them. Hence, dividends in arrears are not reported on the statement of financial position but are disclosed in the notes to the statements. The following note from Lone Star Industries is typical if a company has dividends in arrears:

> The total of dividends in arrears on the $13.50 preferred shares at the end of the year was $11,670,000. The aggregate amount of such dividends must be paid before any dividends are paid on common shares.

REAL WORLD EXCERPT

Lone Star Industries

ANNUAL REPORT

Analysts are particularly interested in information concerning these restrictions because of the impact they have on the company's dividend policy.

FINANCING ACTIVITIES

FOCUS ON CASH FLOWS

Transactions involving share capital have a direct impact on the capital structure of a business. Because of the importance of these transactions, they are reported in a separate section of the statement called "cash flows from financing activities." Examples of cash flows associated with share capital are included in the statement of cash flows for BCE shown in Exhibit 12.6. Remember that shares issued in exchange for assets do not impact cash flow and are disclosed in a note to the statement of cash flows.

LO9

Discuss the impact of share capital transactions on cash flows.

Exhibit **12.6**

Excerpt from Statements of Cash Flows for BCE Inc.

REAL WORLD EXCERPT

BCE Inc.

ANNUAL REPORT

CONSOLIDATED STATEMENTS OF CASH FLOWS
For the Year Ended December 31

(in $ millions)	Note	2009	2008	2007
Cash flows used in financing activities				
(Decrease) increase in notes payable and bank advances		(194)	1	211
Issue of long-term debt		1,348	50	1,071
Repayment of long-term debt		(2,539)	(502)	(3.048)
Issue of common shares	20	2	50	153
Repurchase of common shares	20	(894)	(92)	(227)
Redemption of equity securities by subsidiaries from non-controlling interest		—	—	(333)
Cash dividends paid on common shares	19	(1,201)	(587)	(1,147)
Cash dividends paid on preferred shares		(107)	(129)	(124)
Cash dividends/distributions paid by subsidiaries to non-controlling interest		(369)	(366)	(404)
Other financing activities		(90)	16	(66)
Cash flows used in financing activities		(4,044)	(1,559)	(3,914)

Source: BCE Annual Report 2009.

EFFECT ON STATEMENT OF CASH FLOWS

IN GENERAL → Cash received from owners is reported as an inflow. Cash paid to owners is reported as an outflow. Examples are shown in the following table:

	Effect on Cash Flows
Financing activities	
Issuance of shares	+
Repurchase of shares	−
Payment of cash dividends	−

SELECTED FOCUS COMPANY COMPARISONS: CASH FLOWS FROM FINANCING ACTIVITIES
(in millions)

Nestlé	−€12,361
Home Depot	−US$3,503
Nokia	−€696

FOCUS COMPANY ANALYSIS → BCE has not issued preferred shares recently, but it has issued common shares on exercise of stock options during the years 2008 and 2009. The company repurchased common shares for cancellation during 2008 and 2009, and paid dividends on both common and preferred shares in both years.

ACCOUNTING AND REPORTING FOR UNINCORPORATED BUSINESSES

In this book, we emphasize the corporate form of business because it plays a dominant role in our economy. In fact, there are three forms of business organizations: corporations, sole proprietorships, and partnerships. As we have seen in this chapter, a *corporation* is a legal entity, separate and distinct from its owners. It can enter into contracts in its own name, be sued, and is taxed as a separate entity. A *sole proprietorship* is an unincorporated business owned by one individual. If you started a lawn care business in the summer by yourself, it would be a sole proprietorship. It is not necessary to file any legal papers to create a proprietorship. A *partnership* is an unincorporated business owned by two or more people. Again, it is not necessary to file legal papers to create a partnership, but it is certainly a good idea to have a lawyer draw up a contract between the partners.

Neither partnerships nor proprietorships are separate legal entities. As a result, owners may be directly sued and are individually taxed on the earnings of the business.

Typical Account Structure		
Corporation (Shareholders' Equity)	**Sole Proprietorship (Owner's Equity)**	**Partnership (Partners' Equity)**
Share capital, contributed surplus	Doe, capital	Able, capital; Baker, capital
Retained earnings	Not used	Not used
Dividends paid	Doe, drawings	Able, drawings; Baker, drawings
Revenues, expenses, gains, and losses	Same	Same
Assets and liabilities	Same	Same

Exhibit **12.7**

Comparative Account Structure among Types of Business Entities

The fundamentals of accounting and reporting for unincorporated businesses are the same as for a corporation, except for owners' equity. Typical account structures for the three forms of business organizations are outlined in Exhibit 12.7.

Accounting for sole proprietorships and partnerships is discussed in Appendix 12A.

ACCOUNTING STANDARDS FOR PRIVATE ENTERPRISES

Canadian private enterprises do not issue shares to the public. To finance their growth, most private enterprises turn to banks and other creditors as sources of financing. Because the external users of financial statements prepared by private enterprises are primarily creditors, the Canadian accounting standards for private enterprises have been simplified relative to International Financial Reporting Standards. The main differences in accounting standards related to the equity section of the statement of financial position are summarized below:

- Canadian private enterprises are not required to measure and report other comprehensive income. Their financial statements consist of an income statement, a statement of retained earnings, a balance sheet, and a cash flow statement. They do not have to prepare a statement of changes in equity.
- Canadian private enterprises are permitted to use a simplified valuation model to measure the value of share-based compensation because of the difficulty in determining a fair value for shares that have no public market.
- Canadian private enterprises are not required to report earnings per share because external users do not believe this information is useful. Users, in particular creditors, are most interested in cash flows from operating activities.

DEMONSTRATION **CASE**

This case focuses on the organization and operations for the first year of Mera Corporation, which was organized on January 2, 2011. The laws specify that the legal capital for no par value shares is the full amount of the shares. The corporation was organized by 10 local entrepreneurs for the purpose of operating a business to sell various supplies to hotels. The charter authorized the following share capital:

Common shares, no par value, unlimited number of shares.

Preferred shares, 5 percent, $25 par value, 10,000 shares (cumulative, nonconvertible, and nonvoting; liquidation value, $26).

The following summarized transactions, selected from 2011, were completed during the months indicated:

a. Jan. 5   Sold a total of 7,500 shares of no par value common shares to the 10 entrepreneurs for cash at $52 per share. Credit the common shares account for the total issue amount.

b. Feb. 1   Sold 7,560 preferred shares at $25 per share; cash collected in full.

c. Mar. 10   Purchased land for a store site and made full payment by issuing 400 preferred shares. Early construction of the store is planned. Debit land (store site). The preferred share is selling at $25 per share.

d. Apr. 15   Paid $2,000 cash for organization costs. Debit the intangible asset account, organization costs.

e. May 25   Issued 40 preferred shares to A. B. Cain in full payment of legal services rendered in connection with organization of the corporation. Assume that the preferred share is selling regularly at $25 per share. Debit organization costs.

f. June 10   Sold 500 no par value common shares for cash to C. B. Abel at $54 per share.

g. Nov. 30   The company's board of directors declared the annual dividends on the preferred shares, and a dividend of $0.50 per common share. The dividends are payable on December 20 to shareholders on record at December 15.

h. Dec. 20   Paid the declared dividends on preferred and common shares.

i. Dec. 31   Purchased equipment for $600,000; paid cash. No depreciation expense should be recorded in 2011.

j. Dec. 31   Borrowed $20,000 cash from the City Bank on a one-year, interest-bearing note. Interest is payable at a 12 percent rate at maturity.

k. Dec. 31   Calculated the following for the year: gross revenues, $129,300; expenses, $98,000, including corporation income tax but excluding amortization of organization costs. Assume that these summarized revenue and expense transactions involved cash. Because the equipment and the bank loan transactions were on December 31, no related adjusting entries at the end of 2011 are needed.

l. Dec. 31   Decided that a reasonable amortization period for organization costs, starting as of January 1, 2011, is 10 years. This intangible asset must be amortized to expense.

Required:

1. Prepare appropriate journal entries, with a brief explanation, for each of these transactions.
2. Prepare the required adjusting entry for 2011 to amortize organization costs.
3. Prepare appropriate closing entries at December 31, 2011.
4. Prepare a statement of financial position for Mera Corporation at December 31, 2011. Emphasize full disclosure of shareholders' equity.
5. Assume that, instead of issuing common shares in January for $390,000, the company issued shares for $260,000 and borrowed an amount of $130,000 from its bank, signing a note, payable on December 31, 2013. Interest on the note is 10 percent, payable on December 31 of each year. Is borrowing from the bank more beneficial to the common shareholders, compared with issuing additional common shares? Explain. For the purpose of this analysis, use an income tax rate of 40 percent.

We strongly recommend that you prepare your own answers to these requirements and then check your answers with the suggested solution.

SUGGESTED **SOLUTION**

1. Journal entries:

a. Jan. 5

Cash (A)	390,000	
Common shares (SE)		390,000

Sale of no par value common shares
($52 × 7,500 shares = $390,000).

b. Feb. 1

Cash (A)	189,000	
Preferred shares, 5% (SE)		189,000

Sale of preferred shares ($25 × 7,560 shares = $189,000).

c. Mar. 10	Land (A)		10,000	
	Preferred shares, 5% (SE)			10,000
	Purchased land for future store site; paid in full by issuance *of 100 preferred shares ($25 × 400 shares = $10,000).*			
d. Apr. 15	Organization costs (A)		2,000	
	Cash (A)			2,000
	Paid organization costs.			
e. May 25	Organization costs (A)		1,000	
	Preferred shares 5% (SE)			1,000
	Organization costs (legal services) paid by issuance of *40 preferred shares. The implied market value is* *$25 × 40 shares = $1,000.*			
f. June 10	Cash (A)		27,000	
	Common shares (500 shares) (SE)			27,000
	Sold 500 no par value common shares *($54 × 500 shares = $27,000).*			
g. Nov. 30	Dividends declared—Common (SE)		10,000	
	Dividends declared—Preferred (SE)		4,000	
	Dividends payable—Preferred			10,000
	Dividends payable—Common			4,000
	Declaration of the annual dividend on preferred shares *(8,000 × $25 × 0.05) and a dividend of $0.50 per* *common share.*			
h. Dec. 20	Dividends payable—Preferred		10,000	
	Dividends payable—Common		4,000	
	Cash			14,000
	Payment of the declared dividends.			
i. Dec. 31	Equipment (A)		600,000	
	Cash (A)			600,000
	Purchased equipment.			
j. Dec. 31	Cash (A)		20,000	
	Note payable (L)			20,000
	Borrowed cash and signed a one-year, 12 percent *interest-bearing note.*			
k. Dec. 31	Cash (A)		129,300	
	Revenues (E)			129,300
	Expenses (E)		98,000	
	Cash (A)			98,000
	To record summarized revenues and expenses.			
2. Dec. 31	Expenses (E)		300	
	Organization costs (A)			300
	Adjusting entry to amortize organization costs for one year *[($2,000 + $1,000) ÷ 10 years = $300].*			
3. Closing entries:				
Dec. 31	Revenues (R)		129,300	
	Income summary			129,300
	Income summary		98,300	
	Expenses ($98,000 + $300) (E)			98,300
	Income summary		31,000	
	Retained earnings (SE)			31,000

4. Statement of Financial Position:

MERA CORPORATION
Statement of Financial Position
at December 31, 2011

Assets
Current assets
Cash $ 41,300
Tangible assets
Land $ 10,000
Equipment (no depreciation assumed in the problem) 600,000 610,000
Intangible assets
Organization costs (cost, $3,000 less amortization, $300) 2,700
Total assets $654,000
Liabilities
Current liabilities
Note payable, 12% $ 20,000

Shareholders' Equity
Contributed capital
Preferred shares, 5% (par value $25; authorized 10,000 shares,
issued and outstanding 8,000 shares) $200,000
Common shares (no par value; authorized unlimited, issued and
outstanding 8,000 shares) 417,000
Total contributed capital 617,000
Retained earnings 17,000
Total shareholders' equity 634,000
Total liabilities and shareholders' equity $654,000

5. Interest on the loan equals $13,000 ($130,000 × 10%) for 2011. This expense will reduce the income tax expense by $5,200 ($13,000 × 40%). The profit of $31,000 will then be reduced by $7,800 ($13,000 − $5,200) for a revised profit of $23,200. Profit available to common shareholders equals $13,200 after deducting $10,000 of dividends on preferred shares. The return on *common* shareholders' equity would therefore equal 4.7 percent ($13,200 / $278,100, average common shareholders' equity = [$260,000 + $296,200]/2).

Without the $130,000 loan, the return on *common* shareholders' equity is 5.1 percent ([$31,000 − $10,000] / $412,000). This shows that borrowing an amount of $130,000 at 10 percent is not preferable to issuing additional common shares in this particular case.

Appendix 12A

Accounting for Owners' Equity for Sole Proprietorships and Partnerships

Proprietorships and partnerships are private enterprises that do not issue shares for sale to the public. They normally report their financial information in accordance with the accounting standards for private enterprises. These standards are less complicated than the International Financial Reporting Standards that publicly accountable enterprises must use. For example, private enterprises are not required to report other comprehensive income.

The use of accounting standards for private enterprises does not mean, however, that the standards are less rigorous than those used by publicly accountable enterprises. This simplified set of standards makes the preparation and audit of financial statements affordable for smaller business entities. All of the principles such as economic substance over form and the excess of benefit over cost guided the production of these standards.

OWNER'S EQUITY FOR A SOLE PROPRIETORSHIP

A sole proprietorship is an unincorporated business owned by one person. Only two owner's equity accounts are needed: (1) a capital account for the proprietor (J. Doe, capital), and (2) a drawing (or withdrawal) account for the proprietor (J. Doe, drawings).

The capital account of a sole proprietorship serves two purposes: to record investments by the owner and to accumulate periodic profit or loss. The drawing account is used to record the owner's withdrawals of cash or other assets from the business. The drawing account is closed to the capital account at the end of each accounting period. The capital account reflects the cumulative total of all investments by the owner, plus all earnings of the entity, less all withdrawals of resources from the entity by the owner.

In most respects, the accounting for a sole proprietorship is the same as for a corporation. Exhibit 12.8 presents the recording of selected transactions and the owner's equity section of the statement of financial position of Doe Retail Store to illustrate the accounting for owner's equity for a sole proprietorship.

Selected Transactions during 2011

Exhibit **12.8**

Accounting for Owner's
Equity for a
Sole Proprietorship

January 1, 2011

J. Doe started a retail store by investing $150,000 of personal savings. The journal entry for the business is as follows:

| Cash (A) .... | 150,000 | |
| J. Doe, capital (OE) .... | | 150,000 |

Assets		=	Liabilities	+	Owner's Equity	
Cash	+150,000				J. Doe, capital	+150,000

During 2011

Each month during the year, Doe withdrew $1,000 cash from the business for personal living expenses. Accordingly, the following journal entry was made each month:

| J. Doe, drawings (OE) .... | 1,000 | |
| Cash (A).. | | 1,000 |

Assets		=	Liabilities	+	Owner's Equity	
Cash	−1,000				J. Doe, drawings	−1,000

Note: At December 31, 2011, after the last withdrawal, the drawings account will reflect a debit balance of $12,000.

December 31, 2011

The store's operations for the year resulted in revenues of $128,000 and expenses of $110,000. The revenue and expense accounts are closed to the capital account at the end of the year. The closing entry follows:

Individual revenue accounts (R)	128,000	
Individual expense account (E)		110,000
J. Doe, capital (OE)		18,000

Assets	=	Liabilities	+	Owner's Equity	
				Revenues	−128,000
				Expenses	+110,000
				J. Doe, capital	+18,000

December 31, 2011

The journal entry required to close the drawings account follows:

| J. Doe, capital (OE) .... | 12,000 | |
| J. Doe, drawings (OE) .... | | 12,000 |

Assets	=	Liabilities	+	Owner's Equity	
				J. Doe, capital	−12,000
				J. Doe, drawings	+12,000

Exhibit **12.8**

(Continued)

Statement of Financial Position, December 31, 2011 (partial)

Owner's equity

J. Doe, capital, January 1, 2011	$150,000
Add: Profit for 2011	18,000
Total	168,000
Less: Withdrawals for 2011	(12,000)
J. Doe, capital, December 31, 2011	$156,000

A sole proprietorship does not pay income taxes. Therefore, its financial statements do not reflect income tax expense or income taxes payable. Instead, the profit of a sole proprietorship is taxed when it is included on the owner's personal income tax return. Because an employer/employee contractual relationship cannot exist with only one party involved, a "salary" to the owner is not recognized as an expense of a sole proprietorship. The owner's salary is accounted for as a distribution of profits (i.e., a withdrawal).

OWNERS' EQUITY FOR A PARTNERSHIP

Small businesses and professionals such as accountants, doctors, and lawyers use the partnership form of business. It is formed by two or more persons reaching mutual agreement about the terms of the partnership. The law does not require an application for a charter as it does in the case of a corporation. Instead, the agreement between the partners constitutes a legally enforceable partnership contract. The agreement should specify matters such as division of periodic profit, management responsibilities, transfer or sale of partnership interests, disposition of assets upon liquidation, and procedures to be followed in case of the death of a partner. If the partnership agreement does not specify these matters, the applicable provincial laws are binding.

The primary advantages of a partnership are (1) ease of formation, (2) complete control by the partners, and (3) lack of income taxes on the business itself. The primary disadvantage is the unlimited liability of each partner for the partnership's liabilities. If the partnership does not have sufficient assets to satisfy outstanding debt, its creditors can seize the partners' personal assets.

As with a sole proprietorship, accounting for transactions undertaken by a partnership follows the same underlying fundamentals as any other form of business organization, except for those entries that directly affect owners' equity.

Accounting for partners' equity follows the same pattern as illustrated earlier for a sole proprietorship, except that separate partner capital and drawings accounts must be established for each partner. Investments by each partner are credited to the partner's capital account, and withdrawals from the partnership by each partner are debited to the respective drawings account. The profit for a partnership is divided between the partners in the profit ratio specified in the partnership agreement, and credited to each partner's account. The respective drawings accounts also are closed to the partner capital accounts. After the closing process, each partner's capital account reflects the cumulative total of all investments of that individual partner, plus the partner's share of all partnership earnings, less all the partner's withdrawals.

Exhibit 12.9 presents selected journal entries and partial financial statements for AB Partnership to illustrate the accounting for the distribution of profit and partners' equity.

Exhibit **12.9**

Accounting for
Partners' Equity

Selected Transactions during 2011

January 1, 2011

A. Able and B. Baker organized AB Partnership on this date. Able contributed $60,000 and Baker $40,000 cash to the partnership and agreed to divide profit (and loss) 60% and 40%, respectively. The journal entry for the business to record the investment follows:

Cash (A)	100,000	
A. Able, capital (OE)		60,000
B. Baker, capital (OE)		40,000

Assets		=	Liabilities	+	Owner's Equity	
Cash	+100,000				A. Able, capital	+60,000
					B. Baker, capital	+40,000

During 2011

The partners agreed that Able would withdraw $1,000 and Baker $650 per month in cash. Accordingly, the following journal entry for the withdrawals was made each month:

A. Able, drawings (OE)	1,000	
B. Baker, drawings (OE)	650	
Cash (A)		1,650

Assets		=	Liabilities	+	Owner's Equity	
Cash	−1,650				A. Able, drawings	−1,000
					B. Baker, drawings	−650

December 31, 2011

Assume that the normal closing entries for the revenue and expense accounts resulted in a profit of $30,000 that was distributed between the two partners. The closing entry is as follows:

Individual revenue accounts (R)	150,000	
Individual expense accounts (E)		120,000
A. Able, capital (OE)		18,000
B. Baker, capital (OE)		12,000

Assets	=	Liabilities	+	Owner's Equity	
				Revenues	−150,000
				Expenses	+120,000
				A. Able, capital	+18,000
				B. Baker, capital	+12,000

Profit is divided as follows:

A. Able, $30,000 × 60%	$18,000
B. Baker, $30,000 × 40%	12,000
Total	$30,000

December 31, 2011

The journal entry required to close the drawings accounts follows:

A. Able, capital (OE)	12,000	
B. Baker, capital (OE)	7,800	
A. Able, drawings (OE)		12,000
B. Baker, drawings (OE)		7,800

Assets	=	Liabilities	+	Owner's Equity	
				A. Able, capital	−12,000
				B. Baker, capital	−7,800
				A. Able, drawings	+12,000
				B. Baker, drawings	+7,800

Exhibit **12.9**

(Continued)

A separate statement of partners' capital, similar to the following, is customarily prepared to supplement the statement of financial position:

AB PARTNERSHIP
Statement of Partners' Capital
For the Year Ended December 31, 2011

	A. Able	B. Baker	Total
Investment, January 1, 2011	$60,000	$40,000	$100,000
Add: Additional investments during the year	0	0	0
Profit for the year	18,000	12,000	30,000
Totals	78,000	52,000	130,000
Less: Drawings during the year	(12,000)	(7,800)	(19,800)
Partners' equity, December 31, 2011	$66,000	$44,200	$110,200

The financial statements of a partnership follow the same format as those for a corporation, except that (1) the income statement includes an additional section titled distribution of profit, (2) the partners' equity section of the statement of financial position is detailed for each partner, (3) a partnership has no income tax expense because partnerships do not pay income tax (each partner must report his or her share of the partnership profit on his or her individual tax return), and (4) salaries paid to partners are not recorded as expense but are treated as a distribution of profit (withdrawals).

CHAPTER **TAKE-AWAYS**

1. **Explain the role of share capital in the capital structure of a corporation. p. 639**
   The law recognizes corporations as separate legal entities. Owners invest in a corporation and receive shares that can be traded on established stock exchanges. Shares provide a number of rights, including the right to receive dividends.

2. **Analyze the earnings per share ratio. p. 642**
   The earnings per share ratio facilitates the comparison of a company's earnings over time or with other companies' at a single point in time. By expressing earnings on a per share basis, differences in the size of companies become less important.

3. **Describe the characteristics of common shares and analyze transactions affecting common shares. p. 643**
   A common share is the basic voting share issued by a corporation. Usually it has no par value, but par value shares also can be issued. Preferred shares are issued by some corporations. These shares contain some special rights and may appeal to certain investors.
   A number of key transactions involve share capital: (1) initial sale of shares, (2) cash dividends, (3) stock dividends and stock splits, and repurchase of shares. Each is illustrated in this chapter.

4. **Discuss dividends and analyze related transactions. p. 648**
   The return associated with an investment in shares comes from two sources: appreciation of share price and dividends. Dividends are recorded as a liability when they are declared by the board of directors (i.e., on the date of declaration). The liability is satisfied when the dividends are paid (i.e., the date of payment).

5. **Analyze the dividend yield ratio. p. 651**
   The dividend yield ratio measures the percentage of return on investment from dividends. For most companies, the return associated with dividends is very small.

6. **Discuss the purpose of stock dividends, stock splits, and report transactions. p. 652**
   Stock dividends are distributions of a company's shares to existing shareholders on a pro rata basis. The transaction involves transferring an additional amount into the common shares account from the retained earnings account. A stock split also involves the distribution of

additional shares to shareholders but no additional amount is transferred into the common shares account from the retained earnings account.

7. **Describe the characteristics of preferred shares and analyze transactions affecting preferred shares. p. 654**
Preferred shares provide investors certain advantages, including dividend preferences and a preference on asset distributions in the event the corporation is liquidated.

8. **Measure and report changes in shareholders' equity. p. 657**
The shareholders' equity section of the statement of financial position is affected by many changes that occur over time. These changes are reported in a separate statement of changes in equity that discloses a summary of the effects of transactions and events that affected the various components of equity, including share capital, contributed surplus, retained earnings, and accumulated other comprehensive income (loss).

9. **Discuss the impact of share capital transactions on cash flows. p. 659**
Both inflows (e.g., issuance of share capital) and outflows (e.g., repurchase of shares) are reported in the financing activities section of the statement of cash flows. The payment of dividends is reported as an outflow in this section.

Throughout the preceding chapters, we emphasized the conceptual basis of accounting. An understanding of the rationale underlying accounting is important for both preparers and users of financial statements. In Chapter 13, we bring together our discussion of the major users of financial statements and how they analyze and use them. We discuss and illustrate many widely used analytical techniques discussed in earlier chapters, as well as additional techniques. As you study Chapter 13, you will see that an understanding of accounting rules and concepts is essential for effective analysis of financial statements.

KEY **RATIOS**

The **earnings per share** ratio states the profit of a corporation on a per common share basis. The ratio is computed as follows (p. 642):

$$\text{Earnings per Share} = \frac{\text{Profit Available to Common Shareholders}}{\text{Average Number of Common Shares Outstanding}}$$

The **dividend yield ratio** measures the dividend return on the current share price. The ratio is computed as follows (p. 651):

$$\text{Dividend Yield Ratio} = \frac{\text{Dividends per Share}}{\text{Market Price per Share}}$$

FINDING **FINANCIAL INFORMATION**

STATEMENT OF FINANCIAL POSITION
Under Current Liabilities
Dividends, once declared by the board of directors, are reported as a liability (usually current).

Under Non-current Liabilities
Transactions involving share capital do not usually generate non-current liabilities.

Under Shareholders' Equity
Typical accounts include
Preferred shares
Common shares
Contributed surplus
Retained earnings
Accumulated other comprehensive income (loss)

INCOME STATEMENT
Share capital is never shown on the income statement. Dividends are not an expense. They are a distribution of profit and are, therefore, not reported on the income statement.

STATEMENT OF CASH FLOWS
Under Financing Activities
+ Cash inflows from initial sale of shares
− Cash outflows for dividends
− Cash outflows for repurchase of shares

**STATEMENT OF CHANGES IN
SHAREHOLDERS' EQUITY**

This statement reports detailed information concerning shareholders' equity, including (1) amounts in each equity account, (2) number of shares outstanding, (3) impact of transactions such as declaration of dividends and repurchase of shares.

NOTES
Under Summary of Significant Accounting Policies

Usually, very little information concerning share capital is provided in this summary.

Under a Separate Note

Most companies report information about their stock option plans and information about major transactions such as stock dividends. A historical summary of dividends paid per share is typically provided.

KEY TERMS

Authorized Number of Shares p. 641

Common Shares p. 643

Convertible Preferred Shares p. 655

Cumulative Dividend Preference p. 656

Current Dividend Preference p. 656

Date of Record p. 649

Declaration Date p. 649

Dividends in Arrears p. 656

Issued Shares p. 641

Legal Capital p. 643

No Par Value Shares p. 643

Outstanding Shares p. 641

Par Value p. 643

Payment Date p. 649

Preferred Shares p. 654

Stock Dividend p. 652

Stock Split p. 654

QUESTIONS

1. Define *corporation* and identify its primary advantages.
2. What is the charter of a corporation?
3. Explain each of the following terms: (a) *authorized shares*, (b) *issued shares*, and (c) *outstanding shares*.
4. Name three rights of shareholders. Which of these is most important in your mind? Why?
5. Differentiate between common shares and preferred shares.
6. Explain the distinction between par value shares and no par value shares.
7. What are the usual characteristics of preferred shares?
8. What are the two basic sources of shareholders' equity? Explain each.
9. Owners' equity is accounted for by source. What does *source* mean?
10. What are the two basic requirements to support the declaration of a cash dividend? What are the effects of a cash dividend on assets and shareholders' equity?
11. Differentiate between cumulative and non-cumulative preferred shares.
12. Define *stock dividend*. How does it differ from a cash dividend?
13. What are the primary purposes of issuing a stock dividend?
14. Identify and explain the three important dates with respect to dividends.
15. Define *retained earnings*. What are the primary components of retained earnings at the end of each period?
16. Define *prior period adjustments*. How are they reported?
17. Define *accumulated other comprehensive income (loss)*. Why is it a separate component of shareholders' equity?
18. Your parents have just retired and have asked you for some financial advice. They have decided to invest $100,000 in a company very similar to BCE Inc. The company has issued both common and preferred shares. What factors would you consider in giving them advice? Which type of shares would you recommend?

EXERCISES

E12–1 **Determining the Effects of the Issuance of Common and Preferred Shares**

LO1, 3, 7

Kelly Incorporated was issued a charter on January 15, 2011, that authorized the following share capital:

Common shares, no par value, 100,000 shares.

Preferred shares, $1.50, no par value, 5,000 shares. (*Note:* $1.50 is the dividend rate.)

During 2011, the following selected transactions occurred:

a. Issued 30,000 common shares at $18 cash per share.

b. Issued 2,000 preferred shares at $25 cash per share.

At the end of 2011, the company's profit equalled $42,000.

Required:

1. Prepare the shareholders' equity section of the statement of financial position at December 31, 2011.

2. Assume that you are a common shareholder. If Kelly needed additional capital, would you prefer to have it issue additional common or preferred shares? Explain.

E12–2 **Reporting Shareholders' Equity**

LO1, 2

The financial statements of Sun Media Inc. included the following selected information at December 31, 2012:

Common shares	$6,000,000
Retained earnings	850,000
Profit	1,200,000
Dividends declared	800,000

The common shares were sold at $20 per share.

Required:

1. What was the amount of retained earnings at the beginning of 2012?

2. Compute earnings per share.

3. Prepare the shareholders' equity section of the company's statement of financial position at December 31, 2012.

E12–3 **Reporting Shareholders' Equity and Determining Dividend Policy**

LO1, 3

Sampson Corporation was organized in 2011 to operate a financial consulting business. The charter authorized the issue of 12,000 common shares. During the first year, the following selected transactions were completed:

a. Issued 6,000 common shares for cash at $22 per share.

b. Issued 600 common shares for a piece of land to be used for a facilities site; construction began immediately. Assume that the market price per share was $22 on the date of issuance. Debit land account.

c. Issued 1,000 common shares for cash at $23 per share.

d. At year-end, the income statement showed a loss of $7,000. Because a loss was incurred, no income tax expense was recorded.

Required:

1. Prepare the journal entry required for each of these transactions.

2. Prepare the shareholders' equity section as it should be reported on the statement of financial position at year-end, December 31, 2011.

3. Can Sampson pay dividends at year-end? Explain.

E12–4 **Determining the Effects of Transactions on Shareholders' Equity**

LO1, 3, 7

Nguyen Corporation was organized in January 2012 by 10 shareholders to operate an air-conditioning sales and service business. The charter issued by the government authorized the following no par value shares:

Common shares, 200,000 shares.

Preferred shares, 50,000 shares.

During January and February 2012, the following transactions were completed:

a. Collected $60,000 cash from each of the 10 organizers and issued 3,000 common shares to each of them.

b. Issued 8,000 preferred shares at $25 per share; collected the cash.

c. Issued 500 common shares to a new investor at $25 per share; collected the cash.

The company's operations resulted in profit of $40,000 for 2012. The board of directors declared cash dividends of $25,000 that were paid in December 2012. The preferred shares have a dividend rate of $1 per share.

Required:

1. Prepare the shareholders' equity section of the statement of financial position at December 31, 2012.

2. Why would an investor prefer to buy a preferred share rather than a common share?

3. Is it ethical to sell shares to outsiders at a higher price than the amount paid by the organizers?

LO1, 3

E12–5 **Recording Shareholders' Equity Transactions, Including Non-cash Consideration**
Teacher Corporation obtained a charter at the start of 2011 that authorized 50,000 no par value common shares and 40,000, $1, no par value preferred shares. The corporation was organized by four individuals who "reserved" 51 percent of the common shares for themselves. The remaining shares were to be sold to other individuals at $50 per share on a cash basis. During 2011, the following selected transactions occurred:

a. Collected $25 per share cash from three of the organizers and received two adjoining lots of land from the fourth organizer. Issued 3,000 common shares to each of the four organizers and received title to the land.

b. Issued 6,000 common shares to an investor at $50 cash per share.

c. Issued 8,000 preferred shares at $25 cash per share.

d. At the end of 2011, the accounts reflected profit of $42,000.

Required:

1. Prepare the journal entries to record each of these transactions.

2. Write a brief memo to explain the basis that you used to determine the cost of the land.

3. Is it ethical to sell shares to outsiders at a higher price than the amount paid by the organizers?

LO1, 4

E12–6 **Determining the Ending Balance of Retained Earnings and Evaluating Dividend Policy**
The following account balances were selected from the records of Blake Corporation at December 31, 2011, after all adjusting entries were completed:

Common shares (no par value; authorized 100,000 shares, issued 36,000 shares)	$540,000
Contributed surplus	150,000
Dividends declared and paid in 2011	18,000
Retained earnings, January 1, 2011	67,000
Correction of prior period accounting error (a debit, net of income tax)	8,000
Income summary for 2011 (credit balance)	28,000

The stock price was $17.89 per share on that date.

Required:

1. Identify the amounts that would be reported in the retained earnings column of the statement of change in equity for 2011.

2. Prepare the shareholders' equity section of the statement of financial position at December 31, 2011.

3. Compute and evaluate the dividend yield ratio.

LO4, 6

E12–7 **Analyzing the Impact of Dividend Policy**
McDonald and Associates is a small manufacturer of electronic connections for local area networks. Consider three independent situations.

Case 1: McDonald increases its cash dividends by 50 percent, but no other changes occur in the company's operations.

Case 2: The company's profit and cash flows increase by 50 percent, but this does not change its dividends.

Case 3: McDonald issues a 50 percent stock dividend, but no other changes occur.

Required:

1. How do you think each situation would affect the company's stock price?
2. If the company changed its accounting policies and reported higher profit, would the change have an impact on the stock price?

E12–8   Computing Dividends on Preferred Shares and Analyzing Differences   ■ **LO4**

The records of Hoffman Company reflected the following balances in the shareholders' equity accounts at December 31, 2011:

Common shares, no par value, 40,000 shares outstanding	$800,000
Preferred shares, $2, no par value, 6,000 shares outstanding	150,000
Retained earnings	235,000

On September 1, 2012, the board of directors was considering the distribution of a $62,000 cash dividend. No dividends were paid during 2010 and 2011. You have been asked to determine dividend amounts under two independent assumptions (show computations):

a. The preferred shares are non-cumulative.
b. The preferred shares are cumulative.

Required:

1. Determine the total amounts that would be paid to the preferred shareholders and to the common shareholders under the two independent assumptions.
2. Write a brief memo to explain why the dividend per common share was less under the second assumption.
3. Why would an investor buy Hoffman's common shares instead of its preferred shares if they pay a lower dividend per share? Explain. The market prices of the preferred and common shares were $25 and $40, respectively, on September 1, 2012.

E12–9   Determining the Impact of Dividends   ■ **LO4**

Average Corporation has the following shares outstanding at the end of 2010:

Preferred shares, $4, no par value; 8,000 outstanding shares.

Common shares, no par value; 30,000 outstanding shares.

On October 1, 2011, the board of directors declared dividends as follows:

Preferred shares: Full dividend amount, payable December 20, 2011.

Common shares: 10 percent common stock dividend (i.e., one additional share for each 10 held), issuable December 20, 2011.

On December 20, 2011, the market prices were $50 per preferred share and $32 per common share.

Required:
Explain the effect of each of the dividends on the assets, liabilities, and shareholders' equity of the company at each of the specified dates.

E12–10   Recording the Payment of Dividends   ■ **LO4**

Sun Life Financial Inc. disclosed the following information in a press release: Sun Life Financial Inc.

TORONTO – (February 11, 2010) - The Board of Directors of Sun Life Financial Inc. (TSX/ NYSE: SLF) today announced a quarterly shareholder dividend of $0.36 per common share, payable March 31, 2010, to shareholders of record at the close of business on February 24, 2010. This is the same amount as paid in the previous quarter.

The Board of Directors of Sun Life Financial Inc. also announced the following quarterly dividends on its Class A Non-Cumulative Preferred Shares payable on March 31, 2010, to shareholders of record at the close of business on February 24, 2010: $0.296875 per Series 1 share; $0.30 per Series 2 share; $0.278125 per Series 3 share; $0.278125 per Series 4 share; and $0.28125 per Series 5 share and $0.375 per Series 6R share.

Assume that Sun Life has the following number of shares outstanding at the date of dividend declaration: Common shares, 565 million; Preferred shares, Series 1—16 million, Series 2—13 million, Series 3—10 million, Series 4—12 million, Series 5—10 million, Series 6R—10 million.

Required:

1. Prepare the journal entries to record the declaration and payment of dividends to common shareholders.

2. Prepare the journal entries to record the declaration and payment of dividends to preferred shareholders.

LO6   **E12–11**   **Analyzing Stock Dividends**

On December 31, 2012, the shareholders' equity section of the statement of financial position of R & B Corporation reflected the following:

Common shares (no par value, authorized 60,000 shares, outstanding 25,000 shares)	$250,000
Contributed surplus	12,000
Retained earnings	75,000
Accumulated other comprehensive income	8,000

On February 1, 2013, the board of directors declared a 12 percent stock dividend to be issued April 30, 2013. The market value per share was $18 on the declaration date.

Required:

1. For comparative purposes, prepare the shareholders' equity section of the statement of financial position (a) before the stock dividend and (b) after the stock dividend. (*Hint:* Use two columns for this requirement.)

2. Explain the effects of this stock dividend on the company's assets, liabilities, and shareholders' equity.

LO1, 6   **E12–12**   **Analyzing Stock Dividends**

At the beginning of the year 2012, the shareholders' equity section of the statement of financial position of Ponti Corporation reflected the following:

Common shares, no par value, authorized unlimited number of shares, issued and outstanding 36,000 shares	$360,000
Retained earnings	750,000

On February 1, 2012, the board of directors declared a 100 percent stock dividend to be issued on April 30, 2012. The price per common share was $18 on February 1.

Required:

1. For comparative purposes, prepare the shareholders' equity section of the statement of financial position (a) before the stock dividend and (b) after the stock dividend. (*Hint:* Use two columns to shows amounts for this requirement.)

2. Explain the effects of this stock dividend on assets, liabilities, and shareholders' equity.

LO6   **E12–13**   **Determining the Impact of Stock Dividends and Stock Splits**

Milano Tools Inc. announced a 100 percent stock dividend.

Required:

1. Determine the impact (increase, decrease, no change) of this dividend on the following:

    a. Total assets

    b. Total liabilities

    c. Common shares

    d. Total shareholders' equity

    e. Market value per common share

2. Now assume that the company announced a 2-for-1 stock split. Determine the impact of the stock split on the five items above. Explain why the accounting for stock dividends differs from that of the stock split.

E12–14 Evaluating Dividend Policy

■ **LO4**

H&R Block

H&R Block is a well-known name, especially during income tax time each year. The company serves more than 24 million taxpayers in more than 10,000 offices in Canada, Australia, England, and the United States. The company's news releases for 2010 contained the following announcements:

> **H&R BLOCK REPORTS CONTINUED IMPROVEMENT IN FINANCIAL RESULTS FOR FISCAL 2010 SECOND QUARTER**
>
> KANSAS CITY, MO, Dec 08, 2009 (MARKETWIRE via COMTEX) – H&R Block Inc. (NYSE: HRB) today reported a net loss from continuing operations for the fiscal second quarter ended Oct. 31, 2009, of $126.5 million, or 38 cents per share compared to a loss of $133.2 million, or 40 cents per share in the second quarter a year ago. H&R Block typically reports a second quarter operating loss due to the seasonality of its business.
>
> *Source:* H&R Block News Release.
>
> . . .
>
> **H&R BLOCK ANNOUNCES QUARTERLY CASH DIVIDEND**
>
> KANSAS CITY, MO, Nov 30, 2009 (MARKETWIRE via COMTEX) – The Board of Directors of H&R Block Inc. (NYSE: HRB) has declared a quarterly cash dividend of 15 cents per share, payable Jan. 4, 2010, to shareholders of record Dec. 12, 2009.
>
> *Source:* H&R Block News Release.

Required:

1. Explain why H&R Block can pay dividends despite the loss that it announced for the previous quarter.

2. What factors did the board of directors consider when it declared the dividends?

E12–15 Analyzing the Repurchase of Shares

■ **LO3**

Winnebago

Winnebago is a familiar name on vehicles travelling North American highways. The company manufactures and sells large motor homes for vacation travel. These motor homes can be quickly recognized because of the company's "flying W" trademark. A news article contained the following information:

> The Company's profits have been running double a year ago, revenues were up 27 percent in the May quarter and order backlog stands at 2,229 units. Those are the kind of growth statistics that build confidence in the boardroom. The Company has announced plans to spend $3.6 million to expand its manufacturing facilities and it recently authorized repurchase of $15 million worth of its own shares, the third buyback in two years. The Company's stock is now selling for $25 per share.

Required:

1. Determine the impact of this transaction on the financial statements.

2. Why do you think the board decided to repurchase the company's shares?

3. What impact will this purchase have on Winnebago's future dividend obligations?

■ **LO3**

Danier Leather

E12–16   Repurchase of Shares

Danier Leather Inc. manufactures and retails leather products, earning international recognition as a leader in leather and suede design. The company's annual report for the fiscal year ended June 27, 2009, included the following (all amounts are in thousands):

(d) Normal course issuer bids

On May 5, 2009, the Company received approval from the TSX to commence a normal course issuer bid (the "2009 NCIB"). The Company had a previous Normal Course Issuer Bid that expired on May 5, 2009 (the "2008 NCIB"). The 2009 NCIB permits the Company to acquire up to 267,183 Subordinate Voting Shares, representing approximately 10% of the "public float" of the Subordinate Voting Shares, during the period from May 7, 2009 to May 6, 2010. Under the 2008 NCIB which expired on May 5, 2009, the Company repurchased 100,000 Subordinate Voting Shares for cancellation at a weighted average price per share of $4.60. Under the 2009 NCIB, as of June 27, 2009, the Company had repurchased 267,160 Subordinate Voting Shares for cancellation at a weighted average price per share of $4.24.

The following Subordinate Voting Shares were repurchased for cancellation during year ended June 27, 2009 and June 28, 2008:

	June 27, 2009	June 28, 2008
Number of shares repurchased	367,160	169,000
Amount changed to share capital	$ 1,556	$ 715
Amount charged to retained earnings representing the excess over the average paid-in value	37	950
Total cash consideration	$ 1,593	$ 1,665

Source: Danier Leather Annual Report 2009.

Required:

1. What was the average price that the company paid to repurchase shares in fiscal year 2009?

2. Prepare the journal entry to record a summary of the 2009 repurchase transactions.

PROBLEMS

■ **LO1–4, 6**

P12–1   Finding Missing Amounts (AP12–1)

At December 31, 2011, the records of Nortech Corporation provided the following selected and incomplete data:

Common shares, no par value
   Shares authorized, 200,000.
   Shares issued, _____?_____; issue price $17 per share; cash collected in full, $2,125,000.
Profit for 2011, $118,000.
Dividends declared and paid during 2011, $75,000.
Prior period adjustment, correction of 2010 accounting error, $9,000 (a credit, net of income tax).
Retained earnings balance, January 1, 2011, $155,000.

Required:

1. Complete the following tabulation:
   Shares authorized, _____.
   Shares issued, _____.
   Shares outstanding, _____.

2. Earnings per share, $ _____.

3. Dividend paid per common share, $ _____.

4. The prior period adjustment should be reported on the _____ as an addition to _____ (or a deduction from _____).

5. The amount of retained earnings available for dividends on January 1, 2011, was $_____.

6. Assume that the board of directors voted a 100 percent stock split (the number of shares will double). After the stock split, the average issue price per share will be $_____, and the number of outstanding shares will be _____.

7. Assume that the company declared a 100 percent stock dividend instead of the 100 percent stock split. Compare and contrast the stock dividend and the stock split with regard to their effects on shareholders' equity components.

P12–2 **Recording Transactions Affecting Shareholders' Equity** (AP12–2)

 ▓ **LO1, 3**

Pappas Corporation began operations in January 2012. The charter authorized the following share capital:

Preferred shares: 9 percent, $25 par value, authorized 80,000 shares.

Common shares: no par value, authorized 160,000 shares.

During 2012, the following transactions occurred in the order given:

a. Issued 40,000 common shares to each of the three organizers. Collected $9 cash per share from two of the organizers, and received a plot of land with a small building on it in full payment for the shares of the third organizer and issued the shares immediately. Assume that 30 percent of the non-cash payment received applies to the building.

b. Sold 4,800 preferred shares at $25 per share. Collected the cash and issued the shares immediately.

c. Sold 4,000 preferred shares at $25 and 2,000 common shares at $12 per share. Collected the cash and issued the shares immediately.

d. The operating results at the end of 2012 were as follows:

Revenues	$440,000
Expenses, including income taxes	320,000

Required:

1. Prepare the journal entries to record each of these transactions and to close the accounts.

2. Write a brief memo explaining how you determined the cost of the land and the building in the first journal entry.

3. Prepare the shareholders' equity section of the statement of financial position for Pappas Corporation as at December 31, 2012.

P12–3 **Preparing the Shareholders' Equity Section after Selected Transactions** (AP12–3)

 ▓ **LO1, 3, 4**

Eddie Edwards Limited, a public company, was formed on January 2, 2011, with the following authorized capital structure:

Preferred shares: No par value, $1.00 per share quarterly cumulative dividend, callable at 103, 100,000 shares

Common shares: Unlimited number of shares

The following selected transactions occurred during the first six months of operations:

January 2	Issued 100,000 common shares in exchange for land and building with a combined appraised value of $2,200,000. Sixty percent of the acquisition cost is attributable to the building.
January 3	Issued 50,000 preferred shares for $1,250,000 cash.
April 1	Declared the quarterly cash dividend on the preferred shares, payable on April 25.
April 10	Declared and distributed a 5 percent common stock dividend on all outstanding common shares as of March 31. The market price of the common shares on March 31 was $24 per share.
April 25	Paid the preferred dividend that was declared on April 1.

Required:

1. Prepare journal entries to record the above transactions.

2. Prepare the shareholders' equity section of the statement of financial position for Eddie Edwards Limited as at June 30, 2011. Assume that the company recorded profit of $500,000 for its first six months.

LO5, 6

eXcel

P12–4   **Comparing Stock and Cash Dividends** (AP12–4)

Water Tower Company had the following shares outstanding and retained earnings at December 31, 2011:

Preferred shares, 7% (par value $25; outstanding, 1,200 shares)	$ 30,000
Common shares (outstanding, 30,000 shares)	120,000
Retained earnings	140,000

The board of directors is considering the distribution of a cash dividend to the two groups of shareholders. No dividends were declared during 2009 or 2010. Three independent cases are assumed:

Case A: The preferred shares are non-cumulative; the total amount of dividends is $15,000.

Case B: The preferred shares are cumulative; the total amount of dividends is $6,300.

Case C: Same as Case B, except the amount is $33,000.

Required:

1. Compute the amount of dividends, in total and per share, that would be payable to each class of shareholders for each case. Show computations.

2. Assume that the company issued a 10 percent common stock dividend on the outstanding common shares when the market value per share was $24. Complete the following comparative schedule, including explanation of the differences.

	Amount of Dollar Increase (Decrease)	
Item	**Cash Dividend—Case C**	**Stock Dividend**
Assets	$_____	$_____
Liabilities	$_____	$_____
Shareholders' equity	$_____	$_____

LO4

P12–5   **Analyzing Dividend Policy**

Dana and David, two young financial analysts, were reviewing financial statements for Research In Motion (RIM), a manufacturer of wireless mobile communication devices, including the well-known BlackBerry®. Dana noted that the company did not report any dividends in the financing activity section of the statement of cash flows and said, "I have heard that RIM is one of the best performing companies. If it's so good, I wonder why it isn't paying any dividends." David wasn't convinced that Dana was looking in the right place for dividends but didn't say anything.

Dana continued the discussion and noted, "Sales are nearly up by 50 percent over the previous two years. While profit is up over $600 million compared to last year, cash flow from operating activities increased by nearly $1,500 million compared to the previous year."

At that point, David noted that the statement of cash flows reported that the company had repurchased nearly $800 million in common shares. He commented, "No wonder it can't pay dividends. With cash flows being used to repurchase shares, the board is probably reluctant to obligate itself to dividends."

Required:

1. Correct any misstatements that either Dana or David made. Explain.

2. Which of the factors presented in the case help you understand the company's dividend policy?

LO4

P12–6   **Determining the Financial Statement Effects of Dividends**

Legrand Company has outstanding 45,000 common shares and 25,000, $4, preferred shares. On December 1, 2011, the board of directors voted to distribute a $4 cash dividend per preferred share and a 5 percent common stock dividend on the common shares. At the date of declaration, the common share was selling at $40 and the preferred share at $50. The dividends are to be paid, or issued, on February 15, 2012. The company's fiscal year ends on December 31.

Required:
Explain the comparative effects of the two dividends on the assets, liabilities, and shareholders' equity (a) through December 31, 2011, (b) on February 15, 2012, and (c) the overall effects from December 1, 2011, through February 15, 2012. A schedule similar to the following might be helpful:

	Comparative Effects Explained	
Item	**Cash Dividend on Preferred**	**Stock Dividend on Common**
1. Through December 31, 2011: Assets, etc.		

P12–7 Recording Dividends

RBC Financial Group provides personal and commercial banking, wealth management services, insurance, corporate and investment banking, and transaction processing services on a global basis. On March 3, 2006, a press release announced the following:

> Royal Bank of Canada (RY: TSX, NYSE, SWX) today announced that its Board of Directors has declared a stock dividend, which has the same effect as a two-for-one split of its common shares.
>
> RBC's last stock dividend was paid on October 5, 2000.
>
> The Board of Directors today also declared a quarterly common share cash dividend of $0.72 per share, which represents $0.36 per share on a post-stock dividend basis. This dividend of $0.36 per share is payable on May 24, 2006, to common shareholders of record on April 25, 2006.

Required:
1. Prepare any journal entries that RBC Financial should make as the result of information in the preceding report. Assume that the company has 1.3 million shares outstanding with a market value of $47 per share and an average issue price of $5.60.

2. What do you think happened to the company's stock price after the March 3 announcement?

3. What factors did the board of directors consider in making this decision?

P12–8 Determining the Balance of Retained Earnings and Preparing the Shareholders' Equity Section

The annual report of Andrew Peller Ltd. for fiscal year 2006 included the financial statements for fiscal year 2005, which were restated to reflect the effects of a fraudulent action by a former employee. The restated financial statements included the following items and their account balances:

Share capital	$ 7,375	
Retained earnings, beginning of year	79,260	
Profit	8,467	
Dividends declared	3,109	
Effect of prior period adjustment	593	Debit balance

Required:
1. Determine the balance of retained earnings for the year ending March 31, 2005, and prepare the shareholders' equity section of the statement of financial position as at March 31, 2005.

2. The company provided the following explanation for the prior period adjustment. Use the amounts shown in the "Adjustment" column on the following page to reconstruct the journal entry that was prepared to record the effect of the alleged fraud on the identified income statement and statement of financial position accounts.

PRIOR PERIOD ADJUSTMENT

During fiscal 2006, management uncovered evidence of a misappropriation of certain assets (related to an alleged fraud by a former non-executive employee). As a result, management determined that certain costs, which previously had been included in the cost of inventories, should have been expensed. In addition, certain costs previously included in cost of goods sold have been reclassified as unusual items. Accordingly, the consolidated financial statements for the fiscal year ended March 31, 2005, have been restated as follows from the amounts previously reported:

	As previously reported	Adjustment	As restated
Cost of sales	$ 96,660	$ (1,058)	$ 95,602
Unusual items	—	1,173	1,173
Income tax expense	4,730	(44)	4,686
Profit	8,538	(71)	8,467
Inventories	62,045	(1,072)	60,973
Income taxes recoverable	693	408	1,101
Retained earnings as at March 31, 2005	79,924	(664)	79,260
Retained earnings as at March 31, 2004	74,494	(593)	73,901

LO8

Thomson Reuters Corporation

P12–9 Determining the Balance of Retained Earnings and Preparing the Statement of Changes in Equity (AP12–5)

The consolidated statements of changes in equity of Thomson Reuters Corporation for fiscal years 2009 and 2008 included the following items and their account balances at December 31, 2009 and 2008 (in millions of U.S. dollars). This list shows the balances of the various components of shareholders' equity at the beginning of each year, and changes that affected these components during the year. These changes are presented in a random order.

	2009	2008
Share capital, beginning of year	3,050	2,727
Contributed surplus, beginning of year	156	109
Retained earnings, beginning of year	10,650	10,476
Accumulated other comprehensive income (loss), beginning of year	(2,268)	1
Stock-based compensation	64	218
Profit	840	965
Shares issued under dividend reinvestment plan	22	190
Other comprehensive income (loss), net	797	(2,269)
Dividends declared	929	791
Stock options exercised	57	46
Shares purchased for cancellation	—	9
Shares issued	—	96
Excess of purchase price over carrying value of shares repurchased and cancelled	—	171

Required:

1. Compute the balance of retained earnings at December 31, 2009.

2. Prepare a statement of changes in equity for both fiscal years 2009 and 2008, similar to the statement that appears in Exhibit 12.1.

P12–10 **Analyzing the Repurchase of Shares** (AP12–6)

The Forzani Group Ltd. (FGL) is the largest sporting goods retailer in Canada. The company sells a vast assortment of sports-related products, including athletic footwear, athletic apparel, and equipment required for performing a favourite sport. Its annual report for fiscal year 2009 included the following:

■ **LO3**

Forzani Group

> **11. Share Capital**
>
> (a) Authorized
>   An unlimited number of Class A shares (no par value)
>   An unlimited number of Preferred shares, issuable in series
> (b) Issued
>
> | Class A shares (in thousands) | Number | Consideration |
> |---|---|---|
> | Balance, February 3, 2008 | 32,970 | 157,105 |
> | Shares issued upon employees exercising stock options | 192 | 2,384 |
> | Stock-based compensation related to options exercised | — | 636 |
> | Shares repurchased via normal course issuer bid | (2,694) | (12,964) |
> | Balance, February 1, 2009 | 30,468 | $147,161 |
>
> ...
>
> (e) Normal Course Issuer Bid
>   For the year ended February 1, 2009, 2,694,376 (2008 – 1,802,900) Class A shares
>   were repurchased pursuant to the Company's Normal Course Issuer Bid for a total
>   expenditure of $44,027,000 (2008 – $33,331,000) or $16.34 (2008 – $18.49) per share.
>   The consideration in excess of the stated value of $31,063,000 (2008 – $24,898,000)
>   was charged to retained earnings.

Required:

1. Why do you think FGL's board of directors decided to repurchase the company's shares?

2. Prepare the journal entry to record a summary of the repurchase transactions.

3. Compute the weighted-average issuance price per common share at February 1, 2009, and explain why FGL paid a much higher price for repurchasing its own shares.

4. What impact will this transaction have on FGL's future dividend obligations?

P12–11 **(Appendix 12A) Comparing Owners' Equity Sections for Alternative Forms of Organization**

Assume for each of the following independent cases that the accounting period for NewBiz ends on December 31, 2012, and that the income summary account at that date reflected a debit balance (loss) of $20,000.

■ **LO1**

e**X**cel

Case A: Assume that NewBiz is a *sole proprietorship* owned by Proprietor A. Prior to the closing entries, the capital account reflected a credit balance of $50,000 and the drawings account a balance of $8,000.

Case B: Assume that NewBiz is a *partnership* owned by Partner A and Partner B. Prior to the closing entries, the owners' equity accounts reflected the following balances: A, capital, $40,000; B, capital, $38,000; A, drawings, $5,000; and B, drawings, $9,000. Profits and losses are divided equally.

Case C: Assume that NewBiz is a *corporation*. Prior to the closing entries, the shareholders' equity accounts showed the following: share capital, authorized 30,000 shares, outstanding 15,000 shares, $150,000; contributed surplus, $5,000; retained earnings, $65,000.

Required:

1. Prepare all of the closing entries indicated at December 31, 2012, for each of the three separate cases.

2. Show for each case how the owners' equity section of the statement of financial position would appear at December 31, 2012.

ALTERNATE PROBLEMS

LO1, 3, 4, 5 AP12–1   **Finding Missing Amounts** (P12–1)

At December 31, 2012, the records of Kozmetsky Corporation provided the following selected and incomplete data:

> Common shares, no par value.
>   Shares authorized, unlimited.
>   Shares issued, _____?_____; issue price $75 per share.
> Profit for 2012, $4,800,000.
>   Common shares account, $1,500,000.
> Dividends declared and paid during 2012, $2 per share.
> Retained earnings balance, January 1, 2012, $82,900,000.

Required:

1. Complete the following tabulation:
   Shares issued, _____.
   Shares outstanding, _____.

2. Earnings per share, $_____.

3. Total dividends paid on common shares during 2012, $_____.

4. Assume that the board of directors voted a 100 percent stock split (the number of shares will double). After the stock split, the average issue price per share will be $_____ and the number of outstanding shares will be _____.

5. Disregard the stock split assumed in (4). Assume instead that a 10 percent stock dividend was declared and issued when the market price of the common shares was $91. Explain how the shareholders' equity will change.

LO1, 3 AP12–2   **Recording Transactions Affecting Shareholders' Equity** (P12–2)

Arnold Company was granted a charter that authorized the following share capital:
Preferred shares: 8 percent, par value $25, 20,000 shares
Common shares: No par value, 100,000 shares
During the first year, 2011, the following selected transactions occurred in the order given:

a. Sold 40,000 common shares at $35 cash per share and 10,000 preferred shares at $25 per share. Collected cash and issued the shares immediately.

b. Issued 5,000 preferred shares as full payment for a plot of land to be used as a future plant site. Assume that the share was selling at $25.

c. Declared and paid the quarterly cash dividend on the preferred shares.

d. At December 31, 2011, the accounts reflected profit of $67,000.

Required:

1. Prepare the journal entries to record each of these transactions.

2. Explain the economic difference between acquiring an asset for cash compared with acquiring it by issuing shares. Is it "better" to acquire a new asset without having to give up another asset?

LO1, 3, 4 AP12–3   **Preparing the Shareholders' Equity Section after Selected Transactions** (P12–3)

The shareholders' equity accounts of Freeman Inc. at January 2, 2011, are as follows:

Preferred shares, no par value, cumulative, 6,000 shares issued	$300,000
Common shares, no par value, 250,000 shares issued	500,000
Retained earnings	600,000

The following transactions occurred during the year:

March 10   Purchased a building for $1,000,000. The seller agreed to receive 14,000 preferred shares and 15,000 common shares of Freeman in exchange for the building. The preferred shares were trading in the market at $50 per share on that day.

July 1   Declared a semi-annual cash dividend of $0.50 per common share and the required amount of dividends on preferred shares, payable on August 1, 2011, to shareholders of record on July 21, 2011. The annual dividend of $2 per preferred share had not been paid in either 2010 or 2011.

August 1   Paid the cash dividend declared on July 1 to both common and preferred shareholders.

December 31   Determined that profit for the year was $385,000.

Required:

1. Prepare journal entries to record the above transactions.

2. Prepare the shareholders' equity section of Freeman's statement of financial position as at December 31, 2011.

AP12–4 Comparing Stock and Cash Dividends (P12–4)   ▓ LO5, 6

Ritz Company had the following shares outstanding and retained earnings at December 31, 2012:

Preferred shares, 8% (par value $25; outstanding, 8,400 shares)	$210,000
Common shares (outstanding, 50,000 shares)	500,000
Retained earnings	900,000

The board of directors is considering the distribution of a cash dividend to the two groups of shareholders. No dividends were declared during 2010 or 2011. Three independent cases are assumed:

Case A: The preferred shares are non-cumulative; the total amount of dividends is $25,000.

Case B: The preferred shares are cumulative; the total amount of dividends is $25,000.

Case C: Same as Case B, except the amount is $75,000.

Required:

1. Compute the amount of dividends, in total and per share, payable to each class of shareholders for each case. Show computations.

2. Assume that the company issued a 15 percent common stock dividend on the outstanding common shares when the market value per share was $50. Complete the following comparative schedule, including an explanation of the differences.

	Amount of Dollar Increase (decrease)	
Item	Cash Dividend— Case C	Stock Dividend
Assets	$_____	$_____
Liabilities	$_____	$_____
Shareholders' equity	$_____	$_____

AP12–5 Determining the Balance of Retained Earnings and Preparing the Statement of Changes in Equity (P12–9)   ▓ LO8

The consolidated statements of changes in equity of Alimentation Couche-Tard Inc. for fiscal years 2010 and 2009 included the following items and their account balances at April 25, 2010, and April 26, 2009 (in millions of Canadian dollars). This list shows the balances of the various components of shareholders' equity at the beginning of each year, and the changes that affected these components during the year. These changes are presented in a random order.

Alimentation
Couche-Tard

	2010	2009
Share capital, beginning of year	$329.1	$348.8
Contributed surplus, beginning of year	17.7	15.6
Retained earnings, beginning of year	932.6	775.0
Accumulated other comprehensive income, beginning of year	46.6	114.3
Stock option-based compensation	1.1	2.1
Profit	302.9	253.9
Other comprehensive income (loss), net	62.4	(67.7)
Dividends declared	25.1	24.1
Stock options exercised	3.4	2.4
Shares purchased for cancellation	13.0	22.1
Excess of purchase price over carrying value of Class A multiple voting shares and Class B subordinate voting shares repurchased and cancelled	43.4	72.2

Required:

1. Compute the balance of retained earnings at April 25, 2010.

2. Prepare a statement of changes in equity for both fiscal years 2010 and 2009, similar to the statement that appears in Exhibit 12.1.

LO3   **AP12–6**   **Analyzing the Repurchase of Shares** (P12–10)

Jean Coutu Group

The Jean Coutu Group operates a network of franchised stores in Canada, located in the provinces of Québec, New Brunswick, and Ontario under the banners of PJC Jean Coutu, PJC Clinique, PJC Santé, and PJC Santé Beauté and employs more than 17,000 people. Its annual report for fiscal year 2010 included the following:

13. Capital Stock

. . .

Changes that occurred in capital stock are presented as follows:

| | 2010 | | 2009 | |
| | Shares | | Shares | |
	(in millions)	$	(in millions)	$
Class A subordinate voting shares				
Outstanding shares, beginning of year	118.6	648.1	130.9	715.4
Repurchased and cancelled	—	—	(12.3)	(67.3)
Stock options exercised	0.3	2.7	—	—
Outstanding shares, end of year	118.9	650.8	118.6	648.1

Normal course issuer bid

In July 2008, the Company announced its intention to purchase for cancellation up to 12,311,000 of its outstanding Class A subordinate voting shares. All of these shares were purchased and cancelled during the fiscal year ended February 28, 2009, at an average price of $7.42 per share for a total consideration of $91.4 million including fees. An amount of $24.1 million representing the excess of the purchase price over the carrying value of the acquired shares was deducted from retained earnings. Purchases were made through the facilities of the Toronto Stock Exchange and in accordance with its requirements.

Required:

1. Why do you think Jean Coutu's board of directors decided to repurchase the company's shares?

2. Prepare the journal entry to record a summary of the repurchase transactions.

3. Compute the weighted-average issuance price per common share, and explain why Jean Coutu paid a much higher price for repurchasing its own shares.

4. What impact will this transaction have on Jean Coutu's future dividend obligations?

CASES AND PROJECTS

FINDING AND INTERPRETING FINANCIAL INFORMATION

LO1, 3, 4   **CP12–1**   **Finding Financial Information**

The Nestlé Group

Refer to the financial statements of the Nestlé Group given in Appendix A of this book.

Required:

1. Identify the types of shares that Nestlé is authorized to issue, and their characteristics. Do all types of shares have the same voting rights? If not, explain why.

2. What is the number of shares outstanding on December 31, 2008?

3. Did the company pay dividends during fiscal year 2008? If so, how much per share?

4. Has the company ever issued a stock dividend or declared a stock split? If so, describe.

FINANCIAL REPORTING AND ANALYSIS CASES

LO1, 2, 3, 4

Procter & Gamble

CP12–2 Finding Information Missing from an Annual Report

Procter & Gamble is a multi-billion dollar company that sells a variety of consumer products such as Mr. Clean, Cheer, Crest, Vicks, Scope, Pringles, Folgers, Vidal Sassoon, and Zest. The company's annual report contained the following information (in millions except per share data):

a. Retained earnings at June 30, 2009, totalled $57,309.

b. Profit for the year ended June 30, 2009, was $13,436.

c. The number of common shares outstanding at June 30, 2009, was 2,917 shares.

d. Dividends declared on common shares equalled $1.64 per share.

Required:

1. Compute the total amount of dividends declared by the company.

2. A shareholder observed that P&G has a sizeable amount of retained earnings and wondered why the company accumulated this amount instead of distributing it to its shareholders. Write a brief memo to explain why earnings have been retained by the company.

3. Compute the company's earnings per share, assuming that P&G had not issued preferred shares. Is EPS a useful measure of performance? Explain.

LO3

Power Financial
Corporation

CP12–3 Characteristics of Preferred Shares

Power Financial Corporation is a Canadian diversified international management company that holds interests, directly or indirectly, in companies that are active in the financial services industry in Canada, the United States, and Europe. The company's 2009 annual report included the following information about specific issues of preferred shares:

---

15. Share Capital

The 5.20% Non-Cumulative First Preferred Shares, Series C are entitled to fixed non-cumulative preferential cash dividends at a rate equal to $1.30 per share per annum. The Corporation may redeem for cash the Series C First Preferred Shares in whole or in part, at the Corporation's option, at $25.60 per share if redeemed within the twelve months commencing October 31, 2009, declining by $0.20 per share for each subsequent twelve-month period thereafter to October 31, 2011, $25.20 if redeemed on or after October 31, 2011, and before July 31, 2012, and $25.00 if redeemed on or after July 31, 2012, in each case together with all declared and unpaid dividends to the date of redemption.

On or after July 31, 2012, the Corporation may convert each Series C First Preferred Share into that number of common shares determined by dividing $25.00 together with all declared and unpaid dividends to the date of conversion by the greater of $3.00 and 95% of the weighted average trading price of the common shares for the 20 trading days ending on the last trading day occurring on or before the fourth day immediately prior to the date of conversion.

On or after October 31, 2012, subject to the right of the Corporation to offer the right to convert into a further series of preferred shares, to redeem for cash or to find substitute purchasers for such shares, each Series C First Preferred Share will be convertible at the option of the holder, on the last day of January, April, July, and October of each year into that number of common shares determined by dividing $25.00 together with all declared and unpaid dividends to the date of conversion by the greater of $3.00 and 95% of the weighted average trading price of the common shares for the 20 trading days ending on the last trading day occurring on or before the fourth day immediately prior to the date of conversion.

Required:

1. Identify the various characteristics of these preferred shares.

2. Based on the characteristics of these shares, should they be classified as debt or equity? Explain.

LO5, 6   **CP12–4**   **Analyzing Dividend Policy**

Walmart

Walmart has been one of the most successful retail companies in history with steady growth in earnings over the past eight years. The following information was extracted from the company's annual reports. The market price is an average of the highest and lowest price for the year.

	2010	2009	2008	2007	2006	2005	2004	2003
Dividends	$ 4,217	$ 3,746	$ 3,586	$ 2,802	$ 2,511	$ 2,214	$ 1,569	$ 1,328
Net income (Profit)	14,335	13,346	12,075	11,284	11,231	10,267	9,054	7,955
Dividends per common share	1.21	0.95	0.88	0.67	0.60	0.52	0.36	0.30
Market price per share	53.40	46.92	48.73	47.23	48.00	56.19	53.41	54.18
Dividend yield	2.27%	2.02%	1.81%	1.42%	1.25%	0.93%	0.67%	0.55%

Assume that you are a financial analyst preparing a forecast of Walmart's operating results for fiscal year 2011. Because of a number of factors, you believe that profit for next year will be in the range of $15,000 million to $15,500 million. To complete your financial forecast, you now need to estimate the total amount of dividends that Walmart will pay.

Required:

1. Based on the information above, describe the dividend policy of Walmart, and estimate the dividends that the company will pay in 2011. (*Hint:* the ratio of dividends to profit, called *dividend payout ratio,* may provide useful information about the company's dividend policy.)

2. Walmart's board of directors has increased dividends per share continuously over the past eight years. What would be your expectation of dividends per share for fiscal year 2011? Justify your answer.

3. The dividend yield has also increased steadily over the past eight years. What should be the market price per share for the dividend yield to reach 2.50 percent, assuming a dividend of $1.21 per share? Explain.

CRITICAL THINKING CASES

LO5, 6   **CP12–5**   **Evaluating an Ethical Dilemma**

You are a member of the board of directors of a large company that has been in business for more than 100 years. The company is proud of the fact that it has paid dividends every year that it has been in business. Because of this stability, many retired people have invested large portions of their savings in the company's common stock. Unfortunately, the company has struggled for the past few years as it tries to introduce new products and is considering not paying a dividend this year. The president wants to skip the dividend in order to have more cash to invest in product development, saying, "If we don't invest this money now, we won't get these products to market in time to save the company. I don't want to risk thousands of jobs." One of the most senior board members speaks next: "If we don't pay the dividend, thousands of retirees will be thrown into financial distress. Even if you don't care about them, you have to recognize our stock price will crash when they all sell." The company treasurer proposes this alternative: "Let's skip the cash dividend and pay a stock dividend. We can still say we've had a dividend every year." The entire board now turns to you for your opinion. What should the company do?

LO4   **CP12–6**   **Evaluating an Ethical Dilemma**

You are the president of a very successful Internet company that has had a remarkably profitable year. You have determined that the company has more than $10 million in cash generated by operating activities not needed in the business. You are thinking about paying it out to shareholders as a special dividend. You discuss the idea with your vice-president, who reacts angrily to your suggestion, declaring, "Our stock price has gone up by 200 percent in the last year alone. What more do we have to do for the owners? The people who really earned that money are the employees who have been working 12 hours a day, six or seven days a week to make the company successful. Most of them didn't even take vacations last year. I say we have to pay out bonuses and nothing extra for the shareholders." As president, you know that you are hired by the board of directors, which is elected by the shareholders. What is your responsibility to both groups? To which group would you give the $10 million?

FINANCIAL REPORTING AND ANALYSIS TEAM PROJECT

CP12–7 **Team Project: Examining an Annual Report**   **LO1, 3, 4, 7**

As a team, select an industry to analyze. A list of companies classified by industry can be obtained by accessing www.fpinfomart.ca and then choosing "Companies by Industry." You can also find a list of industries and companies within each industry via http://ca.finance.yahoo.com/investing (click on "Annual Reports" under "Tools"). Using a Web browser, each team member should acquire the annual report for one publicly traded company in the industry, with each member selecting a different company.

Required:

On an individual basis, each team member should then write a short report answering the following questions about the selected company. Discuss any patterns across the companies that you as a team observe. Then, as a team, write a short report comparing and contrasting your companies.

1. *a.* List the accounts and amounts of the company's shareholders' equity.

   b. From the notes to financial statements, identify any unusual features in the contributed capital accounts (e.g., convertible preferred, nonvoting common), if any.

2. Identify the cash flows related to share capital transactions. You will need to refer to the statement of cash flows.

   a. If new shares were issued during the year, what was the average price per share at the time of issuance?

   b. Reconstruct the journal entry for the issuance of shares.

3. What type of dividends did the company declare during the year? How much was paid in cash?

CHAPTER 13

Analyzing Financial Statements

FOCUS COMPANY: **Home Depot**

FINANCIAL ANALYSIS: BRINGING IT ALL TOGETHER

The history of Home Depot (www.homedepot.com) is an unusual success story. Founded in 1978, in Atlanta, Home Depot has grown to be the world's largest home improvement retailer. Its stores are located in major cities in Canada, the United States, Mexico, and China. Home Depot's financial statements are presented in Exhibit 13.1.

Home Depot operates more than 2,200 stores and design centres selling building materials; decor, lawn, and garden products; and home remodelling services. In Canada, Home Depot had 179 stores employing more than 27,000 people as of January 31, 2010. Home Depot's net revenues grew at an average rate of 5.6 percent per year during the period 2003–2009, and its earnings grew at an average annual rate of 1.2 percent during the past 10 years.

Financial analysts evaluate Home Depot's historical performance to determine whether they should recommend that their clients purchase its shares. The analysts want some reasonable assurance that the company will continue to thrive, causing the company's share price to increase, and thereby benefiting their clients. Two analysts looking at the same company, however, may arrive at different conclusions, depending in part on the investors' investment objectives: growth or safety. Some analysts may reject Home Depot because it is too risky relative to other investment opportunities, whereas others may recommend the investment because Home Depot has grown quickly relative to the risk in its business.

As you analyze Home Depot's financial results, it is important to remember that any analysis is understood in the context of what an investor wants to accomplish. Your analysis, in itself, will present neither a good nor a bad picture of Home Depot's performance. This assessment must be made in the context of not only the investor's goals but also of the industry's performance and the economic environment.

Would you want to buy shares in Home Depot? To make a rational decision, you want to consider more factors than just the company's rapid growth in profitability and the recommendation of a financial analyst. The information contained in Home Depot's financial statements and the analytical tools discussed in this chapter provide an important basis to help you decide whether to invest in Home Depot shares.

THE HOME DEPOT, INC., AND SUBSIDIARIES
Consolidated Balance Sheets

amounts in millions, except share and per share data	January 31, 2010	February 1, 2009
Assets		
Current Assets:		
Cash and Cash Equivalents	$ 1,421	$ 519
Short-Term Investments	6	6
Receivables, net	964	972
Merchandise Inventories	10,188	10,673
Other Current Assets	1,321	1,192
Total Current Assets	13,900	13,362
Property and Equipment, at cost:		
Land	8,451	8,301
Buildings	17,391	16,961
Furniture, Fixtures and Equipment	9,091	8,741
Leasehold Improvements	1,383	1,359
Construction in Progress	525	625
Capital Leases	504	490
	37,345	36,477
Less Accumulated Depreciation and Amortization	11,795	10,243
Net Property and Equipment	25,550	26,234
Notes Receivable	33	36
Goodwill	1,171	1,134
Other Assets	223	398
Total Assets	$40,877	$41,164
Liabilities and Stockholders' Equity		
Current Liabilities:		
Accounts Payable	$ 4,863	$ 4,822
Accrued Salaries and Related Expenses	1,263	1,129
Sales Taxes Payable	362	337
Deferred Revenue	1,158	1,165
Income Taxes Payable	108	289
Current Installments of Long-Term Debt	1,020	1,767
Other Accrued Expenses	1,589	1,644
Total Current Liabilities	10,363	11,153
Long-Term Debt, excluding current installments	8,662	9,667
Other Long-Term Liabilities	2,140	2,198
Deferred Income Taxes	319	369
Total Liabilities	21,484	23,387
Stockholders' Equity		
Common Stock, par value $0.05; authorized: 10 billion shares; issued: 1.716 billion shares at January 31, 2010 and 1.707 billion shares at February 1, 2009; outstanding: 1.698 billion shares at January 31, 2010 and 1.696 billion shares at February 1, 2009	86	85
Paid-In Capital	6,304	6,048
Retained Earnings	13,226	12,093
Accumulated Other Comprehensive Income (Loss)	362	(77)
Treasury Stock, at cost, 18 million shares at January 31, 2010 and 11 million shares at February 1, 2009	(585)	(372)
Total Stockholders' Equity	19,393	17,777
Total Liabilities and Stockholders' Equity	$40,877	$ 41,164

See accompanying Notes to Consolidated Financial Statements.
Source: Home Depot Annual Report 2009.

Exhibit **13.1**
(Continued)

THE HOME DEPOT, INC., AND SUBSIDIARIES
Consolidated Statements of Earnings

| | Fiscal Year Ended[1] | | |
amounts in millions, except per share data	January 31, 2010	February 1, 2009	February 3, 2008
Net Sales	$ 66,176	$ 71,288	$ 77,349
Cost of Sales	43,764	47,298	51,352
Gross Profit	22,412	23,990	25,997
Operating Expenses:			
Selling, General and Administrative	15,902	17,846	17,053
Depreciation and Amortization	1,707	1,785	1,702
Total Operating Expenses	17,609	19,631	18,755
Operating Income	4,803	4,359	7,242
Interest and Other (Income) Expense:			
Interest and Investment Income	(18)	(18)	(74)
Interest Expense	676	624	696
Other	163	163	—
Interest and Other, net	821	769	622
Earnings from Continuing Operations Before Provision for Income Taxes	3,982	3,590	6,620
Provision for Income Taxes	1,362	1,278	2,410
Earnings from Continuing Operations	2,620	2,312	4,210
Earnings (Loss) from Discontinued Operations, Net of Tax	41	(52)	185
Net Earnings	$ 2,661	$ 2,260	$ 4,395
Weighted Average Common Shares	1,683	1,682	1,849
Basic Earnings per Share from Continuing Operations	$ 1.56	$ 1.37	$ 2.28
Basic Earnings (Loss) per Share from Discontinued Operations	$ 0.02	$(0.03)	$ 0.10
Basic Earnings per Share	$ 1.58	$ 1.34	$ 2.38
Diluted Weighted Average Common Shares	1,692	1,686	1,856
Diluted Earnings per Share from Continuing Operations	$ 1.55	$ 1.37	$ 2.27
Diluted Earnings (Loss) per Share from Discontinued Operations	$ 0.02	$(0.03)	$ 0.10
Diluted Earnings per Share	$ 1.57	$ 1.34	$ 2.37

(1)Fiscal years ended January 31, 2010 and February 1, 2009 include 52 weeks. Fiscal year ended February 3, 2008 includes 53 weeks.
See accompanying Notes to Consolidated Financial Statements.
Source: Home Depot Annual Report 2009.

THE HOME DEPOT, INC., AND SUBSIDIARIES
Consolidated Statements of Cash Flows

| | Fiscal Year Ended[1] | | |
amounts in millions	January 31, 2010	February 1, 2009	February 3, 2008
Cash Flows from Operating Activities			
Net Earnings	$ 2,661	$ 2,260	$ 4,395
Reconciliation of Net Earnings to Net Cash Provided by Operating Activities:			
Depreciation and Amortization	1,806	1,902	1,906
Impairment Related to Rationalization Charges	—	580	—
Impairment of Investment	163	163	—
Stock-Based Compensation Expense	201	176	207

Exhibit **13.1**

(*Concluded*)

amounts in millions	Fiscal Year Ended[1]		
	January 31, 2010	February 1, 2009	February 3, 2008
Changes in Assets and Liabilities, net of the effects of acquisitions and disposition:			
(Increase) Decrease in Receivables, net	(23)	121	116
Decrease (Increase) in Merchandise Inventories	625	743	(491)
Decrease (Increase) in Other Current Assets	4	(7)	109
Increase (Decrease) in Accounts Payable and Accrued Expenses	59	(646)	(465)
Decrease in Deferred Revenue	(21)	(292)	(159)
(Decrease) Increase in Income Taxes Payable	(174)	262	—
Decrease in Deferred Income Taxes	(227)	(282)	(348)
(Decrease) Increase in Other Long-Term Liabilities	(19)	306	186
Other	70	242	271
Net Cash Provided by Operating Activities	5,125	5,528	5,727
Cash Flows from Investing Activities:			
Capital Expenditures, net of $10, $37 and $19 of non-cash capital expenditures in fiscal 2009, 2008 and 2007, respectively	(966)	(1,847)	(3,558)
Proceeds from Sale of Business, net	—	—	8,337
Payments for Businesses Acquired, net	—	—	(13)
Proceeds from Sales of Property and Equipment	178	147	318
Purchases of Investments	—	(168)	(11,225)
Proceeds from Sales and Maturities of Investments	33	139	10,899
Net Cash (Used in) Provided by Investing Activities	(755)	(1,729)	4,758
Cash Flows from Financing Activities:			
(Repayments of) Proceeds from Short-Term Borrowings, net	—	(1,732)	1,734
Repayments of Long-Term Debt	(1,774)	(313)	(20)
Repurchases of Common Stock	(213)	(70)	(10,815)
Proceeds from Sales of Common Stock	73	84	276
Cash Dividends Paid to Stockholders	(1,525)	(1,521)	(1,709)
Other Financing Activities	(64)	(128)	(105)
Net Cash Used in Financing Activities	(3,503)	(3,680)	(10,639)
Increase (Decrease) in Cash and Cash Equivalents	867	119	(154)
Effect of Exchange Rate Changes on Cash and Cash Equivalents	35	(45)	(1)
Cash and Cash Equivalents at Beginning of Year	519	445	600
Cash and Cash Equivalents at End of Year	$ 1,421	$ 519	$ 445
Supplemental Disclosure of Cash Payments made for:			
Interest, net of interest capitalized	$ 664	$ 622	$ 672
Income Taxes	$ 2,082	$ 1,265	$ 2,524

(1)Fiscal years ended January 31, 2010 and February 1, 2009 include 52 weeks. Fiscal year ended February 3, 2008 includes 53 weeks.
See accompanying Notes to Consolidated Financial Statements.
Source: Home Depot Annual Report 2009.

UNDERSTANDING THE BUSINESS

In Canada and the United States, companies spend billions of dollars each year preparing, auditing, and publishing their financial statements. These statements are then mailed to current and prospective investors. Most companies also make financial information available on the Internet. Home Depot has a particularly interesting website that contains current financial statements, recent news articles about the company, and a variety of other relevant information.

The reason that Home Depot and other companies spend so much money providing information to investors is simple; financial statements help people make better economic decisions. Two broad groups of people use financial statements. One group is the management of the business; it relies on accounting data to make important operating decisions, such as the pricing of products or expansion of productive capacity. The second group is the external decision makers that rely on accounting information to make important investment and credit decisions. In fact, the conceptual framework unequivocally states that the objective of financial reporting is to communicate information primarily to meet the needs of external decision makers, including present and potential owners, investment analysts, and creditors.

Users of financial statements are interested in three types of information:

1. *Information about past performance.* Information concerning items such as profit, sales volume, cash flows, and return earned on the investment helps people assess the success of the business and the effectiveness of its management. Such information also helps the decision maker compare one company with others.

2. *Information about the present condition of a business.* This type of information helps answer the following questions. What types of assets are owned? How much debt does the business owe, and when is it due? What is its cash position? What are its EPS, return on investment, and debt-to-equity ratios? What is the inventory position? Answers to these and similar questions help people assess the successes and failures of the past. More importantly, they provide information useful in assessing the cash flow and profit potentials of the business.

3. *Information about the future performance of the business.* Decision makers select from among several alternative courses of action. Because all decisions are future-oriented, financial statements based on historical cost are not an ideal basis upon which to forecast future performance. Investors are most interested in risk and the potential rewards for accepting risk. In general, as risk in the business environment increases, investors demand higher future returns on their investments to compensate them for that increased risk. Investors prefer to earn maximum return for minimum risk when choosing companies in which to invest.

Reliable accounting measures of past performance are one source of information upon which investors base their assessments of risk and potential return. Analysis of reliable measures indicating financial trends for each company is therefore very important. If investors can reasonably assume that important business factors will in the future be very similar to the current situation, then a reliable historical trend is often a satisfactory basis upon which to predict future financial performance. For example, the recent sales and earnings trends of a business are usually good indicators of what might be expected in the future. In other words, investors must know where the company has been in order to predict where it is likely to go.

ORGANIZATION OF THE CHAPTER

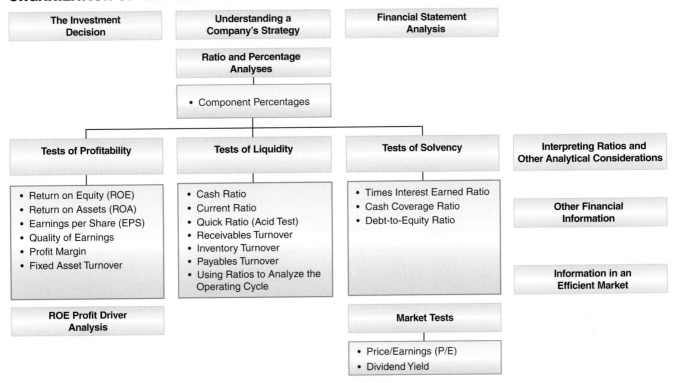

Supplemental material:
Appendix 13A: Expanding the ROE Profit Driver Analysis—The Scott Formula (online)

THE INVESTMENT DECISION

Of the people who use financial statements, current and potential investors are perhaps the single largest group. They often rely on the advice of professional analysts who develop recommendations on widely held stocks, such as Home Depot. Most individual investors use analysts' reports, tracking their recommendations. As this book was being written, professional analysts issued the following investment recommendations for Home Depot:

Analyst Ratings: Home Depot	Current Month	Last Month	Two Months Ago	Three Months Ago
1—Strong Buy	16	16	16	16
2—Moderate Buy	1	1	1	1
3—Hold	10	10	8	8
4—Moderate Sell	0	0	0	0
5—Strong Sell	0	0	2	2

Source: http://moneycentral.msn.com/investor/invsub/analyst/recomnd.asp?Symbol=US%3aHD. Accessed August 24, 2010.

What do these recommendations mean? Analysts are information intermediaries who interpret audited financial information and advise their clients on whether they should buy, hold, or sell shares. It is clear that analysts reach different conclusions despite access to the same set of financial information. Notice also that analysts' recommendations shift over time as new information is released and actual performance becomes observable.

Analysts are expected to have a good understanding of financial statements and the standards that imbue these reports with both relevance and faithful representation. They may disagree, however, on how to interpret the results of their analyses of a company's past performance. Analysts' differing opinions affect their predictions of the future operating performance to the extent that their analyses of a company's past performance is relevant to formulating their predictions. The level of disagreement among financial analysts shows that financial statement analysis is part art and part science.

In addition to analyzing a company's financial statements, analysts consider other factors that might affect the future operating performance of the company and its financial situation. These include global, economic, and industry factors that are not controllable by the company, and management's ability to adapt its business plans in response to the uncertainties and risks associated with these uncontrollable factors. Management success at containing the effects of uncontrollable risks and managing in the face of uncertainties plays a role in analysts' predictions of the future economic health of a specific company. Irrespective of how careful an analyst is, however, the truth about all predictions is that they often prove to be inaccurate.

When considering an investment in shares, the investor should evaluate the future profit and growth potential of the business on the basis of three factors:

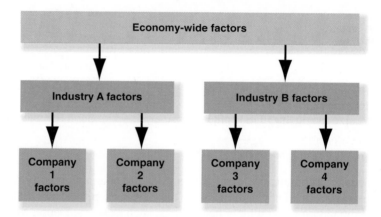

1. *Economy-wide factors.* The overall health of the economy has a direct impact on the performance of an individual business. The dramatic downturn in the global economy that started in 2007 has resulted in reduced demand for goods and services sufficiently severe to bankrupt even extremely large corporations such as General Motors. Prudent investors must consider data such as the unemployment rate, general inflation rate, and changes in interest rates. For example, increases in interest rates often slow economic growth because consumers are less willing to buy merchandise on credit when interest rates are high. Furthermore, companies that wish to expand their operations will find it too expensive to borrow funds.

2. *Industry factors.* Certain events have a major impact on each company within an industry, but have only a minor impact on other companies outside the industry. For example, a major drought will be devastating for food-related industries but will have no effect on the electronics industry.

3. *Individual company factors.* To properly analyze a company, you should learn as much as you can about it. Good analysts do not rely solely on the information contained in the financial statements. They visit the company, buy its products, and read about it in the business press. For example, if you evaluate McDonald's, it is equally important to assess the quality of its statement of financial position and the quality of its McChicken® sandwich.

Besides considering these factors, investors should understand a company's business strategy when evaluating its financial statements. Before discussing analytical techniques, we will show you how business strategy affects financial statement analysis.

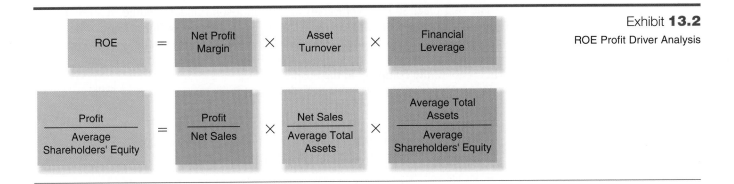

Exhibit **13.2**
ROE Profit Driver Analysis

UNDERSTANDING A COMPANY'S STRATEGY

Financial statement analysis involves more than just "crunching numbers." Before you start looking at numbers, you should know what you are looking for. While financial statements report on transactions, each of these transactions is the result of a company's operating decisions as it implements its business strategy.

LO1

Explain how a company's business strategy affects financial analysis.

A useful starting point for financial statement analysis is the return on equity (ROE) profit driver analysis (also called *ROE decomposition* or *DuPont analysis*), which shows a logical relationship among the three ratios presented in Exhibit 13.2. These ratios are based on financial statement elements that are often called *profit drivers* or *profit levers*, because they describe the three ways that management can improve ROE. The DuPont model helps us understand that a number of business strategies affect the profitability of a business.

Businesses can earn a high rate of return for the owners (i.e., a high ROE) by following different strategies. There are two fundamental strategies:

1. *Product differentiation.* Under this strategy, companies offer products with unique benefits, such as high quality or unusual features or style. These unique benefits allow a company to charge higher prices. In general, higher prices result in higher profit margins, which lead to higher returns on equity (as shown in the ROE model).

2. *Cost advantage.* Under this strategy, companies attempt to operate more efficiently than their competitors, allowing them to offer lower prices to attract customers. The efficient use of resources is captured in the asset turnover ratio, and as the ROE model illustrates, a high asset turnover ratio leads to higher return on investment.

You can probably think of a number of companies that have followed one of these two basic strategies.

The best place to start your analysis is with a solid understanding of a company's business strategy. To evaluate how a company is doing, you must know what managers are trying to do. You can learn a lot about a company's strategy by reading its complete annual report, especially the letter from the president. It also is useful to read articles about the company in the business press.

Home Depot's business strategy is described in its annual report as follows:

REAL WORLD EXCERPT

Home Depot

ANNUAL REPORT

> OPERATING STRATEGY: In fiscal 2009, despite prolonged difficulties in the economy, we continued to focus on our core retail business, investing in our associates and stores and improving our customer service ... we maintained our focus on maximizing the productivity of our existing store base.... we continued to make strategic decisions intended to optimize our capital allocation, control expenses and create long-term value for our shareholders.
>
> *Source:* Home Depot Annual Report 2009.

This strategy has several implications for our analysis of Home Depot:

1. Productivity is critical. Home Depot must be able to generate more earnings per square metre of retail space to improve profits.

2. In response to lower demand for products, Home Depot must stick to what is has done best but improve its sensitivity to customer requirements to increase loyalty and repeated sales.

3. Profitability arises from prudent investment of scarce capital and cost control that provide economies of scale even when volume decreases.

With these implications in mind, we can attach more meaning to the information contained in Home Depot's financial statements.

As the preceding discussion indicates, a company can take different actions to try to affect each of its profit drivers. To understand the impact of these actions, financial analysts disaggregate each of the profit drivers into more detailed ratios. For example, the asset turnover ratio is further disaggregated into turnover ratios for specific assets such as trade receivables, inventory, and fixed assets. We have developed our understanding of these ratios in previous chapters, but we will bring them together in the next few sections as part of a comprehensive review of ratio analysis.

FINANCIAL STATEMENT ANALYSIS

LO2

Discuss how analysts use financial statements.

Analyzing financial data without a basis of comparison is impossible. For example, would you be impressed with a company that earned $1 million last year? You are probably thinking, "It depends." A $1 million profit might be very good for a company that lost money the year before but not good for a company that made $500 million during the previous year. It might be good for a small company but not good for a very large company. And, it might be good if all the other companies in the industry lost money but not good if they all earned much larger profits.

As you can see from this simple example, financial results cannot be evaluated in isolation. To properly analyze the information reported in financial statements, you must develop appropriate comparisons. The task of finding appropriate benchmarks requires judgment and is not always an easy task. For this reason, financial analysis is a sophisticated skill, not a mechanical process.

There are two types of benchmarks for making financial comparisons: time series and comparisons with other companies.

1. *Time series analysis.* In this type of analysis, information for a single company is compared over time. For example, a key measure of performance for a retail company is the change in sales volume each year for its existing stores. The time series chart below shows that Home Depot was able to achieve sales growth in existing stores in fiscal years 2003–2005, but failed to do so in 2006–2009.[1]

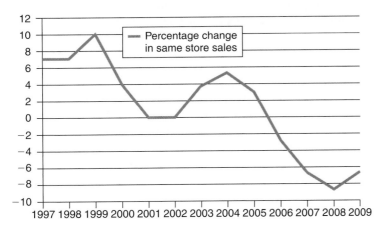

2. *Comparison with similar companies.* Financial results are often affected by industry and economy-wide factors. By comparing a company with another one in the same line of business, an analyst can obtain better insight into its performance. For example, the comparison of profit margin (profit as a percentage of sales) for 2009 and the change in sales for Home Depot, Canadian Tire, and RONA from the previous year, shows that RONA and Canadian Tire suffered decreases in sales of 4.77 and 4.37 percent, respectively, while Home Depot's sales decreased by 7.2 percent. The profit margin for Home Depot grew from 3.2 to 4 percent during the same year, but both RONA and Canadian Tire endured reduced profit margins. Overall, it appears that Home Depot has responded more effectively to a larger decrease in sales and achieved the highest profit margin through difficult years than either of its two competitors.

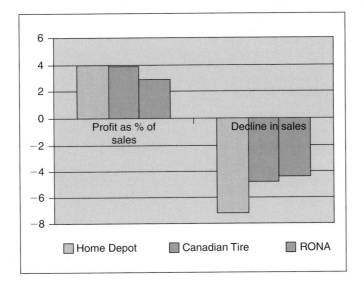

[1] The percentage change in sales for existing stores is computed as follows:

$$\text{Percentage change} = \left[\frac{\text{Sales}_{\text{Current Year}} - \text{Sales}_{\text{Previous Year}}}{\text{Sales}_{\text{Previous Year}}} \times 100 \right]$$

Similar percentage changes can be computed for various elements of financial statements.

Finding comparable companies is often very difficult. Magna International Inc. is a well-known company that supplies automotive components and owns a subsidiary that is the largest operator of thoroughbred race tracks in North America. No other company sells exactly that group of products. Care must be exercised when selecting comparable companies from the same basic industry. Days Inn, Hilton, Holiday Inn, Marriott, and Intrawest are all in the hotel industry, but not all could be considered comparable companies for purposes of financial analysis. These hotels offer different levels of quality and appeal to different types of customers.

The governments of the United States, Canada, and Mexico developed the North American Industry Classification System for use in reporting economic data. The system assigns a specific industry code to each corporation, based on its business operations. Analysts often use these six-digit codes to identify companies that have similar business operations. Financial information services, such as Standard & Poor's, provide averages for many common accounting ratios for various industries as defined by the industrial classification codes. Because of the diversity of companies included in each industry classification, these data should be used with great care. For this reason, some analysts prefer to compare two companies that are very similar instead of using industry-wide comparisons.

RATIO AND PERCENTAGE ANALYSES

RATIO (PERCENTAGE) ANALYSIS is an analytical tool designed to identify significant relationships; it measures the proportional relationship between two financial statement amounts.

All financial analysts use ratio analysis, or percentage analysis, when they review companies. A ratio or percentage expresses the proportionate relationship between two different amounts, allowing for easy comparisons. Assessing a company's profitability is difficult if you know only that it earned a profit of $500,000. Comparing profit to other numbers, such as shareholders' equity, provides additional insights. If shareholders' equity is $5 million, the relationship of profit to shareholder investment is $500,000 ÷ $5,000,000 = 10 percent. This measure indicates a different level of performance than would be the case if shareholders' equity were $50 million. Ratio analysis condenses the large volume of raw financial data and helps decision makers identify significant relationships and make meaningful comparisons between companies.

Ratios may be computed by using amounts in one statement, such as the income statement, or in two different statements, such as the income statement and the statement of financial position. In addition, amounts on a single statement may be expressed as a percentage of a base amount.

LO3

Compute and interpret component percentages.

Component Percentages

A **COMPONENT PERCENTAGE** expresses each item on a particular financial statement as a percentage of a single base amount.

Analysts often compute component percentages, which express each item on a financial statement as a percentage of a single *base amount*, the denominator of the ratio. To compute component percentages for the income statement, the base amount is net sales revenue. Each expense is expressed as a percentage of net sales revenue. On the statement of financial position, the base amount is total assets; each element of the statement of financial position is divided by total assets. This is also known as creating a common-size financial statement.

Discerning important relationships and trends in the Home Depot income statement shown in Exhibit 13.1 is difficult without using component percentages. Profit increased by 15.0 percent between 2008 and 2009,[2] which appears to be good; but it is difficult for an analyst to evaluate the operating efficiency of Home Depot based on the reported numbers on the income statement.

Exhibit 13.3 shows a component percentage analysis for Home Depot's income statement (from Exhibit 13.1). If you simply reviewed the dollar amounts on the

---

[2]The fiscal year of Home Depot ends in January, so its income statement essentially covers the results of the previous calendar year.

income statement, you might be concerned about several significant differences. For example, cost of sales decreased by nearly $3.5 billion between 2008 and 2009. Is this decrease reasonable, relative to the decrease in sales? Should you be concerned, as an analyst? The component percentage indicates that cost of sales actually increased slightly as a percentage of sales revenue during that period. In other words, cost of sales has increased in proportion to sales revenue.

| | **Component Percentages** | | | Exhibit **13.3** |
Income Statement	2009	2008	2007	
Net Sales	100.0%	100.0%	100.0%	Component Percentages for Home Depot
Cost of Sales	66.1	66.3	66.4	
Gross Profit	33.9	33.7	33.6	
Operating Expenses:				
Selling, general and administrative	24.0	25.0	22.0	
Depreciation and amortization	2.6	2.6	2.2	
Total operating expenses	26.6	27.6	24.2	
Operating Income	7.3	6.1	9.4	
Interest and Other (Income) Expense:				
Interest and investment income	—	—	(0.1)	
Interest expense	1.0	0.9	0.9	
Other	0.2	0.2	—	
Interest and Other, net	1.2	1.1	0.8	
Earnings from Continuing Operations				
Before Provision for Income Taxes	6.1	5.0	8.6	
Provision for Income Taxes	2.1	1.8	3.1	
Earnings from Continuing Operations	4.0%	3.2%	5.5%	
Earnings (loss) from Discontinued				
Operations, net of tax	—	—	0.2	
Net Earnings	4.0%	3.2%	5.7%	

The component analysis for Home Depot shown in Exhibit 13.3 helps highlight several additional issues:

1. Profit (net earnings) decreased by 48.6 percent in 2008 compared to 2007, and then increased by 17.7 percent during 2009. Profitability improved despite a continuing decline in revenue. Home Depot's own analysis of operations attributed the turnaround to careful cost control.

2. Some of the changes in percentages may seem immaterial, but they involve very significant amounts of money. The decrease in the ratio of selling, general, and administrative expenses as a percentage of sales from 25 percent in 2008 to 24 percent in 2009 resulted in increased earnings before taxes of $662 million ($66,176 × [25% − 24%]).

3. The gross profit as a percentage of sales increased between 2007 and 2009. The company attributes this increase to fewer markdowns on inventory.

4. Significant stability in all of the income statement relationships indicates a well-run company. Notice that most of the individual income statement items changed by approximately one percentage point over a three-year period. The more stable these relationships are over a long time period, particularly those of economic turbulence, the more confidence analysts will have in their predictions of the company's future based on relationships among the various elements of the company's financial statements.

Many analysts use graphics software in their study of financial results. Graphic representation is especially useful when communicating findings during meetings or in printed form. A graphic summary of key 2009 data from Exhibit 13.3 is shown in the margin chart.

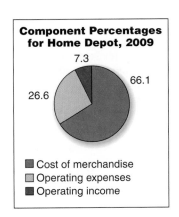

Component Percentages for Home Depot, 2009

7.3
66.1
26.6

■ Cost of merchandise
□ Operating expenses
■ Operating income

In addition to component percentages, analysts use ratios to compare related items from the financial statements. Of the many ratios that can be computed from a single set of financial statements, analysts use only those that are relevant to the analysis of a given situation. Comparing cost of sales to property, plant, and equipment is never useful because these items have no natural relationship. Instead, an analyst will often compute certain widely used ratios and then decide which additional ratios are relevant to the particular decision. For example, research and development costs as a percentage of sales is not a commonly used ratio, but it is useful when analyzing companies that depend on new products, such as pharmaceutical or technology firms.

When you compute ratios, remember a basic fact about financial statements: statement of financial position amounts relate to an instant in time, and income statement amounts relate to a specified period. Therefore, when an income statement amount is compared with a statement of financial position amount, you should express the statement of financial position amount as an average of the beginning and ending balances. In practice, many analysts simply use the ending statement of financial position amount. This approach is appropriate only if no significant changes have occurred in statement of financial position amounts. For consistency, we always use average amounts.

Financial statement analysis is a judgmental process. Not all ratios are relevant to the analysis of a given situation. We will discuss several ratios that are appropriate to most situations. They can be grouped into the five categories shown in Exhibit 13.4.

LO⁴

Compute and interpret profitability ratios.

TESTS OF PROFITABILITY compare profit with one or more primary activities.

TESTS OF PROFITABILITY

Profitability is a primary measure of the overall success of a company. Indeed, it is necessary for a company's survival. Investors and creditors prefer a single measure of profitability that is meaningful in all situations. Unfortunately, no single measure can be devised to meet this comprehensive need. Several tests of profitability focus on measuring the adequacy of profit by comparing it to other items reported on the financial statements.

1. Return on Equity (ROE)

Return on equity (also called *return on owners' investment*) relates profit to the investment made by the owners. It reflects the simple fact that investors expect to earn more money if they invest more money. Two investments that offer a return of $10,000 are not comparable if one requires an investment of $100,000 and the other requires an investment of $250,000. The return on equity ratio is computed as follows:[3]

$$\text{Return on Equity} = \frac{\text{Profit}}{\text{Average Shareholders' Equity}}$$

$$\text{Home Depot, 2009} = \frac{\$2,661}{\$18,585^*} = 14.3\%$$

*($17,777 + $19,393) ÷ 2

Home Depot earned 14.3 percent on the owners' investment. Was that return high or low? We can answer this question by comparing Home Depot's return on equity with the ratios of similar companies. The return on equity for two of Home Depot's competitors follows:

Canadian Tire	9.2%
RONA	8.5
Home Depot	14.3

Return on Equity for Selected Industries, 2009	
Retailing	6.36%
Telecommunication Services	17.32%
Paper and Forest Products	−9.78%
Gold	1.24%

---

[3]The figures for Home Depot used throughout the following ratio examples are taken from the financial statements in Exhibit 13.1.

Ratio	Basic Computation
Tests of Profitability	
1. Return on equity (ROE) (Chapter 4)	$\dfrac{\text{Profit}}{\text{Average Shareholders' Equity}}$
2. Return on assets (ROA) (Chapter 3)	$\dfrac{\text{Profit} + \text{Interest Expense (net of tax)}}{\text{Average Total Assets}}$
3. Earnings per share (Chapter 12)	$\dfrac{\text{Profit Available to Common Shareholders}}{\text{Average Number of Common Shares Outstanding}}$
4. Quality of earnings (Chapter 5)	$\dfrac{\text{Cash Flows from Operating Activities}}{\text{Profit}}$
5. Profit margin (Chapter 4)	$\dfrac{\text{Profit}}{\text{Net Sales}}$
6. Fixed asset turnover (Chapter 9)	$\dfrac{\text{Net Sales}}{\text{Average Net Fixed Assets}}$
Tests of Liquidity	
7. Cash ratio (Chapter 13)	$\dfrac{\text{Cash} + \text{Cash Equivalents}}{\text{Current Liabilities}}$
8. Current ratio (Chapter 10)	$\dfrac{\text{Current Assets}}{\text{Current Liabilities}}$
9. Quick ratio (Chapter 13)	$\dfrac{\text{Quick Assets}}{\text{Current Liabilities}}$
10. Receivables turnover (Chapter 7)	$\dfrac{\text{Net Credit Sales}}{\text{Average Net Trade Receivables}}$
11. Inventory turnover (Chapter 8)	$\dfrac{\text{Cost of Sales}}{\text{Average Inventory}}$
12. Payables turnover (Chapter 10)	$\dfrac{\text{Net Credit Purchases}}{\text{Average Net Trade Payables}}$
Tests of Solvency	
13. Times interest earned (Chapter 11)	$\dfrac{\text{Profit before Interest and Taxes}}{\text{Interest Expense}}$
14. Cash coverage (Chapter 13)	$\dfrac{\text{Cash Flows from Operating Activities (before Interest and Taxes)}}{\text{Interest Paid}}$
15. Debt-to-equity (Chapter 2)	$\dfrac{\text{Total Liabilities}}{\text{Shareholders' Equity}}$
Market Tests	
16. Price/earnings (Chapter 1)	$\dfrac{\text{Current Market Price per Share}}{\text{Earnings per Share}}$
17. Dividend yield (Chapter 12)	$\dfrac{\text{Dividends per Share}}{\text{Market Price per Share}}$

Exhibit **13.4**

Widely Used Accounting Ratios

Note: Most of these ratios have been discussed in previous chapters. The specific chapter appears next to the ratio.

Clearly, Home Depot produced a better return than its competitors.

We gain additional insight by examining Home Depot's ROE over time:

	2009	2008	2007
ROE	14.3	12.7	20.5

This comparison shows that Home Depot's performance, as measured by ROE, followed closely the economic downturn and slow recovery. Home Depot noted the ongoing decrease in new residential construction and increasing unemployment rates as the key causes for its recent performance.

2. Return on Assets (ROA)

Another test of profitability compares profit to the total assets (i.e., total investment) used to earn that profit. Many analysts consider the *return on assets ratio* to be a better measure of management's ability to utilize assets effectively because it is not affected by the way in which the assets were financed. For example, the return on equity could be very large for a company that has a large amount of debt compared to a company that earned the same return based on the same amount of assets but borrowed less money. The return on equity measures profitability from the perspective of the shareholders, whereas the return on assets takes into consideration the resources contributed by both shareholders and creditors. For this reason, the return to shareholders, profit, is augmented by the return to creditors, which is interest expense. Interest expense is measured net of income tax because it represents the net cost of the funds provided by creditors to the corporation.[4]

The return on assets is computed as follows:

$$\text{Return on Assets} = \frac{\textbf{Profit + Interest Expense (net of tax)}}{\textbf{Average Total Assets *}}$$

$$\text{Home Depot, 2009} = \frac{\$2,661 + (\$676 \times 65.8\%)}{\$41,021} = 7.6\%$$

*($41,164 + $40,877) ÷ 2

Home Depot earned 7.6 percent on the total resources it used during the year. The return on assets for Home Depot's competitors is shown below. This comparison indicates that Home Depot utilizes its assets more effectively than its competitors.

Canadian Tire	4.9%
RONA	5.6
Home Depot	7.6

Financial Leverage Percentage

The *financial leverage percentage* measures the advantage or disadvantage that occurs when a company's return on equity differs from its return on assets (i.e., ROE − ROA). In the ROE profit driver analysis discussed earlier in this chapter, financial leverage was defined as the proportion of assets acquired with funds supplied by owners. The *financial leverage percentage* measures a related but different concept. It describes the relationship between the return on equity and the return on assets. Leverage is positive when the rate of return on a company's assets exceeds the average after-tax interest rate on its borrowed funds. Basically, the company borrows at one rate and earns a higher rate of return on its investments. Most companies have positive leverage.

---

[4]To illustrate the net cost of using debt, assume that a company earned $100 in revenue and incurred $70 in operating expenses. Consider two scenarios: (1) the company uses long-term debt that cost $10 in interest expense and (2) the company does not use debt.

	Debt Financing	Equity Financing
Profit before interest and taxes	$30	$30
Interest expense	(10)	0
Profit before income taxes	$20	$30
Income tax expense (@40 percent)	(8)	(12)
Profit	$12	$18

The deduction of interest expense from profit before interest and taxes reduced the income tax expense from $12 to $8, and profit decreased by only $6. Therefore, the net cost of using debt in this case is $6, or $10 × (1 − 0.4, the tax rate).

Financial leverage percentage can be measured by comparing the two return on investment ratios as follows:

$$\textbf{Financial Leverage Percentage = Return on Equity} - \textbf{Return on Assets}$$
$$\textbf{Home Depot, 2009 =} \quad \textbf{14.3\%} \quad - \quad \textbf{7.6\%} \quad = \textbf{6.7\%}$$

When a company is able to borrow funds at an after-tax interest rate and invest those funds to earn a higher after-tax rate of return, the difference benefits the owners. The notes to Home Depot's annual report indicate that the company has borrowed money at rates ranging from 3.75 percent to 5.875 percent and invested this money in assets earning 7.6 percent. The difference between the profit earned on the money it borrows and the interest it paid to creditors is available for Home Depot's shareholders. This benefit of financial leverage is the primary reason that most companies obtain a significant amount of their resources from creditors rather than from the sale of shares. Notice that financial leverage can be enhanced either by investing effectively (i.e., earning a high return on investment) or borrowing effectively (i.e., paying a low rate of interest).

A negative financial leverage percentage means that ROE has decreased relative to ROA or that ROA has increased relative to ROE. The return on equity decreases when profit decreases, signalling a deterioration in the company's profitability, or when equity increases through the issuance of additional shares. An inflow of cash from a new equity issue may indicate that the company is entering a growth phase that is expected to increase profits. Another possibility is that the return on assets may have increased substantially relative to the return on equity because of an increase in after-tax interest expense and in the cost of debt financing. Without careful interpretation of relevant information available on a specific company, investors cannot accurately interpret a decrease in ROE as either good news or bad news.

In general, if a decrease in ROE signals future growth despite a temporarily negative financial leverage percentage, investors may not be too alarmed by negative leverage. If, however, an increase in ROA is the result of borrowing at high interest rates, investors could well interpret negative leverage as reflecting bad news. It is, therefore, important for investors to be cautious when interpreting any increase or decrease in ratios.

Home Depot's financial leverage ratio is higher than those of Canadian Tire (4.3%) and RONA (2.9%).

3. Earnings per Share (EPS)

Earnings per share is a measure of the return on investment that is based on the number of shares outstanding instead of the dollar amounts reported on the statement of financial position. In simple situations, EPS is computed as follows:

$$\textbf{Earnings per Share} = \frac{\textbf{Profit Available to Common Shareholders}}{\substack{\textbf{Average Number of} \\ \textbf{Common Shares Outstanding}}}$$

$$\textbf{Home Depot, 2009} = \frac{\$2,661}{\$1,683^*} = \$1.58 \textbf{ per share}$$

*Reported on the income statement.

This computation of EPS is based on information provided in Note 10 of the company's consolidated financial statements. The additional complexities in the computation of EPS are discussed in advanced accounting courses.

Earnings per share is probably the single most widely watched ratio. Companies' announcements of their net earnings each quarter during the fiscal year are normally reported in the business press. The following news story by Reuters concerning Home

Depot's earnings results for the fourth quarter of 2009 illustrates the importance of earnings per share.

Home Depot sees better year as customers renovate, Tue Feb 23, 2010 1:06pm EST

(Reuters) – Top home-improvement chain Home Depot Inc (HD.N) reported its first quarterly same-store rise in nearly four years and gave an upbeat full-year forecast as customers begin making bigger renovation projects....

"Our expectation is that 2010 will be a transitional year," CEO Frank Blake said on a conference call, adding he expected to see relatively flat growth in the first half of the year, with more momentum in the second half.... Blake said all but two of Home Depot's top 40 markets in the United States showed improvement in the fourth quarter on a same-store sales basis.... Home Depot also raised its quarterly cash dividend 5 percent, the first increase since 2006 and "a testament to our confidence in the company's strategic initiatives," Blake said.

The shares of Home Depot...stocks...rose 2.2 percent in afternoon trading.

Sales Exceed Expectations

Home Depot's net income was $342 million, or 20 cents a share, in the fourth quarter ended January 31, compared with a year-earlier loss of $54 million, or 3 cents a share.

Source: http://www.reuters.com/article/idUSTRE61M2B020100223. Accessed April 10, 2010.

4. Quality of Earnings

Most financial analysts are concerned about the quality of a company's earnings because the use of some accounting procedures can result in higher earnings reports. For example, a company that uses short estimated lives for non-current assets will report lower earnings than will a similar company that uses longer estimated lives. One method of evaluating the quality of a company's earnings is to compare its reported earnings to its cash flows from operating activities, as follows:

$$\text{Quality of Earnings} = \frac{\text{Cash Flows from Operating Activities}}{\text{Profit}}$$

$$\text{Home Depot, 2009} = \frac{\$5,125}{\$2,661} = 1.93$$

A quality of earnings ratio higher than 1 is considered to indicate higher-quality earnings because each dollar of profit is supported by at least one dollar of cash flow. Recall that profit includes both cash and non-cash components that result from accrual of revenues and expenses that will affect cash in future accounting periods. A ratio below 1 indicates that accruals represent a significant portion of profit, which suggests that earnings are of lower quality than if the ratio exceeded 1.

5. Profit Margin

The *profit margin* measures the percentage of each sales dollar, on average, that represents profit. It is computed as follows:

$$\text{Profit Margin} = \frac{\text{Income (before Extraordinary Items)}}{\text{Net Sales Revenue}}$$

$$\text{Home Depot, 2009} = \frac{\$2,661}{\$66,176} = 4.0\%$$

During 2009, each dollar of Home Depot's sales generated 4.0 cents of profit. Care must be used in analyzing the profit margin because it does not consider the amount of resources employed (i.e., total investment) to earn profit. For example, the hypothetical income statements of Home Depot and Canadian Tire might show the following:

	Home Depot	Canadian Tire
a. Sales revenue	$500,000	$150,000
b. Profit	25,000	7,500
c. Profit margin (b ÷ a)	5%	5%
d. Total investment	$250,000	$125,000
e. Return on total investment* (b ÷ d)	10%	6%
*Assuming no interest expense.		

In this example, both companies reported the same profit margin (5 percent). Home Depot, however, appears to be performing much better because it is earning a 10 percent return on the total investment versus the 6 percent earned by Canadian Tire. The profit margin percentages do not reflect the effect of the $250,000 total investment in Home Depot compared to the $125,000 total investment in Canadian Tire. Thus, the profit margin omits one of the two important factors that should be used in evaluating return on the investment.

It is very difficult to compare profit margins for companies in different industries. For example, profit margins are low in the food industry, but they are high in the jewellery business. Both types of businesses can be quite profitable, however, because a high sales volume can compensate for a low profit margin. Grocery stores have low profit margins but generate a large sales volume from their relatively inexpensive stores and inventory. Although jewellery stores earn more profit from each sales dollar, they require a large investment in luxury stores and very expensive inventory.

The trade-off between profit margin and sales volume can be stated in very simple terms: would you prefer to have 5 percent of $1,000,000 or 10 percent of $100,000? As you can see, a larger percentage is not always better.

The operating strength of Home Depot is about the same as Canadian Tire and both are somewhat stronger than RONA when you compare their profit margins for 2009:

Canadian Tire	3.9%
RONA	2.9
Home Depot	4.0

6. Fixed Asset Turnover

Another measure of operating efficiency is the fixed asset turnover ratio, which compares sales volume with a company's investment in fixed assets. The term *fixed assets* is synonymous with *property, plant, and equipment*. The ratio is computed as follows:

$$\text{Fixed Asset Turnover} = \frac{\text{Net Sales}}{\text{Average Net Fixed Assets}}$$

$$\text{Home Depot, 2009} = \frac{\$66,176}{\$25,892^*} = 2.56$$

*($26,234 + $25,550) ÷ 2

The fixed asset turnover ratio for Home Depot is lower than RONA's (5.53) and Canadian Tire's (2.72). In simple terms, this means that both companies have a competitive advantage over Home Depot in terms of their ability to effectively utilize fixed assets to generate revenue. For each dollar that Home Depot invested in property, plant, and equipment, it was able to earn $2.55 in sales revenue, while RONA earned $5.53 and Canadian Tire earned $2.72.

The fixed asset turnover ratio is widely used to analyze capital-intensive companies such as airlines and electric utilities. For companies that have large amounts of inventory and trade receivables, analysts often prefer to use the asset turnover ratio, which is based on total assets rather than fixed assets:

$$\text{Asset Turnover} = \frac{\text{Net Sales}}{\text{Average Total Assets}}$$

$$\text{Home Depot, 2009} = \frac{\$66,176}{\$41,021^*} = 1.61$$

*($41,164 + $40,877) ÷ 2

In 2009, Home Depot was able to generate $1.61 in revenue for each dollar invested in the company's assets. This ratio does not compare favourably to RONA's ratio of 1.79, but it is larger than Canadian Tire's ratio of 1.05.

As we showed with the ROE model earlier in this chapter, one strategy to improve return on equity is to generate more revenue from the company's assets. Many analysts consider this type of improvement to be an important indication of the quality of the company's management.

SELF-STUDY **QUIZ 13-1**

Canadian Tire Corporation Ltd. reported the following data in a recent annual report (in millions of dollars):

	Current Year	Last Year
Net income	$ 335.0	
Sales	8,686.5	
Interest expense (net of tax)	99.9	
Shareholders' equity	3,687.9	$3,565.0
Total assets	8,789.5	7,783.8

1. Compute the following ratios:
   a. Return on equity
   b. Return on assets
   c. Profit margin
2. Does the company use debt effectively to generate returns to shareholders? Explain.

After you complete your answers, go online for the solutions.

ROE PROFIT DRIVER ANALYSIS

Exhibit 13.5 shows a decomposition of Home Depot's ROE profit driver analysis that was presented earlier, in Exhibit 13.2. This analysis shows the sources of the change in ROE and can provide useful insights into Home Depot's business strategy.

Exhibit 13.5 shows a decrease in profit margin in fiscal year 2008, followed by increase in fiscal year 2009. The component percentages (see Exhibit 13.3) suggest that this decrease was caused mainly by the decrease in revenue that outpaced the efforts at cost control during the economic recession. This is consistent with economic hard times when discretionary spending drops quickly, especially when consumers lose their jobs, which leads to excessive inventory and a higher

	Fiscal Year Ended		
	January 31, 2010	**February 1, 2009**	**February 3, 2008**
ROE Profit Drivers			
Profit	$ 2,661	$ 2,260	$ 4,395
Net sales	66,176	71,288	77,349
Average total assets	41,021	42,744	48,294
Average shareholders' equity	18,585	17,746	21,372
ROE Profit Driver Analysis			
Profit/Net sales	0.040	0.037	0.057
× Net sales/Avg. total assets	1.613	1.668	1.602
× Avg. total assets/ Avg. shareholders' equity	2.207	2.409	2.260
= Profit/Avg. shareholders' equity	0.143	0.127	0.206

Exhibit **13.5**

Home Depot ROE Profit Driver Analysis

cost of sales for retailers that make their inventory purchase decisions well in advance of expected sales. Home Depot's statement of financial position shows that merchandise inventories decreased by $485 million or 4.5 percent during 2009, whereas sales decreased by $5.1 billion or 7.2 percent during the same period.

In summary, the improvement in Home Depot's return on equity during 2009 was essentially because of Home Depot's improved productivity and cost management at its existing stores.[5] The decline in the asset turnover ratio during 2009 was not significant enough to offset the effects of the other components of the DuPont model.

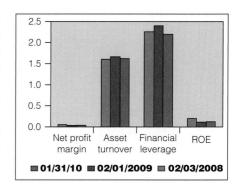

SELF-STUDY **QUIZ 13-2**

We used ROE analysis in Exhibit 13.5 to understand how Home Depot's ROE had changed over the fiscal years 2007–2009. This type of analysis is often called *time series analysis*. ROE analysis can also be used to explain why a company has an ROE that is different from its competitors' at a single point in time. This type of analysis is called *cross-sectional analysis*.

Google Inc. and Yahoo Inc. both supply Internet search services. Both companies have developed reputations for good service. The following is an analysis of their ROEs for the year 2009. Using ROE analysis, explain how Google produced its higher ROE.

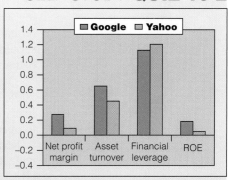

ROE Profit Driver Analysis	Google	Yahoo
Profit/Net sales	0.276	0.094
× Net sales/Avg. total assets	0.654	0.451
× Avg. total assets/Avg. shareholders' equity	1.125	1.206
= Profit/Avg. shareholders' equity	0.180	0.051

After you complete your answers, go online for the solutions.

connect

TESTS OF LIQUIDITY

Liquidity refers to a company's ability to meet its currently maturing debts. Tests of liquidity focus on the relationship between current assets and current liabilities. A company's ability to pay its current liabilities is an important factor in evaluating its

LO5

Compute and interpret liquidity ratios.

TESTS OF LIQUIDITY are ratios that measure a company's ability to meet its currently maturing obligations.

---

[5]An expanded version of the ROE profit driver analysis is provided by the Scott formula. Interested readers are referred to Connect online for a detailed application of the Scott formula to the financial statements of Home Depot Inc.

short-term financial strength. For example, a company that does not have cash available to pay for purchases on a timely basis will lose its cash discounts and run the risk of having its credit discontinued by vendors. Three ratios are used to measure liquidity: cash ratio, current ratio, and quick ratio.

7. Cash Ratio

Cash is the lifeblood of a business. Without cash, a company cannot pay employees or meet obligations to its creditors. Even a profitable business will fail without sufficient cash. One measure of the adequacy of available cash, called the *cash ratio*, is computed as follows:

$$\textbf{Cash Ratio} = \frac{\textbf{Cash} + \textbf{Cash Equivalents}}{\textbf{Current Liabilities}}$$

$$\textbf{Home Depot, 2009} = \frac{\$1,421}{\$10,363} = 0.14$$

Analysts often use this ratio to compare similar companies. The cash ratios for Canadian Tire and RONA indicate that these companies have a larger cash reserve compared to current liabilities.

Canadian Tire	0.31
RONA	0.53
Home Depot	0.14

Would analysts be concerned about the lower ratio for Home Depot? Probably not, because there are other factors to consider. The statement of cash flows for Home Depot shows that the company generates a very large amount of cash from operating activities each year. As a result, it does not have to keep a large amount of cash on hand to meet unexpected needs. Indeed, most analysts believe that the cash ratio should not be too high, because holding excess cash usually is uneconomical. It is far better to invest the cash in productive assets or reduce debt.

The cash ratio for Home Depot has increased from a low of 0.04 at February 3, 2008, to 0.14 at January 31, 2010. Home Depot's relatively low cash ratio is most likely the result of successful efforts by managers to minimize the amount of cash used to operate the business.

Some analysts do not use this ratio because it is very sensitive to small events. The collection of a large trade receivable, for example, would have a significant positive effect on the cash ratio. The current ratio and the quick ratio are much less sensitive to the timing of cash collections from customers.

8. Current Ratio

The *current ratio* measures the relationship between current assets and current liabilities at a specific date. It is computed as follows:

$$\textbf{Current Ratio} = \frac{\textbf{Current Assets}}{\textbf{Current Liabilities}}$$

$$\textbf{Home Depot, 2009} = \frac{\$13,900}{\$10,363} = 1.34$$

The current ratio measures the cushion of working capital that companies maintain to allow for the inevitable unevenness in the flow of funds through the working capital accounts. At the end of 2009, Home Depot had $1.34 in current assets for each $1 of liabilities. Most analysts would judge the ratio to be very strong, given Home Depot's ability to generate cash. By comparison, both Canadian Tire and RONA have higher current ratios than Home Depot.

Canadian Tire	1.99
RONA	2.79
Home Depot	1.34

To properly use the current ratio, analysts must understand the nature of a company's business. Many manufacturing companies have developed sophisticated systems to minimize the amount of inventory they must hold. These systems, called *just-in-time inventory*, are designed so that an inventory item will arrive just as it is needed. While these systems work well in manufacturing processes, they do not work as well in retailing. Customers expect to find merchandise when they want it, and it has proven difficult to precisely forecast consumer behaviour. As a result, most retailers have comparatively large current ratios because they must carry large inventories. With the economic downturn, however, Home Depot initiated a systems approach to inventory management that improves on the distribution of merchandise throughout its supply chain. This process allows improved transportation, simplified order processing at suppliers, and reduced lead time from identification of the products needed by specific stores to replenish inventories. The company now uses centralized Rapid Deployment Centers (RDC) to reduce stock-outs, inventory swell, and distribute products in a more cost-efficient way.

Analysts consider a current ratio of 2 to be financially conservative. Indeed, most companies have current ratios that are below 2. The optimal level for a current ratio depends on the business environment in which a company operates. If cash flows are predictable and stable (as they are for a utility company), the current ratio can even be lower than 1. For a business with highly variable cash flows (such as an airline), a ratio exceeding 1 may be desirable.

Analysts become concerned if a company's current ratio is high compared to those of other companies. A firm is operating inefficiently when it ties up too much money in inventory or trade receivables. There is no reason, for instance, for a Home Depot store to hold 1,000 hammers in stock if it sells only 100 hammers a month.

Current Ratio for Selected Industries, 2009	
Metals and mining	4.50
Pharmaceuticals	5.24
Biotechnology	1.32
Software	3.66
Paper and forest products	2.36
Telecommunication services	0.84

9. Quick Ratio (Acid Test)

The *quick ratio* is a more stringent test of short-term liquidity than the current ratio. The quick ratio compares quick assets, defined as ***cash and near-cash assets***, to current liabilities. Quick assets include cash, short-term investments, and trade receivables (net of the allowance for doubtful accounts). Inventories are omitted from quick assets because of the uncertainty of the timing of cash flows from their sale. Prepayments are also excluded from quick assets. Thus, the quick, or acid test, ratio is a more severe test of liquidity than the current ratio. It is computed as follows:

$$\text{Quick Ratio} = \frac{\text{Quick Assets}}{\text{Current Liabilities}}$$

$$\text{Home Depot, 2009} = \frac{\$2,391}{\$10,363} = 0.23$$

The quick ratio is a measure of the safety margin that is available to meet a company's current liabilities. Home Depot has 23 cents in cash and near-cash assets for every $1 in current liabilities. This value is below the threshold of 0.40 that is considered appropriate for this ratio. Analysts should not be concerned about the magnitude of this ratio because of the large amount of cash that Home Depot generates from operating activities. By comparison, the quick ratios for Canadian Tire and RONA are 1.21 and 1.10, respectively.

SELF-STUDY **QUIZ 13-3**

The current ratios for six industries appear in the margin on page 709. The following quick ratios, presented in a random order, pertain to the same six industries:

	Industries					
	1	**2**	**3**	**4**	**5**	**6**
Quick ratio	3.46	0.58	0.65	1.27	4.61	3.54

Two of these six industries are software and metals and mining. Identify the ratio associated with each of these two industries. On average, the quick assets for the software industry represent 95 percent of the industry's current assets.

connect

After you complete your answers, go online for the solutions.

10. Receivables Turnover Ratio

Trade receivables are closely related to both short-term liquidity and operating efficiency. A company that can quickly collect cash from its customers has good liquidity and does not needlessly tie up funds in unproductive assets. The receivables turnover ratio is computed as follows:

$$\text{Receivables Turnover} = \frac{\text{Net Credit Sales}^*}{\text{Average Net Trade Receivables}}$$

$$\text{Home Depot, 2009} = \frac{\$66,176}{\$968^\dagger} = 68.4 \text{ Times}$$

*When the amount of credit sales is not known, total sales may be used as a rough approximation.
†($972 + $964) ÷ 2

This ratio is called a *turnover* because it reflects how many times the trade receivables were recorded, collected, and then new receivables recorded again during the period (i.e., turned over). Receivables turnover expresses the relationship of the average balance in trade receivables to the transactions (i.e., credit sales) that created those receivables. This ratio measures the effectiveness of the company's credit-granting and collection activities. A high receivables turnover ratio suggests effective collection activities. Granting credit to poor credit risks and making ineffective collection efforts cause this ratio to be low. A very low ratio obviously is a problem, but a very high ratio also can be troublesome because it suggests an overly stringent credit policy that could cause lost sales and profits.

The receivables turnover ratio often is converted to a time basis known as the *average age of trade receivables*. The computation is as follows:

$$\text{Average Age of Trade Receivables} = \frac{\text{Days in a Year}}{\text{Receivables Turnover}}$$

$$\text{Home Depot, 2009} = \frac{365}{68.4} = 5.34 \text{ Average Days to Collect}$$

This computation is equivalent to dividing the average net trade receivables by the average net credit sales per day; that is,

Average collection period = $968 ÷ ($66,176 ÷ 365) = 5.34 days

The effectiveness of credit and collection activities sometimes is judged by the general rule that the average collection period should not exceed 1.5 times the credit terms. For example, if the credit terms require payment in 30 days, the average collection period should not exceed 45 days (i.e., not more than 15 days past due). Like all rules, this one has many exceptions.

When you evaluate financial statements, you should always think about the reasonableness of the numbers you compute. We computed the average age of receivables for

Home Depot as 5.34 days. Is that number reasonable? Probably not. It is very unlikely that Home Depot collects cash from its credit customers on average in just 5.34 days. Because we did not know the amount of Home Depot's credit sales, we used total sales as an approximation. Moreover, Home Depot often uses special promotions offering interest-free credit on its Home Depot credit card for 90 to 180 days on large purchases.

Think about the last time you watched a customer buying merchandise on credit in a retail store. Most customers use a bank credit card such as MasterCard or Visa. From the seller's perspective, a sales transaction involving a bank credit card is recorded in virtually the same manner as a cash sale. A credit sale involving a credit card does not create a trade receivable on the seller's books. Instead, the trade receivable is recorded on the books of the credit card company. In practice, the majority of Home Depot's credit sales involve bank credit cards. As a result, Home Depot's receivables turnover ratio is not meaningful.

11. Inventory Turnover Ratio

Like the receivables turnover, *inventory turnover* is a measure of both liquidity and operating efficiency. It reflects the relationship of inventory to the volume of sales during the period. It is computed as follows:

$$\text{Inventory Turnover} = \frac{\text{Costs of Sales}}{\text{Average Inventory}}$$

$$\text{Home Depot, 2009} = \frac{\$43,764}{\$10,430.5^*} = 4.20 \text{ Times}$$

*($10,673 + $10,188) ÷ 2

Because a company normally realizes a profit each time the inventory is sold, an increase in the ratio is usually favourable. If the ratio is too high, however, it may be an indication that sales were lost because desired items were not in stock. The cost of a lost sale is often much higher than the lost profit. When a business is out of stock on an item desired by a customer, the individual will often go to a competitor to find it. That visit may help the competitor establish a business relationship with the customer. Thus, the cost of being out of stock may be all future profits of a lost customer.

On average, Home Depot's inventory was acquired and sold to customers four times during the year.[6] The inventory turnover ratio is critical for companies that have adopted the Home Depot strategy. They want to be able to offer the customer the right product when it is needed at a price that beats the competition. If Home Depot does not effectively manage its inventory levels, it will incur extra costs that must be passed on to the customer.

Turnover ratios vary significantly from one industry to the next. Companies in the food industry (grocery stores and restaurants) have high inventory turnover ratios because their inventory is subject to rapid deterioration in quality. Companies that sell expensive merchandise (automobiles and high-fashion clothes) have much lower ratios because sales of these items are infrequent but customers want to have a selection to choose from when they do buy.

The turnover ratio often is converted to a time basis called the ***average days' supply in inventory***. The computation is

$$\text{Average Days' Supply in Inventory} = \frac{\text{Days in Year}}{\text{Inventory Turnover}}$$

$$\text{Home Depot, 2009} = \frac{365}{4.20} = 87 \text{ Average Days' Supply in Inventory}$$

---

[6]The inventory turnover ratios for both RONA and Canadian Tire cannot be computed because neither company disclosed its cost of sales on its income statement.

Equivalently, the average days' supply in inventory can be computed by dividing the average inventory by the cost of sales per day—that is,

Average days' supply in inventory = \$10,430.5 ÷ (\$43,764 ÷ 365) = 87 days

12. Payables Turnover Ratio

The *payables turnover ratio* evaluates the company's effectiveness in managing payables to trade creditors. It is computed as follows:

$$\text{Payables Turnover} = \frac{\text{Net Credit Purchases}}{\text{Average Net Trade Payables}}$$

Credit purchases are not usually reported in financial statements; hence, we use total purchases of merchandise inventory as a rough approximation. However, purchases are usually not reported separately in financial statements, but they can be calculated by adjusting the cost of sales for the change in inventory during the period.

Purchases = Cost of sales + Ending inventory − Beginning inventory

The computation of the payables turnover for Home Depot follows:[7]

$$\text{Home Depot, 2009} = \frac{\$43,764 + 10,188 - \$10,673}{\$4,842.5^*} = 8.94 \text{ Times}$$

*(\$4,822 + \$4,863) ÷ 2

This ratio reflects how many times the trade payables were recorded, paid, and then new payables recorded again during the period. The payables turnover expresses the relationship of the average balance in trade payables to the purchase transactions that created those payables. Usually, a low ratio raises questions concerning a company's liquidity. It could also reflect aggressive cash management. By conserving cash with slow payments to trade suppliers, the company minimizes the amount of money it must borrow, and the related interest.

The payables turnover ratio is often converted to a time basis known as the ***average age of payables***. The computation is as follows:

$$\text{Average Age of Payables} = \frac{\text{Days in a Year}}{\text{Payable Turnover}}$$

$$\text{Home Depot, 2009} = \frac{365}{8.94} = 40.8 \text{ Average Days to Pay}$$

This computation is equivalent to dividing the average net trade payables by the average net credit purchases per day.

The payables turnover can be subject to manipulation. Managers may delay payment to creditors during the entire year but catch up at year-end so that the ratio is at an acceptable level.

Using Ratios to Analyze the Operating Cycle

In Chapter 3, we introduced the concept of the operating cycle, which is the time it takes for a company to pay cash to its suppliers, sell goods to its customers, and collect cash from its customers. Analysts are interested in the operating cycle because it helps them evaluate a company's cash needs and is a good indicator of management efficiency.

---

[7]The payable turnover ratios for both RONA and Canadian Tire cannot be computed because neither company disclosed its cost of sales on its income statement.

The operating cycle for most companies involves three distinct phases: acquisition of inventory, sale of inventory, and collection of cash from customers. We have discussed three ratios that are helpful in evaluating a company's operating cycle. They are the payables turnover ratio, inventory turnover ratio, and receivables turnover ratio. Each of these ratios measures the number of days it takes to complete an operating activity. The length of the component parts for Home Depot's operating cycle are

Ratio	Operating Activity	Time
Payables turnover ratio	Purchase of inventory	40.8 days
Inventory turnover ratio	Sale of inventory	87.0 days
Receivables turnover ratio	Collection of cash from customers	5.3 days

The component parts of the operating cycle help us understand the cash needs of the company. Home Depot, on average, pays for its inventory 40.8 days after it receives it. It takes, on average, 92.3 days (87.0 + 5.3) for Home Depot to sell the inventory and collect cash from customers. Therefore, Home Depot must invest cash in its operating activities for nearly 52 days between the time it pays its vendors and the time it collects from its customers. Companies prefer to minimize the time between paying vendors and collecting cash from customers because it frees up cash for other productive purposes. Home Depot could reduce this time by slowing payments to creditors or by increasing the inventory turnover.

Companies that sell products through the Internet may not need to stock merchandise for long periods. In fact, Dell Inc. disclosed in its annual report for fiscal 2009 that its cash conversion cycle was −36 days during that year, indicating that Dell paid suppliers, on average, 36 days after it sold its products and collected from customers. While Home Depot needs money to finance the purchase of inventory, Dell has relied on suppliers to provide the necessary financing.

SELF-STUDY **QUIZ 13-4**

Canadian Tire Corporation Ltd. reported the following data in a recent annual report (in millions of dollars):

Profit	$335.0
Cash and short-term investments	850.0
Trade receivables	835.9
Credit card receivables	2,239.4
Current liabilities	2,564.1
Cash flows from operating activities	418.8

Compute the following ratios:

1. Quality of earnings
2. Quick ratio
3. Cash ratio

After you complete your answers, go online for the solutions.

▦ connect

TESTS OF SOLVENCY

Solvency refers to a company's ability to meet its long-term obligations. Tests of solvency, which are measures of a company's ability to meet these obligations, include the times interest earned, cash coverage, and debt-to-equity ratios.

LO6

Compute and interpret solvency ratios.

TESTS OF SOLVENCY are ratios that measure a company's ability to meet its long-term obligations.

13. Times Interest Earned Ratio

Interest payments are a definite obligation of the borrowing company. If a company fails to make required interest payments, creditors may force it into bankruptcy. Because of the importance of interest payments, analysts often compute a ratio called *times interest earned*:

$$\text{Times Interest Earned} = \frac{\text{Profit before Interest and Taxes}}{\text{Interest Expense}}$$

$$\text{Home Depot, 2009} = \frac{\$3,982 + \$676}{\$676} = 6.89 \text{ Times}$$

This ratio compares the profit that a company generated during one period to its interest expense for the same period. It represents a margin of protection for the creditors. In 2009, Home Depot generated nearly $7 in profit before interest and taxes for each $1 of interest expense, a ratio that indicates a secure position for creditors.

Some analysts prefer to calculate this ratio based on all contractually required payments, including principal payments and rent obligations under lease contracts. Other analysts believe that this ratio is flawed because interest expense and other obligations are paid in cash, not with net profit. These analysts prefer to use the cash coverage ratio.

14. Cash Coverage Ratio

Given the importance of cash flows and required interest payments, it is easy to understand why many analysts use the *cash coverage ratio*. It is computed as follows:

$$\text{Cash Coverage} = \frac{\begin{array}{c}\text{Cash Flows from Operating Activities} \\ \text{before Interest and Taxes}\end{array}}{\text{Interest Paid (from statement of cash flows)}}$$

$$\text{Home Depot, 2009} = \frac{\$5,125 + \$664 + \$2,082}{\$664} = 11.85 \text{ Times}$$

The cash coverage ratio compares the cash generated with the cash obligations of the period. Analysts are concerned about a company's ability to make required interest payments. The cash coverage ratio for Home Depot shows that the company generated $11.85 in cash from operations for every $1 of interest paid, which is strong coverage. Note that the numerator and the denominator of the cash coverage ratio use ***interest paid and income taxes paid*** from the statement of cash flows instead of ***interest expense and income taxes expense*** from the income statement. Accrued interest and interest payments are normally similar in amount, but are not always the same.

15. Debt-to-Equity Ratio

The *debt-to-equity ratio* expresses a company's debt as a proportion of its shareholders' equity.[8] It is computed as follows:

$$\text{Debt-to-Equity} = \frac{\text{Total Liabilities}}{\text{Shareholders' Equity}}$$

$$\text{Home Depot, 2009} = \frac{\$21,484}{\$19,393} = 1.11 \text{ (or 111\%)}$$

---

[8]Alternatively, the relationship between debt and owners' equity may be calculated with the following ratio:

$$\text{Total Liabilities to Total Equities} = \frac{\text{Total Liabilities}}{\text{Total Liabilities and Shareholders' Equity}}$$

$$\text{Home Depot, 2009} = \frac{\$21,484}{\$40,877} = 52.6\%$$

In 2009, for each $1 of shareholders' equity, Home Depot had $1.11 of liabilities. By comparison, RONA and Canadian Tire's debt-to-equity ratios were 0.55 and 1.38, respectively.

Debt is risky for a company because specific interest payments must be made even if the company has not earned sufficient profit. In contrast, dividends are always at the company's discretion and are not legally enforceable until they are declared by the board of directors. Thus, equity capital is usually considered much less risky than debt.

Despite the risk associated with debt, most companies obtain significant amounts of resources from creditors because of the advantages of financial leverage discussed earlier. In addition, interest paid is a deductible expense on the corporate income tax return. In selecting a capital structure, a company must balance the higher returns available through leverage against the higher risk associated with debt. Because of the importance of this risk–return relationship, most analysts consider the debt-to-equity ratio to be a key part of any company evaluation.

Debt-to-Equity Ratio for Selected Industries, 2009	
Paper and forest products	0.98
Telecommunication services	1.17
Software	0.09
Gold	0.13
Retailing	0.21

MARKET TESTS

Several ratios, often called *market tests*, relate the current market price per share to the return that accrues to investors. Many analysts prefer these ratios because they are based on the current value of an owner's investment in a company.

LO7

Compute and interpret market test ratios.

MARKET TESTS are ratios that tend to measure the market worth of a common share.

16. Price/Earnings (P/E)

The *price/earnings (P/E) ratio* measures the relationship between the current market price per share and its earnings per share. Recently, when the price of a Home Depot common share was $33.23, EPS was $1.58, as calculated earlier. The P/E ratio for the company is computed as follows:

$$\text{Price/Earnings} = \frac{\text{Current Market Price per Share}}{\text{Earnings per Share}}$$

$$\text{Home Depot, 2009} = \frac{\$33.23}{\$1.58} = 21.0$$

The P/E ratio indicates that Home Depot's shares were selling at a price that was 21 times its earnings per share. The P/E ratio reflects the stock market's assessment of the company's future business performance. A high ratio indicates that the market expects earnings to grow rapidly. Home Depot's P/E ratio is reasonable and comparable to the ratios of its competitors.

Canadian Tire	13.6
RONA	14.0
Home Depot	21.0

Sometimes the components of the P/E ratio are inverted, giving the *capitalization rate*, a rate at which the stock market apparently is capitalizing the current earnings. The capitalization rate for Home Depot is $1.58 ÷ $33.23 = 4.8 percent.

In economic terms, the share price is related to the present value of the company's future earnings. Thus, a company that expects to increase its earnings in the future is worth more than one that cannot grow its earnings (assuming other factors are the same). But while a high P/E ratio and good growth prospects are considered favourable, there are risks. When a company with a high P/E ratio does not meet the level of earnings expected by the market, the negative impact on its share price can be dramatic.

Average P/E Ratio for Selected Industries, 2009	
Gold	29.7
Software	15.5
Retailing	11.8
Telecommunications	15.5
Transportation	9.3

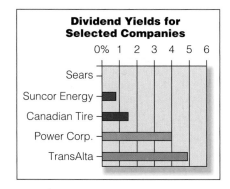

Dividend Yields for Selected Companies

17. Dividend Yield

When investors buy shares, they expect returns from two sources: price appreciation and dividend income. The *dividend yield ratio* measures the relationship between the dividend per share paid to shareholders and the current market price per share. Home Depot paid a dividend of 90 cents per share when the market price per share was $33.23. Its dividend yield ratio is computed as follows:

$$\text{Dividend Yield} = \frac{\text{Dividend per Share}}{\text{Market Price per Share}}$$

$$\text{Home Depot, 2009} = \frac{\$0.90}{\$33.23} = 2.7\%$$

It might seem surprising that Home Depot's dividend yield was rather low, given that an investor could earn similar returns on alternative investments that were risk free. In fact, the dividend yield for shares of most companies is not high compared with returns on alternative investments. Investors may accept low dividend yields if they expect that the price of a company's shares will increase while they own it. Clearly, investors who bought Home Depot's common shares did so with the expectation that their price would increase. In contrast, companies with low growth potential tend to offer much higher dividend yields than do companies with high growth potential. These latter companies usually appeal to retired investors who need current income rather than future growth potential. The chart in the margin shows dividend yields for a selection of companies.

SELF-STUDY **QUIZ 13-5**

Canadian Tire Corporation Ltd. reported the following data in a recent annual report (in millions of dollars):

	Current Year	Last Year
Current assets	$5,112.5	
Current liabilities	2,564.1	
Cost of sales (assumed)	7,788.1	
Inventory	933.6	$917.5
Earnings per share	4.1	
Share price at year-end	61.74	

Compute the following ratios:

1. Current ratio

2. Inventory turnover ratio

3. Price/earnings ratio

After you complete your answers, go online for the solutions.

INTERPRETING RATIOS AND OTHER ANALYTICAL CONSIDERATIONS

Except for earnings per share, the computation of financial ratios has not been standardized by the accounting profession or security analysts. Thus, users of financial statements should compute the various ratios in accordance with their decision objectives. Before using ratios computed by others, the analyst should determine the computational approach that was used.

Ratios can best be interpreted only by comparing them to other ratios or to some threshold value. For example, a very low current ratio may indicate an inability to meet maturing debts, and a very high current ratio may indicate an unprofitable use of funds. Furthermore, an optimal ratio for one company may not be optimal for another. Comparisons of ratios for different companies are appropriate only if the companies

	Years before Bankruptcy					Exhibit **13.6**
	5	**4**	**3**	**2**	**1**	Selected Financial Ratios for
Current ratio	1.20	0.91	0.74	0.60	0.49	Braniff International
Debt-to-equity ratio	2.03	2.45	4.88	15.67	N/A*	

*In the year before bankruptcy, Braniff reported negative owners' equity as a result of a large net loss that produced a negative balance in retained earnings. Total liabilities exceeded total assets.

are indeed comparable in terms of industry, nature of operations, size, and accounting policies.

Because ratios are based on the aggregation of information, they may obscure underlying factors that are of interest to the analyst. For example, a current ratio that is considered optimal may obscure a short-term liquidity problem if the company has a very large amount of inventory but a minimal amount of cash with which to pay debts as they mature. Careful analysis can uncover this type of problem.

In other cases, analysis cannot uncover obscured problems. For example, consolidated statements include financial information about the parent and its subsidiaries. The parent company may have a high current ratio and the subsidiary a low ratio. When the statements are consolidated, the current ratio may fall within an acceptable range. The fact that the subsidiary could have a serious liquidity problem is obscured in this case.

Despite limitations, ratio analysis is a useful analytical tool. For instance, financial ratios are effective for predicting bankruptcy. Exhibit 13.6 gives the current and debt-to-equity ratios for Braniff International Corporation for each year before it filed for bankruptcy. Notice the deterioration of these ratios each year. Analysts who studied the financial ratios probably were not surprised by Braniff's bankruptcy. After selling many of its assets and undergoing a complete financial restructuring, Braniff was able to resume limited flight operations but was forced to file for bankruptcy for a second time after additional financial difficulty.

Financial statements provide information to all investors, both sophisticated and unsophisticated. However, users who understand basic accounting principles and terminology are able to more effectively analyze the information in the financial statements. For example, unsophisticated users who do not understand the cost principle might believe that assets are reported on the statement of financial position at their fair market value. Interpreting accounting numbers without an understanding of the concepts that were used to develop them is impossible.

In analyzing different companies, you will find that they rarely use exactly the same accounting policies. Comparisons among companies are appropriate only if the analyst who is making them understands the impact of various accounting alternatives. For example, one company may be prudent in selecting accounting alternatives such as declining depreciation, while another may use profit-maximizing alternatives such as straight-line depreciation. Those who do not understand the different effects of accounting methods are very likely to misinterpret financial results. Perhaps the most important first step in analyzing financial statements is a review of the company's accounting policies, which are disclosed in a note to the statements.

OTHER FINANCIAL INFORMATION

The ratios we have discussed are useful for most analytical purposes. Because each company is different, you must exercise professional judgment when you conduct each financial analysis. To illustrate, let us look at some special factors that might affect our analysis of Home Depot.

1. *Rapid growth*. Growth in total sales volume does not always indicate that a company is successful. Sales volume from new stores may obscure the fact that existing stores are not meeting customer needs and are experiencing declining sales. In robust economic times, the retail industry often undertakes long-term expansion

plans, which rapidly become unprofitable if the economy slows. For example, Home Depot's annual report shows that the company posted same-store sales increases, ranging from 0 percent to 10 percent in the decade ending 2006, but with the economic recession, this growth rapidly changed to decreases in comparable store sales by 8.7 percent in 2008 and 6.6 percent in 2009. Nevertheless, the management of Home Depot continued to report profit throughout this turbulent period.

2. *Uneconomical expansion*. Some growth-oriented companies open stores in less than desirable locations if good locations cannot be found. These poor locations can cause the company's average productivity to decline. One measure of productivity in the retail industry is sales volume per square foot of selling space. For Home Depot, productivity increased from 2002 to 2005, but has steadily declined since 2005. In response to economic hard times, Home Depot has considerably decreased its new store openings in an effort to improve its productivity.

Year	Sales per Square Foot
2009	$279
2008	298
2007	332
2006	358
2005	377
2004	375
2003	371
2002	370

REAL WORLD EXCERPT

Home Depot

ANNUAL REPORT

NOTES TO CONSOLIDATED FINANCIAL STATEMENTS

2. Rationalization Charges

In fiscal 2008, the Company reduced its square footage growth plans to improve free cash flow, provide stronger returns for the Company, and invest in its existing stores to continue improving the customer experience. As a result of this store rationalization plan, the Company determined that it would no longer pursue the opening of approximately 50 U.S. stores that had been in its new store pipeline. The Company expects to dispose of or sublet these pipeline locations over varying periods. The Company also closed 15 underperforming U.S. stores in the second quarter of fiscal 2008, and the Company expects to dispose of or sublet those locations over varying periods.

Source: Home Depot Annual Report 2009.

3. *Subjective factors*. Remember that vital information about a company is not contained in the annual report. The best way to evaluate Home Depot's strategy of being a price leader, for instance, is to visit its stores and those of competitors.

REAL WORLD EXCERPT

Home Depot

SALOMON SMITH BARNEY
RESEARCH REPORT

On July 15, we surveyed the Boca Raton, Florida, market. The Home Depot store is about two years old and was particularly impressive with respect to its in-stock position, customer service, and total store presentation. We were able to compare Home Depot's pricing on 20 sample items. Our price analysis revealed that Home Depot is the price leader in the market by an average of 11 percent below the average total price of our 20-item market basket. Given the Home Depot's low cost structure, we believe that it will remain the price leader in this important market.

As these examples illustrate, no single approach can be used to analyze all companies. Furthermore, an effective analyst will look beyond the information contained in an annual report.

| INSIDER INFORMATION | A QUESTION OF ACCOUNTABILITY |

Financial statements are an important source of information for investors. Announcement of an unexpected earnings increase or decrease can cause a substantial movement in the price of a company's shares.

A company's accountants are often aware of important financial information before it is made available to the public. This type of data is called *insider information*. Some people may be tempted to buy or sell shares based on insider information, but to do so is a serious criminal offence. Securities commissions have brought charges against a number of individuals who traded on insider information. Their conviction resulted in large fines and time served in jail.

In some cases, it may be difficult to determine whether something is insider information. For example, an individual may simply overhear a comment made in the company elevator by two executives. A well-respected Wall Street investment banker gave good advice when dealing with such situations: "If you are not sure if something is right or wrong, apply the newspaper headline test. Ask yourself how you would feel to have your family and friends read about what you had done in the newspaper." Interestingly, many people who spent time in jail and lost small fortunes in fines because of insider trading convictions say that the most difficult part of the process was telling their families.

To uphold the highest ethical standard, many public accounting firms have rules that prevent members of their professional staff from investing in companies that the firm audits. These rules are designed to ensure that the company's auditors cannot be tempted to engage in insider trading and to maintain independence from the audited firm.

INFORMATION IN AN EFFICIENT MARKET

Considerable research has been performed on the way in which stock markets react to new information. Much of this evidence supports the view that the markets react very quickly to new information in an unbiased manner (i.e., the market does not systematically overreact or under react to new information). A market that reacts to information in this manner is called an *efficient market*. In an efficient market, the price of a security fully reflects all publicly available information.

It is not surprising that the stock markets react quickly to new information. Many professional investors manage stock portfolios valued in the hundreds of millions of dollars. These investors have a large financial incentive to discover new information about a company and trade quickly based on that information.

The research on efficient markets has important implications for financial analysis. It probably is not beneficial to study old information (e.g., an annual report that was released six months earlier) in an effort to identify an undervalued stock. In an efficient market, the price of the stock reflects all of the information contained in the report shortly after it was released. Furthermore, a company cannot manipulate the price of its stock by manipulating its accounting policy. The market should be able to differentiate between a company with increasing earnings because of improved productivity and one that has increased its earnings by changing from prudent to liberal accounting policies.

EFFICIENT MARKETS are securities markets in which prices fully reflect all publicly available information.

ACCOUNTING STANDARDS
FOR PRIVATE ENTERPRISES

As we noted in previous chapters, the Accounting Standards for Canadian Private Enterprises differ from International Financial Accounting Standards with respect to measurement and reporting of specific elements of financial statements, even though both sets of standards are derived from the same conceptual framework for accounting. When analyzing financial statements, users should be aware of the measurement rules that underlie the values reported on these statements, particularly if comparisons are being made between private enterprises and publicly accountable enterprises that use different sets of financial reporting standards.

Appendix 13A: Expanding the ROE Profit Driver Analysis—The Scott Formula (online)

CHAPTER TAKE-AWAYS

1. **Explain how a company's business strategy affects financial analysis. p. 695**
   In simple terms, a business strategy establishes the objectives a business is trying to achieve. Performance is best evaluated by comparing the financial results to the objectives that the business was working to achieve. In other words, an understanding of a company's strategy provides the context for conducting financial statement analysis.

2. **Discuss how analysts use financial statements. p. 696**
   Analysts use financial statements to understand present conditions and past performance as well as to predict future performance. Financial statements provide important information to help users understand and evaluate corporate strategy. The data reported on statements can be used for either time-series analysis (evaluating a single company over time) or in comparison with similar companies at a single point in time. Most analysts compute component percentages and ratios when using statements.

3. **Compute and interpret component percentages. p. 698**
   To compute component percentages for the income statement, the base amount is net sales revenue. Each expense is expressed as a percentage of net sales revenue. On the statement of financial position, the base amount is total assets; the balance of each account is divided by total assets. Component percentages are evaluated by comparing them over time for a single company or by comparing them with percentages for similar companies.

4. **Compute and interpret profitability ratios. p. 700**
   Several tests of profitability focus on measuring the adequacy of profit by comparing it to other items reported on the financial statements. Exhibit 13.4 lists these ratios and shows how to compute them. Profitability ratios are evaluated by comparing them over time for a single company or by comparing them with ratios for similar companies.

5. **Compute and interpret liquidity ratios. p. 707**
   Tests of liquidity measure a company's ability to meet its current maturing debt. Exhibit 13.4 lists these ratios and shows how to compute them. Liquidity ratios are evaluated by comparing them over time for a single company or by comparing them with ratios for similar companies.

6. **Compute and interpret solvency ratios. p. 713**
   Solvency ratios measure a company's ability to meet its long-term obligations. Exhibit 13.4 lists these ratios and shows how to compute them. Solvency ratios are evaluated by comparing them over time for a single company or by comparing them with ratios for similar companies.

7. **Compute and interpret market test ratios. p. 715**
   Market test ratios relate the current price per share to the return that accrues to investors. Exhibit 13.4 lists these ratios and shows how to compute them. Market test ratios are evaluated by comparing them over time for a single company or by comparing them with ratios for similar companies.

FINDING **FINANCIAL INFORMATION**

STATEMENT OF FINANCIAL POSITION

Analysts use information reported on the statement of financial position to compute many ratios. Most analysts use an average of the beginning and ending amounts for statement of financial position accounts when the ratio calculation also includes an amount reported on the income statement.

INCOME STATEMENT

Earnings per share is the only ratio that is required to be reported on the financial statements. It is usually reported at the bottom of the income statement.

STATEMENT OF CASH FLOWS

Some ratios use amounts reported on this statement.

STATEMENT OF CHANGES IN EQUITY

Ratios are not reported on this statement.

NOTES

Under Summary of Significant Accounting Policies

This note has no information pertaining directly to ratios, but it is important to understand differences in accounting policies if you are comparing two companies.

Under a Separate Note

Most companies include a 5-year or a 10-year financial summary as a separate note. This summary includes data for significant financial statement items, some accounting ratios, and non-accounting information.

KEY **TERMS**

Component Percentage p. 698

Efficient Markets p. 719

Market Tests p. 715

Ratio (Percentage) Analysis p. 698

Tests of Liquidity p. 707

Tests of Profitability p. 700

Tests of Solvency p. 713

QUESTIONS

1. What are three fundamental uses of external financial statements by decision makers?
2. What are some of the primary items on financial statements about which creditors usually are concerned?
3. Why are the notes to the financial statements important to decision makers?
4. What is the primary purpose of comparative financial statements?
5. Why are statement users interested in financial summaries covering several years? What is the primary limitation of a 5-year or a 10-year financial summary?
6. What is ratio analysis? Why is it useful?
7. What are component percentages? Why are they useful?
8. Explain the two concepts of return on investment.
9. What is financial leverage? How is it measured as a percentage?
10. Is profit margin a useful measure of profitability? Explain.
11. Compare and contrast the current ratio and the quick ratio.
12. What does the debt-to-equity ratio reflect?
13. What are market tests?
14. Identify two factors that limit the effectiveness of ratio analysis.
15. Doritos Company has prepared draft financial results now being reviewed by the accountants. You notice that the financial leverage percentage is negative. You also note that the current ratio is 2.4 and the quick ratio is 3.7. You remember that these financial relationships are unusual. Does either imply that a mistake has been made? Explain.

EXERCISES

■ **LO3**

Alimentation
Couche-Tard Inc.

E13–1 **Preparing a Schedule by Using Component Percentages**

Alimentation Couche-Tard Inc. is a leading convenience store operator in Canada, with Couche-Tard stores in eastern Canada and Mac's stores in central and western Canada. It also operates Circle K shops in the United States. Complete the component percentage analysis on the company's income statement that follows. Discuss the insights provided by this analysis.

CONSOLIDATED STATEMENTS OF EARNINGS
For the years ended April 26, 2009, April 27, 2008 and April 29, 2007
(in millions of US dollars (Note 2), except per share amounts)

	2009	2008	2007
	$	$	$
Revenues	15,781.1	15,370.0	12,087.4
Cost of sales (excluding depreciation and amortization of property and equipment and other assets as shown separately below)	13,344.5	13,146.5	10,082.9
Gross profit	2,436.6	2,223.5	2,004.5
Operating, selling, administrative and general expenses (Note 6)	1,848.8	1,739.9	1,512.4
Depreciation and amortization of property and equipment and other assets (Note 6)	183.0	172.5	133.8
	2,031.8	1,911.4	1,646.2
Operating income	404.8	312.1	358.3
Financial expenses (Note 6)	36.2	54.6	48.0
Earnings before income taxes	368.6	257.5	310.3
Income taxes (Note 7)	114.7	68.2	113.9
Net earnings	253.9	189.3	196.4

■ **LO5**

E13–2 **Analyzing the Impact of Selected Transactions on the Current Ratio**

Current assets totalled $54,000, and the current ratio was 1.8. Assume that the following transactions were completed: (1) purchased merchandise for $6,000 on short-term credit and (2) purchased a delivery truck for $20,000—paid $4,000 cash and signed a two-year interest-bearing note for the balance.

Required:
Compute the current ratio after each transaction.

■ **LO5**

Procter & Gamble

E13–3 **Analyzing the Impact of Selected Transactions on Trade Receivables and Inventory Turnover**

Procter & Gamble is a multinational corporation that manufactures and markets many products that are probably in your home. Last year, sales for the company were $79,029 (all amounts in millions). The annual report did not disclose the amount of credit sales, so we will assume that 30 percent of sales were on credit. The average gross margin rate was 45 percent on sales. Account balances follow:

	Beginning	Ending
Trade receivables (net)	$6,761	$5,836
Inventory	8,416	6,880

Required:
Compute the turnover for the trade receivables and inventory, the average age of receivables, and the average days' supply of inventory.

E13–4 Analyzing the Impact of Specific Events on Selected Ratios

LO4, 5

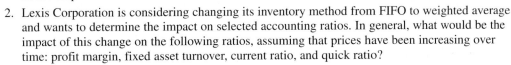

Consider the following two independent situations:

1. A manufacturer reported an inventory turnover ratio of 8.6 during 2010. During 2011, management introduced a new inventory control system that was expected to reduce average inventory levels by 25 percent without affecting sales volume. Given these circumstances, would you expect the inventory turnover ratio to increase or decrease during 2011? Explain.

2. Lexis Corporation is considering changing its inventory method from FIFO to weighted average and wants to determine the impact on selected accounting ratios. In general, what would be the impact of this change on the following ratios, assuming that prices have been increasing over time: profit margin, fixed asset turnover, current ratio, and quick ratio?

E13–5 Computing Financial Leverage

LO4

Nokia

Nokia Corporation is a global leader in providing integrated communications and electronic solutions for businesses. Its financial statements reported the following at year-end (in millions of euro):

Average total assets	€35,738
Average total debt (2% interest)	20,989
Profit (average tax rate 30%)	260

Required:

Compute the financial leverage percentage. Was it positive or negative?

E13–6 Analyzing the Impact of Selected Transactions on the Current Ratio

LO5

Current assets totalled $100,000, and the current ratio was 1.5. Assume that the following transactions were completed: (1) paid $6,000 for merchandise purchased on short-term credit, (2) purchased a delivery truck for $20,000 cash, (3) wrote off a bad trade receivable for $1,000, and (4) paid previously declared dividends in the amount of $20,000.

Required:

Compute the current ratio after each transaction.

E13–7 Inferring Financial Information

LO3

Dollarama

Dollarama is the leading dollar store operator in Canada with over 600 locations in all provinces. In a recent year, the company reported average inventories of $242.1 million and an inventory turnover of 3.35. Average total fixed assets were $134.0 million, and the fixed asset turnover ratio was 9.35. Determine the gross margin for Dollarama.

E13–8 Computing Selected Ratios

LO5

Sales for the year were $500,000, of which one-half was on credit. The average gross margin rate was 40 percent on sales. Account balances follow:

	Beginning	Ending
Trade receivables (net)	$50,000	$60,000
Inventory	50,000	30,000

Required:

Compute and comment on the turnover for the trade receivables and inventory, the average age of receivables, and the average days' supply of inventory.

E13–9 Analyzing the Impact of Selected Transactions on the Current Ratio

LO5

Current assets totalled $1,000,000, the current ratio was 2.0, and the company uses the periodic inventory method. Assume that the following transactions were completed: (1) sold $26,000

in merchandise on account, (2) declared but did not pay dividends of $40,000, (3) paid rent in advance in the amount of $24,000, (4) paid previously declared dividends in the amount of $40,000, (5) collected a trade receivable in the amount of $20,000, and (6) reclassified $90,000 of long-term debt as a short-term liability.

Required:
Compute the current ratio after each transaction.

LO5

E13–10

Cintas

Computing Liquidity Ratios

Cintas designs, manufactures, and implements corporate identity uniform programs that it rents or sells to customers throughout the United States and Canada. The company's stock is traded on the NASDAQ and has provided investors with significant returns on equity over the past few years. Selected information from the company's statement of financial position follows. The company reported revenue of $3,774,685 and cost of sales of $2,223,814 for fiscal year 2009.

Cintas	2009	2008
Statement of Financial Position **(amounts in thousands)**		
Cash and cash equivalents	$129,745	$66,244
Short-term investments	120,393	125,471
Trade receivables, less allowance of $19,532 ($13,139)	357,678	430,078
Inventories, net	202,351	238,669
Prepayments	17,035	12,068
Trade payables	69,965	94,755
Accrued compensation and related liabilities	48,414	50,605
Income taxes, current	—	12,887
Long-term debt due within one year	598	1,070

Required:
Compute the current ratio, quick ratio, inventory turnover, and receivables turnover (assuming that 60 percent of sales was on credit) for 2009, and comment on the liquidity position of the company.

LO5

E13–11

Determining the Impact of Selected Transactions on Measures of Solvency

Three commonly used measures of solvency are the debt-to-equity ratio, the times interest earned ratio, and the cash coverage ratio. For each of the following transactions, determine whether the measure will increase, decrease, or not change. Assume that all ratios are higher than 1.

a. Issued shares in exchange for equipment for $500,000.

b. Issued bonds at par for $1 million cash.

c. Previously declared dividends are paid in cash.

d. Accrued interest expense is recorded.

e. A customer pays money on his trade receivable.

LO3, 5, 6

E13–12

Using Financial Information to Identify Mystery Companies

The following selected financial data pertain to four unidentified companies:

a. Retail fur store

b. Advertising agency

c. Wholesale candy company

d. Car manufacturer

	Companies			
	1	2	3	4
Statement of Financial Position Data				
(component percentage)				
Cash	3.5	4.7	8.2	11.7
Trade receivables	16.9	28.9	16.8	51.9
Inventory	46.8	35.6	57.3	4.8
Property and equipment	18.3	21.7	7.6	18.7
Income Statement Data				
(component percentage)				
Gross profit	22.0	22.5	44.8	N/A*
Profit before taxes	2.1	0.7	1.2	3.2
Selected Ratios				
Current ratio	1.3	1.5	1.6	1.2
Inventory turnover	3.6	9.8	1.5	N/A
Debt-to-equity	2.6	2.6	3.2	3.2
*N/A = Not applicable				

Required:
Match each company with its financial information. Support your choices.

E13–13 Using Financial Information to Identify Mystery Companies   ■ LO3, 5, 6
The following selected financial data pertain to four unidentified companies:

a. Travel agency
b. Hotel
c. Meat packer
d. Drug company

	Companies			
	1	2	3	4
Statement of Financial Position Data				
(component percentage)				
Cash	7.3	21.6	6.1	11.3
Trade receivables	28.2	39.7	3.2	22.9
Inventory	21.6	0.6	1.8	27.5
Property and equipment	32.1	18.0	74.6	25.1
Income Statement Data				
(component percentage)				
Gross profit	15.3	N/A*	N/A	43.4
Profit before taxes	1.7	3.2	2.4	6.9
Selected Ratios				
Current ratio	1.5	1.2	0.6	1.9
Inventory turnover	27.4	N/A	N/A	3.3
Debt-to-equity	1.7	2.2	5.7	1.3
*N/A = Not applicable				

Required:
Match each company with its financial information. Support your choices.

E13–14 Using Financial Information to Identify Mystery Companies   ■ LO3, 5, 6
The following selected financial data pertain to four unidentified companies:

a. Cable TV company
b. Grocery store
c. Accounting firm
d. Retail jewellery store

	Companies			
	1	2	3	4
Statement of Financial Position Data				
(component percentage)				
Cash	5.1	8.8	6.3	10.4
Trade receivables	13.1	41.5	13.8	4.9
Inventory	4.6	3.6	65.1	35.8
Property and equipment	53.1	23.0	8.8	35.7
Income Statement Data				
(component percentage)				
Gross profit	N/A*	N/A	45.2	22.5
Profit before taxes	0.3	16.0	3.9	1.5
Selected Ratios				
Current ratio	0.7	2.2	1.9	1.4
Inventory turnover	N/A	N/A	1.4	15.5
Debt-to-equity	2.5	0.9	1.7	2.3
*N/A = Not applicable				

Required:
Match each company with its financial information. Support your choices.

LO3, 5, 6   **E13–15**   **Using Financial Information to Identify Mystery Companies**

The following selected financial data pertain to four unidentified companies:

a. Full-line department store

b. Wholesale fish company

c. Automobile dealer (new and used cars)

d. Restaurant

	Companies			
	1	2	3	4
Statement of Financial Position Data				
(component percentage)				
Cash	11.6	6.6	5.4	7.1
Trade receivables	4.6	18.9	8.8	35.6
Inventory	7.0	45.8	65.7	26.0
Property and equipment	56.0	20.3	10.1	21.9
Income Statement Data				
(component percentage)				
Gross profit	56.7	36.4	14.1	15.8
Profit before taxes	2.7	1.4	1.1	0.9
Selected Ratios				
Current ratio	0.7	2.1	1.2	1.3
Inventory turnover	30.0	3.5	5.6	16.7
Debt-to-equity	3.3	1.8	3.8	3.1

Required:
Match each company with its financial information. Support your choices.

LO1   **E13–16**   **Inferring Information from the ROE Model**

In this chapter, we discussed the ROE profit driver (or DuPont) model. Using that framework, find the missing amount in each case below:

Case 1: ROE is 10 percent, profit is $300,000; asset turnover is 5, and net sales are $1,000,000. What is the amount of average shareholders' equity?

Case 2: Profit is $440,000; net sales are $8,000,000; average shareholders' equity is $2,000,000; ROE is 22 percent and asset turnover is 8. What is the amount of average total assets?

Case 3: ROE is 15 percent; net profit margin is 10 percent; asset turnover is 5; and average total assets are $1,000,000. What is the amount of average shareholders' equity?

Case 4: Profit is $500,000; ROE is 15 percent; asset turnover is 5; net sales are $1,000,000; and financial leverage is 2. What is the amount of average total assets?

PROBLEMS

P13–1 **Analyzing Comparative Financial Statements by Using Percentages** (AP13–1)

The comparative financial statements prepared at December 31, 2011, for Goldfish Company showed the following summarized data:

◼ LO3

eXcel

	2011	2010
Income Statement		
Sales revenue	$ 195,000*	$165,000
Cost of sales	120,000	100,000
Gross margin	75,000	65,000
Operating expenses and interest expense	60,000	53,000
Profit before taxes	15,000	12,000
Income tax expense	4,000	3,000
Profit	$ 11,000	$ 9,000
Statement of Financial Position		
Cash	$ 4,000	$ 8,000
Trade receivables (net)	15,000	18,000
Inventory	40,000	35,000
Property, plant, and equipment (net)	45,000	38,000
	$ 104,000	$ 99,000
Current liabilities (no interest)	$ 16,000	$ 19,000
Non-current liabilities (10% interest)	45,000	39,000
Common shares (6,000 shares)	30,000	30,000
Retained earnings†	13,000	11,000
	$ 104,000	$ 99,000

*One-third was credit sales.

†During 2011, cash dividends amounting to $9,000 were declared and paid.

Required:

1. Complete the following columns for each item in the preceding comparative financial statements:

Increase (Decrease) 2011 over 2010	
Amount	**Percent**

2. Answer the following:
   a. By what amount did working capital change?
   b. What was the percentage change in the average income tax rate?
   c. What was the amount of cash inflow from revenues for 2011?
   d. What was the percentage change for the average markup realized on sales?

P13–2 **Analyzing Comparative Financial Statements by Using Percentages and Selected Ratios** (AP13–2)

Use the data given in P13–1 for Goldfish Company.

◼ LO3–7

Required:

1. Present component percentages for 2011 only.
2. Answer the following for 2011:
   a. What was the average percentage markup on sales?
   b. What was the average income tax rate?
   c. Compute the profit margin. Was it a good or poor indicator of performance? Explain.
   d. What percentage of total resources was invested in property, plant, and equipment?

e. Compute the debt-to-equity ratio. Does it look good or bad? Explain.

f. What was the return on assets?

g. What was the return on equity?

h. Compute the financial leverage percentage. Did borrowing from creditors benefit shareholders? Explain.

LO3–7

Sears Canada Inc.
and Canadian
Tire Corporation

P13–3   **Analyzing Ratios** (AP13–3)

Sears Canada Inc. and Canadian Tire Corporation are two giants of the Canadian retail industry. Both offer full lines of moderately priced merchandise. Annual sales for Sears total $5.2 billion. Canadian Tire is somewhat larger, with $10 billion in revenues. Compare the two companies as potential investments based on the following ratios:

Ratio	Sears Canada	Canadian Tire
P/E	13.3	14.0
Profit margin	4.5%	3.9%
Quick ratio	1.02	1.54
Current ratio	1.8	1.99
Debt-to-equity	1.05	1.38
Return on equity	14.9%	9.2%
Return on assets	7.6%	5.2%
Dividend yield	0%	0%
Earnings per share	$ 2.18	$ 4.10
Price per share at year-end	$29.0	$57.5
Dividends per share	$ 0	$ 0.84

LO3–7

eXcel

P13–4   **Analyzing a Financial Statement by Using Several Ratios**

Summer Corporation has just completed its comparative statements for the year ended December 31, 2012. At this point, certain analytical and interpretive procedures are to be undertaken. The completed statements (summarized) are as follows:

	2012	2011
Income Statement		
Sales revenue	$480,000[a]	$420,000[a]
Cost of sales	270,000	230,000
Gross margin	210,000	190,000
Operating expenses		
(including interest on bonds)	171,000	168,000
Pretax profit	39,000	22,000
Income tax	12,000	6,000
Profit	$ 27,000	$ 16,000
Statement of Financial Position		
Cash	$ 6,800	$ 3,900
Trade receivables (net)	42,000	28,000
Merchandise inventory	25,000	20,000
Prepayments	200	100
Property, plant, and equipment (net)	130,000	120,000
	$204,000	$172,000
Trade payables	$ 17,000	$ 18,000
Income taxes payable	1,000	2,000
Bonds payable (10% interest rate)	70,000[b]	50,000
Common shares (20,000 shares)	100,000[c]	100,000
Retained earnings	16,000[d]	2,000
	$204,000	$172,000

[a]Credit sales totalled 40 percent of total sales.

[b]$20,000 of bonds were issued on January 2, 2012.

[c]The market price of the stock at the end of 2012 was $18 per share.

[d]During 2012, the company declared and paid a cash dividend of $13,000.

Required:

1. Compute appropriate ratios for 2012 and explain the meaning of each.

2. Answer the following for 2012:

   a. Evaluate the financial leverage. Explain its meaning by using the computed amount(s).

   b. Evaluate the profit margin ratio and explain how a shareholder might use it.

   c. Explain to a shareholder why the current ratio and the quick ratio are different. Do you observe any liquidity problems? Explain.

   d. Assuming that credit terms are 1/10, n/30, do you perceive an unfavourable situation for the company related to credit sales? Explain.

   e. By how much should the balance of trade receivables decrease if the company wishes to reduce its average collection period to 30 days?

P13–5 **Comparing Alternative Investment Opportunities** (AP13–4)

The 2011 financial statements for Armstrong and Blair companies are summarized below:

LO3–7

eXcel

	Armstrong Company	Blair Company
Statement of Financial Position		
Cash	$ 35,000	$ 22,000
Trade receivables (net)	40,000	30,000
Inventory	100,000	40,000
Property, plant, and equipment (net)	140,000	400,000
Other non-current assets	85,000	308,000
Total assets	$400,000	$800,000
Current liabilities	$100,000	$ 50,000
Long-term debt (10%)	60,000	70,000
Share capital	150,000	500,000
Contributed surplus	30,000	110,000
Retained earnings	60,000	70,000
Total liabilities and shareholders' equity	$400,000	$800,000
Income Statement		
Sales revenue (1/3 on credit)	$450,000	$810,000
Cost of sales	(245,000)	(405,000)
Expenses (including interest and income tax)	(160,000)	(315,000)
Profit	$ 45,000	$ 90,000

Selected data from the 2010 statements:

Trade receivables (net)	$20,000	$ 40,000
Inventory	92,000	48,000
Long-term debt	60,000	70,000

Other data:

Share price at end of 2011	$ 18	$ 15
Income tax rate	30%	30%
Dividends declared and paid in 2011	$36,000	$150,000
Number of common shares during 2011	15,000	50,000

The companies are in the same line of business and are direct competitors in a large metropolitan area. Both have been in business approximately 10 years, and each has had steady growth. The management of each has a different viewpoint in many respects. Blair Company is more conservative, and as its president said, "We avoid what we consider to be undue risk." Neither company is publicly held. Armstrong Company has an annual audit by an independent auditor, but Blair Company does not.

Required:

1. Complete a schedule that reflects a ratio analysis of each company. Compute the ratios discussed in the chapter. Use ending balances if average balances are not available.

2. A client of yours has the opportunity to buy 10 percent of the shares in one or the other company at the share prices given and has decided to invest in one of the companies. Based on the data given, prepare a comparative written evaluation of the ratio analyses (and any other available information) and give your recommended choice with supporting explanation.

LO4, 5

P13–6   **Analyzing the Impact of Alternative Inventory Methods on Selected Ratios**
Company A uses the FIFO method to cost inventory, and Company B uses the weighted-average method. The two companies are exactly alike except for the difference in inventory costing methods. Costs of inventory items for both companies have been rising steadily in recent years, and each company has increased its inventory each year. Each company has paid its tax liability in full for the current year (and all previous years), and each company uses the same accounting methods for both financial reporting and income tax reporting, except for inventory valuation.

Required:

Identify which company will report the higher amount for each of the following ratios. If it is not possible, explain why.

1. Current ratio

2. Quick ratio

3. Debt-to-equity ratio

4. Return on equity

5. Earnings per share

LO3–7

The Geox Group

P13–7   **Analyzing Financial Statements by Using Appropriate Ratios** (AP13–5)
The Geox Group creates, produces, promotes, and distributes Geox-brand footwear and apparel, worldwide, through a network of traditional company-owned retail stores and franchised stores. The main feature of its products is the use of innovative and technological solutions that can guarantee the ability to breathe and to remain waterproof at the same time. Its product lines include casual and dress shoes for men, women, and children as well as jackets and coats. The following information was reported in a recent annual report.

GEOX CONSOLIDATED INCOME STATEMENT			
(Thousands of Euro)	Notes	2009	2008 (*)
Net sales	3	865,010	892,513
Cost of sales		(426,957)	(424,461)
Gross profit		438,053	468,052
Selling and distribution costs		(42,409)	(43,248)
General and administrative expenses	4	(214,731)	(185,442)
Advertising and promotion		(46,216)	(66,061)
Special items	7	(5,306)	—
Net asset impairment	5	(12,363)	(1,955)
EBIT	3	117,028	171,346
Net interest	8	(4,154)	(4,297)
PBT		112,874	167,049
Income tax	9	(46,168)	(48,875)
Net income		66,706	118,174
Earnings per share [Euro]	10	0.26	0.46
Diluted earnings per share [Euro]	10	0.26	0.45

(*) Restated in compliance with IAS 38.

Consolidated Statement of Financial Position

(Thousands of Euro)	Notes	Dec. 31, 2009	Dec. 31, 2008*	Jan. 01, 2008*
ASSETS				
Intangible assets	11	74,651	78,231	47,322
Property, plant and equipment	12	71,516	78,020	43,191
Deferred tax assets	13	26,076	26,503	14,862
Non-current financial assets	18–30	1,047	1,229	1,975
Other non-current assets	14	16,947	11,023	7,426
Total non-current assets		**190,237**	**195,006**	**114,776**
Inventories	15	152,387	226,405	183,841
Accounts receivable	16	128,803	124,594	107,997
Other non-financial current assets[a]	17	24,042	23,321	19,492
Current financial assets	18–30	4,402	17,414	637
Cash and cash equivalents	19	107,470	68,672	119,618
Current assets		**417,104**	**460,406**	**431,585**
Total assets		**607,341**	**655,412**	**546,361**
LIABILITIES AND EQUITY				
Share capital	20	25,921	25,920	25,884
Reserves	20	336,124	281,693	207,679
Net income	20	66,706	118,174	121,171
Equity		**428,751**	**425,787**	**354,734**
Employee severance indemnities	21	2,509	3,299	2,834
Provisions for liabilities and charges	22	7,256	3,915	2,457
Long-term loans	23	749	1,145	1,185
Other long-term payables	24	2,316	5,122	1,887
Total non-current liabilities		**12,830**	**13,481**	**8,363**
Accounts payable	25	121,725	149,206	127,559
Other non-financial current liabilities	26	26,023	21,718	16,240
Taxes payable[b]	27	8,428	17,246	25,214
Current financial liabilities	18–30	3,269	1,709	9,278
Bank borrowings and current portion of long-term loans	28	6,315	26,265	4,973
Current liabilities		**165,760**	**216,144**	**183,264**
Total liabilities and equity		**607,341**	**655,412**	**546,361**

*Restated in compliance with IAS 38.
[a]Includes taxes receivable to the parent company of Euro 7,431 thousand in 2009.
[b]Includes taxes payable to the parent company of Euro 4,129 thousand in 2008.

CONSOLIDATED STATEMENT OF CASH FLOWS

(Thousands of Euro)	Notes	2009	2008 (*)
Cash Flow from Operating Activities:			
Net income	20	**66,706**	**118,174**
Adjustments to reconcile net income to net cash provided (used) by operating activities:			
Depreciation and amortization and impairment	5	49,348	29,015
Increase in (use of) deferred taxes and other provisions		13,238	(6,474)
Provision for employee severance indemnities, net		(783)	425
Other non-cash items		10,750	(11,385)
		72,553	11,581
Change in assets/liabilities:			
Accounts receivable		(8,549)	(23,787)
Other assets		(6,382)	(6,720)
Inventories		72,625	(37,112)
Accounts payable		(27,102)	21,164
Other liabilities		961	6,014
Taxes payables		(11,132)	(5,757)
		20,421	(46,198)
Operating cash flow		**159,680**	**83,557**
Cash Flow Used in Investing Activities:			
Capital expenditure on intangible assets	11	(12,030)	(41,624)
Capital expenditure on property, plant and equipment	12	(29,965)	(54,721)
		(41,995)	(96,345)
Disposals		2,957	2,044
(Increase) decrease in financial assets		447	375
Cash flow used in investing activities		**(38,591)**	**(93,926)**
Cash Flow from (used in) Financing Activities:			
Increase (decrease) in short-term bank borrowings, net			
Loans:		(332)	2,905
– Proceeds		21,865	39,168
– Repayments		(41,630)	(22,070)
Dividends	32	(62,210)	(62,199)
Increase in share capital		23	1,648
Cash flow from financing activities		**(82,284)**	**(40,548)**
Increase in cash and cash equivalents		**38,805**	**(50,917)**
Cash and cash equivalents, beginning of the period	19	68,672	119,618
Effect of translation differences on cash and cash equivalents		(7)	(29)
Cash and cash equivalents, end of the period	19	**107,470**	**68,672**
Supplementary information to the cash flow statement:			
Interest paid during the period		2,791	1,652
Interest received during the period		1,436	2,466
Taxes paid during the period		61,748	69,362

(*) Restated in compliance with IAS 38.
Source: Geox Annual Report 2009.

Required:

1. For Geox's past two years, compute the ratios discussed in this chapter. If there is not sufficient information, describe what is missing and explain what you would do.

2. Assume that you work in the loan department of City Bank, and you are evaluating an application from Geox for a two-year loan of €200 million to purchase the shares of another competing company. What specific ratios would you consider in your evaluation, and would you lend Geox the requested amount?

P13–8 **Analyzing an Investment by Comparing Selected Ratios** (AP13–6)

You have the opportunity to invest $10,000 in one of two companies from a single industry. The only information you have follows. The word *high* refers to the top third of the industry, *average* is the middle third, and *low* is the bottom third. Which company would you select? Write a brief report justifying your recommendation.

Ratio	Company A	Company B
Current	High	Average
Quick	Low	Average
Debt-to-equity	High	Average
Inventory turnover	Low	Average
Price/earnings	Low	Average
Dividend yield	High	Average

P13–9 **Analyzing an Investment by Comparing Selected Ratios** (AP13–7)

You have the opportunity to invest $10,000 in one of two companies from a single industry. The only information you have is shown below. The word *high* refers to the top third of the industry, *average* is the middle third, and *low* is the bottom third. Which company would you select? Write a brief report justifying your recommendation.

Ratio	Company A	Company B
Current	Low	Average
Quick	Average	Average
Debt-to-equity	Low	Average
Inventory turnover	High	Average
Price/earnings	High	Average
Dividend yield	Low	Average

P13–10 **Analyzing Financial Statements by Using Appropriate Ratios**

Morksen Corp. has enjoyed modest success in penetrating the personal electronic devices market since it began operations a few years ago. A new line of devices introduced recently has been well received by customers. However, the company president, who is knowledgeable about electronics but not in accounting, is concerned about the future of the company.

Although the company has a line of credit with the local bank, it currently needs cash to continue operations. The bank wants more information before it extends the company's credit line. The president has asked you, as the company's chief accountant, to evaluate the company's performance by using appropriate financial statement analysis, and to recommend possible courses of action for the company. In particular, the president wants to know how the company can obtain additional cash. Summary financial statements for the past three years are available below.

Required:

1. Evaluate the company's performance and its financial condition for the past two years. Select six appropriate ratios to analyze the company's profitability, liquidity, and solvency for 2010 and 2011, and explain to the company's president the meaning of each ratio you calculate.

2. Based on your analysis of the ratios that you computed in (1), what recommendation would you make to the president for obtaining additional cash?

MORKSEN CORP.
Consolidated Income Statements
For the Years Ended December 31

(in thousands of dollars)	2011	2010	2009
Sales	$32,000	$28,000	$23,400
Cost of sales	25,000	21,500	18,000
Gross profit	7,000	6,500	5,400
Operating expenses before interest and income taxes	4,000	3,700	3,310
Interest expense	890	610	0
Profit before income taxes	2,110	2,190	2,090
Income tax expense	950	1,020	970
Profit	$ 1,160	$ 1,170	$ 1,120

MORKSEN CORP. **Consolidated Statements of Financial Position** **At December 31**			
(in thousands of dollars)	**2011**	**2010**	**2009**
Assets			
Current assets			
Cash	$ 190	$ 240	$ 500
Short-term investments	370	370	370
Trade receivables	5,440	4,200	2,570
Merchandise inventory	8,330	5,030	3,610
Total current assets	14,330	9,840	7,050
Property, plant, and equipment			
Land	2,000	2,000	1,000
Buildings and equipment	13,000	13,000	9,000
	15,000	15,000	10,000
Less: accumulated depreciation	4,470	3,720	2,880
Net property, plant, and equipment	10,530	11,280	7,120
Total assets	$24,860	$21,120	$14,170
Liabilities and Shareholders' Equity			
Current liabilities			
Bank loan	$ 8,250	$ 5,700	$ 0
Trade payables	3,000	2,150	1,440
Other liabilities	820	800	750
Income tax payable	480	520	500
Total current liabilities	12,550	9,170	2,690
Shareholders' equity			
Common shares	10,000	10,000	10,000
Retained earnings	2,070	1,760	1,320
Other comprehensive income	240	190	160
Total shareholders' equity	12,310	11,950	11,480
Total liabilities and shareholders' equity	$24,860	$21,120	$14,170

ALTERNATE PROBLEMS

LO3–7

AP13–1   **Analyzing Financial Statements by Using Ratios and Percentage Changes** (P13–1)
Taber Company has just prepared the following comparative annual financial statements
for 2012:

TABER COMPANY **Comparative Income Statement** **For the Years Ended December 31**		
	2012	**2011**
Sales revenue (one-half on credit)	$110,000	$100,000
Cost of sales	52,000	49,000
Gross margin	58,000	51,000
Expenses (including $4,000 interest expense each year)	40,000	37,000
Pretax profit	18,000	14,000
Income tax on operations (30%)	5,400	4,200
Profit	$ 12,600	$ 9,800

TABER COMPANY
Comparative Statement of Financial Position
At December 31, 2012 and 2011

	2012	2011
Assets		
Cash	$ 49,500	$ 18,000
Trade receivables (net; terms 1/10, n/30)	37,000	32,000
Inventory	25,000	38,000
Property, plant, and equipment (net)	95,000	105,000
Total assets	$206,500	$193,000
Liabilities		
Trade payables	$ 42,000	$ 35,000
Income taxes payable	1,000	500
Note payable, long-term	40,000	40,000
Shareholders' equity		
Share capital (9,000 shares)	90,000	90,000
Retained earnings	34,900	25,400
Other comprehensive income (loss)	(1,400)	2,100
Total liabilities and shareholders' equity	$206,500	$193,000

Required (round percentage and ratios to two decimal places):

1. For 2012, compute the tests of (a) profitability, (b) liquidity, (c) solvency, and (d) market. Assume that the quoted price of the stock was $23 per share for 2012. Dividends declared and paid during 2012 were $5,200.

2. Answer the following for 2012:

    a. Compute the percentage changes in sales, profit, cash, inventory, and debt.

    b. What is the pretax interest rate on the note payable?

3. Identify at least two problems facing the company that are suggested by your responses to (1) and (2).

AP13–2 Using Ratios to Analyze Several Years of Financial Data (P13–2)

 LO3, 4, 5

The following information was contained in the annual financial statements of Pine Company, which started business January 1, 2010 (assume account balances only in cash and share capital on this date; all amounts are in thousands of dollars).

	2010	2011	2012	2013
Trade receivables (net; terms n/30)	$11	$12	$18	$ 24
Merchandise inventory	12	14	20	30
Net sales (three-fourths on credit)	44	66	80	100
Cost of sales	28	40	55	62
Profit (loss)	(8)	5	12	11

Required (show computations and round to two decimal places):

1. Complete the following tabulation:

Items	2010	2011	2012	2013
a. Profit margin—percentage				
b. Gross profit percentage				
c. Expenses as percentage of sales, excluding cost of sales				
d. Inventory turnover				
e. Days' supply in inventory				
f. Receivables turnover				
g. Average collection period				

2. Evaluate the results of the related ratios *a*, *b*, and *c* to identify the favourable or unfavourable factors. Give your recommendations to improve the company's operations.

3. Evaluate the results of the last four ratios (*d*, *e*, *f*, and *g*) and identify any favourable or unfavourable factors. Give your recommendations to improve the company's operations.

LO3, 4 **AP13–3**

Coca-Cola and PepsiCo

Analyzing Ratios (P13–3)

Coke and Pepsi are well-known international brands. Coca-Cola sells more than $30 billion worth of beverages each year, while annual sales of Pepsi products exceed $40 billion. Compare the two companies as potential investments based on the following ratios:

Ratio	Coca-Cola	PepsiCo
Price/earnings ratio	19.3	17.8
Gross profit percentage	64.2	53.5
Profit margin	22.0%	13.7%
Quick ratio	0.7	0.5
Current ratio	1.3	1.4
Debt-to-equity	0.9	1.3
Return on equity	29.5%	39.8%
Return on assets	15.9%	16.4%
Dividend yield	2.9%	2.9%

LO3, 4 **AP13–4**

Comparing Loan Requests from Two Companies by Using Several Ratios (P13–5)

The 2011 financial statements for Rand and Tand companies are summarized below:

	Rand Company	Tand Company
Statement of Financial Position		
Cash	$ 25,000	$ 45,000
Trade receivables (net)	55,000	5,000
Inventory	110,000	25,000
Property, plant, and equipment (net)	550,000	160,000
Other assets	140,000	57,000
Total assets	$880,000	$292,000
Current liabilities	$120,000	$ 15,000
Long-term debt (12%)	190,000	55,000
Share capital	480,000	210,000
Contributed surplus	50,000	4,000
Retained earnings	38,000	7,000
Other comprehensive income	2,000	1,000
Total liabilities and shareholders' equity	$880,000	$292,000
Income Statement		
Sales revenue (on credit)	(½) $800,000	(¼) $280,000
Cost of sales	(480,000)	(150,000)
Expenses (including interest and income tax)	(240,000)	(95,000)
Profit	$ 80,000	$ 35,000
Selected Data from the 2010 Statements		
Trade receivables, net	$ 47,000	$ 11,000
Long-term debt (12%)	190,000	55,000
Inventory	95,000	38,000
Other Data		
Share price at end of 2011	$ 14.00	$ 11.00
Income tax rate	30%	30%
Dividends declared and paid in 2011	$ 20,000	$ 9,000
Number of common shares during 2011	24,000	10,500

These two companies are in the same line of business and in the same province but in different cities. Each company has been in operation for about 10 years. Rand Company is audited by a national accounting firm; Tand Company is audited by a local accounting firm. Both companies received an unqualified opinion (i.e., the independent auditors found nothing wrong) on the financial statements. Rand Company wants to borrow $75,000 cash, and Tand Company needs $30,000. The loans will be for a two-year period and are needed for "working capital purposes."

Required:

1. Complete a schedule that reflects a ratio analysis of each company. Compute the ratios discussed in the chapter.

2. Assume that you work in the loan department of a local bank. You have been asked to analyze the situation and recommend which loan is preferable. Based on the data given, your analysis prepared in (1), and any other information, give your choice and provide a supporting explanation.

AP13–5 **Analyzing Financial Statements by Using Appropriate Ratios** (P13–7)
Nokia Corporation is the world's top producer of cell phones. The following information was reported in recent annual reports.

■ **LO3**

Nokia

eXcel

NOKIA CORPORATION AND SUBSIDIARIES Consolidated income statements, IFRS				
Financial year ended December 31	**Notes**	**2009 EURm**	**2008 EURm**	**2007 EURm**
Net sales		40,984	50,710	51,058
Cost of sales		−27,720	−33,337	−33,781
Gross profit		13,264	17,373	17,277
Research and development expenses		−5,909	−5,968	−5,636
Selling and marketing expenses		−3,933	−4,380	−4,379
Administrative and general expenses		−1,145	−1,284	−1,165
Impairment of goodwill	7	−908	—	—
Other income	6	338	420	2,312
Other expenses	6, 7	−510	−1,195	−424
Operating profit	2–9, 23	1,197	4,966	7,985
Share of results of associated companies	14, 30	30	6	44
Financial income and expenses	10	−265	−2	239
Profit before tax		962	4,970	8,268
Tax	11	−702	−1,081	−1,522
Profit		260	3,889	6,746
Profit attributable to equity holders of the parent		891	3,988	7,205
Loss attributable to minority interests		−631	−99	−459
		260	3,889	6,746
Earnings per share (for profit attributable to the equity holders of the parent)	27			
Basic		0.24	1.07	1.85
Diluted		0.24	1.05	1.83
Average number of shares (1,000's shares)	27			
Basic		3,705,116	3,743 622	3,885,408
Diluted		3,721,072	3,780,363	3,932,008

NOKIA CORPORATION AND SUBSIDIARIES
Consolidated statements of financial position, IFRS

December 31	2009 EURm	2008 EURm	2007 EURm
Assets			
Non-current assets			
Capitalized development costs	143	244	378
Goodwill	5,171	6,257	1,384
Other intangible assets	2,762	3,913	2,358
Property, plant and equipment	1,867	2,090	1,912
Investments in associated companies	69	96	325
Available-for-sale investments	554	512	341
Deferred tax assets	1,507	1,963	1,553
Long-term loans receivable	46	27	10
Other non-current assets	6	10	44
	12,125	15,112	8,305
Current assets			
Inventories	1,865	2,533	2,876
Accounts receivable, net of allowances for doubtful accounts (2009: EUR 391 million, 2008: EUR 415 million)	7,981	9,444	11,200
Prepaid expenses and accrued income	4,551	4,538	3,070
Current portion of long-term loans receivable	14	101	156
Other financial assets	329	1,034	239
Investments at fair value through profit and loss, liquid assets	580	—	—
Available-for-sale investments, liquid assets	2,367	1,272	4,903
Available-for-sale investments, cash equivalents	4,784	3,842	4,725
Bank and cash	1,142	1,706	2,125
	23,613	24,470	29,294
Total assets	35,738	39,582	37,599
Shareholders' Equity and Liabilities			
Capital and reserves attributable to equity holders of the parent			
Share capital	246	246	246
Share issue premium	279	442	644
Treasury shares, at cost	-681	-1,881	-3,146
Translation differences	-127	341	-163
Fair value and other reserves	69	62	23
Reserve for invested non-restricted equity	3,170	3,306	3,299
Retained earnings	10,132	11,692	13,870
	13,088	14,208	14,773
Minority interests	1,661	2,302	2,565
Total equity	14,749	16,510	17,338
Non-current liabilities			
Long-term interest-bearing liabilities	4,432	861	203
Deferred tax liabilities	1,303	1,787	963
Other long-term liabilities	66	69	119
	5,801	2,717	1,285
Current liabilities			
Current portion of long-term loans	44	13	173
Short-term borrowings	727	3,578	714
Other financial liabilities	245	924	184
Accounts payable	4,950	5,225	7,074
Accrued expenses	6,504	7,023	7,114
Provisions	2,718	3,592	3,717
	15,188	20,355	18,976
Total shareholders' equity and liabilities	35,738	39,582	37,599

NOKIA CORPORATION AND SUBSIDIARIES
Consolidated statements of cash flows, IFRS

Financial year ended December 31	Notes	2009 EURm	2008 EURm	2007 EURm
Cash flow from operating activities				
Profit attributable to equity holders of the parent		891	3,988	7,205
Adjustments, total	31	3,390	3,024	1,269
Change in net working capital	31	140	−2,546	605
Cash generated from operations		4,421	4,466	9,079
Interest received		125	416	362
Interest paid		−256	−155	−59
Other financial income and expenses, net received		−128	250	−43
Income taxes paid, net received		−915	−1,780	−1,457
Net cash from operating activities		3,247	3,197	7,882
Net cash used in investing activities (details omitted)		−2,148	−2,905	−710
Net cash used in financing activities (details omitted)		−696	−1,545	−3,832
Foreign exchange adjustment		−25	−49	−15
Net increase (+)/decrease (−) in cash and cash equivalents		378	−1,302	3,325
Cash and cash equivalents at beginning of period		5,548	6,850	3,525
Cash and cash equivalents at end of period		5,926	5,548	6,850
Cash and cash equivalents comprise of:				
Back and cash		1,142	1,706	2,125
Current available-for-sale investments, cash equivalents	15, 33	4,784	3,842	4,725
		5,926	5,548	6,850

Source: Nokia Corporation Annual Report 2009.

Required:

1. Compute the ratios discussed in this chapter for the last two years. If there is not sufficient information, describe what is missing and explain what you would do.

2. Assume the role of an investment adviser. A client of yours has the opportunity to invest $1 million in shares of international companies. Prepare a written evaluation of relevant ratios and indicate whether you would recommend to your client that the $1 million be invested in the shares of Nokia Corporation.

AP13–6 Analyzing an Investment by Comparing Selected Ratios (P13–8)

 LO4, 5

You have the opportunity to invest $10,000 in one of two companies from a single industry. The only information you have is shown below. The word *high* refers to the top third of the industry, *average* is the middle third, *low* is the bottom third. Which company would you select? Write a brief report justifying your recommendation.

Ratio	Company A	Company B
Earnings per share	High	Low
Return on assets	Low	High
Debt-to-equity	High	Average
Current	Low	Average
Price/earnings	Low	High
Dividend yield	High	Average

AP13–7 Analyzing an Investment by Comparing Selected Ratios (P13–9)

 LO4, 5, 6, 7

You have the opportunity to invest $10,000 in one of two companies from a single industry. The only information you have is shown on the following page. The word *high* refers to the top third of the industry, *average* is the middle third, *low* is the bottom third. Which company would you select? Write a brief report justifying your recommendation.

Ratio	Company A	Company B
Return on assets	High	Average
Profit margin	High	Low
Financial leverage	High	Low
Current	Low	High
Price/earnings	High	Average
Debt-to-equity	High	Low

CASES AND PROJECTS

FINDING AND INTERPRETING FINANCIAL INFORMATION

LO4, 5, 6, 7 CP13–1

The Nestlé Group

Analyzing Financial Statements

Refer to the financial statements of the Nestlé Group given in Appendix A of this book. From the list of ratios that were discussed in this chapter, select and compute the ratios that help you evaluate the company's operations for fiscal year 2008. Assume a market price of CHF 41.6 per share.

LO4, 5, 6, 7 CP13–2

Cadbury plc

Analyzing Financial Statements

Go to Connect online for the financial statements of Cadbury plc. From the list of ratios that were discussed in this chapter, select and compute the ratios that help you evaluate the company's operations for fiscal year 2008. Assume a market price of £24.4 per share.

FINANCIAL REPORTING AND ANALYSIS CASES

LO1

CP13–3 Interpreting Financial Results Based on Corporate Strategy

In this chapter, we discussed the importance of analyzing financial results based on an understanding of the company's business strategy. Using the ROE model, we illustrated how different strategies could earn high returns for investors. Assume that two companies in the same industry adopt fundamentally different strategies. One manufactures high-quality consumer electronics. Its products employ state-of-the-art technology, and the company offers a high level of customer service both before and after the sale. The other company emphasizes low cost with good performance. Its products utilize well-established technology but are never innovative. Customers buy these products at large, self-service warehouses and are expected to install the products by using information contained in printed brochures. Which of the ratios discussed in this chapter would you expect to differ for these companies as a result of their different business strategies?

CRITICAL THINKING CASES

LO4, 5, 6, 7 CP13–4

Analyzing the Impact of Alternative Depreciation Methods on Ratio Analysis

Speedy Company uses the double-declining-balance method to amortize its property, plant, and equipment, and Turtle Company uses the straight-line method. Both companies use declining-balance depreciation for income tax purposes. The two companies are exactly alike except for the difference in depreciation methods.

Required:

1. Identify the financial ratios discussed in this chapter that are likely to be affected by the difference in depreciation methods.
2. Which company will report the higher amount for each ratio that you have identified? If you cannot be certain, explain why.

LO4, 5 CP13–5

Analyzing the Impact of Alternative Accounting Methods on Ratios

The ratios computed for Home Depot in this chapter are compared with those of RONA Inc. and Canadian Tire Corporation. The comparison of ratios across these three companies assumes that they use the same accounting methods in reporting the various elements of their financial statements.

Required:

1. Access the annual reports of the three companies through their respective websites and identify the method(s) each company uses

    a. to depreciate its long-lived assets, and

    b. to value its inventory at year-end.

2. Are the methods used by these companies similar or different? Explain.

3. If two of these companies use different accounting methods, what impact would the different methods have on the following ratios:

    a. Profit margin

    b. Return on equity

    c. Current ratio

    d. Debt-to-equity

CP13–6 **Evaluating an Ethical Dilemma**

LO4

Bianca Company requested a sizeable loan from Provincial Bank to acquire a large tract of land for future expansion. Bianca reported current assets of $1,900,000 ($430,000 in cash) and current liabilities of $1,075,000. Provincial denied the loan request for a number of reasons, including the fact that the current ratio was below 2. When Bianca was informed of the loan denial, the comptroller of the company immediately paid $420,000 that was owed to several trade creditors. The comptroller then asked Provincial to reconsider the loan application. Based on these abbreviated facts, would you recommend that Provincial approve the loan request? Why? Are the comptroller's actions ethical?

FINANCIAL REPORTING AND ANALYSIS TEAM PROJECT

CP13–7 **Team Project: Examining an Annual Report**

LO3–7

As a team, select an industry to analyze. A list of companies classified by industry can be obtained by accessing **www.fpinfomart.ca** and then choosing "Companies by Industry." You can also find a list of industries and companies within each industry via **http://ca.finance.yahoo.com/ investing** (click on "Annual Reports" under "Tools"). Using a Web browser, each team member should acquire the annual report for one publicly traded company in an industry, with each member selecting a different company. (Library files, the *SEDAR* service at **www.sedar.com**, or the company itself are good resources.)

Required:

On an individual basis, each team member should write a short report providing the following information about the selected company. Discuss any patterns across the companies that you as a team observe. Then, as a team, write a short report comparing and contrasting your companies.

Compute and interpret each of the ratios discussed in this chapter. The most frequently used sections will be the financial statements. Also, you may want to review the notes, the summary of financial information (usually for the past 5 to 10 years), and management's discussion and analysis.

Appendix A

FINANCIAL STATEMENTS OF THE NESTLÉ GROUP

This Appendix includes the financial statements of the Nestlé Group for 2008 and selected notes to these financial statements. The following notes were omitted because of space limitations: 2, 3, 7, 11, 16, 17, 20, and 26 through 32. The complete set of Nestlé's financial statements and related notes is available on the textbook's website.

2008 Financial Statements

Good Food, Good Life

Consolidated Financial
Statements
of the Nestlé Group
Financial Statements
of Nestlé S.A.

Consolidated income statement
for the year ended 31 December 2008

In millions of CHF	Notes	2008	2007
Sales	3	**109 908**	**107 552**
Cost of goods sold		(47 339)	(45 037)
Distribution expenses		(9 084)	(9 104)
Marketing and administration expenses		(35 832)	(36 512)
Research and development costs		(1 977)	(1 875)
EBIT Earnings Before Interest, Taxes, restructuring and impairments	3	**15 676**	**15 024**
Net other income/(expenses)	4		
Other income		9 426	695
Other expenses		(2 124)	(1 285)
		7 302	(590)
Profit before interest and taxes		**22 978**	**14 434**
Net financing cost	5		
Financial income		102	576
Financial expense		(1 247)	(1 492)
		(1 145)	(916)
Profit before taxes and associates		**21 833**	**13 518**
Taxes	7	(3 787)	(3 416)
Share of results of associates	8	1 005	1 280
Profit for the period		**19 051**	**11 382**
of which attributable to minority interests		1 012	733
of which attributable to shareholders of the parent (Net profit)		18 039	10 649
As percentages of sales			
EBIT Earnings Before Interest, Taxes, restructuring and impairments		14.3%	14.0%
Profit for the period attributable to shareholders of the parent (Net profit)		16.4%	9.9%
Earnings per share (in CHF)			
Basic earnings per share (a)	9	4.87	2.78
Fully diluted earnings per share (a)	9	4.84	2.76

(a) 2007 comparatives have been restated following 1-for-10 share split effective on 30 June 2008.

Consolidated balance sheet as at 31 December 2008
before appropriations

In millions of CHF	Notes	2008	2007
Assets			
Current assets			
Cash and cash equivalents	19	5 835	6 594
Short-term investments	19	1 296	2 902
Trade and other receivables	10/19	13 442	14 890
Current income tax receivables		889	531
Assets held for sale		8	22
Inventories	12	9 342	9 272
Derivative assets	11/19	1 609	754
Prepayments and accrued income		627	805
Total current assets		**33 048**	**35 770**
Non-current assets			
Property, plant and equipment	13	21 097	22 065
Investments in associates	8	7 796	8 936
Deferred tax assets	7	2 842	2 224
Financial assets	19	3 868	4 213
Employee benefits assets [a]	16	60	1 513
Goodwill	14	30 637	33 423
Intangible assets	15	6 867	7 217
Total non-current assets		**73 167**	**79 591**
Total assets		**106 215**	**115 361**

[a] 2007 comparatives have been restated following first application of IFRIC 14 (refer to Note 32).

In millions of CHF	Notes	2008	2007
Liabilities and equity			
Current liabilities			
Trade and other payables	19	12 608	14 179
Liabilities directly associated with assets held for sale		–	7
Financial liabilities	19	15 383	24 541
Current income tax payables		824	856
Derivative liabilities	11/19	1 477	477
Accruals and deferred income		2 931	3 266
Total current liabilities		**33 223**	**43 326**
Non-current liabilities			
Financial liabilities	19	6 344	6 129
Employee benefits liabilities	16	5 464	5 165
Deferred tax liabilities (a)	7	1 341	1 558
Other payables		1 264	1 091
Provisions	18	3 663	3 316
Total non-current liabilities		**18 076**	**17 259**
Total liabilities		**51 299**	**60 585**
Equity	21		
Share capital		383	393
Treasury shares		(9 652)	(8 013)
Translation reserve		(11 103)	(6 302)
Retained earnings and other reserves		71 146	66 549
Total equity attributable to shareholders of the parent (a)		**50 774**	**52 627**
Minority interests		4 142	2 149
Total equity		**54 916**	**54 776**
Total liabilities and equity		**106 215**	**115 361**

(a) 2007 comparatives have been restated following first application of IFRIC 14 (refer to Note 32).

Consolidated cash flow statement
for the year ended 31 December 2008

In millions of CHF	Notes	2008	2007
Operating activities [a]			
Profit for the period		19 051	11 382
Non-cash items of income and expense	22	(6 157)	2 097
Decrease/(increase) in working capital	22	(1 787)	82
Variation of other operating assets and liabilities	22	(344)	(122)
Operating cash flow		**10 763**	**13 439**
Investing activities			
Capital expenditure	13	(4 869)	(4 971)
Expenditure on intangible assets	15	(585)	(619)
Sale of property, plant and equipment	13	122	323
Acquisition of businesses	23	(937)	(11 232)
Disposal of businesses	24	10 999	456
Cash flows with associates		266	264
Other investing cash flows		(297)	26
Cash flow from investing activities		**4 699**	**(15 753)**
Financing activities			
Dividend paid to shareholders of the parent	21	(4 573)	(4 004)
Purchase of treasury shares	22	(8 696)	(5 455)
Sale of treasury shares and options exercised		639	980
Cash flows with minority interests		(367)	(205)
Bonds issued	19	2 803	2 023
Bonds repaid	19	(2 244)	(2 780)
Increase in other non-current financial liabilities		374	348
Decrease in other non-current financial liabilities		(168)	(99)
Increase/(decrease) in current financial liabilities		(6 100)	9 851
Decrease/(increase) in short-term investments		1 448	3 238
Cash flow from financing activities		**(16 884)**	**3 897**
Currency retranslations		663	(267)
Increase/(decrease) in cash and cash equivalents		**(759)**	**1 316**
Cash and cash equivalents at beginning of period		6 594	5 278
Cash and cash equivalents at end of period	22	**5 835**	**6 594**

[a] Presentation was amended (refer to section Changes in presentation on page 20).

Consolidated Financial Statements of the Nestlé Group

Consolidated statement of recognised income and expense and changes in equity for the year ended 31 December 2008

Statement of recognised income and expense [a]

In millions of CHF	Notes	2008	2007
Profit for the period recognised in the income statement		19 051	11 382
Currency retranslations		(4 997)	(1 195)
Fair value adjustments on available-for-sale financial instruments			
– Unrealised results		(358)	(15)
– Recognition of realised results in the income statement		(1)	(18)
Fair value adjustments on cash flow hedges			
– Recognised in hedging reserve		(409)	94
– Removed from hedging reserve		52	(168)
Actuarial gains/(losses) on defined benefit schemes [b]	16	(3 139)	273
Changes in equity of associates	8	(853)	(631)
Taxes on equity items [b]	7	1 454	(140)
Income and expense recognised directly in equity		(8 251)	(1 800)
Total recognised income and expense		10 800	9 582
of which attributable to minority interests		798	632
of which attributable to shareholders of the parent		10 002	8 950

[a]   Presentation was amended (refer to section Changes in presentation on page 20).
[b]   2007 comparatives have been restated following first application of IFRIC 14 (refer to Note 32).

Changes in equity

In millions of CHF

	Share capital	Treasury shares	Translation reserve	Retained earnings and other reserves	Total equity attributable to shareholders of the parent	Minority interests	Total equity
Equity as at 31 December 2006 as reported last year	401	(4 644)	(5 205)	60 439	50 991	1 857	52 848
First application of IFRIC 14 [a]				793	793		793
Equity restated as at 1 January 2007	401	(4 644)	(5 205)	61 232	51 784	1 857	53 641
Total recognised income and expense			(1 097)	10 047	8 950	632	9 582
Dividend paid to shareholders of the parent				(4 004)	(4 004)		(4 004)
Dividends paid to minority interests					–	(359)	(359)
Movement of treasury shares (net)		(4 522)		232	(4 290)		(4 290)
Changes in minority interests					–	1	1
Equity compensation plans		14		173	187	18	205
Reduction in share capital	(8)	1 139		(1 131)	–		–
Equity restated as at 31 December 2007	393	(8 013)	(6 302)	66 549	52 627	2 149	54 776
Total recognised income and expense			(4 801)	14 803	10 002	798	10 800
Dividend paid to shareholders of the parent				(4 573)	(4 573)		(4 573)
Dividends paid to minority interests					–	(408)	(408)
Movement of treasury shares (net) [b]		(7 141)		(381)	(7 522)		(7 522)
Changes in minority interests					–	1 574	1 574
Equity compensation plans		223		17	240	29	269
Reduction in share capital	(10)	5 279		(5 269)	–		–
Equity as at 31 December 2008	383	(9 652)	(11 103)	71 146	50 774	4 142	54 916

[a]   Refer to Note 32
[b]   Includes Nestlé S.A. shares exchanged for warrants (refer to Note 19).

Notes

1. Accounting policies

Accounting convention and accounting standards

The Consolidated Financial Statements comply with International Financial Reporting Standards (IFRS) issued by the International Accounting Standards Board (IASB) and with the Interpretations issued by the International Financial Reporting Interpretations Committee (IFRIC).

The consolidated accounts have been prepared on an accrual basis and under the historical cost convention, unless stated otherwise. All significant consolidated companies and associates have a 31 December accounting year-end.

The preparation of the Consolidated Financial Statements requires Group Management to exercise judgement and to make estimates and assumptions that affect the application of policies, reported amounts of revenues, expenses, assets and liabilities and disclosures. These estimates and associated assumptions are based on historical experience and various other factors that are believed to be reasonable under the circumstances. Actual results may differ from these estimates.

The estimates and underlying assumptions are reviewed on an ongoing basis. Revisions to accounting estimates are recognised in the period in which the estimate is revised if the revision affects only that period, or in the period of the revision and future periods if the revision affects both current and future periods. Those areas affect mainly provisions, impairment tests, employee benefits and unrecognised tax losses.

Scope of consolidation

The Consolidated Financial Statements comprise those of Nestlé S.A. and of its affiliated companies, including joint ventures, and associates (the Group). The list of the principal companies is provided in the section "Companies of the Nestlé Group."

Consolidated companies

Companies, in which the Group has the power to exercise control, are fully consolidated. This applies irrespective of the percentage of interest in the share capital. Control refers to the power to govern the financial and operating policies of a company so as to obtain the benefits from its activities. Minority interests are shown as a component of equity in the balance sheet and the share of the profit attributable to minority interests is shown as a component of profit for the period in the income statement.

Proportionate consolidation is applied for companies over which the Group exercises joint control with partners. The individual assets, liabilities, income and expenses are consolidated in proportion to the Nestlé participation in their equity (usually 50%).

Newly acquired companies are consolidated from the effective date of control, using the purchase method.

Associates

Companies where the Group has the power to exercise a significant influence but does not exercise control are accounted for using the equity method. The net assets and results are adjusted to comply with the Group's accounting policies. The carrying amount of goodwill arising from the acquisition of associates is included in the carrying amount of investments in associates.

Venture funds

Investments in venture funds are recognised in accordance with the consolidation methods described above, depending on the level of control or significant influence exercised.

Foreign currencies

The functional currency of the Group's entities is the currency of their primary economic environment.

In individual companies, transactions in foreign currencies are recorded at the rate of exchange at the date of the transaction. Monetary assets and liabilities in foreign currencies are translated at year-end rates. Any resulting exchange differences are taken to the income statement.

On consolidation, assets and liabilities of Group entities reported in their functional currencies are translated into Swiss Francs, the Group's presentation currency, at year-end exchange rates. Income and expense items are translated into Swiss Francs at the annual weighted average rate of exchange or at the rate on the date of the transaction for significant items.

Differences arising from the retranslation of opening net assets of Group entities, together with differences arising from the restatement of the net results for the year of Group entities, are recognised against equity.

The balance sheet and net results of Group entities operating in hyperinflationary economies are restated for the changes in the general purchasing power of the local currency, using official indices at the balance sheet date, before translation into Swiss Francs at year-end rates.

Segmental information

Segmental information is based on two segment formats:
- the primary segment format – by management responsibility and geographic area – reflects the Group's management structure. The Group manages its Food and Beverages business through three geographic Zones and globally for Nestlé Waters and Nestlé Nutrition. The Group's pharmaceuticals activities are also managed on a worldwide basis and are presented separately from Food and Beverages.
- the secondary segment format – by product group – is divided into six product groups (segments).

Segment results represent the contribution of the different segments to central overheads, research and development costs and the profit of the Group. Specific corporate expenses as well as specific research and development costs are allocated to the corresponding segments.

Segment assets comprise property, plant and equipment, intangible assets, goodwill, trade and other receivables, assets held for sale, inventories as well as prepayments and accrued income.

Segment liabilities comprise trade and other payables, liabilities directly associated with assets held for sale as well as accruals and deferred income.

Eliminations represent inter-company balances between the different segments.

Segment assets and liabilities of the primary segment represent the situation at the end of the year. Segment assets of the secondary segment represent the annual average as this provides a better indication of the level of invested capital for management purposes.

Capital additions represent the total cost incurred to acquire property, plant and equipment, intangible assets and goodwill, including those arising from business combinations. Capital expenditure represents the investment in property, plant and equipment only.

Depreciation of segment assets includes depreciation of property, plant and equipment and intangible assets. Impairment of segment assets includes impairment related to property, plant and equipment, intangible assets and goodwill.

Unallocated items represent non-specific items whose allocation to a segment would be arbitrary. They mainly comprise:
- corporate expenses and related assets/liabilities;
- research and development costs and related assets/liabilities;
- some goodwill and intangible assets;
- capital additions related to administration and distribution assets for the secondary segment; and
- assets held for sale and liabilities directly associated with assets held for sale linked to a discontinued operation.

Valuation methods, presentation and definitions

Revenue

Revenue represents amounts received and receivable from third parties for goods supplied to the customers and for services rendered. Revenue from the sales of goods is recognised in the income statement at the moment when the significant risks and rewards of ownership of the goods have been transferred to the buyer, which is mainly upon shipment. It is measured at the list price applicable to a given distribution channel after deduction of all returns, sales taxes, pricing allowances and similar trade discounts. Payments made to the customers for commercial services received are expensed.

Expenses

Cost of goods sold is determined on the basis of the cost of production or of purchase, adjusted for the variation of inventories (which are measured as described in the policy on inventories, below). All other expenses, including those in respect of advertising and promotions, are recognised when the Group has the right of access to the goods or when it receives the services.

Net other income/(expenses)

These comprise all exit costs including but not limited to profit and loss on disposal of property plant and equipment, profit and loss on disposal of businesses, onerous contracts, restructuring costs, impairment of property plant and equipment, intangibles and goodwill.

Restructuring costs are restricted to dismissal indemnities and employee benefits paid to terminated employees upon the reorganisation of a business. Dismissal indemnities paid for normal attrition such as poor performance, professional misconduct, etc. are part of the expenses by functions.

Net financing cost

Net financing cost includes the financial expense on borrowings from third parties as well as the financial income earned on funds invested outside the Group.

Net financing cost also includes other financial income and expense, such as exchange differences on loans and borrowings, results on foreign currency and interest rate hedging instruments that are recognised in the income statement.

Unwind of discount on provisions is presented in net financing cost.

Taxes

The Group is subject to taxes in different countries all over the world. Taxes and fiscal risks recognised in the Consolidated Financial Statements reflect Group Management's best estimate of the outcome based on the facts known at the balance sheet date in each individual country. These facts may include but are not limited to change in tax laws and interpretation thereof in the various jurisdictions where the Group operates. They may have an impact on the income tax as well as the resulting assets and liabilities. Any differences between tax estimates and final tax assessments are charged to the income statement in the period in which they are incurred, unless anticipated.

Taxes include current taxes on profit and other taxes such as taxes on capital. Also included are actual or potential withholding taxes on current and expected transfers of income from Group companies and tax adjustments relating to prior years. Income tax is recognised in the income statement, except to the extent that it relates to items directly taken to equity, in which case it is recognised against equity.

Deferred taxation is the tax attributable to the temporary differences that arise when taxation authorities recognise and measure assets and liabilities with rules that differ from the principles of the Consolidated Financial Statements. It also arises on temporary differences stemming from tax losses carry-forward.

Deferred taxes are calculated under the liability method at the rates of tax expected to prevail when the temporary differences reverse subject to such rates being substantially enacted at the balance sheet date. Any changes of the tax rates are recognised in the income statement unless related to items directly recognised against equity. Deferred tax liabilities are recognised on all taxable temporary differences excluding non-deductible goodwill. Deferred tax assets are recognised on all deductible temporary differences provided that it is probable that future taxable income will be available.

For share-based payments, a deferred tax asset is recognised in the income statement over the vesting period, provided that a future reduction of the tax expense is both probable and can be reliably estimated. The deferred tax asset for the future tax deductible amount exceeding the total share-based payment cost is recognised against equity.

Financial Instruments

Classes of financial instruments

The Group aggregates its financial instruments into classes based on their nature and characteristics. The details of financial instruments by class are disclosed in the notes.

Financial assets

The Group designates its financial assets into the following categories, as appropriate: loans and receivables, held-to-maturity investments, financial assets at fair value through profit and loss and available-for-sale assets.

Financial assets are initially recognised at fair value plus directly attributable transaction costs. Subsequent remeasurement of financial assets is determined by their designation that is revisited at each reporting date.

Derivatives embedded in other contracts are separated and treated as stand-alone derivatives when their risks and characteristics are not closely related to those of their host contracts and the respective host contracts are not carried at fair value.

In case of regular way purchase or sale (purchase or sale under a contract whose terms require delivery within the time frame established by regulation or convention in the market place), the settlement date is used for both initial recognition and subsequent derecognition.

At each balance sheet date, the Group assesses whether its financial assets are to be impaired. Impairment losses are recognised in the income statement where there is objective evidence of impairment. These losses are never reversed unless they refer to a financial instrument measured at fair value and classified as available-for-sale and the increase in fair value can objectively be related to an event occurring after the recognition of the impairment loss.

Financial assets are derecognised (in full or partly) when the Group's rights to cash flows from the respective assets have expired or have been transferred and the Group has neither exposure to the risks inherent in those assets nor entitlement to rewards from them.

Cash and cash equivalents

These are cash balances, deposits at sight as well as time deposits and placements in commercial paper the maturities of which are three months or less at inception.

Loans and receivables

Loans and receivables are non-derivative financial assets with fixed or determinable payments that are not quoted in an active market. This category includes the following three classes of financial assets: loans, trade and other receivables.

Subsequent to initial measurement, loans and receivables are carried at amortised cost using the effective interest rate method less appropriate allowances for doubtful receivables.

Allowances for doubtful receivables represent the Group's estimates of losses that could arise from the failure or inability of customers to make payments when due. These estimates are based on the ageing of customers balances, specific credit circumstances and the Group's historical bad receivables experience.

Loans and receivables are further classified as current and non-current depending whether these will be realised within twelve months after the balance sheet date or beyond.

Held-to-maturity investments

Held-to-maturity investments are non-derivative financial assets with fixed or determinable payments and fixed maturities. The Group uses this designation when it has an intention and ability to hold until maturity and the re-sale of such investments is prohibited.

Subsequent to initial recognition held-to-maturity investments are recognised at amortised cost less impairment losses.

Held-to-maturity investments are further classified as current and non-current depending whether these will mature within twelve months after the balance sheet date or beyond.

Financial assets at fair value through profit and loss

The financial assets at fair value through profit and loss category includes the following two classes of financial assets: held-for-trading assets and undesignated derivatives.

Held-for-trading assets

Held-for-trading assets are marketable securities and other fixed income portfolios that are managed with the aim of delivering performance over agreed benchmarks and are therefore classified as trading. Short-term investments in securities and fixed income instruments are made in line with the Group's liquidity and credit risk management policies.

Subsequent to initial measurement, held-for-trading assets are carried at fair value and all their gains and losses, realised and unrealised, are recognised in the income statement.

Undesignated derivatives

Undesignated derivatives are comprised of two categories. The first includes derivatives for which hedge accounting is not applied because these are either not designated as hedging instruments or not effective as hedging instruments. The second category relates to derivatives that are acquired with the aim of delivering performance over agreed benchmarks of marketable securities portfolios.

Subsequent to initial measurement, undesignated derivatives are carried at fair value and all their gains and losses, realised and unrealised, are recognised in the income statement. In both cases, derivatives are acquired in full compliance with the Group's risk management policies.

Available-for-sale assets

Available-for-sale assets are those non-derivative financial assets that are either designated as such upon initial recognition or are not classified in any of the other financial assets categories. This category includes the following classes of financial assets: cash at bank and in hands, commercial paper, time deposits and other investments.

Subsequent to initial measurement available-for-sale assets are stated at fair value with all unrealised gains or losses recognised against equity until their disposal when such gains or losses are recognised in the income statement.

Interests on available-for-sale assets are calculated using the effective interest rate method and are recognised in the income statement as part of interest income under net financing cost.

Available-for-sale assets are further classified as current and non-current depending whether these will be realised within twelve months after the balance sheet date or beyond.

Financial liabilities at amortised cost

Financial liabilities are initially recognised at the fair value of consideration received less directly attributable transaction costs.

Subsequent to initial measurement, financial liabilities are recognised at amortised cost unless they are part of a fair value hedge relationship (refer to fair value hedges). The difference between the initial carrying amount of the financial liabilities and their redemption value is recognised in the income statement over the contractual terms using the effective interest rate method. This category includes the following four classes of financial liabilities: trade and other payables, commercial paper, bonds and other financial liabilities.

Financial liabilities at amortised cost are further classified as current and non-current depending whether these will fall due within twelve months after the balance sheet date or beyond.

Financial liabilities are derecognised (in full or partly) when either the Group is discharged from its obligation, it expires, is cancelled or replaced by a new liability with substantially modified terms.

Derivative financial instruments

A derivative is a financial instrument that changes its values in response to changes in the underlying variable, requires no or little net initial investment and is settled at a future date. Derivatives are mainly used to manage exposures to foreign exchange, interest rate and commodity price risk. Whilst some derivatives are also acquired with the aim of managing the return of marketable securities portfolios, these derivatives are only acquired when there are underlying financial assets. The classification of derivatives is determined upon initial recognition and is monitored on a regular basis.

Derivatives are initially recognised at fair value, adjusted for directly attributable transaction costs. These are subsequently remeasured at fair value on a regular basis and at each reporting date as a minimum. The fair values of

exchange-traded derivatives are based on market prices, while the fair value of the over-the-counter derivatives are using accepted mathematical models based on market data and assumptions. Derivatives are carried as assets when their fair value is positive and as liabilities when their fair value is negative. Any gains or losses arising from changes in fair values of derivatives that do not qualify for hedge accounting are recognised directly in the income statement.

The Group's derivatives mainly consist of currency forwards, futures, options and swaps; commodity futures and options; interest rate forwards, futures, options and swaps.

The use of derivatives is governed by the Group's policies approved by the Board of Directors, which provide written principles on the use of derivatives consistent with the Group's overall risk management strategy.

Hedge accounting

The Group designates and documents certain derivatives as hedging instruments against changes in fair values of recognised assets and liabilities (fair value hedges), highly probable forecast transactions (cash flow hedges) and hedges of net investments in foreign operations (net investment hedges). The effectiveness of such hedges is demonstrated at inception and verified at regular intervals and at least on a quarterly basis, using prospective and retrospective testing.

Fair value hedges

The Group uses fair value hedges to mitigate foreign currency and interest rate risks of its recognised assets and liabilities.

The changes in fair values of hedging instruments are recognised in the income statement. Hedged items are also stated at fair value in respect of the risk being hedged, with any gain or loss being recognised in the income statement.

Cash flow hedges

The Group uses cash flow hedges to mitigate foreign currency risks of highly probable forecast transactions, such as anticipated future export sales, purchases of equipment and raw materials, as well as the variability of expected interest payments and receipts.

The effective part of the changes in fair value of hedging instruments are recognised against equity, while any ineffective part is recognised immediately in the income statement. When the hedged item results in the recognition of a non-financial asset or liability, the gains or losses previously recognised against equity are included in the measurement cost of the asset or of the liability. Otherwise the gains or losses previously recognised against equity are removed from equity and recognised in the income statement at the same time as the hedged transaction.

Net investment hedges

The Group uses net investment hedges to mitigate translation exposure on its net investments in affiliated companies.

The changes in fair values of hedging instruments are taken directly to equity together with gains or losses on the foreign currency translation of the hedged investments. All of these fair value gains or losses are deferred in equity until the investments are sold or otherwise disposed of.

Fair values

The Group determines the fair values of its financial instruments using market prices for quoted instruments and widely accepted valuation techniques for other instruments.

Valuation techniques include discounted cash flows, standard valuation models based on market parameters, dealer quotes for similar instruments and use of comparable arm's length transactions.

When fair values of unquoted instruments cannot be measured with sufficient reliability, the Group carries such instruments at cost less impairment, if applicable.

Inventories

Raw materials and purchased finished goods are valued at purchase cost. Work in progress and manufactured finished goods are valued at production cost. Production cost includes direct production costs and an appropriate proportion of production overheads and factory depreciation.

Raw material inventories and purchased finished goods are accounted for using the FIFO (first in, first out) method. The weighted average cost method is used for other inventories.

An allowance is established when the net realisable value of any inventory item is lower than the value calculated above.

Prepayments and accrued income

Prepayments and accrued income comprise payments made in advance relating to the following year, and income relating to the current year, which will not be invoiced until after the balance sheet date.

Property, plant and equipment

Property, plant and equipment are shown in the balance sheet at their historical cost. Depreciation is provided on components that have homogenous useful lives by using the straight-line method so as to depreciate the initial cost down to the residual value over the estimated useful lives. The residual values are 30% on head offices and nil for all other asset types. The useful lives are as follows:

Buildings	20–40 years
Machinery and equipment	10–25 years
Tools, furniture, information technology and sundry equipment	3–10 years
Vehicles	3–8 years
Land is not depreciated.	

Useful lives, components and residual amounts are reviewed annually. Such a review takes into consideration the nature of the assets, their intended use including but not limitative to the closure of facilities and the evolution of the technology and competitive pressures that may lead to technical obsolescence.

Depreciation of property, plant and equipment is allocated to the appropriate headings of expenses by function in the income statement.

Financing costs incurred during the course of construction are expensed. Premiums capitalised for leasehold land or buildings are amortised over the length of the lease. Government grants are recognised in accordance with the deferral method, whereby the grant is set up as deferred income which is released to the income statement over the useful life of the related assets. Grants that are not related to assets are credited to the income statement when they are received.

Leased assets

Assets acquired under finance leases are capitalised and depreciated in accordance with the Group's policy on property, plant and equipment unless the lease term is shorter. Land and building leases are recognised separately provided an allocation of the lease payments between these categories is reliable. The associated obligations are included under financial liabilities.

Rentals payable under operating leases are expensed.

The costs of the agreements that do not take the legal form of a lease but convey the right to use an asset are separated into lease payments and other payments if the entity has the control of the use or of the access to the asset or takes essentially all the output of the asset. Then the entity determines whether the lease component of the agreement is a finance or an operating lease.

Business combinations and related goodwill

As from 1 January 1995, the excess of the cost of an acquisition over the fair value of the net identifiable assets, liabilities and contingent liabilities acquired is capitalised. Previously these amounts had been written off through equity.

Goodwill is not amortised but tested for impairment at least annually and upon the occurrence of an indication of impairment. The impairment testing process is described in the appropriate section of these policies.

Goodwill is recorded in the functional currencies of the acquired operations.

All assets, liabilities and contingent liabilities acquired in a business combination are recognised at the acquisition date and measured at their fair value.

Intangible assets

This heading includes intangible assets that are acquired either separately or in a business combination when they are identifiable and can be reliably measured. Intangible assets are considered to be identifiable if they arise from contractual or other rights, or if they are separable i.e. they can be disposed of either individually or together with other assets. Intangible assets comprise indefinite life intangible assets and finite life intangible assets.

Indefinite life intangible assets are those for which there is no foreseeable limit to their useful economic life as they arise from contractual or other legal rights that can be renewed without significant cost and are the subject of continuous marketing support. They are not depreciated but tested for impairment annually or more frequently if an impairment indicator is triggered. They mainly comprise certain brands, trademarks and intellectual property rights. The assessment of the classification of intangible assets as indefinite is reviewed annually.

Finite life intangible assets are those for which there is an expectation of obsolescence that limits their useful economic life or where the useful life is limited by contractual or other terms. They are depreciated over the shorter of their contractual or useful economic lives. They comprise mainly management information systems, patents and rights to carry on an activity (i. e. exclusive rights to sell products or to perform a supply activity). Finite life intangible assets are depreciated on a straight-line basis assuming a zero residual value: management information systems over a period ranging from three to five years; and other finite life intangible assets over five to 20 years. The depreciation period and depreciation method are reviewed annually by taking into account the risk of obsolescence.

Depreciation of intangible assets is allocated to the appropriate headings of expenses by function in the income statement.

Internally generated intangible assets are capitalised, provided they generate future economic benefits and their costs are clearly identifiable.

Research and development

Research costs are charged to the income statement in the year in which they are incurred.

Development costs relating to new products are not capitalised because the expected future economic benefits cannot be reliably determined. As long as the products have not reached the market place, there is no reliable evidence that positive future cash flows would be obtained.

Other development costs (essentially management information system software) are capitalised provided that there is an identifiable asset that will be useful in generating future benefits in terms of savings, economies of scale, etc.

Impairment of goodwill and indefinite life intangible assets

Goodwill and indefinite life intangible assets are tested for impairment at least annually and upon the occurrence of an indication of impairment.

The impairment tests are performed annually at the same time each year and at the cash generating unit (CGU) level. The Group defines its CGUs based on the way that it monitors and derives economic benefits from the acquired goodwill and intangibles. The impairment tests are performed by comparing the carrying value of the assets of these CGUs with their recoverable amount, based on their future projected cash flows discounted at an appropriate pre-tax rate of return. Usually, the cash flows correspond to estimates made by Group Management in financial plans and business strategies covering a period of five years. They are then projected to 50 years using a steady or declining growth rate given that the Group businesses are of a long-term nature. The Group assesses the uncertainty of these estimates by making sensitivity analyses. The discount rate reflects the current assessment of the time value of money and the risks specific to the CGUs (essentially country risk). The business risk is included in the determination of the cash flows. Both the cash flows and the discount rates exclude inflation.

Impairment of property, plant and equipment and finite life intangible assets

Consideration is given at each balance sheet date to determine whether there is any indication of impairment of the carrying amounts of the Group's property, plant and equipment and finite life intangible assets. Indication could be unfavourable development of a business under competitive pressures or severe economic slowdown in a given market as well as reorganisation of the operations to leverage their scale. If any indication exists, an asset's recoverable amount is estimated. An impairment loss is recognised whenever the carrying amount of an asset exceeds its recoverable amount. The recoverable amount is the greater of the fair value less cost to sell and value in use. In assessing value in use, the estimated future cash flows are discounted to their present value, based on the average borrowing rate of the country where the assets are located, adjusted for risks specific to the asset.

Assets held for sale and discontinued operations

Non-current assets held for sale (and disposal groups) are presented separately in the current section of the balance sheet. Immediately before the initial classification of the assets (and disposal groups) as held for sale, the carrying amounts of the assets (or all the assets and liabilities in the disposal groups) are measured in accordance with their applicable accounting policy. Non-current assets held for sale (and disposal groups) are subsequently measured at the lower of their carrying amount and fair value less cost to sell. Non-current assets held for sale (and disposal groups) are no longer depreciated.

Upon occurrence of discontinued operations, the net profit/(loss) on discontinued operations is presented on the face of the Consolidated income statement. Comparative information is restated accordingly. Income statement and cash flow information related to discontinued operations are disclosed separately in the notes.

Provisions

Provisions comprise liabilities of uncertain timing or amount that arise from restructuring plans, environmental, litigation and other risks. Provisions are recognised when there exists a legal or constructive obligation stemming from a past event and when the future cash outflows can be reliably estimated. Obligations arising from restructuring plans are recognised when detailed formal plans have been established and when there is a valid expectation that such plans will be carried out by either starting to implement them or announcing their main features. Obligations under litigations reflect Group Management's best estimate of the outcome based on the facts known at the balance sheet date.

Employee benefits

The liabilities of the Group arising from defined benefit obligations, and the related current service cost, are determined using the projected unit credit method. Actuarial advice is provided both by external consultants and by actuaries employed by the Group. The actuarial assumptions used to calculate the defined benefit obligations vary according to the economic conditions of the country in which the plan is located. Such plans are either externally funded (in the form of independently administered funds) or unfunded.

For the funded defined benefit plans, the deficit or excess of the fair value of plan assets over the present value of the defined benefit obligation is recognised as a liability or an asset in the balance sheet, taking into account any unrecognised past service cost. However, an excess of assets is recognised only to the extent that it represents a future economic benefit which is actually available to the Group, for example in the form of available refunds from the plan or reductions in future contributions to the plan (either effective or possible). When such an excess is not available or does not represent at minimum a possible future economic benefit, it is not recognised but is disclosed in the notes. Impacts of minimum funding requirements in relation to past service are considered when determining pension obligations.

Actuarial gains and losses arise mainly from changes in actuarial assumptions and differences between actuarial assumptions and what has actually occurred. They are recognised in the period in which they occur in the statement of recognised income and expense.

For defined benefit plans, the pension cost charged to the income statement consists of current service cost, interest cost, expected return on plan assets and past service cost. Recycling to the income statement of cumulated actuarial gains and losses recognised against equity is not permitted by IAS 19. The past service cost for the enhancement of pension benefits is accounted for when such benefits vest or become a constructive obligation.

Some benefits are also provided by defined contribution plans; contributions to such plans are charged to the income statement as incurred.

Share-based payment

The Group has equity-settled and cash-settled share-based payment transactions.

Equity-settled share-based payment transactions are recognised in the income statement with a corresponding increase in equity over the vesting period. They are fair valued at grant date and measured using the Black and Scholes model. The cost of equity-settled share-based payment transactions is adjusted annually by the expectations of vesting, for the forfeitures of the participants' rights that no longer satisfy the plan conditions, as well as for early vesting.

Liabilities arising from cash-settled share-based payment transactions are recognised in the income statement over the vesting period. They are fair valued at each reporting date and measured using the Black and Scholes

model. The cost of cash-settled share-based payment transactions is adjusted for the forfeitures of the participants' rights that no longer satisfy the plan conditions, as well as for early vesting.

Accruals and deferred income

Accruals and deferred income comprise expenses relating to the current year, which will not be invoiced until after the balance sheet date and income received in advance, relating to the following year.

Dividends

In accordance with Swiss law and the Company's Articles of Association, dividends are treated as an appropriation of profit in the year in which they are ratified at the Annual General Meeting and subsequently paid.

Contingent assets and liabilities

Contingent assets and liabilities are possible rights and obligations that arise from past events and whose existence will be confirmed only by the occurrence or non-occurrence of one or more uncertain future events not fully within the control of the Group. They are disclosed in the notes.

Events occurring after the balance sheet date

The values of assets and liabilities at the balance sheet date are adjusted if there is evidence that subsequent adjusting events warrant a modification of these values. These adjustments are made up to the date of approval of the Consolidated Financial Statements by the Board of Directors. Other non-adjusting events are disclosed in the notes.

Changes in accounting policies

The Group has applied the following IFRS as from 1 January 2008 onwards:

IFRIC 14 – IAS 19 – The limit on a defined benefit asset, minimum funding requirements and their interaction

This interpretation requires to determine the availability of refunds or reductions in future contributions in accordance with the terms and conditions of the plans and the statutory requirements of the plans of the respective jurisdictions.

The retrospective application of IFRIC 14 impacted the 2007 Consolidated Financial Statements (refer to Note 32).

Reclassification of Financial Assets – Amendments to IAS 39 – Financial Instruments: Recognition and Measurement and IFRS 7 – Financial Instruments: Disclosures

These amendments allow entities to reclassify non-derivative financial assets out of fair value through profit or loss if the assets are no longer held for the purpose of selling or repurchasing and if the entity has the intention and ability to hold them for the foreseeable future or until maturity.

The Group did not reclassify any financial assets out of the fair value through profit or loss category in 2008.

Changes in presentation

Equity

The Group has simplified the presentation of its equity. In line with the income statement, the statement of recognised income and expense discloses in aggregate the allocations to minority interests and shareholders of the parent (previously allocated for each movement). The statement of changes in equity presents the reserves

"Share premium" and "Reserve for treasury shares" together with "Retained earnings." Additionally, all of the movements in respect of equity-settled share-based payment are disclosed together in the statement of changes in equity. Furthermore, the dividends paid to minority interests are shown separately from the other changes in minority interests (previously presented under "Movements with minority interests [net].")

Cash Flow Statement

The Group has enhanced the presentation of its cash flow statement. It presents all of the "Non-cash items of income and expense" in aggregate (previously presented individually or under "Other operating cash flows.") It also discloses separately the variation of the "Other operating assets and liabilities" (previously presented under "Increase/[decrease] in provisions and deferred taxes" and "Other operating cash flows.") These reclassifications have had no impact on the operating cash flow.

Changes in accounting estimates

In accordance with the review of useful lives required by IAS 16, the Group has modified its useful lives as follows in 2008:

- maximum life of buildings increased from 35 to 40 years and deletion of the residual amount of 20% on distribution centres for products stored at ambient temperature,
- maximum useful life of machinery and equipment increased from 20 to 25 years,
- maximum life of tools furniture and sundry equipment increased from 8 to 10 years.

The Group considers that the new maximum lives better reflect the current improved construction techniques and operation conditions of industrial equipment. These changes do no have a material effect on the Group's financial statements.

Changes in IFRS that may affect the Group after 31 December 2008

IFRS 3 Revised – Business combinations

This standard will be effective for the first annual reporting period beginning on or after 1 July 2009. The Group will thus apply it prospectively as from 1 January 2010 onwards. The revised standard will cause the following changes:
– acquisition costs will be expensed;
– for a business combination in which the acquirer achieves control without buying all of the equity of the acquiree, the remaining minority (non-controlling) equity interests are measured either at fair value or at the non-controlling interests' proportionate share of the acquiree's net identifiable assets;
– upon obtaining control in a business combination achieved in stages, the acquirer shall remeasure its previously held equity interest at fair value and recognise a gain or a loss to the income statement; and
– changes in the contingent consideration of an acquisition will be accounted for outside goodwill, in the income statement.

IAS 27 Revised – Consolidated and separate financial statements

This standard will be applicable prospectively for the first annual reporting period beginning on or after 1 July 2009, the Group will thus apply it as from 1 January 2010 onwards. The revised standard stipulates that a change in the minority (non-controlling) interest of an acquiree that does not result in a loss of control shall be recognised in equity.

IFRS 8 – Operating segments

This standard will be applied in 2009. The Group has assessed its impact and determined that it should not significantly change its segments previously identified under IAS 14 – Segment Reporting.

IAS 1 Revised – Presentation of financial statements

The standard includes non-mandatory changes of the titles of the financial statements that the Group may not apply. The standard also introduces a statement of comprehensive income but allows to present an income statement and a statement of recognised income and expense.

IAS 23 Revised – Borrowing costs

The revised standard removes the option of recognising as an expense borrowing costs directly attributable to acquisition, construction or production of a qualifying asset as currently elected by the Group. This standard will not have a material impact on the Group's financial statements.

Improvements to IFRSs

Several standards have been modified on miscellaneous points and are effective in 2009. They are not going to have a material effect on the Group's financial statement. Moreover the Group already complies with the requirement of the change in IAS 38 – Intangible assets whereby expenditure in respect of advertising and promotions is recognised when an entity has the right of access to the goods and when the services are delivered.

IFRIC 13 – Consumer loyalty programmes

The Group will apply this interpretation in 2009. It requires that the fair value of the consideration related to award credits programmes be separately identified as a component of the sales transaction and recognised when the awards are redeemed by the customers and the corresponding obligations are fulfilled by the Group. Such programmes are not numerous in the Group and this interpretation is unlikely to have a material effect on its results.

IFRIC 16 – Hedges of a net investment in a foreign operation

This interpretation deals with the nature of the hedged risk, its designation and where the hedging instrument can be held. This interpretation will have no impact on the Group's financial statements when it is effective in 2009 as the Group already complies with its requirements.

4. Net other income/(expenses)

In millions of CHF	Notes	2008	2007
Other income			
Profit on disposal of property, plant and equipment	13	24	185
Profit on disposal of businesses	24	9 333	318
Other		69	192
		9 426	**695**
Other expenses			
Loss on disposal of property, plant and equipment	13	(6)	(9)
Loss on disposal of businesses	24	(81)	(59)
Restructuring costs	18	(402)	(481)
Impairment of property, plant and equipment	13	(248)	(225)
Impairment of goodwill	14	(561)	(251)
Impairment of intangible assets	15	(1)	(6)
Other [a]		(825)	(254)
		(2 124)	**(1 285)**
Net other income/(expenses)		**7 302**	**(590)**

[a]   In 2008, the significant items are expenses linked to tax litigation claims mainly in South America.

5. Net financing cost

In millions of CHF	2008	2007
Financial income		
Interest income	102	418
Gains on investments at fair value to income statement	–	158
	102	**576**
Financial expense		
Interest expense	(1 102)	(1 481)
Losses on investments at fair value to income statement [a]	(131)	–
Unwind of the discount on provisions	(14)	(11)
	(1 247)	**(1 492)**
Net financing cost	**(1 145)**	**(916)**

[a]   Losses in 2008 are mainly related to fair value losses in trading securities, of which a significant portion is related to Alcon.

6. Expenses by nature

The following items are allocated to the appropriate headings of expenses by function in the income statement:

In millions of CHF	2008	2007
Depreciation of property, plant and equipment	2 625	2 620
Depreciation of intangible assets	624	591
Salaries and welfare expenses	16 129	16 831
Operating lease charges	630	625
Exchange differences	283	146

8. Associates

In millions of CHF	2008	2007
At 1 January	8 936	8 430
Currency retranslations	(986)	90
Investments	116	100
Share of results	1 005	1 280
Dividends received	(382)	(364)
Changes in equity	(853)	(631)
Modification of the scope of consolidation	(40)	31
At 31 December	**7 796**	**8 936**
of which L'Oréal	7 009	8 197

L'Oréal

The Group holds 178 381 021 shares in L'Oréal, representing a 30.6% participation in its equity (considering own shares held by L'Oréal in relation to the employee stock option plans and the share buy-back programmes). At 31 December 2008, the market value of our shares amounts to CHF 16 537 million (2007: CHF 28 961 million).

Key financial data of the main associates

The following items are an aggregate of the Financial Statements of the main associates:

In millions of CHF	2008	2007
Total current assets	10 640	11 153
Total non-current assets	25 130	28 916
Total assets	**35 770**	**40 069**
Total current liabilities	11 791	10 210
Total non-current liabilities	5 714	6 751
Total liabilities	**17 505**	**16 961**
Total equity	**18 265**	**23 108**
Total sales	**29 718**	**29 982**
Total results	**3 155**	**4 305**

9. Earnings per share

	2008	2007 [a]
Basic earnings per share (in CHF)	4.87	2.78
Net profit (in millions of CHF)	18 039	10 649
Weighted average number of shares outstanding	3 704 613 573	3 828 809 470

	2008	2007 [a]
Fully diluted earnings per share (in CHF)	4.84	2.76
Net profit, net of effects of dilutive potential ordinary shares (in millions of CHF)	18 044	10 678
Weighted average number of shares outstanding, net of effects of dilutive potential ordinary shares	3 725 018 002	3 867 876 260

Reconciliation of net profit (in millions of CHF)	2008	2007 [a]
Net profit used to calculate basic earnings per share	18 039	10 649
Elimination of interest expense, net of taxes, related to the Turbo Zero Equity-Link issued with warrants on Nestlé S.A. shares	5	29
Net profit used to calculate diluted earnings per share	18 044	10 678

Reconciliation of weighted average number of shares outstanding	2008	2007 [a]
Weighted average number of shares outstanding used to calculate basic earnings per share	3 704 613 573	3 828 809 470
Adjustment for assumed exercise of warrants, where dilutive	4 182 623	19 666 210
Adjustment for share-based payment schemes, where dilutive	16 221 806	19 400 580
Weighted average number of shares outstanding used to calculate diluted earnings per share	3 725 018 002	3 867 876 260

[a] 2007 comparatives have been restated following 1-for-10 share split effective on 30 June 2008.

10. Trade and other receivables

10.1 By type

In millions of CHF	2008	2007
Trade receivables	10 552	12 025
Other receivables	2 890	2 865
	13 442	**14 890**

The five major receivables represent 9% (2007: 10%) of trade and other receivables, none of them exceeding 3%.

10.2 Past due and impaired receivables

In millions of CHF	2008	2007
Not past due	11 060	12 242
Past due 1–30 days	1 363	1 605
Past due 31–60 days	370	388
Past due 61–90 days	242	173
Past due 91–120 days	144	147
Past due more than 120 days	707	841
Allowance for doubtful receivables	(444)	(506)
	13 442	**14 890**

10.3 Allowance for doubtful receivables

In millions of CHF	2008	2007
At 1 January	506	453
Currency retranslations	(73)	3
Allowance made in the period	151	58
Amounts used and reversal of unused amounts	(141)	(46)
Modification of the scope of consolidation	1	38
At 31 December	**444**	**506**

Based on the historic trend and expected performance of the customers, the Group believes that the above allowance for doubtful receivables sufficiently covers the risk of default.

12. Inventories

In millions of CHF	2008	2007
Raw materials, work in progress and sundry supplies	3 708	3 590
Finished goods	5 901	5 957
Allowance for write-down at net realisable value	(267)	(275)
	9 342	9 272

Inventories amounting to CHF 143 million (2007: CHF 153 million) are pledged as security for financial liabilities.

13. Property, plant and equipment

In millions of CHF					2007
	Land and buildings	Machinery and equipment	Tools, furniture and other equipment	Vehicles	Total
Gross value					
At 1 January	13 245	25 455	7 446	931	47 077
Currency retranslations	(156)	(478)	(171)	(86)	(891)
Capital expenditure	860	2 695	1 209	207	4 971
Disposals	(258)	(884)	(492)	(78)	(1 712)
Reclassified as held for sale	(30)	(38)	(3)	–	(71)
Modification of the scope of consolidation	90	51	3	(44)	100
At 31 December	13 751	26 801	7 992	930	49 474
Accumulated depreciation and impairments					
At 1 January	(5 251)	(15 732)	(5 363)	(501)	(26 847)
Currency retranslations	60	284	60	14	418
Depreciation	(398)	(1 307)	(800)	(115)	(2 620)
Impairments	(26)	(148)	(50)	(1)	(225)
Disposals	165	758	468	67	1 458
Reclassified as held for sale	22	30	3	–	55
Modification of the scope of consolidation	80	228	12	32	352
At 31 December	(5 348)	(15 887)	(5 670)	(504)	(27 409)
Net at 31 December	8 403	10 914	2 322	426	22 065

At 31 December 2007, property, plant and equipment include CHF 1178 million of assets under construction. Net property, plant and equipment held under finance leases amount to CHF 354 million. Net property, plant and equip-ment of CHF 117 million are pledged as security for financial liabilities. Fire risks, reasonably estimated, are insured in accordance with domestic requirements.

	Land and buildings	Machinery and equipment	Tools, furniture and other equipment	Vehicles	Total
Gross value					
At 1 January	13 751	26 801	7 992	930	**49 474**
Currency retranslations	(1 616)	(3 678)	(1 094)	(128)	**(6 516)**
Capital expenditure	1 069	2 615	1 060	125	**4 869**
Disposals	(92)	(733)	(387)	(60)	**(1 272)**
Reclassified as held for sale	(33)	(124)	(29)	–	**(186)**
Modification of the scope of consolidation	26	(170)	(32)	(2)	**(178)**
At 31 December	**13 105**	**24 711**	**7 510**	**865**	**46 191**
Accumulated depreciation and impairments					
At 1 January	(5 348)	(15 887)	(5 670)	(504)	**(27 409)**
Currency retranslations	603	2 225	806	77	**3 711**
Depreciation	(362)	(1 349)	(805)	(109)	**(2 625)**
Impairments	(79)	(131)	(38)	–	**(248)**
Disposals	92	553	371	60	**1 076**
Reclassified as held for sale	33	120	25	–	**178**
Modification of the scope of consolidation	49	148	23	3	**223**
At 31 December	**(5 012)**	**(14 321)**	**(5 288)**	**(473)**	**(25 094)**
Net at 31 December	**8 093**	**10 390**	**2 222**	**392**	**21 097**

At 31 December 2008, property, plant and equipment include CHF 781 million of assets under construction. Net property, plant and equipment held under finance leases amount to CHF 236 million. Net property, plant and equipment of CHF 109 million are pledged as security for financial liabilities. Fire risks, reasonably estimated, are insured in accordance with domestic requirements.

Impairment
Impairment of property, plant and equipment arises mainly from the plans to optimise industrial manufacturing capacities by closing or selling inefficient production facilities.

Commitments for expenditure
At 31 December 2008, the Group was committed to expenditure amounting to CHF 449 million (2007: CHF 442 million).

14. Goodwill

In millions of CHF	Notes	2008	2007
Gross value (a)			
At 1 January		35 142	30 007
Currency retranslations		(2 784)	(1 620)
Goodwill from acquisitions	23	515	6 903
Disposals		(127)	(148)
At 31 December		**32 746**	**35 142**
Accumulated impairments			
At 1 January		(1 719)	(1 494)
Currency retranslations		123	9
Impairments		(561)	(251)
Disposals		48	17
At 31 December		**(2 109)**	**(1 719)**
Net at 31 December		30 637	33 423

(a) In accordance with IFRS 3 – Business Combinations, gross value includes prior years' accumulated amortisation.

14.1 Impairment charge during the period

Nestlé Waters Home and Office Delivery business in Europe

Goodwill related to the 2003 acquisition of Powwow has been allocated for the impairment test to the Cash Generating Unit (CGU) defined as the Nestlé Waters Home and Office Delivery (HOD) business in Europe. As at 31 December 2008, the carrying amounts of all goodwill items allocated to this CGU and expressed in various European currencies represent an equivalent of CHF 836 million before 2008 impairment (2007: CHF 1 119 million).

According to IFRS requirements an annual impairment test was conducted in the second half of the year. Following further deterioration of the business in various countries since the last impairment test and the foreseen disposal of the Italian and UK HOD operations, the present value of future cash flows was revised downwards.

As the recoverable amount of the CGU was lower than its carrying amount, an impairment of goodwill amounting to CHF 442 million has been recognised in 2008 (2007: CHF 210 million).

The recoverable amount of the CGU has been determined based upon a value-in-use calculation. Deflated cash flow projections covering the next 50 years, discounted at a weighted average rate of 6.2%, were used in this calculation. The cash flows for the first five years were based upon financial plans approved by Group Management; years six to ten were based upon Group Management's best expectations. Cash flows were assumed to be flat for years eleven to 50. Cash flows have been adjusted to reflect the specific business risks.

Main assumptions, based on past experiences and current initiatives, were the following:

- sales: annual growth between 1.5 and 8.3% for the first three years, and between 2.2 and 2.3% in the six years afterwards;
- EBIT margin evolution: consistent with sales growth and enhanced cost management and efficiency, with a higher growth during the first three years and then steadily improving ten basis points per year over the following years.

14.2 Yearly impairment tests

Goodwill impairment reviews have been conducted for more than 200 goodwill items allocated to some 50 Cash Generating Units (CGUs). There are no significant carrying values of goodwill that are allocated across multiple CGUs. Detailed results of the impairment tests are presented below for the three significant goodwill items, representing more than 50% of the net book value at 31 December 2008. For the purpose of the tests, they have been allocated to the following CGUs: PetCare, Infant Nutrition and Ice Cream USA.

PetCare

Goodwill related to the 2001 acquisition of Ralston Purina has been allocated for the impairment test to the CGU of the product category PetCare on a worldwide basis. As at 31 December 2008, the carrying amounts, expressed in various currencies, represent an equivalent of CHF 9888 million (2007: CHF 10 618 million) for the goodwill and CHF 29 million (2007: CHF 29 million) for the intangible assets with indefinite useful life.

The recoverable amount of the CGU is higher than its carrying amount. The recoverable amount has been determined based upon a value-in-use calculation. Deflated cash flow projections covering the next 50 years, discounted at a weighted average rate of 6.7%, were used in this calculation. The cash flows for the first five years were based upon financial plans approved by Group Management; years six to ten were based upon Group Management's best expectations, which are consistent with the Group's approved strategy for this period. Cash flows were assumed to be flat for years eleven to 50, although Group Management expects continuing growth. Cash flows have been adjusted to reflect the specific business risks.

Main assumptions, based on past experiences and current initiatives, were the following:

- sales: annual growth between 3.9 and 7.9% for North America and between 3 and 4.5% for Europe over the first ten-year period;
- EBIT margin evolution: steadily improving margin over the period, in a range of 10–30 basis points per year for North America and 10–60 basis points per year for Europe, consistent with sales growth and portfolio rationalisation.

Assumptions used in the calculation are consistent with the expected long-term average growth rate of the PetCare business in the regions concerned.

The key sensitivity for the impairment test is the growth in sales and EBIT margin. Assuming no sales growth and no improvement in EBIT margin over the entire period would not result in the carrying amount exceeding the recoverable amount.

An increase of 100 basis points in the discount rate assumption would not change the conclusions of the impairment test.

Infant Nutrition

Goodwill and intangible assets with indefinite useful life related to the 2007 acquisition of Gerber have been allocated for the impairment test to the CGU of the Infant Nutrition businesses on a worldwide basis. As at 31 December 2008, the carrying amounts, expressed in various currencies, represent an equivalent of CHF 3963 million (2007: CHF 4227 million) for the goodwill and CHF 1405 million (2007: CHF 1497 million) for the intangible assets with indefinite useful life.

The recoverable amount of the CGU is higher than its carrying amount. The recoverable amount has been determined based upon a value-in-use calculation. Deflated cash flow projections covering the next 50 years, discounted at a weighted average rate of 8%, were used in this calculation. The cash flows for the first five years were based upon financial plans approved by Group Management; years six to ten were based upon Group Management's best expectations, which are consistent with the Group's approved strategy for this period. Cash flows were assumed to be flat after, although Group Management expects continuing growth. Cash flows have been adjusted to reflect the specific business risks.

Main assumptions were the following:

- sales: annual growth between 2 and 5% for North America and between 5.2 and 5.7% for the rest of the world over the first five-year period;
- EBIT margin evolution: steadily improving margin over the period, in a range of 10–50 basis points per year for North America and in a range of 60–90 basis points per year for the rest of the world.

The key sensitivity for the impairment test is the growth in sales and EBIT margin. Assuming no sales growth and no improvement in EBIT margin over the entire period would not result in the carrying amount exceeding the recoverable amount.

An increase of 100 basis points in the discount rate assumption would not change the conclusions of the impairment test.

Ice Cream USA

Goodwill and intangible assets with indefinite useful life related to the Group's Ice cream businesses in the USA (Nestlé Ice Cream Company and Dreyer's) has been allocated for the impairment test to the Ice Cream USA CGU. As at 31 December 2008, the carrying amounts, expressed in USD, represent an equivalent of CHF 3096 million (2007: CHF 3301 million) for the goodwill and CHF 76 million (2007: CHF 81 million) for the intangible assets with indefinite useful life.

The recoverable amount of the CGU is higher than its carrying amount. The recoverable amount has been determined based upon a value-in-use calculation. Deflated cash flow projections covering the next 50 years, discounted at 6.4%, were used in this calculation. The cash flows for the first five years were based upon financial plans approved by Group Management; years six to ten were based upon Group Management's best expectations, which are consistent with the Group's approved strategy for this period. Cash flows were assumed to be flat for years eleven to 50, although Group Management expects continuing growth. Cash flows have been adjusted to reflect the specific business risks.

Main assumptions, based on past experiences and current initiatives, were the following:

- sales: annual growth between 2 and 5% over the first ten-year period;
- EBIT margin evolution: steadily improving margin over the period, in a range of 70–270 basis points per year, which is consistent with strong sales growth and enhanced cost management and efficiency.

The key sensitivity for the impairment test is the growth in sales and EBIT margin. Limiting annual growth to only 4% until 2017 and 0% thereafter would not result in the carrying amount exceeding the recoverable amount. Reaching 80% of the expectations in terms of EBIT evolution would not result in the carrying amount exceeding the recoverable amount.

An increase of 100 basis points in the discount rate assumption would not change the conclusions of the impairment test.

15. Intangible assets

In millions of CHF | | | | | 2007

	Brands and intellectual property rights	Operating rights and others	Management information systems	Total	of which internally generated
Gross value					
At 1 January	1 550	753	3 533	**5 836**	3 067
of which indefinite useful life	1 167	–	–	**1 167**	–
Currency retranslations	(153)	(38)	(24)	**(215)**	(8)
Expenditure	11	61	547	**619**	510
Disposals	(8)	(18)	(58)	**(84)**	(3)
Modification of the scope of consolidation	3 129	478	(6)	**3 601**	(6)
At 31 December	**4 529**	**1 236**	**3 992**	**9 757**	**3 560**
of which indefinite useful life	4 133	–	–	**4 133**	–
Accumulated depreciation and impairments					
At 1 January	(224)	(521)	(1 318)	**(2 063)**	(914)
Currency retranslations	–	29	12	**41**	–
Depreciation	(16)	(90)	(485)	**(591)**	(459)
Impairments	(2)	(2)	(2)	**(6)**	–
Disposals	8	14	56	**78**	–
Modification of the scope of consolidation	–	1	–	**1**	–
At 31 December	**(234)**	**(569)**	**(1 737)**	**(2 540)**	**(1 373)**
Net at 31 December	**4 295**	**667**	**2 255**	**7 217**	**2 187**

In millions of CHF   2008

	Brands and intellectual property rights	Operating rights and others	Management information systems	Total	of which internally generated
Gross value					
At 1 January	4 529	1 236	3 992	**9 757**	3 560
of which indefinite useful life	4 133	–	–	**4 133**	–
Currency retranslations	(227)	(65)	(502)	**(794)**	(463)
Expenditure	9	140	436	**585**	362
Disposals	–	(10)	(49)	**(59)**	(18)
Reclassified as held for sale	–	–	(5)	**(5)**	(5)
Modification of the scope of consolidation	184	58	(5)	**237**	(5)
At 31 December	**4 495**	**1 359**	**3 867**	**9 721**	**3 431**
of which indefinite useful life (a)	3 948	–	–	**3 948**	–
Accumulated depreciation and impairments					
At 1 January	(234)	(569)	(1 737)	**(2 540)**	(1 373)
Currency retranslations	10	25	230	**265**	198
Depreciation	(24)	(99)	(501)	**(624)**	(476)
Impairments	–	(1)	–	**(1)**	–
Disposals	–	8	36	**44**	7
Reclassified as held for sale	–	–	1	**1**	1
Modification of the scope of consolidation	–	–	1	**1**	–
At 31 December	**(248)**	**(636)**	**(1 970)**	**(2 854)**	**(1 643)**
Net at 31 December	**4 247**	**723**	**1 897**	**6 867**	**1 788**

(a) Yearly impairment tests are performed together with goodwill items (refer to Note 14).

Internally generated intangible assets consist mainly of management information systems.

Commitments for expenditure
At 31 December 2008, the Group was committed to expenditure amounting to CHF 54 million (2007: none).

18. Provisions and contingencies

18.1 Provisions

In millions of CHF	Restructuring	Environmental	Litigation	Other	Total
At 1 January 2007	1 034	38	1 750	217	3 039
Currency retranslations	2	(2)	(44)	–	(44)
Provisions made in the period	392	7	510	121	1 030
Amounts used	(393)	(4)	(77)	(64)	(538)
Unused amounts reversed	(28)	–	(271)	(47)	(346)
Modification of the scope of consolidation	–	–	131	44	175
At 31 December 2007	1 007	39	1 999	271	3 316
Currency retranslations	(88)	(2)	(175)	(33)	(298)
Provisions made in the period	303	–	994	162	1 459
Amounts used	(313)	(6)	(51)	(80)	(450)
Unused amounts reversed	(51)	–	(283)	(37)	(371)
Modification of the scope of consolidation	–	–	–	7	7
At 31 December 2008	858	31	2 484	290	3 663

Restructuring

Restructuring provisions arise from a number of projects across the Group. These include plans to optimise production, sales and administration structures, mainly in Europe. Restructuring provisions are expected to result in future cash outflows when implementing the plans (usually over the following two to three years) and are generally not discounted.

Litigation

Litigation provisions have been set up to cover tax, legal and administrative proceedings that arise in the ordinary course of business. These provisions concern numerous cases whose detailed disclosure could seriously prejudice the interests of the Group. Reversal of such provisions refer to cases resolved in favour of the Group. The timing of cash outflows of litigation provisions is uncertain as it depends upon the outcome of the proceedings. These provisions are therefore not discounted because their present value would not represent meaningful information. Group Management does not believe it is possible to make assumptions on the evolution of the cases beyond the balance sheet date.

Other

Other provisions are mainly constituted by onerous contracts, liabilities for partial refund of selling prices of divested businesses and various damage claims having occurred during the period but not covered by insurance companies. Onerous contracts result from unfavourable leases or supply agreements above market prices in which the unavoidable costs of meeting the obligations under the contracts exceed the economic benefits expected to be received or for which no benefits are expected to be received. These agreements have been entered into as a result of selling and closing inefficient facilities.

18.2 Contingencies

The Group is exposed to contingent liabilities amounting to a maximum potential payment of CHF 644 million (2007: CHF 1016 million) representing potential litigations of CHF 590 million (2007: CHF 956 million) and other items of CHF 54 million (2007: CHF 60 million).

Contingent assets for litigation claims in favour of the Group amount to a maximum potential recoverable of CHF 296 million (2007: CHF 395 million).

19. Financial assets and liabilities

In millions of CHF	2008	2007
Liquid assets [a]	7 131	9 496
Trade and other receivables	13 442	14 890
Current income tax receivables	889	531
Financial assets – non-current	3 868	4 213
Derivative assets	1 609	754
Total financial assets	**26 939**	**29 884**
Trade and other payables	12 608	14 179
Current income tax payables	824	856
Financial liabilities – current	15 383	24 541
Financial liabilities – non-current	6 344	6 129
Other payables	1 264	1 091
Derivative liabilities	1 477	477
Total financial liabilities	**37 900**	**47 273**
Net financial position	**(10 961)**	**(17 389)**

[a] Liquid assets are composed of cash and cash equivalents and short-term investments.

19.1 By category

In millions of CHF	2008	2007
Loans and receivables	14 932	15 927
Held for trading	854	1 510
Derivative assets [a]	1 609	754
Available-for-sale assets	9 544	11 693
Total financial assets	**26 939**	**29 884**
Financial liabilities at amortised cost	30 341	41 218
Financial liabilities at fair value under hedge accounting	6 082	5 578
Derivative liabilities [a]	1 477	477
Total financial liabilities	**37 900**	**47 273**
Net financial position	**(10 961)**	**(17 389)**

[a] Include derivatives classified as undesignated derivatives (refer to Note 11).

The Group does not apply the fair value option.

19.2 Fair value hierarchy per classes of financial instruments

The Group determines the fair value of its financial instruments on the basis of the following hierarchy. The fair value of instruments that are quoted in active markets is determined based on current market prices. This applies to commodity futures that are traded on terminal exchanges and to listed bonds. The fair value of the other instruments is determined on the basis of valuation techniques such as discounted cash flow calculations or other pricing models. In this category, the fair value of the majority of the instruments is based on parameters stemming from observable market data or by reference to the prices of other instruments, while the fair value of a small number of instruments is based on unobservable input.

19.3 Bonds

In millions of CHF						2008	2007
Issuer	Face value in millions	Interest rates		Year of issue/ maturity	Comments		
		Coupon	Effective				
Nestlé Holdings, Inc., USA	USD 535	0.00%	6.25%	2001–2008	(a)	–	587
	USD 400	3.50%	3.81%	2005–2008	(b)	–	449
	USD 300	5.00%	5.19%	2006–2008	(b)	–	338
	USD 250	3.88%	3.42%	2003–2009	(c)	–	281
	EUR 250	2.13%	2.97%	2005–2009	(b)(d)	367	392
	AUD 300	5.50%	5.68%	2005–2009	(b)(e)	223	286
	GBP 200	5.13%	5.38%	2006–2009	(b)(f)	313	443
	USD 300	4.38%	4.49%	2005–2009	(b)	321	339
	AUD 300	6.00%	6.36%	2006–2010	(b)(g)	225	285
	CHF 625	2.75%	2.69%	2007–2010	(h)	620	398
	HUF 10000	6.88%	7.20%	2007–2010	(b)	53	64
	NOK 1500	4.75%	5.16%	2007–2010	(b)(i)	230	188
	NZD 100	8.25%	8.53%	2008–2010	(b)	62	–
	AUD 600	7.25%	7.63%	2008–2011	(j)	451	–
	CHF 300	2.25%	2.30%	2008–2011	(k)	296	–
	NOK 1000	5.00%	5.55%	2008–2011	(k)	152	–
	USD 750	4.00%	3.87%	2008–2011	(b)	822	–
	USD 500	4.75%	4.90%	2007–2011	(k)	537	572
	CHF 675	3.00%	2.86%	2007–2012	(l)	700	199
	CHF 450	2.50%	2.57%	2006–2013	(b)	454	435
	CHF 250	2.63%	2.66%	2007–2018	(b)	245	235
Nestlé Purina PetCare Company, USA	USD 83	9.25%	5.90%	1989–2009		90	98
	USD 48	7.75%	6.25%	1995–2015		54	59
	USD 63	9.30%	6.46%	1991–2021		83	89
	USD 79	8.63%	6.46%	1992–2022		99	107
	USD 44	8.13%	6.47%	1993–2023		53	57
	USD 51	7.88%	6.45%	1995–2025		62	66
Nestlé Finance International Ltd, Luxembourg	EUR 500	3.50%	3.51%	2003–2008	(b)	–	828
(formerly Nestlé Finance-France S.A., France)	AUD 200	6.00%	6.03%	2004–2008	(b)	–	198
	HUF 25000	7.00%	7.00%	2004–2009	(b)	138	163
	EUR 100	3.50%	3.52%	2006–2009	(b)	149	164
Nestlé (Thai) Ltd, Thailand	THB 5000	2.16%	2.16%	2003–2008		–	167
Other bonds						19	56
Total						**6 818**	**7 543**
of which due within one year						1 607	2 601
of which due after one year						5 211	4 942

Bonds subject to fair value hedges are carried at fair value for CHF 5243 million (2007: CHF 5578 million) and the related derivatives are shown under derivative assets for CHF 377 million (2007: CHF 340 million) and under derivative liabilities for CHF 223 million (2007: none). The full fair value of bonds amounts to CHF 6910 million (2007: CHF 7560 million).

(a) Turbo Zero Equity-Link issue with warrants on Nestlé S.A. shares. The debt component (issue of the notes) was recognised under bonds for USD 451 million at inception, while the equity component (premium on warrants issued) was recognised under equity for USD 123 million. The investors had the option to put the notes to Nestlé Holdings, Inc. and the warrants to Nestlé S.A. at their accreted value in June 2003 and in June 2006.

Exercise conditions of the warrants: 70 000 warrants to purchase Nestlé S.A. shares. Each warrant gives the right to purchase 31.9065 shares. The holders of warrants may exercise their warrants to purchase shares of Nestlé S.A. either:
1) during the note exercise period from July 2001 to June 2008 by tendering a note and a warrant in exchange for shares on the basis that one note is required to exercise each warrant; or
2) on the cash exercise date, 11 June 2008, by tendering warrants together with the exercise price in cash.

The effective initial exercise price per share is USD 261,119 (or CHF 455.–, based on a fixed exchange rate of CHF 1.7425 for each USD), growing by 2.625% per annum, prior to any anti-dilution adjustment. In June 2003, 100 units (at USD 10 000 each) of this issue were put for cash by a holder on the put date at the prescribed price as per the terms and conditions of the issue. In 2006, one warrant was exercised. In 2007, 16 524 warrants were exercised. Notes valued at amortised cost of USD 155 million (nominal USD 165 million) were exchanged for 527 210 Nestlé S.A. shares of nominal value of CHF 1.–. In 2008, 50 765 warrants were exercised. Notes valued at amortised cost of USD 501 million (nominal USD 507 million) were exchanged for 1 619 688 Nestlé S.A. shares of nominal value of CHF 1.–.

(b) Subject to an interest rate and/or currency swap that creates a liability at floating rates in the currency of the issuer.

(c) The step-up fixed rate callable medium term note was called by Nestlé Holdings Inc. in March 2008 in accordance with terms and conditions.

(d) The initial EUR 150 million bond issued in 2005 was increased by EUR 100 million in 2006.

(e) The initial AUD 200 million bond issued in 2005 was increased by AUD 100 million in 2006.

Amounts subject to an interest rate and/or currency swap that creates a liability at floating rates in the currency of the issuer are carried at fair value.

Amounts subject to an interest rate and currency swap that creates a liability at fixed rates in the currency of the issuer are carried at amortised cost.

(f) The initial GBP 100 million bond issued in 2006 was increased by GBP 100 million in 2007.

(g) The initial AUD 200 million bond issued in 2006 was increased by AUD 100 million in 2007.

(h) This bond is composed of:
- CHF 200 million issued in 2007 subject to an interest rate and currency swap that creates a liability at fixed rates in the currency of the issuer;
- CHF 200 million issued in 2007 subject to an interest rate and/or currency swap that creates a liability at floating rates in the currency of the issuer;
- CHF 100 million issued in 2008 subject to an interest rate and currency swap that creates a liability at fixed rates in the currency of the issuer; and
- CHF 125 million issued in 2008 subject to an interest rate and/or currency swap that creates a liability at floating rates in the currency of the issuer.

(i) The initial NOK 1000 million bond issued in 2007 was increased by NOK 500 million in 2008.

(j) This bond is composed of:
- AUD 300 million issued in 2008 subject to an interest rate and currency swap that creates a liability at fixed rates in the currency of the issuer;
- AUD 300 million issued in 2008 subject to an interest rate and/or currency swap that creates a liability at floating rates in the currency of the issuer.

(k) Subject to an interest rate and currency swap that creates a liability at fixed rates in the currency of the issuer.

(l) This bond is composed of:
- CHF 200 million issued in 2007 subject to an interest rate and/or currency swap that creates a liability at floating rates in the currency of the issuer;
- CHF 150 million issued in 2008 subject to an interest rate and currency swap that creates a liability at fixed rates in the currency of the issuer; and
- CHF 325 million issued in 2008 subject to an interest rate and/or currency swap that creates a liability at floating rates in the currency of the issuer.

21. Equity

21.1 Share capital issued

The ordinary share capital of Nestlé S.A. authorised, issued and fully paid is composed of 3 830 000 000 registered shares with a nominal value of CHF 0.10 each (2007: 393 072 500 registered shares with a nominal value of CHF 1.– each). Each share confers the right to one vote. No shareholders may be registered with the right to vote for shares which it holds, directly or indirectly, in excess of 5% of the share capital. Shareholders have the right to receive dividends.

The share capital changed twice in the last two financial years as a consequence of the Share Buy-Back Programmes launched in 2005 and 2007. The cancellation of shares was approved at the Annual General Meetings of 19 April 2007 and 10 April 2008. In 2007, the share capital was reduced by 7 663 200 shares from CHF 401 million to CHF 393 million. In 2008, the share capital was further reduced by 10 072 500 shares from CHF 393 million to CHF 383 million.

Additionally, the shareholders gave their assent at the last Annual General Meeting to a 1-for-10 share split and respective increase of the number of shares. This split aims to increase the liquidity and tradability of the Nestlé S.A. shares. As a consequence, the nominal value of the shares was reduced from CHF 1.– to CHF 0.10.

21.2 Conditional share capital

The conditional capital of Nestlé S.A. amounts to CHF 10 million as in the preceding year. It confers the right to increase the ordinary share capital, through the exercise of conversion or option rights in connection with debentures and other financial market instruments, by a maximum of CHF 10 million by the issue of a maximum of 100 000 000 registered shares with a nominal value of CHF 0.10 each. Thus the Board of Directors has at its disposal a flexible instrument enabling it, if necessary, to finance the activities of the Company through convertible debentures.

21.3 Treasury shares

Number of shares	Notes	2008	2007 (a)
Purpose of holding			
Trading		9 501 554	18 727 050
Share Buy-Back Programme		165 824 000	82 940 000
Warrants on Turbo bond issue of Nestlé Holdings Inc., USA	19	–	17 030 590
Management option rights	17	22 326 896	27 374 110
Restricted Stock Units	17	9 443 950	10 771 260
Freely available for future Long-Term Incentive Plans		7 296 360	11 164 410
		214 392 760	**168 007 420**

(a) 2007 comparatives have been restated following 1-for-10 share split effective on 30 June 2008.

At 31 December 2008, the market value of the treasury shares held by the Group is CHF 8919 million (2007: CHF 8736 million).

21.4 Number of shares outstanding

	Shares issued	Treasury shares	Outstanding shares
2007 (a)			
At 1 January 2007	4 007 357 000	(170 136 260)	3 837 220 740
Purchase of treasury shares		(104 326 920)	(104 326 920)
Sale of treasury shares		8 662 660	8 662 660
Treasury shares delivered in respect of options exercised		15 313 170	15 313 170
Treasury shares delivered in respect of equity compensation plans		575 830	575 830
Treasury shares exchanged for warrants		5 272 100	5 272 100
Treasury shares cancelled	(76 632 000)	76 632 000	–
At 31 December 2007	**3 930 725 000**	**(168 007 420)**	**3 762 717 580**
2008			
Purchase of treasury shares		(183 809 000)	(183 809 000)
Sale of treasury shares		9 575 506	9 575 506
Treasury shares delivered in respect of options exercised		5 740 284	5 740 284
Treasury shares delivered in respect of equity compensation plans		4 502 290	4 502 290
Treasury shares exchanged for warrants		16 880 580	16 880 580
Treasury shares cancelled	(100 725 000)	100 725 000	–
At 31 December 2008	**3 830 000 000**	**(214 392 760)**	**3 615 607 240**

(a) 2007 comparatives have been restated following 1-for-10 share split effective on 30 June 2008.

21.5 Translation reserve

The translation reserve comprises the cumulative gains and losses arising from translating the financial statements of foreign operations that use functional currencies other than Swiss francs. It also includes the changes in the fair value of hedging instruments used for net investments in foreign operations.

21.6 Retained earnings and other reserves

Retained earnings represent the cumulative profits, share premium, as well as actuarial gains and losses on defined benefit plans attributable to shareholders of the parent. Other reserves comprise the fair value reserve and the hedging reserve attributable to shareholders of the parent.

The fair value reserve includes the gains and losses on remeasuring available-for-sale financial instruments. At 31 December 2008, it amounts to CHF 79 million (2007: CHF 436 million).

The hedging reserve consists of the effective portion of the gains and losses on hedging instruments related to hedged transactions that have not yet occurred. At 31 December 2008, the reserve is negative of CHF 378 million (2007: negative of CHF 21 million).

21.7 Minority interests

The minority interests comprise the portion of equity of subsidiaries that are not owned, directly or indirectly, by Nestlé S.A. A significant portion of minority interests relates to Alcon.

21.8 Dividend

The dividend related to 2007 was paid on 16 April 2008 in conformity with the decision taken at the Annual General Meeting on 10 April 2008. Shareholders approved the proposed dividend of CHF 12.20 per share, resulting in a total dividend of CHF 4573 million.

Dividends payable are not accounted for until they have been ratified at the Annual General Meeting. At the meeting on 23 April 2009, a dividend of CHF 1.40 per share will be proposed, resulting in a total dividend of CHF 5127 million. For further details, refer to the Financial Statements of Nestlé S.A.

The Financial Statements for the year ended 31 December 2008 do not reflect this proposed distribution, which will be treated as an appropriation of profit in the year ending 31 December 2009.

22. Cash flow statement

22.1 Non-cash items of income and expense

In millions of CHF	2008	2007
Share of results of associates	(1 005)	(1 280)
Depreciation of property, plant and equipment	2 625	2 620
Impairment of property, plant and equipment	248	225
Impairment of goodwill	561	251
Depreciation of intangible assets	624	591
Impairment of intangible assets	1	6
Net result on disposal of businesses	(9 252)	(259)
Net result on disposal of assets	186	(206)
Non-cash items in financial assets and liabilities	(759)	(113)
Deferred taxes	(1 090)	156
Taxes on equity items	1 454	(140)
Equity compensation plans	250	246
	(6 157)	2 097

22.2 Decrease/(increase) in working capital

In millions of CHF	2008	2007
Inventories	(1 523)	(1 001)
Trade receivables	13	(108)
Trade payables	78	968
Other current assets	(870)	(363)
Other current liabilities	515	586
	(1 787)	**82**

22.3 Variation of other operating assets and liabilities

In millions of CHF	2008	2007
Variation of employee benefits assets and liabilities	(824)	(213)
Variation of provisions	638	146
Other	(158)	(55)
	(344)	**(122)**

22.4 Purchase of treasury shares
In 2008, the Group invested CHF 8685 million on its Share Buy-Back Programme (2007: CHF 4405 million).

22.5 Cash and cash equivalents at end of period

In millions of CHF	2008	2007
Cash at bank and in hand	1 855	2 610
Time deposits [a]	3 174	3 039
Commercial paper [a]	806	945
	5 835	**6 594**

[a] With original maturity of less than three months

22.6 Interest, taxes and dividends
The following items are allocated to the appropriate headings in the cash flow statement:

In millions of CHF	2008	2007
Interest paid	(1 138)	(1 352)
Interest received	231	564
Taxes paid	(3 207)	(3 072)
Dividends paid	(4 981)	(4 363)
Dividends received	399	404

23. Acquisition of businesses

In millions of CHF	2008	2007
Fair value of net assets acquired		
Property, plant and equipment	137	533
Intangible assets	243	3 610
Other assets	53	3 065
Minority interests	(2)	(2)
Purchase of minority interests in existing participations	23	130
Financial liabilities	(21)	(78)
Employee benefits, deferred taxes and provisions	(55)	(1 125)
Other liabilities	(54)	(1 586)
	324	4 547
Goodwill [a]	515	6 903
Total acquisition cost	839	11 450
Cash and cash equivalents acquired	(37)	(132)
Consideration payable	(21)	(132)
Payment of consideration payable on prior years acquisition	156	46
Cash outflow on acquisitions	937	11 232

[a] Of which CHF 95 million (2007: CHF 1006 million) resulting from Alcon's acquisition of own shares to satisfy obligations under the stock option plan of Alcon employees and for shares buy-back programme.

Since the valuation of the assets and liabilities of businesses acquired during the period is still in process, the above values are determined provisionally. Adjustments of values determined provisionally in the preceding year are not significant. The carrying amounts of assets and liabilities determined in accordance with IFRSs immediately before the combination do not differ significantly from those disclosed above except for internally generated intangible assets and goodwill which were not recognised. The goodwill represents elements that cannot be recognised as intangible assets such as synergies, complementary market share and competitive position.

The sales and the profit for the period are not significantly impacted by acquisitions.

24. Disposal of businesses

In millions of CHF	2008	2007
Net assets disposed of		
Property, plant and equipment	92	81
Goodwill and intangible assets	84	139
Other assets	176	297
Minority interests	1 554	(29)
Financial liabilities	(61)	(18)
Employee benefits, deferred taxes and provisions	(5)	36
Other liabilities	(102)	(244)
	1 738	262
Profit/(loss) on current year disposals	9 252	259
Total disposal consideration	10 990	521
Cash and cash equivalents disposed of	(20)	(30)
Consideration receivable	(5)	(41)
Receipt of consideration receivable on prior years disposal	34	6
Cash inflow on disposals	10 999	456

Disposal of Alcon

On 7 July 2008, the Group sold 24.8% of Alcon outstanding capital to Novartis for a total amount of USD 10.4 billion, resulting in a profit on disposal of CHF 9208 million and in an increase of minority interests of CHF 1537 million. Alcon remains fully consolidated.

The agreement further includes the option for Novartis to acquire Nestlé's remaining shareholding in Alcon at a price of USD 181.– per share from January 2010 until July 2011. During the same period, Nestlé will have the option to sell its remaining shareholding in Alcon to Novartis at the lower of either the call price of USD 181.– per share or the average share price during the week preceding the exercise plus a premium of 20.5%. In accordance with IFRS requirements under IAS 39 – Financial Instruments: Recognition and Measurement, contracts between a buyer and a seller in a business combination to buy or sell a business at a later date, are exempt from recognition. Therefore, the outstanding put and call options have not been recognised.

25. Lease commitments

25.1 Operating leases

Lease commitments refer mainly to buildings, industrial equipment, vehicles and IT equipment.

In millions of CHF	2008	2007
	Minimum lease payments	
	Future value	
Within one year	609	559
In the second year	487	425
In the third to the fifth year inclusive	918	859
After the fifth year	524	571
	2 538	**2 414**

25.2 Finance leases

In millions of CHF	2008		2007	
	Minimum lease payments			
	Present value	Future value	Present value	Future value
Within one year	65	67	78	88
In the second year	54	64	100	120
In the third to the fifth year inclusive	101	139	146	208
After the fifth year	74	181	122	264
	294	**451**	**446**	**680**

The difference between the future value of the minimum lease payments and their present value represents the discount on the lease obligations.

Report of the Statutory auditor on the Consolidated Financial Statements

to the General Meeting of Nestlé S.A.

As Statutory auditor we have audited the Consolidated Financial Statements (income statement, balance sheet, cash flow statement, statement of recognised income and expense, changes in equity and notes on pages 3 to 76) of the Nestlé Group for the year ended 31 December 2008.

Board of Directors' responsibility

The Board of Directors is responsible for the preparation and fair presentation of the Consolidated Financial Statements in accordance with International Financial Reporting Standards (IFRS) and the requirements of Swiss law. This responsibility includes designing, implementing and maintaining an internal control system relevant to the preparation and fair presentation of Consolidated Financial Statements that are free from material misstatement, whether due to fraud or error. The Board of Directors is further responsible for selecting and applying appropriate accounting policies and making accounting estimates that are reasonable in the circumstances.

Auditor's responsibility

Our responsibility is to express an opinion on these Consolidated Financial Statements based on our audit. We conducted our audit in accordance with Swiss law and Swiss Auditing Standards and International Standards on Auditing. Those standards require that we plan and perform the audit to obtain reasonable assurance whether the Consolidated Financial Statements are free from material misstatement.

An audit involves performing procedures to obtain audit evidence about the amounts and disclosures in the Consolidated Financial Statements. The procedures selected depend on the auditor's judgment, including the assessment of the risks of material misstatement of the Consolidated Financial Statements, whether due to fraud or error. In making those risk assessments, the auditor considers the internal control system relevant to the entity's preparation and fair presentation of the Consolidated Financial Statements in order to design audit procedures that are appropriate in the circumstances, but not for the purpose of expressing an opinion on the effectiveness of the entity's internal control system. An audit also includes evaluating the appropriateness of the accounting policies used and the reasonableness of accounting estimates made, as well as evaluating the overall presentation of the Consolidated Financial Statements. We believe that the audit evidence we have obtained is sufficient and appropriate to provide a basis for our audit opinion.

Opinion

In our opinion, the Consolidated Financial Statements for the year ended 31 December 2008 give a true and fair view of the financial position, the result of operations and the cash flows in accordance with IFRS and comply with Swiss law.

Report on other legal requirements

We confirm that we meet the legal requirements on licensing according to the Auditor Oversight Act (AOA) and independence (article 728 CO and article 11 AOA) and that there are no circumstances incompatible with our independence.

In accordance with article 728a paragraph 1 item 3 CO and Swiss Auditing Standard 890, we confirm that an internal control system exists, which has been designed for the preparation of Consolidated Financial Statements according to the instructions of the Board of Directors.

We recommend that the Consolidated Financial Statements submitted to you be approved.

 KPMG Klynveld Peat Marwick Goerdeler SA

Mark Baillache
Licensed Audit Expert
Auditor in charge

Stéphane Gard
Licensed Audit Expert

Zurich, 18 February 2009

Financial information – five year review

In millions of CHF (except for per share data and personnel)

	2008	2007	2006	2005 [a]	2004 [b]
Results					
Sales	109 908	107 552	98 458	91 115	84 690
EBIT Earnings Before Interest, Taxes, restructuring and impairments	15 676	15 024	13 302	11 876	10 760
as % of sales	14.3%	14.0%	13.5%	13.0%	12.7%
Taxes	3 787	3 416	3 293	2 647	2 404
Profit for the period attributable to shareholders of the parent (Net profit)	18 039	10 649	9 197	8 081	6 621
as % of sales	16.4%	9.9%	9.3%	8.9%	7.8%
Total amount of dividend	5 127 [d]	4 573	4 004	3 471	3 114
Depreciation of property, plant and equipment	2 625	2 620	2 581	2 382	2 454
Balance sheet and Cash flow statement					
Current assets	33 048	35 770	35 305	41 765	35 285
of which liquid assets	7 131	9 496	11 475	17 393	15 282
Non-current assets	73 167	79 591 [c]	66 500	60 953	51 832
Total assets	106 215	115 361 [c]	101 805	102 718	87 117
Current liabilities	33 223	43 326	32 479	35 854	29 075
Non-current liabilities	18 076	17 259 [c]	16 478	17 796	17 743
Equity attributable to shareholders of the parent	50 774	52 627 [c]	50 991	47 498	39 236
Minority interests	4 142	2 149	1 857	1 570	1 063
Net financial debt	14 596	21 174	10 971	9 725	10 171
Operating cash flow	10 763	13 439	11 676	10 205	10 412
as % of net financial debt	73.7%	63.6%	106.4%	104.9%	102.4%
Free cash flow [e]	5 033	8 231	7 018	6 557	6 640
Capital expenditure	4 869	4 971	4 200	3 375	3 260
as % of sales	4.4%	4.6%	4.3%	3.7%	3.8%
Data per share [f]					
Weighted average number of shares outstanding	3 704 613 573	3 828 809 470	3 848 010 890	3 888 125 640	3 884 499 570
Basic earnings per share from continuing operations	4.87	2.78	2.37	2.08	1.70
Basic earnings per share from discontinued operations	–	–	0.02	(0.00)	0.01
Equity attributable to shareholders of the parent	13.71	13.75 [c]	13.25	12.22	10.10
Dividend	1.40 [d]	1.22	1.04	0.90	0.80
Pay-out ratio based on Total basic earnings per share	28.8% [d]	43.9%	43.5%	43.3%	46.9%
Stock prices (high)	52.95	55.35	44.83	40.43	34.60
Stock prices (low)	38.02	42.65	35.60	29.83	27.60
Yield [g]	2.6/3.7	2.2/2.9	2.3/2.9	2.2/3.0	2.3/2.9
Market capitalisation	150 409	195 661	166 152	152 576	115 237
Number of personnel (in thousands)	283	276	265	250	244

(a) 2005 comparatives restated following first application of the option of IAS 19 – Employee Benefits § 93A ss. and IFRIC 4 – Determining whether an Arrangement contains a Lease, as well as the decision to transfer the fresh cheese activities in Italy to Nestlé Nutrition.

(b) 2004 comparatives restated following first application of IFRS 2 – Share-based Payment and for the discontinued operation following the announcement made in December 2005 for the Chilled dairy activities in Europe.

(c) 2007 comparatives have been restated following first application of IFRIC 14.

(d) As proposed by the Board of Directors of Nestlé S.A.

(e) Operating cash flow less capital expenditure, disposal of tangible assets, purchase and disposal of intangible assets, movements with associates as well as with minority interests.

(f) 2007 and prior years comparatives have been restated following 1-for-10 share split effective on 30 June 2008.

(g) Calculated on the basis of the dividend for the year concerned but which is paid in the following year.

Photo Credits

Index